W9-DCD-935

Building towards a better tomorrow.

Freddie Mac is dedicated to strengthening communities by expanding housing and rental opportunities throughout the U.S. In many ways, we work towards a common goal: a better tomorrow for everyone in America. www.FreddieMac.com

Freddie Mac

We make home possible℠

2006/2007

Contents

ASIAN AMERICAN YEARBOOK

THE US DEPARTMENT OF DEFENSE AND THE INTERNATIONAL SCENE

RELIGION•EDUCATION•HEALTH•ORGANIZATIONS AND MEDIA

DEFINITION OF ASIA*

The continent of Asia is defined by subtracting Europe and Africa from the great land mass of Africa-Eurasia. The boundaries are vague: Asia and Africa meet somewhere near the Suez Canal.

The boundary between Asia and Europe runs via the Dardanelles, the Sea of Marmara, the Hellespont, the Black Sea, the ridges of the Caucasus, the Caspian Sea, the Ural River and the Ural Mountains to Novaya Zemlya. The region of Asia is the continent of Asia plus nearby islands.

DEFINITION OF ASIAN AND PACIFIC ISLANDER**

A person having origins in any of the original peoples of the Far East, Southeast Asia, or the Indian subcontinent including, for example, Cambodia, China, India, Japan, Korea, Malaysia, Pakistan, the Philippine Islands, Thailand, and Vietnam. It includes "Asian Indian," "Chinese," "Filipino," "Korean," "Japanese," "Vietnamese," and "Other Asian."

Native Hawaiian and Other Pacific Islander - A person having origins in any of the original peoples of Hawaii, Guam, Samoa, or other Pacific Islands. It includes people who indicate their race as "Native Hawaiian," "Guamanian or Chamorro," "Samoan,"and "Other Pacific Islander."

*Source: Wikipedia.http://en2.wikipedia.org
**Source: US Census Bureau

ASIANAMERICANYEARBOOK

PUBLISHER
Juan Ovidio Zavala

EDITOR
Angela E. Zavala

ASSOCIATE PUBLISHER
John Zavala

**GOVERNMENT RELATIONS
& CIRCULATION**
Jess Quintero

**ADVERTISING & PUBLIC
RELATIONS**
Evelyn Day
Robert James

PRODUCTION
Ramón Palencia-Calvo
Kim Chi Un
Jordan L. Dansby
Fatoki Olayinka

RESEARCH
Fredalyn Bardaje
Helena V. Pisano
Lorena Quintana

CONTRIBUTING EDITORS
Linda Burnette
Aimée Winegar
Stephen J. Winegar

DESIGN
Caruso Creative, LLC

ADVERTISING SALES
For advertising inquiries, call
DIRECTORY MARKETING INC. (DMI)
(816) 537-7950

Trademark No. 78163199
Library of Congress Control No:
2004209436
ISSN: 1551-0867
ISBN:0-9777254-1-3

GET YOUR COPY! At asianamericanyearbook.com **or** send a check or money order for $29.95 (or $50.00 drawn on a U.S. bank for international postage) payable to TIYM Publishing Co., Inc.
VISA/Mastercard/American Express Accepted

Visit our online edition at asianamericanyearbook.com

ASIAN-AMERICAN YEARBOOK

is an annual publication of
TIYM Publishing Company, Inc. a
current 8(a) certified business, qualified
as a Small Disadvantaged Business
(SDB) under the SBA's Office of Small
Disadvantaged Business Certification
and Eligibility.

TIYM Publishing Company

FOUNDED IN 1985

The Origin of TIYM:

The acronym and commercial name of
the publishing company, TIYM, recalls
its roots in Argentina

Headquarters

6718 Whittier Avenue Suite 130
McLean, Virginia 22101 USA

Tel: (703) 734-1632

Fax: (703) 356-0787

Florida Office

814 Ponce de León Suite 510
Coral Gables, FL 33134 USA

Tel: (305) 442-7003

Fax: (305) 442-7013

tiym@tiym.com

www.tiym.com

Angela E. Zavala, President & CEO
DUNS:161904669

DISTRIBUTION NETWORK
Circulation 50,000
Distributed to many of the groups and
organizations listed in this edition
Throughout the United States:
- US Senate and House of Repr-
  esentatives
- US Department of Defense
- US Marines, Army, Coast Guard,
  and Navy Recruiting Stations
- US Institutions of Higher Education
- High Schools, Community Colleges
- Libraries
- The Congressional Asian Pacific
  American Caucus
- Sponsors of ASIAN-AMERICAN
  YEARBOOK
- Retail Outlets in Association with
  the Independent Publishers Group
  (IPG)

At Conferences and Conventions
- American Council of Education
  (Gear-Up)
- Minority Business Development
  Agency (MED WEEK)
- G.I. Forum
- Asian Pacific American Chambers
  of Commerce
- FAPAC
- HHS & OMH conventions in New
  York, Hawaii, San Francisco, Los
  Angeles, Philadelphia

International:
- US Embassies and Consulates in
  major Asian countries

VERIFIED
AUDIT CIRCULATION

THE WHITE HOUSE

WASHINGTON

November 22, 2005

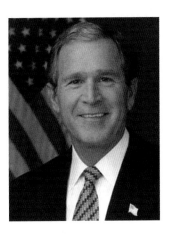

I send greetings to readers of the Asian-American Yearbook.

Throughout our history, America has been a land of diversity and has benefited from the contributions of people of different backgrounds brought together by a love of liberty. Asian Americans have strengthened our country through their achievements in all walks of life, including business, politics, education, the military, community service, the arts, and science. Their hard work, strong values, and devotion to community set a positive example for others and add to the success and prosperity of America.

My Administration is committed to ensuring that our Nation remains the land of hope and opportunity for every citizen. By working to make tax relief permanent, address the growing burden of frivolous lawsuits, reduce excessive Federal regulations, and confront the rising costs of health care, we are building an environment for economic growth and vitality that encourages all Americans to achieve their dreams.

I appreciate all those involved with the Asian-American Yearbook for your efforts to recognize the achievements of Asian Americans and the significant role they have played in making our country prosperous and free. As a resource for business, employment, educational, and health needs, this yearbook helps strengthen the Asian-American community and extend the great promise of America to all our citizens.

Laura and I send our best wishes.

December 13, 2005

It is with pleasure that I extend my heartfelt congratulations to the staff members and supporters of the Asian-American yearbook on the publication of its 2006 edition.

This yearbook will prove invaluable to the Asian-American society by detailing their notable contributions throughout American society and recording the lasting imprint they are making within their local communities. Furthermore, the yearbook provides vital information to facilitate exchanges between Asian American community leaders and will encourage communication between all sectors of society; which in turn will serve our community as a whole.

Let me conclude by expressing my warm appreciation for the hard work and dedication it took to bring this book to print.

With my best wishes,

Lee, Tae-sik
Ambassador of the Republic of Korea

COMMITTEE ON SCIENCE

SUBCOMMITTEES:
RANKING MEMBER
ENERGY
SPACE AND AERONAUTICS

COMMITTEE ON TRANSPORTATION AND
INFRASTRUCTURE
SUBCOMMITTEES:
AVIATION
HIGHWAYS, TRANSIT AND PIPELINES
COAST GUARD AND MARITIME TRANSPORTATION

CHAIR:
CONGRESSIONAL ASIAN PACIFIC AMERICAN CAUCUS
CONGRESSIONAL ETHIOPIA CAUCUS

Congress of the United States
House of Representatives

MICHAEL M. HONDA
15TH DISTRICT, CALIFORNIA

WASHINGTON OFFICE
1713 LONGWORTH BUILDING
WASHINGTON, DC 20515
PHONE: (202) 225-2631
FAX (202) 225-2699

DISTRICT OFFICE
1999 SOUTH BASCOM AVE
SUITE 815
CAMPBELL, CA 95008
PHONE: (408) 558-8085
FAX (408) 558-8086
HTTP://WWW.HOUSE.GOV/HONDA
MIKE.HONDA@MAIL.HOUSE.GOV

January 5, 2006
Message from Congressman Mike Honda
Commemorating the Third Edition of the Asian-American Yearbook

Dear Friends:

It is with great pleasure that I send greetings to all those who helped produce the third edition of the Asian-American Yearbook. The compilation of information, resources, and opportunities contained in this publication serves as an important tool to the Asian and Pacific Islander American (APIA) community, which is the fastest growing ethnic group in the United States.

As Chair of the Congressional Asian Pacific American Caucus, I commend TIYM Publishing for all its efforts in producing this important resource. Its immense contributions to the APIA community are indeed recognized and valued. I wish you all the best in your continuous work to build bridges between the diverse communities in the United States.

Sincerely,

Michael M. Honda

Michael M. Honda, Chair
Congressional Asian Pacific American Caucus

Letter from the Editor

The population outlook for the United States shows our country moving towards more and more diversity. As the White population's growth starts to slow, minority gains will only grow larger. According to estimates released at the turn of the century, by 2050 the racial and ethnic makeup of this country will be notably different.

Asians and Pacific Islanders will be the fastest-growing group during the next fifty years. Turn-of-the-century figures put this group at 12 million—a number that is expected to double by 2010, triple by 2020 and more than quintuple by 2050, surpassing the 40 million mark.

The size and rapid growth of Asians and Pacific Islanders as a group reveals some interesting and noteworthy trends. This community, like all people, seeks a better quality of life, but seems to be achieving it quicker than any other racial or ethnic group. For example, ninety-five percent of Asian Pacific Americans live in suburban areas. Divorce rates are significantly lower among Asians and Pacific Islanders than among the rest of the population. Asian Americans are also exceptionally well educated, with over fifty percent attaining a bachelor's degree or higher. Professionally, they are above the norm—forty-one percent of men and thirty-seven percent of women occupy professional or management positions. Without a doubt, Asian American achievements and prominence, both individually and collectively, will only continue to grow.

Every day at TIYM is a learning experience and each successive Yearbook presents a new challenge—one that requires an ever-expanding search for new and better information in an effort to better serve each community. I present this, the third edition of the ASIAN-AMERICAN YEARBOOK, in the hope that we have reached that goal, but knowing that the bar must always be set higher.

Warmest Regards,

Angela Elizalde Zavala
Editor

Congressman Michael Honda with leaders of the Asian-American community during the 2005 ASIAN-AMERICAN YEARBOOK presentation at the Library of Congress.

Written by:

SAMUEL T. MOK

Mr. Samuel T. Mok was confirmed by the United States Senate in January 2002 as the Chief Financial Officer of the U.S. Department of Labor. Prior to joining the U.S. Department of Labor, Mr. Mok served as the Managing Member of Condor Consulting, LLC, a Washington, D.C.-based international consulting firm. In 1971, he was called to active military duty and served in Okinawa, Japan as a strategic intelligence officer. Upon being promoted to the rank of Captain, he was reassigned to Army Readiness Region 1 at the U.S. Military Academy at West Point. In 1986, he served as a Foreign Service Officer at the Bureau of East Asian and Pacific Affairs at the U.S. Department of State.

Mr. Mok is also very proud of his Chinese heritage. He has held top leadership positions at most major Asian-American community organizations in the greater Washington, D.C. area.

Mr. Mok received his B.S. in Accounting from Fordham University, a master's degree from The Catholic University of America and graduated from the U.S. Foreign Service Institute and the U.S. Army Institute for Administration and Finance. He is a Certified Internal Auditor (CIA) and a Certified Government Financial Manager (CGFM).

President George W. Bush recognizes that the true strength of this country lies in the hearts and souls of its citizens across the country. He has undertaken great efforts to level the playing field for every American, regardless of ethnicity, creed, religious belief, educational background, or social origin. As part of this effort, he has made significant contributions to the advancement of Asian Pacific Americans through political appointments to his administration, the creation of special emphasis programs in different Federal agencies, stepped-up enforcement actions, particularly in the area of employment law, and aggressive outreach projects to promote opportunities for Asian

Pacific Americans in the Federal Government.

Since he took office, President Bush has appointed nearly 290 Asian Pacific Americans to positions in his administration. This is greater than any other President in American history. His appointees include two Cabinet Secretaries and 94 PAS positions (Presidentially Appointed, Senate Confirmed) serving in the highest ranks of the Administration. Twenty-three Asian Pacific Americans, a record number, have served in the White House under President Bush. He also appointed the first Chinese American woman to the President's Cabinet in history, Secretary of Labor Elaine L. Chao, and I am also honored to serve with her as the Chief Financial Officer of the Department of Labor. This is the first time that Chinese Americans have concurrently held such prestigious positions in American history, 57 years after the repeal of the Chinese Exclusion Act.

At the Labor Department, under the leadership of Secretary Chao, more Asian Pacific Americans have been appointed to serve than in any other Cabinet agency. Secretary Chao is committed to improving access to various Federal opportunities for historically underserved communities, including Asian Pacific Americans. The following is a sample of Secretary Chao's accomplishments over the past five years:

Enforcement and Compliance Assistance

To protect the physical and financial security of Asian Pacific Americans, Secretary Chao stepped-up enforcement and compliance assistance in industries with chronic violations, such as garment manufacturing, health care, janitorial services,

> "We must work together to make our voices heard."

restaurants, and hotel industries. These efforts yielded $43,141,911 in back wages for workers, paid to nearly 85,000 workers in fiscal year 2004.

Strategic Partnership

Through partnerships and collaborative activities, the Department of Labor leverages resources and broadens the impact of other strategies and initiatives. Ongoing relationships and outreach programs with Department partners inform low wage and immigrant workers of their rights and the remedies available to them. The Department has developed several successful partnerships in Asian Pacific American communities, such as with The Information Group for Asian American Rights (TIGAAR), Compliance Outreach to the Asian Community and Hispanics (COACH), Grow America Through Entrepreneurship (GATE), and the Rapid Employee Assistance in Chinese Hotline.

Creating Opportunities

To foster a new generation of leaders and promote diversity in the workforce, Secretary Chao established an internship program at the Labor Department. To help Asian Pacific Americans gain better access to careers and leadership opportunities in the Federal Government, Secretary Chao initiated the annual Asian Pacific Federal Career Advancement Summit in

Samuel T. Mok, Chief Financial Officer of the U.S. Department of Labor delivers the keynote address during the U.S. Department of Agriculture's annual Asian Pacific American heritage month celebration.

Samuel T. Mok discusses various Labor Department initiatives with the Zhejiang University Alumni Association in Newark, New Jersey earlier this year.

May 2001. This unprecedented training program has equipped Asian Pacific Americans with better skill sets to become leaders in the American workplace. In 2003, Secretary Chao collaborated with numerous groups and hosted the first annual Opportunity Conference to assist small businesses and entrepreneurs, enhancing their skills in business development, accessing capital, and doing business with Government.

Strengthening the Community
To better serve the Asian Pacific American community, the Labor Department now includes specific data on Asian Pacific Americans in its monthly unemployment reports. The Department has also developed an alliance with the Federal Asian Pacific American Council (FAPAC) to broaden outreach efforts and to improve access to training material critical to career advancement. The Fair Labor Standards Act has been translated into Chinese and an interactive piece, "A Pictorial Walk Through the 20th Century – The Asian American in Mining," is now available at the Labor Department's Mine Safety and Health Administration (MSHA) website, www.msha. gov. In partnership with CVS Pharmacy, the Labor Department is sponsoring a project to assist older women including Asian Pacific Americans obtain jobs with CVS by providing training in basic life and computer skills.

The Labor Department is one of many Federal agencies working hard to improve the well being of Asian Pacific Americans in this country. The private sector is also making great strides by appointing many Asian Pacific Americans to top executive positions. The military now boasts many Asian Pacific American staff rank officers. There is now a vibrant APA Caucus in the U.S. Congress as well. The community is realizing the first step towards total political empowerment in America – a critical mass in leadership positions across economic, political, military, and other sectors. We now have a voice.

We must work together to make our voices heard.

Samuel T. Mok, CFO of the U.S. Department of Labor delivers the key note address at the U.S. Chinese Women Business Leaders Conference in Washington, D.C. earlier this year.

Samuel T. Mok addresses his senior staff at a weekly meeting.

Population

FIG 1. Growth of Population by Population Group: 2000-2004

Between 2000 and 2004, Asian Pacific Americans were the second fastest growing group in the U.S., after Hispanics. The Asian Pacific American population grew almost four times more than the overall U.S. population, which increased only 4.3 percent during this same period.

Source: US Census Bureau. National Population Estimates, 2004.
www.census.gov

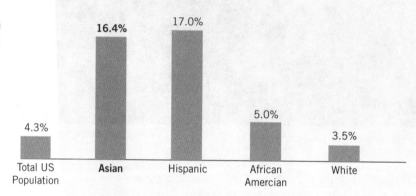

FIG 2. Projected Population of the United States by Race/Ethnicity : 2000-2050
(In thousands except as indicated. As of July 1, 2004. Resident population.)

According to projections by the U.S. Census Bureau, the rapid increase among Asian Pacific Americans will only continue. By 2050, the population is expected to more than triple.

Source: US Census Bureau 2004,
US Interim Projections by Age,
Race, and Hispanic Origin".
www.census.gov

POPULATION AND RACE OR HISPANIC ORIGIN	2000	2010	2020	2030	2040	2050
POPULATION TOTAL	282,125	308,936	335,805	363,584	391,946	419,854
White alone	228,548	244,995	260,629	275,731	289,690	302,626
Black alone	35,818	40,454	45,365	50,442	55,876	61,361
Asian Alone	10,684	14,241	17,988	22,580	27,992	33,430
All other races	7,075	9,246	11,822	14,831	18,388	22,437
Hispanic (of any race)	35,622	47,756	59,756	73,055	87,585	102,560
White alone, not Hispanic	195,729	201,112	205,936	209,176	210,331	210,283

FIG 3. Foreign-Born Population by Region of Birth: 2004

Besides Latin America, Asia was by far the largest region of birth for the United States foreign-born population. Twenty-five percent of the foreign-born population came from Asia. The next largest group was Europe, with fourteen percent.

Source: US Census Bureau. Current Population Survey, Annual Social and Economic Supplement, 2004 www.census.gov

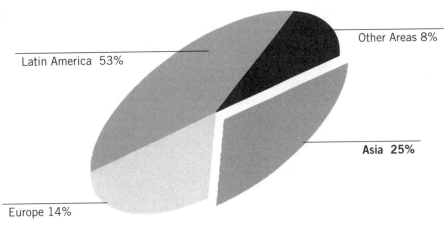

Other Areas 8%

Latin America 53%

Asia 25%

Europe 14%

FIG 4. Asian Foreign-Born Population by Citizenship Status and Year of Entry: 2004

Over half of the Asian Pacific American foreign-born population are citizens.

Source: US Census Bureau. Current Population Survey, Annual Social and Economic Supplement, 2004. www.census.gov

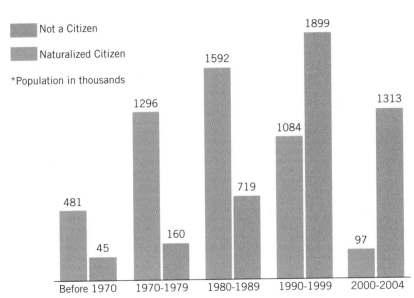

Not a Citizen

Naturalized Citizen

*Population in thousands

	Not a Citizen	Naturalized Citizen
Before 1970	481	45
1970-1979	1296	160
1980-1989	1592	719
1990-1999	1084	1899
2000-2004	97	1313

FIG 5. Asian Pacific American Percentage of State's Population: 2004

The Asian Pacific American population tends to be concentrated in a few states, mostly in the West. The U.S. Census Bureau's 2004 estimates show Hawaii with by far the highest percentage. California and Washington are a distant second and third, respectively.

Source: US Census Bureau, Population Estimates 2004. www.census.gov

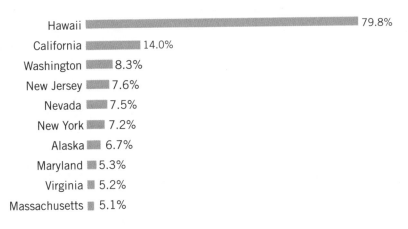

State	Percentage
Hawaii	79.8%
California	14.0%
Washington	8.3%
New Jersey	7.6%
Nevada	7.5%
New York	7.2%
Alaska	6.7%
Maryland	5.3%
Virginia	5.2%
Massachusetts	5.1%

FIG 6. Geographical Distribution of the Asian Pacific American Population: 2004
(Asian alone or in combination with another group or another race)

Almost half of the Asian population lives in the West. These numbers, however, have been changing over the past few years. The West's proportion has decreased slightly (51.1% to 48.1%, 2002-2004), while the South and Northeast have been making up these differences with modest gains over the same period.

Source: US Census Bureau, Population Estimates, 2004. www.census.gov

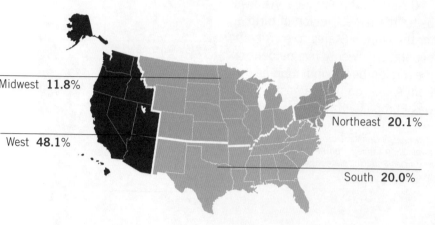

Midwest **11.8%**

Northeast **20.1%**

West **48.1%**

South **20.0%**

FIG 7. Median Age of the U.S. Population by Selected Race/Ethnicity: 2004

Asian Americans were, on average, the second-oldest racial or ethnic group in 2004.

Source: U.S. Census Bureau, 2004 American Community Survey www.census.gov

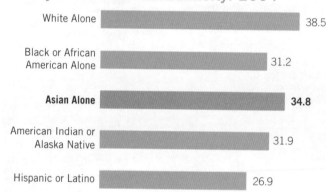

White Alone 38.5

Black or African American Alone 31.2

Asian Alone **34.8**

American Indian or Alaska Native 31.9

Hispanic or Latino 26.9

FIG 8. Top Countries of Birth of the Foreign Born Asian Population: 2000 and 2004
(Numbers in thousands)

The highest number of foreign-born Asian Pacific Americans were from China in both 2000 and 2004. Koreans, however, made the largest percentage gains out of the top five groups.

Source: U.S. Census Bureau, 2004 American Community Survey www.census.gov

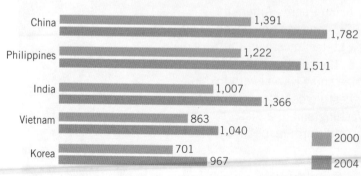

China 1,391 / 1,782

Philippines 1,222 / 1,511

India 1,007 / 1,366

Vietnam 863 / 1,040

Korea 701 / 967

2000
2004

FIG 9. Asian Pacific Americans by Selected Groups: 2004
(Percentage of total Asian Pacific American population)

While Filipinos represented a slightly higher number of foreign-born persons, Asian Indians made up a larger share of the general population of Asian Pacific Americans.

Source: US Census Bureau, 2004 American Community Survey. www.census.gov

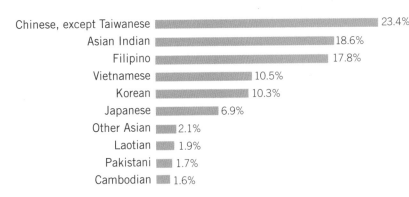

Chinese, except Taiwanese — 23.4%
Asian Indian — 18.6%
Filipino — 17.8%
Vietnamese — 10.5%
Korean — 10.3%
Japanese — 6.9%
Other Asian — 2.1%
Laotian — 1.9%
Pakistani — 1.7%
Cambodian — 1.6%

FIG 10. Asian Pacific American Population by State

Source: US Census Bureau, Population Estimates 2004. www.census.gov

State	Asian alone or in combination*	Native Hawaiian and other Pacific Islander alone or in combination*	State	Asian alone or in combination*	Native Hawaiian and other Pacific Islander alone or in combination*
United States	13,956.61	976.40	Missouri	90.30	7.31
Alabama	45.42	3.54	Montana	7.59	1.11
Alaska	37.92	5.97	Nebraska	31.92	2.06
Arizona	152.11	17.41	Nevada	154.84	21.36
Arkansas	31.58	3.72	New Hampshire	25.63	0.97
California	4,756.18	251.74	New Jersey	647.91	12.99
Colorado	144.32	12.21	New Mexico	31.19	3.87
Connecticut	120.21	5.26	New York	1,346.05	35.14
Delaware	24.37	0.86	North Carolina	171.60	10.61
District of Columbia	19.48	0.79	North Dakota	5.59	0.51
Florida	424.95	31.01	Ohio	187.78	7.86
Georgia	258.37	12.60	Oklahoma	66.22	5.69
Hawaii	727.65	279.65	Oregon	149.75	17.93
Idaho	20.24	3.23	Pennsylvania	295.27	10.43
Illinois	552.64	14.43	Rhode Island	32.56	2.25
Indiana	87.87	5.31	South Carolina	53.95	4.54
Iowa	48.82	2.47	South Dakota	6.99	0.57
Kansas	66.24	3.63	Tennessee	84.40	5.43
Kentucky	45.06	3.68	Texas	797.33	38.71
Louisiana	71.54	3.48	Utah	56.69	23.15
Maine	13.79	0.89	Vermont	7.74	0.33
Maryland	286.14	7.41	Virginia	376.43	11.92
Massachusetts	319.62	10.67	Washington	464.86	47.47
Michigan	253.66	8.70	West Virginia	12.74	0.92
Minnesota	192.54	6.85	Wisconsin	119.63	5.02
Mississippi	26.29	2.09	Wyoming	4.67	0.67

*In thousands

FIG 11. Estimates of Total Asian Pacific Islander Population by State: July 1, 2004*

Source: US Census Bureau.
Population Estimates, 2004
www.census.gov

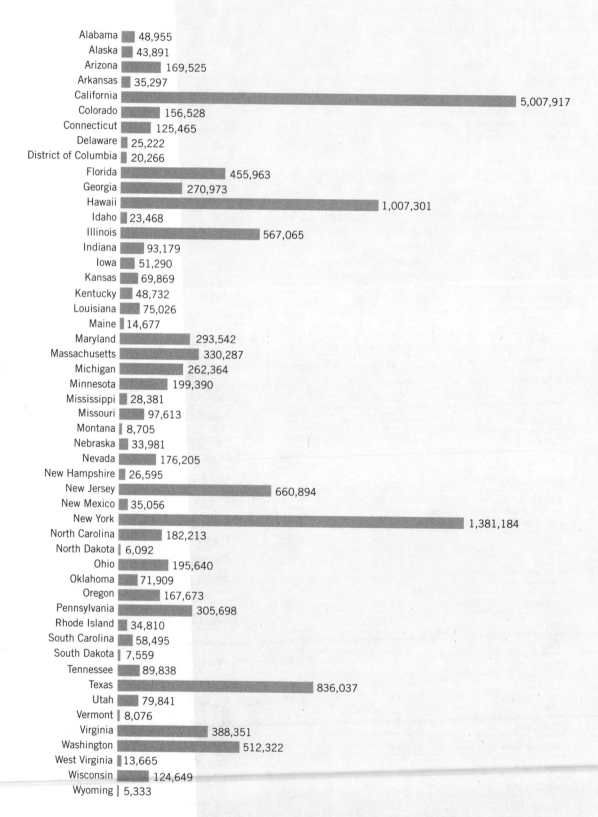

State	Population
Alabama	48,955
Alaska	43,891
Arizona	169,525
Arkansas	35,297
California	5,007,917
Colorado	156,528
Connecticut	125,465
Delaware	25,222
District of Columbia	20,266
Florida	455,963
Georgia	270,973
Hawaii	1,007,301
Idaho	23,468
Illinois	567,065
Indiana	93,179
Iowa	51,290
Kansas	69,869
Kentucky	48,732
Louisiana	75,026
Maine	14,677
Maryland	293,542
Massachusetts	330,287
Michigan	262,364
Minnesota	199,390
Mississippi	28,381
Missouri	97,613
Montana	8,705
Nebraska	33,981
Nevada	176,205
New Hampshire	26,595
New Jersey	660,894
New Mexico	35,056
New York	1,381,184
North Carolina	182,213
North Dakota	6,092
Ohio	195,640
Oklahoma	71,909
Oregon	167,673
Pennsylvania	305,698
Rhode Island	34,810
South Carolina	58,495
South Dakota	7,559
Tennessee	89,838
Texas	836,037
Utah	79,841
Vermont	8,076
Virginia	388,351
Washington	512,322
West Virginia	13,665
Wisconsin	124,649
Wyoming	5,333

*Graph is not to scale

FIG 12. Asian Pacific American Population by Sex and Gender: 2004
(Numbers in thousands)

Age and sex	Total		Asian or Pacific Islander		Non-Hispanic White		Other	
	Number	Percent	Number	Percent	Number	Percent	Number	Percent
Total	285,692	100.0	12,501	100.0	192,363	100.0	80,828	100.0
Under 5 years	20,008	7.0	828	6.6	11,200	5.8	7,980	9.9
5 to 9 years	19,659	6.9	804	6.4	11,365	5.9	7,490	9.3
10 to 14 years	21,085	7.4	801	6.4	12,651	6.6	7,633	9.4
15 to 19 years	19,078	6.7	733	5.9	11,858	6.2	6,487	8.0
20 to 24 years	19,328	6.8	858	6.9	11,830	6.1	6,640	8.2
25 to 29 years	18,771	6.6	1,034	8.3	11,360	5.9	6,378	7.9
30 to 34 years	19,921	7.0	1,268	10.1	12,305	6.4	6,347	7.9
35 to 44 years	43,572	15.3	2,238	17.9	29,237	15.2	12.097	15.0
45 to 54 years	41,219	14.4	1,800	14.4	30,182	15.7	9,238	11.4
55 to 64 years	28,846	10.1	1,117	8.9	22,395	11.6	5,334	6.6
65 to 74 years	18,164	6.4	622	5.0	14,445	7.5	3,097	3.8
75 to 84 years	12,416	4.3	314	2.5	10,439	5.4	1,663	2.1
85 years and over	3,626	1.3	85	0.7	3,096	1.6	445	0.6
Male	139,783	100.0	6,010	100.0	94,272	100.0	39,501	100.0
Under 5 years	10,211	7.3	412	6.9	5,737	6.1	4,062	10.3
5 to 9 years	10,050	7.2	411	6.8	5,848	6.2	3,792	9.6
10 to 14 years	10,789	7.7	411	6.8	6,484	6.9	3,894	9.9
15 to 19 years	9,787	7.0	386	6.4	6,113	6.5	3,288	8.3
20 to 24 years	9,749	7.0	434	7.2	5,930	6.3	3,385	8.6
25 to 29 years	9,347	6.7	488	8.1	5,666	6.0	3,193	8.1
30 to 34 years	9,869	7.1	606	10.1	6,129	6.5	3,135	7.9
35 to 44 years	21,458	15.4	1,073	17.9	14,528	15.4	5,857	14.8
45 to 54 years	20,143	14.4	850	14.1	14,912	15.8	4,381	11.1
55 to 64 years	13,833	9.9	511	8.5	10,891	11.6	2,431	6.2
65 to 74 years	8,284	5.9	270	4.5	6,687	7.1	1,327	3.4
75 to 84 years	5,057	3.6	126	2.1	4,307	4.6	625	1.6
85 years and over	1,206	0.9	33	0.5	1,039	1.1	134	0.3
Female	145,909	100.0	6,491	100.0	98,091	100.0	41,327	100.0
Under 5 years	9,797	6.7	415	6.4	5,463	5.6	3,919	9.5
5 to 9 years	9,609	6.6	393	6.1	5,517	5.6	3,698	8.9
10 to 14 years	10,295	7.1	390	6.0	6,167	6.3	3,739	9.0
15 to 19 years	9,291	6.4	347	5.3	5,745	5.9	3,200	7.7
20 to 24 years	9,579	6.6	424	6.5	5,900	6.0	3,255	7.9
25 to 29 years	9,424	6.5	546	8.4	5,694	5.8	3,184	7.7
30 to 34 years	10,052	6.9	663	10.2	6,177	6.3	3,213	7.8
35 to 44 years	22,113	15.2	1,165	18.0	14,708	15.0	6,240	15.1
45 to 54 years	21,076	14.4	950	14.6	15,269	15.6	4,857	11.8
55 to 64 years	15,013	10.3	606	9.3	11,504	11.7	2,903	7.0
65 to 74 years	9,880	6.8	353	5.4	7,758	7.9	1,770	4.3
75 to 84 years	7,358	5.0	188	2.9	6,132	6.3	1,038	2.5
85 years and over	2,420	1.7	52	0.8	2,057	2.1	311	0.8

Source: US Census Bureau, 2004 American Community Survey. www.census.gov

ASIAN PACIFIC AMERICAN
Politics

FIG 1. Reported Voting and Registration By Citizenship, Race, and Hispanic Orgin: November 2000 and 2004 (Numbers in thousands)

The percentage of Asian Pacific Americans that are registered to vote is among the lowest of any racial or ethnic group. Between 2000 and 2004, this figure actually decreased slightly (from 52.4% to 51.8%). Newly arrived immigrants who are not yet citizens, and therefore ineligible to vote, partially contribute to the lower rate of voter registration. Among the Asian Pacific American population, gains comparable to other racial or ethic groups were made from 2000 to 2004 in the percentage of registered voters who actually voted.

	Total Population				Citizens				Registered	
	Total	Citizen	Reported Registered	Reported Voted	% Reported Registered	Margin of Error[1]	% Reported Voted	Margin of Error[1]	% Reported Voted	Margin of Error[1]
2004										
Total 18 years and over Race and Hispanic Origin	217,694	197,005	142,070	125,736	72.1%	0.3	63.8%	0.3	88.5%	0.3
White	176,618	162,958	119,929	106,588	73.6%	0.2	65.4%	0.3	88.9%	0.3
White non-Hispanic	151,410	148,159	111,318	99,567	75.1%	0.1	67.2%	0.3	89.4%	0.3
Black	24,910	23,346	16,035	14,016	68.7%	0.5	60.0%	1.0	87.4%	1.0
Asian and Pacific Islander	**9,291**	**6,270**	**3,247**	**2,768**	**51.8%**	**1.7**	**44.1%**	**1.8**	**85.2%**	**1.7**
Hispanic (of any race)	27,129	16,088	9,308	7,587	57.9%	1.3	47.2%	1.3	81.5	1.2
2000										
Total 18 years and over Race and Hispanic Origin	202,609	186,366	129,549	110,826	69.5%	0.3	59.5%	0.3	85.5%	0.3
White	168,733	157,291	110,773	95,098	70.4%	0.3	60.5%	0.4	85.8%	0.3
White non-Hispanic	148,035	144,732	103,588	89,469	71.6%	0.4	61.8%	0.4	86.4%	0.3
Black	24,132	22,753	15,348	12,917	67.5%	1.1	56.8%	1.2	84.2%	1.1
Asian and Pacific Islander	**8,041**	**4,718**	**2,470**	**2,045**	**52.4%**	**2.7**	**43.3%**	**2.7**	**82.8%**	**2.9**
Hispanic (of any race)	21,598	13,158	7,546	5,934	57.3%	2.0	45.1%	2.0	78.6%	2.2

[1] This figure added to or subtracted from the estimate provides the 90 percent confidence interval.

Source: US Census Bureau.
Current Population Survey,
November 2000 and 2004
www.census.gov

FIG 2. Citizenship and Reported Voter Registration of the Asian American Population by Age: November 2004*

Among persons eligible to vote, registration in the Asian American community is about fifty-two percent. Older citizens (65 to 74 years old) and women are more likely to be registered. An important challenge for lawmakers and community leaders will be to raise awareness about the benefits and responsibilities of civic participation.

Source: US Census Bureau. Current Population Survey, November 2004 www.census.gov

		U.S. Citizen			Not a Citizen	
	Total	Total Citizens	Reported Registered	Percent of Eligible Voters Registered	Number	Percent of Total
Asian Alone						
BOTH SEXES						
TOTAL 18 YEARS AND OVER	9,291	6,269	3,247	51.8%	3,021	32.5%
18 to 24 years	1,118	766	326	42.6%	353	31.6%
25 to 44 years	4,318	2,563	1,248	48.7%	1,756	40.8%
45 to 64 years	2,790	2,090	1,211	57.9%	700	25.2%
65 to 74 years	600	483	283	58.6%	118	19.7%
75 years and older	464	369	180	48.8%	95	20.5%
MALE						
TOTAL 18 YEARS AND OVER	4,406	3,045	1,542	50.6%	1,361	30.9%
18 to 24 years	571	396	175	44.2%	175	30.6%
25 to 44 years	2,083	1,261	592	46.9%	821	39.4%
45 to 64 years	1,297	1,021	595	55.3%	276	21.3%
65 to 74 years	276	230	134	58.3%	45	16.3%
75 years and over	179	136	76	55.9%	43	24.0%
FEMALE						
TOTAL 18 YEARS AND OVER	4,885	3,224	1,705	52.9%	1,661	34.0%
18 to 24 years	548	370	151	40.8%	178	32.5%
25 to 44 years	2,236	1,302	656	50.4%	934	41.8%
45 to 64 years	1,493	1,069	647	60.5%	424	28.4%
65 to 74 years	324	252	149	59.1%	72	22.2%
75 years and over	285	233	104	44.7%	52	18.2%

*In thousands

FIG 3. Reported Registration and Voting of the Asian American Population by Educational Attainment: 2004 (As a percent of each attainment category)

Voter eligibility again affects the numbers for voting and registration by educational attainment. The important information, however, is the relatively small differences among registered voters and those who voted. This correlation shows that a registered Asian American voter is almost certainly going to vote, highlighting the importance of registration and voter education for those lawmakers and groups who would like to make a difference with this increasingly influential group.

Source: US Census Bureau. Current Population Survey, November 2004 www.census.gov

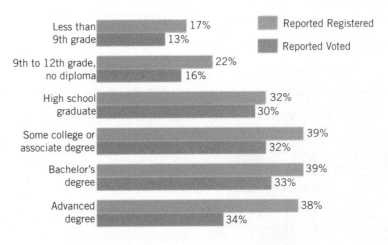

	Reported Registered	Reported Voted
Less than 9th grade	17%	13%
9th to 12th grade, no diploma	22%	16%
High school graduate	32%	30%
Some college or associate degree	39%	32%
Bachelor's degree	39%	33%
Advanced degree	38%	34%

SHU CHIEN, M.D., PH.D.

UNIVERSITY PROFESSOR

Dr. Shu Chien is one of twelve active University Professors of the University of California (UC) system, Founding Director of UCSD Whitaker Institute of Biomedical Engineering (1991-present), Founding Chair of the Department of Bioengineering (1994-99, 2002-05) and Founding Director of UC: Bioengineering Institute in California (2004-present).

After receiving his M.D. at the National Taiwan University and a Ph.D. in Physiology from Columbia University, Dr. Chien was a faculty professor in Physiology at Columbia from 1969 to 1988 and became Professor of Bioengineering and Medicine at UCSD in 1988. He led UCSD Bioengineering to win the Whitaker Foundation Development Award and Leadership Award.

Dr. Chien's research focuses are molecular, cellular and integrative studies on bioengineering; and the physiology of circulation in health and disease. He has received many awards and is a member of the U.S. Institute of Medicine, National Academy of Engineering, and National Academy of Sciences, as well as Academia Sinica (Taiwan) and the American Institute for Medical and Biological Engineering.

He was President of the Microcirculatory Society, American Physiological Society, Federation of American Societies for Experimental Biology, AIMBE, and International Society of Biorheology.

AsAY We wanted to start off by congratulating you on your 2005 Distinguished Lifetime Achievement Award from the Asian American Engineer of the Year (AAEOY) Awards Committee.

Chien Thank you very much. I was very much honored and humbled by that.

AsAY How did you feel after Y.C. Fung received the same award the previous year?

Chien It felt really wonderful. This has been a very fortunate year for me, as I was just elected as a member of the National Academy of Sciences in May. I joined Dr. Fung as one of eight U.S. scientists who are members of all three National Academies: National Academy of Sciences, National Academy of Engineering, and Institute of Medicine. We are in the same bioengineering department at UCSD. In fact, he recruited me from Columbia to UCSD seventeen years ago, in 1988. He is a little more than a decade senior than I. Dr. Fung started the bioengineering program at UCSD in 1966. In 1994 we formed the Department of Bioengineering and I was the Founding Chair of the Department. We've been working together very much and he is my role model, so I'm particularly honored to be in the same distinguished group as he and the many others who are truly outstanding.

AsAY How do you take your achievements and ultimately your image as a nationally renowned scientist and use it to empower the next generation of Asian Americans?

`Chien` We look at education and training of the next generation of scientists as our top priority; and being Asian American myself, I would like to be able to contribute to the education and training of young people of the same heritage. However, education has no boundary and I enjoy training young people of all ethnic backgrounds and am not limited to Asian Americans.

"Being Asian American myself I would like to be able to contribute to the education and training of young people of the same heritage. However, education has no boundary and I enjoy training young people of all ethnic backgrounds and am not limited to Asian Americans."

AsAY What's your approach in educating the next generation of Asian Americans?

`Chien` I think the approach is multifaceted, and this includes educating students in classrooms, in laboratories and on other occasions. In addition to teaching them the knowledge in regards to science and engineering and the way of research, we teach students the importance of learning and mastering the tools of communication-both oral and written-and the importance of understanding what are the needs of society so we can best serve the people. We have to understand the elements of upholding the highest

level of ethics in doing research and in everything we do, whether working in academia, industry, government, or other settings. No matter what walks of life we pursue, we have to always hold the highest ethical standards in caring for people.

AsAY As a premed student at National Peking University, you witnessed firsthand the beginnings of the Communist revolution before your evacuation to Taiwan. You were able to receive higher education at a time when the Cultural Revolution in China was unfolding. How have these experiences allowed you to grasp the significance of education?

`Chien` Asian culture puts great emphasis on education. My parents are among those who regard education very highly. My father was a chemistry professor and our family might have had difficulties during the Cultural Revolution if we had stayed. Fortunately, my parents decided to leave China almost at the last minute, when Beijing was under siege. Their move to Taiwan allowed us to pursue higher education and develop our careers.

AsAY In 1994, you created and continue to chair the Department of Bioengineering

Dr. Chien speaks to potential new bioengineering students at UCSD.

at the University of California, San Diego. Under your leadership, it has flourished to rank second in the nation for biomedical/bioengineering, according to *U.S. News*. What was your vision behind its creation? What leadership styles have you employed in shaping the department as a leading research institution?

Chien The vision behind its creation was an integrative approach. We integrate engineering and biomedical sciences, integrate research and education, and integrate our research across all levels of biological hierarchy, from genes to molecules/cells to tissues/organs. Dr. Fung already had a strong biomechanic program. What I brought was the molecular level of bioengineering. We also fostered tissue engineering and regenerative medicine. Most recently, we have led a new area in bioengineering: systems biology or system bioengineering, i.e., the use of a systems approach to study genes and molecules as an interacting network in regulating the functions of the living system. My leadership styles emphasize the utilization of the collective wisdoms of members of the team and the generation of consensus.

AsAY Asian American culture emphasizes the importance of education as a foundation for success. Your background and achievements reflect this ideal and its tangibility. What other factor, besides education, has played a principal role in your professional success?

Chien Family upbringing. My father was a dedicated scientist and teacher and he held the highest ethical standard. He taught by example.

AsAY In 1988, you were recruited to the bioengineering program by Y.C. Fung, who regards recruiting you as his greatest contribution to UCSD. In turn, what has been your greatest contribution to UCSD?

Chien I am greatly honored that Dr. Fung would regard recruiting

Dr. Yuan-tseh Lee, President of Academia Sinica in Taiwan, presents a plaque to Dr. Chien at a ceremony dedicating a new building for the Institute of Biomedical Sciences (IBMS) of the Academy.

me as his greatest contribution; he has made immense contributions to UCSD, to bioengineering, and to the entire field of science. In terms of my contribution, I regard the creation and development of the Bioengineering Department at UCSD, along with the Whitaker Institute of Biomedical Engineering, as my greatest contributions.

AsAY Throughout your life, you've always taught students who have come behind you. But what has been the greatest lesson you've learned from them?

Chien Young people are creative. They have an ability to come up with original ideas and ways of working with those ideas. I have learned a lot from my students and I have endeavored to foster those creative aspects of people.

AsAY Any closing remarks?

Chien I wish to congratulate and thank the *Asian-American Yearbook* for your wonderful efforts in fostering the activities and the betterment of Asian Americans.

Dr. Chien in a laboratory at MIT.

FEDERAL ASIAN PACIFIC AMERICAN COUNCIL
(FAPAC)

"Promoting Equal Opportunity and Cultural Diversity for APAs in Government"

Federal Asian Pacific American Council
FAPAC

Established 1985

December 7, 2005

President
Linda Tuazon-Miller
Federal Communications Commission
(202) 418-2581
linda.miller@fcc.gov

Sr. Vice-President for Operations
Gerald J. Tiqui
National Aeronautics and Space
Administration
(301) 286-9461
gerald.j.tiqui@nasa.gov

Vice President for Committees
Chau Le Williams
Housing and Urban Development
(202) 708-0614 ext 7491
chaule_williams@hud.gov

Executive Secretary
James Su
National Oceanic and Atmospheric Adm.
(301) 713-0023 ext 139
james.su@noaa.gov

Treasurer
Lily Ho
National Guard Bureau, Army
((703) 607-7634
lily.ho@ngb.army.mil

Website: http://www.fapac.org
E-mail: fapac@fapac.org
Address:
P.O. Box 23184
Washington, D.C. 20026-3184

21st Annual National Leadership Training
Conference and Congressional
Seminar

May 8-12, 2006
Hilton Hawaiian Village Resort and Spa
Honolulu, HI

Greetings:

On behalf of the Executive Board of the Federal Asian Pacific American Council (FAPAC), I am pleased to congratulate TIYM Publishing Co., Inc. on the production of the 2006 Asian American Yearbook, a very valuable resource and referral guide for and about Asian Pacific Americans. Its publication gives the Asian Pacific Americans a valuable tool to boost communication among government agencies, community resources, and America's minority and ethnic groups. The fundamentals are in place for our participation and experience continued growth. This Yearbook illustrates the APA's active presence and as a major contributor in the country's multi-ethnic economy and culture.

FAPAC has been a nationally recognized organization since 1985. FAPAC's mission is to encourage equal opportunity and diversity in the Federal Government through education and recognition of outstanding performance. FAPAC also supports other organizations with the same goal as FAPAC. The annual conference is the flagship of our mission and centers on FAPAC's overall objective, which is:

   Increasing APA participation in government by assisting government agencies in promoting, establishing, and maintaining an effective and equitable participation of APAs in the workforce through education, job fairs, and related events.
   Promoting recognition of APA competencies in the Federal work place. Finding solutions to challenges. Establishing coalitions and good will for APAs in the Federal workforce.
   Training for advancement, leadership and cultural understanding.

FAPAC is the umbrella organization representing the interests of over 130,000 Asian Pacific American (APA) managers and employees in the Federal Government and the Government of the District of Columbia.

I would like to invite TIYM to our 2006 National Leadership Training Conference (NLTC) and Congressional Seminar which will be held in Honolulu, Hawaii from May 8-12, 2006. The NLTC's information is posted on our website at www.fapac.org.

Again, FAPAC congratulates your publication. I also send holiday greetings and best wishes for another successful year ahead.

Linda Tuazon-Miller

Linda Tuazon-Miller
President

The Asian Countries of the World

Country	Area Sq. Km.	Population	Life Expectancy Years	GDP Real Growth (%)	GDP Per Capita	Pop. Below Poverty Line (%)	Unemployment Rate %	Electricity Consumption (kwh) (in thousands)	Exports (in thousands)	Imports (in thousands)
Afghanistan	647,500	29,928,987	42.9	7.5	800	53	NA	652,200	[1] 446,000	3,759,000
Armenia	29,800	2,982,904	71.5	9.0	4,600	50	30.0	5,797,000	850,000	1,300,000
Azerbaijan	86,600	7,911,974	63.3	9.8	3,800	49	1.2	17,370,000	3.168 000	3,622,000
Bahrain	665	688,345	74.2	5.6	19,200	NA	15.0	6,379,000	8.205 000	5,870,000
Bangladesh	144,000	144,319,628	62.0	4.9	2,000	45	40.0	15,300,000	7.478 000	10,030,000
Bhutan	47,000	2,232,291	54.3	5.3	1,400	NA	NA	312,900	154,000	196,000
Brunei	5,770	372,361	74.8	3.2	23,600	NA	3.2	2,286,000	7,700,000	5,200,000
Burma	678,500	42,909,464	60.7	1.3	1,700	25	5.2	3,484,000	2.137 000	1,754,000
Cambodia	181,040	13,607,069	58.9	5.4	2,000	40	2.5	110,600	2.311 000	3,129,000
China	9,596,960	1,306,313,812	72.2	9.1	5,600	10	[2] 9.8	1,630,000,000	583,100,000	552,400,000
Hong Kong	1,092	6,898,686	81.5	7.9	34,200	NA	6.7	38,450,000	268,100,000	275,900,000
Taiwan	35,980	22,894,384	77.2	6.0	25,300	1	4.5	147,400,000	170,500,000	165,400,000
Cyprus (Greek)	5,895	[5] 780133	77.6	3.2	20,300	NA	3.2	3,663,000	1,094,000	5,258,000
Cyprus (Turkish)	3,355	[5] 780133	77.6	2.6	7,135	NA	5.6	602,000	49,300	415,200
East Timor	15,007	1,040,880	65.9	1.0	400	42	50.0	NA	8,000	167,000
Gaza Strip	360	1,376,289	71.7	4.5	600	81	[3] 50.0	NA	[3] 205,000	[3] 1900
Georgia	69,700	4,677,401	75.8	9.5	3,100	54	17.0	6,811,000	909,400	1,806,000
India	3,287,590	1,080,264,388	64.3	6.2	3,100	25	9.2	510,100,000	69,180,000	89,330,000
Indonesia	1,919,440	241,973,879	69.5	4.9	3,500	27	9.2	92,350,000	69,860,000	45,070,000
Iran	1,648,000	68,017,860	69.9	6.3	7,700	40	11.2	119,900,000	38,790,000	31,300,000
Iraq	437,072	26,074,906	68.7	52.3	2,100	NA	25.0	33,700,000	10,100,000	9,900,000
Israel	20,770	6,276,883	79.3	3.9	20,800	18	10.7	38,300,000	34,410,000	36,840,000
Japan	377,835	127,417,244	81.1	2.9	29,400	NA	54.7	971,000,000	538,800,000	401,800,000
Jordan	92,300	5,759,732	78.2	5.1	4,500	30	15.0	7,094,000	3,200,000	7,600,000
Kazakhstan	2,717,300	15,185,844	66.5	9.1	7,800	19	8.0	62,210,000	18,470,000	13,070,000
Korea, North	120,540	22,912,177	71.3	1.0	1,700	NA	NA	31,260,000	1,200,000	2,100,000
Korea, South	98,480	48,422,644	76.8	4.6	19,200	4	3.6	293,600,000	250,600,000	214,200,000
Kuwait	17,820	2,335,648	77.0	6.8	21,300	NA	2.2	30,160,000	22,290,000	11,120,000
Kyrgyzstan	198,500	5,146,281	68.1	6.0	1,700	40	18.0	10,210,000	646,700	775,100
Laos	236,800	6,217,141	55.0	6.0	1,900	40	5.7	3,036,000	365,500	579,500
Lebanon	10,400	3,826,018	72.6	4.0	5,000	28	18.0	8,591,000	1.783 000	8,162,000

Debt External (in thousands)	Telephones, Main Lines in Use	Mobile Telephones	Radio Broadcast Stations	Television Broadcast Stations	Military Expenditures (in thousands)	Inflation % (consumer)	Labor Force	Railways Km.	Country
[9] 8,000,000	33,100	15,000	45	10	188,400	10.3	11,800,000	NA	Afghanistan
905,000	562,600	114,400	16	3	135,000	3.5	1,400,000	845	Armenia
1,832,000	923,800	870,000	28	2	121,000	4.6	5,090,000	2,957	Azerbaijan
6,215,000	185,800	443,100	5	4	628,900	2.1	370,000	NA	Bahrain
19,970,000	740,000	1,365,000	26	15	995,300	6.0	65,490,000	2,706	Bangladesh
245,000	25,200	22,000	2	1	13,700	3.0	[6] NA	NA	Bhutan
0	90,000	137,000	13	2	290,700	0.3	[7] 158,000	NA	Brunei
6,752,000	357,300	66,500	2	2	39,000	17.2	27,010,000	3,955	Burma
2,400,000	35,400	380,000	19	7	112,000	3.1	7,000,000	602	Cambodia
233,300,000	263,000,000	269,000,000	673	3,240	67,490,000	4.1	760,800,000	71,898	China
233,300,000	3,801,300	7,241,400	14	4	[10] NA	-0.3	3,540,000	NA	Hong Kong
55,500,000	13,355,000	25,089,600	601	29	7.574 000	1.7	10,220,000	2,497	Taiwan
8,850,000	427,400	417,900	68	4	[5] 384,000	2.4	330,000	NA	Cyprus (Greek)
7,327,000	86,228	143,178	15	4	[5] 384,000	12.6	95,025	NA	Cyprus (Turkish)
NA	NA	NA	NA	NA	4,400	4.0	NA	NA	East Timor
[3] 108,000	[3] 95,729	[3] 320,000	0	2	NA	[3] 2.2	725,000	NA	Gaza Strip
1,800,000	650,500	522,300	23	12	23,000	5.5	2,100,000	1,612	Georgia
117,200,000	48,917,000	26,154,400	312	562	18,860,000	4.2	482,200,000	63,230	India
141,500,000	7,750,000	11,700,000	803	41	1,300,000	6.1	111,500,000	6,458	Indonesia
13,400,000	14,571,100	3,376,500	82	28	4,300,000	15.5	23,000,000	7,203	Iran
125,000,000	[11] 675,000	20,000	[12] 80	21	1,300,000	25.4	6,700,000	2,200	Iraq
74,460,000	3,006,000	6,334,000	40	17	9,110,000	0.0	2,680,000	640	Israel
NA	71,149,000	86,658,600	325	211	45,841,000	-0.3	66,970,000	23,577	Japan
7,320,000	622,600	1,325,300	12	20	1,460,000	3.2	1,410,000	505	Jordan
26,030,000	2,081,900	1,027,000	86	12	221,800	6.9	7,950,000	13,700	Kazakhstan
12,000,000	1,100,000	NA	45	4	5,217,400	NA	9,600,000	5,214	Korea, North
160,000,000	22,877,000	33,591,800	210	64	20,000,000	3.6	22,920,000	3,472	Korea, South
15,020,000	486,900	1,420,000	18	13	2,585	2.3	1,420,000	NA	Kuwait
1,970,000	394,800	53,100	28	NA	19,200	3.2	2,700,000	470	Kyrgyzstan
2,490,000	61,900	55,200	17	4	10,700	12.3	2,600,000	NA	Laos
15,840,000	678,800	775,100	46	15	541,000	2.0	[8] 2,600,000	401	Lebanon

Country	Area Sq. Km.	Population	Life Expectancy Years	GDP Real Growth (%)	GDP Per Capita	Pop. Below Poverty Line (%)	Unemployment Rate %	Electricity Consumption (kwh) (in thousands)	Exports (in thousands)	Imports (in thousands)
Malaysia	329,750	23,953,136	72.2	7.1	9,700	8.0	3.0	68,400,000	123,500,000	99,300,000
Maldives	300	349,106	64.0	2.3	3,900	NA	NA	115,700	90,000	392,000
Mongolia	1,564,116	2,791,272	64.5	10.6	1,900	36.1	6.7	2,209,000	853,000	1,000,000
Nepal	140,800	27,676,547	59.8	3.0	1,500	42.0	47.0	2,005,000	568,000	1,419,000
Oman	212,460	3,001,583	73.1	1.2	13,100	NA	15.0	9,792,000	13,140,000	6,373,000
Pakistan	803,940	162,419,946	63.0	6.1	2,200	32.0	8.3	52,660,000	15,070,000	14,010,000
Papua New Guinea	462,840	5,545,268	64.9	0.9	2,200	37.0	NA	1,561,000	2,437,000	1,353,000
Philippines	300,000	87,857,473	69.9	5.9	5,000	40.0	11.7	46,050,000	38,630,000	37,500,000
Qatar	11,437	863,051	73.6	8.7	23,200	NA	2.7	9,046,000	15,000,000	6,150,000
Russia	17,075,200	143,420,309	67.1	6.7	9,800	25.0	8.3	894,300,000	162,500,000	92,910,000
Saudi Arabia	1,960,582	26,417,599	75.4	5.0	12,000	NA	25.0	128,500,000	113,000,000	36,210,000
Singapore	692.7	4,425,720	81.6	8.1	27,800	NA	3.4	32,000,000	174,000,000	155,200,000
Sri Lanka	65,610	20,064,776	73.1	5.2	4,000	22.0	7.8	6,228,000	5,306,000	7,265,000
Syria	185,180	18,448,752	70.0	2.3	3,400	20.0	20.0	24,320,000	6,086,000	5,042,000
Tajikistan	143,100	7,163,506	64.5	10.5	1,100	60.0	40.0	14,410,000	1,130,000	1,300,000
Thailand	514,000	65,444,371	71.9	6.1	8,100	10.0	1.5	106,100,000	87,910,000	80,840,000
Turkey	780,580	69,660,559	72.3	8.2	7,400	20.0	[4] 9.3	117,900,000	69,460,000	94,500,000
Turkmenistan	488,100	4,952,081	61.3	20.0	5,700	58.0	60.0	8,908,000	4,000,000	2,850,000
United Arab Em.	82,880	2,563,212	75.2	5.7	25,200	NA	2.4	36,510,000	69,480,000	45,660,000
Uzbekistan	447,400	26,851,195	64.1	4.4	1,800	28.0	0.6	46,660,000	3,700,000	2,820,000
Vietnam	329,560	83,535,576	70.6	7.7	2,700	28.9	1.9	32,060,000	23,720,000	26,310,000
West Bank	5,860	2,385,615	73.0	6.0	800	59.0	[4] 27.2	NA	[4] 205,000	[4] 1,500,000
Yemen	527,970	20,727,063	61.7	1.9	800	45.2	35.0	2,827,000	4,468,000	3,734,000

Debt External (in thousands)	Telephones, Main Lines in Use	Mobile Telephones	Radio Broadcast Stations	Television Broadcast Stations	Military Expenditures (in thousands)	Inflation % (consumer)	Labor Force	Railways Km.	Country
53,360,000	4,571,600	11,124,100	441	1	1,690,000	1.3	10,490,000	1,890	Malaysia
281,000	28,700	41,900	3	1	41,100	1.0	88,000	NA	Maldives
1,191,000	142,300	404,400	72	52	23,100	11.0	1,488,000	1,810	Mongolia
2,700,000	371,800	50,400	12	1	99,200	2.9	[15] 10,000,000	59	Nepal
4,814,000	233,900	464,900	14	13	252,990	-0.3	920,000	NA	Oman
33,970,000	3,982,800	2,624,800	49	22	3,848,000	4.8	45,430,000	8,163	Pakistan
2,463,000	62,000	15,000	55	3	16,900	4.2	3,320,000	NA	Papua New Guinea
55,600,000	3,310,900	15,201,000	957	225	805,500	5.5	35,860,000	897	Philippines
18,620,000	184,500	376,500	12	1	723,000	3.0	140,000	NA	Qatar
169,600,000	35,500,000	17,608,800	923	7,306	NA	11.5	71,830,000	87,157	Russia
34,350,000	3,502,600	7,238,200	76	117	18,000,000	0.8	6,620,000	1,392	Saudi Arabia
19,400,000	1,896,100	35,218,000	19	7	4,470,000	1.7	2,180,000	NA	Singapore
10,850,000	881,400	931,600	72	21	514,800	5.8	7,260,000	1,449	Sri Lanka
4,000,000	2,099,300	400,000	17	44	858,000	2.1	5,120,000	2,711	Syria
888,000	242,100	47,600	20	13	35,400	8.0	3,187,000	482	Tajikistan
50,590,000	6,617,400	26,500,000	544	5	1,775,000	2.8	36,430,000	4,071	Thailand
16,900,000	18,916,700	27,887,500	129	635	12,155,000	9.3	25,300,000	8,697	Turkey
2,400,000	374,000	52,000	26	4	90,000	9.0	2,320,000	2,440	Turkmenistan
5,900,000	1,135,800	29,723,000	23	15	1,600,000	3.2	2,360,000	NA	United Arab Em.
4,351,000	1,717,100	3,208,000	37	4	200,000	3.0	14,640,000	3,950	Uzbekistan
16,550,000	4,402,000	2,742,000	101	7	650,000	9.5	42,980,000	2,600	Vietnam
[4] 108,000	[4] 301,600	[4] 480,000	1	NA	NA	[4] 2.2	364,000	NA	West Bank
5,400,000	542,200	411,100	9	7	885,500	12.2	5,980,000	NA	Yemen

(1) Not including illicit exports.
(2) Substantial unemployment and underemployment in rural areas.
(3) Includes West Bank.
(4) Includes Gaza Strip.
(5) Turkish and Greek areas combined.
(6) Massive lack of skilled labor.
(7) Includes foreign workers and military personnel; temporary residents make up about 40% of labor force.
(8) In addition, there are as many as 1 million foreign workers.
(9) $8 billion in bilateral debt, mostly to Russia; Afghanistan has $500 million in debt to Multilateral Development Banks.
(10) Hong Kong garrison is funded by China.
(11) An unknown number of telephone lines were damaged or destroyed during the March-April 2003 war.
(12) After 17 months of unregulated media growth, there are approximately 80 radio stations on the air inside Iraq
(13) The Palestinian Broadcasting Corporation broadcasts from an AM station in Ramallah on 675 kHz; numerous local, private stations are reported to be in operation.
(14) Extensive export of labor to Saudi Arabia, Kuwait, UAE, Oman, Qatar, and Malaysia; workers' remittances estimated at $1.71 billion in 1998-99.
(15) Severe lack of skilled labor.
(16) Multiple track not included in total.

Abbreviations:
GDP: Gross Domestic Product.

Source: Central Intelligence Agency. The World Factbook 2005, Internet edition. http://www.cia.gov/cia/publications/factbook/

Country	Irrigated Land Sq. Km.	Pop. Growth %	Birth Rate	Death Rate	Literacy	Government Type	Capital	Independence
Afghanistan	23,860	(9)4.77	47.0	20.7	36.0	Transitional	Kabul	August 19, 1919
Armenia	2,870	-0.2	11.7	8.1	98.6	Republic	Yerevan	September 21, 1991
Azerbaijan	14,550	0.5	20.4	9.8	98.8	Republic	Baku	August 30, 1991
Bahrain	50	1.5	18.1	4.0	89.1	Const. Hereditary Monarchy	Manama	August 15, 1971
Bangladesh	38,440	2.0	30.0	8.4	43.1	Parliamentary Democracy	Dhaka	December 16, 1971
Bhutan	400	2.1	34.0	12.9	42.2	Monarchy	Thimphu	August 8, 1949
Brunei	10	1.9	19.0	3.4	93.9	Constitutional Sultanate	Bandar Seri Begawan	January 1, 1984
Burma	15,920	0.4	18.1	12.1	85.3	Military Regime	Rangoon	January 4, 1948
Cambodia	2,700	1.8	27.0	8.9	73.6	Multiparty Democracy	Phnom Penh	November 9, 1953
China	525,800	0.5	13.1	6.9	90.9	Communist State	Beijing	(2)221 BC/1 Oct. 1949
Hong Kong	20	0.6	7.2	5.9	93.5	Limited Democracy	-	None
Taiwan	NA	0.6	12.6	6.3	96.1	Multiparty Democracy Regime	Taipei	January 8, 1904
Cyprus (Greek)	(1)382	0.5	12.5	7.6	97.6	Republic	Nicosia	(3)16 August 1960
Cyprus (Turkish)	(1)382	0.5	12.5	7.6	97.6	Republic	Nicosia	(3)16 August 1960
East Timor	1,065	2.0	27.1	6.3	58.6	Republic	Dili	(4)28 November 1975
Gaza Strip	120	3.7	40.0	3.8	91.9	-	-	-
Georgia	4,700	-0.3	10.2	9.0	99.0	Republic	T'bilisi	April 9, 1991
India	590,000	1.4	22.3	8.2	59.5	Federal Republic	New Delhi	August 15, 1947
Indonesia	48,150	1.4	20.7	6.2	87.9	Republic	Jakarta	August 17, 1945
Iran	75,620	0.8	16.8	5.5	79.4	Theocratic Republic	Tehran	April 1, 1979
Iraq	35,250	2.7	32.5	5.4	40.4	Transitional	Baghdad	October 3, 1932
Israel	1,990	1.2	18.2	6.1	95.4	Parliamentary Democracy	Jerusalem	May 14, 1948
Japan	26,790	0.0	9.4	8.9	99.0	Const. Monarchy w/Parliament	Tokyo	660 BC
Jordan	750	2.5	21.7	2.6	91.3	Constitutional Monarchy	Amman	May 25, 1946
Kazakhstan	23,320	0.3	15.7	9.4	98.4	Republic	Astana	December 16, 1991
Korea, North	14,600	0.9	16.0	7.0	99.0	Communist State	Pyongyang	August 15, 1945
Korea, South	11,590	0.3	10.0	6.2	97.9	Republic	Seoul	August 15, 1945
Kuwait	60	(10)3.44	21.8	2.4	83.5	Nominal Const. Monarchy	Kuwait	June 19, 1961
Kyrgyzstan	10,740	1.2	22.4	7.1	98.7	Republic	Bishkek	August 31, 1991
Laos	(8)1640	2.4	35.9	11.8	66.4	Communist State	Vientiane	July 19, 1949
Lebanon	1,200	1.2	18.8	6.2	87.4	Republic	Beirut	November 22, 1943

National Holiday	GDP (in thousands)	Electricity Production (in thousands)	Currency	Currency Code	Internet Country Code	Internet Users	Total Fertility Rate	Country
Independence Day	21,500,000	540,000	afghani	AFA	.af	1,000	6.7	**Afghanistan**
Independence Day	13,650,000	6,492,000	dram	AMD	.am	150,000	1.3	**Armenia**
Founding Day	30,010,000	17,550,000	Azerbaijani manat	AZM	.az	300,000	2.4	**Azerbaijan**
National Day	13,010,000	6,860,000	Bahraini dinar	BHD	.bh	195,700	2.6	**Bahrain**
Independence Day	275,700,000	16,450,000	taka	BDT	.bd	243,000	3.1	**Bangladesh**
National Day	2,900,000	2,001,000	ngultrum/Indian rupee	BTN/INR	.bt	15,000	4.8	**Bhutan**
National Day	6,842,000	2,458,000	Bruneian dollar	BND	.bn	35,000	2.3	**Brunei**
Independence Day	74,300,000	5,068,000	kyat	MMK	.mm	28,000	2.0	**Burma**
Independence Day	26,990,000	122,000	riel	KHR	.kh	30,000	3.4	**Cambodia**
Anniv. of Founding Day	7,262,000,000	1,910,000,000	yuan	CNY	.cn	94,000,000	1.7	**China**
National Day	234,500,000	35,510,000	Hong Kong dollar	HKD	.hk	3,212,800	0.9	**Hong Kong**
Republic Day	576,200,000	158,500,000	new Taiwan dollar	TWD	.tw	13,800,000	1.5	**Taiwan**
Independence Day	15,710,000	4,000,000	Cypriot pound	CYP	.cy	(1) 210,000	1.8	**Cyprus (Greek)**
Independence Day	4,540,000	NA	Turkish lira	TRL	.cy	(1) 210,000	1.8	**Cyprus (Turkish)**
Independence Day	370,000	NA	US dollar	USD	.tl	NA	3.6	**East Timor**
-	768,000	NA	new Israeli shekel	ILS	.ps	(5) 145,000	5.9	**Gaza Strip**
Independence Day	14,450,000	6,732,000	lari	GEL	.ge	150,500	1.4	**Georgia**
Republic Day	3,319,000,000	547,200,000	Indian rupee	INR	.in	18,481,000	2.7	**India**
Independence Day	827,400,000	110,200,000	Indonesian rupiah	IDR	.id	8,000,000	2.4	**Indonesia**
Republic Day	516,700,000	129,000,000	Iranian rial	IRR	.ir	4,300,000	1.8	**Iran**
Revolution Day	54,400,000	32,600,000	New Iraqui dinar	NID	.iq	25,000	4.2	**Iraq**
Independence Day	129,000,000	42,670,000	new Israeli shekel	ILS	.il	2,000,000	2.4	**Israel**
Birthday of Emperor	3,745,000,000	1,044,000,000	yen	JPY	.jp	57,200,000	1.3	**Japan**
Independence Day	25,500,000	7,307,000	Jordanian dinar	JOD	.jo	457,000	2.7	**Jordan**
Republic Day	118,400,000	66,820,000	tenge	KZT	.kz	250,000	1.8	**Kazakhstan**
Founding Day	40,000,000	33,620,000	N. Korean won	KPW	.kp	NA	2.1	**Korea, North**
Liberation Day	925,100,000	322,500,000	S. Korean won	KRW	.kr	29,220,000	1.2	**Korea, South**
National Day	48,000,000	32,430,000	Kuwaiti dinar	KD	.kw	567,000	2.9	**Kuwait**
Independence Day	8,495,000	11,720,000	Kurgyzstani som	KGS	.kg	152,000	2.7	**Kyrgyzstan**
Republic Day	11,280,000	3,560,000	kip	LAK	.la	15,000	4.7	**Laos**
Independence Day	18,830,000	8,066,000	Lebanese pound	LBP	.lb	400,000	1.9	**Lebanon**

Country	Irrigated Land Sq. Km.	Pop. Growth %	Birth Rate	Death Rate	Literacy	Government Type	Capital	Independence
Malaysia	3,650	1.8	23.0	5.0	88.7	Constitutional Monarchy	Kuala Lumpur	August 31, 1957
Maldives	NA	2.8	35.4	7.2	97.2	Republic	Male	July 26, 1965
Mongolia	840	1.4	21.5	7.0	97.8	Parliamentary	Ulaanbaatar	July 11, 1921
Nepal	11,350	2.2	31.4	9.4	45.2	Const. Monarchy/Par. Democracy	Kathmandu	November 3, 1908
Oman	620	3.3	36.7	3.8	75.8	Monarchy	Muscat	July 8, 1908
Pakistan	180,000	2.0	30.4	8.4	48.7	Federal Republic	Islamabad	August 14, 1947
Papua New Guinea	NA	2.2	29.9	7.3	64.6	Const. Monarchy/Par. Democracy	Port Moresby	September 16, 1975
Philippines	15,500	1.8	25.3	5.4	92.6	Republic	Manila	June 12, 1898
Qatar	130	2.6	15.5	4.6	89.0	Traditional Monarchy	Doha	September 3, 1971
Russia	46,630	-0.3	9.8	14.5	99.6	Federation	Moscow	August 24, 1991
Saudi Arabia	16,200	2.3	29.5	2.6	78.8	Monarchy	Riyadh	September 23, 1932
Singapore	NA	1.5	9.4	4.1	92.5	Parliamentary Republic	Singapore	August 9, 1965
Sri Lanka	6,510	0.7	15.6	6.4	92.3	Republic	Colombo	February 4, 1948
Syria	12,130	2.3	28.2	4.8	76.9	Republic/Military Regime	Damascus	April 17, 1946
Tajikistan	7,200	2.1	32.5	8.3	99.4	Republic	Dushanbe	September 9, 1991
Thailand	47,490	0.8	15.7	7.0	92.6	Const. Monarchy	Bangkok	[7]1238
Turkey	42,000	1.0	16.8	5.9	86.5	Rep. Parliamentary Democracy	Ankara	October 29, 1923
Turkmenistan	17,500	1.8	27.6	8.7	98.8	Republic	Ashgabat	October 27, 1991
United Arab Em.	720	1.5	18.7	4.2	77.9	Federation	Abu Dhabi	December 2, 1971
Uzbekistan	42,810	1.6	26.2	7.9	99.3	Republic	Tashkent	September 1, 1991
Vietnam	30,000	1.0	17.0	6.2	90.3	Communist State	Hanoi	September 2, 1945
West Bank	NA	3.1	32.3	3.9	91.9	-	-	-
Yemen	4,900	3.4	43.0	8.5	50.2	Republic	Sanaa	[6]May 22, 1990

National Holiday	GDP (in thousands)	Electricity Production (in thousands)	Currency	Currency Code	Internet Country Code	Internet Users	Total Fertility Rate	Country
Independence Day	229,300,000	75,330,000	ringgit	MYR	.my	8,692,100	3.0	**Malaysia**
Independence Day	1,250,000	124,400	rufiyaa	MVR	.mv	15,000	5.0	**Maldives**
Independence Day	5,332,000	2,692,000	togrog/tugrik	MNT	.mn	220,000	2.2	**Mongolia**
Birthday of King	39,530,000	2,054,000	Nepalese rupee	NPR	.np	80,000	4.1	**Nepal**
Birthday of Sultan	38,090,000	9,896,000	Omani real	OMR	.om	180,000	5.8	**Oman**
Republic Day	347,300,000	75,270,000	Pakistani rupee	PKR	.pk	1,500,000	4.1	**Pakistan**
Independence Day	11,990,000	1,679,000	kina	PGK	.pg	75,000	3.9	**Papua New Guinea**
Independence Day	430,600,000	52,860,000	Philippine peso	PHP	.ph	3,500,000	3.1	**Philippines**
Independence Day	19,490,000	9,727,000	Qatari rial	QAR	.qa	126,000	2.8	**Qatar**
Russia Day	1,408,000,000	915,000,000	Russian ruble	RUR	.ru/.su	6,000,000	1.2	**Russia**
Unif. of the Kingdom	310,200,000	138,200,000	Saudi riyal	SAR	.sa	1,500,000	4.0	**Saudi Arabia**
Independence Day	120,900,000	35,330,000	Singapore dollar	SGD	.sg	2,310,000	1.0	**Singapore**
Independence Day	80,580,000	6,697,000	Sri Lankan rupee	LKR	.lk	200,000	1.8	**Sri Lanka**
Independence Day	60,440,000	26,150,000	Syrian pound	SYP	.sy	220,000	3.5	**Syria**
Independence Day	7,950,000	15,080,000	somoni	TJS	.tj	4,100	4.0	**Tajikistan**
Birthday of King	524,800,000	118,900,000	baht	THB	.th	6,971,500	1.8	**Thailand**
Independence Day	508,700,000	139,700,000	New Turkish lira	YTL	.tr	5,500,000	1.9	**Turkey**
Independence Day	27,600,000	11,410,000	Turkmen manat	TMM	.tm	8,000	3.4	**Turkmenistan**
Independence Day	63,670,000	45,120,000	Emirati dirham	AED	.ae	1,110,200	2.9	**United Arab Em.**
Independence Day	47,590,000	47,700,000	Uzbekistani sum	UZS	.uz	492,000	2.9	**Uzbekistan**
Independence Day	227,200,000	34,480,000	dong	VND	.vn	3,500,000	1.9	**Vietnam**
-	1,800,000	(11)NA	new Israeli shekel/Jordanian dinar	ILS/JOD	.ps	(5) 145,000	4.4	**West Bank**
Unification Day	16,250,000	3,040,000	Yemeni rial	YER	.ye	100,000	6.6	**Yemen**

(1) Turkish and Greek areas combined.
(2) 221 BC (unification under the Qin or Ch'in Dynasty 221 BC; Qing or Ch'ing Dynasty replaced by the Republic on 12 February 1912; People's Republic established 1 October 1949).
(3) 16 August 1960 (from UK); Turkish Cypriot area proclaimed self-rule on 13 February 1975.
(4) 28 November 1975 (date of proclamation of independence from Portugal); 20 May 2002 is the official date of international recognition of East Timor's independence from Indonesia.
(5) Gaza Strip and West Bank.
(6) 22 May 1990, Republic of Yemen was established with the merger of the Yemen Arab Republic (Yemen) (Sanaa or North Yemen) and the Marxist-dominated People's Democratic Republic of Yemen (Yemen) (Aden or South Yemen); previously North Yemen had become independent on November 1918 (from the Ottoman Empire) and South Yemen had become independent on 30 November 1967 (from the UK).
(7) Traditional founding date, never colonized.
(8) Rainy season irrigation - 2,169 sq km; dry season irrigation - 750 sq km.
(9) This rate does not take into consideration the recent war and its continuing impact.
(10) This rate reflects a return to pre-Gulf crisis immigration of expatriates.
(11) Most electricity imported from Israel; East Jerusalem Electric Company buys and distributes electricity to Palestinians in East Jerusalem and its concession in the West Bank; the Israel Electric Company directly supplies electricity to most Jewish residents and military facilities; some Palestinian municipalities, such as Nablus and Janin, generate their own electricity from small power plants.

Abbreviations:
GDP: Gross Domestic Product.

Source: Central Intelligence Agency. The World Factbook 2005, Internet edition. http://www.cia.gov/cia/publications/factbook/

A Message From General Schoomaker, United States Army
For the TIYM 2006 Asian-American Yearbook

America is proud of its cultural and ethnic mix and has benefited from each group's contributions. Publications like this Yearbook help raise the awareness of the contributions of Asian-Americans in our Nation's history, while highlighting opportunities for personal and professional growth.

As an institution that embraces its diverse background, the Army salutes the Asian-American Soldiers that have honorably served our Nation. Their contributions include the heroic efforts of the Japanese-American 100th Infantry Battalion and the 442nd Regimental Combat Team in World War II, and the appointment of the 34th, and first Asian-American, Chief of Staff, Army—General Eric Shinseki.

While diversity in our force fosters creativity and new ideas, the Army aspires to one set of unifying ideals--the seven Army Values of loyalty, duty, respect, selfless service, honor, integrity and personal courage. As we fight the war on terror, Soldiers of all religions, races, and creeds are now sacrificing to ensure the blessings of freedom for people around the world and to preserve America's limitless opportunities. Embodying the essence of our Nation, our Soldiers stand strongly together so that people around the world may benefit.

Thank you to TIYM Publishing Company for your continued programs to promote racial equality and for providing a comprehensive tool to serve members of diverse communities.

Sincerely,

Peter J. Schoomaker
General, United States Army

CHIEF OF NAVAL OPERATIONS

TO ANGELA ZAVALA AND THE TEAM AT TIYM PUBLISHING

It is with great pleasure that I extend congratulations to you on the 20th anniversary of your publishing enterprise. Through hard work and diligence you have etched an indelible mark upon the African American, Hispanic, and Asian American communities by producing a quality resource. Your yearbooks not only inform and educate, but also strengthen and elevate the cause of diversity.

The value of diversity to the nation has always been important, perhaps more now than at any point in our history. The rapidly changing global economy requires us all to embrace people with different perspectives, backgrounds, and experiences in order to remain competitive. For our part, the Navy is making a concerted effort to seek out, challenge, and develop leaders from---and for---all parts of our great country. The Navy recognizes that diversity strengthens us as evidenced by the tremendous contributions of people like 1915 Medal of Honor recipient Fireman 1st Class Telesforo Trinidad, an Asian Pacific American who demonstrated extraordinary heroism despite severe personal injuries. Modern day achievers include Rear Admiral Cecil D. Haney, an African American submarine officer serving as Deputy Chief of Staff for Policy, Plans, and Requirements for the U.S. Pacific Fleet, and Captain Kathlene Contres, the highest ranking Latina on active duty in the United States Navy and who was selected to become Commandant of the Defense Equal Opportunity Management Institute, a joint service school.

These pioneers and so many others have shown us that like the motto engraved upon our coins--- *e pluribus unum* ---our rich diversity serves to truly strengthen the fabric of our nation, and bolsters our values of faith, freedom, family, work and country. They have taught us that while accommodating diversity is essential to ensure every citizen has the opportunity to excel, we gain so much more when we genuinely embrace and invest in the broad talents of all our people. Your yearbooks do a great service by highlighting those talents.

Again, congratulations on 20 terrific years. It is indicative of the esteem in which your company is held and the value accorded to your publications that you have not only survived in a highly competitive industry, but thrived. I wish you and your staff my very best and look forward to seeing you succeed for many years to come.

Sincerely,

M. G. MULLEN
Admiral, U. S. Navy

Asian Pacific American
U.S. Senators

DANIEL KAHIKINA AKAKA
U.S. Senator, Hawaii (D)

Senator Akaka was first elected to Congress in 1976 to represent Hawaii's Second Congressional District. He won seven consecutive elections by wide margins. He has served in the United States Senate since 1990. Senator Akaka handily won a spirited special election in November 1990 to complete the unexpired four-year term of the late Senator Spark M. Matsunaga. Elected to a six-year term in 1994, he was reelected in November 2000 with over 70 percent of the popular vote.

Senator Akaka serves on the Armed Services, Energy and Natural Resources, Governmental Affairs (GAC), Veterans' Affairs, and Indian Affairs committees. He is also a member of the Select Committee on Ethics. He is the first U.S. Senator of Native Hawaiian ancestry and is the only Chinese American member of the Senate. He is chairman of the Hawaii Congressional Task Force on Native Hawaiian Issues that is working to address longstanding issues concerning the relationship between Native Hawaiians and the United States.

On the Energy and Natural Resources Committee, Senator Akaka is a leader in renewable energy research and development; park and wildlife issues, tropical agriculture and coral reef conservation, ocean sciences and technology, aquaculture research, and marine protection and environmental preservation. Senator Akaka is Ranking Member on the Subcommittee on National Parks. In his assignment on the Armed Services Committee, and as Ranking Member of the Readiness and Management Support Subcommittee, Senator Akaka aims to continue Hawaii's excellent relationship with the military, and works with the Defense Department to meet our nation's security interests in the Pacific and around the world.

DANIEL K. INOUYE
U.S. Senator, Hawaii (D)

Daniel K. Inouye, the third most senior member of the U.S. Senate, is known for his distinguished record as a legislative leader, and as a World War II combat veteran who earned the nation's highest award for military valor, the Medal of Honor.

As the ranking Democrat on the Senate Defense Appropriations Subcommittee, Senator Inouye has been able to focus on defense matters that strengthen national security, and enhance the quality of life for military personnel and their families. This reflects his hope for a more secure world, and his desire to provide the best possible assistance to the men and women who put their lives at risk to protect the United States.

Senator Inouye has also championed the interests of Hawaii's people throughout his career. He was instrumental in engineering the restoration and return of Kahoolawe, the island that had been used for target practice by the U.S. military, to the State of Hawaii.

Senator Inouye was first elected to the U.S. Senate in 1962 and is now serving his eighth consecutive term. When Hawaii became a state in 1959, he was elected the first Congressman from the new state, and was re-elected to a full term in 1960.

The son of Japanese immigrants, Dan Inouye was born and raised in Honolulu. Exactly three months after he had celebrated his 17th birthday, the Japanese attacked Pearl Harbor on December 7, 1941. Young Dan Inouye, who had medical aid training, rushed into

service as the head of a first-aid litter team. He saw a "lot of blood."

After losing his right arm, Dan Inouye spent 20 months in an Army hospital in Battle Creek, Michigan. On May 27, 1947, he was honorably discharged with the rank of Captain, and returned home with a Distinguished Service Cross, the nation's second highest award for military valor, along with a Bronze Star, Purple Heart with cluster, and 12 other medals and citations.

His Distinguished Service Cross was upgraded to the Medal of Honor, and that medal was presented to him by the President of the United States on June 21, 2000.

DEPARTMENTS OF THE ARMY AND THE AIR FORCE
NATIONAL GUARD BUREAU
1411 JEFFERSON DAVIS HIGHWAY
ARLINGTON VA 22202-3231

A MESSAGE FROM THE DIRECTOR OF THE AIR NATIONAL GUARD

Embracing diversity at all levels in our organization will be the key to our success. We must continue to build upon a strong foundation, which entails vision, and demonstrated commitment from the Air National Guard's senior leadership.   We must continue to win the war for talent by aggressively recruiting and retaining a high-quality military and civilian workforce that reflects the diverse talents of our citizenry, within key critical occupational skills.

In today's world of multiple priorities and taskings, and doing more with less, it is easy to be involved in activities that don't result in enhancing performance. The ANG diversity concept is a way of thinking that suggests if the ANG is to truly become a diverse organization it must do business differently. As such, our diversity philosophy seeks to re-clarify the roles of the major components of the ANG Diversity Initiative, develop a sound strategy for success, and create a web based measuring tool that indicates the level of goal attainment.

The Air National Guard's concept on diversity embraces the idea that it is critical to see the world, organizations, teams, and individuals as they truly are; complex, constantly adapting living systems that defy easy categorization. Being able to see the organization as it truly is provides agents the ability to navigate the environment in a more effective way. Additionally, collective collaboration between interested groups and enlightened guidance by ANG senior leadership can provide a sincere path toward effective objective achievement.

By thinking strategically about diversity and culture transformation, we can articulate, demonstrate, and detail the ANG commitment to achieving full participation to achieve the highest quality total defense and readiness: "Ready, Reliable, Relevant – Needed Now and in the Future". This strategy affirms our commitment to being at the vanguard of protecting and defending our communities, states and nation.

The Air National Guard's civilian and military personnel join me in congratulating your publication. I also send holiday greetings and best wishes for another successful milestone in your storied history. Establishing a climate that embraces diversity is a strategic goal the Air National Guard can not afford to miss. I invite you to learn more about the climate and transformation of our Air Guard at: http://angdiversity.ang.af.mil/home/index.asp.

Sincerely,

DANIEL JAMES III
Lieutenant General, USAF
Director, Air National Guard

Asian Pacific American Federal Officials and Presidential Appointees

AMERICAN SAMOA
Congressman Eni F.H. Faleomavaega
Washington, DC Office
2422 Rayburn House Office Bldg.
Washington, DC 20515
Tel: (202) 225-8577 Fax: (202) 225-8757
Email: faleomavaega@mail.house.gov
Web: www.house.gov/faleomavaega

Pago Pago Office
P.O. Drawer X
Executive Office Bldg., 1st Fl., Utulei, AS
Pago Pago, AS 96799
Tel: (684) 633-1372 Fax: (684) 633-2680
Email: faleomavaega@mail.house.gov
Web: www.house.gov/faleomavaega

CALIFORNIA
Congressman Mike Honda
California-15th District
Washington, DC Office
1713 Longworth House Office Bldg.
Washington, DC 20515
Tel: (202) 225-2631 Fax: (202) 225-2699
Email: mike.honda@mail.house.gov
Web: www.house.gov/honda

Campbell Office
1999 S. Bascom Ave. #815
Campbell, CA 95008
Tel: (408) 558-8085 Fax: (408) 558-8086
Email: mike.honda@mail.house.gov
Web: www.house.gov/honda

Congresswoman Doris Matsui
California-5th District
Washington DC Office
2310 Rayburn HOB
Washington , DC 20515-0505
Tel: (202) 225-7163 Fax: (202) 225-0566
Web: www.matsui.house.gov

Sacramento Office
501 I Street, Suite 12-600
Sacramento, CA 95814-7305
Tel: (916) 498-5600 Fax: (916) 444-6117
Web: www.matsui.house.gov

OREGON
Congressman David Wu
Oregon-1st District
Washington, DC Office
1023 Longworth House Office Bldg.
Washington, DC 20515
Tel: (202) 225-0855 Fax: (202) 225-9497
Web: www.house.gov/wu

Portland Office
620 SW Main St. #606
Portland , OR 97205

Tel: (503) 326-2901 Fax: (503) 326-5066
Web: www.house.gov/wu

VIRGINIA
Congressman Robert C. "Bobby" Scott
Virginia 3rdDistrict
Washington Office
1201 Longworth HOB
Washington , DC 20515
Tel: (202) 225-8351 Fax: (202) 225-8354
Email: bobby.scott@mail.house.gov
Web: www.house.gov/scott/

New Port Office
2600 Washington Ave Suite 1010
New Port News , VA 23607
Tel: (757) 380-1000 Fax: (757) 928-6694
Email: bobby.scott@mail.house.gov
Web: www.house.gov/scott/

Richmond Office
The Jackson Center, 501 N 2nd St. #401
Richmond, VA 23219-1321
Tel: (804) 644-4845 Fax: (804) 648-6026
Email: bobby.scott@mail.house.gov
Web: www.house.gov/scott/

Norfolk Office
700 Park Avenue Norfolk State University
Harrison B. Wilson Administration Building
2nd Floor Conference Room
Norfolk, VA 23504
Email: bobby.scott@mail.house.gov
Web: www.house.gov/scott/

Walter Liang, Regional Administrator
Labor, US Dept. of
Region X
1111 3rd Ave. #920
Seattle , WA 98101
Tel: (206) 553-0574 Fax: (206) 553-2086
Web: www.dol.gov

Bj Gorgen, Executive Assistant to the Senior Advisor to the President
The White House
Washington, DC 20520
Tel: (202) 456-1414
Web: www.whitehouse.gov

Edmund Moy, Special Assistant to the President/Associate Director of Presidential Personnel
The White House
Washington, DC 20520
Tel: (202) 456-1414
Web: www.whitehouse.gov

Catherine Martin, Assistant to the Vice President/Staff Secretary
The White House
Office of the Vice President
The White House
Washington, DC 20520
Tel: (202) 456-1414
Web: www.whitehouse.gov

Lisa Walsh, Acting Associate Director
The White House
White House Fellows Program
1900 E. St. NW #B-431
Washington, DC 20415
Tel: (202) 395-4522 Fax: (202) 395-6179
Web: www.whitehouse.gov/fellows

Debra W.Yang, US Attorney
Justice, US Dept. of
US Attorney's Office
312 N. Spring St. NW #1200
Los Angeles, CA 90012
Tel: (213) 894-2434 Fax: (213) 894-0141
Web: www.usdoj.gov/usao/cac

Carol Chien-Hua Lam, US Attorney
Justice, US Dept. of
US Attorney's Office
Federal Office Bldg., 880 Front St. #6293
San Diego, CA 92101-8893
Tel: (619) 557-5610 Fax: (619) 557-5551
Web: www.usdoj.gov/usao/cas

Phyllis Fong, Inspector General
Agriculture, US Dept. of
Office of Inspector General
1400 Independence Ave. SW, Whitten Bldg. #117W
Washington, DC 20250
Tel: (202) 720-8001 Fax: (202) 690-1278
Web: www.usda.gov/oig

Dr. Joseph J. Jen, Under Secretary
Agriculture, US Dept. of
Research Education & Economics
1400 Independence Ave. SW #216-W,
Jamie L. Whitten Bldg.
Washington, DC 20250
Tel: (202) 720-5923 Fax: (202) 690-2842
Email: joseph.jen@usda.gov
Web: www.reeusda.gov/ree

Dr. Margaret S.Y. Chu, Director
Energy, US Dept. of
Office of Civilian Radioactive Waste Management
1000 Independence Ave SW, Forrestal
Bldg. HQ, M/C RW-1 #5A-085
Washington, DC 20585

Tel: (202) 586-6842 Fax: (202) 586-6638
Web: www.ocrwm.doe.gov

Michael M.F. Liu, Assistant Secretary for Public & Indian Housing
Housing and Urban Development, US Dept. of
Public and Indian Housing
451 7th St. SW #4100
Washington, DC 20410
Tel: (202) 708-0950 Fax: (202) 619-8478
Web: www.hud.gov

Elaine L. Chao, Secretary of Labor
Labor, US Dept. of
Office of the Secretary of Labor
200 Constitution Ave. NW #S-2018
Washington, DC 20210
Tel: (202) 693-6000 Fax: (202) 693-6111
Email: secretaryelainechao@dol.gov
Web: www.dol.gov

Samuel T. Mok, Chief Financial Officer
Labor, US Dept. of
Office of the Chief Financial Officer
200 Constitution Ave. NW #S-4030
Washington, DC 20210
Tel: (202) 693-6800 Fax: (202) 693-6963
Email: contact.ocfo@dol.gov
Web: www.dol.gov/ocfo

Shinae Chun, Director
Labor, US Dept. of
Women's Bureau
200 Constitution Ave. NW #S-3002
Washington, DC 20210
Tel: (202) 693-6710 Fax: (202) 693-6725
Web: www.dol.gov/wb

Dr. David Chu, Under Secretary
Defense, US Dept. of
Office of Personnel and Readiness
4000 Defense Pentagon #3E-764
Washington, DC 20301-4000
Tel: (703) 697-5001 Fax: (703) 697-8256
Web: www.defenselink.mil

Shirin Raziuddin Tahir-Kheli, Representative
State, US Dept. of
United Nations Economic and Social Council
John Hopkins University, School of Advanced International Studies, 1619
Massachusetts Ave. NW
Washington, DC 20036

Norman Mineta, Secretary of Transportation
Transportation, US Dept. of
Office of the Secretary of Transportation
400 7th St. SW, Nassif Bldg. #10200
Washington, DC 20590
Tel: (202) 366-1111 Fax: (202) 366-7202
Web: www.dot.gov

Dr. Edward Hachiro Kubo, Jr., US Attorney
Justice, US Dept. of
US Attorney's Office
PJKK Federal Bldg., 300 Ala Moana Blvd.
#6-100
Honolulu, HI 96850
Tel: (808) 541-2850 Fax: (808) 541-2958
Email: usa-hi-publicreport@usdoj.gov
Web: www.usdoj.gov/usao/hi

Mark Moki Hanohano, US Marshal
Justice, US Dept. of
US Marshals
300 Ala Moana Blvd., PJKK Federal Bldg.
Honolulu, HI 96850
Tel: (808) 541-3000 Fax: (808) 541-3056
Web: www.usdoj.gov/marshals/district/hi

Daniel K. Inouye, Senator
United States Senate
Honolulu Office
300 Ala Moana Blvd. #7-212
Honolulu, HI 96850-4975
Tel: (808) 541-2542 Fax: (808) 541-2549
Email: senator@inouye.senate.gov
Web: http://inouye.senate.gov

Sichan Siv, Ambassador
State, US Dept. of
US Mission to the United Nations
799 United Nations Plz.
New York, NY 10017
Tel: (212) 415-4278 Fax: (212) 415-4299

PRESIDENTIAL APPOINTEES TO BOARDS AND COMMISSIONS (PT)

Pablo J. Wong, Advisory Board
Community Development Advisory Board

Matthew Fong, Chairman
Pension Benefit Guaranty Corporation
Advisory Board
Strategic Advisory Group

Rei Cheryl Takemoto, Commissioner
President's Commission on Excellence in
Special Education

Dr. David Lee, Council Member
President's Council on the 21st Century
Workforce

Dr. Moon Chen, Jr., Member
National Cancer Institute
National Cancer Advisory Board
4501 X St. #3010
Sacramento, CA 95817
Tel: (916) 734-1191
Email: moon.chen@ucdmc.ucdavis.edu
Web: www.cancer.gov

Lawrence Okamura, Council Member
National Council on the Humanities
1100 Pennsylvania Ave. NW
Washington, DC 20506
Tel: (202) 606-8400
Email: info@neh.gov
Web: www.neh.gov

Chi Ming Lee, Committee Member
President's Advisory Committee on the Arts
John F. Kennedy Center for the Performing
Arts
2700 F St. NW
Washington, DC 20566
Tel: (202) 416-8070 Fax: (202) 416-8076
Web: www.kennedy-center.org

William Marumoto, Committee Member
President's Advisory Committee on the Arts
John F. Kennedy Center for the Performing
Arts
2700 F St. NW
Washington, DC 20566

Tel: (202) 416-8070 Fax: (202) 416-8076
Web: www.kennedy-center.org

Dr. Vijayalakshmi Appareddy, Vice Chairperson
President's Committee for People with
Intellectual Disabilities
370 L'Enfant Promenade SW
Washington, DC 20447
Web: www.acf.hhs.gov/programs/pcpid

Dr. Larke Nahme Huang, Commissioner
President's New Freedom Commission on
Mental Health
Center for Child Health and Mental Health
Policy
Georgetown University, 3307 M. St. NW
#401
Washington, DC 20007
Tel: (202) 687-8855
Web: www.mentalhealthcommission.gov

Frank Jao, Member
Vietnam Education Foundation
Board of Directors
2111 Wilson Blvd. #700
Arlington, VA 22201
Tel: (703) 351-5053 Fax: (703) 351-1423
Email: infomation@vef.gov
Web: www.vef.gov

Marilyn Pattillo, Member
Vietnam Education Foundation
Board of Directors
2111 Wilson Blvd. #700
Arlington, VA 22201
Tel: (703) 351-5053 Fax: (703) 351-1423
Email: infomation@vef.gov
Web: www.vef.gov

Robert L. Bryant, Member
Vietnam Education Foundation
Board of Directors
2111 Wilson Blvd. #700
Arlington, VA 22201
Tel: (703) 351-5053 Fax: (703) 351-1423
Email: infomation@vef.gov
Web: www.vef.gov

THE EXECUTIVE BRANCH

Roger K. Minami , Confidential Assistant to the Under Secretary
Agriculture, US Dept. of
Marketing & Regulatory Programs
Jamie L. Whitten Federal Bldg.,1400
Independence Ave. SW
Washington, DC 20250
Tel: (202) 720-7835
Email: roger.minami@usda.gov
Web: www.usda.gov/mrp

Tim Wang, Special Assistant to the Assistant Secretary for International Trade
Commerce, US Dept. of
International Trade Administration
Herbert C. Hoover Bldg., 14th St. &
Constitution Ave. NW #2067
Washington, DC 20230
Tel: (202) 482-2540 Fax: (202) 482-0980
Email: tim_wang@ita.doc.gov
Web: www.ita.doc.gov

Chiling Tong, Deputy Assistant Secretary for Market Compliance
Commerce, US Dept. of
Minority Business Development Agency
14th St. and Constitution Ave. NW #5090
Washington, DC 20230
Tel: (202) 482-6279 Fax: (202) 482-4206
Email: ctong@mbda.gov
Web: www.mbda.gov

Mary Jin K. Choi, Senior Advisor
Commerce, US Dept. of
Minority Business Development Agency
14th St. and Constitution Ave. NW #5063
Washington, DC 20230
Tel: (202) 482-5061 Fax: (202) 482-5117
Email: mchoi@mbda.gov
Web: www.mbda.gov

Benjamin H. Wu, Deputy Under Secretary for Technology
Commerce, US Dept. of
Technology Administration
1401 Constitution Ave. NW #4824
Washington, DC 20230
Tel: (202) 482-1091 Fax: (202) 501-2595
Email: public_affairs@technology.gov
Web: www.technology.gov

Anh-Chau Truong, Confidential Assistant
Education, US Dept. of
Office of English Language Acquisition
Potomac Center Plz., 550 12th St. SW
#10088
Washington, DC 20065
Tel: (202) 245-7135
Email: anh-chau.truong@ed.gov
Web: www.ed.gov/offices/oela

Marina Tse, Principal Associate Deputy Under Secretary
Education, US Dept. of
Office of English Language Acquisition,
Language Enhancement & Academic
Achievement (OELA)
Potomac Center Plz., 550 12th St. SW
Washington, DC 20065-6510
Tel: (202) 245-7100 .Fax: (202) 245-7168
Email: marina.tse@ed.gov
Web: www.ed.gov/about/offices/list/oela

Tori Hatada, Confidential Assistant to the Under Secretary
Education, US Dept. of
Office of the Under Secretary
400 Maryland Ave. SW, Federal Office Bldg.
6 #7W228
Washington, DC 20202
Tel: (202) 205-7779 Fax: (202) 401-9027
Web: www.ed.gov

Dr. Nguyen Van Hanh, Director
Health and Human Services, US Dept. of
Administration for Children and Families
370 L'Enfant Promenade SW, 6th Fl. East,
Aerospace Center Bldg.
Washington, DC 20447
Tel: (202) 401-9246 Fax: (202) 401-1022
Web: www.acf.hhs.gov/programs/orr

David Leaverton, Special Assistant
Health and Human Services, US Dept. of
Office of the Assistant Secretary for
Legislation
200 Independence Ave. SW #415-H
Washington, DC 20201
Tel: (202) 690-6311 Fax: (202) 690-5760
Email: david.leaverton@hhs.gov
Web: www.hhs.gov/asl

Michael O'Grady, Assistant Secretary for Planning and Evaluation
Health and Human Services, US Dept. of
Office of the Assistant Secretary for
Planning and Evaluation
200 Independence Ave. SW
Washington, DC 20201
Tel: (202) 619-0257
Email: michael.ogrady@hhs.gov
Web: http://aspe.hhs.gov

David B. Cohen, Deputy Assistant Secretary for Insular Affairs
Interior, US Dept. of
Office of Insular Affairs
1849 C. St. NW, M/S 4311-A
Washington, DC 20240

Tel: (202) 208-4736 Fax: (202) 219-1989
Web: www.doi.gov/oia

Daniel J. Bryant, Assistant Attorney General
Justice, US Dept. of
Office of Legal Policy
Main Justice Bldg. #4234, 950
Pennsylvania Ave. NW
Washington, DC 20530-0001
Tel: (202) 514-4601 Fax: (202) 514-2424
Web: www.usdoj.gov/olp

Luis A. Reyes, Counselor to the Assistant Attorney General for Civil Rights
Justice, US Dept. of
Office of the Assistant Attorney General
950 Pennsylvania Ave. NW, Main Bldg.
Washington, DC 20530
Tel: (202) 514-2151 Fax: (202) 514-0293
Web: www.usdoj.gov

Anna Hui, Special Assistant to the CFO
Labor, US Dept. of
Office of the Chief Financial Office
200 Constitution Ave. NW #S-4030
Washington, DC 20210
Tel: (202) 693-6800 Fax: (202) 693-6963
Email: hui.anna@dol.gov
Web: www.dol.gov/ocfo

Eddy Badrina, Investment Development Associate
Overseas Private Investment Corporation
Office of Investment Development and
Economic Growth
1100 New York Ave. NW
Washington, DC 20527
Tel: (202) 336-8639 Fax: (202) 408-9859
Web: www.opic.gov

Gopal Khanna, CFO
Peace Corps
1111 20th St. NW
Washington, DC 20526
Tel: (202) 692-1600 Fax: (202) 692-1601
Web: www.peacecorps.gov

Manny Cuan, Special Assistant to the Director of Policy
Transportation, US Dept. of
Federal Highway Administration
400 7th St. SW, A-1 #10414
Washington, DC 20590
Tel: (202) 366-4570 Fax: (202) 366-6337
Email: manny.cuan@ost.dot.gov
Web: www.dot.gov

Suhail Khan, Legal Counsel
Transportation, US Dept. of
Federal Highway Administration
400 7th St. SW #10406
Washington, DC 20590
Tel: (202) 366-6681 Fax: (202) 366-3675
Email: suhail.khan@fhwa.dot.gov
Web: www.fhwa.dot.gov

Stephen Fong, Staff Assistant to the Administrator
Transportation, US Dept. of
Federal Transit Administration
400 7th St. SW #9400
Washington, DC 20590
Tel: (202) 366-1215 Fax: (202) 366-3472
Email: webmaster@fta.dot.gov
Web: www.fta.dot.gov

Michael Trujillo, Director
Transportation, US Dept. of
Office of Civil Rights
400 7th St. SW #10215
Washington, DC 20590
Tel: (202) 366-4648 Fax: (202) 366-9371
Web: www.dot.gov

Jane Pak, Deputy Director of Scheduling
US Small Business Administration
Office of the Administrator
409 3rd St. SW, M/C 2110 #7000
Washington, DC 20416
Tel: (202) 205-6392 Fax: (202) 481-0220
Email: jane.pak@sba.gov
Web: www.sba.gov

John Quoc Duong, Executive Director
White House Initiative on Asian Americans
and Pacific Islanders
5600 Fishers Ln. #10-42
Rockville, MD 20857
Tel: (301) 443-2492 Fax: (301) 443-0259

Angie Tang, Regional Representative
Labor, US Dept. of
Region II
201 Varick St. #605
New York, NY 20014
Tel: (212) 337-2387 Fax: (212) 337-2386
Web: www.dol.gov

Dr. Paul Kyo Jhin, Director
Peace Corps
Office of Planning, Policy and Analysis
8350 Greensboro Dr. #203
McLean, VA 22102
Tel: (202) 692-2134 Fax: (202) 692-2131
Web: www.peacecorps.gov

Norm Proctor, Regional Administrator
US Small Business Administration
Region X
1200 6th Ave., Park Place Bldg. #1805
Seattle, WA 98101-1128
Tel: (206) 553-5676 Fax: (206) 553-4155
Web: www.sba.gov/wa/seattle

THE PRESIDENT'S ADVISORY COMMISSION ON ASIAN AMERICANS AND PACIFIC ISLANDERS

Akshay Desai, Commissioner
President's Advisory Commission on Asian
Americans and Pacific Islanders
5600 Fisher's Ln. #10-42
Rockville , MD 20857
Tel: (301) 443-2492 Fax: (301) 443-0259
Email: aapi@hrsa.gov
Web: www.aapi.gov

Betty Wu, Chair
President's Advisory Commission on Asian
Americans and Pacific Islanders
5600 Fisher's Ln. #10-42
Rockville , MD 20857
Tel: (301) 443-2492 Fax: (301) 443-0259
Email: aapi@hrsa.gov
Web: www.aapi.gov

Derrick H. Nguyen, Commissioner
President's Advisory Commission on Asian
Americans and Pacific Islanders
5600 Fisher's Ln. #10-42
Rockville, MD 20857
Tel: (301) 443-2492 Fax: (301) 443-0259
Email: aapi@hrsa.gov
Web: www.aapi.gov

Jeffrey B. Sakaguchi, Commissioner
President's Advisory Commission on Asian
Americans and Pacific Islanders
5600 Fisher's Ln. #10-42
Rockville, MD 20857
Tel: (301) 443-2492 Fax: (301) 443-0259
Email: aapi@hrsa.gov
Web: www.aapi.gov

Jimmy Lee, Commissioner
President's Advisory Commission on Asian
Americans and Pacific Islanders

5600 Fisher's Ln. #10-42
Rockville, MD 20857
Tel: (301) 443-2492 Fax: (301) 443-0259
Email: aapi@hrsa.gov
Web: www.aapi.gov

John C. Kim, Commissioner
President's Advisory Commission on Asian
Americans and Pacific Islanders
5600 Fisher's Ln. #10-42
Rockville , MD 20857
Tel: (301) 443-2492 Fax: (301) 443-0259
Email: aapi@hrsa.gov
Web: www.aapi.gov

Joseph Melookaran, Commissioner
President's Advisory Commission on Asian
Americans and Pacific Islanders
5600 Fisher's Ln. #10-42
Rockville, MD 20857
Tel: (301) 443-2492 Fax: (301) 443-0259
Email: aapi@hrsa.gov
Web: www.aapi.gov

Kenneth Wong, Commissioner
President's Advisory Commission on Asian
Americans and Pacific Islanders
5600 Fisher's Ln. #10-42
Rockville, MD 20857
Tel: (301) 443-2492 Fax: (301) 443-0259
Email: aapi@hrsa.gov
Web: www.aapi.gov

Martha Cruz Ruth, Commissioner
President's Advisory Commission on Asian
Americans and Pacific Islanders
5600 Fisher's Ln. #10-42
Rockville, MD 20857
Tel: (301) 443-2492 Fax: (301) 443-0259
Email: aapi@hrsa.gov
Web: www.aapi.gov

Nina Nguyen Collier, Commissioner
President's Advisory Commission on Asian
Americans and Pacific Islanders
5600 Fisher's Ln. #10-42
Rockville , MD 20857
Tel: (301) 443-2492 Fax: (301) 443-0259
Email: aapi@hrsa.gov
Web: www.aapi.gov

Rudy Pamintuan, Commissioner
President's Advisory Commission on Asian
Americans and Pacific Islanders
5600 Fisher's Ln. #10-42
Rockville, MD 20857
Tel: (301) 443-2492 Fax: (301) 443-0259
Email: aapi@hrsa.gov
Web: www.aapi.gov

Vellie Dietrich-Hall, Commissioner
President's Advisory Commission on Asian
Americans and Pacific Islanders
5600 Fisher's Ln. #10-42
Rockville, MD 20857
Tel: (301) 443-2492 Fax: (301) 443-0259
Email: aapi@hrsa.gov
Web: www.aapi.gov

William Kil, Commissioner
President's Advisory Commission on Asian
Americans and Pacific Islanders
5600 Fisher's Ln. #10-42
Rockville, MD 20857
Tel: (301) 443-2492 Fax: (301) 443-0259
Email: aapi@hrsa.gov
Web: www.aapi.gov

William P. Afeaki, Commissioner
President's Advisory Commission on Asian
Americans and Pacific Islanders
5600 Fisher's Ln. #10-42
Rockville, MD 20857
Tel: (301) 443-2492 Fax: (301) 443-0259
Email: aapi@hrsa.gov
Web: www.aapi.gov

The Congressional Asian Pacific American Caucus

AMERICAN SAMOA

HOUSE OF REPRESENTATIVES

The Hon. Eni F.H. Faleomavaega (D)
2422 Rayburn HOB
Washington, DC 20515
Tel: (202) 225-8577 Fax: (202) 225-8757
Email: faleomavaega@mail.house.gov
Web: www.house.gov/faleomavaega

District Office
Executive Office Bldg., 1st Fl.
P.O. Drawer X, Utulei
Pago Pago, AS 96799
Tel: (684) 633-1372 Fax: (684) 633-2680

ARIZONA

HOUSE OF REPRESENTATIVES

The Hon. Raul M. Grijalva (D-7th District)
1440 Longworth HOB
Washington, DC 20515
Tel: (202) 225-2435 Fax: (202) 225-1541
Email: raul.grijalva@mail.house.gov
Web: www.house.gov/grijalva

District Office
810 E. 22nd St. #102
Tucson, AZ 85713
Tel: (520) 622-6788 Fax: (520) 622-0198

District Office
1455 S. 4th Ave. #4
Yuma, AZ 85364
Tel: (928) 343-7933 Fax: (928) 343-7949

The Hon. Ed Pastor (D-4th District)
2465 Rayburn HOB
Washington, DC 20515
Tel: (202) 225-4065 Fax: (202) 225-1655
Web: www.house.gov/pastor

District Office
411 N. Central Ave. #150
Phoenix, AZ 85004
Tel: (602) 256-0551

CALIFORNIA

HOUSE OF REPRESENTATIVES

The Hon. Joe Baca (D-42nd District)
328 Cannon HOB
Washington, DC 20515-0542
Tel: (202) 225-6161 Fax: (202) 225-8671
Email: joe.baca@mail.house.gov
Web: www.house.gov/baca

District Office
201 N. E St. #102
San Bernardino, CA 92401
Tel: (909) 885-2222

The Hon. Xavier Becerra (D-30th District)
1119 Longworth HOB
Washington, DC 20515
Tel: (202) 225-6235 Fax: (202) 225-2202
Email: xavier.becerra@mail.house.gov
Web: www.house.gov/becerra

District Office
1910 Sunset Blvd. #560
Los Angeles, CA 90026
Tel: (213) 483-1425

The Hon. Howard L. Berman (D-28th District)
2221 Rayburn HOB
Washington, DC 20515
Tel: (202) 225-4695 Fax: (202) 225-3196
Email: howard.berman@mail.house.gov
Web: www.house.gov/berman

District Office
14546 Hamlin St. #202
Van Nuys, CA 91411
Tel: (818) 994-7200

The Hon. Lois Capps (D-22nd District)
1707 Longworth HOB
Washington, DC 20515
Tel: (202) 225-3601 Fax: (202) 225-5632
Email: lois.capps@mail.house.gov
Web: www.house.gov/capps

District Office
1216 State St. #403
Santa Barbara, CA 93101
Tel: (805) 730-1710 Fax: (805) 730-9153

District Office
1411 Marsh St. #205
San Luis Obispo, CA 93401
Tel: (805) 546-8348 Fax: (805) 546-8368

District Office
141 S. A St. #204
Oxnard, CA 93030
Tel: (805) 385-3440 Fax: (805) 385-3399

The Hon. Susan A. Davis (D-53rd District)
1224 Longworth HOB
Washington, DC 20515
Tel: (202) 225-2040 Fax: (202) 225-2948
Email: susan.davis@mail.house.gov
Web: www.house.gov/susandavis

District Office
4305 University Ave. #515
San Diego, CA 92105
Tel: (619) 280-5353 Fax: (619) 280-5311

The Hon. Anna G. Eshoo (D-14th District)
205 Cannon HOB
Washington, DC 20515
Tel: (202) 225-8104 Fax: (202) 225-8890
Web: www-eshoo.house.gov

District Office
698 Emerson St.
Palo Alto, CA 94301
Tel: (650) 323-2984 Fax: (650) 323-3498

The Hon. Sam Farr (D-17th District)
1221 Longworth HOB
Washington, DC 20515
Tel: (202) 225-2861 Fax: (202) 225-6791
Web: www.house.gov/farr

District Office
100 W. Alisal St.
Salinas, CA 93901
Tel: (831) 424-2229 Fax: (831) 424-7099

District Office
701 Ocean St. #318
Santa Cruz, CA 95060
Tel: (831) 429-1976

The Hon. Bob Filner (D-51st District)
2428 Rayburn HOB
Washington, DC 20515
Tel: (202) 225-8045 Fax: (202) 225-9073
Web: www.house.gov/filner

District Office
333 F St. #A
Chula Vista, CA 91910
Tel: (619) 422-5963 Fax: (619) 422-7290

District Office
1101 Airport Rd. #D
Imperial, CA 92251
Tel: (760) 355-8800 Fax: (760) 355-8802

The Hon. Michael Honda (D-15th District)
1713 Longworth HOB
Washington, DC 20515
Tel: (202) 225-2631 Fax: (202) 225-2699
Email: mike.honda@mail.house.gov
Web: www.house.gov/honda

District Office
1999 S. Bascom Ave. #815
Campbell, CA 95008
Tel: (408) 558-8085 Fax: (408) 558-8086

The Hon. Tom Lantos (D-12th District)
2413 Rayburn HOB
Washington, DC 20515
Tel: (202) 225-3531 Fax: (202) 226-9789
Web: www.house.gov/lantos

District Office
400 S. El Camino Real #410
San Mateo, CA 94402
Tel: (650) 342-0300 Fax: (650) 375-8270

The Hon. Barbara Lee (D-9th District)
1724 Longworth HOB
Washington, DC 20515
Tel: (202) 225-2661 Fax: (202) 225-9817
Email: barbara.lee@mail.house.gov
Web: www.house.gov/lee

District Office
1301 Clay St. #1000 North
Oakland, CA 94612
Tel: (510) 763-0370 Fax: (510) 763-6538

The Hon. Zoe Lofgren (D-16th District)
102 Cannon HOB
Washington, DC 20515
Tel: (202) 225-3072 Fax: (202) 225-3336
Email: zoe.lofgren@mail.house.gov
Web: http://zoelofgren.house.gov

District Office
635 N. 1st St. #B
San Jose, CA 95112
Tel: (408) 271-8700 Fax: (408) 271-8713

The Hon. Doris Matsui (D-5th District)
2310 Rayburn HOB
Washington, DC 20515-0505
Tel: (202) 225-7163 Fax: (202) 225-0566
Web: http://matsui.house.gov

District Office
Robert T. Matsui United States Courthouse,
501 I St. #12-600
Sacramento, CA 95814-7305
Tel: (916) 498-5600 Fax: (916) 444-6117

The Hon. Juanita Millender-McDonald (D-37th District)
1514 Longworth HOB
Washington, DC 20515
Tel: (202) 225-7924 Fax: (202) 225-7926
Email: millender-mcdonald@mail.house.gov
Web: www.house.gov/millender-mcdonald

District Office
970 W. 190th St., East Tower #900
Torrance, CA 90502
Tel: (310) 538-1190

The Hon. George Miller (D-7th District)
2205 Rayburn HOB
Washington, DC 20515
Tel: (202) 225-2095 Fax: (202) 225-5609
Email: george.miller@mail.house.gov
Web: www.house.gov/georgemiller

District Office
1333 Willow Pass Rd. #203
Concord, CA 94520
Tel: (925) 602-1880

District Office
3220 Blume Dr. #281
Richmond, CA 94806
Tel: (510) 262-6500

District Office
375 G St. #1
Vallejo, CA 94592
Tel: (707) 645-1888 Fax: (707) 645-1870

The Hon. Gary Miller (R-42nd District)
1037 Longworth HOB
Washington, DC 20515
Tel: (202) 225-3201 Fax: (202) 226-6962
Email: gary.miller@mail.house.gov
Web: www.house.gov/garymiller

District Office
1800 E. Lambert Rd. #150
Brea, CA 92821
Tel: (714) 257-1142 Fax: (714) 257-9242

District Office
200 Civic Center Dr.
Mission Viejo, CA 92691
Tel: (949) 470-8484

The Hon. Grace F. Napolitano (D-38th District)
1609 Longworth HOB
Washington, DC 20515
Tel: (202) 225-5256 Fax: (202) 225-0027
Web: www.napolitano.house.gov

District Office
11627 E. Telegraph Rd. #100
Sante Fe Springs, CA 90670
Tel: (562) 801-2134 Fax: (562) 949-9144

The Hon. Nancy Pelosi (D-8th District)
2371 Rayburn HOB
Washington, DC 20515
Tel: (202) 225-4965 Fax: (202) 225-8259
Email: sf.nancy@mail.house.gov
Web: www.house.gov/pelosi

District Office
450 Golden Gate Ave. #145378
San Francisco, CA 94102
Tel: (415) 556-4862 Fax: (415) 861-1670

The Hon. Lucille Roybal-Allard (D-34th District)
2330 Rayburn HOB
Washington, DC 20515
Tel: (202) 225-1766 Fax: (202) 226-0350
Web: www.house.gov/roybal-allard

District Office
255 E. Temple St. #1860
Los Angeles, CA 90012-3334
Tel: (213) 628-9230 Fax: (213) 628-8578

The Hon. Linda T. Sanchez (D-39th District)
1007 Longworth HOB
Washington, DC 20515
Tel: (202) 225-6676 Fax: (202) 226-1012
Web: www.house.gov/lindasanchez

District Office
4007 Paramount Blvd. #106
Lakewood, CA 90712
Tel: (562) 429-8499 Fax: (562) 938-1948

The Hon. Loretta Sanchez (D-47th District)
1230 Longworth HOB
Washington, DC 20515
Tel: (202) 225-2965 Fax: (202) 225-5859
Email: loretta@mail.house.gov
Web: www.house.gov/sanchez

District Office
12397 Lewis St. #101
Garden Grove, CA 92840
Tel: (714) 621-0102 Fax: (714) 621-0401

The Hon. Adam Schiff (D-29th District)
326 Cannon HOB
Washington, DC 20515
Tel: (202) 225-4176 Fax: (202) 225-5828
Web: www.house.gov/schiff

District Office
35 S. Raymond Ave. #205
Pasadena, CA 91105
Tel: (626) 304-2727 Fax: (626) 304-0572

The Hon. Brad Sherman (D-27th District)
1030 Longworth HOB
Washington, DC 20515-0524
Tel: (202) 225-5911 Fax: (202) 225-5879
Web: www.house.gov/sherman

District Office
5000 Van Nuys Blvd. #420
Sherman Oaks, CA 91403
Tel: (818) 501-9200 Fax: (818) 501-1554

The Hon. Hilda L. Solis (D-32nd District)
1725 Longworth HOB
Washington, DC 20515
Tel: (202) 225-5464 Fax: (202) 225-5467
Email: hilda@mail.house.gov
Web: http://solis.hilda.gov

District Office
4401 Santa Anita Ave. #211
El Monte, CA 91731
Tel: (626) 448-1271 Fax: (626) 448-8062

District Office
4716 Cesar Chavez Ave. Bldg. A
East Los Angeles, CA 90022
Tel: (323) 307-9904 Fax: (323) 307-9906

The Hon. Fortney H. "Pete" Stark (D-13th District)
239 Cannon HOB
Washington, DC 20515
Tel: (202) 225-5065 Fax: (202) 226-3805
Email: petemail@stark.house.gov
Web: www.house.gov/stark

District Office
39300 Civic Center Dr. #220
Fremont, CA 94538
Tel: (510) 494-1388

The Hon. Ellen O. Tauscher (D-10th District)
1034 Longworth HOB
Washington, DC 20515
Tel: (202) 225-1880 Fax: (202) 225-5914
Web: www.house.gov/tauscher

District Office
2121 N. California Blvd. #555
Walnut Creek, CA 94596
Tel: (925) 932-8899 Fax: (925) 932-8159

District Office
420 W. 3rd St.
Antioch, CA 94509
Tel: (925) 757-7187

District Office
2000 Cadenasso Dr. #A
Fairfield, CA 94533
Tel: (707) 428-7792

The Hon. Diane E. Watson (D-33rd District)
125 Cannon HOB
Washington, DC 20515-0533
Tel: (202) 225-7084 Fax: (202) 225-2422
Email: diane.watson@mail.house.gov
Web: www.house.gov/watson

District Office
4322 Wilshire Blvd. #302
Los Angeles, CA 90010
Tel: (323) 965-1422 Fax: (323) 965-1113

The Hon. Henry Waxman (D-30th District)
2204 Rayburn HOB
Washington, DC 20515
Tel: (202) 225-3976 Fax: (202) 225-4099
Web: www.house.gov/waxman

District Office
8436 W. 3rd St. #600
Los Angeles, CA 90048
Tel: (323) 651-1040 Fax: (323) 655-0502

The Hon. Lynn Woolsey (D-6th District)
2263 Rayburn HOB
Washington, DC 20515
Tel: (202) 225-5161 Fax: (202) 225-5163
Web: http://woolsey.house.gov

District Office
1050 Northgate Dr. #354
San Rafael, CA 94903
Tel: (415) 507-9554 Fax: (415) 507-9601

District Office
1101 College Ave. #200
Santa Rosa, CA 95404
Tel: (707) 542-7182 Fax: (707) 542-2745

COLORADO

HOUSE OF REPRESENTATIVES

The Hon. Diana L. DeGette (D-1st District)
1530 Longworth HOB
Washington, DC 20515
Tel: (202) 225-4431 Fax: (202) 225-5657
Email: degette@mail.house.gov
Web: www.house.gov/degette

District Office
600 Grant St. #202
Denver, CO 80203
Tel: (303) 844-4988 Fax: (303) 844-4996

The Hon. Mark Udall (D-2nd District)
115 Cannon HOB
Washington, DC 20515
Tel: (202) 225-2161 Fax: (202) 226-7840
Web: wwwa.house.gov/markudall

District Office
8601 Turnpike Dr. #206
Westminster, CO 80031
Tel: (303) 650-7820 Fax: (303) 650-7827

District Office
P.O. Box 325
Minturn, CO 81645
Tel: (970) 827-4154 Fax: (970) 827-4138

CONNECTICUT

HOUSE OF REPRESENTATIVES

The Hon. John B. Larson (D-1st District)
1005 Longworth HOB
Washington, DC 20515
Tel: (202) 225-2265 Fax: (202) 225-1031
Web: www.house.gov/larson

District Office
221 Main St., 2nd Fl.
Hartford, CT 06106
Tel: (860) 278-8888 Fax: (860) 278-2111

FLORIDA

HOUSE OF REPRESENTATIVES

The Hon. Alcee L. Hastings (D-23rd District)
2235 Rayburn HOB
Washington, DC 20515
Tel: (202) 225-1313 Fax: (202) 225-1171
Email: alcee.pubhastings@mail.house.gov
Web: www.house.gov/alceehastings

District Office
2701 W. Oakland Park Blvd. #200
Fort Lauderdale, FL 33311
Tel: (954) 733-2800 Fax: (954) 735-9444

District Office
5725 Corporate Way #208
West Palm Beach, FL 33407
Tel: (561) 684-0565 Fax: (561) 684-3613

GUAM

HOUSE OF REPRESENTATIVES

The Hon. Madeleine Z. Bordallo (D)
427 Cannon HOB
Washington, DC 20515-5301
Tel: (202) 225-1188 Fax: (202) 226-0341
Email: madeleine.bordallo@mail.house.gov
Web: www.house.gov/bordallo

District Office
120 Father Duenas Ave. #107
Hagatna, GU 96910
Tel: (671) 477-4272 Fax: (671) 477-2587

HAWAII

SENATE

The Hon. Daniel Akaka (D)
141 Hart SOB
Washington, DC 20510
Tel: (202) 224-6361 Fax: (202) 224-2126
Email: senator@akaka.senate.gov
Web: http://akaka.senate.gov

District Office
Prince Kuhio Federal Bldg., 300 Ala Moana
Blvd. #3-106, Box 50144
Honolulu, HI 96850
Tel: (808) 522-8970 Fax: (808) 545-4683

District Office
101 Aupuni St.
Hilo, HI 96720
Tel: (808) 935-1114 Fax: (808) 935-9064

The Hon. Daniel K. Inouye (D)
722 Hart HOB
Washington, DC 20510-1102
Tel: (202) 224-3934 Fax: (202) 224-6747
Web: www.senate.gov/~inouye

District Office
300 Ala Moana Blvd. #7-212
Honolulu, HI 96850-4975
Tel: (808) 541-2542 Fax: (808) 541-2549

District Office
24 N. Church St. #407
Maui, HI 96793
Tel: (808) 242-9702 Fax: (808) 242-7233

District Office
101 Aupuni St. #205
Hilo, HI 96720
Tel: (808) 935-0844 Fax: (808) 961-5163

HOUSE OF REPRESENTATIVES

The Hon. Neil Abercrombie (D-1st District)
1502 Longworth HOB
Washington, DC 20515
Tel: (202) 225-2726 Fax: (202) 225-4580
Email: neil.abercrombie@mail.house.gov
Web: www.house.gov/abercrombie

District Office
Prince Kuhio Federal Bldg., 300 Ala Moana
Blvd. #4-104
Honolulu, HI 96850
Tel: (808) 541-2570 Fax: (808) 533-0133

The Hon. Ed Case (D-2nd District)
128 Cannon HOB
Washington, DC 20515
Tel: (202) 225-4906 Fax: (202) 225-4987
Email: ed.case@mail.house.gov
Web: wwwc.house.gov/case

District Office
5104 Prince Kuhio Federal Bldg.
Honolulu, HI 96850
Tel: (808) 541-1986 Fax: (808) 538-0233

ILLINOIS

HOUSE OF REPRESENTATIVES

The Hon. Danny K. Davis (D-7th District)
1222 Longworth HOB
Washington, DC 20515
Tel: (202) 225-5006 Fax: (202) 225-5641
Web: www.house.gov/davis

District Office
3333 W. Arthington St.
Chicago, IL 60624
Tel: (773) 533-7520 Fax: (773) 533-7530

District Office
2301 Roosevelt Rd.
Broadview, IL 60155
Tel: (708) 345-6857

The Hon. Lane Evans (D-17th District)
2211 Rayburn HOB
Washington, DC 20515
Tel: (202) 225-5905 Fax: (202) 225-5396
Email: lane.evans@mail.house.gov
Web: www.house.gov/evans

District Office
1535 47th Ave. #5
Moline, IL 61265
Tel: (309) 793-5760 Fax: (309) 762-9193

District Office
261 N. Broad St. #5
Galesburg, IL 61401
Tel: (309) 342-4411 Fax: (309) 342-9749

District Office
236 N. Water St. #765
Decatur, IL 62523
Tel: (217) 422-9150 Fax: (217) 422-9245

The Hon. Bobby L. Rush (D-1st District)
2416 Rayburn HOB
Washington, DC 20515
Tel: (202) 225-4372 Fax: (202) 226-0333
Web: www.house.gov/rush

District Office
700-706 E. 79th St.
Chicago, IL 60619
Tel: (773) 224-6500 Fax: (773) 224-9624

District Office
3235 W. 147th St.
Midlothian, IL 60445
Tel: (708) 385-9550 Fax: (708) 385-3860

The Hon. Janice Schakowsky (IL-9th District)
515 Cannon HOB
Washington, DC 20515
Tel: (202) 225-2111 Fax: (202) 226-6890
Email: jan.schakowsky@mail.house.gov
Web: www.house.gov/schakowsky

District Office
5533 Broadway
Chicago, IL 60640
Tel: (773) 506-7100 Fax: (773) 506-9202

District Office
820 Davis St. #105
Evanston, IL 60201
Tel: (847) 328-3399 Fax: (847) 328-3425

District Office
1420 Renaissance Dr. #102
Park Ridge, IL 60068
Tel: (847) 298-2128 Fax: (847) 298-2173

KANSAS

HOUSE OF REPRESENTATIVES

The Hon. Dennis Moore (D-3rd District)
431 Cannon HOB
Washington, DC 20515
Tel: (202) 225-2865 Fax: (202) 225-2807
Web: www.house.gov/moore

District Office
8417 Santa Fe Dr. #101
Overland Park, KS 66212
Tel: (913) 383-2013 Fax: (913) 383-2088

District Office
500 State Ave. #176
Kansas City, KS 66101
Tel: (913) 621-0832 Fax: (913) 621-1533

District Office
647 Massachusetts St. #212
Lawrence, KS 66044
Tel: (785) 842-9313 Fax: (785) 843-3289

LOUISIANA

HOUSE OF REPRESENTATIVES

The Hon. William Jefferson (D-2nd District)
240 Cannon HOB
Washington, DC 20515
Tel: (202) 225-6636 Fax: (202) 225-1988
Email: jeffersonmc@mail.house.gov
Web: www.house.gov/jefferson

District Office
501 Magazine St. #1012
New Orleans, LA 70130
Tel: (504) 589–2274

MARYLAND

HOUSE OF REPRESENTATIVES

The Hon. Elijah Cummings (D-7th District)
1632 Longworth HOB
Washington, DC 20515
Tel: (202) 225-4741 Fax: (202) 225-3178
Web: www.house.gov/cummings

District Office
1010 Park Ave. #105
Baltimore, MD 21201
Tel: (410) 685-9199 Fax: (410) 685-9399

District Office
754 Frederick Rd.
Catonsville, MD 21228
Tel: (410) 719-8777 Fax: (410) 455-0110

The Hon. Steny H. Hoyer (D-5th District)
1705 Longworth HOB
Washington, DC 20515
Tel: (202) 225-4131 Fax: (202) 225-4300
Web: www.hoyer.house.gov

District Office
6500 Cherrywood Ln. #310
Greenbelt, MD 20770
Tel: (301) 474-0119 Fax: (301) 474-4697

District Office
401 Post Office Rd. #202
Waldorf, MD 20602
Tel: (301) 843-1577 Fax: (301) 843-1331

The Hon. Dutch Ruppersberger (D-2nd District)
1630 Longworth HOB
Washington, DC 20515-2002

Tel: (202) 225-3061 Fax: (202) 225-3094
Web: http://dutch.house.gov

District Office
5 West Padonia Rd. #200
Timonium, MD 21093
Tel: (410) 628-2701 Fax: (410) 628-2708

The Hon. Chris Van Hollen (D-8th District)
1419 Longworth HOB
Washington, DC 20515
Tel: (202) 225-5341 Fax: (202) 225-0375
Email: chris.vanhollen@mail.house.gov
Web: www.house.gov/vanhollen

District Office
51 Monroe St. #507
Rockville, MD 20850
Tel: (301) 424-3501 Fax: (301) 424-5992

District Office
3409 Rhode Island Ave.
Mount Rainier, MD 20712
Tel: (301) 927-5223 Fax: (301) 927-6122

The Hon. Albert Wynn (D-4th District)
434 Cannon HOB
Washington, DC 20515-2004
Tel: (202) 225-8699 Fax: (202) 225-8714
Web: www.wynn.house.gov

District Office
18200 Georgia Ave. #E
Olney, MD 20832
Tel: (301) 929-3462 Fax: (301) 929-3466

District Office
9200 Basil Ct. #221
Largo, MD 20774
Tel: (301) 773-4094 Fax: (301) 925-9694

MASSACHUSETTS

HOUSE OF REPRESENTATIVES

The Hon. Michael E. Capuano (D-8th District)
1232 Longworth HOB
Washington, DC 20515
Tel: (202) 225-5111 Fax: (202) 225-9322
Email: michael.e.capuano@mail.house.gov
Web: www.house.gov/capuano

District Office
110 1st St.
Cambridge, MA 02141
Tel: (617) 621-6208 Fax: (617) 621-8628

The Hon. William Delahunt (D-10th District)
1317 Longworth HOB
Washington, DC 20515
Tel: (202) 225-3111 Fax: (202) 225-5658
Email: william.delahunt@mail.house.gov
Web: www.house.gov/delahunt

District Office
146 Main St.
Hyannis, MA 02601
Tel: (508) 771-0666 Fax: (508) 790-1959

District Office
1250 Hancock St. #802-N
Quincy, MA 02169
Tel: (617) 770-3700 Fax: (617) 770-2984

The Hon. Stephen F. Lynch (D-9th District)
319 Cannon HOB
Washington, DC 20515
Tel: (202) 225-8273 Fax: (202) 225-3984
Email: stephen.lynch@mail.house.gov
Web: www.house.gov/lynch

District Office
88 Black Falcon Ave. #340

Boston, MA 02210
Tel: (617) 428-2000 Fax: (617) 428-2011

District Office
Brockton Federal Bldg., 166 Main St.
Brockton, MA 02301
Tel: (508) 586-5555 Fax: (508) 580-4692

The Hon. John F. Tierney (D-6th District)
120 Cannon HOB
Washington, DC 20515
Tel: (202) 225-8020 Fax: (202) 225-5915
Web: www.house.gov/tierney

District Office
17 Peabody Sq.
Peabody, MA 01960
Tel: (978) 531-1669 Fax: (978) 531-1996

MICHIGAN

HOUSE OF REPRESENTATIVES

The Hon. Bart Stupak (D-1st District)
2352 Rayburn HOB
Washington, DC 20515
Tel: (202) 225-4735 Fax: (202) 225-4744
Email: stupak@mail.house.gov
Web: www.house.gov/stupak

District Office
111 E. Chisholm
Alpena, MI 49707
Tel: (989) 356-0690 Fax: (989) 356-0923

District Office
Iron County Courthouse, 2 S. 6th St. #3
Crystal Falls, MI 49920-1413
Tel: (906) 875-3751 Fax: (906) 875-3889

District Office
902 Ludington St.
Escanaba, MI 49829
Tel: (906) 786-4504 Fax: (906) 786-4534

MINNESOTA

HOUSE OF REPRESENTATIVES

The Hon. Betty McCollum (D-4th District)
1029 Longworth HOB
Washington, DC 20515
Tel: (202) 225-6631 Fax: (202) 225-1968
Web: www.house.gov/mccollum

District Office
165 Western Ave. North #17
St. Paul, MN 55102
Tel: (651) 224-9191 Fax: (651) 224-3056

The Hon. Collin C. Peterson (D-7th District)
2159 Rayburn HOB
Washington, DC 20515
Tel: (202) 225-2165 Fax: (202) 225-1593
Web: http://collinpeterson.house.gov

District Office
714 Lake Ave. #107
Detroit Lakes, MN 56501
Tel: (218) 847-5056

District Office
Minnesota Wheat Growers Bldg., 2603 Wheat Dr.
Red Lake Falls, MN 56750
Tel: (218) 253-4356

District Office
320 4th St. SW, Centre Point Mall
Willmar, MN 56201
Tel: (320) 235-1061

MISSISSIPPI

HOUSE OF REPRESENTATIVES

The Hon. Gene Taylor (D-4th District)
2311 Rayburn HOB
Washington, DC 20515-2405
Tel: (202) 225-5772 Fax: (202) 225-5772
Web: www.house.gov/genetaylor

District Office
2424 14th St.
Gulfport, MS 39501
Tel: (228) 864-7670

District Office
701 Main St. #215
Hattiesburg, MS 39401
Tel: (601) 582-3246

District Office
1314 Government St.
Ocean Springs, MS 39564
Tel: (228) 872-7950

The Hon. Bennie G. Thompson (D-2nd District)
2432 Rayburn HOB
Washington, DC 20515
Tel: (202) 225-5876 Fax: (202) 225-5898
Email: thompsonms2nd@mail.house.gov
Web: www.house.gov/thompson

District Office
107 W. Madison St.
Bolton, MS 39041
Tel: (601) 866-9003 Fax: (601) 866-9036

District Office
910 Courthouse Ln.
Greenville, MS 38701
Tel: (662) 335-9003 Fax: (662) 334-1304

District Office
509 Hwy. 82 West
Greenwood, MS 38930
Tel: (662) 455-9003 Fax: (662) 453-0118

MISSOURI

HOUSE OF REPRESENTATIVES

The Hon. William Lacy Clay, Jr. (D-1st District)
131 Cannon HOB
Washington, DC 20515
Tel: (202) 225-2406 Fax: (202) 225-1725
Web: www.house.gov/clay

District Office
625 N. Euclid St. #200
St. Louis, MO 63108
Tel: (314) 367-1970 Fax: (314) 367-1341

District Office
8525 Page Blvd.
St. Louis, MO 63114
Tel: (314) 890-0349 Fax: (314) 427-6320

NEVADA

HOUSE OF REPRESENTATIVES

The Hon. Shelley Berkley (D-1st District)
439 Cannon HOB
Washington, DC 20515-4708
Tel: (202) 225-5965 Fax: (202) 225-3119
Email: shelley.berkley@mail.house.gov
Web: www.house.gov/berkley

District Office
2340 Paseo Del Prado #D-106
Las Vegas, NV 89102
Tel: (702) 220-9823 Fax: (702) 220-9841

NEW JERSEY

HOUSE OF REPRESENTATIVES

The Hon. Robert E. Andrews (D-1st District)
2439 Rayburn HOB
Washington, DC 20515
Tel: (202) 225-6501 Fax: (202) 225-6583
Email: rob.andrews@mail.house.gov
Web: www.house.gov/andrews

District Office
506-A White Horse Pike
Haddon Heights, NJ 08035
Tel: (856) 546-5100

District Office
63 N. Broad St.
Woodbury, NJ 08096
Tel: (856) 546-5100

The Hon. Rush Holt (D-12th District)
1019 Longworth HOB
Washington, DC 20515
Tel: (202) 225-5801 Fax: (202) 225-6025
Web: http://holt.house.gov

District Office
50 Washington Rd.
West Windsor, NJ 08550
Tel: (609) 750-9365 Fax: (609) 750-0618

The Hon. Frank Pallone, Jr. (D-6th District)
420 Cannon HOB
Washington, DC 20515-3006
Tel: (202) 225-4671 Fax: (202) 225-9665
Email: frank.pallone@mail.house.gov
Web: www.house.gov/pallone

District Office
67/69 Church St., Kilmer Sq.
New Brunswick, NJ 08901
Tel: (732) 249-8892

District Office
504 Broadway
Long Branch, NJ 07740
Tel: (732) 571-1140

District Office
1390 Hwy. 36 #104
Hazlet, NJ 07730
Tel: (732) 264-9104

The Hon. Bill Pascrell, Jr. (D-8th District)
1722 Longworth HOB
Washington, DC 20515
Tel: (202) 225-5751 Fax: (202) 225-5782
Web: www.pascrell.house.gov

District Office
Robert A. Roe Federal Bldg., 200 Federal Plz. #500
Paterson, NJ 07505
Tel: (973) 523-5152 Fax: (973) 523-0637

The Hon. Steven R. Rothman (D-9th District)
1607 Longworth HOB
Washington, DC 20515
Tel: (202) 225-5061 Fax: (202) 225-5851
Web: http://rothman.house.gov

District Office
25 Main St.
Hackensack, NJ 07601
Tel: (201) 646-0808 Fax: (201) 646-1944

District Office
130 Central Ave.
Jersey City, NJ 07306
Tel: (201) 798-1366 Fax: (201) 798-1725

NEW MEXICO

HOUSE OF REPRESENTATIVES

The Hon. Tom Udall (D-3rd District)
1414 Longworth HOB
Washington, DC 20515
Tel: (202) 225-6190 Fax: (202) 226-1331
Web: www.tomudall.house.gov

District Office
811 St. Michael's Dr. #104
Santa Fe, NM 87505
Tel: (505) 984-8950 Fax: (505) 986-5047

District Office
Rio Rancho City Hall, 3900 Southern Blvd. SE
Rio Rancho, NM 87124
Tel: (505) 994-0499 Fax: (505) 994-0550

District Office
P.O. Box 88102
Clovis, NM 88102
Tel: (505) 763-7616 Fax: (505) 763-7642

NEW YORK

HOUSE OF REPRESENTATIVES

The Hon. Gary L. Ackerman (D-5th District)
2243 Rayburn HOB
Washington, DC 20515
Tel: (202) 225-2601 Fax: (202) 225-1589
Email: gary.ackerman@mail.house.gov
Web: www.house.gov/ackerman

District Office
218-14 Northern Blvd.
Bayside, NY 11361
Tel: (718) 423-2154 Fax: (718) 423-5053

The Hon. Joseph Crowley (D-7th District)
312 Cannon HOB
Washington, DC 20515
Tel: (202) 225-3965 Fax: (202) 225-1909
Email: joseph.crowley@mail.house.gov
Web: http://crowley.house.gov

District Office
74-09 37th Ave. #306-B
Jackson Heights, NY 11372
Tel: (718) 779-1400

District Office
177 Dreiser Loop #3
Bronx, NY 10475
Tel: (718) 320-2314

District Office
3425 E. Tremont Ave. #1-3
Bronx, NY 10465
Tel: (718) 931-1400

The Hon. Maurice Hinchey (D-22nd District)
2431 Rayburn HOB
Washington, DC 20515
Tel: (202) 225-6335 Fax: (202) 226-0774
Web: www.house.gov/hinchey

District Office
City Hall, 3rd Fl., 16 James St.
Middletown, NY 10940
Tel: (845) 344-3211

District Office
100-A Federal Bldg.
Binghamton, NY 13901
Tel: (607) 773-2768

District Office
291 Wall St.
Kingston, NY 12401
Tel: (845) 331-4466

The Hon. Steve Israel (D-2nd District)
429 Cannon HOB
Washington, DC 20515
Tel: (202) 225-3335 Fax: (202) 225-4669
Web: www.house.gov/israel

District Office
150 Motor Pkwy. #108
Hauppauge, NY 11788
Tel: (631) 951-2210 Fax: (631) 951-3308

The Hon. Carolyn B. Maloney (D-14th District)
2331 Rayburn HOB
Washington, DC 20515-3214
Tel: (202) 225-7944 Fax: (202) 225-4709
Email: rep.carolyn.maloney@mail.house.gov
Web: www.house.gov/maloney

District Office
1651 3rd Ave. #311
New York, NY 10128-3679
Tel: (212) 860-0606 Fax: (212) 860-0704

District Office
28-11 Astoria Blvd.
Astoria, NY 11102-1933
Tel: (718) 932-1804 Fax: (718) 932-1805

The Hon. Carolyn McCarthy (D-4th District)
106 Cannon HOB
Washington, DC 20515
Tel: (202) 225-5516 Fax: (202) 225-5758
Web: www.house.gov/carolynmccarthy

District Office
200 Garden City Plz. #320
Garden City, NY 11530
Tel: (516) 739-3008

The Hon. Gregory W. Meeks (D-6th District)
1710 Longworth HOB
Washington, DC 20515
Tel: (202) 225-3461 Fax: (202) 226-4169
Email: congmeeks@mail.house.gov
Web: www.house.gov/meeks

District Office
196-06 Linden Blvd.
St. Albans, NY 11412
Tel: (718) 949-5600 Fax: (718) 949-5972

District Office
1931 Mott Ave. #305
Far Rockaway, NY 11691
Tel: (718) 327-9791 Fax: (718) 327-4722

District Office
106-11 Liberty Ave., 2nd Fl.
Richmond Hill, NY 11417
Tel: (718) 738-4200 Fax: (718) 738-5588

The Hon. Jerrold Nadler (NY-8)
2334 Rayburn House Office Building
Washington, DC 20515
Tel: (202) 225-5635 Fax: (202) 225-6923
Web: www.house.gov/nadler/

District Office
201 Varick St. #669
New York, NY 10014
Tel: (212) 367-7350

District Office
445 Neptune Ave.
Brooklyn, NY 11224
Tel: (718) 373-3198

The Hon. Major R. Owens (D-11th District)
2309 Rayburn HOB
Washington, DC 20515
Tel: (202) 225-6231 Fax: (202) 226-0112
Web: www.house.gov/owens

District Office
289 Utica Ave.
Brooklyn, NY 11213
Tel: (718) 773-3100 Fax: (718) 735-7143

District Office
1414 Cortelyou Rd.
Brooklyn, NY 11226

The Hon. José E. Serrano (D-16th District)
2227 Rayburn HOB
Washington, DC 20515-3216
Tel: (202) 225-4361 Fax: (202) 225-6001
Email: jserrano@mail.house.gov
Web: www.house.gov/serrano

District Office
788 Southern Blvd.
Bronx, NY 10455
Tel: (718) 620-0084 Fax: (718) 620-0658

The Hon. Edolphus Towns (D-10th District)
2232 Rayburn HOB
Washington, DC 20515
Tel: (202) 225-5936 Fax: (202) 225-1018
Email: edolphus.towns@mail.house.gov
Web: www.house.gov/towns

District Office
1110 Pennsylvania Ave. #5
Brooklyn, NY 11207
Tel: (718) 272-1175

District Office
1670 Fulton St.
Brooklyn, NY 11213
Tel: (718) 774-5682

District Office
26 Court St. #1510
Brooklyn, NY 11241
Tel: (718) 855-8018

The Hon. Nydia M. Velazquez (D-12th District)
2241 Rayburn HOB
Washington, DC 20515-2104
Tel: (202) 225-2361 Fax: (202) 226-0327
Email: nydia.velazquez@mail.house.gov
Web: www.house.gov/velazquez

District Office
268 Broadway, 2nd Fl.
Brooklyn, NY 11211
Tel: (718) 599-3658

District Office
173 Avenue B
New York, NY 10009
Tel: (212) 673-3997

District Office
16 Court St. #1006
Brooklyn, NY 11241
Tel: (718) 222-5819

The Hon. Anthony D. Weiner (D-9th District)
1122 Longworth HOB
Washington, DC 20515
Tel: (202) 225-6616 Fax: (202) 226-7253
Email: weiner@mail.house.gov
Web: www.house.gov/weiner

District Office
80-02 Kew Gardens Rd. #5000
Kew Gardens, NY 11415
Tel: (718) 520-9001

District Office
1800 Sheepshead Bay Rd.
Brooklyn, NY 11235
Tel: (718) 743-0441

District Office
90-16 Rockaway Beach Blvd.
Rockaway, NY 11693
Tel: (718) 318-9255

NORTH CAROLINA

HOUSE OF REPRESENTATIVES

The Hon. David E. Price (D-4th District)
2162 Rayburn HOB
Washington, DC 20515
Tel: (202) 225-1784 Fax: (202) 225-2014
Web: www.house.gov/price

District Office
5400 Trinity Rd. #205
Raleigh, NC 27607
Tel: (919) 859-5999 Fax: (919) 859-5998

District Office
411 W. Chapel Hill St., NC Mutual Bldg., 6th Fl.
Durham, NC 27701
Tel: (919) 688-3004 Fax: (919) 688-0940

District Office
88 Vilcom Ctr. #140
Chapel Hill, NC 27514
Tel: (919) 967-7924 Fax: (919) 967-8324

The Hon. Melvin L. Watt (D-12th District)
2236 Rayburn HOB
Washington, DC 20515-0001
Tel: (202) 225-1510 Fax: (202) 225-1512
Email: nc12.public@mail.house.gov
Web: www.house.gov/watt

District Office
1230 W. Morehead St. #306
Charlotte, NC 28208-5214
Tel: (704) 344-9950 Fax: (704) 344-9971

District Office
301 S. Greene St. #210
Greensboro, NC 27401-2615
Tel: (336) 275-9950 Fax: (336) 379-9951

OHIO

HOUSE OF REPRESENTATIVES

The Hon. Sherrod Brown (D-13th District)
2332 Rayburn HOB
Washington, DC 20515
Tel: (202) 225-3401 Fax: (202) 225-2266
Email: sherrod.brown@mail.house.gov
Web: www.house.gov/sherrodbrown

District Office
St. Joseph's Community Ctr., 205 W. 20th St. #M230
Lorain, OH 44052
Tel: (440) 245-5350 Fax: (440) 245-5355

District Office
1655 W. Market St. #E
Akron, OH 44313
Tel: (330) 865-8450 Fax: (330) 865-8470

The Hon. Stephanie Tubbs Jones (D-11th District)
1009 Longworth HOB
Washington, DC 20515
Tel: (202) 225-7032 Fax: (202) 225-1339
Email: stephanie.tubbs.jones@mail.house.gov
Web: www.house.gov/tubbsjones

District Office
3645 Warrensville Center Rd. #204
Shaker Heights, OH 44122
Tel: (216) 522-4900 Fax: (216) 522-4908

OREGON

HOUSE OF REPRESENTATIVES

The Hon. Earl Blumenauer (D-3rd District)
2446 Rayburn HOB
Washington, DC 20515
Tel: (202) 225-4811 Fax: (202) 225-8941
Email: earl.blumenauer@mail.house.gov
Web: www.house.gov/blumenauer

District Office
729 NE Oregon St. #115
Portland, OR 97232
Tel: (503) 231-2300 Fax: (503) 230-5413

The Hon. Peter A. DeFazio (D-4th District)
2134 Rayburn HOB
Washington, DC 20515
Tel: (202) 225-6416 Fax: (202) 225-0032
Email: peter.defazio@house.mail.gov
Web: www.house.gov/defazio

District Office
151 W. 7th #400
Eugene, OR 97401
Tel: (541) 465-6732

District Office
125 Central #250
Coos Bay, OR 97420
Tel: (541) 269-2609

District Office
612 SE Jackson St. #9
Roseburg, OR 97470
Tel: (541) 440-3523

The Hon. Darlene Hooley (D-5th District)
2430 Rayburn HOB
Washington, DC 20515
Tel: (202) 225-5711 Fax: (202) 225-5699
Web: www.house.gov/hooley

District Office
315 Mission St. SE #101
Salem, OR 97302
Tel: (503) 588-9100 Fax: (503) 588-5517

District Office
21570 Willamette Dr.
West Linn, OR 97068
Tel: (503) 557-1324 Fax: (503) 557-1981

The Hon. David Wu (D-1st District)
1023 Longworth HOB
Washington, DC 20515
Tel: (202) 225-0855 Fax: (202) 225-9497
Web: www.house.gov/wu

District Office
620 SW Main #606
Portland, OR 97205
Tel: (503) 326-2901 Fax: (503) 326-5066

PENNSYLVANIA

HOUSE OF REPRESENTATIVES

The Hon. Robert A. Brady (D-1st District)
206 Cannon HOB
Washington, DC 20515
Tel: (202) 225-4731 Fax: (202) 225-0088
Email: robert.a.brady@mail.house.gov
Web: www.house.gov/robertbrady

District Office
1907 S. Broad St.
Philadelphia, PA 19148
Tel: (215) 389-4627 Fax: (215) 389-4636

District Office
The Colony Bldg., 511-13 Welsh St., 1st Fl.
Chester, PA 19013
Tel: (610) 874-7094 Fax: (610) 874-7193

The Hon. Tim Holden (PA-17th District)
2417 Rayburn HOB
Washington, DC 20515
Tel: (202) 225-5546 Fax: (202) 226-0996
Web: www.holden.house.gov

District Office
Berks Corporate Dr., 280 Corporate Dr.
Reading, PA 19605
Tel: (610) 916-6363 Fax: (610) 916-6337

District Office
1721 N. Front St.
Harrisburg, PA 17102
Tel: (717) 234-5904 Fax: (717) 234-5918

District Office
47 S. 8th St.
Lebanon, PA 17042
Tel: (717) 270-1395 Fax: (717) 270-1095

The Hon. John P. Murtha (PA-12th District)
2423 Rayburn HOB
Washington, DC 20515
Tel: (202) 225-2065 Fax: (202) 225-5709
Email: murtha@mail.house.gov
Web: www.house.gov/murtha

District Office
P.O. Box 780
Johnstown, PA 15907-0780
Tel: (814) 535-2642 Fax: (814) 539-6229

RHODE ISLAND

HOUSE OF REPRESENTATIVES

The Hon. Patrick J. Kennedy (D-1st District)
407 Cannon HOB
Washington, DC 20515
Tel: (202) 225-4911 Fax: (202) 225-3290
Email: patrick.kennedy@mail.house.gov
Web: www.house.gov/patrickkennedy

District Office
249 Roosevelt Ave. #200
Pawtucket, RI 02860
Tel: (401) 729-5600 Fax: (401) 729-5608

SOUTH CAROLINA

HOUSE OF REPRESENTATIVES

The Hon. James E. Clyburn (D-6th District)
2135 Rayburn HOB
Washington, DC 20515
Tel: (202) 225-3315 Fax: (202) 225-2313
Email: jclyburn@mail.house.gov
Web: www.house.gov/clyburn

District Office
1703 Gervais St.
Columbia, SC 29201
Tel: (803) 799-1100 Fax: (803) 799-9060

District Office
P.O. Box 6286
Florence, SC 29506
Tel: (843) 662-1212 Fax: (843) 662-8474

District Office
8833 Old Number Six Hwy.
Santee, SC 29142
Tel: (803) 854-4700 Fax: (843) 965-5581

TEXAS

HOUSE OF REPRESENTATIVES

The Hon. Lloyd Doggett (D-10th District)
201 Cannon HOB
Washington, DC 20515-0001
Tel: (202) 225-4865 Fax: (202) 225-3073
Email: lloyd.doggett@mail.house.gov
Web: www.house.gov/doggett/

District Office
300 E. 8th St. #763
Austin, TX 78701-3275
Tel: (512) 916-5921 Fax: (512) 916-5108

District Office
311 N. 15th St.
McAllen, TX 78501
Tel: (956) 687-5921 Fax: (956) 683-1301

The Hon. Charles A. Gonzalez (D-20th District)
327 Cannon HOB
Washington, DC 20515
Tel: (202) 225-3236 Fax: (202) 225-1915
Web: www.house.gov/gonzalez

District Office
727 E. Durango #B-124, Federal Bldg.
San Antonio, TX 78206
Tel: (210) 472-6195 Fax: (210) 472-4009

The Hon. Al Green (10-TX)
1529 Longworth House Office Building
Washington, DC 20515-4309
Tel: (202) 225-7508 Fax: (202) 225-2947
Web: www.house.gov/algreen/index.shtml

District Office
3003 South Loop West Suite 460
Houston, TX 77054
Tel: (713) 383-9234 Fax: (713) 383-9202

The Hon. Gene Green (D-29th District)
2335 Rayburn HOB
Washington, DC 20515
Tel: (202) 225-1688 Fax: (202) 225-9903
Web: www.house.gov/green

District Office
256 N. Sam Houston Pkwy. East #29
Houston, TX 77060
Tel: (281) 999-5879 Fax: (281) 999-5716

District Office
11811 I-10 E. #430
Houston, TX 77029
Tel: (713) 330-0761 Fax: (713) 330-0807

The Hon. Ralph M. Hall (D-4th District)
2405 Rayburn HOB
Washington, DC 20515
Tel: (202) 225-6673 Fax: (202) 225-3332
Email: rmhall@mail.house.gov
Web: www.house.gov/ralphhall

District Office
104 N. San Jacinto St.
Rockwall, TX 75087-2508
Tel: (972) 771-9118 Fax: (972) 722-0907

District Office
101 E. Pecan St.
Sherman, TX 75090-5917
Tel: (903) 892-1112 Fax: (903) 868-0264

District Office
211 W. Ferguson St. #211
Tyler, TX 75702-7222
Tel: (903) 597-3729 Fax: (903) 597-0726

The Hon. Rubén E. Hinojosa (D-15th District)
2463 Rayburn HOB
Washington, DC 20515
Tel: (202) 225-2531 Fax: (202) 225-5688
Web: www.house.gov/hinojosa

District Office
311 N. 15th St.
McAllen, TX 78501
Tel: (956) 682-5545 Fax: (956) 682-0141

District Office
107 S. St. Mary's St.
Beeville, TX 78102
Tel: (361) 358-8400 Fax: (361) 358-8407

The Hon. Sheila Jackson-Lee (D-18th District)
2435 Rayburn HOB
Washington, DC 20515
Tel: (202) 225-3816 Fax: (202) 225-3317
Web: www.jacksonlee.house.gov

District Office
1919 Smith St. #1180
Houston, TX 77002
Tel: (713) 655-0050 Fax: (713) 655-1612

District Office
420 W. 19th St.
Houston, TX 77008
Tel: (713) 861-4070

District Office
6719 W. Montgomery #204
Houston, TX 77091
Tel: (713) 691-4882

The Hon. Eddie Bernice Johnson (D-30th District)
1511 Longworth HOB
Washington, DC 20510
Tel: (202) 225-8885 Fax: (202) 226-1477
Email: per.e.b.johnsom@mail.house.gov
Web: www.house.gov/ebjohnson

District Office
Cedar Springs Plz., 2501 Cedar Springs Rd. #550
Dallas, TX 75201
Tel: (214) 922-8885

District Office
1634-B W. Irving Blvd.
Irving, TX 75061
Tel: (972) 253-8885

The Hon. Solomon P. Ortiz (D-27th District)
2470 Rayburn HOB
Washington, DC 20515
Tel: (202) 225-7742 Fax: (202) 226-1134
Web: www.house.gov/ortiz

District Office
3649 Leopard St. #510
Corpus Christi, TX 78408
Tel: (361) 883-5868 Fax: (361) 884-9201

District Office
1805 Ruben Torres #B-27
Brownsville, TX 78526
Tel: (956) 541-1242 Fax: (956) 544-6915

VERMONT

HOUSE OF REPRESENTATIVES

The Hon. Bernie Sanders (Ind.)
2233 Rayburn HOB
Washington, DC 20515
Tel: (202) 225-4115 Fax: (202) 225-6790

Email: bernie@mail.house.gov
Web: http://bernie.house.gov

District Office
1 Church St., 2nd Fl.
Burlington, VT 05401
Tel: (802) 862-0697 Fax: (802) 860-6370

District Office
167 Main St. #410
Brattleboro, VT 05301
Tel: (802) 254-8732 Fax: (802) 254-9207

VIRGINIA

HOUSE OF REPRESENTATIVES

The Hon. Robert C. "Bobby" Scott (D-3rd District)
2464 Rayburn HOB
Washington, DC 20515
Tel: (202) 225-8351 Fax: (202) 225-8354
Email: bobby.scott@mail.house.gov
Web: www.house.gov/scott

District Office
2600 Washington Ave. #1010
Newport News, VA 23607
Tel: (757) 380-1000 Fax: (757) 928-6694

District Office
The Jackson Ctr., 501 N. 2nd St. #401
Richmond, VA 23219-1321
Tel: (804) 644-4845 Fax: (804) 648-6026

WASHINGTON

SENATE

The Hon. Maria Cantwell (D)
717 Hart SOB
Washington, DC 20510
Tel: (202) 224-3441 Fax: (202) 228-0514
Web: http://cantwell.senate.gov

District Office
915 2nd Ave. #3206
Seattle, WA 98174
Tel: (206) 220-6400 Fax: (206) 220-6404

District Office
US Federal Courthouse, W. 920 Riverside #697
Spokane, WA 99201
Tel: (509) 353-2507 Fax: (509) 353-2547

District Office
Marshall House, 1313 Officers Row
Vancouver, WA 98661
Tel: (360) 696-7838 Fax: (360) 696-7844

The Hon. Patty Murray (D)
173 Russell SOB
Washington, DC 20510
Tel: (202) 224-2621 Fax: (202) 224-0238
Web: http://murray.senate.gov

District Office
2988 Jackson Federal Bldg., 915 2nd Ave.
Seattle, WA 98174
Tel: (206) 553-5545 Fax: (206) 553-0891

District Office
2930 Wetmore Ave. #903
Everett, WA 98201
Tel: (425) 259-6515 Fax: (425) 259-7152

District Office
601 W. Main Ave. #1213
Spokane, WA 99201
Tel: (509) 624-9515 Fax: (509) 624-9561

HOUSE OF REPRESENTATIVES

The Hon. Jay Inslee (D-1st District)
308 Cannon HOB
Washington, DC 20515-4701
Tel: (202) 225-6311 Fax: (202) 226-1606
Web: www.house.gov/inslee

District Office
21905 64th Ave. West #101
Mountlake Terrace, WA 98043-2278
Tel: (425) 640-0233 Fax: (425) 776-7168

District Office
17791 Fjord Dr. NE #112
Poulsbo, WA 98370-8481
Tel: (360) 598-2342 Fax: (360) 598-3650

The Hon. Rick Larsen (D-2nd District)
1529 Longworth HOB
Washington, DC 20515
Tel: (202) 225-2605 Fax: (202) 225-4420
Email: rick.larsen@mail.house.gov
Web: www.house.gov/larsen

District Office
2930 Wetmore Ave. #9E
Everett, WA 98201
Tel: (425) 252-3188 Fax: (425) 252-6606

District Office
104 W. Magnolia #303
Bellingham, WA 98225
Tel: (360) 733-4500 Fax: (360) 733-5144

The Hon. Jim McDermott (D-7th District)
1035 Longworth HOB
Washington, DC 20515
Tel: (202) 225-3106 Fax: (202) 225-6197
Web: www.house.gov/mcdermott

District Office
1809 7th Ave. #1212
Seattle, WA 98101-1399
Tel: (206) 553-7170 Fax: (206) 553-7175

WISCONSIN

HOUSE OF REPRESENTATIVES

The Hon. Tammy Baldwin (D-2nd District)
1022 Longworth HOB
Washington, DC 20515
Tel: (202) 225-2906 Fax: (202) 225-6942
Email: tammy.baldwin@mail.house.gov
Web: http://tammybaldwin.house.gov/index.asp

District Office
10 E. Doty St. #405
Madison, WI 53703
Tel: (608) 258-9800 Fax: (608) 258-9808

District Office
400 E. Grand Ave. #402
Beloit, WI 53511
Tel: (608) 362-2800 Fax: (608) 362-2838

Prominent Asian Pacific Americans

Arts

HENRY CHO
Comedian

For Comedian Henry Cho, making the most of who he is has not been a problem. "I'm an Asian with a Southern accent," remarks Cho. "To a lot of people, that right there is funny." Cho, who is Korean American, was born in Knoxville, Tennessee, and speaks with a Southern accent. To a lot of people, that right there is comedic.

In 1994, Henry got the call from NBC to host NBC's *Friday Night Videos*, which he did weekly for two years. While in LA, Cho became a regular guest/comedian on such shows as *The Tonight Show* and *The Arsenio Hall Show*. His TV credits also include guest roles on various sitcoms such as CBS' *Designing Women* and *The New WKRP in Cincinnati* and a starring role in FOX's TV movie, *Revenge of the Nerds* III: The *Next Generation*. Cho's many comedy credits include NBC's *Bob Hope's Young Comedians Special*, MTV's 1/2 Hour Comedy Hour, and *Comedy Central*.

He has starred opposite Tom Arnold and David Allen Grier in Universal's *McHale's Navy* and the Farrelly brothers' movie *Say It Isn't So*, with Sally Field, Heather Graham and Chris Klein.

This past summer, Cho was the keynote entertainer for the fitfy ninth Annual Radio & Television Correspondents' Dinner. Then, over the holiday season, Cho joined Amy Grant and Vince Gill on their annual Christmas Tour.

Just recently, Cho inked a deal with ABC and Touchstone Studios to develop his own sitcom in which he will also be co-creator and co-storywriter.

FRED HO
Founder, Composer, Musician, Writer, Producer & Activist, Big Red Media, Inc.

Fred Ho is a one-of-a-kind revolutionary Chinese American baritone saxophonist, composer, writer, producer, political activ-

ist and leader of the Afro Asian Music Ensemble and the Monkey Orchestra. For two decades, he has innovated an Afro Asian New American Multicultural Music imbedded in the swingest, most soulful and transgressive forms of African American music with the musical influences of Asia and the Pacific Rim.

Ho is a prodigious composer, having written over a half dozen operas, music/theater epics, cutting edge multimedia performance works, martial arts ballet, and oratorios. In the mid-1980s, Ho created the Asian Pacific American performance art trilogy, Bamboo that Snaps Back, presented at the Whitney Museum, and for which the music/spoken word score was released on Finnadar/WEA records. He wrote the first contemporary Chinese American opera, *A Chinaman's Chance*, staged at the Brooklyn Academy of Music, featuring a bilingual libretto and which signaled his ground-breaking combination of traditional Chinese and western instrumentation. In 1988 he conceived and composed the music/theater epic, *A Song for Manong* as a tribute to Filipino workers. He composed and created a multimedia bilingual oratorio, *Turn Pain Into Power*!

His music/theater/opera/dance-ballet epic *Journey Beyond the West: The New Adventures of Monkey* was commissioned by the Joseph Papp Public Theater, developed by the Guggenheim Museum Works and Process Series, and presented at the Brooklyn Academy of Music 1997 Next Wave Festival. Joining with librettist Ann T. Greene, Ho created the opera *Warrior Sisters: The New Adventures of African and Asian Womyn Warriors*, commissioned by the Mary Flagler Cary Charitable Trust, Aaron Davis Hall, the National Endowment for the Arts Opera/Musical Theater program, Dance Theater Workshop and Arizona State University-Tempe and premiered at The Kitchen in NYC. The opera was released as a double CD by Koch Jazz. In collaboration with librettist Ruth Margraff, Fred Ho created *Night Vision: A Third to First World Vampyre* Opera, supported by the New York State Council on the Arts and the Rockefeller Foundation. This opera was presented at Cooper Union and the HERE Arts Center in NYC, with development by The Joseph Papp Public Theater New Work Now Festival and New York Theater Workshop. The book and double CD was published and released by Autonomedia and Big Red Media. The Mary Flager Cary Charitable Trust with the World Music Institute, the New

York State Council on the Arts and the John Harms Center for the Arts commissioned the world premiere of Ho's blockbuster *Once Upon a Time in Chinese America*, a martial arts ballet and music theater epic, presented at the Guggenheim Museum, the JVC Jazz Festival, the Seattle International Children's Festival and the Brooklyn Academy of Music 2001. The soundtrack is released on the Innova label. Re-titled *Voice of the Dragon: Once Upon a Time in Chinese America, The Martial Arts Epic*, the show was signed to Columbia Artists Management Inc. for a tour to 33 U.S. cities in 2002 to 2003. In 2003/04, the Caribbean Cultural Center, the Mary Flagler Cary Charitable Trust, the Apollo Theater Foundation, Mutable Music and the New York State Council on the Arts commissioned Fred Ho to compose and conceive the sequel to this highly successful show, *Voice of the Dragon 2: Shaolin Secret Stories*, which premiered in January 2004 at the world famous Apollo Theater.

Fred Ho received numerous awards, including the McKnight Foundation Composer/ Residency award; five Rockefeller Foundation Multi-Arts Project grants, two National Endowment for the Arts Fellowships; three New York Foundation for the Arts Music Composition fellowships; a 1988 Duke Ellington Distinguished Artist Lifetime Achievement Award from the Black Musicians Conference; the 1987 Harvard University Peter Ivers Visiting Artist award; and many others. He has been a Master Artist at the Atlantic Center for the Arts, an Artist Fellow at the Djerassi Resident Artists Program; resident artist at the Civitelli Ranieri center in Umbria, Italy; and resident scholar and visiting artist at Rockefeller Foundation Bellagio Study and Conference Center in Bellagio, Italy.

As a life-long activist, Ho helped to found the East Coast Asian Students Union, the Asian American Resource Workshop, the Asian American Arts Alliance, among many others. Ho co-edited with Ron Sakolsky Sounding Off! Music as Subversion/ Resistance/ Revolution which won the 1996 American Book Award; he edits the popular and best-selling annual Sheroes/ Womyn Warriors calendar. He also was lead editor of the anthology *Legacy to Liberation: Politics and Culture of Revolutionary Asian Pacific America*, considered by many to be a milestone work. In 2005 Duke University Press will publish Ho's landmark anthology *Afro/Asia: Revolutionary Political and Cultural Connections Between African Americans and Asian Americans* co-edited with Bill V. Mullen. Fred Ho resides in Brooklyn, New York.

MING TSAI
Chef & Host, Simply Ming, East Meets West, Cooking with Ming Tsai & Ming's Quest

Ming Tsai grew up in Dayton, Ohio, spending countless hours cooking alongside his parents at their family-owned restaurant, Mandarin Kitchen. As a teenager, Ming headed East to attend school at Andover, continuing to Yale University and earning his degree in Mechanical Engineering. During this time, Ming never strayed far from the kitchen; while at Yale, he spent his sophomore summer at Le Cordon Bleu cooking school in Paris. Upon graduating, Ming decided to focus on food. In Paris he trained under renowned Pastry Chef Pierre Herme and in Osaka

with Sushi Master Kobayashi. Ming then enrolled in graduate school at Cornell University, earning his Master's Degree in Hotel Administration and Hospitality Marketing. In February of 1998, Ming's dream became reality. He and his wife, Polly, opened Blue Ginger, a bistro-style restaurant dedicated to East-West cuisine. Located in Wellesley, Massachusetts, Blue Ginger brings urban dining and sophistication to the Boston suburbs.

Since opening, Blue Ginger has impressed diners from Boston and beyond with its unique East-West cuisine. In its first year, Blue Ginger received three stars from the *Boston Globe*, was named 'Best New Restaurant' by *Boston Magazine*, was nominated by the James Beard Foundation as "Best New Restaurant 1998" and *Esquire Magazine* honored Ming as 'Chef of the Year 1998.' Five years later, the popularity continues. The James Beard Foundation crowned Ming as the "2002 Best Chef Northeast," while the 2002-2003, 2003-2004 & 2004-2005 *Zagat Restaurant Guide* rated Blue Ginger as the 2nd Most Popular Boston Restaurant. In 2005, Ming was honored as "Restaurateur of the Year" by the Massachusetts Restaurant Association.

Ming is currently the host of the Public Television cooking show *Simply Ming* and one of three celebrity judges on PBS's 'reality' cooking show, *Cooking Under Fire*. Ming began cooking for television audiences on the Food Network, where he was the 1998 Emmy-Award winning host of East Meets West, Cooking with Ming Tsai and Ming's Quest. In 2005, *Simply Ming* was awarded the prestigious Cine Golden Eagle Award. In addition to television, Ming is also the author of three cookbooks: *Blue Ming* and *Ming's Master Recipes*.

Business

JOHN S. CHEN
Chairman, CEO and President, Sybase, Inc.

John S. Chen was born in Hong Kong in 1955. He came to the United States as a student in 1973, where he attended the coveted Northfield Mount Herman College Preparatory in Northfield, Massachusetts. In 1978, Mr. Chen graduated from Brown University with a Bachelor of Science degree in Electrical Engineering and Magna Cum Laude, Sigma Xi and Tau Beta Pi honors. In 1979, he received his Master of Science degree in Electrical Engineering from the California Institute of Technology.

In 1979, Mr. Chen began a thirteen-year career at Unisys/ Burroughs in Pasadena, California, where he held a variety of engineering and management positions, including Vice President and General Manager of the $500 million Unisys Convergent

UNIX Systems Group and Vice President and General Manager of the $125 million Unisys Convergent RISC Platform Division. Furthering his engineering and management leadership, Mr. Chen joined Pyramid Technology Corporation as executive Vice President in 1991. In 1993, he became President, Chief Operating Officer and Board Member, where he was responsible for all aspects of the $275 million, high-end UNIX-based systems company. In 1995, Mr. Chen's proven leadership and operational expertise led to the successful negotiation of the sale of Pyramid Technology to Siemens Nixdorf Informationssysteme, AG of Munich Germany. He became one of the first Asian Americans to join the Siemens Nixdorf's Executive Board of Directors. In 1996, Mr. Chen was elevated to President and CEO of Siemens Nixdorf's $3 billion Open Enterprise Computing Division.

Mr. Chen's successful career led him in 1997 to Sybase, Inc., where he was recruited as President and Chief Operating Officer to help restore growth and profitability, and build a long term, sustainable management team for the billion dollar software company. Under Mr. Chen's first year of leadership, he refocused the company on high-growth market initiatives and reported three quarters of operating profit as well as a 13% increase in cash. He was named Chairman, CEO and President of Sybase in October 1998 and later unveiled a new business strategy to divisionalize the company as part of a move toward providing customers with targeted, market-driven business solutions.

Mr. Chen currently serves as a member of the board of directors for CIT, and TurboLinux. Committee of 100, a powerful group of nationally visible Asian Americans, recruited Mr. Chen to become a member of this prestigious think-tank in 1997. The organization's mission is to help strengthen relationships between the U.S. and China by promoting greater collaboration and enhanced understanding of issues faced by Asian Americans. Its membership includes some of the nation's most influential Asian American business leaders, musicians, medical researchers, lawyers, academics, Supreme Court justices, authors, and Nobel Peace Prize winners.

In 1998, Committee of 100 awarded Mr. Chen as 'Entrepreneur of the Year'; and the Overseas Chinese Association awarded him as 'Distinguished Asian American Businessman' for his professional accomplishments in the high technology industry.

ANDREA JUNG
Chairman & CEO, Avon Products, Inc.

As Chairman of the Board and Chief Executive Officer, Andrea Jung has directed the successful transformation of Avon Products, Inc., by defining its vision as the company for women. She is revitalizing Avon's reputation as the world's foremost direct seller of beauty products while leading the company into exciting new lines of business, launching a series of bold and image-enhancing initiatives, and expanding career opportunities for women around the world.

She was elected Chairman in September 2001 and has been CEO since November 1999. Previously, she was President and Chief

Operating Officer, responsible for all Avon business units worldwide. She has been a member of the Board of Directors since January 1998.

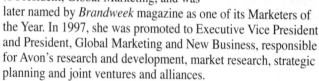

Ms. Jung joined Avon in January 1994 as President, Product Marketing Group, Avon U.S. In 1996, she was promoted to President, Global Marketing, and was later named by *Brandweek* magazine as one of its Marketers of the Year. In 1997, she was promoted to Executive Vice President and President, Global Marketing and New Business, responsible for Avon's research and development, market research, strategic planning and joint ventures and alliances.

Before joining Avon, Ms. Jung was Executive Vice President at Neiman Marcus, responsible for accessories, cosmetics and women's intimate apparel and children's apparel. Earlier in her career, she was Senior Vice President, General Merchandising Manager, for I. Magnin in San Francisco.

In March 2001, Ms. Jung became the first woman elected Chair of the Cosmetic, Toiletry, and Fragrance Association, a role she held until early 2005. She currently serves on the Board of Directors of the General Electric Company and is a member of the New York Presbyterian Hospital Board of Trustees and the Catalyst Board of Directors.

In 1997, *Advertising Age* magazine bestowed on Ms. Jung the National Outstanding Mother Award and named her one of the "25 Women to Watch." In 1998, the American Advertising Federation inducted her into the Advertising Hall of Fame. In 2001, *Time Magazine*/CNN declared her one of the 25 Most Influential Global Executives, and in January 2003, she was featured in *Business Week* as one of the best managers of the year. She has been ranked #3 among *Fortune* magazine's "50 most powerful women in business" for the past two years. In 2004, the *Wall Street Journal* named Ms. Jung one of "50 people to watch in business" and in December 2004 she was named one of "10 prominent people to watch in 2005" by *Newsweek* magazine.

Ms. Jung is a magna cum Laude graduate of Princeton University and is fluent in Chinese (Mandarin).

JEONG H. KIM, PH.D
President, Lucent Technologies' Bell Laboratories

As a notable technologist and businessman, Jeong H. Kim has broad professional experience and wide-ranging interests. He is currently president of Lucent Technologies' Bell Laboratories, overseeing the communication industry's most heralded R&D organization. Dr. Kim is also a strong entrepreneur, having successfully led a high technology start-up as Chairman & CEO, and provided strategic direction and leadership as a key senior executive with a Fortune 50 corporation.

Dr. Kim's early career encompassed computer design, satellite systems design and data communications, and included seven years as a Nuclear Submarine Officer in the U.S. Navy. He founded Yurie Systems, a high-tech communications equipment company, in 1992, and served as Chairman and CEO until its acquisition by Lucent Technologies in 1998 for $1.1 billion. As Group President of the Optical Networking Group at Lucent, Dr. Kim led a successful turnaround effort and returned the business unit to profitability within a short period while recapturing market segment leadership. Prior to rejoining Lucent as the President of Bell Labs, Dr. Kim was an active professor at the University of Maryland Clark School of Engineering, and served as Chairman of CIBERNET Corporation, an emergent wireless technology services company.

He holds a Ph.D. in Reliability Engineering from the University of Maryland, and a Master's Degree in Technical Management from Johns Hopkins University, where he also earned Bachelor's degrees in Electrical Engineering and Computer Science.

Among his many service commitments, Dr. Kim served on an eight member Presidential Commission on Review of U.S. Intelligence and as a member of the Board of Regents for the University System of Maryland. At present, Dr. Kim holds Board positions with several organizations, including In-Q-Tel, Stanford University's Institute for International Studies, Johns Hopkins University, University of Maryland College Park Foundation, McLeod USA, MTI MicroFuel Cells Inc., and GIV Global Private Equity. Additionally, he was elected as a member to the prestigious National Academy of Engineering for his distinguished contributions to the field.

VYOMESH JOSHI

Executive Vice President, Imaging & Printing Group, Hewlett-Packard Company

Vyomesh Joshi is Executive Vice President of HP's Imaging and Printing Group, with worldwide responsibility for all printing, scanning and digital camera platforms, for ensuring the greatest leverage from the company's investments in inkjet, laser and LEP printing technologies, and for key initiatives to transform the commercial printing market through digital publishing. VJ became the Vice President and General Manager of the former Inkjet Imaging Solutions Personal Imaging and Printing organization in 1999. In that position, he had worldwide responsibility for all inkjet printing and imaging platforms, which included inkjet printers, imaging products and associated supplies. He also led the HP company-wide initiative on digital imaging appliances, infrastructure and services.

Under VJ's leadership as General Manager in the spring of 1997, the Home Imaging Division introduced a complete digital photography system that included a digital camera, photo scanner and photo printer. In 1995, HP entered into the digital color copier business with the introduction of an affordable color copier/printer appliance. VJ became Operations Manager of the San Diego Imaging Operation in 1994 after serving four years as Research-and-Development Manager of two new HP businesses: large format color printing and fax/multifunction products.

In 1989, VJ was given Section Manager responsibility for color printer connectivity solutions, which included the development of HP's PCL 5C color printer language and color device drivers. In 1984, he became Project Manager for the Inkjet Components Division, where he served as section manager and Program Manager for the first color inkjet cartridge developed by HP. VJ joined HP in 1980 as a Research and Development Engineer for pen plotters in San Diego.

VJ holds a Master's Degree in Electrical Engineering from Ohio State University.

Community

DALE MINAMI

Advocate/Lawyer, Minami, Lew & Tamaki

Dale Minami, a partner with Minami, Lew & Tamaki in San Francisco, specializes in personal injury and entertainment law. He received a B.A. in 1968 with Honors in Political Science from the University of Southern California and graduated magna cum laude and Phi Beta Kappa. He received his J.D. in 1971 from Boalt Hall School of Law, University of California.

Mr. Minami was a co-founder of the Asian Law Caucus, Inc., the Asian American Bar Association of the Greater Bay Area, the Asian Pacific Bar of California and the Coalition of Asian Pacific Americans. He has been involved in significant litigation involving the civil rights of Asian Pacific Americans and other minorities, including *Korematsu v. United States* (overturning 40 year-old conviction upheld by Supreme Court in 1942 for refusal to obey military orders aimed at Japanese Americans during World War II) and class actions for employment discrimination (*United Pilipinos for Affirmative Action v. California Blue Shield*), the first class action employment lawsuit brought by Asian Pacific Americans on behalf of Asian Pacific Americans, and educational discrimination (*Spokane JACL v. Washington State University*). He also represented Don Nakanishi in his claim for unfair denial of tenure at UCLA which resulted in the granting of tenure. Mr. Minami also represents clients in the entertainment industry including Kristi Yamaguchi, the 1992 Olympic Gold Medal skater, playwright Philip Kan Gotanda; CNN's Erica Hill; KRON's Wendy Tokuda and Vic Lee, KPIX's anchor Sydnie Kohara; and numerous other newscasters in the Bay Area. He is counsel to the National Asian American Telecommunications Association and the Asian American Journalists' Association.

Mr. Minami has served as a member of the California Fair Employment and Housing Commission; the California Attorney General's Asian Pacific Advisory Committee; the State Bars Commission on Judicial Nominee's Evaluation; Senator Barbara Boxer's Judicial Screening Committee which made recommendations for Federal Judicial Appointments; and was appointed by President Clinton as Chair of the Civil Liberties Public Education Fund. He now serves on the Board of Kristi Yamaguchi's Always Dream Foundation and the Advisory Board of the Angel Island Immigration Station Foundation. He has taught at U.C. Berkeley and Mills College in Oakland and was Co-Executive Producer (with Philip Kan Gotanda) of *Drinking Tea* and *Life Tastes Good*, both of which were screened at the Sundance Film Festival.

Mr. Minami has received numerous awards, including the American Bar Association's 2003 Thurgood Marshall Award, the 2003 ACLU Civil Liberties Award, the State Bar President's Pro Bono Service Award, an honorary Juris Doctor degree from the McGeorge School of Law, designation of a dormitory at the University of California at Santa Cruz as the "Queen Liliuokalani-Minami" Dormitory, awards from the Coro Foundation, the Harry Dow Memorial Fellowship in Boston, the Fred Korematsu Civil Rights Fund Award, the Organization of Chinese Americans, the Japanese American Youth Center and Centro Legal de la Raza.

JAMES ZOGBY
Founder & President, Arab American Institute

Dr. James J. Zogby is founder and President of the Arab American Institute (AAI), a Washington, D.C.-based organization which serves as the political and policy research arm of the Arab American community. Since 1985, Dr. Zogby and AAI have led Arab American efforts to secure political empowerment in the U.S. Through voter registration, education and mobilization, AAI has moved Arab Americans into the political mainstream.

For the past three decades, Dr. Zogby has been involved in a full range of Arab American issues. A co-founder and Chairman of the Palestine Human Rights Campaign in the late 1970s, he later co-founded and served as the Executive Director of the American-Arab Anti-Discrimination Committee. In 1982, he co-founded Save Lebanon, Inc., a private non-profit, humanitarian and non-sectarian relief organization which funds health care for Palestinian and Lebanese victims of war, and other social welfare projects in Lebanon. In 1985, Zogby founded AAI.

In 1993, following the signing of the Israeli-Palestinian peace accord in Washington, Dr. Zogby was asked by Vice President Al Gore to lead Builders for Peace, a private sector committee, to promote U.S. business investment in the West Bank and Gaza. In his capacity as co-president of Builders, Zogby frequently traveled to the Middle East with delegations led by Vice President Gore and late Secretary of Commerce Ron Brown. In 1994, with former U.S. Congressman Mel Levine, his colleague as co-president of Builders, Zogby led a U.S. delegation to the signing of the Israeli-Palestinian agreement in Cairo. Zogby also chaired a forum on the Palestinian economy at the Casablanca Economic Summit in 1994. After 1994, through Builders, Zogby worked with a number of U.S. agencies to promote and support Palestinian economic development, including AID, OPIC, USTDA, and the Departments of State and Commerce.

Dr. Zogby has also been personally active in U.S. politics for many years. Most recently, Zogby was elected a co-convener of the National Democratic Ethnic Coordinating Committee (NDECC), an umbrella organization of Democratic Party leaders of European and Mediterranean descent. On September 24, 1999, the NDECC elected Dr. Zogby as its representative to the DNC's Executive Committee.

A lecturer and scholar on Middle East issues, U.S.-Arab relations, and the history of the Arab American community, Dr. Zogby appears frequently on television and radio. He has appeared as a regular guest on all the major network news programs. After hosting the popular *A Capital View* on the Arab Network of America for several years, he now hosts Viewpoint with James Zogby on Abu Dhabi Television, LinkTV, Dish Network, and DirecTV [broadcast schedule].

Since 1992, Dr. Zogby has also written a weekly column on U.S. politics for the major newspapers of the Arab world. The column, *Washington Watch*, is currently published in fourteen Arab countries. He has authored a number of books including two recent publications, "What Ethnic Americans Really Think" and "What Arabs Think: Values, Beliefs and Concerns."

Dr. Zogby has testified before U.S. House of Representatives and Senate committees, has been guest speaker on a number of occasions in the Secretary's Open Forum at the U.S. Department of State, and has addressed the United Nations and other international forums. He recently received a Distinguished Public Service Award from the U.S. Department of State "in recognition of outstanding contributions to national and international affairs."

Dr. Zogby is also active professionally beyond his involvement with the Arab American community. He currently serves on the Human Rights Watch Middle East Advisory Committee and on the national advisory boards of the American Civil Liberties Union and the National Immigration Forum, and is a member of the Council on Foreign Relations. In January 2001, he was selected by the President to be a member of the Central Asian-American Enterprise Fund and serves on its Board of Directors. Additionally, he recently attained a position with polling firm Zogby International as Senior Analyst.

In 1975, Dr. Zogby received his doctorate from Temple University's Department of Religion, where he studied under the Islamic scholar Dr. Ismail al-Faruqi. He was a National Endowment for the Humanities Post-Doctoral Fellow at

Princeton University in 1976, and on several occasions was awarded grants for research and writing by the National Endowment for the Humanities, the National Defense Education Act, and the Mellon Foundation. Dr. Zogby received a Bachelor of Arts from Le Moyne College. In 1995, Le Moyne awarded Zogby an honorary doctoral of laws degree, and in 1997 named him the college's outstanding alumnus.

Dr. Zogby is married to Eileen Patricia McMahon and is the father of five children. Zogby's mother, Cecilia Ann, was a woman committed to religion, family, education, and service of others.

Education

AMY CHUA

Professor of Law, Yale University

Professor Chua was an executive editor of the Harvard Law Review and after graduation clerked for Chief Judge Patricia Wald of the United States Court of Appeals for the D.C. Circuit. Prior to entering the academy in 1994, she practiced with the Wall Street firm of Cleary, Gottlieb, Steen & Hamilton, where she worked on international transactions throughout Asia, Europe, and Latin America, including the privatization of Teléfonos de México. Professor Chua has taught at Duke, Columbia, NYU, and Stanford; she joined the Yale Law School faculty in 2001. Her recent book World on Fire: How Exporting Free Market Democracy Breeds Ethnic Hatred and Global Instability (Doubleday, 2003) was a New York Times bestseller. It was also selected by both The Economist and the U.K.'s Guardian as one of the Best Books of 2003. World on Fire has been translated into Chinese, Finnish, Japanese, Korean, Italian, Spanish, and Indonesian.

Professor Chua has addressed numerous government and policymaking institutions, including the World Bank, the Brookings Institution, the United Nations, and the CIA. She has also lectured widely outside the United States, including in Argentina, Bolivia, Chile, China, Mexico, Taiwan, Turkey, and South Africa. She teaches in the areas of contracts, law and development, international business transactions, and law and globalization.

VIET D. DINH

Professor of Law & Co-Director of Asian Law and Policy Studies, Georgetown University Law Center

Viet D. Dinh is Professor of Law and Co-Director of Asian Law and Policy Studies at the Georgetown University Law Center.

A regular commentator on policy issues and a public affairs consultant, Dinh served as U.S. Assistant Attorney General for Legal Policy from 2001 to 2003. As the official responsible for federal legal policy, Dinh helped develop initiatives to reduce demand for illicit drugs, eliminate racial profiling in federal law enforcement, protect children from exploitation, combat human trafficking, develop DNA technology, reduce gun violence, and reform civil and criminal justice procedures. After 9/11, Dinh conducted a comprehensive review and revision of Department of Justice priorities, policies and practices to ensure that all available resources are dedicated to protecting America against terrorist acts. He played a key role in developing the USA Patriot Act and revising the Attorney General's Guidelines, which govern federal law enforcement activities and national security investigations. Dinh also represented the Department of Justice in selecting and confirming federal judges, contributing to the appointment of 100 district judges and twenty-three appellate judges during his tenure.

Dinh specializes in constitutional law, corporations law, and the law and economics of development. His representative publications include *Defending Liberty: Terrorism and Human Rights, 14 Helsinki Monitor 328 (2003); Codetermination and Corporate Governance in a Multinational Business Enterprise, 24 J. Corp. L. 975 (1999); and Financial Sector Reform and Economic Development in Vietnam, 28 L. & Pol. Int'l Bus. 857 (1997).*

Dinh serves on the boards of the News Corporation, Liberty's Promise, the American Judicature Society, the Transition Committee for California Governor Arnold Schwarzenegger, the Section on National Security Law of the Association of American Law Schools, and the ABA Section on Administrative Law. Dinh graduated magna cum laude from both Harvard College and Harvard Law School, where he was a Class Marshal and an Olin Research Fellow in Law and Economics. He was a law clerk to Judge Laurence H. Silberman of the U.S. Court of Appeals for the D.C. Circuit and to U.S. Supreme Court Justice Sandra Day O'Connor. He served as Associate Special Counsel to the U.S. Senate Whitewater Committee, as Special Counsel to Senator Pete V. Domenici for the Impeachment Trial of the President, and as counsel to the Special Master in *In re Austrian and German Bank Holocaust Litigation.* He is a member of the District of Columbia and U.S. Supreme Court bars.

Born on February 22, 1968, in Saigon, Vietnam, Dinh came to America as a refugee in 1978. After two years in Portland, Oregon, his family settled in Fullerton, California. He resides in Washington, D.C.

Government

DAVID C. CHU
Under Secretary of Defense for Personnel and Readiness

David S. C. Chu was sworn in as the Under Secretary of Defense for Personnel and Readiness on June 1, 2001. A Presidential appointee confirmed by the Senate, he is the Secretary's senior policy advisor on recruitment, career development, pay and benefits for 1.4 million active duty military personnel, 1.3 million Guard and Reserve personnel and 680,000 DoD civilians and is responsible for overseeing the state of military readiness.

The Under Secretary of Defense for Personnel and Readiness also oversees the $15 billion Defense Health Program, Defense Commissaries and Exchanges with $14.5 billion in annual sales, the Defense Education Activity which supports over 100,000 students, and the Defense Equal Opportunity Management Institute, the nation's largest equal opportunity training program.

Dr. Chu earlier served in government as the Director and then Assistant Secretary of Defense (Program Analysis and Evaluation) from May 1981 to January 1993. In that capacity, he advised the Secretary of Defense on the future size and structure of the armed forces, their equipment, and their preparation for crisis or conflict.

From 1978 to 1981, Dr. Chu served as the Assistant Director for National Security and International Affairs, Congressional Budget Office, providing advice to the Congress on the full range of national security and international economic issues.

Dr. Chu began his service to the nation in 1968 when he was commissioned in the Army and became an instructor at the U.S. Army Logistics Management Center, Fort Lee, Virginia. He later served a tour of duty in the Republic of Vietnam, working in the Office of the Comptroller, Headquarters, 1st Logistical Command. He obtained the rank of captain and completed his service with the Army in 1970.

Prior to rejoining the Department of Defense, Dr. Chu served in several senior executive positions with RAND, including Director of the Arroyo Center, the Army's federally funded research and development center for studies and analysis and Director of RAND's Washington Office.

Dr. Chu received a Bachelor of Arts Degree, magna cum laude, in Economics and Mathematics from Yale University in 1964 and a Doctorate in Economics, also from Yale, in 1972. He is a fellow of the National Academy of Public Administration and a recipient of its National Public Senior Award. He holds the Department of Defense Medal for Distinguished Public service with silver palm.

SHINAE CHUN
Director, Women's Bureau, U.S. Dept. of Labor

On May 9, 2001, Shinae Chun was confirmed by the U.S. Senate as the 15th Director of the Women's Bureau. Serving under Secretary of Labor Elaine L. Chao, Ms. Chun is President Bush's highest-ranking Korean American appointee, and heads the only Federal agency charged with advocating on behalf of women in the workforce.

During her tenure, Ms. Chun has transformed the way the Women's Bureau does business by implementing innovative demonstration projects, increasing partnerships, and enhancing the Bureau's visibility. Under her leadership, the Women's Bureau strives to advance the status of 21st Century Working Women in the pursuit of Better Jobs! Better Earnings! Better Living!

In 1991, Governor James Edgar appointed her Director of the Illinois Department of Labor, a position she held until 1999. Two years prior to this appointment, she made Illinois history when Governor James R. Thompson appointed her Director of the Illinois Department of Financial Institutions, making her Illinois' first ever Asian American cabinet member.

In 1982, Ms. Chun was one of the founding members of the Asian American Advisory Council to Governor Thompson. In 1984, the Governor appointed her Special Assistant to the Governor on Asian American Affairs, the first such position in the country.

From 1976 to 1983, through the Title VII Bilingual Education Program and the Title IX Multiethnic Studies Program, Ms. Chun developed a teacher inservice training program to heighten the sensitivity of public school teachers to cultural diversity in the classroom.

Ms. Chun completed her undergraduate degree at Ewha Womans University in Seoul, Korea, and her Master's degree in Education and Social Policy at Northwestern University In 1992, she received a fellowship to the Harvard University, John F. Kennedy School of Government, Program for Senior Executives in State and Local Government.

She has received the Alumni Merit Award from Northwestern University and the Outstanding Alumni Award from Ewha Womans University; the Business Women's Network Special Achievement for Leadership Award; the Southern Women in Public Service Pacesetter Award; and the Asian American Coalition of Chicago Excellence in Public Service Award. She is author of *From the Mountains of Masan to the Land of Lincoln* (1996).

Ms. Chun and her husband, Dr. Kyong Chul Chun, have two sons.

STUART J. ISHIMARU
Commissioner, U.S. Equal Employment Opportunity Commission

Stuart J. Ishimaru was sworn in on November 17, 2003, as a Commissioner of the U.S. Equal Employment Opportunity Commission (EEOC) to serve the remainder of a term expiring July 1, 2007. Mr. Ishimaru was nominated by President George W. Bush on October 14 and confirmed by the full U.S. Senate on October 31, 2003.

As a member of the Commission, he participates with the other Commissioners on all matters which come before it, including the development and approval of enforcement policies, authorization of litigation, issuance of Commissioner's charges of discrimination, and performance of such other functions as may be authorized by law, regulation, or order.

Mr. Ishimaru previously served as Deputy Assistant Attorney General in the Civil Rights Division of the U.S. Department of Justice between 1999 and 2001, where he served as a principal advisor to the Assistant Attorney General for Civil Rights, advising on management, policy, and political issues involving the Civil Rights Division. He supervised more than 100 attorneys in high-profile litigation, including employment discrimination cases, fair housing and fair lending cases, criminal police misconduct, hate crime and slavery prosecutions, and enforcement of the Americans with Disabilities Act.

Prior to this, as Counsel to the Assistant Attorney General in the Civil Rights Division for five years, Mr. Ishimaru provided advice on a broad range of issues, including legislative affairs, politics and strategies. He maintained liaison between the office and Members of Congress, and supervised fair housing and fair lending, equal employment opportunity, education, and Voting Rights Act litigation. He also testified before Congressional Committees on fair housing issues.

In 1993, Mr. Ishimaru was appointed by President Clinton to be the Acting Staff Director of the U.S. Commission on Civil Rights, and from 1984-1993 served on the professional staffs of the House Judiciary Subcommittee on Civil and Constitutional Rights and two House Armed Services Subcommittees of the U.S. Congress.

Mr. Ishimaru, a native of San Jose, California received his A.B. in Political Science and in Economics from the University of California, Berkeley, and his law degree from the George Washington University. He is married to Agnieszka Fryszman, an attorney, and they have two sons, Matthew and Benjamin.

RAMESH K. PUNWANI
Chief Financial Officer, Federal Aviation Administration

Ramesh K. Punwani was named as the Federal Aviation Administration (FAA) chief financial officer (CFO) on March 26, 2004. As CFO, Punwani oversees the FAA's $14 billion operating budget as well as the development and agency-wide application of cost accounting and financial management systems. Punwani joined the agency following his work as senior vice president for global strategy at the Cendant Corp.

Punwani's background in aviation and the travel industry spans over three decades that includes CFO and vice president positions for Pan American World Airways, Tower Air, and Trans World Airlines. Prior to joining Cendant Corp, Punwani was the executive vice president and CFO of Travelocity.com as the innovative internet travel company grew to become a $3 billion enterprise and the largest public e-travel company. Punwani was also vice president of tour and cruise relations and director of business development for American Express before joining Travelocity.com. From September 1993 to 1996, Punwani was senior vice president and CFO for Empire Blue Cross and Blue Shield.

Punwani received a Master of Business Administration degree from New York University in 1978 and a Master of Engineering in management science from Cornell University in 1966. Punwani also holds a Bachelor of Technology degree in industrial engineering from the Indian Institute of Technology in Mumbai, India.

Literature/Media

KHALED HOSSEINI
Author, The Kite Runner

Khaled Hosseini was born in Kabul, Afghanistan, in 1965. His father was a diplomat with the Afghan Foreign Ministry and his mother taught Farsi and History at a large high school in Kabul. In 1970, the Foreign Ministry sent his family to Tehran, where his father worked for the Afghan embassy. They lived in Tehran until 1973, at which point they returned to Kabul. In July of 1973, on the night Hosseini's youngest brother was born, the Afghan king, Zahir Shah, was overthrown in a bloodless coup by the king's cousin, Daoud Khan. At the time, Hosseini was in fourth grade and was already drawn to poetry and prose; he read a great deal of Persian poetry as well as Farsi translations of novels ranging from Alice in Wonderland to Mickey Spillane's Mike Hammer series.

In 1976, the Afghan Foreign Ministry once again relocated the Hosseini family, this time to Paris. They were ready to return to Kabul in 1980, but by then Afghanistan had already witnessed a bloody communist coup and the invasion of the Soviet army. The Hosseinis sought and were granted political asylum in the United States. In September of 1980, Hosseini's family moved to San Jose, California. They lived on welfare and food stamps for a short while, as they had lost all of their property in Afghanistan. His father took multiple jobs and managed to get his family off welfare. Hosseini graduated from high school in 1984 and enrolled at Santa Clara University where he earned a bachelor's degree in Biology in 1988. The following year, he entered the University of California-San Diego's School of Medicine, where he earned a Medical Degree in 1993. He completed his residency at Cedars-Sinai Hospital in Los Angeles.

Hosseini has been in practice (Internal Medicine) since 1996, but his first love has always been writing. Hosseini's vivid, and fond, memories of peaceful pre-Soviet era Afghanistan led partially to the writing of this novel, as well as his personal experiences with Afghan Hazaras. One Hazara man in particular was a thirty-year-old man named Hossein Khan, who worked for the Hosseinis when they were living in Iran. When Hosseini was in the third grade, he taught Khan to read and write. Though his relationship with Hossein Khan was brief and rather formal, Hosseini always remembered the fondness that developed between them, and those memories served as an inspiration of sorts for the relationship between Amir and Hassan in *The Kite Runner*.

RINKU SEN

Publisher, ColorLines Magazine & Communications Director, Applied Reserach Center

Rinku Sen, the Publisher of ColorLines magazine and Communications Director of the Applied Research Center, has a rich history of organizing, writing and lecturing on issues of race, gender and activism. She started her organizing career as a student activist at Brown University, fighting race, gender and class discrimination on campuses. She received a B.A. in Women's Studies from Brown University in 1988 and an M.S. in Journalism at Columbia University.

Her latest book, Stir It Up: Lessons in Community Organizing, a guide for community organizations of all orientations was released in the fall of 2003. The book was a finalist for the 2004 Nautilus Book Award in the social change category.

From 1988-2000, she was on the staff of the Center for Third World Organizing (CTWO), a national network of organizations of color. As a staff member, then Co-Director of CTWO, she trained new organizers of color and crafted public policy campaigns around poverty, education, racial and gender equity, health care and immigration issues. She is a board member of the Center for Third World Organizing, Speak Out Speakers and Artists, and is a member on the advisory board of the Philanthropic Initiative for Racial Equity. She is formerly a member of the board of the Independent Press Association and the Tides Center.

She was recognized by Ms. Magazine as one of 21 feminists to watch in the 21st century in 1996, the same year that she received the Ms. Foundation for Women's Gloria Steinem Women of Vision award. She was a Gerbode Fellow in 1999 and was selected as a 2004 Charles H. Revson Fellow on the Future of New York.

Military

ANTONIO M. TAGUBA

Deputy Assistant Secretary of Defense for Reserve Affairs (Readiness, Training and Mobilization)

Major General Antonio M. Taguba is the second Filipino American to attain the rank of US Army General. He was born on October 31, 1950 in Sampaloc, Manila, the Philippines and received a Bachelor of Arts degree in history from the Armor Officer Basic and Advanced Course, the Army Command and General Staff College, the College of Naval Command and Staff, and the Army War College. He received his master's degree in public administration at Webster University international relations from Salve Regina College, and a masters in national security and strategic studies from the Naval War College.

Major General Taguba served in the 1st. Battalion, 72d Armor, 2nd. Infantry Division, Eight United States Army in South Korea from January 1991 to August 1992. From June 1995 to July 1997, Taguba served as Commander in the 2d Brigade, 4th Infantry Division on Fort Hood, Texas. He acted as Commanding General of the United States Army Community and Family Support Center in Alexandria, and served as the Vice Director of the Army Staff/Director, Management, Office of the Chief Staff for the US Army in Washington DC' until November 2002. He then served as Acting Director of the Army Staff, Office of the Chief of Staff from November 2002 to July 2003 and as Deputy Commanding General (Support) for the Third US Army in Fort McPherson, Georgia until July 2004.
Major General Taguba has been awarded the Distinguished Service Medal, Legion of Merit with 3 Oak Leaf Clusters, Bronze Star Medal, Meritorious Service Medal with 5 Oak Leaf Clusters, Army Commendation Medal with 2 Oak Leaf Clusters, Army Achievement Medal with Oak Leaf Cluster, Army Staff Identification Badge and Office of the Secretary of Defense Identification Badge.

Science

CHARLES ELACHI
Director, Advanced Planning and Jet Propulsion Laboratory

Dr. Elachi was born April 18, 1947 in Lebanon. Dr. Elachi received a B.S. in physics from the University of Grenoble, France and the Diplome in Engineering from the Polytechnic Institute, in 1968 where he graduated first in the class, and M.S. and Ph.D. degrees in Electrical Sciences from the California Institute of Technology, Pasadena in 1969 and 1971. He later received an MBA from USC and an M.S. degree in geology from UCLA.

He is currently the Director of the Jet Propulsion Laboratory and Vice President of the California Institute of Technology, where he is also a Professor of Electrical Engineering and Planetary Science. He taught "The Physics of Remote Sensing" at Caltech from 1982 to 2000. Elachi was Principal Investigator on numerous research and development studies and flight projects sponsored by the National Aeronautics and Space Administration. He was Principal Investigator for the Shuttle Imaging Radar series (SIR-A in 1981, SIR-B in 1984 and SIR-C in 1994), was a Co-Investigator on the Magellan imaging radar, and is presently the Team Leader of the Cassini Titan Radar experiment and a co-investigator on the Rosetta Comet Nucleus Sounder Experiment. He is the author of over 230 publications in the fields of space and planetary exploration, Earth observation from space, active microwave remote sensing, electromagnetic theory, and integrated optics, and he holds several patents in those fields. In addition, he has authored three textbooks in the field of remote sensing. One of these textbooks has been translated into Chinese.

In his 30 year career at JPL, Dr. Elachi played the lead role in developing the field of spaceborne imaging radar from a small research area to a major field of scientific research and application. As a result, JPL and NASA became the world leaders in the field of spaceborne imaging radars, and over the last decade, developed Seasat, SIR-A, SIR-B, SIR-C, Magellan, SRTM and the Cassini Radar. He received numerous national and international awards for his leadership in this field. During the late 80's and 90's Dr. Elachi was responsible for the definition and development of JPL flight instruments and missions for Solar System Exploration, the Origins program, Earth Observation and Astrophysics. During this period more than 45 flight missions and instruments were conceived, developed, and flown.

In January 2001, Dr. Elachi was appointed as the Director of the Jet Propulsion Laboratory and Vice President of Caltech. Dr. Elachi has received numerous awards, including the Takeda Award (2002), the NASA Outstanding Leadership Medal (2002), the Wernher Von Braun Award (2002), the UCLA Department of Earth and Space Science Distinguished Alumni Award (2002), Dryden Award (2000,), the NASA Distinguished Service Medal (1999), the COSPAR Nordberg Medal (1996), the Nevada Medal (1995), NASA Outstanding Leadership Medal (1994), the IEEE Medal of Engineering Excellence (1992), the IEEE Geoscience and Remote Sensing Distinguished Achievement Award (1987), the W.T. Pecora Award (1985), the NASA Exceptional Scientific Medal (1982), and the ASP Autometric Award (1980 and 1982).

In 1989, at the age of 42, he was elected to the National Academy of Engineering. In 1993-1995 he was a member of the NAE 4th Decadal Committee. In 1995, he chaired the NAE membership committee. He served on numerous NAE committees. He is a fellow of IEEE and the American Institute of Aeronautics and Astronautics, and is a member of the International Academy of Astronautics.

He is married to Valerie Gifford and has two daughters, Joanna and Lauren. His outside interests include skiing, woodworking, history and travel. He is a member of the Pasadena Twilight Club and chaired the JPL United Way Campaign in 1988-1989.

Sports

RENA INOUE
Figure Pair Skater

Inoue is a two-time Olympian for Japan in singles and pairs. She previously competed in pairs with Tomoaki Koyama from 1987-1992. Inoue began skating at the age of 4 when her doctor suggested it might help her asthma. She is also pursuing a medical degree, perhaps as a pediatrician. Inoue Enjoys reading, knitting, sewing, swimming and camping, and has one cat, "Madonna". She describes herself as "short, shy, and polite" and says she loves eating and sleeping. Her Favorite movie is "Monsters Inc." and her motto is to be happy and enjoy everything. After her skating career she would like to drive across the country.

John Baldwin is a veteran of the State Farm U.S. Championships dating back to 1986 as a novice competitor. He claimed the U.S. novice title in 1987. Baldwin enjoys tennis, jet-skiing and gardening. In spring 2004 the pair donated all of fees they earned while touring with the Champions on Ice Tour to the U.S. Figure Skating Memorial Fund. The Memorial Fund provides qualified U.S. Figure Skating athletes who are in need of financial aid with monetary assistance to pursue their goals both inside and outside the competitive arena. Both Inoue and Baldwin received aid from the program in the past. Both of them appeared in a skating exhibition at the 2004 HBO All Star Family Sport Jam fundraiser for Children's Hospital Los Angeles.

Asian Pacific American Conventions and Events 2006

JANUARY

ASIAN PACIFIC AMERICAN DISPUTE RESOLUTION CENTER
2006 Mediation Training Emphasizing Cross-Cultural Competency
January 4-6, 9-10, 2006/Los Angeles, CA
Tel: (213) 250-8190 Fax: (213) 250-8195
Emial: info@apadrc.org
Web: www.apadrc.org

ASIAN AMERICAN BUSINESS DEVELOPMENT CENTER, INC.
2006 Lunar New Year Festival
January 29, 2006/New York City, NY
Contact: Wing Shung
Tel: (212) 966-0100 Fax: (212) 966-2786
Emial: general.info@aabdc.com
Web: www.aabdc.com

WOW PRODUCTIONS
2007 National Multicultural Conference and Summit
January, 2006 TBA
Contact: Wendy Anderson
Tel: (626) 683-8243
Emial: wowproductions2@earthlink.net
Web: www.multiculturalsummit.org

FEBRUARY

SAN DIEGO CHINESE-AMERICAN SCIENTISTS AND ENGINEERS ASSOCIATION
Annual Banquet
February 5, 2006/Delmar, CA
Contact: Iwen Yao
Tel: (858) 651-0262
Emial: sdcasea2k@yahoo.com
Web: www.sdcasea.com

AMERICAN ADVERTISING FEDERATION
10th Annual Most Promising Minority Students Program
February 7-9, 2006/New York City, NY
Contact: Karen Cohn
Tel: (202) 898-0089 Fax: (202) 898-0159
Emial: aaf@aaf.org
Web: www.aaf.org

AMERICAN COUNCIL ON EDUCATION
88th Annual Meeting
February 11-14, 2006/Los Angeles, CA
Contact: Wendy Bresler

Tel: (202) 939-9410 Fax: (202) 833-4730
Emial: annualmeeting@ace.nche.edu
Web: www.acenet.edu

NATIONAL MINORITY BUSINESS COUNCIL, INC.
26th Annual Awards Luncheon
February 14, 2006
Tel: (212) 997-4753 Fax: (212) 997-5102
Emial: nmbc@msn.com
Web: www.nmbc.org

CENTER FOR SOUTH ASIA STUDIES
21st Annual South Asia Conference
February 17-18, 2006/Berkeley, CA
Tel: (510) 642-3608 Fax: (510) 643-5793
Emial: csasevnt@berkeley.edu
Web: http://ias.berkeley.edu/southasia

MARCH

DIVERSIFIED BUSINESS COMMUNICATIONS
International Complementary and Natural Healthcare Conference and Expo
March 3-5, 2006/New York, NY
Contact: Nancy Hasselback
Tel: (207) 842-5500 Fax: (207) 842-5503
Emial: info@camexpo.com
Web: www.divbusiness.com

CATALYST WOMEN
2006 Catalyst Awards Conference
March 16, 2006/New York City, NY
Contact: Jesal Mehta
Tel: (212) 514-7600 Fax: (212) 514-8470
Email: info@catalystwomen.org
Web: www.catalystwomen.org

CENTER FOR DEMOCRATIC RENEWAL
International Day Against Racism
March 21, 2006/Atlanta, GA
Contact: Keith Jennings
Tel: (404) 392-9562 Fax: (404) 221-0045
Emial: info@thecdr.org
Web: www.thecdr.org

AMERICAN DIABETES ASSOCIATION
11th Annual Rainbow Gala Fighting Diabetes Among Diverse Communities
March 24, 2006/Livingston, NJ
Contact: Pam Cooper
Tel: (732) 469-7979 Fax: (732) 469-3906
Web: www.diabetes.org

DIVERSITYBUSINESS.COM
6th Annual National Multicultural Business Conference
March 29-31, 2006/Las Vegas, NV
Contact: Bill Stokes
Tel: (203) 255-8966 Fax: (203) 255-8501
Emial: wstokes@ccaii.com
Web: www.div2000.com

APRIL

ASSOCIATION FOR ASIAN STUDIES
AAS Annual Meeting
April 6-9, 2006/San Francisco, CA
Contact: Karen Fricke
Tel: (734) 665-2490 Fax: (734) 665-3801
Emial: annmtg@aasianst.org
Web: www.aasianst.org

LINKAGE, INC.
7th Summit on Leading Diversity
April 10-13, 2006/Atlanta, GA
Contact: Karina Wilhelms
Tel: (781) 402-5461 Fax: (781) 402-5556
Emial: info@linkageinc.com
Web: www.linkageinc.com

CHICAGO MINORITY BUSINESS DEVELOPMENT COUNCIL, INC.
39th Annual Chicago Business Opportunity Fair
April 11-13, 2006/Chicago, IL
Contact: Cynthia Jordan
Tel: (312) 755-8880 X19 Fax: (312) 755-8890
Emial: cjordan@cmbdc.org
Web: www.cmbdc.org

ASIAN WOMEN IN BUSINESS
Conference on Certification and Procurement Opportunities for Minority/Women Business Enterprises
April 19, 2006/New York , NY
Contact: Bonnie Wong
Tel: (212) 868-1368 Fax: (212) 868-1373
Emial: info@awib.org
Web: www.awib.org

COMMITTEE OF 100
15th Annual Conference
April 20-22, 2006/San Francisco, CA
Contact: Alice Mong
Tel: (212) 371-6565 Fax: (212) 371-9009
Emial: c100@committee100.org
Web: www.committee100.org

AMERICAN ASSOCIATION FOR AFFIRMATIVE ACTION
32nd Annual Conference
April 21-30, 2006/Tampa, FL
Contact: Shirley J. Wilcher
Tel: (800) 252-8952 Fax: (202) 355-1399
Emial: execdir@affirmativeaction.org
Web: www.affirmativeaction.org

NATIONAL ASSOCIATION OF MINORITY MEDIA EXECUTIVES
NAMME Awards Banquet
April 27, 2006/Seattle, WA
Contact: Toni F. Laws
Tel: (703) 893-2410 Fax: (703) 893-2414
Emial: tlaws@namme.org
Web: www.namme.org

NEW YORK UNIVERSITY CENTER FOR MARKETING
Marketing to the New Majority: How to Reach the Multicultural Consumer
April 28-29, 2006/New York, NY
Contact: Lisa Skrilloff
Tel: (212) 242-3351 Fax: (212) 691-5969
Emial: lisa@multicultral.com
Web: www.multicultural.com

ASIAN AMERICAN COALITION OF FLORIDA
AsiaFest 2006
April 29, 2006/Tampa, FL
Contact: Kimi Springsteen
Tel: (813) 276-8623 Fax: (813) 272-5851
Emial: springsteenk@hillsboroughcounty.org

ASIAN PACIFIC AMERICAN HERITAGE ASSOCIATION
2006 Annual Heritage Festival
April 29, 2006/Houston, TX
Contact: Jerome Vielman
Tel: (713) 784-1112 Fax: (832) 201-8228
Emial: jerome@apaha.org
Web: www.apaha.org

ASIAN PROFESSIONAL EXTENSION, INC.
13th Anniversary Gala Benefit
April, 2006 TBA/New York, NY
Contact: Sunny Kim
Tel: (212) 748-1225 Fax: (212) 748-1250
Emial: apex@apex-ny.org
Web: www.apex-ny.org

IQPC
4th Annual Multicultural Branding Conference
April 2006 TBA/New York City, NY
Tel: (212) 885-2700 Fax: (212) 885-2703
Emial: info@iqpc.com
Web: www.iqpc.com

MAY

ASIAN DIVERSITY, INC.
5th Annual Asian Diversity Career Expo 2006
May 5, 2006/New York City, NY
Contact: Jino Ahn
Tel: (212) 465-8777 Fax: (212) 465-8396
Emial: jino.ahn@adiversity.com
Web: www.adiversity.com

MULTICULTURAL EDUCATION DEPARTMENT
Ethnic Festival 2006
May 6, 2006/Oak Park, IL
Contact: Lynn Allen
Tel: (708) 524-7700 Fax: (708) 524-7703
Emial: lallen@op97.org
Web: www.op97.org

THE COALITION OF ASIAN PACIFIC AMERICANS
27th Annual Asian Pacific American Heritage Festival
May 7, 2006/New York, NY
Contact: Ning Zhang
Tel: (212) 989-3610 Fax: (702) 993-5316
Emial: nzhang@capaonline.org
Web: www.capaonline.org

FEDERAL ASIAN PACIFIC AMERICAN COUNCIL
21st Annual Congressional Seminar, National Leadership Training Conference & Exhibits
May 8-12, 2006/Honolulu, HI
Contact: Linda Tuazon-Miller
Tel:
Emial: fapac@fapac.org
Web: www.fapac.org

ASIAN AMERICAN FEDERATION OF NEW YORK
12th Annual Benefit Gala
May 9, 2006/New York City, NY
Contact: Kendra Lee
Tel: (212) 344-5878 Fax: (212) 344-5636
Emial: kendra@aafny.org
Web: www.aafny.org

US PAN ASIAN AMERICAN CHAMBER OF COMMERCE
CelebrAsian 2006, 18th Annual Conference
May 15-17, 2006/Chicago, IL
Contact: Susan Au Allen
Tel: (202) 296-5221 Fax: (202) 296-5225
Emial: administrator@uspaacc.com
Web: www.uspaacc.com

ASIAN PACIFIC AMERICAN INSTITUTE FOR CONGRESSIONAL STUDIES
12th Annual APAICS Gala Dinner
May 16, 2006/Washington, DC
Contact: William H. Marumoto
Tel: (202) 296-9200 Fax: (202) 296-9236
Emial: apaics@apaics.org
Web: www.apaics.org

CORNELL'S DIVERSITY MANAGEMENT PROGRAM
Advanced Diversity Strategies
May 17-18, 2006/New York, NY
Contact: Christopher J. Metzler
Tel: (212) 340-2852 Fax: (212) 340-2890
Emial: cm277@cornell.edu
Web: www.ilr.cornell.edu/mgmtprog/dm/
certificates.html

NATIONAL MULTICULTURAL INSTITUTE
Cultural Liberty: The Elusion of Inclusion Beyond Heroic to Sustainable Future
May 18-21, 2006/Bethesda, MD
Contact: Melinda Chow
Tel: (202) 483-0700 X232 Fax: (202) 483-5233
Emial: nmci@nmci.org
Web: www.nmci.org

ASIAN ENTERPRISE MAGAZINE
12th Annual National Asian Entrepreneur of the Year Awards Banquet
May 27, 2006/Kona, HI
Contact: Gelly Borromeo
Tel: (909) 860-3316 Fax: (909) 865-4915
Emial: gellyb@asianenterprise.com
Web: www.asianenterprise.com

JUNE

FILIPINO AMERICAN CULTURAL EVENT
Philippine Independence Day Celebration, Daly City Fil-Am Festival
June 3, 2006/Vallejo, CA
Contact: Jenny Montenegro
Tel: (650) 697-6619 Fax: (650) 697-6233
Emial: filipino.insider@gmail.com

THE LAGRANT FOUNDATION
8th Annual Recognition Reception/Awards Program
June 12, 2006/New York, NY
Contact: Melissa Lopez
Tel: (323) 469-8680 Fax: (323) 469-8683
Emial: melissalopez@lagrant.com
Web: www.lagrantfoundation.org

JAPANESE AMERICAN CITIZENS LEAGUE
2006 National Convention
June 21-24, 2006/Phoenix, AZ
Contact: John Tateishi
Tel: (415) 921-5225 Fax: (415) 931-4671
Emial: jacl@jacl.org
Web: www.jacl.org

JULY

CONFERENCE OF MINORITY TRANSPORTATION OFFICIALS
2006 National Meeting & Training Conference
July 8-12, 2006/Austin, TX
Contact: Patrea' Cheatham-Logan
Tel: (202) 530-0551 Fax: (202) 530-0617
Emial: comto@comto.org
Web: www.comto.org

SOUTH ASIAN JOURNALISTS ASSOCIATION
SAJA Convention
July 13-16, 2006/New York City, NY
Contact: S. Mitra Kalita
Tel: (212) 854-5979
Emial: saja@columbia.edu
Web: www.saja.org

ORGANIZATION OF CHINESE AMERICANS
2006 Convention
July 20-23, 2006/Philadelphia, PA
Contact: Vicki Shu
Tel: (202) 223-5500 Fax: (202) 296-0540
Emial: vshu@ocanatl.org
Web: www.ocanatl.org

AUGUST

NATIONAL MEDICAL ASSOCIATION
2006 Annual Convention and Scientific Assembly
August 5-10, 2006/Dallas, TX
Tel: (202) 347-1895 X250
Fax: (202) 783-5193
Emial: pnorman@nmanet.org
Web: www.nmanet.org

FEDERATION OF SOUTHERN COOPERATIVES LAND ASSISTANCE FUND
39th Annual Meeting
August 17-19, 2006/Epes, AL
Contact: Jackie Ward
Tel: (404) 765-0991 Fax: (404) 765-9178
Emial: fsc@mindspring.com
Web: www.federationsoutherncoop.com

PHILIPPINE FIESTA, INC.
Philippine Fiesta in America
August 19-20, 2006/Secaucus, NJ
Contact: Mila Mendez
Tel: (201) 946-0328 Fax: (212) 682-2038
Emial: milamendez@aol.com
Web: www.philippinefiesta.com

SEPTEMBER

INTERNATIONAL ECONOMIC DEVELOPMENT COUNCIL
2006 Annual Conference
September 17-20, 2006/New York, NY
Contact: Jeff Stone
Tel: (202) 223-7800 Fax: (202) 223-4745
Emial: jstone@iedconline.org
Web: www.iedconline.org

NATIONAL COLLEGE ACCESS NETWORK
2006 Annual Conference
September 25-27, 2006/Orlando, FL
Contact: Christina R. Milano
Tel: (216) 241-6122 Fax: (216) 241-6140
Web: www.collegeaccess.org

OCTOBER

ASIAN AMERICAN JUSTICE CENTER
10th Annual American Courage Awards
October 5, 2006/Washington, DC
Contact: Adlai J. Amor
Tel: (202) 296-2300 Fax: (202) 296-2318
Emial: aamor@napalc.org
Web: www.napalc.org

ASIAN PACIFIC AMERICAN MEDICAL STUDENT ASSOCIATION
2006 APAMSA National Conference
October 6-8, 2006/Washington, DC
Contact: Annie Lee
Tel: (520) 626-3269 Fax: (520) 621-7574
Emial: annie@md.northwestern.edu
Web: www.apamsa.org

DIVERSITY BEST PRACTICES
2006 Diversity and Women Summit & Gala
October 25-26, 2006/Washington, DC
Contact: Edie Fraser
Tel: (202) 466-8209 Fax: (202) 833-1808
Emial: inquire@tpag.com
Web: www.diversitybestpractices.com

ASIAN TASK FORCE
2006 Annual Silk Road Gala
October 28, 2006/Boston, MA
Contact: Ki Perry
Tel: (617) 338-0012 Fax: (617) 338-2354
Emial: asiandv@atask.org
Web: www.atask.org

NATIONAL MINORITY SUPPLIER DEVELOPMENT COUNCIL, INC.
NMSDC Conference
October 29-November 1, 2006/San Diego, CA
Contact: Suzannet Eaddy
Tel: (212) 944-2430 Fax: (212) 719-9611
Web: www.nmsdcus.org

CHINESE INSTITUTE OF ENGINEERS, GREAT NEW YORK AREA CHAPTER
Annual Chapter Convention
October, 2006 TBA/Newark, NJ
Contact: David An
Tel: (732) 939-2810
Web: www.cie-gnyc.org

NOVEMBER

MINORITY CORPORATE COUNSEL ASSOCIATION
Creating Pathways to Diversity Conference
November 8, 2006/New York City, NY
Contact: Shawn Boynes
Tel: (202) 739-5909 Fax: (202) 216-9040
Emial: info@mcca.com
Web: www.mcca.com

ASSOCIATION OF NATIONAL ADVERTISERS, INC.
2006 Multicultural Marketing Conference
November 12-14, 2006/Los Angeles, CA
Contact: Patricia Hanlon
Tel: (212) 697-5950 Fax: (212) 661-8057
Emial: phanlon@ana.net
Web: www.ana.net

DECEMBER

GLOBAL DIVERSITY GROUP, INC.
Business Exchange 2006 Tour for Success
December 8, 2006/Miami, FL
Tel: (410) 730-6906 Fax: (410) 730-6908
Emial: corporate@globaldiversitygroup.com
Web: www.mpbnetwork.com

ARTISTIC

ASIAN AMERICAN ARTS ALLIANCE
www.aaartsalliance.org

To raise public awareness of Asian American arts.

ASIAN AMERICAN WOMEN ARTISTS ASSOCIATION
www.aawaaart.com

Supports and promotes Asian American women artists in the visual, literary, and performing arts.

ASIAN CINEVISION
www.asiancinevision.org

Dedicated to promoting and preserving Asian and Asian American media expressions.

ASIAN CULTURAL ASSOCIATION
www.aca-florida.org

To preserve and promote the performing and visual arts traditions of Asia.

FOUNDATION FOR CHINESE PERFORMING ARTS
www.chineseperformingarts.net

To enhance the understanding and appreciation of Eastern heritage through music and performing arts.

BUSINESS

ASIAN AMERICAN ALLIANCE
www.asianamericanalliance.com

To increase the economic potential of small businesses by providing technical knowledge to entrepreneurs.

ASIAN AMERICAN BUSINESS DEVELOPMENT CENTER, INC.
www.aabdc.com

To advance the capacity of Asian-owned businesses in areas needed to compete in the mainstream marketplace.

ASIAN AMERICAN MANUFACTURING ASSOCIATION
www.aamasv.com

To recognize and publicize the achievements of Asian Americans.

ASIAN BUSINESS ASSOCIATION OF SAN DIEGO
www.abasd.org

Provides networking opportunities, professional development, and business advocacy for the ever-increasing Asian Pacific American business community.

ASIANINFO.ORG
www.asianinfo.org

The leading provider of telecom network and software solutions in China.

ASSOCIATION OF CHINESE FINANCE PROFESSIONALS
www.acfp.net

Promote across the board business opportunities by bringing together American and Chinese financial institutions.

ASSOCIATION OF NIST-ASIAN PACIFIC AMERICANS
www.nist.gov/anapa

Providing advice and supporting management efforts toward creating a diverse NIST workforce at all levels.

DETROIT CHINESE BUSINESS ASSOCIATION
www.dcba.com

To foster beneficial business relationships between Chinese and American business.

DIVERSITY NEWS
www.diversitynews.com

Serves as the link between women and minority-owned businesses and their professional peers.

COMMUNICATIONS

CROSSWAVE COMMUNICATIONS, INC.
www.cwc.co.jp

The first company dedicated to data communications in Japan.

CULTURAL

JAPANESE AMERICAN CULTURAL & COMMUNITY CENTER
www.jaccc.org

Dedicated to presenting, perpetuating, transmitting and promoting Japanese, and Japanese American Art and Culture.

KOREAN AMERICAN MUSEUM
www.kamuseum.org

Dedicated to preserving Korean American History and Culture.

NATIONAL COUNCIL OF ASIAN PACIFIC AMERICANS
www.ncapaonline.org

To promote understanding and appreciation of Asian Pacific American cultures, traditions, customs, and heritage.

ENTERTAINMENT

ASIA STUDIOS
www.asiastudios.com

The world's leading Asian online entertainment company.

FUJI TELECAST
www.ktsf.com

Not only serves the Asian-American market but provides research as well.

KIKU-TV
www.kikutv.com

Over 120 hours of fascinating programming from around the world in 8 different languages.

KSCI-TV
www.kscitv.com

The leading over-the-air Asian language television station in the United States.

RUPOSHI BANGLA TELEVISION
www.banglatv.com

Home for Ruposhi Bangla Television.

THE ASIA NETWORK
www.kbfd.com

Devoted to entertaining the fastest growing viewer segment, Asian Americans.

TV ASIA
www.i-channel.com

Provides a wide range of programming produced for South Asian Americans.

GENEALOGY

ASIAGEN WEB PROJECT
www.rootsweb.com/~asiagw

Gives access to multiple sources about Asian American Genealogy.

GOVERNMENT

ASIAN AMERICAN GOVERNMENTS EXECUTIVE NETWORK
www.aagen.org

Promote, expand, and support Asian Pacific American leadership in public service.

ASIAN AND PACIFIC ISLANDER AMERICAN VOTE
www.apiavote.org

Encourages civic participation and promotes a better understanding of public policy and the electoral process.

ISP

PACIFIC INTERNET
www.pacnet.com

The largest Telco-independent Internet service provider in the Asia Pacific region.

LITERARY

ASIAN AMERICAN WRITERS' WORKSHOP
www.aaww.org

The record of Asian American Literature and the writers that give life to it.

ASIAN ENTERPRISE MAGAZINE
www.asianenterprise.com

Asian Enterprise is the largest small-business-focus publication.

ASIAN JOURNAL USA
www.asianjournalusa.com

The leading Asian American publication in Southern California today.

ASIAN PACIFIC AMERICAN TIMES
www.apatimes.com

Provides coverage of a wide variety of topics that appeal to Filipino-Americans.

ASIAN REPORTER NEWSPAPER
www.asianreporter.com

Pacific Northwest based weekly newspaper.

ASIANWEEK
www.asianweek.com

A national English-language news weekly for the Asian Pacific American community.

CALIFORNIA EXAMINER
www.californiaexaminer.net

The leading Filipino-American newspaper in Southern California.

CHINESE CLASSICAL POETRY
www.chinapage.com/poetry9.html

Collections of the complete works of Li Bai, Li Qingzhao, and Jiang Ye.

CHINESE JOURNAL CORPORATION
www.chinesejournal.com

A bilingual community newspaper with a volunteer staff of young Chinese Americans, the Journal was the voice of the Chinese community.

DESI TALK
www.desitalk.com

Premiere Asian Indian Newspaper.

FILIPINO REPORTER
www.filipinoreporter.com

The only ethnic newspaper belonging to the New York Press Club.

INDIA ABROAD
www.indiaabroad.com

The oldest Asian Indian publication in North America.

INDIA WEST
www.indiawest.com

The largest and most prestigious weekly newspaper on the West Coast.

INDIAN EXPRESS
www.iexpressusa.com

Fills a need for Indians who want to stay connected to their motherland and the community.

MULTI-PURPOSE

ARAB AMERICAN AND CHALDEAN COUNCIL
www.arabacc.org

Acts as a bridge for Middle Eastern communities through employment, training, and educational programs.

LAO FAMILY COMMUNITY OF FRESNO, INC.
www.laofamilyfresno.org

To promote educational, economical, employment, and resettlement services.

NEWS

CALIFORNIA JOURNAL FOR FILIPINO AMERICANS
www.cjfilam.com

Provides readers with news from the Philippines, consumer and business news, SBA updates, and community events.

HMONG TIMES
www.hmongtimes.com

Leader in delivering Hmong news.

80-20 INITIATIVE
www.80-20initiative.net

Dedicated to working for equality and justice for all Asian Americans.

AMERICAN MUSLIM ALLIANCE
www.amaweb.org

To organize the American Muslim community in mainstream public affairs, civic discourse, and party politics all across the United States.

AMERICAN-ARAB ANTI-DISCRIMINATION COMMITTEE
www.adc.org

A civil rights organization committed to defending the rights of people of Arab descent.

API LEGAL OUTREACH
www.apilegaloutreach.org

To work against the long-standing barriers which have denied Asian and Pacific Islander people equal justice.

ASIAN AMERICAN FEDERATION OF NEW YORK
www.aafny.org

A not-for-profit organization that provides public policy and community service leadership.

ASIAN PACIFIC AMERICAN INSTITUTE FOR CONGRESSIONAL STUDIES
www.apaics.org

To build a politically empowered Asian Pacific American population.

POLITICAL ACTION

ASIAN PACIFIC POLICY AND PLANNING COUNCIL
www.a3pcon.org

To initiate action of major policy and planning issues that affect the APIA community.

CENTER FOR ASIAN AMERICANS UNITED FOR SELF EMPOWERMENT
www.causeusa.org

To advance the political empowerment of our community through voter registration and education, along with community outreach.

CHINESE FOR AFFIRMATIVE ACTION
www.caasf.org

To defend and promote the civil and political rights of Chinese and Asian Americans.

INDIAN AMERICAN CENTER FOR POLITICAL AWARENESS
www.iacfpa.org

To increase political awareness in the Indian American community and to encourage participation.

KOREAN AMERICAN COALITION
www.kacdc.org

To facilitate the Korean American community's participation in civic, legislative, and political affairs.

MAUREEN AND MIKE MANSFIELD FOUNDATION
www.mansfieldfdn.org

A public policy organization committed to promoting understanding and cooperation between the United States and Asia.

MIDDLE EAST POLICY COUNCIL
www.mepc.org

To expand public discussion and understanding of issues affecting U.S. policy in the Middle East.

ORANGE COUNTY ORGANIZATION OF CHINESE AMERICANS
www.oca-orangecounty.org

Dedicated to securing the rights of Chinese American and Asian American citizens.

PROJECT IMPACT
www.project-impact.org

To enhance the civic responsibility and community leadership of South Asian Americans.

U.S. COMMISSION ON CIVIL RIGHTS
www.usccr.gov

This commission is part of the Executive Branch of the U.S. Government. Investigates complaints alleging that citizens are being deprived of their right to vote by reason of their race, color, religion, sex, age, disability, or national origin.

PORTAL

ASIAN AMERICAN NET
www.asianamerican.net

Serves all Asian American communities to promote and strengthen cultural, educational, and commercial ties.

ASIANAVENUE.COM
www.asianavenue.com

The Top Asian-American Network on the Web.

ASIANCONNECTIONS.COM
www.asianconnections.com

The leader in providing comprehensive Asian content.

BOLLYWOOD WORLD
www.bollywoodworld.com

Latest Bollywood News, Star Interviews, and Bollywood Chat.

CONTACT PAKISTAN
www.contactpakistan.com

World's largest virtual welfare organization for Pakistanis.

GOLDSEA
www.goldsea.com

Everything Asian, very useful portal access.

IMAGE IN ASIAN CYBERLAND
www.image-in-asian.com

Your link to all kinds of South Asian stuff.

INDOLINK
www.indolink.com

The first Ethnic portal serving Asian-Indians worldwide.

SIFY.COM
www.sify.com

India's premier portal.

PROFESSIONAL

AMERICAN SOCIETY OF ENGINEERS OF INDIAN ORIGIN
www.aseio.org

An international nonprofit professional organization of engineers, students, and professionals primarily engaged in the pursuit of the enhancement of technical, professional, educational, and economic benefits.

ASIAN AMERICAN HOTEL OWNERS ASSOCIATION
www.aahoa.com

The fastest-growing hospitality organization in the United States.

ASIAN AMERICAN JOURNALISTS ASSOCIATION
www.aaja.org

To increase employment of Asian-American print and broadcast journalists.

ASIAN AMERICAN SOCIETY OF ENGINEERS
www.columbia.edu/cu/aase

To promote minority involvement in the professional industry.

ASIAN PROFESSIONAL EXCHANGE
www.apex.org

Premier membership organization for Asian Pacific Americans in Southern California who have a strong commitment to excellence in professional development.

ASSOCIATION OF PAKISTANI PHYSICIANS OF NORTH AMERICA
www.appna.org

To facilitate a greater and better understanding of relations amongst Pakistani physicians.

CHINESE AMERICAN MEDICAL SOCIETY
www.camsociety.org

Promoting the scientific association of medical professionals of Chinese descent.

INDUS ENTREPRENEURS
www.tie.org

A not-for-profit global network of entrepreneurs and professionals.

KOREAN AMERICAN SOCIETY OF ENTREPRENEURS
www.kase.org

To foster and support a growing network of Korean Americans interested in starting or playing key roles in professionally managed high growth companies in the United States.

NATIONAL ARAB AMERICAN MEDICAL ASSOCIATION
www.naama.com

Medical professionals of Arab descent.

NATIONAL ASIAN PACIFIC AMERICAN BAR ASSOCIATION
www.napaba.org

Provides financial assistance to Asian Pacific American law students who have demonstrated academic excellence and social leadership.

NATIONAL ASSOCIATION OF ASIAN AMERICAN PROFESSIONALS
www.naaap.org

Asian American professionals across the country that work together to enhance Asian American leadership.

NETWORK OF INDIAN PROFESSIONALS
www.netip.org

Dedicated to the overall achievement and advancement of South Asian American professionals.

SOUTH ASIAN JOURNALISTS ASSOCIATION
www.saja.org

Promoting journalism amongst South Asian Americans.

TIBETAN YOUTH CONGRESS
www.tibetanyouthcongress.org

A worldwide organization of Tibetans united in our common struggle for the restoration of complete independence for the whole of Tibet.

RELIGIOUS

JAPANESE EVANGELICAL MISSIONARY SOCIETY
www.jems.org

A nonprofit Christian Organization.

VIETNAMESE CHRISTIAN RESOURCE CENTER
www.vcrc.org

An electronic library which provides resource materials and online information for the Vietnamese Christian ministries and services.

RESEARCH

PHILIPPINE-AMERICAN ACADEMY OF SCIENCE AND ENGINEERING
www.paase.org

To encourage collaborative work among scientists and engineers in research and development.

SHOPPING

ASIANMALL.COM
www.asianmall.com

A great selection of Asian-inspired goods.

CHINASPROUT
www.chinasprout.com

Chinese books, Chinese music, and Chinese clothing.

SPEC. INT., EDUCATION

ASIAN AMERICAN STUDIES DEPARTMENT
www.csun.edu/AsianAmericanStudies

To promote student learning and intellectual growth, including the development of problem-solving skills and habits of lifelong education.

CALIFORNIA JAPANESE AMERICAN ALUMNI ASSOCIATION
www.cjaaa.org

To provide academic scholarships, fellowships, and internships to undergraduate and graduate students of Japanese American ancestry.

CENTER FOR SOUTH ASIA STUDIES
www.ias.berkeley.edu/southasia

To provide active support for the teaching and research activities of South Asia-related faculty.

CHINESE AMERICAN POLITICAL ASSOCIATION
www.capa-news.org

Education of Chinese Americans in the area of public affairs.

KOREAN AMERICAN SCHOLARSHIP FOUNDATION
www.kasf.org

Established to help meet the financial needs of Korean-American students seeking higher education.

KOREAN CENTER, INC.
www.koreannet.org

Offers educational opportunities in English as a Second Language, computers, and Korean studies.

SCHOLARSITE.COM
www.scholarsite.com

An interactive database tool with an extensive list of educational institutions awarding scholarships to minority groups in the U.S.

SPEC. INT., EMPLOYMENT

CHINATOWN MANPOWER PROJECT
www.cmpny.org

To provide vocational training, employment services, educational programs, and economic development programs to disadvantaged Asian Americans.

HIREDIVERSITY.COM
www.hirediversity.com

The leading online service for diversity recruitment.

NATIONAL ASIAN PACIFIC AMERICAN LAW STUDENT ASSOCIATION
www.napalsa.org

To promote legal education and legal employment opportunities for Asian Americans.

PACIFIC ASIAN CONSORTIUM IN EMPLOYMENT
www.pacela.org

To address the employment and job training needs of the Asian Pacific Islander communities.

SPEC, INT., HEALTH SERVICES

ASIAN HEALTH SERVICES
www.ahschc.org

Assures access to health care services regardless of income, insurance status, language, or culture.

ASIAN PACIFIC AMERICAN MEDICAL STUDENTS ASSOCIATION
www.apamsa.org

Directly promoting the health and well-being of the Asian community.

ASSOCIATION OF ASIAN PACIFIC COMMUNITY HEALTH ORGANIZATIONS
www.aapcho.org

Improving the health status and access of Asian Americans.

CHARLES B. WANG COMMUNITY HEALTH CENTER
www.cbwchc.org

Community health center that is a division of Chinatown Health Clinic.

VIETNAM HEALTH EDUCATION LITERATURE PROJECT
www.vnhelp.org

Dedicated to helping street children by providing medical care and supplies.

SPEC. INT., HUMAN RELATIONS

ASIA FOUNDATION
www.asiafoundation.org

To build leadership, improve policy and regulation, and strengthen institutions to foster greater openness.

SPEC. INT., MENTAL HEALTH

ASIAN AMERICAN FAMILY SERVICES
www.aafcc.org

Serving the mental health needs of the Asian American community.

ASIAN AMERICAN PSYCHOLOGICAL ASSOCIATION
www.aapaonline.org

Addresses Asian American mental health issues.

SPEC. INT., SOCIAL INTEREST

ASIAN AMERICAN INSTITUTE
www.aaichicago.org

To empower the Asian American community through advocacy by utilizing research, education, and coalition building.

FESTIVALS.COM
www.festivals.com

This site contains worldwide festivals and events. It has a comprehensive list of festivals by country of origin.

SPEC. INT., SPORTS

ASIANATHLETE.COM
www.asianathlete.com

Dedicated to providing information and news about Asian athletes.

MIXEDFOLKS.COM
www.mixedfolks.com/aathletes.htm

Mixed athletes from the Asian continent.

SPEC. INT., WOMEN

ASIAN PACIFIC AMERICAN WOMEN'S LEADERSHIP INSTITUTE
www.apawli.org

Address the challenges facing Asian American and Pacific Islander women and to nurture trust within our communities.

TECHNOLOGY

JAPAN INFORMATION ACCESS PROJECT
www.jiaponline.org

To strengthen international understanding of Japanese and Northeast Asian science, technology, economic, and security policy.

WEBINDIA INTERNET SERVICES
www.webindia.com

Provides business related information and services like web hosting, web designing, web promotions, chennai website development, etc.

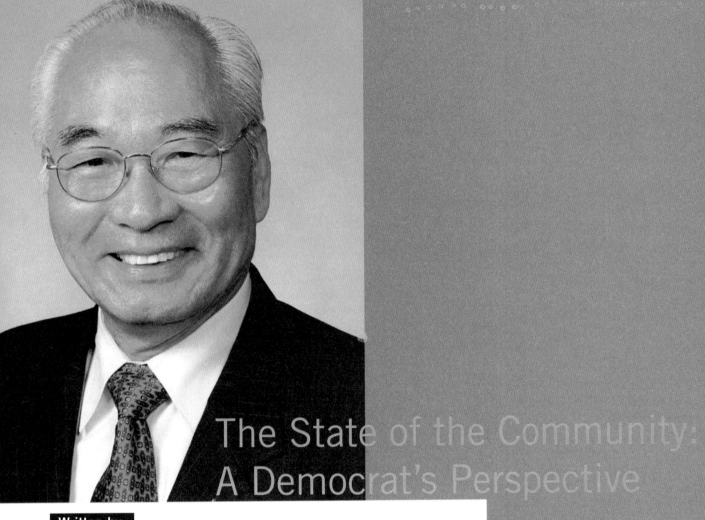

The State of the Community: A Democrat's Perspective

Written by:

SENATOR PAULL SHIN, PH.D.

Senator Paull Shin serves the twenty-first Legislative District of Washington State, which includes Mukilteo, Lynnwood, parts of Edmonds, Mountlake Terrace, and unincorporated Snohomish County. Senator Shin was born in 1935 and adopted by an American GI during the Korean War. Brought to the United States by his adoptive family, he began his education with a GED and went on to earn a Ph.D. in History from the University of Washington. He retired after teaching at the college level for thirty-one years, the last twenty years at Shoreline Community College in Seattle. Senator Shin serves as Chair of the International Trade and Economic Development Committee, Vice Chair of the Agriculture and Rural Economic Development Committee, and as a member of the Early Learning, K-12 and Higher Education Committee. Senator Shin and his wife Donna have lived in Edmonds for more than thirty years. They have two children and five grandsons.

I have lived the American Dream. From my roots in pre-war Korea living on the street as an orphan, I was fortunate to come to the United States where I could achieve my goals of getting a formal education and having a family of my own. And because I am so grateful to those who helped me along my path, I have committed my adult life to giving back to my community as an educator, a state legislator and an Asian-American.

I was born in Korea in 1935. My mother died when I was four years old and my father walked out of my life shortly thereafter. Having no place to go, I was reduced to standing on the street corners of Seoul, begging for food to stay alive. I led the life of a street urchin until the age of fifteen.

When the Korean War broke out in 1950, I fled south like so many other refugees. But when I heard the rumor that U.S. forces were landing in Inchon, I decided to walk up to the front line and greet the arriving American troops. Not long after, for reasons I can't imagine, one of the soldiers reached out his hand and pulled me into their truck. It was the beginning of my new life.

I worked for several Army officers, polishing their shoes, washing and ironing their clothes, and doing other household duties. Dr. Ray Paull, an Army dentist, became a true friend and decided to adopt me into his family. In honor of my adopted father's gift, I changed my first name to Paull. After nearly two years of bureaucratic paperwork, I was able to join my new family in the United States. I was eighteen years old.

After dinner on my first night in the United States, my dad asked me what I would like to do. I

"In 2000, the Legislature adoted my bill to declare May of each year Asian-Pacific Islander Heritage Month in our Washington. It's a powerful symbol, and a beautiful time for schools, communities and the state government to recognize the accomplishments of Asian and Pacific Islander Americans."

always regretted never having the opportunity to go to school in Korea, so I immediately told him I wanted to get an education. I knew I could not succeed in my new homeland without it.

We headed down to the local school the next day. It stung when I was told I didn't have the educational background to attend high school with the other children. But I jumped at the opportunity to learn with a tutor to earn my GED. And I certainly wasn't going to let that hard-earned diploma go to waste. After earning my high school equivalency, I went on to university and graduate school, eventually earning a Ph.D.

When I saw how doors were opened to me because I had an education, I knew I had to give that gift to others. There is an old Chinese proverb, "If you are planning for a year, sow rice; if you are planning for a decade, plant trees; if you are planning for a lifetime, educate people." I embarked on a teaching career that spanned more than thirty-one years, teaching Asian history and international relations to students all around the United States. It was a very rewarding path, and I encourage everyone to be a teacher, whether they do it as a profession or as a mentor.

Throughout my teaching career, I was called on by the governors of Washington State to serve as an advisor on trade issues. I served four governors and led several trade missions with them to various Asian countries. I was grateful that I was able to render service to the people of the United States and Asia, and I felt I made a worthwhile contribution in promoting trade that benefits our state.

I had prospered in the United States, and I knew I had more energy to give to my community. Benjamin Franklin wrote, "A grateful person is one who realizes blessings and reciprocates by serving." In 1992, I

VICE PRESIDENT PRO TEM
PAULL SHIN

Senator Paull Shin in his role as Vice President Pro Tem. January 24, 2005.

Senator Paull Shin listens as Matthew Landon testifies on SB6122 before the Senate Commerce and Trade committee in Olympia. Fifth and sixth grade students in Mountlake Terrace proposed the legislation which would prohibit smoking within thirty-five feet of public places.

ran against an entrenched incumbent for a seat in the Washington State House of Representatives and won.

My commitment to education has only deepened while serving in the state House and Senate. The central goal of our K-12 and higher education system is to give students the skills they need to find a place in the work force and become productive members of society. And our state Constitution calls it the "paramount duty of the state" to make sure we have a strong education system. It's a duty I take seriously.

This past year, the Legislature significantly expanded education funding. We adopted the largest school construction budget in history, lowered K-12 class sizes and increased pay for teachers. We also added nearly 8,000 new places for students at our state universities and colleges, while addressing nagging inequities in our compensation system for college teachers. I'm living proof of the value of education. These are investments that will pay huge

dividends when these students become full members of society.

As the first Korean-American legislator to serve in Washington, I felt a responsibility to promote cultural awareness and understanding. In 2000, the Legislature adopted my bill to declare May of each year Asian-Pacific Islander Heritage Month in our Washington. It's a powerful symbol, and a beautiful time for schools, communities and the state government to recognize the accomplishments of Asian and Pacific Islander Americans. Asians first came to Washington more than 150 years ago, enduring physical hardships and painful discrimination. Asian-Pacific Islanders fought for their civil rights for decades and we still must teach against ignorance and bigotry.

But today we can also celebrate many success stories and inspirational Asian-American leaders such as Wing Luke, our first Asian-American elected official in the Pacific Northwest, and Gary Locke, the first Chinese-American

governor in the United States. And through API Heritage Month, each year we recognize the contributions of Asian-Pacific Islanders, both prominent individuals and the community as a whole.

Early in my tenure in the Legislature, I was shocked to learn that our state still used the painful term "oriental" to describe Asians. Although we had come a long way from the days of "For Whites Only," clearly there was more work to be done. Many of my colleagues didn't understand why I found it so offensive; my concern was for the young people who were exposed to this obsolete racial terminology. In 2002, my colleagues unanimously approved my measure to eliminate this pejorative word from our laws and regulations, and I have heard from other states' legislators who would like to follow suit.

Today, I continue my work to promote the American Dream in my state. As the state Senate's leader in promoting international trade

Senator Paull Shin speaks on the Senate floor. February 18, 2003.

and economic development, I fully recognize that a good education leading to a reliable family-wage job is the key to that American Dream. I want to make Washington an even better place to start or grow a business. We need to create another 100,000 family-wage jobs in our state in the next five years. And we must take advantage of our strategic location on the Pacific Rim to narrow the trade gap between imports to and exports from our state. I continue to attract more foreign investment in Washington and promote Washington products overseas. The goal is a better life for everyone in our state.

If my story proves anything, it is that as you search for the answers to the questions of identity, you can overcome any obstacle with determination and the support of a caring family, whether or not you are an adoptee. I truly believe in the power of positive thinking. When you love yourself and believe that you are equal in capacity and potential to anyone else, you can achieve anything you can visualize.

UNITED STATES DEPARTMENT OF COMMERCE
Minority Business Development Agency
Washington, D.C. 20230

NOV 2 5 2005

Dear Colleagues:

Each year as TIYM publishes its ASIAN AMERICAN YEARBOOK, the Minority Business Development Agency (MBDA) looks forward to the opportunity to send greetings to its readers.

MBDA considers this publication to be an excellent resource for information on minority establishments in the United States. In fact, MBDA has ties to many individuals and organizations featured in this YEARBOOK, as we share a common goal of promoting the growth of Asian American businesses and communities.

As the only federal agency created solely to foster the establishment and growth of minority businesses in this country, MBDA is delighted to report that there are now over 4.1 million minority firms in the United States. The number of Asian American firms has grown 24% since 1997 and now exceeds 1.1 million firms. Their receipts are $343.3 billion, and together they employ over 2.3 million people. These numbers indicate that Asian American businesses have a significant impact on the economic landscape of our Nation. MBDA predicts even greater growth ahead for minority enterprises.

Everyone at TIYM is to be commended for your dedication to strengthening the foundation upon which Asian American entrepreneurs can build powerful business collaborations. Thank you for your commitment, and you have our best wishes for many more years of success with the YEARBOOK.

Sincerely,

Ronald N. Langston
National Director

JERROLD ASAO HIURA

ARTIST

Jerry Hiura was appointed to the California Arts Council in 2002 by Governor Gray Davis and currently serves as its Vice-Chair. He is only the fourth Asian American appointment in over thirty years of the council's existence. Prior to this he served and chaired the San Jose Fine Arts Commission (1985-1993) and presided over the Arts Council of Silicon Valley (1993-2001). His government and private/public sector arts involvement is driven by a strong need to represent people of color and ethnic communities in public policy creation in the community-based arts and cultural arenas. In 1994 he founded Contemporary Asian Theater Scene in San Jose which is today a leading platform in Silicon Valley for Asian American theater and independently produced Asian and Asian American filmmakers, mounting an annual film festival which draws thousands to its screenings. As a principle fashion jewelry design partner with Sharyn Yoshida in the early eighties, their 'Shibui' collection was featured in all the Neiman Marcus and Saks Fifth Avenue stores across the country. The collection accessorized designer collections from Geoffrey Beene to Bill Blass and was seen in Estee Lauder ads, Vogue and Women's Wear Daily. He attended UC, Berkeley, Harvard University and Washington University in St. Louis, and has a full time dental practice in San Jose's Japantown. He lives with his wife, Lucia Cha in Los Gatos, California.

AsAY As a dentist by trade, how did you become an artist in costume jewelry design? When did you first become interested in the arts?

Hiura In the early 1980s after moving to San Jose from St. Louis, Missouri following my graduation from Washington University's School of Dental Medicine, I teamed up with another visual artist and began a collection of costume jewelry we called "Shibui" that was picked up by Neiman Marcus Stores. The Shibui Collection was big, hand-painted laquerware that caught the eye of several couture designers including Geoffrey Beene and Bill Blass. The collection was eventually carried in all the Nieman Marcus and Saks Fifth Avenue stores throughout the US and featured in advertisements in Vogue, Women's Wear Daily and Estee Lauder.

AsAY In 1994 you founded the Contemporary Asian Theatre Scene. What were your motivations and ultimately your vision behind its creation?

Hiura Contemporary Asian Theater Scene was founded in 1994 to platform APA theatric arts in Silicon Valley. We were motivated by the dearth of cultural arts organizations in the region particularly ones that served the APA population which to this day is the fastest growing demographic in California. The founders had also befriended many APA playwrights, actors and film makers and came to understand that access to stages and venues to mount productions and resources that support development of new work were practically non-existent in Silicon Valley. What CATS has successfully launched over the past 11 years is a convergence of diversified funding, professional marketing and stage production and most importantly, a strong APA community base that is aimed at presenting and producing APA theater and film to a mainstream audience. CATS historically plays to SRO audiences for most of its dramatic stage productions as well as the International Asian Film Festival in San Jose, which is a collaboration with the National Asian American Telecommunications Association.

We hope as a model APA cultural arts platform, CATS can open up a commitment with APA cultural workers and artists in finding, expressing and mounting the most relevant, provocative creative voices for the entire APA community.

AsAY As former chair of the Arts Council of Silicon Valley and the Arts Commission of San Jose, what did those experiences

teach you? What else can be done in terms of advancing and promoting the arts in the state of California? On a national level?

Hiura The APA arts and cultural sector is part of a broader multicultural arts front which in turn underpins a more comprehensive mainstream arts base. That mainstream arts platform is a significant item in the cultural tourism/hospitality industry which all falls under the mantle of the Creative Society/Creative Industries. This is the layered equation that APA arts and cultural issues must engage in. The arguments that make these issues compelling are one, a fascination by mainstream America's younger population with popular media and culture arising from China , Korea, the Phillipines and in a fundamental way with Japan; two, significant participation by APA and MCAO (multicultural arts organizations) in outreach to the schools and exposure at a grass roots level with arts education initiatives, a universally held high

priority area by the general public and increasingly, by both public and private funders, three, the rapid growth of immigration from Asian countries (Japan being the exception) particularly from China and Asian India; four, the explosive APA population growth rates: the 2000 US Census found a 71.7% growth rate amongst APAs in Santa Clara County and a 48.3% APA increase bay area wide. In 2000, APA's made up 11.1% of the state population (3.7 million) while Hispanic totaled 32.4% (11 million): five, the alarming historic 'lack' of support for APA non-profits. For example, throughout the '90s, bay area foundations' funding to APA concerns stood at a meager 0.77% while the bay area's APA population during that period grew to represent 19.3% of the total; finally, six, the accepted reality that multicultural and cross cultural art forms are critical components of urban center revitalization creation of destination hubs and carry much of the hub's 'commercial attraction' through

Dr. Hiura (front row center) with guests at KQED and Union Bank of California's Asian Pacific American Heritage event: Five Outstanding Local Heroes, on May 10, 2005.

festivals, parades etc. This converts to measurable economic outcomes and tax generation and this in turn arms arts leaders with rationales to provoke more inclusive arts policies and a greater share of public support for APA and MCAOs. This does not happen in a vacuum. APA communities are immigrant heavy and culturally rich. These communities value their cultural heritage and its concomitant artistic expression as a sort of motherboard of pride, historical memory and sense of self. The value proposition this makes with the community is palpable. As a result there is deep support and involvement from a multigenerational base of leaders, patrons, participants and most importantly, volunteerism.

Jerrold Asao Hiura at KQED and Union Bank of California's Asian Pacific American Heritage event: Five Outstanding Local Heroes, on May 10, 2005.

rose to over 50% of all those funded. It was critical for the commission to develop arts policies that addressed squarely the issues of cultural equality, diversity and

"In the coming years, Asian Pacific Americans will have a larger impact. The census projects that by 2050, that segment of the population will double. Therefore, there needs to be more Asian Americans in government positions and executive boardrooms."

My two terms (1985-93) on the San Jose Arts Commission was an eye-opener. In the mid-80s almost 92% of all grant allocations went to six large budgeted institutions (Symphony, Ballet, Museum of Art, etc.) and 8% was spread out to 40 or so mid sized and small budget arts organizations. Two of those arts groups were APR. By the early 90s, [these traditional institutions] accounted for less then 60% of all city funding to the arts and multicultural arts organizations

the importance of arts in our ethnic neighborhoods and multicultural communities as economic engines.

AsAY As a member of the California Arts Council and taking into account the large Asian American population in your state, are you satisfied with the involvement of the Asian American community in the arts?

Hiura The National Endowment for the Arts allocates annually over

$1 million to the California Arts Council. This funding is directed to arts education programs. The CAC over its thirty-year history has been the model of enlightened arts policies and programs and as a state, ranked in the top tiers of funding and granting dollars when compared to state art agencies across the US. Over the past 3 years, we've witnessed General Funds to CAC decrease from $33m in 2001 to 3m today. The agency has literally been gutted. The NEA support and the leadership of Dana Goia have been absolutely crucial to the survival of the CAC. Goia has made it a point to work proactively with arts leaders across the country to craft a Cultural Literacy Movement that has implications for Asian Americans.

ASIANPACIFICAMERICAN
Business

FIG 1. U.S. Buying Power by Race: 1990-2009 (Numbers in billions)

According to the Selig Center for Economic Growth at the University of Georgia, Asian Americans' share of U.S. buying power increased more than any other specific racial or ethnic group between 1990 and 2000. During this period, that number shot up 127 percent. The Center projects that by 2009, Asian buying power in the U.S. will reach $528 billion, a further increase of almost ninety-seven percent. Appealing to and capturing a share of this increasingly important consumer group will be a continuing goal for marketers. One factor that makes this market especially appealing is the fact that Asian Americans are, according to the U.S. Census Bureau, more educated than the rest of the country. Among other factors, education contributes to a higher income and therefore more buying power on an individual and household basis. Indeed, the U.S. Census Bureau estimated the average Asian household's income at $57,518 in 2004 — significantly higher than the nationwide figure ($44,389).

Race or Ethnicity	1990	2000	Percent Increase 1990 - 2000	2009	Percent Increase 2000 - 2009
Total	4,277.20	7,113.60	66.3%	11,068.80	55.6%
White	3,736.40	5,919.90	58.4%	8,967.50	51.5%
Black	318.3	584.9	83.8%	964.6	64.9%
Hispanic	221.9	503.9	127.1%	992.3	96.9%
Asian	118.2	268.7	127.3%	528.2	96.6%
Other	85.0	195.7	130.2%	371.8	90.0%
American Indian	19.3	37.2	92.7%	65.6	76.3%
Multiracial	NA	107.2	NA	170.9	59.4%

Source: Selig Center for Economic Growth, Terry College of Business, The University of Georgia, May 2004

FIG 2. States with the Largest Number of Asian American-Owned Firms: 2002

In 2002, Asian Americans owned 4.8 percent of the total firms in the United States. In sheer numbers, the leading states for Asian-owned businesses were California, New York and Texas. Although it came in fifth place for total firms, Hawaii had by far the highest percentage of Asian American-owned firms.

State	Asian-Owned	Percent of Total Firms
United States	1,105,329	4.8%
California	372,221	12.9%
New York	145,626	8.5%
Texas	78,018	4.5%
New Jersey	51,974	7.3%
Hawaii	44,980	45.3%
Illinois	44.501	4.6%
Florida	41,342	2.7%
Virginia	30,470	5.8%
Georgia	26,923	4.0%
Washington	26,872	5.8%

Source: U.S. Census Bureau, 2002 Survey of Business Owners www.census.gov

Federal and State Employment Offices

ALABAMA

AGRICULTURE, DEPT. OF
Alabama State Office
4121 Carmichael Rd. #601
Montgomery, AL 36106-3683
Martha Davis, Asian American Program
Manager
Tel: (334) 279-3400 Fax: (334) 279-3403
Email: martha.davis@al.usda.gov
Web: www.usda.gov

AIR FORCE, DEPT. OF THE
Maxwell AFB
Maxwell AFB, AL 36112-6334
Tel: (800) 423-8723
Web: www.airforce.com

ARMY, DEPT. OF THE
US Army Recruiting Battalion Montgomery
775 McDonald St., Bldg. 1510
MAFB Gunter Annez, AL 36114
Tel: (334) 271-3059

EQUAL EMPLOYMENT OPPORTUNITY
COMMISSION
Birmingham District Office
1130 22nd St. South #2000
Birmingham, AL 35205
Beverly B. Hinton, Outreach Coordinator
Tel: (205) 212-2082 Fax: (205) 212-2105
Email: beverly.hinton@eeoc.gov
Web: www.eeoc.gov

HOMELAND SECURITY, DEPT. OF
USCG Recruiting Office Birmingham
Eastwood Festival Ctr., 7001 Crestwood
Blvd. #612
Birmingham, AL 35201
BMC Jose Rodriquez, Recruiter in Charge
Tel: (205) 592-8923 Fax: (205) 592-9826
Email: jrodriquez@cgrc.uscg.mil
Web: www.gocoastguard.com

USCG Recruiting Office Mobile
Mobile Festival Ctr., 3725 Airport Blvd.
#148
Mobile, AL 36608-1633
SKC Charles L. Miles, Recruiter in Charge
Tel: (251) 441-5171 Fax: (251) 441-5173
Email: cmiles@cgrc.uscg.mil
Web: www.gocoastguard.com

USCG Recruiting Office Montgomery
Armed Forces Career Ctr., 2933 Eastern
Blvd.
Montgomery, AL 36116
AMTC Tim Lucas, Recruiter in Charge
Tel: (334) 279-4880 Fax: (334) 279-3129
Email: tlucas@cgrc.uscg.mil
Web: www.gocoastguard.com

NAVY, DEPT. OF THE
Navy Recruiting District, Montgomery
2400 President Dr. South
Montgomery, AL 36116
Tel: (334) 279-8543

USMC Recruiting Station, Montgomery
2853 Fairlane Dr. #64, Bldg. G
Montgomery, AL 36116-1698
Tel: (334) 647-3110
Web: www.marines.com

POSTAL SERVICE
Alabama District
351 24th St. North
Birmingham, AL 35203-9989
April M. Williams, Diversity Development
Specialist
Tel: (205) 521-0256 Fax: (205) 521-0935
Email: april.m.williams@usps.gov
Web: www.usps.gov

ALASKA

AIR FORCE, DEPT. OF THE
Eielson AFB
Eielson AFB, AK 99702-1720
Tel: (800) 423-8723
Web: www.airforce.com

Elmendorf AFB
Elmendorf AFB, AK 99506-2400
Tel: (800) 423-8723
Web: www.airforce.com

HOMELAND SECURITY, DEPT. OF
USCG Recruiting Office Anchorage
800 Diamond Blvd. Space 3-205
Anchorage, AK 99515
AETC Frank L. Brown, Recruiter in Charge
Tel: (907) 271-2447 Fax: (907) 271-5075
Email: flbrown@cgrc.uscg.mil
Web: www.gocoastguard.com

INTERIOR, DEPT. OF THE
National Park Service
Alaska Region
240 W. 5th Ave. #114
Anchorage, AK 99501
Darwin Aho, Human Resources Manager
Tel: (907) 644-3336
Email: darwin_aho@nps.gov
Web: www.nps.gov

ARIZONA

AIR FORCE, DEPT. OF THE
Davis-Monthan AFB
Davis-Monthan AFB, AZ 85707-3018
Tel: (800) 423-8723
Web: www.airforce.com

Luke AFB
Luke AFB, AZ 85309-1514
Tel: (800) 423-8723
Web: www.airforce.com

ARMY, DEPT. OF THE
US Army Recruiting Battalion Phoenix
1 N. 1st St. #400
Phoenix, AZ 85004-2357
Tel: (602) 254-1981

EQUAL EMPLOYMENT OPPORTUNITY
COMMISSION
Phoenix District Office
Equal Employment Opportunity Office
3300 N. Central Ave. #690
Phoenix, AZ 85012-2504
Chester Bailey, Director
Tel: (602) 640-5000 Fax: (602) 640-5071
Email: chester.bailey@eeoc.gov
Web: www.eeoc.gov

HOMELAND SECURITY, DEPT. OF
USCG Recruiting Office Phoenix
826 N. Central Ave.
Phoenix, AZ 85004-2003
SKC Zeke Witherspoon, Recruiter in Charge
Tel: (602) 379-3834 Fax: (602) 379-3843
Email: zwitherspoon@cgrc.uscg.mil
Web: www.gocoastguard.com

USCG Recruiting Office Tucson
Mission Plz., 4679 E. Speedway
Tucson, AZ 85714
AMT1 Mickey Winchel, Recruiter in Charge
Tel: (520) 323-5546 Fax: (520) 323-5587
Email: mwinchel@cgrc.uscg.mil
Web: www.gocoastguard.com

INTERIOR, DEPT. OF THE
Bureau Indian Affairs
Western Region, Personnel Office
400 N. 5th St. 12th Fl.
Phoenix, AZ 85004
Marcelnia Hills, Acting Personnel Officer
Tel: (602) 379-6739 Fax: (602) 379-4966
Web: www.bia.gov

NAVY, DEPT. OF THE
Navy Recruiting District, Phoenix
P.O. Box 25368
Phoenix, AZ 85002
Tel: (602) 256-6026

USMC Recruiting Station, Phoenix
1 N. 1st St. #302
Phoenix, AZ 85004
Tel: (602) 256-7819
Web: www.marines.com

POSTAL SERVICE
Arizona District
4949 E. VanBuren
Phoenix, AZ 85026
Aida Murrieta-Penn, Diversity Development
Specialist
Tel: (602) 225-5451 Fax: (602) 225-5432
Email: amurrieta@email.usps.gov
Web: www.usps.gov

STATE OF ARIZONA
Governors Office
Governors Office on Equal Opportunity
1700 W. Washington St. #156
Phoenix, AZ 85007
Patti Campbell, Specialist
Tel: (602) 542-3711 Fax: (602) 542-3712
Email: pcampbell@az.gov
Web: www.governor.state.az.us

ARKANSAS

AGRICULTURE, DEPT. OF
Natural Resources
3416 Federal Building
2898 Point Cr. #2
Fayetteville, AR 72704
Rhonda Foster, Asian American Program
Manager
Tel: (479) 442-4160 Fax: (479) 444-8726
Email: rhonda.foster @ar.usda.gov
Web: www.ar.nrcs.usda.gov

AIR FORCE, DEPT. OF THE
Little Rock AFB
Little Rock AFB, AR 72099-5052
Tel: (800) 423-8723
Web: www.airforce.com

EQUAL EMPLOYMENT OPPORTUNITY
COMMISSION
Little Rock Area Office
Equal Employment Opportunity Office
820 Louisiana St. #200
Little Rock, AR 72201
Kay Klugh, Director
Tel: (501) 324-5060 Fax: (501) 324-5991
Email: kay.klugh@eeoc.gov
Web: www.eeoc.gov

HOMELAND SECURITY, DEPT. OF
USCG Recruiting Office Little Rock
Ashley Sq. Shopping Ctr., 9108 N. Rodney
Parham Rd.
Little Rock, AR 72205-1648

AMTC James Lawson, Recruiter in Charge
Tel: (501) 217-9446 Fax: (501) 217-3858
Email: jlawson@cgrc.uscg.mil
Web: www.gocoastguard.com

POSTAL SERVICE
Arkansas District
420 Natural Resources Dr.
Little Rock, AR 72205-9001
Judy E. Gurkin, Diversity Development
Specialist
Tel: (501) 228-4263 Fax: (501) 228-4249
Email: judith.e.gurkin@usps.gov
Web: www.usps.com

STATE OF ARKANSAS
Department of Finance & Administration
Office of Administrative Services
1515 W. 7th St. #102
Little Rock, AR 72201
Jenette S. Manno, DSA Manager of Human
Resources
Tel: (501) 371-6009 Fax: (501) 683-2174
Email: jenette.manno@dfa.state.ar.us
Web: www.arkansas.gov/dfa

CALIFORNIA

AGRICULTURE, DEPT. OF
Forest Service
Region 5, Pacific Southwest Region
1323 Club Dr.
Vallejo, CA 94592
Sandra Wallace, Civil Rights, Director
Tel: (707) 562-8752 Fax: (707) 562-9044
Email: swallace@fs.fed.us
Web: www.fs.fed.us

Forest Service
Supervisor Office, Lassen National Forest
2550 Riverside Dr.
Susanville, CA 96130
Daniel Gonzalez, Equal Employment
Manager
Tel: (530) 257-2151 Fax: (530) 252-6428
Email: dgonzalez@fs.fed.us
Web: www.fs.fed.us

AIR FORCE, DEPT. OF THE
Beale AFB
Beale AFB, CA 95903-1533
Tel: (800) 423-8723
Web: www.airforce.com

Edwards AFB
Edwards AFB, CA 93524-1470
Tel: (800) 423-8723
Web: www.airforce.com

Los Angeles AFB
Los Angeles AFB, CA 90245-4677
Tel: (800) 423-8723
Web: www.airforce.com

March AFB
March AFB, CA 92518-1723
Tel: (800) 423-8723
Web: www.airforce.com

Onizuka Air Station
Sunnyvale, CA 94089-1233
Tel: (800) 423-8723
Web: www.airforce.com

Travis AFB
Travis AFB, CA 94535-2406
Tel: (800) 423-8723
Web: www.airforce.com

Vandeburg AFB
Vandeburg AFB, CA 93437-6252

Tel: (800) 423-8723
Web: www.airforce.com

ARMY, DEPT. OF THE
US Army Recruiting Battalion Los Angeles
5051 Rodeo Rd., Rm. 2087
Los Angeles, CA 90016-4793
Tel: (323) 293-7317

US Army Recruiting Battalion Sacramento
2880 Sunrise Blvd. #230
Rancho Cordova, CA 95742-6549
Tel: (916) 638-0970

US Army Recruiting Battalion Southern California
27401 Los Altos #330
Mission Viejo, CA 92691-6316
Tel: (949) 367-1159

CITY OF LOS ANGELES
LA Unified School District
Teaching Recruitment and Personnel Office
P.O. Box 3307
Los Angeles, CA 90051
Debby Ignagni, Director
Tel: (213) 241-5300 Fax: (213) 241-8412
Web: www.teachinla.com

ENVIRONMENTAL PROTECTION AGENCY
Human Resources Office, Region 9
75 Hawthorne St. PMD-12
San Francisco, CA 94105
Kim Driver, Outreach and Recruitment
Coordinator
Tel: (415) 972-3830 Fax: (415) 947-8024
Email: driver.kim@epa.gov
Web: www.epa.gov

EQUAL EMPLOYMENT OPPORTUNITY COMMISSION
Fresno Local Office
Equal Employment Opportunity Office
1265 W. Shaw Ave. #103
Fresno, CA 93711
Tel: (559) 487-5793 Fax: (559) 487-5053
Web: www.eeoc.gov

Los Angeles District Office
Roybal Federal Bldg., 255 E. Temple St.,
4th Fl.
Los Angeles, CA 90012
Olophius Perry, Director
Tel: (213) 894-1000 Fax: (213) 894-1118
Email: olophius.perry@eeoc.gov
Web: www.eeoc.gov

Oakland Local Office
1301 Clay St. #1170-N
Oakland, CA 94612-5217
Joyce Hendy, Director
Tel: (510) 637-3230 Fax: (510) 637-3235
Email: joyce.hendy@eeoc.gov
Web: www.eeoc.gov

San Francisco District Office
Equal Employment Opportunity Office
350 The Embarcadero #500
San Francisco, CA 94105-1260
Joan Ehrlich, Director
Tel: (415) 625-5600 Fax: (415) 625-5609
Email: joan.ehrlich@eeoc.gov
Web: www.eeoc.gov

San Jose Local Office
Equal Employment Opportunity Office
96 N. 3rd St. #200
San Jose, CA 95112
Joyce Endy, Acting Director
Tel: (408) 291-7352 Fax: (408) 291-4539
Email: joyce.endy@eeoc.gov
Web: www.eeoc.gov

GENERAL SERVICES ADMINISTRATION
Office of Equal Employment Opportunity
Region 9, 10
450 Golden Gate Ave. #6577
San Francisco, CA 94102-3434
Antoinette B. Brady, Regional Officer
Tel: (415) 522-2711 Fax: (415) 522-2710
Email: antoinette.brady@gsa.gov
Web: www.gsa.gov

HOMELAND SECURITY, DEPT. OF
USCG Recruiting Office Fresno
3749 W. Shaw Ave.
Fresno, CA 93711
HSC Richard Garcia, Recruiter in Charge
Tel: (559) 221-6600 Fax: (559) 229-5608
Email: rgarcia@cgrc.uscg.mil
Web: www.gocoastguard.com

USCG Recruiting Office Hawthorne
12620 Hawthorne Plz. #C
Hawthorne, CA 90250
YNC Rodney Weiss, Recruiter in Charge
Tel: (310) 675-7562 Fax: (310) 675-7739
Email: twilbert@cgrc.uscg.mil
Web: www.gocoastguard.com

USCG Recruiting Office Humboldt Bay
Victoria Place Shopping Ctr., 3220 S.
Broadway St. #A-4
Eureka, CA 95501-3854
SK1 Tim Crothers, Recruiter in Charge
Tel: (707) 268-2471 Fax: (707) 268-2473
Email: tcrothers@cgrc.uscg.mil
Web: www.gocoastguard.com

USCG Recruiting Office Lakewood
Lakewood Center., 4431 Candlewood St.
Lakewood, CA 90712
HSC James Anderson, Recruiter in Charge
Tel: (562) 790-2318 Fax: (562) 790-2478
Email: wbulman@cgrc.uscg.mil
Web: www.gocoastguard.com

USCG Recruiting Office Montebello
2350 W. Beverly Blvd. #100
Montebello, CA 90640
HSC Diana Bullwinkle, Recruiter in Charge
Tel: (323) 887-7558 Fax: (323) 887-7576
Email: dbullwikle@cgrc.uscg.mil
Web: www.gocoastguard.com

USCG Recruiting Office Riverside
1090 E. Washington St. #A
Colton, CA 92324-8180
AMTCS Wayne Campbell, Recruiter in
Charge
Tel: (909) 783-2772 Fax: (909) 783-3158
Email: wcampbell@cgrc.uscg.mil
Web: www.gocoastguard.com

USCG Recruiting Office Sacramento
Antelope Plz., 6456 Tupelo Dr. #A-5
Citrus Heights, CA 95621
MKC Thomas Pitock, Recruiter in Charge
Tel: (916) 721-6877 Fax: (916) 721-7857
Email: tpitock@cgrc.uscg.mil
Web: www.gocoastguard.com

USCG Recruiting Office San Diego
Point Loma Plz., 3663 E. Midway Dr.
San Diego, CA 92110-3224
FSCS Randy Washington, Recruiter in
Charge
Tel: (619) 226-8222 Fax: (619) 226-8234
Email: rwashington@cgrc.uscg.mil
Web: www.gocoastguard.com

USCG Recruiting Office San Diego South
703 H St. #3
Chula Vista, CA 91910-4056

FSCS Randy Washington, Recruiter in
Charge
Tel: (619) 427-1678 Fax: (619) 427-0585
Email: rwashington@cgrc.uscg.mil
Web: www.gocoastguard.com

US Coast Guard
USCG Recruiting Office San Francisco
14410 Washington Ave. #118
San Leandro, CA 94578
GMC Rick Ward, Recruiter in Charge
Tel: (510) 352-8992 Fax: (510) 352-0359
Email: rickward@cgrc.uscg.mil
Web: www.gocoastguard.com

USCG Recruiting Office San Jose
3381 Stevens Creek Blvd.
San Jose, CA 95117-1070
YNC Carlos Rosario, Recruiter in Charge
Tel: (408) 246-8724 Fax: (408) 246-8729
Email: crosario@cgrc.uscg.mil
Web: www.gocoastguard.com

USCG Recruiting Office Ventura
4202 S. Victoria Ave.
Oxnard, CA 93035
OSCS Thomas Buccowich, Recruiter in
Charge
Tel: (805) 984-6893 Fax: (805) 984-5925
Email: tbuccowich@cgrc.uscg.mil
Web: www.gocoastguard.com

INTERIOR, DEPT. OF THE
Bureau of Land Management, California State Office
Equal Employment Opportunity Office
2800 Cottage Wy. #W-1834
Sacramento, CA 95825-1886
Mario Gonzalez, Manager
Tel: (916) 978-4492 Fax: (916) 978-4498
Web: www.ca.blm.gov

Bureau of Reclamation
Mid-Pacific Region
2800 Cottage Way
Sacramento, CA 95825
Leila Horibata, Special Emphasis
Coordinator
Tel: (916) 978-5032 Fax: (916) 978-5496
Email: lhoribata@mp.usbr.gov
Web: www.usbr.gov/mp

LABOR, DEPT. OF
Employment and Training Administration
Office of Youth Programs and Job Corps
71 Stevenson St. #1015
San Francisco, CA 94105-2970
Erine Priesley, Regional Director
Tel: (415) 975-4680 Fax: (415) 975-4715
Email: priespley.erine@dol.gov
Web: www.jobcorps.gov

NAVY, DEPT. OF THE
Naval Reserve Recruiting Command Area Pacific
960 N. Harbor Dr.
San Diego, CA 92132-5000
Tel: (619) 532-3157

Navy Recruiting District, Los Angeles
5051 Rodeo Rd.
Los Angeles, CA 90016
Tel: (800) 252-1588

Navy Recruiting District, San Diego
33055 Nixie Way
San Diego, CA 92147
Tel: (619) 524-6683

USMC Recruiting Station, Los Angeles
5051 Rodeo Rd. #2061
Los Angeles, CA 90016-4794

Tel: (323) 294-3679
Web: www.marines.com

USMC Recruiting Station, Orange County
1921 E. Alton Ave. #150
Santa Anna, CA 92705
Tel: (949) 261-0331
Web: www.marines.com

USMC Recruiting Station, Sacramento
3870 Rosin Ct. #110
Sacramento, CA 95834-1633
Tel: (916) 646-6980
Web: www.marines.com

USMC Recruiting Station, San Diego
2221 Camino del Rio South #212
San Diego, CA 92108-3610
Tel: (619) 688-1508
Web: www.marines.com

USMC Recruiting Station, San Francisco
Moffet Federal Airfield, 546 Vernon Ave. #212
Mountain View, CA 94043
Tel: (650) 603-8953
Web: www.marines.com

POSTAL SERVICE
Oakland District
1675 7th St. #306
Oakland, CA 94615-9992
Elmira A. Walton, Diversity Development Specialist
Tel: (510) 874-8665 Fax: (510) 433-7643
Email: ewalton@usps.gov
Web: www.usps.gov

Pacific Area Office
1675 7th St.
Oakland, CA 94615-9998
Tel: (510) 874-8650 Fax: (510) 874-8596
Web: www.usps.gov

San Diego District
11251 Rancho Carmel Dr. #253
San Diego, CA 92199-9461
Ed Carmona, Diversity Development Specialist
Tel: (858) 674-2713 Fax: (619) 674-2711
Email: ed.carmona@usps.gov
Web: www.usps.com

San Francisco District
P.O. Box 885348
San Francisco, CA 94188-5348
Abel E. Sanchez, Diversity Development Specialist
Tel: (415) 550-5710 Fax: (415) 550-5283
Email: asanche4@email.usps.gov
Web: www.usps.gov

Santa Ana District
15421 Gale Ave.
City of Industry, CA 91715-9347
Norma Diaz, Diversity Development Specialist
Tel: (626) 855-6354 Fax: (626) 855-5964
Email: norma.diaz@usps.gov
Web: www.usps.gov

Van Nuys District
28201 Franklin Pkwy.
Santa Clarita, CA 91383-9994
Tyrone Washington, Diversity Development Specialist
Tel: (661) 775-7055 Fax: (661) 775-7181
Email: tyrone.d.washington@usps.gov
Web: www.usps.com

STATE OF CALIFORNIA
Employment Development Department
Equal Employment Opportunity Office
P.O. Box 826880
Sacramento, CA 94280-0001
Walter Johnson, Chief
Tel: (916) 654-8434 Fax: (916) 654-9371
Email: wjohnson@edd.ca.gov
Web: www.edd.ca.gov

COLORADO

AGRICULTURE, DEPT. OF
Forest Service
Rocky Mountain Region (R-2)
P.O. Box 25127
Lakewood, CO 80225-0127
Rick Cables, Regional Forester
Tel: (303) 275-5343 Fax: (303) 275-5671
Email: rcables@fs.fed.us

NRCS, State of Colorado
655 Parfet St. #E200C
Lakewood, CO 80215-5517
Tel: (720) 544-2860 Fax: (720) 544-2862
Web: www.co.nrcs.usda.gov

AIR FORCE, DEPT. OF THE
Buckley AFB
Buckley AFB, CO 80011-9542
Tel: (800) 423-8723
Web: www.airforce.com

Schriever AFB
Schriever AFB, CO 80912
Tel: (800) 423-8723
Web: www.airforce.com

USAF Academy
USAF Academy, CO 80840-2215
Tel: (800) 423-8723
Web: www.airforce.com

ARMY, DEPT. OF THE
US Army Recruiting Battalion Denver
225 E. 16th Ave. #400
Denver, CO 80203-1620
Tel: (303) 894-9804

COMMERCE, DEPT. OF
Oceanic & Atmospheric Research
Equal Employment Opportunity Office
325 Broadway, Bldg. 22
Boulder, CO 80305
Tony Tafoya, Manager
Tel: (303) 497- 6731 Fax: (303) 497-7283
Email: anthony.j.tafoya@noaa.gov
Web: www.noaa.gov

EQUAL EMPLOYMENT OPPORTUNITY COMMISSION
Denver District Office
Equal Employment Opportunity Office
303 E. 17th Ave. #510
Denver, CO 80203
Janet Leno, Director
Tel: (303) 866-1300 Fax: (303) 866-1085
Email: janet.leno@eeoc.gov
Web: www.eeoc.gov

HOMELAND SECURITY, DEPT. OF
USCG Recruiting Office Denver
7355 W 88th Ave. #H
Westminister, CO 80021
MKC Charles Rowland, Recruiter in Charge
Tel: (303) 252-0919 Fax: (303) 252-1763
Email: crowland@cgrc.uscg.mil
Web: www.gocoastguard.com

INTERIOR, DEPT. OF THE
Bureau of Reclamation

Human Resources Office
P.O. Box 25007
Denver, CO 80225-0007
Laurie Johnson, Manager
Tel: (303) 445-2656 Fax: (303) 445-6349
Email: ljohnson@do.usbr.gov
Web: www.usbr.gov

Bureau of Reclamation
Workforce Diversity Office
P.O. Box 25007 #D-7300
Denver, CO 80225-0007
Karen Megorden, Officer
Tel: (303) 445-2658 Fax: (303) 445-6705
Email: kmegoreden@pn.usbr.gov
Web: www.usbr.gov

Geological Survey, Central Region
P.O. Box 25046
Denver, CO 80225-0046
Deborah Douglas, Human Resources Officer
Tel: (303) 236-9562 Fax: (303) 236-5973
Email: ddouglas@usgs.gov
Web: www.usgs.gov

National Park Service
Intermountain Region, Office of Human Resources
P.O. Box 25287
Denver, CO 80225
John Crowley, Assistant Regional Director
Tel: (303) 969-2506 Fax: (303) 969-2785
Email: john_crowley@nps.gov
Web: www.nps.gov

NAVY, DEPT. OF THE
Naval Reserve Recruiting Command Area West
791 Chambers Rd. #502
Aurora, CO 80011-7152
Tel: (303) 361-0631 Fax: (303) 361-0648

Navy Recruiting District, Denver
225 E. 16th Ave.
Denver, CO 80203
Tel: (303) 866-1984

USMC Recruiting Station, Denver
225 E. 16th Ave. #500
Denver, CO 80203-9860
Tel: (303) 832-2515
Web: www.marines.com

CONNECTICUT

HOMELAND SECURITY, DEPT. OF
USCG Recruiting Office Hartford
William Cotter Bldg.,135 High St. #G
Hartford, CT 06103
ETC Randall Davidson, Recruiter in Charge
Tel: (860) 240-4260 Fax: (860) 240-4302
Email: rdavidson@cgrc.uscg.mil
Web: www.gocoastguard.com

USCG Recruiting Office New London
New London Shopping Plz., 260 Frontage Rd. #202
New London, CT 06320
AETI Darrin Merrill, Recruiter in Charge
Tel: (860) 444-4947 Fax: (860) 444-4946
Email: dmerrill@cgrc.uscg.mil
Web: www.gocoastguard.com

POSTAL SERVICE
Connecticut District
141 Weston St.
Hartford, CT 06101-9998
Karen Kucharczyk, Acting Diversity Development Specialist
Tel: (860) 524-6137 Fax: (860) 524-6446

Email: karen.m.kucharczyk@usps.gov
Web: www.usps.gov

Northeast Area Office
6 Griffin Rd. North
Windsor, CT 06006-7110
Michelle D. Collins, Senior Diversity Program Coordinator
Tel: (860) 285-7246 Fax: (860) 285-1203
Email: michelle.d.collins@usps.gov
Web: www.usps.gov

DELAWARE

AGRICULTURE, DEPT. OF
NRCS, East Region
1221 College Park Dr. #100
Dover, DE 19904-8713
Manager
Tel: (302) 678-4160 Fax: (302) 678-0843
Web: www.de.nrcs.usda.gov

AIR FORCE, DEPT. OF THE
Dover AFB
Dover AFB, DE 19902-5520
Tel: (800) 423-8723
Web: www.airforce.com

DISTRICT OF COLUMBIA

AGRICULTURE, DEPT. OF
Office of Civil Rights
300 7th St. SW #250
Washington, DC 20250
Versha Kumar, Asian American Program Manager
Tel: (202) 720-4845 Fax: (202) 619-0853
Email: versha.kumar@usda.gov
Web: www.usda.gov/cr

Office of Civil Rights
1400 Independence Ave. SW #9403
Washington, DC 20250
Jack E. Nelson, Departmental African American Manager
Tel: (202) 401-1880 Fax: (202) 690-2345
Email: jacke.nelson@usda.gov
Web: www.usda.gov/cr

Office of Operations
South Bldg., 1400 Independence Ave. SW. #1456
Washington, DC 20250
Sandy Ellixson, Human Resources Liaison
Tel: (202) 720-3937 Fax: (202) 690-0761
Email: sandra.ellixson@usda.gov
Web: www.usda.gov

Agricultural Marketing Service
Office of Civil Rights
South Bldg., 1400 Independence Ave. SW #3074
Washington, DC 20250
Tel: (202) 720-0583 Fax: (202) 690-0476
Web: www.ams.usda.gov
Agricultural Research Service
South Bldg., 1400 Independence Ave. SW #3552
Washington, DC 20250
Mary Ward, Program Specialist
Tel: (202) 690-0166 Fax: (202) 690-0109
Email: mward@ars.usda.gov
Web: www.ars.usda.gov

Cooperative State Research, Education, & Extension Service
Equal Employment
800 9th St. SW #1230
Washington, DC 20250-2201
Curtiland Deville, Director

Tel: (202) 720-2700 Fax: (202) 720-6954
Email: cdeville@csrees.usda.gov
Web: www.csrees.usda.gov

Economic Research Service
1800 M St. NW #2185
Washington, DC 20036-5831
Ram Chandram, Asian American Program
Manager
Tel: (202) 694-5446 Fax: (202) 694-5757
Email: chandran@ers.usda.gov
Web: www.ers.usda.gov

**Employment Compliance & Technical
Assistance Division**
Office of Civil Rights
300 7th St. SW #250
Washington, DC 20250
Robert Day, Chief Employment Program
Compliance
Tel: (202) 720-7314 Fax: (202) 690-2345
Email: robert.day@usda.gov
Web: www.usda.gov

Food Safety & Inspection Service
South Bldg., 1400 Independence Ave. SW
#0131
Washington, DC 20250
Carolyn Scales, African American Program
Manager
Tel: (202) 720-8124 Fax: (202) 690-3738
Email: carolyn.scales@fsis.usda.gov
Web: www.fsis.usda.gov

Foreign Agricultural Service
Outreach and Exporter Assistance Office
1400 Independence Ave. SW, South Bldg.
#4949
Washington, DC 20250
Karl Hampton, Foreign Service Officer
Tel: (202) 690-0188 Fax: (202) 205-9728
Email: hamptonk@fas.usda.gov
Web: www.fas.usda.gov

Forest Service
201 14th St. SW
Washington, DC 20024
Larry Sandoval, Asian American Program
Manager
Tel: (202) 205-1080 Fax: (202) 690-1025
Email: s.sandoval@fs.fed.us
Web: www.fs.fed.us

**Grain Inspection, Packers, & Stockyards
Administration**
South Bldg., 1400 Independence Ave. SW
#1627
Washington, DC 20250-3620
Ellie Speelman, Asian American Program
Manager
Tel: (202) 690-3479 Fax: (202) 690-3951
Email: ellie.d.speelman@usda.gov
Web: www.usda.gov/gipsa

Marketing & Regulatory Programs
Agricultural Marketing Service (AMS)
South Bldg., 1400 Independence Ave. SW
#3074
Washington, DC 20250
Crystal Sutherland, Asian American
Program Manager
Tel: (202) 720-8219 Fax: (202) 690-0476
Email: crystal.sutherland@usda.gov
Web: www.ams.usda.gov

Research, Education & Economics
Cooperative State Research, Education, and
Economics, EEO Staff
South Bldg., 1400 Independence Ave.,
SW #3912
Washington, DC 20250

Maria Goldberg, Executive Director
Tel: (202) 720-6506 Fax: (202) 720-5336
Email: mgoldberg@ars.usda.gov
Web: www.ars.usda.gov

Research, Education & Economics
National Agricultural Statistical Service
(NASS)
South Bldg., 1400 Independence Ave. SW
#5041A
Washington, DC 20250-2000
Rafael Sanchez, Civil Rights, Director
Tel: (202) 720-8257 Fax: (202) 720-9013
Email: rsanchez@nass.usda.gov
Web: www.nass.usda.gov

Research, Education & Economics
National Agricultural Statistical Service
(NASS)
South Bldg., 1400 Independence Ave. SW
#4133
Washington, DC 20250-2000
Sylvia Magbanua, Asian Pacific American
Special Emphasis Program Manager
Tel: (202) 720-6488 Fax: (202) 720-0507
Email: smagbanua@nass.usda.gov
Web: www.nass.usda.gov

Risk Management Agency
Equal Employment Opportunity Office
1400 Independence Ave. SW
Washington, DC 20250
Sae Mi Hong, Specialist
Tel: (202) 690-1687 Fax: (202) 690-2496
Email: sae.mi.hong@rma.usda.gov
Web: www.rma.usda.gov

AIR FORCE, DEPT. OF THE
Headquarters US Air Force
1040 Air Force Pentagon #4E235 HQ
USAF/DPDF
Washington, DC 20330-1040
Coleen Corcoran, Affirmative Action
Program Manager
Tel: (703) 693-2699 Fax: (703) 695-4083
Email: ccorcoran@pentagon.af.mil
Web: www.pentagon.mil

**AMTRAK (NATIONAL RAILROAD
PASSENGER CORPORATION)**
Business Diversity and Strategic Initiatives
60 Massachusetts Ave. NE
Washington, DC 20002
Rodney Ruffin, Director External Affairs
Tel: (202) 906-3753 Fax: (202) 906-2889
Web: www.amtrak.com

COMMERCE, DEPT. OF
Office of the Inspector General
1401 Constitution Ave. NW #7898C
Washington, DC 20230
Tel: (202) 482-4948 Fax: (202) 482-3006
Web: www.oig.doc.gov

Bureau of the Census
Equal Employment Opportunity Office
4700 Silver Hill Rd. Bldg. 3 #1229
Washington, DC 20233
Kathy Shelton, Special Emphasis Program
Manager
Tel: (301) 763-2853 Fax: (301) 457-1160
Email: kathy.e.shelton@census.gov
Web: www.census.gov

International Trade Administration
Human Resource Management
14th & Constitution Ave. NW
Washington, DC 20230
Tina James, Recruitment Manager
Tel: (202) 482-0653
Web: www.ita.doc.gov

Policy & Evaluation Division
Office of Civil Rights
14th & Constitution Ave. NW #6012
Washington, DC 20230
Tel: (202) 482-8189 Fax: (202) 482-5375
Web: www.oig.doc.gov

COMMISSION ON CIVIL RIGHTS
Office of Human Resources
624 9th St. NW #510
Washington, DC 20425
Myrna Hernandez, Human Resources
Specialist
Tel: (202) 376-8364 Fax: (202) 376-7577
Email: mhernandez@usccr.gov
Web: www.usccr.gov

**COMMODITY FUTURES TRADING
COMMISSION**
Office of EEO
3 Lafayette Ctr., 1155 21st St. NW
Washington, DC 20581
Sandra J. Canery, Director
Tel: (202) 418-5400 Fax: (202) 418-5546
Email: scanery@cftc.gov
Web: www.cftc.gov

CORPORATION FOR NATIONAL SERVICE
Equal Opportunity Office
Office of Civil Right and Exclusivness
1201 New York Ave. NW #10800
Washington, DC 20525
Jonathan Williams, Director
Tel: (202) 606-5000 Fax: (202) 565-2816
Email: jwilliams@cns.gov
Web: www.nationalservice.org

DEFENSE, DEPT. OF
Defense Intelligence Agency
Equal Employment Opportunity Office
Bolling Air Force Base, Bldg. 6000, Attn:
3100 Clarendon (DTS).
Washington, DC 20340
Council Chairman
Tel: (202) 231-4928 Fax: (703) 907-2921
Web: www.dia.mil

**Office of Deputy Assistant Secretary of
Defense for Equal Opportunity**
Room 5D641, Pentagon
Washington, DC 20301-4000
Judith C. Gilliom, Asian American Program
Manager
Tel: (703) 571-9330 Fax: (703) 571-9339
Email: judy.gilliom@osd.mil
Web: www.osd.mil

**DEFENSE NUCLEAR FACILITIES SAFETY
BOARD**
625 Indiana Ave. NW #700
Washington, DC 20004
Kenneth Pusateri, EEO Director
Tel: (202) 694-7000 Fax: (202) 208-6515
Email: kenp@ dnfsb.gov
Web: www.dnfsb.gov

DISTRICT OF COLUMBIA
Office of Human Rights
441 4th St. NW #570 North
Washington, DC 20001
Kenneth L. Saunders, Director
Tel: (202) 727-4559 Fax: (202) 727-9589
Email: kenneth.saunders@dc.gov
Web: www.ohr.dc.gov

Fire Department
Equal Employment Opportunity Office
1923 Vermont Ave. NW #201 South
Washington, DC 20001
Adrian H. Thompson, Officer & Diversity
Program Manager
Tel: (202) 673-3320 Fax: (202) 462-0807

Email: adrian.thompson@dc.gov
Web: www.dc.gov

Office of Asian & Pacific Islander Affairs
441 4th St. NW #805-S
Washington, DC 20001
Greg Chen, Director
Tel: (202) 727-3120 Fax: (202) 727-9655
Email: apia@dc.gov
Web: www.apia.dc.gov

DC Office of Personnel
Office of Asian and Pacific Islander Affairs
441 4th St. NW #805 South
Washington, DC 20001
Gregory Chen, Executive Director
Tel: (202) 727-3120 Fax: (202) 727-9655
Email: greg.chen@dc.gov
Web: www.dc.gov

EDUCATION, DEPT. OF
Equal Employment Opportunity Group
400 Maryland Ave. SW FOB-6 #2W228
Washington, DC 20202
James R. White, Director
Tel: (202) 205-0518 Fax: (202) 205-5760
Web: www.ed.gov

Equal Employment Opportunity Group
Complaints Processing
400 Maryland Ave. SW #2W-228
Washington, DC 20202
Gwendolyn Washington, Diversity and
Workforce Planning
Tel: (202) 401-3560 Fax: (202) 205-5760
Email: gwendolyn.washington@ed.gov
Web: www.ed.gov

ELECTION ASSISTANCE COMMISSION
1225 New York Ave. NW #1100
Washington, DC 20005
Tel: (202) 566-3100 Fax: (202) 566-3127
Email: www.eac.gov
Web: havainfo@eac.gov

ENVIRONMENTAL PROTECTION AGENCY
Office of Civil Rights
1200 Pennsylvania Ave. NW, M/C 1201-A
Washington, DC 20004
June Turner, Asian American Program
Manager
Tel: (202) 564-7272 Fax: (202) 501-1836
Email: turner.june@epa.gov
Web: www.epa.gov

**EQUAL EMPLOYMENT OPPORTUNITY
COMMISSION**
Washington Field Office
Equal Employment Opportunity Office
1801 L St. NW #100
Washington, DC 20005
Dana Hutter, Director
Tel: (202) 419-0700 Fax: (202)
Email: dana.hutter@eeoc.gov
Web: www.eeoc.gov

EXECUTIVE OFFICE OF THE PRESIDENT
Office of Administration
EEO Office
725 17th St. NW #2200
Washington, DC 20503
Linda Sites, Director
Tel: (202) 395-3996 Fax: (202) 395-3613

**EXPORT-IMPORT BANK OF THE UNITED
STATES**
Equal Employment Opportunity and
Diversity Programs Office
811 Vermont Ave. NW #753
Washington, DC 20571
Patrease Jones-Brown, Director
Tel: (202) 565-3300 Fax: (202) 565-3595

Email: patrease.brown@exim.gov
Web: www.exim.gov

FEDERAL COMMUNICATIONS COMMISSION
Office of Workplace Diversity
445 12th St. SW
Washington, DC 20554
Barbara J. Douglas, Director
Tel: (202) 418-1799 Fax: (866) 418-0232
Email: ccinfo@fcc.gov
Web: www.fcc.gov

FEDERAL COURTS-ADMINISTRATIVE OFFICE
Employee Relations Office
1 Columbus Cir. NE #5-265
Washington, DC 20544
Trudi M. Morrison, Chief, Employee Relations Office
Tel: (202) 502-1380 Fax: (202) 502-1433
Email: trudi_morrison@ao.uscourts.gov
Web: www.uscourts.gov

FEDERAL DEPOSIT INSURANCE CORPORATION
Office of Diversity and Economic Opportunity
FDIC Rm. 201-1215
Washington, DC 20434-0001
Janice Williams, Specialist
Tel: (202) 416-2475 Fax: (202) 416-2841
Email: jwilliams@fdic.gov
Web: www.fdic.gov

FEDERAL ELECTION COMMISSION
Equal Employment Opportunity Office
999 E St. NW #436
Washington, DC 20463
Lola Hatcher-Capers, Officer
Tel: (202) 694-1228 Fax: (202) 219-0260
Email: eeo@fec.gov
Web: www.fec.gov

FEDERAL HOUSING FINANCE BOARD
Department of Human Resources
1625 Eye St. NW
Washington, DC 20006
David Lee, Associate Director
Tel: (202) 408-2514 Fax: (202) 408-2530
Email: david.lee@fhfb.gov
Web: www.fhfb.gov

FEDERAL LABOR RELATIONS AUTHORITY
EEO
1400 K St. NW, 2nd Fl.
Washington, DC 20424-0001
Bridget Sisson, Director
Tel: (202) 218-7919 Fax: (202) 482-6629
Email: bsisson@flra.gov
Web: www.flra.gov

FEDERAL MARITIME COMMISSION
EEO Office
800 N. Capitol St. NW #1052
Washington, DC 20573
Carmen Cantor, Director
Tel: (202) 523-5806 Fax: (202) 523-4224
Email: ccantor@fmc.gov
Web: www.fmc.gov

FEDERAL MEDIATION AND CONCILIATION SERVICE
Office of Human Resources
2100 K St. NW 7th Fl.
Washington, DC 20427
Dan Ellerman, Director
Tel: (202) 606-5460 Fax: (202) 606-4216
Email: dellerman@fmcs.gov
Web: www.fmcs.gov

FEDERAL MINE SAFETY AND HEALTH REVIEW COMMISSION
Office of EO
200 Constitution Ave. NW

Washington, DC 20210
Daliza Salas, Director
Tel: (202) 693-7719 Fax: (202) 693-7716
Web: www.msha.gov

FEDERAL RETIREMENT THRIFT INVESTMENT BOARD
Personnel Office
1250 H St. NW #200
Washington, DC 20005
Susan Smith, Director
Tel: (202) 942-1600 Fax: (202) 942-1674
Email: ssmith@tsp.gov
Web: www.frtib.gov

GENERAL ACCOUNTING OFFICE
Recruitment Office
441 G St. NW #1165
Washington, DC 20548
Phillis Hughes, Recruitment and Employment Services, Director
Tel: (202) 512-3000 Fax: (202) 512-2539
Email: phughes@gao.gov
Web: www.gao.gov

GENERAL SERVICES ADMINISTRATION
National Central Region
Office of Equal Employment Opportunity
7th & D St. SW #7002
Washington, DC 20407
Avis Johnson, Officer
Tel: (202) 708-8588 Fax: (202) 205-0656
Email: avis.johnson@gsa.gov
Web: www.gsa.gov

Office of Civil Rights
Central Office
1800 F St. NW
Washington, DC 20405
Madeline Caliendo, Associate Administrator
Tel: (202) 501-0767 Fax: (202) 219-3369
Email: madeline.caliendo@gsa.gov
Web: www.gsa.gov

Office of Civil Rights
Office of EEO
1800 F St. NW #5123
Washington, DC 20405
Bernadette Butler, EE Officer
Tel: (202) 501-0767 Fax: (202) 219-3369
Email: bernadette.butler@gsa.gov
Web: www.gsa.gov

GOVERNMENT PRINTING OFFICE
Small & Disadvantaged Business Office
Human Capital Office M/S HC
Washington, DC 20401
Jennifer B. Dooley, Recruiter
Tel: (202) 512-1051 Fax: (202) 512-2139
Email: jdooley@gpo.gov
Web: www.gpo.gov

HEALTH AND HUMAN SERVICES, DEPT. OF
Administration for Children & Families
370 L'Enfant Promenade SW
Washington, DC 20447
Carl Montoya, Community Outreach Coordinator
Tel: (202) 205-8557 Fax: (202) 401-5727
Email: cmontoya@acf.hhs.gov
Web: www.acf.dhhs.gov

Office of the Secretary
EEO Office
200 Independence Ave. SW, HHS Bldg.
Washington, DC 20201
Bonita V. White, Esq., Director
Tel: (202) 690-6555 Fax: (202) 690-8328
Email: bonita.white@hhs.gov
Web: www.hhs.gov

Office of the Secretary
EEO Office
200 Independence Ave. SW #709-D, HHS Bldg.
Washington, DC 20201
David L. Shorts, Manager
Tel: (202) 690-8215 Fax: (202) 619-0823
Email: david.shorts@hhs.gov
Web: www.hhs.gov

HOMELAND SECURITY, DEPT. OF
USCG Recruiting Office Washington DC
3204A Pennsylvania Ave. SE
Washington, DC 20020
MKC Joseph Geter, Recruiter in Charge
Tel: (202) 583-3641 Fax: (202) 583-3645
Email: jgeter@cgrc.uscg.mil
Web: www.gocoastguard.com

US Coast Guard, Headquarters
Civil Rights Office
2100 2nd St. SW #2400
Washington, DC 20593
Arlene J. Gonzalez, Director
Tel: (202) 267-0042 Fax: (202) 267-4282
Email: agonzalez@comdt.uscg.mil
Web: www.uscg.mil

US Customs and Border Protection
Office of the Special Assistant to the Commissioner (EEO)
1300 Pennsylvania Ave. NW #3 2D
Washington, DC 20229
Senora Coggs, API Program Manager
Tel: (202) 344-1463 Fax: (202) 927-1476
Email: senora.coggs@dhs.gov
Web: www.dhs.gov

HOUSING AND URBAN DEVELOPMENT, DEPT. OF
EEO Office
451 7th St. SW #2134
Washington, DC 20410
Linda Bradford Washington, Acting Director
Tel: (202) 708-3362 Fax: (202) 401-2843
Email: linda_b_washington@hud.gov
Web: www.hud.gov

INSTITUTE OF MUSEUM AND LIBRARY SERVICES
Office of Administration and Budget
1800 M St. NW, 9th Fl.
Washington, DC 20036-5802
Teresa LaHaie, Director
Tel: (202) 653-4633 Fax: (202) 653-4625
Web: www.imls.gov

INTERIOR, DEPT. OF THE
Equal Employment Opportunity Office
1849 C St. NW, M/S 5214
Washington, DC 20240
Sharon Eller, Director
Tel: (202) 208-5693 Fax: (202) 208-6112
Email: sharon_eller@ios.doi.gov
Web: www.doi.gov

Bureau of Reclamation
Commissioner's Office
1849 C St. NW #7060-MIB
Washington, DC 20240-0001
Janice Johnson, Chief of Administrative Services
Tel: (202) 513-0522 Fax: (202) 513-0310
Email: jjohnson@usbr.gov
Web: www.usbr.gov

National Capital Region-NPS
Department of Human Resources
1100 Ohio Dr. SW
Washington, DC 20242

Kym Elder, Special Emphasis Recruitment Officer
Tel: (202) 619-7246 Fax: (202) 619-7244
Email: kym_elder@nps.gov
Web: www.nps.gov

National Park Service
Employment Office
1849 C St. NW
Washington, DC 20240
Tel: (202) 354-1993 Fax: (202) 219-1786
Web: www.nps.gov

National Park Service
WAFO Area, Office of Human Resources
1201 Eye St. NW, 12th Fl.
Washington, DC 20240
Adele Singer, Personnel Specialist
Tel: (202) 354-1985 Fax: (202) 371-1762
Email: adele_singer@nps.gov
Web: www.nps.gov

Office of Surface Mining
Equal Employment Opportunity Office
1951 Constitution Ave. NW #20240
Washington, DC 20240
James Joiner, Officer
Tel: (202) 208-5897 Fax: (202) 219-3109
Email: jjoiner@osmre.gov
Web: www.osmre.gov

Office of Surface Mining
Equal Employment Opportunity Office
1951 Constitution Ave. NW #138
Washington, DC 20240
Diane Wood-Medley, Diversity Program Manager
Tel: (202) 208-2997 Fax: (202) 219-3109
Email: dwood@osmre.gov
Web: www.osmre.gov

INTERNATIONAL BROADCASTING BUREAU
Office of Civil Rights
Equal Employment Opportunity Office
330 C St. SW #1086
Washington, DC 20237
Delia L. Johnson, Director
Tel: (202) 619-5157 Fax: (202) 260-0406
Email: djohnso@ibb.gov
Web: www.ibb.gov

JUSTICE, DEPT. OF
Bureau of Alcohol, Tobacco, Firearms & Explosives
Equal Employment Opportunity Office
650 Massachusetts Ave. NW #8210
Washington, DC 20226
Dora Salas, Special Emphasis Programs Manager
Tel: (202) 927-7760 Fax: (202) 927-8835
Web: www.atf.gov

Executive Office for US Attorneys
Equal Employment Opportunity Office
1331 Pennsylvania Ave. NW #524
Washington, DC 20530
Hilda Hudson, Specialist
Tel: (202) 514-3982 Fax: (202) 305-1431
Web: www.usdoj.gov/usao/eousa/

Executive Office for US Attorneys
Equal Employment Opportunity Office
1331 Pennsylvania Ave. NW #524
Washington, DC 20530
Hilda Hudson, Asian American Program Manager
Tel: (202) 514-3982 Fax: (202) 305-1431
Email: askdoj@usdoj.gov
Web: www.usdoj.gov

Federal Bureau of Investigation
Equal Employment Opportunity Office

935 Pennsylvania Ave. NW #7901
Washington, DC 20535
Kimberlee Swain, Program Manager
Tel: (202) 324-6603 Fax: (202) 324-3976
Web: www.fbi.gov

Federal Bureau of Prisons
Discriminations, Complaints and Ethics
320 1st St. NW #437
Washington, DC 20534
Carlos V. Rivera, Diversity Management
Administrator
Tel: (202) 307-3175 Fax: (202) 307-0828
Web: www.bop.gov

Federal Bureau of Prisons
Discriminations, Complaints and Ethics
320 1st St. NW #770
Washington, DC 20534
Sandra Burks-Farrior, Chief, Affirmative
Action Programs
Tel: (202) 307-3175 Fax: (202) 514-9650
Email: sfarrior@bop.gov
Web: www.bop.gov

Headquarters
Equal Employment Opportunity Office
1110 Vermont Ave. NW #620
Washington, DC 20530
Carmen Mendez, Asian/Hispanic Program
Manager
Tel: (202) 616-4812 Fax: (202) 616-4823
Email: carmen.g.mendez@smojmd.usdoj.
gov
Web: www.usdoj.gov/jmd/eeos

Marshals Service
Equal Employment Opportunity Office
US Marshals Services Office Washington
DC, Department of EEO
Washington, DC 20530-1000
Annalisa Lee, Affirmative Employment
Manager
Tel: (202) 307-9048 Fax: (202) 307-8765
Email: annalisa.lee@usdoj.gov
Web: www.usdoj.gov/marshals

Office of Justice Programs
Equal Employment Opportunity Office
810 7th St. NW #6103
Washington, DC 20531
Robyn Russ, Asian Pacific Program
Manager
Tel: (202) 514-1938 Fax: (202) 514-1938
Email: russr@usdoj.gov
Web: www.usdoj.gov

LABOR, DEPT. OF
Bureau of Labor Statistics
Office of Human Resources Equal
Employment Opportunity Office
2 Massachusetts Ave. NE #4280
Washington, DC 20212
Dorothy Wigglesworth, Officer
Tel: (202) 691-6604 Fax: (202) 691-6610
Email: wigglesworth_d@bls.gov
Web: www.bls.gov

Employment Standards Administration
Equal Employment Opportunity Office
200 Constitution Ave. NW #C-3315
Washington, DC 20210
Tel: (202) 693-0328 Fax: (202) 693-1455
Web: www.dol.gov

Occupational Safety & Health Administration
Equal Employment Opportunity Office
200 Constitution Ave. NW #N-3425
Washington, DC 20210
William Burke, Acting Director
Tel: (202) 693-2150 Fax: (202) 693-1626

Email: william.burke@bol.gov
Web: www.osha.gov

Office of the Assistant Secretary for Administration & Management
Business Operation Center, EEO Office
200 Constitution Ave. NW #S1514
Washington, DC 20210
Milton Blount, Manager
Tel: (202) 693-4031 Fax: (202) 219-5138
Email: blount.milton@dol.gov
Web: www.dol.gov

Office of the Assistant Secretary for Administration & Management
Worklife Center
200 Constitution Ave. NW #C5515
Washington, DC 20210
Thomasina McPhail, Events Program
Manager
Tel: (202) 693-7774 Fax: (202) 693-7611
Email: tmcphail@dol.gov
Web: www.dol.gov

MERIT SYSTEM PROTECTION BOARD
Equal Employment Opportunity Office
1615 M St. NW
Washington, DC 20419
Janice Pirkle, Director
Tel: (202) 653-6180 Fax: (202) 653-7130
Email: janice.pirkle@mspb.gov
Web: www.mspb.gov

METROPOLITAN POLICE DEPT.
Office of Police Recruiting
Equal Employment Opportunity Office
#6 DC Village Ln. SW, Bldg. #1A
Washington, DC 20032
Kevin Anderson, Director
Tel: (202) 645-0445 Fax: (202) 645-0444
Email: mpd@dc.gov
Web: www.mpdc.dc.gov

NATIONAL AERONAUTICS AND SPACE ADMINISTRATION
Equal Employment Opportunity Office
300 E St. SW, #4W39
Washington, DC 20546
Dr. Dorothy Hayden-Watkins, Assistant
Administrator
Tel: (202) 358-2167 Fax: (202) 358-3336
Web: www.hq.nasa.gov

NATIONAL CAPITAL PLANNING COMMISSION
401 9th St. NW, North Lobby #500
Washington, DC 20004
Barry Socks, Executive Office
Tel: (202) 482-7200 Fax: (202) 482-7272
Email: info@ncpc.gov
Web: www.ncpc.gov

NATIONAL COUNCIL ON DISABILITY
1331 F St. NW #850
Washington, DC 20004
Tel: (202) 272-2004 Fax: (202) 272-2022
Email: info@ncd.gov
Web: www.ncd.gov

NATIONAL ENDOWMENT FOR THE ARTS
Office of Human Resources
Equal Employment Opportunity Office
1100 Pennsylvania Ave. NW #627
Washington, DC 20506
Craig McCord, Director
Tel: (202) 682-5470 Fax: (202) 682-5666
Email: mccordc@arts.endow.gov
Web: www.arts.endow.gov

NATIONAL ENDOWMENT FOR THE HUMANITIES
Administrator Services
Equal Employment Opportunity Office

1100 Pennsylvania Ave. NW #202
Washington, DC 20506
Willie V. McGhee, Jr., Officer
Tel: (202) 606-8233 Fax: (202) 606-8243
Email: wmcghee@neh.gov
Web: www.neh.fed.us

Office of Human Resources
Equal Employment Opportunity Office
1100 Pennsylvania Ave. NW #418
Washington, DC 20506
Tim Connelly, Director
Tel: (202) 606-8415 Fax: (202) 606-8656
Email: tconnelly@neh.gov
Web: www.neh.gov

NATIONAL LABOR RELATIONS BOARD
Equal Employment Opportunity Office
1099 14th St. NW #6300
Washington, DC 20570
Robert Poindexter, Director
Tel: (202) 273-3891 Fax: (202) 273-4473
Email: robert.poindexter@nlrb.gov
Web: www.nlrb.gov

NATIONAL TRANSPORTATION SAFETY BOARD
EEO Office
490 L'Enfant Plz. SW
Washington, DC 20594
Tel: (202) 314-6190 Fax: (202) 314-6018
Web: www.ntsb.gov

NAVY, DEPT. OF THE
Computer and Telecommunications Command
EEO Office
1014 N. St. SE #1
Washington, DC 20374-5050
Tel: (202) 685-1879 Fax: (202) 433-2653
Web: www.navy.mil

Military Sealift Command
EEO Office
914 Charles Morris Ct. SE
Washington, DC 20398
Wanda Watson-Mays, Command Deputy
EEO Officer
Tel: (202) 685-5563 Fax: (202) 685-5514
Email: wanda.watson-mays@navy.mil
Web: www.navy.mil

Secretariat/HQ Human Resources Office
Office EEO
2 Navy Annex #2052
Washington, DC 20370-5240
Deborah McCormick, Command Deputy
EEO Officer
Tel: (703) 693-0202 Fax: (703) 693-1333

OCCUPATIONAL SAFETY & HEALTH REVIEW COMMISSION
1120 20th St. NW, 9th Fl.
Washington, DC 20036
Barbara Ligon, Administrative Assistant
Tel: (202) 606-5380 Fax: (202) 606-5050
Email: Lg_gpo@oshrc.gov
Web: www.oshrc.gov

OFFICE OF GOVERNMENT ETHICS
1201 New York Ave. NW #500
Washington, DC 20005-3917
Tel: (202) 482-9300
Email: contactoge@oge.gov
Web: www.usoge.gov

OFFICE OF PERSONNEL MANAGEMENT
EEO Office
1900 E St. NW #6460
Washington, DC 20415
Terry Coleman, EEO Specialist
Tel: (202) 606-2460 Fax: (202) 606-1841
Web: www.opm.gov

EEO Office
1900 E St. NW #6460
Washington, DC 20415
Stephen Shih, Director
Tel: (202) 606-2460 Fax: (202) 606-1841
Web: www.opm.gov

OFFICE OF SPECIAL COUNSEL
EEO
1730 M St. NW #218
Washington, DC 20036-4505
Bill Reukauf, Director
Tel: (202) 254-3600 Fax: (202) 653-5161
Web: www.osc.gov

OFFICE OF THE NATIONAL COUNTERINTELLIGENCE EXECUTIVE
National Counterintelligence Executive
(NCIX), CS5 #380
Washington, DC 20505
Ann Johnson, Director of Administration
Tel: (703) 682-4555 Fax: (703) 682-4510
Email: aannfj@ncix.gov
Web: www.ncix.gov

PEACE CORPS
Minority Recruitment
Equal Employment Opportunity Office
1111 20th St. NW, 6th Fl.
Washington, DC 20526
Wilfredo Sauri, Director
Tel: (202) 692-1819 Fax: (202) 692-1801
Email: wsauri@peacecorps.gov
Web: www.peacecorps.gov

PENSION BENEFIT GUARANTY CORPORATION
EEO
1200 K St. NW #1080
Washington, DC 20005
Lori Bledsoe, EEO Manager
Tel: (202) 326-4000 Fax: (202) 326-4016
Web: www.pbgc.gov

POSTAL SERVICE
Affirmative Employment Program
475 L'Enfant Plz. SW #3821
Washington, DC 20260-3821
Young Chung-Hall, Special Emphasis
Program Specialist
Tel: (202) 268-5844 Fax: (202) 268-6573
Email: ychung@email.usps.gov
Web: www.usps.gov

Diversity Development
475 L'Enfant Plz. SW #3821
Washington, DC 20260-3821
Jean Fu Trezza , Special Emphasis Program
Specialist
Tel: (202) 268-5692 Fax: (202) 268-6573
Email: jeanfu.trezza@usps.gov
Web: www.usps.gov

Affirmative Employment
475 L'Enfant Plaza SW #3821
Washington, DC 20260-3821
Chester S. Cross, Jr., Manager
Tel: (202) 268-7456 Fax: (202) 268-6573
Email: chester.s.cross@usps.gov
Web: www.usps.com

Employee Development & Diversity
475 L'Enfant Plaza SW #3901
Washington, DC 20260-5600
Susan M. LanChance, Vice President
Tel: (202) 268-6566 Fax: (202) 268-4263
Email: susan.m.lanchance@usps.gov
Web: www.usps.com

SECURITIES AND EXCHANGE COMMISSION
Equal Employment Opportunity Office
100 F St. NE #212
Washington, DC 20549

Deborah Balducchi, Director
Tel: (202) 551-6006 Fax: (202) 942-9547
Email: deborahbalducchi@sec.gov
Web: www.sec.gov

SMALL BUSINESS ADMINISTRATION
Equal Employment Opportunity Office
409 3rd St. SW #5100
Washington, DC 20416
Harriett Tyler, Specialist
Tel: (202) 205-6750 Fax: (202) 205-7580
Email: hariett.tyler@sba.gov
Web: www.sba.gov

Office of Personnel
409 3rd St. SW #5300
Washington, DC 20416
Judy Mitchell, Lead Human Resource
Specialist
Tel: (202) 205-6786 Fax: (202) 205-6172
Email: judy.mitchell@sba.gov
Web: www.sba.gov/dc

SMITHSONIAN INSTITUTION
Office of Equal Employment Opportunity
and Minority Affairs
750 9th St. NW #8100
Washington, DC 20013-7012
Pauline Fletemeyer, Special Emphasis
Program Manager
Tel: (202) 275-0145 Fax: (202) 275-2055
Email: fletemey@si.edu
Web: www.si.edu

Office of Human Resources & Recruitment
Chief Executive Resources Branch
750 9th St. NW #6100, MRC 912
Washington, DC 20560-0912
Darrell Caldwell, Chief Executive Resources
Officer
Tel: (202) 275-1055 Fax: (202) 275-1115
Email: caldwelld@hr.si.edu
Web: www.si.edu

TRANSPORTATION, DEPT. OF
Federal Highway Administration
Office of Human Resources
400 7th St. SW #4317
Washington, DC 20590
Patrica Tool, Director
Tel: (202) 366-0530 Fax: (202) 366-3749
Email: patricia.tool@fhwa.dot.gov
Web: www.fhwa.dot.gov

Office of the Secretary
Departmental Office of Civil Rights
400 7th St. SW #5420A
Washington, DC 20590
Roger Peralta, Program Manager AAPI
Tel: (202) 366-8964 Fax: (202) 366-7717
Email: roger.peralta@ost.dot.gov
Web: www.dot.gov/ost/docr

TREASURY, DEPT. OF THE
Bureau of Engraving & Printing
Equal Employment Opportunity Office &
Employee Counseling Services
14th & C St. SW #639-17 PD
Washington, DC 20228
Arthur W. Hicks, Chief Officer
Tel: (202) 874-2460 Fax: (202) 874-3311
Email: arthurw.hicks@bep.trea.gov
Web: www.bep.treas.gov

Internal Revenue Service
Equal Employment Opportunity Office
1111 Constitution Ave. NW #2422
Washington, DC 20224
John M. Robinson, Chief EEO and Diversity
Tel: (202) 622-5400 Fax: (202) 622-6529
Email: john.m.robinson@irs.gov
Web: www.irs.gov

Office of the Comptroller of the Currency
250 E St. SW
Washington, DC 20219
Joyce Cofield, Employment & Diversity
Management, Director
Tel: (202) 874-5359 Fax: (202) 874-4656
Email: joyce.cofield@occ.treas.gov
Web: www.occ.treas.gov

Office of Thrift Supervision
1700 G St. NW 5th Fl.
Washington, DC 20552
Douglas Mason, Senior Contract Specialist
and Advocate, Outreach Program
Tel: (202) 906-7624 Fax: (202) 906-5648
Email: douglas.mason@ots.treas.gov
Web: www.ots.treas.gov

UNITED STATES INTERNATIONAL TRADE COMMISSION
Office EEO
500 E St. SW #4000
Washington, DC 20436
Jacqueline Waters, Director
Tel: (202) 205-2240 Fax: (202) 205-3004
Web: www.usitc.gov

WASHINGTON METRO TRANSIT AUTHORITY
Office of Human Resources
600 5th St. NW #806-A
Washington, DC 20001
Cassandra Graves, Employee Programs &
Worklife Coordinator
Tel: (202) 962-1365 Fax: (202) 962-2263
Email: cgraves@wmata.com
Web: www.wmata.com

FLORIDA

AGRICULTURE, DEPT. OF
Natural Resources & Conservation Service
6191 Orange Dr. #6183Q
Davis, FL 33314
Thaddeus Hamilton , NRCS Urban
Conservationist
Tel: (954) 792-1984 Fax: (954) 792-4919
Web: www.nrcs.usda.gov

AIR FORCE, DEPT. OF THE
Eglin AFB
Eglin AFB, FL 32542-6825
Tel: (800) 423-8723
Web: www.airforce.com

Homestead AFB
Homestead AFB, FL 33039-1299
Tel: (800) 423-8723
Web: www.airforce.com

Macdill AFB
Macdill AFB, FL 33621-5321
Tel: (800) 423-8723
Web: www.airforce.com

Patrick AFB
Patrick AFB, FL 32925-3303
Tel: (800) 423-8723
Web: www.airforce.com

Tyndall AFB
Tyndall AFB, FL 32403-5538
Tel: (800) 423-8723
Web: www.airforce.com

ARMY, DEPT. OF THE
US Army Recruiting Battalion Jacksonville
1851 Executive Center Dr. #130
Jacksonville, FL 32207-2350
Tel: (904) 396-2673/2673

US Army Recruiting Battalion Miami
The Augusta Bldg., 8685 NW 53rd Terr.
#200
Miami, FL 33166-4611
Tel: (305) 591-1833

US Army Recruiting Battalion Tampa
3350 Buschwood Park Dr. #140
Tampa, FL 33618-4312
Tel: (813) 935-5657/8955

EQUAL EMPLOYMENT OPPORTUNITY COMMISSION
Miami District Office
Equal Employment Opportunity Office
1 Biscayne Tower, 2 S. Biscayne Blvd.
#2700
Miami, FL 33131
Federico Costales, Director
Tel: (305) 536-4491 Fax: (305) 536-4011
Email: federico.costales@eeoc.gov
Web: www.eeoc.gov

Tampa Area Office
Equal Employment Opportunity Office
501 E. Polk St. #1000
Tampa, FL 33602
Manuel Zurita, Director
Tel: (813) 228-2310 Fax: (813) 228-2841
Email: manuel.zurita@eeoc.gov
Web: www.eeoc.gov

HOMELAND SECURITY, DEPT. OF
USCG Recruiting Office Daytona
Ormond Interchange Complex., 1568 W.
Granada Blvd.
Ormond Beach, FL 32174
YNC David DePietro, Recruiter in Charge
Tel: (386) 672-2945 Fax: (386) 672-8104
Email: ddepietro@cgrc.uscg.mil
Web: www.gocoastguard.com

USCG Recruiting Office Jacksonville
Manderini Landing Shopping Ctr., 10601
San Jose Blvd. #215
Jacksonville, FL 32257
TCC Julius Tatum, Recruiter in Charge
Tel: (904) 232-1561 Fax: (904) 232-2760
Email: jtatum@cgrc.uscg.mil
Web: www.gocoastguard.com

USCG Recruiting Office Miami Central-
Lakes
Royal Oak Plaza Ctr., 15466 NW 77th Ct.
Miami Lakes, FL 33016
PAC Harry Craft, Recruiter in Charge
Tel: (305) 819-3330 Fax: (305) 819-7484
Email: hcraft@cgrc.uscg.mil
Web: www.gocoastguard.com

USCG Recruiting Office Miami North-
Broward
West Broward Shopping Ctr., 3939 W.
Broward Blvd.
Ft. Lauderdale, FL 33312
SKC Jim Council, Recruiter in Charge
Tel: (954) 321-8172 Fax: (954) 321-8776
Email: jcouncil@cgrc.uscg.mil
Web: www.gocoastguard.com

USCG Recruiting Office Miami South-Dade
18867 S. Dixie Hwy.
South Miami, FL 33157
MSTC Miguel Flores, Recruiter in Charge
Tel: (786) 242-2148 Fax: (305) 255-7956
Email: mflores@cgrc.uscg.mil
Web: www.gocoastguard.com

USCG Recruiting Office Orlando
8427 S. John Young Pkwy.
Orlando, FL 32819
ETC Jeffery Locklair, Recruiter in Charge

Tel: (407) 352-3897 Fax: (407) 352-9017
Email: jlocklair@cgrc.uscg.mil
Web: www.gocoastguard.com

USCG Recruiting Office Panama City
1714 W. 23rd St. #C
Panama City, FL 32405-2928
BMC Daniel J. Undieme, Recruiter in
Charge
Tel: (850) 763-1950 Fax: (850) 763-9018
Email: dundieme@cgrc.uscg.mil
Web: www.gocoastguard.com

USCG Recruiting Office Tampa Bay
Bayview Shopping Ctr., 11022 4th St. North
St. Petersburg, FL 33716-2945
MSTC Rodolpho Lopez, Recruiter in Charge
Tel: (727) 579-3849 Fax: (727) 579-8079
Email: rlopez@cgrc.uscg.mil
Web: www.gocoastguard.com

NATIONAL AERONAUTICS AND SPACE ADMINISTRATION
Employee Services
Mail Code BA-C Kennedy Space Center
Kennedy Space Center, FL 32899
Steve Chance, Recruiting and College
Relations
Tel: (321) 867-4194 Fax: (321) 867-8135
Email: steven.h.chance@nasa.gov

NAVY, DEPT. OF THE
Naval Reserve Recruiting Area Southeast
5850 T.G. Lee Blvd. #210
Orlando, FL 32822-4437
Tel: (407) 856-4424 Fax: (407) 856-4424

Navy Recruiting District, Miami
8523 53rd Terr., Savannah Bldg. #201
Miami, FL 33166-4521
Tel: (954) 845-0101

USMC Recruiting Station, Ft. Lauderdale
7820 Peters Rd. Rm. 109, Bldg. E
Plantation, FL 33324-4006
Tel: (954) 452-0113
Web: www.marines.com

USMC Recruiting Station, Jacksonville
3728 Phillips Hwy. #229
Jacksonville, FL 32207
Tel: (904) 858-9698
Web: www.marines.com

USMC Recruiting Station, Orlando
5886 S. Semoran Blvd., Air Business Ctr.
Orlando, FL 32822-4817
Tel: (407) 249-5870
Web: www.marines.com

PANAMA CANAL AUTHORITY
P.O. Box 526725
Miami, FL 33152-6725
Web: www.pancanal.com

POSTAL SERVICE
Central Florida District
P.O. Box 999237
Mid Florida, FL 32799-9237
Annie P. Seabrooks, Diversity Development
Specialist
Tel: (407) 333-4892 Fax: (407) 333-8467
Email: annie.p.seabrooks@usps.gov
Web: www.usps.gov

South Florida District
2200 NW 72nd Ave. #204
Miami, FL 33152-9461
Dorothy Johnson, Diversity Development
Manager
Tel: (305) 470-0622 Fax: (305) 470-0647
Email: dorothy.johnson@usps.gov
Web: www.usps.gov

Sun Coast District
2203 N. Lois Ave. #1070
Tampa, FL 33607-7170
Regla M. Watts, Diversity Development
Specialist
Tel: (813) 354-6023 Fax: (813) 877-8656
Email: rwatts@email.usps.gov
Web: www.usps.gov

GEORGIA

AGRICULTURE, DEPT. OF
NRCS, Southeast Region
355 E. Hancock Ave. #200
Athens, GA 30601
Delores Almand, Asian American Program
Manager
Tel: (706) 546-2067 Fax: (706) 546-2120
Email: delores.almand@ga.usda.gov
Web: www.ga.nrcs.usda.gov

AIR FORCE, DEPT. OF THE
Dobbins AFB
Dobbins AFB, GA 30069-5010
Tel: (800) 423-8723
Web: www.airforce.com

Headquarters Air Force Reserve Command
Robins AFB, GA 31098
Tel: (800) 423-8723
Web: www.airforce.com

Moody AFB
Moody AFB, GA 31699-1518
Tel: (800) 423-8723
Web: www.airforce.com

Robins AFB
Robins AFB, GA 31098-1662
Tel: (800) 423-8723
Web: www.airforce.com

ARMY, DEPT. OF THE
US Army 2nd Recruiting Brigade
Southeast Region
1295 Hood Ave.
Forest Park, GA 30297-5104
Tel: (404) 469-3192/3194

US Army Recruiting Battalion Atlanta
2400 Herodian Way #490
Smyrna, GA 30080-8500
Tel: (770) 951-2815/2834

ENERGY, DEPT. OF
Southeastern Power Administration
1166 Athens Tech Rd.
Elberton, GA 30635-6711
Joel Seymour, Diversity Program Manager
Tel: (706) 213-3822 Fax: (706) 213-3884
Email: joels@sepa.doe.gov
Web: www.sepa.doe.gov

ENVIRONMENTAL PROTECTION AGENCY
Human Capitol Management Branch
Office of Civil Rights Equal Employment
Opportunity Office
61 Forsyth St. SW
Atlanta, GA 30303-3104
Freda Lockhart, Officer
Tel: (404) 562-8142 Fax: (404) 562-9772
Email: lockheart.freda@epa.gov
Web: www.epa.gov

EQUAL EMPLOYMENT OPPORTUNITY COMMISSION
Atlanta District Office
Equal Employment Opportunity Office
100 Alabama St. #4R30
Atlanta, GA 30303

Bernice Williams-Kimbrough, Director
Tel: (404) 562-6800 Fax: (404) 562-6909
Email: bernice.williams@eeoc.gov
Web: www.eeoc.gov

Savannah Local Office
Equal Employment Opportunity Office
410 Mall Blvd. #G
Savannah, GA 31406-4821
Tel: (912) 652-4234 Fax: (912) 652-4248
Web: www.eeoc.gov

FEDERAL RESERVE BANK
Atlanta Region
1000 Peachtree St. NE
Atlanta, GA 30309-4470
Mary Keplar, Human Resources, Director
Tel: (404) 498-8500 Fax: (404) 498-8997
Email: mkeplar@frbatlanta.org
Web: www.frbatlanta.org

GENERAL SERVICES ADMINISTRATION
Office of Equal Employment Opportunity
Region 4
77 Forsyth St. #660
Atlanta, GA 30303
Ouida Cosey, Officer
Tel: (404) 331-5127 Fax: (404) 331-7080
Email: ouida.cosey@gsa.gov
Web: www.gsa.gov

HOMELAND SECURITY, DEPT. OF
Federal Law Enforcement Training Center
1131 Chapel Crossing Rd. Bldg 29
Glynco, GA 31524
Gretchen Waley-Wong, Special Emphasis
Program Manager
Tel: (912) 267-3702 Fax: (912) 280-5390
Email: gretchen.wong@dsh.gov
Web: www.fletc.gov

Federal Law Enforcement Training Center
Equal Employment Opportunity & Diversity
Division
1131 Chapel Crossing Rd. Townhouse #379
Glynco, GA 31524
Alison Delcore, Senior Specialist
Tel: (912) 261-3766 Fax: (912) 267-4586
Email: alison.delcore@dsh.gov
Web: www.fletc.gov

USCG Recruiting Office Atlanta East
2375 Westley Chapel Rd. #9
Decatur, GA 30035
YNC Dexter Lindsey, Recruiter in Charge
Tel: (770) 808-0329 Fax: (770) 808-0794
Email: dlindsey@cgrc.uscg.mil
Web: www.gocoastguard.com

USCG Recruiting Office Atlanta North
3983 Lavista Rd. #189
Tucker, GA 30084
YNC Dexter Lindsey, Recruiter in Charge
Tel: (770) 934-9686 Fax: (770) 934-7022
Email: clindsey@cgrc.uscg.mil
Web: www.gocoastguard.com

USCG Recruiting Office Savannah
46 Abercorn St.
Savannah, GA 31401
AMTC David Medeiros, Recruiter in Charge
Tel: (912) 447-0832 Fax: (912) 352-9748
Email: dmedeiros@cgrc.uscg.mil
Web: www.gocoastguard.com

INTERIOR, DEPT. OF THE
Geological Survey, Southeast Region
Personnel Office
3850 Holcomb Bridge Rd. #160
Norcross, GA 30092

Connie Smith, Chief Human Resources
Officer
Tel: (770) 409-7706 Fax: (770) 409-7771
Email: connie.smith@usgs.gov
Web: www.usgs.gov

National Park Service
Southeast Region, Office of EEO and
Diversity Programs
100 Alabama St. SW, Bldg.1924, 5th Fl.
Atlanta, GA 30303
Gwen Evans, Special Emphasis Program
Manager
Tel: (404) 562-3103 Fax: (404) 562-3269
Email: gwen_evans@nps.gov
Web: www.nps.gov

LABOR, DEPT. OF
Atlanta Regional Office
Personnel Office
61 Forsyth St. SW #6B50
Atlanta, GA 30303
Betty McPherson, Personnel Manager
Specialist
Tel: (404) 562-2008 Fax: (404) 562-2050
Web: www.dol.gov

Employment and Training Administration
South East Job Corps
61 Forsyth St. SW #6T95
Atlanta, GA 30303
Wenomia Person, Outreach Coordinator
Tel: (404) 562-2382 Fax: (404) 562-2396
Email: person.wenomia@dol.gov
Web: www.doleta.gov

NAVY, DEPT. OF THE
Navy Recruiting District, Atlanta
2400 Herodian #400
Smyrna, GA 30080
Tel: (770) 612-4384

US Marine Corps Logistics Base, Albany
814 Radford Blvd. #20319
Albany, GA 31704-0319
Deborah Faulkner, Asian American
Program Manager
Tel: (229) 639-7268 Fax: (229) 639-5525
Email: faulknerdc@logcom.usmc.mil
Web: www.usmc.gov

USMC Recruiting Station, Atlanta
4855 Peachtree Industrial Rd. #225
Norcross, GA 30071-1251
Tel: (770) 246-9029
Web: www.marines.com

POSTAL SERVICE
Atlanta District
P.O. Box 599390
Duluth, GA 30026-9390
Barbara Danzy, Diversity Development
Specialist
Tel: (770) 717-2992 Fax: (770) 717-2993
Email: barbara.a.danzy@usps.gov
Web: www.usps.gov

South Georgia District
451 College St. #414
Macon, GA 31213-9904
Alberta Lawson, Diversity Development
Specialist
Tel: (478) 752-8494 Fax: (478) 752-8685
Web: www.usps.com

SMALL BUSINESS ADMINISTRATION
Disaster Personnel Office-Disaster Area 2
1 Baltimore Pl. #300
Atlanta, GA 30308
Henriquetta Wessman, Acting Personnel
Officer

Tel: (404) 347-3771 Fax: (404) 347-5487
Email: henriquetta.wessman@sba.gov
Web: www.sba.gov/ga

GUAM

AIR FORCE, DEPT. OF THE
Andersen AFB
Andersen AFB, GU 96543-4001
Tel: (800) 423-8723
Web: www.airforce.com

HOMELAND SECURITY, DEPT. OF
US Coast Guard
USCG Recruiting Office Guam
Baltej Pavillion., 415 Chalan San Antonio
Rd. #314
Tamuning, GU 96911
CPO Kevin Hiro, Recruiter in Charge
Tel: (671) 647-6156 Fax: (671) 647-6169
Email: khiro@cgrc.uscg.mil
Web: www.gocoastguard.com

HAWAII

AIR FORCE, DEPT. OF THE
Hickam AFB
Hickam AFB, HI 96853-5411
Tel: (800) 423-8723
Web: www.airforce.com

EQUAL EMPLOYMENT OPPORTUNITY COMMISSION
Honolulu Local Office
Equal Employment Opportunity Office
P.O. Box 50082
Honolulu, HI 96850-0051
Timothy A. Riera, Director
Tel: (808) 541-3120 Fax: (808) 541-3390
Email: timothy.riera@eeoc.gov
Web: www.eeoc.gov

HOMELAND SECURITY, DEPT. OF
USCG Recruiting Office Honolulu
Pearl Ridge Mall Phase III., 98-151 Pali
Momi St. #106
Aiea, HI 96701
BMC Calvin Williams, Recruiter in Charge
Tel: (808) 486-8677 Fax: (808) 487-3640
Email: cwilliams@cgrc.uscg.mil
Web: www.gocoastguard.com

IDAHO

AIR FORCE, DEPT. OF THE
Mountain Home AFB
Mountain Home AFB, ID 83648-5298
Tel: (800) 423-8723
Web: www.airforce.com

ENERGY, DEPT. OF
Idaho Operations Office
Equal Employment Opportunity Office
1955 N. Freemont M/S 1240
Idaho Falls, ID 83401
Jan Ogilvie, Diversity Program Manager
Tel: (208) 526-9272 Fax: (208) 526-7407
Email: ogilvie@id.doe.gov
Web: www.id.doe.gov

HOMELAND SECURITY, DEPT. OF
USCG Recruiting Office Boise
Overland Park., 6907 Overland Rd.
Boise, ID 83709-1908
PO Gary Armstrong, Recruiter in Charge
Tel: (208) 376-7655 Fax: (208) 376-1180
Email: garmstrong@cgrc.uscg.mil
Web: www.gocoastguard.com

INTERIOR, DEPT. OF THE
Bureau of Land Management
Office of Human Resources
3833 S. Development Ave.
Boise, ID 83705-5354
Wendy Little, Human Resources Specialist
Tel: (208) 387-5564 Fax: (208) 387-5723
Web: www.nifc.gov

Bureau of Reclamation
Pacific Northwest Region, Human Resources
1150 N. Curtis Rd. #100
Boise, ID 83706-1234
Max Gallegos, Human Resources Officer
Tel: (208) 378-5140 Fax: (208) 378-5023
Email: mgallegos@pn.usbr.gov
Web: www.usbr.gov

ILLINOIS

AGRICULTURE, DEPT. OF
NRCS, Midwest Region
2301 Hoffman Dr.
Effingham, IL 62401
Manuel Wei, Asian American Employment Program Manager
Tel: (217) 347-7107 Fax: (217) 342-9855
Email: manny.wei@il.usda.gov
Web: www.il.nrcs.usda.gov

AIR FORCE, DEPT. OF THE
Scott AFB
Scott AFB, IL 62225-5037
Tel: (800) 423-8723
Web: www.airforce.com

ARMY, DEPT. OF THE
US Army Recruiting Battalion Chicago
P.O. Box 1130
Sheridan US Army Reserve Ctr., Bldg. 142
Highland Park, IL 60035-7130
Tel: (847) 266-1359/1360

EQUAL EMPLOYMENT OPPORTUNITY COMMISSION
Chicago District Office
Equal Employment Opportunity Office
500 W. Madison St. #2800
Chicago, IL 60661
John P. Rowe, District Director
Tel: (312) 353-2713 Fax: (312) 886-1168
Email: john.rowe@eeoc.gov
Web: www.eeoc.gov

FEDERAL RESERVE BANK
Chicago District Office
Office of Human Resources
230 S. La Salle St.
Chicago, IL 60604-1413
Michael H. Moskow, President/CEO
Tel: (312) 322-5322 Fax: (312) 322-5332
Email: information.chi@chi.frb.org
Web: www.chicagofed.org

HOMELAND SECURITY, DEPT. OF
USCG Recruiting Office Chicago
Chatham Village Sq., 716 E. 87th St.
Chicago, IL 60619
DCC Tyrone Hughes, Recruiter in Charge
Tel: (773) 723-8751 Fax: (773) 994-3857
Email: thughes@cgrc.uscg.mil
Web: www.gocoastguard.com

LABOR, DEPT. OF
Employment & Training Administration
Office of Youth Programs and Job Corps
Federal Bldg., #676, 230 S. Dearborn St.
Chicago, IL 60604
Tom Deuschle, Regional Director
Tel: (312) 596-5475 Fax: (312) 596-5471

Email: tdeuschle@doleta.gov
Web: www.doleta.gov

NAVY, DEPT. OF THE
Naval Reserve Recruiting Command Area Central
2834B Green Bay Rd., Bldg. 3400, Rm. 266
Great Lakes, IL 60088-5709
Tel: (847) 688-2548

USMC Recruiting Station, Chicago
1700 S. Wolfe Rd.
Des Plaines, IL 60018-5912
Tel: (847) 803-6371
Web: www.marines.com

POSTAL SERVICE
Central Illinois District
6801 W. 73rd St.
Bedford Park, IL 60499-9311
Sharon Murphy, Diversity Development Specialist
Tel: (708) 563-7343 Fax: (708) 563-7638
Email: sharon.t.murphy@usps.gov
Web: www.usps.com

Chicago District
433 W. Harrison St., 4th Fl.
Chicago, IL 60607-3296
Iloma Perkins , Diversity Development Specialist
Tel: (312) 983-8039 Fax: (312) 983-8033
Email: iperkins@usps.gov
Web: www.usps.gov

Great Lakes Area Office
244 Knollwood Dr., 4th Fl.
Bloomingdale, IL 60117-3060
Jaime Claudio, Jr., Senior Diversity Program Coordinator
Tel: (630) 539-8338 Fax: (630) 539-7095
Email: jaime.claudio@usps.gov
Web: www.usps.com

Northern Illinois District
500 E. Fullerton Ave.
Carol Stream, IL 60199-9601
Efren Anguiano, Acting Diversity Development Specialist
Tel: (630) 260-5203 Fax: (630) 260-5841
Email: efren.z.anguiano@usps.gov
Web: www.usps.com

RAILROAD RETIREMENT BOARD
Equal Employment Opportunity Office
844 N. Rush St. #60611-2092
Chicago, IL 60611-2092
Lynn Cousins, Director
Tel: (312) 751-4942 Fax: (312) 751-7136
Email: lynn.cousins@rrb.gov
Web: www.rrb.gov

STATE OF ILLINOIS
Department of Commerce & Community Affairs
Equal Employment Opportunity Office
620 E. Adams St.
Springfield, IL 62701
Victoria Benn-Rochelle, Compliance Manager
Tel: (217) 524-2997 Fax: (217) 524-0189
Email: vbennroc@commerce.state.il.us
Web: www.commerce.state.il.us

INDIANA

AGRICULTURE, DEPT. OF
NRCS, Indiana Office
109 S. Grant Ave. #A
Fowler, IN 47944
Mani Phengrasmy, Asian American Employment Program Manager
Tel: (765) 884-1090 Fax: (765) 888-1030
Email: mani.phengrasmy@in.usda.gov
Web: www.in.nrcs.usda.gov

AIR FORCE, DEPT. OF THE
Grissom ARB
Grissom ARB, IN 46971-5000
Tel: (800) 423-8723
Web: www.airforce.com

ARMY, DEPT. OF THE
US Army Recruiting Battalion Indianapolis
9152 Kent Ave.
Indianapolis, IN 46216
Tel: (317) 549-0338/1738

EQUAL EMPLOYMENT OPPORTUNITY COMMISSION
Indianapolis District Office
Equal Employment Opportunity Office
101 W. Ohio St. #1900
Indianapolis, IN 46204-4203
Danny G. Harter, Director
Tel: (317) 226-7212 Fax: (317) 226-7953
Email: danny.harter@eeoc.gov
Web: www.eeoc.gov

HOMELAND SECURITY, DEPT. OF
USCG Recruiting Office Indianapolis
Metroplex Ctr., 8255 Craig St. #130
Indianapolis, IN 46250-4583
DCC Thomas Huffman, Recruiter in Charge
Tel: (317) 596-0833 Fax: (317) 596-1097
Email: thuffman@cgrc.uscg.mil
Web: www.gocoastguard.com

NAVY, DEPT. OF THE
Naval Reserve Recruiting Center Indianapolis
3010 White River Pkwy.
Indianapolis, IN 46208
Tel: (317) 921-2024
Email: d2s20007@cnrrc.nola.navy.mil

Navy Recruiting District, Indianapolis
9152 Kent Ave., Bldg. 401 #352
Indianapolis, IN 46216
Tel: (317) 554-0701

USMC Recruiting Station, Indianapolis
9152 Kent Ave. #C-200
Indianapolis, IN 46216-2036
Tel: (317) 554-0506
Web: www.marines.com

POSTAL SERVICE
Greater Indiana District
3939 Vincennes Rd.
Indianapolis, IN 46298-9855
Patricia A. Proctor, Diversity Development Specialist
Tel: (317) 870-8562 Fax: (317) 870-8686
Email: patricia.proctor@usps.gov
Web: www.usps.com

INDIANA (IOWA)

AGRICULTURE, DEPT. OF
NRCS, Midwest Region
210 Wallnut St. #693
Des Moines, IA 50309
James Zeigler, Asian American Employment Program Manager
Tel: (515) 284-4519 Fax: (515) 284-4767
Email: james.zeigler@ia.usda.gov
Web: www.ia.nrcs.usda.gov

ARMY, DEPT. OF THE
US Army Recruiting Battalion Des Moines
Federal Bldg. 557, 210 Walnut St.
Des Moines, IA 50309-2108
Tel: (515) 280-7401

HOMELAND SECURITY, DEPT. OF
USCG Recruiting Office Davenport
Old Town Mall., 901 E Kimberly Rd. #20
Davenport, IA 52807-1622
AST1 Kirk Machovec, Recruiter in Charge
Tel: (563) 388-2002 Fax: (319) 388-1090
Email: kmachovec@cgrc.uscg.mil
Web: www.gocoastguard.com

NAVY, DEPT. OF THE
USMC Recruiting Station, Des Moines
4725 Merle Hay Rd. #209
Des Moines, IA 50322
Tel: (515) 253-9508
Web: www.marines.com

KANSAS

AIR FORCE, DEPT. OF THE
McConnell AFB
McConnell AFB, KS 67221-3614
Tel: (800) 423-8723
Web: www.airforce.com

ENVIRONMENTAL PROTECTION AGENCY
Human Resources Office, Region 7
Equal Employment Opportunity Office
901 N. 5th St.
Kansas City, KS 66101
Jackie Beard, Director
Tel: (913) 551-7407 Fax: (913) 551-7267
Email: beard.jackie@epa.gov
Web: www.epa.gov

EQUAL EMPLOYMENT OPPORTUNITY COMMISSION
Kansas City Area Office
Equal Employment Opportunity Office
4th & State Ave. 9th Fl.
Kansas City, KS 66101
Billy Asheton , Acting Director
Tel: (913) 551-5655 Fax: (913) 551-6957
Email: billy.asheton@eeoc.gov
Web: www.eeoc.gov

KENTUCKY

ARMY, DEPT. OF
Headquarters, 2nd Region (ROTC)
US Army Cadet Command
Attn: Public Affairs Office
Fort Knox, KY 40121-5610
Tel: (502) 624-8149

US Army 3rd Recruiting Brigade
Upper Midwest Region
Bldg. 6580
Fort Knox, KY 40121-2726
Tel: (502) 626-1030/1041

US Army Recruiting Command G5
1307 3rd Ave., Rm. 3078
Fort Knox, KY 40121-2726
Julia Bobick, Public Information Specialist
Tel: (502) 626-0172 Fax: (502) 626-0924
Email: julia.bobick@usarec.army.mil

EQUAL EMPLOYMENT OPPORTUNITY COMMISSION
Louisville Area Office
Equal Employment Opportunity Office
600 Dr. Martin Luther King Jr. Pl. #268
Louisville, KY 40202
Marcia Hall-Craig, Director
Tel: (502) 582-6082 Fax: (502) 582-5895
Email: marcia.hall@eeoc.gov
Web: www.eeoc.gov

HOMELAND SECURITY, DEPT. OF
USCG Recruiting Office Louisville
3201 Fern Valley Rd. #112
Louisville, KY 40213-3535
BMC Jess W. Farmer, Recruiter in Charge
Tel: (502) 969-4006 Fax: (502) 969-3572
Email: jfarmer@cgrc.uscg.mil
Web: www.gocoastguard.com

NAVY, DEPT. OF THE
Naval Reserve Center Lexington
151 Votech Rd.
Lexington, KY 40511
Tel: (859) 422-8767

USMC Recruiting Station, Louisville
600 Martin Luther King Jr. Pl. #221
Louisville, KY 40202-2269
Tel: (502) 582-6601
Web: www.marines.com

LOUISIANA

AGRICULTURE, DEPT. OF
Office of the Chief Financial Officer
13800 Old Gentilly Rd.
New Orleans, LA 70129
Patricia A. Bachemin, Asian American Program Manager
Tel: (504) 426-6206 Fax: (504) 426-9710
Email: patricia.bachemin@usda.gov
Web: www.usda.gov

AIR FORCE, DEPT. OF THE
Barksdale AFB
Barksdale AFB, LA 71110-2073
Tel: (800) 423-8723
Web: www.airforce.com

ARMY, DEPT. OF THE
US Army Recruiting Battalion New Orleans
4400 Dauphine St., Bldg. 602-2C
New Orleans, LA 70146-1699
Tel: (504) 678-8531/8533

COMMERCE, DEPT. OF
National Weather Service, Southern Region
Equal Employment Opportunity Office
5655 Hollywood Ave.
Shreveport, LA 71109
Bill Parker, Program Manager
Tel: (318) 631-3669 Fax: (318) 636-9620
Email: bill.parker@noaa.gov
Web: www.noaa.gov

EQUAL EMPLOYMENT OPPORTUNITY COMMISSION
New Orleans District Office
Equal Employment Opportunity Office
701 Loyola Ave. #600
New Orleans, LA 70113-9936
Keith Hill, Acting Director
Tel: (504) 589-2329 Fax: (504) 589-6861

Email: keith.hill@eeoc.gov
Web: www.eeoc.gov

INTERIOR, DEPT. OF THE
Minerals Management Service
Personnel Office
1201 Elmwood Park Blvd. M/S 2620
New Orleans, LA 70123-2394
Sarah Schlumbrecht, Personnel Staffing Classification Specialist
Tel: (504) 736-2884 Fax: (504) 736-2478
Email: sarah.schlumbrecht@mms.gov
Web: www.mms.gov

NAVY, DEPT. OF THE
Navy Recruiting District, New Orleans
4400 Dauphine St.
New Orleans, LA 70146
Tel: (504) 678-5520

USMC Recruiting Station, New Orleans
Naval Support Station, 4400 Dauphine St. 602-2-C
New Orleans, LA 70146-0800
Tel: (504) 678-5095
Web: www.marines.com

POSTAL SERVICE
Louisiana District
701 Loyola Ave. #10021
New Orleans, LA 70113-9813
Hedy H. Duplessis, Diversity Development Specialist
Tel: (504) 589-1283 Fax: (504) 589-1467
Email: hduples1@email.usps.gov
Web: www.usps.com

MAINE

ARMY, DEPT. OF THE
US Army Recruiting Battalion New England
33 Canam Dr.
Topsham, ME 04086-1117
Tel: (207) 725-8637

HOMELAND SECURITY, DEPT. OF
USCG Recruiting Office Portland
Brighton Avenue Plz., 1041 Brighton Ave.
Portland, ME 04102
YNC Don Hodgdon, Recruiter in Charge
Tel: (207) 761-4307 Fax: (207) 874-6058
Email: dhodgdon@cgrc.uscg.mil
Web: www.gocoastguard.com

NAVY, DEPT. OF THE
Naval Reserve Center Brunswick
500 Sewall St.
Brunswick, ME 04011
Tel: (207) 921-1534

POSTAL SERVICE
Maine District
380 Riverside St.
Portland, ME 04103-7000
Debbie Woods, Diversity Development Specialist
Tel: (207) 828-8400 Fax: (207) 828-8446
Email: debra.a.woods@usps.com
Web: www.usps.com

MARYLAND

AGRICULTURE, DEPT. OF
Marketing & Regulatory Programs
Animal and Plant Health Inspection Service (APHIS)
4700 River Rd. Unit 92, #5C17
Riverdale, MD 20737
Sophia Kirby, Asian American Program Manager

Tel: (301) 734-5366 Fax: (301) 734-3698
Email: sophia.l.kirby@aphis.usda.gov
Web: www.aphis.usda.gov

Natural Resources Conservation Service
Office of Civil Rights
5601 Sunnyside Ave. #1-1120
Beltsville, MD 20705-5000
Andrew Johnson, Director
Tel: (301) 504-2182 Fax: (301) 504-2175
Email: andrew.johnson@usda.gov
Web: www.usda.gov

AIR FORCE, DEPT. OF THE
Andrews AFB
Andrews AFB, MD 20762-7002
Tel: (800) 423-8723
Web: www.airforce.com

ARMY, DEPT. OF THE
US Army 1st Recruiting Brigade
Northeast Region
4550 Llewelyn Ave.
Fort George Meade, MD 20755-5380
Tel: (301) 677-2380/2378

US Army Recruiting Battalion Baltimore
4550 Llewelyn Ave.
Fort George G. Meade, MD 20755-5390
Tel: (301) 677-7034/7029

COMMERCE, DEPT. OF
National Institute of Standards & Technology
100 Bureau Dr. #1740
Gaithersburg, MD 20899
Cynthia Snipes, Acting Diversity Program Manager
Tel: (301) 975-5481 Fax: (301) 926-7203
Email: cynthia.snipes@nist.gov
Web: www.nist.gov

National Oceanic & Atmospheric Administration
Office of Civil Rights
1305 East-West Hwy. Bldg. SSMC4 #12222
Silver Spring, MD 20910
Michelle Moore, Asian American Coordinator
Tel: (301) 713-0500 Fax: (301) 713-0983
Email: michelle.t.moore@noaa.gov
Web: www.noaa.gov

CONSUMER PRODUCT SAFETY COMMISSION
Equal Employment Opportunity Office & Minority Enterprise
4330 East-West Hwy. # 712
Bethesda, MD 20814
Kathleen Buttrey, Director
Tel: (301) 504-7771 Fax: (301) 504-0107
Email: kbuttrey@cpsc.gov
Web: www.cpsc.gov

Office of EEO and Minority Enterprise
4330 East-West Hwy.
Bethesda, MD 20814-4408
Kathleen Buttrey, Director
Tel: (301) 504-7904 Fax: (301) 504-0107
Email: kbuttrey@cpsc.gov
Web: www.cpsc.gov

DEFENSE, DEPT. OF
National Security Agency
9800 Savage Rd. #6659
Ft. Meade, MD 20755-1100
Pam Brown, Special Emphasis Program Manager
Tel: (301) 688-6961 Fax: (443) 479-6690
Email: pbrown1@nsa.gov
Web: www.nsa.gov

Uniformed Services University of the Health Services
Equal Employment Opportunity Office
4301 Jones Bridge Rd.
Bethesda, MD 20814-4799
Patricia Burke, Officer
Tel: (301) 295-3032 Fax: (301) 295-3916
Email: pburke@usuhs.mil
Web: www.usuhs.mil

EQUAL EMPLOYMENT OPPORTUNITY COMMISSION
Baltimore District Office
Equal Employment Opportunity Office
City Crescent Bldg., 10 S. Howard St.
3rd Fl.
Baltimore, MD 21201
James L. Le, Director
Tel: (410) 962-3932 Fax: (410) 962-4270
Email: james.le@eeoc.gov
Web: www.eeoc.gov

HEALTH AND HUMAN SERVICES, DEPT. OF
Centers for Medicare & Medicaid Services
Office of Equal Opportunity and Civil Rights
7500 Security Blvd. #N2-22-17
Baltimore, MD 21244-1850
Angela Davis-Putty, Affirmative Employment / Special Emphasis
Tel: (410) 786-5112 Fax: (410) 786-9549
Email: adavisputty@cms.hhs.gov
Web: www.cms.hhs.gov

Centers for Medicare & Medicaid Services
Office of Equal Opportunity and Civil Rights
7500 Security Blvd. #N2-22-17
Baltimore, MD 21244-1850
Patricia Lamond, Director
Tel: (410) 786-5110 Fax: (410) 786-9549
Email: patricia.lamond@cms.hhs.gov
Web: www.cms.hhs.gov

Food and Drug Administration
Equal Employment Opportunity Office
Parklawn Bldg., 5600 Fishers Ln. #883
Rockville, MD 20857
Cheryl Kelley, Specialist
Tel: (301) 827-6737 Fax: (301) 827-9675
Web: www.fda.gov

Office of Minority Health
Resource Center
1101 Wootton Pkwy. #650
Rockville, MD 20852
José T. Carneiro, Project Director
Tel: (800) 444-6472 Fax: (301) 251-2160
Email: jcarneiro@omhrc.gov
Web: www.omhrc.gov

Substance Abuse and Mental Health Services Administration
Office of Equal Opportunity and Civil Rights
Parklawn Bldg., 5600 Fishers Ln. Rm. 12-105
Rockville, MD 20857
Carmen Martinez, Director
Fax: (301) 443-0839
Email: info@samhsa.gov
Web: www.samhsa.gov

HOMELAND SECURITY, DEPT. OF
USCG Recruiting Office Baltimore
6499 Baltimore National Pike
Catonsville, MD 21228-3904
YNC Kenneth Starnes, Recruiter in Charge
Tel: (410) 747-3963 Fax: (410) 747-9264
Email: kstarnes@cgrc.uscg.mil
Web: www.gocoastguard.com

USCG Recruiting Office Salisbury
1506 S. Salisbury Blvd. #7
Salisbury, MD 21801

MKC Bernard Graham, Recruiter in Charge
Tel: (410) 742-3778 Fax: (410) 543-2621
Email: bgraham@cgrc.uscg.mil
Web: www.gocoastguard.com

MONTGOMERY COUNTY GOVERNMENT
Minority & Multi-Cultural Affairs
99 Maryland Ave.
Rockville, MD 20850
Betty Valdes, Community Affairs Officer for
Montgomery County Public Libraries
Tel: (240) 777-0017 Fax: (301) 217-2517
Email: betty.valdes@montgomerycountymd.gov
Web: www.montgomerylibrary.org

Montgomery County Department of Police
Personnel Section
2350 Research Blvd. #203
Rockville, MD 20850
Brian Walker, Recruitment Officer
Tel: (240) 773-5310 Fax: (240) 773-5302
Email: brian.walker@montgomerycountymd.gov
Web: www.montgomerycountymd.gov

NATIONAL ARCHIVES AND RECORDS ADMINISTRATION
EEO and Diversity Programs
8601 Adelphi Rd. #4400
College Park, MD 20740-6001
Robert D. Jew, Director
Tel: (301) 837-1849 Fax: (301) 837-0869
Email: robert.jew@nora.gov
Web: www.archives.gov

EEO and Diversity Programs
8601 Adelphi Rd. #4400
College Park, MD 20740-6001
Allison Darnaby, AEP/Diversity Manager
Tel: (301) 837-0295 Fax: (301) 837-0869
Web: www.archives.gov

NAVY, DEPT. OF THE
Naval Reserve Center Baltimore
Ft. McHenry
Baltimore, MD 21230-5392
Tel: (410) 547-1915
Email: d5s20006@cnrrc.nola.navy.mil

USMC Recruiting Station, Baltimore
6845 Deerpath Rd., Dorsey Business Ctr.
Elk Ridge, MD 21227-6221
Tel: (410) 379-0800
Web: www.marines.com

USMC Recruiting Station, Frederick
5112 Pegasus Ct. #B
Frederick, MD 21704
Tel: (301) 668-2025
Web: www.marines.com

NUCLEAR REGULATORY COMMISSION
Office of Human Resources
11555 Rockville Pike
Rockville, MD 20852-2738
Peggy Etheridge, Recruitment Manager
Tel: (301) 415-2294 Fax: (301) 415-3818
Email: opa@nrc.gov
Web: www.nrc.gov

POSTAL SERVICE
Baltimore District
900 E. Fayette St. #327
Baltimore, MD 21233-9989
Thomasine A. Adams, Diversity
Development Specialist
Tel: (410) 347-4265 Fax: (410) 234-8620
Email: thomasine.a.adams@usps.gov
Web: www.usps.com

Capital District
16501 Shady Grove Rd.

Gaithersburg, MD 20898-9998
Penny L. Fleury, Manager, Diversity &
Human Capital Management
Tel: (301) 548-1432 Fax: (301) 548-1434
Email: penny.l.fleury@usps.gov
Web: www.usps.gov

SOCIAL SECURITY ADMINISTRATION
Center for Personnel Policy & Staffing
Annex Bldg., 6401 Security Blvd. #G-120, 2720
Baltimore, MD 21235
Sandy Eckert, Director
Tel: (410) 965-4506
Email: general@opm.gov
Web: www.opm.gov

MASSACHUSETTS

AIR FORCE, DEPT. OF THE
Hanscom AFB
Hanscom AFB, MA 01731-2800
Tel: (800) 423-8723
Web: www.airforce.com

Otis ANGB
Otis ANGB, MA 02542-5028
Tel: (800) 423-8723
Web: www.airforce.com
Westover AFB
Westover AFB, MA 01022-1843
Tel: (800) 423-8723
Web: www.airforce.com

ENVIRONMENTAL PROTECTION AGENCY
Region 1
Human Resources Office
1 Congress St. #1100
Boston, MA 02114-2023
Byron Mah, Asian American Program
Manager
Tel: (617) 918-1249 Fax: (617) 918-0395
Email: mah.byron@epa.gov
Web: www.epa.gov

EQUAL EMPLOYMENT OPPORTUNITY COMMISSION
Boston Area Office
Equal Employment Opportunity Office
John F. Kennedy Federal Bldg., 4th Fl. #475
Boston, MA 02203
Robert L. Sanders, Director
Tel: (617) 565-3200 Fax: (617) 565-3196
Email: robert.sanders@eeoc.gov
Web: www.eeoc.gov

HOMELAND SECURITY, DEPT. OF
USCG Recruiting Office Boston
Capt. John Foster Williams Bldg., 408
Atlantic Ave. #548
Boston, MA 02110-3350
ETC William Slauenwhite, Recruiter in
Charge
Tel: (617) 565-8656 Fax: (617) 565-8460
Email: wslauenwhite@cgrc.uscg.mil
Web: www.gocoastguard.com

USCG Recruiting Office Springfield
New Federal Office Bldg., 1550 Main St. #110
Springfield, MA 01103-1422
MSTC Timothy Ryan, Recruiter in Charger
Tel: (413) 785-0324 Fax: (413) 785-0326
Email: tryan@cgrc.uscg.mil
Web: www.gocoastguard.com

LABOR, DEPT. OF
Employment & Training Administration
Office of Youth Programs and Job Corps
JFK Federal Bldg., #E-350

Boston, MA 02203
Tel: (617) 788-0170 Fax: (617) 788-0101
Web: www.doleta.gov

Employment & Training Administration
Office of Youth Programs and Job Corps,
Region I
JFK Federal Center Bldg., #E-350
Boston, MA 02203
Joseph Semansky, Regional Director
Tel: (617) 788-0197 Fax: (617) 788-0189
Email: semansky.joseph@dol.gov
Web: www.nejobcorps.org

NAVY, DEPT. OF THE
Naval Reserve Center Quincy
85 Sea St.
Quincy, MA 02169
Tel: (617) 753-4669 Fax: (617) 753-4642
Email: d5s20001@cnrrc.nola.navy.mil

Navy Recruiting District, New England
495 Summer St.
New England, MA 02210
Tel: (800) 792-9099

USMC Recruiting Station, Springfield
105 East St.
Chicopee Falls, MA 01020-3400
Tel: (413) 594-2033
Web: www.marines.com

POSTAL SERVICE
Middlesex-Central Cluster
74 Main St.
North Reading, MA 01889-9402
Andrea Marshall, Diversity Development
Specialist
Tel: (978) 664-7652 Fax: (978) 664-5998
Email: andrea.v.marshall@usps.gov
Web: www.usps.com

SOCIAL SECURITY ADMINISTRATION
Boston Region
Equal Employment Opportunity Office
JFK Federal Bldg., #1900
Boston, MA 02203
Linda Tuttle, Manager
Tel: (617) 565-2879 Fax: (617) 723-0460
Email: linda.tuttle@ssa.gov
Web: www.ssa.gov

MICHIGAN

AIR FORCE, DEPT. OF THE
Selfridge ANGB
Selfridge ANGB, MI 48045-5399
Tel: (800) 423-8723
Web: www.airforce.com

ARMY, DEPT. OF THE
US Army Recruiting Battalion Great Lakes
Holiday Office Park North, 6545 Mercantile
Way #11
Lansing, MI 48911-5974
Tel: (517) 887-5782

EQUAL EMPLOYMENT OPPORTUNITY COMMISSION
Detroit District Office
Equal Employment Opportunity Office
477 Michigan Ave. #865
Detroit, MI 48226-9704
James R. Neely, Jr., Director
Tel: (313) 226-4600 Fax: (313) 226-4610
Email: james.neely@eeoc.gov
Web: www.eeoc.gov

HOMELAND SECURITY, DEPT. OF
USCG Recruiting Office Detroit
26097 John R. Rd.

Madison Heights, MI 48071-3607
OSC Fred Napoleon, Recruiter in Charge
Tel: (248) 582-8364 Fax: (248) 582-8375
Email: fnapoleon@cgrc.uscg.mil
Web: www.gocoastguard.com

USCG Recruiting Office Lansing
2515 E. Jolly Rd. #1
Lansing, MI 48910
MKC Andrew Hiester, Recruiter in Charge
Tel: (517) 377-1719 Fax: (517) 377-1731
Email: ahiester@cgrc.uscg.mil
Web: www.gocoastguard.com

INTERIOR, DEPT. OF THE
National Park Service
Sleeping Bear Dunes National Lake Shore
9922 Front St.
Empire, MI 49630-9797
Gale Purifoy, Personnel Management
Specialist
Tel: (231) 326-5134 Fax: (231) 326-5382
Email: gale_purifoy@nps.gov
Web: www.nps.gov

NAVY, DEPT. OF THE
Naval Reserve Center Detroit
Bldg. 1410, 25154 Plattsburg
Selfridge Angb, MI 48045-4911
Tel: (586) 307-6638 Fax: (586) 307-6985

Navy Recruiting District, Michigan
1155 Brewery Park Blvd. #320
Detroit, MI 48207
Tel: (313) 259-1004

USMC Recruiting Station, Detroit
580 Kirts Blvd. #307
Troy, MI 48084
Tel: (248) 269-9058
Web: www.marines.com

USMC Recruiting Station, Lansing
6545 Mercantile Way #12
Lansing, MI 48933
Tel: (517) 882-8762
Web: www.marines.com

POSTAL SERVICE
Detroit District
1401 W. Fort St. #1020
Detroit, MI 48233-9998
Alzana Braxton, Diversity Development
Specialist
Tel: (313) 226-8131 Fax: (313) 226-8005
Email: alzana.braxton@usps.gov
Web: www.usps.gov

Greater Michigan District
678 Front St. NW, 3rd Fl.
Grand Rapids, MI 49599-9997
Timothy Quigley, Diversity Development
Specialist
Tel: (616) 776-6139 Fax: (616) 336-5399
Email: timothy.p.quigley@usps.gov
Web: www.usps.com

MINNESOTA

ARMY, DEPT. OF THE
US Army Recruiting Battalion Minneapolis
BHW Federal Bldg. #3700, 1 Federal Dr.
Fort Snelling, MN 55111-4007
Tel: (612) 725-3122/3121

EQUAL EMPLOYMENT OPPORTUNITY COMMISSION
Minneapolis Area Office
Equal Employment Opportunity Office
Towle Bldg., 330 S. 2nd St. #430
Minneapolis, MN 55401-2224
Anastacia Belladonna, Director

Tel: (612) 335-4040 Fax: (612) 335-4044
Email: anastacia.belladonna@eeoc.gov
Web: www.eeoc.gov

HOMELAND SECURITY, DEPT. OF
USCG Recruiting Office Minneapolis
8575 Lyndale Ave. South
Bloomington, MN 55420
AMTC Tad Gentile, Recruiter in Charge
Tel: (612) 725-3222 Fax: (612) 725-3238
Email: tgentile@cgrc.uscg.mil
Web: www.gocoastguard.com

NAVY, DEPT. OF THE
Navy Recruiting District, Minneapolis
6020 28th Ave. South
Minneapolis, MN 55450
Tel: (612) 725-0414

USMC Recruiting Station, Twin Cities
Bishop Henry Whipple Federal Bldg., 1
Federal Dr. #1
Ft. Snelling, MN 55111
Tel: (612) 725-3193
Web: www.marines.com

POSTAL SERVICE
Northland District
P.O. Box 645001
St. Paul, MN 55164-5001
Andrew S. Fisher, Diversity Development
Specialist
Tel: (651) 293-3716 Fax: (651) 293-3000
Email: andrew.s.fisher@usps.gov
Web: www.usps.gov

MISSISSIPPI

AIR FORCE, DEPT. OF THE
Columbus AFB
Columbus AFB, MS 39710-6801
Tel: (800) 423-8723
Web: www.airforce.com

Keesler AFB
Keesler AFB, MS 39534-2547
Tel: (800) 423-8723
Web: www.airforce.com

ARMY, DEPT. OF THE
US Army Recruiting Battalion Jackson
Howie Bldg., 3780 I-55 N. Frontage Rd.
Jackson, MS 39211-6323
Tel: (601) 366-0895

EQUAL EMPLOYMENT OPPORTUNITY COMMISSION
Jackson Area Office
Equal Employment Opportunity Office
100 W. Capitol St. #207
Jackson, MS 39269
Benjamin Bradley, Area Director
Tel: (601) 965-4537 Fax: (601) 965-5272
Email: benjamin.bradley@eeoc.gov
Web: www.eeoc.gov

HOMELAND SECURITY, DEPT. OF
USCG Recruiting Office Jackson
4229 Lakeland Dr.
Flowood, MS 39232
AMTC Don Fortin, Recruiter in Charge
Tel: (601) 933-4901 Fax: (601) 939-9757
Email: dfortin@cgrc.uscg.mil
Web: www.gocoastguard.com

NAVY, DEPT. OF THE
Naval Reserve Center
434 Rosenbaum Ave.
Meridian, MS 39309
Tel: (601) 679-7105 Fax: (601) 679-8609

MISSOURI

AIR FORCE, DEPT. OF THE
Jefferson Barracks ANGS
Jefferson Barracks ANGS, MO 63125-4193
Tel: (800) 423-8723
Web: www.airforce.com

Whiteman AFB
Whiteman AFB, MO 65305-5021
Tel: (800) 423-8723
Web: www.airforce.com

ARMY, DEPT. OF THE
US Army Recruiting Battalion Kansas City
10300 NW Prairie View Rd.
Kansas City, MO 64153-1350
Tel: (816) 891-8721/8729

US Army Recruiting Battalion St. Louis
Robert Young Bldg., 1222 Spruce St.,
10th Fl.
St. Louis, MO 63102-2815
Tel: (314) 331-4131/4145

COMMERCE, DEPT. OF
National Oceanic & Atmospheric Administration, Central Administrative Support Center
Office of Human Resources
601 E. 12th St. #1737
Kansas City, MO 64106
Paul Kountzman, Manager
Tel: (816) 426-3044 Fax: (816) 426-7085
Email: p.j.kountzman@noaa.gov
Web: www.noaa.gov

EQUAL EMPLOYMENT OPPORTUNITY COMMISSION
St. Louis District Office
Equal Employment Opportunity Office
Robert A. Young Bldg., 1222 Spruce St.
#8-100
St. Louis, MO 63103
Lynn Bruner, Director
Tel: (314) 539-7800 Fax: (314) 539-7894
Email: lynn.bruner@eeoc.gov
Web: www.eeoc.gov

FEDERAL RESERVE BOARD
Office of Human Resources
Kansas City Region
925 Grand Blvd.
Kansas City, MO 64198
Esther George, Senior Vice President
Tel: (816) 881-2000 Fax: (816) 881-2281
Web: www.kc.frb.org

GENERAL SERVICES ADMINISTRATION
Office of Equal Employment Opportunity, Region 6
1500 E. Bannister Rd. #1181
Kansas City, MO 64131
Pinkie Mason, Officer
Tel: (816) 926-7349 Fax: (816) 823-1970
Email: pinkie.mason@gsa.gov
Web: www.gsa.gov

HOMELAND SECURITY, DEPT. OF
USCG Recruiting Office Kansas City
6228 NW Barry Rd.
Kansas City, MO 64154-2530
MSTC Thomas Kimberling, Recruiter in
Charge
Tel: (816) 746-9924 Fax: (816) 746-9927
Email: tkimberling@cgrc.uscg.mil
Web: www.gocoastguard.com

USCG Recruiting Office St. Louis
5445 Telegraph Rd. #125
St. Louis, MO 63129-3500
MSTC Greg Cable, Recruiter in Charge

Tel: (314) 845-0807 Fax: (314) 845-1805
Email: gcable@cgrc.uscg.mil
Web: www.gocoastguard.com

NAVY, DEPT. OF THE
Navy Recruiting District, Kansas City
10306 Prairie View Rd.
Kansas City, MO 64153
Tel: (816) 880-1105

Navy Recruiting District, St. Louis
1222 Spruce St., 10th Fl.
St. Louis, MO 63103
Tel: (314) 331-4296

USMC Recruiting Station, Kansas City
10302 NW Prairie View Rd.
Kansas City, MO 64153-1350
Tel: (816) 891-7577
Web: www.marines.com

USMC Recruiting Station, St. Louis
1222 Spruce St. #1031
St. Louis, MO 63103-2817
Tel: (314) 331-4555
Web: www.marines.com

POSTAL SERVICE
Gateway District
1720 Market St. #2022
St. Louis, MO 63155-9756
Glenda Fields, Diversity Development
Specialist
Tel: (314) 436-3868 Fax: (314) 436-6424
Email: glenda.d.fields@usps.gov
Web: www.usps.com

Mid-America District
300 W. Pershing Rd. #223
Kansas City, MO 64108-9403
Rita A. Hamilton, Diversity Development
Specialist
Tel: (816) 374-9131 Fax: (816) 374-9487
Email: rita.a.hamilton@usps.gov
Web: www.usps.gov

MONTANA

AIR FORCE, DEPT. OF THE
Malmstrom AFB
Malmstrom AFB, MT 59402-6857
Tel: (800) 423-8723
Web: www.airforce.com

INTERIOR, DEPT. OF THE
Bureau of Indians Affairs
Rocky Mountain Region, Personnel Office
316 N. 26th St.
Billings, MT 59101
Sharon Limberhand, Human Resource
Officer
Tel: (406) 247-7956 Fax: (406) 247-7902
Email: sharonlimberhand@bia.gov
Web: www.bia.gov

Bureau of Reclamation
Great Plains Region
P.O. Box 36900
Billings, MT 59107-6900
Sue McCannel, Personnel Manager
Tel: (406) 247-7614 Fax: (406) 247-7741
Web: www.usbr.gov/gp

POSTAL SERVICE
Big Sky District
841 S. 26th St.
Billings, MT 59101-9437
Leslie L. Denny, Diversity Development
Specialist

Tel: (406) 657-5660 Fax: (406) 657-5788
Email: leslie.l.denny@usps.gov
Web: www.usps.com

NEBRASKA

AIR FORCE, DEPT. OF THE
Offutt AFB
Offutt AFB, NE 68113-4015
Tel: (800) 423-8723
Web: www.airforce.com

HOMELAND SECURITY, DEPT. OF
USCG Recruiting Office Omaha
Montclair Ctr., 2758 S. 129th Ave.
Omaha, NE 68144
SKC Mark G. Floerchinger, Recruiter in
Charge
Tel: (402) 334-0607 Fax: (402) 334-0260
Email: mfloerchinger@cgrc.uscg.mil
Web: www.gocoastguard.com

NAVY, DEPT. OF THE
Navy Recruiting District, Omaha
6910 Pacific St. #400
Omaha, NE 68106
Tel: (402) 558-7909

STATE OF NEBRASKA
Equal Opportunity Commission
Equal Employment Opportunity Office
P.O. Box 94934
Lincoln, NE 68509-4934
Anne Hobbs, Executive Director
Tel: (402) 471-2024 Fax: (402) 471-4059
Email: ahobbs@neoc.state.ne.us
Web: www.neoc.state.ne.us

NEVADA

AIR FORCE, DEPT. OF THE
Nellis AFB
Nellis AFB, NV 89191-6526
Tel: (800) 423-8723
Web: www.airforce.com

ARMY, DEPT. OF THE
US Army 6th Recruiting Brigade
Western Region
4539 N. 5th St.
North Las Vegas, NV 89031
Tel: (702) 639-2071/2072

ENVIRONMENTAL PROTECTION AGENCY
Human Resources Office
Environmental Sciences Division
P.O. Box 93478
Las Vegas, NV 89193-3478
May Fong, Asian American Program
Manager
Tel: (702) 798-2624
Email: fong.may@epa.gov
Web: www.epa.gov

HOMELAND SECURITY, DEPT. OF
USCG Recruiting Office Las Vegas
Tropicana Gardens., 3510 E Tropicana
Blvd. #L
Las Vegas, NV 89121-7341
AMT1 JD Lawrence, Recruiter in Charge
Tel: (702) 898-2226 Fax: (702) 898-3026
Email: jlawrence@cgrc.uscg.mil
Web: www.gocoastguard.com

INTERIOR, DEPT. OF THE
Bureau of Reclamation
Lower Colorado Region, Personnel Office
P.O. Box 61470
Boulder City, NV 89006-1470
Bob Johnson, Regional Director

Tel: (702) 293-8412 Fax: (702) 293-8614
Web: www.usbr.gov

NAVY, DEPT. OF THE
Armed Forces Reserve Center Las Vegas
Navy Reserve, Area III
Nellis Air Force Base, 5095 Range Rd.
Las Vegas, NV 89115
Tel: (702) 632-1468

NEW HAMPSHIRE

HOUSING AND URBAN DEVELOPMENT, DEPT. OF
New Hampshire State Office
1000 Elm St., 8th Fl.
Manchester, NH 03101-1730
Robert A. Grenier, Operations Specialist
Tel: (603) 666-7510 Fax: (603) 666-7667
Email: Robert_Grenier@hud.gov
Web: www.hud.gov

NAVY, DEPT. OF THE
USMC Recruiting Station, Portsmouth
875 Greenland Rd. #A9
Portsmouth, NH 03801-4123
Tel: (603) 436-0890
Web: www.marines.com

POSTAL SERVICE
New Hampshire District
955 Goffs Falls Rd.
Manchester, NH 03103-9990
Harry Figueroa, Diversity Development Specialist
Tel: (603) 644-3890 Fax: (603) 644-3896
Email: harry.figueroa@usps.gov
Web: www.usps.gov

NEW JERSEY

AIR FORCE, DEPT. OF THE
McGuire AFB
McGuire AFB, NJ 08641-5000
Tel: (800) 423-8723
Web: www.airforce.com

ARMY, DEPT. OF THE
US Army Recruiting Battalion Mid-Atlantic
Lakehurst Naval Air Station, Hwy. 547, Bldg. 120
Lakehurst, NJ 08733
Tel: (732) 323-7380/7376

EQUAL EMPLOYMENT OPPORTUNITY COMMISSION
Newark Area Office
Equal Employment Opportunity Office
1 Newark Ctr. 21st Fl.
Newark, NJ 07102-5233
Corrado Gigante, Director
Tel: (973) 645-6383 Fax: (973) 645-4524
Email: corrado.gigante@eeoc.gov
Web: www.eeoc.gov

HOMELAND SECURITY, DEPT. OF
USCG Recruiting Office Atlantic City
1333 New Rd. #8
Northfield, NJ 08225-1202
FSC George Lopez, Recruiter in Charge
Tel: (609) 484-8260 Fax: (609) 484-9471
Email: glopez@cgrc.uscg.mil
Web: www.gocoastguard.com

NAVY, DEPT. OF THE
Naval Reserve Center Fort Dix
5994 New Jersey Ave.
Fort Dix, NJ 08650-7810
Tel: (609) 723-6582 Fax: (609) 723-4832

USMC Recruiting Station, New Jersey
Naval Weapons Station Earle, 201 Hwy. 34 South
Colts Neck, NJ 07722
Tel: (732) 866-2933
Web: www.marines.com

POSTAL SERVICE
Northern New Jersey District
494 Broad St.
Newark, NJ 07102-9300
Florina Cordero, Diversity Development Specialist
Tel: (973) 468-7203 Fax: (973) 468-7254
Email: fcordero@email.usps.gov
Web: www.usps.gov

NEW MEXICO

AIR FORCE, DEPT. OF THE
Cannon AFB
Cannon AFB, NM 88103-5326
Tel: (800) 423-8723
Web: www.airforce.com

Holloman AFB
Holloman AFB, NM 88330-8060
Tel: (800) 423-8723
Web: www.airforce.com

Kirtland AFB
Kirtland AFB, NM 87117-5625
Tel: (800) 423-8723
Web: www.airforce.com

ENERGY, DEPT. OF
NNSA Service Center
Equal Employment Opportunity Office
P.O. Box 5400
Albuquerque, NM 87185-5400
Yolanda Ruiz, Diversity Program Manager
Tel: (505) 845-4243 Fax: (505) 845-4963
Email: yruiz@doeal.gov
Web: www.doeal.gov/eeo

EQUAL EMPLOYMENT OPPORTUNITY COMMISSION
Albuquerque Area Office
505 Marquette NW #900
Albuquerque, NM 87102
Georgia M. Marchbanks, Enforcement Manager
Tel: (505) 248-5201 Fax: (505) 248-5239
Email: georgia.marchbanks@eeoc.gov
Web: www.eeoc.gov

HOMELAND SECURITY, DEPT. OF
USCG Recruiting Office Albuquerque
6001 San Mateo Blvd. NE #B-2A
Albuquerque, NM 87109-3348
EMCS James Richey, Recruiter in Charge
Tel: (505) 883-5396 Fax: (505) 883-5721
Email: jrichey@cgrc.uscg.mil
Web: www.gocoastguard.com

INTERIOR, DEPT. OF THE
Bureau of Indian Affairs
Southwest Region, Personnel Office
P.O. Box 26567
Albuquerque, NM 87102
Karen Tarrish, Personnel Officer
Tel: (505) 563-3170 Fax: (505) 563-3040
Web: www.bia.gov

NAVY, DEPT. OF THE
USMC Recruiting Station, Albuquerque
5338 Montgomery Blvd. NE #300
Albuquerque, NM 87109
Tel: (505) 248-5274
Web: www.marines.com

STATE OF NEW MEXICO
Energy Minerals & Natural Resources
New Mexico State Parks Division-Personnel Office
1220 S. Saint Francis Dr.
Santa Fe, NM 87505
Faye Barela, Personnel Officer
Tel: (505) 476-3375 Fax: (505) 476-3361
Email: fbarela@state.nm.us
Web: www.state.nm.us

NEW YORK

AIR FORCE, DEPT. OF THE
Niagara Falls ARS
Niagara Falls ARS, NY 14304-5001
Tel: (800) 423-8723
Web: www.airforce.com

ARMY, DEPT. OF THE
US Army Recruiting Battalion Albany
21 Aviation Rd.
Albany, NY 12205-1131
Tel: (518) 438-5536/1615

US Army Recruiting Battalion New York
407 Pershing Loop, North
Fort Hamilton, NY 11252-7000
Tel: (718) 630-4386/4387

US Army Recruiting Battalion Syracuse
The Atrium, 2 Clinton Sq. #230
Syracuse, NY 13202-1042
Tel: (315) 479-8534

ENVIRONMENTAL PROTECTION AGENCY
Human Resources Office, Region 2
290 Broadway, 16th Fl.
New York, NY 10007-1866
Jeannie Yu, Asian American Program Manager
Tel: (212) 637-3205 Fax: (212) 637-3535
Email: yu.jeannie@epa.gov
Web: www.epa.gov

EQUAL EMPLOYMENT OPPORTUNITY COMMISSION
Buffalo Local Office
Equal Employment Opportunity Office
6 Fountain Plz. #350
Buffalo, NY 14202
Elizabeth Cadle, Director
Tel: (716) 551-4441 Fax: (716) 551-4387
Email: elizabeth.cadle@eeoc.gov
Web: www.eeoc.gov

New York District Office
Equal Employment Opportunity Office
33 Whitehall St.
New York, NY 10014
Spencer H. Lewis, Jr., Director
Tel: (212) 336-3620 Fax: (212) 336-3621
Email: spencer.lewis@eeoc.gov
Web: www.eeoc.gov

FEDERAL RESERVE BOARD
Office of Human Resources
New York Region
33 Liberty St.
New York, NY 10045-0001
Robert Scrivani, Senior Vice President
Tel: (212) 720-6040 Fax: (212) 720-6947
Email: robert.scrivani@ny.frb.org
Web: www.newyorkfed.org

HOMELAND SECURITY, DEPT. OF
USCG Recruiting Office Albany
Loudon Plz., 324 Northern Blvd.
Albany, NY 12204-1028
Troy Timmons,
Tel: (518) 465-6182 Fax: (518) 465-6319

Email: ttimmons@cgrc.uscg.mil
Web: www.gocoastguard.com

USCG Recruiting Office Bronx
46 Westchester Square Plz.
Bronx, NY 10461
OSC Paul Gladding, Recruiter in Charge
Tel: (718) 904-8585 Fax: (718) 904-1900
Email: pgladding@cgrc.uscg.mil
Web: www.gocoastguard.com

USCG Recruiting Office Brooklyn
7810 Flatlands
Brooklyn, NY 11236
PO Craig Reid, Recruiter in Charge
Tel: (718) 251-1636 Fax: (718) 251-1660
Email: creid@cgrc.uscg.mil
Web: www.gocoastguard.com

USCG Recruiting Office Buffalo
1526 Walden Ave. #500
Cheektowaga, NY 14225
MKC Bernard Tobolski, Recruiter in Charge
Tel: (716) 893-2429 Fax: (716) 893-0570
Email: btobolski@cgrc.uscg.mil
Web: www.gocoastguard.com

USCG Recruiting Office Long Island
Wantagh Plz., 747 Wantagh Ave.
Wantagh, NY 11793-3133
FSC Dana Jewett, Recruiter in Charge
Tel: (516) 796-3339 Fax: (516) 796-3344
Email: djewett@cgrc.uscg.mil
Web: www.gocoastguard.com

USCG Recruiting Office New York
Battery Park Bldg., 1 South St. #109
New York, NY 10004-1466
YN1 Kevin Brathwaite, Recruiter in Charge
Tel: (212) 668-7036 Fax: (212) 668-7866
Email: kbrathwaite@cgrc.uscg.mil
Web: www.gocoastguard.com

USCG Recruiting Office Queens
116-18 Queens Blvd.
Forest Hills, NY 11375
PO Esther Martinez, Recruiter in Charge
Tel: (718) 793-4962 Fax: (718) 793-0540
Email: emartinez@cgrc.uscg.mil
Web: www.gocoastguard.com

USCG Recruiting Office Syracuse
Shop City Shopping Ctr., 386 Grant Blvd.
Syracuse, NY 13206
ETC Lawrence McLaren, Recruiter in Charge
Tel: (315) 437-6135 Fax: (315) 437-2953
Email: lmclaren@cgrc.uscg.mil
Web: www.gocoastguard.com

NAVY, DEPT. OF THE
Naval Reserve Recruiting Center Brooklyn
Floyd Bennett Field
Brooklyn, NY 11234-7097
Tel: (718) 258-0324 Fax: (718) 258-0780
Email: d5s20012@cnrrc.nola.navy.mil

Navy Recruiting District, Buffalo
300 Pearl St. #200
Buffalo, NY 14202
Tel: (716) 551-5816

Navy Recruiting District, New York
1975 Hempstead Turnpike
East Meadow, NY 11554
Tel: (800) 451-8758

USMC Recruiting Station, Albany
US Army Watervliet Arsenal Bldg. 40-3, 2nd Fl.
Watervliet, NY 12189-4050

Tel: (518) 266-6113
Web: www.marines.com

USMC Recruiting Station, Buffalo
100 Corporate Pkwy.
Buffalo, NY 14226
Tel: (716) 551-4915
Web: www.marines.com

USMC Recruiting Station, New York
605 Stewart Ave.
Garden City, NY 11530-4761
Tel: (516) 228-3684
Web: www.marines.com

POSTAL SERVICE
Albany District
30 Old Karner Rd.
Albany, NY 12288-9291
Josephine D. Grimes, Diversity
Development Specialist
Tel: (518) 452-2219 Fax: (518) 452-2492
Email: jgrimes@usps.gov
Web: www.usps.gov

Long Island District
P.O. Box 7700
Islandia, NY 11760-9997
Celina Lopez, Diversity Development
Specialist
Fax: (516) 582-7595
Email: celina.lopez@usps.gov
Web: www.usps.com

New York District
421 8th Ave. #3018
New York, NY 10199-9994
Evette Corchado, Diversity Development
Specialist
Tel: (212) 330-3935 Fax: (212) 330-3934
Web: www.usps.com

New York Metro Area Office
142-02 20th Ave.
Flushing, NY 11351-0600
Hector J. Borges, Senior Diversity Program
Coordinator
Tel: (718) 321-5723 Fax: (718) 321-7149
Email: hborges@email.usps.gov
Web: www.usps.gov

Triboro District
142-02 20th Ave. #3145
Flushing, NY 11351-9702
Judith N. Matzio, Diversity Development
Specialist
Tel: (718) 321-5081 Fax: (718) 321-5999
Email: jmatzio@usps.gov
Web: www.usps.com

Westchester District
1000 Westchester Ave. #3130
White Plains, NY 10610-9411
Enid M. Samuels, Diversity Development
Specialist
Tel: (914) 697-7102 Fax: (914) 697-7152
Email: enid.m.samuels@usps.gov
Web: www.usps.com

Western New York District
1200 William St. #304
Buffalo, NY 14240-9431
Mary Quin, Diversity Development Specialist
Tel: (716) 846-2484 Fax: (716) 846-2407
Email: mary.quin@usps.gov
Web: www.usps.com

SMALL BUSINESS ADMINISTRATION
Office of Disaster Assistance-Disaster Area 1
130 S. Elmwood Ave.
Buffalo, NY 14202

Jina M. Koop, Personnel Management
Specialist
Tel: (716) 843-4100 Fax: (716) 282-6151
Email: da1.hr@sba.gov
Web: www.sba.gov

TRANSPORTATION, DEPT. OF
St. Lawrence Seaway Development
Corporation
180 Andrews St.
Massena, NY 13662-0520
Jill Hamilton, Employment Program
Manager
Tel: (315) 764-3210 Fax: (315) 764-3235
Email: jill.hamilton@sls.dot.gov
Web: www.seaway.dot.gov

NORTH CAROLINA

AIR FORCE, DEPT. OF THE
Pope AFB
Pope AFB, NC 28308-2372
Tel: (800) 423-8723
Web: www.airforce.com

Seymour Johnson AFB
Seymour Johnson AFB, NC 27531-2469
Tel: (800) 423-8723
Web: www.airforce.com

ARMY, DEPT. OF
Headquarters, 1st Region (ROTC)
US Army Cadet Command
Attn: Public Affairs Office
Fort Bragg, NC 28307-5000
Tel: (910) 396-9415

US Army Recruiting Battalion Raleigh
Cypress Bldg., 3117 Poplarwood Ct. #218
Raleigh, NC 27604-1041
Tel: (919) 872-9147/3441

EQUAL EMPLOYMENT OPPORTUNITY
COMMISSION
Charlotte District Office
Equal Employment Opportunity Office
129 W. Trade St. #400
Charlotte, NC 28202
Reuben Daniels, Jr., Director
Tel: (704) 344-6682 Fax: (704) 344-6734
Email: reuben.daniels@eeoc.gov
Web: www.eeoc.gov

Greensboro Local Office
Equal Employment Opportunity Office
2303 W. Meadowview Rd. #201
Greensboro, NC 27407
Thomas Colclough, Acting Director
Tel: (336) 547-4188 Fax: (336) 547-4032
Email: thomascolclough@eeoc.gov
Web: www.eeoc.gov

HOMELAND SECURITY, DEPT. OF
USCG Recruiting Office Charlotte
Sugar Creek Professional Bldg., 537 W
Sugar Creek Rd.
Charlotte, NC 28213-6159
PAC Renee E. Gordon, Recruiter in Charge
Tel: (704) 598-2424 Fax: (704) 598-2426
Email: rgordon@cgrc.uscg.mil
Web: www.gocoastguard.com

USCG Recruiting Office Greensboro
4411 High Point Rd. #103
Greensboro, NC 27407-4315
MST1 Daniel Moore, Recruiter in Charge
Tel: (336) 294-6975 Fax: (336) 323-0592
Email: dmoore@cgrc.uscg.mil
Web: www.gocoastguard.com

USCG Recruiting Office Raleigh

2917 Brentwood Rd.
Raleigh, NC 27604-2464
ETC Chad Willits, Recruiter in Charge
Tel: (919) 878-4303 Fax: (919) 878-4460
Email: cwillits@cgrc.uscg.mil
Web: www.gocoastguard.com

USCG Recruiting Office Wilmington
Cornerstone Shopping Ctr., 1616 Shipyard
Blvd. #15
Wilmington, NC 28412
MKC Richard Lyons, Recruiter in Charge
Tel: (910) 791-2593 Fax: (910) 791-5247
Email: rlyons@cgrc.uscg.mil
Web: www.gocoastguard.com

NAVY, DEPT. OF THE
Navy Recruiting District, Raleigh
801 Oberlin Rd.
Raleigh, NC 27605
Tel: (919) 831-4158

NAVY, DEPT. OF THE
USMC Recruiting Station, Raleigh
5000 Falls of Neuse Rd. #404
Raleigh, NC 27609-5408
Tel: (919) 790-3039
Web: www.marines.com

POSTAL SERVICE
Greensboro District
P.O. Box 27499
Greensboro, NC 27498-9000
Patricia H. Gray, Diversity Development
Specialist
Tel: (336) 668-1268 Fax: (336) 668-1218
Web: www.usps.gov

NORTH DAKOTA

AIR FORCE, DEPT. OF THE
Grand Forks AFB
Grand Forks AFB, ND 58205-6338
Tel: (800) 423-8723
Web: www.airforce.com

AIR FORCE, DEPT. OF THE
Minot AFB
Minot AFB, ND 58705-5038
Tel: (800) 423-8723
Web: www.airforce.com

OHIO

AIR FORCE, DEPT. OF THE
Wright Patterson AFB
Wright Patterson AFB, OH 45433-5006
Tel: (800) 423-8723
Web: www.airforce.com

Youngstown Air Reserve Station
Vienna, OH 44473-5904
Tel: (800) 423-8723
Web: www.airforce.com

ARMY, DEPT. OF THE
US Army Recruiting Battalion Cleveland
1240 E. 9th St. #1269
Cleveland, OH 44199
Tel: (216) 802-1409

US Army Recruiting Battalion Columbus
New Federal Bldg., 200 N. High St., Rm.
114
Columbus, OH 43215-2483
Tel: (614) 469-2343/2345

ENVIRONMENTAL PROTECTION AGENCY
Office of Human Resources
26 W. Martin Luther King Dr.

Cincinnati, OH 45268
Sheila Gilliam, Specialist
Tel: (513) 569-7941 Fax: (513) 569-7530
Email: gilliam.sheila@epa.gov
Web: www.epa.gov

EQUAL EMPLOYMENT OPPORTUNITY
COMMISSION
Cincinnati Area Office
Equal Employment Opportunity Office
Federal Office Bldg., 550 Main St.10th Fl.
Cincinnati, OH 45202
Wilma L. Javey, Director
Tel: (513) 684-2851 Fax: (513) 684-2361
Email: wilma.javey@eeoc.gov
Web: www.eeoc.gov

Cleveland District Office
Equal Employment Opportunity Office
Tower City-Skylight Office Tower., 1660 W.
2nd St. #850
Cleveland, OH 44113-1412
James R. Neely, Jr., Director
Tel: (216) 522-2003 Fax: (216) 522-7395
Email: james.neely@eeoc.gov
Web: www.eeoc.gov

FEDERAL RESERVE BANK
Office of Human Resources
Cleveland District
1455 E. 6th St.
Cleveland, OH 44114
Elizabeth Robinson, Asst. Vice Pres.
Tel: (216) 579-2000 Fax: (216) 579-3198
Web: www.clevelandfed.org

HOMELAND SECURITY, DEPT. OF
USCG Recruiting Office Cincinnati
7255 Dixie Hwy.
Fairfield, OH 45014-8504
ETC Randy Evans, Recruiter in Charge
Tel: (513) 942-3145 Fax: (513) 942-3149
Email: revans@cgrc.uscg.mil
Web: www.gocoastguard.com

USCG Recruiting Office Cleveland
912 Great Northern Mall
North Olmstead, OH 44070-3394
ETC Kevin Riggs, Recruiter in Charge
Tel: (440) 734-4400 Fax: (440) 734-1643
Email: kriggs@cgrc.uscg.mil
Web: www.gocoastguard.com

USCG Recruiting Office Columbus
6046 Huntley Rd.
Columbus, OH 43229-2508
SCPO Harry Rosa, Recruiter in Charge
Tel: (614) 431-0270 Fax: (614) 431-0368
Email: hrosa@cgrc.uscg.mil
Web: www.gocoastguard.com

NAVY, DEPT. OF THE
Naval Reserve Center Cleveland
1089 E. 9th St.
Cleveland, OH 44114
Tel: (216) 861-3406
Email: d2s20005@cnrrc.nola.navy.mil

Navy Recruiting District, Ohio
200 N. High St. #609
Columbus, OH 43215
Tel: (614) 469-6672

USMC Recruiting Station, Cleveland
7261 Engle Rd. #110
Middleburg Heights, OH 44130-3479
Tel: (440) 243-4010
Web: www.marines.com

POSTAL SERVICE
Cincinnati District
1623 Dalton St. #423

Cincinnati, OH 45234-9431
Jo Ann Hutton, Diversity Development
Specialist
Tel: (513) 684-5250 Fax: (513) 684-5242
Email: jo.a.hutton@usps.gov
Web: www.usps.com

Cleveland District
2200 Orange Ave. #239
Cleveland, OH 44101
Gloria Jennings, Diversity Development
Specialist
Tel: (216) 443-4235 Fax: (216) 443-4879
Email: gloria.m.jennings@usps.gov
Web: www.usps.gov

Columbus District
850 Twin River Dr.
Columbus, OH 43216-9402
Deborah O'Neal, Diversity Development
Specialist
Tel: (614) 722-9629 Fax: (614) 722-9649
Email: debra.y.oneal@usps.gov
Web: www.usps.gov

STATE OF OHIO
Attorney General's Office
Equal Employment Opportunity Office
30 E. Broad St., 16th Fl.
Columbus, OH 43215-3428
Megan Kish, Director
Tel: (614) 466-8911 Fax: (614) 728-7582
Email: mkish@ag.state.oh.us
Web: www.ag.state.oh.us

OKLAHOMA

AIR FORCE, DEPT. OF THE
Altus AFB
Altus AFB, OK 73523-5001
Tel: (800) 423-8723
Web: www.airforce.com

Tinker AFB
Tinker AFB, OK 73145-3014
Tel: (800) 423-8723
Web: www.airforce.com

Vance AFB
Vance AFB, OK 73705-5011
Tel: (800) 423-8723
Web: www.airforce.com

ARMY, DEPT. OF THE
US Army Recruiting Battalion Oklahoma City
301 NW 6th St. #218
Oklahoma City, OK 73102
Tel: (405) 609-8792/8794

EQUAL EMPLOYMENT OPPORTUNITY COMMISSION
Oklahoma Area Office
Equal Employment Opportunity Office
210 Park Ave. #1350
Oklahoma City, OK 73102-2265
Donald T. Stevens, Director
Tel: (405) 231-4911 Fax: (405) 231-4140
Email: donald.t.stevens@eeoc.gov
Web: www.eeoc.gov

HOMELAND SECURITY, DEPT. OF
USCG Recruiting Office Oklahoma City
7329 S. Western Ave.
Oklahoma City, OK 73139
MKC Brent Divine, Recruiter in Charge
Tel: (405) 231-4483 Fax: (405) 231-4486
Email: bdivine@cgrc.uscg.mil
Web: www.gocoastguard.com

INTERIOR, DEPT. OF THE
Bureau of Indian Affairs

Southern Plains Region, Personnel Office
P.O. Box 1487
Anadarko, OK 73005
Jeannie Cooper, Human Resources Officer
Tel: (405) 247-6673 Fax: (405) 247-3920
Web: www.bia.gov

NAVY, DEPT. OF THE
Naval Reserve Center Oklahoma City
5316 Douglas Blvd.
Oklahoma City, OK 73150-9702
Tel: (405) 733-3368
Email: d3s20002@cnrrc.nola.navy.mil

USMC Recruiting Station, Oklahoma City
301 NW 6th St. #211
Oklahoma City, OK 73102
Tel: (405) 787-1635
Web: www.marines.com

POSTAL SERVICE
Oklahoma District
3030 NW Expressway St. #1042
Oklahoma City, OK 73198-9807
Eugene Talley, Diversity Development
Specialist
Tel: (405) 553-6217 Fax: (405) 553-6107
Email: eugene.talley@usps.gov
Web: www.usps.com

OREGON

AIR FORCE, DEPT. OF THE
Portland IAP
Portland IAP, OR 97218-2797
Tel: (800) 423-8723
Web: www.airforce.com

ARMY, DEPT. OF THE
US Army Recruiting Battalion Portland
6130 NE 78th Ct.
Portland, OR 97218-2853
Tel: (503) 256-1436/1433

NAVY, DEPT. OF THE
Navy Recruiting District, Portland
Airport Business Ctr.,7028 NE 79th Ct.,
Bldg. 2
Portland, OR 97218
Tel: (503) 258-2017

USMC Recruiting Station, Portland
Federal Bldg., 1220 SW 3rd Ave. #519
Portland, OR 97204-2888
Tel: (503) 326-3016
Web: www.marines.com

PENNSYLVANIA

AIR FORCE, DEPT. OF THE
Pittsburgh IAP-ARS
Pittsburgh IAP-ARS, PA 15108-4403
Tel: (800) 423-8723
Web: www.airforce.com

Willowgrove ARS
Willowgrove ARS, PA 19090-5203
Tel: (800) 423-8723
Web: www.airforce.com

ARMY, DEPT. OF THE
US Army Recruiting Battalion Harrisburg
M Ave., Bldg. 54 #11, New Cumberland
Army Depot
New Cumberland, PA 17070-5099
Tel: (717) 770-6721/7252

US Army Recruiting Battalion Pittsburgh
Wm. Moorhead Federal Bldg., Rm. 1404,
1000 Liberty Ave.

Pittsburgh, PA 15222-4197
Tel: (412) 395-5879/5786

COMMONWEALTH OF PENNSYLVANIA
Department of Banking
Office of Human Resources
333 Market St. 16th Fl.
Harrisburg, PA 17101
Kevin Hoffman, Director
Tel: (717) 787-4129 Fax: (717) 787-8773
Email: cdondero@state.pa.us
Web: www.banking.state.pa.us

Department of Community & Economic Development
Equal Employment Opportunity Office
Commonwealth Keystone Bldg., 400 N. St.
Harrisburg, PA 17120
Brenda Longacre, Human Resources
Analyst
Tel: (717) 346-7786 Fax: (717) 787-6939
Email: blongacre@state.pa.us
Web: www.state.pa.us

Department of Corrections
Equal Employment Opportunity Office
P.O. Box 598
Camp Hill, PA 17001-0598
Rafael Chieke, Director
Tel: (717) 975-4905 Fax: (717) 731-7115
Email: rchieke@state.pa.us
Web: www.cor.state.pa.us

Department of Labor & Industry
Equal Employment Opportunity Office
L & I Bldg. #514
Harrisburg, PA 17120
Merry-Grace Majors, Director
Tel: (717) 787-1182 Fax: (717) 772-2321
Email: mmajors@state.pa.us
Web: www.state.pa.us

Department of Public Welfare
Equal Employment Opportunity Office
P.O. Box 2675
Harrisburg, PA 17120
Merry-Grace Majors, Director
Tel: (717) 787-1127 Fax: (717) 772-4366
Email: mgmajors@state.pa.us
Web: www.state.pa.us

Department of the Treasury
Office of Human Resources
103 Finance Bldg.
Harrisburg, PA 17120
Patrick Tighe, Director
Tel: (717) 787-5979 Fax: (717) 787-3026
Email: ptighe@tre.state.pa.us
Web: www.state.pa.us

Insurance Department, Bureau of Administration
Human Resources Office
1326 Strawberry Sq.
Harrisburg, PA 17120
Jeffrey Wallace, Director
Tel: (717) 705-4194 Fax: (717) 705-3873
Email: jewallace@state.pa.us
Web: www.state.pa.us

Office of Administration
Equal Employment Opportunity Office
Finance Bldg., #506
Harrisburg, PA 17120
Tel: (717) 772-5085 Fax: (717) 787-4105
Web: www.state.pa.us

Pennsylvania Board of Probation & Parole
Equal Employment Opportunity Office
1101 S. Front St. #5600
Harrisburg, PA 17104-2522
Brenda Kates, Specialist

Tel: (717) 787-6897 Fax: (717) 772-4185
Email: lingram@state.pa.us
Web: www.parole.state.pa.us

Pennsylvania Fish & Boat Commission
Equal Employment Opportunity Office
1601 Elmerton Ave.
Harrisburg, PA 17110
Vicki Wadel, Officer
Tel: (717) 705-7820 Fax: (717) 705-7821
Email: vwadel@state.pa.us
Web: www.fish.state.pa.us

Pennsylvania Human Relations Commission
Office of Human Resources
301 Chestnut St. #300
Harrisburg, PA 17101
Richard Fairfax, Director
Tel: (717) 783-8483 Fax: (717) 214-0584
Email: webmaster@pa.state.us
Web: www.phrc.state.pa.us

Pennsylvania Liquor Control Board
Equal Employment Opportunity Office
Northwest Office Bldg., #408
Harrisburg, PA 17124
Kathy Blatt, Specialist
Tel: (717) 705-6958 Fax: (717) 787-8820
Email: mblatt@state.pa.us
Web: www.lcb.state.pa.us

Pennsylvania Milk Marketing Board
Agriculture Bldg., #110
Harrisburg, PA 17110
Tim Moyer, Personnel Analyst
Tel: (717) 787-4231 Fax: (717) 783-6492
Email: tmoyer@state.pa.us
Web: www.mmb.state.pa.us

Public TV Network Commission
Equal Employment Opportunity Office
24 Northeast Dr.
Hershey, PA 17033
Barbara Frantz, Officer
Tel: (717) 533-6011 Fax: (717) 533-4236
Email: bfrantz@state.pa.us
Web: www.state.pa.us

Securities Commission
Personnel Office
1010 N. 7th St. 2nd Fl.
Harrisburg, PA 17102
Peggy Hivner, Director
Tel: (717) 787-8061 Fax: (717) 783-5122
Email: phivner@state.pa.us
Web: www.state.pa.us

DEPARTMENT OF COMMUNITY AND ECONOMIC DEVELOPMENT
Commonwealth of Pennsylvania
Personnel Office
Commonwealth Keystone Bldg., 400 North St.
Harrisburg, PA 17120
George Spiess, Director
Tel: (717) 720-1468 Fax: (717) 787-6939
Web: www.state.pa.us

EDUCATION, DEPT. OF
Office of Human Resources
333 Market St., 11th Fl.
Harrisburg, PA 17126-0333
Susan Shatto, Representative
Tel: (717) 705-2672 Fax: (717) 783-9348
Email: sshatto@state.pa.us
Web: www.psp.state.pa.us

ENERGY, DEPT. OF
Federal Energy Technology Center
Equal Employment Opportunity Office
P.O. Box 10940, M/S CO2
Pittsburgh, PA 15236-0940

Nancy Vargas, Diversity Officer
Tel: (412) 386-4654 Fax: (412) 386-6014
Email: nancy.vargas@netl.doe.gov
Web: www.netl.doe.gov

ENVIRONMENTAL PROTECTION AGENCY
Human Resources Management Branch, Region 3
1650 Arch St. M/C 3HS22
Philadelphia, PA 19103-2029
Raj Sharma, Asian American Program Manager
Tel: (215) 814-3260 Fax: (215) 814-3002
Email: raj.sharma@epa.gov
Web: www.epa.gov

EQUAL EMPLOYMENT OPPORTUNITY COMMISSION
Philadelphia District Office
Equal Employment Opportunity Office
The Bourse Bldg., 21 S. 5th St. #400
Philadelphia, PA 19106
Marie M. Tomasso, Director
Tel: (215) 440-2600 Fax: (215) 440-2632
Email: marie.tomasso@eeoc.gov
Web: www.eeoc.gov

Pittsburgh Area Office
Liberty Center 1001 Liberty Ave. #300
Pittsburgh, PA 15222-4187
Eugene V. Nelson, Director
Tel: (412) 644-3444 Fax: (412) 644-2664
Email: eugene.nelson@eeoc.gov
Web: www.eeoc.gov

GENERAL SERVICES ADMINISTRATION
Region 1 & 3
Office of Equal Employment Opportunity
The Strawbridges Bldg., 20 N. 8th St. 9th Fl.
Philadelphia, PA 19107
Kelly Ann Williams, Officer
Tel: (215) 446-4906 Fax: (215) 446-5126
Email: kellyann.williams@gsa.gov
Web: www.gsa.gov

HOMELAND SECURITY, DEPT. OF
USCG Recruiting Office Harrisburg
4337A Union Deposit Rd., Union Ct.
Harrisburg, PA 17111-2883
BMC Joe Colonna, Recruiter in Charge
Tel: (717) 561-0972 Fax: (717) 561-0975
Email: bcolonna@cgrc.uscg.mil
Web: www.gocoastguard.com

USCG Recruiting Office Philadelphia North
Haverford Avenue Shops., 2327 Cottman Ave. #48
Philadelphia, PA 19149
BMC Marshall Miller, Recruiter in Charge
Tel: (215) 331-2788 Fax: (215) 473-8956
Email: mmiller@cgrc.uscg.mil
Web: www.gocoastguard.com

USCG Recruiting Office Philadelphia West
Haverford Avenue Shops., 7567 Haverford Ave.
Philadelphia, PA 19151
BMC Marshal Miller, Recruiter in Charge
Tel: (215) 473-8497 Fax: (215) 473-8956
Email: mmiller@cgrc.uscg.mil
Web: www.gocoastguard.com

USCG Recruiting Office Pittsburgh
7206 McKnight Rd. #104
Pittsburgh, PA 15237-3510
AMTC Troy Klabach, Recruiter in Charge
Tel: (412) 369-2870 Fax: (412) 369-2873
Email: ssnyder@cgrc.uscg.mil
Web: www.gocoastguard.com

INTERIOR, DEPT. OF THE
National Park Service
Northeast Region, Office of Human Resources, Staffing Division
200 Chestnut St., 3rd Fl.
Philadelphia, PA 19106
Delores Dyer, Special Emphasis Program Manager
Tel: (215) 597-7067 Fax: (215) 597-5747
Email: delores_dyer@nps.gov
Web: www.nps.gov

LABOR, DEPT. OF
Employment & Training Administration
Office of Youth Programs and Job Corps
The Curtis Center #815 E., 170 Independence Mall West
Philadelphia, PA 19106-3315
Lynn Intrepidi, Regional Director
Tel: (215) 861-5501 Fax: (215) 861-5520
Email: Intrepidi.lynn@dol.gov
Web: www.dol.gov

MILITARY VETERANS AFFAIRS, DEPT. OF
Bureau of Administrative Services
Equal Employment Opportunity Office
DMVA Fishers Ave.
Annville, PA 17003-5002
Kristy L. Smith, Director
Tel: (717) 861-8796 Fax: (717) 861-8628
Email: krsmith@state.pa.us
Web: www.state.pa.us

NAVY, DEPT. OF THE
Navy Recruiting District, Philadelphia
700 Robbins Ave., Bldg. 2D
Philadelphia, PA 19111
Tel: (215) 697-3984

Navy Recruiting District, Pittsburgh
1000 Liberty Ave. #713
Pittsburgh, PA 15222
Tel: (412) 395-6824

USMC Recruiting Station, Harrisburg
Bldg. 54, #5DDC
New Cumberland, PA 17070-5006
Tel: (717) 770-4227
Web: www.marines.com

USMC Recruiting Station, Pittsburgh
New Federal Bldg., 1000 Liberty Ave. #1512
Pittsburgh, PA 15222-4179
Tel: (412) 395-4917
Web: www.marines.com

PENNSYLVANIA HISTORICAL AND MUSEUM COMMISSION
Division of Personnel Services
300 N. St.
Harrisburg, PA 17120
Jane Peyton, Personnel Director
Tel: (717) 787-3362 Fax: (717) 783-9924
Email: ra-phmc-webmaster@state.pa.us
Web: www.phmc.state.pa.us

PENNSYLVANIA PUBLIC SCHOOL EMPLOYMENT RETIREMENT SYSTEM
Human Resources Division
5 N. 5th St.
Harrisburg, PA 17101-1905
Maribel Laluz, Director
Tel: (717) 720-4737 Fax: (717) 783-7275
Email: ra-ps-contact@state.pa.us
Web: www.psers.state.pa.us

PENNSYLVANIA STATE POLICE COMMISSION
Equal Employment Opportunity Office
1800 Elmerton Ave.
Harrisburg, PA 17110
Martin L. Henry III, Officer
Tel: (717) 787-7220 Fax: (717) 705-2185
Email: marthenry@state.pa.us
Web: www.pcp.state.pa.us

POSTAL SERVICE
Eastern Area Office
5315 Campbells Run Rd.
Pittsburgh, PA 15277-7050
Sue Marsh, Diversity Human Capitol Development, Manager
Tel: (412) 494-2567 Fax: (650) 357-6375
Email: susan.l.marsh@usps.gov
Web: www.usps.com

Erie District
2709 Legion Rd.
Erie, PA 16515-9741
Wendy Nelson-Smith, Acting Diversity Development Specialist
Tel: (814) 836-7209 Fax: (814) 836-7215
Email: wendy.l.nelson-smith@usps.gov
Web: www.usps.com

Harrisburg District
1425 Crooked Hill Rd.
Harrisburg, PA 17107-0041
Bobbi Reid, Diversity Development Specialist
Tel: (717) 257-5380 Fax: (717) 257-2168
Email: bobbi.reid@usps.gov
Web: www.usps.com

Philadelphia District
P.O. Box 7237
Philadelphia, PA 19101-7237
Belinda Kelley, Diversity Development Specialist
Tel: (215) 895-8040 Fax: (651) 406-5549
Email: belinda.s.kelley@usps.gov
Web: www.usps.com

Pittsburgh District
1001 California Ave. #2300
Pittsburgh, PA 15290-9600
Tel: (412) 359-7510 Fax: (412) 359-7535
Web: www.usps.gov

SOCIAL SECURITY ADMINISTRATION
Philadelphia Region
Civil Rights and Equal Employment Opportunity Office
P.O. Box 8788
Philadelphia, PA 19101
Agnes T. Sampson, Manager
Tel: (215) 597-1694 Fax: (215) 597-2827
Web: www.ssa.gov

STATE EMPLOYEES RETIREMENT SYSTEM
Office of Human Resources
30 N. 3rd St., 3rd Fl.
Harrisburg, PA 17108-1147
Cheryl Krchnar, Personnel Officer
Tel: (717) 783-8085 Fax: (717) 783-0581
Email: ckrchnar@state.pa.us
Web: www.sers.state.pa.us

PUERTO RICO

HOMELAND SECURITY, DEPT. OF
USCG Recruiting Office Aguadilla
USCG Air Station Borinquen, 260 Guard Rd.
Aguadilla, PR 00603
GM1 Reynaldo Gonzalez, Recruiter in Charge
Tel: (787) 890-8400 X8020 Fax: (787) 890-8407
Email: rgonzalez@cgrc.uscg.mil
Web: www.gocoastguard.com

USCG Recruiting Office San Juan
100 Gran Bulevar Los Paseos. #102
San Juan, PR 00926
SKC Alfredo Rodríguez, Recruiter in Charge
Tel: (787) 292-0210 Fax: (787) 292-0405
Email: arodriguez@cgrc.uscg.mil
Web: www.gocoastguard.com

OFFICE OF PERSONNEL MANAGEMENT
San Juan Service Center
Torre de Plaza Las Americas #1114., 525 F.D. Roosevelt Ave.
San Juan, PR 00918-8026
Vivian Fernandez, Senior Personnel Specialist
Tel: (787) 766-5620 Fax: (787) 766-5598
Email: lxrodrig@opm.gov
Web: www.opm.gov

RHODE ISLAND

HOMELAND SECURITY, DEPT. OF
USCG Recruiting Office Providence
380 Westminster St.
Providence, RI 02903-3246
AET1 Darrin Merrill, Recruiter in Charge
Tel: (401) 421-1291 Fax: (401) 528-4371
Email: dmerrill@cgrc.uscg.mil
Web: www.gocoastguard.com

POSTAL SERVICE
Southeast New England District
24 Corliss St.
Providence, RI 02904
Mary Hahnen, Diversity Development Specialist
Tel: (401) 276-6905 Fax: (401) 276-6968
Email: mary.e.hahnen@usps.gov
Web: www.usps.gov

STATE OF RHODE ISLAND
Equal Employment Opportunity Office
1 Capitol Hill
Providence, RI 02908
A. Vincent Igliozzi, Administrator
Tel: (401) 222-3090 Fax: (401) 222-2490

SOUTH CAROLINA

AIR FORCE, DEPT. OF THE
Charleston AFB
Charleston AFB, SC 29404-5021
Tel: (800) 423-8723
Web: www.airforce.com

Shaw AFB
Shaw AFB, SC 29152-5028
Tel: (800) 423-8723
Web: www.airforce.com

ARMY, DEPT. OF THE
US Army Recruiting Battalion Columbia
Strom Thurmond Federal Bldg., 1835 Assembly St. #733
Columbia, SC 29201-2491
Tel: (803) 765-5640

EQUAL EMPLOYMENT OPPORTUNITY COMMISSION
Greenville Local Office
Equal Employment Opportunity Office
301 N. Main St. #1402
Greenville, SC 29601-9916
Patricia B. Fuller, Director
Tel: (864) 241-4400 Fax: (864) 241-4416
Email: patricia.fuller@eeoc.gov
Web: www.eeoc.gov

HOMELAND SECURITY, DEPT. OF
USCG Recruiting Office Charleston
1650 Sam Rittenberg Blvd. #1
Charleston, SC 29407-4933
SC Charles Franklin, Recruiter in Charge
Tel: (843) 766-7315 Fax: (843) 766-7630
Email: cfranklin@cgrc.uscg.mil
Web: www.gocoastguard.com

USCG Recruiting Office Columbia
Capitol Center Shopping Ctr., 201 Columbia Mall Blvd. #207
Columbia, SC 29223
SKCS Glenda Smith-Leeth, Recruiter in Charge
Tel: (803) 699-7230 Fax: (803) 699-6149
Email: gleeth@cgrc.uscg.mil
Web: www.gocoastguard.com

NAVY, DEPT. OF THE
Naval Reserve Center Columbia
513 Pickens St.
Columbia, SC 29201-4198
Tel: (803) 256-7167 Fax: (803) 156-7096
Email: d4s20007@cnrrc.nola.navy.mil

USMC Recruiting Station, Columbia
9600 2 Notch Rd. #17
Columbia, SC 29223-4379
Tel: (803) 788-9251
Web: www.marines.com

POSTAL SERVICE
Greater South Carolina District
P.O. Box 929801
Columbia, SC 29292-9801
Mary Ellen Padin, Diversity Development Specialist
Tel: (803) 926-6429 Fax: (803) 926-6434
Email: maryellen.padin@usps.gov
Web: www.usps.gov

SOUTH CAROLINA STATE WIDE
Minority Business Development Center
Columbia MBDC
1515 Richland St. #C
Columbia, SC 29201
Greg Davis, Director
Tel: (803) 779-5905 Fax: (803) 779-5915
Email: davisg@desainc.com
Web: www.scmbdc.com

SOUTH DAKOTA

AGRICULTURE, DEPT. OF
Natural Resources
1820 N. Kimball
Mitchell, SD 57301-1114
Steve Vlieger, Asian American Program Manager
Tel: (605) 996-1564 Fax: (605) 996-4708
Email: steven.vlieger@sd.usda.gov
Web: www.sd.nrcs.usda.gov

AIR FORCE, DEPT. OF THE
Ellsworth AFB
Ellsworth AFB, SD 57706-4700
Tel: (800) 423-8723
Web: www.airforce.com

TENNESSEE

AIR FORCE, DEPT. OF THE
Arnold AFB
Arnold AFB, TN 37389-3314
Tel: (800) 423-8723
Web: www.airforce.com

ARMY, DEPT. OF THE
US Army Recruiting Battalion Nashville
2517 Perimeter Place Dr.
Nashville, TN 37214
Tel: (615) 871-4172

EQUAL EMPLOYMENT OPPORTUNITY COMMISSION
Memphis District Office
Equal Employment Opportunity Office
1407 Union Ave. #621
Memphis, TN 38104
Chirley Richardson, Director
Tel: (901) 544-0115 Fax: (901) 544-0111
Email: chirley.richardson@eeoc.gov
Web: www.eeoc.gov

Nashville Area Office
Equal Employment Opportunity Office
50 Vantage Wy. #202
Nashville, TN 37228-9940
Sarah L. Smith, Director
Tel: (615) 736-5820 Fax: (615) 736-2107
Email: sarah.smith@eeoc.gov
Web: www.eeoc.gov

HOMELAND SECURITY, DEPT. OF
USCG Recruiting Office Knoxville
Blue Grass Landing., 9321 Northshore Dr.
Knoxville, TN 37922
OSCS Paul Hunyady, Recruiter in Charge
Tel: (865) 690-1164 Fax: (865) 690-4544
Email: phunyady@cgrc.uscg.mil
Web: www.gocoastguard.com

USCG Recruiting Office Memphis
2830 Coleman Rd. #G
Memphis, TN 38128
OSC Gerald Jett, Recruiter in Charge
Tel: (901) 380-9873 Fax: (901) 380-1395
Email: gjett@cgrc.uscg.mil
Web: www.gocoastguard.com

USCG Recruiting Office Nashville
The Market at Bell Forge., 5308 Mount View Rd. #C
Antioch, TN 37013-2307
BMC Randy L. Price, Recruiter in Charge
Tel: (615) 731-3408 Fax: (615) 731-4992
Email: rprice@cgrc.uscg.mil
Web: www.gocoastguard.com

NAVY, DEPT. OF THE
Naval Reserve Center Memphis
5722 Integrity Dr., Bldg. N-930
Millington, TN 38128
Tel: (901) 874-5056 Fax: (901) 874-5841
Email: d4s20006@cnrrc.nola.navy.mil

Navy Recruiting District, Nashville
640 Grassmere Park #104
Nashville, TN 37211
Tel: (615) 332-0824

USMC Recruiting Station, Nashville
2519 Perimeter Place Dr.
Nashville, TN 37214-3681

Tel: (615) 627-1526
Web: www.marines.com

POSTAL SERVICE
Area Office
225 N. Humphreys Blvd.
Memphis, TN 38166-0840
Betty J. Davis-Smith, Manager, Diversity & Human Capital Development
Tel: (901) 747-7209 Fax: (901) 747-7206
Email: betty.j.davis-smith@usps.gov
Web: www.usps.gov

Tennessee District
811 Royal Pkwy.
Nashville, TN 37229-9771
Yvonne Walker, Acting Diversity Development Specialist
Tel: (615) 872-5693 Fax: (615) 885-9374
Email: yvonne.walker@usps.gov
Web: www.usps.gov

TENNESSEE VALLEY AUTHORITY
400 W Summit Hill Dr.
Knoxville, TN 37902-1499
Tel: (865) 632-8981
Email: tvainfo@tva.com
Web: www.tva.gov

TEXAS

AIR FORCE, DEPT. OF THE
Air Force Personnel Center
Randolph AFB, TX 78150-4759
Tel: (800) 423-8723
Web: www.airforce.com

Brooks AFB
Brooks AFB, TX 78235-5358
Tel: (800) 423-8723
Web: www.airforce.com

Dyess AFB
Dyess AFB, TX 79607-1517
Tel: (800) 423-8723
Web: www.airforce.com

Goodfellow AFB
Goodfellow AFB, TX 76908-3216
Tel: (800) 423-8723
Web: www.airforce.com

Lackland AFB
Lackland AFB, TX 78236-5226
Tel: (800) 423-8723
Web: www.airforce.com

Laughlin AFB
Laughlin AFB, TX 78843-5230
Tel: (800) 423-8723
Web: www.airforce.com

Randolph AFB
Randolph AFB, TX 78150-4308
Tel: (800) 423-8723
Web: www.airforce.com

Sheppard AFB
Sheppard AFB, TX 76311-2927
Tel: (800) 423-8723
Web: www.airforce.com

ARMY, DEPT. OF THE
US Army 5th Recruiting Brigade
South Central Region
P.O. Box 8277
Bldg. 2064, Fort Sam Houston Wainwright Station, TX 78277
Tel: (210) 221-1900/0176

US Army Recruiting Battalion Dallas

1350 Walnut Hill Ln. #150
Irving, TX 75038-3025
Tel: (972) 756-0842

US Army Recruiting Battalion Houston
1919 Smith St. #1529
Houston, TX 77002
Tel: (713) 209-3220/3222

US Army Recruiting Battalion San Antonio
1265 Buck Rd., Bldg. 2003
Fort Sam Houston, TX 78234-5034
Tel: (210) 295-0624/0626

EQUAL EMPLOYMENT OPPORTUNITY COMMISSION
Dallas District Office
Equal Employment Opportunity Office
207 S. Houston St., 3rd Fl.
Dallas, TX 75202-4726
Mike Fetzer, Director
Tel: (214) 253-2700 Fax: (214) 253-2720
Email: mike.fetzer@eeoc.gov
Web: www.eeoc.gov

El Paso Area Office
Equal Employment Opportunity Office
300 E. Main St. #500
El Paso, TX 79901
Roberto Calderon, Director
Tel: (915) 534-6700 Fax: (915) 534-6701
Email: roberto.calderon@eeoc.gov
Web: www.eeoc.gov

Houston District Office
Equal Employment Opportunity Office
Mickey Leland Federal Bldg., 1919 Smith St. #600
Houston, TX 77002-8049
Mike Fetzer, Director
Tel: (713) 209-3320 Fax: (713) 209-3381
Email: mike.fetzer@eeoc.gov
Web: www.eeoc.gov

San Antonio District Office
Equal Employment Opportunity Office
Mockingbird Plz. II., 5410 Fredericksburg Rd. #200
San Antonio, TX 78229-3555
Pedro M. Esquivel, Director
Tel: (210) 281-7600 Fax: (210) 281-7690
Email: pedro.esquivel@eeoc.gov
Web: www.eeoc.gov

FEDERAL RESERVE BANK
Office of Human Resources
Dallas Region
2200 N. Pearl St.
Dallas, TX 75201-2272
Bob Williams, Assistant Vice President
Tel: (214) 922-5270 Fax: (214) 922-6355
Email: info@dallasfed.org
Web: www.dallasfed.org

GENERAL SERVICES ADMINISTRATION
Office of Equal Employment Opportunity
Region 7, 8
819 Taylor St. #7A12
Fort Worth, TX 76102-6105
James Hood, Officer
Tel: (817) 978-3838 Fax: (817) 978-4179
Email: james.hood@gsa.gov
Web: www.gsa.gov

HOMELAND SECURITY, DEPT. OF
Office of Human Resources
2301 S. Main St.
McAllen, TX 78503
Cynthia Garcia, Personnel Specialist
Tel: (956) 984-3813 Fax: (956) 984-3990
Email: cynthia.garcia@dhs.gov
Web: www.dhs.gov

Immigration & Naturalization Services
San Antonio District Office, Administrative Office
8940 Fourwinds Dr.
San Antonio, TX 78239
Annie Ross, Program Manager, Special Emphasis Programs
Tel: (210) 967-7125 Fax: (210) 967-7099
Email: annie.ross@dhs.gov
Web: www.dhs.gov

USCG Recruiting Office Corpus Christi
Wind Chase Shopping Ctr., 2033 Airline Rd. #E-4
Corpus Christi, TX 78412
AET1 David Ozuna, Recruiter in Charge
Tel: (361) 993-6977 Fax: (361) 993-9810
Email: dozuna@cgrc.uscg.mil
Web: www.gocoastguard.com

USCG Recruiting Office Dallas
Beltline Village Shopping Center., 3455 N. Beltline Road
Irving, TX 75062
BMC Brian Lee, Recruiter in Charge
Tel: (972) 255-0165 Fax: (972) 255-6397
Email: blee@cgrc.uscg.mil
Web: www.gocoastguard.com

USCG Recruiting Office El Paso
9100 Viscount Blvd. #E
El Paso, TX 79925
ETC Jarrod Purseglove, Recruiter in Charge
Tel: (915) 591-6741 Fax: (915) 591-6766
Email: jpurseglove@cgrc.uscg.mil
Web: www.gocoastguard.com

USCG Recruiting Office Houston Central
Gulfgate Center Mall., 3111 Woodridge Ave. #160
Houston, TX 77087
HSC Travis Biggerstaff, Recruiter in Charge
Tel: (713) 641-3559 Fax: (713) 641-5341
Email: tbiggerstaff@cgrc.uscg.mil
Web: www.gocoastguard.com

USCG Recruiting Office Houston West
12807 Westheimer Rd.
Houston, TX 77077
PS1 Patrick Zinck, Recruiter in Charge
Tel: (281) 556-1460 Fax: (281) 556-1534
Email: pzinck@cgrc.uscg.mil
Web: www.gocoastguard.com

USCG Recruiting Office San Antonio East
River Oaks Plz., 8347 Perrin Beitel
San Antonio, TX 78218
YNC Bruce Crawford, Recruiter in Charge
Tel: (210) 590-9760 Fax: (210) 590-9763
Email: bcrawford@cgrc.uscg.mil
Web: www.gocoastguard.com

USCG Recruiting Office San Antonio West
Ingram Place Shopping Ctr., 3227 Wurzbach Rd.
San Antonio, TX 78238
YNC Bruce Crawford, Recruiter in Charge
Tel: (210) 680-5475 Fax: (210) 680-5509
Email: bcrawford@cgrc.uscg.mil
Web: www.gocoastguard.com

INTERIOR, DEPT. OF THE
National Park Service
San Antonio Missions National Historical Parks
2202 Roosevelt Ave.
San Antonio, TX 78210-4919
Karen Steed, Human Resources Specialist
Tel: (210) 534-8875 X240 Fax: (210) 534-1106
Email: karen_steed@nps.gov
Web: www.nps.gov/saan

JUSTICE, DEPT. OF
Attorney's Office
816 Congress Ave. #1000
Austin, TX 78701
Barbara Brown, Asian American Employment Program Manager
Tel: (512) 916-5858 Fax: (512) 916-5854
Email: barbara.brown@usdoj.gov
Web: www.usdoj.gov

LABOR, DEPT. OF
Employment & Training Administration
Office of Youth Programs and Job Corps
525 Griffin St. #403
Dallas, TX 75202
Joan Boswell, Regional Director
Tel: (214) 767-2114 Fax: (214) 767-2148
Web: www.dallasregioncdss.org

NAVY, DEPT. OF THE
Naval Reserve Recruiting Command Area South
1564 Headquarters Ave.
Ft. Worth, TX 76127-1564
Tel: (817) 782-6131/69

Navy Recruiting District, Dallas
6440 N. Beltline Rd. #150
Irving, TX 75063
Tel: (972) 714-8300

USMC Recruiting Station, Dallas
207 S. Houston St. #146
Dallas, TX 75202-4703
Tel: (214) 655-3481
Web: www.marines.com

USMC Recruiting Station, Ft. Worth
3313 Pioneer Pkwy.
Pantego, TX 76013
Tel: (817) 303-3488
Web: www.marines.com

USMC Recruiting Station, Houston
701 San Jacinto St. #230
Houston, TX 77002-3622
Tel: (713) 718-4282
Web: www.marines.com

USMC Recruiting Station, San Antonio
1265 Buck Rd. #MC
Fort Sam Houston, TX 78234-5034
Tel: (210) 295-1006
Web: www.marines.com

POSTAL SERVICE
Dallas District
951 W. Bethel Rd.
Coppell, TX 75099-9852
Gail Lofton, Diversity Development Specialist
Tel: (972) 393-6665 Fax: (972) 393-6502
Web: www.usps.gov

Rio Grande District
1 Post Office Dr.
San Antonio, TX 78284-9425
Alice A. Orta, Diversity Development Specialist
Tel: (210) 368-5563 Fax: (210) 368-8409
Email: alice.orta@usps.gov
Web: www.usps.com

Southwest Area Office
P.O. Box 225459
Dallas, TX 75222-5459
Vickie Tovar, Senior Diversity Program Coordinator
Tel: (214) 819-8736 Fax: (214) 819-8956
Email: vickie.a.tovar@usps.gov
Web: www.usps.com

SMALL BUSINESS ADMINISTRATION
Disaster Assistance-Disaster Area 3
14925 Kingsport Dr.
Ft. Worth, TX 76155
Kandye Wells, Personnel Officer
Tel: (817) 868-2300 Fax: (817) 684-5621
Email: kandye.wells@sba.gov
Web: www.sba.gov

SOCIAL SECURITY ADMINISTRATION
Dallas Region
Equal Employment Opportunity Office
1301 Young St. #500
Dallas, TX 75202
Emerson Lattimore, Manager
Tel: (214) 767-3036 Fax: (214) 767-4338
Email: emerson.lattimore@ssa.gov
Web: www.ssa.gov

STATE OF TEXAS
Office of the Governor
Office of Human Resources
P.O. Box 12428
Austin, TX 78711
Edna Jackson, Director
Tel: (512) 463-1740 Fax: (512) 463-8464
Email: humanresources@governor.state.tx.us
Web: www.governor.state.tx.us

Texas Workforce Commission
Office of Human Resources
101 E. 15th St. #230
Austin, TX 78778-0001
Brenda Nickles, Acting Director
Tel: (512) 463-2314 Fax: (512) 463-2832
Email: brenda.nickles@twc.state.tx.us
Web: www.twc.state.tx.us

VETERANS AFFAIRS, DEPT. OF
South Texas Veterans Health Care System
Equal Employment Opportunity Office
Audie L. Murphy VA., 7400 Merton Minter Blvd.
San Antonio, TX 78229
Laura Faust, Manager
Tel: (210) 617-5300 Fax: (210) 949-3304
Email: laura.faust@med.va.gov
Web: www.vasthcs.med.va.gov

UTAH

AIR FORCE, DEPT. OF THE
Hill AFB
Hill AFB, UT 84056-5819
Tel: (800) 423-8723
Web: www.airforce.com

ARMY, DEPT. OF THE
US Army Recruiting Battalion Salt Lake City
2830 S. Redwood Rd.
Salt Lake City, UT 84119-4708
Tel: (801) 974-9518/9519

DEPARTMENT OF COMMUNITY AND CULTURE
State of Utah
State Office of Asian Affairs
324 S. State St. #500
Salt Lake City, UT 84111
Edith Mitko, Director
Tel: (801) 538-8691 Fax: (801) 538-8678
Email: emitko@utah.gov
Web: http://ethnicoffice.utah.gov

HOMELAND SECURITY, DEPT. OF
USCG Recruiting Office Salt Lake City
Roy Shopping Ctr., 5639 S. 1900 W. #302
Roy, UT 84067-2301
HSC David Holcomb, Recruiter in Charge
Tel: (801) 525-1904 Fax: (801) 525-1925
Email: dholcomb@cgrc.uscg.mil
Web: www.gocoastguard.com

INTERIOR, DEPT. OF THE
Bureau of Reclamation
Upper Colorado Regional Office
125 S. State St. #6107
Salt Lake City, UT 84138-1147
Kathy Nicholson, Acting Human Resources Officer
Tel: (801) 524-3656 Fax: (801) 524-3187
Email: knicholson@uc.usbr.gov
Web: www.usbr.gov

NAVY, DEPT. OF THE
USMC Recruiting Station, Salt Lake City
1279 W. 2200 South Bldg. #A
West Valley City, UT 84119-1471
Tel: (801) 954-0418
Web: www.marines.com

POSTAL SERVICE
Salt Lake City District
1760 W. 2100 South
Salt Lake City, UT 84199-2922
Pania Heimuli, Diversity Development Specialist
Tel: (801) 974-2922 Fax: (801) 974-2975
Email: pania.heimuli@usps.gov
Web: www.usps.com

VIRGINIA

AGRICULTURE, DEPT. OF
Department of Human Resources
2100 Clarendon Blvd. #511
Arlington, VA 22201
Hilaria Heilman, Personnel Analyst/ Outreach Specialist
Tel: (703) 228-3506 Fax: (703) 228-3265
Email: hheilm@arlingtonva.us
Web: www.arlingtonva.us

Food and Nutrition Service
3101 Park Center Dr. #222
Alexandria, VA 22302
Candice Johnson, Asian American Program Manager
Tel: (703) 305-2231 Fax: (703) 305-1102
Email: candice.johnson@fns.usda.gov
Web: www.usda.gov

AIR FORCE, DEPT. OF THE
Langley AFB
Langley AFB, VA 23665-2773
Tel: (800) 423-8723
Web: www.airforce.com

ARMY, DEPT. OF
Headquarters, US Army Cadet Command
Attn: Public Affairs Office
Bldg. 56 Patch Rd.
Fort Monroe, VA 23651-5000
Tel: (757) 788-4610

Ft. Myers
Equal Employment Opportunity Office
204 Lee Ave.

Ft. Myers, VA 22211-1199
Hazel Barnes, Assistant
Tel: (703) 696-6258 Fax: (703) 696-8588
Email: hazel.barnes@fmmc.army
Web: www.fmmc.army.mil

COMMERCE, DEPT. OF
Patent and Trademark Office
Office of Civil Rights
2011 Crystal Dr. #608
Arlington, VA 22202
Maria Campo, Acting Director
Tel: (703) 305-8255 Fax: (703) 305-9154
Email: maria.campo@uspto.gov
Web: www.uspto.gov

DEFENSE, DEPT. OF
Defense Commissary Agency
1300 E Ave.
Ft. Lee, VA 23801-1800
Karen Swindell, Affirmative Action
Employment Program Manager
Tel: (804) 734-8620 Fax: (804) 734-8028
Email: karen.swindell@deca.mil
Web: www.commissaries.com

Defense Contract Audit Agency, Headquarters
Equal Employment Opportunity Office
8725 John J. Kingman Rd. #2135
Ft. Belvoir, VA 22060-6219
Vicki O'Donnell, Director
Tel: (703) 767-1240 Fax: (703) 767-1228
Email: vicki.o'donnell@dcaa.mil
Web: www.dcaa.mil

Defense Security Service
Office of Diversity Management
1340 Braddock Pl.
Alexandria, VA 22314
Thomas A. Beber, Asian American Program Manager
Tel: 703-325-5472 Fax: 703-325-5341
Email: thomas.beber@dss.mil
Web: www.dss.mil

National Guard Bureau
Equal Opportunity Division
1411 Jefferson Davis Hwy. #2400
Arlington, VA 22202
Phyllis Brantley, Special Emphasis Program Manager
Tel: (703) 607-0782 Fax: (703) 607-0790
Email: phyllis.brantley@ngb.ang.af.mil
Web: www.ngb.army.mil

Office of the Inspector General
Equal Employment Opportunity Office
400 Army Navy Dr. #754
Arlington, VA 22202
Linda Lee, Asian American Pacific Program Manager
Tel: (703) 604-9647 Fax: (703) 604-9608
Email: llee@dodig.osd.mil
Web: www.dodig.osd.mil

EQUAL EMPLOYMENT OPPORTUNITY COMMISSION
Norfolk Area Office
Equal Employment Opportunity Office
Federal Bldg., 200 Granby St. #739
Norfolk, VA 23510
Herbert Brown, Director
Tel: (757) 441-3470 Fax: (757) 441-6720
Email: herbert.brown@eeoc.gov
Web: www.eeoc.gov

Richmond Area Office
Equal Employment Opportunity Office
830 E.Main St., 6th Fl.
Richmond, VA 23219
Tel: (804) 771-2200 Fax: (804) 771-2222
Web: www.eeoc.gov

FAIRFAX COUNTY PUBLIC SCHOOLS
Human Resources Recruitment Office
6815 Edsall Rd.
Springfield, VA 22151
Pamela Mcknight, Recruitment Coordinator
Tel: (703) 750-8519 Fax: (703) 750-8593
Email: pamela.mcknight@fcps.edu
Web: www.fcps.edu

FARM CREDIT ADMINISTRATION
EEO and Office of the Ombudsman
1501 Farm Credit Dr.
McLean, VA 22102-5090
Eric Howard, Director
Tel: (703) 883-4481 Fax: (703) 734-5784
Email: howarde@fca.gov
Web: www.fca.gov

HOMELAND SECURITY, DEPT. OF
USCG Recruiting Office Fredericksburg
4300 Plank Rd. #160
Fredericksburg, VA 22408
BMC Howard McCarthy, Recruiter in Charge
Tel: (540) 785-4068 Fax: (540) 785-4085
Email: cthompson@cgrc.uscg.mil
Web: www.gocoastguard.com

USCG Recruiting Office Hampton Roads
1011 Eden Wy. North #A
Chesapeake, VA 23320-2768
YNC Rhonda Killmon, Recruiter in Charge
Tel: (757) 312-0514
Email: jhoesli@cgrc.uscg.mil
Web: www.gocoastguard.com

USCG Recruiting Office Potomac Mills
2700 Potomac Mills Cir. #832
Woodbridge, VA 22193
YN1 Justin Batton, Recruiter in Charge
Tel: (703) 492-3949
Email: jbatton@cgrc.uscg.mil
Web: www.gocoastguard.com

USCG Recruiting Office Richmond
10447 Midlothian Trnpk.
Richmond, VA 23235
MK2 Jeffery Keim, Recruiter in Charge
Tel: (804) 771-8635 Fax: (804) 771-8076
Email: jkeim@cgrc.uscg.mil
Web: www.gocoastguard.com

INTER-AMERICAN FOUNDATION
901 N. Stuart St., 10th Fl.
Arlington, VA 22203
Tel: (703) 306-4301 Fax: (703) 306-4365
Email: info@iaf.gov
Web: www.iaf.gov

INTERIOR, DEPT. OF THE
Bureau of Land Management
Equal Employment Opportunity Office
7450 Boston Blvd.
Springfield, VA 22153
Lynda Nix, Manager
Tel: (703) 440-1593 Fax: (703) 440-1797
Email: lynda_nix@es.blm.gov
Web: www.blm.gov

Fish & Wildlife Service
Directorate of Civil Rights

4401 N. Fairfax Dr. #200
Arlington, VA 22203
Pedro De Jesus, Manager
Tel: (703) 358-2552 Fax: (703) 358-2030
Email: pedro_dejesus@fws.gov
Web: www.fws.gov

Minerals Management Service
Equal Employment Opportunity Office
381 Elden St. M/S 2900
Herndon, VA 20170
Rosa Thomas, Specialist
Tel: (703) 787-1314 Fax: (703) 787-1601
Email: rosa.thomas@mms.gov
Web: www.mms.gov

Minerals Management Service
Equal Employment Opportunity Office
Pkwy Atrium Bldg., 381 Elden St. M/S 2900
Herndon, VA 20170
Patricia Callis, Director
Tel: (703) 787-1313 Fax: (703) 787-1601
Email: patricia.callis@mms.gov
Web: www.mms.gov

JUSTICE, DEPT. OF
Drug Enforcement Administration
Equal Employment Opportunity Office
600 Army-Navy Dr. #E11275
Arlington, VA 22202
Tel: (202) 307-8895 Fax: (202) 307-8942
Web: www.usdj.gov

Executive Office for Immigration Review
Equal Employment Opportunity Office
5107 Leesburg Pike #1902
Falls Church, VA 22041
Wanda Owens, Manager
Tel: (703) 305-0994 Fax: (703) 605-0367
Email: wanda.owens@usdoj.gov
Web: www.usdoj.gov

Executive Office for US Attorneys
Equal Employment Opportunity Office
2401 Jefferson Davis Hwy.
Alexandria, VA 22301
Tel: (202) 307-8888 Fax: (202) 307-8942
Web: www.usdj.gov

LABOR, DEPT. OF
Mine Safety & Health Administration
Office of Diversity Outreach and Employee Safety
1100 Wilson Blvd. #2407
Arlington, VA 22209-3939
Michael Thompson, Director
Tel: (202) 693-9882 Fax: (202) 693-9881
Email: thompson.michael@dol.gov
Web: www.msha.gov

NATIONAL CREDIT UNION ADMINISTRATION
Equal Employment Opportunity Office
1775 Duke St. #4093
Alexandria, VA 22314
Marilyn Gannon, Director
Tel: (703) 518-6325 Fax: (703) 518-6319
Email: mggannon@ncua.gov
Web: www.ncua.gov

NATIONAL SCIENCE FOUNDATION
Equal Opportunity Programs
Equal Employment Opportunity Office
255 S. Wilson Blvd.
Arlington, VA 22230

Ronald Branch, Director
Tel: (703) 292-8020 Fax: (703) 292-9072
Email: rbranch@nsf.gov
Web: www.nsf.gov

NAVY, DEPT. OF THE
Navy Recruiting District, Richmond
411 E. Franklin St.
Richmond, VA 23219
Tel: (804) 771-2001

USMC Recruiting Station, Richmond
9210 Arboretum Pkwy. #220
Richmond, VA 23236-3472
Tel: (804) 272-0227
Web: www.marines.com

PERSONNEL MANAGEMENT, OFFICE OF
Norfolk Service Center
Federal Bldg., 200 Granby St. #500
Norfolk, VA 23510-1886
Alan Nelson, Director
Tel: (757) 441-3373 Fax: (757) 441-6280
Email: norfolk@opm.gov
Web: www.opm.gov

POSTAL SERVICE
Northern Virginia District
8409 Lee Hwy.
Merrifield, VA 22081-9996
Andrea Bufford, Acting Diversity Development Specialist
Tel: (703) 698-6614 Fax: (703) 204-3004
Email: jbufford@usps.gov
Web: www.usps.gov

Richmond District
1801 Brook Rd.
Richmond, VA 23232-9998
Doreen Anglero, Diversity Development Specialist
Tel: (804) 775-6362 Fax: (804) 897-4703
Email: doreen.anglero@usps.gov
Web: www.usps.com

SELECTIVE SERVICE SYSTEM
Equal Employment Opportunity Office
1515 Wilson Blvd. #400
Arlington, VA 22209-2425
Richard S. Flahavan, Officer
Tel: (703) 605-4100 Fax: (703) 605-4106
Email: richard.flahavan@sss.gov
Web: www.sss.gov

TRADE AND DEVELOPMENT AGENCY
1000 Wilson Blvd. #1600
Arlington, VA 22209-3901
Tel: (703) 875-4357 Fax: (703) 875-4009
Email: info@ustda.gov
Web: www.tda.gov

WASHINGTON

AIR FORCE, DEPT. OF THE
Fairchild AFB
Fairchild AFB, WA 99011-8524
Tel: (800) 423-8723
Web: www.airforce.com

McChord AFB
McChord AFB, WA 98438-1109
Tel: (800) 423-8723
Web: www.airforce.com

ARMY, DEPT. OF
Headquarters, 4th Region (ROTC)
US Army Cadet Command
Attn: Public Affairs Office
Fort Lewis, WA 98433-7100
Tel: (253) 967-7473

US Army Recruiting Battalion Seattle
P.O. Box 3957
4735 E. Marginal Way South
Seattle, WA 98124-3957
Tel: (206) 764-3599

COMMERCE, DEPT. OF
National Oceanic & Atmospheric Administration
Human Resources Division-WC2
Western Administrative Support Ctr., 7600
Sand Point Wy. NE
Seattle, WA 98115-6349
Mary Berklund, Human Resources
Specialist
Tel: (206) 526-6059 Fax: (206) 526-6673
Email: mary.j.berklund@noaa.gov
Web: www.noaa.gov

EDUCATION, DEPT. OF
Commonwealth of Pennsylvania
Office of Human Resources
Jackson Federal Bldg., 915 2nd Ave.
#3388
Seattle, WA 98174
Ike Gilbert, Human Resources Officer
Tel: (206) 220-7813 Fax: (206) 220-7949
Email: ike.gilbert@ed.gov
Web: www.ed.gov

ENVIRONMENTAL PROTECTION AGENCY
Civil Rights, Calma Enforcement and Environmental Justice
Equal Employment Opportunity Office
1200 6th Ave., M/C CRE-164
Seattle, WA 98101
Victoria Plata, Officer
Tel: (206) 553-8580 Fax: (206) 553-7176
Email: plata.victoria@epa.gov
Web: www.epa.gov

Human Resources, Region 10
Office of Air, Waste & Toxics
1200 6th Ave. M/S OAQ-107
Seattle, WA 98101
Lucita Valiere, AAPI Manager & National
Chair
Tel: (206) 553-8087 Fax: (206) 553-0110
Email: valiere.lucita@epa.gov
Web: www.epa.gov

EQUAL EMPLOYMENT OPPORTUNITY COMMISSION
Seattle District Office
Equal Employment Opportunity Office
Federal Office Bldg., 909 1st Ave. #400
Seattle, WA 98104-1061
Jeanette M. Leino, Director
Tel: (206) 220-6883 Fax: (206) 220-6911
Email: jeanette.leino@eeoc.gov
Web: www.eeoc.gov

HOMELAND SECURITY, DEPT. OF
USCG Recruiting Office Portland
8109 F NE Vancouver Mall Dr.
Vancouver, WA 98662-6422
AMTC Thomas F. Brunney, Recruiter

Tel: (360) 699-1047 Fax: (360) 699-1048
Email: tbrunney@cgrc.uscg.mil
Web: www.gocoastguard.com

USCG Recruiting Office Seattle
10712 5th Ave. NE
Seattle, WA 98125
BMC Randall Dennis, Recruiter in Charge
Tel: (206) 364-4667 Fax: (206) 365-0866
Email: rdennis@cgrc.uscg.mil
Web: www.gocoastguard.com

USCG Recruiting Office Spokane
11516-A E. Sprague Ave.
Spokane, WA 99206-5135
GMC Mark Brown, Recruiter in Charge
Tel: (509) 927-0993 Fax: (509) 927-8026
Email: mebrown@cgrc.uscg.mil
Web: www.gocoastguard.com

USCG Recruiting Office Tacoma
Tacoma Office Mall Bldg., 4301 S. Pine
St. #102
Tacoma, WA 98409-7264
MKC Steve Fisk, Recruiter in Charge
Tel: (253) 476-5939 Fax: (253) 476-8382
Email: sfisk@cgrc.uscg.mil
Web: www.gocoastguard.com

USCG Recruiting Office Yakima
1200 Chesterly Dr. #110, Plz. II
Yakima, WA 98902-7338
AMTC Russel Kirkham, Recruiter in Charge
Tel: (509) 452-1356 Fax: (509) 452-1375
Email: rkirkham@cgrc.uscg.mil
Web: www.gocoastguard.com

LABOR, DEPT. OF
Employment and Training Administration
Office of Youth Programs and Job Corps
1111 3rd Ave. #800
Seattle, WA 98101-3212
Fax: (206) 553-4009
Web: www.dol.gov

NAVY, DEPT. OF THE
Navy Recruiting District, Seattle
2901 3rd Ave.
Seattle, WA 98121
Tel: (800) 832-0258

USMC Recruiting Station, Seattle
South Federal Center South, 4735 E.
Marginal Way
South Seattle, WA 98134-2379
Tel: (206) 762-1645
Web: www.marines.com

POSTAL SERVICE
Seattle District
Diversity Development Office
415 1st Ave. North
Seattle, WA 98109-9997
Carol V. Peoples-Procter, Diversity
Development Specialist
Tel: (206) 442-6293 Fax: (206) 378-2537
Email: carol.v.peoples-procter@usps.gov
Web: www.usps.com

Spokane District
707 W. Main #600
Spokane, WA 99299-1000

Gail Meredith, Diversity Development
Specialist
Tel: (509) 626-6714 Fax: (509) 626-6918
Email: gmeredi1@email.usps.gov
Web: www.usps.com

STATE OF WASHINGTON
Department of Social & Health Services
Aging & Adult Services Administration-State
Unit on Aging
P.O. Box 45600
Olympia, WA 98504-5600
Patty McDonald, Diversity Program
Manager
Tel: (360) 725-2559 Fax: (360) 438-8633
Email: mcdonpm@dshs.wa.gov
Web: www.aasa.dshs.wa.gov

WEST VIRGINIA

ARMY, DEPT. OF THE
US Army Recruiting Battalion Beckley
21 Mallard Ct.
Beckley, WV 25801-3615
Tel: (304) 252-0422/0459

INTERIOR, DEPT. OF THE
National Park Service
Harpers Ferry Center, Equal Employment
Opportunity Office
P.O. Box 50
Harpers Ferry, WV 25425
Magaly M. Green , Manager
Tel: (304) 535-6003 Fax: (304) 535-6295
Email: Magaly_green@nps.gov
Web: www.nps.gov

NAVY, DEPT. OF THE
USMC Recruiting Station, Charleston
4216 State Rt. 34
Hurricane (Teays Valley), WV 25526
Tel: (304) 757-5028
Web: www.marines.com

POSTAL SERVICE
Appalachian District
P.O. Box 59000
Charleston, WV 25350-9000
Lora M. Moles, Diversity Development
Specialist
Tel: (304) 561-1269 Fax: (304) 561-1268
Email: lora.m.moles@usps.gov
Web: www.usps.com

TREASURY, DEPT. OF THE
Bureau of Public Debt
Equal Employment Opportunity Office
200 3rd St. #415
Parkersburg, WV 26106
Cheryl D. Adams, Officer
Tel: (304) 480-6527 Fax: (304) 480-6074
Email: cheryl.adams@bpd.treas.gov
Web: www.publicdebt.treas.gov

WISCONSIN

ARMY, DEPT. OF THE
US Army Recruiting Battalion Milwaukee
310 W. Wisconsin Ave. #600
Milwaukee, WI 53203-2211
Tel: (414) 297-4596/1193

EQUAL EMPLOYMENT OPPORTUNITY COMMISSION
Milwaukee District Office
Equal Employment Opportunity Office
Reuss Federal Plz., 310 W. Wisconsin Ave.
#800
Milwaukee, WI 53203-2292
John P. Rowe, Director
Tel: (414) 297-1111 Fax: (414) 297-4133
Email: john.p.rowe@eeoc.gov
Web: www.eeoc.gov

HOMELAND SECURITY, DEPT. OF
USCG Recruiting Office Milwaukee
Woodland Ct., 3953 S. 76th St.
Milwaukee, WI 53220-2320
MKC David Shuart, Recruiter in Charge
Tel: (414) 321-4220 Fax: (414) 321-3527
Email: dshuart@cgrc.uscg.mil
Web: www.gocoastguard.com

NAVY, DEPT. OF THE
USMC Recruiting Station, Milwaukee
310 Wisconsin Ave. #480
Milwaukee, WI 53203-2216
Tel: (414) 297-1796
Web: www.marines.com

POSTAL SERVICE
Milwaukee District
P.O. Box 5027
Milwaukee, WI 53201-5027
Terri Jordan, Diversity Development
Specialist
Tel: (414) 287-2577 Fax: (414) 287-2296
Email: terri.l.jordan@usps.gov
Web: www.usps.com

WYOMING

AIR FORCE, DEPT. OF THE
FE Warren AFB
FE Warren AFB, WY 82005-3905
Tel: (800) 423-8723
Web: www.airforce.com

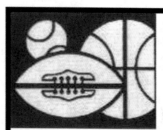

Private Sector Minority Business Opportunities

ALABAMA

REGIONS FINANCIAL
Corporate Heaquarters
471 N. 20th St.
Birmingham, AL 35203
Tel: (205) 944-1300
Web: www.regions.com

SAKS
Corporate Headquarters
750 Lakeshore Pkwy
Birmingham, AL 35211
Barbara Webb,
Tel: (205) 940-4010
Web: www.saksincorporated.com

ARIZONA

ALLIED WASTE INDUSTRIES
Procurement
15880 N. Greenway-Hayden Loop
Scottsdale, AZ 85260
Jennifer Bryant, Manager, Corporate
Procurement
Tel: (480) 627-2700
Web: www.alliedwaste.com

KB HOME
Purchasing
432 N. 44th st #400
Pheonix, AZ 85008
Derek Bowen, Purchasing Manager
Tel: 602-567-4800

ARKANSAS

ALLTEL
Vendor Relations
1 Allied Dr.
Little Rock, AR 72202
Tel: (501) 905-8000
Email: corp.corporate.
communications@alltel.com
Web: www.alltel.com

AVNET
Corporate Headquarters
2211 S. 47th St.
Phoenix, AR 85034
Greg Frazier, Executive Vice President,
Supply Chain Services
Tel: (480) 643-2000
Web: www.avnet.com

DILLARD'S
Corporate Headquarters
1600 Cantrell Rd.
Little Rock, AR 72201

Tel: (501) 376-5200
Web: www.dillards.com

MURPHY OIL
Vendor Relations
200 Peach St.
El Dorado, AR 71731
Kelly Hammock, Manager, Purchasing
Tel: (870) 862-6411
Web: www.murphyoilcorp.com

PHELPS DODGE
Supply Chain Management
1 N. Central Ave.
Phoenix, AR 85004
Chuck Wargo, Global Supply Chain
Tel: (602) 366-8456
Web: www.phelpsdodge.com

TYSON FOODS
Corporate Headquarters
2210 W. Oaklawn Dr
Springdale, AR 72762
Donnie Smith, Senior Vice President Supply
Chain Management
Tel: (479) 290-4000
Web: www.tysonfoodsinc.com

WAL-MART STORES
Arkansas
702 S.W. Eighth St.
Bentonville, AR 72716
Chris Rasche, Director, Supplier Diversity
Tel: (479) 277-2326
Web: www.walmartstores.com

CALIFORNIA

ADVANCED MICRO DEVICES
Corporate Headquarters
1 AMD Place
Sunnyvale, CA 94088
Tel: (408) 749-4000
Web: www.amd.com

AGILENT TECHNOLOGIES
Supplier Diversity
M/S 54L-BB, 5301 Stevens Creek Blvd.
Santa Clara, CA 95051-7295
Supplier Diversification Process Manager
Tel: (650) 752-5000
Email: supplier_diversity@agilent.com
Web: www.agilent.com

AMGEN
Corporate Headquarters
1 Amgen Center Dr.
Thousand Oaks, CA 91320
Tel: (805) 447-3600
Web: www.amgen.com

APPLE COMPUTER
Supplier Diversity
1 Infinite Loop
Cupertino, CA 95014
Tel: (408) 996-1010
Email: supplierdiversity@apple.com
Web: www.apple.com

APPLIED MATERIALS
Corporate Headquarters
3050 Bowers Ave.
Santa Clara, CA 95054
Mark R. Pinto, Chief Technology Officer and
Senior Vice President New Business and
New Product Group
Tel: (408) 727-5555
Web: www.appliedmaterials.com

AVERY DENNISON
Purchasing
150 N. Orange Grove Blvd
Pasadena, CA 91103
Juan Guerrero, Manager Purchasing
Tel: (626) 304-2000
Web: www.averydennison.com

CALPINE
Vendor Relations
50 W. San Fernando St.
San Jose, CA 95113
Tel: (408) 995-5115
Email: isvendor@calpine.com
Web: www.calpine.com

CHARLES SCHWAB
Procurement
120 Kearny St.
San Francisco, CA 94108
Ann Arhontes, Director, Procurement
Tel: (415) 627-7000
Web: www.schwab.com

CHEVRONTEXACO
Headquarters
6001 Bollinger Canyon Rd.
San Ramon, CA 94583
Audrey Goins Brichi, Supplier Diversity
Manager
Tel: (925) 842-1000 Fax: (925) 790-3987
Web: www.chevrontexaco.com

CISCO SYSTEMS
Corporate Headquarters
170 W. Tasman Dr.
San Jose, CA 95134
Kate D'camp, Senior Vice President,
Supplier Diversity and Human Resources
Tel: (408) 526-4000
Web: www.cisco.com

CLOROX
Corporate Headquarters
1221 Broadway

Oakland, CA 94612
Tel: (510) 271-7000
Web: www.clorox.com

CNF INC.
Purchasing
3240 Hillview Ave.
Palo Alto, CA 94304
D. Wayne Byerley, Jr., Vice President,
Purchasing
Tel: (650) 424-2900
Web: www.cnf.com

COMPUTER SCIENCES
Corporate Headquarters
2100 E. Grand Ave.
El Segundo, CA 90245
Steve Goble, Manager Supply Chain
Tel: (214) 523-5552
Email: sgoble@csc.com
Web: www.csc.com

COUNTRYWIDE FINANCIAL
Corporate Headquarters
4500 Park Granada
Calabasas, CA 91302
Michael Keating, Senior Managing Director,
Global Operations
Web: www.countrywide.com

DIRECTV GROUP
Corporate Headquarters
2250 E. Imperial Highway
El segundo, CA 90245
Tel: (310) 964-5000
Web: www.directv.com

DOLE FOOD
Corporate Headquarters
1 Dole Dr.
Westlake Village, CA 91362
Tel: (818) 879-6600
Web: www.dole.com

EDISON INTERNATIONAL
Corporate Headquarters
2244 Walnut Grove Ave.
Rosemead, CA 91770
Tel: (626) 302-2222
Web: www.edison.com

FIRST AMERICAN CORP.
Corporate Headquarters
1 First American Way
Santa Ana, CA 92707
Tel: (714) 800-3000
Web: www.firstam.com

FLUOR
Supplier Diversity
1 Enterprise Dr.
Aliso Viejo, CA 92656
Lisa Harley, Supplier Diversity Executive,
Procurement

Tel: (949) 349-2000
Email: supplier.diveristy@fluor.com
Web: www.fluor.com

GAP
Corporate Headquarters
2 Folson St.
San Francisco, CA 94105
Nick J. Cullen, Executive Vice President,
Supply Chain
Tel: (650) 952-4400
Web: www.gapinc.com

GATEWAY
New Vendor Relations
7565 Irvine Center Dr.
Irvine, CA 92618
Dan Stevenson, Vice President, Direct
Tel: (949) 491-7000
Web: www.gateway.com

GOLDEN WEST FINANCIAL
Corporate Headquarters
1901 Harrison St.
Oakland, CA 94612
Tel: (510) 446-3420
Web: www.worldsavings.com

HEALTH NET
Corporate Headquarters
26150 Oxnard St.
Woodland Hills, CA 91367
Strategic Sourcing and Procurement
Tel: (800) 590-1848
Email: supplierhotline@healthnet.com
Web: www.healthnet.com

HEWLETT-PACKARD
Headquarters
3000 Hanover St
Palo Alto, CA 94304
Jon Flaxman, Senior Vice President and
Controller Accounting and Financial
Reporting
Tel: (650) 857-1501 Fax: (650) 857-5518
Web: www.hp.com

INGRAM MICRO
1600 E. St. Andrews Pl.
Santa Ana, CA 92705
Terry Tysseland, Senior Vice President,
Supply Chain
Tel: (714) 566-1000 x22040
Web: www.ingrammicro.com

INTEL
Corporate Headquarters
2200 Mission College Blvd
Santa Clara, CA 95052
Rosalin Hudnell, Director of Diversity
Tel: (408) 765-8080
Web: www.intel.com

JACOBS ENGINEERING GRP.
Corporate Headquarters
1111 S. Arroyo Pkwy
Pasadena, CA 91105
Tel: (865) 220-4800
Web: www.jacobs.com

LEVI STRAUSS
Corporate Headquarters
1155 Battery St.
San Francisco, CA 94111
Tel: (415) 501-6000
Web: www.levistrauss.com

LONGS DRUG STORES
Supplier Diversity
141 N. Civic Dr.
Walnut Creek, CA 94596
Tony Dickens, Supplier Diversity
Tel: (925) 937-1170
Web: www.longs.com

MATTEL
Corporate Headquarters
333 Continental Blvd
El Segundo, CA 90245
Tel: (310) 252-2000
Web: www.mattel.com

MAXTOR
Corporate Headquarters
500 McCarthy Blvd
Milpitas, CA 95035
Tel: (408) 894-5000
Web: www.maxtor.com

MCKESSON
Corporate Headquarters
1 Post St.
San Francisco, CA 94104
Susan Jee, Small Business Liaison Officer
Tel: (415) 983-7170
Email: supplier.diveresity@mckesson.com
Web: www.mckesson.com

NORTHROP GRUMMAN
Corporate Headquarters
1840 Century Park E.
Los Angeles, CA 90067
Katie Gray , Vice President, Materials
Management and Procurement
Tel: (310) 553-6262 Fax: (310) 814-0660
Web: www.northropgrumman.com

OCCIDENTAL PETROLEUM
Corporate Headquarters
10889 Wilshire Blvd
Los Angeles, CA 90024
Tel: (310) 208-8800
Web: www.oxy.com

ORACLE
Corporate Headquarters
500 Oracle Pkwy
Redwood City, CA 94065
Tel: (650) 506-7200
Web: www.oracle.com

PACIFIC LIFE
Corporate Headquarters
700 Newport Center Dr.
Newport Beach, CA 92660
Tel: (949) 219-3011
Web: www.pacificlife.com

PACIFICARE HEALTH SYS.
Corporate Headquarters
5995 Plaza Dr.
Cypress, CA 90630
Tel: (714) 952-1121
Web: www.pacificare.com

PG&E CORP.
Supplier Diversity
1 Market St.
San Francisco, CA
Jane Jansen, Director Supplier Diversity
Tel: (415) 973-4853
Web: www.pgecorp.com

QUALCOMM
Diversity
5775 Morehouse Dr.
San Diego, CA 92121
Tel: (858) 587-1121
Email: diversity.info@qualcomm.com
Web: www.qualcomm.com

ROSS STORES
Purchasing
4440 Rosewood Dr.
Pleasanton, CA 94588
Rosanna Berger, Manager, Purchasing
Tel: (925) 965-4400
Web: www.rossstores.com

RYLAND GROUP
Purchasing
24025 park Sorrento
Calabasas, CA 91302
Steven M. Dwyer, Vice President,
Purchasing
Tel: (818) 223-7500
Web: www.ryland.com

SAFEWAY
Corporate Headquarters
5918 Stoneridge Mall Rd.
Pleasanton, CA 94588
Sherrie Ysunza, Director, Supplier Diversity
Tel: (925) 467-3000 Fax: (925) 951-4709
Web: www.safeway.com

SANMINA-SCI
Corporate Headquarters
2700 N. First St
San Jose, CA 95143
Tel: (408) 964-3504 Fax: (408) 964-3636
Web: www.sanmina-sci.com

SCIENCE APPLICATIONS INTL.
Corporate Headquarters
10260 Campus Point Dr.
San Diego, CA 92121
George Otchere, Senior Vice President,
Corporate Development and Small Business
Development
Tel: (858) 826-6000
Web: www.saic.com

SEMPRA ENERGY
Corporate Headquarters
101 Ash St.
San Diego, CA 92101
Shawn Ferrar, Director, Diverse Business
Enterprises
Tel: (877) 555-1212
Web: www.sempra.com

SOLECTRON
Corporate Headquarters
847 Gibralter Dr.
Milpitas, CA 95053
Tel: (408) 957-8500
Web: www.solectron.com

STATER BROS. HOLDINGS
Purchasing
21700 Barton Rd.
Cotton, CA 92324
Ed Segura, Purchasing
Tel: (909) 783-5000
Web: www.starterbros.com

SUN MICROSYSTEMS
Supplier Diversity
4150 Network Circle
Santa Clara, CA 95054
Tel: (650) 960-1300 Fax: (510) 315-6072
Email: supplier_diversity@sun.com
Web: www.sun.com

UNOCAL CORPORATION
Vendor Relations
6001 Bollinger Canyon Rd. #H3040
San Ramon, CA 94583
Janet Winter Smith,
Tel: (925) 790-3947
Web: www.unocal.com

WALT DISNEY
Corporate Headquarters
500 S. Buena Vista Dr.
Burbank, CA 91521
Sandra Picaro, Director, Supplier Diversity
Tel: (818) 560-1000
Web: www.disney.com

WELLS FARGO
Corporate Headquarters

420 Montgomery Rd.
San Francisco, CA 94104
Tel: (800) 333-0343 Fax: (415) 975-6260
Email: www.suppdive@wellsfargo.com
Web: www.wellsfargo.com

COLORADO

BALL
Corporate Headquarters
10 Longs Peak Dr.
Broomfield, CO 80021
Tel: (303) 469-3131
Web: www.ball.com

ECHOSTAR COMMUNICATIONS
Procurement
9601 S. Meridian Blvd.
Englewood, CO 80112
Julie Peters
Tel: (303) 723-1000
Web: www.echostar.com

FIRST DATA
Corporate Procurement
6200 S. Quebec St.
Greenwood Village, CO 80111
Tel: (303) 488-8000
Email: corporate.procurement@firstdata.com
Web: www.firstdata.com

LEVEL 3 COMMUNICATIONS
Corporate Headquarters
1025 Eldorado Blvd.
Broomfield, CO 80021
Tel: (720) 888-1000 Fax: (720) 888-8296
Web: www.level3.com

LIBERTY MEDIA
12300 Liberty Blvd.
Englewood, CO 80112
Tel: (720) 875-5400
Web: www.libertymedia.com

MDC HOLDINGS
Purchasing
3600 S. Yosemite St.
Denver, CO 80237
Rob Wagner, Manager, Purchasing
Tel: (303) 773-1100
Web: www.richmondamerican.com

MOLSON COORS BREWING
Corporate Headquarters
311 Tenth St.
Golden, CO 80401
Tel: (303) 279-6565
Web: www.molsoncoors.com

NEWMONT MINING
Vendor Relations
1700 Lincoln St.
Denver, CO 80203
Debbie Robinson, Facilities Manager
Tel: (303) 863-7414
Web: www.newmont.com

QWEST COMMUNICATIONS
Supplier Diversity
1801 California St.
Denver, CO 80202
Angela Norris, Supplier Diversity
Tel: (303) 707-5572 Fax: (303) 707-9155
Email: supplier@qwest.com
Web: www.quest.com

TRANSMONTAIGNE
Corporate Headquarters
1670 Broadway
Denver, CO 80202
Tel: (303) 626-8200 Fax: (303) 626-8228
Web: www.transmontaigne.com

CONNECTICUT

AETNA
Corporate Headquarters
151 Farmington Ave
Hartford, CT 06156
Luz Calderon, Assistant Head of Diversity
Tel: (860) 273-0123
Email: supplierdiversity@aetna.com
Web: www.aetna.com

EMCOR GROUP
Corporate Headquarters
301 Merritt 7 Corporate Pk.
Norwalk, CT 06851
Tel: (203) 849-7800
Web: www.emcorpgroup.com

GENERAL ELECTRIC
Corporate Headquarters
3135 Easton Turnpike
Fairfield, CT 06828
Tel: (203) 373-2211
Email: newsuppliers@ge.com
Web: www.ge.com

HARTFORD FINANCIAL SERVICES
Corporate Headquarters
690 Asylum Ave.
Hartford, CT 06115
Tel: (860) 547-5000
Web: www.thehartford.com

INTERNATIONAL PAPER
Coporate Headquarters
400 Atlantic St.
Stamford, CT 06921
Deborah Wilson, Supplier Diversity
Tel: (901) 419-9000
Web: www.ipaper.com

NORTHEAST UTILITIES
Purchasing
107 Selden St.
Berlin, CT 06037
Cheryl Clark, Supplier Diversity Manager
Tel: (860) 665-5000
Web: www.nu.com

PITNEY BOWES
Business Diversity
1 Elmcroft Rd.
Stamford, CT 06926
Kevin Beirne, Manager, Business Diversity
Development
Tel: (203) 356-6265
Web: www.pb.com

PRAXAIR TECHNOLOGY INC.
Corporate Headquarters
39 Old Ridgebury Rd.
Danbury, CT 06810
John P. Stevens, Vice President,
Procurement and Material Management
Tel: (203) 837-2000
Web: www.praxair.com

PREMCOR
Corporate Headquarters
1700 E. Putnam Ave.
Old Greenwich, CT 06870
Tel: (203) 698-7500 Fax: (203) 698-7925
Web: www.premcor.com

TEREX
Supplier Services
500 Post Rd. E.
Westport, CT 06880
Edward Lutz, Corporate Supplier
Commodity Manager
Tel: (203) 222-7170 Fax: (203) 227-1647
Email: supplier@terex.com
Web: www.terex.com

UNITED TECHNOLOGIES
Corporate Headquarters
1 Financial Plaza
Hartford, CT 06103
Casandra Charles-Gerst, Minority Small
Business
Tel: (860) 678-4554
Web: www.utc.com

W.R. BERKLEY
Purchasing
475 Steamboat Rd.
Greenwich, CT 06830
Ann Thompson, Manager, Purchasing
Tel: (203) 629-3000
Web: www.wrbc.com

XEROX
Corporate Headquarters
800 Long Ridge Rd.
Stamford, CT 06904
Wim Appelo, Vice President, Paper,
Supplies and Supply Chain Operations
Business Group Operations
Tel: (203) 968-3000
Web: www.xerox.com

DELAWARE

DUPONT
Corporate Headquarters
1007 Market St.
Wilmington, DE 19898
Willie C. Martin, Vice President, Global
Diversity
Tel: (302) 774-1000
Web: www.dupont.com

MBNA
Corporate Headquarters
1100 N. King St.
Wilmington, DE 19884
Linda Dealing, Manager, Purchasing
Fax: (302) 458-1171
Web: www.mbna.com

DISTRICT OF COLUMBIA

DANAHER
Corporate Headquarters
2099 Pennsylvannia Ave, N.W
Washington, DC 20006
Tel: (202) 828-0850
Web: www.danaher.com

PEPCO HOLDINGS
Supplier Diversity
701 Ninth St. N.W.
Washington, DC 20068
Gerry Harsha, Coordinator of Supplier
Diversity
Tel: 202-872-2141
Web: www.pepcoholdings.com

FLORIDA

AUTONATION
Corporate Headquarters
110 S.E. Sixth St.
Fort Lauderdale, FL 33301
Lorraine Varese, Manager, Procurement
Tel: (954) 769-7000
Web: www.autonation.com

CSX
Corporate Headquarters
500 Water St.
Jacksonville, FL 32202

Fran Chinnici, Vice President, Purchasing
and Material
Tel: (904) 359-3109
Web: www.csx.com

DARDEN RESTAURANTS
Supplier Diversity
5900 Lake Ellenor Dr.
Orlando, FL 32809
Norma Sica, Supplier Diversity
Tel: (407) 245-5930
Email: nsica@darden.com
Web: www.darden.com

FIDELITY NATIONAL FINANCIAL
601 Riverside Ave.
Jacksonville, FL 32204
Pete Pennella, Staffing Manager
Tel: (904) 854-8100 Fax: (904) 854-4282
Web: www.fnf.com

FPL GROUP
Corporate Headquarters
700 Universe Blvd
Juno Beach, FL 33408
Tel: (561) 691-7827
Web: www.fplgroup.com

HUGHES SUPPLY
Supplier Diversity
1 Hughes Way
Orlando, FL 32805
Tamara V. Hall, Coordinator, Supplier
Diversity
Tel: (407) 822-2219 Fax: (407) 426-9173
Email: tamara.hall@hughessupply.com
Web: www.hughessupply.com

ITT INDUSTRIES
Corporate Purchasing
2 Corporate Dr.
Palm Coast, Fl 32137
Donna J. Bucci, Senior Buyer
Tel: (386) 446-6161 Fax: (386) 445-4012
Email: donna.bucci@itt.com
Web: www.itt-tds.com

JABIL CIRCUIT
Supply Chain
10560 Dr. Martin Luther King Jr. St. N.
St. Petersburg, FL 33716
Courtney J. Ryan, Senior Vice President,
Global Supply Chain
Tel: (727) 577-9749
Web: www.jabil.com

LENNAR
Corporate Headquarters
700 N.W. 107th Ave.
Miami, FL 33172
Kirk Younans, Manager, Purchasing
Tel: (305) 559-4000
Web: www.lennar.com

OFFICE DEPOT
Corporate Headquarters
2200 Old Germantown Rd.
Delray Beach, FL 33445
John Skinner, Director, Internal
Procurement Services
Tel: (561) 438-4800
Email: supplierdiversity@officedepot.com
Web: www.officedepot.com

PUBLIX SUPER MARKETS
Corporate Headquarters
3300 Publix Corporate Pkwy
Lakeland, FL 33811
Dave Duncan, Vice President, Facilities
Tel: (863) 688-1188
Web: www.publix.com

RYDER SYSTEM
Supplier Diversity
3600 N.W. 82nd Ave
Miami, FL 33166
Tel: (305) 500-3726
Email: supplier_diversity_program@ryder.
com
Web: www.ryder.com

TECH DATA
Corporate Headquarters
5350 Tech Data Dr.
Clearwater, FL 33760
William K. Todd Jr, Senior Vice President of
Logistics and Integration
Tel: (727) 539-7429
Web: www.techdata.com

WINN-DIXIE STORES
Corporate Headquarters
5050 Edgewood Ct
Jacksonville, FL 32254
Dick Judd, Senior Vice President, Sales and
Procurement
Tel: (904) 370-6890
Web: www.winn-dixie.com

WORLD FUEL SERVICES
Vendor Relations
9800 N.W. 41st St.
Miami, FL 33178
Tel: (305) 428-8000
Web: www.wfscorp.com

GEORGIA

AFLAC
Corporate Headquarters
1932 Wynnton Rd.
Columbus, GA 31999
Kay Mason, Director, Materials
Management
Tel: (706) 323-3431
Web: www.aflac.com

AGCO
Corporate Headquarters
4205 River Green Pkwy
Duluth, GA 30096
Greg Turnerman,
Tel: (770) 813-9200
Web: www.agcocorp.com

BEAZER HOMES USA
Corporate Headquarters
1000 Abernathy Rd
Atlanta, GA 30328
Tel: (770) 829-3700
Web: www.beazer.com

BELLSOUTH
Corporate Headquarters
1155 Peachtree St. NE
Atlanta, GA 30309
Valencia I. Adams, Vice President, Chief
Diversity Officer
Tel: (404) 249-2000
Email: supplier.qual@bellsouth.com
Web: www.bellsouth.com

COCA-COLA
Corporate Headquarters
1 Coca-Cola Plaza
Atlanta, GA 30313
Johnny B. Booker, Director, Supplier
Diversity
Tel: (404) 676-2121
Web: www.coca-cola.com

COCA-COLA ENTERPRISES
Corporate Headquarters
2500 Windy Ridge Pkwy.

Atlanta, GA 30339
Edward L. Sutter, Vice President
Tel: (770) 989-3000
Web: www.cokecce.com

COX COMMUNICATIONS
Purchasing
1400 Lake Hearn Dr.
Atlanta, GA 30319
Beverly Keith, Purchasing Coordinator
Tel: (404) 843-5000 Fax: (404) 269-1133
Web: www.cox.com

DELTA AIR LINES
Corporate Headquarters
1030 Delta Blvd
Atlanta, GA 30320
Lee Macenczak, Senior Vice President and
Chief Customer Service Officer
Tel: (404) 715-2600 Fax: (404) 677-1257
Email: supplier.diveresity@delta.com
Web: www.delta.com

GENUINE PARTS
Corporate Headquarters
2999 Circle 75 Pkwy.
Atlanta, GA 30339
Bob Thomley, Vice President, Wholesale
Management
Tel: (770) 953-1700
Web: www.genpt.com

GEORGIA-PACIFIC
Corporate Headquarters
133 Peachtree St. N.E.
Atlanta, GA 30303
Lissa J. Owens, Manager, Supplier Diversity
Tel: (404) 652-4000
Web: www.gp.com

HOME DEPOT
Corporate Headquarters
2455 Paces Ferry Rd., N.W.
Atlanta, GA 30339
John Costelo, Executive Vice President,
Marketing and Merchandising
Tel: (770) 433-8211
Web: www.homedepot.com

MIRANT
Procurement
1155 Perimeter Center W.
Atlanta, GA 30338
Tel: (678) 579-5000
Email: procurement@mirant.com
Web: www.mirant.com

MOHAWK INDUSTRIES
Purchasing
160 S. Industrial Blvd
Calhoun, GA 30701
Connie Layson, Manager, Purchasing
Tel: (800) 241-4072
Web: www.mohawkind.com

NEWELL RUBBERMAID
Purchasing
10 B GlenlakePkwy, #600
Atlanta, GA 30328
Paul Box, Vice President, Corporate
Purchasing
Tel: (770) 407-3800
Web: www.newellrubbermaid.com

SOUTHERN
Supplier Diversity
270 Peachtree St. N.W.
Atlanta, GA 30303
Tel: (404) 506-5000
Email: supplierdiversity@powersource.com
Web: www.southernco.com

SUNTRUST BANKS
Supplier Diversity

303 Peachtree St. N.E.
Atlanta, GA 30308
Tel: (404) 588-7711
Email: supplier.diversity@suntrust.com
Web: www.suntrust.com

UNITED PARCEL SERVICE
Corporate Headquarters
55 Glenlake Pkwy, N.E
Atlanta, GA 30328
Bob Stoffel, Senior Vice President, Supply
Chain Group
Tel: (404) 828-6000
Web: www.ups.com

IDAHO

ALBERTSON'S
Corporate Headquarters
250 Parkcenter Blvd.
Boise, ID 83642
Ana Marie Rodriguez, Supplier Diversity
Tel: (208) 914-3445
Web: www.albertsons.com

MICRON TECHNOLOGY
Corporate Headquarters
8000 S. Federal Way
Boise, ID 83716
Tel: (208) 368-4000
Web: www.micron.com

ILLINOIS

ABBOTT LABORATORIES
Corporate Headquarters
100 Abbott Park Rd.
Abbott Park, IL 60064
John Landgraf, Senior Vice President,
Pharmaceutical Supply
Tel: (847) 937-6100
Web: www.abbott.com

ALLSTATE
Corporate Headquarters
2775 Sanders Rd.
Northbrook, IL 60062
Erika Hatwig, Executive Assistant to the Vice
President
Tel: (847) 402-5600
Web: www.allstate.com

AON
Supplier Diversity
200 E. Randolph St.
Chicago, IL 60601
Jay Skiar, Director, Supplier Diversity
Tel: (312) 381-1000
Web: www.aon.com

ARCHER DANIELS MIDLAND
Corporate Headquarters
4666 Faries Pkwy
Decatur, IL 62525
John Taylor, Director, Corporate Supplier
Diversity
Tel: (800) 637-5843 Fax: (217) 451-4383
Email: supplier_diversity@admworld.com
Web: www.admworld.com

BAXTER INTERNATIONAL
Corporate Headquarters
1 Baxter Pkwy
Deerfield, IL 60015
Tel: (847) 948-2000
Web: www.baxter.com

BOEING
Corporate Headquarters
100 N. Riverside Park
Chicago, IL 60606

Walter Skowronski, Senior Vice President,
Boeing Capital Corporation
Tel: (312) 544-2000
Web: www.boeing.com

BRUNSWICK
Purchasing
1 N. Field Court
Lake Forest, IL 60045
Anna Baker, Manager, Purchasing
Tel: (847) 735-4700
Web: www.brunswick.com

CATERPILLAR
Corporate Headquarters
100 N.E. Adams St
Peoria, IL 61629
Mary H. Bell, Vice President, Logistics
Services and Supply Chain
Tel: (309) 675-1000
Web: www.cat.com

CDW
Purchasing
200 N. Milwaukee Ave.
Vernon Hills, IL 60061
Matthew A. Troka, Vice President,
Purchasing
Tel: (847) 465-6000
Web: www.cdw.com

EXELON
Corporate Headquarters
10 S. Dearborn St.
Chicago, IL 60680
Craig Adams, Chief Supply Officer
Tel: (312) 394-7398
Web: www.exeloncorp.com

FORTUNE BRANDS
Purchasing
300 Tower Pkwy
Lincolnshire, IL 60069
Christine Feltner, Manager, Purchasing
Tel: (847) 484-4400
Web: www.fortunebrands.com

ILLINOIS TOOL WORKS
Corporate Headquarters
3600 W. Lake Ave.
Glenview, IL 60026
Gary Anton, Vice President, Strategic
Sourcing
Tel: (847) 724-7500
Web: www.itw.com

JOHN DEERE
Corporate Headquarters
1 John Deere Pl.
Moline, IL 61265
William Norton, Senior Vice President,
Worldwide Supply Management
Tel: (309) 765-8000
Web: www.deere.com

LAIDLAW INTERNATIONAL
Corporate Headquarters
55 Shuman Blvd.
Naperville, IL 60563
Tel: (630) 848-3000
Web: www.laidlaw.com

MCDONALD'S
Corporate Headquarters
1 McDonald's Plaza
Oak Brook, IL 60523
Marcella Allen, Director, Supplier Diversity
Tel: (630) 623-3000
Web: www.mcdonalds.com

MOTOROLA
Corporate Headquarters
1303 E. Algonquin Rd.
Schaumburg, IL 60196

Theresa Metty, Senior VP and Chief
Procurement Officer
Tel: (847) 576-5000
Web: www.motorola.com

NAVISTAR INTERNATIONAL
Supplier Diversity
4201 Winfield Rd.
Warrenville, IL 60555
Tel: (630) 753-5000
Email: supplierdiversity@nav-international.
com
Web: www.navistar.com

OFFICEMAX
Corporate Headquarters
150 Pierce Rd.
Itasca, IL 60143
Reuben Slone, Executive Supply Chain
Tel: (630) 438-7800
Web: www.officemax.com

R.R. DONNELLEY & SONS
Supply Chain Management
3075 Highland Parkway
Downers Grove, IL 60515
Eva Chess, Supplier Diversity
Tel: 630-322-6335
Web: www.rrdonnelley.com

SARA LEE
Corporate Headquarters
3 First National Plaza
Chicago, IL 60602
Gary Berryman, Manager, Procurement
and Supply
Tel: (312) 726-2600
Web: www.saralee.com

SEARS ROEBUCK
Corporate Headquarters
3333 Beverly Rd.
Hoffman Estates, IL 60179
Carol Neltan, Supplier Diversity Director
Tel: (847) 286-2500
Web: www.sears.com

SERVICEMASTER
Corporate Headquarters
3250 Lacey Rd.
Downers Grove, IL 60515
Tel: (630) 663-2000
Web: www.svm.com

SMURFIT-STONE CONTAINER
Vendor Relations
150 N. Michigan Ave.
Chicago, IL 60601
Mark A. Polivka, Vice President,
Procurement
Tel: (312) 346-6600
Email: supplierzone@smurfit.com
Web: www.smurfit-stone.com

STATE FARM INSURANCE COS
Corporate Headquarters
1 State Farm Plz.
Bloomington, IL 61710
Leonard Bell, Manager, Supplier Diversity
Tel: (309) 766-2342
Web: www.statefarm.com

TELEPHONE & DATA SYS.
New Vendor Relations
30 N. LaSalle St.
Chicago, IL 60602
Meredith Roane, Legal Assistant, New
Vendor Relations
Tel: (312) 630-1990
Web: www.teldta.com

TENNECO AUTOMOTIVE
Supply Chain
500 N. Field Dr.

Lake Forest, IL 60045
Paul Schultz, Senior Vice President, Global Supply Chain Management
Tel: (847) 482-5000
Web: www.tenneco-automotive.com

TRIBUNE
Purchasing
435 N. Michigan Ave.
Chicago, IL 60611
Andy Magaley, Purchasing Manager
Tel: (312) 222-9100
Web: www.tribune.com

UNITED AIRLINE INC.
Corporate Headquarters
1200 E. Algonquin Rd.
ElkGrove Township, IL 60007
Sandra Rand, Director Supplier Diversity
Tel: (847) 700-5121 Fax: (847) 700-5861
Email: sandra.rand@united.com
Web: www.united.com

UNITED STATIONERS
Purchasing
2200 E. Golf Rd.
Des Plaines, IL 60016
Doug Nash, Vice President, Purchasing
Tel: (847) 699-5000
Web: www.unitedstationers.com

USG
Purchasing
125 S. Franklin St.
Chicago, IL 60606
Michelle Shaw, Purchasing
Tel: (312) 606-4000
Web: www.usg.com

W.W. GRAINGER
Supplier Diversity
100 Grainger Pkwy
Lake Forest, IL 60045
Nancy Conner, Manager, Supplier Diversity
Tel: (847) 535-4471
Email: diversity.s@grainger.com
Web: www.grainger.com

WALGREENS
Corporate Headquarters
200 Wilmot Rd.
Deerfield, IL 60015
Roger Anderson, Director, Diversity Services
Tel: (847) 914-5165
Web: www.walgreens.com

WM. WRIGLEY JR.
Procurement
410 N. Michigan Ave.
Chicago, IL 60611
Patrick D. Mitchell, Vice President, Procurement
Tel: (312) 644-1212
Web: www.wrigley.com

INDIANA

CONSECO
Corporate Headquarters
11825 N. Pennsylvania St.
Carmel, IN 46032
Tel: (317) 817-6100
Web: www.conseco.com

CUMMINS
Vendor Relations
500 Jackson St. M/C 6004
Columbus, IN 47201
Becky Speaker, Procurement Director
Tel: 812-377-5315

ELI LILLY
Corporate Headquarters
Lilly Corporate Center
Indianapolis, IN 46285
Steven R. Plump, Vice President, Global Marketing and Sales
Tel: (317) 276-2000
Web: www.lilly.com

GUIDANT
Purchasing
111 Monument Circle
Indianapolis, IN 46204
Alice Gomez, Manager, Purchasing
Tel: (317) 971-2000
Web: www.guidant.com

NISOURCE
Supplier Diversity
801 E. 86th Ave.
Merrillville, IN 46410
Mike Law, Supplier Diversity
Tel: (219) 647-6200
Web: www.nisource.com

WELLPOINT
Supplier Diversity
120 Monument Circle
Indianapolis, IN 46204
Tel: (317) 488-6000
Email: supplierdiveresity@wellpoint.com
Web: www.wellpoint.com

IOWA

MAYTAG
Corporate Headquarters
403 W. Fourth St. N.
Newton, IA 50208
Tel: (641) 792-7000
Web: www.maytagcorp.com

PRINCIPAL FINANCIAL
Supplier Diversity
711 High St.
Des Moines, IA 50392
Lisa Sandos, Supplier Diversity
Tel: (515) 247-5111 Fax: (515) 248-4171
Web: www.principal.com

KANSAS

HUMANA
Supplier Diversity
500 W. Main St.
Louisville, KS 40202
Sandra Harper, Manager, Supplier Diversity
Tel: (502) 580-1000
Web: www.humana.com

SPRINT
Corporate Headquarters
6200 Sprint Pkwy
Overland Park, KS 66251
David P. Thomas, Vice President and Chief Divesity Office
Tel: (800) 829-0965
Email: supplier.diversity@mail.sprint.com
Web: www.sprint.com

YELLOW ROADWAY
Supplier Diversity
10990 Roe Ave
Overland Park, KS 66211
Tel: (913) 696-6100
Email: supplier.diversity@yellowcorp.com
Web: www.yellowroadway.com

KENTUCKY

ASHLAND
Supplier Diversity
50 E. RiverCenter Blvd.
Covington, KY 41012
Mary Miller, Supplier Diversity
Tel: (859) 815-3333
Email: mmiller@ashland.com
Web: www.ashland.com

KINDRED HEALTHCARE
Purchasing
680 S. Fourth St.
Louisville, KY 40202
John Cowgill, Vice President, Facilities Management
Tel: (502) 596-7300
Web: www.kindredhealthcare.com

LEXMARK INTERNATIONAL
Corporate Headquarters
740 W. New Circle Rd.
Lexington, KY 40550
Tel: (859) 232-2000
Web: www.lexmark.com

OMNICARE
Purchasing
100 E. RiverCenter Blvd
Covington, KY 41011
Daniel J. Maloney, R.Ph, Vice President, Purchasing
Tel: (859) 392-3300
Web: www.omnicare.com

YUM BRANDS
Corporate Headquarters
1441 Gardiner Ln.
Louisville, KY 40213
Tel: (502) 874-2885 Fax: (502) 874-8662
Web: www.yum.com

LOUISIANA

ENTERGY
Corporate Headquarters
639 Loyola Ave.
New Orleans, LA 70113
Walter Rhodes, Vice President, Chief Procurement
Tel: (504) 576-4000
Web: www.entergy.com

MARYLAND

BLACK & DECKER
Vendor Relations
701 E. Joppa Rd.
Towson, MD 21286
Tel: (410) 716-3900
Web: www.bdk.com

CONSTELLATION ENERGY
Corporate Headquarters
750 E. Pratt St.
Baltimore, MD 21202
Thomas F. Brady, Executive Vice President, Corporate Strategy and Retail Competitive Supply
Tel: (410) 783-2800
Web: www.constellation.com

COVENTRY HEALTH CARE
Purchasing
6705 Rockledge Dr.
Bethesda, MD 20817
Amy Nees, Manager, Purchasing
Tel: (301) 581-0600 Fax: (301) 493-0751

Web: www.cvty.com

HOST MARRIOTT
Purchasing
6903 Rockledge Rd.
Bethesda, MD 20817
Michelle Montano, Manager
Tel: (240) 744-1000
Web: www.hostmarriott.com

LOCKHEED MARTIN
Corporate Headquarters
6801 Rockledge Dr.
Bethesda, MD 20817
Meghan Mariman, Supplier Diversity
Tel: (301) 897-6195
Email: meghan.mariman@lmco.com
Web: www.lockheedmartin.com

MARRIOTT INTERNATIONAL
Corporate Headquarters
10400 Fernwwod Rd.
Bethesda, MD 20817
Tel: (877) 276-0249 Fax: (301) 380-1550
Web: www.marriott.com

MASSACHUSETTS

BJ'S WHOLESALE CLUB
Vendor Relations
1 Mercer Rd.
Natick, MA 01760
Tel: (508) 651-7400
Web: www.bjs.com

BOSTON SCIENTIFIC
Purchasing
1 Boston Scientific Pl.
Natick, MA 01760
Karen Winestin, Purchasing
Tel: (508) 650-8000
Web: www.bostonscientific.com

EMC
Supplier Diversity
176 South St.
Hopkinton, MA 01748
Aida Sabo, Senior Operations Manager
Tel: (508) 435-1000
Email: supplierdiversity@emc.com
Web: www.emc.com

LIBERTY MUTUAL INS. GROUP
Corporate Headquarters
175 Berkeley St.
Boston, MA 02116
Contract Manager
Tel: (617) 654-3950 Fax: (617) 574-5618
Email: supplier_contact@libertymutual.com
Web: www.libertymutual.com

MASSMUTUAL FINANCIAL GROUP
Corporate Headquarters
1295 State St.
Springfield, MA 01111
Tel: (413) 788-8411
Email: mmtechnology@massmutual.com
Web: www.massmutual.com

RAYTHEON
Corporate Headquarters
870 Winter St.
Waltham, MA 02451
Jim Schuster, Executive Director Diversity
Tel: (781) 522-3000
Web: www.raytheon.com

REEBOK INTERNATIONAL
Purchasing
1891 J.W. Foster Blvd
Canton, MA 02021
Bill Bailey, Director, Purchasing

Tel: (781) 401-5000
Web: www.reebok.com

STAPLES
Corporate Headquarters
500 Staples Dr.
Framingham, MA 01702
Dorren Nichols, Director, Associate
Relations and Diversity
Tel: (508) 253-5000
Web: www.staples.com

STATE STREET CORPORATION
Purchasing
1 Lincoln St.
Boston, MA 02111
Tel: (617) 786-3000
Web: www.statestreet.com

THE GILLETTE COMPANY
Corporate Headquarters
Prudential Tower Bldg.
Boston, MA 02199
Jaime Van Celev-Troiano, Manager,
Strategic Sourcing/Supplier Diversity
Tel: (617) 421-8282 Fax: (617) 421-8002
Email: jamie_van_cleve@gillette.com
Web: www.gillette.com

THE TJX COMPANIES, INC.
Corporate Headquarters
770 Cochituate Rd.
Framingham, MA 01701
Ruth Johnson, Manager, Supplier Diversity
Tel: (508) 390-3043
Email: supplier_diversity@tjx.com
Web: www.tjx.com

MICHIGAN

ARVINMERITOR
Corporate Headquarters
2135 W. Maple Rd.
Troy, MI 48084
Tel: (248) 435-1000 Fax: (248) 435-1393
Web: www.arvinmeritor.com

AUTO-OWNERS INSURANCE
Procurement
6101 Anacapri Blvd
Lansing, MI 48917
Michael Storay, Manager
Tel: (517) 323-1200
Web: www.auto-owners.com

BORDERS GROUP
Corporate Headquarters
100 Phoenix Dr.
Ann Arbor, MI 48108
Tel: (734) 477-1100 Fax: (734) 477-1616
Web: www.bordersgroupinc.com

CMS ENERGY
Vendor Relations
1 Energy Plaza
Jackson, MI 49201
Eric Beda, New Vendor Relations
Tel: (517) 788-0550
Web: www.cmsenergy.com

COLLINS & AIKMAN
Corporate Headquarters
250 Stephenson Hwy
Troy, MI 48083
Tel: (248) 824-2500
Web: www.collinsaiken.com

DELPHI
Corporate Headquarters
5725 Delphi Dr.
Troy, MI 48098

R. David Nelson, Vice President Global
Supply Management
Tel: (248) 813-2000
Web: www.delphi.com

DOW CHEMICAL
Corporate Headquarters
2030 Dow Center
Midland, MI 48674
Tel: (989) 636-1000
Web: www.dow.com

DTE ENERGY
Diversity Management
2000 Second Ave.
Detroit, MI 48226
Nikki Moss
Tel: (313) 235-9363
Web: www.dteenergy.com

FEDERAL-MOGUL
Diversity
26555 Northwestern Hwy.
Southfield, MI 48034
Pam Mitchell, Director, Diversity
Web: www.federal-mogul.com

FORD MOTOR
Corporate Office
1 American Rd.,
Dearborn, MI 48126
Ray M. Jensen, Director, Supplier Diversity
Tel: (313) 390-3879 Fax: (313) 845-4713
Email: rjensen@ford.com
Web: www.ford.com

GENERAL MOTORS
Corporate Headquarters
300 Renaissance Center
Detroit, MI 48265
Bo I. Anderson, Vice President, Global
Purchasing and Supply Chain
Tel: (313) 556-5000 Fax: (517) 272-3709
Web: www.gm.com

KELLOGG
Supplier Diversity
1 Kellogg Square
Battle Creek, MI 49016
Cathy Kutch, Director, Supplier Diversity
Tel: (269) 961-2000 Fax: (269) 961-3687
Email: supplier.diversity@kellogg.com
Web: www.kelloggcompany.com

KELLY SERVICES
Supplier Diversity
999 W. Big Beaver Rd.
Troy, MI 48084
Amy Grudman, Supplier Diversity
Tel: (248) 244-5630
Web: www.kellyservices.com

KMART HOLDING
Corporate Headquarters
3100 W. Big Beaver Rd.
Troy, MI 48084
Tel: (248) 463-1000
Web: www.searsholdings.com

LEAR
Corporate Headquarters
21557 Telegraph Rd.
Southfield, MI 48034
Chuck White, Director, Supplier Diversity
Program
Tel: (248) 447-5137 Fax: (248) 447-5944
Web: www.lear.com

MASCO
Corporate Headquarters
21001 Van Born Rd.
Taylor, MI 48180
Tel: (313) 274-7400

Web: www.masco.com

PULTE HOMES
Corporate Headquarters
100 Bloomfield Hill Pkwy
Bloomfield, MI 48304
Tel: (248) 647-2750
Web: www.pulte.com

STRYKER
Purchasing
2725 Fairfield Rd.
Kalamazoo, MI 49002
Caroline Ridderman, Director, Purchasing
Tel: (269) 323-7700
Web: www.stryker.com

TRW AUTOMOTIVE HOLDINGS
Corporate Heaquarters
12025 Tech Center Dr.
Livonia, MI 48150
Renita Donladson, Cost Planning Manager
N.A. Procurement
Tel: (734) 855-2600
Email: MBE.diversity@trw.com
Web: www.trwauto.com

UNITED AUTO GROUP
Purchasing
2555 Telegraph Rd.
Bloomfield Hills, MI 48302
Jeff Edward, Vice President, Purchasing
Tel: (248) 648-2500
Web: www.unitedauto.com

VISTEON
Corporate Headquarters
1 Village Center Dr.
Van Buren Township, MI 48111
Henry Martin Jr., Associate Director,
Supplier Diversity Development
Tel: (800) 847-8366
Web: www.visteon.com

WHIRLPOOL
Corporate Headquarters
2000 North M-63
Benton Harbor, MI 49022
Tel: (269) 923-5000
Web: www.whirlpoolcorp.com

MINNESOTA

3M
Corporate Headquarters
3M Center
St. Paul, MN 55144
Tel: (888) 364-3577
Web: www.3m.com

BEST BUY
Corporate Headquarters
7601 Penn Ave., S.
Richfield, MN 55423
Susan Busch, Director, Corporate Public
Relations
Tel: (621) 291-1000
Web: www.bestbuy.com

C.H. ROBINSON WORLDWIDE
Purchasing
8100 Mitchell Rd.
Eden Prairie, MN 55344
Patrick Trombley, Manager, Purchasing
Tel: (952) 937-8500
Web: www.chrobinson.com

CHS INC.
Corporate Headquarters
5500 Cenex Cr.
Inver Grove Hghts., MN 55077
Tel: (651) 355-6000
Web: www.chsinc.com

ECOLAB
Supplier Diversity
370 Wabasha St. N.
St. Paul, MN 55102
Mitzy Lutz, Manager, Supplier Diversity
Tel: (651) 293-2233

GENERAL MILLS
Corporate Headquarters
1 General Mills Blvd
Minneapolis, MN 55426
Jana Goldenman, Supplier Diversity
Tel: (763) 764-7600
Web: www.generalmills.com

HORMEL FOODS
Purchasing
1 Hormel Place
Austin, MN 55912
Bradley Lindberg, Corporate Purchasing
Buyer
Tel: (507) 437-5611
Web: www.hormel.com

LAND O'LAKES
Purchasing
P.O. Box 64101
St. Paul, MN 55164
Tel: (651) 481-2222
Web: www.landolakesinc.com

MEDTRONIC
Supplier Diversity
710 Medtronic Pkwy.
Minneapolis, MN 55423
Gretchen Ebert, Manager, Supplier Diversity
Tel: (763) 514-4000
Email: gretchen.ebert@medtronic.com
Web: www.medtronic.com

NASH FINCH
Corporate Headquarters
7600 France Ave S.
Minneapolis, MN 55432
Tel: (952) 832-0534
Web: www.nashfinch.com

NORTHWEST AIRLINES
Corporate Headquarters
2700 Lone Oak Pkwy,
Eagan, MN 55121
Tel: (612) 726-2111
Email: general.purchasing@nwa.com
Web: www.nwa.com

ST. PAUL TRAVELERS COS.
Corporate Headquarters
385 Washington St.
St. Paul, MN 55102
Larry Gill, Personal Analyst, Supplier
Diversity
Tel: (860) 277-3220
Web: www.stpaultravelers.com

SUPERVALU
Corporate Headquarters
11840 Valley View Rd.
Eden Prairie, MN 55344
James Oesinger, Manager, Marketing
Tel: (717) 232-6821 X4006
Web: www.supervalu.com

TARGET
Corporate Headquarters
1000 Nicollet Mall
Minneapolis, MN 55403
Patricia Adams, Senior Vice President,
Merchandising
Tel: (612) 761-6500
Web: www.target.com

THRIVENT FINANCIAL FOR LUTHERANS
Corporate Headquarters
625 Fourth Ave S.
Minneapolis, MN 55415-1624

Tel: (800) 847-4836
Email: mail@thrivent.com
Web: www.thrivent.com

U.S. BANCORP
Supplier Diversity
800 Nicolett Mall
Minneapolis, MN 55402
Mary Andersen, Manager, Supplier Diversity
Tel: (651) 466-3000 Fax: (515) 245-6363
Web: www.usbank.com

UNITED HEALTH GROUP
Corporate Headquarters
9900 Bren Rd. E.
Minnetonla, MN 55343
Tel: (952) 936-1300
Web: www.unitedhealthgroup.com

XCEL ENERGY
Supplier Diversity
414 Nicollet Mall
Minneapolis, MN 55402
Ramona Wilson, Manager of Supplier
Diversity
Tel: (612) 330-5500

MISSOURI

AMEREN
Minority Business Development
1901 Chouteua Ave.
St. Louis, MO 63103
Bran Montgomery, Minority Business
Development Specialist
Tel: (314) 554-2709
Web: www.ameren.com

ANHEUSER-BUSCH
Corporate Headquarters
1 Busche Pl.
St. Louis, MO 63118
Arturo Corral, Director, Supplier Diversity
Tel: (314) 577-2000
Web: www.anheuser-busch.com

CHARTER COMMUNICATIONS
Purchasing
12405 Powerscourt Dr.
St. Louis, MO 63131
Dave Demming, Director, Purchasing
Tel: (314) 965-0555
Web: www.charter.com

EMERSON ELECTRIC
Corporate Headquarters
8000 W. Florissant Ave.
St. Louis, MO 63136
Larry Kremer, Vice President, Procurement
Tel: (314) 553-2000
Web: www.gotoemerson.com

EXPRESS SCRIPTS
Corporate Headquarters
13900 Riverport Rd.
Maryland Heights, MO 63043
Deborah Heck, Director Procurement
Tel: (314) 770-1666
Web: www.express-scripts.com

GRAYBAR ELECTRIC
Purchasing
34 N. Meramec Ave.
St. Louis, MO 63105
Mike Pooansky, Director, Purchasing
Tel: (314) 573-9200
Web: www.graybar.com

H&R BLOCK
Corporate Headquarters
4400 Main St.
Kansas City, MO 64111

Tel: (816) 753-6900
Web: www.hrblock.com

LEGGETT & PLATT
Purchasing
1 Leggett Rd.
Carthage, MO 64836
Kiley Williams, Contract Administration
Manager
Tel: (417) 358-8131
Web: www.leggett.com

MAY DEPT. STORES
Corporate Headquarters
611 Olive St.
St. Louis, MO 63101
Judy Schultz, Director, Purchasing
Tel: (314) 554-7100
Web: www.mayco.com

MONSANTO
Diversity
800 N. Lindergh Blvd
St. Louis, MO 63167
Deborah Brick, Supplier Diversity
Tel: (314) 694-1000 Fax: (314) 694-4696
Email: monsanto.diversity@monsanto.com
Web: www.monsanto.com

PEABODY ENERGY
Purchasing
701 Market St.
St. Louis, MO 63101
Jennie Horton, Director, Purchasing
Tel: (314) 342-3400
Web: www.peabodyenergy.com

NEBRASKA

BERKSHIRE HATHAWAY
Corporate Headquarters
1440 Kiewit Plz.
Omaha, NE 68131
Tel: (402) 346-1400
Web: www.berkshirehathaway.com

CONAGRA FOODS
Corporate Headquarters
1 ConAgra Dr.
Omaha, NE 68102
Pam Reynolds, Manager, Supplier Diversity
Program
Tel: (402) 595-4000 Fax: (402) 595-5304
Email: mwbe@conagrafoods.com
Web: www.conagrafoods.com

MUTUAL OF OMAHA INSURANCE
Procurement
Mutual of Omaha Plaza
Omaha, NE 38175
Gloria Raven, Manager, Procurement
Tel: (402) 342-7600
Web: www.mutualofomaha.com

UNION PACIFIC
Supplier Diversity
1400 Douglas St.
Omaha, NE 68179
Robert B. Morgan, Director, Supplier
Diversity
Tel: (402) 271-3091
Web: www.up.com

NEVADA

CAESARS ENTERTAINMENT
Supplier Diversity
3930 Howard Hughes Pkwy
Las Vegas, NV 89109

Diane Michel, Supplier Diversity
Tel: (702) 699-5000
Web: www.caesars.com

HARRAH'S ENTERTAINMENT
Supplier Diversity
1 Harrah's Court
Las Vegas, NV 89119
Diane Michel, Supplier Diversity
Tel: (702) 407-6000 Fax: (706) 407-6079
Email: sshelpdesk@harrahs.com
Web: www.harrah's.com

MGM MIRAGE
Supplier Diversity
3600 las Vegas Blvd S.
Las Vegas, NV 89109
Tel: (702) 693-7120 Fax: (702) 891-1606
Email: supplierdiversity@mgmmirage.com
Web: www.mgmmirage.com

NEW HAMPSHIRE

FISHER SCIENTIFIC INTL.
New Business Services
1 Liberty Lane
Hampton, NH 03842
Dan Defelice, Manager, New Business
Services
Tel: (412) 490-8300
Web: www.fisherscientific.com

NEW JERSEY

AMERICAN STANDARD
Corporate Headquarters
1 Centennial Ave.
Piscataway, NJ 08855
Tel: (732) 980-6000
Web: www.americanstandard.com

AT&T
Corporate Headquarters
1 AT&T
Bedminster, NJ 07921
Fred Lona, Manager, Supplier Diversity
Tel: (212) 944-2430
Email: flona@att.com
Web: www.att.com

AUTOMATIC DATA PROC.
Corporate Headquarters
1 ADP Blvd
Roseland, NJ 07068
Kathy Carpini, Corporate Purchasing
Tel: (973) 974-5000
Web: www.adp.com

AVAYA
Purchasing
211 Mount Airy Rd.
Basking Ridge, NJ 07920
Patricia R. Hume, Global Vice President,
Small and Medium Business Solutions
Tel: (908) 953-6000
Web: www.avaya.com

BANK OF NEW YORK CO.
Procurement
925 Patterson Plank Rd.
Secaucus, NJ 07094
Thomas Raffa, VP for Procurement
Tel: (201) 325-7730
Web: www.bankofny.com

BECTON DICKINSON
Purchasing
1 Becton Dr.
Franklin Lakes, NJ 07417
Michael Pichano, Purchasing

Tel: (201) 847-6800
Web: www.bd.com

BED BATH & BEYOND
Purchasing
650 Liberty Ave
Union, NJ 07083
Teresa Miller, Vice President, Purchasing
Tel: (908) 688-0888
Web: www.bedbathandbeyond.com

CAMPBELL SOUP
Supplier Diversity
1 Campbell Place
Camden, NJ 08103
Harry Perales, Senior Procurement
Manager
Tel: (856) 342-4800 Fax: (856) 342-3759
Email: Harry_perales@campbellsoup.com
Web: www.campbellsoupcompany.com

CHUBB
Corporate Headquarters
15 Mountain View Rd.
Warren, NJ 07061
Kathleen P. Marvel, Chief Diversity Officer
Tel: (908) 903-2000
Web: www.chubb.com

CIT GROUP
Vendor Relations
1 CIT Dr.
Livingston, NJ 07039
Tel: (973) 740-5000
Email: citcorporategiving@cit.org
Web: www.cit.com

ENGLEHARD
Corporate Headquarters
101 Wood Ave
Iselin, NJ 08830
Tel: (732) 205-5000
Web: www.englehard.com

HONEYWELL INTL.
Corporate Headquarters
101 Columbia Rd.
Morristown, NJ 07962
Mike Glass, Liaison Officer, SSEC Small
Buiness
Tel: (973) 455-2000 Fax: (973) 455-4807
Web: www.honeywell.com

HOVNANIAN ENTERPRISES
Purchasing
10 Highway 35
Red Bank, NJ 07701
Lou Molinaro, Director, Purchasing
Tel: (732) 225-4001
Web: www.khov.com

JOHNSON & JOHNSON
Corporate Headquarters
1 Johnson & Johnson Plz.
New Brunswick, NJ 08933
Tel: (732) 524-0400
Email: purchasing@corus.jnj.com
Web: www.jnj.com

LUCENT TECHNOLOGIES
Diversity Business
600 Mountain Ave.
Murray Hill, NJ 07974
Jorge Valdes, Executive Director, Diversity
Business Management
Tel: (908) 582-8500
Web: www.lucent.com

MEDCO HEALTH SOLUTIONS
Corporate Headquarters
100 Parsons Pond Dr.
Franklin Lakes, NJ 07417
Tel: (201) 269-3400
Web: www.medco.com

MERCK
Supplier Diversity
1 Merck Rd.
Whitehouse Station, NJ 08889
Silvana Demers, Procurement
Tel: (908) 423-4107
Email: supplier_diversity@merck.com

PATHMARK STORES
Corporate Headquarters
200 Milk St.
Carteret, NJ 07008
Tel: (732) 499-3000
Web: www.pathmark.com

PRUDENTIAL FINANCIAL
Corporate Headquarters
751 Broad st.
Newark, NJ 07102
Beth Canning, Manager, Supplier Diversity
Tel: (973) 367-7125 Fax: (973) 367-7138
Email: beth.canning@prudential.com
Web: www.prudential.com

PUBLIC SERVICE ENTERPRISE GROUP
Corporate Headquarters
80 Park Plaza
Newark, NJ 07102
Diane Stenburg, Supplier Diversity
Tel: (973) 430-5839
Web: www.pseg.com

QUEST DIAGNOSTICS
Supplier Diversity
1290 Wall St. W.
Lyndhurst, NJ 07071
Gladys Daniel, Director, Supplier Diversity
Tel: (610) 454-4158
Web: www.questdiagnostics.com

SCHERING-PLOUGH
Corporate Headquarters
2000 Galloping Hill Rd.
Kenilworth, NJ 07033
Tel: (908) 298-4000
Web: www.Schering-Plough.com

SEALED AIR
Corporate Headquarters
Park 80 E.
Saddle Brook, NJ 07663
Tel: (201) 791-7600
Web: www.sealedair.com

TOYS `R` US
Corporate Headquarters
1 Geoffrey Way
Wayne, NJ 07470
Amanda Allen, Procurement
Tel: (973) 617-3500
Web: www.toyrusinc.com

WYETH
Corporate Headquarters
5 Giralda Farms
Madison, NJ 07940
Greg Bobyock, Vice President, Global New Products
Tel: (973) 660-5000
Web: www.wyeth.com

NEW YORK

ALTRIA GROUP
Corporate Headquarters
120 Park Ave.
New York, NY 10017
Corey Smith, ALCS Procurement
Tel: (917) 663-2358 Fax: (917) 663-5317
Web: www.altria.com

AMERADA HESS
Corporate Headquarters
1185 Sixth Ave.
New York, NY 10036
John Garbarino, Director, Procurement
Tel: (212) 997-8500
Web: www.hess.com

AMERICAN EXPRESS
Corporate Headquarters
200 Vesey St.
New York, NY 10285
Jeff Kaiser, Director, Procurement
Tel: (212) 640-2390
Web: www.americanexpress.com

AMERICAN INTL. GROUP
Corporate Headquarters
70 Pine St.,
New York, NY 10270
Director Supplier Diversity
Tel: (212) 770-7000
Web: www.aig.com

ARROW ELECTRONICS
Corporate Headquarters
50 Marcus Dr.
Melville, NY 11747
Irene Staiton, Director, Purchasing
Tel: (631) 847-2000
Web: www.arrow.com

ASBURY AUTOMOTIVE GROUP
Vendor Relations
622 Third Ave
New York, NY 10017
Joe Moccia, New Vendor Relations
Tel: (212) 885-2500
Web: www.ashburyauto.com

ASSURANT
Corporate Headquarters
1 Chase Manhattan Center
New York, NY 10005
Tel: (212) 859-7000
Web: www.assurant.com

AVON PRODUCTS
Supplier Diversity
1345 Sixth Ave.
New York, NY 10105
Donna Westerman, Director, Supplier Diversity and Social Accountability North America
Tel: 212-282-7352
Web: www.avoncompany.com

BARNES & NOBLE
Corporate Headquarters
122 Fifth Ave
New York, NY 10011
Tel: (212) 633-3300
Web: www.barnesandnobleinc.com

BEAR STEARNS
Corporate Headquarters
383 Madison Ave.
New York, NY 10179
Tel: (212) 272-2000
Web: www.bearstearns.com

BRISTOL-MYERS SQUIBB
Corporate Headquarters
345 Park Ave.
New York, NY 10154
Ingrid M. Sheremeta, Associate Director, Supplier Diversity Procurement
Tel: (212) 546-4000
Email: Ingrid.Sheremeta@bms.com
Web: www.bms.com

CABLEVISION SYSTEMS
Corporate Headquarters
1111 Stewart Ave.

Bethpage, NY 11714
Tel: (516) 803-2300
Web: www.cablevision.com

CENDANT
Corporate Headquarters
9 W. 57th St.
New York, NY 10019
Scott Welsh, Cendant Corporation
Tel: (212) 413-1800
Email: Scott.Welsh@cendant.com
Web: www.cendant.com

CITIGROUP
Corporate Headquarters
399 Park Ave.,
New York, NY 10043
Simon Williams, Chief Risk Officer, Global Consumer Group
Tel: (212) 559-1000

COLGATE-PALMOLIVE
Product Supply Chain
300 Park Ave.
New York, NY 10022
David R. Groener, Vice President, Global Product Supply Chain
Tel: (212) 310-2000
Web: www.colgate.com

CONSOLIDATED EDISON
Supplier Diversity
4 Irving Pl.
New York, NY 10003
Joy Crichlow, Director, Supplier Diversity
Tel: (212) 460-4600
Web: www.conedison.com

CORNING
Diversity Program
1 Riverfront Plaza
Corning, NY 14831
Gail Baity, Manager, Diversity Programs
Tel: (607) 974-9000
Web: www.corning.com

DOVER
Vendor Relations
280 Park Ave.
New York, NY 10017
Tel: (212) 922-1640
Web: www.dovercorporation.com

EASTMAN KODAK
Corporate Headquarters
343 State St.
Rochester, NY 14650
Armond Kane, Supplier Diversity Manager
Tel: (585) 477-8288
Web: www.kodak.com

ENERGY EAST
Corporate Headquarters
Albany, NY 12212
Tel: (518) 434-3049
Web: www.energyeast.com

ESTÉE LAUDER
Corporate Headquarters
767 Fifth Ave.
New York, NY 10153
Tel: (212) 572-4200
Web: www.elcompanies.com

FOOT LOCKER
Corporate Headquarters
112 W. 34th St.
New York, NY 10120
Tel: (212) 720-3700
Web: www.footlocker-inc.com

GOLDMAN SACHS GROUP
Corporate Headquarters
85 Broad St.

New York, NY 10004
Liz Hyman, Supplier Diversity
Tel: (212) 902-1000 Fax: (212) 463-0220
Email: supplier.diversity@gm.com
Web: www.gs.com

GUARDIAN LIFE OF AMERICA
Human Resources Department
7 Hanover Square
New York, NY 10004
Steven Smith, Recruitment Manager
Tel: (212) 598-8000

HENRY SCHEIN
Purchasing
135 Duryea Rd.
Melville, NY 11747
Frank Audia, Manager, Purchasing
Tel: (631) 843-5500 Fax: (631) 843-5698
Web: www.henryschein.com

IAC/INTERACTIVE
Purchasing
152 W. 57th St.
New York, NY 10019
Joe Listo, Purchasing
Tel: (212) 314-7300
Web: www.iac.com

INTERPUBLIC GROUP
Human Resource
1114 Sixth Ave.
New York, NY 10036
James Simmons, Manager, Diversity Performance
Tel: (212) 704-1200
Web: www.interpublic.com

INTL. BUSINESS MACHINES (IBM)
Corporate Headquarters
New Orchard Rd.
Armock, NY 10504
I. Javette Jenkins, Minority Supplier Programs Director
Tel: (914) 499-1900
Email: javette@us.ibm.com
Web: www.ibm.com

J.P. MORGAN CHASE & CO.
Corporate Headquarters
270 Park Ave.,
New York, NY 10017
Harvey Butler, Vice President, Corporate Supplier Diversity
Tel: (201) 595-5264
Email: harvey.butler@jpmchase.com
Web: www.jpmorganchase.com

KEYSPAN
Diversity
1 Metro Tech Center
Brooklyn, NY 11201
Terrence McBeth, Diversity Manager
Tel: (718) 403-1000
Web: www.keyspanenergy.com

L-3 COMMUNICATIONS
Procurement
600 Third Ave
New York, NY 10016
Ralph DeNino, Vice President, Procurement
Tel: (212) 697-1111
Web: www.L-3com.com

LEHMAN BROTHERS HLDGS.
Supplier Diversity
745 Seventh Ave.
New York, NY 10019
Aaron Blumenthal, Manager, Supplier Diversity
Tel: (212) 526-7000 Fax: (646) 758-3146
Email: ablument@lehman.com
Web: www.lehman.com

LIZ CLAIBORNE
Corporate Headquarters
1441 Broadway
New York, NY 10018
Tel: (212) 354-4900
Web: www.lizclaiborne.com

LOEWS CORPORATION
Corporate Headquarters
667 Madison Ave
New York, NY 10021
Jackie Pineiro, Purchasing Manager,
National Program
Tel: (212) 521-2000 Fax: (212) 521-2996
Web: www.loews.com

MARSH & MCLENNAN
Corporate Headquarters
1166 Sixth Ave.
New York, NY 10036
Linda Creighton, Director, Purchasing
Tel: (212) 345-5000
Web: www.mmc.com

MCGRAW-HILL
Purchasing
1221 Sixth Ave.
New York, NY 10020
Evelyn Lowinsten, Manager, Purchasing
Tel: (212) 512-2000
Web: www.mcgraw-hill.com

MERRILL LYNCH
Corporate Headquarters
4 Financial Center
New York, NY 10080
Tamra Luckett, Supplier Diversity Director
Tel: (212) 449-1000 Fax: (609) 282-3557
Email: tamara_luckett@ml.com
Web: www.ml.com

METLIFE
Corporate Headquarters
200 Park Ave.
New York, NY 10166
Denise Singleton, Manager, Minority
Diversity
Tel: (908) 253-1068
Web: www.metlife.com

MORGAN STANLEY
Corporate Headquarters
1585 Broadway
New York, NY 10036
Jennifer Rosa, Executive Director, Supplier
Diversity
Tel: (212) 762-2034
Email: supdiversity@morganstanley.com
Web: www.morganstanley.com

NEW YORK LIFE INSURANCE
Supplier Diversity
51 Madison Ave
New York, NY 10010
Annette Fucucello, Director of Supplier
Diversity
Tel: (212) 576-7000
Email: nylsupplierdiversity@newyorklife.com
Web: www.newyorklife.com

NEWS CORP.
Corporate Headquarters
1211 Sixth Ave.
New York, NY 10036
Tel: (212) 852-7000
Web: www.newscorp.com

NTL
Corporate Headquarters
909 Third Ave
New York, NY 10022
Tel: (212) 906-8440
Web: www.ntl.com

OMNICOM GROUP
Vendor Relations
437 Madison Ave.
New York, NY 10022
Tel: (212) 415-3600 Fax: (212) 415-3530
Web: www.omnicompgroup.com

PEPSI BOTTLING
Corporate Headquarters
1 Pepsi Way
Somers, NY 10589
J. Frederick Canady, Director, Minority
Business
Tel: (914) 767-6000
Web: www.pbg.com

PEPSICO
700 Anderson Hill Rd.
Purchase, NY 10577
James Kozlowski, Senior Vice President,
Global Procurement
Tel: (914) 253-2000
Web: www.pepsico.com

PFIZER
235 E. 2nd St.
New York, NY 10017
Gwendolyn Turner, Supplier Diversity
Tel: (212) 573-2323
Web: www.pfizer.com

STARWOOD HOTELS & RSRTS.
Diversity
1111 Westchester Ave.
White Plains, NY 10604
Randal Tucker, Manager MBE and Diversity
Tel: (914) 640-8100
Web: www.starwoodhotels.com

TIAA-CREF
Corporate Headquarters
730 Third Ave.
New York, NY 10017
Joan Watson, Manager, Suppliers Diversity
Tel: (212) 490-9000 X3039 Fax: (212)
916-6030
Web: www.tiaa-cref.org

TIME WARNER
Corporate Headquarters
1 Time Warner Center
New York, NY 10019
Greta Davis, National Director, Supplier
Diversity
Tel: (212) 484-8000
Email: greta.davis@timewarner.com
Web: www.timewarner.com

VERIZON COMMUNICATIONS
Corporate Headquarters
1095 Sixth Ave.
New York, NY 10036
Lawrence T. Babbio, Jr., Vice Chairman and
President
Tel: (212) 395-2121 Fax: (212) 921-2917
Web: www.verizon.com

VIACOM
Corporate Headquarters
1515 Broadway
New York, NY 10036
Tel: (212) 258-6000
Web: www.viacom.com

WELLCHOICE
Vendor Relations
11 W. 42nd St.
New York, NY 10036
Tel: (888) 476-7245
Web: www.wellchoice.com

NORTH CAROLINA

BANK OF AMERICA CORP.
Corporate Headquarters
100 N. Tryon St.
Charlotte, NC 28255
Kim Yu, Supplier Diveristy Manager
Tel: (415) 241-3428 Fax: (415) 241-5386
Email: kim.t.vu@bankofamerica.com
Web: www.bankofamerica.com

BB&T CORP.
Vendor Relations
200 W. Second St.
Winston-Salem, NC 27101
Tel: (336) 733-2000
Web: www.bbandt.com

DUKE ENERGY
Corporate Headquarters
526 S. Church St.
Charlotte, NC 28202
Richard Williams, Vice President, Diversity
and Employment Services
Tel: (704) 594-6200
Web: www.duke-energy.com

FAMILY DOLLAR STORES
Supply Chain
10401 Monroe Rd.
Matthews, NC 28105
Charles S. Gibson Jr., Executive Vice
President, Supply Chain
Tel: (704) 847-6961
Web: www.familydollar.com

GOODRICH
Procurement
2730 W. Tyvola Rd.
Charlotte, NC 28217
Jim Burfield, Procurement Specialist
Tel: (704) 423-7000
Web: www.goodrich.com

JEFFERSON-PILOT
Purchasing
100 N. Greene St.
Greensboro, NC 27401
Theresa Darcy, Vice President,
Administrative Services
Tel: (336) 691-3000
Web: www.jpfinancial.com

LOWE'S
Supplier Diversity
100 Loews Blvd
Mooresville, NC 28117
Gil Galigos, Supplier Diversity Manager
Tel: (704) 758-2653
Web: www.loews.com

NUCOR
Corporate Headquarters
2100 Rexford Rd.
Charlotte, NC 28211
Tel: (704) 366-7000 Fax: (704) 362-4208
Web: www.nucor.com

PROGRESS ENERGY
Vendor Relations
410 S. Wilmington St.
Raleigh, NC 27601
Tel: (919) 546-6111
Email: psn-vendors@pgnmail.com
Web: www.progress-energy.com

REYNOLDS AMERICAN
Corporate Headquarters
401 N. Main St.
Winston-Salem, NC 27102
Tel: (336) 741-5500
Web: www.reynoldsamerican.com

SONIC AUTOMOTIVE
Corporate Headquarters
6415 Idlewild Rd
Charlotte, NC 28212
Tel: (704) 566-2400
Web: www.sonicautomotive.com

SPX CORPORATION
Corporate Headquarters
13515 Ballantyne Corporate Place
Charlotte, NC 28277
Tel: (704) 752-4400
Web: www.spx.com

VF CORPORATION
Corporate Headquarters
105 Corporate Center Blvd
Greensboro, NC 27408
Boyd Rogers, Vice President, Supply Chain
Tel: (336) 424-6000 Fax: (336) 424-7668
Web: www.vfc.vom

WACHOVIA CORP.
Corporate Headquarters
301 S. College St.
Charlotte, NC 28288
Ann Prock, Manager, Supplier Diversity
Tel: (704) 374-6807
Email: supplierdiversity@wachovia.com
Web: www.wachovia.com

OHIO

AK STEEL HOLDING
Supply Chain
703 Curtis St.
Middletown, OH 45043
John F. Kaloski, Senior Vice President,
Supply Chain
Tel: (513) 425-5000
Web: www.aksteel.com

AMERICAN ELECTRIC POWER
Corporate Headquarters
1 Riverside Rd
Columbus, OH 43215
Gloria Hines, Diversified Business
Coordinator
Tel: (614) 716-1955 Fax: (866) 705-9689
Web: www.aep.com

AMERICAN FINANCIAL GRP.
Purchasing
1 E. Fourth St.
Cincinnati, OH 45202
Fran Hall, Purchasing
Tel: (513) 579-2121
Web: www.afginc.com

BIG LOTS
Purchasing
300 Phillipi Rd.
Columbus, OH 43228
Debbie Sandol, Director, Purchasing
Tel: (614) 278-6800
Email: sell2us@biglots.com
Web: www.biglots.com

CARDINAL HEALTH
Corporate Headquarters
7000 Cardinal Pl.
Dublin, OH 43017
Kathy Benn, Vice President, Supplier
Diversity
Tel: (614) 757-5000
Web: www.cardinal.com

CINCINNATI FINANCIAL
Purchasing
6200 Gilmore Rd.
Fairfield, OH 45014

Stacey Hall, Manager, Purchasing
Tel: (513) 870-2000
Web: www.cinfin.com

CINERGY
Purchasing
139 E. 4th St.
Cincinnati, OH 45202
April Collins, Purchasing
Tel: (513) 421-9500 X3018
Web: www.cinergy.com

COOPER TIRE & RUBBER
Supplier Relations
701 Lima Ave
Findlay, OH 45840
Lynn Maag, Manager, Supplier Performance
and Material Control
Tel: (419) 420-6161
Web: www.coopertire.com

DANA
Corporate Heaquarters
4500 Dorr St.
Toledo, OH 43615
Felissa Parker, Director, Minority Supplier
Development
Tel: (248) 324-6762
Web: www.dana.com

EATON
Supplier Diversity
1111 Superior Ave
Cleveland, OH 44114
Deborah R. Pickens, Director, Supplier
Diversity
Tel: (216) 523-4226
Web: www.eaton.com

FEDERATED DEPT. STORES
Corporate Headquarters
7 W. Seventh St.
Cincinnati, OH 45202
Tom Knott, Director, Diversity Vendor
Relations
Tel: (513) 579-7803
Web: www.fds.com

FIFTH THIRD BANCORP
Diversity
38 Fountain Square Pl.
Cincinnati, OH 45263
Ann Lazarus-Barnes, Vice President,
Diversity
Tel: (513) 534-8204

FIRSTENERGY
Corporate Headquarters
76 S. Main St.
Akron, OH 44308
Michael J. Dowling, Chief Procurement
Officer, Vice President Supply Chain
Tel: (800) 736-3402
Web: www.firstenergycorp.com

GOODYEAR TIRE & RUBBER
Corporate Headquarters
1144 E. Market St.
Akron, OH 44316
Dave Stoltz, Global Diversity Initiatives
Manager
Tel: (330) 796-2121 Fax: (330) 796-2222
Web: www.goodyear.com

INTERNATIONAL STEEL GROUP
Corporate Headquarters
4020 Kinross Lakes Pkwy.
Richfield, OH 44286
Tel: (219) 399-1200
Web: www.intlsteel.com

KEYCORP
Vendor Relations
127 Public Square

Cleveland, OH 44114
Tel: (216) 689-6300
Web: www.key.com

KROGER
Corporate Headquarters
1014 Vine St.
Cincinnati, OH 45202
Denise Thomas, Director, Corporate
Supplier
Tel: (513) 762-4000
Web: www.kroger.com

LIMITED BRANDS
Corporate Headquarters
3 Limited Pkwy.
Columbus, OH 43230
Tel: (614) 415-7000
Web: www.limitedbrands.com

NATIONAL CITY CORP.
Vendor Diversity
1900 E. Ninth St.
Cleveland, OH 44114
Tel: (216) 222-2000
Email: vendordiversity@nationalcity.com
Web: www.nationalcity.com

NATIONWIDE
Corporate Headquarters
1 Nationwide Plaza
Columbus, OH 43215
Tel: (614) 249-7111 X92977
Web: www.nationwide.com

NCR
Purchasing
1700 S. Patterson Blvd
Dayton, OH 45479
Tel: (937) 445-5000
Web: www.ncr.com

OWENS CORNING
Purchasing
1 Owens Corning Pkwy
Toledo, OH 43659
Doug Pontsler, Manager, Purchasing
Tel: (419) 248-8000
Web: www.owenscorning.com

OWENS-ILLINOIS
Procurement
1 SeaGate
Toledo, OH 43666
Ryan C. Schlaff, Vice President,
Procurement
Tel: (419) 247-5000
Web: www.o-i.com

PARKER HANNIFIN
Procurement
6035 Parkland Blvd.
Cleveland, OH 44124
John Dedinsky, VP Procurement
Tel: (216) 896-2761 Fax: (216) 896-4057
Web: www.parker.com

PROCTER & GAMBLE
1 Procter & Gamble Plz.
Cincinnati, OH 45202
Tel: (513) 983-1100
Email: hodnett.dm@pg.com
Web: www.pg.com

PROGRESSIVE
Corporate Headquarters
6300 Wilson Mills Rd.
Mayfield Village, OH 44143
Tel: (440) 461-5000
Web: www.progressive.com

SHERWIN-WILLIAMS
Purchasing
101 Prospect Ave. N.W.

Cleveland, OH 44115
Simi Gane, Manager, Purchasing
Tel: (216) 566-2000
Web: www.sherwin.com

TIMKEN
Supply Chain
1835 Dueber Ave S.W
Canton, OH 44706
Donna J. Demerling, Senior Vice President,
Supply Chain Transformation
Tel: (330) 438-3000
Web: www.timken.com

WENDY'S INTERNATIONAL, INC.
Corporate Headquarters
1 Dave Thomas Blvd.
Dublin, OH 43017
Tel: (614) 764-3100
Web: www.wendys.com

WESTERN & SOUTHERN FINANCIAL
Corporate Headquarters
400 Broadway
Cincinnati, OH 45202
Tel: (513) 629-1800
Web: www.westernsouthern.com

OKLAHOMA

DEVON ENERGY CORPORATION
Corporate Headquarters
20 N. Broadway
Oklahoma City, OK 73102
Tel: (405) 235-3611

KERR-MCGEE
Purchasing
Kerr-McGee Center
Oklahoma, OK 73125
Mat Thorton, Purchasing
Tel: (405) 270-1313
Web: www.kerr-mcgee.com

OGE ENERGY
Purchasing
321 N. Harvey Ave.
Oklahoma City, OK 73102
Earl Farmer, Purchasing
Tel: (405) 553-5868
Web: www.oge.com

ONEOK
Purchasing
100 W. Fifth St.
Tulsa, OK 74103
Gary Bradshaw, Manager, Purchasing
Tel: (918) 588-7000
Web: www.oneok.com

WILLIAMS
Corporate Headquarters
1 Williams Center
Tulsa, OK 74172
Kelly Swan, Purchasing
Tel: (918) 573-2000
Web: www.williams.com

OREGON

NIKE
Corporate Headquarters
1 Bowerman Dr.
Beaverton, OR 97005
Nicholas Athanasakos, Vice President,
Supply Chain
Web: www.nike.com

PENNSYLVANIA

AIR PRODUCTS & CHEM.
7201 Hamilton Blvd.
Allentown, PA 18195
Joe Troller
Tel: (610) 481-4911
Web: www.airproducts.com

ALCOA
Corporate Headquarters
201 Isabella St.
Pittsburgh, PA 15212
Mark Straszheim, Procurement
Tel: (213) 894-7395 Fax: (412) 553-4498
Web: www.alcoa.com

AMERISOURCEBERGEN
Corporate Headquarters
1300 Morris Dr.
Chesterbrook, PA 19087
Len Decandia, Manager, Procurement
Tel: (610) 727-7211
Email: pcerula@amerisourcebergen.com
Web: www.amerisourcebergen.com

ARAMARK
Corporate Headquarters
1101 Market St.
Philadelphia, PA 19107
John Orobono, Vice President, Vending
Services
Tel: (215) 238-3000
Web: www.aramark.com

CIGNA
Corporate Headquarters
1 Liberty Pl.
Philadelphia, PA 19192
Tel: (215) 761-1000
Email: vendorDA@cigna.com
Web: www.cigna.com/itvendors

COMCAST
Supplier Diversity
1500 Market St.
Philadelphia, PA 19102
Debbie Grossman, Vice President, Supplier
Diversity
Tel: (215) 665-1700 Fax: (215) 655-8113
Email: supplierinfo@cable.comcast.com
Web: www.comcast.com

CROWN HOLDINGS
Sourcing Department
1 Crown Way
Philadelphia, PA 19154
Alan Stott, Director of Sourcing Dept.
Tel: (215) 698-5100
Web: www.crowncork.com

ERIE INSURANCE GROUP
Corporate Headquarters
100 Erie Insurance Pl.
Erie, PA 16530
Cheryl Ferrie, Purchasing Director
Tel: (814) 870-2000
Web: www.erieinsurance.com

H.J. HEINZ
Supplier Diversity
Attn: Supplier Profile Questionnaire
P.O. Box 57
Pittsburgh, PA 15230
Tel: (412) 456-5700
Email: supplierdiversity@hjheinz.com
Web: www.heinz.com

HERSHEY FOODS
Purchasing
14 E. Chocolate Ave.
Hershey, PA 17033

Purchasing
Tel: (717) 534-6799
Web: www.hersheys.com

IKON OFFICE SOLUTIONS
Supplier Diversity
70 Valey Stream Pkwy
Malvern, PA 19355
Betsy Parrish, Diversity Program
Administrator
Tel: (610) 722-1520 Fax: (610) 727-2995
Email: supplierdiversity@ikon.com
Web: www.ikon.com

JONES APPAREL GROUP
Purchasing
250 Rittenhouse Circle
Bristol, PA 19007
Liz Raddi, Manager, Purchasing
Tel: (215) 785-4000
Web: www.jny.com

LINCOLN NATIONAL
Corporate Headquarters
1500 Market St.
Philadelphia, PA 19102
Tel: (215) 448-1400
Web: www.lfg.com

MELLON FINANCIAL CORP.
Corporate Headquarters
1 Melon Center
Pittsburgh, PA 15258
Tel: (412) 234-5530
Email: tech.info@mellon.com
Web: www.mellon.com

PILGRIM'S PRIDE
Purchasing
110 S. Texas St.
Pittsburg, PA 75686
Ron Pittington, Director, Purchasing
Tel: (903) 434-1122
Web: www.pilgrimspride.com

PNC FINANCIAL SERVICES
Purchasing
249 Fifth Ave
Pittsburgh, PA 15222
Tel: (412) 762-2000
Web: www.pnc.com

PPG INDUSTRIES
Corporate Headquarters
1 PPG St.
Pittsburgh, PA 15272
Kathleen A. McGuire, Vice President
Purchasing and Distribution
Tel: (412) 434-3131
Web: www.ppg.com

PPL CORPORATION
Supplier Diversity
2 N. Ninth St.
Allentwon, PA 18101
Gloria E. Collins, Administrator, Supplier
Diversity
Tel: (610) 774-5151
Web: www.pplweb.com

RITE AID
Corporate Headquarters
30 Hunter Lane
Camp Hill, PA 17011
Wilson A Lester, Jr., Senior Vice President
Supply Chain
Tel: (717) 761-2633
Web: www.riteaid.com

ROHM & HAAS
Vendor Relations
100 Independence Mall W.
Philadelphia, PA 19106

Jean-Francois Mayer, Vice President,
Procurement
Tel: (212) 592-3000 Fax: (212) 592-3377
Web: www.rohmhaas.com

SUNOCO
Corporate Headquarters
1801 Market Pl.
Philadlphia, PA 19103
Joel H. Maness, Senior Vice President,
Refining and Supply
Tel: (215) 977-6764
Web: www.sunocoinc.com

TOLL BROTHERS
Corporate Headquarters
250 Gibraltar Rd
Horsham, PA 19044
Tel: (215) 938-8000
Web: www.tollbrothers.com

UGI CORPORATION
Purchasing
460 N. Gulph Rd
King of Prussia, PA 19406
James Siege, Manager, Purchasing
Tel: (610) 337-1000
Web: www.unicorp.com

UNISYS
Supplier Diversity
Unisys Way
Blue Bell, PA 19424
Murray Schooner, Corporate Director,
Supplier Diversity
Tel: (703) 439-5098
Web: www.unisys.com

UNITED STATES STEEL
Corporate Headquarters
600 Grant St.
Philadelphia, PA 15219
Christopher J. Navetta, Senior Vice
President, Procurement, Logistics, and
Diversified Business
Tel: (412) 433-1121
Web: www.ussteel.com

UNIVERSAL HEALTH SVCS.
Purchasing
367 S. Gulph Rd.
King of Prussia, PA 19406
Clark Sailor, Director, Purchasing
Tel: (610) 768-3300
Web: www.uhsinc.com

WESCO INTERNATIONAL
Minority Business Relations
225 West Station Square Dr.
Pittsburgh, PA 15219
Mike Ludwig, Director, Minority Business
Relations
Tel: (412) 454-2200
Web: www.wesco.com

YORK INTERNATIONAL
Sourcing Dept.
631 S. Richland Ave.
York, PA 17403
Tel: (717) 771-7890
Email: sourcing@york.com
Web: www.york.com

RHODE ISLAND

CVS
Corporate Headquarters
1 CVS Dr.
Woonsocket, RI 02895
Tel: (401) 765-1500
Web: www.cvs.com

TEXTRON
Corporate Headquarters
40 Westminster St.
Providence, RI 02903
Tel: (401) 421-2800
Web: www.textron.com

SOUTH CAROLINA

SCANA
Procurement
1426 Main St.
Columbia, SC 29201
Sarena D. Burch, Senior Vice President,
Fuel Procurement and Asset Management
Tel: (803) 217-9000
Web: www.scana.com

TENNESSEE

AUTOZONE
Supply Chain
123 S. Front St.
Memphis, TN 38103
Michael E. Longo, Executive Vice President,
Supply Chain
Tel: (901) 495-6500
Web: www.autozone.com

CAREMARK RX
Corporate Headquarters
211 Commerce St.
Nashville, TN 37201
Ruben Hamilton, Director Procurement
and Supply
Tel: (847) 559-4700
Web: www.caremark.com

DOLLAR GENERAL
Supply Chain Management
100 Mission Ridge
Goodlettsville, TN 37072
Lloyd Davis, Senior Vice President, Supply
Chain Operations
Tel: (615) 855-4000
Web: www.dollargeneral.com

EASTMAN CHEMICAL
Vendor Relations
100 N. Eastman Rd.
Kingsport, TN 37660
Tom Mcpherson
Tel: (423) 229-2000
Web: www.eastman.com

FEDEX
Corporate Headquarters
924 S. Shady Grove Rd.
Memphis, TN 38120
Douglas E. Witt, President, Chief Executive
Officer Supply Chain Services
Tel: (901) 818-7500
Web: www.fedex.com

HOSPITAL CORPORATION OF AMERICA
Corporate Headquarters
1 Park Plz.
Nashville, TN 37203
James A. Fitzgerald , Senior Vice President,
Supply Chain Operations
Tel: (615) 344-9551
Web: www.hcahealthcare.com

UNUMPROVIDENT
Corporate Headquarters
1 Fountain Sq.
Chattanooga, TN 37402
Stacey Custeau, Director, Purchasing

Tel: (423) 755-1011
Web: www.unumprovident.com

TEXAS

AFFILIATED COMPUTER SVCS.
Purchasing
2828 N. Haskell Ave
Dallas, TX 75204
Brad Lawrenson, Manager, Purchasing
Tel: (214) 841-6111
Web: www.acs-inc.com

AMERICAN AIRLINES
Diversity Supplier Program
4333 Amon Carter Blvd.
Fort Worth, TX 76155-2664
Luis Gomez, Manager for Supplier Diversity
Tel: (817) 963-1234
Email: luis.gomez@aa.com
Web: www.aa.com/supplierdiversity

US Hispanic National Organizations and
Promotions
4255 Amon Carter Blvd. M/D 4412
Fort Worth, TX 76155
Juan J. Rios, Manager
Tel: (817) 931-4243
Email: juan.rios@aa.com
Web: www.aa-pro.com

ANADARKO PETROLEUM
Purchasing
1201 Lake Robbins Dr.
The Woodlands, TX 77380
Steve Englehardt, Manager, Purchasing
Tel: (832) 636-1000 Fax: (832) 636-5097
Email: steve_englehardt@anadarko.com
Web: www.anadarko.com

APACHE
Purchasing
2000 Post Oak Blvd
Houston, TX 77056
Joe Augustine, Corporate Purchasing,
Manager
Tel: (713) 296-6436
Web: www.apachecorp.com

BAKER HUGHES
Purchasing
3900 Essex Lane
Houston, TX 77027
Brenda Schelsteder, Manager, Purchasing
Tel: (713) 625-5700
Web: www.bakerhughes.com

BRINKER INTERNATIONAL
Purchasing
6820 L.B.J. Freeway
Dallas, TX 75240
Janine McShane, Director, Purchasing
Tel: (972) 980-9917
Web: www.brinker.com

BURLINGTON NO. SANTA FE
Corporate Headquarters
2650 Lou Menk Dr.
Fort Worth, TX 76131
Mary Escobar, Director, Procurement
Tel: (785) 676-3830 X31 Fax: (785)
676-3094
Web: www.bnsf.com

BURLINGTON RESOURCES
Purchasing
717 Texas Ave
Houston, TX 77002
Tel: (817) 347-2000
Web: www.br-inc.com

CENTERPOINT ENERGY
Supplier Diversity
1111 Louisiana St.
Houston, TX 77002
Jewel Smith, Manager, Supplier Diversity
Tel: (713) 207-6951 Fax: (713) 207-9347
Web: www.centerpointenergy.com

CLEAR CHANNEL COMMUNICATIONS
Diversity
200 E. Basse Rd.
San Antonio, TX 78209
M. Helen Cavazos, Diversity Manager
Tel: (210) 822-2828
Web: www.clearchannel.com

COMMERCIAL METALS
Corporate Headquarters
6565 N. MacArthur Blvd
Irving, TX 75039
Tel: (214) 689-4300
Web: www.commercialmetals.com

CONOCOPHILLIPS
Corporate Headquarters
600 N. Dairy Ashford Rd.
Houston, TX 77079
Jim W. Nokes, Executive Vice President
Refining, Marketing, Supply and
Transportation
Tel: (281) 293-1000
Web: www.conocophillips.com

CONTINENTAL AIRLINES
Supplier Diversity
1600 Smith St.
Houston, TX 77002
Phyllis Graham, Supplier Diversity Program
Liaison
Tel: (713) 324-5000
Email: sdp@coair.com
Web: www.continental.com

D.R. HORTON
Corporate Headquarters
301 Commerce St.
Fort Worth, TX 76102
Tel: (817) 390-8200
Web: www.drhorton.com

DEAN FOODS
Corporate Headquarters
2515 McKinney Ave.
Dallas, TX 75201
Tel: (214) 303-3400
Web: www.deanfoods.com

DELL
Corporate Headquarters
1 Dell Way
Round Rock, TX 78682
Fred Hayes, Supplier Diversity
Tel: (512) 338-4400 Fax: (512) 283-6161
Web: www.dell.com

DYNEGY
Purchasing
1000 Louisiana St.
Houston, TX 77002
Brenda Valladares, Manager, Purchasing
Tel: (713) 507-6400
Email: scm@dynegy.com
Web: www.dynegy.com

EL PASO
Materials and Contracts Management
1001 Louisiana St.
Houston, TX 77002
Helda Longoria, Coordinator, Supplier
Diversity Program
Tel: (713) 420-2600 Fax: (713) 420-7464
Web: www.elpaso.com

ELECTRONIC DATA SYSTEMS
Supplier Diversity
5400 Legacy Dr.
Plano, TX 75024
Mike Mussy, Manager, Supplier Diversity
Tel: (972) 604-6000
Web: www.eds.com

ENBRIDGE ENERGY PARTNERS
Corporate Headquarters
1100 Louisiana St.
Houston, TX 77002
Tel: (713) 821-2000
Web: www.enbridgepartners.com

ENTERPRISE PRODUCTS
Vendor Relations
2727 N. Loop West
Houston, TX 77008
Kim McKenny, Sourcing and Procurement
Tel: (713) 880-6500

EXXON MOBIL
Exxon Mobil Corporation
5959 Las Colinas Blvd
Irving, TX 75039-2298
Nancy Swartout, Supplier Diversity
Tel: (972) 444-1000 Fax: (972) 444-1883
Web: www.exxon.mobil.com

GROUP 1 AUTOMOTIVE
Corporate Headquarters
950 Echo Lane
Houston, TX 77024
Tel: (713) 647-5700
Web: www.group1auto.com

HALLIBURTON
Corporate Headquarters
1401 McKinney
Houston, TX 77010
Ien Cooper, Director, Procurement
Tel: (281) 575-3270
Web: www.haliburton.com

J.C. PENNEY
Corporate Headquarters
6501 Legacy Dr.
Plano, TX 75024
James W. LaBounty, Senior Vice President,
Director Supply Chain
Tel: (973) 431-1000
Web: www.jcpenney.net

KIMBERLY-CLARK
Corporate Headquarters
351 Phelps Dr.
Irving, TX 75038
Shannon Styker, Supplier Diversity and
Procurement
Tel: (920) 721-2000
Email: supplierdiversity@kcc.com
Web: www.kimberly-clark.com

KINDER MORGAN ENERGY
Contracting Department
500 Dallas St. #1000
Houston, TX 77002
Jenny Brown, Senior Contract Administrator
Tel: (713) 369-9296
Web: www.kindermorgan.com

LYONDELL CHEMICAL
Supply Management
1221 McKinney St.
Houston, TX 77010
Tel: (713) 652-7200
Web: www.lyondell.com

MARATHON OIL
Corporate Headquarters
5555 San Felipe Rd.
Houston, TX 77056

Donna Nichols-Carr, Supplier Diversity
Tel: (713) 296-4361
Email: dnicholscarr@marathon.com
Web: www.marathon.com

PLAINS ALL AMERICAN PIPELINE
Corporate Headquarters
333 Clay St.
Houston, TX 77002
Sky Cheney, Purchasing Manager
Tel: (713) 646-4100
Web: www.paalp.com

RADIOSHACK
Supply Chain
300 Radio Shack Circle
Fort Worth, TX 76102
Mike Kowal, Senior Vice President, Supply
Chain
Web: www.radioshackcorporation.com

RELIANT ENERGY
Corporate Headquarters
P.O. Box 4932
Houston, TX 77210-4932
Tel: (713) 497-3000
Web: www.reliantenergy.com

SBC COMMUNICATIONS
Corporate Headquarters
175 E. Houston St.
San Antonio, TX 78205
Tel: (210) 821-4105
Web: www.sbc.com

SMITH INTERNATIONAL
Supplier Diversity
411 N. Sam Houston Pkwy
Houston, TX 77060
Judy Fulton, Supplier Diversity
Tel: (281) 233-5582
Email: jfulton@smith.com
Web: www.smith.com

SOUTHWEST AIRLINES
Supplier Relations
2705 Love Field Dr.
Dallas, TX 75235
Lourdes Romero, Manager of Compliance
Tel: (214) 792-4000 Fax: (214) 792-5015
Email: lourdesromero@wnco.com
Web: www.southwest.com

SYSCO
Corporate Headquarters
1390 Enclave Pkwy
Houston, TX 77077
Cameron L. Blakely, Vice President,
eBusiness and BSCC Supplier Services
Tel: (281) 584-1390
Web: www.sysco.com

TEMPLE-INLAND
Supplier Diversity
1300 MoPac expressway S.
Austin, TX 78746
Novell Eustey, Director, Supplier Diversity
Tel: (512) 434-5800
Web: www.templeinland.com

TENET HEALTHCARE
Corporate Headquarters
13737 Noel Rd.
Dallas, TX 75240
Ken Newman, Manager, Purchasing
Tel: (469) 893-2200
Web: www.tenethealth.com

TESORO
Corporate Headquarters
300 Concord Plaza Dr.
San Antonio, TX 78216
C.A. Flagg, Senior Vice President, Supply
and Optimization

Tel: (210) 828-8484
Web: www.tsocorp.com

TEXAS INSTRUMENTS
Minority and Women supplier
12500 TI Blvd
Dallas, TX 75266
Shirely Smith, Minority and Women
Supplier Director
Tel: (972) 995-3773
Email: mwbd@list.ti.com
Web: www.ti.com

TRIAD HOSPITALS
Supply Chain
5800 Tennyson Pkwy
Plano, TX 75024
Corris Boyd, Vice President, Supply Chain
Optimization
Tel: (214) 473-7000
Web: www.triadhospitals.com

TXU
Supplier Diversity
1601 Bryan St.
Dallas, TX 75201
Sharon Rowlett, Procurement Specialist
Tel: (214) 812-6923 Fax: (214) 812-5597
Email: supplierdiversity@txu.com
Web: www.txucorp.com

USAA
Supplier Relations
9800 Fredericksburg Rd.
San Antonio, TX 78288
Tel: (210) 498-2211
Email: supplier.relations@usaa.com
Web: www.usaa.com

VALERO ENERGY
Corporate Headquarters
1 Valero Way
San Antonio, TX 78249
Tel: (210) 345-2000 Fax: (210) 345-2646
Web: www.valero.com

WASTE MANAGEMENT
Supplier Diversity
1001 Fannin St.
Houston, TX 77002
Betty Banks, Director, Supplier Diversity
Tel: (713) 265-1567 Fax: (713) 328-7604
Web: www.wm.com

WHOLE FOODS MARKET
Purchasing
550 Bowie St.
Austin, TX 78703
Tamara Gillary, Director, Purchasing
Tel: (512) 477-4455
Web: www.wholefoodsmarket.com

UTAH

AUTOLIV
Purchasing
3350 Airport Rd.
Ogden, UT 84405
Halvar Jonzon, Vice President, Purchasing
Tel: (801) 625-9200
Web: www.autoliv.com

VIRGINIA

ADVANCE AUTO PARTS
Corporate Headquarters
5673 Airport Rd.
Roanoke, VA 24012
Tel: (540) 362-4911 Fax: (540) 561-4104

Web: www.advanceautoparts.com

AES
Corporate Headquarters
4300 Wilson Blvd
Arlington, VA 22203
Ali Naqvi, Vice President, Chief
Procurement Officer
Tel: (703) 522-1315
Web: www.aes.com

BRINK'S
Corporate Headquarters
1801 Bayberry Ct.
Richmond, VA 23226
Tel: (804) 289-9700
Email: info@brinkscompany.com
Web: www.brinkscompany.com

CAPITAL ONE FINANCIAL
Corporate Headquarters
1680 Capital One Dr.
McLean, VA 22102
Tel: (703) 720-1000
Web: www.capitalone.com

CARMAX
Corporate Headquarters
4900 Cox Rd.
Glen Allen, VA 23060
Tel: (888) 601-5567
Web: www.carmax.com

CIRCUIT CITY STORES
Corporate Headquarters
9950 Maryland Dr.
Richmond, VA 23233
Ronald G. Cuthberton, Senior Vice
President, Supply Chain and Inventory
Management
Tel: (804) 527-4000
Web: www.circuitcity.com

DOMINION RESOURCES
Supplier Diversity
120 Tredegar St.
Richmond, VA 23219
Larry Taylor, Supplier Diversity
Tel: (804) 819-2000
Email: supplier_diversity@dom.com
Web: www.dom.com

GANNETT
Diversity
7950 Jones Branch Dr.
McLean, VA 22107
Jose Berrios, Vice President, Diversity
Tel: (703) 854-6000
Web: www.gannett.com

GENERAL DYNAMICS
Corporate Headquarters
2941 FairView Park Dr
Falls Church, VA 22042
Tel: (703) 876-3000 Fax: (703) 876-3125
Web: www.gd.com

MCI
Corporate Headquarters
22001 Loundon County Pkwy
Ashburn, VA 20147
John N. Marshall, Program Director,
Corporate Supplier Diversity
Tel: (703) 866-5600
Web: www.mci.com

MEADWESTVACO
Supplier Diversity
1011 Boulder Spring Dr
Richmond, VA 23225
Sally Crook, Manager, Supplier Diversity
Tel: (804) 327-7900 Fax: (804) 327-6334

Web: www.meadwestvaco.com

NEXTEL COMMUNICATIONS
Corporate Headquarters
2001 Edmund Halley Dr.
Reston, VA 20191
Ben Lusvy, Director, Purchasing
Tel: (703) 433-4000
Web: www.nextel.com

NORFOLK SOUTHERN
Corporate Headquarters
3 Commercial Pl.
Norfolk, VA 23510
Doug Clary, Manager, Purchasing
Tel: (540) 981-3086
Email: nsdbe@nscorp.com

NVR
Purchasing
7601 Lewinsville Rd
McLean, VA 22102
Paul Huber, Director, Purchasing
Tel: (703) 956-4000
Web: www.nvrinc.com

OWENS & MINOR
Supplier Diversity
4800 Cox Rd.
Glen Allen, VA 23060
Angela T. Wilkes, Director, Supplier Diversity
Tel: (804) 965-5874 Fax: (804) 965-5403
Email: angela.wilkes@owens-minor.com
Web: www.owens-minor.com

PERFORMANCE FOOD GROUP
Procurement
12500 W. Creek Pkwy.
Richmond, VA 23238
Scott Barnewolt, Director of Procurement
Tel: (804) 484-7700 Fax: (804) 484-7760
Email: sbarnewolt@pfgc.com
Web: www.pfgc.com

SALLIEMAE
Corporate Headquarters
12061 Bluemont Way
Reston, VA 20190
Tel: (703) 810-3000
Web: www.salliemae.com

SMITHFIELD FOODS
Purchasing
200 Commerce St.
Smithfield, VA 23430
Elaine C. Abicht, Vice President
Tel: (757) 365-3000
Web: www.smithfieldfoods.com

US AIRWAYS GROUP
Corporate Headquarters
2345 Crystal Dr.
Arlington, VA 22227
Jamie Jackson
Tel: (703) 872-7000
Web: www.usairways.com

WASHINGTON

AMAZON.COM
Corporate Headquarters
P. O. Box 81226
Seattle, WA 98108
Tel: (800) 201-7575
Web: www.amazon.com

COSTCO WHOLESALE
Corporate Headquarters
999 Lake Dr.
Issaquah, WA 98027
James P. Murphy, Senior Vice President,
International Operations

Tel: (425) 313-8100
Web: www.costco.com

MICROSOFT
Corporate Headquarters
1 Microsoft Way
Redmond, WA 98052
Tel: (425) 882-8080 Fax: (425) 936-7329
Web: www.microsoft.com

NORDSTROM
Supplier Diversity Program
1617 Sixth Ave.
Seattle, WA 98101
Chrinstine Young, Supplier Diversity Affairs
Tel: (206) 628-2111
Web: www.nordstrom.com

PACCAR
Corporate Headquarters
777 106th Ave.
Bellevue, WA 98004
Tel: (425) 468-7368 Fax: (425) 468-8235
Web: www.paccar.com

SAFECO
Diversity
Safeco Plaza
Seattle, WA 98185
Kevin Carter, Director of Diversity
Tel: (206) 545-5000 Fax: (206) 925-0165
Web: www.safeco.com

STARBUCKS
Vendor Relations
2401 Utah Ave.
Seattle, WA 98134
Dorothy Kim, Executive Vice President,
Supply Chain and Coffee Operations
Tel: (206) 447-1575
Web: www.starbucks.com

WASHINGTON MUTUAL
Corporate Headquarters
1201 Thrid Ave.
Seattle, WA 98101
Strategic Sourcing/Purchasing
Tel: (206) 461-2000
Web: www.wamu.com

WEYERHAEUSER
33633 Weyerhaeuser Way St.
Federal Way, WA 98063
Tel: (253) 924-4577 Fax: (253) 924-4692
Email: purchasing.contact@weyerhaeuser.com
Web: www.weyerhaeuser.com

WISCONSIN

AMERICAN FAMILY INSURANCE GROUP
Supplier Relations
6000 American Pkwy.
Madison, WI 53783
Tel: (608) 249-2111
Email: suppliercontact@amfam.com
Web: www.amfam.com

HARLEY-DAVIDSON
Purchasing
3700 Juneau Ave.
Milwaukee, WI 53208
Mary Evans, Purchasing
Tel: (414) 342-4680
Web: www.harley-davidson.com

JOHNSON CONTROLS
Corporate Headquarters
5757 N. Green Bay Ave
Milwaukee, WI 53201

Larry Alles, Vice President, Global Corporate
Procurement
Tel: (414) 524-1200
Email: diversitybusiness@jci.com
Web: www.johnsoncontrols.com

KOHL'S
Corporate Headquarters
N56 W. 17000 Ridewood Dr.
Menomonee Falls, WI 53051
Tel: (262) 703-7000 Fax: (262) 703-7115
Web: www.kohls.com

MANPOWER
Corporate Headquarters
5301 N. Ironwood Rd.
Milwaukee, WI 53217
Pico Senboutaraj, Manager Supplier
Diversity
Tel: (414) 961-1000
Web: www.manpower.com

NORTHWESTERN MUTUAL
Corporate Headquarters
720 E. Wisconsin Ave
Milwaukee, WI 53202
Tel: (414) 271-1444
Web: www.northwesternmutual.com

ROCKWELL AUTOMATION, INC.
Supplier Diversity
777 E. Wisconsin Ave.
Milwaukee, WI 53202
Dan Buecheo, Supplier Diversity
Tel: (414) 382-0510 Fax: (414) 382-0666
Email: rasupplierdiversity@ra.rockwell.com
Web: www.rockwellautomation.com

ROUNDY'S
Procurement
875 E. Wisconsin Ave
Milwaukee, WI 53202
Joe Becker, Director, Procurement
Tel: (414) 231-5000
Web: www.roundys.com

WISCONSIN ENERGY
Supplier Diversity
231 W. Michigan St.
Milwaukee, WI 53203
Jerry Fulmer, Director, Supplier Diversity
Tel: (414) 221-2345
Web: www.wisconsinenergy.com

WPS RESOURCES
Purchasing
700 N. Adams St.
Green Bay, WI 54307
Carrie Kugel, Manager, Purchasing
Tel: (920) 433-4901
Web: www.wpsr.com

Private Sector Employment Opportunities

ALABAMA

REGIONS FINANCIAL
Human Resources
471 N. 20th St.
Birmingham, AL 35203
John M. Daniel, Director, Human Resources
Tel: (205) 944-1289
Web: www.regions.com

SAKS INCORPORATED
Human Resources
750 Lakeshore Pkwy
Birmingham, AL 35211
Marilyn Tipton, Director of Trainer
Tel: (601) 968-5348
Web: www.saksincorporated.com

ARIZONA

ALLIED WASTE INDUSTRIES
Human Resources
15880 N. Greenway-Hayden Loop
Scottsdale, AZ 85260
Stephanie Kalivas, Recuiter, Human Resources
Tel: (480) 627-2700
Web: www.alliedwaste.com

ARKANSAS

ALLTEL
Human Resources
1 Allied Dr.
Little Rock, AR 72202
C. J. Duvall, Human Resources
Tel: (501) 905-8000 Fax: (501) 905-5444
Web: www.alltel.com

AVNET
Human Resources
2211 S. 47th St.
Phoenix, AR 85034
Tel: (480) 643-2000
Web: www.avnet.com

DILLARD'S
Human Resources
1600 Cantrell Rd
Little Rock, AR 72201
Tel: (501) 376-5200
Web: www.dillards.com

MURPHY OIL CORPORATION
200 Peach St.
El Dorado, AR 71731
Matt Angelette, Manager Personnel
Tel: (870) 864-6435 Fax: (870) 864-6511
Email: matt_angelette@murphyoilcorp.com
Web: www.murphyoilcorp.com

PHELPS DODGE
Human Resources
1 N. Central Ave.
Phoenix, AR 85004
David L. Pulatie, Senior Vice President, Human Resources
Tel: (602) 366-8100
Web: www.phelpsdodge.com

TYSON FOODS INC.
Human Resources
2210 W. Oaklawn Dr.
Springdale, AR 72762
Kenneth J. Kimbro, Senior Vice President, Human Resources
Tel: (479) 290-4000
Web: www.tysonfoodsinc.com

WAL-MART STORES
Arkansas
702 S.W. Eighth St
Bentonville, AR 72716
Lawrence V. Jackson, Executive Vice President People Division
Tel: (479) 273-4000 Fax: (479) 273-4329
Web: www.walmart.com

CALIFORNIA

ADVANCED MICRO DEVICES
Human Resources
1 AMD Place
Sunnyvale, CA 94088
Tel: (408) 749-4000
Web: www.amd.com

AGILENT TECHNOLOGIES
Human Resources
395 Page Mill Rd.
Palo Alto, CA 94306
Jean M. Halloran, Senior Vice President, Human Resources
Tel: (650) 752-5000
Web: www.agilent.com

AMGEN
Human Resources
1 Amgen Center Dr.
Thousand Oaks, CA 91320
Brian McNamee, Senior Vice President, Human Resources
Tel: (805) 447-1000 Fax: (805) 447-1010
Web: www.amgen.com

APPLE COMPUTER
Human Resources
1 Infinite Loop #301-1RC
Cupertino, CA 95014
Shelly Hoefer, Director of Human Resources
Tel: (408) 974-2852 Fax: (408) 996-1010
Email: college@apple.com
Web: www.apple.com/jobs

APPLIED MATERIALS
Human Resources
3050 Bowers Ave.
Santa Clara, CA 95054
Jeannette Liebman, Vice President, Global Human Resources
Tel: (408) 727-5555
Web: www.appliedmaterials.com

AVERY DENNISON
Human Resources
150 N. Orange Grove Blvd.
Pasadena, CA 91103
Tel: (626) 304-2000
Web: www.averydennison.com

CALPINE
Human Resources
50 W. San Fernando St.
San Jose, CA 95113
John Miller, Senior Vice President, Human Resources and Safety
Tel: (408) 995-5115 Fax: (408) 995-0505
Web: www.calpine.com

CHARLES SCHWAB
Human Resources
120 Kearny St.
San Francisco, CA 94108
Tel: (415) 627-7000
Web: www.schwab.com

CHEVRONTEXACO
Chevron Headquarters
6001 Bollinger Canyon Rd.
San Ramon, CA 94583
Candy Gubauich, Head of Human Resources
Tel: (888) 825-5247 Fax: (888) 239-8647
Web: www.chevrontexaco.com

CISCO SYSTEMS
Human Resources
170 W. Tasman Dr.
San Jose, CA 95134
Kate D'camp, Senior Vice President, Human Resources
Tel: (408) 526-4000
Web: www.cisco.com

CLOROX
Human Resources
1221 Broadway
Oakland, CA 94612
Tel: (510) 271-7000
Web: www.clorox.com

CNF
Human Resources
3240 Hillview Ave.
Palo Alto, CA 94304
David L. Slate, Vice President, Human Resources
Tel: (650) 424-2900
Web: www.cnf.com

COMPUTER SCIENCES
Corporate Headquarters
2100 E. Grand Ave.
El Segundo, CA 90245
Tel: (310) 615-0311
Web: www.csc.com

COUNTRYWIDE FINANCIAL
Corporate Headquarters
4500 Park Granada
Calabasas, CA 91302
Leora I. Goren, Senior Managing Director and Chief Human Resources Officer
Web: www.countrywide.com

DIRECTV GROUP
Corporate Headquarters
2250 E. Imperial Highway
El Segundo, CA 90245
Tel: (310) 964-5000
Web: www.directv.com

DOLE FOOD
Human Resources
1 Dole Dr
Westlake Village, CA 91362
Yvonne Myenon, Recruiter, Human Resources
Tel: (818) 879-6600
Web: www.dole.com

EDISON INTERNATIONAL
Corporate Headquarters
2244 Walnut Grove Ave.
Rosemead, CA 91770
Tel: (626) 302-2222
Web: www.edison.com

FIRST AMERICAN CORP.
Human Resources
1 First American Way
Santa Ana, CA 92707
Tel: (714) 800-3000
Web: www.firstam.com

FLUOR
Human Resources
1 Enterprise Dr.
Aliso Viejo, CA 92656
H. Steven Gilbert, Senior Vice President, Human Resources and Administration
Tel: (949) 349-2000 Fax: (949) 349-2585
Web: www.fluor.com

GAP
Corporate Headquarters
2 Folson St.
San Francisco, CA 94105
Eva Sage-Gavin, Executive Vice President, Human Resouces
Tel: (650) 952-4400
Web: www.gapinc.com

GATEWAY
Human Resources
7565 Irvine Center Dr.
Irvine, CA 92618
Mike Tyler, Vice President, Administration
Tel: (949) 491-7000
Web: www.gateway.com

GOLDEN WEST FINANCIAL
Human Resources
1901 Harrison St.
Oakland, CA 94612
Tel: (510) 446-3420
Web: www.worldsavings.com

HEALTH NET
Corporate Headquarters
21650 Oxnard St.
Woodland Hills, CA 91367
Steven Sell, Vice President, Employer
Services
Tel: (818) 676-6000
Web: www.healthnet.com

HEWLETT-PACKARD
Headquarters
3000 Hanover St
Palo Alto, CA 94304
Marcela Perez de Alonso, Executive Vice
President, Human Resources
Tel: (650) 857-1501 Fax: (650) 857-5518
Web: www.hp.com

INGRAM MICRO
Human Resources
1600 E. St. Andrews Pl.
Santa Ana, CA 92705
Matthew A Suaer, Senior Vice President,
Human Resources
Tel: (714) 566-1000
Web: www.ingrammicro.com

INTEL
Corporate Headquarters
2200 Mission College Blvd
Santa Clara, CA 95052
Patricia Murray, Senior Vice President,
Human Resources
Tel: (408) 765-8080
Web: www.intel.com

JACOBS ENGINEERING GRP.
Human Resources
1111 S. Arroyo Pkwy
Pasadena, CA 91105
Tel: (626) 578-3500
Web: www.jacobs.com

KB HOME
Human Resources
10990 Wilshire Blvd.
Los Angeles, CA 90024
Laurel Osborne, Client Service Manager
Email: losborne@kbhome.com
Web: www.kbhome.com

LEVI STRAUSS
Human Resources
1155 Battery St.
San Francisco, CA 94111
Fred Paulenich, Senior Vice President,
Human Resources
Tel: (415) 501-6000
Web: www.levistrauss.com

LONGS DRUG STORES
Human Resources
141 N. Civic Dr.
Walnut Creek, CA 94596
Linda M. Watt, Senior Vice President,
Human Resources
Tel: (925) 937-1170
Web: www.longs.com

MATTEL
Human Resources
333 Continental Blvd
El Segundo, CA 90245
Alan Kaye, Senior Vice President, Human
Resources
Tel: (310) 252-2000 Fax: (310) 252-2180
Web: www.mattel.com

MAXTOR
Human Resources
500 McCarthy Blvd
Milpitas, CA 95035
Lina George, Senior Vice President, Human
Resources
Tel: (408) 894-5000
Web: www.maxtor.com

MCKESSON
Corporate Headquarters
1 Post St.
San Francisco, CA 94104
Paul E. Kirincic, Executive Vice President,
Human Resources
Tel: (415) 983-8300
Web: www.mckesson.com

NORTHROP GRUMMAN
Corporate Headquarters
1840 Century Park E.
Los Angeles, CA 90067
J. Michael Hately, Corporate Voice
President and Chief Human Resources and
Administrative Officer
Tel: (310) 553-6262
Web: www.northropgrumman.com

OCCIDENTAL PETROLEUM
Corporate Headquarters
10889 Wilshire Blvd
Los Angeles, CA 90024
Tel: (310) 208-8800
Web: www.oxy.com

ORACLE CORPORATION
Corporate Headquarters
500 Oracle Pkwy
Redwood City, CA 94065
Tel: (650) 506-7000
Web: www.oracle.com

PACIFIC LIFE
Human Resources
700 Newport Center Dr.
Newport Beach, CA 92660
Anthony J. Bonno, Senior Vice President,
Human Resources
Tel: (949) 219-3011
Web: www.pacificlife.com

PACIFICARE HEALTH SYS.
Human Resources
5995 Plaza Dr.
Cypress, CA 90630
Carol Black, Senior Vice President, Human
Resources
Tel: (714) 952-1121
Web: www.pacificare.com

PG&E CORP.
Corporate Headquarters
1 Market St.
San Francisco, CA 94105
Russell M. Jackson, Senior Vice President,
Human Resources
Tel: (415) 267-7000
Web: www.pgecorp.com

QUALCOMM
Human Resources
5775 Morehouse Dr.
San Diego, CA 92121
Dr. Daniel L. Sullivan, Executive Vice
President, Human Resources

Tel: (858) 587-1121
Web: www.qualcomm.com

ROSS STORES
Human Resources
4440 Rosewood Dr
Pleasanton, CA 94588
D. Jane Marvin, Senior Vice President,
Human Resources
Tel: (925) 965-4400
Web: www.rossstores.com

RYLAND GROUP
Human Resources
24025 Park Sorrento
Calabasas, CA 91302
Robert J. Cunnion, III, Senior Vice
President, Human Resources
Tel: (818) 223-7500
Web: www.ryland.com

SAFEWAY
Corporate Headquarters
5918 Stoneridge Mall Rd.
Pleasanton, CA 94588
James Derosier, Manager Supplier Human
Resources
Tel: (925) 467-3000
Web: www.safeway.com

SANMINA-SCI
Corporate Headquarters
2700 N. First St.
San Jose, CA 95143
Carmine Renzilli, Senior Vice President,
Global Human Resources
Tel: (408) 964-3500 Fax: (408) 964-3779
Web: www.sanmina-sci.com

SCIENCE APPLICATIONS INTL.
Human Resources Dept.
102260 Campus Point Dr.
San Diego, CA 92121
Tel: (858) 826-6000
Web: www.saic.com

SEMPRA ENERGY
Human Resources
101 Ash St.
San Diego, CA 92101
G. Joyce Rowling, Senior Vice President,
Human Resources
Tel: (619) 696-2000
Web: www.sempra.com

SOLECTRON
Human Resources
847 Gibratlar Dr.
Milpitas, CA 95053
Kevin O'Connor, Executive Vice President,
Human Resources
Tel: (408) 957-8500
Web: www.solectron.com

STARTER BROS. HOLDINGS
Human Resources
21700 Barton Rd.
Cotton, CA 92324
Cathy Finazzo, Vice President Diversity and
Corporate EEO
Tel: (909) 783-5000
Web: www.starterbros.com

SUN MICROSYSTEMS
Human Resources
4150 Network Circle
Santa Clara, CA 95054
Bill MacGowan, Senior Vice President,
Human Resources
Tel: (650) 960-1300
Web: www.sun.com

UNOCAL CORPORATION
Corporate Headquarters

2141 Rosecrans Ave.
El Segundo, CA 90245
Tel: (310) 726-7600
Web: www.unocal.com

WALT DISNEY
Corporate Headquarters
500 S. Buena Vista Dr.
Burbank, CA 91521
John M. Rentro, Senior Vice President and
Chief Human Resources
Tel: (818) 560-1000
Web: www.disney.com

WELLS FARGO
Corporate Headquarters
420 Montgomery Rd.
San Francisco, CA 94104
Avid Modtjabai, Executive Vice President,
Human Resources
Tel: (800) 333-0343
Web: www.wellsfargo.com

COLORADO

BALL
Human Resources
10 Longs Peak Dr.
Broomfield, CO 80021
Tel: (303) 469-3131
Web: www.ball.com

ECHOSTAR COMMUNICATIONS
Human Resources
9601 S. Meridian Blvd.
Englewood, CO 80112
Tel: (303) 723-1000
Web: www.echostar.com

FIRST DATA
Human Resources
6200 S. Quebec St.
Greenwood Village, CO 80111
Mike D'Ambrose, Executive Vice President,
Human Resources
Tel: (303) 488-8000
Web: www.firstdata.com

LEVEL 3 COMMUNICATIONS
Human Resources
1025 Eldorado Rd
Broomfield, CO 80021
Tel: (720) 888-1000
Web: www.level3.com

LIBERTY MEDIA
Human Resources
12300 Liberty Blvd.
Englewood, CO 80112
Tel: (720) 875-5400
Web: www.libertymedia.com

MDC HOLDINGS
Human Resources
3600 S. Yosemite St.
Denver, CO 80237
Sharon S. Brown, Vice President, Human
Resources
Tel: (303) 773-1100
Web: www.richmondamerican.com

MOLSON COORS BREWING
Human Resources
311 Tenth St.
Golden, CO 80401
Tel: (303) 279-6565
Web: www.molsoncoors.com

NEWMONT MINING
Human Resources
1700 Lincoln St.
Denver, CO 80203

Darla Caudie, Vice President, Human
Resources
Tel: (303) 863-7414
Web: www.newmont.com

QWEST COMMUNICATIONS
Corporate Headquarters
1801 California St.
Denver, CO 80202
Teresa Taylor, Executive Vice President/
Chief Human Resources
Tel: (303) 992-1400 Fax: (303) 896-8515
Web: www.quest.com

TRANSMONTAIGNE
Human Resources
1670 Broadway
Denver, CO 80202
Nico Soreno, Human Resources
Tel: (303) 626-8200 Fax: (303) 626-8228
Web: www.transmontaigne.com

CONNECTICUT

AETNA
Corporate Headquarters
151 Farmington Ave
Hartford, CT 06156
Elease Wright, Head of Human Resources
Tel: (860) 273-0123
Web: www.aetna.com

EMCOR GROUP
Human Resources
301 Merritt 7 Corporate Pk.
Norwalk, CT 06851
Christine Names, Vice President, Human
Resources
Tel: (203) 849-7800
Web: www.emcorpgroup.com

GENERAL ELECTRIC
Corporate Headquarters
3135 Easton Turnpike
Fairfield, CT 06828
Julie Grzee, Managing Director, Human
Resources
Tel: (203) 373-2211
Web: www.ge.com

HARTFORD FINANCIAL SERVICES
Human Resources
690 Asylum Ave.
Hartford, CT 06115
Ann M. de Raismes, Executive Vice
President, Human Resources
Tel: (860) 547-5000
Web: www.thehartford.com

INTERNATIONAL PAPER
Corporate Headquarters
400 Atlantic st.
Stamford, CT 06921
Jerome N. Carter, Senior Vice President,
Human Resources
Tel: (203) 451-8000
Web: www.ipaper.com

NORTHEAST UTILITIES
Human Resources
107 Selden St.
Berlin, CT 06037
Jean M. LaVecchia, Vice President, Human
Resources
Tel: (860) 665-5000
Web: www.nu.com

PITNEY BOWES
Human Resources
1 Elmcroft Rd.
Stamford, CT 06926
Johnna G. Torsone, Senior Vice President,
Human Resources

Tel: (203) 356-5000
Web: www.pb.com

PRAXAIR
Human Resources
39 Old Ridgebury Rd.
Danbury, CT 06810
Sally A. Savoia, Vice President, Human
Resources
Tel: (203) 837-2000
Web: www.praxair.com

PREMCOR
Corporate Headquarters
1700 E. Putnam Ave.
Old Greenwich, CT 06870
Peter Terenzio, Vice President, Human
Resources
Tel: (203) 698-7500 Fax: (203) 698-7925
Web: www.premcor.com

TEREX
Human Resources
500 Post Rd. E.
Westport, CT 06880
Kevin A. Barr, Vice President, Human
Resources
Tel: (203) 222-7170
Web: www.terex.com

UNITED TECHNOLOGIES
Corporate Headquarters
1 Financial Plz.
Hartford, CT 06103
William L. Bucknall Jr., Senior Vice
President, Human Resources and
Organization
Tel: (860) 678-5454
Web: www.utc.com

W.R. BERKLEY
Human Resources
475 Steamboat Rd.
Greenwich, CT 06830
Joseph M. Pennachio, Vice President,
Human Resources
Tel: (203) 629-3000
Web: www.wrbc.com

XEROX
Corporate Headquarters
800 Long Ridge Rd.
Stamford, CT 06904
Patricia M. Nazemetz, Vice President,
Human Resources
Tel: (203) 968-3000
Web: www.xerox.com

DELAWARE

DUPONT
Corporate Headquarters
1007 Market St.
Wilmington, DE 19898
James C. Borel, Senior VP- Dupont Global
Human Resources
Tel: (302) 774-1000
Web: www.dupont.com

MBNA
Corporate Headquarters
1100 N. King St.
Wilmington, DE 19884
Tel: (800) 362-6255
Web: www.mbna.com

DISTRICT OF COLUMBIA

DANAHER
Human Resources
2099 Pennsylvannia Ave, N.W.

Washington, DC 20006
Tel: (202) 828-0850
Web: www.danaher.com

PEPCO HOLDINGS, INC.
Corporate Headquarters
701 9th St. NW
Washington, DC 20068
Freda Gray, Staffing Supervisor
Tel: (202) 872-2101 Fax: (202) 331-6850
Web: www.pepcoholdings.com

FLORIDA

AUTONATION
Human Resources
110 S.E. Sixth St.
Fort Lauderdale, FL 33301
Andrea Dawkins, Manager, Human
Resources
Tel: (954) 769-2757
Web: www.autonation.com

CSX
Human Resources
500 Water St.
Jacksonville, FL 32202
Robert J. Haulter, Senior Vice President,
Human Resources and Labor Relations
Tel: (904) 359-3200
Web: www.csx.com

DARDEN RESTAURANTS
Human Resources
5900 Lake Ellenor Dr.
Orlando, FL 32809
Daniel M. Lyons, Senior Vice President,
Human Resources
Tel: (407) 245-4000
Web: www.darden.com

FIDELITY NATIONAL FINANCIAL
Human Resources
601 Riverside Ave.
Jacksonville, FL 32204
Pete Pennella, Staffing Manager
Tel: (904) 854-8100 Fax: (904) 854-4282
Web: www.fnf.com

FPL GROUP
Corporate Headquarters
700 Universe Blvd
Juno Beach, FL 33408
Robert H. Escoto, Vice President, Human
Resources
Tel: (561) 694-4000
Web: www.fplgroup.com

HUGHES SUPPLY
Human Resources
1 Hughes Way
Orlando, FL 32805
Jay Romans, Senior Vice President, Human
Resources
Tel: (407) 841-4755
Web: www.hughessupply.com

JABIL CIRCUIT
Human Resources
10560 Dr. Martin Luther King Jr. St. N.
St. Petersburg, FL 33716
Thomas T. O'Connor, Vice President,
Human Resources-Americas
Tel: (727) 577-9749
Web: www.jabil.com

LENNAR
Corporate Headquarters
700 N.W. 107th Ave.
Miami, FL 33172
Frank Matthews, Director, Human
Resources

Tel: (305) 559-4000
Web: www.lennar.com

OFFICE DEPOT
Human Resources
2200 Old Germantown Rd.
Delray Beach, FL 33445
Frank Scruggs, Executive Vice President,
Human Resources
Tel: (561) 438-4800
Web: www.officedepot.com

PUBLIX SUPER MARKETS
Corporate Headquarters
3300 Publix Corporate Pkwy.
Lakeland, FL 33811
John Harabusa, Vice President, Human
Resources
Tel: (863) 688-1188
Web: www.publix.com

RYDER SYSTEM
Human Resources
3600 N.W. 82nd Ave.
Miami, FL 33166
Jennifer Thomas, Senior Vice President,
Human Resources
Tel: (305) 500-3726
Web: www.ryder.com

TECH DATA
Corporate Headquarters
5350 Tech Data Dr.
Clearwater, FL 33760
Lawrence W. Hamilton, Senior Vice
President, Human Resources
Tel: (727) 539-7429
Web: www.techdata.com

WINN-DIXIE STORES
Corporate Headquarters
5050 Edgewood Ct
Jacksonville, FL 32254
Tel: (904) 783-5000
Web: www.winn-dixie.com

WORLD FUEL SERVICES
Human Resources
9800 NW 41st St.
Miami, FL 33178
Tel: (305) 428-8000 Fax: (305) 392-5600
Web: www.wfscorp.com

GEORGIA

AFLAC
Human Resources
1932 Wynnton Rd.
Columbus, GA 31999
Audrey Tillman, Director, Human Resources
Tel: (706) 323-3431
Web: www.aflac.com

AGCO
Human Resources
4205 River Green Pkwy.
Duluth, GA 30096
Norman L. Boyd, Senior Vice President,
Human Resources
Tel: (770) 813-9200 Fax: (770) 232-8001
Web: www.agcocorp.com

BEAZER HOMES USA
Human Resources
1000 Abernathy Rd.
Atlanta, GA 30328
Fred Fratto, Senior Vice President, Human
Resources
Tel: (770) 829-3700
Web: www.beazer.com

BELLSOUTH
Corporate Headquarters

1155 Peachtree St. N.E.,
Atlanta, GA 30309
Tel: (404) 249-2000
Web: www.bellsouth.com

COCA-COLA
Corporate Headquarters
1 Coca-Cola Plz.
Atlanta, GA 30313
Cynthia P. McCague, Director, Human
Resources
Tel: (404) 676-2121
Web: www.coca-cola.com

Human Resources
2500 Windy Ridge Pkwy.
Atlanta, GA 30339
Daniel S. Bowling, III, Senior Vice President,
Human Resources
Tel: (770) 989-3000
Web: www.cokecce.com

COX COMMUNICATIONS
Human Resources
1400 Lake Hearn Dr.
Atlanta, GA 30319
Monica Johnson, Director of Recruiting
Tel: (404) 843-5000
Web: www.cox.com

DELTA AIR LINES
Corporate Heaquarters
1030 Delta Blvd
Atlanta, GA 30320
Lee Macenczak, Senior Vice President and
Chief Customer Service Officer
Tel: (404) 715-2600
Web: www.delta.com

GENUINE PARTS
Human Resources
2999 Circle 75 Pkwy.
Atlanta, GA 30339
Kathy McCort, Human Resources
Tel: (770) 953-1700
Web: www.genpt.com

GEORGIA-PACIFIC
Corporate Headquarters
133 Peachtree St. N.E.
Atlanta, GA 30303
Patricia A. Bernard, Executive Vice
President, Human Resources
Tel: (404) 652-4000
Web: www.gp.com

HOME DEPOT
Corporate Headquarters
2455 Paces Ferry Rd. N.W.
Atlanta, GA 30339
Dennis Donovan, Executive Vice President,
Human Resources
Tel: (770) 433-8211
Web: www.homedepot.com

MIRANT
Human Resources
1155 Perimeter Center W.
Atlanta, GA 30338
Tel: (678) 579-5000
Web: www.mirant.com

MOHAWK INDUSTRIES
Human Resources
160 S. Industrial Blvd
Calhoun, GA 30701
Tel: (706) 629-7721
Web: www.mohawkind.com

NEWELL RUBBERMAID
Human Resources
10 B Glenlake Pkwy. #600
Atlanta, GA 30328

James M. Sweet, Vice President, Human
Resources
Tel: (770) 407-3800
Web: www.newellrubbermaid.com

SOUTHERN
Corporate Headquarters
270 Peachtree St. N.W.
Atlanta, GA 30303
Tel: (404) 506-5000
Web: www.southernco.com

SUNTRUST BANKS
Human Resources
303 Peachtree St. N.E.
Atlanta, GA 30308
Mary T. Steele, Director, Human Resources
Tel: (404) 588-7711
Web: www.suntrust.com

UNITED PARCEL SERVICE
Corporate Headquarters
55 Glenlake Pkwy, N.E.
Atlanta, GA 30328
Lea N. Soupata, Senior Vice President,
Human Resources
Tel: (404) 828-6000
Web: www.ups.com

IDAHO

ALBERTSON'S
Corporate Headquarters
250 Parkcenter Blvd
Boise, ID 83642
Jennifer Giro, Director of Corporate Human
Resources
Tel: (208) 395-3853
Web: www.albertsons.com

MICRON TECHNOLOGY
Human Resources
8000 S. Federal Way
Boise, ID 83716
Jo Anne S. Arnold, Vice President, Human
Resources
Tel: (208) 368-4000
Web: www.micron.com

ILLINOIS

ABBOTT LABORATORIES
Corporate Headquarters
100 Abbott Park Rd.
Abbott Park, IL 60064
Stephen R. Fusell, Senior Vice President,
Human Resources
Tel: (847) 937-6100
Web: www.abbott.com

ALLSTATE
Corporate Headquarters
2775 Sanders Rd.
Northbrook, IL 60062
Joan M. Crockett, Senior Vice President,
Human Resources
Tel: (847) 402-5000
Web: www.allstate.com

AON
Corporate Headquarters
200 E. Randolph St.
Chicago, IL 60601
Jeremy G.O. Farmer, Senior Vice President
and Head, Human Resources
Tel: (312) 381-1000
Web: www.aon.com

ARCHER DANIELS MIDLAND
Corporate Headquarters
4666 Faries Pkwy

Decatur, IL 62525
Randy Moon, Human Resources
Tel: (217) 424-5200 Fax: (217) 451-4383
Web: www.admworld.com

BAXTER INTERNATIONAL
Human Resources
1 Baxter Pkwy
Deerfield, IL 60015
Karen J. May, Corporate Vice President,
Human Resources
Tel: (847) 948-2000
Web: www.baxter.com

BOEING
Corporate Headquarters
100 N. Riverside Park
Chicago, IL 60606
Richard Stephens, Senior Vice President,
Internal Services
Tel: (312) 544-2000
Web: www.boeing.com

BRUNSWICK
Human Resources
1 N. Field Court
Lake Forest, IL 60045
B. Russell Lockridge, Vice President and
Chief Human Resources Officer
Tel: (847) 735-4700
Web: www.brunswick.com

CATERPILLAR
Corporate Headquarters
100 N.E. Adams St.
Peoria, IL 61629
Sidney C. Bandwart, Vice President Human
Resources
Tel: (309) 675-1000
Web: www.cat.com

CDW
Corporate Headquarters
200 N. Milwaukee Ave.
Vernon Hills, IL 60061
Maria M. Sullivan , Vice President, Learning
and Development
Tel: (847) 465-6000
Web: www.cdw.com

EXELON
Corporate Headquarters
10 S. Dearborn St.
Chicago, IL 60680
S. Gary Snodgrass, Executive Vice President
and Chief Human Resources Officer
Tel: (312) 394-7398
Web: www.exeloncorp.com

FORTUNE BRANDS
Human Resources
300 Tower Pkwy
Lincolnshire, IL 60069
Tel: (847) 484-4400
Web: www.fortunebrands.com

ILLINOIS TOOL WORKS
Human Resources
3600 W. Lake Ave.
Glenview, IL 60026
Barbara Morris, Manager, Human
Resources
Tel: (847) 724-7500
Web: www.itw.com

JOHN DEERE
Corporate Headquarters
1 John Deere Pl.
Moline, IL 61265
Mertroe B. Hornbuckle, VP of Human
Resources
Tel: (309) 765-8000
Web: www.deere.com

LAIDLAW INTERNATIONAL
Human Resources
55 Shuman Blvd.
Naperville, IL 60563
Alice Wright, Human Resources
Tel: (630) 848-3000
Web: www.laidlaw.com

MCDONALD'S
Corporate Headquarters
1 McDonald's Plaza
Oak Brook, IL 60523
Richard Floersch, Executive Vice President,
Worldwide Human Resources
Tel: (630) 623-3000
Web: www.mcdonalds.com

MOTOROLA
Corporate Headquarters
1303 E. Algonquin Rd.
Schaumburg, IL 60196
Ruth Fattori, Executive Vice President,
Human Resources
Tel: (847) 576-5000
Web: www.motorola.com

NAVISTAR INTERNATIONAL
Corporate Headquarters
4201 Winfield Rd.
Warrenville, IL 60555
Tel: (630) 753-5000
Web: www.navistar.com

OFFICEMAX
Corporate Headquarters
150 Pierce Rd.
Itasca, IL 60143
Lorene Flewellen, Senior Vice President,
Human Relations
Tel: (630) 438-7800
Web: www.officemax.com

R.R. DONNELLEY & SONS
Human Resources Department
111 S.Wacker Dr.
Chicago, IL 60601
Stan Jaworski
Tel: 312-326-8396
Web: www.rrdonnelley.com

SARA LEE
Human Resources
3 First National Plaza
Chicago, IL 60602
Lois M. Huggins, Senior Vice President,
Global Human Resources
Tel: (312) 726-2600
Web: www.saralee.com

SEARS ROEBUCK
Corporate Headquarters
3333 Beverly Rd
Hoffman Estates, IL 60179
Tel: (847) 286-2500
Web: www.sears.com

SERVICEMASTER
Human Resources
3250 Lacey Rd.
Downers Grove, IL 60515
Lisa Goettel, Senior Vice President, Human
Resources
Tel: (630) 663-2000
Web: www.svm.com

SMURFIT-STONE CONTAINER
Human Resources
150 N. Michigan Ave.
Chicago, IL 60601
Marissia Ayala, Human Resources
Tel: (312) 346-6600
Web: www.smurfit-stone.com

STATE FARM INSURANCE COS
Corporate Headquarters
1 State Farm Plaza
Bloomington, IL 61710
Margie Southard, Assistant Vice President,
Diversity/Human Resources
Tel: (309) 766-2311
Web: www.statefarm.com

TELEPHONE & DATA SYS.
Human Resources
30 N. LaSalle St.
Chicago, IL 60602
C. Theordore Herbert, Vice President,
Human Resources
Tel: (312) 630-1990
Web: www.teldta.com

TENNECO AUTOMOTIVE
Human Resources
500 N. Field Dr.
Lake Forest, IL 60045
Barb Kluch, Director, Human Resources
Tel: (847) 482-5000
Web: www.tenneco-automotive.com

TRIBUNE
Human Resources
435 N. Michigan Ave.
Chicago, IL 60611
Luis E. Lewin, Senior Vice President,
Human Resources
Tel: (312) 222-9100
Web: www.tribune.com

UNITED AIRLINES INC.
Corporate Headquarters
1200 E. Algonquin Rd.
Elk Grove Township, IL 60007
Sara A. Fields, Senior Vice President,
People
Tel: (847) 700-4000
Web: www.united.com

UNITED STATIONERS
Human Resources
2200 E. Golf Rd.
Des Plaines, IL 60016
John T. Sloan, Senior Vice President,
Human Resources
Tel: (847) 699-5000
Web: www.unitedstationers.com

USG
Human Resources
125 S. Franklin St.
Chicago, IL 60606
Brian J. Cook, Senior Vice President,
Human Resources
Tel: (312) 606-4000
Web: www.usg.com

W.W. GRAINGER
Human Resources
100 Grainger Pkwy
Lake Forest, IL 60045
Tel: (847) 535-1000
Web: www.grainger.com

WALGREEN
Corporate Headquarters
200 Wilmot Rd.
Deerfield, IL 60015
Jennifer Briscoe, Human Resources
Recruiting Manager
Tel: (847) 914-2500
Web: www.walgreens.com

WM. WRIGLEY JR.
Human Resources
410 N. Michigan Ave.
Chicago, IL 60611

Dushan Petrovich, Senior Vice President,
Administrative
Tel: (312) 644-1212
Web: www.wrigley.com

INDIANA

CONSECO
Human Resources
11825 N. Pennsylvania St.
Carmel, IN 46032
Susan L. Menzel, Executive Vice President,
Human Resources
Tel: (317) 817-6100
Web: www.conseco.com

CUMMINS
Human Resources
500 Jackson St.
Columbus, IN 47201
Felecia Roseburgh, Manager, Corporate
Compliance
Tel: (317)-610-2481

ELI LILLY
Corporate Headquarters
Lilly Corporate Center
Indianapolis, IN 46285
Anthony Murphy, Senior Vice President
Tel: (317) 276-2000
Web: www.lilly.com

GUIDANT
Human Resources
111 Monument Circle
Indianapolis, IN 46204
Roger Marchetti, Vice President, Human
Resources
Tel: (317) 971-2000
Web: www.guidant.com

NISOURCE
Human Resources
801 E. 86th Ave.
Merrillville, IN 46410
S. LaNette Zimmerman, Executive Vice
President, Human Resources
Tel: (219) 647-6200
Web: www.nisource.com

WELLPOINT
Human Resources
120 Mounment Circle
Indianapolis, IN 46204
Randy Brown, Senior Vice President,
Human Resources
Tel: (317) 523-6000
Web: www.wellpoint.com

IOWA

MAYTAG
Human Resources
403 W. Fourth St. N.
Newton, IA 50208
Mark W. Krivoruchka, Senior Vice President,
Human Resources
Tel: (641) 792-7000 Fax: (641) 787-8376
Web: www.maytagcorp.com

PRINCIPAL FINANCIAL
Human Resources
711 High St.
Des Moines, IA 50392
James D. DeVries, Senior Vice President,
Human Resources
Tel: (571) 247-5111
Web: www.principal.com

KANSAS

HUMANA
Human Resources
500 W. Main St.
Louisville, KS 40202
Bonita C. Hathcock, Senior Vice President,
Chief Human Resources Officer
Tel: (502) 580-1000
Web: www.humana.com

SPRINT
Corporate Headquarters
6200 Sprint Pkwy
Overland Park, KS 66251
Jim Kessinger, Vice President, Human
Resources
Tel: (800) 829-0965
Web: www.sprint.com

YELLOW ROADWAY
Human Resources
10990 Roe Ave.
Overland Park, KS 66211
Steven T. Yamasaki, Senior Vice President,
Human Resources
Tel: (913) 696-6100
Web: www.yellowroadway.com

KENTUCKY

KINDRED HEALTHCARE
Human Resources
680 S. Fourth St.
Louisville, KY 40202
Terry Montgomery, Recruiting Services
Tel: (502) 596-7300
Web: www.kindredhealthcare.com

LEXMARK INTERNATIONAL
Human Resources
740 W. Circle Rd.
Lexington, KY 40550
Jeri Stromquist, Vice President, Human
Resources
Tel: (859) 232-2000
Web: www.lexmark.com

OMNICARE
Human Resources
100 E. River Center Blvd.
Covington, KY 41011
J. Michael Roberts, Vice President, Human
Resources
Tel: (859) 392-3300
Web: www.omnicare.com

YUM BRANDS
Human Resources
1441 Gardiner Ln.
Louisville, KY 40213
Anne P. Byerlein, Chief People Officer
Tel: (502) 874-8300
Web: www.yum.com

LOUISIANA

ENTERGY
Human Resources
639 Loyola Ave.
New Orleans, LA 70113
William E. Madison, Senior Vice President,
Human Resources and Adminsitration
Tel: (504) 576-4000
Web: www.entergy.com

MARYLAND

BLACK & DECKER
Human Resources
701 E. Joppa Rd.
Towson, MD 21286
Paul F. McBride, Senior Vice President,
Human Resources and Corporate Initiatives
Tel: (410) 716-3900
Web: www.bdk.com

CONSTELLATION ENERGY
Human Resources
750 E. Pratt St.
Baltimore, MD 21202
Marc L. Ugol, Senior Vice President
Tel: (410) 783-2800
Web: www.constellation.com

COVENTRY HEALTH CARE
Human Resources
6705 Rockledge Dr.
Bethesda, MD 20817
Clarie Connors, Director, Executive
Recruiting Human Resources
Tel: (301) 581-0600
Web: www.cvty.com

HOST MARRIOTT
Human Resources
6903 Rockledge Rd.
Bethesda, MD 20817
Pamela K. Wagoner, Senior Vice President,
Human Resources and Leadership
Development
Tel: (240) 744-1000
Web: www.hostmarriott.com

LOCKHEED MARTIN
Corporate Headquarters
6801 Rockledge Dr.
Bethesda, MD 20817
Jean Carr, Diversity, Human Resources
Manager
Tel: (301) 897-6000
Web: www.lockheedmartin.com

MARRIOTT INTERNATIONAL
Corporate Headquarters
10400 Fernwood Rd.
Bethesda, MD 20817
Brendan M. Keegan, Executive Vice
President, Human Resources
Tel: (301) 380-3000
Web: www.marriott.com

MASSACHUSETTS

BJ'S WHOLESALE CLUB
Human Resources
1 Mercer Rd.
Natick, MA 01760
Tel: (508) 651-7400
Web: www.bjs.com

BOSTON SCIENTIFIC
Human Resources
1 Boston Scientific Pl.
Natick, MA 01760
Tel: (508) 650-8000
Web: www.bostonscientific.com

EMC CORPORATION
Human Resources
176 South St.
Hopkinton, MA 01748
John T. Mollen, Senior VP, Human
Resources
Tel: (508) 435-1000 Fax: (508) 497-6912
Web: www.emc.com

LIBERTY MUTUAL INS. GROUP
Corporate Headquarters
175 Berkeley St.
Boston, MA 02116
Helen E.R. Sayles, Senior Vice President,
Human Resources and Administration
Tel: (617) 357-9500
Web: www.libertymutual.com

MASS. MUTUAL LIFE INS.
Corporate Headquarters
1295 State St.
Springfield, MA 01111
Tel: (413) 788-8411
Web: www.massmutual.com

RAYTHEON
Human Resources
870 Winter St.
Waltham, MA 02451
David Freeman, Director, Human
Resources
Tel: (781) 522-3000
Web: www.raytheon.com

REEBOK INTERNATIONAL
Human Resources
1891 J.W. Foster Blvd
Canton, MA 02021
Tel: (781) 401-5000
Web: www.reebok.com

STAPLES
Corporate Headquarters
500 Staples Dr.
Framingham, MA 01702
Tel: (508) 253-5000 Fax: (508) 305-1300
Web: www.staples.com

STATE ST. CORP.
Human Resources
1 Lincoln St.
Boston, MA 02111
Luis J. de Ocejo, Executive Vice President,
Human Resources and Organizational
Performance
Tel: (617) 786-3000
Web: www.statestreet.com

THE GILLETTE COMPANY
Human Resources
Prudential Tower Bldg.
Boston, MA 02199
Edward E. Guillet, Vice President, Human
Resources
Tel: (617) 421-7000
Web: www.gillette.com

THE TJX COMPANIES INC.
Human Resources
770 Cochituate Rd.
Framingham, MA 01701
Mary Beth Kelly, Manager Human
Resources
Tel: (508) 390-1000
Web: www.tjx.com

MICHIGAN

ARVINMERITOR
Human Resources
2135 W. Maple Rd.
Troy, MI 48084
Ernie Whitus, Senior Vice President, Human
Resources
Tel: (248) 435-1000 Fax: (248) 435-1393
Web: www.arvinmeritor.com

AUTO-OWNERS INSURANCE
Human Resources
6101 Anacapri Blvd
Lansing, MI 48917

Amy Baker, Manager, Recruiting Services
Tel: (517) 323-1200 Fax: (512) 323-8796
Web: www.auto-owners.com

BORDERS GROUP
Human Resources
100 Phoenix Dr.
Ann Arbor, MI 48108
Daniel Smith, Senior Vice President,
Human Resources
Tel: (734) 477-1100
Web: www.bordersgroupinc.com

CMS ENERGY
Human Resources
1 Energy Plaza
Jackson, MI 49201
John F. Drake, Senior Vice President,
Human Resources and Administrative
Services
Tel: (517) 788-0550
Web: www.cmsenergy.com

COLLINS & AIKMAN
Human Resources
250 Stephenson Hwy
Troy, MI 48083
Tel: (248) 824-2500 Fax: (248) 824-1613
Web: www.collinsaikman.com

DELPHI
Corporate Headquarters
5725 Delphi Dr.
Troy, MI 48098
Mark R. Weber, Executive Vice President,
Operations, Human Resources
Management and Corporate Affairs
Tel: (248) 813-2000
Web: www.delphi.com

DOW CHEMICAL
Corporate Headquarters
2030 Dow Center
Midland, MI 48674
Luciano Respini, Corporate Vice President,
Geography, Human Resources and Public
Affairs
Tel: (989) 636-1000
Web: www.dow.com

DTE ENERGY
2000 2nd Ave.
Detroit, MI 48226
Theresa Alfafara, Director of Human
Resources
Tel: (313) 235-6520
Email: theresaalfafara@dtenergy.com
Web: www.dtenergy.com

FEDERAL-MOGUL
Human Resources
26555 Northwestern Hwy.
Southfield, MI 48034
Pam Mitchell, Director, Diversity
Tel: (248) 354-7700 Fax: 248-354-8100
Web: www.federal-mogul.com

FORD MOTOR
Corporate Office
1 American Rd.
Dearborn, MI 48126
Felicia J. Fields, Vice President, Human
Resources
Tel: (313) 322-3000
Web: www.ford.com

GENERAL MOTORS
300 Renaissance Center
Detroit, MI 48265
Kathleen S. Barclay, Human Resources
Tel: (313) 556-5000 Fax: (517) 272-3709
Web: www.gm.com

KELLOGG
Human Resources

1 Kellogg Square
Battle Creek, MI 49016
Annuciata Cerioli, Vice President, Human
Resources
Tel: (269) 961-2000
Web: www.kelloggcompany.com

KELLY SERVICES
Human Resources
999 W. Big Beaver Rd.
Troy, MI 48084
Michael L. Durik, Executive Vice President,
Administration.
Tel: (248) 362-4444
Web: www.kellyservices.com

KMART HOLDING
Human Resources
3100 W. Big Beaver Rd.
Troy, MI 48084
Robert Luse, Senior Vice President, Human
Resources
Tel: (248) 463-1000
Web: www.searsholdings.com

LEAR
Human Resources
21557 Telegraph Rd.
Southfield, MI 48034
Mary-Ann Churchwell, Director Human
Resources
Tel: (248) 447-1500 Fax: (248) 447-5944
Web: www.lear.com

MASCO
Corporate Headquarters
21001 Van Born Rd.
Taylor, MI 48180
Tel: (313) 274-7400
Web: www.masco.com

PULTE HOMES
Corporate Headquarters
100 Bloomfields Hill Pkwy
Bloomfield Hills, MI 48304
Tel: (248) 647-2750
Web: www.pulte.com

STRYKER
Human Resources
2725 Fairfield Rd.
Kalamazoo, MI 49002
Michael W. Rude, Vice President, Human
Resources
Tel: (269) 385-2600 Fax: (269) 385-1062
Web: www.stryker.com

TRW AUTOMOTIVE HOLDINGS
Human Resources
12025 Tech Center Dr.
Livonia, MI 48150
Neil Marchuk, Human Resources
Tel: (734) 855-2600
Web: www.trwauto.com

UNITED AUTO GROUP
Corporate Headquarters
2555 Telegraph Rd.
Bloomfield Hills, MI 48302
Randolph Johnson, Vice President, Human
Resources
Tel: (248) 648-2500
Web: www.unitedauto.com

VISTEON
Corporate Headquarters
1 Village Center Dr.
Van Buren Township, MI 48111
Charles Hudson, Vice President, Corporate
Human Resources
Tel: (800) 847-8366
Web: www.visteon.com

WHIRLPOOL
Corporate Headquarters

2000 North M-63
Benton Harbour, MI 49022
David A. Binkley, Senior Vice President,
Global Human Resources
Tel: (269) 923-5000
Web: www.whirlpoolcorp.com

MINNESOTA

3M
Human Resources
3M Center
St. Paul, MN 55144
M. Kay Grenz, Senior Vice President,
Human Resources
Tel: (651) 733-1110
Web: www.3m.com

BEST BUY
Corporate Headquarters
7601 Penn Ave. South
Richfield, MN 55423
Shari Ballard, Executive Vice President,
Human Capital and Leadership
Tel: (621) 291-1000
Web: www.bestbuy.com

C.H. ROBINSON WORLDWIDE
Human Resources
8100 Mitchell Rd.
Eden Prairie, MN 55344
Laura Guillund, Vice President, Human
Resources
Tel: (952) 937-8500
Web: www.chrobinson.com

CHS INC.
Corporate Headquarters
5500 Cenex Dr.
Inver Grove Hghts., MN 55077
John Schmitz, Executive ViP/CFO
Tel: (651) 355-6000
Web: www.chsinc.com

ECOLAB
Human Resources
370 Wabasha St. N.
St. Paul, MN 55102
Tel: (651) 293-2233
Web: www.ecolab.com

GENERAL MILLS
Human Resources
1 General Mills Blvd.
Minneapolis, MN 55426
Michael A. Peel, Senior Vice President,
Human Resources and Corporate Services
Tel: (763) 764-7600
Web: www.generalmills.com

HORMEL FOODS
Corporate Headquarters
1 Hormel Place
Austin, MN 55912
Tel: (507) 437-5611
Web: www.hormel.com

LAND O'LAKES
Human Resources
4001 Lexington Ave. North
Arden Hills, MN 55126
Kasey Comnick, Recruitment Coordinator
Tel: (651) 766-1778 Fax: (651) 766-1376
Web: www.landolakesinc.com

MEDTRONIC
Human Resources
710 Medtronic Pkwy.
Minneapolis, MN 55423
Janet Fiola, Senior Vice President, Human
Resources
Tel: (763) 514-4000
Web: www.medtronic.com

NASH FINCH
Human Resources
7600 France Ave. S.
Minneapolis, MN 55435
Joe R. Eulberg , Senior Vice President,
Human Resources
Tel: (952) 832-0534
Web: www.nashfinch.com

NORTHWEST AIRLINES
Human Resources
2700 Lone Oak Pkwy.
Eagan, MN 55121
Michael J. Becker, Senior Vice President,
Human Resources and Labor Relations
Tel: (612) 726-2111
Web: www.nwa.com

ST. PAUL TRAVELERS COS.
Corporate Headquarters
385 Washington St
St. Paul, MN 55102
John Clifford, Senior Vice President, Human
Resources
Tel: (651) 310-7911
Web: www.stpaultravelers.com

SUPERVALU
Human Resources
11840 Valley View Rd
Eden Prairie, MN 55344
Rick Talmersheim, Manager, Human
Resources
Tel: (952) 828-4000
Web: www.supervalu.com

TARGET
Corporate Headquarters
1000 Nicollet Mall
Minneapolis, MN 55403
Todd V. Blackwell, Executive Vice President,
Human Resources, Assets Protection,
Target Sourcing Services
Tel: (612) 304-6073
Web: www.target.com

THRIVENT FINANCIAL FOR LUTHERANS
Human Resources
625 Fourth Ave. S.
Minneapolis, MN 55415
Deb Palmer, Staffing Manager
Tel: (800) 847-4836 Fax: (612) 340-6897
Email: deb.palmer@thrivent.com
Web: www.thrivent.com

U.S. BANCORP
Corporate Headquarters
800 Nicolett Mall
Minneapolis, MN 55402
Jennie P. Carlson, Executive vice
President, Human Resources
Tel: (651) 466-3000
Web: www.usbank.com

UNITEDHEALTH GROUP
Corporate Headquarters
9900 Bren Rd. E.
Minnetonka, MN 55343
L. Robert Dapper, Senior Vice President,
Human Capital
Tel: (952) 936-1300
Web: www.unitedhealthgroup.com

XCEL ENERGY
Human Resources
414 Nicollet Mall
Minneapolis, MN 55402
Mark Sauerbrey, Corporate Recruiter
Tel: (612) 330-5724 Fax: (612) 330-7935
Email: mark.w.sauerbrey@xcelenergy.com
Web: www.xcelenergy.com

MISSOURI

AMEREN
Human Resources
1901 Chouteau Ave.
St. Louis, MO 63103
Donna K. Martin, Senior Vice President,
Human Resources
Tel: (314) 621-3222
Web: www.ameren.com

ANHEUSER-BUSCH
Human Resources
1 Busche Pl.
St. Louis, MO 63118
Tel: (314) 577-2000
Web: www.anheuser-busch.com

CHARTER COMMUNICATIONS
Human Resources
12405 Powerscourt Dr.
St. Louis, MO 63131
Lynne F. Ramsey, Senior Vice President,
Human Resources
Tel: (314) 965-0555
Web: www.charter.com

EMERSON ELECTRIC
Human Resources
8000 W. Florissant Ave.
St. Louis, MO 63136
Charles Kelly, Vice President, Human
Resources
Tel: (314) 553-2000
Web: www.gotoemerson.com

EXPRESS SCRIPTS
Corporate Headquarters
13900 Riverport Rd.
Maryland Heights, MO 63043
Glenda Knebel, Director Human Resources
Tel: (314) 770-1666
Web: www.express-scripts.com

GRAYBAR ELECTRIC
Human Resources
34 N. Meramec Ave.
St. Louis, MO 63105
Kathleen M. Mazzarella, Vice President,
Human Resources and Strategic Planning
Tel: (314) 573-9200
Web: www.graybar.com

H&R BLOCK
Human Resources
4400 Main St.
Kansas City, MO 64111
Tammy S Serati, Senior Vice President,
Human Resources
Tel: (816) 753-6900
Web: www.hrblock.com

LEGGETT & PLATT
Human Resources
1 Leggett Rd.
Carthage, MO 64836
Cathleen Garrison, Recruiting Manager,
Human Resources
Tel: (417) 358-8131
Web: www.leggett.com

MAY DEPT. STORES
Human Resources
611 Olive St.
St. Louis, MO 63101
Marian Wagner, Vice President, Human
Resources
Tel: (314) 342-6300
Web: www.mayco.com

MOSANTO
Human Resources
800 N. Lindbergh Blvd

St. Louis, MO 63167
Steven C. Mizell, Senior Vice President,
Human Resources
Tel: (314) 694-1000
Web: www.mosanto.com

PEABODY ENERGY
Human Resources
701 Market St.
St. Louis, MO 63101
Sharon D. Fiehler, Executive Vice President,
Human Resources
Tel: (314) 342-3400
Web: www.peabodyenergy.com

NEBRASKA

BERKSHIRE HATHAWAY
Corporate Headquarters
1440 Kiewit Plaza
Omaha, NE 68131
Tel: (402) 346-1400
Web: www.berkshirehathaway.com

CONAGRA FOODS
Human Resources
1 ConAgra Dr.
Omaha, NE 68102
Peter M. Perez, Senior Vice President,
Human Resources
Tel: (402) 595-4000
Web: www.conagrafoods.com

MUTUAL OF OMAHA INS.
Human Resources
Mutual of Omaha Plaza
Omaha, NE 38175
Deborah Woods, Diversity Program
Coordinator
Tel: (402) 351-3044
Web: www.mutualofomaha.com

UNION PACIFIC
Corporate Headquarters
1400 Douglas St.
Omaha, NE 68179
Barbara W. Schaefer, Senior Vice President,
Human Resources and Corporate Secretary
Tel: (402) 544-5000
Web: www.up.com

NEVADA

CAESARS ENTERTAINMENT
Human Resources
3930 Howard Hughes Pkwy
Las Vegas, NV 89109
Jerry Boone, Senior Vice President, Human
Resources
Tel: (702) 699-5000
Web: www.caesars.com

HARRAH'S ENTERTAINMENT
Human Resources
1 Harrah's Court
Las Vegas, NV 89119
Jerry Boone, Senior Vice President, Human
Resources
Tel: (702) 407-6000
Web: www.harrah's.com

MGM MIRAGE
Human Resources
3600 Las Vegas Blvd S.
Las Vegas, NV 89109
Tel: (702) 693-7120
Web: www.mgmmirage.com

NEW HAMPSHIRE

FISHER SCIENTIFIC INTL.
Human Resources
1 Liberty Lane
Hampton, NH 03842
Mariam Quast, Recruiter
Tel: (603) 926-5911
Web: www.fisherscientific.com

NEW JERSEY

AMERICAN STANDARD
Human Resources
1 Centennial Ave.
Piscataway, NJ 08855
Lawrence B. Costello, Senior Vice
President, Human Resources
Tel: (732) 980-6000
Web: www.americanstandard.com

AT&T
Corporate Headquarters
1 AT&T Way
Bedminster, NJ 07921
Mirian Graddick-Weir, Executive Vice
President, Human Resources
Tel: (908) 221-2000
Web: www.att.com

AUTOMATIC DATA
1 ADP Blvd
Roseland, NJ 07068
Tel: (973) 974-5000 Fax: (973) 422-4323
Web: www.adp.com

AVAYA
Human Resources
211 Mount Airy Rd.
Basking Ridge, NJ 07920
Maryanne DiMarzo, Senior Vice President,
Human Resources
Tel: (908) 953-6000
Web: www.avaya.com

BECTON DICKINSON
Human Resources
1 Becton Dr.
Franklin Lakes, NJ 07417
Jean-Marc Dageville, Vice President,
Human Resources
Tel: (201) 847-6800
Web: www.bd.com

BED BATH & BEYOND
Human Resources
650 Liberty Ave.
Union, NJ 07083
Concetta Van Dyke, Vice President, Human
Resources
Tel: (908) 688-0888
Web: www.bedbathandbeyond.com

CAMPBELL SOUP
Human Resources
1 Campbell Place
Camden, NJ 08103
Marlon Doles, Sr. Manager Global Staffing
and Diversity
Tel: (856) 342-4800 Fax: 856-342-3765
Email: marlon_doles@campbellsoup.com
Web: www.campbellsoupcompany.com

CHUBB
Corporate Headquarters
15 Mountain View Rd.
Warren, NJ 07061
Tel: (908) 903-2000 Fax: (908) 903-2027
Web: www.chubb.com

CIT GROUP
Human Resources

1 CIT Dr.
Livingston, NJ 07039
Gail Hardenburg, Manager, Human
Resources
Tel: (973) 740-5000
Web: www.cit.com

ENGELHARD
Human Resources
101 Wood Ave
Iselin, NJ 08830
Shamika Williams, Manager, Human
Resources
Tel: (732) 205-5000
Web: www.englehard.com

HONEYWELL INTL.
Corporate Headquarters
101 Columbia Rd.
Morristown, NJ 07962
Thomas W. Weidenkopf, Senior Vice
President, Human Resources and
Communication
Tel: (973) 455-2000 Fax: (973) 455-4807
Web: www.honeywell.com

HOVNANIAN ENTERPRISES
Human Resources
10 Highway 35
Red Bank, NJ 07701
Robyn T. Mingle, Senior Vice President,
Human Resources
Tel: (732) 747-7800
Web: www.khov.com

JOHNSON & JOHNSON
Corporate Headquarters
1 Johnson & Johnson Plz.
New Brunswick, NJ 08933
Tel: (732) 524-0400
Web: www.jnj.com

LUCENT TECHNOLOGIES
Human Resources
600 Mountain Ave.
Murray Hill, NJ 07974
Pamela Kimmet, Senior Vice President,
Human Resources
Tel: (908) 582-8500
Web: www.lucent.com

MEDCO HEALTH SOLUTIONS
Corporate Headquarters
100 Parsons Pond Dr.
Franklin Lakes, NJ 07417
Laury Lawsky, Recruiter, Human Resources
Tel: (201) 269-3400 Fax: (201) 269-1204
Web: www.medco.com

MERCK
Corporate Headquarters
I Merck Rd.
Whitehouse Station, NJ 08889
Marcia J. Avedon, Senior Vice President,
Human Resources
Tel: (908) 423-1000
Web: www.merck.com

PATHMARK STORES
200 Milk St.
Carteret, NJ 07008
Tony Parisi, Manager for Employment/
Recruiting
Tel: (732) 499-3000 Fax: (732) 499-3500
Web: www.pathmark.com

PRUDENTIAL FINANCIAL
Corporate Headquarters
751 Broad St.
Newark, NJ 07102
Peter Rienzi, Director, Human Resources
Tel: (973) 802-6000
Web: www.prudential.com

PUBLIC SERVICE ENTERPRISE GROUP
Corporate Headquarters
80 Park Plaza
Newark, NJ 07102
Tel: (973) 430-7565
Web: www.pseg.com

QUEST DIAGNOSTICS
Human Resources
1290 Wall St. W.
Lyndhurst, NJ 07071
Tel: (201) 393-5000
Web: www.questdiagnostics.com

SCHERING-PLOUGH CORPORATION
Human Resources
2000 Galloping Hill Rd.
Kenilworth, NJ 07033
Carmelina Passante, HR Coordinator
Tel: (908) 298-2728 Fax: (908) 298-6756
Web: www.Schering-Plough.com

SEALED AIR
Human Resources
Park 80 E.
Saddle Brook, NJ 07663
Nadine Maffucci, Recruiter, Human
Resources
Tel: (201) 791-7600
Web: www.sealedair.com

TOYS `R` US
Human Resources
1 Geoffrey Way.
Wayne, NJ 07470
Deborah Derby, Executive Vice President,
Human Resources
Tel: (973) 617-3500
Web: www.toysrusinc.com

WYETH
Corporate Headquarters
5 Giraida Farms
Madison, NJ 07940
Rene R. Lewin, Senior Vice President
Tel: (973) 660-5000
Web: www.wyeth.com

NEW YORK

ALTRIA GROUP
Corporate Headquarters
120 Park Ave.
New York, NY 10017
Kenneth Murphy, Senior Vice President,
Human Resources and Administration
Tel: (917) 663-2144 Fax: (917) 663-5544
Web: www.altria.com

AMERADA HESS
Corporate Headquarters
1185 6th Ave
New York, NY 10036
Lawrence Fox, Director of Human
Resources
Tel: (212) 997-8500
Web: www.hess.com

AMERICAN EXPRESS
Corporate Headquarters
200 Vesey St.
New York, NY 10285
Bet Franzone, Manager, Public Affairs and
Communications, Human Resources
Tel: (212) 640-1850 Fax: (212) 640-0332
Email: betfranzone@aexp.com
Web: www.americanexpress.com

AMERICAN INTL. GROUP
Corporate Headquarters
70 Pine St.,
New York, NY 10270

Alex I. Freudmann, Senior Vice President,
Human Resources
Tel: (212) 770-7000
Web: www.aig.com

ARROW ELECTRONICS
Human Resources
50 Marcus Dr.
Melville, NY 11747
Susan M. Suver, Senior Vice President,
Global Human Resources
Tel: (631) 847-2000
Web: www.arrow.com

ASBURY AUTOMOTIVE GROUP
Human Resources
622 Third Ave.
New York, NY 10017
Mr. Phil Johnson, Vice President, Human
Resources
Tel: (212) 885-2500
Web: www.ashburyauto.com

ASSURANT
Human Resources
1 Chase Manhattan Center
New York, NY 10005
Robert Haertel, Senior Vice President,
Compensation and Benefits
Tel: (212) 859-7000
Web: www.assurant.com

AVON PRODUCTS
Human Resources
1345 Sith Ave.
New York, NY 10105
Mae Eng, Global Recruiting
Tel: (212) 282-5000
Web: www.avoncompany.com

BANK OF NEW YORK CO.
Human Resources
1 Wall St.
New York, NY 10286
Gerry Gallashaw, Manager of Affirmative
Action and Diversity
Tel: (212) 635-7479 Fax: (212) 635-7470
Email: ggallashaw@bankofny.com
Web: www.bankofny.com

BARNES & NOBLE
Human Resources
122 Fifth Ave.
New York, NY 10011
Michelle Smith, Vice President, Human
Resources
Tel: (212) 633-3300
Web: www.barnesandnobleinc.com

BEAR STEARNS
Human Resources Department
383 Madison Ave.
New York, NY 10179
Tony Brown, Senior Managing Director
Tel: (212) 272-2000
Email: hresources_internetbear.com@bear.
com
Web: www.bearstearns.com

BRISTOL-MYERS SQUIBB
Corporate Headquarters
345 Park Ave.
New York, NY 10154
Stephen E. Bear, Senior Vice President,
Human Resources
Tel: (212) 546-4000
Web: www.bms.com

CABLEVISION SYSTEMS
Human Resources
1111 Stewart Ave.
Bethpage, NY 11714
Cara Mancini, Recruiting Manager, Human
Resources

Tel: (516) 803-2300
Web: www.cablevision.com

CENDANT
Corporate Headquarters
9 W. 57th St.
New York, NY 10019
Terence P. Conley, Executive Vice President,
Human Resources and Corporate Services
Tel: (212) 413-1800
Web: www.cendent.com

CITIGROUP
Corporate Headquarters
399 Park Ave.
New York, NY 10043
Michael Schlein, Senior Vice President,
Global Corporate Affairs, Human Resources
and Business Practices Citigroup Inc.
Tel: (212) 559-1000
Web: www.citigroup.com

COLGATE-PALMOLIVE
Human Resources
300 Park Ave.
New York, NY 10022
Paul T. Parker, Vice President, Human
Resources
Web: www.colgate.com

CONSOLIDATED EDISON
Human Resources
4 Irving Pl.
New York, NY 10003
Claude Trahan, Vice President, Human
Resources
Tel: (212) 460-4600
Web: www.conedison.com

CORNING
1 Riverfront Plz.
Corning, NY 14831
Tel: (607) 974-9000
Web: www.corning.com

DOVER
Human Resources
280 Park Ave.
New York, NY 10017
Tel: (212) 922-1640
Web: www.dovercorporation.com

EASTMAN KODAK COMPANY
Corporate Headquarters
343 State St.
Rochester, NY 14650
Tel: (800) 254-7923
Web: www.kodak.com

ENERGY EAST
Human Resources
Albany, NY 12212
Tel: (518) 434-3049
Web: www.energyeast.com

ESTÉE LAUDER
Human Resources
767 Fifth Ave.
New York, NY 10153
May Digeso, Senior Vice President, Human
Resources
Tel: (212) 572-4200
Web: www.elcompanies.com

FOOT LOCKER
Human Resources
112 W. 34th St.
New York, NY 10120
Paticia A. Peck, Vice President, Human
Resources
Tel: (212) 720-3700
Web: www.footlocker-inc.com

GOLDMAN SACHS GROUP
Corporate Headquarters
85 Broad St.
New York, NY 10004
Tel: (212) 902-1900
Web: www.gs.com

GUARDIAN LIFE OF AMERICA
Human Resources Department
7 Hanover Square
New York, NY 10004
Steven Smith, Recruitment Manager
Tel: (212) 598-8407
Web: www.guardianlife.com

HENRY SCHEIN
Human Resources
135 Duryea Rd.
Melville, NY 11747
Gerald A. Benjamin, Vice President
Tel: (631) 843-5500
Web: www.henryschein.com

IAC/INTERACTIVE
Human Resources
152 W. 57th St.
New York, NY 10019
Tel: (212) 314-7300
Web: www.iac.com

INTERPUBLIC GROUP
Human Resources
1114 Sixth Ave.
New York, NY 10036
James Simmons, Manager
Tel: (212) 704-1200
Web: www.interpublic.com

INTL. BUSINESS MACHINES
Corporate Headquarters
New Orchard Rd.
Armock, NY 10504
J. Randall McDonald, Human Resources
Tel: (914) 499-1900
Web: www.ibm.com

ITT INDUSTRIES
Human Resources
4 W. Red Oak Ln.
White Plains, NY 10604
Lucille Hill, Manager, Human Resources
Tel: (914) 641-2077
Web: www.itt.com

J.P. MORGAN CHASE & CO.
Corporate Headquarters
270 Park Ave.,
New York, NY 10017
John Farrell, Human Resources
Tel: (212) 270-6000
Web: www.jpmorganchase.com

L-3 COMMUNICATIONS
Human Resources
600 Third Ave
New York, NY 10016
Kenneth W. Manne, Human Resources
Tel: (212) 697-1111
Web: www.L-3com.com

LEHMAN BROTHERS HLDGS.
Human Resources
745 Seventh Ave.
New York, NY 10019
Lori Blankstein, Human Resources
Tel: (212) 526-7000
Email: humanresources.us@lehman.com
Web: www.lehman.com

LIZ CLAIBORNE
Human Resources
1441 Broadway
New York, NY 10018
Lawrence D. McClure, Senior Vice
President, Human Resources
Tel: (212) 354-4900
Web: www.lizclaiborne.com

LOEWS CORPORATION
Human Resources
655 Madison Ave. 7th Fl.
New York, NY 10021
Alan Moneyer, Director, Human Resources
Tel: (212) 521-2000 Fax: (212) 521-2466
Email: hrrep@newposition.com
Web: www.loews.com

MARSH & MCLENNAN
Corporate Headquarters
1166 Sixth Ave.
New York, NY 10036
Brian M. Storms, President/CEO
Tel: (212) 345-5000
Web: www.mmc.com

MCGRAW-HILL
Human Resources
1221 Sixth Ave.
New York, NY 10020
David L. Murphy, Executive Vice President,
Human Resources
Tel: (212) 512-2000
Web: www.mcgraw-hill.com

MERRILL LYNCH
Corporate Headquarters
4 Financial Center
New York, NY 10080
Terry Kasel, Head of Human Resources
Tel: (212) 449-1000
Web: www.ml.com

METLIFE
Corporate Headquarters
200 Park Ave.
New York, NY 10166
Denise Singleton, Minority Diversity
Manager
Tel: (908) 253-1068
Web: www.metlife.com

MORGAN STANLEY
Corporate Headquarters
1585 Broadway
New York, NY 10036
Marilyn Booker, Global Head of Diversity
Tel: (212) 761-4000
Email: diversityrecruiting@morganstanley.
com
Web: www.morganstanley.com

NEW YORK LIFE INSURANCE
Corporate Headquarters
51 Madison Ave
New York, NY 10010
Craig Gill, Senior Vice President, Human
Resources
Tel: (212) 576-7000
Web: www.newyorklife.com

NEWS CORP.
Human Resources
1211 Sixth Ave.
New York, NY 10036
Margaret Smith, Manager, Human
Resources
Tel: (212) 852-7000
Web: www.newscorp.com

NTL
Human Resources
909 Third Ave
New York, NY 10022
Carloyn Walker, Director, Human Resources
Tel: (212) 906-8440
Web: www.ntl.com

OMNICOM GROUP
Human Resources
437 Madison Ave.
New York, NY 10022
Tel: (212) 415-3600 Fax: (212) 415-3530
Web: www.omnicompgroup.com

PEPSI BOTTLING
Corporate Headquarters
1 Pepsi Way
Somers, NY 10589
John L. Berisford, Senior Vice President,
Human Resources
Tel: (914) 767-6000
Web: www.pbg.com

PEPSICO
700 Anderson Hill Rd.
Purchase, NY 10577
Margaret D. Moore, Senior Vice President,
Human Resources
Tel: (914) 253-2000
Web: www.pepsico.com

PFIZER
Corporate Headquarters
235 E. 42nd St.
New York, NY 10017
Sylvia M. Montero, Senior Vice President,
Human Resources
Tel: (212) 573-2323 Fax: (212) 573-7851
Web: www.pfizer.com

STARWOOD HOTELS & RSRTS.
Human Resources
1111 Westchester Ave.
White Plains, NY 10604
Randal Tucker, Manager MBE and Diversity
Tel: (914) 640-8100
Web: www.starwoodhotels.com

TIAA-CREF
Corporate Headquarters
730 Third Ave.
New York, NY 10017
Dermot J. O'Brien, Executive Vice
President, Human Resources
Tel: (212) 490-9000
Web: www.tiaa-cref.org

TIME WARNER
Corporate Headquarters
1 Time Warner Center
New York, NY 10019
Patricia Fili-Krushel, Executive Vice
President, Administration
Tel: (212) 484-8000
Web: www.timewarner.com

VERIZON COMMUNICATIONS
Corporate Headquarters
1095 Sixth Ave.
New York, NY 10036
Marc C. Reed, Executive Vice President,
Human Resources
Tel: (212) 395-1525 Fax: (212) 597-2721
Web: www.verizon.com

VIACOM
Corporate Headquarters
1515 Broadway
New York, NY 10036
William A. Roskin, Executive Vice President,
Human Resources
Tel: (212) 258-6000
Web: www.viacom.com

WELLCHOICE
Human Resources
11 W. 42nd St.
New York, NY 10036
Robert Lawrence, Senior Vice President,
Human Resources and Services
Tel: (212) 476-7800
Web: www.wellchoice.com

NORTH CAROLINA

BANK OF AMERICA CORP.
Corporate Headquarters
100 N. Tryon St.
Charlotte, NC 28255
Steele Alphin, Global Personnel Executive
Tel: (704) 386-8486
Web: www.bankofamerica.com

BB&T CORP.
200 W. 2nd St.
Winston-Salem, NC 27101
Laura Wingate, Administrator Assistance
Tel: (336) 733-2000
Web: www.bbandt.com

DUKE ENERGY
Corporate Headquarters
526 S. Church St.
Charlotte, NC 28202
Jim. W. Moggs, Group Vice President and
Chief Development Officer
Tel: (704) 594-6200
Web: www.duke-energy.com

FAMILY DOLLAR STORES
Human Resources
10401 Monroe Rd.
Matthews, NC 28105
Samuel N. McPherson, Senior Vice
President, Human Resources
Tel: (704) 847-6961
Web: www.familydollar.com

GOODRICH
Human Resources
2730 W. Tyvola Rd.
Charlotte, NC 28217
Jennifer Pollino, Senior Vice President,
Human Resources
Tel: (704) 423-7000
Web: www.goodrich.com

JEFFERSON-PILOT
Human Resources
100 N. Greene St.
Greensboro, NC 27401
Brenda Lawrence, Manager, Recruiting
Tel: (336) 691-4061
Email: gsojobs@jpfinancial.com
Web: www.jpfinancial.com

LOWE'S
Corporate Headquarters
100 Loews Blvd
Mooresville, NC 28117
Maureen Ausura, Senior Vice President,
Human Resources
Tel: (704) 758-1000
Web: www.loews.com

NUCOR
Human Resources
2100 Rexford Rd.
Charlotte, NC 28211
James M. Coblin, Vice President, Human
Resources
Tel: (704) 366-7000 Fax: (704) 362-4208
Web: www.nucor.com

PROGRESS ENERGY
Human Resources
410 S. Wilmington St.
Raleigh, NC 27601
Anne M. Huffman, Vice President, Human
Resources
Tel: (919) 546-6111
Web: www.progress-energy.com

REYNOLDS AMERICAN
Corporate Headquarters
401 N. Main St.

Winston-Salem, NC 27102
Ann A. Johnston, Executive Vice President,
Human Resources
Tel: (336) 741-5500
Web: www.reynoldsamerican.com

SONIC AUTOMOTIVE
Human Resources
6415 Idlewild Rd
Charlotte, NC 28212
Tel: (704) 566-2400 Fax: (704) 536-4665
Web: www.sonicautomotive.com

SPX
Human Resources
13515 Ballantyne Corporate Place
Charlotte, NC 28277
Robert B. Foreman, Senior Vice President,
Human Resources
Tel: (704) 752-4400
Web: www.spx.com

VF CORPORATION
Human Resources
105 Corporate Center Blvd.
Greeensboro, NC 27408
Joann Otto, Manager, Human Resources
Tel: (336) 332-4143 Fax: (336) 332-4118
Email: joann_otto@vfc.com
Web: www.vfc.com

WACHOVIA CORP.
Corporate Headquarters
301 S. College St.
Charlotte, NC 28288
Shannon McFayden, Head of Human
Resources and Corporate Relations
Tel: (704) 374-6161
Web: www.wachovia.com

OHIO

AK STEEL HOLDING
Human Resources
703 Curtis St.
Middletown, OH 45043
Lawrence Zizzo, Human Resources
Tel: (513) 425-5000
Web: www.aksteel.com

AMERICAN ELECTRIC POWER
Human Resources
1 Riverside Rd.
Columbus, OH 43215
Steven Jamison, Human Resources
Tel: (614) 716-1000 Fax: (614) 716-1864
Web: www.aep.com

AMERICAN FINANCIAL GRP.
Human Resources
1 E. Fourth St.
Cincinnati, OH 45202
Michelle Young, Recruiting Manager
Tel: (513) 579-2121
Web: www.afginc.com

ASHLAND
Human Resource Department
PO Box 2219
Columbus, OH 43216
Tel: (800) 782-4669 Fax: (614) 790-3973
Web: www.ashland.com

BIG LOTS
Human Resources
300 Phillipi Rd.
Columbus, OH 43228
Paulie McCormick, Manager
Tel: (614) 278-6800
Web: www.biglots.com

CARDINAL HEALTH
Corporate Headquarters

7000 Cardinal Pl.
Dublin, OH 43017
Carole Watkins, Human Resources
Tel: (614) 757-5000
Web: www.cardinal.com

CINCINNATI FINANCIAL
Human Resources
6200 Gilmore Rd.
Fairfield, OH 45014
Dave Karas, Manager, Recruiting
Tel: (513) 870-2000
Web: www.cinfin.com

CINERGY
139 E. 4th St.
Cincinnati, OH 45202
Tel: (513) 421-9500
Web: www.cinergy.com

COOPER TIRE & RUBBER
Human Resources
701 Lima Ave
Findlay, OH 45840
Linda Gallant, Recruiting Manager
Tel: (419) 423-1321
Web: www.coopertire.com

DANA
Corporate Headquarters
4500 Dorr St.
Toledo, OH 43615
Richard W. Spriggle, Vice President,
Human Resources
Web: www.dana.com

EATON
Human Resources
1111 Superior Ave.
Cleveland, OH 44114
Susan J. Cook, Vice President, Human
Resources
Tel: (216) 523-5000
Web: www.eaton.com

FEDERATED DEPT. STORES
Human Resources
7 W.Seventh St.
Cincinnati, OH 45202
David W. Clark, Human Resources
Tel: (513) 579-7000
Web: www.fds.com

FIFTH THIRD BANCORP
Human Resources
38 Fountain Square Pl.
Cincinnati, OH 45263
Rachel Klink, Employment Process
Manager
Tel: (513) 534-5300 Fax: (534) 534-8621

FIRST ENERGY
Human Resources
76 S. Main St.
Akron, OH 44308
Renee Spino, Director, Human Resources
Tel: (800) 736-3402 Fax: (330) 384-2455
Web: www.firstenergycorp.com

GOODYEAR TIRE & RUBBER
Human Resources
1144 E. Market St.
Akron, OH 44316
Kathleen T. Geier, Senior Vice President,
Human Resources
Tel: (330) 796-2121 Fax: (330) 796-2222
Web: www.goodyear.com

INTERNATIONAL STEEL GROUP
Human Resources
4020 Kinross Lakes Pkwy.
Richfield, OH 44286
Karen A. Smith, Vice President, Human
Resources
Tel: (330) 659-9100

Web: www.intlsteel.com

KEYCORP
Human Resources
127 Public Square
Cleveland, OH 44114
Thomas E. Helfrich, Executive Vice
President, Human Resources
Tel: (216) 689-6300
Web: www.key.com

KROGER
Corporate Headquarters
1014 Vine St.
Cincinnati, OH 45202
Caroline Growl, Human Resources
Tel: (513) 762-4000 Fax: (513) 762-1160
Web: www.kroger.com

LIMITED BRANDS
Human Resources
3 Limited Pkwy.
Columbus, OH 43230
Sandra West, Executive Vice President
Tel: (614) 415-7000
Web: www.limitedbrands.com

NATIONAL CITY CORP.
Corporate Headquarters
1900 E. 9th St.
Cleveland, OH 44114
Jon N. Couture, Senior Vice President
Tel: (216) 222-2000
Web: www.nationalcity.com

NATIONWIDE
Human Resources
1 Nationwide Plaza
Columbus, OH 43215
Tel: (614) 249-7111
Web: www.nationwide.com

NCR CORPORATION
Human Resources
1700 S. Patterson Blvd.
Dayton, OH 45479
Tel: (937) 445-5000
Web: www.ncr.com

OWENS CORNING
Human Resources
1 Owens Corning Pkwy
Toledo, OH 43659
Joseph C. High, Senior Vice President
Tel: (419) 248-8000
Web: www.owenscorning.com

OWENS-ILLINOIS
Human Resources
1 Seagate
Toledo, OH 43666
Stephen Malia, Senior Vice President
Tel: (419) 247-5000
Web: www.o-i.com

PARKER HANNIFIN
Human Resources
6035 Parkland Blvd.
Cleveland, OH 44124
Patti Sfero, HR Manager
Tel: (216) 896-3000 Fax: (216) 896-4024
Web: www.parker.com

PROCTER & GAMBLE
1 Procter & Gamble Plz.
Cincinnati, OH 45202
Richard L. Antoine, Global Human
Resources Officer
Tel: (513) 983-1100
Web: www.pg.com

PROGRESSIVE
Human Resources
6300 Wilson Mills Rd.

Mayfield Village, OH 44143
Susan Patricia Griffith, COO
Tel: (440) 461-5000
Web: www.progressive.com

SHERWIN-WILLIAMS
Human Resources
101 Prospect Ave. N.W.
Cleveland, OH 44115
Neil Ghanen, Human Resources Manager
Tel: (216) 566-2000 Fax: (216) 566-3670
Web: www.sherwin.com

TIMKEN
Human Resources
1835 Dueber Ave S.W.
Canton, OH 44706
Donald L. Walker, Human Resources
Tel: (330) 438-3000
Web: www.timken.com

WENDY'S INTERNATIONAL
Human Resources
4288 W. Dublin-Granville Rd.
Dublin, OH 43017
Kim Anderson, Administrator
Tel: (614) 764-3100
Web: www.wendys.com

WESTERN & SOUTHERN FINANCIAL
Human Resources
400 Broadway
Cincinnati, OH 45202
Noreen J. Hayes, Senior Vice President
Tel: (513) 629-1800 Fax: (513) 629-1220
Web: www.westernsouthern.com

OKLAHOMA

DEVON ENERGY CORPORATION
Human Resources
20 N. Broadway
Oklahoma City, OK 73102
Paul R. Poley, Human Resources
Tel: (405) 235-3611 Fax: (405) 552-4550
Web: www.devonenergy.com

KERR-MCGEE
Human Resources
Kerr-McGee Center
Oklahoma, OK 73125
Fran G. Heartwell, Vice President, Human
Resources
Tel: (405) 270-1313
Web: www.kerr-mcgee.com

OGE ENERGY
Human Resources
321 N. Harvey Ave.
Oklahoma City, OK 73102
Kevin Maxwell, Recruiting Coordinator
Tel: (405) 553-3000
Web: www.oge.com

ONEOK
Human Resources
100 W. Fifth St.
Tulsa, OK 74103
Manning, Manager, Human Resources
Tel: (918) 588-7000
Web: www.oneok.com

WILLIAMS
Human Resources
1 Williams Center
Tulsa, OK 74172
John C. Fischer, Vice President, Human
Resources
Tel: (918) 573-2000
Web: www.williams.com

OREGON

NIKE
Human Resources
1 Bowerman Dr.
Beaverton, OR 97005
Julia Law, Vice President
Web: www.nike.com

PENNSYLVANIA

AIR PRODUCTS & CHEM.
Central Staffing Group
7201 Hamilton Blvd.
Allentown, PA 18195
Robin Lysek, Director of Central Staffing
Tel: (610) 481-4911 X8787
Web: www.airproducts.com

ALCOA
Corporate Headquarters
201 Isabella St.
Pittsburgh, PA 15212
Regina M. Hitchery, Human Resources
Tel: (412) 553-4545 Fax: (412) 553-4498
Web: www.alcoa.com

AMERISOURCEBERGEN
Corporate Headquarters
1300 Morris Dr.
Chesterbrook, PA 19087
Gab Holdman, Human Resources Manager
Tel: (610) 727-7000 Fax: (617) 727-3611
Web: www.amerisourcebergen.com

ARAMARK
Human Resources
1101 Market St.
Philadelphia, PA 19107
Lynn B. McKee, Human Resources
Tel: (215) 238-3000
Web: www.aramark.com

CIGNA
Corporate Headquarters
1 Liberty Pl.
Philadelphia, PA 19192
John M. Murabito, Executive Vice
President, Human Resources and Services
Tel: (215) 761-1000
Web: www.cigna.com

COMCAST
Human Resources
1500 Market St.
Philadelphia, PA 19102
Chaisse Lillie, Vice President, Human
Resources
Tel: (215) 665-1700
Web: www.comcast.com

CROWN HOLDINGS
Human Resources
1 Crown Way
Philadelphia, PA 19154
Douglass McLaughlin, Cooporate Manager
Tel: (215) 698-5100 Fax: (215) 676-7245

ERIE INSURANCE GROUP
Human Resources
100 Erie Insurance Pl.
Erie, PA 16530
Ann Scott, Manager, Human Resources
Tel: (814) 870-2000
Web: www.erieinsurance.com

H.J. HEINZ
World Headquarters
357 6th Ave.
Pittsburgh, PA 152222
Thomas DiDonato, Chief People Officer

Tel: (412) 456-5700
Web: www.heinz.com/jsp/careers_f.jsp

HERSHEY FOODS
Human Resources
100 Crystal A Dr.
Hershey, PA 17033
Marcella K. Arline, Senior Vice President
Tel: (717) 534-6799

IKON OFFICE SOLUTIONS
Human Resources
70 Valley Stream Pkwy
Malvern, PA 19355
Beth B. Sexton, Senior Vice President
Tel: (610) 296-8000
Web: www.ikon.com

JONES APPAREL GROUP
Human Resources
250 Rittenhouse Circle
Bristol, PA 19007
Jackie Mallory, Recruiting Manager
Tel: (215) 785-4000
Web: www.jny.com

LINCOLN NATIONAL
Human Resources
1500 Market St.
Philadelphia, PA 19102
Elizabeth L. Reeves, Senior Vice President
Tel: (215) 448-1400
Web: www.lfg.com

MELLON FINANCIAL CORP.
Human Resources
1 Melon Center
Pittsburgh, PA 15258
Tel: (412) 234-5000
Web: www.mellon.com

PNC FINANCIAL SERVICES
249 5th Ave.
Pittsburgh, PA 15222
Tel: (412) 762-2000
Web: www.pnc.com

PPG INDUSTRIES
Human Resources
1 PPG St.
Pittsburgh, PA 15272
Charles W. Wise, Vice President, Human
Resources
Tel: (412) 434-3131
Web: www.ppg.com

PPL
Human Resources
2 N. Ninth St.
Allentown, PA 18101
Tel: (610) 774-5836
Web: www.pplweb.com

RITE AID
Corporate Headquarters
30 Hunter Lane
Camp Hill, PA 17011
Stephanie Naito, Human Resources
Tel: (717) 761-2633
Web: www.riteaid.com

ROHM & HAAS
Human Resources
100 Independence Mall W.
Philadelphia, PA 19106
Tel: (212) 679-0000
Web: www.rohmhaas.com

SUNOCO
Corporate Headquarters
1801 Market Pl.
Philadelphia, PA 19103
Rolf D. Naku, Human Resources
Tel: (215) 977-6106
Web: www.sunocoinc.com

TOLL BROTHERS
250 Gibraltar Rd.
Horsham, PA 19044
Jay Lehnan, Director of Recruiting
Tel: (215) 938-8130 Fax: (215) 938-3060
Web: www.tollbrothers.com

UGI
Human Resources
460 N. Gulph Rd.
King of Prussia, PA 19406
Rose Mary
Tel: (610) 337-1000
Web: www.unicorp.com

UNITED STATES STEEL
Human Resources
600 Grant St.
Pittsburgh, PA 15219
Thomas W. Sterling, Senior Vice President
Tel: (412) 433-6748
Web: www.ussteel.com

UNIVERSAL HEALTH SVCS.
Human Resources
367 S. Gulph Rd.
King of Prussia, PA 19406
Coleen Johns, Recruiter, Human Resources
Tel: (610) 768-3300
Web: www.uhsinc.com

WESCO INTERNATIONAL
Human Resources
225 West Station Square Dr.
Pittsburgh, PA 15219
Bob Henshaw, Director, Human Resources
Tel: (412) 454-2200
Web: www.wesco.com

YORK INTERNATIONAL
Human Resources
631 S. Richland Ave.
York, PA 17403
Jeffret Gard, Vice President, Human
Resources
Tel: (717) 771-7890
Web: www.york.com

RHODE ISLAND

CVS
Corporate Headquarters
1 CVS Dr.
Woonsocket, RI 02895
V. Michael Ferdinandi, Senior Vice
President, Human Resources
Tel: (401) 765-1500
Web: www.cvs.com

TEXTRON
Human Resources
40 WestMinster St.
Providence, RI 02903
George E. Metzger, Vice President
Tel: (401) 421-2800
Web: www.textron.com

SOUTH CAROLINA

SCANA
Human Resources
1426 Main St.
Columbia, SC 29201
Joseph C. Bouknight, Human Resources
Tel: (803) 217-9000
Web: www.scana.com

TENNESSEE

AUTOZONE
Human Resources
123 S. Front St.
Memphis, TN 38103
Daisy L. Vanderlinde, Senior Vice President
Tel: (901) 495-6500
Web: www.autozone.com

CAREMARK RX
Human Resources
211 Commerce St.
Nashville, TN 37201
Kirk McConnell, Executive Vice President
Tel: (615) 743-6600
Web: www.caremark.com

DOLLAR GENERAL
Human Resources
100 Mission Ridge
Goodlettsville, TN 37072
Jeffrey Rice, Vice President
Tel: (615) 855-4000
Web: www.dollargeneral.com

EASTMAN CHEMICAL
Human Resources
100 N. Eastman Rd.
Kingsport, TN 37660
Norris P. Sneed, Senior Vice President,
Human Resources
Tel: (423) 229-2000
Web: www.eastman.com

FEDEX
Corporate Headquarters
924 S. Shady Grove Rd.
Memphis, TN 38120
Larry C. Miller, President, Chief Executive
Officer, FedEx Freight East
Tel: (901) 369-3600
Web: www.fedex.com

HCA
Corporate Headquarters
1 Park Plz.
Nashville, TN 37203
John M. Steele, Senior Vice President,
Human Resources
Tel: (615) 344-9551
Web: www.hcahealthcare.com

UNUMPROVIDENT
Human Resources
1 Fountain Sq.
Chattanooga, TN 37402
Aileen Farrah, Director, Human Resources
Tel: (423) 755-1011
Web: www.unumprovident.com

TEXAS

AFFILIATED COMPUTER SVCS.
Human Resources
2828 N. Haskell Ave
Dallas, TX 75204
Denettra Quintanilla, Manager, Recruiting
Tel: (214) 841-6111
Web: www.acs-inc.com

AMR
Corporate Headquarters
4333 Amon Carter Dr.
Fort Worth, TX 76155
Jeffery J. Brunage, Senior Vice President,
Human Resources
Tel: (817) 963-1234
Web: www.aa.com

ANADARKO PETROLEUM
Human Resources
1201 Lake Robbins Dr.
The Woodlands, TX 77380
Susan Cleveland, Staff Specialist
Tel: (832) 636-1000 Fax: (832) 636-5653
Email: susan_cleveland@andarko.com
Web: www.anadarko.com

APACHE
Human Resources
2000 Post Oak Blvd.
Houston, TX 77056
Jeffrey M. Bender, Human Resources
Tel: (713) 296-6000
Web: www.apachecorp.com

BAKER HUGHES
Human Resources
3900 Essex Lane
Houston, TX 77027
Greg Nakanishi, Vice President
Tel: (713) 439-8600
Web: www.bakerhughes.com

BRINKER INTERNATIONAL
Human Resources
6820 L.B.J. Freeway
Dallas, TX 75240
Valerie L. Davisson, Executive Vice
President, Human Resources
Tel: (972) 980-9917
Web: www.brinker.com

BURLINGTON NO. SANTA FE
Corporate Headquarters
2650 Lou Menk Dr.
Fort Worth, TX 76131
Jeanna E. Michalski, Vice President
Tel: (800) 795-2673
Web: www.bnsf.com

BURLINGTON RESOURCES
Human Resources
717 Texas Ave.
Houston, TX 77002
William Usher, Vice President
Tel: (817) 347-2000 Fax: (817) 347-2229
Web: www.br-inc.com

CENTERPOINT ENERGY
Corporate Headquarters
1111 Louisiana St.
Houston, TX 77002
Preston Johnson, Jr., Senior Vice President
Tel: (713) 207-1111
Web: www.centerpointenergy.com

CENTEX
Human Resources
2728 N. Harwood St.
Dallas, TX 75201
Wilemia Shaw, Director, Human Resources
Tel: (214) 981-5000
Web: www.centex.com

CLEAR CHANNEL COMMUNICATIONS
Human Resources
200 E. Basse Rd.
San Antonio, TX 78209
Bill Hamersly, Senior Vice President
Tel: (210) 822-2828
Email: billhamersly@clearchannel.com
Web: www.clearchannel.com

COMMERCIAL METALS
Human Resources
6565 N. MacArthur Blvd
Irving, TX 75039
Keith Shull, Vice President, Human
Resources
Tel: (214) 689-4300
Web: www.commercialmetals.com

CONOCOPHILLIPS
Corporate Headquarters
600 N. Dairy Ashford Rd.
Houston, TX 77079
Carin S. Knickel, Vice President, Human
Resources
Tel: (281) 293-1000
Web: www.conocophillips.com

CONTINENTAL AIRLINES
Human Resources
1600 Smith St.
Houston, TX 77002
Mike Bonds, Senior Vice President
Tel: (713) 324-5000
Web: www.continental.com

D.R. HORTON
Corporate Headquarters
301 Commerce St.
Fort Worth, TX 76102
Tel: (817) 390-8200
Web: www.drhorton.com

DEAN FOODS
Human Resources
2515 McKinney Ave.
Dallas, TX 75201
Robert Dunn, Senior Vice President
Tel: (214) 303-3400
Web: www.deanfoods.com

DELL
Corporate Headquarters
1 Dell Way
Round Rock, TX 78682
Paul D. McKinnon, Senior Vice President
Tel: (512) 338-4400
Web: www.dell.com

DYNEGY
Human Resources
1000 Louisiana St.
Houston, TX 77002
R. Blake Young, Executive Vice President,
Administration and Technology
Tel: (713) 507-6400
Web: www.dynegy.com

EL PASO
Human Resources
1001 Louisana St.
Houston, TX 77002
Tel: (713) 420-2600
Email: staffing@elpaso.com
Web: www.elpaso.com

ELECTRONIC DATA SYSTEMS
Human Resources
5400 Legacy Dr.
Plano, TX 75024
Tina M. Sivinski, Executive Vice President,
Human Resources
Tel: (972) 604-6000
Web: www.eds.com

ENBRIDGE ENERGY PARTNERS
Human Resources
1100 Louisiana St.
Houston, TX 77002
Tel: (713) 821-2000 Fax: (713) 821-2229
Web: www.enbridgepartners.com

ENTERPRISE PRODUCTS
Human Resources
2727 N. Loop West
Houston, TX 77008
David Scott, Manager of Benefits
Tel: (713) 880-6500
Web: www.epplp.com

EXXON MOBIL
Exxon Mobil Corporation
5959 Las Colinas Blvd.
Irving, TX 75039-2298

L. J. Cavanaugh, Vice President
Tel: (972) 444-1000 Fax: (972) 444-1883
Web: www.exxon.mobil.com

GROUP 1 AUTOMOTIVE
Human Resources
950 Echo Lane
Houston, TX 77024
J. Brooks O'Hara, Vice President, Human
Resources
Tel: (713) 647-5700 Fax: (713) 647-5858
Web: www.group1auto.com

J.C. PENNEY
Corporate Headquarters
6501 Legacy Dr.
Plano, TX 75024
Gary L. Davis, Executive Vice President,
Chief Human Resources and Administrative
Office
Tel: (973) 431-1000
Web: www.jcpenney.net

KIMBERLY-CLARK
Corporate Headquarters
351 Phelps Dr.
Irving, TX 75038
Lizanne C. Gottung, Senior Vice President,
Human Resources
Tel: (972) 281-2000
Web: www.kimberley-clark.com

KINDER MORGAN ENERGY
Human Resources
500 Dallas St. #1000
Houston, TX 77002
Roger Mosby, VP of HR
Tel: (713) 369-9000 Fax: (713) 369-9411
Web: www.kindermorgan.com

LYONDELL CHEMICAL
Human Resources
1221 McKinney St.
Houston, TX 77010
John A. Hollinshead, Vice President,
Human Resources
Tel: (713) 652-7200
Web: www.lyondell.com

MARATHON OIL
Corporate Headquarters
5555 San Felipe Rd.
Houston, TX 77056
Eileen Campbell, Vice-President, Human
Resources
Tel: (713) 629-6600
Web: www.marathon.com

PILGRIM'S PRIDE
Human Resources
110 S. Texas St.
Pittsburg, TX 75686
Peg Patton, Recuiter, Human Resources
Tel: (903) 855-1000
Web: www.pilgrimspride.com

PLAINS ALL AMERICAN PIPELINE
Human Resources
333 Clay St.
Houston, TX 77002
Connie Emerson, Recuitment, Human
Resources
Tel: (713) 646-4100 Fax: (713) 646-4147
Web: www.paalp.com

RADIO SHACK
Human Resources
300 Radio Shack Circle
Fort Worth, TX 76102
James R. Fredericks, Senior Vice President,
Human Resources
Web: www.radioshackcorporation.com

RELIANT ENERGY
Human Resources
1000 Main St.
Houston, TX 77002
Karen D. Taylor, Senior Vice President,
Human Resources and Administration
Tel: (713) 497-3000 Fax: (713) 488-5925
Web: www.reliant.com

SBC COMMUNICATIONS
Corporate Headquarters
175 E. Houston St.
San Antonio, TX 78205
Karen Jennings, Senior Executive Vice
President, Human Resources and
Communications
Tel: (210) 821-4105
Web: www.sbc.com

SMITH INTERNATIONAL
Human Resources
411 N. Sam Houston Pkwy.
Houston, TX 77060
Malcolm W. Anderson, Vice President,
Human Resources
Tel: (281) 443-3370
Web: www.smith.com

SOUTHWEST AIRLINES
Human Resources
2702 Love Field Dr.
Dallas, TX 75235
Willie Edwards, Director, Human Resources
Tel: (214) 792-6192 Fax: (214) 792-5015
Email: willieedwards@wnco.com
Web: www.southwest.com

SYSCO
Corporate Headquarters
1390 Enclave Pkwy
Houston, TX 77077
K. Susan Billiot, Assistant Vice President,
Human Resources
Tel: (281) 584-1390
Web: www.sysco.com

TEMPLE-INLAND
Human Resources
1300 MoPac Expressway S.
Austin, TX 78746
Tel: (512) 434-5800
Web: www.templeinland.com

TENET HEALTHCARE
Human Resources
13737 Noel Rd.
Dallas, TX 75240
Joseph A. Bosch, Senior Vice President,
Human Resources
Tel: (469) 893-2200 Fax: (469) 893-8600
Web: www.tenethealth.com

TESORO
Corporate Headquarters
300 Concord Plaza Dr.
San Antonio, TX 78216
Susan A. Lerette, Vice President, Human
Resources
Tel: (210) 828-8484
Web: www.tsocorp.com

TEXAS INSTRUMENTS
Corporate Headquarters
12500 TI Blvd
Dallas, TX 75266
Steve Leven, Senior Vice President,
Manager of Worldwide Human Resources
Web: www.ti.com

TRIAD HOSPITALS
Human Resources
5800 Tennyson Pkwy
Plano, TX 75024
Rick Thomason, Vice President

Tel: (214) 473-7000
Web: www.triadhospitals.com

TXU
Diversity
1601 Bryan St.
Dallas, TX 75201
Cheryl Stevens, Vice President, Workforce
and Supplier Diversity
Tel: (214) 812-6923 Fax: (214) 812-5597
Web: www.txucorp.com

VALERO ENERGY
Human Resources
1 Valero Way
San Antonio, TX 78249
Pat Dullie, Human Resources
Tel: (210) 345-2000 Fax: (210) 345-2646
Web: www.valero.com

WASTE MANAGEMENT
Human Resources
1001 Fannin St.
Houston, TX 77002
Carlton Yearwood, Vice President
Tel: (713) 512-6200
Web: www.wm.com

WHOLE FOODS MARKET
Human Resources
550 Bowie St.
Austin, TX 78703
Mark Ehrstein, Director, Human Resources
Tel: (512) 477-4455
Web: www.wholefoodsmarket.com

UTAH

AUTOLIV
Human Resources
3350 Airport Rd.
Ogden, UT 84405
Brian Peterson, Human Resources
Manager
Tel: (801) 625-9200
Web: www.autoliv.com

VIRGINIA

ADVANCE AUTO PARTS
Human Resources
5673 Airport Rd.
Roanoke, VA 24012
Keith A. Oreson, Senior Vice President
Tel: (540) 362-4911
Web: www.advanceautoparts.com

AES
Human Resources
4300 Wilson Blvd
Arlington, VA 22203
Jay Kloosterboer, Vice President
Tel: (703) 522-1315
Web: www.aes.com

BRINK'S
Human Resources
1801 Bayberry Ct
Richmond, VA 23226
Joe Verostic, Director Human Resources
Tel: (804) 289-9700 Fax: (804) 289-9758
Web: www.brinkscompany.com

CAPITAL ONE FINANCIAL
Corporate Headquarters
1680 Capital One Dr.
McLean, VA 22102
Tel: (703) 720-1000
Web: www.capitalone.com

CARMAX
Human Resources
4900 Cox Rd.
Glen Allen, VA 23060
Scott Rivas, Vice President
Tel: (804) 747-0422
Web: www.carmax.com

CIRCUIT CITY STORES
Human Resources
9950 Maryland Dr.
Richmond, VA 23233
Eric A. Jonas, Jr., Senior Vice President
Tel: (804) 527-4000
Web: www.circuitcity.com

DOMINION RESOURCES
Corporate Heaquarters
120 Tredegar St
Richmond, VA 23219
Tel: (804) 819-2000
Web: www.dom.com

GANNETT
Human Resources
7950 Jones Branch Dr.
McLean, VA 22107
Jose Berrios, VP of Leadership
Tel: (703) 854-6224 Fax: (703) 854-2009
Web: www.gannett.com

GENERAL DYNAMICS
Human Resources
2941 Fairview Park Dr
Falls Church, VA 22042
Walter M. Oliver, Senior Vice President
Tel: (703) 876-3000 Fax: (703) 876-3125
Web: www.gd.com

MCI
Human Resources
22001 Loundon County Pkwy,
Ashburn, VA 20147
Daniel Casaccia, Executive Vice President
Tel: (703) 866-5600
Web: www.mci.com

MEADWESTVACO CORPORATION
Human Resources/Staffing
1011 Boulder Spring Dr.
Richmond, VA 23225
Cynda Berger, Staffing Director
Tel: (804) 327-7900 Fax: (804) 327-7205
Web: www.meadwestvaco.com

NEXTEL COMMUNICATIONS
Human Resources
2001 Edmund Halley Dr
Reston, VA 20191
Randy Harris, Senior Vice President
Tel: (703) 433-4000
Web: www.nextel.com

NORFOLK SOUTHERN
Human Resources
3 Commercial Pl.
Norfolk, VA 23510
Ricky Morris, Management Recruiting
Tel: 757-664-5066 Fax: 757-664-5069
Email: ricky.morris@nscorp.com
Web: www.nscorp.com

NVR
Human Resources
7601 Lewinsville Rd
McLean, VA 22102
Tel: (703) 956-4000 Fax: (703) 956-4750
Web: www.nvrinc.com

OWENS & MINOR
Human Resources
4800 Cox Rd.
Glen Allen, VA 23060
Erika T. Davis, Senior Vice President

Tel: (804) 747-9794 Fax: (804) 270-7281
Web: www.owens-minor.com

PERFORMANCE FOOD GROUP
Human Resources
12500 W. Creek Pkwy.
Richmond, VA 23238
Pauline Donato, Regional Vice President
Tel: (804) 484-7700 Fax: (804) 484-7940
Email: pdonato@pfgc.com
Web: www.pfgc.com

SLM
Human Resources
12061 Bluemont Way
Reston, VA 20190
Joni Reich, Senior Vice President
Tel: (703) 810-3000
Web: www.salliemae.com

SMITHFIELD FOODS
Corporate Headquarters
200 Commerce St.
Smithfield, VA 23430
Denise Sweat, Employee Relations Manager
Tel: (757) 365-3000
Web: www.smithfieldfoods.com

WASHINGTON

AMAZON.COM
Human Resources
1200 12th Ave. South
Seattle, WA 98144
Tel: (206) 266-2171 Fax: (206) 266-1355
Web: www.amazon.com

COSTCO WHOLESALE
Corporate Headquarters
999 Lake Dr.
Issaquah, WA 98027
John Matthews, Senior Vice President,
Human Resources and Risk Management
Tel: (425) 313-8100
Web: www.costco.com

MICROSOFT
Corporate Headquarters
1 Microsoft Way
Redmond, WA 98052
Lisa Brummel, Corporate Vice President,
Human Resources
Tel: (425) 882-8080
Web: www.microsoft.com

NORDSTROM
Human Resources
1671 Sixth Ave.
Seattle, WA 98101
Johnnetta Rowsey, Washing/Alaska Diversity
Affairs Director
Tel: (206) 628-2111
Web: www.nordstrom.com

SAFECO
Human Resources
Safeco Plaza
Seattle, WA 98185
Kevin Carter, Director of Diversity
Tel: (206) 545-5000 Fax: (206) 925-0165
Web: www.safeco.com

STARBUCKS
Human Resources
2401 Utah Ave.
Seattle, WA 98134
Tel: (206) 447-1575
Web: www.starbucks.com

WASHINGTON MUTUAL
Human Resources
1201 Third Ave.
Seattle, WA 98101

Daryl D. David, Executive Vice President,
Human Resources
Tel: (206) 461-2000
Web: www.wamu.com

WEYERHAEUSER
Human Resources
33633 Weyerhaeuser Way St.
Federal Way, WA 98063
Edward Rogel, Senior Vice President,
Human Resources
Tel: (253) 924-2345
Web: www.weyerhaeuser.com

WISCONSIN

AMERICAN FAMILY INS. GRP.
Strategic Staffing
6000 American Pkwy.
Madison, WI 53783
Tel: (608) 249-2111 Fax: (608) 243-6529
Web: www.amfam.com

HARLEY-DAVIDSON
Human Resources
3700 Juneau Ave.
Milwaukee, WI 53208
Ryan Smith, Recuiter, Human Resources
Tel: (414) 342-4680
Web: www.harley-davidson.com

JOHNSON CONTROLS
Corporate Headquarters
5757 N. Green Bay Ave.
Milwaukee, WI 53201
Susan Davis, Vice President, Human
Resources
Tel: (414) 524-1200
Web: www.johnsoncontrols.com

KOHL'S
Human Resources
N56 W. 17000 Ridgewood Dr.
Menomonee Falls, WI 53051
Genny Shields, Vice President, Human
Resources
Tel: (262) 703-7000 Fax: (262) 703-7115
Web: www.kohls.com

MANPOWER
Human Resources
5301 N. Ironwood Rd.
Milwaukee, WI 53217
Charles Pugh, Director of Human
Resources
Tel: (414) 961-1000 Fax: (414) 961-7985
Web: www.manpower.com

NORTHWESTERN MUTUAL
Corporate Headquarters
720 E. Wisconsin Ave.
Milwaukee, WI 53202
Susan A. Lueger, Vice President
Tel: (414) 271-1444
Web: www.northwesternmutual.com

ROUNDY'S
Human Resources
875 E. Wisconsin Ave.
Milwaukee, WI 53202
John Quincannon, Senior Recruiter
Tel: (414) 231-5000
Web: www.roundys.com

WISCONSIN ENERGY
Human Resources
231 W. Michigan St.
Milwaukee, WI 53203
Arthur A. Zintek, Vice President, Human
Resources
Tel: (414) 221-2345
Web: www.wisconsinenergy.com

A MESSAGE FROM THE COMMANDANT OF THE MARINE CORPS

It is an honor to congratulate TIYM Publishing on the third edition of the Asian American Yearbook. This publication is a valued resource that includes the many achievements of Asian Americans in our nation.

A number of the Corps' finest leaders are Asian American. One distinguished leader is Colonel Leo A. Mercado, Chief of Staff for the Marine Corps University at Quantico, Va. Colonel Mercado is one of the highest-ranking Filipino Americans in the Marine Corps. Another outstanding Asian American Marine is Sergeant Jeffrey Chao, a Marine reservist who received the 2005 Federal Asian Pacific American Council Service Award for promoting equal opportunity and cultural diversity by encouraging participation and advancement of Asian Pacific Americans within the government.

The dedication and faithful service of these Marines and countless other Asian American Marines honor the proud heritage of Asian Americans.

Again, congratulations to the leadership of TIYM Publishing for developing this invaluable resource guide. The United States Marine Corps commends you for recognizing the accomplishments of Asian Americans throughout our nation. I wish you the very best for future success with this endeavor.

Semper Fidelis,

M. W. Hagee

General, U.S. Marine Corps

The call "Send in the Marines!" has been sounded over 200 times since the end of World War II — an average of once every 90 days. Our nation's leaders have great confidence in the Marine Corps' ability to succeed anytime, anywhere, and in any situation. The warfighting excellence and warrior culture displayed by today's Marine Corps is part of a legacy that extends back 230 years.

United States Marines have defended and fought for the American people since before the Continental Congress approved the Declaration of Independence. Congress authorized the formation of two battalions of Marines on November 10, 1775 — the official birth date of the Marine Corps.

The foresight of Congress to mandate the existence of an always ready, combined-arms expeditionary force seems particularly discerning in light of the current Global War on Terrorism.

The ongoing Global War on Terrorism is different than any war America has ever fought, and the stakes are high. In this new kind of conflict our military must be responsive, agile, decisive and expeditionary in order to quickly respond to crises and conflict when needed.

Every Marine and Marine unit is trained and ready to rapidly task-organize and deploy from the United States or while stationed abroad. When crises erupt anywhere in the world, the nation may call upon the Marine Corps to rapidly carry out the nation's foreign policy and security objectives. Throughout our history, the Marine Corps has been the force most ready when the nation is least ready.

Marines are warriors. We are comprised of smart, tough, highly adaptable men and women who serve as the nation's force-in-readiness. Ours is a smaller, more dynamic force than any other in the American arsenal, and the only forward-

Leading by example
Colonel Rose Marie Favors

Colonel Rose Marie Favors is the senior female Asian American officer in the Marine Corps. She is a graduate of the University of South Carolina with a Bachelors Degree in International Studies and a juris doctor. Colonel Favors joined the Marine Corps in 1979, during her second year of law school and upon completion of training at The Basic School and Naval Justice School began a career as a Judge Advocate. Over the course of her 25-year career, Favors has served as trial counsel, defense counsel and various positions as a Judge Advocate in the military legal system. Currently, Favors serves as the Staff Judge Advocate for the Marine Corps Combat Development Command. Colonel Favors is admitted to practice law before the Supreme Court of the United States, the United States Court of Appeals for the Armed Forces, and the Supreme Court of South Carolina.

"With approximately 7,600 Asians and Pacific Islanders in the Marine Corps, Asian Americans play an important role not only in our country's economic and cultural development, but also in our security and safety," Favors said. "I believe the Marine Corps awakens in the young Asian American important personal and cultural attributes – honor, courage, commitment, loyalty, discipline and respect. In our heritage as Asian Americans, the Marine Corps wakens those traits and reinforces what our mothers and fathers taught us as children."

deployed force designed for expeditionary operations by air, land or sea. It is our size and expertise that allow us to move faster and adapt to rapidly changing situations. Working to overcome disadvantage and turn conflict into victory, we accomplish great things, and we do it as a team.

While innovations and new technology are critical for improving readiness and combat and support capabilities, the Marine Corps never underestimates the importance and value of the individual Marine. We recognize that the individual Marine, with a diverse range of experiences and traditions, is the strength of our Corps.

Everyone who joins the Marine Corps has chosen an extremely challenging route. Marines – officer and enlisted – rise to challenges, becoming more innovative and creative when faced with problems. Each Marine is encouraged to maximize leadership potential through practice and evaluation, leading to better decisions in real-world situations.

The common denominator is leadership. Marines are required to be leaders and advance based on their potential leadership qualities. Our training is tough. It has to be as Marines take on responsibilities well beyond their years.

As we move into the 21st century, we face a rapidly changing world with complex situations. Our focus must be on training people to make sound decisions under rapidly changing conditions. The Marine Corps must be prepared for what may be called a "three-block war." On one block we may deliver humanitarian assistance to help people survive. Moments later, on the next block, we may be called upon to take a harder line as a peacekeeping force. Finally, if hostilities do erupt, we must be able to win mid-intensity battles on a third block. To effectively make the right decision for the situations we face on each block requires a sharp and agile mind, and the ability to take charge.

TO THINK OF OURSELVES FIRST IS HUMAN NATURE, **BUT TO PUT OTHERS FIRST IS THE NATURE OF A MARINE.**

Today's Marines

Asian Americans find many opportunities in the service of our Nation. They make up a growing number of our Marines in service around the globe with more than 7,600 Asian Americans in today's Marine Corps.

If you are interested in developing your decision-making abilities and cultivating your leadership skills, consider joining the Marine Corps team. For more information about opportunities to serve in the United States Marine Corps, log on to Marines. com, MarineOfficer.com or call 1-800-MARINES. Keep an open mind. The Marine Corps is unlike anything you have ever experienced. We offer no excuses, and we take none. We make Marines and win battles. No compromises.

The Strength of Our Corps

"Our Marines have always been our greatest strength. Indeed, the Corps' enduring contribution to America is the development of Marines who embrace our service values and warrior culture, selflessly serve their country, and then return to society as outstanding private citizens."

— General Michael W. Hagee,

Commandant of the Marine Corps

Sergeant Marvie V. Paje
Reproduction Chief
II Marine Expeditionary Force

As a combat camera Marine, Paje is in charge of the print reproduction department. He designs letterhead, signs, and other artwork requested by units deployed to Iraq. Some examples of his daily reproduction jobs are memorial service bulletins, medical forms and training manuals essential to the Marine Corps mission. "I felt at the time I joined, I could do more with my life," said Paje. "I knew the Marine Corps would develop my sense of responsibility, positive character, and my education."

Lance Corporal Joon-Hyun Ryu
8th Communication Battalion
II Marine Expeditionary Force

Lance Corporal Joon-Hyun Ryu, 20, was born in Korea, but moved to the United States with his mother to grasp the opportunities available in America. "My parents wanted me to have a better opportunity for education," said Ryu, a refrigeration mechanic. "I started learning the alphabet on the plane to America."

Joining the United States Marine Corps was his way of paying tribute to his father, a Republic of Korea Marine, giving back to the United States and gaining life experience.

Gunnery Sergeant Elmer Pagaragan
Recruiting Station, Orange
12th Marine Corps District

Gunnery Sergeant Pagaragan, who is of Filipino descent, is currently stationed at Recruiting Substation Hawaii. A Honolulu native, Pagaragan attended three different high schools and graduated from Ellison High School in Killeen, Texas, in 1994.

Pagaragan set three goals for himself while on recruiting duty; to be meritoriously promoted, to be Recruiter of the Year and to enlist 100 people into the Marine Corps. So far, Pagaragan has been meritoriously promoted and has been named Recruiter of the Year.

Captain Kimberly Johnson
Aide de Camp
Marine Corps Recruiting Command

Born in Seoul, Korea and raised in the United States, Captain Johnson joined the Marine Corps for the challenge and opportunity. The Tulane University graduate set out to make a difference, locally and globally.

"My major accomplishment as a Marine is just that, being a Marine," said Johnson.

Johnson has deployed three times with the 11th Marine Expeditionary Unit, twice to Iraq.

2nd Lieutenant Clark Hsu Lo
Supply Officer
CSSG-3, Kaneohe Bay, Hawaii

2nd Lt. Clark Hsu Lo is a University of Central Florida graduate. Lo, who is of Chinese descent, feels that being a Marine holds several meanings.

"There are multiple reasons why I became a Marine," said Lo. "I joined because I wanted to serve my country and have a job that held meaningful challenges in store for me. I wanted to do something different than what everyone back home expected of me."

Colonel Leo A. Mercado
Chief of Staff
Marine Corps University

Colonel Mercado is responsible for ensuring the development, delivery, and evaluation of professional military education and training. Through the resident and distant education programs of the Marine Corps University, Mercado helps prepare leaders to meet the challenges of operational environments.

Mercado, who is of Filipino descent, was the Marine Corps Aide to President Clinton and holds a Master's of Public Administration from Shippensburg University.

THEY CAME FROM SMALL TOWNS AND BIG CITIES **TO PROVE THEY BELONG IN THIS PROUD FAMILY**
WHOSE HERITAGE TRAVELS BACK MORE THAN TWO CENTURIES

ARLINGTON, Va. (June 2, 2005) -- The Department of Defense (DoD) in collaboration with the Federal Asian Pacific American Council (FAPAC), honored nine military service members during the DoD Asian Pacific American Heritage Month Luncheon June 2, for their significant contributions in positively impacting the Asian Pacific American community.

This year's event gathered more than 550 special guests and FAPAC members to pay tribute to military service members from the U. S. Armed Services, both past and present. Two of the awardees were United States Marines.

The Marines honored were Staff Sgt. Jonathan E. Flick, a recruiter stationed in Guam, and Sergeant Jeffrey Chao, a platoon sergeant for 2nd Battalion, 23rd Marines in Encino, California. Both Marines were nominated by their commands and selected by an awards board at Headquarters, United States Marine Corps.

The awardees' selection not only recognized the significant contributions made in fostering positive relations between the military and the Asian Pacific American community but also highlighted their efforts in promoting diversity and equal opportunity employment in the federal work force. Making a direct impact for the federal work force, Flick's recruiting effort stood out among top DoD officials.

"We are very proud of what Marines do across the board, both in service and in the local communities," said the Honorable Dr. David S. Chu, Under Secretary of Defense, Personnel and Readiness. "As for recruiting, the Marines do it right. They send some of the best people on recruiting duty and it shows in their consistent results."

Flick was an accomplished steward of the Corps while on recruiting duty. He helped 90 qualified Asian Pacific Americans find promising careers as Marines. His involvement with local youth organizations, government-sponsored events and the promotion of physical fitness among his applicants made him a befitting recipient for this year's award.

"Looking back, I think I made a good impact and influence on the Asian Pacific American community," Flick said. "I worked hard to meet people and build professional relationships, and along the way I made several long-lasting friendships."

Flick, a native of Manchester, Connecticut, was meritoriously promoted to his current rank and was the Western Recruiting Region's recruiter of the year for 2004.

"Not only is he a role model, he is a leader - and they have seen that in the Asian Pacific community and have responded by joining the Marine Corps," said Brigadier General Walter E. Gaskin, commanding general, Marine Corps Recruiting Command. "He is a Marine who has what we look for in those that become Marines - the ability to interact with the community they live in and can tell the Marine Corps story."

Chao, a Marine reservist, has also made an indelible impact for Asian Pacific Americans. The 21-year-old native of Los Angeles has been a voice in his community and a promoter of military awareness. He recently demonstrated his support for Asian and veteran citizens by running for city councilman in Monterey Park, Calif., where he resides. Chao initially ran for city council because of his concern for improving the processes of educational benefits for

veterans. He attributes his focus in politics to what he has experienced and learned as a Marine.

"The values we learn as Marines can help you to become more focused and instills in you the ability to solve problems better," Chao said.

As a student at California State, Chao tries to dispel the negativity surrounding the military in general with those who seem to have varying opinions about serving their country.

"I try to tell them there are a lot of people making sacrifices for their freedom and they have to understand that," Chao said.

His efforts did not go unnoticed as Chu expressed his delight after presenting Chao with his award.

"Chao was honored for his community service and how he was successful in reaching out," Chu said. "By him helping to bring the whole country together is just a joy."

In addition to the awards presentation, a tribute to fallen Asian Pacific heroes was presented with the playing of Taps followed by a moment of silence from all who were present in the banquet room.

(Story and Photo by Staff Sergeant Marc Ayalin)

THE DEPUTY SECRETARY OF DEFENSE
WASHINGTON

JAN 1 3 2006

Congratulations on the 20th anniversary edition of the Anuario Hispano – Hispanic Yearbook. This annual guide, together with the African and Asian yearbooks that followed, have effectively highlighted the vital contributions to peace, prosperity and progress made by our friends around the world and by Americans of many diverse backgrounds. Year after year, these reference resources have played an important role in connecting leaders in business, government, education and the public to build the close personal relationships that are the foundation of strong international ties and to provide a roadmap to opportunities in employment, business and education.

From the first edition, the Armed Forces of the United States have been part of each of these yearbooks. The yearbooks have aided in our recruiting efforts and highlighted the work of the many thousands of Soldiers, Sailors, Airmen, Marines, Coast Guardsmen and civilian employees who proudly serve in the defense of freedom and liberty.

America's military reflects the diverse people and intrinsic values of our blessed country. Our men and women in uniform protect and defend all Americans, our friends and allies, and our way of life. The Armed Services have earned the respect and admiration of a grateful Nation.

My very best wishes to the readers of these informative yearbooks and my thanks to the dedicated staff who each year compiles these valuable guides.

Again, congratulations on 20 years of success!

ASIANPACIFICAMERICAN
DEFENSE

FIG 1. Active Duty Military Personnel and Total U.S. Population by Race/Ethnicity: 2004

Across all branches of the United States military there are racial and ethnic disparities among active servicemen and women when compared with the total population. Asian Pacific Islanders, however, are represented remarkably well. In contrast to African Americans and Hispanics—which showed significant differences between general population and active military percentages—the Asian Pacific Islander population matched perfectly at 4.4 percent in both categories.

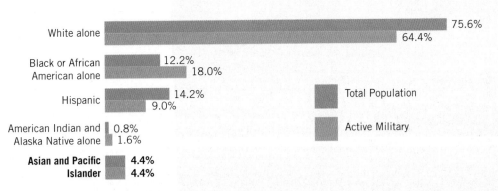

Source: U.S. Census Bureau, Current Population Survey, 2004
and Defense Manpower Data Center Report 3035EO

FIG 2. Active Duty Officers and Total Active Personnel by Race/Ethnicity: 2004

It is important to examine officer statistics because these data reflect promotion trends, and likelihood, for each of the different groups. According to the U.S. Department of Defense's own figures, the percentage of officers that are White is more than fourteen percent higher than that group's overall representation in the military. Asian Pacific Islanders are slightly underrepresented, but are generally much better off than other non-White ethnic or racial groups.

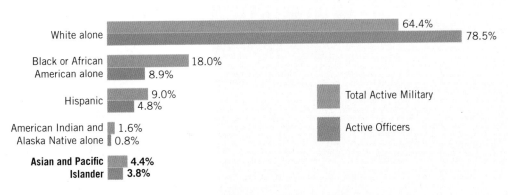

Source: U.S. Census Bureau, Current Population Survey, 2004
and Defense Manpower Data Center Report 3035EO

US Embassies and Consulates in Asian Countries

AFGHANISTAN

KABUL (E)
Great Masoud Rd.
Kabul, Afghanistan
Tel: [93] (20) 230-0436
Fax: [93] (20) 230-1364
Web: http://usembassy.state.gov/
afghanistan

AMB: Ronald E. Neumann
AMB OMS: Carolee A. Cooper
DCM: Richard B. Norland
DCM OMS: Jeanne Kincaid (Acting)
POL: Mary N. Townswick (Acting)
CON: Adrienne Harchick
MGT: Rosemary E. Hansen
AID: Alonzo Fulghum
DAO: Ray Hodgkins
DEA: Joseph Remenar
ECO: Douglas P. Climan
FIN: Vickie R. Lawrence
FMO: Craig Flanagan
GSO: Elizabeth Thompson
IMO: R. Vance Blakely
IPO: Bradley Gabler
PAO: Michael Macy
RSO: James McDermott

ARMENIA

YEREVAN (E)
1 American Ave.
Yerevan, Armenia
Tel: (37410) 46-47-00
Fax: (37410) 46-47-42
Email: usinfo@usa.am
Web: http:// yerevan.usembassy.gov

AMB: John Evans
AMB OMS: Pauline Maurantonio
DCM: Anthony Godfrey
DCM OMS: Leslie David
POL: Aaron Sherinian
POL/ECO: Cynthia Doell
CON: Mary Stickles
MGT: Lawrence Richter
AGR: Randall Hager (Moscow)
AID: Robin Phillips
CLO: Gino De Luca
CUS: James Homan
DAO: Russel Grimley
ECO: Vacant
ECO/COM: David Letteney
FMO: Christiana Foreman
GSO: Robert Ruehle

IMO: Bryon Hallman
IPO: Vacant
ISO/ISSO: Brian Jetter
NAS: Edward Schack
PAO: Kimberly Hargan

AZERBAIJAN

BAKU (E)
83 Azadlig Prospect
Baku, Azerbaijan
Tel: [9] (9412) 498-0335
Fax: [9] (9412) 465-6671
Web: www.usembassybaku.org

AMB: Reno L. Harnish, III
AMB OMS: Jamuna Harris
DCM: Jason P. Hyland
POL/ECO: Caryn McClelland
CON: Tristram & Elizabeth Perry
MGT: Robert Hensley
AFSA: Tristram Perry
AID: James Goggin
CLO: Michelle McAloon
DAO: Brendan McAloon
ECO/COM: Robert Burgess
EEO/PAO/State ICASS: Theresa Markiw
FMO: Kit Junge
GSO: Robert Burnett
IMO: Don Greer
ISO/ISSO: Jonathan Kirkpatrick
RSO: Fred Stolper

BAHRAIN

MANAMA (E)
PSC 451, Box 660, FPO AE
Bldg. 979, Rd. 3119, Block 331
Zinj District, Bahrain 09834
Tel: (973) 1724-2700
Fax: (973) 1727-2594
Web: http://bahrain.usembassy.gov

AMB: William T. Monroe
AMB OMS: Phyllis Williams
DCM: Susan L. Ziadeh
DCM OMS: Barbara Hayden
POL/ECO: Steve Bondy
CON: Larilyn Reffett
MGT: Raymond Kengott
ATO: Mike Henney (resident Dubai)
CLO: April Rodriguez
DAO: Ivar S. Tait
DEA: Jeffery J. Fitzpatrick (resident Islamabad)
ECO: Steve Simpson
FAA: Paul H. Feldman (resident Brussels)
FAA/CASLO: Karl R. Brown (resident Rome)

FMO: Sherrie Szymeczek
GSO: Peter Hayden
IMO: Kenneth Mack
IPO/ISSO: Brian Ahern
IRS: Frederick Pablo (resident Rome)
ISO: Greg Liddle
LEGATT: Fred Brink (resident Riyadh)
PAO: Wyn Hornbuckle
RSO: Keith Swinehart

BANGLADESH

DHAKA (E)
Madani Avenue, Baridhara
Dhaka, Bangladesh
Tel: [880] (2) 885-5500
Fax: [880] (2) 882-3744
Web: http://dhaka.usembassy.gov

DCM: Judith A. Chammas
DCM OMS: Martha K. Dunkley
POL: Dundas C. McCullough
CON: Elizabeth P. Gourlay
MGT: Vincent P. Raimondi
AID: Gene George
CLO: Agnes Maria Manzie
DAO: Brian K. Hedrick
ECO: David W. Renz
EEO: Sheri-Nouane Johnson
FMO: David H. Howard
GSO: Carlos M. Bras
IMO: Richard Hewitt
ISO/ISSO: Krishnan S. Sridhar
PAO: Jonathan D. Cebra
RSO: Dominic A. Sabruno

BRUNEI

BANDAR SERI BEGAWAN (E)
PSC 470 (BSB), FPO AP 96507
Teck Guan Plz.
Bandar Seri Begawan, Brunei
Tel: [673] (2) 229-670
Fax: [673] (2) 225-293
Web: http://bandar.usembassy.gov

AMB: Gene Christy
DCM: Jeff Hawkins
CON/MGT: Christa Dupuis
DAO: Col. John Bordwell (Singapore)
EEO/RSO: Judy Clark
FMO: Robert Wert (Singapore)
GSO/IMO/ISSO: Harry Clark
INS/IRS: (Singapore)

BURMA

RANGOON (E)
581 Merchant St. (GPO 521)
Rangoon, Burma
Tel: [95] (1) 379-880
Fax: [95] (1) 256-018

AMB: Carmen Martinez
AMB OMS: Judy Groves
DCM: Ron MCMullen
DCM OMS: Karen Heinrich
POL: Patrick Murphy
CON: Kerry Brougham
MGT: Laura Eppers
AFSA: William Brown, III
CLO: Angela Shepherd
DAO: Mike Norton
DEA: Joseph Shepherd
ECO/State ICASS: Ben Wohlaeur
EEO: Judith Groves
FMO: James Wickersham
GSO: Thomas Favret
ICASS Chair: Deanna Merriman
IMO/IPO: Monte Marchant
ISO/ISSO: James H. Johnson
PAO: Mary Ellen Countryman
RSO: Alfred Vincent

CAMBODIA

PHNOM PENH (E)
Unit 8166, Box P, APO AP
#16-18
Phnom Penh, Cambodia 96546
Tel: [855] (23) 216-436
Fax: [855] (23) 216-437
Web: http://cambodia.usembassy.gov

DCM: Mark C. Storella
POL: Donald B. Coleman
CON: Terrence West
MGT: Richard A. Johnson
AID: Jonathan S. Addleton
CLO: Hoang Oanh
DAO: Terence M. Tidler
FMO: Pericles M. Hernandez
GSO: Dana R. Williams
IMO: Robert R. Popchak
IPO: Craig A. Bowman
PAO: David Gainer
RSO: John P. Davis

Source: US Department of State, www.foia.state.gov

CHINA

BEIJING (E)
3 Xiu Shui Bei Jie
Beijing, China 100600
Tel: [86] (10) 6532-3831
Fax: [86] (10) 6532-6929
Web: www.usembassy-china.org.cn

AMB: Clark T. Randt, Jr.
AMB OMS: Penny Grayson
DCM: David S. Sedney
DCM OMS: Joan Bower
CG: Michael Regan
POL: Daniel L. Shields
MGT: James R. Van Laningham
AGR: Maurice W. House
APHIS: Theresa Boyle
ATO: Laverne Brabant
CLO: Pamela T. Ayoung
COM/ADB: Craig Allen
CUS: Andy Yu
DAO: Ralph Jodice
DEA: James Tse
ECO: Robert S. Wang
EEO: Katherine Lawson
EST: Deborah J. Seligsohn
FAA: Joseph Tymczyszyn
FMO: Mazhar Ahson
GSO: Charles G. Krips
ICASS Chair: Brad Fribley
IMO: Heywood Miller
INS: Carlton Ayoung
IPO: Jim Wojciechowski
ISO: Thomas Martin
ISSO: Nancy Yoas
LAB: Helen C. Hudson
LEGATT: William Liu
PAO: Donald M. Bishop
RSO: Bob Eckert

CHENGDU (CG)
4 Lingshiguan Lu
Chengdu, Sichuan, China 610041
Tel: [86] (28) 8558-3992
Fax: [86] (28) 8558-3520
Web: www.usembassy-china.org.cn/chengdu

CG: Jeffrey A. Moon
CG OMS/AFSA: Deborah Vaughn
PO: Jeffrey A. Moon
POL: Kate Pongonis
POL/ECO: Krista Neumann
CON: Dave Hillon
MGT/State ICASS: Jeannette Juricic
CLO: Vacant
ECO: G.A. Donovan
EEO: Vacant
EST: Marc Abramson
FCS: Vacant
GSO: Ed Waters
IMO/IPO/ISSO: David Foster
ISO: CJ Baltz
OMS: Nomsa Gonzales
PAO: John Louton
RSO: Monica Byler

GUANGZHOU (CG)
1 Shamian St. South
Guangzhou, China 510133
Tel: [86] (20) 8121-8000
Fax: [86] (20) 8184-6296
Web: www.usembassy-china.org.cn/guangzhou

CG: Edward K.H. Dong

COM: Robert Murphy
CON: William J. Martin
MGT: Jeffrey Rock
AGR: Keith Schneller
ECO: Harvey A. Somers
GSO: Kenneth L. Meyer
INS: Thomas Wong
IPO: Frank Landymore
PAO: Wendy Lyle
RSO: Michael Brenn

SHANGHAI (CG)
1469 Huai Hai Zhong Lu
Shanghai, China 200031
Tel: [86] (21) 6433-3936
Fax: [86] (21) 6433-4122
Web: www.usembassy-china.org.cn/shanghai

CG: Kenneth Jarrett
CG OMS: Kellee Farmer
PO: Kenneth Jarrett, CG
POL/ECO: Mary Tarnowka
COM: Ira Kasoff
CON: George Hogeman
MGT/State ICASS: Andrea Baker
AFSA: Paul Thomas
ATO: Ross Kreamer
CLO: Kimberly Albright
EEO: Jean-Pierre Louis
ICASS Chair: Sub Group Only
IPO: vacant
ISO: Thomas Lacy
ISSO: Troy Jackson
PAO: Jennifer Galt
RSO: Brendan Murray

SHENYANG (CG)
52, 14th Wei Rd., Heping District
Shenyang, China 110003
Tel: [86] (24) 2322-0848
Fax: [86] (24) 2322-1733
Web: www.usembassy-china.org.cn/shenyang

CG: David A. Kornbluth
CG OMS: Kathy Kong
COM: Soching Tsai
CON: Douglas Kelly
MGT: Joseph E. Zadrozny
CLO: Vacant
ECO: Laurel Steele
EEO: Vacant
GSO: Colleen E. Altstock
IPO/ISSO: John Meradith
ISO: Vacant
PAO: Cynthia Caples
RSO: John Young

CYPRUS

NICOSIA (E)
P.O. Box 24536
Metochiou and Ploutarchou St.
Engomi, Nicosia, Cyprus 2407
Tel: [357] (22) 393-939
Fax: [357] (22) 780-944
Web: www.americanembassy.org.cy

AMB OMS: Ginny Phillips
DCM/CHG: Jane Zimmerman
DCM OMS: Carol Hazzard
POL/State ICASS: Matthew A. Palmer

CON: Henry H. Hand
MGT: Katherine A. Muchmeyer
AID: Thomas Dailey
CLO: Kathy Boukedes
CUS: Robert Granico
DAO: Steve G. Boukedes
DEA: Richard Hudon
ECO: Michael S. Dixon
EEO: Karen Rezek
FAA: Vacant
GSO: Kurt J. Hoyer
ICASS Chair: Janet Newby
IMO: Robert P. MCumber
IPO/ISSO: James Rezek
IRS: Fred Pablo (resident in Rome)
PAO: Tom Miller
RSO: Joan Andrews

EAST TIMOR

DILI (E)
Unit 8129, Box D
Ave. de Portugal, Pantai Kelapa
Dili, East Timor
Tel: [670] 332-4684
Fax: [670] 331-3206

AMB: Grover Joseph Rees, III
AMB OMS: Myrna F. Farmer
DCM/ICASS Chair/RSO: Sean B. Stein
DCM OMS: Midori Oliver
AID: Flynn Fuller
ECO/COM/POL/ADV: Curtis Ried
FMO: Ralph Hamilton
GSO/IMO: Daniel Reagan

GEORGIA

TBILISI (E)
25 Atoneli
Tbilisi, Georgia
Tel: [995] (32) 989-967
Fax: [995] (32) 938-951

AMB: Richard Miles
AMB OMS: Linda Price
DCM: Patricia N. Moller
DCM OMS: Jessica Haynie
CON: Kim Richter
MGT: Carol Stricker
AID: Denny Robertson
CLO: Claudia Ostrowski
CUS: Jon Trumble
DAO: Alan Hester
FIN: Jason Orlando
FMO: Louis Nelli
GSO: Deane Parker
ICASS Chair/PAO/State
ICASS: Rowena Cross-Najafi
IMO: Lester Brayshaw
LEGATT: Bryan Paarmann
RSO: Ronnie Catipon

HONG KONG

HONG KONG (M)
PSC 461, Box 1, FPO AP 96521
26 Garden Rd. Central
Hong Kong, Hong Kong
Tel: [852] 2523-9011
Fax: [852] 2845-1598
Web: http://hongkong.usconsulate.gov

AMB: James B. Cunningham
AMB OMS: Kyla J. Seals
DCM: Marlene J. Sakaue
DCM OMS: Linda M. Mason-Witt
POL/ECO: Simon J. Schuchat
CON: Richard F. Gonzalez
MGT: Lewis R. Atherton
ATO/ICASS Chair: Lloyd S. Harbert
CLO: Jennifer A. Eckert/Kathleen M. Grabruck
CUS: Thomas J. Howe
DAO: George T. Foster
DEA: Thomas Ma
EEO: Michael Pascual
FCS: Stewart J. Ballard
FMO: Laurence A. Rigg
GSO: William H. Boyle (Acting SGSO)
IMO: Janifer K. Sulaiman
IPO: Bryan W. Berry (Acting)
ISO: Wenyi Shu
LEGATT: Kingman K. Wong
PAO: Richard W. Stites
RSO: Robert A. Eckert, Jr. (Acting)

INDIA

NEW DELHI (E)
Shanti Path, Chanakaya
New Delhi, India 110021
Tel: [91] (11) 2419-8000
Fax: [91] (11) 2419-90017
WEB: http://newdelhi.usembassy.gov

AMB: David C. Mulford
AMB OMS: Susanne Ames
DCM: Robert O. Blake
DCM OMS: Irvina Wallace
CG/CON: William Bartlett
POL: Geoffrey Pyatt
COM: John Peters
MGT: James Forbes
AGR: Chad Russell
AID: George Deikun
APHIS: Marvin Felder
CLO: Fatima Brown
CUS: James Dozier
DAO: Steven Sboto
DEA: Ronald Khan
ECO: Lee A. Brudvig
EST: Marco DiCapua
FAA: Howard W. Nesbitt
FIN: David Sarisky
FMO: William Hedges
GSO: Stephen Ames
ICASS Chair: Ron Olsen
IMO: James L. Cleveland
INS: Henry Eager
IPO: Robert Hall
IRS: Elizabeth Kinney
ISO: Sherril Pavin
ISSO: Bill Price
LEGATT: David Ford
MLO: Mark Ericson
NAS: Laura Livingston
PAO/State ICASS: Michael Anderson
RSO: George Lambert

CALCUTTA (C)
5/1 Ho Chi Minh Sarani
Calcutta, India 700071
Tel: [91] (33) 2282-3611
Fax: [91] (33) 2282-2335
Web: http://calcutta.usconsulate.gov

CG: George N. Sibley
CON: Sarah A. Nelson
MGT: William L. Smith
IMO: James L. Cleveland
IPO: Robert A. Hall (New Delhi)
ISO: Sherril L. Pavin (New Delhi)
PAO: Susan M. Shultz
RSO: Dominic A. Sabruno (Chennai)

CHENNAI (C)
220 Anna Salai Rd.
Chennai, India 600006
Tel: [91] (44) 2811-2000
Fax: [91] (44) 2811-2020
Email: chennaics@state.gov
Web: http://chennai.usconsulate.gov

CG: David Hopper
CG OMS: Sumita Gupta
PO: David Hopper
POL: Robert King
COM: Mark Russell
CON: Michael D. Thomas
MGT: Kelly Buenrostro
GSO: Mary Lou Gonzales
IPO/ISO/ISSO: James J. Foster
PAO: Ravi Candidai
RSO: Dominick Sabruno

MUMBAI (CG)
78 Bhulabhai Desai Rd.
Mumbai, India
Tel: [91] (22) 2363-3611
Fax: [91] (22) 2363-0350
Web: http://usembassy.state.gov/mumbai

CG: Angus T. Simmons
CG OMS: Mirtea Starkey
PO: Angus T. Simmons
POL: William Klein
COM: Richard Rothman
CON: Joseph Pomper
MGT: James Leaf
CLO: Joan Luethi
ECO: Rebecca Frerichs
GSO: Phyllis Desmet-Howard
ISO: Bill Mains
PAO: Linda Cheatham
RSO: Scott Messick

INDONESIA

JAKARTA (E)
Medan Merdeka Selatan 5
Jakarta, Indonesia 96520-8129
Tel: [62] (21) 3435-9000
Fax: [62] (21) 386-2259
Web: http://jakarta.usembassy.gov

AMB: B. Lynn Pascoe
DCM: W. Lewis Amselem
CG/CON: Mary Grandfield
POL: Marc Desjardins
COM/FCS: Margaret Keshishian
MGT: Lawrence Mandel
AGR/ICASS Chair: Fred Kessel
AID: William Frej
CLO: Anne Luehrs
DAO: Col. Joseph Judge (USA)
ECO: William Heidt
EEO: Max Kwak
EST: Anthony Woods
FMO: Ralph Hamilton
GSO: Wade Leahy
IMO: David Yeutter
IPO: Timmie Chatelain
ISO/ISSO: Ron Lay
LAB: Mark D. Clark

PAO/State ICASS: Charles Silver
RSO: Earl R. Miller

SURABAYA (CG)
Jl. Dr. Soetomo #33
Surabaya, Indonesia 60264
Tel: [62] (31) 295-6400
Fax: [62] (31) 567-4492

PO: Phillip L. Antweiler
POL: Steven J. Whitaker
POL/ECO: Mara A. Kaplan
CON: Sabin M. Hinton
MGT: Susan Cheatham
GSO: Cheryl Hepburn
PAO: Mary Beth Polley
RSO: Kevin T. Whitson

ISRAEL

TEL AVIV (E)
71 Hayarkon St.
Tel Aviv, Israel
Tel: [972] (3) 519-7575
Fax: [972] (3) 517-3227
Email: nivtelaviv@state.gov
Web: http:usembassy-israel.org.il

AMB: Daniel C. Kurtzer
AMB OMS: Deborah M. Burns
DCM: Gene A. Cretz
DCM OMS: Dahlene C. Sprague
CG OMS: Christopher Call
POL: Norman H. Olsen
COM: Ronald Soriano
MGT: Brian H. McIntosh
AID: James Bever
CLO: Kristi Lund/Patricia Schultz
ECO: William Weinstein
EEO/IPO: Tom Robilotta
EST: Robert Tansey
FMO: John M. Gieseke
GSO: Vacant
ICASS Chair: Vacant
IMO: James C. Norton
ISO: R. Curt Rhea
ISSO: Jack D. West
LEGATT: Cary Gleicher
PAO: Helena K. Finn
RSO: Mark J. Hipp

HAIFA(CA)
12 Jerusalem St.
Haifa, Israel 33132
Tel: [972] (04) 670615

JERUSALEM (CG)
PSC 98 Box 0039 APO AE 09830
18 Agron Rd.
Jerusalem, Israel 94190
Tel: [972] (2) 622-7230
Fax: [972] (2) 625-9270
Email: uscongenjerusalem@state.gov
Web: http://jerusalem.usconsulate.gov

CG: David Pearce
DCM: Maura Connelly-DPO
PO: David D. Pearce
POL: John C. Stevens
COM: David J Ranz
CON: Mary D. Draper
MGT: Sylvie L. Martinez
AFSA: John C. Stevens
AGR: Yolanda Parra
AID: Thomas Dailey
CLO: Valerie Franchi
ECO: David J Ranz

EEO: Alison E. Dilworth
FMO: Yolanda Parra
GSO: Elias Parra
ICASS Chair: Charles F. Hunter
IMO: Stephen P. Provencal
ISO: Billy D. Feely
ISSO: Douglas E. Haidle
PAO: Charles F. Hunter
RSO: Keith A. Swinehart
State ICASS: Charles F. Hunter

JAPAN

TOKYO (E)
10-5 Akasaka, 1 Chome
Tokyo, Japan 1078420
Tel: [81] (3) 3224-5000
Fax: [81] (3) 3505-1862
Web: http://tokyo.usembassy.gov

AMB: John Thomas Schieffer
DCM: Joseph R. Donovan
CG: Edward McKeon
POL: Michael Meserve
CON: Patty L. Hill
MGT: James Van Derhoff
AFSA: Joel Ehrenreich
AGR: Daniel Berman
AID: Charles R. Aanenson
APHIS: Robert Tanaka
ATO: Mark A. Dries
CLO: Marilynn Fulcher/Raul Alferez
CUS: Michael R. Cox
DAO: Mark Welch
DEA: Daniel Moore
ECO: James P. Zumwalt
EEO: Sheila Pannell
EST: Joyce Rabens
FAA/ICASS Chair: Christopher S. Metts
FAA/CASLO: Cornell Russell
FCS: Samuel H. Kidder
FIN: Richard Johnston
FMO: Francis M. Conte
GSO: Paul Wedderien
IMO: Kay E. Gotoh
IPO: Robert L. Adams
ISO/ISSO: David Mango
LAB: Ann M. Kambara
LEGATT: Lawrence J. Futa
MLO: John V. Robson
PAO: William M. Morgan
RSO: Gentry Smith

FUKUOKA (C)
5-26 Ohori 2-Chome, Chuo-ku
Fukuoka, Japan 810-0052
Tel: [81] (92) 751-9331
Fax: [81] (92) 713-9222
Web: http://fukuoka.usconsulate.gov

PO: Joyce S. Wong
CON/MGT/FMO/GSO/IMO/ISSO: Eric R. Kettner
MGT: Blair R. Kettner
PAO: John A. Dyson

NAGOYA (C)
Nishiki SIS Bldg., 6th Fl. 10-33 Nishiki
3-chome, Naka-ku
Nagoya, Japan 460-0003
Tel: [81] (52) 203-4011
Fax: [81] (52) 201-4612
Web: http://nagoya.usconsulate.gov

PO: Gary G. Oba

CUS: George Wakayama
FCS: Stephen J. Anderson
PAO: Michael R. Turner

NAHA (CG)
2564 Nishihara, Urasoe City
Okinawa, Japan 901-2101
Tel: [81] (98) 876-4211
Fax: [81] (98) 876-4243
Web: http://naha.usconsulate.gov

CG: Thomas G. Reich
POL: Patricia M. Stigliani
CON: Jason McInerney
MGT/EEO/IMO/ISSO: Dan O. Fulwiler
PAO: Frank W. Stanley

OSAKA-KOBE (CG)
11-5 Nishitenma, 2 Chome, Kita-Ku
Osaka, Japan 530-8543
Tel: [81] (6) 6315-5900
Fax: [81] (6) 6315-5915

PO: Alexander Almasov
POL/ECO: Patrick L. Chow
COM: Alan Long
CON: Paul J. Howard
MGT: Robert J. Dupalo
ATO: Emiko Purdy
IPO: Peter A. Steitz
ISSO: Peter A. Steitz/Stephen S. Wheeler
PAO: John Laycock

SAPPORO (CG)
Kita 1-Jo Nishi 28-Chome, Chuo-ku
Sapporo, Japan 064-0821
Tel: [81] (11) 641-1115
Fax: [81] (11) 643-1283
Web: http://sapporo.usconsulate.gov

CG: Marrie Y. Schaefer
CON/MGT/ISO: Elise J. Fox
IMO: Shinji Hosokawa (FSN)
PAO: Marrie Y. Schaefer

YOKOHAMA
152-3 Yamate-cho, Naka-ku
Yokohama, Japan 231-0862
Tel: [81] (45) 622-6514
Fax: [81] (45) 622-6516
PO: Lawrence J. Mire

JORDAN

AMMAN (E)
P.O. Box 354
Amman, Jordon 11118
Tel: [962] (6) 590-6000
Fax: [962] (6) 592-0163
Web: www.usembassy-amman.org.jo

AMB: Vacant
DCM: David Hale
DCM OMS: Virginia Bladwin
CG/CON: Daniel Goodspeed
CG OMS: Erin Dibiasi
POL: Christopher Henzel
COM: Laurie Farris
MGT: Perry Adair
AGR/APHIS/ATO: Hala Khoury
AID: Anne Aarnes
ATF/DEA/RSO: Robert Goodrich
CLO: Jane Paddock & Cherie Steinkampf
CUS: Greg Lawless
DAO: David MacLean

ECO: Richard Eason
EEO/ISO: Cecilia Blue
EPA/EST/NAS: John Whittlesey
FMO: Richard Boohaker
GSO: Victor E. Manley
ICASS Chair: Sheryle Robinson
IMO: Howard Copeland
ISSO: Tacla Boohaker
LEGATT: Andre Khoury
PAO: Michael Pelletier

KAZAKHSTAN

ALMATY (E)
99/97A Furmanov St.
Almaty, Kazakhstan
Tel: [7] (3272) 50-48-02
Fax: [7] (3272) 50-24-77
Web: www.usembassy-kazakhstan.freenet.kz

AMB: John M. Ordway
AMB OMS: Janet Van Der Zalm
DCM: Mark L. Asquino
DCM OMS: Diane Rogers
POL: Karen Kitsman
POL/ECO: Deborah Mennuti
CON: Jeffrey Lodinsky
MGT: Russell W. Jones, Jr.
AFSA/GSO: Ramon Best
AGR: James J. Higgiston (Turkey)
AID: Michael Fritz
CLO: Jennifer Donnelly
CUS: Andrew Offenbacher
DAO: Matthew Brand
DEA: Steven Monaco (Tashkent)
EEO: Angela Lord
FAA: Sandi Rohrbach (Brussels)
FCS: Mitchel Auerbach
FMO: Frederick J. Miller
ICASS Chair: Margaret McCarthy
IMO: Gregory E. Davis
IRS: Margaret Lullo (Berlin)
ISO/ISSO: Joshua Walde
LEGATT: Jeffrey Iverson
NAS: Clifford Sorensen
PAO: Ann Welden
RSO: Elizabeth Murphy

ASTANA (BO)
62 Kosmonavtov St.
Astana, Kazakhstan
Tel: [7] (3) 172-58-08-90
Fax: [7] (3) 172-58-08-99

AMB: John M. Ordway
AMB OMS: Janet Van Der Zalm
DCM : Mark L. Asquino
DCM OMS: Diane Rogers
PO: Lynne Tracy
POL: Elizabeth Webster
POL/ECO/ECO: Peter Andreoli
EEO/GSO/PAO: Suzanne Bodoin
RSO: Elizabeth Murphy

KOREA, SOUTH

SEOUL (E)
U.S. Embassy Seoul, Unit 15550, APO AP
96205-5550
32 Sejongno, Jong-gu
Seoul, Korea 110-710
Tel: [82] (2) 397-4114
Fax: [82] (2) 738-8845
Email: seoulniv@state.gov
Web: http://seoul.usembassy.gov

AMB: Christopher R. Hill
AMB OMS: Gretchen M. Miranda-Velez
DCM CHG: Mark C. Minton
DCM OMS: Donna J. Snead
CG: Michael D. Kirby
CG OMS: Dul Lim Lee
POL: Joseph Y. Yun
MGT: An T. Le
AFSA: Michael H. Young
AGR: Larry M. Senger
APHIS: George A. Ball
ATO: Susan B. Phillips
CLO: Paul F. Mazeika
CUS: Barry Tang
DAO: Steven F. Beal
DEA: Christopher Browning
ECO: Kurt W. Tong
EEO/FMO: Michael J. Browning
EST: Milton L. Charlton
FAA: Joseph Tymczyszyn
FCS: Carmine D'Aloisio
GSO: George T. Novinger
ICASS Chair: Thomas J. Castle
IMO: Timothy C. Lawson
INS: Jose R. Olivares
IPO: Rudolph R. Garcia
IRS: Stanley Beesley
ISO: Michael A. Bricker
LAB: Michael F. Kleine
LEGATT: J. Sung Maeng
PAO: Don Q. Washington
RSO: David J. Schnorbus
State ICASS: Paul G. Gilmer

KUWAIT

KUWAIT (E)
P.O. Box 77
Al-Masjed Al-Aqsa St.
Bayan Plot, Kuwait
Tel: [965] 259-1001
Fax: [965] 538-0282
Email: consularkuwaitm@state.gov
Web: http://usembassy.state.gov/kuwait

AMB: Richard B. LeBaron
AMB OMS: Janice G. Smith
DCM: Matthew H. Tueller
DCM OMS: Malgorzata Lamot
POL/EEO: Natalie E. Brown
CON: Charles L. Glatz, Jr.
MGT: Marjorie R. Phillips
CLO: Beth U. Alois
CUS: James C. Piatt
DAO: Lt. Colonel Robert Friedenberg US Army
DEA: Embassy Cairo
ECO: Stephen J. Carrig
FAA/CASLO: FAA-Amemb Manama
FCS: Peter B. Alois
FMO: James C. Maher
GSO: Beverly Rochester-Johnson
IBB: Walter Patterson
ICASS Chair: Daniel Robers
IMO: George M. Navadel
IPO: Ricardo Garcia
ISO/ISSO: Anup Y. Shah
LAB: Joseph Porto
MLO: Brig General John Mullholland US Army
PAO: DCM-Matthew Tueller

RSO: Mark S. Conord
State ICASS: Vicki L. Adair

KYRGYZSTAN

BISHKEK (E)
171 Prospect Mira
Bishkek, Kyrgyzstan 720016
Tel: [996] (312) 551-241
Fax: [996] (312) 551-264

AMB: Stephen M. Young
AMB OMS: Susan Christy
DCM: Donald Lu
DCM OMS: Vacant
POL/ECO: Salvatore Amodeo
CON/AFSA/ICASS Chair/State ICASS: John Gimbel
MGT: Mona Kuntz
AGR: James Higgiston (Ankara)
AID: Clifford Brown
CLO: Mary Spatz
CUS: John Krob
DAO: Mark Hallisey
DEA: Doug Cortinovis (Tashkent)
FAA: James Nasiatka (Moscow)
FMO: Patrick Spatz
GSO: Dan McCullough
IMO: Joel Wisner
IPO/ISSO: Ralph T. Pollard
IRS: Susan Stanley (Berlin)
LEGATT: Jeffrey Iverson (Almaty)
NAS: J. Michael Stiers
PAO: William James
RSO: David Eberhardt

LAOS

VIENTIANE (E)
Rue Bartolonie, B.P. 114
Vientiane, Laos 96546-0001
Tel: [856] (21) 26-7000
Fax: [856] (21) 26-7190
Web: http://usembassy.state.gov/laos

AMB: Patricia M. Haslach
AMB OMS: Linda Wood
DCM: Kristen F. Bauer
POL/ECO: Gregory D. Chapman
CON: Gregory J. Adamson
MGT: Marilyn R. Mattke
CLO: Susan M. Ritter (Admin. Assistant)
DEA: Richard Gommert
ECO: Scott L. Rolston
GSO: Erin A. Sawyer
ICASS Chair/IMO/ISSO: David K. Frazee
NAS: Clifford D. Heinzer
PAO: James A. Warren
RSO: Thomas Van Den Brink

LEBANON

BEIRUT (E)
P.O. Box 70-840 Antelias
Beirut, Lebanon
Tel: [961] (4) 542-600
Fax: [961] (4) 544-136
Web: http://lebanon.usembassy.gov

AMB: Jeffrey Feltman
AMB OMS: Laura Craynon
DCM: Christopher Murray
DCM OMS: Georgeanne Ranzino
POL: Edward Messmer

POL/ECO: George Fredrick
CON: William Gill
MGT: Barbara McCarthy
AID: Raouf Youssef
DAO: Kazimierz Kotlow
DEA: Tom Varvitsiotis
GSO: Edward Quinn
IMO/ISSO: Celestine Quinn
LEGATT: Andre Khoury
MLO: Benjamin Crockett
PAO: Juliet Wurr
RSO: Arthur Balek

MALAYSIA

KUALA LUMPUR (E)
376 Jalan Tun Razak
Kuala Lumpur, Malaysia
Tel: [6] (03) 2168-5000
Fax: [6] (03) 2142-2207
Web: http://usembassymalaysia.org.my

AMB: Christopher J. LaFleur
AMB OMS: Wendy R. Gralnek
DCM: Robert A. Pollard
DCM OMS: Shirley J. Crowley
POL: Thomas F. Daughton
MGT: Francisca T. Helmer
AFSA/IPO: William H. Lanzet
AGR/ICASS Chair: Jonathan P. Gressel
CLO: Janet C. Gresham
DAO: Jason Weintraub
ECO: Colin S. Helmer
FCS: Joseph Kaesshaefer
FMO: Dianne M. Hand
GSO: Ellen Langston
IMO: Meredith B. Donaway
ISSO: David A. Hansen
LEGATT: Timothy C. Haught
PAO: Phillip P. Hoffmann
RSO: Brian F. Duffy
LEGATT: Timothy Haught
PAO: Karl Stoltz
RSO: Brian F. Duffy
State ICASS: Virginia Murray

MONGOLIA

ULAANBAATAR (E)
P.O. Box 1021
Micro District 11, Big Ring Rd.
Ulaanbaatar, Mongolia
Tel: [976] (11) 329-095
Fax: [976] (11) 320-776
Web: http://www.us-mongolia.com/home

AMB: Pamela J.H. Slutz
AMB OMS: Jane Lopez
DCM: Mark A. Tokola
POL/State ICASS: Patrick Freemen
COM/ECO/EEO: Megan Myers
CON: Joan Kane
MGT: J. Denver Herren
AFSA/PAO: Scott Weinhold
AGR: Beijing
AID/ICASS Chair: Leon Waskin
APHIS: Beijing
ATF: Beijing
ATO: Beijing
CLO: Jamie Weinhold
CUS: Beijing
DAO/MLO: Mark Gillette
DEA: Beijing
EPA: Beijing

EST: Beijing
FAA: Beijing
FAA/CASLO: Beijing
FMO: Thomas Galloway
GSO: Danielle Wood
IMO/IPO/ISO/ISSO: Leo Parpart
INS: Beijing
IRS: Tokyo
LAB: Beijing
LEGATT: Beijing
NAS: Beijing
RAMC: Bangkok
RSO: Craig Reistad

NEPAL

KATHMANDU (E)
Panipokhari
Kathmandu, Nepal
Tel: [977] (1) 441-1179
Fax: [977] (1) 441-9963
Web: http://nepal.usembassy.gov

AMB: James F. Moriarty
AMB OMS: Meredith K. Katterson
DCM: Elisabeth I. Millard
DCM OMS: Claire Berger
POL: Grace W. Shelton
CON: Robert N. Farquhar
MGT: Michelle M. Esperdy
AID: Donald Clark
CLO: David Stum
DAO: Scott R. Taylor
FIN: Patricia Miller
FMO: David Wall
GSO: Alan Monetta
IMO: E. Alex Copher
MLO: Randall L. Koehlmoos
PAO: Laura D. Lucas
RSO: James W. Gayhart

OMAN

MUSCAT (E)
P.O. Box 202, Code No. 115, Medinat Al
Suitan Qaboos
Muscat, Oman
Tel: (968) 24-698-989
Fax: (968) 24-696-928
Web: http://oman.usembassy.gov

AMB: Richard L. Baltimore, III
AMB OMS: Jennifer Schaaf
DCM: William R. Stewart
POL: Michael G. Snowden
CON: Lia N. Miller
MGT: Vivian M. Lesh
CLO: Linda G. Ammons
DAO: Mark A. Avery
ECO/COM: Brian M. Grimm
EEO/ISO: Kevin Rubesh
FMO: Javier A. Araujo
GSO: Alex Fleming
ICASS Chair: Dennis Long
IMO: Karen A. Finer
ISSO: Timothy Hinman
LEGATT: Martin Reardon (resident in
Riyadh)
PAO: Christopher P. Quade
RAMC: FSC Bangkok
RSO: Peter M. Riva

PAKISTAN

ISLAMABAD (E)
Diplomatic Enclave, Ramna 5
Islamabad, Pakistan
Tel: [92] (51) 208-0000
Fax: [92] (51) 227-6427
Web: http://islamabad.usembassy.gov

AMB: Ryan C. Crocker
AMB OMS: Beverly A. Oliver
DCM: Patricia A. Butenis
DCM OMS: Suzann Reynolds
CG: Zandra Flemister
POL/NAS: Lisa Johnson
MGT: Judith A. Futch
AID: Lisa Chiles
CLO: Claudia Coleman, HRO
DAO: Mark Boettcher
DEA: Thomas Nuse
ECO: Christian DeAngelis
EEO: Michael Spring
FIN: Lois E. Simms
FMO: Morris Williams
GSO: Deborah Esteves
IMO: Mel Rollins
IPO: Art Hermanson
ISO: Keith Houk
ISSO: Lynne Hermanson
LEGATT: Ralph Horton
MLO: Craig McDonald
PAO: Gregory Crouch
RSO: Scott Farquar

KARACHI (CG)
8 Abdullah Haroon Rd.
Karachi, Pakistan
Tel: [92] (21) 568-5170
Fax: [92] (21) 568-0496
Web: http://usembassy.state.gov/karachi

CG: Mary H. Witt
CON/EEO: Fredric W. Stern
MGT: Robert Pitre
FMO: Dennis J. Springhetti
GSO: Rekha N. Stern
IPO: Jorge Viscal
ISSO: Ellis M. McVea
RSO: Thomas V. Gallagher

LAHORE (C)
50 Empress Rd.
Lahore, Pakistan 54000
Tel: [92] (42) 603-4000
Fax: [92] (42) 603-4200
Web: http://usembassy.state.gov/lahore

AMB: Ryan C. Crocker (Islamabad)
DCM: Pat A. Butenis (Islamabad)
PO: Brian G. Heath
CON/POL/ECO: Brian J. George
ICASS Chair: Tom Nuse (Islamabad)
RSO: Wayne T. Mastriano

PESHAWAR (C)
11 Hospital Rd.
Peshawar, Pakistan
Tel: [92] (91) 279-801
Fax: [92] (91) 284-171
Web: http://usembassy.state.gov/peshawar

AMB: Ryan Crocker (Islamabad)
DCM: Patricia Butenis (Islamabad)
PO: Michael A. Spangler
POL/CON/AFSA: Partha Mazumdar
MGT: Mary Elizabeth Madden
DAO: Lloyd Somers (Islamabad)
DEA: Tracy Haig

ECO/PAO: Allison D. Dyess
FMO: Lois Simms (Islamabad)
IMO: Mel Rollins (Islamabad)
ISSO: Keith Houk (Islamabad)
LEGATT: Chuck Finley (Islamabad)
NAS: Robert Traister
RSO: Kristen Sivertson

PAPUA NEW GUINEA

PORT MORESBY (E)
P.O. Box 1492, NCD
Douglas St.
Port Moresby, Papua New Guinea
Tel: (675) 321-1455
Fax: (675) 320-0637

AMB: Robert Fitts
AMB OMS: Vacant
DCM: Thomas Niblock
MGT: Margaret L. Genco
AFSA/GSO: Guy Margalith
CLO: Angela M. Niblock
ECO/COM: Eric Catalfamo
IPO/ISSO: Ken Kobilarcik
RSO: A.D. Aderinto

PHILIPPINES

MANILA (E)
P.O. Box 151
1201 Roxas Rd.
Manila, Philippines 1000
Tel: (632) 528-6300
Fax: (632) 522-4361
Web: http://manila.usembassy.gov

AMB: Vacant
AMB OMS: Vacant
DCM: Joseph A. Mussomeli, CDA
DCM OMS/EEO: Maria T. De Veyra
CG: Richard D. Haynes
POL: Scott D. Bellard
MGT: Sharon E. Ludan
US EXEC DIR: Paul W. Speltz
US ALT EXEC DIR: Troy Wray
AFSA: Leon W. Gendin
AGR: David C. Miller
AID: Jon Lindborg
APHIS: Leonides L. Cardenas
ATO: Dennis B. Voboril
CLO: Carola B. Mcelligott
COM/ADB: C. Franklin Foster, Jr.
CUS: Kevin R. Peters
DAO: Terry P. Cook
DEA: Timothy C. Teal
ECO: Robert P. Ludan
FAA: Bert Williams
FCS: Judy Reinke
FIN: Robert J. Ripley
FMO: William E. Barnhart
GSO: Stephen B. Hogard
IBB: Terence J. Donovan
ICASS Chair/LEGATT: Stephen P. Cutler
IMO: Roger W. Johnson
INS: Corazon Licerio, Acting
IPO: Steven G. Ackerman
ISO: Bradley L. Summers
ISSO: Romeo O. Ballesteros/David C.
Pillman
LAB: Joseph L. Novak
PAO: M. Lee McClenny
RAMC: John C. Bedwell
RSO: William H. Lamb

QATAR

DOHA (E)
22 February St.
Doha, Qatar
Tel: [974] 488-4101
Fax: [974] 488-4298
Web: http://qatar.usembassy.gov

AMB: Chase Untermeyer
AMB OMS: Nichole Walton
DCM: Scott McGehee
DCM OMS: Gina Miller
POL: Farah Chery-Medor
POL/ECO/State ICASS: Albert R. Pyott
CON: Larry Mitchell
MGT: Anne G. Molyneaux
AFSA/EEO/ICASS Chair/PAO: Patricia Kabra
CLO: Rana Nmair
DAO: John Arnold
ECO: Shante Moore
FMO: Robert Kingman
GSO: Chris Volciak
IMO/IPO: Frederick Ogg
ISSO: Neil Brans
RSO: Pat Capriglione

RUSSIA

MOSCOW (E)
8 Bolshoy Devyatinskiy
Moscow, Russia 121099
Tel: [7] (095) 728-5000
Fax: [7] (095) 728-5090
Web: http://moscow.usembassy.gov

AMB: Joseph Burns
AMB OMS: Karen Pennington
DCM: John R. Beyrle
DCM OMS: Joan Odean
CG: James Pettit
DPO/PAO: James Kenney
POL: Bruce Donahue (Acting)
MGT: Edward Alford
AFSA: Randy Kreft
AGR: Allan Mustard
AID: Terry Myers
ATO: Jeffrey Hesse
CLO: Joy Salpini
CUS: Edgar Lacy (Dept. of Homeland
Security)
DAO: Miles B. Wachendorf
DEA: Christopher Ogilvie
ECO: Pamela Quanrud
EEO: Jenny O'Connor and Naomi Lyew
EST: Sandra Dembski
FAA: James Nasiatka
FCS: Dorothy Lutter
FMO: Dirk Richards
GSO: Naomi Lyew
ICASS Chair: Kelsey Harris-Smith
IMO: William Curry
INS: Karen Landsness
IPO: Bryan Martin
ISO: William Mains
ISSO: Egan Wang
LAB: Nathan Lane
LEGATT: John DiStasio
NAS: Philip Cleary
OMS: Olga Pavlova
PAO: Laurence Wohlers
RSO: Robert Barton
State ICASS: Steven Rider

US Embassies and Consulates in Asian Countries - Russia

ST. PETERSBURG (CG)
Furshtadskaya Ulitsa 15
St. Petersburg, Russia 191028
Tel: [7] (812) 331-2600
Fax: [7] (812) 331-2852

PO: Karen Malzahn
POL/ECO: Rafik Mansour
COM: William Czajkowski
CON: Jeff Vick
CLO: Laura Perry
GSO: Bill Hunt
IPO: Rod Rajkovich
ISO: Marcus Anderson
PAO: Jeff Murray
RSO: Noelle Licari

VLADIVOSTOK (CG)
32 Pushkinskaya
Vladivostok, Russia
Tel: (7) 4232-30-00-70
Fax: (7) 4232-49-93-72/71
Web: http://vladivostok.usconsulate.gov/

CG/PO: John Mark Pommersheim
POL/ECO: Randall Houston
COM: Vacant
CON: Ken Zurcher
MGT/FMO/RSO/State ICASS: Matthew E. Johnson
AGR: Svetlana Ily'ina
AID: Irina Isaeva
GSO: Vacant
GSO: Vacant
ISO/ISSO: David Stansbury
PAO: Tara Rougle

YEKATERINBURG (CG)
Gogolya, 15 Yekaterinburg
Yekaterinburg, Russia 620151
Tel: [7] (343) 379-3001
Fax: [7] (343) 379-4515
Web: www.uscgyekat.ur.ru

POL/ECO: Matt Purl
CON: Chris Beard
MGT/ISSO: David Shao
CLO: Jana Beard
ISO: Scott McKnight
PAO: Brad Hurst

SAUDI ARABIA

RIYADH (E)
Diplomatic Quarter
Riyadh, Saudi Arabia
Tel: [966] (1) 488-3800
Fax: [966] (1) 488-7360
Web: http://riyadh.usembassy.gov

AMB: James C. Oberwetter
AMB OMS: Nancy Carpenter
DCM: Gary Grappo
DCM OMS: Lucia Keegan
POL: Michael Gfoeller
CON: Dennis Hankins
MGT: Alberta G.J. Mayberry
AFSA: Jacqueline Dacus
CLO: Vacant
DAO: Kenneth D. Shive
ECO: David Rundell
EEO/State ICASS: Victor Hurtado
FCS: Nancy Charles Parker
FMO: William Lauritsen
GSO: Tom Gray, Acting SGSO
ICASS Chair: David Slyman
IMO: Howard Keegan

IPO: James McRea
ISO/ISSO: Joyce Clark
LEGATT: Fred Brink
PAO: Carol Kalin
RSO: Jan Abbott

DHAHR (CG)
P.O. Box 38955
Dhahran, Saudi Arabia
Tel: [966] (3) 330-3200
Fax: [966] (3) 330-2123
Web: http://usembassy.state.gov/riyadh

CG: Alfred F. Fonteneau
CG OMS: Mary Clark
PO: Alfred F. Fonteneau
POL: Bryan Koontz
CON: Carolina Melara
MGT: Jonathan B. Korach
ECO: John Miner
ISSO/RSO: James Reynolds
PAO: Erin Eddy

JEDDAH (CG)
Palestine St. Unit 62112
Jeddah, Saudi Arabia 21411
Tel: [966] (2) 667-0080
Fax: [966] (2) 669-3074
Email: usconsjeddahwebsite@state.gov
Web: http://jeddah.usconsulate.gov

CG/PO: Tatiana Volkoff-Gfoeller
POL: Heather Kalmbach
POL/ECO: Jerry Ismail
CON: Diane Shelby
MGT: Hector Morales
ATO: James Williams
GSO: Anis Puckett
IMO/IPO/ISSO: Rahima Kandahari
ISO: Tariq Islam
PAO: Erin Eddy
RSO: Lance Leveque

SINGAPORE

SINGAPORE (E)
27 Napier Rd.
Singapore, Singapore 258508
Tel: (65) 6476-9100
Fax: (65) 6476-9340
Web: http://singapore.usembassy.gov/index.shtml

AMB: Franklin L. Lavin
AMB OMS: Margaret McDermott
DCM: Judith R. Fergin
DCM OMS: Elizabeth Babroski
POL/ECO: Laurent D. Charbonnet
CON: Julie L. Kavanagh
MGT: Karen C. Stanton
AFSA: Susan W. Wong
AGR: Jonathan Gressel
CLO: Vacant
CUS: Matthew H. King
DAO: C. Rivers Cleveland
DEA: Russell Holske
EEO: L. Gabrielle Cowan
FAA: Nancy J. Graham
FCS: George Ruffner
FMO: Robert A. Wert
GSO: Michelle A. Burton
ICASS Chair: Vacant
IMO/ISSO: Thomas C. Proctor
IPO: Arthur T. Day
ISO: Robert S. Blankenship
LEGATT: Vacant
PAO: Valerie C. Fowler
RSO/State ICASS: Aurelia L. Fedenisn

SRI LANKA

COLOMBO (E)
210 Galle Rd.
Colombo, Sri Lanka 3
Tel: [94] (11) 244-8007
Fax: [94] (11) 243-7345
Web: http://usembassy.state.gov/srilanka

AMB: Jeffrey J. Lunstead
DCM : James F. Entwistle
PO: Patricia A. Mahoney
COM/EEO: Teresa L. Manlowe
CON: Marc H. Williams
MGT: Jane Ross
AFSA: Chris J. Long
AID: Carol Becker
CLO: Elizabeth Sugermeyer
DAO/ICASS Chair: Richard S. Girven, LTC
ECO: Dean R. Thompson
FMO: James E. Hostetler
GSO: James P. Stover
IMO/ISSO: Craig A. Zimmerman
PAO: Philip A. Frayne
RSO/State ICASS: Alex Moore

SYRIA

DAMASCUS (E)
P.O. Box 29
2 Al-Mansour St.
Damascus, Syria
Tel: [963] (11) 333-1342
Fax: [963] (11) 224-7938
Web: http://damascus.usembassy.gov

AMB: Margaret Scobey
AMB OMS: Mika McBride
DCM CHG: Steve Seche
DCM OMS: Joyce Cobb
POL/State ICASS: William Roebuck
CON: Patricia Fietz
MGT: Kathy Johnson-Casares
AFSA: Christian Lynch
CLO: Susan Canning
DAO: Norman Larson
ECO: Todd Holmstrom
FMO: Jeffrey Perkinson
GSO: Mary Oliver
ICASS Chair: Brian O'Rourke
IMO: James Lyne
IPO: Ray Ahring
ISO/ISSO: Nancy Chaudhry
PAO: Arthur C. Eccel
RSO: Michael Mack

TAJIKISTAN

DUSHANBE (E)
10 Pavlova St.
Dushanbe, Tajikistan
Tel: [992] (372) 21-03-48
Fax: [992] (372) 51-00-29
http://tajikistan.usembassy.gov

AMB: Richard E. Hoagland
AMB OMS: Helena Reca
DCM: Thomas Armbruster
POL/EEO: Amanda Cranmer
POL/ECO/ICASS Chair: Joseph Chamberlain
CON: Evan McCarthy
MGT: Bruce Wilson
AID: Peter Argo
CLO: Patsy Wilson
DAO: Taft Blackburn
DEA: Steve Monaco (Embassy of Tashkent)

FMO: Michael Berryman
GSO: Marissa Martin
IMO: David Wills
IPO: William Hamer
LEGATT: Regional Coverage from Almaty
PAO: Jeni Washeleski
RSO: James Rowe

THAILAND

BANGKOK (E)
120/122 Wireless Rd.
Bangkok, Thailand 96546
Tel: [66] (2) 205-4000
Fax: [66] (2) 205-4306
Web: http://bangkok.usembassy.gov

AMB: Ralph Boyce
AMB OMS: Patricia Hart
DCM: Alex A. Arvizu
DCM OMS: Lavay Miller
POL: James F. Cole (Acting)
COM: Judy Reinke
CON/State ICASS: Edward J. Wehrli
MGT: Cornelis M. Keur
AFSA: Roy A. Perrin
AGR: S. Rodrick McSherry
AID: Timothy Beans
ATO: Jeff Ressin
CLO: Marilyn Tarter/Catherine McSherry
CUS: Mark Robinson
DAO: Scott W. Page
DEA: Michael Chapman (Acting)
ECO: Michael Delaney
EEO: Rafael Rodriguez
FAA: Sharon Sharon Walloppillai
FMO: Michael Mullins
GSO: Dennis A. Droney
IBB: Jack A. Fisher
ICASS Chair: Rod S. McSherry
IMO: Patrick Meagher
INS: Jean M. Christiansen
IPO: Eric Milstead
ISO/ISSO: Mike Bretz
LEGATT: Robert H. Cahill, Jr.
MLO: Jack Dibrell
NAS: Douglas Rasmussen
PAO: Mark Larsen
RAMC: Thomas J. Quinzio
RSO: Larry Salmon

CHIANG MAI (CG)
Box C
387 Wichayanond Rd.
Chiang Mai, Thailand 50300
Tel: [66] (53) 252-629
Fax: [66] (53) 252-633
Web: http://bangkok.usembassy.gov/consulcm/consulcm.htm

CG: Beatrice A. Camp
CON: John Aloia
MGT: Henry V. Jardine
CLO: Margaret Flynn
CON/POL/ECO: Scott W. Hansen
DEA: Richard D. Gommert

TURKEY

ANKARA (E)
Ataturk Bulvari 110
Ankara, Turkey
Tel: [90] (312) 455-5555
Fax: [467] 2532, 468-6138
http://ankara.usembassy.gov

AMB: Vacant
DCM: James R. Moore, Acting
DCM/CHG: Nancy E. McEldowney
DCM OMS: Anna Thomas
POL: John Kunstadter
COM: Erik Hunt
CON: Laura Dogu
MGT: Gerri O'Brien
AGR/ICASS Chair: James Higgiston
CLO: Melissa Sagun
DAO: Roman Hrycaj
DEA: James Cloonan
ECO: Thomas Goldberger
EEO: Jonathan Jenkins
EST: Kurt Donnelly
FAA: Gregory Joyner (Resident in Rome)
FMO: Georgienne Bednar
GSO: David Drinkard
IMO/IPO: William McManus
LAB: Mary Jane Bushnaq
PAO: James Moore
RSO: Jeffrey Breed
State ICASS: Andrew Snow

ADANA (C)
Girne Bulvari #212 Guzelevler Mahallesi
Yuregir
Adana, Turkey
Tel: [90] (322) 346-6262
Fax: [90] (322) 346-7916
Web: www.usconadana.org.tr

PO: Walter S. Reid, III
CON/MGT/EEO/GSO: Telside Manson

ISTANBUL (CG)
Kaplicalar Mevkii Sokak #2
Istanbul, Turkey 34460
Tel: [90] (212) 335-9000
Fax: [90] (212) 335-9107
Web: http://istanbul.usconsulate.gov

CG: Deborah K. Jones
CG OMS: Louise A. Nash
POL: Stuart M. Smith
CON: John A. Lowell
MGT: Lewis K. Elbinger
AGR: James Higgiston-Ankara
CLO: Stacey L. Williams
FMO: Richard W. Boera
GSO: Vanessa Brooks
IMO: Vacant
IPO: Mark A. Zerwas
ISO/ISSO: John Fellingham
LEGATT: E. Keith Owens
PAO: Walter Douglas
RSO: Thomas A. Huey

TURKMENISTAN

ASHGABAT (E)
Pushkin St. #9
Ashgabat, Turkmenistan 744000
Tel: [9] (9312) 35-00-45
Fax: [9] (9312) 39-26-14
Web: www.usemb-ashgabat.rpo.at

AMB: Tracey Jacobson
AMB OMS: Carole Akgun
DCM: Jennifer Brush
DCM OMS: Kathy Stewart
POL: Jason Wemhoener-Cuite
POL/ECO: Carla Gonneville
CON: Ian Turner
MGT: Gary Anderson
AID: Ashley Moretz
CUS: Michael Kirk
DAO: Padraig Clark
FMO: Fred Mauren
GSO: Joshua Baker
IMO/ISSO: Mike Brown
PAO: Ilya Levin
RSO: Don Gonneville

UNITED ARAB EMIRATES

ABU DHABI (E)
P.O. Box 4009
Abu Dhabi, United Arab Emirates
Tel: [971] (2) 414-2200
Fax: [971] (2) 414-2469
Email: consularabudha@state.gov
Web: http://usembassy.state.gov/uae

AMB: Michele J. Sison
AMB OMS: Kam Wong
DCM: Martin Quinn
DCM OMS: Carol Bourne
POL: Joel Maybury
CON: Robert Dolce
MGT: Debra Smoker-Ali
ATO: Mike Henney
CLO: Nejla B. Zary
DAO: Brian Kerins
ECO: Oliver John
FCS: Christian Reed
FMO: David Thomas
GSO: Mary Davis
IMO: Bruce Chaplin
IPO/ISSO: Mahmud Khan
LEGATT: Daniel Roggenbuck
PAO: Hilary Olsin-Windecker
RSO: Thomas Barnard

DUBAI (CG)
P.O. Box 9343
Dubai World Trade Ctr., 21st Fl.
Dubai, United Arab Emirates
Tel: [971] (4) 311-6000
Fax: [971] (4) 311-6166
Web: http://dubai.usconsulate.gov

PO: Jason Davis
POL: Alan Eyre
COM: Patrick Wall
CON: Cynthia Ebeid
MGT: Johanna Schoeppl

AGR: Mike Henney
CLO: Vacant
ECO: Michael Carver
GSO: Jennifer Johnson
PAO: Peter Neisuler
RSO: Frank Theus

UZBEKISTAN

TASHKENT (E)
82 Chilanzarskaya St.
Tashkent, Uzbekistan 700115
Tel: [998] (71) 120-5450
Fax: [998] (71) 120-6335
Web: www.usembassy.uz

AMB: John Purnell
AMB OMS: Penny O'Brien
DCM: David Appleton
DCM OMS: Karen Landherr
POL/ECO: Sylvia Curran
POL/ECO: Erika Olson
COM/IMO: Gary Harral
CON: John Ballard
MGT: Brent Bohne
AFSA: Linda Recht
AID/ICASS Chair: James Bonner
CLO: Donna Lupton/Michael Goddard
DAO: Todd Brown
DEA: Steve Monaco
EEO: Tracy Newell
EST: Evelyn Putnam
FMO: Cathie Roberts
GSO: Juliana Ballard/Cathie Roberts
IPO: Scott Branks
PAO/State ICASS: D. Michael Reinert
RSO: Ivan Wray

VIETNAM

HANOI (E)
7 Lang Ha, Ba Dinh District
Hanoi, Vietnam
Tel: [84] (4) 772-1500
Fax: [84] (4) 772-1510
Web: http://hanoi.usembassy.gov

AMB: Michael W. Marine
AMB OMS/CM OMS: Victoria Q. Spiers
CM: Michael W. Marine
DCM: John S. Boardman
DCM OMS: Janet Seung
CG: Seth D. Winnick
CG OMS: Karie Ennis
DPO: Kenneth Chern
POL: Marc E. Knapper
CON/CA/EEO: Mai-Thao Nguyen
MGT: Gregory S. Stanford
AFSA: Marilou B. Endermuhle
AGR: John Wade
AID: Dennis Zvinakis
APHIS: Dale Maki
CLO: Michelle M. Quick
CUS: Mark Robinson
DAO: Mark B. Chakwin
DEA: Jeffrey P. Wanner
ECO: Samuel R. Watson
EST: Vacant
FAA: Elizabeth Erickons
FCS: Miguel Pardo de Zela

FIN: Charles E. Bullington
FMO: Dario Mann
GSO: Lilian R. Murphy
ICASS Chair: David T. Rockey
IMO: Joseph Smith
INS: Rick P. Sell
ISO: Vacant
ISSO: Vacant
LAB: TBD
OMS: Tara A. Bell
PAO: Louis P. Lantner
RSO: Mark C. Malhoyt
State ICASS: TBD

HO CHI MINH CITY (CG)
4 Le Duan St., District 1
Ho Chi Minh City, Vietnam
Tel: [84] (8) 822-9433
Fax: [84] (8) 822-9434
Email: uscongenhcmc@state.gov
Web: http://hochiminh.usconsulate.gov

CG: Seth D. Winnick
CG OMS: Karie L. Ennis
PO: Seth D. Winnick
DPO/State ICASS: Kenneth S. Chern
POL: Robert Silberstein
COM/FCS: Robert D. Bannerman
CON: Jeff C. Schwenk
MGT: Lonnie Kelley
AFSA/GSO: Rodrigo Garza
AGR/ICASS Chair: John Wilson (resident in Hanoi)
CLO: Uyen Nguyen
ECO: Heather C. Variava
EEO: Yan Li
INS: Rick P. Sell
IPO/ISSO: Christopher C. Lawson
PAO: Robert Ogburn
RSO: John M. Milkiewixz

YEMEN

SANAA (E)
P.O. Box 22347
Sa'awan St.
Sanaa, Yemen
Tel: [967] (1) 303-155
Fax: [967] (1) 303-182
Web: http://usembassy.state.gov/yemen

AMB: Thomas C. Krajeski
DCM: Nabeel Khoury
DCM OMS: Mariam Abdulle
POL/ECO: Shayna Steinger
CON: William Lesh
MGT: Thomas Weinz
AFSA/FMO: Christian Charette
AGR: Ali Abdi (Cairo)
AID: Doug Heisler
CLO: Kate Griffin
DAO: Maj. David Alley (Acting)
DEA: Robert Shannon (Cairo)
EEO: Susan Alexander
FAA: Lynn Osmus (Brussels)
GSO: Mary Oliver
ICASS Chair: Col. Mark Devlin
IMO/ISSO: Joseph Rizcallah
IRS: Margaret Lullo (Berlin)
LEGATT: Stephen Gaudin
PAO: John Balian
RSO: Tim Laas

Asian Embassies in the US

AFGHANISTAN

EMBASSY OF AFGHANISTAN
2341 Wyoming Ave. NW
Washington, DC 20008
Tel: (202) 483-6410 Fax: (202) 483-6488
Web: www.embassyofafghanistan.com

Ambassador E. and P.
His Excellency Tayeb JAWAD; Mrs. Shamim Jawad
Political Counsellor
Mr. Fazel R. FAZEL
Second Secretary
Mr. Abdul Jamil AHMADZAI; Mrs. Fahima Ahmadzai

ARMENIA

EMBASSY OF THE REPUBLIC OF ARMENIA
2225 R St. NW
Washington, DC 20008
Tel: (202) 319-1976 Fax: (202) 319-2982
Web: www.armeniaemb.org

Ambassador E. and P.
His Excellency Tatoul MARKARIAN; Mrs. Anahit Markarian
Counsellor
Mr. Arman ISRAELIAN; Mrs. Lianna Israelian
Counsellor (Consular)
Mr. Armen YEGANIAN; Mrs. Maria Yeganian
Defense, Military, Naval & Air Attaché
Colonel Armen SARGSYAN; Mrs, Susanna Sargsyan
Assistant (Press & Public Affairs)
Mr. Haik GUGARATS
Assistant (Finance & Personnel)
Mrs. Narine Petrosyan

AZERBAIJAN

EMBASSY OF THE REPUBLIC OF AZERBAIJAN
2741 34th St. NW
Washington, DC 20008
Tel: (202) 337-3500 Fax: (202) 337-5911
Web: www.azembassy.com

Ambassador E. and P.
His Excellency Hafiz Mir Jalal PASHAYEV; Mrs. Rena Pashayeva
Counsellor (Political)
Mr. Tahir Pirali Oglu KARIMOV; Mrs. Svetlana Nadir Qizi Karimova

Counsellor (Economic)
Mr. Fikrat Mammadali PASHAYEV; Mrs. Elmira Rafiq Qizi Pashayeva
First Secretary
Mr. Sultan Habil Oglu MALIKOV; MRS. Malahat Saleh Gizi Malikova
Second Secretary & Consul
Mr. Huseyn Ismayil Oglu HUSEYNOV; Mrs. Zenab Sadikh Gizi Huseynova
Second Secretary
Mr. Iglar Yusif MUKHTAROV; Mrs. Nargiz Fikret Rahimkhanova
Third Secretary
Mr. Elchin Ragub Oglu BASHIROV; Mrs. Konul Tariyel Gizi Bashirova
Third Secretary
Mr. Khazar Zafir Oglu IBRAHIM
Attaché
Ms. Aysel Shakir Gizi YAGUBOVA
Defense, Military, Naval & Air Attaché
Colonel Dashdamir Mammadaga Oglu MAMMADOV; Mrs. Yegana Qudrut Qizi Mammadova

BAHRAIN

EMBASSY OF THE KINGDOM OF BAHRAIN
3502 International Dr. NW
Washington, DC 20008
Tel: (202) 342-0741 Fax: (202) 362-2192
Web: www.bahrainembassy.org

Ambassador E. and P.
His Excellency Sheikh Khalifa Ali ALKHALIFA; Sheikha Maryam Mubarak Alkhalifa
Second Secretary (Deputy Chief of Mission)
Mr. Yasser Ghanim SHAHEEN; Mrs. Nahla Abdulrahman Abualfath Ali
Second Secretary (Administrative)
Mr. Husain Mohamed Mahmood ALMAHMOOD; Mrs. Khulood Jasim Mohamed Mohamed
Second Secretary
Mr. Jamal Fares Al ROWAIEI; Mrs. Sama Ali Jasim Ali Alkhaja
Attaché (Cultural)
Mr. Faisal Al. HASAN; Mrs. Fatema Hasan Alqadhi
Attaché (Economic)
Mr. Naser Mohamed Al BALOOSHI; Mrs. Sharifa Mohamed Benammour
Defense, Military, Naval & Air Attaché
Lieutenant Colonel Ahmed Khalifa Al KHALIFA; Sheikha Aysha Ali Al Khalifa
Asst. Defense, Military, Naval & Air Attaché
Major Hamed Abdulla Al THAWADI; Mrs. Kawtharyusuf Ismaeel

BANGLADESH

EMBASSY OF THE PEOPLE'S REPUBLIC OF BANGLADESH
3510 International Dr. NW
Washington, DC 20008
Tel: (202) 244-0183 Fax: (202) 244-2771
Web: www.bangladoot.org

Ambassador E. and P.
His Excellency Shamsher M. CHOWDHURY
Minister (Political & Deputy Chief of Mission)
Mr.Shahidul ISLAM
Minister (Consular)
Vacant
Minister (Economics)
Mr. MD Abdul Kalam AZAD; Mrs. Ferdous Banu
Minister
Mr. MD. Shahidul ISLAM; Mrs. Jesmeen Islam
Counsellor (Economic)
Mr. Fakrul AHSAN; Mrs. Riti Ibrahim Ahsan
Minister
Mr. Md. Shahidul ISLAM; Mrs. Jesmeen Islam
Counsellor
Mr. Chowdhury Ahmed NUR; Mrs. Sonia Ahmed
First Secretary
Mr. Muhammad Zulqar NAIN; Mrs. Afsana Bulbul
Second Secretary
Mr. Kazi Asif AHMED
Defense, Military, Naval & Air Attaché
Bridgadier General Muhammed F. MIAN; Mrs. Nasreen Firdaus

BRUNEI

EMBASSY OF THE STATE OF BRUNEI DARUSSALAM
3520 International Ct. NW
Washington, DC 20008
Tel: (202) 237-1838 Fax: (202) 885-0560
Web: www.bruneiembassy.org

Ambassador E. and P.
His Excellency Pengiran Anak Dato PUTEH; Mrs. Datin Kamilah Abdullah
Minister-Counsellor (Deputy Chief of Mission)
Ms. Janeh SUKAIMI
Second Secretary
Mr. Zuffri Abdull SANI
Second Secretary
Ms. Megawati MANAN
Third Secretary (Administrative & Finance)
Mr. Haji Mohammad Nafiah Haji YUSOP; Mrs. Hismawaty Hitam

Attaché
Mr. Haji Saini CHUCHU; Mrs. Serimah Ahmad
Attaché
Miss Zabaidah DAUD

BURMA

EMBASSY OF THE UNION OF BURMA
2300 S St. NW
Washington, DC 20008
Tel: (202) 332-3344 Fax: (202) 332-4351
Web: www.rangoon.usembassy.gov

Ambassador of E. and P.
Vacant
Minister (Deputy Chief of Mission)
Ms. YINYINMYINT
Minister-Counsellor
Mr. Min LWIN; Mrs. Sabai Win
Counsellor
Mr. Ye Tun MYAT; Mrs. May Than Tun
Second Secretary
Mr. Aung Kyaw THUYA; Mrs. Khine Moe Naing
Attaché
Sergeant Thet Naing AYE; Mrs. Pa Pa Win
Attaché
Mr. Than HLAING; Mrs. Ohn Mar Kyaw
Attaché
Corporal Min OO; Mrs. Tin Tin Lin
Attaché
Warrent Officer Soe NAING; Mrs. Tin May Aye
Attaché
Mr. San OO; Mrs. Thit Thit Htay
Attaché
Mr. Win THEIN; Mrs. Aye Aye Than
Attaché
Mr. Zaw Lin OO
Attaché
Mr. Zaw THET
Defense, Military, Naval & Air Attaché
Brigadier General Soe HTAY; Mrs. Aye Aye Thain

CAMBODIA

ROYAL EMBASSY OF CAMBODIA
4530 16th St. NW
Washington, DC 20011
Tel: (202) 726-7742 Fax: (202) 726-8381
Web: www.embassy.org/cambodia

Ambassador E. and P.
His Excellency Sereywath EK; Mrs. Sang Khov
Minister-Counsellor (Deputy Chief of Mission)
H.E. Meng Eang NAY

Source: US Department of State. www.state.gov

Second Secretary
Mr. Samrattanak CHIN; Mrs. Sopheak Seng
Second Secretary
Mrs. Leakhena KUN; Mr. Sambath Seang
Economic Counsellor
Mr. Chantaphal YEM
Consular Service
Mrs. Sor SAMEN
Accounting Attaché
Mrs. Syani THEANH

CHINA

EMBASSY OF THE PEOPLE'S REPUBLIC OF CHINA
2300 Connecticut Ave. NW
Washington, DC 20008
Tel: (202) 328-2500 Fax: (202) 328-2582

Ambassador E. and P.
His Excellency Wen Zhong Zhou YANG;
Mrs. Shu Minxie
Minister (Deputy Chief of Mission)
Mr. Li Jun LAN; Mrs. Lang Lin Gu
Minister
Mr. Yi LIU; Ms. Liwen Xu
Minister-Counsellor
Mr. Yun Lou DAI; Mrs. Yan Geng
Minister-Counsellor
Mr. Xiao Ming JIN; Mrs. Qun Li Song
Minister-Counsellor
Mr. Dong Wen LI
Minister-Counsellor
Mrs. Chuan Sheng LIU; Mr. Zhong Hua Xia
Minister-Counsellor
Mr. Ge SU; Mrs. Jing Li
Minister-Counsellor
Mr. Bing Xi ZHEN; Ms.Jian Qing Zhang
Counsellor
Mr. Hong Bo DENG; Ms. Ling Shi
Counsellor
Mr. Chang Lin GUO; Mrs. Yunmeihu
Counsellor
Mr. Guang Feng HAO; Ms. Wei Kong
Counsellor
Mr. Liang Liang Kuang
Counsellor
Ms. Aimei LE
Counsellor & Consul General
Mr. Rui You LI
Counsellor
Mr. Dong LIAO; Ms. Chun Mei Li
Counsellor & Consul
Ms. Jian Ping LUO; Mr. Ya Fei He
Counsellor
Mr. Qing Bao NIU; Mrs. Jun Yuan
Counsellor
Mr. Yun Dong PAN; Mrs. Yu Zhu
Counsellor
Mr. Ang SUN; Mrs. Li Yu Wang
Counsellor
Mr. Wei De SUN; Mrs. Jun Xu
Counsellor
Mr. Jun TIAN; Mrs. Hong Han
Counsellor
Mr. Xian WANG; Mrs. Jian Fen Hu
Counsellor & Deputy Consul General
Mr. Dong XU; Mrs. Lin Hong Zong
Counsellor
Mr. Jie XU; Mrs. Jun Mei Guan
Counsellor
Mrs. Jian YANG
Counsellor
Mr. You Ming YANG; Mrs. Hai Ling Geng
Counsellor & Deputy Consul General
Ms. Jian Qing ZHANG; Mr. Bing Xi Zhen
Counsellor
Mr. Weiping ZHAO; Mrs. Mei Gong
First Secretary
Mr. Wei Min CHANG; Mrs. Qing Yan Yang

First Secretary
Mr. Lei CHEN
First Secretary
Mr. Yu Ming DAI; Mrs. Ping Li
First Secretary
Mr. Da Qi DUAN; Mrs. Yan Mei Yang
First Secretary
Mr. Zhong Hua FAN; Mrs. Jun Qu
First Secretary
Mr. Qing Chao FANG; Ms. Shu Fen Guo
First Secretary (Economic &Trade)
Mr. Li Gao; Mrs. Ping Wei
First Secretary
Mr. Shengwu GUO; Ms. Yan Wang
First Secretary
Mrs. Hong HAN; Mr. Jun Tian
First Secretary
Mr. Chun Hai JIAO; Mrs. Chune Deng
First Secretary
Ms. Wei KONG; Mr. Guang Feng Hao
First Secretary
Mrs. Mei Yun LE; Mr. Yi Qun Zhang
First Secretary
Mr. Jian Hua LI
First Secretary & Consul
Mr. Si Ning LI
First Secretary
Ms. Wei Kun LI
First Secretary
Mr. Yun Lin LI; Mrs. Shang Li Ni
First Secretary
Mr. Feng Kui LIANG; Mrs. Hai Yun Zhao
First Secretary
Mr. Ru Hai LIN; Mrs. Wei Dong
First Secretary
Mr. Hai Yan LIU; Mrs. Pei Shu Wang
First Secretary
Mr. Jian Giao LIU; Ms. Xiao Lian Sun

CYPRUS

EMBASSY OF THE REPUBLIC OF CYPRUS
2211 R St. NW
Washington, DC 20008
Tel: (202) 462-5772 Fax: (202) 483-6710
Web: www.cyprusembassy.net

Ambassador of E. and P.
His Excellency Euripides L. EVRIVIADES;
Mrs. Anastasia Iacovidou Evriviades
Counsellor (Deputy Chief of Mission)
Mr. Haralambos KAFKARIDES; Mrs. Eleni
Agathocleous
Counsellor
Mr. Basil POLEMITIS; Ms. Erine Petrides
Polemitis
Second Secretary
Mr. Andreas NICOLAIDES

EAST TIMOR

EMBASSY OF THE DEMOCRATIC REPUBLIC OF TIMOR LESTE
4201 Connecticut Ave. NW #504
Washington, DC 20008
Tel: (202) 966-3202 Fax: (202) 966-3205

Ambassador E. and P.
His Excellency Jose Luis GUTERRES
Minister-Counsellor
Mr. Constancio C. PINTO; Mrs. Gabriela
Pinto

GEORGIA

EMBASSY OF THE REPUBLIC OF GEORGIA
1101 15th St. NW #602
Washington, DC 20005
Tel: (202) 387-2390 Fax: (202) 393-4537
Web: www.georgiaemb.org

Ambassador E. and P.
His Excellency Levan MIKELADZE; Mrs. Lali
Chikvaidze
Minister
Mr. David SOUMBADZE; Mrs. Inga
Diasamidze
Counsellor
Mr. Beka DVALI; Mrs. Nino Lezhava
Counsellor
Mr. Mamuka MURJIKNELI; Mrs. Natalia
Pipia
Counsellor
Mr. Alex PETRIASHVILI; Mrs. Ketevan
Kavteladze
Counsellor (Consular)
Mr. Zurab TINIKASHVILI; Mrs. Zalina
Kazakova
Counsellor
Mr. David ZALKALIANI; Mrs. Tamara
Kemoklidze
First Secretary & Vice Consul
Ms. Ketevan GOGOLASHVILI
Second Secretary
Mr. Lasha ARVELADZE
Second Secretary
Mrs. Tamar DARCHIA; Mr. Levan Shanidze
Second Secretary
Mr. Irakli JGENTI; Mrs. Maka Panjikdze
Defense, Military, Naval & Air Attaché
Major Lasha Beridze; Mrs. Diana
Natenadze

INDIA

EMBASSY OF INDIA
2107 Massachusetts Ave. NW
Washington, DC 20008
Tel: (202) 939-7000 Fax: (202) 483-3972

Ambassador E. and P.
His Excellency Ronen SEN
Minister (Deputy Chief of Mission)
Mr. Rakesh SOOD
Minister
Mr. Anil Kumar GUPTA; Mrs. Uma Gupta
Minister (Director of Audit)
Mr. Rakesh JAIN; Mrs. Lovelina Jain
Minister
Mr. Sunil JAIN; Mrs. Gargi Jain
Minister (Economic)
Mr. Yogesh KHANNA; Mrs. Indu Khanna
Minister (Consular)
Mr. Jayadeva RANADE; Mrs. Vinita Ranade
Minister (Political)
Mr. Ashok SAJJANHAR; Mrs. Madhu
Sajjanhar
Minister (Commerce)
Dr. Villur S. SESHADRI; Mrs. Vidya Seshadri
Counsellor
Mr. Francis ARANHA; Mrs. Marie Aranha
Counsellor
Mr. Rupinder Singh BHATIA; Mrs.
Manmohan Kaur Bhatia
Counsellor (Science & Technology)
Dr. Kamal Kant DWIVEDI; Dr. Rekha
Dwivedi
Counsellor (Political & Head of Chancery)
Mr. Sunil Kumar LAL; Mrs. Gitanjali Lal
Counsellor
Mr. Vikram MISRI; Mrs. Dolly Misri
Counsellor
Mr. Manik MUKHERJEE; Mrs. Seema
Mukherjee
Counsellor (Political)
Mr. Devendra Nath SRIVASTAVA; Mrs.
Saroj Srivastava
Counsellor (Special Assistant to Ambassador)
Mr. Tirunelvelli S. TIRUMURTI; Mrs. Gowri
Tirumurti
First Secretary (Audit)
Mr. Anand Mohan BAJAJ; Mrs. Madhu Bajaj

First Secretary (Consular)
Mr. Raj Kumar CHHIBBER; Mrs. Usha
Chhibber
First Secretary
Mr. Venkateswara Rao VADAPALLI; Mrs.
Malathi Rao Vadapalli
Second Secretary
Mr. Chander Lal RANGA; Mrs. Usha Ranga
Third Secretary
Ms. Sumitra CHOWDHURI
Attaché
Mr. Rajender Krishan DANYAL; Mrs. Seema
Krishan Danyal
Attaché
Mr. Amar JEET; Mrs. Lalita Jeet
Attaché
Mr. Hakumat Rai KAPOOR; Mrs.
Shakuntala Kapoor
Attaché
Mr. Vinod KELKAR; Mrs. Anita Kelkar
Attaché
Mr. Sita Ram MEENA; Mrs. Gayatri Meena
Attaché
Mr. Om Parkash NERWAL; Mrs. Erwal Ram
Murti
Attaché
Mr. Sita Rama Das PISIPATI
Attaché (Administrative)
Mr. Mohd Raghib QURESHI; Mrs. Chandini
Qureshi
Attaché
Mr. Gurdas Ram RANGRA; Mrs. Kamla
Rangra
Attaché
Mr. Kulbhushan SHARMA; Mrs. Neeta
Sharma
Attaché
Mr. Mahabir S. RAWAT; Mrs. Sarveshwari
Rawat
Attaché (Consular)
Mr. Shyam K. SHARMA; Mrs. Karuna
Sharma
Attaché (Accounts)
Mr. Surendra VELEGALETI; Mrs. Mary
Sridevi Velegaleti
Attaché
Mr. Perumal VENKATASAMY; Mrs.
Srirenganatchiyar Perumal
Defense & Military Attaché
Brigadier Shankar Ranjan GHOSH; Mrs.
Bulbul Ghosh
Naval Attaché
Commodore Ashok SAWHNEY; Mrs. Geeta
Sawhney
Air Attaché
Air Commodore Sumit MUKERJI; Mrs.
Nandita Mukerji

COMMERCIAL AND SUPPLY, PASSPORT AND VISA SECTION
2536 Massachusetts Ave. NW
Washington, DC 20008
Tel: (202) 939-9806

INDONESIA

EMBASSY OF THE REPUBLIC OF INDONESIA
2020 Massachusetts Ave. NW
Washington, DC 20036
Tel: (202) 775-5200 Fax: (202) 775-5365
Web: www.embassyofindonesia.org

Ambassador E. and P.
His Excellency Soemadi Djoko M.
BROTODININGRAT; Mrs. Suharti
Brotodiningrat
Minister (Deputy Chief of Mission)
Mr. Andri Hadi
Counsellor (Economic)
Mr. Ibnu HADI; Mrs. Dyah Prastyawati Hadi

Counsellor (Information)
Mr. Suhardjono SASTROMIHARDJO; Mrs. Theresia M. A. Sastromihardjo
Counsellor
Mr. Teguh WARDOYO; Mrs. Binta Rizkiyati
Counsellor (Administrative)
Mr. Ade Wismar WIJAYA; Mrs. Nungkie Rusminny Wijaya
First Secretary (Econmics)
Ms. Wita Sri MAJANGWOELAN
Second Secretary (Political)
Mr. Arko Hananto BUDIADI; Mrs. Yani Nurbayani
Second Secretary (Economics)
Mrs. Tuti Wahyuningsih IRMAN; Mrs. Herdiana Kurnia Irman
Second Secretary
Mr. Riaz Januar Putra SAEHU
Second Secretary
Mr. Heru SANTOSO; Mrs. Rita Agustina
Second Secretary (Administration)
Mrs. Ita MARIA; Mr. Markis Ismail
Second Secretary
Mr. Irwan SINAGA; Mrs. Onny Hotmaida Simatupang
Second Secretary
Mr. Iwan Freddy Hari SUSANTO; Mrs. Riviana Pasah
Third Secretary
Ms. Elleonora TAMBUNAN
Attaché (Administration)
Mr. ERMAWAN; Mrs. Nurwulan Oktarini
Attaché (Education & Culture)
Mr. Harris ISKANDAR; Mrs. Ooslyndiani
Attaché (Administration)
Mr. Yuda GUNADI; Mrs. Wiendaru Nurasasi
Attaché (Industry & Trade)
Mr. Iman PAMBAGYO; Mrs. Radnyawati
Attaché (Transportation & Communication)
Mr. Tri SuriadJjie SUNOKO; Mrs. Adinda Sunoko
Attaché (Agriculture)
Mrs. Metrawinda TUNUS; Mr. Rabin Drasiregar
Defense & Military Attaché
Colonel Ashory Tadjudin; Mrs. Anta Uwatie
Air Attaché
Lieutenant Colonel Mochammad SOFIUDIN; Mrs. Dwi Kurniawati Iriany
Naval Attaché
Captain Desi Albert MAMAHIT; Mrs. Franca Aebelona Mamahit Malkan

IRAN

INTERESTS SECTION OF THE ISLAMIC REPUBLIC OF IRAN
2209 Wisconsin Ave. NW
Washington, DC 20007
Tel: (202) 965-4990 Fax: (202) 965-1073

IRAQ

EMBASSY OF THE REPUBLIC OF IRAQ
1801 P St. NW
Washington, DC 20036
Tel: (202) 483-7500 Fax: (202) 462-5066
Web: www.iraqembassy.org
Minister
Mr. Faiza K. ALGAILANI; Mrs. Gulala D. A. Babab
Attaché (Administrative)
MR. FARIS A. ABDUL WAHAB; MRS. THEKRA S. NAJI

ISRAEL

EMBASSY OF ISRAEL
3514 International Dr. NW
Washington, DC 20008
Tel: (202) 364-5500 Fax: (202) 364-5607
Email: ask@israelemb.org
Web: www.israelemb.org

Ambassador E. and P.
His Excellency Daniel AYALON; Mrs. Anne Ayalon
Minister (Deputy Chief of Mission)
Mr. Rafael BARAK; Mrs. Miriam Barak
Minister (Interreligious, Jewish & Public) & Consul General
Mr. Moshie FOX; Mrs. Helen Patricia Fox
Minister (Public and Academic Affairs)
Mr. Aviva Raz-SHECHTER
Minister (Congressional)
Mr. Alon USHPIZ; Mrs. Inbar Ushpiz
Minister-Counsellor
Mr. Naor GILON
Minister-Counsellor (Middle Eastern Affairs)
Mr. Eynat Shlein-MICHAEL
Counsellor (Political Affairs)
Mr. Reuven AZAR
Counsellor (Press)
Mr. David SIEGEL
Minister Counsellor & Consul
Mr. Aliza EZRA
Minister (Economic)
Mr. Ron DERMER
Minister (Agriculture and Scientific Affairs)
Dr. Mordehai COHEN
Defense and Armed Forces Attaché
Major General Amos YADLIN

JAPAN

EMBASSY OF JAPAN
2520 Massachusetts Ave. NW
Washington, DC 20008
Tel: (202) 238-6700 Fax: (202) 328-2187
Web: www.embjapan.org

Ambassador E. and P.
His Excellency Ryozo KATO; Mrs. Hanayo Kato
Minister (Deputy Chief of Mission)
Mr. Jynich IHARA
Minister
vacant
Minister
Mr. Hiroaki ISHII
Minister
Mr. Kimihiro ISHIKANE; Mrs. Kaoru Ishikane
Minister
Mr. Nobukatsu KANEHARA
Minister
Mr. Satoru SATOH; Mrs. Reiko Sato
Minister (Finance)
Mr. Rintaro TAMAKI; Mrs. Natalia Tamaki
Minister (Trade, Industry, & Energy)
Mr. Katsuhiko UMEHARA; Mrs. Naoko Umehara
Minister
Mr. Hitoshi NODA; Mrs. Chiyoe Noda
Counsellor
Mr. Yasuo ANDO; Mrs. Yuko Ando
Counsellor
Mr. Tetsuo KABE; Mrs. Noriko Kabe
Counsellor (Science)
Mr. Hiroshi IKUKAWA; Mrs. Tomoko Ikukawa
Counsellor
Mr. Kenji KANASUGI; Mrs. Yasuko Kanasugi
Counsellor

MR. Yoshiki KOBAYASHI; Mrs. Sonoko Kobayashi
Counsellor
Mr. Hiroki MATSUMOTO
Counsellor
Mr. Yasuhiro KAWAGUCHI; Mrs. Toshie Kawaguchi
Counsellor
Mr. Noriyuki MITA; Ms. Etsuko Mita
Counsellor
Mr. Takashi MURATA; Mrs. Hirono Murata
Counsellor
Mr. Kazuya NASHIDA; Mrs. Mari Nashida
Counsellor
Mr. Yasuhiro OKANISHI; Ms. Atsuko Okanishi
Counsellor
Mr. Yasuhiko TANIWAKI; Mrs. Kyoko Taniwaki
Counsellor
Ms. Chiyoko TERANISHI
Counsellor
Mr. Hiroshi TSUBOUCHI; Mrs. Masami Tsubouchi
Counsellor (Economic)
Mr. Jun YAMADA; Mrs. Satoyo Yamada
Counsellor
Mr. Hideaki YAMAZAKI; Mrs. Masako Yamazaki
Counsellor
Mr. Shoji YASAKA; Mrs. Saeko Yasaka
First Secretary
Mr. Atsushi ANDO
First Secretary
Mr. Yoshiyuki CHIHARA; Mrs. Takako Chihara
First Secretary
Mr. Takehiro FUNAKOSHI
First Secretary (Protocol)
Mr. Hiroshi FURUSAWA; Mrs. Kayoko Furusawa
First Secretary (Managements, Coordination)
Mr. Keiichi ICHIKAWA; Mrs. Sachiko Ichikawa
First Secretary
Mr. Hirotuki IKEDA; Ms. Atsuko Ikeda
First Secretary
Mr. Yoshihisa ISHIKAWA; Mrs. Mary Cherry Pie Ishikawa
First Secretary
Mr. Keiichi IAWMOTO; Mrs. Miyuki Iwamoto
First Secretary
Mr. Takehiro KANO; Mrs. Shinako Kano
First Secretary (Science)
Mr. Hiroyuki KOBAYASHI; Mrs. Kuniyo Kobayashi
First Secretary
Mr. Yasuji KOMIYAMA
First Secretary
Mr. Yoshiyuki KURASHIMA; Mrs. Keiko Kurashima
First Secretary
Mr. Mamoru KUROKAMI
First Secretary (Economics)
Mr. Tsuyoshi KUROKAWA; Mrs. Aiko Kurokawa
First Secretary
Mr. Makoto MATSUDA; Mrs. Satoko Matsuda
First Secretary
Mr. Yoichi MIKAMI; Mrs. Kumi Mikami
First Secretary
Mr. Osamu MIZUI; Mrs. Yukie Mizui
First Secretary
Mr. Mitsuhiro MOCHIZUKI; Ms. Maya Mochizuki
First Secretary
Mr. Katsuro NAGAI; Mrs. Azusa Nagai
First Secretary
Mr. Hidemasa NAKAMURA; Mrs. Tokiko Nakamura
First Secretary (Political)

Mr. Koichiro NAKAMURA; Mrs. Keiko Nakamura
First Secretary
Mr. Yasushi NOGUCHI; Mrs. Yuko Noguchi

INFORMATION AND CULTURE CENTER
1155 21st St. NW
Washington, DC 20036
Tel: (202) 238-6900 Fax: (202) 822-6524

JORDAN

EMBASSY OF HASHEMITE KINGDOM OF JORDAN
3504 International Dr. NW
Washington, DC 20008
Tel: (202) 966-2664 Fax: (202) 966-3110
Email: hkjembassydc@aol.com
Web: www.jordanembassyus.org

Ambassador E. and P.
His Excellency Karim KAWAR; Mrs. Luma Karim Kawar
Counsellor (Deputy Chief of Mission)
Mr. Jafar Abed A. HASSAN
First Secretary
Mr. Samer NABER
First Secretary
Mr. Muhib NIMRAT
First Secretary
Mr. Samer DABBAS
Consul
Miss Abeer JARRAR
Director (Press Attaché & Information Bureau)
Miss Merissa KHURMA
Press Attaché/Information Bureau
Mr. Omar OBEIDAT
Director (Economic & Commerce Bureau)
Mr. Maher MATALKA
Trade Representative (Economic & Commerce Bureau)
Mr. Yanal BEASHA

INFORMATION BUREAU
3504 International Dr. NW
Washington, DC 20008
Tel: (202) 265-1606 Fax: (202) 667-0777

KAZAKHSTAN

EMBASSY OF THE REPUBLIC OF KAZAKHSTAN
1401 16th St. NW
Washington, DC 20036
Tel: (202) 232-5488 Fax: (202) 232-5845
Email: kazakh.embusa@verizon.net
Web: www.kazakhembus.com

Ambassador E. and P.
His Excellency Dr. Kanat B. SAUDABAYEV; Mrs. Kullikhan B. Saudabayeva
Counsellor (Deputy Chief of Mission)
Mr. Talgat G. KALIYEV; Mrs. Assel E. Kaliyeva
Counsellor (Economic)
Dr. Mainura S. MURZAMADIEVA
Counsellor (Education & Culture)
Dr. Khadisha N. DAIROVA
Counsellor (Legal)
Mr. Zhunus K. YERGALIYEV
Counsellor (Political)
Mr. Askar S. TAZHIYEV
First Secretary (Political)
Mr. Talgat K. BAZARBEKOV
First Secretary (Press, Assistant to Ambassador)
Mr. Roman Y. VASSILENKO
Second Secretary (Consul)
Mr. Samat K. ZHANABAI
Second Secretary (Science & Technology)

Mr. Galymzhan B. NURMAGAMBETOV
Second Secretary (Economic)
Ms. Aigul N. MOLDABEKOVA
Third Secretary (Congressional)
Mr. Aibek K. NURBALIN
Attaché (Political)
Mr. Amir K. BASHBAYEV
Attaché (Consular)
Mr. Bolat S. TEMIRBAYEV
Defense, Military & Air Attaché
Colonel Assylbek A. MENDYGALIYEV; Mrs.
Raushan K. Mendygaliyev
Asst. Defense, Military & Air Attaché
Captain Zhandos Zhaksylykuly
USHKEMPIROV; Mrs. Aigul Seidikasymovna
Baibekova

KOREA, SOUTH

EMBASSY OF THE REPUBLIC OF KOREA
2450 Massachusetts Ave. NW
Washington, DC 20008
Tel: (202) 939-5600 Fax: (202) 387-0250
Web: www.koreaembassyusa.org

Ambassador E. and P.
vacant
Minister (Deputy Chief in Mission)
Mr. Jong Hwa CHOE; Mrs. Kyu Sook Choe
Minister (Public Affairs)
Mr. Soo Dong O; Mrs. Sung Sim Lee O
Minister
Mr. Yong Jin KIM; MRS. Hong Sun Kim
Minister (Counsellor)
Mr. Byoung Lip CHO; Mrs. Sung Boon KIM
Counsellor (Political)
Mr. Sung Lac WI; Mrs. Sang Hak Wi
Counsellor-Minister & Consul General
Mr. Byung KOOCHOI; Mrs. Kyung Soo Kim
Counsellor & Consul
Mr. Chongghee AHN; Mrs. Soh Young
Ahn Kim
Counsellor (Education)
Mr. Ki Won JANG; Mrs. Jung Sun Jang Yoo
Counsellor
Mr. Hyeyang Ji; Mrs. Hyosook Ji Lee
Counsellor
Mr. Eun SEOKKIM; Mrs. Mi Hy Nam
Counsellor (Education)
Mr. Wang Bok KIM; Mrs. Eun Suk Kim
Counsellor (Legal)
Mr. Young June KIM; Mrs. Kye Hyun Park
Kim
Counsellor
Mr. Chang Ho LEE; Mrs. Ok Kyung Lee Kim
Counsellor & Consul General
Mr. Hyun Ju Lee; Mrs. So Hee Lee Lee
Counsellor
Mr. Jae Hoon LEE; Mrs. Song Kyoung Lee
Kim
Counsellor
Mr. Jong Chil Lee; Mrs. Mi Hee Kim Lee
Counsellor
Mr. Kee Woo LEE; Mrs. Jung Hee Lee
Counsellor
Mr. Muberm LIM; Mrs. Kui Bok Lim Hwang
Counsellor
Mr. Sungnam LIM
Counsellor (Finance)
Mr. Dae Lae NOH; Mrs. Hay Li Noh Park
Counsellor (Communications)
Mr. Jeong Seon SEOL; Mrs. Kyung Hee
Seol Jin
Counsellor (Finance & Economy)
Mr. Dong Kyu SHIN; Mrs. Hyun Sook Park
Counsellor (Health & Welfare)
Mr. Young Hak YOO; Mrs. Hyun Kyong
Yoo Youk
First Secretary
Mr. Young Tae BYUN; Mrs. Young Ja Cho
First Secretary
Mr. Gyuwan CHOI; Mrs. Junghwa Kim

First Secretary
Mr. Jeong Ho CHOI; Mrs. In Sook Jin
First Secretary & Consul
Mr. Jeong Moon CHOI; Mrs. Soon Jue Choi
First Secretary
Mr. Sangchol CHOI, Mrs. Sunhee Choi
First Secretary
Mr. Sang Wha CHUNG; Mrs. Sun Kyung
Chung Choi
First Secretary
Mr. Joon Ki HONG; Mrs. Kwang Ok Hong
Park
First Secreatry
Mr. Woon Bae JEON; Mrs. Won Hee Park
First Secretary
Mr. Hye Yang JI; Mrs. Hyo Sook Ji Lee
First Secretry
Mr. Seuk Jun KANG; Mrs. Jeong Ok Kang
Yu
First Secreaty & Consul
Mr. Byeong Tae KIM; Mrs. Mee La Kim Jin
First Secretary
Mr. Chang Beom KIM; Mrs. Hyun Mee Kim
First Secretary
Mr. Hae Yong KIM; Mrs. Jeeya Kim
First Secretary
Mr. Se Gon KIM; Mrs. Kyung Im Park
First Secretary & Consul
Mr. Won Jik KWON; Mrs. Eun Jung Kwon
Jang
First Secretary
Mr. Heon LEE; Mrs. Hye Jung Lee
First Secretary
Mr. Hoseung LEE; Mrs. Kuemjeong Lee Kim
First Secretary
Mr. Jeong Kyu LEE; Mrs. Sang Hee Lee
Yoon
First Secretary
Mr. Woongsoon LIM; Mrs. Eun Sun Lim Lee
First Secretary
Mr. Song OH; Mrs. Jee Won Oh
First Secretary
Mr. Won Sup PARK; Mrs. Mee Sook Moon
First Secretary
Mr. Chae Hyun SHIN; Mrs. Bong Hee
Shin Son
First Secretary
Mr. Jae Hak SON; Mrs. Eun Joo Son Cha
First Secretary
Mr. Jeong Sun SUH; Mrs. Moon Sook Suh
Jeong
First Secretary
Mr. Seung Bae YEO; Mrs. Sung Hee Yeo
Choi

CHANCERY ANNEX
2400 Wilson Blvd.
Arlington, VA 22201
Tel: (703) 524-5505 Fax: (703) 524-9273

EDUCATION OFFICE
2320 Massachusetts Ave. NW
Washington, DC 20008
Tel: (202) 939-5679 Fax: (202) 265-2127

INFORMATION OFFICE
2370 Massachusetts Ave. NW
Washington, DC 20008
Tel: (202) 797-6343 Fax: (202) 387-0413

OFFICE OF THE DEFENSE AND LOGISTICS
2400 Wilson Blvd.
Arlington, VA 22201
Tel: (703) 524-5505 Fax: (703) 524-9273

KUWAIT

EMBASSY OF THE STATE OF KUWAIT
2940 Tilden St. NW
Washington, DC 20008
Tel: (202) 966-0702 Fax: (202) 966-0517

Ambassador E. and P.
His Excellency Sheikh Salem Abdullah Al
Jaber AL-SABAH; Mrs. Rima Al -Sabah
Counsellor (Deputy Chief of Mission)
Mr. Ahmad Bader Mahmood RAZOUQI;
Mrs. Hessah Abdulaziz A. Al Mulaifi
Counsellor (Cultural)
Dr. Merza H. M. HASAN; Mrs. Wajeeha R.
H. M. Ali
First Secretary
Mr. Jasem Mohamed A. A. Al BUDAIWI;
Mrs. Mona Saleh M. S. Al Mohhamad
First Secretary
Mr. Nabeel Al DAKHEEL; Mrs. Wejdan D
S.M. Al Busairi
Third Secretary
Mr. Nawaf A. S. A. Al AHMAD; Mrs. Nouf F.
A. J. Boodai
Second Secretary
Mr. Talal S. S. S. Al FASSAM; Mrs. Halah Ali
A. A. Al Shayeji
Third Secretary
Mr. Zeyad Al MASHAN; Mrs. Yasmeen M.
A. M. H. Al ATIQI
Attaché
Major Tareq A. Al ASFOUR; Mrs. Khaledah
H. Al Ansari
Attaché
Major Hamed H. Al AYAR; Mrs. Soha A.
Al Refai
Attaché (Health)
Dr. Ahdi Yousef Al GHANIM; Mrs. Ibtihaj
Abdullah Al Ghanim
Attaché (Media)
Dr. Fatma Sh. Hasan Al KHALIFA; Dr.
Musaed Rashed A. Al Haroun
Attaché (Media)
Ms. Taha ni Noori Al TERKATE
Attaché (Cultural)
Mr. Abdullah M. F. Al WOTAID; Mrs.
Pamela Sue Al Wotaid
Attaché (Media)
Mr. Tareq Eid AL-MEZREM; Mrs. Bashaer
J.S.T. Al-Dawi
Attaché
Mr. Salem Abdulrahman Jasem
ALGHANEM
Attaché
Brigadier General Ahmed S. J. ALNASER;
Mrs. Muna S. M. N. Alnajadi
Attaché (Consular Affairs)
Mr. Nasser A. BEHBEHANI; Mrs. Fariha
Mohialdin Safa
Attaché (Media)
Ms. Sarah A. A. M. DEYYAIN
Attaché
Lieutenant Colonel Faraj H. ESMAIL; Mrs.
Basimah S. Al Lahaw
Attaché (Cultural)
Dr. Fatima A. H. NAZAR

CULTURAL, UNIVERSITY, LIAISON OFFICES
3500 International Dr. NW
Washington, DC 20008
Tel: (202) 363-8055 Fax: (202) 537-3253

HEALTH OFFICE
4201 Connecticut Ave. NW #502
Washington, DC 20008
Tel: (202) 686-4304

INFORMATION OFFICE
2600 Virginia Ave. NW #404
Washington, DC 20037
Tel: (202) 338-0211 Fax: (202) 338-0957

KYRGYZSTAN

EMBASSY OF THE KYRGYZ REPUBLIC
1732 Wisconsin Ave. NW
Washington, DC 20007
Tel: (202) 338-5141 Fax: (202) 338-5139

Ambassador E. and P.
Her Excellency Zamira SYDYKOVA
Counsellor
Mrs. Gulnara KYSKARAEVA
First Secretary
Mr. Emil KAIKIEV
Attaché (Economic Affairs)
Mrs. Sarina ABDYSHEVA
Attaché (Culture and Education)
Ms. Chinara MAMBETOVA

LAOS

**EMBASSY OF THE LAOS PEOPLE'S
DEMOCRATIC REPUBLIC**
2222 S St. NW
Washington, DC 20008
Tel: (202) 332-6416 Fax: (202) 332-4923
Web: www.laosembassy.com

Ambassador E. and P.
His Excellency Phanthong
PHOMMAHAXAY; Mrs. Amphanh
Phommahaxay
**Minister-Counsellor (Deputy Chief of
Mission)**
Mr. Seng SOUKHATHIVONG; Mrs. Somdy
Soukhathivong
Counsellor
Mr. Vanhesa SENGMEUANT
First Secretary
Mr. Bounneme CHOUANGHOM; Mrs.
Katemany Chouanghom
First Secretary
Mr. Thonglung SAYAVONG
First Secretary
Mr. Sisavath INPHACHANH
Third Secretary
Mr. Amphayvanh CHANTHAVONG
Third Secretary
Mr. Phousavanh SOUPHANY
Third Secretary (Administrative & Financial)
Mr. Kongthong BRIANENG

LEBANON

EMBASSY OF LEBANON
2560 28th St. NW
Washington, DC 20008
Tel: (202) 939-6300 Fax: (202) 939-6324
Email: info@lebanonembassyus.org
Web: www.lebanonembassyus.org

Ambassador E. and P.
His Excellency Dr. Farid ABBOUD; Mrs.
Rim Hilal
Deputy Chief of Mission
Ms. Carla JAZZAR
First Secretary (Consular Affairs)
Mr. Ziad ATALLAH
First Secretary (Congressional Affairs)
Miss Rola NOUREDDINE
Second Secretary
Mr. Marwan FRANCIS

MALAYSIA

EMBASSY OF MALAYSIA
3516 International Ct. NW
Washington, DC 20008
Tel: (202) 572-9700 Fax: (202) 572-9882

Ambassador E. and P.
HIS Excellency Ghazzli S.A. KHALID
**Minister- Counsellor (Deputy Chief of
Mission)**
Mr. Ahmad Izlan Bin IDRIS; Mrs. Rose Binti
Abdullah
Minister-Counsellor
Mr. Rohani Bin WALAT; Mrs. Zainab Binti
Ismail

Minister-Counsellor (Economics)
Mr. Seng Foo WONG; Mrs. Hooi Ping Foo
Counsellor
Mr. Kennedy JAWAN; Mrs. Josephine Anak Dagang
First Secretary
Mr. Ahmad Hamizan Mohd YUSOF; Mrs. Suziana Masni Majid
First Secretary
Mr. Wan Ashbi Bin LEMAN; Mrs. Norashikin Binti Mohamad Ashari
Second Secretary (Administrative & Financial)
Mr. Mohd Noor Bin Mat ISA
Third Secretary
Mr. Nordin Bin ISMAIL; Mrs. Rosmidah Binti Nordin
Attaché (Education)
Dr. Zahratul Kamar Binti MAHMUD; Dr. Azahari Bin Ismail
Attaché (Science)
Dr. Thiagarajan TANGAVELU; Mrs. Pavany Periasamy
Asst. Attaché (Education)
Mr. Latip Bin Abdul RANI; Mrs. Norliza Binti Nordin
Asst. Attaché (Education)
Miss Norina JAMALUDIN
Asst. Attaché (Education)
Mr. Mohamad Hamidi MAZLAN; Mrs. Yusnaili Yusoff
Asst. Attaché (Education)
Mrs. Radziah MOHAMED; Mr. Mohd Razali Jadi
Defense, Military, Naval & Air Attaché
Colonel Latip Bin ISMAIL; Mrs. Che Norsiah Binti Mohammad
Asst. Defense, Military, Naval & Air Attaché
Lieutenant Colonel Muhammad Anwar ABDULLAH; Mrs. Marina Mohd Shariff

MALDIVES

EMBASSY OF THE REPUBLIC OF MALDIVES
800 2nd Ave. #400E
New York, NY 10017
Tel: (212) 599-6195 Fax: (212) 661-6405

Ambassador E. and P.
His Excellency Dr. Mohamed LATHEEF; Mrs. Shakeela Hameed

MONGOLIA

EMBASSY OF MONGOLIA
2833 M St. NW
Washington, DC 20007
Tel: (202) 333-7117 Fax: (202) 298-9227
Email: esyam@mongolianembassy.us
Web: www.mongolianembassy.us

Ambassador E. and P.
His Excellency Ravdan BOLD; Mrs. Oyuun Mijiddorj
Minister Counsellor & Deputy Chief of Mission
Mr. Banzragch ODONJILL
Defense Attaché
Mr. Jargalsaikhan MENDEE
Counsellor & Consul General
Mr. Gonchig SESEER
Trade and Economic Counsellor
Mr. Sodnom GANBOLD
Second Secretary
Mrs. Sukhbaatar ALTANTSETSEG
Third Secretary & Consul
Mr. Galsan ALTANSUKH

NEPAL

ROYAL NEPALESE EMBASSY
2131 Leroy Pl. NW
Washington, DC 20008
Tel: (202) 667-4550 Fax: (202) 667-5534
Web: www.nepalembassyusa.org

Ambassador E. and P.
His Excellency Kedar B. SHRESTHA; Mrs. Shanta Shrestha
Minister-Counsellor (Deputy Chief of Mission)
Mr. Rudra Kumar NEPAL; Mrs. Karuna Nepal
First Secretary
Mr. Krishna Chandra ARYAL; Mrs. Ganga Aryal
Third Secretary
Mr. Netra Bahadur TANDAN; Mrs. Kauseela Tandan
Defense & Military Attaché
Lieutenant Colonel Bijendra GAUTAM; Mrs. Rima Gautam

OMAN

EMBASSY OF THE SULTANATE OF OMAN
2535 Belmont Rd. NW
Washington, DC 20008
Tel: (202) 387-1980 Fax: (202) 745-4933

Ambassador E. and P.
His Excellency Mohamed Ali Al KHUSAIBY
First Secretary
Mr. Ahmed Mohamed Nasser Al ARAIMI; Mrs. Hana Ibrahim Saleem Al Rahbi
First Secretary
Mr. Mahmood Khamis Mohamed Al HINAI; Mrs. Mahfoodha Hamed Mohamed Al Hinai
First Secretary
Mr. Nasser Khamis Al KALBANI
First Secretary
Mr. Abdullah Khalid Al SULEIMANI; Mrs. Salma Khamis Nasser Al Gheilani
Attaché (Information)
Mr. Ali Ismail Ali Al BULUSHI; Mrs. Atifa Mustafa Saleem Al Ward
Attaché (Cultural)
Dr. Talib Issa Zahran Al SALMI; Mrs. Fatma Mohamed Zahran Al Salmi
Defense, Military, Naval & Air Attaché
Colonel Ahmed Saif Bashir Al GHAFRI; Mrs. Naela Hamed Hamood Al Ghafri
Asst. Defense, Military, Naval & Air Attaché
Lieutenant Colonel Nasser Saif Yahya Al HADDABI

CULTURAL OFFICE
8381 Old Courthouse Rd. #130
Vienna, VA 22182
Tel: (571) 722-0000 Fax: (571) 722-0001

DEFENSE OFFICE
2535 Belmont Rd. NW
Washington, DC 20008
Tel: (202) 387-1980 Fax:

PAKISTAN

EMBASSY OF PAKISTAN
3517 International Ct. NW
Washington, DC 20008
Tel: (202) 243-6500 Fax: (202) 686-1544
Email: info@embassyofpakistan.org
Web: www.embassyofpakistan.org

Ambassador E. and P.
His Excellency Jehangir KARAMAT; Mrs. Nilofar Jehangir
Minister (Deputy Chief of Mission)

Mr. Mohammad SADIQ; Mrs. Sadia Sadiq
Minister (Political)
Mr. Aslam KHAN
Counsellor (Political)
Mr. Farukh AMIL
Counsellor
Mr. Sohail KHAN
Counsellor
Mr. Shahid AHMED
Counsellor
Mr. Zulfiqar GARDEZI
First Secretary
Mr. Zahid Hafeez CHAUDHRI
Second Secretary
Ms. Ayesha Abbas AHSAN
Consular & Administration Attaché
Mr. Gul Khatab ABBASI
Defense & Military Attaché
Brig Khawar HANIF
Minister (Economics)
Mr. Mushtaq MALIK
Minister (Trade)
Mr. Ashraf HAYAT
Press Minister
Mrs. Talat WASEEM
Press Attaché
Mr. Nadeem Haider KIANI
Naval & Air Attaché
Group Captain Nadeem JAVED
Attaché Defense Procurement
Group Captain Kamran SHAHID
Attaché (Defense & Procurement)
Col Omar Mahmood HAYAT
Army Tech Liaison Officer
Col Khalid MAHMOOD
Finance & Accounts Officer
Mr. Aamir Nazir GONDAL

CHANCERY ANNEX
3517 International Ct. NW
Washington, DC 20008
Tel: (202) 243-6500 Fax: (202) 686-1544

COMMERCIAL OFFICE
3517 International Ct. NW
Washington, DC 20008
Tel: (202) 243-6500 Fax: (202) 686-1544

PAPUA NEW GUINEA

EMBASSY OF PAPUA NEW GUINEA
1779 Massachusetts Ave. NW #805
Washington, DC 20036
Tel: (202) 745-3680 Fax: (202) 745-3679
Email: info@pngembassy.org
Web: www.pngembassy.org

Ambassador E. and P.
His Excellency Evan Jeremy PAKI
First Secretary
Mr. Wasser Vincent SUMALE; Mrs. Mary SUMALE

PHILIPPINES

EMBASSY OF THE REPUBLIC OF THE PHILIPPINES
1600 Massachusetts Ave. NW
Washington, DC 20036
Tel: (202) 467-9300 Fax: (202) 467-9417
Web: www.philippineembassy-usa.org

Ambassador E. and P.
His Excellency Albert Ferreros Del ROSARIO; Mrs. Margaret Gretchen Del Rosario
Minister & Consul General (Deputy Chief Of Mission)
Mrs. Jocelyn Batoon GARCIA; Mr. Evan P. Garcia
Minister & Consul

Mr. Evan P. GARCIA; Mrs. Jocelyn Batoon Garcia
Minister & Consul
Ms. Lourdes Ortiz YPARRAGUIRRE
Counsellor
Mr. Joselito A. Jimeno; Ms. Araceli Cuesta Jimeno
First Secretary & Consul
Mr. Henry S. BENSURTO; Mrs. Ann Mariza N. Sanchez Bensurto
First Secretary & Consul
Ms. Hjayceelyn Mancenido QUINTANA
First Secretary & Consul
Ms. Patricia Ann PAEZ
Second Secretary & Consul
Mr. Enrico Trinidad FOS; Mrs. Myla Antonette Fabre Fos
Attaché (Commercial)
Mr. Romeo Gamboa BORILLO
Attaché
Mr. Ramon M. EBALO; Ms. Hideko Shimoji
Attaché (Police)
Mr. Dante Tamayo FERRER
Attaché
Mrs. Janeth Zulita FALSIS; Mr. Darwin Balingcongan Falsis
Attaché
Mrs. Fe Cuevas GENOTA
Attaché
Mr. Roger Rosal GONZALES; Mrs. Estela Rimas Gonzales
Attaché
Mr. Jose Edgar E. LEDONIO; Mrs. Maria Angelica Beatriz A. Ledonio
Attaché (Agriculture)
Mr. Victoriano B. LEVISTE; Mrs. Florina Gener Leviste
Attaché
Mrs. Filomena M. MANAOIS; Mr. Jose Rivera Manaois
Attaché
Ms. Rosa Guadalupe Angela R. PARAISO
Attaché
Ms. Nenita Parulan PARTOSAN; Mr. Esteban Artates, Jr Partosan
Attaché
Mrs. Vivian Mancia PASCUA; Mr. Rodolfo Antalan Pascua
Attaché
Ms. Angelica H. RAMOS
Attaché
Ms. Sylvia Montallana REYES
Attaché (Labor)
Mr. Arturo SODUSTA
Attaché (Financial)
Mrs. Cynthia Doroja TAYAM; Mr. Domingo Manlangit Tayam
Attaché
Mr. Renie Pascual TOMAS
Attaché (Cultural)
Ms. Gracia Divina Valera JARAMILLO
Asst. Attaché (Agriculture)
Mr. Lucio Castillo,Jr MANGHINANG; Mrs. Jennifer M. Manghinang
Defense Attaché
Brigadier General Delfin Negrillo LORENZANA; Mrs. Editha Aguilar Lorenzana
Military Attaché & Asst. Defense Attaché
Colonel Nestor Reyno SADIARIN; Ms. Ligaya Martin Sadiarin
Naval Attaché
Commander Victor Emmanuel Carr MARTIR; Mrs. Ma Stella Sarmiento Martir
Air Attaché
Lieutenant Colonel Romeo Cabacungan PRESTOZA; Mrs. Lilian Obillo Prestoza

QATAR

EMBASSY OF THE STATE OF QATAR
2555 M St. NW
Washington, DC 20037-1305
Tel: (202) 274-1600 Fax: (202) 237-0061
Web: www.qatarembassy.net

Ambassador E. and P.
His Excellency Nasser Bin Hamad M. AL KHALIFA
Minister (Deputy Chief of Mission)
Mr. Hamad Mohamed Al KHALIFA
Counsellor
Mr. Abdulla Yousef Al MANA
Counsellor
Mr. Mohamed Abdulaziz Al NASSR
First Secretary
Sheikh Ali Jassim Al THANI; Mrs. Eiman Hamad A. Al Kawari
First Secretary
Sheikh Meshal Hamad M. Al THANI
First Secretary
Mr. Fahad M. KAFOUD; Mrs. Tamather Mohamednoor Al Obaidly
Third Secretary
Mr. Hamad Mohamed Abdulla Al DOSARI; Mrs. Sheikha Noora Hamad F. Al Thani
Attaché (Medical)
Mr. Hamad Mahanna Ali Al DOSARI; Mrs. Aisha A. Al Dossari
Attaché (Cultural)
Mr. Nasser Ali Mohamed Al SAADI; Mrs. Fatma Hassan Abdulla Al Banna
Defense, Military, Naval & Air Attaché
Colonel Abdulrahman Ibrahim Al HEMAIDI; Mrs. Hend M. Al Qatari

CULTURAL ATTACHÉ OFFICE
2555 M St. NW
Washington, DC 20037
Tel: (202) 274-1627 Fax: (202) 966-8211

MEDICAL ATTACHÉ OFFICE
2555 M St. NW
Washington, DC 20037
Tel: (202) 274-1630 Fax: (202) 237-8393

RUSSIA

EMBASSY OF THE RUSSIAN FEDERATION
2650 Wisconsin Ave. NW
Washington, DC 20007
Tel: (202) 298-5700 Fax: (202) 298-5735
Web: www.russianembassy.org

Ambassador E. and P.
His Excellency Yury V. USHAKOV; Mrs. Svetlana M. Ushakova
Minister-Counsellor (Deputy Chief of Mission)
Mr. Sergey A. RYABKOV; Mrs.Marina N. Ryabkova
Senior Counsellor
Mr. Nikolay Y. BABICH
Senior Counsellor
Mr. Vadim N. GRISHIN
Senior Counsellor
Mr. Aleksandr S. KOZHURIN
Senior Counsellor
Mr. Andrey M. KUZIN
Senior Counsellor
Mr. Aleksandr K. LUKASHEVICH
Senior Couselor
Mr. Boris Y. MARCHUK
Senior Counsellor
Mr. Aleksandr S. STRIGANOV
Senior Counsellor
Mr. Yevgeniy ZVEDRE
Senior Counsellor
Mr. Vladimir I. YERMAKOV
Counsellor

Mr. Iskander K. AZIZOV
Counsellor
Mr. Georgiy Y. BORISENKO
Counsellor
Mr. Aleksandr M. DEYNEKO
Counsellor
Mr. Petr V. ILICHEV
Counsellor
Mr. Aleksey V. ISAKOV
Counsellor
Mr. Oleg A. NOVIKOV
Counsellor
Mr. Aleksey A. OSTROVSKIY
Counsellor
Mr. Vladimir I. RYBACHENKOV
Counsellor
Mr. Boris I. SOKOLOV
First Secretary
Mr. Roman Y. AMBAROV
First Secretary
Mr. Aleksandr Y. BARABANOV
First Secretary (Press)
Mr. Yevgeniy V. KHORISHKO
First Secretary
Mr. Yuriy S. KORNEYEV
First Secretary
Mr. Vladimir S. KRASNOV
First Secretary
Mr. Anatoliy N. KUTYAVIN
First Secretary
Mr. Andrey V. KUZNETSOV
First Secretary
Mr. Vasiliy S. MAKAROV
First Secretary
Mr. Igor Y. POLOZKOV
First Secretary (Cultural Attaché)
Mrs. Irina V. POPOVA
First Secretary
Mr. Elmir T. TAGIROV
First Secretary
Mr. Yevgeniy N. YELIZAROV
Second Secretary
Mr. Nikolay I. DEGTYAREV
Second Secretary
Ms. Tamara A. GOLOVETSKAYA
Second Secretary
Mr. Yuriy V. GORODNICHEV
Second Secretary
Mr. Kirill M. KOROBOV
Second Secretary
Mr. Andrey V. KROSHKIN
Second Secretary
Mr. Gennadiy Y. PELESHCHAK
Second Secretary
Mr. Yuriy V. PETROV
Second Secretary
Mr. Oleg V. POZDNYAKOV
Second Secretary
Mr. Ruslan Y. SHMELEV
Second Secretary
Mr. Vladlen V. YEPIFANOV
Second Secretary
Mr. Oleg A. ZVEREV
Third Secretary
Ms. Tatyana A. BALYKINA
Third Secretary
Mr. Aleksey G. DOMOCHKIN
Third Secretary
Mr. Aleksandr V. IVASHCHENKO
Third Secretary
Ms. Irina A. KHORTONEN
Third Secretary
Mr. Roman R. MALYGIN
Third Secretary
Mr. Aleksandr V. POLYANTSEV

DEFENSE MILITARY, NAVAL AND AIR ATTACHÉ OFFICE
2552 Belmont Rd. NW
Washington, DC 20008
Tel: (202) 965-1181 Fax: (202) 298-5742

Defense Attaché
Rear Admiral Alexander Agapov

FISHERIES ATTACHÉ OFFICE
1609 Decatur St. NW
Washington, DC 20011
Tel: (202) 726-3838

INFORMATION OFFICE
1706 18th St. NW
Washington, DC 20009
Tel: (202) 232-6020

RUSSIAN CULTURAL CENTRE
1825 Phelps Pl. NW
Washington, DC 20008
Tel: (202) 265-3840 Fax: (202) 265-6040

Director
Mr. Alexey Lunkov

TRADE REPRESENTATIVE OF THE RUSSIAN FEDERATION
2001 Connecticut Ave. NW
Washington, DC 20008
Tel: (202) 234-7170 Fax: (202) 232-2917

SAUDI ARABIA

EMBASSY OF SAUDI ARABIA
601 New Hampshire Ave. NW
Washington, DC 20037
Tel: (202) 342-3800 Fax: (202) 944-3113
Web: www.saudiembassy.net

Ambassador E. and P. & Consul General
His Royal Highness Prince Turki AL-FAISAL
Minister (Deputy Chief of Mission)
Vacant
Minister
Mr. Zain M. K. Al ZAHIRY; Mrs. Asia Hussein M. Murad.
Minister
Mr. Adel A. Al-JUBEIR
Minister
His Royal Highness Mohammed Faisal Turki AL-SAUD; Mrs. Wafa Fayyad Al-Saud
Minister
Mr. Rehab M. MASSOUD
Minister
First Lieutenant Salman Bin Sultan Bin ABDULAZIZ;Princess Folwah Bint Ahmad Bin A. Al Saud
Counsellor
Mr. Abdul Rahman I. Al NOAH; Mrs. Hessah Saleh N. Al Hatlani
Counsellor
Mr. Mesfer A. ALGHASEB; Mrs. Fatima M. H. Al Kahtany
Counsellor
Mr. Tala A. BARRI; Mrs.Sabah M. Zaitoni
First Secretary
Mr. Khaleel Y. A. AFFAN
First Secretary
Mr. Omar Ali Saleh Al OYAIDI; Mrs.Hoda Omar S. Al Oyaidi
First Secretary
Mr. Saad S. Al SALEH; Mrs. Nadia A. Al Saleh
First Secretary
Mr. Saud F.M. Al SUWELIM; Mrs. Fatma A. Al Shehri
First Secretary
Mr. Azzam A. AL-GAIN; Mrs.Ahlam N. Basrawi
First Secretary
Mr. Reda A. AlNUZHA; Mrs. Hana Kh ALHOSAINY
First Secretary
Mr. Taha M.A. BAKHSH; Mrs. Amal M. A. Khadem

First Secretary
Mr. Emad A. MADANI; Mrs. Sahar Madani
First Secretary
Mr. Yousef A. SHAZLE; Mrs.Hyfa M. A. Bakhsh
Second Secretary
Mr. Abdullah O. AL AJROUSH
Second Secretary
Mr. Muzahim A. Al HAMOUD; Mrs.Sana S. Malak
Second Secretary
Mr. Nail Ahmed Al JUBEIR
Second Secretary
His Royal Highness Prince Faisal Bin Turki Bin N. Al SAUD; Princess Rema Bandar Al Sahud
Second Secretary
Mr. Abdulmohsen F. ALYAS; Mrs. Rouaa M. Atyah
Second Secretary
Mr. Khaled M. BADAWI; Mrs. Sarah A. Fadaak
Second Secretary
Mr. Hamzah Ahmad EDREES; Mrs. Khadijah Ahmad Al-Sawi
Second Secretary
Mr. Sameer H. QUTAB; Mrs. Samiah J. Qutab
Third Secretary
Mr. Hamad M. Al JEBREEN; Mrs. Moneerah A. Al Qahtani
Third Secretary
Mr. Saud A. Al SUDAIRY; Mrs. Ebtesam A Al Qubali
Attaché (Administrative)
Captain Abdulah Abdulaziz Al DAHLAWY; Mrs.Hend S. Baasiem
Attaché (Administrative)
Brigadier General Saleh A. Al JAWINI; Mrs. Mariam A. Al Jawini
Attaché (Cultural)
Dr. Mazyed I. Al MAZYED; Mrs. Wendy M. Al Mazyed
Attaché (Cultural)
Mr. Iehab A. Al RASSAN; Mrs. Abeer H. Al Hamoudi
Attaché (Head of National Guard Office)
Mr. Shakir A. Al SALEH; Mrs. Albandary S. Kathiry
Attaché (Administrative)
Lieutenant Colonel Naef Ahmed A. Al SAUD; Mrs. Fahdah Bint Khaled Al-Saud
Attaché (Commercial)
Mr. Ibrahim A. Al SAYGH
Attaché
Mr. Ahmed M. Sh. Al SHOMAR; Mrs. Fatimah S. H. Al Hilwah
Attaché
Mr. Abdulaziz H. Al WASIL
Attaché (Administrative)
Mr. Nassir Kh. AL-AJMI; Mrs. Al Joharah M. Al Sudairi
Attaché (Administrative)
Mr. Omar A. AL-BASSAM; Mrs. Fawziah Rashid Al-Ashban
Attaché (Administrative)
Colonel Sulaiman S.S. AL-BASSAM; Mrs. Hend Al-Faris
Attaché (Administrative)
Dr. Majed H. N. AL-GHESHEYAN; Mrs. Badria Fahad Al-Ghesheyan
Attaché (Administrative)
Mr. Fahad S. AL-GHOFAILY; Mrs. Mariam Al Ashban
Attaché (Administrative)
Mr. Fahd S. AL-MHQANI; Mrs. Ghazwa E. Al-Otaibi
Attaché
Mr. Saud Saleh AL-MUHANNA; Mrs. Amal Mohammed Al-Nejaidi
Attaché
Mr. Khalid M. ALSAIF
Attaché

Mr. Adel A. S. ALTAHINI
Attaché (Administrative)
Brigadier General Abdulaziz Saleh M. ASEEL; Mrs. Thoria Ali Etaiwi
Attaché (Administrative)
First Lieutenant Salman Bin ABDULAZIZ; Mrs. Folwah Bint Ahmad Bin A. Al Saud

DEFENSE AND ARMED FORCES ATTACHÉ OFFICE
1001 30th St. NW
Washington, DC 20007
Tel: (202) 857-0122 Fax: (202) 342-0588

Defense Attaché
Col. Ali ALRAKAS

SAUDI ARABIAN CULTURAL MISSION
2600 Virginia Ave. #800
Washington, DC 20037
Tel: (202) 337-9450 Fax:

SAUDI ARABIAN NATIONAL GUARD OFFICE
601 New Hampshire Ave. NW
Washington, DC 20037
Tel: (202) 944-3344 Fax: (202) 944-3340

SINGAPORE

EMBASSY OF THE REPUBLIC OF SINGAPORE
3501 International Pl. NW
Washington, DC 20008
Tel: (202) 537-3100 Fax: (202) 537-0876

Ambassador E. and P.
Her Excellency Heng Chee CHAN
Minister-Counsellor (Deputy Chief of Mission)
Ms. L. K. Susan SIM
Counsellor (Administrative/Consular)
Mr. Ngee Seng Roy KHO; Mrs. Lee Cheng Pauline Tan
Counsellor (Economic)
Mr. Rossman ITHNAIN
Counsellor
Mr. Kah Meng NG
Counsellor (Political)
Mr. C.T. Samuel TAN; Ms. S. Y. Alice Ho
Counsellor (Defense Technology)
Mr. Peng Yam TAN; Mrs. Huey Lih Heng
First Secretary
Mr. Jaime Chun Wei HO; Mrs.Hwee Peng Ong
First Secretary (Information)
Mr. Yuin Chien LIM; Ms. Yun May Chan
First Secretary (Defense Technology)
Mr. George LOH; Mrs. Audrey Tan
First Secretary (Defense and Technical)
Mr. Chung Hoe NG; Mrs. Soo Ching Mavis Chong
First Secretary (Political)
Ms. Ariel Eunice Hwi Tiang TAN
First Secretary
Mr. Gabriel Ee Chung WONG; Mrs. Wei Yuen Angelina Hing
Second Secretary (Political)
Ms. Su Yin Tracy CHAN
Second Secretary
Miss Gerardine JONG
Attaché
Ms. Yong Mei LI
Defense, Military, Naval and Air Attaché
Brigadier General Tse Chow VOON; Mrs. Seok Pin Josephine Lee
Asst. Defense, Military, Naval and Air Attaché.
Llieutenant Solonel Pee Nian CHOO; Mrs. Lay Kuan Ang

SRI LANKA

EMBASSY OF THE DEMOCRATIC SOCIALIST REPUBLIC OF SRI LANKA
2148 Wyoming Ave. NW
Washington, DC 20008
Tel: (202) 483-4025 Fax: (202) 232-7181
Email: slembassy@slembassyusa.org
Web: www.slembassyusa.org

Ambassador E. and P.
His Excellency Bernard GOONETILLEKE; Mrs. Maria G.J. Goonetilleke
Minister (Deputy Chief of Mission)
Mr. BANDARA
Minister (Commercial)
Mr. Saman UDAGEDARA
Minister (Political & Information)
Mr. Ravinatha ARYASINHA
Defense Attaché
Brigadier Milinda PEIRIS
First Secretary (Economic)
Ms. Dhammika SEMASINGHE
Second Secretary (Commerce)
Mrs. Ameena MOHIN
Third Secretary
Ms. Prabashini PONNAMPERUMA
Attaché
Mr. Padmasiri EKANAYAKE

SYRIA

EMBASSY OF THE SYRIAN ARAB REPUBLIC
2215 Wyoming Ave. NW
Washington, DC 20008
Tel: (202) 232-6313 Fax: (202) 234-9548
Web: www.syrianembassy.us

Ambassador E. and P.
His Excellency Dr. Imad MOUSTAPHA; Mrs. Rafif Alsayed
Minister
Mr. Zouheir JABBOUR
Counsellor
Mr. Samir BASHOUR; Mrs. Omayazeitoun
First Secretary
Mr. Jawdat ALI; Mrs. Soumaya Matouk
First Secretary
Mr. Mhd Hasanein KHADDAM; Mrs. Louiza Zorpa
Second Secretary
vacant
Third Secretary
Mr. Ammar Al ARSAN; Mrs. Lama Al Assas
Attaché (Administrative Affairs)
Mr. Mohammad Al IBRAHIM; Mrs. Amal Al Asa Ad
Attaché (Media Affairs)
Ms. Maryam SHAQRA
Attaché
Ms. Joumana HAZIM

TAJIKISTAN

EMBASSY OF THE REPUBLIC OF TAJIKISTAN
1005 New Hampshire Ave. NW
Washington, DC 20037
Tel: (202) 223-6090 Fax: (202) 223-6091
Web: www.tjus.org

Ambassador E. and P.
His Excellency Khamrohon ZARIPOV
First Secretary & Consul
Mr. Bakhtier EROV

THAILAND

EMBASSY OF THAILAND
1024 Wisconsin Ave. NW
Washington, DC 20007
Tel: (202) 944-3600 Fax: (202) 944-3611
Web: www.thaiembdc.org

Ambassador E. and P.
vacant
Minister (Deputy Chief of Mission)
Mr. Chirachai PUNKRASIN; Mrs. Kanyaratana Punkrasin
Minister (Commercial)
Mrs. Chaveevarn CHANDANABHUMMA; Mr. Pipat Chandanabhumma
Minister-Counsellor
Mr. Chombhala CHAREONYING; Mrs. Chuthatip Chareonying
Minister-Counsellor (Commercial)
Ms. Tiptida NIYAMOSOTHA
Minister-Counsellor (Education)
Mr. Visoot PRASITSIRIWONGSE; Mrs. Kamonthip Prasitsiriwongse
Minister-Counsellor
Ms. Malinee PUNKA
Minister-Counsellor
Mr. Songsak SAICHEUA; Mrs. Yupadee Saicheua
Minister-Counsellor (Economic & Finance)
Ms. Ubolwan USAWATTANAGUL
Minister-Counsellor (Science & Technology)
Mr. Sonthi VANNASAENG; Mrs. Nuntarath Vannasaeng
Minister-Counsellor (Agriculture)
Mr. Prakarn VIRAKUL; Mrs. Chintana Virakul
Counsellor (Commercial)
Mr. Supat TANGTRONGCHIT; Mrs. Usavan Tangtrongchit
First Secretary (Procurement)
Commander Thumanoon HONGKIT; Mrs. Siwanee Hongkit
First Secretary
Mrs. Teerada KERDSUWAN; Mr. Vacharachai Kerdsuwan
First Secretary
Miss Samana KRISANATHEVIN
First Secretary
Mr. Natapanu NOPAKUN; Mrs. Nitima Nopakun
First Secretary
Mr. Totsapol RONGWAREE; Mrs. Oranit Rongwaree
First Secretary
Mr. Sorasak SAMONKRAISORAKIT; Mrs. Rachadaporn Samonkraisorakit
First Secretary
Miss Siriporn SUPANIMITWISETKUL
First Secretary (Agricultural)
Ms. Bhibhatra SUWANABATR
First Secretary
Mr. Sasiwat WONGSINSAWAT
Second Secretary
Mrs. Penmas LUSANANON
Second Secretary
Mr. Veerasakdi Prem AREE; Mrs. Choonhanate Prem Aree
Second Secretary
Miss Anintita VATCHARASIRITHAM
Third Secretary
Mr. Satien KODKANTA; Mrs. Areewalya Kodkanta
Third Secretary
Mrs. Supaporn MANEENOI; Mr. Seneemaneenoi
Defense & Military Attaché
Colonel Naretrak THITATHAN; Mrs. Wipawee Thitathan
Air Attaché & Asst. Defense Attaché
Group Captain Chakrit WUTHIKARN; Mrs. Sirijantrarat Wuthikarn
Asst. Defense & Military Attaché
Colonel Natee WONGISSARES; Mrs. Atiporn Wongissares
Asst. Naval & Defense Attaché
Captain Chonlathis NAVANUGRAHA; Mrs. Pornsiri Navanugraha

CULTURAL OFFICE
1024 Wisconsin Ave. NW
Washington, DC 20007
Tel: (202) 944-3600 Fax: (202) 944-3611

EDUCATION AFFAIRS
1906 23rd St. NW
Washington, DC 20008
Tel: (202) 667-9111 Fax: (202) 265-7239

EDUCATION COUNSELLOR OFFICE
1906 23rd St. NW
Washington, DC 20008
Tel: (202) 667-0675

TURKEY

EMBASSY OF THE REPUBLIC OF TURKEY
2525 Massachusetts Ave. NW
Washington, DC 20008
Tel: (202) 612-6700 Fax: (202) 612-6744
Web: www.turkishembassy.org

Ambassador E. and P.
His Excellency Dr. Osman Faruk LOGOGLU; Mrs. Mevhibe Logoglu
Minister-Counsellor (Deputy Chief of Mission)
MR. Engin SOYSAL; Mrs. Tulay SOYSAL
Minister-Counsellor (Special Assistant to Ambassador)
Mr. Tuluy TANC; Mrs. Feride Tanc
Counsellor (Commercial)
Mr. Salih CICEK
Counsellor
Mr. Yunus DEMIRER
Counsellor (Press)
Mr. Osman Bulent ERDEMGIL; Mrs. Fatma Sirindilek Erdemgil
Counsellor (Head of the Chancery)
Mr. U. Kenan IPEK
Counsellor (Planning)
Mr. Akin IZMIRLIOGLU
Counsellor
Mr. Burak OZUGERGIN
Counsellor (Agricultural)
Mr. Kemal SANDIK; Mrs. Fatma Sandak
Counsellor (Commercial)
Mr. Bilgehan SASMAZ; Mrs. Aysegul Sasmaz
Counsellor
Mr. Engin SOYSAL; Mrs. Tulay Soysal
First Secretary
Mr. Oguzhan ERTUGRUL; Mrs. Ozge Ertugrul
First Secretary
Mr. Murut LUTEM; Mrs. Gulsum Idil Lutem
First Secretary
Mr. Timur T. SOYLEMEZ; Mrs. Huma S. Ulgen Soylemez
Third Secretary
Mr. Semih Lutfu TURGUT; Mrs. Leyla Turgut
Attaché
Ms. Ayfer ALPTEKIN
Attaché
Mr. Mehmet Tarik ASKIN
Attaché
Mrs. Begum ATAY; Mr. Ugur Atay
Attaché
Mr. Sinan AYVACI; Mrs. Ilknur Ayvaci
Attaché
Mr. Hamza Ramazan CAGLAR; Mrs. Ebru Caglar
Attaché

Mr. Mehmet DEMIREL; Mrs. Sidika Derya Demirel
Attaché
Mr. Ilhami DIKMEN; Mrs. Firdes Dikmen
Attaché
Ms. Betul DUMAN
Attaché
Mr. Bunyamin ERGISI
Attaché
Mr. Huseyin Hilmi GURPINAR; Mrs. Fahriye Gurnipar
Attaché
Mrs. Guldan KALEM; Mr. Yucel Kalem
Attaché
Mr. Turgut KARAGOZ
Attaché & Vice Consul
Mr. Mahmut KUSMEZ
Attaché
Mr. Cosar PALA
Attaché (Medical)
Major Onur SUER; Mrs. Ayla Suer
Attaché
Mr. Said TURER
Attaché (Education)
Mrs. Aynur UZER; Mr. Suleyman Uzer
Asst. Attaché (Army Supply)
Major Ibrahim ARSLAN; Mrs. Binnaz Seher Arslan
Asst. Attaché (Air Supply)
Major Seyfettin ERYILMAZ; Mrs. Murvet Eryilmaz
Asst. Attaché (Naval Supply)
Lieutenant Teoman YILDIRIM
Defense & Air Attaché
Brigadier General Beyazit KARATAS; Mrs. Binnur Karatas
Military Attaché
Colonel Ziya BATUR; Mrs. Ferdane Batur
Naval Attaché
Captain Alaettin SEVIM; Mrs. Ebru Sevim
Asst. Military Attaché (Army Supply)
Major Ali Ozcan GUMUSTEKIN; Mrs. Gulhan Gumustekin
Asst. Air Attaché
Lieutenant Colonel Murat NURCAN; Mrs. Mehtap Nurcan

DEFENSE ATTACHÉ OFFICE
2202 Massachusetts Ave. NW
Washington, DC 20008
Tel: (202) 939-1860

TURKMENISTAN

EMBASSY OF TURKMENISTAN
2207 Massachusetts Ave. NW
Washington, DC 20008
Tel: (202) 588-1500 Fax: (202) 588-0697
Email: turkmen@mindspring.com
Web: www.turkmenistanembassy.org

Ambassador E. and P.
His Excellency Meret Bairamovich ORAZOV; Mrs. Irina Borisovna Orazova
Minister-Counsellor & Consul
Mr. Parakhat DURDYEV; Mrs. Bakhar Durdyeva

UNITED ARAB EMIRATES

EMBASSY OF THE UNITED ARAB EMIRATES
3522 International Ct. NW #400
Washington, DC 20008
Tel: (202) 243-2400 Fax: (202) 243-2432
Web: www.uae-embassy.org

Ambassador E. and P.
His Excellency Alasri Saeed ALDHAHRI; Mrs. Maryam A. Aldhahri
Counsellor
Mr. Jassim Mohd ALHOUSANI; Mrs. Maryam Jaber Alhousani
First Secretary
Mr. Khalifa Saif ALMAZROOEI; Mrs. Moza Mohd Almazrooei
Third Secretary
Mr. Abdulla Ali ALSABOOSI; Mrs. Hissa J. Alromaithi
Attaché (Administrative)
Major Ghazi Al BAKRI; Mrs. Hasna Al Bakri
Attaché (Administrative)
Mayor Jasim Mohamed Al HOSANI; Mrs. Maysoon Awani Awani
Attaché (Administrative)
Sergeant Ahmed ALALAWI; Mrs. Shaikha Belhoon
Attaché (Administrative)
Warrant Officer Abdulla ALALI; Mrs. Maryam Alali
Attaché (Administrative)
First Lieutenant Hamad Mubarak Abdulla Alaryani
Attaché (Administrative)
Corporal Nassir Abdullatif M.F. ALBALOOSHI; Mrs. Hudaaliali
Attaché (Administrative)
Warrant Officer Saeed Darweish Ali A. ALDHAHRI; Mrs. Nabeilah Ali Aldhahri
Attaché (Administrative)
Sergeant Khaled Salem Saie ALFALASI
Attaché (Cultural)
Dr. Abdulla Juma ALHAJ; Mrs. Muna Salim
Attaché (Administrative)
Mr. Mohamed Hamad ALHAMELI; Mrs. Fatima Khadim Alhameli
Attaché (Administrative)
Captain Mohammed ALJUNAIBI
Attaché (Administrative)
Warrant Officer Khaled Mohammed Matar ALKAABI; Mrs. Mariam Khamis Al Kaabi
Attaché (Administrative)
Mr. Maktoum Abdulla ALKAABI
Attaché (Administrative)
Mr. Nazem Fawwaz ALKUDSI; Mrs.Rala Mohamed Kinan
Attaché (Administrative)
Mr. Mohamed Hamad ALKUWAITI; Mrs. Amna Ahmed
Attaché (Administrative)
Mr. Salem Ali ALMAZROOEI; Mrs. Mariam Almazrooei
Attaché (Administrative)
First Lieutenant Rashed Hamad Rashed Z. ALNUAIMI
Attaché (Administrative)
Mr. Khalifa Darwish ALRUMAITHI; Mrs. Mariam T. Alrumaithi
Attaché (Administrative)
Mr. Saif Mubarak ALSHAMISI; Mrs. Hamda Adeel Alshamisi
Attaché (Administrative)
First Lieutenant Ahmed Khalfan Mohamed ALSHAMSI
Attaché (Administrative)
Mr. Ahmed Ali ALSHEHHI
Attaché (Administrative)
Mr. Khaled Abdulla ALSHEHHI; Mrs. Asma Ahmed Alshehhi
Attaché (Administrative)
Mr. Mohammed Humaid R. ALSUWAIDI; Mrs. Qumza Saeed Alhajeri
Attaché (Administrative)
Ms. Muna Rashed OWAIDHA
Attaché (Administrative)
Sergeant Ali Ahmed QADOUR; Mrs. Fatmah Saeed Qaddur
Attaché (Administrative)
Mr. Wesam Hassan RAQAQI

Defense, Military, Naval & Air Attaché
Brigadier General Mohammed Ahmed Hamel ALQUBAISI; Mrs. Eida Mohammed Alqubaisi

CULTURAL OFFICE
1010 Wisconsin Ave. NW #700
Washington, DC 20007
Tel: (202) 672-1050 Fax: (202) 672-1082

UZBEKISTAN

EMBASSY OF THE REPUBLIC OF UZBEKISTAN
1746 Massachusetts Ave. NW
Washington, DC 20036-1903
Tel: (202) 887-5300 Fax: (202) 293-6804
Web: www.uzbekistan.org

Ambassador E. and P.
His Excellency Abdulaziz KAMILOV; Mrs. Gulnora Rashidova
Counsellor (Deputy Chief of Mission)
Mr. Bakhtier IBRAGIMOV; Mrs. Manzura Ibragimov
Counsellor (Trade & Economic)
Mr. Bakhtiyor ABDULLAKHANOV
Counsellor
Mr. Sherzod ABDULLAEV; Mrs. Muborakkhon Abdullaev
First Secretary (Political)
Mr. Ismatulla FAIZULLAEV; Mrs. Motabar Fayzullaeva
First Secretary
Mr. Eldor ARIPOV; Mrs. Shakhnoza Shaakhrarovna Aripov
Second Secretary
Mr. Alisher AZAMATOV; Mrs.Yulduzkhon Azamatova
Attaché (Assistant to Ambassador)
Mr. Bekhruz ABDUVALIEV; Mrs. Govkhar Abduvaliev
Attaché
Mr. Furkat SIDIKOV; Mrs. Gulchekhra Sidikova
Attaché (Assistant to Ambassador)
Me. Erkin HAMRAEV
Attaché
Mr. Ashirbek YUSUPOV
Defense, Military, Naval & Air Attaché
Lieutenant Colonel Ilkhomjon BEKMIRZAEV; Mrs. Gulnora Bekmirzayeva

VIETNAM

EMBASSY OF VIETNAM
1233 20th St. NW #400
Washington, DC 20036
Tel: (202) 861-0737 Fax: (202) 861-0917
Email: info@vietnamembassy.us
Web: www.vietnamembassy-usa.org

Ambassador E. and P.
His Excellency Tam Chien NGUYEN; Mrs. Huong Thi Lien Nguyen
Deputy Chief of Mission
Mr. Dang Dzung VU
Counsellor (Political)
Mr. Dinh Quy DANG
Counsellor (Consular)
Mr. Cong Dzung NGUYEN
Counsellor (Congressional Liaison)
Mr. Vu Tu NGUYEN
Counsellor (Economic)
Mr. Quang Minh VU
Counsellor (Political)
Mr. Ho Phat DANG
Counsellor (Education & Science)
Mr. Xuan Phong HO
Couselor (Investment)
Mr. Quoc Trung BUI

Counsellor
Mr. Minh Dzung TRAN
First Secretary (Administrative)
Mr. Dinh Chien TRAN
First Secretary
Mr. Dan LE
First Secretary (Consular)
Mrs. Mai Phuong DANG
First Secretary (Consular)
Mr. Van Dinh PHAM
First Secretary
Mr. Trong Khanh HOANG
First Secretary
Mr. Van Minh DO
Second Secretary (Consular)
Mr. Truong Giang PHAM
Second Secretary
Ms. Phuong Anh PHAM
Second Secretary
Mr. Viet Dzung VU
Second Secretary
Mr. Tran Phuong VU
Third Secretary
Mr. Thanh Tam TRAN
Attaché (Press and Cultural Affairs)
Mr. Ngoc Chien BACH
Attaché (Administrative)
Ms. Le Thanh DANG
Attaché (Consular)
Mr. Kim Chi NGO

TRADE OFFICE
1730 M St. NW #501
Washington, DC 20036
Tel: (202) 463-9419

YEMEN

EMBASSY OF THE REPUBLIC OF YEMEN
2319 Wyoming Ave. NW
Washington, DC 20008
Tel: (202) 965-4760 Fax: (202) 337-2017
Email: ambassador@yemenembassy.org
Web: www.yemenembassy.org

Ambassador E. and P.
His Excellency Abdulwahab A. AL-HAJJRI; Mrs. Saboura H. Al-Mahfadi
Minister (Deputy Chief of Mission)
Mr. Abdulhakim ALERYANI
Military Attaché
Mr. B.G. Abdullah ABULREJAL
Minister
Mr. Abdulmalik A. Al HAJRI
Minister
Mr. Hassan Al SHAMI; Mrs. Amat Alrazag M. Al Shami
Minister
Mr. Ibrahim M. A. ALKIBSI; Mrs. Ilham Ali Alssiraji
Minister
Mr. Ahmed Mohamed LUQMAN; Mrs. Amatalrahim A. M. Ishak
Counsellor
Mrs. Amat Alghafoor A. Al WADI
First Secretary
Mr. Yahya Y. GHOBAR; Mrs. Kother M. Takialdeen
Second Secretary
Mr. Abdulla M. Al SOCOTRY; Mrs. Mona Saad Hgiry Ahmed
Attaché
Mr. Bakeel Mohamed A'ATEF
Attaché (Cultural)
Mr. Yassin Saaif Abdulla SHAIBANY; Mrs. Raddiah Ahmed Alhobaishi
Attaché
Mr. Jamal Ali Nasser MOHAMED
Defense, Military, Naval & Air Attaché
Brigadier General Abdullah A. Yahya ABULREJAL; Mrs. Faoziah Ahmed Saleh Gaid

Asian Consulates in the US

AFGHANISTAN

NEW YORK
New York (CG)
360 Lexington Ave., 11th Fl.
New York, NY 10017
Tel: (212) 972-2277 Fax: (212) 972-9046

Consul General
Vacant
Consul
Mr. Saved Sardar Ahmad AHMADI
Vice Consul
Mr. Abdul M. DANISHYAR

ARMENIA

CALIFORNIA
Los Angeles (CG)
50 N. La Cienega Blvd. #210
Beverly Hills, CA 90211
Tel: (310) 657-6102

Consul General
Mr. Gagik KIRAKOSIAN
Deputy Consul General
Mr. Harutyun KOJOYAN
Vice Consul
Mr. Artur MADOYAN
Consul
Mr. Vahagn Vachagan HOVSEPYAN

AZERBAIJAN

WASHINGTON
District of Columbia (EMB)
2741 34th St. NW
Washington, DC 20008
Tel: (202) 337-3500 Fax: (202) 337-5911

Consul
Mr. Huseyn Ismayil Oglu HUSEYNOV

BAHRAIN

CALIFORNIA
San Diego (HCG)
1101 1st St. #302
Coronado, CA 92118
Tel: (619) 437-0044 Fax: (619) 437-0066

Honorary Consul General
Mr. Charles W. HOSTLER

NEW YORK

New York (CG)
44th St., 25th Fl. East
New York, NY 10017
Tel: (212) 223-6200 Fax: (212) 319-0687

BANGLADESH

CALIFORNIA
Los Angeles (CG)
4201 Wilshire Blvd. #605
Los Angeles, CA 90010
Tel: (323) 932-0100 Fax: (323) 932-9703

Consul General
Mr. Mdshamsul HAQUE
Consul
Mr. Shah AHMED

HAWAII
Honolulu (HCG)
3785 Old Pali Rd.
Honolulu, HI 96817
Tel: (808) 521-5353

Honorary Consul General
Mr. Raymond Y. HO

LOUISIANA
New Orleans (HCG)
321 St. Charles Ave.
New Orleans, LA 70130
Tel: (504) 586-8300

Honorary Consul General
Mr. Thomas Blaise COLEMAN

NEW YORK
New York (CG)
211 E. 43rd St. #502
New York, NY 10017
Tel: (212) 599-6767 Fax: (212) 682-9211

Consul General
Mr. Rafiq Ahmed KHAN
Deputy Consul General
Mr. Chowdhury Golam MOWLA
Consul
Mr. Kazi Imtiaz HOSSAIN
Consul
Mr. Abu M. FERDOUS
Vice Consul
Mr. Khandker Habib AHMED
Vice Consul
Mr. M. Amanul HAQ

TEXAS
Houston (HCG)
35 N. Wynden Dr.
Houston, TX 77056
Tel: (713) 621-8462

Honorary Consul General
Mr. Edward J. HUDSON, Jr.

BHUTAN

DISTRICT OF COLUMBIA
Washington (HC)
1325 18th St. NW #806
Washington, DC 20036

Honorary Consul
Mr. William David HOPPER

NEW YORK
New York (CG)
2 United Nations Plz., 27th Fl.
New York, NY 10017

Consul General
Mr. Sonam Tobgay DORJI

BURMA

NEW YORK
New York (CG)
10 E. 77th St.
New York, NY 10021
Tel: (212) 535-1310 Fax: (212) 737-2421

CAMBODIA

CALIFORNIA
Los Angeles (HC)
422 Ord St. #G
Los Angeles, CA 90012

Honorary Consul
Mr. Hay YANG

WASHINGTON
Seattle (HC)
1818 Westlake Ave. North #315
Seattle, WA 98109
Tel: (206) 217-0830

Honorary Consul
Mr. Daravuth HUOTH

CHINA

CALIFORNIA
Los Angeles (CG)
443 Shatto Pl.
Los Angeles, CA 90020
Tel: (213) 807-8088 Fax: (213) 380-1961

Consul General
Mr. Jian Hua ZHONG
Deputy Consul General
Mr. Yi Ping LI
Deputy Consul General
Mr. Zi Xian CAI
Consul
Ms. Luo Mei SHU
Consul
Mr. Hui Jun WU
Consul
Mr. Yong Shan CHEN
Consul
Mr. Jian Long DONG
Consul
Mr. Hua YU
Consul
Mr. Ya Dong LI
Consul
Mr. Yao Sheng LI
Consul
Mr. Bo LAI
Consul
Mr. Kai Bin ZHANG
Consul
Mr. Jin Wang PAN
Consul
Mr. Qin ZHOU
Consul
Mr. Baq Qi ZHANG
Consul
Ms. Li Ying WANG
Consul
Mr. Wan Sheng LIU
Consul
Mr. Zhi Geng HE
Vice Consul
Mr. Yi YANG
Vice Consul
Mr. Jian YAO
Vice Consul
Mr. Yong ZHANG

CALIFORNIA
San Francisco (CG)
1450 Lacuna St.
San Francisco, CA 94115
Tel: (415) 674-2900

Consul General
Mr. Yun Xiang WANG
Deputy Consul General
Mr. Xue Jun QIU
Deputy Consul General
Mrs. Chun Yan TIAN
Consul
Mr. Fei GUO
Consul
Mr. Xiao Min WU
Consul

Source: US Department of State. www.state.gov

Ms. Xiao Ru MA
Consul
Mr. Yu Xi WANG
Consul
Mr. Qi Yao WANG
Consul
Mr. Lei HONG
Consul
Ms. Jin Hua XIN
Consul
Mr. Mian Shuo WANG
Consul
Mr. Xiu Sheng YAN
Consul
Mr. Jun HE
Consul
Ms. Xu LU
Consul
Mr. Jun WEN
Consul
Mr. Ling TIAN
Consul
Mr. Yue CHEN
Consul
Mr. Wei Wei ZHANG
Consul
Mr. Zhongnan WANG
Consul
Mr. Yong Pu WANG
Consul
Mr. Zeng Bo GAO

CONSULAR AFFAIRS
Washington (CON)
2300 Connecticut Ave. NW
Washington, DC 20008
Tel: (202) 328-2518

Consul
Mr. Si Ning LI

DISTRICT OF COLUMBIA
Washington (EMB)
2300 Connecticut Ave. NW
Washington, DC 20008
Tel: (202) 328-2500 Fax: (202) 328-2582

Consul General
Mr. Rui You LI
Deputy Consul General
Ms. Jian Qing ZHANG
Consul
Ms. Ling SHI
Consul
Mr. Yi Gong WANG
Consul
Ms. Jian Ping LUO

EDUCATION OFFICE
Chicago (EDC)
3322 W. Peterson Ave.
Chicago, IL 60659

Consul
Dr. Bo JIANG
Consul
Mr. Jia Cai CHENG
Consul
Mr. Yu Hua TANG
Consul
Mr. Hong Qing ZHU
Consul
Ms. Cui Ying XU
Consul
Mr. Zhi Gang ZHANG
Vice Consul
Mrs. Qiao Mei HE

ILLINOIS
Chicago (CG)

100 W. Erie St.
Chicago, IL 60610
Tel: (312) 803-0095 Fax: (312) 803-0105
Web: www.chinaconsulatechicago.org

Consul General
Mr. Jin Zhong XU
Deputy Consul General
Mr. Ying TANG
Vice Consul
Ms. Zhiyuan JI
Consul
Mr. Heqing ZHANG
Consul
Mr. Sai Po ZHOU
Vice Consul
Mr. Xiaoce YAN
Consul
Mr. Ren Liang WANG
Consul
Mr. Jun LIU
Consul
Mr. Zhi Min CAO
Consul
Mr. Zhen Cai WEN
Consul
Mr. De You TIAN
Consul
Mr. Huixun ZHANG
Consul
Mr. YI ZHAO
Consul
Mr. Gang LIANG
Consul
Mr. De Cun ZHAN
Consul
Ms. Hong ZHU
Consul
Mr. Xiao Dong FAN
Consul
Mr. Xin Jie LI
Consul
Mr. Hongzheng PAN
Vice Consul
Mr. Bin XUN
Vice Consul
Mr. Weija WANG**NEW YORK**
New York (CG)
520 12th Ave.
New York, NY 10036
Tel: (212) 244-9456 X9001
Fax: (212) 279-4275

Consul General
Mr. Bi Wei LIU
Deputy Consul General
Mr. Sheng Wu QU
Deputy Consul General
Mrs. Wang XiA CHEN
Deputy Consul General
Mr. Hui Kang HUANG
Consul
Mr. Er Jun LIANG
Consul
Mr. Hui Chun SUN
Consul
Mr. Kang Lin YU
Consul
Mr. Xiong Feng CHEN
Consul
Mr. Li Bin SHEN
Consul
Mr. Yue Cheng LI
Consul
Ms. Jun CHEN
Consul
Mr. Zhi LIN
Consul
Mrs. Jing Bo LIU
Consul

Ms. Gui Zhi TANG
Consul
Ms. Jin Lan SHI
Consul
Ms. Kang LI
Consul
Mr. Yue Jin SONG
Consul
Mr. Hong Shan GAO
Consul
Ms. Jian Dong SHI
Consul
Mr. Xiao Hua ZENG
Consul
Mr. Shu Jing SUN

TEXAS
Houston (CG)
3417 Montrose Blvd. #700
Houston, TX 77006

Consul General
Mr. Yeshun HU
Deputy Consul General
Mr. Bi GANG
Consul
Mr. Yuan Quan LI
Consul
Mr. Xiao Ping MI
Consul
Mr. Lin Ying MA
Consul
Mr. Jian Guang LU
Consul
Mr. Jia Hai XU
Consul
Mr. Yan Sheng MA
Consul
Mr. Zhuo Fan YANG
Consul
Mr. Chen Qi YANG
Consul
Ms. Fu Ling YANG
Consul
Ms. Liru YAN
Consul
Mr. Jian Ping CHEN
Consul
Mr. Jian Lei SHEN
Consul
Mr. Xi Yan YANG
Consul
Mr. Yanzhou LI
Consul
Mr. Hai Sheng ZHAO
Consul
Mr. Kuang XU
Vice Consul
Mr. Chang Qing KE
Vice Consul
Mr. Jian Bin LI
Vice Consul
Mr. Zhen Shan WANG

CYPRUS

ARIZONA
Phoenix (HC)
1277 E. Missouri
Phoenix, AZ 85014
Tel: (602) 264-9701

Honorary Consul
Mr. Stanley J. DRU

CALIFORNIA
Los Angeles (HCG)
4219 Coolidge Ave.

Los Angeles, CA 90066
Tel: (310) 397-0771

Honorary Consul General
Mr. Andreas C. KYPRIANIDES

CALIFORNIA
San Francisco (HC)
75 Silverwood Dr.
Lafayette, CA 94549
Tel: (925) 284-1060

Honorary Consul
Mr. Nicolaos Costas THEOPHANOUS

DISTRICT OF COLUMBIA
Washington (EMB)
2211 R St. NW
Washington, DC 20008
Tel: (202) 462-5772 Fax: (202) 483-6710

Consul
Mr. Andreas NICOLAIDES

FLORIDA
Jacksonville (HC)
112 Paddock Pl.
Ponte Vedra Beach, FL 32082
Tel: (904) 953-2802

GEORGIA
Atlanta (HC)
895 Somerset Dr.
Atlanta, GA 30327
Tel: (770) 941-3764

Honorary Consul
Mr. Kyriakos M. MICHAELIDES

ILLINOIS
Chicago (HC)
1875 Dempster St. #555
Park Ridge, IL 60068
Tel: (847) 698-5500 Fax: (847) 685-1182

Honorary Consul
Dr. Charles KANAKIS, Jr.

LOUISIANA
New Orleans (HC)
2 Canal St. #2146
New Orleans, LA 70130
Tel: (504) 568-9300

Honorary Consul
Mr. Thomas MANTIS

MASSACHUSETTS
Boston (HC)
70-7 Kirkland St.
Cambridge, MA 02138
Tel: (617) 497-0219

Honorary Consul
Mr. John C. PAPAJOHN

MICHIGAN
Detroit (HC)
15706 Michigan Ave.
Dearborn, MI 48126
Tel: (313) 582-1411

Honorary Consul
Mr. Steve G. STYLIANOU

NEW YORK
Maritime Office (CG)
13 E. 40th St., 5th Fl.
New York, NY 10016
Tel: (212) 447-1790

NEW YORK
New York (CG)
13 E. 40th St.
New York, NY 10016
Tel: (212) 686-6016

Consul General
Mrs. Martha A. MAVROMMATIS
Consul
Mr. Cleanthis ORPHANOS

NEW YORK
Tourist Office (CON)
13 E. 40th St.
New York, NY 10016
Tel: (212) 683-5280

NORTH CAROLINA
Jacksonville (HC)
412 Country Club Dr.
Jacksonville, NC 28546
Tel: (910) 353-4970 Fax: (910) 353-0126

Honorary Consul
Dr. Takey CRIST

OREGON
Portland (HC)
1130 Morrison St. SW #510
Portland, OR 97205
Tel: (503) 227-1411

Honorary Consul
Mr. Alexander CHRISTY

PENNSYLVANIA
Philadelphia (HC)
7714 Langdon St.
Philadelphia, PA 19111
Tel: (215) 728-6980

Honorary Consul
Mr. James ORATIS

TEXAS
Houston (HCG)
1128 River Glen Dr.
Houston, TX 77063
Tel: (713) 465-2091

Honorary Consul General
Mr. William C. CRASSAS

VIRGINIA
Virginia Beach (HC)
2973 Shore Dr. #102
Virginia Beach, VA 23451-1248
Tel: (757) 481-3583

Honorary Consul
Mr. Thomas C. KYRUS

WASHINGTON
Seattle (HC)
5555 Lakeview Dr. #200
Kirkland, WA 98033
Tel: (425) 827-1700 Fax: (425) 889-0308

Honorary Consul
Mr. Vassos Michael DEMETRIOU

INDIA

CALIFORNIA
San Francisco (CG)
540 Arguello Blvd.
San Francisco, CA 94118
Tel: (415) 668-0662 Fax: (415) 668-9764

Consul General
Mr. B.S. PRAKASH
Consul
Mr. Soumen BAGCHI
Consul
Mr. Vijay KUMAR
Consul
Mr. Prabhat K. SINGH
Vice Consul
Mr. Machingal VIJAYAN

GEORGIA
Atlanta (HC)
1201 W. Peachtree St. #2000
Atlanta, GA 30309-3400
Tel: (404) 898-8172 Fax: (404) 881-0470

Honorary Consul
Mr. Kenneth Andrew CUTSHAW

HAWAII
Honolulu (HCG)
2051 Young St.
Honolulu, HI 96826
Tel: (808) 732-7692

Honorary Consul General
Mrs. Sheila H. WATUMULL

ILLINOIS
Chicago (CG)
455 N. Cityfront Plaza Dr. #850
Chicago, IL 60611
Tel: (312) 595-0405 Fax: (312) 595-0416

Consul General
Mr. Arun KUMAR
Consul
Mr. Kedar Singh GUSAIN

LOUISIANA
New Orleans (HC)
1525 Webster St.
New Orleans, LA 70118

Honorary Consul
Mr. George DENEGRE

NEW YORK
New York (CG)
3 E. 64th St.
New York, NY 10021

Consul General
Mr. Pramathesh RATH
Deputy Consul General
Mr. Ashok TOMAR
Consul
Mr. Santosh JHA
Consul
Mr. Rattan SINGH
Consul
Mr. Amarendra KHATUA
Consul
Mr. Rabindra Nath PANDA
Consul
Mr. Surinder K. NANGIA
Consul
Mr. Vinod BHANDARI
Consul
Mr. Sandeep Mohan BHATNAGAR
Vice Consul
Mr. Subhash CHANDER
Vice Consul
Mr. Sushil KUMAR
Vice Consul
Mr. Arun Kumar SHARMA

TEXAS
Houston (CG)
1990 Post Oak Blvd. #600
Houston, TX 77056
Tel: (713) 626-2148 Fax: (713) 626-2450

Consul General
Mr. S.M. GAVAI
Deputy Consul General
Mr. K.P. PILLAI
Vice Consul
Mr. Vijay Kumar MEHTA
Vice Consul
Mr. Shri Muraleedhar BABU
Vice Consul
Mr. Shri B. ASEEJA

INDONESIA

CALIFORNIA
Los Angeles (CG)
3457 Wilshire Blvd.
Los Angeles, CA 90010
Tel: (213) 383-5126

Consul General
Mr. Handriyo Kusumo PRIYO
Consul
Mr. Manginar SIMBOLON
Consul
Mr. Bambang Tarsanto SUMOSUTARGIO
Consul
Mr. Rahmat PRAMONO
Consul
Mr. Adhy SOESANTO
Consul
Mr. UCHDOR
Vice Consul
Mr. Yudi ALAMIN
Vice Consul
Mr. Prasetyo HADI
Vice Consul
Ms. Hendro Retno WULAN

CALIFORNIA
San Francisco (CG)
1111 Columbus Ave.
San Francisco, CA 94133
Tel: (415) 474-9571 Fax: (415) 441-4320

Consul
Mr. Nur Syahrir RAHARDJO
Vice Consul
Mrs. Suwartini Sukardi WIRTA
Vice Consul
Mr. Krishna Kesuma Utama HANNAN
Vice Consul
Mr. Nelson SIMORANGKIR
Vice Consul
Ms. Dwi Ayu ARIMAMI

HAWAII
Honolulu (HC)
1001 Bishop St. #2970
Honolulu, HI 96813
Tel: (808) 531-3017

Honorary Consul
Mr. Patrick Kevin SULLIVAN

ILLINOIS
Chicago (CG)
540 N. Laselle
Chicago, IL 60610
Tel: (312) 595-1777 Fax: (312) 595-9952

Consul General
Vacant
Consul
Mr. Hidayat HAIMADJA
Consul
Mrs. Enda Ng IRAWAN
Consul
Mr. Yudho SASONGKO
Vice Consul
Mrs. Nunung Nurwulan WIBOWO

NEW YORK
New York (CG)
5 E. 68th St.
New York, NY 10021
Tel: (212) 879-0600

Acting Consul General
Mr. Harbang NAPITUPULU
Consul
Mr. Eek SLAMET
Consul
Mr. AYERFAS
Vice Consul
Mrs. Sahadatun DONATIRIN
Vice Consul
Mr. Yohpy Ichsan WARDANA

TEXAS
Houston (CG)
10900 Richmond Ave.
Houston, TX 77042
Tel: (713) 785-1691 Fax: (713) 780-9644

Consul General
Mr. Benny Permadi SURYAWINATA
Consul
Mr. Abdul Rachman DUDUNG
Consul
Mr. Basyiruddin Ahmad HIDAYAT
Vice Consul
Mr. Lingga SETIAWAN

TRADE PROMOTION CENTER OF INDONESIA
New York (CON)
1328 Broadway Ave. #510
New York, NY 10001

ISRAEL

CALIFORNIA
Economic Mission of Israel San Francisco (CON)
456 Montgomery St. #2100
San Francisco, CA 94104
Tel: (415) 844-7509 Fax: (415) 844-7555

Consul
Mr. Tzach SEGAL

CALIFORNIA
Los Angeles (CG)
6380 Wilshire Blvd. #1700
Los Angeles, CA 90048
Tel: (323) 852-5500 Fax: (323) 852-5555
Email: admin@losangeles.mfa.gov.il

Consul General
Mr. Yuval ROTEM
Consul
Mr. Yehoshua AVIGDOR
Consul
Mr. Zvi Aviner VAPNI
Consul
Mr. Nathan ABRAHAMI
Consul
Ms. Rachel NIR
Consul
Mr. Avraham Eliezer RUSEK
Vice Consul
Mr. Yuval GEFEN
Vice Consul
Mr. Yariv OVADIA
Vice Consul
Mr. Snir VARSAVYAK
Vice Consul
Mr. Moshe Miki BIZAOUI

**DEFENSE PROCUREMENT MISSION OF
NEW YORK (CON)**
800 2nd Ave., 10-12th Fls.
New York, NY 10017
Tel: (212) 551-0444 Fax: (212) 551-0482

Consul
Mr. Yekutiel MOR
Vice Consul
Mr. Yossef NATAN
Vice Consul
Mr. Erez Ben DOV
Vice Consul
Mr. Meir ARBER
Vice Consul
Mr. Shaul AHARON
Vice Consul
Mr. Amos KEDAR
Vice Consul
Mr. Arie Ben ARI
Vice Consul
Mr. Dani SHACHAR
Vice Consul
Mr. Erez EINAV
Vice Consul
Mr. Eytan Kedar COSTO
Vice Consul
Mr. Ronen ZAGORSKY
Vice Consul
Mr. Jakob MEIR
Vice Consul
Mr. Offer Alfred RONEN
Vice Consul
Mr. Pini HALFON
Vice Consul
Mr. Albert GODELMAN
Vice Consul
Mr. Avner Haim DVASH
Vice Consul
Mr. Haim GANZER
Vice Consul
Mr. Judah Shasha COHEN
Vice Consul
Mr. Michael ARWAS
Vice Consul
Mr. Ouri GOEL
Vice Consul
Mr. Yosef DAYAN

DISTRICT OF COLUMBIA
Washington (EMB)
3514 International Dr. NW
Washington, DC 20008
Tel: (202) 364-5500 Fax: (202) 364-5607

Consul General
Mr. Moshe FOX
Consul
Ms. Aliza EZRA

ECONOMIC MISSION OF ATLANTA (CON)
1100 Spring St. #440
Atlanta, GA 30309-2823
Tel: (404) 487-6500 Fax: (404) 487-6555

**ECONOMIC MISSION OF LOS ANGELES
(ECN)**
6380 Wilshire Blvd. #1700
Los Angeles, CA 90048
Tel: (323) 658-7924 Fax: (323) 651-0572

Consul
Mr. Shai AIZIN

ECONOMIC MISSION OF NEW YORK (CON)
800 2nd Ave., 17th Fl.
New York, NY 10017
Tel: (212) 499-5716 Fax: (212) 499-5715

Consul
Mr. Zvi CHALAMISH
Consul
Mr. Yarden YOFFE
Consul
Mr. Zohar PERI

FLORIDA
Miami (CG)
100 N. Biscayne Blvd. #1800
Miami, FL 33132

Consul General
Mr. Michael ARBEL
Consul
Mr. Mattanya COHEN
Consul
Mr. Shmuel MICHA
Vice Consul
Mr. Tomer Israel SADE

GEORGIA
Atlanta (CG)
1100 Spring St. NW #440
Atlanta, GA 30309
Tel: (404) 487-6500 Fax: (404) 487-6555

Consul General
Mr. Shmuel Ben SHMUEL
Vice Consul
Mr. Aviv EZRA
Vice Consul
Mr. Sagiv OFRI

ILLINOIS
Chicago (CG)
111 E. Wacker Dr., 13th Fl.
Chicago, IL 60601
Tel: (312) 297-4800 Fax: (312) 297-4855

Consul General
Mr. Barukh BINAH
Deputy Consul General
Mr. Andy DAVID
Consul
Mr. Eliahu LEVY
Vice Consul
Mr. Avishai ROZNER

ILLINOIS
Economic Mission of Israel (CON)
55 E. Monroe St. #2020
Chicago, IL 60603
Tel: (312) 332-2160 Fax: (312) 332-2163

Consul
Mr. Moshe Zeev SHOHAM

MASSACHUSETTS
Boston (CG)
20 Park Plz. #1020
Boston, MA 02116
Tel: (617) 535-0200 Fax: (617) 535-0255

Consul General
Mr. Meir SHLOMO
Consul
Mr. Hillel NEWMAN
Consul
Mr. Joseph ABRAHAM
Vice Consul
Mr. Oren POLEG
Vice Consul
Mr. Ron LAVI

NEW YORK
New York (CG)
800 2nd Ave., 13th, 14th, 15th Fls.

New York, NY 10017
Tel: (212) 499-5477 Fax: (212) 499-5455

Consul General
Mr. Alon PINKAS
Consul
Mr. Yigal TZARFATI
Consul
Mr. Ido AHARONI
Consul
Ms. Simona FRANKEL
Consul
Ms. Ofra Ben YAACOV
Consul
Mr. Amir Shmuel OFEK
Vice Consul
Mr. Shmuel Sharon RAVE
Vice Consul
Mr. Yoel PRESMAN
Vice Consul
Mr. Yosef WURMBRAND
Vice Consul
Mr. Addy SANDLER
Vice Consul
Mr. Addy SANDLER
Vice Consul
Mr. Amihai Ben HORIN
Vice Consul
Mr. Israel GORODISTIAN
Vice Consul
Mr. Yaron SCHNABEL
Vice Consul
Mr. Gali SNIR
Vice Consul
Mr. Danny ZALEWSKI
Vice Consul
Mr. Gal WAINTROB
Vice Consul
Mr. Nir OHAYON
Vice Consul
Mr. Tsoock Simon HAZIZA

OFFICE OF TOURISM MISSION OF ISRAEL
New York (CON)
800 2nd Ave., 16th Fl.
New York, NY 10017
Tel: (212) 499-5660 Fax: (212) 499-5665

Consul
Mr. Arie SOMMER
Vice Consul
Mr. Haim Golan GUTIN

OFFICE OF TOURISM OF ISRAEL
Chicago (CON)
111 E. Wacker Dr. #1230
Chicago, IL 60601
Tel: (312) 938-3885 Fax: (312) 938-3668

PENNSYLVANIA
Philadelphia (CG)
230 S. 15th St., 8th Fl.
Philadelphia, PA 19102
Tel: (215) 546-5556 Fax: (215) 545-3986

Consul General
Mr. Uriel PALTI
Vice Consul
Mr. Amit COHEN
Vice Consul
Mr. Shachar SHELES
Vice Consul
Mr. Nissan LEVY

TEXAS
Houston (CG)
24 Greenway Plz. #1500
Houston, TX 77046
Tel: (713) 627-3780 Fax: (713) 627-0149

Consul General
Vice Consul
Mr. Leonid KALMANOVICH
Vice Consul
Mr. Belaynesh Zevadia-ADIGEH
Vice Consul
Mr. Nir GREENBERG

TOURIST OFFICE OF ISRAEL
Atlanta (CON)
1100 Spring St. #440
Atlanta, GA 30309-2823
Tel: (404) 487-6500 Fax: (404) 487-6555

JAPAN

ALABAMA
Birmingham (HCG)
80 Bulldog Cir.
Cropwell, AL 35054
Tel: (205) 879-5004 Fax: (205) 252-4417

Honorary Consul General
Mr. Elmer B. HARRIS

ALASKA
Anchorage (CG)
3601 C St. #1300
Anchorage, AK 99503-5925
Tel: (907) 562-8424 Fax: (907) 562-8434

Consul General
Mr. Akihiro AOKI
Consul
Mr. Shuji INOUE
Consul
Mr. Takashi YAMAMOTO
Vice Consul
Mr. Satoshi TOYAMA

ARIZONA
Phoenix (HCG)
4635 S. Lakeshore Dr.
Tempe, AZ 85282
Tel: (480) 241-8245 Fax: (480) 345-4526

Honorary Consul General
Mr. Kelly MOEUR

CALIFORNIA
Los Angeles (CG)
350 S. Grand Ave. #1700
Los Angeles, CA 90071
Tel: (213) 617-6700 Fax: (213) 617-6727
Web: www.la.us.emb-japan.go.jp

Consul General
Mr. Yoshio NOMOTO
Deputy Consul General
Mr. Masahiro KOHARA
Consul
Mr. Masaru DEKIBA
Consul
Mr. Yoshiyuki ISODA
Consul
Mrs. Yuko KAIFU
Consul
Mr. Tomohide TOYAMA
Consul
Mr. Yoshiki NAKAMATA
Consul
Mr. Takeshi MATSUMOTO
Consul

Mr. Yasuhiko KAMADA
Consul
Mr. Nozomu KIKUCHI
Consul
Mr. Toshinori MATSUSHIO
Vice Consul
Mr. Norihisa SUCHIRO
Vice Consul
Mr. Tomonori MINOWA
Vice Consul
Mr. Shinichi YAMAMOTO
Vice Consul
Ms. Yurika ARINO
Vice Consul
Ms. Mieko ISHIMARU
Vice Consul
Mr. Yosuke KOMATSU
Vice Consul
Mr. Keiichi ICHIKAWA

CALIFORNIA
San Diego (HCG)
10455 Pomerado Rd.
San Diego, CA 92131
Tel: (619) 635-4537

San Francisco (CG)
50 Fremont St., 23rd Fl.
San Francisco, CA 94105
Tel: (415) 777-3533 Fax: (415) 974-3660

Consul General
Mr. Shigeru NAKAMURA

COLORADO
Denver (CG)
1225 17th St. #3000
Denver, CO 80202
Tel: (303) 534-1151 Fax: (303) 534-3393

Consul General
Mr. Yuzo OTA
Deputy Consul General
Mr. Kenichi KIMIYA
Consul
Mr. Kenjiro MORI
Consul
Mr. Haruo YAMAGAMI
Consul
Mr. Tatsuya FURUKAWA
Vice Consul
Ms. S. Yasuyo KOMINE

CONNECTICUT
Avon (HCG)
175 Century Dr.
Bristol, CT 06010
Tel: (860) 583-9100 Fax: (860) 583-9111

Honorary Consul General
Mr. Louis AULETTA, Sr.

DISTRICT OF COLUMBIA
Washington (EMB)
2520 Massachusetts Ave. NW
Washington, DC 20008
Tel: (202) 238-6700 Fax: (202) 328-2187

Consul
Mr. Toshiaki IGARASHI
Vice Consul
Mr. Yasutoshi TANIMOTO

FLORIDA
Miami (CG)
80 SW 8th St. #3200
Miami, FL 33130
Tel: (305) 530-9090 Fax: (305) 530-0950
Email: cgjfl@cofs.net

Consul General
Mr. TOSHIKAGE
Consul
Mr. Masani OHNO
Consul
Mr. Noriyasu SHUDO
Consul
Mr. Hitoshi KOGA
Consul
Mr. Takayuki KOIKE
Vice Consul
Mr. Suguru YAMANOUE
Vice Consul
Mr. Yoshinori ASANO
Vice Consul
Ms. Reiko KITATOCHI

GEORGIA
Atlanta (CG)
1 Alliance Ctr., 3500 Lenox Rd. #1600
Atlanta, GA 30326
Tel: (404) 240-4300 Fax: (404) 240-4311

Consul General
Mr. Shoji OGAWA
Deputy Consul General
Mr. Takeshi ISHII
Consul
Mr. Yoshihiro TSUJIMOTO
Consul
Ms. Michiyo TAKEMOTO
Vice Consul
Mr. Yoshihi ko MACHIDA
Vice Consul
Mr. Yosuke SAKATANI
Consul
Mr. Yoshimitsu TAMURA
Consul
Mr. Shinichi FUJIMARA
Vice Consul
Mr. Toshinori MATSUDA

GUAM
Agana (CG)
590 S. Marine Dr. #604
Tamuning, Guam 96911

Consul General
Mr. Kennosuke IRIYAMA
Consul
Mr. Toshiyuki HARA
Consul
Mr. Akinori TAKEMORI
Vice Consul
Mr. Yumi KANETAKA
Vice Consul
Mr. Yuichi HIRAO
Vice Consul
Mr. Kazutaka KOMATSU

HAWAII
Honolulu (CG)
1742 Nuuanu Ave.
Honolulu, HI 96817
Tel: (808) 543-3111 Fax: (808) 543-3170

Acting Consul General
Mr. Makoto HINEI
Consul
Mr. Hayasaka Toyonori
Consul
Mr. Iwao KOYAMA
Consul
Ms. Hiroko TANIGUCHI
Consul
Mr. Takashi HATORI
Consul
Mr. Hitoshi TSUNODA
Consul
Mr. Makoto HINEI

Consul
Mr. Kazuhiro HIDA
Consul
Mr. Hironori MAEDA
Vice Consul
Mr. Hiromichi ONODA
Vice Consul
Ms. Miyako KAYAMORI

HAWAII
Honolulu (HCG)
1104 Ainko Ave.
Hilo, HI 96720
Tel: (808) 935-5477

Honorary Consul General
Mr. Tommy HIRANO

ILLINOIS
Chicago (CG)
737 N. Michigan Ave. #1100
Chicago, IL 60611
Tel: (312) 280-0400 Fax: (312) 280-9568

Consul General
Mr. Yutaka YOSHIZAWA
Deputy Consul General
Mr. Hachiro ISHIDA
Consul
Mr. Masaru IGAWAHARA
Consul
Ms. Hiroko MATSUO
Consul
Mr. Masaru HATTORI
Consul
Mr. Masahito SAITO
Consul
Mr. Keiichi SUGITA
Consul
Mr. Satoru HAMAGUCHI
Vice Consul
Mr. Massaki KAWAHARA
Vice Consul
Mr. Akihito KOBAYASHI
Vice Consul
Ms. Junko TAMAKI
Vice Consul
Mr. Ryusuke SHIMADA

INDIANA
Indianapolis (HCG)
11 S. Meridian St.
Indianapolis, IN 46204
Tel: (317) 231-7227

Honorary Consul General
Mr. Robert Hugh REYNOLDS

JAPAN INFORMATION CENTER OF JAPAN
Chicago (CON)
737 N. Michigan Ave. #1000
Chicago, IL 60611
Tel: (312) 280-0430

KENTUCKY
Lexington (HCG)
400 E. College St.
Georgetown, KY 40324
Tel: (859) 258-3139 Fax: (859) 233-0658

Honorary Consul General
Mrs. Martha Layne COLLINS

LOUISIANA
New Orleans (CG)
639 Loyola Ave. #2050
New Orleans, LA 70113
Tel: (504) 529-2101 Fax: (504) 836-7411

Consul General
Mr. Masaru SAKATO
Consul
Mr. Shigeki MAKANAE
Consul
Mr. Tsuneyoshi HIGASHI
Consul
Mr. Kenji INOUE
Vice Consul
Ms. Ritsu SATO
Vice Consul
Mr. Koco KOJIMA
Vice Consul
Ms. Saori NAGASE
Vice Consul
Mr. Hironori NAKASHIMA
Vice Consul
Miss Yukiko OKAYASU

MASSACHUSETTS
Boston (CG)
600 Atlantic Ave., 14th Fl.
Boston, MA 02210
Tel: (617) 973-9772 Fax: (617) 542-1329

Consul General
Mr. Masuo NISHIBAYASHI
Deputy Consul General
Mr. Yoshimasa IWATA
Consul
Mr. Takahiko WATABE
Consul
Mr. Masaki KAWAGUCHI
Consul
Mr. Tetsuo OKUBO
Vice Consul
Ms. Tomoko AKASHI
Vice Consul
Mr. Kazuhito OMIYA
Vice Consul
Mr. Shoji HIRANO
Vice Consul
Mr. Takuya NAKANE
Vice Consul
Mr. Kazuhiro YANAGAWA
Vice Consul
Mr. Takuya KODERA

MICHIGAN
Detroit (CG)
400 Renaissance Ctr. #1600
Detroit, MI 48243
Tel: (313) 567-0120 Fax: (313) 567-7086

Consul General
Mr. Yoshiyuki SADAOKA
Deputy Consul General
Mr. Keiji MIURA
Consul
Mr. Toshikazu KOBAYASHI
Consul
Mr. Takahiro OMORI
Vice Consul
Mr. Yuji KONOSHIMA
Vice Consul
Ms. Sayaka MARUYAMA
Vice Consul
Mr. Tainosuke MATSUMURA

MINNESOTA
Minneapolis (HCG)
16 Woodland Rd.
Minneapolis, MN 55424
Tel: (952) 925-3807

Honorary Consul General
Mr. William R. STRANG

MISSOURI
St. Louis (HCG)
46 Briarcliff St.
St. Louis, MO 63124
Tel: (314) 994-1133 Fax: (314) 994-1133

Honorary Consul General
Mr. Bruce S. BUCKLAND

NEBRASKA
Omaha (HCG)
412 N. 85th St.
Omaha, NE 68114
Tel: (402) 399-0928 Fax: (402) 399-1796

Honorary Consul General
Dr. Ronald W. ROSKENS

NEW YORK
Buffalo (HCG)
45 Tudor Pl.
Buffalo, NY 14222
Tel: (716) 868-7899

Honorary Consul General
Mr. P. Joseph KOESSLER
New York (CG)
299 Park Ave., 18-19th Fls.
New York, NY 10171
Tel: (212) 371-8222 Fax: (212) 319-6357

Consul General
Mr. Hiroyasu ANDO
Consul
Mr. Mitsuo KAWAGUCHI
Consul
Ms. Midori TAKEUCHI
Consul
Mr. Hiroki KIMURA
Consul
Mr. Jun KOHNO
Consul
Mr. Akihiko ISHIMOTO
Consul
Mr. Ikuyo TAKAHATA
Consul
Mr. Satoshi WAKUYA
Consul
Mr. Kazuhiko KOSHIKAWA
Consul
Mr. Katsumi FUNAYAMA
Consul
Mr. Masahiro FUKUKAWA
Consul
Mr. Shuji YAMASHITA
Consul
Mr. Akira HAYASHI
Consul
Mr. Hideo MATSUBARA
Consul
Mr. Takato FURUTACHI
Consul
Mr. Masaaki TANINO
Consul
Mr. Futoshi HOSHINA
Consul
Mr. Ryoichi OIKE
Consul
Mr. Takashi NAKAYAMA
Consul
Mr. Takashi OSADA
Consul
Mr. Takashi NAKAMARU

NORTH CAROLINA
High Point (HCG)
305 W. High St. #416
High Point, NC 27260
Tel: (336) 883-0392 Fax: (336) 883-0392

Honorary Consul General
Mr. O. William FENN, Jr.

OHIO
Columbus (HCG)
1712 Neil Ave. #325
Columbus, OH 43210

OKLAHOMA
Oklahoma City (HCG)
906 W. Timberdell Rd.
Norman, OK 73072
Tel: (405) 321-3602 Fax: (405) 321-5800

Honorary Consul General
Dr. Yoshi K. SASAKI

OREGON
Portland (CG)
1300 SW 5th Ave. #2700
Portland, OR 97201
Tel: (503) 221-1811

Consul General
Mr. Akio EIGAWA
Senior Consul
Mr. Shigenobu KOBAYASHI
Consul
Mr. Takeshi MORISHITA
Consul
Mr. Hideki MAKINO
Consul
Mr. Yayoi KANEKO
Vice Consul
Mr. Yuko SATO
Vice Consul
Mr. Hideo YAMAMURA
Vice Consul
Mr. Yu TAMURA

PENNSYLVANIA
Philadelphia (HCG)
1701 Market St.
Philadelphia, PA 19103
Tel: (215) 963-5513

Honorary Consul General
Mr. Dennis J. MORIKAWA

PUERTO RICO
San Juan (HCG)
530 Constitution Ave.
San Juan, PR 00901-2304
Tel: (787) 289-8725 Fax: (787) 289-8726

Honorary Consul General
Mr. Manuel MORALES, JR.

TENNESSEE
Nashville (HCG)
3401 West End Bldg. #300
Nashville, TN 37203
Tel: (615) 292-8787

Honorary Consul General
Mr. Edward G. NELSON

TEXAS
Houston (CG)
1000 Louisiana St. #2300
Houston, TX 77002
Tel: (713) 652-2977 Fax: (713) 651-7822

Consul General
Mr. Yoshi KAMO
Consul
Ms. Mika SATO
Consul
Mr. Kunio NAKAMURA
Consul
Mr. Hirosiya NOMURA
Consul
Mr. Shinichi KURITA
Vice Consul

Mr. Hirokazo SAYASHI
Vice Consul
Mr. Aki SHAIMAIDA
Vice Consul
Mr. Naoto YAMAURA
Vice Consul
Mr. Takashi MISHIMA

WASHINGTON
Seattle (CG)
601 Union St. #500
Seattle, WA 98101
Tel: (206) 682-9107 Fax: (206) 624-9097

Consul General
Mr. Kazuo TANAKA
Consul
Mr. Kiyoshi FURUOYA
Consul
Mr. Ayumu KITAZAWA
Consul
Mr. Koichi SANO
Consul
Mr. Yoshiyuki KIMURA
Consul
Mr. Katsutoshi TAKEDA
Consul
Mr. Masakazu OHASHI
Consul
Mr. Junji MATSUMOTO
Vice Consul
Mr. Noriyasu YOSHINAKA
Vice Consul
Ms. Tomoko HASUIKE
Vice Consul
Mr. Minoru ISHII

WYOMING
Casper (HCG)
111 W. 14th St.
Casper, WY 82601
Tel: (307) 234-2317

Honorary Consul General
Mrs. Mariko T. MILLER

JORDAN

CALIFORNIA
San Francisco (HC)
972 Mission St., 4th Fl.
San Francisco, CA 94103
Tel: (415) 546-1111

Honorary Consul
Mr. Kamel J. AYOUB

ILLINOIS
Chicago (HCG)
12559 S. Holiday Dr.
Alsip, IL 60803
Tel: (708) 272-6665

Honorary Consul General
Mr. Ihsan G. SWEISS

MICHIGAN
Detroit (HC)
28551 Southfield Rd. #203
Lathrup, MI 48076

Honorary Consul
Mr. Habib I. FAKHOURI

TEXAS
Houston (HCG)

P.O. Box 3727
Houston, TX 77253
Tel: (713) 224-2911

Honorary Consul General
Mr. Sabir Muhammad AMAWI

KAZAKHSTAN

NEW YORK
New York (CON)
866 United Nations Plz. #586A
New York, NY 10017
Tel: (212) 888-3024 Fax: (212) 888-3025

Consul General
Mr. Raushan YESBULAGOVA

KOREA, SOUTH

ALASKA
Anchorage (HCG)
1127 W. 7th Ave.
Anchorage, AK 99501
Tel: (907) 263-7225

Honorary Consul General
Mr. William H. BITTNER

CALIFORNIA
Cultural Center of Korea Los Angeles (CON)
5505 Wilshire Blvd.
Los Angeles, CA 90036
Tel: (323) 936-7141 Fax: (323) 936-5712

Consul
Mr. Soon Tae PARK

Los Angeles (CG)
3243 Wilshire Blvd.
Los Angeles, CA 90010
Tel: (213) 385-9300 Fax: (213) 385-1849

Consul General
Mr. Lee Youn-BOK
Deputy Consul General
Mr. Byong Man CHUNG
Deputy Consul General
Mr. Jeong Gwan LEE
Consul
Mr. Chong Seok LEE
Consul
Mrs. Soon Dong KIM
Consul
Mr. Jung Soo KIM
Consul
Mr. Min RYU
Consul
Mr. Sung Kong KANG
Consul
Mr. Won Ik LEE
Consul
Mr. Hong Kee SHON
Consul
Mr. Sung Yeon KIM
Consul
Mr. Yong KIM
Consul
Mr. Young Yong LEE
Consul
Mrs. Young Ran Choi YANG
Consul
Mr. Dong Sook LEE
Consul
Mr. Dong Ho OH
Consul
Mr. Young Jae JUN

Consul
Mr. Man Ho KIM
Consul
Mr. Bong Woo KO
Consul
Mr. Jong Yul LEE
Consul
Mr. Sung Ho LEE

CALIFORNIA
San Francisco (CG)
3500 Clay St.
San Francisco, CA 94118
Tel: (415) 921-2251 Fax: (415) 921-5946

Consul General
Mr. Jong Hoon KIM
Deputy Consul General
Mr. Byung Jae CHO
Consul
Mr. Tae Won LEE
Consul
Mr. Jun Youl TAE
Consul
Mr. In Ki LEE
Consul
Mrs. Eun Ji SEO
Consul
Mr. Yeong Han CHOI
Consul
Mr. Jin Hyung KIM
Consul
Mr. Heon Kyu LEE
Consul
Mr. Kang Choo PARK

DISTRICT OF COLUMBIA
Washington (EMB)
2450 Massachusetts Ave. NW
Washington, DC 20008
Tel: (202) 939-5600 Fax: (202) 387-0250

Consul General
Mr. Byung Koo CHOI

FLORIDA
Miami (HCG)
1 SE 3rd Ave., 27th Fl.
Miami, FL 33131
Tel: (305) 982-5690 Fax: (305) 374-5095

Honorary Consul General
Mr. Burton A. LANDY

GEORGIA
Atlanta (CG)
229 Peachtree St. #500
Atlanta, GA 30303
Tel: (404) 522-1611 Fax: (404) 521-3169

Consul General
Mr. Kwang-Jae LEE

GUAM
Agana (C)
125C Tun Jose Camacho St. Tamuning
Tamuning, Guam 96911
Tel: (671) 647-6488 Fax: (671) 649-1336

Consul
Mr. Byung Kuck JHUNG
Vice Consul
Mr. Tae Yeol KWAK

HAWAII
Honolulu (CG)
2756 Pali Hwy.
Honolulu, HI 96817
Tel: (808) 595-6109 Fax: (808) 595-3046

Consul General
Mr. Dae Hyun KANG

Deputy Consul General
Mr. Wahn Seong JEONG
Consul
Mr. Si Jung PARK
Consul
Mr. Chang Muk LIM
Consul
Mr. Kyung Ho CHOI
Consul
Mr. Chang Soo HAN

ILLINOIS
Chicago (CG)
455 N. Cityfront Plaza Dr. #2700
Chicago, IL 60611
Tel: (312) 822-9485 Fax: (312) 822-9849

Consul General
Mr. Wook KIM
Deputy Consul General
Mr. Young Suck DO

LOUISIANA
New Orleans (HCG)
321 St. Charles Ave.
New Orleans, LA 70130
Tel: (504) 524-0757 Fax: (504) 525-9464

Honorary Consul General
Mr. James Julian COLEMAN

MASSACHUSETTS
Boston (CG)
1 Gateway Ctr., 2nd Fl.
Boston, MA 02258
Tel: (617) 641-2830 Fax: (617) 641-2831

Consul General
Mr. Won Sun CHOI
Deputy Consul General
Mr. Dal Young MAENG
Deputy Consul General
Mr. Taesoojung CHOI
Consul
Mr. Han JUNG

MICHIGAN
Detroit (HC)
40400 E. Ann Arbor Rd.
Plymouth, MI 48170

Honorary Consul
Mr. Alphonse V. TABAKA

MINNESOTA
Minneapolis (HCG)
2222 Park Ave.
Minneapolis, MN 55404

Honorary Consul General
Mr. Allison R. MERCER

MONTANA
Helena (HC)
1601 N. Benton Ave.
Helena, MT 59625
Tel: (406) 447-4331

Honorary Consul
Mr. Robert Ray SWARTOUT, JR.

NEW YORK
New York (CG)
335 E. 45th St., 4th, 5th, 6th Fl.
New York, NY 10017
Tel: (646) 674-6001 Fax: (646) 674-6038

Consul General
Mr. WONILCHO

Deputy Consul General
Mr. Joon Il LEE
Deputy Consul General
Mr. Dae Wan JUN
Deputy Consul General
Mr. Seok Chin PARK
Deputy Consul General
Mr. Hyun Myung KIM
Consul
Mr. Kun Woong PARK
Consul
Mr. Kwang Il HARN
Consul
Mr. Han Jin BAE
Consul
Mr. Im Gi SU
Consul
Mr. Seong Won KIM
Consul
Mr. Doo Soon PARK
Consul
Mr. Duk Ho MOON
Consul
Mr. Joo Hyeon BAIK
Consul
Mr. Tae Hee WOO
Consul
Mr. Eung Soo HAN
Consul
Mr. Joon Soo KIM
Consul
Mr. Yang Woo PARK
Consul
Mr. Wan Joo JEON
Consul
Mr. Min JUNG
Consul
Mr. Dong Man HAN
Consul
Mr. Hi Su LEE

Passport, Visa Section & Cultural Service
New York (CON)
460 Park Ave., 6th Fl.
New York, NY 10022
Tel: (646) 674-6075

Consul
Mr. Ki Hong KIM

OKLAHOMA
Oklahoma City (HC)
1200 NW 63rd #500
Oklahoma City, OK 73116
Tel: (405) 767-3636 Fax: (405) 840-2946

Honorary Consul
Mr. John E. KIRKPATRICK

PUERTO RICO
San Juan (HCG)
255 Ponce De Leon Ave., 10th Fl.
San Juan, PR 00917
Tel: (787) 758-8888 Fax: (787) 765-4225

Honorary Consul General
Mr. Hector REICHARD

TEXAS
Dallas (HC)
13111 N. Central Expressway
Dallas, TX 75243
Tel: (214) 454-1112 Fax: (214) 454-1212

Honorary Consul
Mr. Kenneth R. MARVEL

Houston (CG)
1990 Post Oak Blvd. #1250
Houston, TX 77056

Tel: (713) 961-0186 Fax: (713) 961-3340

Consul General
Mr. Dongseok MIN
Consul
Mr. Bonyul KOU
Consul
Mr. Hae Nam KIM
Consul
Mr. Sang Ho LEE
Vice Consul
Mr. Chun Sik PARK
Vice Consul
Mr. Shin Seung KI

WASHINGTON
Seattle (CG)
2033 6th Ave. #1125
Seattle, WA 98121
Tel: (206) 441-1011 Fax: (206) 441-7912

Consul General
Mr. Jae Gouk KIM
Consul
Mr. Yong-Ho KIM
Consul
Mr. Sung Yong OH
Consul
Mr. Changboo MOON
Consul
Mr. Jehak JANG

KYRGYZSTAN

CALIFORNIA
Los Angeles (HC)
800 W. 6th St. #1600
Los Angeles, CA 90017
Tel: (213) 891-9564 Fax: (213) 891-9562

Honorary Consul
Mr. S. Chic WOLK

DISTRICT OF COLUMBIA
Washington (EMB)
1732 Wisconsin Ave. NW
Washington, DC 20007
Tel: (202) 338-5141 Fax: (202) 338-5139

Consul
Mr. Emil KAIKIEV

TEXAS
Houston (HCG)
15600 Barkers Landing Rd. 1
Houston, TX 77079
Tel: (281) 920-1841 Fax: (281) 920-1823

Honorary Consul General
Mr. Darrell D. LUTHI

LEBANON

CALIFORNIA
Los Angeles (CG)
660 S. Figueroa St. #1050
Los Angeles, CA 90017
Tel: (213) 243-0990 Fax: (213) 612-5070

Consul General
Mr. Charbel WEHBI

FLORIDA
Miami (HC)
6600 SW 57th Ave. #200
Miami, FL 33143

Tel: (305) 665-3004 Fax: (305) 666-8905

Honorary Consul
Mr. Anthony R. ABRAHAM

MICHIGAN
Detroit (CG)
3031 W. Grand Blvd. #560
Detroit, MI 48202
Tel: (313) 393-5874

Consul General
Mr. ALIAJAMI
Consul
Mr. Milad Hanna NAMMOUR

TEXAS
Houston (HC)
2400 Agusta #308
Houston, TX 77057
Tel: (713) 268-1640 Fax: (713) 268-1641
Email: mabohsali@sbcglobal.net

Honorary Consul
Mr. Amin BOHSALI

MALAYSIA

CALIFORNIA
Los Angeles (CG)
550 S. Hope St. #400
Los Angeles, CA 90071
Tel: (213) 892-1238 Fax: (213) 892-9031

Consul General
Mr. Mohd Zulkephli Mohd NOOR
Consul
Mr. Mohd Adnan Bin Haji Md SAAID
Consul
Mr. Ahmad Bin AKIM
Consul
Mrs. Tengku Ashaharina Tengku AHMAD
Vice Consul
Mrs. Roslawati Binti Abdul WAHAB
Vice Consul
Mr. Karunanithi Al RANOO
Vice Consul
Mr. Masri Zohaini Bin IDRIS

HAWAII
Honolulu (HC)
P.O. Box 3200
Honolulu, HI 96847-0001
Tel: (808) 525-7702 Fax: (808) 525-5016

Honorary Consul
Mr. Herbert E. WOLFF

NEW YORK
New York (CG)
313 E. 43rd St.
New York, NY 10017
Tel: (212) 490-2722 Fax: (212) 490-2049

Consul General
Mr. Mohamad Sadik Bin KETHERGANY
Consul
Mr. Jamaludin HUSSAIN
Consul
Mr. Ah Tong PHANG
Consul
Mrs. Nuryante Binti Mohd YAZID
Vice Consul
Mr. Mohd Fadzil Bin Mohd OTHMAN
Vice Consul
Mr. Shahrol Bin SHAHABUDIN

NEW YORK
Trade and Investment Office of Malaysia New York (CON)
313 E. 43rd St., 2nd Fl.
New York, NY 10017

Tel: (212) 682-0232 Fax: (212) 983-1987

OREGON
Portland (HC)
18697 SE Semple
Clackamas, OR 97015
Tel: (503) 658-3633 Fax: (503) 658-2210
Email: forte@pcez.com

Honorary Consul
Mr. Jay A. KILLEEN

MONGOLIA

CALIFORNIA
San Francisco (HCG)
909 Montgomery St. #400
San Francisco, CA 94133
Tel: (415) 434-1111

Honorary Consul General
Mr. Richard C. BLUM

COLORADO
Denver (HC)
1700 Broadway #1202
Denver, CO 80290-1201
Tel: (303) 832-6511

Honorary Consul
Mr. James Frederick WAGENLANDER

DISTRICT OF COLUMBIA
Washington (EMB)
2833 M St. NW
Washington, DC 20007
Tel: (202) 333-7117 Fax: (202) 298-9227

Consul General
Mr. Seseer GONCHIG
Consul
Mr. Bat-Ochir MNAVAANTAYA

NEW YORK
New York (CG)
6 E. 77th St.
New York, NY 10021

Consular Agent
Mr. Jagir SUHEE

TEXAS
Houston (HCA)
P.O. Box 328
Houston, TX 77001
Tel: (713) 759-1922

Honorary Consular Agent
Mr. Edward T. STORY, Jr.

NEPAL

CALIFORNIA
San Francisco (HCG)
909 Montgomery St. #400
San Francisco, CA 94133
Tel: (415) 434-1111

Honorary Consul General
Mr. Richard C. BLUM

ILLINOIS
Chicago (HCG)
100 W. Monroe St. #500
Chicago, IL 60603
Tel: (312) 263-1250

Honorary Consul General
Mr. Marvin A. BRUSTIN

NEW YORK
New York (CG)

820 2nd Ave. #17B
New York, NY 10017
Tel: (212) 370-4188

OHIO
Cleveland (HCG)
310 E. Market St.
Cleveland, OH 44883

Honorary Consul General
Dr. WIlliam C. CASSELL

PAKISTAN

CALIFORNIA
Los Angeles (CG)
10850 Wilshire Blvd. #1250
Los Angeles, CA 90024
Tel: (310) 441-5114 Fax: (310) 441-9256

Consul General
Mr. Noor Muhammad JADMANI
Vice Consul
Mr. Ahmad FAROOQ
Consular Agent
Mr. Muhammad BASHIR

CALIFORNIA
Sunnydale (CG)
5150 El Camino Real #A32
Los Altos, CA 94022

Trade Office (TRA)
10850 Wilshire Blvd. #1250
Los Angeles, CA 90024
Tel: (310) 474-6861 Fax: (310) 474-4871

Consul
Mr. Shahid TARAR

MAINE
Portland (HC)
19 South St.
Portland, ME 04101
Tel: (207) 253-5000 Fax: (207) 253-5560

Honorary Consul
Mr. Jacob Daniel HOFFMAN

MASSACHUSETTS
Boston (HCG)
20 Chestnut St.
Needham, MA 02492
Tel: (617) 267-9000 Fax: (617) 266-6666

Honorary Consul General
Mr. Barry D. HOFFMAN

NEW YORK
New York (CG)
12 E. 65th St.
New York, NY 10021
Tel: (212) 879-5800 Fax: (212) 517-7541

Consul General
Mr. Muhammad Haroon SHAUKAT
Consul
Mr. Muhammad ASLAM
Vice Consul
Mr. Irfan AHMED
Consular Agent
Mr. Arif RASHID

PAPUA NEW GUINEA

CALIFORNIA
Los Angeles (HCG)
1308 Banyan Dr.
Fallbrook, CA 92028
Tel: (760) 731-0436

Honorary Consul General
Mr. Charles CHEATHEM

TEXAS
Houston (HCG)
4900 Woodway Dr. #825
Houston, TX 77056
Tel: (713) 966-2500

Honorary Consul General
Mr. Nathan M. AVERY

PHILIPPINES

CALIFORNIA
Los Angeles (CG)
3600 Wilshire Blvd. #500
Los Angeles, CA 90010
Tel: (213) 639-0980 Fax: (213) 639-0990

Consul General
Mr. Marciano Aguirre PAYNOR, Jr.
Consul
Ms. Maria Hellen BARBER
Vice Consul
Mr. Gines GALLAGA
Vice Consul
Ms. Noemi DIAZ

CALIFORNIA
San Diego (C)
600 B St. #1200
San Diego, CA 92101

San Francisco (CG)
447 Sutter St., 6th Fl.
San Francisco, CA 94108
Tel: (415) 433-6666

Consul General
Ms. Rowena Mendoza SANCHEZ
Deputy Consul General
Consul
Mr. Wilfredo C. SANTOS
Vice Consul
Mr. Anthony A.L. MANDAP
Vice Consul
Mr. Rafael SC HERMOSA

COMMERCIAL OFFICE
Los Angeles (U)
3660 Wilshire Blvd. #216-218
Los Angeles, CA 90010

DISTRICT OF COLUMBIA
Washington (EMB)
1600 Massachusetts Ave. NW
Washington, DC 20036
Tel: (202) 467-9300 Fax: (202) 467-9417

Consul General
Mrs. Jocelyn Batoon GARCIA
Consul
Mr. Evan P. GARCIA
Consul
Mr. Henry S. BENSURTO
Consul
Ms. Lourdes Ortiz YPARRAGUIRRE

Consul
Ms. Patricia Ann PAEZ
Consul
Ms. Hjayceelyn Mancenido QUINTANA
Vice Consul
Mr. Enrico Trinidad FOS

GEORGIA
Atlanta (HCG)
3340 Peachtree Rd. NE #850
Atlanta, GA 30326
Tel: (404) 239-5740 Fax: (404) 233-4041

Honorary Consul General
Mr. Raoul R. DONATO

GUAM
Tamuning (CG)
20 Marine Dr. #601-602
Tamuning, GUAM 96931
Tel: (671) 646-4620 Fax: (671) 649-1868

Consul General
Mrs. Teresita Lopez MENDIOLA
Consul
Ms. Rosario P. LEMQUE
Vice Consul
Ms. Charmaine Rowena C. AVIQUIVIL

HAWAII
Honolulu (CG)
2433 Pali Hwy.
Honolulu, HI 96817
Tel: (808) 595-6316 Fax: (808) 595-2581

Acting Consul General
Mrs. Eva G. BETITA
Vice Consul
Mrs. Arlene Gonzales MACAISA

ILLINOIS
Chicago (CG)
30 N. Michigan Ave. #2100
Chicago, IL 60602
Tel: (312) 332-6458

Consul General
Mrs. Blesila C. CABRERA
Consul
Mr. Patrick John U. HILADO
Vice Consul
Mr. Roberto T. BERNARDO

LOUISIANA
New Orleans (HCG)
2144 World Trade Ctr.
New Orleans, LA 70130
Tel: (504) 529-7561 Fax: (504) 529-7562

Honorary Consul General
Ms. Cielo Tolentino MARTINEZ

NEW YORK
New York (CG)
556 5th Ave.
New York, NY 10036
Tel: (212) 764-1330

Consul General
Mrs. Cecilia Baltazar REBONG
Deputy Consul General
Mrs. Melita Sta. Maria-THOMECZEK
Consul
Mrs. Millicent Cruz PAREDES
Consul
Ms. Maria Lourdes Cruz LEGASPI
Vice Consul
Mr. Edgar Barrairo BADAJOS

SAIPAN
Trust Territories of the Pacific Islands
Mariana Islands (CG)
P.O. Box 500731CK
5th Fl. Nauru Bldg.
San Jose, Saipan 96950
Tel: (670) 234-1848 Fax: (670) 234-1849

Consul General
Mr. Wilfredo L. MAXIMO

TOURISM OFFICE
Los Angeles (U)
3660 Wilshire Blvd. #216
Los Angeles, CA 90010

QATAR

TEXAS
Houston (CG)
1990 Post Oak Blvd. #810
Houston, TX 77056
Tel: (713) 355-8221 Fax: (713) 355-8184

Consul General
Mr. Rashid ALKHATER
Vice Consul
Mr. Abdulla Jassim Al MAADADI

RUSSIA

ALASKA
Anchorage (HCG)
3581 Kachemak Cir.
Anchorage, AK 99515
Tel: (907) 349-5481

Honorary Consul General
Mr. Steve R. SMIRNOFF

CALIFORNIA
San Francisco (CG)
2790 Green St.
San Francisco, CA 94123
Tel: (415) 928-6878 Fax: (415) 929-0306

Consul General
Mr. Viktor Nikolayevich LIZUN
Deputy Consul General
Mr. Yuriy Vartanoich BEDZHANYAN
Consul
Mr. Stanislav Semenovich SMIRNOV
Consul
Mr. Vladimir Aleksandrovich NEBYVAYEV
Consul
Mr. Andrey Leonidovich PODYELYSHEV
Consul
Mr. Vladimir Alekseyevich MARKOV
Consul
Mr. Viktor Ivanovich MARTYNOV
Consul
Mr. Igor Yuryevich KOCHETKOV
Vice Consul
Mr. Aleksey Vitalyevich KARMALITO
Vice Consul
Mr. Nikolay Yuryevich LYASHCHENKO
Vice Consul
Mr. Viktor Aleksandrovich KOZLOV
Vice Consul
Mr. Sergey Viktorovich KUZNETSOV
Vice Consul
Mr. Andrey Mikhaylovich KABASHKO
Vice Consul
Mr. Sergey Anatolyevich PSHENICHNIY
Vice Consul
Mr. Pavel Nikolayevich KSENOFONTOV

DISTRICT OF COLUMBIA
Consular Division Washington (U)
2641 Tunlaw Rd. NW
Washington, DC 20007
Tel: (202) 939-8907 Fax: (202) 939-8917

Consul General
Mr. Vadim SAVELIEV
Consul
Mr. Georgiy V. KOCHETOV

Washington (EMB)
2650 Wisconsin Ave. NW
Washington, DC 20007
Tel: (202) 298-5700 Fax: (202) 298-5735

Consul
Mr. Roman Y. AMBAROV
Consul
Mr. Vladimir V. TITARENKO
Vice Consul
Mr. Andrey Y. DANILOV

HAWAII
Honolulu (HCG)
4117 Kahala Ave.
Honolulu, HI 96816
Tel: (808) 956-8007

Honorary Consul General
Ms. Natasha B. OWEN

NEW YORK
New York (CG)
9 E. 91st St.
New York, NY 10128
Tel: (212) 348-0926 Fax: (212) 831-9162

Consul General
Mr. Vyacheslava A. PAVLOVSKIY
Consul
Mr. Nikolay N. PASHCHENKO
Consul
Mr. Vyacheslavv V. SLAVKIN
Consul
Mr. Aleksandr S. GRIGORYEV
Consul
Mr. Nikolay N. LAVILIN
Consul
Mr. Yuriy Yuryevich NAUMOV
Vice Consul
Mr. Vage R. YENGIBARYAN
Vice Consul
Mr. Aleksandr V. PRUSOV
Vice Consul
Mr. Aleksandr V. DEMKIN
Vice Consul
Mr. Aleksey Aleksandrovich ROGOV
Vice Consul
Mr. Igor V. SOLOVYEV
Vice Consul
Mr. Artem Viktorovich BARKOV

Trade Office New York (TRA)
400 Madison Ave. #901
New York, NY 10017

UTAH
Salt Lake City (HCG)
5244 S. Highland Dr. #201
Salt Lake City, UT 84117

Honorary Consul General
Dr. Ross E. BUTLER, Jr.

WASHINGTON
Seattle (CG)
Weston Bldg., 2001 6th Ave. #2323
Seattle, WA 98121

Tel: (206) 728-1910 Fax: (206) 728-1871

Consul General
Mr. Vladimir I. VOLNOV
Consul
Mr. Dmitry REPKOV
Consul
Mr. Aleks andr V. DORONIN
Vice Consul
Mr. Andrey VLADIMIR
Vice Consul
Mr. Satunkin MIKHAIL

SAUDI ARABIA

CALIFORNIA
Los Angeles (CG)
2045 Sawtelle Blvd.
Los Angeles, CA 90025
Tel: (310) 479-6000 Fax: (310) 478-6646

Consul General
Mr. Abdullah S.A. AL-HARTHI
Deputy Consul General
Mr. Faisal A.A. Al SUDAIRY
Deputy Consul General
Mr. Waleed A. BUKHARI
Vice Consul
His Highness Prince Mohamed Saud Al-Faisal AL-SAUD
Vice Consul
Mr. Hassan M.A. SHAWAF
Vice Consul
Mr. Riad SOLH
Vice Consul
Mr. Nasser A. Al GHANOOM
Vice Consul
Mr. Sultan M. Al KAHTANI
Vice Consul
Mr. Abdulkarim Saad Bin BAZ
Vice Consul
Mr. Waleed S. Al NATHEER
Vice Consul
Mr. Amer A. Al SHEHRY

DISTRICT OF COLUMBIA
Washington (EMB)
601 New Hampshire Ave. NW
Washington, DC 20037
Tel: (202) 342-3800 Fax: (202) 944-3113

Ambassador
His Royal Highness Prince BIN SULTAN

NEW YORK
New York (CG)
866 United Nations Plz. #480
New York, NY 10017
Tel: (212) 752-2740

Consul General
Dr. Abdulrahman M. GDAIA
Deputy Consul General
Mr. Faisal A. AMODI
Vice Consul
Mr. Essam SALGETAEL
Vice Consul
Mr. Abdulaziz R. Al MOTAIEB
Vice Consul
Mr. Zaid M. Zal HARBI
Vice Consul
Mr. Mohammed Sh Al HARBI

TEXAS
Houston (CG)
5718 Westheimer #1500
Houston, TX 77057
Tel: (713) 785-5577

Consul General
Mr. Abdulaziz A. Al DRISS

SINGAPORE

CALIFORNIA
Los Angeles (HCG)
609 Deep Valley Dr. #200
Rolling Hills Estate, CA 90274

Honorary Consul General
Mr. Robert Gilway Van DINE

San Francisco (CG)
595 Market St. #2450
San Francisco, CA 94105
Tel: (415) 543-4775 Fax: (415) 543-4788

Consul General
Mr. J. Singh SOHAN
Consul
Mr. Julian Hsu Hin ONG

ILLINOIS
Chicago (HCG)
10 S. Dearborn St. #4800
Chicago, IL 60603
Tel: (312) 853-7555

Honorary Consul General
Mr. Newton MINOW

NEW YORK
New York (C)
231 E. 51st St.
New York, NY 10022
Tel: (212) 223-3331 Fax: (212) 826-5028

Consul
Mr. Richard GROSSE
Consul
Mr. Lip Cheng HOW

SRI LANKA

ARIZONA
Phoenix (HC)
329 W. Cypress St.
Phoenix, AZ 85003
Tel: (602) 254-1899

Honorary Consul
Dr. Jeremy Robert TORSTVEIT

CALIFORNIA
Los Angeles (CG)
3250 Wilshire Blvd. #1405
Los Angeles, CA 90010
Tel: (213) 387-0210 Fax: (213) 387-0216

Consul General
Mr. Gamini PEMASIRI
Consular Agent
Mr. Cyril Gunaratne Hikkaduwe W. DON

GEORGIA
Atlanta (HCG)
1201 W. Peachtree St.
Atlanta, GA 30309-3424
Tel: (404) 881-7000 Fax: (404) 881-4777

Honorary Consul General
Mr. Keven E. GRADY

HAWAII
Honolulu (HC)
60 N. Beretania St. #410
Honolulu, HI 96817-4754
Tel: (808) 524-6738 Fax: (808) 524-6738

Honorary Consul
Mrs. Kusuma C. COORAY

LOUISIANA
New Orleans (HC)
401 Veterans Blvd. #102
Metairie, LA 70005
Tel: (504) 455-7600 Fax: (504) 455-7605

Honorary Consul
Mr. David R. BURRUS

NEW JERSEY
Newark (HC)
2 E. Glen Rd.
Denville, NJ 07834
Tel: (973) 627-7855 Fax: (973) 586-3411

Honorary Consul
Mr. Jayasiri Parakrama LIYANAGE

NEW MEXICO
Santa Fe (HC)
7610 Old Santa Fe Trail
Santa Fe, NM 87505
Tel: (505) 983-9582 Fax: (505) 989-7252

Honorary Consul
Dr. Althea GRAY

NEW YORK
New York (CON)
630 3rd Ave., 20th Fl.
New York, NY 10017
Tel: (212) 986-7040

Consul
Mr. Wijesiri PADUKKAGE

SYRIA

CALIFORNIA
Los Angeles (HCG)
3 Civic Plz. #190
Newport Beach, CA 92660
Tel: (949) 640-9888 Fax: (949) 640-9292

Honorary Consul General
Dr. Hazem Hikmat CHEHABI

MICHIGAN
Detroit (HCG)
1750 Birmingham Blvd.
Birmingham, MI 48009
Tel: (248) 593-5943 Fax: (248) 598-5944

Honorary Consul General
Dr. Naji ARWASHAN

TEXAS
Houston (HCG)
5433 Westheimer Rd. #1020
Houston, TX 77056
Tel: (713) 622-8860 Fax: (713) 622-8872

Honorary Consul General
Mr. Ayman M. MIDANI

THAILAND

ALABAMA
Montgomery (HCG)
919 Bell St.
Montgomery, AL 36104
Tel: (334) 269-2518 Fax: (334) 269-4678

Honorary Consul General
Mr. Robert F. HENRY

CALIFORNIA
Los Angeles (CG)
611 N. Larchmont Blvd.
Los Angeles, CA 90004
Tel: (323) 962-9574 Fax: (323) 962-2128

Consul General
Mr. Isinthorn SORNVAI
Deputy Consul General
Mrs. Nantana SIVAKUA
Consul
Mr. Songseen SUSEVI
Consul
Mr. Wasin DHAMAVASI
Consul
Mr. Paitoon SONGKAEO
Consul
Mr. Sakeson SAROBOL
Consul
Mr. Satid SIRISAWADDI
Consul
Mrs. Sumittra Na RANONG
Consul
Miss Kanokwan PIBALCHON
Consul
Mr. Chana MIENCHAROEN
Vice Consul
Mrs. Somthavil SITTISA
Vice Consul
Mr. Amonsak PARARAMAN

Thai Trade Office Los Angeles (TRA)
611 N. Larchmont Blvd., 3rd Fl.
Los Angeles, CA 90004
Tel: (323) 466-9645

Consul
Mr. Song Seen SUFVIRI

COLORADO
Denver (HCG)
1123 Auraria Pkwy. #200
Denver, CO 80204
Tel: (303) 892-0118 Fax: (303) 892-0119

Honorary Consul General
Mr. Donald William RINGSBY

FLORIDA
Coral Gables (HCG)
2199 Ponce de Leon Blvd. #301
Coral Gables, FL 33134
Tel: (305) 445-7577 Fax: (305) 444-0487

Honorary Consul General
Mr. George M. CORRIGAN
Honorary Consul
Mr. Louis STINSON, JR.

GEORGIA
Atlanta (HCG)
900 Ashwood Pkwy. #300
Atlanta, GA 30338

Honorary Consul General
Mr. Robert M. HOLDER

HAWAII
Honolulu (HCG)
1287 Kalani St. #103
Honolulu, HI 96817
Tel: (808) 845-7332 Fax: (808) 848-0022

Honorary Consul General
Mr. Colin T. MIYABARA

ILLINOIS
Chicago (CG)
700 N. Rush St.
Chicago, IL 60611
Tel: (312) 664-3129 Fax: (312) 664-3230

Consul General
Mr. Chet DHERAPATTANA
Deputy Consul General
Ms. Narota SANGKAMANEE
Consul
Ms. Dhama Dhama VASI

Thai Trade Center Chicago (TRA)
500 N. Michigan Ave. #1920
Chicago, IL 60611
Tel: (312) 467-0044 Fax: (312) 467-1690

Consul
Mr. Piramol CHAROENPAO

MASSACHUSETTS
Boston (HCG)
41 Union St.
Boston, MA 02108
Tel: (617) 227-2750

Honorary Consul General
Mr. Joseph A. MILANO

MICHIGAN
Gross Pointe (HVC)
280 Moross Rd.
Gross Pointe, MI 48236
Tel: (313) 884-7075

Honorary Vice Consul
Mr. Thomas Benton STEVENS

MISSOURI
Kansas City (HC)
3906 W. 103rd St.
Overland Park, MO 66207
Tel: (913) 385-5555 Fax: (913) 385-5558

Honorary Consul
Ms. Mary Frances Taylor-KIRKPATRICK

NEW YORK
New York (CG)
351 E. 52nd St.
New York, NY 10022
Tel: (212) 754-1770 Fax: (212) 754-1907

Consul General
Ms. Vipawan NIPATAKUSOL
Deputy Consul General
Mr. Mongkol PROMPAYUCK
Consul
Mr. Atthapong KIATPONG
Consul
Mr. Pupcharee SANGIEM

NEW YORK
Thai Commercial/Economic/Investment Offices New York (COM)
61 Broadway #2810
New York, NY 10006
Tel: (212) 422-9009 Fax: (212) 422-9119

Consul
Mrs. Vasana MUTUTANONT
Vice Consul
Mr. Audsitti SROITHONG

OKLAHOMA
Tulsa (HC)
25900 E. 81st St.
Broken Arrow, OK 74014
Tel: (918) 357-2886

Honorary Consul General
Ms. Nora GORDON

OREGON
Portland (HCG)
121 SW Salmon St. #1430
Portland, OR 97204-2924
Tel: (503) 221-0440 Fax: (503) 221-0550

Honorary Consul
Mr. Nicholas John STANLEY

PUERTO RICO
Hato Rey (HCG)
159 Costa Rica St. #11-F
Hato Rey, PR 00917
Tel: (787) 565-9617 Fax: (787) 753-7276

Honorary Consul General
Mr. Rolando J. Piernes ALFONSO
Honorary Consul
Mrs. Carmen V. MENENDEZ-PIERNES

TEXAS
Dallas (HCG)
3232 McKinney Ave. #1400
Dallas, TX 75204-2429
Tel: (214) 740-1498 Fax: (214) 740-1499

Honorary Consul General
Mr. W. Forrest SMITH

El Paso (HCG)
6305 Franklin View
El Paso, TX 79912
Tel: (915) 526-3503

Honorary Consul General
Mrs. Mary Lee Leavell PINKERTON

Houston (HCG)
600 Travis St. #2800
Houston, TX 77002-3094
Tel: (713) 229-8733 Fax: (713) 228-1303

Honorary Consul General
Mr. Charles C. FOSTER
Honorary Vice Consul
Ms. Julie M. RICHARDSON

TURKEY

CALIFORNIA
Los Angeles (CG)
6300 Wilshire Blvd. #2010
Los Angeles, CA 90048
Tel: (323) 655-8832 Fax: (323) 655-8681

Consul General
Mr. Ahmet Engin ANSAY
Vice Consul
Mr. Ozgur Kivanc ALTAN
Consular Agent
Mr. Osman Gonen KARADENIZ

Consular Agent
Mrs. Hilal YUCEL

CALIFORNIA
Oakland (HCG)
PMB 345, 19229 Sonoma Hwy.
Sonoma, CA 95476
Tel: (415) 362-0912 Fax: (707) 939-1433

Honorary Consul General
Mrs. Bonnie Joy KASLAN

DISTRICT OF COLUMBIA
Washington (EMB)
2525 Massachusetts Ave. NW
Washington, DC 20008
Tel: (202) 612-6700 Fax: (202) 612-6744

Vice Consul
Mr. Huseyin H. GURPINAR

GEORGIA
Atlanta (HCG)
4287 Parlen Wolk
Atlanta, GA 30327
Tel: (404) 262-9524

Honorary Consul General
Ms. Mona DIAMOND

ILLINOIS
Chicago (CG)
360 N. Michigan Ave. #1405
Chicago, IL 60601
Tel: (312) 263-0644

Consul General
Mr. Ali Naci KORU
Vice Consul
Mr. Bahri BATU
Consular Agent
Mr. Dursun AKDOGAN

KANSAS
Mission Hills (HCG)
8436 Somerset Dr.
Shanee Mission, KS 66207

Honorary Consul General
Mr. Jeffrey P. HILLELSON

MARYLAND
Baltimore (HCG)
313 Wendover Rd.
Baltimore, MD 21218

Honorary Consul General
Mr. Cenap Remzi KIRATLI

NEW YORK
New York (CG)
821 United Nations Plz.
New York, NY 10017
Tel: (212) 949-0160 Fax: (212) 983-1293

Consul General
Mr. Omer ONHON
Consul
Mrs. Hatun DEMIRER
Vice Consul
Mrs. Gulcan Akoguz KARAGOZ
Consular Agent
Mr. Levent KADIOGLU
Consular Agent
Mr. Yuksel AKCA

Consular Agent
Mr. Mehmet Cuneyt YENER
Consular Agent
Mrs. Melahat OZAY
Consular Agent
Mr. Hasan Serdar OZTURK
Consular Agent
Mr. Mustafa TEKIN
Consular Agent
Mr. Bulent BARAN
Consular Agent
Mr. Hasan OZDEMIR
Consular Agent
Ms. Mehtap GUNDUZ
Consular Agent
Mr. Mustafa ZEYBEK
Consular Agent
Mrs. Serpil OGUZ

NEW YORK
Office of Education New York (EDC)
821 United Nations Plz., 7th Fl.
New York, NY 10017
Tel: (212) 687-8395 Fax: (212) 557-1632

Educational Attaché
Dr. Samil OCAL

Turkish Culture Tourist and Information Office
New York (CUL)
821 United Nations Plz., 4th Fl.
New York, NY 10017
Tel: (212) 687-2194 Fax: (212) 599-7568

Consular Agent
Mr. Meltem ONHON

TEXAS
Houston (CG)
1990 Post Oak Blvd. #1300
Houston, TX 77056
Tel: (713) 622-5849

Consul General
Vacant
Deputy Consul General
Vacant
Vice Consul
Ms. Emriye Bagdagul ORMANCI
Consular Agent
Mrs. Azize Tijen YILDIZ

WASHINGTON
Seattle (HCG)
12328 NE 97th St.
Kirkland, WA 98033
Tel: (425) 739-6722

Honorary Consul General
Mr. John U. GOKCEN

TURKMENISTAN

DISTRICT OF COLUMBIA
Washington (EMB)
2207 Massachusetts Ave. NW
Washington, DC 20008
Tel: (202) 588-1500 Fax: (202) 588-0697

Consul
Mr. Parakhat DURDYEV

UZBEKISTAN

COLORADO
Denver (HCG)
948 Hamilton Creek Rd.
Silverthorne, CO 80498
Tel: (970) 513-8000

Honorary Consul General
Mr. Lawrence T. KURLANDER

NEW YORK
New York (CG)
801 2nd Ave., 20th Fl.
New York, NY 10017
Tel: (212) 754-6178 Fax: (212) 486-7998

Consul General
Mr. Khasan IKRAMOV
Vice Consul
Mr. Salokhitdin SIDIKOV

WASHINGTON
Seattle (HCG)
800 5th Ave. #4000
Seattle, WA 98104
Tel: (206) 625-1199 Fax: (206) 292-9736

Honorary Consul General
Mr. Gary C. FURLONG

VIETNAM

CALIFORNIA
San Francisco (CG)
1700 California St. #430
San Francisco, CA 94109
Tel: (415) 922-1577 Fax: (415) 922-1848

Consul General
Mr. Tran Tuan ANH
Deputy Consul General
Mr. Dang The HUNG
Consul
Mr. Bui Van THINH
Consul
Mr. Le Manh CUONG
Consul
Mrs. Nguyen Thuy DZUONG
Consul
Mr. Bui Xuan LINH
Consul
Mr. Lai Xuan HUNG
Consul
Mr. Nguyen Khac MAI
Consul
Ms. Le Thu SON
Consul
Mr. Le Kim LAM
Vice Consul
Mr. Nguyen Thanh VINH

Missions of Asian Countries to the United Nations

The United Nations works to maintain peace and provide humanitarian assistance throughout the world. It was founded on October 24, 1945 and includes 191 member states.

AFGHANISTAN

PERMANENT MISSION OF AFGHANISTAN TO THE UNITED NATIONS
360 Lexington Ave., 11th Fl.
New York, NY 10017
Tel: (212) 972-1212 Fax: (212) 972-1216
Email: afgwatan@aol.com
National Holiday: August 19th

Ambassador E. and P.
His Excellency Ravan A. G. Farhâdi; Mrs. Adéla Hachémi Farhâdi
Minister Plenipotentiary
Mr. Mohammad Yunus Bâzel; Mrs. Gulalai Bâzel
Minister Counsellor
Mr. M. Erfâni Ayoob; Mrs. Jamila Ayoob
Counsellor
Mr. Adib Farhâdi
Counsellor
Mr. Salhuddin Rabbâni; Mrs. Amina Bârakzai Rabbâni
Counsellor
Mr. Mohammad Wali Naeemi; Mrs. Hakima Naeemi
Counsellor (Political Affairs)
Mr. Ahmad Seyar Zafar
First Secretary
Mr. Mohammad Ali; Mrs. Mariam Ali
First Secretary
Ms. Ariâ Seljuki
First Secretary
Mr. Shah Mohammad Niazi; Mrs. Razia Niazi
Second Secretary
Mr. Enâyat Nooristani; Mrs. Lida Nooristani
Second Secretary
Mr. Youssof Ghafoorzai
Third Secretary
Ms. Raihana Bashir

ARMENIA

PERMANENT MISSION OF THE REPUBLIC OF ARMENIA TO THE UNITED NATIONS
119 E. 36th St.
New York, NY 10016
Tel: (212) 686-9079 Fax: (212) 686-3934
Email: armenia@un.int
Web: www.un.int/armenia
National Holiday: September 21st

Ambassador E. and P.
His Excellency Armen Martirosian; Mrs. Anahit Martirosian
Minister Counsellor, Deputy Permanent Representative
Ms. Dziunik Aghajanian
First Secretary
Ms. Marine Davtyan
Counsellor
Ms. Anouschka Izmirlian

AZERBAIJAN

PERMANENT MISSION OF THE REPUBLIC OF AZERBAIJAN TO THE UNITED NATIONS
866 United Nations Plz. #560
New York, NY 10017
Tel: (212) 371-2559 Fax: (212) 371-2784
Email: azerbaijan@un.int
National Holiday: May 28th

Ambassador E. and P.
His Excellency Yashar Aliyev; Mrs. Neegiar Aliyeva
Counsellor
Mr. Ilgar Mammadov; Mrs. Pari Mammadova
First Secretary
Mr. Elshad Iskandarov; Mrs. Maleyka Iskandarova
Second Secretary
Ms. Husniyya Mammadova
Third Secretary
Ms. Farah Adjalova
Attaché
Mr. Surkhay Shukurov
Attaché
Mr. Mehdi Mammadov
Attaché
Ms. Rana Salayeva

BAHRAIN

PERMANENT MISSION OF THE KINGDOM OF BAHRAIN TO THE UNITED NATIONS
866 2nd Ave., 14 & 15th Fl.
New York, NY 10017
Tel: (212) 223-6200 Fax: (212) 319-0687
Email: bahrain@un.int
National Holiday: December 16th

Ambassador E. and P.
His Excellency Tawfeeq Ahmed Almansoor; Mrs. Awatif Al-Khaja
First Secretary
Mr. Ahmed Ali Yousif Arrad
Second Secretary
Mr. Abdul-Rahman Hasan Yusuf Hashem
Second Secretary
Mr. Ebrahim Mustafa Husain Aamer
Third Secretary
Mr. Ahmed Al-Muharraqi

BANGLADESH

PERMANENT MISSION OF THE PEOPLE'S REPUBLIC OF BANGLADESH TO THE UNITED NATIONS
227 E. 45th St., 14th Fl.
New York, NY 10017-3520
Tel: (212) 867-3434 Fax: (212) 972-4038
Email: bangladesh@un.int
Web: www.un.int/bangladesh
National Holiday: March 26th

Ambassador E. and P.
His Excellency Iftekhar Ahmed Chowdhury; Mrs. Nicole Sherin Chowdhury
Counsellor
Mr. Md. Zulfiqur Rahman; Mrs. Shameem Akhter
Counsellor
Mr. Muhammad A. Muhith; Mrs. Ruby Parveen
Counsellor
Mr. Khondker Mohammad Talha; Mrs. Masuma Haque
First Secretary
Mr. Md. Abdul Alim; Mrs. Shamima Akhter
First Secretary
Ms. Ishrat Jahan Ahmed
First Secretary
Mr. Tariq Md. Ariful Islam; Ms. Aliya Najma Nur
Minister (Press)
Mr. Mohamed Muhaddes; Mrs. Regina Muhaddes
Minister (Economic Affairs)
Mr. Mahmudul Karim; Mrs. Kazi Momtaz Shireen
Defence Adviser
Brigadier General Ilyas Iftekhar Rasul; Ms. Bahali Ifekhar

BHUTAN

PERMANENT MISSION OF THE KINGDOM OF BHUTAN TO THE UNITED NATIONS
343 E. 43rd St.
New York, NY 10017
Tel: (212) 682-2268 Fax: (212) 661-0551
National Holiday: December 17th

Ambassador E. and P.
His Excellency Daw Penjo; Mrs. Daw Zam
Minister Counsellor
Mr. Kinga Singye; Mrs. Kesang Choki
Counsellor
Mr. Sangye Rinchhen
First Secretary
Mr. Sonam Tobgay Dorji; Mrs. Rinzin Dorji
First Secretary
Mrs. Sangay Zangmo; Lt. Col. Kado
First Secretary
Mr. Letho; Mrs. Tshering Yudon
Attaché
Mrs. Dechhen Jamyang

BRUNEI

PERMANENT MISSION OF BRUNEI DARUSSALAM TO THE UNITED NATIONS
771 United Nations Plz.
New York, NY 10017
Tel: (212) 697-3465 Fax: (212) 697-9889
Email: info@bruneimission-ny.org
National Holiday: February 23rd

Ambassador E. and P.
Vacant
Minister Counsellor, Deputy Permanent Representative
Mr. Adnan Jaafar; Mrs. Salina Alli
First Secretary
Ms. Florence Chong Siew Hui
Second Secretary
Mr. Muhammad Shahrul Nizzam Umar; Mrs. Nor Hayati Ismail
Second Secretary
Mrs. Noni Zurainah Ismi
Second Secretary
Mr. Sheikh Abdul Mahdani
Third Secretary
Mr. Metussin Aji; Mrs. Zaiton Rahmat
Attaché
Ms. Masni Ahmad
Attaché
Mr. Ibrahim Rajap

CAMBODIA

PERMANENT MISSION OF THE KINGDOM OF CAMBODIA TO THE UNITED NATIONS
866 United Nations Plz. #420
New York, NY 10017
Tel: (212) 223-0676 Fax: (212) 223-0425
Email: cambodia@un.int
National Holiday: November 9th

Ambassador E. and P.
His Excellency Chem Widhya; Mrs. Sulivann Chem
Ambassador, Deputy Permanent Representative
His Excellency Sea Kosal
Minister Counsellor
Mr. Say Kheang; Mrs. Mao Sovana
First Secretary
Mr. Ok Sara
Second Secretary
Mr. Phyna Preap; Mrs. Prak Sitha
Third Secretary
Mr. Hoy Sopheap; Mrs. Ny Sok

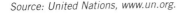

Third Secretary
Mr. Chanveasna Rath; Mrs. Moa Chhayheang
Third Secretary
Mr. Yaung Chan Sophea
Attaché
Mrs. Yos Chantika; Mr. Yos Rothana

CHINA

PERMANENT MISSION OF THE PEOPLE'S REPUBLIC OF CHINA TO THE UNITED NATIONS
350 E. 35th St.
New York, NY 10016
Tel: (212) 655-6100 Fax: (212) 634-7626
Email: chinamission_un@mfa.gov.cn
Web: www.china-un.org
National Holiday: October 1st

Ambassador E. and P.
His Excellency Wang Guangya; Mrs. Wang (Ms. Cong Jun)
Ambassador Extraordinary and Plenipotentiary, Deputy Permanent Representative
His Excellency Zhang Yishan; Mrs. Zhang (Mrs. Zhai Jinrong)
Minister
Mr. Liu Pei
Minister Counsellor
Mrs. Cong Jun; His Excellency Wang Guangya
Minister Counsellor
Mr. Liu Hanming
Minister Counsellor
Mr. Cheng Jingye
Minister Counsellor
Mr. Yao Wenlong; Mrs. Yao (Ms. Zhang Libin)
Counsellor
Mr. Ge Songxue; Mrs. Ge (Ms. Xing Jiping)
Counsellor
Mr. Xu Bu; Mrs. Xu (Ms. Zhu Yongfeng)
Counsellor
Mr. Xie Yunliang; Mrs. Xie (Ms. Wu Yan)
Counsellor
Mr. Hu Ping
Counsellor
Ms. Wang Tieli
Counsellor
Mr. Mu Changlin
Counsellor
Mr. Ju Fangqun; Mrs. Ju (Ms. Yang Xu)
Counsellor
Mr. Yu Shihao; Mrs. Yu (Ms. Yang Qiuju)
Counsellor
Mr. Li Junhua; Mrs. Li (Ms. Bai Yongjie)
Counsellor
Mr. Xie Bohua; Mrs. Xie (Ms. Zhao Yan)
Counsellor
Mr. Hong Xiaoyong
Counsellor
Ms. Bai Yongjie; Mr. Li Junhua
Counsellor
Mr. Zhang Benliang
Counsellor
Mr. Liu Hongyang; Mrs. Liu (Ms. Mao Jingqiu)
Counsellor
Ms. Wang Xinxia
Counsellor
Mr. Shen Yanjie
Counsellor (Legal Adviser)
Mr. Guan Jian; Mrs. Guan (Ms. Wang Hong)
Counsellor
Mr. Zhang Jianwen; Mrs. Zhang (Ms. Sun Qiuhuan)

First Secretary
Mr. Li Song; Mrs. Li (Ms. Wang Xiaolin)
First Secretary
Ms. Zhai Jinrong; His Excellency Zhang Yishan
First Secretary
Ms. Mao Jingqiu; Mr. Liu Hongyang
First Secretary
Mr. Shen Cong
First Secretary
Mr. Shang Hong
First Secretary
Mr. Li Tianwu; Mrs. Li (Ms. Zhang Yin)
First Secretary
Mr. Zhao Lianghua; Mrs. Zhao (Ms. Gao Meiping)
First Secretary
Mr. Sun Xudong; Mrs. Sun (Ms. Zhang Qiaozhi)
First Secretary
Ms. Xian Weiyi; Mr. Chen Xiang
First Secretary
Ms. Li Jijuan; Mr. Wu Zhiwe
First Secretary
Ms. Yan Jarong
First Secretary
Ms. Wang Xiaolin; Mr. Li Song
First Secretary
Mr. Tian Lixian; Mrs. Tian (Ms. Li Ping)
Second Secretary
Ms. Li Yanni; Mr. Qi Jianmin
Second Secretary
Mr. Wang Ximao
Second Secretary
Mr. Jin Lansheng; Mrs. Jin (Ms. Li Liya)
Second Secretary
Ms. Wang Yanqun
Second Secretary
Mr. Dong Fashui
Third Secretary
Mr. Wei Xuehui; Mrs. Wei (Ms. Chen Yu)
Third Secretary
Mr. Zhou Zhe; Mrs. Zhou (Ms. Huang Jun)
Third Secretary
Mr. Zhou Bo
Third Secretary
Mr. Shen Bo
Third Secretary
Ms. Yang Ningning; Mr. Xiong Biao
Third Secretary
Mr. Yao Shaojun

CYPRUS

PERMANENT MISSION OF THE REPUBLIC OF CYPRUS TO THE UNITED NATIONS
13 E. 40th St.
New York, NY 10016
Tel: (212) 481-6023 Fax: (212) 685-7316
Email: pmccyprus.un@verizon.net
Web: www.un.int/cyprus
National Holiday: October 1st

Ambassador E. and P.
His Excellency Andreas D. Mavroyiannis; Mrs. Calliopi Efthyvoulou-Mavroyiannis
Counsellor, Deputy Permanent Representative
Mr. Andreas Hadjichrysanthou
First Secretary
Mrs. Penelope Erotokritou; Mr. Vaios Liapis
Second Secretary
Ms. Polly Ioannou
Attaché (Administration)
Mrs. Eleni Vassiliadou; Mr. Christodoulos Michael
Attaché (Administration)
Mrs. Eleni Cosma Fatouros; Mr. Peter Fatouros

Counsellor (Press)
Mrs. Maria G. Zoupaniotis; Mr. Apostolis Zoupaniotis
Attaché (Press)
Miss Elena Panayides
Counsellor (Economic)
Mr. Dennis C. Droushiotis; Mrs. Mary Margaret Droushiotis

GEORGIA

PERMANENT MISSION OF GEORGIA TO THE UNITED NATIONS
1 United Nations Plz., 26th Fl.
New York, NY 10017
Tel: (212) 759-1949 Fax: (212) 759-1832
National Holiday: May 26th

Ambassador E. and P.
His Excellency Revaz Adamia; Mrs. Nino Chachua
Minister Plenipotentiary, Deputy Permanent Representative
Mr. Kaha Chitaia; Mrs. Manana Gotsiridze
Minister
Mr. Erasti Kitsmarishvili; Mrs. Imaze Kitsmarishvili
Senior Counsellor
Mr. George Kaladze
Counsellor
Ms. Tamar Tchitanava
First Secretary
Ms. Shalva Tsiskarashvili
Attaché
Mrs. Nina G. Sologashvili

INDIA

PERMANENT MISSION OF INDIA TO THE UNITED NATIONS
235 E. 43rd St.
New York, NY 10017
Tel: (212) 490-9660 Fax: (212) 490-9656
Email: india@un.int
National Holiday: January 26th

Ambassador E. and P.
His Excellency Nirupam Sen; Mrs. Grazyna Sen
Ambassador, Deputy Permanent Representative
His Excellency Ajai Malhotra; Mrs. Ira Malhotra
Minister
Mrs. Ruchi Ghanashyam; Mr. A. R. Ghanashyam
Minister
Mr. Harsh Vardhan Shringla; Mrs. Hemal Store
Counsellor
Mr. Alok K. Sinha; Mrs. Mamta Sinha
Counsellor
Mrs. Ruchira Kamboj; Mr. Diwaker Kamboj
Counsellor
Mr. Jaideep Mazumdar; Mrs. Parvati C. Mazumdar
Counsellor
Mr. Amreet Ahluwalia; Mrs. Madhu Bhalla Ahluwalia
Counsellor
Mr. Manimuthu Gandhi; Mrs. Caroline Gandhi
Counsellor
Mr. Taranjit Singh Sandhu
First Secretary
Mr. Sanjiv Ranjan; Mrs. Smita Ranjan
First Secretary
Mr. Nagabhushana Reddy Bollavaram; Mrs. Lalita Devi Bollavaram

Second Secretary
Mr. Raj Kishore Chawla; Mrs. Neelam Chawla
Second Secretary
Mr. Joginder Pal; Mrs. Veena Kumari
Second Secretary
Mr. Harsh Vardhan Singh Negi; Mrs. Usha Negi
Second Secretary
Mr. Amarjeet Singh Takhi; Mrs. Gurinder Kaur Takhi
Second Secretary
Mr. Dharam Vir Singh; Mrs. Sheela Singh
Second Secretary
Mr. Vijai Kumar; Mrs. Indira Chauhan
Attaché
Mr. Pradeep Dixit; Mrs. Shobha Dixit
Attaché
Mr. Scaria Thekkadasseril Augustine; Mrs. Shineese Scaria Augustine
Attaché
Mr. Surender Kumar; Mrs. Kiran Kumar
Attaché
Mr. Gobind Lal Narang; Mrs. Rukman Devi Narang
Attaché
Mr. Ashok Kumar Khera

INDONESIA

PERMANENT MISSION OF THE REPUBLIC OF INDONESIA TO THE UNITED NATIONS
325 E. 38th St.
New York, NY 10016
Tel: (212) 972-8333 Fax: (212) 972-9780
National Holiday: August 17th

Ambassador E. and P.
His Excellency Rezlan Ishar Jenie; Mrs. Sally Yukari Budiardjo Jenie
Ambassador, Deputy Permanent Representative
Her Excellency Adiyatwidi Adiwoso Asmady; Mr. Asmady Parman
Minister Counsellor
Mr. Prayono Atiyanto; Mrs. Tariyanti Dewi Yulita
Minister Counsellor (Military Adviser)
Rear Admiral Willem Rampangilei; Mrs. Antharina Patricia Paago
Minister Counsellor (Political Affairs)
Mr. Desra Percaya; Mrs. Evy Widajanti Percaya
First Secretary (Political Affairs)
Mr. Fikry Cassidy; Mrs. Lusia Veniokta
First Secretary (Economic and Social Affairs)
Mr. Dicky Komar
First Secretary (Economic Affairs)
Mr. Sanga Panggabean; Mrs. Luisa Prasanti
First Secretary (Economic Affairs)
Mr. Tri Tharyat; Mrs. Rina Saribanon
First Secretary (Economic and Social Affairs)
Miss Nina Saraswati Djajaprawira
First Secretary (Political Affairs)
Mr. Adam Mulawarman Tugio; Mrs. Irna Eka Mauliyanti
First Secretary (Political Affairs)
Mr. Andy Rachmianto; Mrs. Ismi Rohimaningsih
First Secretary
Mr. Muhammad Anshor; Mrs. Tantri Rukmini Dewi
First Secretary (Economic Affairs)
Mr. Mohamad Siradj Parwito; Mrs. Feria Damayanti
First Secretary (Administrative Affairs)
Mr. Hariyanta Soetarto; Mrs. Ramadhani Iskandarrini Soetarto
First Secretary (Economic and Social Affairs)
Mrs. Yuni Suryati; Mr. Suprapto

First Secretary
Mr. Witjaksono Adji; Mrs. Utami Astar Witjaksono
Second Secretary (Economic Affairs)
Mr. Jehezkiel Stephanus George Lantu
Second Secretary (Administrative Affairs)
Mr. Fernando Alwi; Mrs. Elly Zulkarnaini Alwi
Second Secretary (Political Affairs)
Mr. Mohammed Ichsan
Third Secretary (Political Affairs)
Miss Carolina Tinangon
Third Secretary (Economic and Social Affairs)
Mr. Bonanza Perwira Taihitu
Third Secretary (Economic Affairs)
Mr. Andre Omer Siregar; Mrs. Eurika Putri Anindhita
Attaché (Administrative Affairs)
Mr. Dadan Subarnas; Mrs. Neny Handayani

IRAN

PERMANENT MISSION OF THE ISLAMIC REPUBLIC OF IRAN TO THE UNITED NATIONS
622 3rd Ave., 34th Fl.
New York, NY 10017
Tel: (212) 687-2020 Fax: (212) 867-7086
Email: iran@un.int
National Holiday: February 11th

Ambassador E. and P.
His Excellency M. Javad Zarif; Mrs. Ashraf Zarif
Ambassador, Deputy Permanent Representative
His Excellency Mehdi Danesh-Yazdi; Mrs. Seddigheh Danesh-Yazdi
Ambassador
His Excellency Hossein Fereidoun; Mrs. Azar Fereidoun
First Counsellor
Mr. Mehdi Mirafzal; Mrs. Zahra Mirafzal
First Counsellor
Mr. Bahman Naimiarfa; Mrs. Vida Naimiarfa
First Counsellor
Mr. Javad Amin Mansour; Mrs. Tayebeh Amin Manzour
Second Counsellor (Protocol)
Mr. Reza Najafi; Mrs. Ameneh Najafi
Second Counsellor
Mr. Ali Hajmohammadian
Second Counsellor
Mr. Hossein Maleki; Mrs. Fouzieh Maleki
Third Counsellor
Mr. Mostafa Dolatyar; Mrs. Sharareh Dolatyar
Third Counsellor
Mr. Ahmad Sadeghi; Mrs. Soghra Sadeghi
Third Counsellor
Mr. Reza Afshar
First Secretary
Mr. Mansour Sadeghi; Mrs. Azam Sadeghi
First Secretary
Mr. Gholamhossein Mohammadnia; Mrs. Omeleyla Mohammadnia
First Secretary
Mr. Morteza Shafaghi; Mrs. Pouran Shafaghi
Second Secretary
Mr. Mohammad Hossein Nosrat; Mrs. Mansoureh Nosrat
Second Secretary (Press)
Mr. Morteza Darzi Ramandi; Mrs. Shahnaz Darzi Ramandi

Third Secretary
Mr. Abbas Bagherpour Ardekani; Mrs. Khadijeh Bagherpour Ardeka
Attaché
Mr. Alireza Ghaedali; Mrs. Maryam Ghaedali
Attaché
Mr. Ali Asgari Yazdi; Mrs. Fatemeh Asgari Yazdi
Attaché
Mr. Mehdi Babakazemi Meymi; Mrs. Zahra Babakazemi Meymi
Attaché
Mr. Mahdi Vahidi Asil
Special Adviser
Mrs. Paimaneh Hasteh; Mr. Kasra Barkeshli

IRAQ

PERMANENT MISSION OF IRAQ TO THE UNITED NATIONS
14 E. 79th St.
New York, NY 10021
Tel: (212) 737-4433 Fax: (212) 772-1794
Email: iraqmission@nyc.rr.com

Ambassador E. and P.
His Excellency Samir Shakir Mahmood Sumaida'ie; Mrs. Yang Ying
Ambassador Extraordinary and Plenipotentiary, Deputy Permanent Representative
His Excellency Feisal Amin al-Istrabadi; Mrs. Juliet Rose al-Istrabadi
Minister Plenipotentiary
Mr. Said Shihab Ahmad; Mrs. Saadiya Khamis
Minister Plenipotentiary
Mr. Ahmad Kadhim Ibrahim
First Secretary
Mr. Abdul Karim Shwaikh; Mrs. Sadyah M. Hummady
First Secretary
Ms. Jwan H. Tawfiq
Second Secretary
Mr. Mohammed Karim Mahmoud; Mrs. Aseel S. Al-Nejim
Attaché
Mr. Saleh F. Humadi; Mrs. Sahira Mohamad
Attaché
Ms. Manat H. I. Al-Shawi

ISRAEL

PERMANENT MISSION OF ISRAEL TO THE UNITED NATIONS
800 2nd Ave.
New York, NY 10017
Tel: (212) 499-5510 Fax: (212) 499-5515
Email: un@israel.org
Web: www.israel-un.org
National Holiday: May 12th

Ambassador E. and P.
His Excellency Dan Gillerman; Mrs. Janice Gillerman
Ambassador, Deputy Permanent Representative
His Excellency Daniel Carmon; Ms. Ditza Froim
Ambassador
His Excellency Elazar Saar; Mrs. Nurit Shuali
Minister (Administration)
Mrs. Stella Rapp; Mr. Itzhak Rapp
Counsellor
Mr. Moshe Sermoneta
Counsellor

Mr. Gilad Cohen; Mrs. Kinneret Cohen
Counsellor
Mr. Ilan Shapira; Mrs. Vardit Shapira Kaplan
Counsellor
Mrs. Eilon Shahar; Mr. Ran Shahar
First Secretary
Mr. Ilan Melamed
Second Secretary
Mr. Ori Barshishat; Mrs. Meirav Barshishat
Second Secretary
Mr. Ronen Levi; Mrs. Hagit Levy
Attaché (Legal Adviser)
Mr. Tal Becker; Mrs. Naomi Becker
Attaché (Coordinator, Candidatures)
Mr. Itai Eithan Shamir
Attaché
Ms. Keren Tenenbaum
Attaché (Spokeperson)
Ms. Anat Friedman
Attaché
Mr. Alon Malkai; Mrs. Yonit Malkai
Attaché
Mr. Gabriel Cohen; Mrs. Talmore Rafali Cohen
Attaché
Ms. Dana Wolf
Attaché
Mr. Gregory Levey

JAPAN

PERMANENT MISSION OF JAPAN TO THE UNITED NATIONS
866 United Nations Plz., 2nd Fl.
New York, NY 10017
Tel: (212) 223-4300 Fax: (212) 751-1966
Email: mission@un-japan.org
Web: www.un.int/japan
National Holiday: December 23rd

Ambassador E. and P.
His Excellency Kenzo Oshima
Ambassador Extraordinary and Plenipotentiary, Deputy Permanent Representative
His Excellency Shinichi Kitaoka; Mrs. Rieko Kitaoka
Ambassador
His Excellency Toshiro Ozawa; Mrs. Shizuko Ozawa
Minister (Political Affairs)
Mr. Koji Haneda; Mrs. Ihoko Haneda
Minister (Administrative and Budgetary Affairs)
Mr. Jun Yamazaki; Mrs. Junko Yamazaki
Minister (Economic Affairs)
Mr. Kazuo Sunaga; Mrs. Yukari Sunaga
Minister (Social Affairs)
Mr. Yasushi Takase; Mrs. Asako Takase
Minister (General Affairs)
Mr. Jiro Kodera; Mrs. Hiroko Kodera
Counsellor (Political Affairs)
Mr. Takahisa Kawakami; Mrs. Chieko Kawakami
Counsellor (Economic Affairs)
Mr. Yoshiaki Ito; Mrs. Noriko Ito
Counsellor (Political Affairs)
Mr. Hiroshi Ishikawa; Mrs. Yuko Ishikawa
Counsellor (Economic Affairs)
Ms. Naoko Yamamoto
Counsellor (Political Affairs)
Mr. Hiroshi Matsuura
Counsellor (Political Affairs)
Mr. Shutaro Omura; Mrs. Saho Omura
First Secretary (Political Affairs)
Mr. Hiroshi Tajima; Mrs. Yuki Tajima

First Secretary (Administrative and Budgetary Affairs)
M. Takeshi Matsunaga; Mrs. Miho Matsunaga
First Secretary (Administrative Affairs)
Mr. Fumiyoshi Omi
First Secretary (Administrative and Budgetary Affairs)
Mr. Akira Yamamoto; Mrs. Chieko Yamamoto
First Secretary (Political Affairs)
Mr. Shinichi Iida; Mrs. Norika Iida
First Secretary (Social Affairs)
Mr. Shigeyuki Shimamori; Mrs. Yuko Shimamori
First Secretary (Political Affairs)
Col. Motohide Yamamoto; Mrs. Kazumi Yamamoto
First Secretary (Political Affairs), Defence Attaché
Mr. Tadayuki Miyashita; Mrs. Yuka Miyashita
First Secretary (Political Affairs)
Ms. Kikuko Kato
First Secretary (Special Assistant to the Permanent Representative)
Mr. Kenji Nakano
First Secretary (Politcal Affairs)
Mr. Hiroshi Waguri; Mrs. Hiromi Waguri
First Secretary (Political Affairs)
Mr. Masahiro Nakata
First Secretary (Administrative Affairs)
Mr. Masahiro Matsuzawa; Mrs. Agnes Matsuzawa
First Secretary (Social Affairs)
Ms. Hitomi Sato
First Secretary (Administrative Affairs)
Mr. Masakazu Takahashi; Mrs. Yoshie Takahashi
First Secretary (Administrative Affairs)
Mr. Hironari Nemoto; Mrs. Eiko Nemoto
First Secretary (General Affairs)
Mr. Moyoyuki Ishize; Mrs. Stoko Ishize
First Secretary (Administrative Affairs)
Ms. Akiko Sugita
Second Secretary (Administrative Affairs)
Mr. Toshihiko Nakagami; Mrs. Yumie Nakagami
Second Secretary (Administrative Affairs)
Mr. Kazuhiro Ishikawa; Mrs. Mariko Ishikawa
Second Secretary (Social Affairs)
Mr. Makoto Hashizume
Second Secretary (Social Affairs)
Ms. Satomi Saito
Second Secretary (Economic Affairs)
Mr. Go Shimada; Mrs. Megumi Shimada
Second Secretary (Administrative Affairs)
Ms. Kotono Hara
Second Secretary (Administrative and Budgetary Affairs)
Mr. Hitoshi Kozaki; Mrs. Tomoko Kozaki
Second Secretary (Administrative Affairs)
Mr. Masahiro Nagayoshi; Mrs. Yoko Nagayoshi
Second Secretary (Protocol)
Mr. Kenichi Nishizawa; Mrs. Yoshie Nishizawa
Second Secretary (Protocol)
Ms. Chika Imaizumi
Second Secretary (Political Affairs)
Mr. Takeomi Yamamoto; Mrs. Satoko Yamamoto
Second Secretary (Political Affairs)
Ms. Yukiko Murai
Third Secretary (Administrative Affairs)
Ms. Ai Saito
Third Secretary (Economic Affairs)

Mrs. Sachiyo Seya
Attaché (Administrative Affairs)
Ms. Noriko Yamazaki
Attaché (Administrative Affairs)
Ms. Aoi Mihara
Attaché (Administrative Affairs)
Ms. Kimie Suzuki

JORDAN

PERMANENT MISSION OF THE HASHEMITE KINGDOM OF JORDAN TO THE UNITED NATIONS
866 Second Ave., 4th Fl.
New York, NY 10017
Tel: (212) 832-9553 Fax: (212) 832-5346
Email: missionun@jordanmissionun.com
National Holiday: May 25th

Ambassador E. and P.
His Royal Highness Prince Zeid Ra'ad Zeid Al-Hussein; Her Royal Highness Princess Sarah Zeid
Counsellor, Deputy Permanent Representative
Mr. Basheer F. Zoubi; Mrs. Dina Zoubi
Counsellor
Miss Saja Sattam Habes Majali
First Secretary
Mr. Mahmoud Hmoud
First Secretary
Mr. Mohammad Tal; Mrs. Hoda Moh'd Mostafa Tal
Second Secretary
Mr. Haron Hassan
Second Secretary
Mr. Mu'taz Hyassat
Counsellor, Military Adviser (Peacekeeping Affairs)
Col. Mohammad M. Z. Alhoqel; Mrs. Wedad Alhoqel
Second Secretary (Police Adviser)
Major Wael Jamil Yousef Shabsough; Mrs. Sineh Yousef Asad Janbout

KAZAKHSTAN

PERMANENT MISSION OF THE REPUBLIC OF KAZAKHSTAN TO THE UNITED NATIONS
866 United Nations Plz. #586
New York, NY 10017
Tel: (212) 230-1900 Fax: (212) 230-1172
Email: kazakhstan@un.int
Web: www.un.int/kazakhstan
National Holiday: December 16th

Ambassador E. and P.
His Excellency Yerzhan Kh. Kazykhanov; Mrs. Danara M. Kazykhanova
Counsellor
Mr. Murat A. Smagulov; Mrs. Nailya Mukanova
Counsellor
Mr. Serik Zhanibekov; Mrs. Saule Zhanibekova
Counsellor
Mr. Dulat Bakishev
First Secretary
Mr. Arman Issetov; Mrs. Asemgul Issetova
First Secretary
Mr. Zhanat Shaimerdenov; Mrs. Milana Shaimerdenova
First Secretary
Mr. Yevgeniy Kokovin
First Secretary (Consul)
Ms. Raushan K. Yesbulatova
Attaché
Mr. Sergey Viktorov

KOREA, NORTH

PERMANENT MISSION OF THE DEMOCRATIC PEOPLE'S REPUBLIC OF KOREA TO THE UNITED NATIONS
820 2nd Ave., 13th Fl.
New York, NY 10017
Tel: (212) 972-3105 Fax: (212) 972-3154
Email: dpr.korea@verizon.net
National Holiday: September 9th

Ambassador E. and P.
His Excellency Pak Gil Yon; Mrs. Pak
Ambassador, Deputy Permanent Representative
His Excellency Kim Chang Guk; Mrs. Kim
Ambassador, Deputy Permanent Representative
His Excellency Han Song Ryol
Ambassador
His Excellency Ri Song Hyon; Mrs. Ri
Counsellor
Mr. Pak Pu Ung; Mrs. Pak
Counsellor
Mr. Jo Kil Hong; Mrs. Jo
First Secretary
Mr. Sin Song Chol; Mrs. Sin
First Secretary
Mr. Song Se Il; Mrs. Song

KOREA, SOUTH

PERMANENT MISSION OF THE REPUBLIC OF KOREA TO THE UNITED NATIONS
335 E. 45th St.
New York, NY 10017
Tel: (212) 439-4000 Fax: (212) 986-1083
Email: korea@un.int
National Holiday: August 15th

Ambassador E. and P.
His Excellency Choi Young-jin
Ambassador, Deputy Permanent Representative
His Excellency Shin Kak-soo; Mrs. Shin So-san
Ambassador, Deputy Permanent Representative
His Excellency Oh Joon; Mrs. Oh Miri
Minister
Mr. Suh Dong-gu; Mrs. Suh Yoon-jeong
Minister
Ms. Kang Kyung-wha; Mr. Lee Yillbyung
Minister Counsellor
Mr. Lew Kwang-chul; Mrs. Lew Kyung-hai
Minister Counsellor
Mr. Song Young-wan; Mrs. Song Sang-mi
Counsellor
Mr. Lee Beom-chan; Mrs. Lee Eun-hee
Counsellor
Mr. Hwang Joon-kook; Mrs. Hwang Shil
Counsellor
Mr. Choi Hong-ghi; Mrs. Choi Eun-mi
Counsellor
Mr. Park Yoon-june
Counsellor
Mr. Yoon Yeocheol; Mrs. Yoon So-young
Counsellor
Mr. Choi Kwang-mook; Mrs. Choi Kwan-soon
Counsellor
Mr. Shin Yoo-chul; Mrs. Shin Yoon-kyoung
Counsellor
Mr. Kang Byung-koo; Mrs. Kang Kyung-hee
Counsellor
Mr. Shin Donk-ik; Mrs. Shin Jung-wha
First Secretary
Mr. Yoo Dae-jong; Mrs. Yoo Soo-kyung
First Secretary
Mr. Bahk Sahng-hoon; Mrs. Bahk Jong-hee

First Secretary
Mr. Moon Seoung-hyun; Mrs. Moon Myung-ji
First Secretary
Mr. Kim Kiejoo; Mrs. Kim Tae-jung
First Secretary
Mr. Ham Sang-wook; Mrs. Ham Ja-ok
First Secretary
Mr. Kweon Ki-hwan; Mrs. Kweon So-hyun
First Secretary
Mr. Kang Seok-hee; Mrs. Kang Sang-hee
First Secretary
Mr. Park Chun-kyoo; Mrs. Park Sang-mee
First Secretary
Mr. Lee Jang-keun; Mrs. Lee Song-lim
First Secretary
Mr. Lee Tae-woo; Mrs. Lee Mi-hyun
Second Secretary
Ms. Ahn Eun-ju
Second Secretary
Mr. Sa Jin-woo; Mrs. Sa Jung-un
Second Secretary
Mr. Kim Il-bum
Second Secretary
Mr. Yoon Hee-chan; Mrs. Yoon Jung-ah
Second Secretary
Mr. Lee Bumho
Third Secretary
Mr. Kim Young-chol; Mrs. Kim Young-a
Attaché, Military Adviser
Lt. Colonel Kim Il-suk; Mrs. Kim Chul-soon

KUWAIT

PERMANENT MISSION OF THE STATE OF KUWAIT TO THE UNITED NATIONS
321 E. 44th St.
New York, NY 10017
Tel: (212) 973-4300 Fax: (212) 370-1733
Email: kuwait@kuwaitmission.com
Web: www.kuwaitmission.com
National Holiday: Feburary 25th

Ambassador E. and P.
Her Excellency Nabeela Abdulla Al-Mulla
Counsellor, Deputy Permanent Representative
Mr. Mansour Ayyad Sh. A. Al-Otaibi; Mrs. Al-Otaiba
First Secretary
Mr. Jasem Ibrahim J. M. Al-Najem; Mrs. Al-Najem
First Secretary
Mr. Naser Abdullah H. M. Al-Hayen
Second Secretary
Mr. Nasser S. A. Sh. Al-Ghanim; Mrs. Al-Ghanim
Second Secretary
Mr. Meshal A. M. A. Al-Mansour; Mrs. Al-Mansour
Third Secretary
Mr. Nawaf N. M. Al-Enezi
Attaché
Miss Reham Al-Ghanem
Attaché
Mr. Ahmed M. Al-Khamees; Mrs. Al-Khamees
Attaché
Mr. Ebrahim Al-Rubaian; Mrs. Al-Rubaian

KYRGYZSTAN

PERMANENT MISSION OF THE KYRGYZ REPUBLIC TO THE UNITED NATIONS
866 United Nations Plz. #477
New York, NY 10017
Tel: (212) 486-4214 Fax: (212) 486-5259
National Holiday: August 31st

Ambassador E. and P.

His Excellency Nurbek Jeenbaev; Mrs. Lola Jusupbekova
Minister Plenipotentiary, Deputy Permanent Representative
Mr. Kainarbek Toktomushev; Mrs. Irina Toktomusheva
First Secretary
Mr. Aibek B. Moldogaziev; Mrs. Gulzat Abdyldaeva
Attaché
Ms. Jyldyz T. Kasymova

LAOS

PERMANENT MISSION OF THE LAO PEOPLE'S DEMOCRATIC REPUBLIC TO THE UNITED NATIONS
317 E. 51st St.
New York, NY 10022
Tel: (212) 832-2734 Fax: (212) 750-0039
National Holiday: December 2nd

Ambassador E. and P.
His Excellency Alounkèo Kittikhoun; Mrs. Kongpadith Kittikhoun
Minister Counsellor, Deputy Permanent Representative
Mr. Ounseng Vixay; Mrs. Kesone Vixay
Counsellor
Mr. Phomma Khammanichanh
First Secretary
Mrs. Viengsavanh Sipraseuth
Second Secretary
Mrs. Khanhxay Pholsena
Second Secretary
Mr. Asoka Rasphone; Mrs. Simalay Rasphone
Third Secretary
Mr. Vongvilay Thiphalangsy
Attaché
Miss Daosavanh Boulommavong

LEBANON

PERMANENT MISSION OF LEBANON TO THE UNITED NATIONS
866 United Nations Plz. #531-533
New York, NY 10017
Tel: (212) 355-5460 Fax: (212) 838-2819
Email: lebanon@nyct.net
National Holiday: November 22nd

Ambassador E. and P.
Vacant
Counsellor, Deputy Permanent Representative
Mr. Ibrahim Assaf
Counsellor
Mr. Majdi Ramadan
Counsellor
Mr. Sami Zeidan

MALAYSIA

PERMANENT MISSION OF MALAYSIA TO THE UNITED NATIONS
313 E. 43rd St.
New York, NY 10017
Tel: (212) 986-6310 Fax: (212) 490-8576
Email: malaysia@un.int
National Holiday: August 31st

Ambassador E. and P.
His Excellency Hamidon Ali; Mrs. Amy Low Abdullah
Ambassador, Alternate Permanent Representative

His Excellency Mohd. Radzi Abdul
Rahman; Mrs. Jazliza Jalaludin
Counsellor
Mr. Yoke Heng Yean; Mrs. Tutu Dutta Yean
Counsellor, Defence Adviser
Col. Mohammad Perang Haji Musa; Mrs.
Zafeena Hamzah al-Rashid
Counsellor
Mr. Norzuhdy Mohammad Nordin; Mrs. Lili
Mardiana Samsudin
Counsellor
Mr. Ganeson Sivagurunathan; Mrs. Gowri
Kirubamoorthy
Counsellor
Mr. Mohamad Razif Haji Abd. Mubin; Mrs.
Norasmah Mustapha
First Secretary
Mr. Ikram Mohd Ibrahim; Mrs. Noor Azida
Azmi
First Secretary
Mr. Westmoreland Palon; Mrs. Elvinna
Luhum
Second Secretary
Mr. Riedzal Abdul Malek
Second Secretary
Ms. Sharon Ho Swee Peng
Third Secretary
Mr. Abdul Rahim Ibrahim; Mrs. Zainatul
Husniah Hussain

MALDIVES

**PERMANENT MISSION OF THE REPUBLIC
OF MALDIVES TO THE UNITED NATIONS**
800 2nd Ave. #400E
New York, NY 10017
Tel: (212) 599-6194 Fax: (212) 661-6405
Email: maldives@un.int
National Holiday: July 26th

Ambassador E. and P.
His Excellency Mohamed Latheef; Mrs.
Shakeela Hameed
**Counsellor, Deputy Permanent
Representative**
Mr. Ahmed Khaleel; Ms. Yasmin Adam
Khaleel
Attaché
Mr. Muruthala Moosa
Attaché
Mr. Ahmed Shifaz
Attaché
Mr. Hussain Jahhaz

MONGOLIA

**PERMANENT MISSION OF MONGOLIA TO
THE UNITED NATIONS**
6 E. 77th St.
New York, NY 10021
Tel: (212) 861-9460 Fax: (212) 861-9464
Email: mongolia@un.int
National Holiday: July 11th

Ambassador E. and P.
His Excellency Baatar Choisuren; Mrs.
Enkhjargal Bekh-Ochir
Counsellor
Mr. Tulga Narkhuu
Counsellor, Military Adviser
Mr. Gur Ragchaa
Second Secretary
Mr. Nemuun Gal
Attaché
Mr. Ganbold Dambajav; Mrs. Tserennadmid
Erdenesoyol

NEPAL

**PERMANENT MISSION OF THE KINGDOM
OF NEPAL TO THE UNITED NATIONS**
820 2nd Ave., 17th Fl. #17B
New York, NY 10017
Tel: (212) 370-3988 Fax: (212) 953-2038
Email: nepal@un.int
National Holiday: July 7th

Ambassador E. and P.
His Excellency Madhu Raman Acharya;
Mrs. Geeta Sharma Acharya
**Minister Plenipotentiary, Deputy Permanent
Representative**
Mr. Arjun Bahadur Thapa; Mrs. Pabitra
Thapa
Minister Counsellor
Mr. Arun Kurnar Dhital
Counsellor, Military Adviser
Colonel Devendra Bahadur Medhasi
First Secretary
Mr. Durga Bahadur Subedi; Mrs. Poonam
Subedi
First Secretary
Mr. Ram Babu Dhakal; Mrs. Rita Dhakal
First Secretary
Mr. Tirtha Raj Wagle; Mrs. Bimala Wagle
Third Secretary
Mr. Ghanashyam Lal Joshi
Third Secretary
Mr. Prakash Adhikari

OMAN

**PERMANENT MISSION OF THE SULTANATE
OF OMAN TO THE UNITED NATIONS**
866 United Nations Plz. #540
New York, NY 10017
Tel: (212) 355-3505 Fax: (212) 644-0070
Email: oman@un.int
National Holiday: November 18th

Ambassador E. and P.
His Excellency Fuad al-Hinai; Mrs. Hunaina
S. Al-Mughairy
First Secretary
Mr. Abdul Mohsin Shaban Salim Al-Ojaili;
Mrs. Al-Ojaili
First Secretary
Mr. Khalid Yaqoob Hamed Al-Harthy
First Secretary
Mr. Abdullah Mohammed Abdulla Al-Araimi
First Secretary
Mr. Mohammed Aqeel Omar Ba-Omar
Second Secretary
Mr. Omar Said Omar Al-Kathiri
Attaché (Commercial Adviser)
Mrs. Hunaina S. Al-Mughairy; His
Excellency Fuad Al-Hinai

PAKISTAN

**PERMANENT MISSION OF PAKISTAN TO
THE UNITED NATIONS**
8 E. 65th St.
New York, NY 10021
Tel: (212) 879-8600 Fax: (212) 744-7348
Email: pakistan@un.int
Web: www.un.int/pakistan
National Holiday: March 23rd

Ambassador E. and P.
His Excellency Munir Akram; Mrs. Christine
M. Akram
**Ambassador, Deputy Permanent
Representative**
His Excellency Aizaz Ahmad Chaudhry;
Mrs. Najia Aizaz Ahmad

Counsellor
Mr. Asad Majeed Khan; Mrs. Zunaira Asad
Khan
Counsellor
Mr. Imtiaz Hussain
First Secretary
Mr. Asim Iftikhar Ahmad; Mrs. Asma
Ahmad
First Secretary
Mr. Khalil-ur-Rahman Hashmi; Mrs.
Marium Mahmood
First Secretary
Mr. Syed Haider Shah; Mrs. Palwasha
Haider
Second Secretary
Mr. Bilal Hayee; Mrs. Shamyla Bilal
Second Secretary
Mr. Ahmed Farooq
Third Secretary
Ms. Madiha Mohyuddin Ali
Third Secretary
Miss Farhat Ayesha
Minister (Press)
Mr. Mansoor Suhail; Mrs. Lubna Suhail
Counsellor, Military Adviser
Col. Muhammad Asim; Mrs. Nighat Naz
Malik

PALESTINE

**PERMANENT OBSERVER MISSION OF
PALESTINE TO THE UNITED NATIONS**
115 E. 65th St.
New York, NY 10021
Tel: (212) 288-8500 Fax: (212) 517-2377
Email: mission@palestine-un.org

Ambassador, Permanent Observer
His Excellency Riyad H. Mansour
First Counsellor
Mrs. Somaia S. Barghouti; Mr. Anis
Barghouti
First Counsellor
Mr. Muin Burhan Shreim; Mrs. Khalida
Shreim
First Counsellor
Ms. Feda Abdelhady-Nasser; Mr. Tarik
Nasser
First Secretary
Ms. Nadya Rifaat Rasheed
Second Secretary
Mr. Ammar M. B. Hijazi; Mrs. Nour Odeh

PAPUA NEW GUINEA

**PERMANENT MISSION OF PAPUA NEW
GUINEA TO THE UNITED NATIONS**
201 E. 42nd St. #405
New York, NY 10017
Tel: (212) 557-5001 Fax: (212) 557-5009
Email: png@un.int
National Holiday: September 16th

Ambassador E. and P.
His Excellency Robert Guba Aisi; Mrs.
Susan Iamonama Aisi
**Minister Counsellor, Deputy Permanent
Representative**
Ms. Mathilda Jacinta Takaku
Second Secretary
Mr. Sakias Tameo; Mrs. Mary Wanefai

PHILIPPINES

**PERMANENT MISSION OF THE REPUBLIC
OF THE PHILIPPINES TO THE UNITED
NATIONS**
556 5th Ave., 5th Fl.
New York, NY 10036

Tel: (212) 764-1300 Fax: (212) 840-8602
Email: misunphil@aol.com
Web: www.un.int/philippines
National Holiday: June 12th

Ambassador E. and P.
His Excellency Lauro L. Baja, Jr.; Mrs.
Norma C. Baja
**Ambassador, Deputy Permanent
Representative**
His Excellency Bayani S. Mercado; Mrs.
Nida Montallana Mercado
Minister
Mr. Leslie B. Gatan; Mrs. Lydia Debbie M.
Gatan
Minister
Mr. Anacleto Rei A. Lacanilao III; Mrs.
Vivian J. Lacanilao
Minister
Ms. Maria Teresa L. Taguiang
Minister
Mr. Meynardo Montealegre
First Secretary
Miss Maria Rosario C. Aguinaldo
Second Secretary
Mr. Jimmy D. Blas; Mrs. Milagros L. Blas
Third Secretary
Mr. Patrick A. Chuasoto
Third Secretary
Mrs. Marie Yvette Banzon Abalos
Third Secretary
Mr. Elmer G. Cato; Mrs. Melanie Gliceria
R. Cato
Third Secretary
Ms. Emma Romano Sarne
Attaché
Mr. Apolonio L. Garcia; Mrs. Lolita S. Garcia
Attaché
Mr. Tomas A. Valerio, Jr.; Mrs. Susan P.
Valerio
Attaché
Mr. Arturo V. Romua; Mrs. Antonieta
Romua
Attaché
Mr. Bayani G. Sibug, Jr.; Mrs. Amalia R.
Sibug
Attaché
Mrs. Michelle M. Jayag; Mr. Reynon Jayag
Attaché
Ms. Christina T. Trinidad
Attaché
Mr. Normandy U. Macadangdang; Mrs.
Maria Rosario S. Macadangdang
Attaché
Mrs. Camille M. Macalintal; Mr. Albert A.
Macalintal
Attaché
Mrs. Olivia S. Osias-Magpile; Mr. Zoilo A.
Magpile
Attaché
Mr. Felix V. de Leon; Mrs. Rosemarie de
Leon
Attaché
Mrs. Amalia R. Sibug; Mr. Bayani G. Sibug.
Jr.
Attaché
Ms. Barbara O. Gison
Attaché
Mr. Eric R. Cruz
Attaché
Mr. Romero Seguis; Mrs. Lourdes C. Seguis

QATAR

**PERMANENT MISSION OF THE STATE OF
QATAR TO THE UNITED NATIONS**
809 United Nations Plz., 4th Fl.
New York, NY 10017
Tel: (212) 486-9335 Fax: (212) 758-4952
Email: qatar-e@qatarmission.org
National Holiday: September 3rd

Ambassador E. and P.
His Excellency Nassir Abdulaziz Al-Nasser
Minister Plenipotentiary, Deputy Permanent Representative
Mr. Mohamad Ahmed Mohamed H. Al-Hayki
Minister Plenipotentiary
Mr. Jamal Nasser Al-Bader; Mrs. Maria Teresa García
Counsellor
Mr. Abdullah Eid Salman Al-Sulaiti; Mrs. Hanadi Ahmed Rashid A. Al-Naimi
First Secretary
Mr. Jassim Ali Abdulla Al-Obaidli
First Secretary
Mr. Faisal Abdulla Hamad A. Al-Athba
Second Secretary
Mr. Sultan Ibrahim Yousuf Al-Mahmoud
Second Secretary
Mr. Mishal Mohammed Ali Ahmed Al-Ansari

RUSSIA

PERMANENT MISSION OF THE RUSSIAN FEDERATION TO THE UNITED NATIONS
136 E. 67th St.
New York, NY 10021
Tel: (212) 861-4900 Fax: (212) 628-0252
National Holiday: June 12th

Ambassador E. and P.
His Excellency Andrey I. Denisov; Mrs. Natalia A. Denisova
Envoy Extraordinary and Minister Plenipotentiary, First Deputy Permanent Representative
Mr. Alexander V. Konuzin; Mrs. Marina V. Konuzina
Envoy Extraordinary and Minister Plenipotentiary, Deputy Permanent Representative
Mr. Konstantin K. Dolgov; Mrs. Natalia V. Dolgova
Envoy Extraordinary and Minister Plenipotentiary, Deputy Permanent Representative
Mr. Nikolay V. Chulkov
Envoy Extraordinary and Minister Plenipotentiary, Deputy Permanent Representative
Mr. Ilya I. Rogachev; Mrs. Elena V. Vysotskaya
Senior Counsellor
Mr. Vladimir A. Iosifov; Mrs. Elena N. Iosifova
Senior Counsellor
Mr. Sergey Trepelkov; Mrs. Irina G. Trepelkova
Senior Counsellor
Mr. Alexander V. Ananiev; Mrs. Elena V. Ananieva
Senior Counsellor, Military Adviser
Mr. Nikolay M. Uvarov; Mrs. Tatiana M. Uvarova
Senior Counsellor
Mr. Dmitry A. Lobach; Mrs. Antonina M. Lobach
Senior Counsellor
Mr. Vadim S. Smirnov; Mrs. Galina V. Smirnova
Senior Counsellor
Mr. Nikolay I. Kolpakov; Mrs. Irina A. Kolpakova
Senior Counsellor
Mr. Alexey A. Novikov; Mrs. Alina B. Novikova
Senior Counsellor
Mr. Vitaliy A. Leplinskiy; Mrs. Elena B. Leplinskaya
Senior Counsellor
Mr. Dmitry I. Maksimychev; Mrs. Elena V. Maksimycheva

Counsellor
Mr. Vladimir V. Zagoskin; Mrs. Leila O. Zagoskina
Counsellor
Mr. Oleg N. Kulikov; Mrs. Tatiana Y. Kulikova
Counsellor
Mr. Oleg A. Shamanov; Mrs. Galina B. Shamanova
Counsellor
Mr. Andrey A. Nikiforov; Mrs. Irina A. Nikiforova
Counsellor
Mr. Pavel R. Knyazev
Counsellor
Mr. Aleksandr A. Putsenko; Mrs. Tatiana A. Putsenko
Counsellor
Mr. Alexandr A. Musienko; Mrs. Tatiana I. Sorokina
Counsellor
Mr. Sergey M. Tarasenko; Mrs. Elena E. Tarasenko
Counsellor
Mr. Nikolay N. Popikov; Mrs. Svetlana A. Popikova
Counsellor
Mr. Vladimir P. Salov; Mrs. Vera G. Alekseeva
Counsellor
Mr. Andrey V. Kovalenko
Counsellor
Mr. Gleb F. Desyatnikov; Mrs. Tatiana I. Desyatnikova
Counsellor
Mr. Dmitry V. Feoktistov; Mrs. Maria G. Feoktistova
Counsellor
Mr. Vladimir V. Tolkachev; Mrs. Irina P. Tolkacheva
Counsellor
Mr. Nikolay G. Baygushev; Mrs. Lyubov M. Baygusheva
Counsellor
Mr. Eduard A. Sinitsyn; Mrs. Anna A. Sinitsyna
Counsellor
Mr. Igor A. Alekseev; Mrs. Marina V. Alekseeva
First Secretary
Mr. Yuri M. Rudakov
First Secretary
Mr. Dmitry V. Tolbuzin; Mrs. Tatiana V. Tolbuzina
First Secretary
Mr. Albert V. Sitnikov; Mrs. Galina V. Sitnikova
First Secretary
Mr. Aleksandr A. Kislov; Mrs. Oksana V. Kislova
First Secretary
Mr. Maxim V. Ershov; Mrs. Zhanna Y. Chesnokova
First Secretary
Mr. Vyacheslav G. Fomichev; Mrs. Tatania I. Fomicheva
First Secretary
Mr. Vladimir Y. Zheglov; Mrs. Tatiana G. Zheglova
First Secretary
Mr. Alexander S. Alimov; Mrs. Tatiana R. Alimova
First Secretary
Mr. Sergey A. Sizov; Mrs. Irina S. Sizova
First Secretary
Mr. Mkhail V. Noskov; Mrs. Margarita V. Noskova
Second Secretary
Mr. Igor A. Malyshev; Mrs. Tatiana L. Malysheva
Second Secretary
Mr. Evgeny V. Prokopenko; Mrs. Natalia D. Prokopenko

Second Secretary
Mr. Dmitry I. Grigoriev; Mrs. Svetlana Y. Grigorieva
Second Secretary
Mr. Stepan Y. Kuzmenkov; Mrs. Alla V. Kuzmenkova
Second Secretary
Mr. Boris V. Chernenko; Mrs. Yulia V. Chernenko
Second Secretary
Mr. Oleg V. Solomatin; Mrs. Elena V. Solomatina
Second Secretary
Mr. Alexander A. Ilchenko

SAUDI ARABIA

PERMANENT MISSION OF SAUDI ARABIA TO THE UNITED NATIONS
809 United Nations Plz., 10 & 11th Fl.
New York, NY 10017
Tel: (212) 557-1525 Fax: (212) 983-4895
Email: saudi-mission@un.int
National Holiday: September 23rd

Ambassador E. and P.
His Excellency Fawzi A. Shobokshi; Mrs. Shobokshi
Counsellor
Mr. Abdullatif H. Sallam; Mrs. Sallam
Counsellor
Mr. Saud M. A. Shawwaf; Mrs. Aida Ahmed O. Sharabati
First Secretary
Mr. Abdullah S. Al-Anazi; Mrs. Al-Anazi
First Secretary
Mr. Abdullah M. Al-Rasheed; Mrs. Al-Rasheed
Second Secretary
Mr. Abdulaziz M. Al-Badi; Mrs. Al-Badi
Second Secretary
Mr. Haytham H. Al-Malki; Mrs. Al-Malki
Second Secretary
Mr. Ehab M. Al-Najjar; Mrs. Al-Najjar
Second Secretary
Mr. Khalid M. R. H. Al Wafi
Third Secretary
Mr. Fawaz A. Al-Shubaili; Mrs. Al-Shubaili
Third Secretary
Mr. Munasser Salem Nasser Lasloom
Attaché
Mr. Abdulfattah Ahmed Saleh Emam; Mrs. Emam
Attaché
Mr. Hussam Jamel Ahmed Mukhtar; Mrs. Mukhtar
Adviser
Mr. Ahmed Farid
Adviser
Mr. Jamal T. Alotaibi

SINGAPORE

PERMANENT MISSION OF THE REPUBLIC OF SINGAPORE TO THE UNITED NATIONS
231 E. 51st St.
New York, NY 10022
Tel: (212) 826-0840 Fax: (212) 826-2964
Email: singapore@un.int
Web: www.mfa.gov.sg/newyork
National Holiday: August 9th

Ambassador E. and P.
His Excellency Vanu Gopala Menon; Mrs. Jayanthi Menon
Minister Counsellor, Deputy Permanent Representative
Mr. Tan York Chor; Mrs. Lim Boon Siang
Counsellor, Military Adviser
Brigadier General Leong Yue Kheong

Counsellor
Mr. Raziff Aljunied; Mrs. Caroline Martha Klibingaitis
First Secretary (Administration)
Mr. Tong Tek Liong
First Secretary
Mr. Chew Ming Charles Christian
First Secretary
Ms. Melissa Wong Chin Hui

SRI LANKA

PERMANENT MISSION OF THE DEMOCRATIC SOCIALIST REPUBLIC OF SRI LANKA TO THE UNITED NATIONS
630 3rd Ave., 20th Fl.
New York, NY 10017
Tel: (212) 986-7040 Fax: (212) 986-1838
Email: slpmny@aol.com
National Holiday: February 4th

Ambassador E. and P.
His Excellency Prasad Kariyawasam; Mrs. Kanthi Kariyawasam
Minister, Deputy Permanent Representative
Mr. A. L. Abdul Azeez; Mrs. Mahira Abdul Azeez
Minister
Mr. Vijayasiri Padukkage; Mrs. Jayamini Dhammika Padukkage
First Secretary
Ms. Yasoja Gunasekera
Second Secretary
Mrs. Varuni Hewavitharana; Mr. Manjula Hewavitharana
Attaché
Mr. D. M. U. N. Dassanayake; Mrs. Padmini T. Dassanayake
Attaché
Mr. Galle Liyanage Senarath; Mrs. K. P. S Rupika Karunanayake

SYRIA

PERMANENT MISSON OF THE SYRIAN ARAB REPUBLIC TO THE UNITED NATIONS
820 2nd Ave., 15th Fl.
New York, NY 10017
Tel: (212) 661-1313 Fax: (212) 983-4439
Email: syrianmission@verizonmail.com
National Holiday: April 17th

Ambassador E. and P.
His Excellency Fayssal Mekdad; Mrs. Shkrieh Mekdad
Minister Counsellor, Deputy Permanent Representative
Mr. Milad Atieh; Mrs. Faten Istanbouly
Counsellor
Mr. Bassam Sabagh
Second Secretary
Mr. Ahmad Alhariri
Second Secretary
Mr. Mhd. Najib Elji
Second Secretary
Ms. Warif Halabi
Third Secretary
Mr. Haydar Ali Ahmad
Third Secretary
Mr. Hussein Sabbagh; Mrs. Samah Al Khatib Alsabsabi Al Rifaai
Attaché
Ms. Laila Baba
Attaché
Mr. Mhd. Nael Al-Mahrous
Attaché
Mr. Yassar Diab
Attaché
Mr. Manar Taleb

TAJIKISTAN

PERMANENT MISSION OF THE REPUBLIC OF TAJIKISTAN TO THE UNITED NATIONS
136 E. 67th St.
New York, NY 10021
Tel: (212) 744-2196 Fax: (212) 472-7645
Email: tajikistanun@aol.com
National Holiday: September 9th

Ambassador E. and P.
Vacant
Counsellor
Mr. Khomidjon T. Nazarov; Mrs. Mahbuba Jumankulova
Third Secretary
Mr. Firdavs Alimov
Adviser
Mrs. Lyudmila Lapshina

THAILAND

PERMANENT MISSION OF THAILAND TO THE UNITED NATIONS
351 E. 52nd St.
New York, NY 10022
Tel: (212) 754-2230 Fax: (212) 688-3029
Email: thailand@un.int
National Holiday: December 5th

Ambassador E. and P.
Her Excellency Laxanachantorn Laohaphan
Minister, Deputy Permanent Representative
Mr. Pravit Chaimongkol; Mrs. Siriporn Chaimongkol
Minister Counsellor
Mr. Ittiporn Boonpracong; Mrs. Suteera Boonpracong
Minister Counsellor
Mr. Biravij Suwanpradhes; Mrs. Supinya Suwanpradhes
Minister Counsellor, Military Adviser
Col. Sakda Sangsnit; Mrs. Pornthip Sangsnit
Minister Counsellor, Military Adviser
Col. Ruampon Meechoo-Arrth
Counsellor
Mrs. Kanchana Patarachoke
First Secretary
Miss Wanalee Lohpechra
First Secretary
Mr. Tull Traisorat
First Secretary
Mr. Phuchphop Mongkolnavin; Mrs. Phantuma Mongkolnavin
First Secretary
Mr. Kudatara Nagaviroj
First Secretary
Mrs. Nadariya Phromyothi
Second Secretary
Ms. Malinee Numchaisrika
Second Secretary
Mr. Jak Sangchai
Second Secretary
Ms. Somjai Klaipetch
Second Secretary
Mr. Kosol Satithamajit; Mrs. Wipapat Satithamajit
Attaché
Master Sergeant Surakit Keannukul; Mrs. Atcharawan Keannukul
Attaché
Mr. Saksit Promthong

TIMOR-LESTE

PERMANENT MISSION OF THE DEMOCRATIC REPUBLIC OF TIMOR-LESTE TO THE UNITED NATIONS
866 United Nations Plz. #441
New York, NY 10017
Tel: (212) 759-3675 Fax: (212) 759-4196
Email: timor-leste@un.int
National Holiday: May 20th

Ambassador E. and P.
His Excellency José Luís Guterres; Ms. Ana Maria J. M. Valerio
First Secretary
Ms. Natercia Coelho de Silva
Counsellor
Ms. Sofia Borges; Mr. Hansjoerg Strohmeyer

TURKEY

PERMANENT MISSION OF TURKEY TO THE UNITED NATIONS
821 United Nations Plz., 10th Fl.
New York, NY 10017
Tel: (212) 949-0150 Fax: (212) 949-0086
Email: turkuno-dt@un.int
National Holiday: October 29th

Ambassador E. and P.
His Excellency Baki Ilkin; Mrs. Nur Ilkin
Minister Counsellor, Deputy Permanent Representative
Mr. Ersin Erçin; Mrs. Jülide Kayöhan Erçin
Counsellor, Military Adviser
Mr. Metin Tokel; Mrs. Zennure Tokel
Counsellor (Financial Affairs)
Mr. Cihan Terzi
First Counsellor
Mr. Kerim Uras; Mrs. Zeynep Saylan Uras
First Counsellor
Mr. Ömer Gücük
Counsellor
Ms. Damla Yesim Say
Counsellor
Mr. Çagatay Erciyes; Mrs. Aytaç Erciyes
Counsellor (Legal Affairs)
Ms. Emine Gökçen Tugral
First Secretary
Mr. Serhat Aksen; Mrs. Meltem Aksen
First Secretary
Ms. Ayse Berris Ekinci
First Secretary
Mr. Haldun Tekneci
First Secretary
Mr. Mustafa Levent Bilgen; Mrs. Ayse Zerif Bilgen
Attaché
Mr. Mehmet Kürsat Öztürk; Mrs. Nursen Öztürk
Attaché
Mr. Fatih Yagiz ; Mrs. Asli Barut-Yagiz
Attaché
Mr. Ugur Yilmaz
Attaché
Mrs. Hülya Dogan; Mr. Nuri Dogan
Attaché
Mr. Aytaç Özenç; Mrs. Seval Özenç

TURKMENISTAN

PERMANENT MISSION OF TURKMENISTAN TO THE UNITED NATIONS
866 United Nations Plz. #424
New York, NY 10017
Tel: (212) 486-8908 Fax: (212) 486-2521
Email: turkmenistan@un.int

National Holiday: October 27th

Ambassador E. and P.
Her Excellency Aksoltan T. Ataeva; Mr. Tchary Pirmoukhamedov
Counsellor, Deputy Permanent Representative
Mr. Esen M. Aydogdyev; Mrs. Nurgozel Aydogdyeva
First Secretary
Mr. Dovletmyrat Bozaganov; Mrs. Merdjen Bozaganova

UNITED ARAB EMIRATES

PERMANENT MISSION OF THE UNITED ARAB EMIRATES TO THE UNITED NATIONS
3 Dag Hammarskjöld Plz., 305 E. 47th St., 7th Fl.
New York, NY 10017
Tel: (212) 371-0480 Fax: (212) 371-4923
National Holiday: December 2nd

Ambassador E. and P.
His Excellency Abdulaziz Nasser Al-Shamsi; Mrs. Hissa Al-Otaiba Al-Shamsi
First Secretary
Mr. Mohammed Al-Otaiba
Second Secretary
Mr. Salim Ibrahim Ahmed Al-Naqbi; Mrs. Muna Ali Al-Naqbi
Third Secretary
Mr. Saeed Rashed S. Alwan Al-Hebsi
Third Secretary
Mr. Mohamed Issa Hamad Abushahab; Mrs. Amna Ali Hamad Al-Muhairy
Attaché (Administrative Affairs)
Mrs. Amna Ali Hamad Al-Muhairy; Mr. Mohamed Issa Hamad Abushahab

UZBEKISTAN

PERMANENT MISSION OF THE REPUBLIC OF UZBEKISTAN TO THE UNITED NATIONS
801 2nd Ave., 20th Fl.
New York, NY 10017
Tel: (212) 486-4242 Fax: (212) 486-7998
National Holiday: September 1st

Ambassador E. and P.
His Excellency Alisher Vohidov; Mrs. Svetlana Vohidova
Counsellor
Mrs. Gulzara Tuyunbayeva
Second Secretary
Mr. Farhod Arziev; Mrs. Rano Arzieva
Third Secretary
Mr. Rustam Kayumov; Mrs. Nilufar Kayumova

VIETNAM

PERMANENT MISSION OF THE SOCIALIST REPUBLIC OF VIET NAM TO THE UNITED NATIONS
866 United Nations Plz. #435
New York, NY 10017
Tel: (212) 644-0594 Fax: (212) 644-5732
Email: vietnamun@vnmission.com
Web: www.un.int/vietnam
National Holiday: September 2nd

Ambassador E. and P.
His Excellency Le Luong Minh; Mrs. Nguyen Thanh Huong
Minister Counsellor, Deputy Permanent Representative

Mr. Nguyen Duy Chien; Mrs. Nguyen Thi Hoa
Minister Counsellor, Deputy Permanent Representative
Mr. Nguyen Tat Thanh; Mrs. Nguyen Tu Huyen
Counsellor
Mr. Nguyen Dinh Hai; Mrs. Nguyen Thi Thu Ha
First Secretary (Head of Chancery)
Mr. Nguyen Manh Hung; Mrs. Ninh Thi Binh
First Secretary
Mr. Nguyen Minh Thanh; Mrs. Nguyen Thi Bich Hoa
First Secretary
Mr. Nguyen Quoc Thang; Mrs. Nguyen Thi Thu Huong
First Secretary
Mr. Vu Tran Phong; Mrs. Nguyen Thi Phu
Second Secretary
Mr. Nguyen Ha An
Third Secretary
Mr. Duong Hoai Nam; Mrs. Nguyen Linh Hhan
Third Secretary
Mrs. Nguyen Thi Van Anh
Third Secretary
Mr. Pham Hai Anh
Third Secretary
Mrs. Nguyen Thi Lan; Mr. Nghiem Xuan Cai
Attaché
Mr. Dang Hoang Giang
Attaché
Mr. To Anh Tuan
Attaché
Mr. Vu Quang Huy; Mrs. Co Minh Huyen

YEMEN

PERMANENT MISSION OF THE REPUBLIC OF YEMEN TO THE UNITED NATIONS
413 E. 51st St.
New York, NY 10022
Tel: (212) 355-1730 Fax: (212) 750-9613
Email: yemun@un.int
National Holiday: May 22th

Ambassador E. and P.
His Excellency Abdullah M. Alsaidi; Mrs. Amirah A. Alsaidi
Ambassador, Deputy Permanent Representative
His Excellency Ahmed Hassan Hassan Mohamed
Counsellor
Mr. Mohammed M. Ali Al-Otmi; Mrs. Arma A. M. Al-Mahfadi
Counsellor
Mr. Abdulkader Ahmed Saeed Alsubeihi
First Secretary
Mr. Ismail Mohamed Yahya Almaabri
Second Secretary
Mr. Tarek M. Mutahar; Mrs. Soha Loft H. Alkohlani
Second Secretary
Mr. Abdulmalik Motahar A. Alshabibi
Second Secretary
Ms. Arwa Ali Noman
Third Secretary
Mr. Najeeb Ali Mohamed Al-Jabowbi

Wondering how to pay for college?

The Coast Guard has the money to help.

Coast Guard Academy:

A free college education and guaranteed job after graduation as a Coast Guard officer.

College Student Pre-Commissioning Initiative:

Receive full tuition for your junior and senior years, books and educational fees, a monthly stipend of approximately $2,000, plus guaranteed job after graduation as a Coast Guard officer

Active Duty Montgomery GI Bill:

Up to $1034 per month for 36 months.

Reserve Montgomery GI Bill:

Up to $297 per month for 36 months.

Tuition Assistance:

Up to $297 per semester hour, up to $4,500 per year.

Coast Guard Foundation Grant:

$350 per student per year for books and other education-related expenses

Coast Guard Mutual Assistance:

Grants of $160 per student per year for the cost of college textbooks, plus interest free loans loans are available.

Servicemember's Opportunity College Coast Guard:

An affiliation of colleges, that assists members in earning an associate degree or a bachelor's degree, and allow Coast Guard members to transfer college credits between schools and reduce their requirements for residency.

For more information, call us toll-free at

1-877-NOW-USCG (1-877-669-8724).

or visit:

Active Duty & Reserve
www.gocoastguard.com

Civilian
www.uscg.mil.civilian jobs

These programs may have additional requirements for participation. Amounts and availability of programs are subject to change. Contact your local Coast Guard recruiter for more information.

A MESSAGE FROM THE COMMANDANT OF THE COAST GUARD

Congratulations on the third edition of the Asian American Yearbook. Since its creation, this publication has been a valuable resource for Americans to obtain a better understanding of resources and leaders in the Asian American community nationwide. It also serves to broaden the interest of youth and to ensure success in advancing their academic aspirations…which ultimately serves our organization in meeting our mission to obtain and sustain a diverse workforce.

The Coast Guard is a military, multi-mission and maritime service. Though we are America's smallest armed service, we perform an astonishingly broad range of services for our country. Never was that more evident than in the preparation and response last year to the worst hurricane season on record. In the aftermath of Hurricane Katrina the Coast Guard saved more than 24,000 people and evacuated almost 9,500 hospital patients to safety. For example, Coast Guard Flight Surgeon Lieutenant Commander John Hariadi's tireless efforts over a seven day period in arduous conditions allowed him to treat 133 patients and conduct 50 medical evacuations. The Coast Guard also responded to more than 3800 marine pollution cases, and reopened affected waterways to restart commerce in most areas within a week. The Coast Guard's unique abilities and missions allowed us to respond quickly and decisively, balancing our simultaneous roles of lifesavers, environmental responders, and law enforcement officers within our military command and control structure.

The Coast Guard succeeds because of our terrific and diverse people. We seek the best talent America has to offer to keep our Service strong. We draw on the strengths of our differences and similarities to create an environment that places high value on individual dignity, respect, and professional growth so that all members can achieve their full potential and make their greatest contribution to the mission.

Coast Guard people are unsung heroes that make up our American community. They are your neighbors who make the extraordinary things look ordinary every day. They are active duty and reserve military personnel, civilian employees, and even volunteers from the Coast Guard Auxiliary. Our people are what make the Coast Guard great. We invite you to join us and share in a lifelong affiliation with a noble service.

Semper Paratus – Always Ready.

THOMAS H. COLLINS
Admiral, United States Coast Guard

Interview

DONNA SHALALA

PRESIDENT OF THE UNIVERSITY OF MIAMI

Donna E. Shalala became Professor of Political Science and President of the University of Miami on June 1, 2001. Born in Cleveland, Ohio, President Shalala received her A.B. degree in History from Western College for Women and her Ph.D. degree from The Maxwell School of Citizenship and Public Affairs at Syracuse University. A leading scholar on the political economy of state and local governments, she has also held tenured professorships at Columbia University, the City University of New York (CUNY), and the University of Wisconsin-Madison. She served as President of Hunter College of CUNY from 1980 to 1987 and as Chancellor of the University of Wisconsin-Madison from 1987 to 1993. She is a Director of Gannett Co., Inc.; UnitedHealth Group, Inc.; and the Lennar Corporation. She also serves as a Trustee of the Henry J. Kaiser Family Foundation.

President Shalala has more than three dozen honorary degrees and a host of other honors, including the 1992 National Public Service Award, the 1994 Glamour magazine Woman of the Year Award, the National Conference for Community and Justice (NCCJ) 2005 Silver Medallion Award for Service to Humanity, and in 2005, was named one of America's Best Leaders by U.S. News & World Report and the Center for Public Leadership at Harvard University's Kennedy School of Government. She has been elected to the Council on Foreign Relations; National Academy of Education; the National Academy of Public Administration; the American Academy of Arts and Sciences; the National Academy of Social Insurance; the American Academy of Political and Social Science; and the Institute of Medicine of the National Academy of Sciences.

AsAY What areas are you focused on improving for the University of Miami and its students during your presidency? Also, what do you hope will take place in terms of the higher education landscape in this country?

Shalala All of us have to learn how to manage diverse populations, because that's what the future is, and be more responsive to the kinds of diverse student bodies we're going to have in the future.

AsAY Diversity at the University of Miami is phenomenal, with

President Shalala's inauguration with Jeb Bush and Sebastian on November 2, 2001.

39 percent minority freshmen and 45 percent minority undergraduates, according to statistics from 2004. To what do you atribute this success in terms of creating a diverse environment? How do you work to enhance an already diverse campus?

Shalala Well, we are lucky because of location, but we work very hard in creating an atmosphere in which students are comfortable no matter what their background. And you have to work at it.

The second point I would make is that students come here because of the diversity and so they're pretty conscious about it. It's not everybody's cup of tea–some students are overwhelmed by it, but the vast majority of our students celebrate it and are excited by the diversity.

AsAY Asian Americans constitute 7 percent of undergraduates as opposed to Hispanics who represent 27 percent. What accounts for this disparity aside from the large Hispanic community in South Florida? What is being done to create a more balanced population within the minority community?

Shalala That's a location phenomenon. If you were at USC, it would be the opposite. It's just a location issue. We also have a large South Asian population in South Florida and I think our numbers reflect that. We're always recruiting talented minority students.

AsAY Asian Americans have statistically higher academic achievement levels. How do you explain the relatively high academic attainment of the Asian American community? What needs to be done to raise the academic achievement levels of the other minority groups?

Shalala In general, it's a question of providing opportunity and comfort.

AsAY In your opinion, what impact will the rapidly-growing Asian American population have on the academic community in the United States over the next decade?

Shalala I think the impact will be improving the quality and opening up opportunities for more minorities as the population becomes the majority.

AsAY As President of the University of Miami, what would you like your legacy to be?

Shalala That we demonstrated that you can be both diverse and excellent.

President Shalala delivered the keynote address on March 18, 2002 at a "Send-Off" celebration for 34 new Peace Corps volunteers traveling to Haiti for two years. President Shalala was also in the Peace Corps, spending two years in Iran beginning in 1962.

FIG 1. Educational Attainment of Asian and Pacific Islanders 25 Years and Over: 2004

The collective level of education for any group is an important measurement that reflects a number of other socioeconomic and cultural trends. According to the U.S. Census Bureau's 2004 American Community Survey, 47.3 percent of Asian and Pacific Islanders in the United States age 25 years and over have earned a bachelor's degree or higher.

Source: US Census Bureau, 2004 American Community Survey www.census.gov

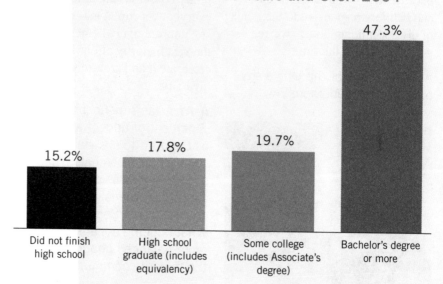

FIG 2. Post-Secondary Educational Attainment of the Asian and Pacific Islander Population 25 Years and Over: 2004

As of 2004, twenty-eight percent of Asian and Pacific Islander Americans over the age of 24 had completed a bachelor's degree. Among the same group, almost nineteen percent had attained an advanced degree of some kind.

Source: US Census Bureau, 2004 American Community Survey www.census.gov

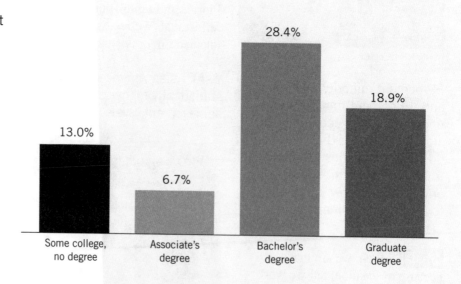

FIG 3. Educational Attainment of Asian American Population 25 Years and Over, by Nativity: 2004

Foreign-born Asian Americans are highly educated. The percentage of non-natives that earned a bachelor's degree or higher was only 0.5 percent lower than their native-born counterparts.

Source: US Census Bureau, Current Population Survey, 2004 www.census.gov

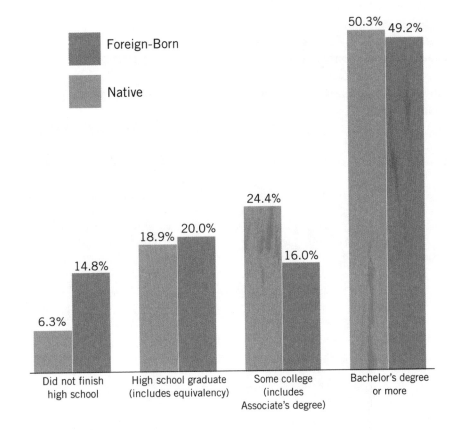

FIG 4. Educational Attainment of Asian and Pacific Islander Population Age 25 and Over, by Sex: 2004

Asian Pacific American men age 25 and older were more likely than women of the same group to have a bachelor's degree or higher. There was virtually no difference between men and women for completing at least some college or an associate's degree.

Source: US Census Bureau, 2004 American Community Survey www.census.gov

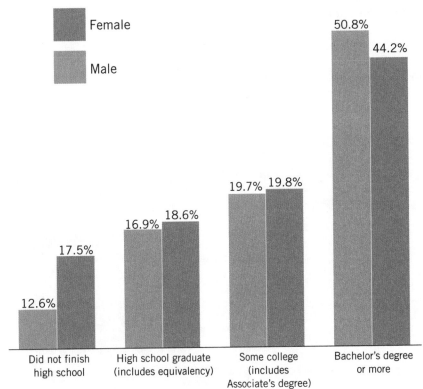

FIG 5a. Women's Educational Attainment for Selected Groups 25 Years and Over: 2004

Asian women far outperformed non-Hispanic White women in higher education. Forty-six percent of Asian women earned a bachelor's degree or higher compared with only twenty-eight percent of non-Hispanic Whites.

Source: US Census Bureau, Current Population Survey, 2004 www.census.gov

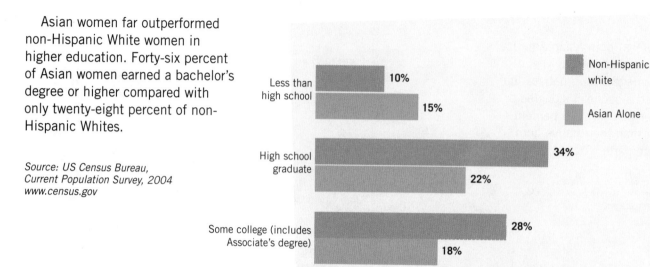

Non-Hispanic white

Asian Alone

Less than high school — 10% / 15%

High school graduate — 34% / 22%

Some college (includes Associate's degree) — 28% / 18%

Bachelor's degree or more — 28% / 46%

FIG 5b. Men's Educational Attainment for Selected Groups 25 Years and Over: 2004

Asian men were also much more likely to have a post-secondary degree than their non-Hispanic White counterparts.

Source: US Census Bureau, Current Population Survey, 2004 www.census.gov

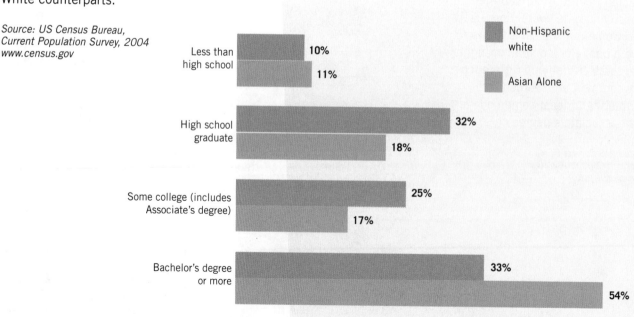

Non-Hispanic white

Asian Alone

Less than high school — 10% / 11%

High school graduate — 32% / 18%

Some college (includes Associate's degree) — 25% / 17%

Bachelor's degree or more — 33% / 54%

ScholarSite.com Financial Aid for Asian Pacific Americans

Approximately 75 student financial aid opportunities are listed below. They were selected for their focus on Asian Pacific American students at the undergraduate level. For more detailed information on conditions and restrictions for these and thousands of other opportunities, please visit TIYM's financial aid website. www.scholarsite.com.

Award

W

WESTERN ILLINOIS UNIVERSITY
Office of Financial Aid
1 University Circle
Macomb, IL 61455-1396

Donald Poindexter Research Award Fund
Janice Owens, Director of University
Scholarship Activities
Tel: (309) 298-2001 Fax: (309) 298-2432
Email: info@wiu.edu
Web: www.wiu.edu
Requirements: Student must be an American ethnic minority, and have a research proposal approved. Priority will be given to undergraduates but graduate students are also eligible. Contact the Department of Psychology.
Disciplines: Psychology
Award: $150
Eligible Inst.: Western Illinois University

Fellowship

A

AMERICAN BAR FOUNDATION
750 N. Lake Shore Dr., 4th Fl.
Chicago, IL 60611

Montgomery Summer Research Diversity Fellowships in Law and Social Science for Undergraduate Students
Tim Watson, Program Associate
Tel: (312) 988-6560 Fax: (312) 988-6579
Email: fellowships@abfn.org
Web: www.abf-sociolegal.org
Requirements: Eligible are American citizens and lawful permanent residents including, but not limited to, persons who are African American, Hispanic/Latino, Native American, or Puerto Rican, as well as other individuals who will add diversity to the field of law and social science. Applications will be considered only from sophomores and juniors, that is, students who have completed at least the sophomore year and who have not received a bachelor's degree by the time the fellowship begins. Applicants must have a Grade Point Average of at least 3.0 (on a 4.0 scale) and be moving toward an academic major in the social sciences or humanities.
Disciplines: Law, Social Sciences, Humanities Research
Eligible Inst.: US schools
Deadline: March 15

U

UNIVERSITY OF CALIFORNIA AT BERKELEY
Graduate Division
312 Mcluaghlin Hall #1702
Berkeley, CA 94720

UC-Berkeley Summer Research for Minority Undergraduates
Pamela D. Jennings, Coordinator
Tel: (510) 643-6443 Fax: (510) 643-5600
Email: cblf@berkeley.edu
Web: www.berkeley.edu
Requirements: A 10-week summer research and professional development program is available for disadvantaged and underrepresented minority students interested in careers as physican scientists. The program is designed for students in their freshman, sophmore or junior years of college.
Disciplines: Natural Sciences, Social Sciences, Humanities & Liberal Arts, Biology
Award: $1,600
Eligible Inst.: University of California Berkeley

Grant

P

PAGE EDUCATION FOUNDATION
P.O. Box 581254
Minneapolis, MN 55458-1254

Page Education Foundation Grant
Ramona Harristhal, Administrative Director
Tel: (612) 332-0406 Fax: (612) 332-0403
Email: info@page-ed.org
Web: www.page-ed.org
Requirements: Are students of color, show financial need, demonstrate a positive attitude toward education and community service, attend post-secondary school in Minnesota, and be willing to complete 50 hours of service to children each year.
Disciplines: Any
Award: $1,000-2,500
Eligible Inst.: US schools
Deadline: May 1

PRESBYTERIAN CHURCH (USA)
Office of Financial Aid for Studies
100 Witherspoon St.
Louisville, KY 40202-1396

Racial Ethnic Supplemental Grant
Frances Cook
Tel: (502) 569-5776 Fax: (502) 569-5018

Email: fcook@ctr.pcusa.org
Web: www.pcusa.org
Requirements: Studying full-time in a PC (USA) seminary or accredited theological institution approved by the student's Committee on Preparation for Ministry. M.Div. students must be enrolled as an inquirer or candidate by a PC (USA) presbytery prior to the application deadline date eligible for the award a maximum of two years as an Inquirer,eligible for the award in their third/final year as a Candidate, MACE students must be seeking a degree to pursue a church occupation.Recommended by the financial aid officer at theological institution. Funding allocated for first professional degree for a church occupation. Students already awarded an M.Div. or MACE will not be considered for grants, but may apply for a theological student loan. For African American, Alaska Native, Asian American, Hispanic American, or Native American students who have been awarded the Presbyterian Study Grant and have remaining need.
Disciplines: Religion & Theology
Award: $500-$1,000
Eligible Inst.: US schools

Internship

N

NEWS JOURNAL
P.O. Box 15505
Wilmington, DE 19850

Internship Program
John Sweeney, Public Editor
Tel: (302) 324-2500 Fax: (302) 324-2578
Web: www.delawareonline.com/
Requirements: Internship programs are available in info graphics and layout/design. The internship is available for the summer. Send resume, sample of works, references, and a cover letter.
Disciplines: Graphic Communications, Design
Award: Varies

U

U.S. DEPARTMENT OF ENERGY

Historically Black Colleges and Universities and Minority Institutions Collaborative Research Project
Christina Budwine
Tel: (925) 422-5460

Web: www.doe.gov
Requirements: The program gives minority students valuable hands-on experience in developing technologies to promote the efficient and environmentally safe use of coal, oil and natural gas.
Disciplines: Natural Sciences
Award: Varies
Eligible Inst.: US schools

UNIVERSITY CORPORATION FOR ATMOSPHERIC RESEARCH
P.O. Box 3000
Boulder, CO 80307-3000

Significant Opportunities in Atmosphere Research and Science (SOARS)
Tel: (303) 497-1000 Fax: (303) 497-1654
Email: jwhite@ucar.edu
Web: www.ucar.edu/soars
Requirements: This is for a four-year undergraduate and graduate program for underrepresented students interested in careers in the atmospheric and related sciences. Provides summer research internships, ongoing mentoring, and financial support for graduate school study.
Disciplines: Natural Sciences
Award: Varies

Scholarship

A

ALABAMA SPACE GRANT CONSORTIUM
c/o University of Alabama in Huntsville
Materials Science Bldg. #205
Huntsville, AL 35899

Teacher Education Scholarship Program
Tel: (256) 824-6800 Fax: (256) 890-6061
Web: www.uah.edu
Requirements: The Teacher Education Scholarship Program, is designed to attract and encourage talented individuals to enter a course of study leading to pre-college secondary teaching certification in the sciences, mathematics and technology education. Applications are solicited from high school seniors and community college students in their final year who have been accepted at one of the seven Alabama Space Grant Universities.
Disciplines: Education
Award: $1,000
Eligible Inst.: University of Alabama
Deadline: March 1

ALBERTUS MAGNUS COLLEGE

Financial Aid
700 Prospectus St.
New Haven, CT 06511

Nationwide Insurance Scholarship

Tel: (203) 773-8505 Fax: (203) 773-8972
Email: admissions@albertus.edu
Web: www.albertus.edu
Requirements: This scholarship is available to minority students who demonstrate financial need.
Disciplines: Any
Award: $1,250
Eligible Inst.: Albertus Magnus College
Deadline: April 15

AMERICAN NUCLEAR SOCIETY

555 N. Kensington Ave.
La Grange Park, IL 60525

Undergraduate Scholarship

Tony Bishop, Scholarship Coordinator
Tel: (708) 352-6611 Fax: (708) 352-0499
Email: tbishop@ans.org
Web: www.ans.org
Requirements: This scholarship is available to a sophomore student enrolled in a course of study relating to a degree in nuclear science or nuclear engineering in a U.S. institution and must be either a U.S citizen or permanent resident.
Disciplines: Nuclear Science, Engineering
Award: $2,000
Eligible Inst.: US schools
Deadline: February 1

ARKANSAS STATE UNIVERSITY

College of Communications
P.O. Box 540
State University, AR 72467

William Randolph Hearst Minority Scholarship in Journalism and Radio-Television

Tel: (870) 972-2310 Fax: (870) 972-2794
Email: admissions@chickasaw.astate.edu
Web: www.astate.edu
Requirements: This scholarship is available to the most outstanding recent graduate or graduate senior student and above majoring in journalism or radio-television.
Disciplines: Journalism, Radio Broadcasting, TV Broadcasting, Broadcasting, Communications,
Eligible Inst.: Arkansas State University
Deadline: April 1

B

BIOLA UNIVERSITY

Office of Admissions
13800 Biola Ave.
La Mirada, CA 90639-4652

Scholarships for Underrepresented Groups of Ethnicity (SURGE)

Scholarship Administrator
Tel: (562) 903-4752 Fax: (562) 906-4541
Web: www.biola.edu
Requirements: These scholarships are available to African-American, Hispanic-American or Native American full time undergraduate students showing merit and involvement in cultural activities. Applicant must maintain GPA of 3.0.
Disciplines: Any
Award: $6,500
Eligible Inst.: Biola University
Deadline: February 15

BROWN FOUNDATION FOR EDUCATIONAL EQUITY, EXCELLENCE, AND RESEARCH

P.O. Box 4862
Zip Topeka, KS 66604

Brown Scholar

Chelsey Smith, Administrative Assistant
Tel: (785) 235-3939 Fax: (785) 235-1001
Email: brownfound@juno.com
Web: www.brownvboard.org
Requirements: Applicants must be a minority student and admitted to a teacher education program at a 4-year college or university. In addition, applicant must submit two letters of recommendation: one from a teacher, counselor, or other school official and one from a person familar with the applicant's skills and abilities who is not a family member.
Disciplines: Education
Award: $1,000
Eligible Inst.: US schools
Deadline: March 30

BUCKNELL UNIVERSITY

Financial Aid Office
621 St. George St.
Lewisburg, PA 17837

Berlin Family Scholarship

Andrea C.A. Leithner, Director
Tel: (570) 577-1331 Fax: (570) 577-1481
Email: finaid@bucknell.edu
Web: www.bucknell.edu
Requirements: The Berlin Family Scholarship was established by George R. Berlin, Class of 1965, his mother, Elizabeth Smith Berlin, Class of 1935, and his sons, Bradley J. Berlin, Class of 1993, and William B. Berlin, Class of 1993 (M.A.), in recognition of George R. Berlin's father, William H. Berlin, Class of 1935. Preference for the scholarship award shall be given to students whose racial, ethnic, cultural, economic or other characteristics enhance the diversity of Bucknell's student group.
Disciplines: Any
Award: Varies
Eligible Inst.: Bucknell University

Bott-Jennings Family Scholarship

Andrea C.A. Leithner, Director
Tel: (570) 577-1331 Fax: (570) 577-1481
Email: finaid@bucknell.edu
Web: www.bucknell.edu
Requirements: The Bott-Jennings Family Scholarship was established by Robert L. Jennings Jr., Class of 1973, and Barbara H. Bott, Class of 1973. The scholarship shall be awarded to students with demonstrated financial need, whose ethnic, racial, economic or national origins add to the diversity of Bucknell.
Disciplines: Any
Award: Varies
Eligible Inst.: Bucknell University

Catherine Vaughan Hellerman Scholarship

Andrea C.A. Leithner, Director
Tel: (570) 577-1331 Fax: (570) 577-1481
Email: finaid@bucknell.edu
Web: www.bucknell.edu
Requirements: The Catherine Vaughan Hellerman Scholarship was established by Stephen W. Vittorini, Class of 1979, in memory of his grandmother and great-grandfather, Charles P. Vaughan, acting president of Bucknell University in 1931. Preference for the scholarship award shall be given to a student or students from the Philadelphia area whose ethnic and economic origins add to the diversity of the university. It is the donor's wish that the scholarship

recipient(s), upon graduation, expect to use their learned skills and knowledge to enhance the economic and cultural well-being of communities similar to those from which they were selected.
Disciplines: Any
Award: Varies
Eligible Inst.: Bucknell University

Charles E. Howell Memorial Scholarship

Andrea C.A. Leithner, Director
Tel: (570) 577-1331 Fax: (570) 577-1481
Email: finaid@bucknell.edu
Web: www.bucknell.edu
Requirements: The Charles E. Howell Memorial Scholarship was established by Bucknell students under the auspices of the Bucknell Student Government, and by the friends and family of Charles Howell, a member of Bucknell's Class of 1990. As a minority student, an academically superior engineering student, football player, and outstanding citizen of the university community, Charles Howell set an example for all Bucknellians. This scholarship will be awarded annually to a student who best represents the qualities Charles exhibited before his untimely death in 1987.
Disciplines: Engineering, Athletics
Award: Varies
Eligible Inst.: Bucknell University

Ekedahl Family Scholarship

Andrea C.A. Leithner, Director
Tel: (570) 577-1331 Fax: (570) 577-1481
Email: finaid@bucknell.edu
Web: www.bucknell.edu
Requirements: The Ekedahl Family Scholarship was established by Dave Ekedahl, Class of 1956, and his wife, Patty Ekedahl. Preference for the scholarship award shall be given to students whose ethnic, racial, economic, or national origins add to the diversity of Bucknell.
Disciplines: Any
Award: Varies
Eligible Inst.: Bucknell University

Joanne E. Lewis Forsyth and Family Scholarship

Andrea C.A. Leithner, Director
Tel: (570) 577-1331 Fax: (570) 577-1481
Email: finaid@bucknell.edu
Web: www.bucknell.edu
Requirements: The Joanne E. Lewis Forsyth and Family Scholarship was established in 1998 by Kenneth J. and Nancy J. Lewis, parents of Joanne E. Lewis Forsyth, Class of 1995. The scholarship shall be awarded to students with demonstrated financial need. Preference shall be given to talented student-athletes, with special consideration given to student-athletes from California or the West Coast, whose ethnic, racial, economic, or national origins add to the diversity of Bucknell. The scholarship award shall be made without other restriction.
Disciplines: Athletics
Award: Varies
Eligible Inst.: Bucknell University

John H. and Susan B. Mathias Scholarship

Andrea C.A. Leithner, Director
Tel: (570) 577-1331 Fax: (570) 577-1481
Email: finaid@bucknell.edu
Web: www.bucknell.edu
Requirements: The John H. and Susan B. Mathias Scholarship was established by John H. '69 and Susan B. Mathias '69, and honors the extensive ties of the Mathias family to Bucknell University. Preference for the

scholarship award shall be given to students whose ethnic, racial, economic, or national origins add to the diversity of Bucknell.
Disciplines: Any
Award: Varies
Eligible Inst.: Bucknell University

Tague Family Scholarship

Andrea C.A. Leithner, Director
Tel: (570) 577-1331 Fax: (570) 577-1481
Email: finaid@bucknell.edu
Web: www.bucknell.edu
Requirements: The Tague Family Scholarship was established by Barry E. Tague, Class of 1960, and his wife, Dorothy Tague. Preference for the scholarship award shall be given to students from the greater Philadelphia area, with demonstrated financial need, whose ethnic, racial, economic or national origins add to the diversity of Bucknell.
Disciplines: Any
Award: Varies
Eligible Inst.: Bucknell University

C

CHICAGO SUN-TIMES

401 N. Wabash Ave.
Chicago, IL 60611

Minority Scholarship Program

Assistant to the Executive Editor
Tel: (312) 321-3000 Fax: (312) 321-3084
Web: www.suntimes.com
Requirements: This scholarship is available to minority students from the Chicago area who have graduated from a Chicago-area high school or have been residents of the area for at lest five years. Applicants must submit two letters of recommendation from adults familiar with their journalism skills and interests, and must write a 500-word essay about themselves. Applicants may also submit non-returnable samples of their writing, editing, or photography. Applicants may be called in for an interview.
Disciplines: Communications, Journalism
Eligible Inst.: US schools

CHICAGO URBAN LEAGUE

4510 S. Michigan Ave.
Chicago, IL 60653-3898

Anheuser-Busch Scholarship and Coors of Excellence Program

Leticia Ransom, Education Specialist
Tel: (773) 285-5800 Fax: (773) 285-7772
Email: scholarships@cul-chicago.org
Web: www.cul-chicago.org
Requirements: Renewable scholarships are offered to Illinois students with a minimum GPA of 2.5.
Disciplines: Any
Award: $2,500
Eligible Inst.: US schools
Deadline: March 1

COLLEGE OF SAINT ELIZABETH

Financial Aid Office
2 Convent Rd.
Morristown, NJ 07960-6989

William E. Simon Scholarship

Vincent Tunstall, Director
Tel: (800) 210-7900 Fax: (973) 290-4421
Email: vtunstall@cse.edu
Web: www.cse.edu
Requirements: This scholarship is for students that are high school graduates, enrolled at least half time at the College of Saint Elizabeth in a degree granting program. Be a US citizen or eligible non-citizen; be making satisfactory academic progress toward a degree, for minority students.

Disciplines: Any
Award: Varies
Eligible Inst.: College of Saint Elizabeth

CREIGHTON UNIVERSITY
Financial Aid Office
2500 California Plz.
Omaha, NE 68178

Frederick J. de la Vega Scholarship
Robert Walker, Director
Tel: (800) 282-5835 Fax: (402) 280-2895
Email: finaid@creighton.edu
Web: www.creighton.edu
Requirements: Students in the three undergraduate colleges are eligible for these highly competitive awards. Academic achievement is the main selection criterion, but the financial need of applicants may be considered. Between equally eligible applicants, a preference is given to students of color. This award is renewable by maintaining a 3.0 GPA.
Disciplines: Any
Award: Varies
Eligible Inst.: Creighton University
Deadline: February 1

John L. and Carol V. Maginn Scholarship
Robert Walker, Director
Tel: (800) 282-5835 Fax: (402) 280-2895
Email: finaid@creighton.edu
Web: www.creighton.edu
Requirements: This scholarship is designed to assist students enrolled in Creighton's College of Business Administration who are academically qualified and have financial need. Preference is given to women and students of color. The award is renewable with a 2.5 minimum grade average.
Disciplines: Business
Award: Varies
Eligible Inst.: Creighton University
Deadline: January 15

Union Pacific Corporation Foundation Affirmative Action Scholarship
Robert Walker, Director
Tel: (800) 282-5835 Fax: (402) 280-2895
Email: finaid@creighton.edu
Web: www.creighton.edu
Requirements: Applications for this scholarship are accepted from women and minority students in the College of Business Administration and the Masters in Business Administration Program. Applicants must have at least a 3.0 GPA and have demonstrated financial need and extracurricular involvement.
Disciplines: Business
Award: Varies
Eligible Inst.: Creighton University
Deadline: January 15

Union Pacific Corporation Foundation Minority Accounting Scholarship
Deborah L. Wells, Acting Dean
Tel: (402) 280-2850 Fax: (402) 280-2172
Email: dwells@creighton.edu
Web: http://cobweb.creighton.edu
Requirements: This scholarship is awarded to a minority senior accounting major who has evidenced an interest in internal auditing and who has maintained a high scholastic average.
Disciplines: Accounting
Award: $1,000
Eligible Inst.: Creighton University
Deadline: January 15

Walter J. and Ruth C. Maginn Scholarship
Robert Walker, Director
Tel: (800) 282-5835 Fax: (402) 280-2895
Email: finaid@creighton.edu

Web: www.creighton.edu
Requirements: This scholarship is designed to assist students enrolled in Creighton's College of Business Administration who are academically qualified and have financial need. Preference is given to students of color. The award is renewable with a 2.5 GPA.
Disciplines: Business
Award: Varies
Eligible Inst.: Creighton University
Deadline: January 15

William Randolph Hearst Foundation Scholarship
Robert Walker, Director
Tel: (800) 282-5835 Fax: (402) 280-2895
Email: finaid@creighton.edu
Web: www.creighton.edu
Requirements: A scholarship is awarded to provide financial support to a student in one of Creighton's undergraduate colleges who demonstrates financial need. Preference is given to multicultural students and the scholarship is renewable.
Disciplines: Any
Award: Varies
Eligible Inst.: Creighton University
Deadline: January 15

DR. SYNGMAN RHEE SCHOLARSHIP FUND
96-129 Ala Ike
Pearl City, HI 96782

Dr. Syngman Rhee Scholarship
Tel: (808) 454-4700 Fax: (808) 453-6075
Web: www.uhwo.hawaii.edu/s
Requirements: This program is for Korean students who are residents of Hawaii.
Disciplines: Any
Award: $1250/yr
Eligible Inst.: US schools
Deadline: June

DUKE UNIVERSITY
Financial Aid Office
2122 Campus Dr.
Durham, NC 27708

United Methodist Minority Scholarship
James A. Belvin, Jr., Director
Tel: (919) 684-6225 Fax: (919) 660-9811
Email: finaid@duke.edu
Web: www.duke.edu
Requirements: This scholarship is available to Methodist students who have shown financial need and minority students.
Disciplines: Any
Award: $500
Eligible Inst.: Duke University

EASTERN ILLINOIS UNIVERSITY
Journalism Department
600 Lincoln Ave.
Charleston, IL 61920-3099

James C. Copley Foundation Award for Minority Students
James Tidwell, Acting Chair of Journalism Dept.
Tel: (217) 581-6003 Fax: (217) 581-2923
Email: admissns@eiu.edu
Web: www.eiu.edu
Requirements: This scholarship is available to a minority journalism major who intends to pursue a career in journalism. Candidates should have made a significant contribution to campus media.

Disciplines: Journalism
Eligible Inst.: Eastern Illinois University
Deadline: March 10

EASTERN ILLINOIS UNIVERSITY
Journalism Department
600 Lincoln Ave.
Charleston, IL 61920-3099

James Saunders Minority Scholarship
James Tidwell, Acting Chair of Journalism Dept.
Tel: (217) 581-6003 Fax: (217) 581-7188
Email: journal@eiu.edu
Web: www.eiu.edu/~journal
Requirements: This scholarship seeks to recognize minority students who will serve as role models in the journalism profession or in related fields. Nominees must have completed 30-89 semester hours with at least a 2.0 GPA and submit a 250-word statement of career objectives and proof of work on one or more student publications or other media.
Disciplines: Journalism
Award: $500
Eligible Inst.: Eastern Illinois University
Deadline: March 10

ELMHURST COLLEGE
Office of Admission and Financial Aid
190 Prospect Ave.
Elmhurst, IL 60126

Enrichment Scholarship
Ruth Pusich, Director, Financial Aid
Tel: (630) 617-3400 Fax: (630) 617-5501
Email: admit@elmhurst.edu
Web: www.elmhurst.edu
Requirements: This scholarship is available to academically eligible Asian, African American, Hispanic, or Native American students. Recipients are required to apply for financial aid.
Disciplines: Any
Award: $5,000
Eligible Inst.: Elmhurst College
Deadline: April 15

HERCULES, INC.
1313 N. Market St.
Wilmington, DE 19894-0001

Minority Engineering Development Program
Tel: (302) 594-5000 Fax: (302) 594-5400
Web: www.herc.com
Requirements: The Hercules MinD Program is designed to increase the availability of under-represented minority group members in professions found in the Chemical Industry, especially the engineering fields. The program involves a combination of student scholarships, work experiences and grants to participating institutions.
Disciplines: Engineering
Eligible Inst.: US schools

IDAHO STATE BOARD OF EDUCATION
Scholarship Programs
P.O. Box 83720
Boise, ID 83720-0037

Idaho Minority and "At-Risk" Student Scholarship
Dana Kelly
Tel: (208) 334-2270 Fax: (208) 334-2632
Email: dkelly@osbe.state.id.us

Web: www.idahoboardofed.org
Requirements: Be a U.S. citizen and a resident of Idaho, be a graduate of an Idaho high school, be a first-generation college student, be disabled, be a migrant farm worker or the dependent of a migrant farm worker, have substantial financial need, be a member of an ethnic minority historically underrepresented in higher education in Idaho.
Disciplines: Any
Award: $3,000
Eligible Inst.: US schools

KOREAN AMERICAN GROCERS ASSOCIATION
3055 Wilshire Blvd. # 680
Los Angeles, CA 90010

KAGRO Foundation Scholarship
Tel: (213) 388-0114 Fax: (213) 388-2489
Email: juhankim@comcast.net
Web: www.kagro.org
Requirements: Applicants must be at least 16 years of age, of Asian heritage, a U.S citizen or permanent resident and beginning full time study at an accredited post-secondary educational institution in the United States. Must be able to attend the Awards program at each award ceremony and have a GPA of 3.3 with a financial need.
Disciplines: Any
Award: Varies
Eligible Inst.: US schools

L

LEE ELDER SCHOLARSHIP FUND
1725 K St. NW #1201
Washington, DC 20006

Lee Elder Scholarship
Web: www.auburn.edu/student_info/naacp/minorityscholarshipspage.htm
Requirements: This organization was founded by the noted golfer, the Fund makes grants to help minority and other students meet educational expenses. The acceptable majors are in sports management, promotion, and event coordinating.
Disciplines: Athletics, Recreation
Award: Varies
Eligible Inst.: US schools

M

MARTIN LUTHER KING, JR. MEMORIAL SCHOLARSHIP FUND
P.O. Box 921
Burlingame, CA 94011

Martin Luther King, Jr. Memorial Scholarship
Tel: (949) 824-5461 Fax: (949) 824-2092
Email: scholarships@cta.org
Web: www.scholars.uci.edu
Requirements: In order to be eligible an applicant must be pursuing a teaching-related career in public education and be a member of a defined ethnic minority group. Applicant must also be an active member of CTA, or a dependent child of an active, retired-life or deceased CTA member, or a member of Student CTA (SCTA).
Disciplines: Education
Award: Varies
Eligible Inst.: US schools
Deadline: March 15

METROPOLITAN STATE COLLEGE OF DENVER
Office of Financial Aid
P.O. Box 173362
Denver, CO 80217-3362

E.B. Jeppesen Endowed Memorial Scholarship
Tel: (303) 556-2983 Fax: (303) 556-4927
Web: www.mscd.edu
Requirements: Applicants must be full-time students with financial need, and have a declared major in Aerospace Science, with a GPA of 3.0 in the major and overall. Student would need to write an essay.
Disciplines: Aerospace Science, Management, Technology
Eligible Inst.: Metropolitan State College of Denver
Deadline: March 1

William T. Blackburn, Jr. Endowed Memorial Scholarship
Tel: (303) 556-3130 Fax: (303) 556-4927
Web: www.mscd.edu
Requirements: Applicants must have a declared major in the Health Professions Department, have completed 12 credit hours in the department, carry 6 credit hours and show financial need.
Disciplines: Nursing
Eligible Inst.: Metropolitan State College of Denver
Deadline: March 1

N

NATIONAL HISPANIC UNIVERSITY
14271 Story Rd.
San Jose, CA 95127

NHU Scholarships
Dr. B. Roberto Cruz, President
Tel: (408) 254-6900 Fax: (408) 254-7629
Email: rcruz@nhu.edu
Web: www.nhu.edu
Requirements: Financial aid is available to students who have received a high school diploma or GED; have a minimum GPA of 2.0; plan to attend NHU towards completion of a degree in Business, Liberal Studies, Education, Health, or Computer Science. Applicants must supply two letters of recommendation from teachers or counselors.
Disciplines: Education, Business, Humanities & Liberal Arts, Health Care, Computer & Information Science,
Award: Varies
Eligible Inst.: National Hispanic University

NATIONAL MINORITY JUNIOR GOLF SCHOLARSHIP ASSOCIATION
4950 E. Thomas rd
Phoenix, AZ 85018

NMJGSA Scholarship
Tel: (602) 258-7851 Fax: (602) 258-3412
Web: www.nmjgsa.org
Requirements: This scholarship is available to a college-bound or continuing minority golfer who already exists in the database.
Disciplines: Athletics
Award: $1,000-$6,000
Eligible Inst.: US schools

NOVA SOUTHEASTERN UNIVERSITY
Office of Student Financial Aid
3301 College Ave.
Fort Lauderdale, FL 33314-7796

Chancellor's Scholarship
Tel: (954) 262-3380 Fax: (954) 262-3533
Web: www.nova.edu
Requirements: Candidates must be currently enrolled or accepted for enrollment. (Currently enrolled students must be in good academic standing and must be permanent residents of Florida.) Candidates must be from a disadvantaged background and demonstrate financial need. Consideration will be given to those from families where few or no members have previously attended college.
Disciplines: Medical Sciences, Medical Doctor, Health Care, Nursing
Award: Tuition
Eligible Inst.: Nova Southeastern University
Deadline: May 30

S

SAN DIEGO STATE UNIVERSITY
School of Communication
5500 Campanile Dr.
San Diego, CA 92182-4516

KFMB Scholarship
Tel: (619) 594-5200 Fax: (619) 594-4268
Web: www.sdsu.edu
Requirements: This scholarship is available to minority students in the fields of news-editorial and radio-TV news.
Disciplines: Editing/Reporting, TV Broadcasting, Broadcasting
Award: Varies
Eligible Inst.: San Diego State University
Deadline: March 1

Reggie Smith Memorial Scholarship
Dr. Glen Broom, Professor & Chair
Tel: (619) 594-5200 Fax: (619) 594-4268
Web: www.sdsu.edu
Requirements: Candidates must be in good academic standing. Preference is given to underrepresented minority students. For application materials, contact the Department of Communication.
Disciplines: Journalism
Award: Varies
Eligible Inst.: San Diego State University
Deadline: March 1

SAN FRANCISCO STATE UNIVERSITY
Student Financial Aid Office
HSS 120, 1600 Holloway Ave.
San Francisco, CA 94132

Rosa Parks Scholarship
Evelyn Hooker
Tel: (415) 338-2032 Fax: (415) 338-0949
Email: ehooker@sfsu.edu
Web: www.sfsu.edu
Requirements: This scholarship is available to students who have been accepted into a graduate or credential program at SFSU; Enrolled in at least 8 units. Applicant must be a U.S. citizen.
Disciplines: Any
Award: $750
Eligible Inst.: San Francisco State University

SAN JUAN COLLEGE
Financial Aid Office
4601 College Blvd.
Farmington, NM 87402

San Juan Generating Station of the Public Service Company of New Mexico Scholarship

Roger Evans, Director
Tel: (505) 566-3323 Fax: (505) 566-3568
Email: evansr@sanjuancollege.edu
Web: www.sanjuancollege.edu
Requirements: This scholarship is awarded to full-time students residing in San Juan County. Preference is given to students who are minority or female. Applicants must plan to enroll in a minimum of 12 credit hours; have obtained a minimum high school GPA of 2.8 (or college GPA of 3.0).
Disciplines: Any
Award: Varies
Eligible Inst.: San Juan College
Deadline: April 15

T

TAYLOR UNIVERSITY
236 W. Reade Ave.
Upland, IN 46989

Ethnic Student Scholarship
Tel: (765) 998-5358
Email: admissions_u@tayloru.edu
Web: www.tayloru.edu
Requirements: This scholarship is available to students who have the ability to demonstrate exceptional leadership skills or who contribute to cultural diversity.
Disciplines: Any
Award: 25% Tuition
Eligible Inst.: Taylor University

U

UNIVERSITY OF ALABAMA
College of Communication and Information Sciences
P.O. Box 870172
Tuscaloosa, AL 35487-0172

Cooper, Mitch, Crawford, Kuykendall and Whatley Forensics Scholarship
Tel: (205) 348-6756 Fax: (205) 348-6544
Web: www.ua.edu
Requirements: This scholarship is available to a minority undergraduate or graduate student participating in forensics and/or purusing a degree in the Communications Department.
Disciplines: Speech Communications, Debate/Public Speaking
Award: $1,500
Eligible Inst.: University of Alabama
Deadline: December 1

Ione Hendrick Roche Memorial Endowed Scholarship
Jim Oakley
Tel: (205) 348-8594 Fax: (205) 348-6544
Email: joakley@ccom.ua.edu
Web: www.ua.edu
Requirements: This scholarship is available to minority women who demonstrate academic excellence, interest in social concerns and the intention to pursue a degree in the College of Communication and Information Sciences.
Disciplines: Communications
Award: $1,000/yr
Eligible Inst.: University of Alabama
Deadline: December 1

James T. and Joanne Lynagh Endowed Minority Scholarship
Jim Oakley
Tel: (205) 348-8594 Fax: (205) 348-6544
Email: joakley@ccom.ua.edu
Web: www.ua.edu
Requirements: This scholarship is available to outstanding minority students majoring

in communication, freshman through junior enrolled full-time. Priority is given to telecommunication and film majors.
Disciplines: Communications
Award: $1,000/yr
Eligible Inst.: University of Alabama
Deadline: December 1

John S. and James L. Knight Minority Scholarship
Jim Oakley, Placement Director
Tel: (205) 348-8594 Fax: (205) 348-3836
Email: joakley@ua.edu
Web: www.ua.edu
Requirements: This scholarship is available to outstanding minority students majoring in journalism. Applicants must be full-time freshmen through juniors.
Disciplines: Journalism
Award: $1,000/Yr.
Eligible Inst.: University of Alabama
Deadline: December 1

WBMG-TV Endowed
Jim Oakley
Tel: (205) 348-8594 Fax: (205) 348-6544
Email: joakley@ccom.ua.edu
Web: www.ua.edu
Requirements: This scholarship is available to entering full-time telecommunication major (entering freshman through junior), with priority given to minority students.
Disciplines: Telecommunications
Award: $500
Eligible Inst.: University of Alabama
Deadline: February 15

UNIVERSITY OF IDAHO
Office of Student Financial Aid Services
875 Perimeter Dr
Moscow, ID 83844-4291

Minority at Risk Scholarship
Tel: (208) 885-6312 Fax: (208) 885-4477
Email: finaid@uidaho.edu
Web: www.uidaho.edu/sfas/
Requirements: This scholarship is available to first generation college students who either have a disablity or have an ethnic background of Hispanic American, African American or Native American descent demonstrating substantial financial need or be a son or daughter of a migrant farm family. Must also be a graduate of an Idaho high school.
Disciplines: Any
Eligible Inst.: University of Idaho

Multi-Cultural Scholars in Agriculture Scholarship
Tel: (208) 885-6312 Fax: (208) 885-4477
Email: finaid@uidaho.edu
Web: www.uidaho.edu/sfas/
Requirements: This scholarship is available to undergraduate students in the field of agricultural and life sciences.
Disciplines: Agriculture
Eligible Inst.: University of Idaho

UNIVERSITY OF IOWA
School of Art and Art History
E100 Art Bldg.
Iowa City, IA 52242

Emma McAllister Novel Scholarship
Tel: (319) 335-1450 Fax: (319) 335-3060
Email: financial-aid@uiowa.edu
Web: www.uiowa.edu
Requirements: This scholarship is available to undergraduate or graduate minority students.
Disciplines: Arts
Award: $1,000
Eligible Inst.: University of Iowa
Deadline: February 1

UNIVERSITY OF MIAMI

School of Business Administration
P.O. Box 248027
Coral Gables, FL 33146

Morgan-Stanley Scholarship/Internship

Tel: (305) 284-4643 Fax: (305) 284-2507
Email: admission@miami.edu
Web: www.miami.edu/admission-information/
Requirements: This scholarship is available to undergraduate juniors, with preference given to minorities.
Disciplines: Business
Award: Varies
Eligible Inst.: University of Miami
Deadline: April 11

UNIVERSITY OF MISSOURI-KANSAS CITY

School of Nursing
2220 Holmes
Kansas City, MO 64110-2499

George Hedgepeth Trust Scholarship Fund

Tel: (816) 235-1154 Fax: (816) 235-5511
Web: www.umkc.edu
Requirements: Undergraduates and graduates; preference to minorities; 3.0 GPA or above.
Disciplines: Nursing
Award: Varies
Eligible Inst.: University of Missouri-Kansas City

UNIVERSITY OF MONTEVALLO

Office of Admissions
Station 6030
Montevallo, AL 35115

Minority Teachers' Scholarship Program

Tel: (205) 665-6030 Fax: (205) 665-6032
Email: admissions@um.montevallo.edu
Web: www.montevallo.edu
Requirements: This scholarship is available to minority students in education with the intent to teach in Alabama.
Disciplines: Education
Award: Varies
Eligible Inst.: University of Montevallo
Deadline: April 1

UNIVERSITY OF NEBRASKA AT OMAHA

Office of Multicultural Affairs
Milo Bail Student Ctr., 1st Fl.
Omaha, NE 68182

Davis Memorial Scholarship

James Freeman, Director
Tel: (402) 554-2248 Fax: (402) 554-2000
Email: jfreeman@mail.unomaha.edu
Web: www.unomaha.edu
Requirements: This scholarship is available to outstanding minority students wishing to pursue a post-secondary education.
Disciplines: Any
Award: $2,000-4,000
Eligible Inst.: University of Nebraska at Omaha
Deadline: February 1

Isaacson Inventive Scholarship

James Freeman, Director
Tel: (402) 554-2248 Fax: (402) 554-2000
Email: jfreeman@mail.unomaha.edu
Web: www.unomaha.edu
Requirements: The Isaacson Incentive Scholarship Program, funded by the Jacob J. and Dottie M. Isaacson estate, was established to recognize the academic achievements of talented students throughout the Omaha area, while encouraging their enrollment at the University of Nebraska at Omaha. Applicants must reside in the Omaha metropolitan area for one year prior to applying for this scholarship. Up to ten Isaacson Incentive scholarships can be awarded to First Year students on an annual basis. Each scholarship is awarded in the amount of $1,000 per academic year to recipients admitted to UN Omaha.
Disciplines: Any
Award: $1,000
Eligible Inst.: University of Nebraska at Omaha
Deadline: January 15

UNIVERSITY OF SOUTHERN CALIFORNIA

Asian Pacific American Support Group (USC-APASG)
55 Fair Dr.
Los Angeles, CA 90089-4851

Asian Pacific American Support Group Scholarship

Tel: (213) 740-4923 Fax: (213) 749-9781
Web: www.usc.edu
Requirements: This scholarship is available to full-time USC students who are U.S. citizens or permanent residents. Applicants must have a stong sense of ethnic identity or commitment to the Asian Pacific community. Selected on the basis of academic achievement.
Disciplines: Any
Award: $1,000-$2,500
Eligible Inst.: University of Southern California
Deadline: February

UNIVERSITY OF TEXAS-PAN AMERICAN

Office of Financial Aid
1201 W. University Dr. SSB 186
Edinburg, TX 78539-2999

Adolph Coors Scholarship

Tel: (210) 381-2501 Fax: (210) 381-2392
Web: www.panam.edu/finaid
Requirements: This scholarship is intended to increase the number of minority college graduates with management and leadership potential. Juniors and seniors are eligible to apply. Selection is based on academic achievement. The UTPA Scholarship Application may be used to apply.
Disciplines: Business
Award: $300/yr
Eligible Inst.: University of Texas-Pan American
Deadline: January 14

W

WALSH UNIVERSITY

Financial Aid Office
2020 Easton St. NW
North Canton, OH 44720-3396

Timken Foundation Endowed Scholarship

Tel: (216) 490-7165 Fax: (216) 490-7165
Email: admissions@alex.walsh.edu
Web: www.walsh.edu
Requirements: This scholarship is available to minority students enrolled full-time.
Disciplines: Any
Award: Varies
Eligible Inst.: Walsh University

WAYNE STATE UNIVERSITY

Engineering Building
5050 Anthony Wayne Dr.
Detroit, MI 48202

Chrysler Corporation Minority Scholarship

Tel: (313) 577-3780
Email: admissions@wayne.edu
Web: www.wayne.edu
Requirements: Minority students in Mechanical Engineering, Electrical Engineering, Industrial Management or Business Administration. The student must also demonstrate financial need, outstanding scholastic achievement and leadership qualities.
Disciplines: Mechanical Engineering, Electrical Engineering, Business Administration
Award: Varies depending on funds available.
Eligible Inst.: Wayne State University

WAYNE STATE UNIVERSITY

Office of Scholarships and Financial Aid
Student Services Ctr., 3 West
Detroit, MI 48202

Ford EEOC Scholarship

Kevin J. Culler, Interim Director of Financial Aid
Tel: (313) 577-3378 Fax: (313) 577-6648
Email: admissions@wayne.edu
Web: www.wayne.edu
Requirements: This scholarship is available to minority or female students who are either a Ford Motor Company employee, or a spouse or child of a Ford Motor Company employee; certification of Ford employment required.
Disciplines: Any
Award: Varies depending on funds available.
Eligible Inst.: Wayne State University
Deadline: April 28

Howard Baker Foundation General Scholarship

Kevin J. Culler, Interim Director of Financial Aid
Tel: (313) 577-3378 Fax: (313) 577-6648
Email: admissions@wayne.edu
Web: www.wayne.edu
Requirements: This scholarship is available to full-time undergraduate minority students. Recipients must be Detroit high school graduates, residents of the city of Detroit and U.S. citizens, and have a minimum cumulative GPA of 2.5. Students must submit a brief, written biographical statement. Recipients are chosen on the basis of financial need by the Howard Baker Foundation Selection Committee. Preference is given to students majoring in nursing or in a natural science curriculum.
Disciplines: Natural Sciences, Nursing
Award: Tuition+books
Eligible Inst.: Wayne State University
Deadline: April 30

MichCon-Leon Atchison Scholarship

Kevin J. Culler, Interim Director of Financial Aid
Tel: (313) 577-3378 Fax: (313) 577-6648
Email: admissions@wayne.edu
Web: www.wayne.edu
Requirements: This scholarship is available to minority students from the MichCon service area majoring in accounting, chemical engineering, mechanical engineering, or computer science. Applicants must maintain a 2.5 GPA, demonstrate financial need, and be US citizens.
Disciplines: Accounting, Chemical Engineering, Computer & Information Science, Mechanical Engineering
Award: Varies
Eligible Inst.: Wayne State University
Deadline: April 30

WESTERN CAROLINA UNIVERSITY

Financial Aid Office
242 H.F. Robinson Administration Bldg.
Cullowhee, NC 28723

C.D. Spangler Jr. Scholarship for Minority Students

Nancy B. Dillard, Director
Tel: (828) 227-7290 Fax: (828) 227-7042
Email: finaid@wcu.edu
Web: www.wcu.edu
Requirements: This endowed scholarship program's purpose is to provide financial support for deserving young minority students. Awards are based upon high academic achievement, successful participation in various school activities, overall social and civic contributions, and financial need. Contact the Office of Financial Aid.
Disciplines: Any
Award: Varies
Eligible Inst.: Western Carolina University
Deadline: March 31

Religion in Asian Countries

COUNTRY/RELIGION	TOTAL POP./ FOLLOWERS	%
Afghanistan	29,928,987	
Sunni Muslim	23,943,190	80.0%
Shi'a Muslim	5,686,507	19.0%
Other	299,289	1.0%
Armenia	2,982,904	
Armenian Apostolic	2,833,758	94.7%
Other Christian	119,316	4.0%
Yezidi (Zoroastrian/Animist)	29,829	1.3%
Azerbaijan	7,911,974	
Muslim	7,389,783	93.4%
Russian Orthodox	197,799	2.5%
Armenian Orthodox	181,975	2.3%
Other	142,415	1.8%
Bahrain	688,345	
Muslim (Shi'a and Sunni)	558,936	81.2%
Christian	61,951	9.0%
Other	67,457	9.8%
Bangladesh	144,319,628	
Muslim	119,785,291	83.0%
Hindu	23,091,140	16.0%
Other	1,443,196	1.0%
Bhutan	2,232,291	
Lamaistic Buddhist	1,674,218	75.0%
Indian and Nepalese-influenced Hinduism	558,072	25.0%
Brunei	372,361	
Muslim (official)	249,481	67.0%
Buddhist	48,406	13.0%
Christian	37,236	10.0%
Indigenous beliefs and Other	37,236	10.0%
Burma	42,909,464	
Buddhist	38,189,422	89.0%
Christian	1,716,378	4.0%
Muslim	1,716,378	4.0%
Animist	429,094	1.0%
Other	858,189	2.0%

COUNTRY/RELIGION	TOTAL POP./ FOLLOWERS	%
Cambodia	13,607,069	
Theravada Buddhist	12,926,715	95.0%
Other	680,353	5.0%
China	1,306,313,812	
Officially atheist		
Daoist (Taoist), Buddhist, Muslim		1-2%
Christian		3-4%
Hong Kong	6,898,686	
Eclectic mixture of local religions	620,881,740	90.0%
Christian	689,868	10.0%
Taiwan	22,894,384	
Mixture of Buddhist, Confucian, and Taoist	21,291,777	93.0%
Christian	1,030,247	4.5%
Other	572,359	2.5%
Cyprus	780,133	
Greek Orthodox	608,503	78.0%
Muslim	140,423	18.0%
Maronite, Armenian Apostolic, and other	31,205	4.0%
East Timor	1,040,880	
Roman Catholic	936,792	90.0%
Muslim	41,635	4.0%
Protestant	31,226	3.0%
Hindu	5,204	0.5%
Buddhist, Animist		
Gaza Strip	1,376,289	
Muslim (predominantly Sunni)	1,358,397	98.7%
Christian	9,634	0.7%
Jewish	8,257	0.6%
Georgia	4,677,401	
Orthodox Christian	3,924,339	83.9%
Armenia-Gregorian	182,418	3.9%
Catholic	37,419	0.8%
Muslim	463,062	9.9%
Other	37,419	0.8%
None	66,820	0.7%

Source: Central Intelligence Agency. The World Factbook 2005, Internet edition. http://www.cia.gov/cia/publications/factbook

COUNTRY/RELIGION	TOTAL POP./ FOLLOWERS	%
India	1,080,264,388	
Hindu	869,612,832	80.5%
Muslim	144,755,428	13.4%
Christian	24,846,080	2.3%
Sikh	2,052,502,337	1.9%
Other	19,444,758	1.8%
Unspecified	1,080,264	0.1%
Indonesia	241,973,879	
Muslim	212,937,013	88.0%
Protestant	12,098,693	5.0%
Roman Catholic	7,259,216	3.0%
Hindu	4,839,477	2.0%
Buddhist	2,419,738	1.0%
Other	2,419,738	1.0%
Iran	68,017,860	
Shi'a Muslim	60,535,895	89.0%
Sunni Muslim	6,121,607	9.0%
Zoroastrian, Jewish, Christian, and Baha'i	1,360,357	2.0%
Iraq	26,074,906	
Muslim	25,292,658	97.0%
Shi'a Muslim		60-65%
Sunni Muslim		32-37%
Christian or other	782,247	3.0%
Israel	6,276,883	
Jewish	4,801,815	76.5%
Muslim	998,024	15.9%
Arab Christian	106,707	1.7%
Other Christian	25,107	0.4%
Druze	100,430	1.6%
Unspecified	244,798	3.9%
Japan	127,417,244	
Observe both Shinto and Buddhist	107,030,485	84.0%
Other (including Christian 0.7%)	20,386,759	16.0%
Jordan	5,759,732	
Sunni Muslim	5,298,953	92.0%
Christian denominations	345,583	6.0%
Other (Shi'a Muslim and Druze populations)	115,194	2.0%
Kazakhstan	15,185,844	
Muslim	7,137,346	47.0%
Russian Orthodox	6,681,771	44.0%
Protestant	303,716	2.0%
Other	1,063,009	7.0%
Korea, North	22,912,177	
Traditionally Buddhist and Confucianist, Christian and Syncretic Chondogyo		
Korea, South	48,422,644	
Non affiliation	22,274,416	46.0%

COUNTRY/RELIGION	TOTAL POP./ FOLLOWERS	%
Christian	12,589,887	26.0%
Buddhist	12,589,887	26.0%
Confucianist	484,226	1.0%
Other	484,226	1.0%
Kuwait	2,335,648	
Muslim	1,985,300	85.0%
Christian, Hindu, Parsi, and other	350,347	15.0%
Kyrgyzstan	5,146,281	
Muslim	3,859,710	75.0%
Russian Orthodox	1,029,256	20.0%
Other	257,314	5.0%
Laos	6,217,141	
Buddhist	3,730,284	60.0%
Animist and other	2,486,856	40.0%
Lebanon	3,826,018	
Muslim	2,284,132	59.7%
Christian	1,492,147	39.0%
Other	49,738	1.3%
Malaysia	23,953,136	
Muslim, Buddhist, Daoist, Hindu, Christian, Sikh		
Maldives	349,106	
Sunni Muslim		
Mongolia	2,791,272	
Buddhist Lamaism	1,395,636	50.0%
None	1,116,508	40.0%
Shamanism, and Christian	167,476	6.0%
Muslim	111,650	4.0%
Nepal	27,676,547	
Hinduism	22,307,296	80.6%
Buddhism	2,961,390	10.7%
Muslim	1,162,414	4.2%
Kirant	996,355	3.6%
Other	249,088	0.9%
Oman	3,001,583	
IBadhi Muslim	2,251,187	75.0%
Sunni Muslim, Shi'a Muslim, Hindu		
Pakistan	162,419,946	
Muslim	157,547,347	97.0%
Sunni, Shi'a	157,547,347	97.0%
Christian, Hindu, and other	4,872,598	3.0%
Papua New Guinea	5,545,268	
Roman Catholic	1,219,958	22.0%
Lutheran	887,242	16.0%
Presbyterian/Methodist/London Missionary Soc.	443,621	8.0%
Anglican	277,263	5.0%
Evangelical Alliance	221,810	4.0%

COUNTRY/RELIGION	TOTAL POP./ FOLLOWERS	%	COUNTRY/RELIGION	TOTAL POP./ FOLLOWERS	%
Seventh-Day Adventist	55,452	1.0%	**Tajikistan**	7,163,506	
Other Protestant	554,526	10.0%	Sunni Muslim	6,088,980	85.0%
Indigenous beliefs	1,885,391	34.0%	Shi'a Muslim	358,175	5.0%
Philippines	87,857,473		Other	716,350	10.0%
Roman Catholic	71,076,695	80.9%	**Thailand**	65,444,371	
Evangelical	2,460,009	2.8%	Buddhist	61,910,374	94.6%
Iglesia ni Kristo	2,020,721	2.3%	Muslim	3,010,441	4.6%
Aglipayan	1,757,149	2.0%	Christian	458,110	0.7%
Other Christian	3,953,586	4.5%	Other	65,444	0.1%
Muslim	4,392,873	5.0%	**Turkey**	69,660,559	
Other	1,581,434	1.8%	Muslim (mostly Sunni)	69,521,237	99.8%
Unspecified	527,144	0.6%	Other (mostly Christians and Jews)	139,321	0.2%
None	87,857	0.1%	**Turkmenistan**	4,952,081	
Qatar	863,051		Muslim	4,407,352	89.0%
Muslim	819,898	95.0%	Eastern Orthodox	44,568	0.9%
Russia	143,420,309		Unknown	9,904	0.2%
Russian Orthodox, Muslim, Other			**United Arab Emirates**	2,563,212	
Saudi Arabia	26,417,599		Muslim	2,460,683	96.0%
Muslim	2,641,759	100%	Christian, Hindu, and Other	102,528	4.0%
Singapore	4,425,720		**Uzbekistan**	26,851,195	
Buddhist	1,880,931	42.5%	Muslim (mostly Sunnis)	23,629,051	88.0%
Muslim	659,432	14.9%	Eastern Orthodox	2,416,607	9.0%
Taoist	376,186	8.5%	Other	805,535	3.0%
Hindu	177,028	4.0%	**Vietnam**	83,535,576	
Catholic	212,434	4.8%	Buddhist	776,880,856	9.3%
Other Christian	433,720	9.8%	Catholic	5,596,883	6.7%
Other	30,980	0.7%	Hoa Hao	1,253,033	1.5%
None	655,006	14.8%	Cao Dai	918,891	1.1%
Sri Lanka	20,064,776		Protestant	417,677	0.5%
Buddhist	13,864,760	69.1%	Muslim	83,535	0.1%
Muslim	1,524,922	7.6%	None	67,496,745	80.8%
Hindu	1,424,599	7.1%	**Yemen**	20,727,063	
Christian	1,244,016	6.2%	Muslim including Shaf'I (Sunni) and Zaydi (Shi'a)		
Unspecified	2,006,477	10.0%	Small numbers of Jewish, Christian and Hindu		

ASIANPACIFICAMERICAN
Health

FIG 1. Leading Causes of Death per 100,000 for Asian Americans and Pacific Islanders: 2002

The major causes of death in the U.S. Asian Pacific Islander population corresponded closely with those of the general population. In both groups cancer, heart disease and stroke were the top three killers. Heart disease, however, was more prevalent in the general population than it was with Asian Pacific Islanders, for whom cancer was the number one cause of death. Looking at causes of death by gender in the Asian Pacific Islander group shows some interesting differences. Neither suicide nor homicide—the eighth and tenth highest causes in males respectively—made the top ten list for females. Alzheimer's disease, which was number nine on the women's list, did not show up anywhere among the top ten causes of death for men.

Source: Center for Disease Control (CDC): Health, United States, 2004.
www.omhrc.gov

Asian/Pacific Islander All Ages/Both Sexes	Asian/Pacific Islander Males All Ages	Asian/Pacific Islander Females All Ages
Cancer: 9,998	Heart Disease: 5,523	Cancer: 4,805
Heart Disease: 9,983	Cancer: 5,193	Heart Disease: 4,460
Stroke: 3,530	Stroke: 1,599	Stroke: 1,931
Accidents: 1,875	Accidents: 1,175	Diabetes: 711
Diabetes: 1,359	Chronic Lower Respiratory Disease: 743	Accidents: 700
Chronic Lower Respiratory Disease: 1,138	Influenza and Pneumonia: 636	Influenza and Pneumonia: 535
Influenza and Pneumonia: 1,171	Diabetes: 648	Chronic Lower Respiratory Disease: 395
Suicide: 661	Suicide: 469	Kidney Disease: 329
Kidney Disease: 649	Homicide: 277	Hypertension: 221
Septicemia: 423	Kidney Disease: 320	Alzheimer's Disease: 231

FIG 2. Health Insurance Coverage for the Entire Year and Type of Coverage: 2004

In 2004, according to the U.S. Census Bureau almost 17 percent of Asian Americans (alone or in combination) were completely uninsured. This rate of uninsured persons was down just slightly from 2002. These same data showed that a majority (72 percent) of people classified as Asian alone or in combination were covered by privately purchased health insurance, mostly coming from the workplace.

Source: US Census Bureau, Current Population Survey, 2005 Annual Social and Economic Supplement.
www.census.gov

	Population*	Percentage
Asian Alone or in Combination	13,373	100.0%
Government Insurance		
Medicaid	1,377	10.3%
Medicare	1,127	8.4%
Military	433	3.2%
Government Total	2,937	22.0%
Private Health Insurance		
Employment Based	8,305	62.0%
Direct Purchase	1,324	9.9%
Private Total	9,629	72.0%
Not Covered	2,217	16.6%

*In thousands

Federal and State Departments of Health and Minority Health Offices

ALABAMA

ALABAMA DEPARTMENT OF PUBLIC HEALTH
Minority Health Section
201 Monroe St. #710, RSA Tower
Montgomery, AL 36104
Tel: (334) 206-5396 Fax: (334) 206-5434
Web: www.adph.org/minorityhealth

AMERICAN SAMOA

AMERICAN SAMOAN GOVERNMENT
P.O. Box LBJ
LBJ Tropical Medical Ctr.
Pago Pago, AS 96799
Tel: (684) 633-1222 Fax: (684) 633-5379

ARIZONA

ARIZONA DEPARTMENT OF HEALTH SERVICES
Office of Health Systems Development, Center for Minority Health
1740 W. Adams St. #410
Phoenix, AZ 85007
Tel: (602) 542-1219 Fax: (602) 542-2011

ARKANSAS

ARKANSAS DEPARTMENT OF HEALTH
Arkansas Minority Health Commission
1123 S. University #312
Little Rock, AR 72204
Tel: (501) 686-2720 Fax: (501) 686-2722
Web: www.arminorityhealth.com

Office of Minority Health & Health Disparities
P.O. Box 1437, Slot H-22
Little Rock, AR 72203-1437
Tel: (501) 661-2193 Fax: (501) 661-2414
Web: www.healthyarkansas.com

CALIFORNIA

DEPARTMENT OF HEALTH SERVICES
Office of Multicultural Health
P.O. Box 997413, M/S 0022
Sacramento, CA 95899-7413
Tel: (916) 440-7562 Fax: (916) 440-7565

COLORADO

COLORADO DEPARTMENT OF PUBLIC HEALTH & ENVIRONMENT
Office of Health Disparities
4300 Cherry Creek Dr. South #B1
Denver, CO 80246-1530
Tel: (303) 692-2329 Fax: (303) 691-7746

CONNECTICUT

CONNECTICUT DEPARTMENT OF PUBLIC HEALTH
Office of Multicultural Health
410 Capitol Ave., MS-11GCT
Hartford, CT 06134
Tel: (860) 509-8098 Fax: (860) 508-7227

DELAWARE

DELAWARE DEPARTMENT OF HEALTH
Office of Minority Health, Division of Public Health
P.O. Box 637
Federal & Waters Sts.
Dover, DE 19903
Tel: (302) 744-4700 Fax: (302) 739-6659
Web: www.state.de.us/dhss/dph

DISTRICT OF COLUMBIA

DISTRICT OF COLUMBIA DEPARTMENT OF HEALTH
State Center for Health Statistics Administration, Research & Analysis Division
825 N. Capitol St. NE, 2nd Fl.
Washington, DC 20002
Tel: (202) 442-9039 Fax: (202) 442-4833
Web: www.dchealth.dc.gov

FLORIDA

FLORIDA STATE DEPARTMENT OF HEALTH
Office of Minority Health
4052 Bald Cypress Way, #A00
Tallahassee, FL 32399-1701
Tel: (850) 245-4012 Fax: (850) 487-2168

GEORGIA

GEORGIA DEPARTMENT OF COMMUNITY HEALTH
Office of Minority Health, Health Improvement Programs
2 Peachtree St. NW, 36th Fl.
Atlanta, GA 30303-3159
Tel: (404) 457-6707 Fax: (404) 657-2769

Georgia Department of Community Health Office of Minority Health
2 Peachtree St. NW, 38th Fl.
Atlanta, GA 30303-3159
Tel: (404) 463-3450 Fax: (404) 657-2769

GUAM

GOVERNMENT OF GUAM
Department of Public Health & Social Services
P.O. Box 2816
Agana, Guam 96932
Tel: (671) 734-7102 Fax: (671) 734-5910

HAWAII

HAWAII STATE DEPARTMENT OF HEALTH
Office of Health Equity
1250 Punchbowl St. #257
Honolulu, HI 96813
Tel: (808) 586-4673 Fax: (808) 586-8252

IDAHO

IDAHO DEPARTMENT OF HEALTH & WELFARE
State Office of Rural Health & Primary Care
450 W. State St., 4th Fl.
Boise, ID 83720
Tel: (208) 332-7212 Fax: (208) 332-7262

ILLINOIS

COOK COUNTY DEPARTMENT OF PUBLIC HEALTH
Health Promotion Unit
1010 Lake St. #300
Oak Park, IL 60301
Tel: (708) 492-2079 Fax: (708) 492-2913
Web: www.idph.state.il.us

ILLINOIS DEPARTMENT OF PUBLIC HEALTH
Center for Minority Health Services
535 W. Jefferson, 5th Fl.

Springfield, IL 62761
Tel: (217) 785-4311 Fax: (217) 558-7181
Web: www.idph.state.il.us

INDIANA

INDIANA MINORITY HEALTH COALITION, INC.
3737 N. Meridian St. #300
Indianapolis, IN 46208
Tel: (317) 926-4011 Fax: (317) 926-4012
Web: www.imhc.org

INDIANA STATE DEPARTMENT OF HEALTH
Office of Minority Health
2 N. Meridian St. #2-K
Indianapolis, IN 46204
Tel: (317) 233-3006 Fax: (317) 233-7943
Web: www.in.gov/isdh

IOWA

IOWA DEPARTMENT OF HEALTH
Office of Multicultural Health
321 E. 12th St., 4th Fl.
Des Moines, IA 50319-0075
Tel: (515) 281-4904 Fax: (515) 242-6384
Web: www.idph.state.ia.us

KANSAS

KANSAS DEPARTMENT OF HEALTH & ENVIRONMENT
1000 SW Jackson St. #540
Topeka, KS 66612-1368
Tel: (785) 291-3219 Fax: (785) 368-6368

LOUISIANA

LOUISIANA DEPARTMENT OF HEALTH & HOSPITALS
Bureau of Minority Health Access
1201 Capitol Access Rd., 3rd Fl.
Baton Rouge, LA 70821
Tel: (225) 342-9500 Fax: (225) 342-5568
Web: www.dhh.state.la.us/lamha

MAINE

MAINE DEPARTMENT HEALTH & HUMAN SERVICES
Office of Minority Health
161 Capitol St. #11
Augusta, ME 04333-0011
Tel: (207) 287-5503 Fax: (207) 287-5431

MARSHALL ISLANDS

REPUBLIC OF THE MARSHALL ISLANDS
Minister of Health & Environment
P.O. Box 16
Majuro, Marshall Islands 96960
Tel: (692) 625-3432 Fax: (692) 625-4543

MARYLAND

MARYLAND DEPARTMENT OF HEALTH & MENTAL HYGIENE
Office of Minority Health & Health Disparities
201 W. Preston St. #500
Baltimore, MD 21201
Tel: (410) 767-0094 Fax: (410) 333-5100
Web: www.dhmh.state.md.us

MASSACHUSETTS

MASSACHUSETTS DEPARTMENT OF PUBLIC HEALTH
Office of Multicultural Health
250 Washington St., 5th Fl.
Boston, MA 02108
Tel: (617) 624-5471 Fax: (617) 624-6062
Web: www.state.ma.us/dph/omh/omh.htm

MICHIGAN

MICHIGAN DEPARTMENT OF COMMUNITY HEALTH
Health Disparities Reduction & Minority Health Section, Division of Health, Wellness & Disease Control
109 Michigan Ave., 10th Fl.
Lansing, MI 48913
Tel: (517) 241-0854 Fax: (517) 241-0875

MINNESOTA

MINNESOTA DEPARTMENT OF HEALTH
Office of Minority & Multicultural Health
625 Robert St. North
St. Paul, MN 55155-2538
Tel: (651) 201-5813 Fax: (651) 201-4986
Web: www.health.state.mn.us/ommh

MICRONESIA

FEDERATED STATES OF MICRONESIA DEPARTMENT OF HEALTH, EDUCATION & SOCIAL SERVICES
P.S. 70
Palikir, Pohnpei State, FM 96941
Tel: (691) 320-2872 Fax: (691) 320-5263

MISSISSIPPI

MISSISSIPPI DEPARTMENT OF HEALTH
Office of Health Disparity
570 E. Woodrow Wilson Blvd. #120
Jackson, MS 39215
Tel: (601) 576-8102 Fax: (601) 576-7270
Web: www.msdh.state.ms.us

MISSOURI

MISSOURI DEPARTMENT OF HEALTH & SENIOR SERVICES
Office of Minority Health
P.O. Box 570
912 Wildwood Dr.
Jefferson City, MO 65102
Tel: (573) 751-6064 Fax: (573) 522-1599
Web: www.health.state.mo.us

MONTANA

MONTANA DEPARTMENT OF PUBLIC HEALTH & HUMAN SERVICES
1400 Broadway, #C202
Helena, MT 59620
Tel: (406) 444-3583 Fax: (406) 444-0272
Web: www.dphhs.state.mt.us

NEBRASKA

NEBRASKA HEALTH & HUMAN SERVICES SYSTEM
Nebraska Health & Human Services System, Office of Minority Health
P.O. Box 95044
301 Centennial Mall South
Lincoln, NE 68509-5007
Tel: (402) 471-0152 Fax: (402) 471-0383
Web: www.hhs.state.ne.us/omh

NEVADA

STATE DEPARTMENT OF HEALTH & HUMAN RESOURCES
Office of Minority Health
505 E. King St. #201
Carson City, NV 89701
Tel: (775) 684-4200 Fax: (775) 684-4046

NEW HAMPSHIRE

NEW HAMPSHIRE DEPARTMENT OF HEALTH & HUMAN SERVICES
Office of Minority Health
129 Pleasant St.
Concord, NH 03301
Tel: (603) 271-8459 Fax: (603) 271-4727
Web: www.dhhs.state.nh.us/DHHS/MHO/default.htm

NEW JERSEY

NEW JERSEY DEPARTMENT OF HEALTH & SENIOR SERVICES
Office of Minority & Multicultural Health
P.O. Box 360
Trenton, NJ 08625-0360
Tel: (609) 292-6962 Fax: (609) 292-8713
Web: www.state.nj.us/health/commiss/omh/index.html

NEW MEXICO

NEW MEXICO DEPARTMENT OF HEALTH
Office of Policy & Multicultural Health
1190 St. Francis Dr. #S-4260
Santa Fe, NM 87502-6110
Tel: (505) 827-2280 Fax: (505) 827-2942

NEW YORK

NEW YORK CITY DEPARTMENT OF HEALTH & MENTAL HYGIENE
Office of Minority Health Programs
485 Throop Ave. #1460
Brooklyn, NY 11221
Tel: (646) 253-5800 Fax: (646) 253-7502

NEW YORK STATE DEPARTMENT OF HEALTH
Office of Minority Health
ESP-Corning Tower Bldg. #780
Albany, NY 12237-0092
Tel: (518) 474-2180 Fax: (518) 473-4695

NORTH CAROLINA

NORTH CAROLINA DEPARTMENT OF HEALTH & HUMAN SERVICES
Office of Minority Health & Health Disparities
1110 Navaho Dr. #510, 1906 Mail Service Ctr.
Raleigh, NC 27699-1906
Tel: (919) 431-1613 Fax: (919) 850-2758
Web: http://www.ncminorityhealth.org/omhhd/index.html

NORTHERN MARIANA ISLANDS

COMMONWEALTH OF THE NORTHERN MARIANA ISLANDS
Secretary of Health
P.O. Box 500-409 CK
Saipan, MP 96950-0409
Tel: (670) 234-8950 Fax: (670) 234-8930

OHIO

COLUMBUS HEALTH DEPARTMENT
Office of Minority Health
240 Parsons Ave.
Columbus, OH 43215
Tel: (614) 645-7159 Fax: (614) 645-5888
Web: www.cmhhealth.org

COMBINED HEALTH DISTRICT OF MONTGOMERY COUNTY
117 S. Main St.
Dayton, OH 45402
Tel: (937) 225-4403

OHIO COMMISSION ON MINORITY HEALTH
Vern Riffe Center for Government and the Performing Arts, 77 S. High St. #745
Columbus, OH 43215
Tel: (614) 466-4000 Fax: (614) 752-9049
Web: www.state.oh.us/mih

OKLAHOMA

OKLAHOMA STATE DEPARTMENT OF HEALTH
Office of Minority Health
1000 NE 10th St. #211
Oklahoma City, OK 73117-1299
Tel: (405) 271-1337 Fax: (405) 271-9228
Web: www.health.state.ok.us

OREGON

DEPARTMENT OF HUMAN SERVICES
Office of Multicultural Health
800 NE Oregon St. #930
Portland, OR 97232
Tel: (971) 673-1285 Fax: (971) 673-1299
Web: www.healthoregon.org/omh/index.cfm

PENNSYLVANIA

PENNSYLVANIA DEPARTMENT OF HEALTH
7th and Forster Sts., Health & Welfare Bldg. #802
Harrisburg, PA 17102-0090
Tel: (717) 787-6436 Fax: (717) 7870191

PUERTO RICO

PUERTO RICO DEPARTMENT OF HEALTH
Office of Special Racial/Ethnic Health Issues
P.O. Box 70139
Bldg. A, Medical Center
San Juan, PR 00936
Tel: (787) 274-7735 Fax: (787) 759-6864

REPUBLIC OF PALAU

REPUBLIC OF PALAU
Minister of Health
P.O. Box 6027
Koror, Republic of Palau 96940
Tel: (680) 488-5552 Fax: (680) 488-1215

RHODE ISLAND

RHODE ISLAND DEPARTMENT OF HEALTH
Office of Minority Health, Ctr. for Healthy People
3 Capitol Hill #401
Providence, RI 02908
Tel: (401) 222-2901 Fax: (401) 273-4350

SOUTH CAROLINA

SOUTH CAROLINA DEPARTMENT OF HEALTH & ENVIRONMENT CONTROL
Office of Minority Health
2600 Bull St.
Columbia, SC 29201
Tel: (803) 898-3808 Fax: (803) 898-3810
Web: www.scdhec.gov/omh

SOUTH DAKOTA

SOUTH DAKOTA DEPARTMENT OF HEALTH
600 E. Capitol Ave.
Pierre, SD 57501
Tel: (605) 773-5303 Fax: (605) 773-5683

TENNESSEE

TENNESSEE DEPARTMENT OF HEALTH
Office of Minority Health
425 5th Ave. North, Cordell Hull Bldg., 3rd Fl.
Nashville, TN 37247
Tel: (615) 741-9443 Fax: (615) 253-1434
Web: www2.state.tn.us/health/minorityhealth

continued on p. 306

ALABAMA

ARTISTIC

JAPANESE GARDEN FOUNDATION, INC.
P.O. Box 91572
Mobile, AL 36691-1572
Charles Wood, President
Email: azubanora@aol.com

CULTURAL

HUNTSVILLE TAIWANESE ASSOCIATION
P.O. Box 6955
Huntsville, AL 35824
Charles Chen, President
Email: CCChen123@charter.net
Web: www.geocities.com/taa_huntsville/

INDIAN CULTURAL ASSOCIATION OF BIRMINGHAM
3029 English Oaks Cir.
Birmingham, AL 35226
Nalini Sathiakumar, Vice President
Tel: (205) 934-3719 Fax: (205) 975-7058
Email: nalini@uab.edu

POLITICAL ACTION

FEDERAL ASIAN PACIFIC AMERICAN COUNCIL
Alabama Chapter
Marshall Space Flight Ctr.
Huntsville, AL 35812
Dr. Alan Chow, Chapter Chairperson
Tel: (256) 544-7107
Email: alan.s.chow@nasa.gov
Web: www.fapac.org

RELIGIOUS

FAIRHOPE TIBETAN SOCIETY, INC.
P.O. Box 617
Fairhope, AL 36533
Geshe Thupten Dorjee
Email: info@fairhopetibetansociety.org
Web: www.fairhopetibetansociety.org

TEMPLE BETH-EL
2179 Highland Ave.
Birmingham, AL 35295
Laura Benjaminson, Executive Director
Tel: (205) 933-2740 Fax: (205) 933-2747
Email: execdirector@templebeth-el.net
Web: www.templebeth-el.net

TEMPLE EMANU-EL
2100 Highland Ave.
Birmingham, AL 35255
Judi Drew, Executive Director
Tel: (205) 933-8037 Fax: (205) 933-8099
Email: jdrew@ourtemple.org
Web: www.ourtemple.org

TUSCALOOSA CHINESE CHRISTIAN FELLOWSHIP
P.O. Box 862492
Tuscaloosa, AL 35486
Email: tccf@bama.ua.edu
Web: http://bama.ua.edu/~tccf/

COLLAT JEWISH FAMILY SERVICES OF BIRMINGHAM
3940 Montclair Rd. #205
Birmingham, AL
Esther Schuster, Executive Director
Tel: (205) 879-3438 Fax: (205) 871-5939
Email: jfs@cjfsbham.org
Web: www.cjfsbham.org

SPEC. INT., SOCIAL INTEREST

BIRMINGHAM JEWISH FEDERATION
3966 Montclair Rd.
Birmingham, AL 35213
Tel: (205) 879-0416 Fax: (205) 803-1526
Email: federation@bjf.org
Web: www.bjf.org

CENTRAL ALABAMA ASSOCIATION FOR CHINESE
9660 Bentbrook Dr.
Montgomery, AL 36117
Yingyue Zhang, President
Tel: (334) 270-8737
Email: tzhang999@yahoo.com

JAPAN AMERICA SOCIETY OF ALABAMA
500 Beacon Pkwy. West
Birmingham, AL 35209
Teresa Wilson, Executive Director
Tel: (205) 943-4730 Fax: (205) 943-4760
Email: jasa@mindspring.com
Web: www.jasaweb.net

STUDENT ORGANIZATION

INDIAN STUDENT ORGANIZATION
University of Alabama in Huntsville
University Center Bldg. UAH
Huntsville, AL 35899
Shine Pillai, President
Email: iso@uah.edu
Web: http://iso.uah.edu

MUSLIM STUDENT ASSOCIATION
University of South Alabama
Islamic Society of Mobile, 63 East Dr.
Mobile, AL 36608
Br. Arshad Anwar, President
Tel: (251) 343-4695 Fax: (251) 343-4695
Email: ism@islamicsocietyofmobile.com
Web: www.southalabama.edu/msa

TAIWANESE STUDENT ASSOCIATION
Auburn University
203 Foy Student Union
Auburn, AL 36849-5134
Quincy Chiu, President

Tel: (334) 442-4511
Email: chiuqui@auburn.edu
Web: www.auburn.edu/student_info/csa

ALASKA

CULTURAL

FILIPINO COMMUNITY, INC.
251 S. Franklin St.
Juneau, AK 99801-1894
Morris Carrillo, President
Tel: (907) 586-4116
Email: filcomjnu@gci.net
Web: www.filcomalaska.org

SPEC. INT., SOCIAL INTEREST

JAPAN-AMERICA SOCIETY OF ALASKA
200 W. 34th Ave. PMB 1232
Anchorage, AK 99501
Tel: (907) 278-7233

SPEC. INT., SPORTS

INTERNATIONAL SHOTOKAN KARATE CLUB
Alaska Region
P.O. Box 81710
Fairbanks, AK 99708
Tony Nakazawa, Regional Director
Tel: (907) 457-4918 Fax: (907) 457-4913
Email: nakazawa@alaska.com
Web: www.iskf-alaska.com

ARIZONA

ARTISTIC

TARA DHATU
P.O. Box 367
Flagstaff, AZ 86002
Tel: (337) 584-2119
Email: taradhatu@flagstaff.org
Web: www.taradhatu.org

CHAMBER OF COMMERCE

ASIAN CHAMBER OF COMMERCE
1219 E. Glendale Ave. #25
Phoenix, AZ 85020
James Rocky Tang, President
Tel: (602) 222-2009 Fax: (602) 870-7562
Web: www.asianchamber.org

PHILIPPINE AMERICAN CHAMBER OF COMMERCE OF ARIZONA
13065 W. McDonald Rd. #C-114
Avondale, AZ 85323
Pricilla Chesler, President
Tel: (602) 625-2947 Fax: (623) 535-1999

ARIZONA ASIAN AMERICAN ASSOCIATION
P.O.E. Box 62224

Phoenix, AZ 85082-2224
Bernard Woo, President
Tel: (480) 998-9325 Fax: (480) 998-9325
Email: info@aaaa-az.org
Web: www.aaaa-az.org

1375 W. Island Cir.
Chandler, AZ 85248
Arif Kazmi P.E., PhD, President
Tel: (480) 722 2996 Fax: (623) 572-9527
Email: Kazmiarif@hayoo.com
Web: www.pakistaninformation.org

POLITICAL ACTION

MIDDLE EAST STUDIES ASSOCIATION OF NORTH AMERICA
University of Arizona
1219 N. Santa Rita Ave.
Tucson, AZ 85721
Mark J. Lowder, Assistant Director
Tel: (520) 621-5850 Fax: (520) 626-9095
Email: mesana@u.arizona.edu
Web: http://fp.arizona.edu/mesassoc

ORGANIZATION OF CHINESE AMERICANS
Phoenix Chapter
223 W. Palmaire Ave.
Phoenix, AZ 85021
Charles Psui, Advisor
Tel: (602) 330-5300 Fax: (602) 997-8881
Email: cpsui1@netscape.net
Web: www.ocanatl.org

PROFESSIONAL

ASIAN AMERICAN JOURNALISTS ASSOCIATION
Arizona Chapter
200 E. Van Buren St.
Phoenix, AZ 85004
Christina Leonard, President
Tel: (602) 444-4845 Fax: (602) 444-8044
Email: christina.leonard@arizonarepublic.com
Web: www.aajaz.org

CHINESE AMERICAN SEMICONDUCTOR PROFESSIONAL ASSOCIATION
Phoenix Chapter
Phoenix, AZ
Lee Zou, Chair of Phoenix Branch
Tel: (480) 554-3728 Fax: (480) 554-7490
Email: phoenixcaspa@yahoo.com
Web: www.caspa-phoenix.com

NATIONAL ARAB AMERICAN MEDICAL ASSOCIATION
Arizona Chapter
2532 N. 20th St.
Phoenix, AZ 85006
Dr. Marwan Bahu, Chapter President
Tel: (602) 240-5811
Email: naama@naama.com
Web: www.naama.com

RELIGIOUS

ARIZONA TEACHINGS, INC.
P.O. Box 43997
Tucson, AZ 85733-3997
Tel: (520) 327-7187 Fax: (520) 882-8831
Email: azteachings@earthlink.net
Web: www.arizonateachings.org

CAMBODIAN BAPTIST FELLOWSHIP
c/o Corona Baptist Church, 4450 W. Ray Rd.
Chandler, AZ 85226
Mr. Savong Ker
Tel: (480) 786-9208 Fax: (480) 838-3197
Email: cambodian_baptist@coronabc.org
Web: http://coronabc.org/cambodian_baptist

CHINESE CHRISTIAN INTERNET MISSION
P.O. Box 11263
Tempe, AZ 85284-0022
Tel: (480) 768-1780
Email: webservant@ccim.org
Web: www.ccim.org

FIRST ARABIC BAPTIST MISSION
2232 W. Campbell
Phoenix, AZ 85031
Jamal Bishara, Pastor
Tel: (602) 863-9244
Email: jamalbishara@qwest.net
Web:

FIRST CHINESE BAPTIST CHURCH
4910 E. Earll Dr.
Phoenix, AZ 85017
Nathan Pillow, Interim Senior Pastor
Tel: (602) 955-3114
Email: office@fcbcphx.org
Web: www.fcbcphx.org

GREATER PHOENIX CHINESE CHRISTIAN CHURCH
890 W. Ray Rd.
Chandler, AZ 85225
Kuang-Fu Yang, Senior Pastor
Tel: (480) 786-4977 Fax: (480) 786-4978
Email: kfyang@gpccc.org
Web: www.gpccc.org

JEWISH VOICE MINISTRIES INTERNATIONAL
P.O. Box 30990
Phoenix, AZ 85046-0990
Jonathan Bernis, Director
Tel: (602) 971-8501 Fax: (602) 971-6486
Email: mail@jewishvoicetoday.org
Web: www.jewishvoicetoday.org

KOREA CHRISTIAN GOSPEL MISSION
P.O. Box 25886
Tempe, AZ 85285
Lee Shafer, Chairman
Tel: (480) 730-1231
Email: lemayll@yahoo.com
Web: www.kcgm.org

SIKH RELIGIOUS SOCIETY OF ARIZONA
1129 E Sheridan St.
Phoenix, AZ 85006
Ranjit S. Bisla, Chairman
Tel: (602) 716-0408
Web: www.arizonasikhgurdwara.com

TEMPLE BETH SHOLOM
3400 N. Dobson Rd.
Chandler, AZ 85224
Barbara Gold, President
Tel: (480) 897-3636
Email: mjbgjjaj@cox.net
Web: www.templebethsholomaz.org

TEMPLE EMANU-EL
225 N. Country Club
Tucson, AZ 85716
Samuel M. Cohon, Senior Rabbi
Tel: (520) 327-4501 Fax: (520) 327-4504
Email: rabbi@templeemanueltucson.org
Web: www.templeemanueltucson.org

TEMPLE EMANUEL OF TEMPE
5801 S. Rural Rd.
Tempe, AZ 85283
Andrew Straus, Rabbi
Tel: (480) 838-1414 Fax: (480) 838-2192
Email: contact@emanueloftempe.org
Web: www.emanueloftempe.org

TUCSON CHINESE CHRISTIAN CHURCH
307 E. Helen St.
Tucson, AZ 85705
Tai Zhang, Elder
Tel: (520) 319-8333
Email: taizhang@aol.com
Web: http://tccf.ccim.org/

VALLEY CHINESE CHURCH
3960 N. 24th Ave.
Phoenix, AZ 85015
Rev. Terry Fung, Pastor
Tel: (480) 421-9115
Email: terrykafung@cox.net
Web: www.valleychinesechurch.com

SCIENTIFIC

AMERICAN COMMITTEE FOR THE WEIZMANN INSTITUTE OF SCIENCE
7975 N. Hayden Rd. #A-108
Scottsdale, AZ 85258
Irene Rosenblum, Regional Chair
Tel: (480) 556-0620
Email: arizona@acwis.org
Web: www.weizmann-usa.org

SPEC. INT., CHILD CARE

CHILD RELIEF AND YOU AMERICA, INC.
CRY-Phoenix
408 N. Sicily Place
Chandler, AZ 85226
Hrushikesh Vasuki, Chapter Coordinator
Tel: (480) 329-9993
Email: hrushikesh.vasuki@microchip.com
Web:

SOUTHERN ARIZONA FAMILIES WITH CHILDREN FROM CHINA
5352 E. Calle Vista De Colores
Tucson, AZ 85711
Cathy Lee, President
Tel: (520) 299-3033
Email: cathylee5@yahoo.com
Web: http://mywebpages.comcast.net/
jknorman/fcc/index.html

SPEC. INT., COUNSELING

JEWISH FAMILY AND CHILDREN'S SERVICES OF SOUTHERN ARIZONA, INC.
4301 E. 5th St.
Tucson, AZ 85711-2005
Susan Rubin, Executive Director
Tel: (520) 795-0300 Fax: (520) 795-8206
Email: jfcsinfo@jfcstucson.org
Web: www.jfcstucson.org

SPEC. INT., EDUCATION

ASHA FOR EDUCATION
Arizona Chapter
P.O. Box 873001 ASU #17 Student
Development Office
Tempe, AZ 85287-3001
Radhika Rao, Coordinator
Email: radhika.rao@intel.com
Web:

CENTER FOR MIDDLE EASTERN STUDIES
University of Arizona
P.O. Box 210158B
Tucson, AZ 85721-0158
Tel: (520) 621-5450 Fax: (520) 621-9257
Email: mideast@u.arizona.edu
Web: www.cmes.arizona.edu

NATIONAL ASIAN PACIFIC AMERICAN LAW STUDENT ASSOCIATION
Asian Law Students Association @ ASU (Arizona State University)
P.O. Box 877906

Tempe, AZ 85287
Jason Wong
Tel: (480) 965-6181 Fax: (480) 965-2427
Email: alsassoc@asu.edu
Web: www.asu.edu/clubs/alsa

TAIWANESE COLLEGIAN
P.O. Box 24652
Tempe, AZ 85285-4652
Shihmin Ho, Secretary General
Email: tcmikeho@hotmail.com
Web: http://tc.formosa.org

US CHINA PEOPLES FRIENDSHIP ASSOCIATION
Mountain States Subregion
7506 E. Via Cornucopia
Tucson, AZ 85715
Sue Rux, President
Tel: (520) 298-0570 Fax: (520) 298-1380
Web: www.uscpfa.org

US CHINA PEOPLES FRIENDSHIP ASSOCIATION
Tucson Chapter
P.O. Box 41598
Tucson, AZ 85717
Iris C. Veomett, Contact
Tel: (520) 795-1682
Web: www.uscpfa.org

SPEC. INT., HEALTH SERVICES

ARIZONA DEPARTMENT OF HEALTH SERVICES
Office of Local and Minority Health
150 N. 18th Ave.
Phoenix, AZ 85007
Tel: (602) 542-2906 Fax: (602) 542-0883
Web: www.hs.state.az.us

SPEC. INT., HUMAN RELATIONS

ARIZONA FRIENDS OF TIBET
P.O. Box 31956
Tucson, AZ 85751-1956
Emily Danies, Board of Director
Tel: (520) 885-6527 Fax: (520) 751-2671
Email: judytbrewer@msn.com
Web: www.arizona-friends-of-tibet.org

COUNCIL ON AMERICAN-ISLAMIC RELATIONS
Arizona Chapter
202 E. McDowell #170
Phoenix, AZ 85004
Deedra Abboud, Director
Tel: (602) 262-2247 Fax: (602) 262-2249
Email: director@cairaz.org
Web: www.cairaz.org

PAN ASIAN COMMUNITY ALLIANCE
940 S. Craycroft Rd.
Tucson, AZ 85711
Dorothy Lew, Executive Director
Tel: (520) 512-0144 Fax: (520) 512-0189
Email: pacacenter@aol.com

PHYSIOTHERAPY & REHABILITATION SUPPORT FOR AFGHANISTAN
P.O. Box 255
Bisbee, AZ 85603
Bob MacMakin
Tel: (520) 432-7711 Fax: (520) 432-7711
Email: macmakin@theriver.com
Web: www.parsa-afghanistan.org

THE AMERICAN JEWISH COMMITTEE
Arizona Chapter
4725 N. Scottsdale Rd. #243

Scottsdale, AZ 85251-7622
Ken C. Smith, Chapter President
Tel: (480) 970-6363 Fax: (480) 970-6464
Email: phoenix@ajc.org
Web: www.ajc.org

SPEC. INT., LEGAL ASSISTANCE

JEWISH LABOR COMMITTEE
Arizona Chapter
10044 E. Champagne Dr.
Sun Lakes, AZ 85248
Herman Brown
Tel: (480) 883-9291
Email: JLCArizona@aol.com
Web: www.jewishlabor.org

SPEC. INT., MENTAL HEALTH

ASIAN AMERICAN PSYCHOLOGICAL ASSOCIATION
5025 N. Central Ave., PMB #527
Phoenix, AZ 85012
Alvin Alvarez, President
Tel: (602) 230-4257
Web: www.aapaonline.org

CHINESE SENIOR CITIZENS ASSOCIATION
734 W. Elm St.
Phoenix, AZ 85013
Ken Szeto, President
Tel: (602) 262-6411 Fax: (602) 534-4251

SPEC. INT., SOCIAL INTEREST

ARIZONA JEWISH HISTORICAL SOCIETY
4710 N. 16th St. #201
Phoenix, AZ 85016
Beryl S. Morton, Executive Director
Tel: (602) 241-7870 Fax: (602) 264-9773
Email: azjhs@aol.com
Web: http://aspin.asu.edu/azjhs/links.html

ASIAN AMERICAN CULTURAL ASSOCIATION
University of Arizona
Tucson, AZ 85721
Henry Yau, President
Email: AACAinfo@hotmail.com
Web: http://clubs.arizona.edu/~aaca/

EMAHO FOUNDATION, INC.
1402 N. Miller Rd. #B1
Scottsdale, AZ 85257
ZaChoeje Rinpoche
Tel: (877) 495-9959 Fax: (877) 495-9959
Email: rinpoche@emahofoundation.org
Web: www.emahofoundation.org

INDIA ASSOCIATION OF PHOENIX
P.O. Box 60121
Phoenix, AZ 85082
Girija Krishnamurthy, President
Tel: (480) 940-7153
Email: info@azindiaassociation.com
Web: www.azindiaassociation.com

INDO-AMERICAN FOUNDATION OF ARIZONA
P.O. Box 82756
Phoenix, AZ 85071
Achut Kumar, President
Web: www.azindia.com/iafoa/iafoa.asp

ASIAN AMERICAN FACULTY, STAFF, AND ALUMNI ASSOCIATION
P.O. Box 43975
Tucson, AZ 85722
Susan Chan, Board Member
Tel: (520) 620-5350
Web:

CHINESE AMERICAN CITIZENS ALLIANCE
Tucson Chapter
P.O. Box 27942
Tucson, AZ 85726
Dorothy Lew, Grand Representative

Tel: (520) 297-1042 Fax: (520) 297-5304
Email: dorothylew@aol.com
Web:

CHINESE UNITED ASSOCIATION OF GREATER PHOENIX
P.O. Box 40413
Phoenix, AZ 85067
John Tang, President
Tel: (623) 939-7717
Email: tangyou@msn.com
Web: www.chineseunitedphoenix.com

EAST VALLEY JEWISH COMMUNITY CENTER
1521 S. Indian Bend Rd.
Tempe, AZ 85281
Ilene Blau, Executive Director
Tel: (480) 897-0588 Fax: (480) 517-0124
Email: tricityjcc@aol.com
Web: www.evjcc.org

NEPALIS AND FRIEND ASSOCIATION
Phoenix, AZ
Madan Poudel, President
Email: nafa@asu.edu
Web: www.west.asu.edu/Nafa/

JAPANESE AMERICAN SOCIETY OF TUCSON
5160 N. Hacienda Del Sol
Tucson, AZ 85718
M. Craig, President
Tel: (520) 331-0602 Fax: (520) 299-9297
Email: morigami2@yahoo.com
Web:

JEWISH COMMUNITY FOUNDATION OF GREATER PHOENIX
12701 N. Scottsdale Rd. #202
Scottsdale, AZ 85254
Tel: (480) 699-1717 Fax: (480) 699-1807
Email: info@jcfphoenix.org
Web: www.jcfphoenix.org

JEWISH COMMUNITY OF SEDONA AND THE VERDE VALLEY
P.O. Box 10242
Sedona, AZ
Joseph Knauer, President
Tel: (928) 204-1286 Fax: (928) 204-2616
Email: jcsvv@esedona.net
Web: www.sedonajewishcommunity.org

JEWISH FEDERATION OF GREATER PHOENIX
12701 N. Scottsdale Rd. #201
Scottsdale, AZ 85254
Tel: (480) 634-4900 Fax: (480) 634-4588
Email: info@jewishphoenix.org
Web: www.jewishphoenix.org

JEWISH FEDERATION OF SOUTHERN ARIZONA
3822 E. River Rd.
Tucson, AZ 85718
Shawn Green, CEO
Tel: (520) 577-9393 Fax: (520) 577-0734
Email: cbaldwin@jfsa.org
Web: www.jewishtucson.org

PAKISTAN AMERICAN CULTURAL SOCIETY
P.O. Box 10575
Glendale, AZ 85318
Khizer Hayat, President
Tel: (602) 299-0017
Email: pacs@pacspacs.com
Web: www.pacspacs.com

THE EAST VALLEY JEWISH COMMUNITY CENTER
1521 S. Indian Bend Rd.
Tempe, AZ 85281
Ilene Blau, Executive Director
Tel: (480) 897-0588 Fax: (480) 517-0124
Email: tricityjcc@aol.com
Web: www.evjcc.org

TUCSON CHINESE ASSOCIATION
P.O. Box 27025
Tucson, AZ 85726-7025
Peter Chang, President
Tel: (520) 620-5309 Fax: (520) 622-7482
Email: yslai@ft.newyorklife.com
Web:

TUCSON JEWISH COMMUNITY CENTER
3800 E. River Rd.
Tucson, AZ 85718
Ken Light, President/CEO
Tel: (520) 299-3000 Fax: (520) 299-0373
Email: info@tucsonjcc.org
Web: www.tucsonjcc.org

TURKISH AMERICAN ASSOCIATION OF ARIZONA
P.O. Box 373
Tempe, AZ 85281
Suat Ozdemir, President
Tel: (602) 332-7670
Email: info@taaaz.org
Web: www.taaaz.org

VALLEY OF THE SUN JEWISH COMMUNITY CENTER
12701 N. Scottsdale Rd. #203
Scottsdale, AZ 85254
Tel: (480) 483-7121 Fax: (480) 483-8441
Web: www.vosjcc.org

SPEC. INT., SPORTS

ARABIAN HORSE OWNERS FOUNDATION
P.O. Box 30924
Tucson, AZ 85751
Howard Shenk, Executive Director
Tel: (800) 892-0682
Email: info@ahof.org
Web: www.arabianhorseowners.org

INTERNATIONAL SHOTOKAN KARATE CLUB
Western
6326 N. 7th St.
Phoenix, AZ 85014
Shojiro Koyama, Instructor
Tel: (602) 274-1136 Fax: (602) 943-3350
Email: azkarate@earthlink.net
Web: www.iskf.com

STUDENT ORGANIZATION

ASIAN PACIFIC AMERICAN MEDICAL STUDENTS ASSOCIATION
National Office
1200 E. University Ave., Old Main Bldg. #104
Tucson, AZ 85721-0001
Celeste Ming Chu, President
Tel: (520) 626-3269 Fax: (520) 621-7574
Email: mvp_apamsa@hotmail.com
Web: www.apamsa.org

CONTEMPORARY CHINESE SCHOOL OF ARIZONA
P.O. Box 25668
Tempe, AZ 85285-5668
Ying Gao, Principal
Tel: (480) 892-6301
Email: ccsarizona@yahoo.com
Web: www.dreamschool.com/ccsa

PHILIPPINE AMERICAN STUDENT ASSOCIATION
Arizona State University
ASU PASA #215
Tempe, AZ 85287-3001
Jose Valdez, President
Email: asu_pasa@hotmail.com
Web: www.asupasa.tk

ARKANSAS

CULTURAL

ARKANSAS INTERNATIONAL CENTER
University of Arkansas at Little Rock
2801 S. University
Little Rock, AR 72204
Dr. Walter Nunn, Director
Tel: (501) 569-3282 Fax: (501) 569-8347
Email: whnunn@ualr.ued
Web: www.ualr.edu/aic/

SPEC. INT., SOCIAL INTEREST

ARKANSAS PHILIPPINE ASSOCIATION
3708 N. Hills Blvd.
N. Little Rock, AR 72116
Elsa Bayani, Chairman
Tel: (501) 758-8998
Email: ebayani@aol.com
Web:

JAPAN AMERICA SOCIETY OF ARKANSAS
2801 S. University Ave.
Little Rock, AR 72204
Vicki Gonterman, President
Tel: (501) 569-3282 Fax: (501) 569-8347
Email: txsuzuki@ualr.edu
Web: www.freewebs.com/jasarkansas/index.htm

JEWISH FEDERATION ARKANSAS
425 North University Ave.
Little Rock, AR 72205
Tel: (501) 663-3571 Fax: (501) 663-7286
Email: jfar@jewisharkansas.org
Web: www.jewisharkansas.org

CALIFORNIA

ARTISTIC

AL-FUNUN AL-ARABIYA
1147 Beverwil Dr.
Los Angeles, CA 90035
Fadwa El Guindi, Founder
Web: www-bcf.usc.edu/~elguindi/Funun.htm

ARMENIAN ALLIED ARTS ASSOCIATION
3063 Dona Marta Dr.
Studio City, CA 91604
Kathleen K. Kurkjian, President
Tel: (310) 838-1949 Fax: (818) 553-1133
Email: info@armenianalliedarts.com
Web: www.armenianalliedarts.org

ASIA AMERICA SYMPHONY ASSOCIATION
608 Silver Spur Rd. #320
Rolling Hills, CA 90274
Dr. Seng-Hsiu Lee, Operations Director
Tel: (310) 377-8977 Fax: (310) 377-8949
Web:

ASIAN AMERICAN REPERTORY THEATRE
P.O. Box 81796
San Diego, CA 92138-1796
Anne Tran, Marketing Manager
Tel: (888) 568-2278
Email: atran@asianamericanrep.org
Web: www.asianamericanrep.org

ASIAN AMERICAN THEATER COMPANY
690 5th St. #211
San Francisco, CA 94107
Sean Lim, Artistic Director
Tel: (415) 543-5738 Fax: (415) 543-5638
Email: slim@asianamericantheater.org
Web: www.asianamericantheater.org

ASIAN AMERICAN WOMEN ARTISTS ASSOCIATION
Kearny Street Workshop at SomArts
934 Brannan St.
San Francisco, CA 94103
Terry Acebo Davis, Member

Email: aawaa2000@yahoo.com
Web: www.aawaaart.com

ASIAN ART MUSEUM
200 Larkin St.
San Francisco, CA 94102
Emily Sano, Museum Director
Tel: (415) 581-3500 Fax: (415) 581-4700
Email: pr@asianart.org
Web: www.asianart.org

ASIAN IMPROV
1375 Sutter St. #110
San Francisco, CA 94109
Dina Shek
Tel: (415) 353-5732 Fax: (415) 353-5733
Email: contact@asianimprov.com
Web: www.asianimprov.com

ASIAN IMPROV ARTS
201 Spear St. #1650
San Francisco, CA 94105
Francis Wong, Creative Director
Tel: (415) 908-3636 Fax: (415) 442-0994
Email: contact@asianimprov.com
Web: www.asianimprov.com

ASIAN STORY THEATER
1250 Weaver St.
San Diego, CA 92114
Gingerlily Lowe, Education Director
Tel: (619) 527-2816
Email: ast@asianstorytheater.com
Web: http://la.znet.com/~ast/

ASSOCIATION FOR VIET ARTS
P.O. Box 90088
San Jose, CA 95109-3088
Lan Nguyen, Contact
Tel: (408) 586-9006
Email: info@vietarts.org
Web: www.vietarts.org

BAY AREA SOUTH ASIAN ARTIST RESOURCE
Berkeley, CA 94701
Email: basaar2000@yahoo.com
Web: www.basaar.org

CHINESE FOLK DANCE ASSOCIATION
619 Kearny St.
San Francisco, CA 94108
Tel: (415) 834-1359
Web: www.cfdasf.org

CHINESE PERFORMING ARTISTS OF AMERICA
San Francisco Chapter
456 10th St.
San Francisco, CA 94118
Tel: (415) 386-3571 Fax: (415) 978-5380
Email: CPAA@comcast.net
Web: www.chineseperformingarts.org

San Jose Chapter
377 S. 1st St.
San Jose, CA 95113
Tel: (408) 973-8276 Fax: (408) 973-8276
Email: CPAA@comcast.net
Web: www.chineseperformingarts.org

CHUNG NGAI DANCE TROUPE
724 Commercial St.
San Francisco, CA 94108
Tel: (415) 398-8738
Email: chungngaitroupe@yahoo.com
Web: www.geocities.com/chungngaitroupe/chungngaidancetroupe.html

CONTEMPORARY ASIAN THEATER SCENE
565 N. 5th St.
San Jose, CA 95112
Christine Padilla, Executive Director
Tel: (408) 298-2287 Fax: (408) 280-0407
Email: info@asiantheater.org
Web: http://asiantheater.org

EAST WEST PLAYERS
120 N. Judge John Aiso St.
Los Angeles, CA 90012
Tim Dang, Producing Artistic Director
Tel: (213) 625-7000 Fax: (213) 625-7111
Email: info@eastwestplayers.org
Web: www.eastwestplayers.org

ETH-NOH-TEC
977 S. Van Ness Ave.
San Francisco, CA 94110
Nancy Wang, Co-Director
Tel: (415) 282-8705 Fax: (415) 282-8795
Email: info@ethnohtec.org
Web: www.ethnohtec.org

GREAT LEAP, INC.
1145 Wilshire Blvd. #100-D
Los Angeles, CA 90017
Nobuko Miyamoto, Founder/Artistic Director
Tel: (213) 250-8800 Fax: (213) 250-8801
Email: luke@greatleap.org
Web: www.greatleap.org

JAPANESE MUSIC INSTITUTE OF AMERICA
5074 Bissett Way
Sacramento, CA 95835
Masayuki Koga, Director
Tel: (916) 419-6456
Email: mkoga@sbcglobal.net
Web: www.jmia.org

KAYAMANAN NG LAHI PHILIPPINE FOLK ARTS
11338 Braddock Dr.
Culver City, CA 90230
Joel F. Jacinto, Founder
Tel: (310) 391-2357 Fax: (413) 702-8228
Email: kayamanan@earthlink.net
Web: www.kayamanan.org

KHAM AID FOUNDATION
556 S. Fair Oaks Ave. #309
Pasadena, CA 91105
Pamela Logan, President
Tel: (626) 449-7505 Fax: (626) 628-3109
Email: khamaid@khamaid.org
Web: www.khamaid.org

KOREAN AMERICAN MUSIC SUPPORTERS ASSOCIATION
P.O. Box 2063
Cupertino, CA 95015-2063
Key T. Kim, President
Email: info@kamsa.org
Web: www.kamsa.org

KOREAN DANCE ACADEMY
1010 S. Fedora St. #203
Los Angeles, CA 90006
Jung Im Lee, Director
Tel: (213) 487-2957
Email: jungimlee@yahoo.com
Web: www.koreandanceacademy.com

MUSIC CIRCLE
625 S. Madison Ave.
Pasadena, CA 91106
Harihar Rao, President & Artistic Director
Tel: (626) 449-6987
Email: info@musiccircle.org
Web: www.musiccircle.org

NIOSHA DANCE ACADEMY
604 Pinot Blanc Way
Fremont, CA 94539
Tel: (510) 573-2804 Fax: (408) 943-9292
Email: niosha@niosha.com
Web: www.niosha.com

PACIFIC ASIA MUSEUM
46 N. Los Robles Ave.
Pasadena, CA 91101
Tel: (626) 449-2742
Web: www.pacificmuseum.org

PURNA DAS BAUL ACADEMY
P.O. Box 16381
San Diego, CA 92176-0381
Email: info@purnadasbaul.org

RAAG AND TAAL ACADEMY
5528 Caminito Vista Lujo
San Diego, CA 92130
Anupam Talapatra
Tel: (858) 254-2366 Fax: (858) 793-1864
Email: anupamt2000@yahoo.com
Web: www.raagandtaal.org

SAN DIEGO ASIAN FILM FOUNDATION
7969 Engineer Rd. #206
San Diego, CA 92111-0212
Lee Ann Kim, Executive Director
Tel: (858) 650-3459 Fax: (858) 650-3459
Email: info@sdaff.org
Web: www.sdaff.org

SAN JOSE TAIKO
P.O. Box 26895
San Jose, CA 95159
Roy Hirabayashi, Managing Director
Tel: (408) 293-9344 Fax: (408) 293-9366
Email: sjtaiko@taiko.org
Web: www.taiko.org

TEADA PRODUCTIONS
1653 18th St. #2
Santa Monica, CA 90404
Leilani Chan, Founder Artistic Director
Tel: (310) 998-8765 Fax: (310) 453-4347
Email: teada@teada.org
Web: www.teada.org

THE CAMBODIAN DANCERS OF SAN DIEGO
4191 Colts Way #B.5
San Diego, CA 92115
Tel: (619) 287-0894 Fax: (619) 229-8915
Email: cyouth@cambodiandancers.org
Web: www.cambodiandancers.org

THE JAPANESE TRADITIONAL PERFORMING ARTS ORGANIZATION
221 Via Los Miradores
Redondo Beach, CA 90277
Mikko Haggott Henson, Founder & President
Tel: (310) 378-3550 Fax: (310) 378-6990
Email: Mikko@jtpao.org
Web: www.jtpao.org

THE JEWISH MUSIC FOUNDATION
8241 Quiet Hills Ct.
West Hills, CA 91304
Neal Brostoff, Contact
Email: jewishmusicfoundation@yahoo.com
Web: www.jewishmusicfoundation.org

VISUAL COMMUNICATIONS, SOUTHERN CALIFORNIA ASIAN AMERICAN STUDIES CENTRAL,INC.
120 Judge John Aiso St.
Los Angeles, CA 90012-3805
Leslie Ito, Executive Director
Tel: (213) 680-4462 Fax: (213) 687-4848
Email: info@vconline.org
Web: http://vconline.org

BUSINESS

ARMENIAN TECHNOLOGY GROUP,INC.
1300 E. Shaw Ave. #149
Fresno, CA 93710
Tel: (559) 224-1000 Fax: (559) 224-1002
Email: info@atgusa.org
Web: www.atgusa.org

ASIA AMERICA MULTITECHNOLOGY ASSOCIATION
3300 Zanker Rd. M/D SJ2F8
San Jose, CA 95134
Roberta M. Lee, Executive Director
Tel: (408) 955-4505 Fax: (408) 955-4516
Email: aama@aamasv.com
Web: www.aamasv.com

ASIA SILICON VALLEY CONNECTION
268 Bush St. #88
San Francisco, CA 94104
Thomas T.H. Chou, Director & President
Email: info@asvc.org
Web: www.asvc.org

ASIAN AMERICAN BUSINESS ASSOCIATION
University of Southern California
Bridge Hall 103
Los Angeles, CA 90089
Email: aaba@usc.edu

ASIAN AMERICAN ECONOMIC DEVELOPMENT ENTERPRISES,INC.
216 W. Garvey Ave. #E
Monterey Park, CA 91754
William Chang, Vice President
Tel: (626) 572-7021 Fax: (626) 572-6533
Email: info@aaede.org
Web: www.aaede.org

ASIAN BUSINESS ASSOCIATION
41 Sutter St. PMB #1080
San Francisco, CA 94104
Basilio Chen, President
Tel: (415) 284-6765 Fax: (415) 284-6767
Email: info@abainc.org
Web: www.abainc.org

ASIAN BUSINESS ASSOCIATION OF ORANGE COUNTY
2960 S. Daimler St.
Santa Ana, CA 92705
Thi Nguyen, Executive Manager
Tel: (949) 222-2291 Fax: (949) 222-2293
Email: info@abaoc.org
Web: www.abaoc.org

ASIAN BUSINESS ASSOCIATION OF SAN DIEGO
7808 Clairemont Mesa Blvd. #A
San Diego, CA 92111
Fabiola M. Fujiwara, Marketing Executive
Tel: (858) 277-2822 Fax: (858) 277-2622
Email: fabiola@abasd.org
Web: www.abasd.org

ASIAN BUSINESS LEAGUE OF SAN FRANCISCO
564 Market St. #404
San Francisco, CA 94104
Kitty So, Executive Director
Tel: (415) 788-4664 Fax: (415) 788-4756
Email: info@ablsf.org
Web: www.asianbusinessleague.org

ASIAN BUSINESS LEAGUE OF SOUTHERN CALIFORNIA
505 S. Flower St. #C23
Los Angeles, CA 90071
Tel: 213-624-9975

ASIAN PACIFIC COMMUNITY FUND
5318 S. Crenshaw Blvd.
Los Angeles, CA 90043
Judy M. Asazawa, President
Tel: (323) 293-6284 Fax: (323) 295-4075
Email: general@apcf.org
Web: www.apcf.org

ASIAN PACIFIC ISLANDER SMALL BUSINESS PROGRAM
231 E. 3rd St. #G106
Los Angeles, CA 90013
H. Cooke Sunoo, Director
Tel: (213) 473-1605 Fax: (213) 473-1601
Email: csunoo@ltsc.org
Web: www.apisbp.org

BERKELEY ROUNDTABLE ON THE INTERNATIONAL ECONOMY
2234 Piedmont Ave. #2322
Berkeley, CA 94720
Noriko Katagiri, Administrative Assistant
Tel: (510) 642-3067 Fax: (510) 643-6617
Email: brie@socrates.berkeley.edu
Web: http://brie.berkeley.edu

CALIFORNIA ASIA BUSINESS COUNCIL
1919 Clement Ave., Bldg. 11
Alameda, CA 94501
Jeremy Potash, Executive Director
Tel: (510) 523-8188 Fax: (510) 865-0812
Email: jeremy@calasia.org
Web: www.calasia.org

CALIFORNIA COMMUNITY ECONOMIC DEVELOPMENT ASSOCIATION
Southern California Office
1055 Wilshire Blvd. #1475
Los Angeles, CA 90017
Ralph Lippman, Executive Director
Tel: (213) 353-1676 Fax: (213) 207-2780
Email: ralph@cceda.com
Web: www.cceda.com

CHINESE ENTERPRISE ASSOCIATION, INC.
4675 Stevens Creek Blvd. #125B
Santa Clara, CA 95051
ZongRui Xia, President
Tel: (408) 248-6016 Fax: (408) 286-6126
Email: cea@cea-usa.org
Web: www.cea-usa.org

CHINESE PROFESSIONAL SERVICES
8825 Aero Dr. #110
San Diego, CA 92123
Sally Wong-Abry, Director
Tel: (858) 565-0068 Fax: (858) 571-6867

COUNCIL OF ASIAN AMERICAN BUSINESS ASSOCIATIONS
1 Kaiser Plz., Ordway Bldg. #1333
Oakland, CA 94612
Edward W. Chin, President/CEO
Tel: (510) 893-5331 Fax: (510) 893-4445
Email: info@ais-insurance.com
Web: www.ais-insurance.com

DECCA ENTERPRISES
1324 E. Katella Ave.
Anaheim, CA 92805
Eric Chung, President
Tel: (714) 939-9480 Fax: (714) 939-9717

HONG KONG ASSOCIATION OF NORTHERN CALIFORNIA
41 Sutter St. #1748
San Francisco, CA 94104
Thomas Wu, President
Tel: (415) 398-4506 Fax: (415) 392-2964
Email: ed@hkanc.com
Web: www.hkanc.com

HONG KONG ECONOMIC AND TRADE OFFICE
San Francisco Office
130 Montgomery St.
San Francisco, CA 94104
Doris Cheung, Director
Tel: (415) 835-9300 Fax: (415) 421-0646
Email: doris_cheung@hketosf.gov.hk
Web: www.hketosf.gov.hk/sf

HONG KONG-SILICON VALLEY
130 Montgomery St.
San Francisco, CA 94101
Pauline Lo Alker, Chairman & President
Tel: (415) 835-9316 Fax: (415) 392-2963
Web: www.hongkong-sv.com

INTERNATIONAL ENTERPRISE SINGAPORE
San Francisco Office
595 Market St. #2450
San Francisco, CA 94105
Hoo Hoe Keat, Director
Tel: (415) 543-0488 Fax: (415) 543-0484
Email: enquiry@iesingapore.gov.sg
Web: www.iesingapore.gov.sg

IRANIAN TRADE ASSOCIATION
P.O. Box 927743
San Diego, CA 92192
Shahriar Afshar, President
Tel: (619) 368-6790 Fax: (858) 547-0823
Email: info@iraniantradetrade.org
Web: www.iraniantrade.org

JAPAN BUSINESS ASSOCIATION OF SOUTHERN CALIFORNIA
1411 W. 190th St. #270
Gardena, CA 90248
Kuniaki Seto, Executive Director
Tel: (310) 515-9522 Fax: (310) 515-9722
Email: jba@jba.org
Web: www.jba.org

JAPAN EXTERNAL TRADE ORGANIZATION
San Francisco Chapter
235 Pine St. #1700
San Francisco, CA 94104
Osamu Watanabe, Chairman/CEO
Tel: (415) 392-1333 Fax: (415) 788-6927
Email: sfc@jetro.go.jp
Web: www.jetrosf.org

JOSHUA VENTURE
28 2nd St. #500
San Francisco, CA 94105
Emily Freed, Director of Operations
Tel: (415) 777-4500 Fax: (415) 777-4045
Email: fellowship@joshuaventure.org
Web: http://joshuaventure.org

KOREAN AMERICAN BUSINESS ASSOCIATION
3400 W. 6th St. #209
Los Angeles, CA 90020
Jong Min Kang, President
Tel: (213) 368-0848 Fax: (213) 368-0846
Email: yohngsohk@yahoo.com

KOREAN AMERICAN GARMENT INDUSTRY ASSOCIATION
1830 W. Olympic Blvd. St. 219
Los Angeles, CA 90006
Tel: (213) 389-7776 Fax: (213) 389-6093

KOREAN APPAREL MANUFACTURERS ASSOCIATION
420 E. 11th St. #312
Los Angeles, CA 90015
David Choi, President
Tel: (213) 746-5362 Fax: (213) 746-0728
Email: kama@sbcglobal.net

KOREAN DRYCLEANERS & LAUNDRY ASSOCIATION OF SOUTHERN CALIFORNIA
14909 Crenshaw Blvd. #204
Gardena, CA 90249
Young Shinn, President
Tel: (310) 679-1300 Fax: (310) 679-6890
Email: kdla@kdla.org
Web: www.kdla.org

MALAYSIAN PROFESSIONAL AND BUSINESS ASSOCIATION
226 Airport Pkwy. #480
San Jose, CA 95110
Bunny Chuah, President
Tel: (408) 392-0617 Fax: (408) 392-0619
Email: president@mpba.org
Web: www.mpba.org

NATIONAL COUNCIL OF ASIAN AMERICAN BUSINESS ASSOCIATIONS
23824 Twin Pine Ln.
Diamond Bar, CA 91765
Jelly Borromeo, Executive Director
Tel: (909) 861- 9670 Fax: (909) 861-7896
Email: ana@national-caaba.org
Web: www.national-caaba.org

NATIONAL UNIVERSITY OF SINGAPORE ENTREPRENEURS ASSOCIATION
100 View St. #102
Mountain View, CA 94041
John Lim, VP of External Affairs
Email: john@nusea.org
Web: www.nusea.org

PAKISTANI AMERICAN BUSINESS EXECUTIVES
23105 Kashiwa Ct.
Torrance, CA 90505
Tel: (310) 534-1505 x141

Fax: (310) 534-1424
Email: info@pabe.org
Web: www.pabe.org

SILICON VALLEY-CHINA WIRELESS TECHNOLOGY ASSOCIATION
P.O. Box 360184
Milpitas, CA 95036-0184
Gary Wang, Chairman
Tel: Fax: (408) 549-9886
Email: garysvc@yahoo.com
Web: http://svcwireless.org

SINGAPORE AMERICAN BUSINESS ASSOCIATION
333 Twin Dolphin Dr. #112
Redwood City, CA 94065
Grace Yu, Executive Director
Tel: (415) 252-1150 Fax: (415) 252-1160
Email: sabausa@aol.com
Web: www.saba-usa.org

TAIWAN TRADE CENTER-SAN FRANCISCO
5201 Great America Pkwy. #307
Santa Clara, CA 95054
Tel: (408) 988-5018 Fax: (408) 988-5029
Email: office@taiwantradesf.org
Web: www.taiwantradesf.org

THE INDUS ENTREPRENEUR
Silicon Valley Office
2903 Bunker Hill Ln. #108
Santa Clara, CA 95054
Raj Desai, Executive Director
Tel: (408) 567-0700 Fax: (408) 567-0777
Email: tieadmin@tie.org
Web: www.tiesv.org

THE U.S.-IRAN BUSINESS COUNCIL
Iranian trade Association
P.O. Box 927743
San Diego, CA 92192
Shahriar Afshar, President
Tel: (858) 564-0560 Fax: (858) 564-0561
Email: info@iraniantrade.org
Web: www.iraniantrade.org/usibc

TURKISH AMERICAN BUSINESS FORUM
California
P.O. Box 885
Cupertino, CA 95015
Aydin Koc, Executive Committee Member
Tel: (650) 743-1424
Email: info@calforum.org
Web: www.calforum.org

US-CHINA EXCHANGE ASSOCIATION
Los Angeles Office
11100 Valley Blvd. #340-6
El Monte, CA 91731
Tel: (626) 279-2981 Fax: (626) 279-5779
Web: www.usachina.org

AFGHAN CHAMBER OF COMMERCE
39270 Paseo Padre Pkwy. #343
Fremont, CA 94538
Tariq Saifi, President
Tel: (800) 435-8795
Email: info@afghanchamber.org
Web: www.afghanchamber.org

AMERICAN LEBANESE CHAMBER OF COMMERCE OF NORTH AMERICA
1400 San Miguel Dr.
Corona del Mar, CA 92625
Tel: (949) 644-2153 Fax: (949) 759-9539
Email: mikefarah1@aol.com
Web: www.ltio.org

ARMENIAN AMERICAN CHAMBER OF COMMERCE
417 W. Arden Ave. #112-B
Glendale, CA 91203
Joe Dermenjian, President
Tel: (818) 247-0196 Fax: (818) 247-7668

Email: aacc@armchamber.com
Web: www.armenianchamber.com

ASIAN PACIFIC-USA CHAMBER OF COMMERCE
150 S. Los Robles Ave. #490
Pasadena, CA 91101
Gene Lu, President
Tel: (626) 795-9486 Fax: (626) 795-9452
Email: info@apucc.org
Web: www.apucc.org

CALIFORNIA ISRAEL CHAMBER OF COMMERCE
10725 N. De Anza Blvd.
Cupertino, CA 94015
Shuly Galili, Executive Director
Tel: (408) 343-0917 Fax: (408) 343-1197
Email: shuly@ca-israelchamber.org
Web: www.ca-israelchamber.org

CHINESE AMERICAN CHAMBER OF COMMERCE
2021 The Alameda
San Jose, CA 95126-1110
Dennis Wan, Executive Director
Tel: (408) 615-7300 Fax: (408) 984-6682
Email: denis@dwinvestment.com

CHINESE CHAMBER OF COMMERCE
730 Sacramento St.
San Francisco, CA 94108
Wayne Hu, President
Tel: (415) 982-3000 Fax: (415) 982-4720

CHINESE CHAMBER OF COMMERCE OF LOS ANGELES
977 N. Broadway G/F #E
Los Angeles, CA 90012
Henry Leong, President
Tel: (213) 617-0396 Fax: (213) 617-2128
Email: info@lachinesechamber.org
Web: www.lachinesechamber.org

FEDERATION OF PHILIPPINE AMERICAN CHAMBER OF COMMERCE, INC.
2887 College Ave. No. 1 Box #106
Berkeley, CA 94705
Yolanda O. Stern, President
Tel: (510) 664-9952 Fax: (510) 841-5008
Email: fpacc@aol.com
Web: www.fpacc.com

FILIPINO AMERICAN CHAMBER OF COMMERCE OF ORANGE COUNTY
215 E. Orangethorpe Ave. # 288
Fullerton, CA 92832-3017
Erlinda Sarno, President
Tel: (714) 280-4729 Fax: (714) 525-0208
Email: lindasarno@aol.com
Web: www.faccoc.org

FILIPINO AMERICAN CHAMBER OF COMMERCE OF SAN DIEGO COUNTY
3131 Camino del Rio #1580 North
San Diego, CA 92108
Willie D. Racelis, President
Tel: (619) 641-0014 Fax: (619) 641-0014
Email: wracelis@foresters.biz
Web: www.faccsd.com

FILIPINO AMERICAN CHAMBER OF COMMERCE OF SAN FRANCISCO
135 Darien Way
San Francisco, CA 94127
Carmen Colet, Executive Director
Tel: (415) 726-8816 Fax: (510) 494-5308
Email: president@filamccsf.org
Web: www.filamccsf.org

FILIPINO AMERICAN CHAMBER OF COMMERCE OF SANTA CLARA COUNTY,INC.
1046 W. Taylor St. #206
San Jose, CA 95126
Elvie De La Vega, Executive Director
Tel: (408) 283-0833 Fax: (408) 998-1252
Email: tvegafilchamber@aol.com
Web: www.filchamber.org

HAWAI'I CHAMBER OF COMMERCE OF NORTHERN CALIFORNIA
1375 Sutter St. #300
San Francisco, CA 94109
Eric Tao, President
Tel: (415) 845-5196 Fax: (415) 775-7002
Email: webmaster@hccnc.com
Web: www.hccnc.com

INDO-AMERICAN CHAMBER OF COMMERCE
3095 Greentree Way
San Jose, CA 95128
Vimu Rajdev, President
Tel: (408) 261-6400
Email: info@icccchamber.org
Web: www.icccganber.org

INDO-AMERICAN CHAMBER OF COMMERCE OF NORTHERN CALIFORNIA
1616 University Ave.
Berkeley, CA 94703
Manjul Batra, Director/Treasurer
Tel: (510) 841-1513 Fax: (510) 841-4756
Web: www.icccchamber.org

IRANIAN AMERICAN CHAMBER OF COMMERCE
3239 Ramos Cir.
Sacramento, CA 95827
Mina Nakreini, Treasurer
Tel: (916) 363-9283
Web:

San Francisco Bar Area
P.O. Box 190813
San Francisco, CA 94119
Shiva Pakdel, Board of Director
Tel: Fax: (415) 512-8289
Email: iacc@iranianchamber..org
Web: www.iranianchamber.com

IRAQI AMERICAN CHAMBER OF COMMERCE AND INDUSTRY
4813 Lowell Ave.
La Crescenta, CA 91214
Nadia, Executive Assistant
Tel: (818) 249-1525 Fax: (818) 249-3032
Email: nadia@i-acc.org
Web: itali@i-acci.org

ISLAMIC CHAMBER OF COMMERCE & INDUSTRY
1338 Ridder Park Dr.
San Jose, CA 95131
Amr Mohsen, Chairman
Tel: (408) 453-2485 Fax: (408) 453-2485
Email: info@islamic-commerce.org
Web: www.islamic-commerce.org

JAPANESE AMERICAN CHAMBER OF COMMERCE OF SILICON VALLEY
95 S. Market St. #520
San Jose, CA 95113
Denise Kawahara, Director of Operations
Tel: (408) 288-5222 Fax: (408) 298-7554
Email: info@jaccsv.org
Web: www.jaccsv.org

JAPANESE CHAMBER OF COMMERCE OF NORTHERN CALIFORNIA
1875 S. Grant St. #760
San Mateo, CA 94402
Kaz Sugiura, Executive Director
Tel: (650) 522-8500 Fax: (650) 522-8300
Email: mail@jccnc.org
Web: www.jccnc.org

JAPANESE CHAMBER OF COMMERCE OF SOUTHERN CALIFORNIA
244 San Pedro St. #504
Los Angeles, CA 90012
Shinji Abe, President
Tel: (213) 626-3067 Fax: (213) 626-3067
Email: office@jccsc.com
Web: www.jccsc.com

KOREAN AMERICAN CHAMBER OF COMMERCE OF LOS ANGELES
3440 Wilshire Blvd. #520
Los Angeles, CA 90010
Edward Moon Sik, President
Tel: (213) 480-1115 Fax: (213) 480-7521
Email: info@koraminsurance.com
Web: www.koreanchamberla.org

KOREAN AMERICAN CHAMBER OF COMMERCE OF SILICON VALLEY
1530 The Alameda #305
San Jose, CA 95126
Tak Chang, President
Tel: (408) 975-0189 Fax: (408) 975-9100
Email: info@kacc-sv.com
Web: www.kacc-sv.org

NATIONAL US-ARAB CHAMBER OF COMMERCE
Los Angeles Office
8929 S. Sepulveda Blvd. #310
Los Angeles, CA 90045
Elie Atallah, Program Director
Tel: (310) 646-1499 Fax: (310) 646-2462
Email: nusacc@aol.com
Web: www.nusacc.org

OAKLAND CHINATOWN CHAMBER OF COMMERCE
388 9th St. #258
Oakland, CA 94607
Jennie Ong, Executive Director
Tel: (510) 893-8979 Fax: (510) 893-8988
Email: oklandctchamber@aol.com
Web: www.oaklandchinatownstreetfest.com

PAKISTAN AMERICAN CHAMBER OF COMMERCE
24439 E. Gold Point Pl.
Diamond Bar, CA 91765
Waqar Khan, President
Tel: (909) 612-1138 Fax: (714) 612-1132
Email: info@safeerepakistan.com

SACRAMENTO ASIAN PACIFIC CHAMBER OF COMMERCE
1331 T. St. #3
Sacramento, CA 95814
Pat Fong Kushida, President
Tel: (916) 446-7883 Fax: (916) 446-7098
Email: sacasiancc@aol.com
Web: www.asiancc.org

SEATTLE CHINESE CHAMBER OF COMMERCE
675 S. King St.
Seattle, CA 98104
Benjamin Lee, President
Tel: (206) 332-1933 Fax: (206) 650-8337
Email: info@chinesechamber.net
Web: www.chinesechamber.net

SOUTHERN CALIFORNIA ISRAEL CHAMBER OF COMMERCE
6300 Wilshire Blvd. #1010
Los Angeles, CA 90048
Teri Cohan-Link, Chairperson
Tel: (323) 951-0990 Fax: (323) 651-5938
Email: admin@scicc.biz
Web: www.scicc.biz

TAIWANESE CHAMBER OF COMMERCE OF SAN DIEGO
7170 Convoy Ct.
San Diego, CA 92111
Joe Chou, President
Tel: (858) 560-8884 Fax: (858) 560-9276
Email: joe@tccsd.com
Web: www.tccsd.com

US PAN ASIAN AMERICAN CHAMBER OF COMMERCE
West Coast Chapter
8907 Warner Ave. #163
Huntington Beach, CA 92647
Frank Jao, Chapter President/Founder

Tel: (714) 842-7332 Fax: (714) 596-8663
Email: info@uspaaccwest.org
Web: www.uspaaccwest.org

VIETNAMESE AMERICAN CHAMBER OF COMMERCE OF SANTA CLARA VALLEY
255 N. Market St. #110
San Jose, CA 95110
Thuan Nguyen, Executive Director
Tel: (408) 288-7602 Fax: (408) 288-7604
Email: vacc@ix.netcom.com

COMMUNICATIONS

ARAB AMERICAN MEDIA CENTER
1939 Divisadero #3
San Francisco, CA 94115
Tel: (415) 457-8269
Email: info@arabmediacenter.org
Web: www.arabmediacenter.org

MINORITY MEDIA SERVICES,INC.
1580 Bryant St.
Daly City, CA 94105
Greg Macabenta, President
Tel: (650) 992-4001 Fax: (650) 992-4002
Email: mmsi13@aol.com
Web: www.minoritymedia.com

CULTURAL

AFGHAN CENTER
37416 Joseph St.
Fremont, CA 94536
Tel: (510) 794-1050

AMERICA-NEPAL SOCIETY OF CALIFORNIA, INC.
20734 Saticoy
Winnetka, CA 91306
Anil Pradhan, President
Email: president@ansca.org
Web: www.ansca.org

ANGEL ISLAND IMMIGRATION STATION FOUNDATION
P.O. Box 29237
San Francisco, CA 94129-0237
Charles Greene, Executive Director
Tel: (415) 561-2160 Fax: (415) 561-2162
Email: info@aiisf.org
Web: www.aiisf.org

ARAB AMERICAN CULTURAL OF SILICON VALLEY
416 Park Ave.
San Jose, CA 95110
Joseph Louis, President
Tel: (408) 279-2722 Fax: (408) 279-3322
Email: arabcenter_sj@sbcglobal.net
Web: www.arabcentersv.org

ARAB CULTURAL AND COMMUNITIY CENTER
2 Plaza St.
San Francisco, CA 94116
Abeer Fedrafiti, Director
Tel: (415) 664-2200 Fax: (415) 664-2280
Email: info@arabculturalcenter.org
Web: www.arabculturalcenter.org/home.html

ARARAT-ESKIJIAN MUSEUM AND LIBRARY
15105 Mission Hills Rd.
Mission Hills, CA 91345
Luther Eskijian, Founder
Tel: (818) 838-4862
Web: www.ararat-eskijian-museum.com

ARMENIAN FOUNDATION FILM, MUSIC & ART
2919 Maxwell St.
Los Angeles, CA 90027
Sylvia Minassian, Chairperson
Tel: (323) 663-1882 Fax: (323) 663-1882
Email: affma_filmfestival@yahoo.com
Web: www.affma.org

ARMENIAN GENERAL BENEVOLENT UNION
Los Angeles Chapter
2495 E. Mountain St.
Pasadena, CA 91104
Tel: (626) 794-7942 Fax: (626) 794-2622
Email: info@agbuypla.org
Web: www.agbuypla.org

ASIAN AMERICAN CURRICULUM PROJECT INC., ASIAN AMERICAN BOOKS
83 37th Ave.
San Mateo, CA 94403
Florence M. Hongo, President/General Manager
Tel: (800) 874-2242 Fax: (650) 357-6908
Email: aacpinc@asianamericanbooks.com
Web: www.asianamericanbooks.com

ASIAN AMERICAN DANCE PERFORMANCES
1840 Sutter St. #206
San Francisco, CA 94115
Jez Kuono'ono Lee, Director
Tel: (415) 441-8831 Fax: (415) 440-5597
Email: aadp@unboundspirit.org
Web: www.unboundspirit.org

ASIAN PACIFIC ISLANDER CULTURAL CENTER
934 Brannan St.
San Francisco, CA 94103
Tel: (415) 864-4120 Fax: (415) 864-4134
Email: info@apiculturalcenter.org
Web: www.apiculturalcenter.org

AU CO VIETNAMESE CULTURAL CENTER
P.O. Box 347042
San Francisco, CA 94134
Email: auco@aucocenter.org
Web: www.aucocenter.org

BALBHARTI INDO-AMERICAN CULTURAL ACADEMY
P.O. Box 263
Fremont, CA 94537-0263
Web: www.balbharti.org

CHAKSAM-PA TIBETAN DANCE & OPERA COMPANY
P.O. Box 581
Sonoma, CA 95476
Tashi Dhondup
Tel: (707) 935-8172
Email: sapana@vom.com
Web: www.tibet.org/chaksampa/

CHINATOWN REVITALIZATION, INC. OF FRESNO
1433 Kern St.
Fresno, CA 93706
Michael Yada, President
Tel: (559) 441-7915
Email: admin@fresno-chinatown.org
Web: www.fresno-chinatown.org

CHINESE AMERICAN MUSEUM
425 N. Los Angeles St.
Los Angeles, CA 90012
Tel: (213) 485-8567 Fax: (213) 473-4224
Web: www.camla.org

CHINESE CULTURAL CENTER OF THE TECO IN LOS ANGELES
9443 Telstar Ave.
El Monte, CA 91731
Tel: (626) 443-9999 Fax: (626) 443-7777
Web: www.ccclaroc.org

CHINESE CULTURE CENTER OF LOS ANGELES
420 Bernard St.
Los Angeles, CA 90012
Tel: (213) 626-7295 Fax: (213) 617-7656
Email: la1@ocac.net
Web: www.ocac.gov.tw/la1

CHINESE CULTURE FOUNDATION OF SAN FRANCISCO
750 Kearny St., 3rd Fl.
San Francisco, CA 94108-1809
Mike Curtis, Administrative Assistant
Tel: (415) 986-1822 Fax: (415) 986-2825
Email: info@c-c-c.org
Web: www.c-c-c.org

CHINESE HISTORICAL AND CULTURAL PROJECT
P.O. Box 5366
San Jose, CA 95150-5366
Rodney Lum O.D., President
Tel: (408) 366-0688 Fax: (408) 773-8885
Email: chcp@chcp.org
Web: www.chcp.org

CHINESE HISTORICAL SOCIETY OF AMERICA
965 Clay St.
San Francisco, CA 94108
Sue Lee, Executive Director
Tel: (415) 391-1188 Fax: (415) 391-1150
Email: info@chsa.org
Web: www.chsa.org

CHINESE HISTORICAL SOCIETY OF GREATER SAN DIEGO & BAJA CALIFORNIA
Chinese Museum
404 3rd Ave.
San Diego, CA 92101
Alexander Chuang, Executive Director
Tel: (619) 338-9888 Fax: (619) 338-9889
Email: info@sdchm.org
Web: www.sdchm.org

CHINESE HISTORICAL SOCIETY OF SOUTHERN CALIFORNIA
P.O. Box 862647
Los Angeles, CA 90086-2647
Kenneth Chan, President
Tel: (323) 222-0856
Email: chssc@chssc.org
Web: www.chssc.org

COMMITTEE OF 100 FOR TIBET
P.O. Box 60612
Palo Alto, CA 94306-0612
Email: info@c100tibet.org
Web: www.c100tibet.org

CONEJO CHINESE CULTURAL ASSOCIATION
1728 Moorpark Rd. #416
Thousand Oaks, CA 91360
Web: www.ccca-tocs.org

DIMENSION PERFORMING ARTS, INC.
1173-D S. De Anza Blvd.
San Jose, CA 95129
Maria Chen, Board of Director
Email: info@dimensionarts.org
Web: www.dimensionarts.org

FILIPINO AMERICAN ASSOCIATION OF SAN DIEGO NORTH COUNTY
P.O. Box 26014
San Diego, CA 92126
Patricia Tejada Feaster, President
Email: filamsdnc@cs.com
Web: www.faasdnc.org

FILIPINO AMERICAN NATIONAL HISTORICAL SOCIETY
Los Angeles Chapter
16557 Nordhoff St.
North Hills, CA 91343
Johann Diel, President
Tel: (323) 256-7178
Email: lafanhs@fanhsla.org
Web: www.fanhsla.org
San Diego Chapter
P.O. Box 7135
Chula Vista, CA 91912
Judy Patacsil, President
Email: fanhs18@yahoo.com
Web: www.geocities.com/fanhs18/

Stockton Chapter
P.O. Box 4616
Stockton, CA 95204
Mel LaGasca, President
Tel: (209) 462-3489
Email: StocktonFANHS@aol.com
Web: www.geocities.com/fanhs_stkn/

FULLERTON CHINESE CULTURAL ASSOCIATION
P.O. Box 2370
La Habra, CA 90632
Tel: (714) 525-2726
Email: info@fullertonchinese.org
Web: www.fullertonchinese.org

GARDENA VALLEY JAPANESE CULTURAL INSTITUTE
1964 W. 162nd St.
Gardena, CA 90247
Alison Kochiyama, Interim Executive Director
Tel: (310) 324-6611 Fax: (310) 324-3223
Email: info@jci-gardena.org

INDIA COMMUNITY CENTER
Milpitas Office
555 Los Coches St.
Milpitas, CA 95035
Anil Godhwani, President
Tel: (408) 934-1130 Fax: (408) 934-1150
Email: info@indiacc.org
Web: www.indiacc.org

INDO-AMERICAN CULTURAL CENTER
2210 Lincoln Blvd.
Venice, CA 90291
Sarita Vasa, Executive Director
Tel: (310) 391-3330 Fax: (310) 391-1066
Email: sarita@artwallah.org
Web: www.iacc-la.org/prism

INSTITUTE OF VIETNAMESE STUDIES
P.O. Box 11900
Westminster, CA 92685-1900
Minh-Lan Nguyen, Secretary General
Tel: (714) 775-2050 Fax: (714) 775-3550
Email: info@viethoc.org
Web: www.viethoc.org

IRAN ALLIANCE
P.O. Box 3388
Alhambra, CA 91803
Mohammad Ala, Executive Board Member
Email: mala@teacher.com
Web: www.iranalliance.org

IRANIAN COMMUNITY SERVICE CENTER
P.O. Box 2288
Cupertino, CA 95015
Mona Khatami, Contact
Tel: (408) 289-1449
Email: ircs@yahoo.com

IRANIAN MUSLIM ASSOCIATION OF NORTH
3376 Motor Ave.
Los Angeles, CA 90034
Dr. Mohammad Sadegh Namazikhah, President/CEO
Tel: (310) 202-8181 Fax: (310) 202-0878
Email: iman@iman.org
Web: www.iman.org

JAPAN AMERICAN CITIZENS LEAGUE
Ventura County Chapter
P.O. Box 1092
Camarillo, CA 93011
Email: vcjacl@hotmail.com
Web: www.vcjacl.org

JAPANESE AMERICAN CULTURAL & COMMUNITY CENTER
244 S. San Pedro St. #505
Los Angeles, CA 90012
Cora Mirikitani, President/CEO
Tel: (213) 628-2725 Fax: (213) 617-8576
Email: info@jaccc.org
Web: www.jaccc.org

JAPANESE AMERICAN HISTORICAL SOCIETY OF SAN DIEGO
P.O. Box 20988
San Diego, CA 92162-0988
Vernon Yoshioka, President
Email: contact@jahssd.org
Web: www.jahssd.org

JAPANESE AMERICAN MUSEUM OF SAN JOSÉ
535 N. 5th St.
San Jose, CA 95112
Joseph Yasutake, President
Tel: (408) 294-3138 Fax: (408) 294-6157
Email: mail@jamsj.org
Web: www.jamsj.org

JAPANESE AMERICAN NATIONAL MUSEUM
369 E. 1st St.
Los Angeles, CA 90012
Irene Y. Hirano, President/CEO
Tel: (213) 625-0414 Fax: (213) 625-1770
Email: thashimoto@janm.org
Web: www.janm.org

JAPANESE AMERICAN NETWORK
231 E. 3rd St. #G-104
Los Angeles, CA 90013
Email: janet-info@janet.org
Web: www.janet.org

JAPANESE AMERICAN RELIGIOUS AND CULTURAL CENTER
3165 Treat Blvd.
Concord, CA 94518
Tel: (925) 682-5299
Web: www.diablojaclub.org

JAPANESE CULTURAL AND COMMUNITY CENTER OF NORTHERN CALIFORNIA
1840 Sutter St.
San Francisco, CA 94115
Paul Osaki, Executive Director
Tel: (415) 567-5505 Fax: (415) 567-4222
Email: jcccnc@jcccnc.org
Web: www.jcccnc.org

JAPANESE CULTURAL ARTS CENTER
1249 Marin Ave.
Albany, CA 94706
Tel: (510) 524-9283 Fax: (510) 528-8914
Web: www.kiaikido.org/JCAC/

JAPANESE CULTURAL FAIR
Santa Cruz, CA
Chieko Yoshikawa, Executive Committee
Tel: (831) 462-4589
Web: www.jcfsc.org

JAPANESE INSTITUTE OF SAWTELLE
2110 Corinth Ave.
Los Angeles, CA 94107
Tel: (310) 479-2477

JAPANESE SPEAKING SOCIETY OF AMERICA
1759 Sutter St.
San Francisco, CA 94115
Kiyoshi Naito, President
Tel: (415) 921-1782
Web:

JAPANTOWN TASK FORCE,INC.
1765 Sutter St., 1st Fl.
San Francisco, CA 94115
Linda Jofuku, Executive Director
Tel: (415) 346-1239 Fax: (415) 346-6703
Email: linda@jtowntaskforce.org
Web: www.jtowntaskforce.org

JEWEL OF PERSIA, INC.
14252 Culver Dr. #916
Irvine, CA 92604
Darr Hashempour, President
Tel: (866) 473-7742 Fax: (714) 389-9700
Email: info@jewelofpersia.org
Web: www.jewelofpersia.org

JEWISH FAMILY HISTORY FOUNDATION
P.O. Box 16305
Encino, CA 91416
David B. Hoffman, President
Email: gdlpproject@aol.com
Web: www.jewishfamilyhistory.org

JUDAH L. MAGNES MUSEUM
2911 Russell St.
Berkeley, CA 94705
Terry Pink Alexander, Executive Director
Tel: (510) 549-6950 Fax: (510) 849-3673
Email: info@magnes.org
Web: www.magnes.org

KAISAHAN
19 N. 2nd St. #102
San Jose, CA 95113
Raymundo Moreno, President/Chairman
Tel: (408) 298-3787 Fax: (408) 280-0407
Email: kaisahan@hotmail.com
Web: www.kaisahan.org

KEARNY STREET WORKSHOP
934 Brannan St.
San Francisco, CA 94103
Truong Tran, Executive Director
Tel: (415) 503-0520 Fax: (415) 503-0547
Email: info@kearnystreet.org
Web: www.kearnystreet.org

KOREAN AMERICAN MUSEUM
3727 W. 6th St. #400
Los Angeles, CA 90020
Susan Choi, Program Coordinator
Tel: (213) 388-4229 Fax: (213) 381-1288
Email: info@kamuseum.org
Web: www.kamuseum.org

KOREAN CULTURAL CENTER
5505 Wilshire Blvd.
Los Angeles, CA 90036
Jun Young Jae, Director
Tel: (323) 936-7141 Fax: (323) 936-5712
Email: info@kccla.org
Web: www.kccla.org

KOREAN INDEPENDENCE HISTORICAL ASSOCIATION
1954 Redesdale Ave.
Los Angeles, CA 90039
David Hyun, Chairman
Tel: (323) 666-6044 Fax: (323) 666-0199
Email: kihai@earthlink.net

LAO COMMUNITY CULTURAL CENTER
1988 Hazelwood Pl.
San Diego, CA 92105
Nham Infisienmay, President
Tel: (619) 266-8109 Fax: (619) 264-3809

LEBANESE AMERICAN ASSOCIATION
P.O. Box 4464
Burlingame, CA 94010-4464
Fuad Freiha, President
Tel: (650) 259-9871 Fax: (650) 259-9874
Email: laa@laa.org
Web: www.laa.org

LOS ANGELES FRIENDS OF TIBET
P.O. Box 641066
Los Angeles, CA 90064
Tao Tenzing Dhamcho, President
Tel: (310) 289-4654
Email: friends@latibet.org
Web: www.latibet.org

LOS ANGELES KOREAN FESTIVAL FOUNDATION
680 Wilshire Pl. #411
Los Angeles, CA 90005
Young C. Kim, Executive Director
Tel: (213) 487-9696 Fax: (213) 487-5234
Email: info@lakoreanfestival.com
Web: www.lakoreanfestival.com

LOS ANGELES-GUANGZHOU SISTER CITY ASSOCIATION
800 N. Broadway #L

Los Angeles, CA 90012-2379
Caroline L. Ahmanson, Chairman
Tel: (213) 626-8368 Fax: (213) 626-8361
Email: info@lagsca.com
Web: www.lagsca.com

MANILATOWN HERITAGE FOUNDATION
953 Mission St. #30
San Francisco, CA 94103
Emil A. De Guzman, President
Tel: (415) 777-1130
Web: www.manilatown.org

MARIN CHINESE CULTURAL ASSOCIATION
P.O. Box 2053
Novato, CA 94948
Eddy Lo, President
Tel: (415) 491-0724
Email: eddylo@fairissic.com

MEHRGAN FOUNDATION
11932 Bernardo Plaza Dr.
San Diego, CA 92128
Tel: (858) 673-7000 Fax: (858) 451-9086
Email: admin@mehrgan.us
Web: www.mehrgan.us

MINGEI INTERNATIONAL MUSEUM
1439 El Prado
San Diego, CA 92101
Martha Ehringer, Director of Public Relations
Tel: (619) 239-0003 Fax: (619) 239-0605
Email: mingei@mingei.org
Web: www.mingei.org

NATIONAL FOUNDATION FOR JEWISH CULTURE
West Coast Office
3807 Wilshire Blvd. #717
Los Angeles, CA 90010
Emily Hodos, West Coast Program Director
Tel: (2123) 387-0990 Fax: (213) 387-0987
Email: nfjcla@jewishculture.org
Web: www.jewishculture.org

NATIONAL JAPANESE AMERICAN HISTORICAL SOCIETY
1684 Post St.
San Francisco, CA 94115
Rosalyn Tonai, Executive Director
Tel: (415) 921-5007 Fax: (415) 921-5087
Email: njahs@njahs.org
Web: www.njahs.org

NIKKEI BRIDGE
P.O. Box 6522
Torrance, CA 90504
Hayato Tamura, President
Web: www.nikkeibridge.org

NORTH ORANGE COUNTY CHINESE CULTURE ASSOCIATION
P.O. Box 17065
Anaheim Hills, CA 92807
David Liu, President
Email: webmaster@noccca.org
Web: www.noccca.org

OAKLAND ASIAN CULTURAL CENTER
288 9th St. #290
Oakland, CA 94607
Anne Huang, Executive Director
Tel: (510) 637-0455
Email: ahuang@oacc.cc
Web: www.oacc.cc

ORGANIZATION OF ISTANBUL ARMENIANS
19726 Sherman Way
Winnetka, CA 91306
Dr. Arto Ersan-Hatcherian, President
Tel: (818) 342-6378 Fax: (818) 342-9804
Web: www.oia.net

PACIFIC ISLANDERS' CULTURAL ASSOCIATION
1016 Lincoln Blvd. #5
San Francisco, CA 94129
Shirley Avilla, President
Tel: (415) 281-0221

Email: info@pica-org.org
Web: www.pica-org.org

PACIFIC LINKS FOUNDATION
5236 Claremont Ave.
Oakland, CA 94618
Sue Chan, Advisory Board Member
Tel: (510) 435-3035 Fax: (510) 658-2057
Email: info@pacificlinks.org
Web: www.pacificlinks.org

PASADENA JAPANESE CULTURAL INSTITUTE
595 Lincoln Ave.
Pasadena, CA 91103
Bryan Takeda, Board Member
Tel: (626) 449-5487 Fax: (626) 396-9862
Email: afinity2000@earthlink.net

PERSIAN CENTER
P.O. Box 5363
Redwood City, CA 94063
Hamid Taeb, Director
Tel: (510) 848-0264 Fax: (510) 848-2537
Email: info@persiancenter.org
Web: www.persiancenter.org

PERSIAN CULTURAL CENTER
P.O. Box 500914
San Diego, CA 92150
Tel: (858) 653-0336 Fax: (619) 374-7335
Email: pcc@pccsd.org
Web: www.pccsd.org

PHILIPPINE AMERICAN SOCIETY AND CULTURAL ARTS TROUPE
102 E. 16th St.
National City, CA 91950
Tess Abella, President
Tel: (619) 477-3383
Email: booking@pasacat.org
Web: www.pasacat.org

PRABASI
Bay Area Prabasi Inc.
P.O. Box 2116
Fremont, CA 94536
Surajit Sengupta, Chairman
Tel: (408) 973-1294
Web: www.prabasi.org

ROOTS IN CHINA EDUCATION INTERNATIONAL
P.O. Box 51801
Palo Alto, CA 94303
John Chou, President
Tel: (630) 366-1085 Fax: (650) 366-1755
Email: info@rice.ws
Web: www.rice.ws

SAN DIEGO CHINESE CENTER
428 3rd Ave.
San Diego, CA 92101
Cham Louie, President
Tel: (619) 234-4447 Fax: (619) 234-0442
Email: sdcc1972@yahoo.com
Web: www.geocities.com/
sandiegochinesecenter

SAN DIEGO CHINESE HISTORICAL MUSEUM
404 3rd Ave.
San Diego, CA 92101
Patrice Yagen, Administrative Assistant
Tel: (619) 338-9888 Fax: (619) 338-9889
Email: pyagen@sdchm.org
Web: www.sdchm.org

SAN FRANCISCO TAIKO DOJO
1581 Webster St. #200
San Francisco, CA 94115
Ryuma Tanaka, General Manager
Tel: (415) 928-2456 Fax: (415) 928-2456
Email: taikodojo@earthlink.net
Web: www.taikodojo.org

SILKROAD FOUNDATION
P.O. Box 2275
Saratoga, CA 95070
Email: info@silk-road.com
Web: www.silk-road.com

SOUTH BAY VIETNAMESE CULTURAL CENTER
P.O. Box 1512
Redondo Beach, CA 90278
Dien Van Nguyen, President
Tel: (310) 634-6468 Fax: (310) 702-2213
Email: info@sbvcc.org
Web: www.sbvcc.org

SOUTHEAST ASIAN CULTURE AND EDUCATION FOUNDATION
17212 Blue Fox Cir.
Huntington Beach, CA 92647-2441
Tel: (714) 842-7589 Fax: (714) 847-4009
Email: SEACAEF@socal.rr.com
Web: www.seacaef.org

SPEAK OUT - INSTITUTE FOR DEMOCRATIC EDUCATION AND CULTURE
P.O. Box 99096
Emeryville, CA 94662
Felicia Gustin, Co-Director
Tel: (510) 601-0182 Fax: (510) 601-0183
Email: info@speakoutnow.org
Web: www.speakoutnow.org

SRI LANKA AMERICA ASSOCIATION OF SOUTHERN CALIFORNIA
4021 Rosewood Ave. #212
Los Angeles, CA 90004
Keshini Wijegoonarathna, President
Tel: (909) 618-4677
Email: shir@prodigy.net
Web: www.slaasc.com

TAIWANESE AMERICAN CITIZENS LEAGUE
National Headquarters
3001 Walnut Grove Ave. #7
Rosemead, CA 91770
Morgan Lin, Chairman
Tel: (626) 571-7197 Fax: (626) 571-7197
Email: tacl@tacl.org
Web: www.tacl.org

San Francisco Chapter
4988 Paseo Padre Pkwy. #101
Fremont, CA 94555
Victoria Tseng, President
Email: tacl-sf@tacl.org
Web: www.tacl-sf.org

TAIWANESE UNITED FUND
3001 Walnut Grove Ave. #7
Rosemead, CA 91770
Tel: (626) 569-0692
Email: info@tufusa.org
Web: www.tufusa.org

THE SINO-JUDAIC INSTITUTE
232 Lexington Dr.
Menlo Park, CA 94025
Al Dien, President
Email: aldien@leland.stanford.edu
Web: www.sino-judaic.org

THE SRI LANKA FOUNDATION
1930 Wilshire Blvd. # 1100
Los Angeles, CA 90057
Walter Jayasinghe, Founder
Tel: (213) 483-2620
Email: adrian@lamedcenter.com
Web: www.srilankafoundation.org

TURKISH AMERICAN ASSOCIATION OF CALIFORNIA
2053 Grant Rd. PMB 123
Los Altos, CA 94024
Ahmet Toprak, Executive Vice President
Tel: (415) 646-0946 Fax: (586) 461-5929
Email: taac@taaca.org
Web: www.taaca.org

UNITED VIETNAMESE AMERICANS
P.O. Box 794
San Jose, CA 95108-0974
Nhat Ngo, President
Email: info@uvaus.com
Web: www.uvaus.com

VENTURA COUNTY CHINESE AMERICAN ASSOCIATION
P.O. Box 806
Camarillo, CA 93011-0806
Hillary Ling, President
Tel: (805) 386-4188
Email: info@vccaa.org
Web: www.vccaa.org

VIETNAM FRIENDSHIP VILLAGE PROJECT USA, INC.
P.O. Box 3805
Santa Cruz, CA 95063
Email: info@vietnamfriendship.org
Web: www.vietnamfriendship.org

VIETNAMESE AMERICAN NATIONAL GALA
P.O. Box 21130
San Jose, CA 95151-1130
Ryan Hubris, Executive Director
Tel: (408) 238-7780 Fax: (408) 238-0107
Email: info@vangusa.com
Web: www.vangusa.com

WILDFLOWERS INSTITUTE
354 Pine St., 7th Fl.
San Francisco, CA 94104
Dr. Hanmin Liu, President/CEO
Tel: (415) 399-1199 Fax: (415) 399-1599
Email: wizard@wildflowers.org
Web: www.wildflowers.org

3RD I LOS ANGELES
c/o 617 Cabrillo Villas
Los Angeles, CA 90042
Email: thirdi_losangeles@yahoo.com
Web: www.thirdi.org/~la/

3RD I SAN FRANCISCO
c/o Ivan Jaigirdar 992 Valencia St.
San Francisco, CA 94110
Email: thirdi_sf@yahoo.com
Web: www.thirdi.org/~sf/index.html

ARAB FILM FESTIVAL
2 Plz. Ave.
San Francisco, CA 94116
Dina Saba, Director and Founder
Tel: (415) 564-1100
Email: amera@aff.org
Web: www.aff.org

CENTER FOR ASIAN AMERICAN MEDIA
145 9th St. #350
San Francisco, CA 94103
Eddie Wong, Executive Director
Tel: (415) 863-0814
Email: info@naatanet.org
Web: www.naatanet.org

CHINESE KWUN OPERA SOCIETY
602 N. Huntington Ave. #3
Monterey Park, CA 91754
William Kin, Secretary
Email: kunqu@hotmail.com
Web: www.angelfire.com/ca2/RedwallRules/
kwunopera.html

COALITION OF ASIAN PACIFICS IN ENTERTAINMENT
P.O. Box 251855
Los Angeles, CA 90025
Adele Yoshioka, Co-President
Tel: (310) 278-2313 Fax: (310) 910-8883
Email: info@capeusa.org
Web: www.capeusa.org

ASIAN PACIFIC AMERICAN LEGISLATIVE STAFF NETWORK
1217 El Prado Ave.
Torrance, CA 90501
Stacey Toda, Field Representative
Tel: (310) 782-1553 Fax: (310) 782-2566
Email: stacey.toda@asm.ca.gov

ASIAN GANG INVESTIGATORS' ASSOCIATION OF CALIFORNIA
P.O. Box 4241
West Covina, CA 91791-0241
Edward Yee, Secretary
Email: EdwardYee@agiaconline.org
Web: www.agiaconline.org

ASIAN PEACE OFFICERS ASSOCIATION
P.O. Box 221251
Sacramento, CA 95822
Dean Louie, President
Email: apoasac@aol.com
Web: www.napoa.org

CHINATOWN PUBLIC SAFETY ASSOCIATION
823 N. Hill St.
Los Angeles, CA 90012
Tony Sperl, Executive Director
Tel: (213) 621-3043 Fax: (213) 621-1650
Email: cpsa90012@yahoo.com
Web: www.cpsala.com

LAW ENFORCEMENT ASSOCIATION OF ASIAN PACIFICS
P.O. Box 11336
Glendale, CA 91226
Daniel Wong, President
Email: dwonglapd@yahoo.com
Web: www.leaap.org

NATIONAL ASSOCIATION OF ASIAN AMERICAN LAW ENFORCEMENT COMMANDERS
P.O. Box 1822
Camarillo, CA 93011
Dante Honorico, President
Email: dante.honorico@mail.co.ventura.ca.us
Web: www.naaalec.org

NORTHERN CALIFORNIA ASIAN PEACE OFFICERS ASSOCIATION
P.O. Box 144
San Bruno, CA 94066
Richard Hong, President
Email: hong75sfda@juno.com
Web: www.ncapoa.org

PAN PACIFIC LAW ENFORCEMENT ASSOCIATION
P.O. Box 126156
San Diego, CA 92112-6156
Mike Shiraishi, President
Email: president@panpac.org
Web: www.panpac.org

AMERASIAN NETWORK, INC.
9432 Portsmouth Dr.
Huntington Beach, CA 92646
Tel: Fax: (714) 965-0564
Web: www.amerasiannetwork.org

ASIA FOUNDATION
Headquarters
465 California St., 9th Fl.
San Francisco, CA 94104
Barnett Baron, Executive Vice President
Tel: (415) 982-4640 Fax: (415) 392-8863
Email: info@asiafound.org
Web: www.asiafoundation.org

ASIAN AMERICAN COALITION
247 W. Ferguson Ave.
Visalia, CA 93291
Paul Chao, Executive Director
Tel: (559) 713-4203 Fax: (559) 713-4830
Email: chaospy@juno.com
Web: http://aacoalition.org.tripod.com

ASIAN AMERICAN CONTRACTORS ASSOCIATION
1670 Pine St.
San Francisco, CA 94109
Frank Fung, Chair
Tel: (415) 928-5910 Fax: (415) 921-0182
Email: info@asianinc.org
Web: www.asianinc.org

ASIAN AMERICAN PUBLIC POLICY INSTITUTE
Associate of Asian Aids Action (AAA)
4546 El Camino Real #B10-129
Los Altos, CA 94022
Kim Singh, Director
Tel: (650) 346-5998 Fax: (925) 892-0871
Email: policyinstitute@juno.com

ASIAN PROFESSIONAL EXCHANGE
207 E. Franklin Ave. # B
El Segundo, CA 90254
Michelle JiYun Meadows, President
Email: michelle@apex.org
Web: www.apex.org

BAY AREA FRIENDS OF ARMENIA
1558 25th Ave
San Francisco, CA 94122
John Haleblian, Ph.D., Executive Director
Tel: (415) 681-7148
Email: janigh@ix.netcom.com
Web: www.bafa.org

CAMBODIAN COMMUNITY OF STOCKTON
4212 N. Pershing Ave. #A9
Stockton, CA 95207
Tel: (209) 951-7087

CHINA FOUNDATION, INC.
Western Regional Office
546 Clement St. #C
San Francisco, CA 94118
Christine Uong, Regional Director
Tel: (415) 377-9909
Email: us-west@chinafoundation.net
Web: www.chinafoundation.net

CHINATOWN SERVICE CENTER
Main Office
767 N. Hill St. #400
Los Angeles, CA 90012
Debbie Ching, President
Tel: (213) 808-1700 Fax: (213) 680-0787
Email: csc-info@cscla.org
Web: www.cscla.org

CHINESE AMERICAN POLITICAL ASSOCIATION COMMUNITY EDUCATION FUND
P.O. Box 4314
Walnut Creek, CA 94596-0314
Emily Chang, Executive Director
Tel: (925) 945-1901 Fax: (925) 938-2961
Email: capa@capacommunity.org
Web: www.capacommunity.org

CULTURE, HEALTH, EDUCATION AND ENVIRONMENTAL RESOURCES FOR VIETNAM
P.O. Box 341
Culver City, CA 90232
Doan thi Nam-Hue, Director
Tel: (310) 836-6410
Email: cheervietnam@hotmail.com
Web: www.geocities.com/Tokyo/Flats/5111/CHEER1.htm

DEAF ASIA FOUNDATION
1313 N. Grand Ave.
Walnut, CA 91789
George Taylor, President

Tel: Fax: (951) 346-5678
Email: info@deafasia.org
Web: www.deafasia.org

EAST BAY VIETNAMESE ASSOCIATION, INC.
1218 Miller Ave.
Oakland, CA 94601
Lai Van Luu, Executive Director
Tel: (510) 533-4224 Fax: (510) 533-4219
Email: ebviet@ebva.org

FILIPINO AMERICAN COMMUNITY DEVELOPMENT COUNCIL
Northside Community Center
2352 Alum Rock Ave.
San Jose, CA 95116
Ben Menor, President & CEO
Tel: (408) 928-1100 Fax: (408) 928-1105
Email: northsidecenter@sbcglobal.net
Web: www.filamnorthside.org

FRIENDS OF NEPAL
10410 Palm Blvd. PMB 22
Los Angeles, CA 90034
Tel: (310) 842-6100 Fax: (310) 815-9197
Email: friendsofnepal@usa.com
Web: www.fonnj.org

GLOBAL KOREAN NETWORK OF LOS ANGELES
11432 South St. #301
Cerritos, CA 90703
Michael Won, CPA
Tel: (501) 640-8133 Fax: (626) 628-3246
Email: postmaster@gkn-la.net
Web: www.gkn-la.net

SACRAMENTO CHINESE COMMUNITY SERVICE CENTER
915 T St.
Sacramento, CA 95814
Henry Kloczkowski, Executive Director
Tel: (916) 442-2523 Fax: (916) 442-1089
Email: sccsc915@hotmail.com
Web: http://pages.sbcglobal.net/cchiang/sccsc.htm

SAMOAN COMMUNITY DEVELOPMENT CENTER
2055 Sunnydale Ave.
San Francisco, CA 94134
Patsy Tito, Executive Director
Tel: (415) 841-1086 Fax: (415) 333-1658
Email: scdc_sf@packbell.net

SANTA BARBARA FRIENDS OF TIBET
119 Cooper Rd.
Santa Barbara, CA 93109
Kevin Young
Tel: (805) 564-3400 Fax: (805) 564-3400
Email: kyoung@sbre.com
Web: www.sbre.com/tibet/index.html

TAIWANESE AMERICAN FOUNDATION OF SAN DIEGO
Taiwanese American Community Center
7170 Convoy Ct.
San Diego, CA 90013
Ted Fan, Executive Director
Tel: (858) 560-8884 Fax: (858) 560-9276
Email: tedfan@taiwancenter.com
Web: www.taiwancenter.com

TIBETAN ASSOCIATION OF NORTHERN CALIFORNIA
P.O. Box 9128
Berkeley, CA 94709
Chimmy Gonpo, President
Tel: (916) 638-8347
Email: chimmy@tanc.org
Web: www.tanc.org

TZU CHI
California Office
175 Dempsey Rd.
Milpitas, CA 95035
Cheng Yen, Founder

Tel: (408) 262-3389 Fax: (408) 262-3390
Email: northerncal@us.tzuchi.org
Web: http://northerncal.us.tzuchi.org

Main Office
222 E. Palm Ave.
Monrovia, CA 91016
Cheng Yen, Founder
Tel: (626) 305-1188 Fax: (626) 305-1185
Email: info@us.tzuchi.org
Web: www.tzuchi.org

VIETNAMESE AMERICAN COUNCIL
1115 E. Santa Clara St. #8
San Jose, CA 95116
Dat Nguyen, Executive Director
Tel: (408) 971-8280 Fax: (408) 971-8285
Email: hvietmy@viet-nam.org
Web: www.viet-nam.org

VIETNAMESE COMMUNITY
Los Angeles County
1710 S. Del Mar Ave. #216
San Gabriel, CA 91776
Long Bui, President
Tel: (626) 288-0908 Fax: (626) 288-4624
Email: longbui216@sbcglobal.net

VIETNAMESE COMMUNITY OF ORANGE COUNTY, INC.
Asian Health Center
5015 K-L W. Edinger Ave.
Santa Ana, CA 92704
Karen Nguyen, Manager
Tel: (714) 418-2040 Fax: (714) 418-2045
Email: vncoc@aol.com
Web: www.vncoc.org

Headquarters
1618 W. 1st St.
Santa Ana, CA 92703
Mai Cong, President/CEO
Tel: (714) 558-6009 Fax: (714) 558-6120
Email: vncoc@aol.com
Web: www.vncoc.org

Little Saigon Social and Cultural Services Center
14541 Brookhurst St. #C9-11
Westminster, CA 92683
Mai Cong, President/CEO
Tel: (714) 839-4441 Fax: (714) 839-6668
Email: vncoc@aol.com
Web: www.vncoc.org

Phu Dong Early Childhood Development Center
12421 Magnolia St.
Garden Grove, CA 92841
Kaycee Nguyen, Manager
Tel: (714) 534-9060 Fax: (714) 534-9049
Email: vncoc@aol.com
Web: www.vncoc.org

WEST BAY PILIPINO MULTI SERVICE CENTER
180 7th St.
San Francisco, CA 94103
Edwin Jocson, Executive Director
Tel: (415) 431-9336 Fax: (415) 431-7324
Email: info@pilipinocenter.org
Web: www.pilipinocenter.org

POLITICAL ACTION

AMERICAN MUSLIM ALLIANCE
39675 Cedar Blvd. #220-E
Newark, CA 94560
Dr. Agha Saeed, National Chairman
Tel: (510) 252-9858 Fax: (510) 252-9863
Email: ama@amaweb.org
Web: www.amaweb.org

AMERICAN MUSLIMS INTENT ON LEARNING AND ACTIVISM
P.O. Box 2216
Los Gatos, CA 95031

Moina Noor, Director
Email: director@amila.org
Web: www.amila.org

AMERICAN-ARAB ANTI DISCRIMINATION COMMITTEE
San Francisco Bay Area Chapter
522 Valencia
San Francisco, CA 94110
Tel: (415) 861-7444
Email: adcsf@hotmail.com
Web: www.adcsf.org

AMERICANS FOR PEACE NOW
Los Angeles Office
5870 W. Olympic Blvd.
Los Angeles, CA 90036
Tel: (323) 934-3480 Fax: (323) 934-3550
Email: apnwest@netzero.net
Web: www.peacenow.org

API LEGAL OUTREACH
1188 Franklin St. #202
San Francisco, CA 94109
Dean Ito Taylor, Executive Director
Tel: (415) 567-6255 Fax: (415) 567-6248
Email: info@apilegaloutreach.org
Web: www.apilegaloutreach.org

ARMENIAN ASSEMBLY OF AMERICA
Western Office
50 N. La Cienega Blvd. #202
Beverly Hills, CA 90211
Peter Abajian, Deputy Executive Director
Tel: (310) 360-0091 Fax: (310) 360-0094
Email: laoffice@aaainc.org
Web: www.aaainc.org

ARMENIAN NATIONAL COMMITTEE
ANC-San Gabriel Valley/Montebello Chapter
95 N. Marengo Ave. #105
Pasadena, CA 91101
Seto Boyadjian
Tel: (626) 568-8616 Fax: (626) 568-0144
Email: setobesq@yahoo.com
Web: www.anca.org

ANC-Torrance/South Bay Chapter
2222 Lomita Blvd.
Lomita, CA 90717
Khachig Khachadourian
Tel: (310) 325-8616
Email: southbayanc@yahoo.com
Web: www.anca.org

San Francisco - Bay Area Chapter
51 Commonwealth Ave.
San Francisco, CA 94118
Tel: (415) 387-3433 Fax: (415) 751-0617
Email: mail@ancsf.org
Web: www.ancsf.org

ARMENIAN NATIONAL COMMITTEE OF AMERICA
Western Region
104 N. Belmont #200
Glendale, CA 91206
Ardashes Kassakhian, Executive Director
Tel: (818) 500-1918 Fax: (818) 246-7353
Email: ancawr@anca.org
Web: www.anca.org

ASIAN PACIFIC AMERICAN LABOR ALLIANCE
Los Angeles Chapter
2130 James Wood Blvd.
Los Angeles, CA 90006
John Delloro, President
Tel: (213) 387-1744
Email: johndelloro@hotmail.com
Web: www.apalanet.org

San Diego Chapter
c/o SEIU 2028, 222 S. Wisconsin St., P.O. Box 1134
Fallbrook, CA 92088
Rose Marie C. Peralta
Tel: (760) 723-6300 x3681

Fax: (760) 728-2420
Email: rperalta@fuhsd.net

San Francisco Chapter
c/o SEIU 790, 1390 Market St. #1118
San Francisco, CA 94102
Mary Anne Ahtye, President
Tel: (415) 956-8373 Fax: (415) 431-6241
Email: mahtye@uesf.org
Web: www.apalanet.org

San Jose Pre-Chapter
2302 Zankar Rd.
San Jose, CA 95131
Shaw San Liu
Tel: (408) 954-8715 x175
Email: apala@apalanet.org
Web: www.apalanet.org

2616 8th Ave.
Oakland, CA 94606
Monica Flores Lodise, Executive Director
Tel: (510) 508-1535
Email: APAFP@apaforprogress.org
Web: www.apaforprogress.org

BAY AREA IRANIAN AMERICAN DEMOCRATS
6363 Christie Ave. #2611
Emeryville, CA 94608
Tel: (510) 595-3684
Email: info@baiad.org
Web: www.baiad.org

BAY AREA IRANIAN-AMERICAN VOTER ASSOCIATION
P.O. Box 1105
Burlingame, CA 94011-1105
Email: info@baivoter.org
Web: www.baivoter.org

CENTER FOR ASIAN AMERICANS UNITED FOR SELF-EMPOWERMENT
260 S. Los Robles Ave. #118
Pasadena, CA 91101
Kathy Hassan, Director of Administration
Tel: (626) 356-9838 Fax: (626) 356-9878
Email: info@causeusa.org
Web: www.causeusa.org

CHINESE AMERICAN CIVIL RIGHTS ORGANIZATION
108 N. Ynez Ave. #200
Monterey Park, CA 91754
David Ma, Chairman
Tel: (626) 288-3915 Fax: (626) 288-9160
Email: thma@hotmail.com
Web: www.caciro.org

CHINESE FOR AFFIRMATIVE ACTION
Chinatown Office
17 Walter U. Lum Pl.
San Francisco, CA 94108
Brian H. Cheu, Interim Executive Director
Tel: (415) 274-6750 Fax: (415) 397-8770
Email: caa@caasf.org
Web: www.caasf.org

Visitation Valley Office
1099 Sunnydale Ave. #325
San Francisco, CA 94134
Brian H. Cheu, Interim Executive Director
Tel: (415) 587-5779
Email: caa@caasf.org
Web: www.caasf.org

GREATER LOS ANGELES FEDERATION FOR A DEMOCRATIC CHINA
P.O. Box 548
South Pasadena, CA 91031
Tel: (626) 285-7767 Fax: (626) 285-7767
Email: lafdc@hotmail.com
Web: www.lafdc.org

IRANIAN AMERICAN DEMOCRATS OF LOS ANGELES
11901 Santa Monica Blvd. #428
Los Angeles, CA 90025
Tel: (310) 252-9818

Email: info@iadla.com
Web: http://iadla.com

IRANIANS FOR INTERNATIONAL COOPERATION
P.O. Box 3388
Alhambra, CA 91803
Mohammad Ala, Executive Board Member
Email: info@iic.org
Web: www.iic.org

JAPAN POLICY RESEARCH INSTITUTE
California Office
2138 Via Tiempo
Cardiff, CA 92007
Chalmers Johnson, President
Tel: (760) 944-3950 Fax: (760) 944-9022
Email: info@jpri.org
Web: www.jpri.org

KOREAN AMERICAN COALITION
Los Angeles
3727 W. 6th St. #515
Los Angeles, CA 90020
Charles Kim, Executive Director
Tel: (213) 365-5999 Fax: (213) 380-7990
Email: charles@kacla.org
Web: www.kacla.org

Sacramento Chapter
P.O. Box 277925
Sacramento, CA 95827
Karen Kim, President
Tel: (916) 368-4200
Email: kar_bear777@yahoo.com

San Francisco Bay Area Chapter
1070 Marina Village Pkwy. #203
Alameda, CA 94501
David Hong, President
Tel: (415) 430-2161 x 2475
Email: info@kacsf.org
Web: www.kacsf.org

MUSLIM PUBLIC AFFAIRS COUNCIL
MPAC Los Angeles
3010 Wilshire Blvd. #217
Los Angeles, CA 90010
Salam Al-Marayati, Executive Director
Tel: (213) 383-3443 Fax: (213) 383-9674
Email: salam@mpac.org
Web: www.mpac.org

NATIONAL KOREAN AMERICAN SERVICE & EDUCATION CONSORTIUM, INC.
900 S. Crenshaw Blvd.
Los Angeles, CA 90019
Eun Sook Lee, Executive Director
Tel: (323) 937-3703 Fax: (323) 937-3526
Email: nakasec@nakasec.org
Web: www.nakasec.org

ORGANIZATION OF CHINESE AMERICANS
Peninsula Chapter of San Mateo County,
P.O. Box 218
San Mateo, CA 94401
Tel: (650) 376-1019
Email: info@ocasanmateo.org
Web: www.ocasanmateo.org

ORGANIZATION OF CHINESE AMERICANS- GREATER LOS ANGELES
Asian Pacific American Legal Center
1145 Wilshire Blvd., 1st Fl.
Los Angeles, CA 90017
Stacey Toda, President
Tel: (213) 250-9888 Fax: (213) 977-7595
Email: ray.louie@oca-gla.org
Web: www.oca.gla.org

ORGANIZATION OF CHINESE AMERICANS, INC.
East Bay
363 13th St.
Oakland, CA 94612
Y. H. Lee, President
Tel: (510) 836-6688 Fax: (510) 836-6689
Email: yuihay@yhla.net
Web: www.ocanatl.org

Greater Sacramento Chapter
P.O. Box 904
Sacramento, CA 95812
Linda Ng, President
Tel: (916) 322-1949 Fax: (916) 393-2785
Email: lngjmh@sbcglobal.net
Web: www.ocanatl.org

PACIFIC COUNCIL ON INTERNATIONAL POLICY
3502 Trousdale Pkwy., SOS B-15
Los Angeles, CA 90089
Cynthia L. Hogle, External Affairs Officer
Tel: (213) 740-4296 Fax: (213) 740-9498
Email: pcip@usc.edu
Web: www.pacificcouncil.org

RAND
Center for Asia Pacific Policy
1700 Main St.
Santa Monica, CA 90407-2138
Nina Hachigian, Director
Tel: (310) 393-0411 x6030 Fax: (310) 451-6960
Email: nina_hachigian@rand.org
Web: www.rand.org/nsrd/capp

THE HMONG AMERICAN REPUBLIC NATIONAL REFORM UNION, INC.
167 W. Rialto Ave.
Clovis, CA 93612-4312
Hendg Vang, Founder
Tel: (559) 291-1027 Fax: (559) 292-1701
Web: www.hndlink.org/org-calf.htm

VIETNAMESE-AMERICAN PUBLIC AFFAIRS COMMITTEE
P.O. Box 2113
Saratoga, CA 95070
Binh Vo, President
Tel: (408) 904-4617 Fax: (408) 904-4617
Email: vpac@vpac-usa.org
Web: www.vpac-usa.org

PROFESSIONAL

AMERICA NEPAL MEDICAL FOUNDATION
4420 Alpine Rd. #108
Portola Valley, CA 94028-8005
Sanjaya Khanal, Chairperson
Email: anmf@anmf.net
Web: www.anmf.net

ARMENIAN ENGINEERS AND SCIENTISTS OF AMERICA, INC.
417 W. Arden Ave. #112C
Glendale, CA 91203
Tel: (818) 547-3372
Email: office1@aesa.org
Web: www.aesa.org

ASIAN AMERICAN ARCHITECTS AND ENGINEERS ASSOCIATION
8320 Lincoln Blvd. #108
Los Angeles, CA 90045
Shelley Santo, President
Tel: (213) 896-9270 Fax: (213) 896-9271
Email: aaaesc@earthlink.net
Web: www.aaaesc.com

ASIAN AMERICAN BAR ASSOCIATION OF THE GREATER BAY AREA
1188 Franklin St. #202
San Francisco, CA 94109
Victor Hwang, Management Attorney
Tel: (415) 567-6255
Email: info@apilegaloutreach.org
Web: www.apilegaloutreach.org

ASIAN AMERICAN JOURNALISTS ASSOCIATION
San Francisco Bay Area
1182 Market St. #320
San Francisco, CA 94102
Rene Astudillo, Executive Director
Tel: (415) 346-2051 Fax: (415) 346-6343
Email: aaja@aajasf.org
Web: www.aajasf.org

ASIAN BAR OF CALIFORNIA
700 Civic Center Dr. West
Santa Ana, CA 92701
Andrew H. Do, President
Tel: (714) 834-3203 Fax: (714) 773-4487
Email: andrew.do@da.ocgov.com
Web: www.napaba.org

ASIAN EMPLOYEES ASSOCIATION
530 Water St.
Oakland, CA 94607
Tony Chu, Secretary
Tel: (510) 627-1239
Email: tchu@portoakland.com
Web: www.portaea.org

ASIAN PACIFIC AMERICAN BAR ASSOCIATION OF LOS ANGELES COUNTY
12021 Wilshire Blvd. #603
Los Angeles, CA 90025
Paul J. Estuar, President-Elect
Email: email@apabala.org
Web: www.apabala.org

ASIAN PACIFIC STATE EMPLOYEES ASSOCIATION
P.O. Box 22909
Sacramento, CA 95822
Honey Lum, President
Tel: (916) 962-6309
Email: hxlum@comcast.net
Web: www.apsea.org

ASIAN/PACIFIC BAR ASSOCIATION OF SACRAMENTO
P.O. Box 2215, Metro Station
Sacramento, CA 95812-2215
Lara D. Dunbar, President
Tel: (916) 431-2773
Email: lara_dunbar@comcast.net
Web: www.sacramentoasianbar.com

ASSOCIATION OF CHINESE FINANCE PROFESSIONALS
240 Hazelwood Ave.
San Francisco, CA 94127
William Ren, President
Tel: Fax: (925) 949-7560
Email: acfp_us@yahoo.com
Web: www.acfp.net

ASSOCIATION OF PHILIPPINES PHYSICIANS IN AMERICA
P.O. Box 452164
Los Angeles, CA 90045
Renato Judalena,M.D., President
Tel: (310) 889-7131
Email: masmd@aboutappa.org
Web: www.aboutappa.org

ASSOCIATION OF PROFESSORS AND SCHOLARS OF IRANIAN HERITAGE
P.O. Box 4175
Diamond Bar, CA 91765
Dr. Mohamad Navab, President
Email: sparisay@csupomona.edu
Web: www.apsih.org

BURMESE AMERICAN PROFESSIONALS SOCIETY
220 Mariposa Ave.
Daly City, CA 94015
Maurice Chee, President
Email: danielm@alum.mit.edu
Web: www.bapsusa.org

BURMESE AMERICAN SCIENCE AND ENGINEERING SOCIETY
10200 Sepulveda Blvd. #380
Mission Hills, CA 91345
Dr. Christopher Lee, President
Web: www.basesusa.org

CALIFORNIA CHINESE ENGINEERS ASSOCIATION
Headquarters Office
419 Rivergate Way
Sacramento, CA 95831

Jason Fan, President
Tel: (916) 227-9875
Email: president@cccea.org
Web: www.cccea.org

CHINESE AMERICAN LIBRARIANS ASSOCIATION

P.O. Box 4992
Irvine, CA 92616
Sally C. Tseng, Executive Director
Tel: (949) 552-5615 Fax: (949) 857-1988
Email: sctseng888@yahoo.com
Web: www.cala-web.org

CHINESE AMERICAN PHYSICIANS' SOCIETY

817 Harrison St.
Oakland, CA 94607
David Der, M.D., Executive Director
Tel: (510) 451-8089 Fax: (510) 451-6360
Email: society@caps-ca.org
Web: www.caps-ca.org

CHINESE AMERICAN SEMICONDUCTOR PROFESSIONAL ASSOCIATION

3555 Ryder St.
Santa Clara, CA 95051
David W. Wang, President
Tel: (408) 245-5638 Fax: (408) 245-5638
Email: caspa@ix.netcom.com
Web: www.caspa.com

CHINESE INSTITUTE OF ENGINEERS

San Francisco Bay Area Chapter
P.O. Box 2880
Cupertino, CA 95015
David Fong, Chairman
Tel: (408) 738-4024 Fax: (408) 296-6628
Email: david_fong@forteconnections.com
Web: www.cie-sf.org

CHINESE INSTITUTE OF ENGINEERS/USA

Su-Syin Chou, President
Tel: (415) 749-2453
Email: su-syin.chou@sfgov.org
Web: www.cie-usa.org

CHINESE MUSIC TEACHERS ASSOCIATION OF NORTHERN CALIFORNIA

1194 Donington Dr.
San Jose, CA 95129
Tel: (408) 446-0309
Web: www.cmtanc.org

CHINESE SOFTWARE PROFESSIONALS ASSOCIATION

P.O. Box 700249
San Jose, CA 95170-0249
Keng Lim, President/CEO
Email: info@cspa.com
Web: www.cspa.com

CHINESE-AMERICAN ENGINEERS AND SCIENTISTS ASSOCIATION OF SOUTHERN CALIFORNIA

216 W. Garvey Ave. #E
Monterey Park, CA 91754
William Chang, Chairman of Board
Tel: (626) 572-7021 Fax: (626) 572-6533
Email: chasccw@yahoo.com
Web: www.cesasc.org

EAST BAY ASIAN DESIGN PROFESSIONALS

211 10th St. #328
Oakland, CA 94607
Colland Jang
Tel: (510) 839-2820 Fax: (510) 839-7828
Email: colland@aol.com

FILIPINO AMERICAN LAWYERS OF SAN DIEGO

P.O. Box 81537
San Diego, CA 92138
Marty B. Lorenzo, President
Tel: (858) 677-1430
Email: falsd@cox.net
Web: www.falsd.org

FILIPINO ARCHITECTS CONTRACTORS & ENGINEERS

25 Kearny St. #100
San Francisco, CA 94108
Dan Valiao, President
Tel: (415) 765-0451 Fax: (415) 421-2770
Email: dan@polainc.com

HONG KONG ASSOCIATION OF SOUTHERN CALIFORNIA

350 S. Figueroa St. #139
Los Angeles, CA 90071
Raymond Cheng, President
Tel: (213) 622-9446 Fax: (213) 622-9554
Email: info@hkasc.org
Web: www.hkasc.org

HUA YUAN SCIENCE AND TECHNOLOGY ASSOCIATION

P.O. Box 60753
Palo Alto, CA 94306
Min Zhu, President
Email: huayuansta@yahoo.com
Web: www.huayuan.org

INDIAN MEDICAL ASSOCIATION OF GREATER LOS ANGELES

3400 W. Lomita Blvd. #100
Torrence, CA 90505
Manish Mehta, M.D., President
Tel: (310) 541-1930 Fax: (310) 530-5550
Web: www.aapiusa.net/pacific.htm#ima

INDIAN MEDICAL ASSOCIATION OF SOUTHERN CALIFORNIA

26075 Dumont Rd.
Hemet, CA 92544
Ajeet Singhvi, M.D., President
Tel: (909) 929-0124 Fax: (909) 929-4567
Email: asinghvi@aol.com
Web: www.aapiusa.net/pacific.htm#ima

INDIAN PHYSICIANS OF CENTRAL CALIFORNIA

6089 N. 1st St. #102
Fresno, CA 95710
Harcharan Chann, M.D., President
Tel: (559) 449-9100
Web: www.aapiusa.net/pacific.htm#ima

INDONESIAN PROFESSIONALS ASSOCIATION

Foster City, CA 94404-9991
Kevin Kokadir, President
Email: info@ipanet.org
Web: www.ipanet.org

IRANIAN AMERICAN DENTAL ASSOCIATION

11301 W. Olympic Blvd. #501
Los Angeles, CA 90272
Dr. Stephan Moradians, President
Tel: (805) 497-6009
Email: info@iada.us
Web: www.iada.us

KEIZAI SOCIETY

220 State St. #B
Los Altos, CA 94022
Nadine Kazuko Grant, President
Tel: (650) 969-8393 Fax: (650) 968-3526
Email: nadine@keizai.org
Web: www.keizai.org

KOREAN AMERICAN BAR ASSOCIATION OF SOUTHERN CALIFORNIA

c/o First Capitol Consulting, Inc., 3530 Wilshire Blvd. #1460
Los Angeles, CA 90010
Robert S. Sheen, President
Tel: (213) 382-1115 Fax: (213) 382-1161
Email: rsheen@fccila.net
Web: www.kabasocal.org

KOREAN AMERICAN MEDICAL ASSOCIATION OF SOUTHERN CALIFORNIA

3807 Wilshire Blvd. #901
Los Angeles, CA 90010

Grace Park, Secretary
Tel: (213) 272-5762
Email: gracepark@kamasc.org
Web: www.kamasc.org

KOREAN AMERICAN PROFESSIONAL SOCIETY

445 Milan Dr. #107
San José, CA 95134
Jackie Shin, President
Email: jackie@kaps.org
Web: www.kaps.org

KOREAN AMERICAN SOCIETY OF ENTREPRENEURS

2882 Sand Hill Rd. #100
Menlo Park, CA 94025
Keibobk Lee, Chairman
Email: kasesv@kase.org
Web: www.kase.org

KOREAN INFORMATION TECHNOLOGY NETWORK

3003 N. 1st St.
San Jose, CA 95134
Charles C. Koo, President
Tel: (408) 432-5000 Fax: (408) 432-5056
Email: info@koreait.org
Web: www.koreanit.org

MONTE JADE SCIENCE AND TECHNOLOGY ASSOCIATION

Southern California Chapter
3011 Malibu Canyon Rd.
Malibu, CA 90265-4797
K.C. Wang, Chairman
Tel: (805) 906-8388 Fax: (805) 492-3118
Email: kc.wang@ieee.org
Web: www.scmj.org

NATIONAL ARAB AMERICAN MEDICAL ASSOCIATION

California Chapter
9645 Monte Vista Ave. #302
Mount Claire, CA 91763
Laura Solorio, Secretary
Tel: (905) 624-8366
Email: naama@naama.com
Web: www.naama.com

NATIONAL ASIAN PACIFIC AMERICAN BAR ASSOCIATION

Los Angeles Office
725 S. Figueroa St. #1690
Los Angeles, CA 90017
Grace Yoo, Executive Director
Tel: (213) 955-8022 Fax: (213) 955-9250
Email: ed@napaba.org
Web: www.napaba.org

NATIONAL ASSOCIATION OF VIETNAMESE NURSES

P.O. Box 9692
Fountain Valley, CA 92728-9692
Diep Pham, President
Tel: (714) 330-1243 Fax: (775) 320) 9758
Email: info@navn.us
Web: www.navn.us

NETWORK OF INDIAN PROFESSIONALS-LOS ANGELES

Network of Indian Professionals of North America
Los Angeles, CA
Kunal Gorakshakar, President
Tel: (562) 307-4076
Email: president@netipla.org
Web: www.netipla.org

NETWORK OF INDIAN PROFESSIONALS-SAN DIEGO

Network of Indian Professionals of North America
San Diego, CA
Saad Ilyas, President
Email: saad@netipsd.org
Web: www.netipsd.org

NETWORK OF INDIAN PROFESSIONALS-SAN FRANCISCO BAY AREA

Network of Indian Professionals of North America
39120 Argonaut Way #528
Fremont, CA 94538
Hari Kommaraju, President
Email: president@netip-sfba.org
Web: www.netip-sfba.org

NETWORK OF IRANIAN-AMERICAN PROFESSIONALS OF ORANGE-COUNTY

2182 Dupont Dr. #22
Irvine, CA 92612
Dr. Hossein Hosseini, President
Tel: (949) 851-3993
Email: info@nipoc.org
Web: www.@nipoc.org

NORTH AMERICA TAIWANESE ENGINEERS' ASSOCIATION

P.O. Box 360776
Milpitas, CA 95036
Shinn-Horng Lee, President
Email: sv@natea.org
Web: www.natea.org

NORTHERN CALIFORNIA ASSOCIATION OF VIETNAMESE AMERICAN DENTISTS

P.O. Box 610442
San Jose, CA 95161-0442
Giang Chu, President
Tel: (408) 710-3024
Email: giangchu@yahoo.com
Web: www.ncavad.org

ORANGE COUNTY ASIAN AMERICAN BAR ASSOCIATION

5319 University Dr. #212
Irvine, CA 92612
Vladimir Khiterer, President
Tel: (949) 440-6700 x254 Fax: (714) 784-4016
Email: ocaaba@cox.net
Web: www.ocaaba.org/index.html

ORANGE COUNTY JAPANESE AMERICAN LAWYERS' ASSOCIATION

P.O. Box 17777
Irvine, CA 92623-7777
John Yasuda, President
Tel: (949) 453-0300 Fax: (714) 564-1600
Email: ocjala@onebox.com
Web: www.ocjala.org

PAN ASIAN LAWYERS OF SAN DIEGO

P.O. Box 82784
San Diego, CA 92138-2784
Jerrilyn T. Malana, President
Email: palsd@hotmail.com
Web: www.palsd.org

PHILIPPINE AMERICAN BAR ASSOCIATION

P.O. Box 70267
Los Angeles, CA 90070
Allison Aquino, President
Tel: (626) 339-1424 Fax: (626) 339-3484
Email: aaquino@aquinolaw.net
Web: www.pabala.org

SAN DIEGO CHINESE-AMERICAN SCIENTISTS AND ENGINEERS ASSOCIATION

P.O. Box 720126
San Diego, CA 92172
Lily Shieh, President
Email: sdcasea2k@yahoo.com
Web: www.sdcasea.com

SILICON VALLEY CHINESE ENGINEERS ASSOCIATION

P.O. Box 612283
San Jose, CA 95161
Email: info@scea.org
Web: www.scea.org

SILICON VALLEY INDIAN PROFESSIONALS ASSOCIATION
P.O. Box 3533
Santa Clara, CA 95055
Avinash Vaidya, President
Tel: (510) 589-6906
Email: contact@sipa.org
Web: www.sipa.org

SOCIETY OF AFGHAN PROFESSIONALS
P.O. Box 486
Fremont, CA 94537
Tel: (866) 841-9139 X2013
Email: info@sapweb.org
Web: www.sapweb.org

SOCIETY OF IRANIAN PROFESSIONALS
P.O. Box 3753
Santa Clara, CA 95055
Dr. Mohammad Mortazavi, President
Tel: (408) 235-0558
Email: president@anjoman.org
Web: www.anjoman.org

SOUTH ASIAN BAR ASSOCIATION OF NORTHERN CALIFORNIA
c/o Day Casebeer Madrid & Batchelder, LLP.,
20300 Stevens Creek Blvd. #400
Cupertino, CA 95014
Paul Grewal, President
Tel: (408) 342-4543
Email: pgrewal@daycasebeer.com
Web: www.southasianbar.org

SOUTHERN CALIFORNIA CHINESE LAWYERS ASSOCIATION
c/o Los Angeles City Attorney's Office, 200 N. Main St. #700
Los Angeles, CA 90012
Philip H. Lam, President
Tel: (213) 978-8138 Fax: (213) 978-8211
Email: plam@atty.lacity.org
Web: www.sccla.org

THAI AMERICAN YOUNG PROFESSIONALS ASSOCIATION
600 Laurel St. #4
San Francisco, CA 94118
Joe Wana, President
Email: taypa@taypa.org
Web: www.taypa.org

THE ASSOCIATION OF IRANIAN AMERICAN PROFESSIONALS OF SAN DIEGO, INC.
P.O. Box 503944
San Diego, CA 92150
Javed Rostami, Chairperson
Tel: (619) 645-7253 Fax: (309) 285-9762
Email: admin@aiap.org
Web: www.aiap.org

THE NATIONAL ASSOCIATION OF ASIAN AMERICAN PROFESSIONALS
NAAAP-San Francisco
P.O. Box 60322
Sunnyvale, CA 94088-0322
David Ching, President
Tel: (408) 569-3785
Email: david_ching@naaap.org
Web: www.naaapsf.org

VIETNAMESE AMERICAN PROFESSIONALS ALLIANCE
P.O. Box 70804
Sunnyvale, CA 94086
Vy Tran, Board Member
Tel: (877) 705-6671 Fax: (877) 705-6671
Email: contact@vapaonline.org
Web: www.vapaonline.org

VIETNAMESE MEDICAL ASSOCIATION OF THE USA
6255 University Ave. #A2
San Diego, CA 92115
Ton Duy Tran, President
Tel: (619) 583-0553 Fax: (619) 583-5702
Email: tontran10@yahoo.com
Web: www.vmausa.org

VIETNAMESE PROFESSIONALS SOCIETY
Northern California Chapter
3542 Corte Bella Dr.
San Jose, CA 95148
Tony Nguyen, President
Tel: (408) 270-7754 Fax: (408) 705-7414
Email: atsnguyen@yahoo.com
Web: www.vps.org

Southern California Chapter
3114 S. Maddock St.
Santa Ana, CA 92704
John Nguyen, President
Tel: (714) 979-6692
Email: south_ca@hcgvn.net
Web: www.vps.org

VIRTUAL THINK TANK PAKISTAN
P.O. Box 64310
Los Angeles, CA 90064
Athar Osama, Doctor Fellow in Policy Studies
Email: athar@vttp.org
Web: www.vttp.org

RELIGIOUS

AGAPE CHINESE ALLIANCE CHURCH
7250 Convoy Ct. #B
San Diego, CA 92111
Patrick Chow, Senior Pastor
Tel: (858) 277-0055 Fax: (858) 277-0039
Email: chowpatrick@yahoo.com
Web: www.agapecac.org

ANAHEIM KOREAN PRESBYTERIAN CHURCH ENGLISH MINISTRY
1408 S. Euclid St.
Anaheim, CA 92802
David Kang, Pastor
Tel: (714) 956-8491
Web: www.akpcem.org

ARABIC BIBLE CHRISTIAN CHURCH
3000 E. 3rd St.
Long Beach, CA 90814
Latif Marcos, Pastor
Tel: (562) 438-5328 Fax: (562) 434-9239
Web: www.abcc.org

ARMENIAN BIBLE CHURCH
P.O. Box 40322
Pasadena, CA 91114
Tel: (626) 345-9841
Email: email19@armenianbiblechurch.org
Web: www.armenianbiblechurch.org

ARMENIAN BROTHERHOOD BIBLE CHURCH
P.O. Box 40069
Pasadena, CA 91104
Rev. Calvin Sagherian, Pastor
Tel: (626) 797-8985 Fax: (626) 791-7773
Email: info@abbcpas.org
Web: www.abbcpas.org

ARMENIAN CHURCH OF THE NAZARENE
411 E. Acacia
Glendale, CA 91205
Rev. Habib Alajaji, Pastor
Tel: (818) 244-9920
Web: www.ganc.org

ARMENIAN CHURCH YOUTH MINISTRIES
Youth Ministry Church & Center
632 W. Stocker
Glendale, CA 91202
Fr. Vazken Movsesian
Tel: (818) 558-7474 Fax: (818) 558-6333
Email: dervaz@acyministries.org
Web: www.acyministries.org

ARMENIAN EVANGELICAL BRETHREN CHURCH
3200 London St.
Los Angeles, CA 90026-3725
Rev. Dikran Shanlian, Pastor
Tel: (213) 483-7265 Fax: (213) 483-7002
Email: aebcministries@aol.com
Web: www.aebcm.org

ARPC KOREAN PRESBYTERIAN CHURCH
1204 W. 163rd St.
Gardena, CA 90247
Joseph I. Paek, Pastor
Tel: (310) 538-4876
Email: paek@church4u.org

ASIA EVANGELISTIC FELLOWSHIP
18333 Dolan Way #111
Canyon Country, CA 91351
Dr. G.D. James, Founder/President
Email: john316@aapt.net.au
Web: www.aefi.org.au/Aef_USA.htm

ASIAN AMERICAN CHRISTIAN FELLOWSHIP
948 E. 2nd St.
Los Angeles, CA 90012
Tel: (213) 613-0022 Fax: (213) 613-0211
Web: www.aacf.org

BAY AREA CHINESE BIBLE CHURCH
750 Fargo Ave.
San Leandro, CA 94579
Stephen Gregg Quen, Senior Pastor
Tel: (510) 351-4936 Fax: (510) 351-1789
Email: squen@bacbc.org
Web: www.bacbc.org

BETH SHIR SHOLOM
1827 California Ave.
Santa Monica, CA 90403
Nika Galperin, Executive Director
Tel: (310) 453-3361 Fax: (310) 453-6827
Email: nika@bethshirsholom.com
Web: www.bethshirsholom.com

BETHEL KOREAN CHURCH
18700 Harvard Ave.
Irvine, CA 92612
Sandy Ro, Pastor
Tel: (949) 854-4010 Fax: (949) 854-4018
Email: webmaster@bkc.org
Web: www.bkc.org

BURMA BUDDHIST MONASTERY
710 Grandview Ln.
La Puente, CA 91744
Tel: (626) 336-3419 Fax: (626) 961-8951
Email: burmesetemple@bigplanet.com

BURMESE CHRISTIAN COMMUNITY CHURCH OF SILICON VALLEY
30 Kirk Ave.
San Jose, CA 95127
Dorothy D'Vaz, Advisory Council Member
Email: bcccsv@yahoo.com
Web: www.bcccsv.org

CALVARY ARMENIAN CONGREGATIONAL CHURCH
725 Brotherhood Way
San Francisco, CA 94132
Tel: (415) 586-2000 Fax: (415) 333-1076
Email: cacc@cacc-sf.org
Web: www.cacc-sf.org

CALVARY CHAPEL CHINESE FELLOWSHIP
520 S. Lark Ellen Ave.
West Covina, CA 91791-2552
Tel: (621) 917-0688
Email: webservant-westcovina@calvarychapel.com
Web: www.calvarychapel.org/westcovina

CAMBODIAN BUDDHIST SOCIETY OF POMONA
1145 W. 10th St.
Pomona, CA 91766
Tel: (909) 623-1639

CAMBODIAN BUDDHIST SOCIETY OF SAN DIEGO INC.
3616 47th St.
San Diego, CA 92105
Tel: (619) 282-0613

CAMBODIAN BUDDHIST TEMPLE OF LONG BEACH
2625 E. 3rd St.
Long Beach, CA 90814
Tel: (562) 434-4343

CAMBODIAN EVANGELICAL CHURCH
12722 Woods Ave.
Norwalk, CA 90650
Tel: (562) 863-4949

CANAAN TAIWANESE CHRISTIAN CHURCH
1904 Silverwood Ave.
Mountain View, CA 94043
Rev. Daniel Cheng, Pastor
Tel: (650) 969-2822 Fax: (650) 969-8222
Email: canaanenglish@yahoo.com
Web: www.ecanaan.org

CAPITAL KOREAN PRESBYTERIAN CHURCH
11427 Fair Oaks Blvd.
Fair Oaks, CA 95628
Jong Choon Kim, Senior Pastor
Tel: (916) 536-1878 Fax: (916) 536-1880
Email: office@sckpc.org
Web: www.sckpc.org

CENTRAL CHINESE CHRISTIAN CHURCH
18381 Lake Chabor Rd.
Castro Valley, CA 94546
Tel: (510) 888-1331
Web: www.cccc-cv.org

CHINA EVANGELISTIC MISSION, INC.
1040 Oak Grove Rd. #204
Concord, CA 94518
Tel: (925) 689-9874 Fax: (925) 689-9931
Email: cemusa@pacbell.ne
Web: www.cemhk.org.hk/mid.htm

CHINA MINISTRIES INTERNATIONAL, INC.
P.O. Box 40489
Pasadena, CA 91114-7489
Tel: (626) 398-0145 Fax: (626) 398-2361
Email: cmius@compuserve.com
Web: http://ourworld.compuserve.com/homepages/cmius/

CHINA SOUL FOR CHRIST FOUNDATION
P.O. Box 450
Petaluma, CA 94953-0450
Tel: (707) 782-9588 Fax: (707) 782-9586
Email: info@chinasoul.org
Web: www.chinasoul.org

CHINESE BAPTIST CHURCH OF CENTRAL ORANGE COUNTY
12012 Yale Ct.
Irvine, CA 92620
Darryl Fong, Assistant English Pastor
Tel: (714) 669-1700
Web: www.cbccoc.org

CHINESE BAPTIST CHURCH OF SAN JOSE
2215 Curtner Ave.
Campbell, CA 95008
Rev. Wah-Yiu Fu, Pastor
Tel: (408) 371-6200 Fax: (408) 371-3124
Email: info@cbcsj.org
Web: www.cbcsj.org

CHINESE BAPTIST CHURCH OF WEST LOS ANGELES
1925 Sawtelle Blvd.
West Los Angeles, CA 90025
Rev. Warren Wang, Pastor
Tel: (310) 479-8394 Fax: (310) 479-8394
Email: cbcwla@cbcwla.org
Web: http://come.to/cbcwla

CHINESE BIBLE CHURCH
12335 World Trade Dr. #2
San Diego, CA 92128
Rev. Albert Lam, Senior Pastor
Tel: (858) 675-8777
Email: admin@cbcsd.org
Web: www.cbcsd.org

CHINESE CHRISTIAN ALLIANCE CHURCH
18827 Roscoe Blvd.
Northridge, CA 91324-4545
Tel: (818) 718-2282
Email: info@ccac.ws
Web: www.ccac.ws

CHINESE CHRISTIAN CHURCH OF THOUSAND OAKS
218 W. Janss Rd.
Thousand Oaks, CA 91360
Tel: (805) 379-0882 Fax: (805) 379-0373
Web: www.cccto.org

CHINESE CHRISTIAN MISSION, INC.
P.O. Box 750759
Petaluma, CA 94975-0759
Rev. Paul Chan, President
Tel: (707) 762-1314 Fax: (707) 762-1713
Email: ccmusa@ix.netcom.com
Web: www.ccmusa.org

CHINESE CHRISTIAN TESTIMONY MINISTRY
P.O. Box 292
Alhambra, CA 91801
Tel: (626) 281-5781 Fax: (626) 293-8704
Email: weiszu@juno.com
Web: www.cctrmweb.net

CHINESE CHRISTIANS FOR JUSTICE
P.O. Box 374
San Gabriel, CA 91778
Tel: Fax: (626) 309-1223
Email: pfccj@aol.com

CHINESE CHURCH IN CHRIST
920 Sierra Vista Ave.
Mountain View, CA 94043
Jessie Peng, Administrative Assistant
Tel: (650) 968-2900 Fax: (650) 968-3392
Email: jpengla@yahoo.com
Web: www.ccic.org

CHINESE CHURCH IN CHRIST NORTH VALLEY
399 S. Main St.
Milpitas, CA 95035
Elder Chris Chen
Tel: (408) 945-1301 Fax: (408) 945-1341
Email: webmaster@ccinv.org
Web: www.ccinv.org

CHINESE CHURCH IN CHRIST SAN JOSE
1490 Saratoga Ave.
San Jose, CA 95129
Arthur Lum, English Minister
Tel: (408) 364-2242 Fax: (408) 364-2226
Email: artlumccic@aol.com
Web: www.ccic-sj.org

CHINESE CHURCH IN CHRIST SOUTH VALLEY
6601 Camden Ave.
San Jose, CA 95120
Tom Chow, Pastor
Tel: (408) 997-1982 Fax: (408) 997-1983
Email: tomchow@ccic-sv.org
Web: www.ccic-sv.org

CHINESE COMMUNITY CHURCH
1750 47th St.
San Diego, CA 92102
Rev. Steve Leong, International Interim Pastor
Tel: (619) 262-5433 Fax: (619) 262-5474
Web: www.chinesechurch-sandiego.com

CHINESE EVANGELICAL CHURCH OF SAN DIEGO
2585 Judson St.
San Diego, CA 92111
Rev. Steven Siu, Associate Pastor
Tel: (858) 277-9622
Email: admin@cec-sd.org
Web: www.cec-sd.org

CHINESE EVANGELICAL FREE CHURCH
1111 S. Atlantic Blvd.

Monterey Park, CA 91754
Henry Chiu, Senior Pastor
Tel: (626) 570-8971 Fax: (626) 570-1248
Web: www.cefc.org

SANTA BARBARA OFFICE
15 W. Calle Crepis
Santa Barbara, CA 93105
Rev. Adrian Lim, Pastor
Tel: (805) 569-7159

CHINESE FAMILIES FOR CHRIST
3350 Scott Blvd. #57
Santa Clara, CA 95054
Peter Chiu, President
Tel: (408) 886-6086 Fax: (408) 886-6088
Email: mailroom@cffc.org
Web: www.cffc.org

CHINESE FOR CHRIST BERKELEY CHURCH
2715 Prince St.
Berkeley, CA 94705
Rev. Kenneth Carlson, Pastor
Tel: (510) 654-4823
Email: pastor.ken@cfcberkeley.org
Web: www.cfcberkeley.org

CHINESE FOR CHRIST CHURCH OF SAN JOSE
4255 Williams Rd.
San Jose, CA 95129
Job K. Lee, Pastor
Tel: (408) 725-8733
Email: cfccsj@hotmail.com
Web: www.cfcsj.com

CHINESE GRACE BIBLE CHURCH
6656 Park Riviera Way
Sacramento, CA 95831
Dr. Alan K. Ginn, Pastor
Tel: (916) 422-4253 Fax: (916) 422-6547
Email: akginn@sbcglobal.net
Web: www.sac-cgbc.org

CHINESE IMMANUEL CHURCH
9350 Kiefer Blvd.
Sacramento, CA 95826
Tel: (916) 363-1256
Email: info@chineseimmanuel.org
Web: www.chineseimmanuel.org

CHINESE INDEPENDENT BAPTIST CHURCH OF FREMONT
37365 Centralmont Pl.
Fremont, CA 94536
Pastor Glenn Pon, Lead Pastor
Tel: (510) 796-9882
Email: pastorglenn@cibcfremont.org
Web: www.cibcfremont.org

CHINESE INDEPENDENT BAPTIST CHURCH OF OAKLAND
280 8th St.
Oakland, CA 94607
Dr. Alvin Louie, Lead Pastor
Tel: (510) 452-1772 Fax: (510) 452-5467
Email: info@cibc-oakland.org
Web: www.cibc-oakland.org

CHINESE MARANATHA BIBLE CHURCH
2400 Old Crow Canyon Rd. #A4
San Ramon, CA 94583
Tel: (925) 820-0383
Email: chinesemaranathabible@yahoo.com
Web: www.cmbc-web.org

CHINESE PRESBYTERIAN CHURCH OF OAKLAND
265 8th St.
Oakland, CA 94607
Rev. James Shum, Pastor
Tel: (510) 452-4963
Email: JamesShum@aol.com
Web: http://oaklandcpc.presbychurch.org/

CHINESE PRESBYTERIAN CHURCH OF ORANGE COUNTY
14614 Magnolia St.
Westminster, CA 92683

Pastor Wayland Wong
Tel: (714) 893-5500
Email: info@cpcoc.org
Web: www.cpcoc.org

CHINESE UNITED METHODIST CHURCH
825 N. Hill St.
Los Angeles, CA 90012
Rev. Judith Portinga, Pastor
Tel: (213) 626-8570 Fax: (213) 687-0264
Web: www.cumcla.org

CHRIST COMMUNITY CHINESE ALLIANCE CHURCH
19741 Hathaway Ave.
Hayward, CA 94541
Clement Lam, Pastor
Tel: (510) 481-0410 Fax: (510) 481-8034
Email: info@cccac.org
Web: www.cccac.org

CONCORD KOREAN BAPTIST CHURCH
5000 Hiller Ln.
Martinez, CA 94553
Loren Chong, Pastor
Tel: (925) 228-3769 Fax: (925) 228-3719
Web: www.ckbch.org/em

CONGREGATION BETH ISRAEL
9001 Towne Centre Dr.
San Diego, CA 92122
Stuart Simmons, Executive Director
Tel: (858) 535-1111 Fax: (858) 535-1130
Email: ssimmons@cbisd.org
Web: www.cbisd.org

CONGREGATION BETH SHALOM
P.O. Box 1027
Corona, CA 92878-1024
Gail Koren, President
Email: gailkatcbs@aol.com
Web: www.cbsofcorona.org

CONGREGATION EMANU-EL
2 Lake St.
San Francisco, CA 94118
Ann Blumlein Lazarus, President
Tel: (415) 751-2535 Fax: (415) 751-2511
Email: mail@emanuelsf.org
Web: www.emanuelsf.org

CONGREGATION KOL AMI
1200 N. La Brea Ave.
West Hollywood, CA 90038
Lee Werbel, Executive Director
Tel: (323) 606-0996 Fax: (323) 606-0997
Email: execdie@kol-ami.org
Web: www.kol-ami.org

CONGREGATION SHERITH ISRAEL
2266 California St.
San Francisco, CA 94123
Nancy Drapin, Executive Director
Tel: (415) 346-1720
Email: ndrapin@sherithisrael.org
Web: www.sherithisrael.org

CONTRA COSTA KOREAN PRESBYTERIAN CHURCH
2449 Buena Vista Ave.
Walnut Creek, CA 94596
Tel: (925) 932-2963 Fax: (925) 932-2359
Web: www.cckpc.org

CROSSPOINT CHINESE CHURCH OF SILICON VALLEY
680 E. Calaveras Blvd.
Milpitas, CA 95035
Pastor Chiu
Tel: (408) 586-8688
Email: info@crosspointchinese.com
Web: www.crosspointchinese.com

CUMBERLAND PRESBYTERIAN CHINESE CHURCH
865 Jackson St.
San Francisco, CA 94133
Lawrence Fung, Senior Pastor

Tel: (415) 421-1624 Fax: (415) 421-1874
Email: church@cumberlandsf.org
Web: www.cumberlandsf.org

DHARMA REALM BUDDHIST ASSOCIATION
1825 Murchison Dr.
Burlingame, CA 94010-4504
Tel: (415) 421-6117
Web: www.drba.org

Gold Wheel Monastery
235 N. Ave. 58
Los Angles, CA 90042
Tel: (323) 258-6668 Fax: (323) 258-6668
Web: www.goldwheel.org

Institute for World Religions & Berkeley Buddhist Monastery
2304 McKinley Ave.
Berkeley, CA 94703
Tel: (510) 848-3440 Fax: (510) 548-4551
Web: www.drba.org/branches/

EMMANUEL CAMBODIAN EVANGELICAL CHURCH
825 Highmoor Ave.
Stockton, CA 95210
Tel: (209) 952-1672

EVANGELIZE CHINA FELLOWSHIP
437 S. Garfield Ave.
Monterey Park, CA 91754
Tel: (626) 288-8828
Email: info@ecfusa.org
Web: www.ecfusa.org

FILIPINO INTERNATIONAL FELLOWSHIP
Reseda
7855 Lindley Ave.
Reseda, CA 91335
Email: andrew.afable@filchurch.org
Web: www.filchurch.org/Hamlin.
html?tag=hamlin

Winneteka
20600 Roscoe Blvd.
Winneteka, CA 91306
Email: andrew.afable@filchurch.org
Web: www.filchurch.org/Winnetka.html

FIRST CHINESE BAPTIST CHURCH
942 Yale St.
Los Angeles, CA 90012
Timothy Lin, Pastor Emeritus
Tel: (213) 687-0814 Fax: (213) 687-4954
Email: info@fcbc.org
Web: www.fcbc.org

16835 Brookhurst St.
Fountain Valley, CA 92708
Dr. Murphy Lum, Pastor
Tel: (714) 964-3697 Fax: (714) 964-2160
Email: fcbcfv@fcbcfv.org
Web: www.fcbcfv.org

1 Waverly Pl.
San Francisco, CA 94108
Rev. Donald Ng, Senior Pastor
Tel: (415) 362-4139 Fax: (415) 362-7644
Email: office@fcbc-sf.org
Web: www.fcbc-sf.org

1555 Fairway Dr.
Walnut, CA 91789
Tel: (909) 468-0098 Fax: (909) 468-1098
Email: webservants@fcbcwalnut.org
Web: www.fcbcwalnut.org

FIRST CHINESE SOUTHERN BAPTIST MISSION
3325 Clairemont Mesa Blvd.
San Diego, CA 92117
Peter Sun, Pastor
Tel: (858) 270-6111 Fax: (858) 483-3218
Email: info@fcsbcsd.org
Web: www.fcsbcsd.org

FIRST FIL-AM CHRISTIAN CHURCH
1200 W. Hammer Ln.
Stockton, CA 95209
Rev. Johnny Danganan, Pastor
Tel: (209) 957-3674
Email: ffacc@ffacc.org
Web: www.ffacc.org

FREMONT CHINESE EVANGELICAL FREE CHURCH
505 Driscoll Rd.
Fremont, CA 94539
Melvin Wong, Deacon Chair
Tel: (510) 668-0929
Email: info@fcefc.org
Web: www.fcefc.org

FRESNO CAMBODIAN BUDDHIST SOCIETY INC.
2533 N. Valentine Ave.
Fresno, CA 93722
Tel: (559) 276-2901

GOSPEL CHINESE CHRISTIAN CHURCH
137 Dempsey Rd.
Milpitas, CA 95035
Rev. Jack Chen, Senior Pastor
Tel: (408) 935-8477 Fax: (408) 935-8478
Web: www.chinesegospel.org

GOSPEL OPERATION INTERNATIONAL FOR CHINESE CHRISTIANS
561 San Mateo Ave.
San Bruno, CA 94066
Rev. Mark Cheng, Chaplain
Tel: (650) 866-4450
Email: gointl@pacbell.net
Web: www.gointl.org

GRACE KOREAN CHURCH
1645 W. Valencia Dr.
Fullerton, CA 92833
David Kwangshin Kim, Senior Pastor
Tel: (714) 446-6200 Fax: (714) 446-6207
Email: info@gracemi.com
Web: www.gkc.org

HANA CHURCH
7951 Commonwealth Ave.
Buena Park, CA 90621
Joshua Park, Senior Pastor
Tel: (714) 232-8888 Fax: (714) 232-8889
Email: info@hanachurch.org
Web: www.hanachurch.org

IRANIAN AMERICAN JEWISH CENTER
1317 N. Crescent Heights Blvd.
West Hollywood, CA 90046
Mark Cohen, Executive Director
Tel: (323) 654-1791 Fax: (323) 654-1791

IRANIAN CHRISTIAN CHURCH
4265 Kirk Rd.
San Jose, CA 95124
Hormoz Shariat, Pastor
Tel: (408) 267-4520 Fax: (408) 267-9145
Email: iranchurch@yahoo.com
Web: www.iranchurch.org

ISRAELITE HERITAGE INSTITUTE
P.O. Box 418147
Sacramento, CA 95841-8147
Mitchell Greenbaum
Email: ihbsc@yahoo.com

JAPANESE BIBLE AND THEOLOGY MINISTRY
P.O. Box 623
Weimar, CA 95736
Masao Uenuma
Tel: (530) 823-1977 Fax: (530) 823-1977
Email: muenuma@earlink.net
Web: www.jbtm.org

JAPANESE EVANGELICAL MISSIONARY SOCIETY
948 E. 2nd St.
Los Angeles, CA 90012
Rev. Sam Tonomura, Executive Director, Minister at Large
Tel: (213) 613-0022 Fax: (213) 613-0211
Email: info@jems.org
Web: www.jems.org

JEWS FOR JESUS
International Headquarters
60 Haight St.
San Francisco, CA 94102
David Brickner, Executive Director
Tel: (415) 864-2600 Fax: (415) 552-8325
Email: jfj@jewsforjesus.org
Web: www.jfjonline.org

Los Angeles
10962 Le Conte Ave.
Los Angeles, CA 90024
Tuvya Zaretsky, Leadership Team
Tel: (310) 443-9553 Fax: (310) 443-9555
Email: la@jewsforjesus.org
Web: www.jfjonline.org

San Francisco
2103 Clement
San Francisco, CA 94121
Robyn Wilk
Tel: (415) 387-9980 Fax: (415) 387-9982
Email: sf@jewsforjesus.org
Web: www.jfjonline.org

KOREA CAMPUS CRUSADE FOR CHRIST IN AMERICA
Los Angeles Office
505 S. Virgil Ave.
Los Angeles, CA 90020
Tel: (213) 389-5222 Fax: (213) 389-5200
Email: laoffice@kcccusa.org
Web: www.kcccusa.org

KOREAN BUDDHIST SAMBOSA
28110 Robinson Canyon Rd.
Carmel, CA 93923
Tel: (831) 624-3686 Fax: (831) 624-1482
Email: bhsnim@hotmail.com
Web: www.maum.net/sambosa

KOREAN CENTRAL PRESBYTERIAN CHURCH
6154-6160 Mission St.
Daly City, CA 94014
Rev. Ryan Kim, Pastor
Tel: (650) 550-0071 Fax: (650) 550-0072
Email: revryankim@hotmail.com
Web: www.sfkcpc.org

KOREAN CHURCHES FOR COMMUNITY DEVELOPMENT
3550 Wilshire Blvd. #500
Los Angeles, CA 90010
Hyepin Im, President/CEO
Tel: (213) 805-4216
Email: kccdonline@yahoo.com
Web: www.kccd3300.org

KOREAN COVENANT CHURCH OF SAN FRANCISCO
5260 E. Lincoln Ave.
Los Angeles, CA 90042
Rev. Dr. John Ahn, Pastor
Tel: (323) 349-0699
Email: jostaylor@hotmail.com

KOREAN MARTYRS CATHOLIC CHURCH
7655 Trask Ave.
Westminster, CA 92889
Fax: (714) 897-0832
Web: www.kmccoc.org

KOREAN UNITED METHODIST CHURCH OF SANTA CLARA VALLEY
1001 Ginger Ln.
San Jose, CA 95128
Rev. Eric C. Cho, Pastor
Tel: (408) 295-6004
Email: Ericccho@juno.com
Web: www.santaclaraumc.org/elm/

KOREAN-AMERICAN CAMPUS MISSION
12413 E. 195th St.
Cerritos, CA 90703
Richard Kim, Director
Tel: (562) 809-7575 Fax: (562) 809-6445
Email: richardkim@kcmonline.org
Web: www.kcmonline.org

LAGUNA CHINESE BAPTIST CHURCH
9215 Neosho Dr.
Elk Grove, CA 95758
Wesley Ong, Senior Pastor
Tel: (916) 683-3233 Fax: (916) 683-3233
Email: pastorwes@lagunabaptist.com
Web: www.sacbaptist.com

LONG BEACH CAMBODIAN EVANGELICAL CHURCH
2416 E. 11th St.
Long Beach, CA 90804
Tel: (562) 433-0250

LORD'S GRACE CHRISTIAN CHURCH
1101 San Antonio Rd. #409
Mountain View, CA 94043
Rev. David Poon, Senior Pastor
Tel: (650) 623-0917 Fax: (650) 623-0920
Email: office@lordsgrace.org
Web: www.lordsgrace.org

MARYKNOLL JAPANESE CATHOLIC CENTER
222 S. Hewitt St.
Los Angeles, CA 90012
Father David L. Doerner, Clergy
Tel: (213) 626-2279 Fax: (213) 628-1757
Email: info@japanesecatholiccenter.com
Web: www.japanesecatholiccenter.com

MONTEREY PARK CHINESE BAPTIST CHURCH OF ALHAMBRA
302 W. Commonwealth Ave.
Alhambra, CA 91801
Alan Chow, Senior Pastor
Tel: (626) 289-1284 Fax: (626) 289-0772
Email: achow@mpcbc.org
Web: www.mpcbc.org

MOUNTAIN VIEW CHINESE CHRISTIAN CHURCH
175 E. Dana Ave.
Mountain View, CA 94041
Rev. William Sun, Pastor
Tel: (650) 964-1591 Fax: (650) 964-8491
Email: mvccc2001@yahoo.com
Web: www.mvccc.org

NEW LIFE CHINESE LUTHERAN CHURCH
395 Addison St.
San Francisco, CA 94131
Rev. Chip Fox, Pastor
Tel: (415) 586-6525 Fax: (415) 586-6526
Email: PastorChip@aol.com
Web: www.newlifechinese.org

NEW LIFE KOREAN PRESBYTERIAN CHURCH
23662 Birtcher Dr.
Lake Forest, CA 92630
David Choe, English Minister
Tel: (949) 458-9191 Fax: (949) 458-9158
Email: info@newlifekpc.org
Web: www.newlifekpc.org

OAKLAND KOREAN UNITED METHODIST CHURCH ENGLISH MINISTRY
737 E. 17th St.
Oakland, CA 94606
Uriah Kim, Pastor
Tel: (510) 451-9076
Email: yonghwan@earthlink.net
Web: www.geocities.com/okumcem

PATHWAY BIBLE CHURCH
Christian Center of San Jose
1515 Kooser Rd.
San Jose, CA 95118
David J. Park, Senior Pastor
Tel: (408) 712-7228

Email: pastordavidpark@yahoo.com
Web: www.pathwaybible.org

PENINSULA CHINESE ALLIANCE CHURCH
1299 Bayshore Hwy. #100
Burlingame, CA 94010
Tel: (650) 343-7677 Fax: (650) 343-7577
Email: pcac@sbcglobal.net
Web: www.p-cac.org/index.html

PENINSULA TEMPLE BETH EL
1700 Alameda de las Pulgas
San Mateo, CA 94403
Alan L. Berg, Senior Rabbi
Tel: (650) 341-7701 Fax: (650) 570-7183
Email: mail@templebethel.org
Web: www.templebethel.org

PENINSULA TEMPLE SHOLOM
1655 Sebastian Dr.
Burlingame, CA 94010
Marie Barkoff, President
Tel: (650) 697-2266 Fax: (650) 697-2544
Email: president@sholom.org
Web: www.sholom.org

PILGRIM ARMENIAN CONGREGATIONAL CHURCH
3673 N. 1st St.
Fresno, CA 93726-6870
Tel: (559) 229-2915 Fax: (559) 229-6431
Web: www.pilgrimchurch.com

RIVERSIDE CHINESE ALLIANCE CHURCH
9640 Jurupa Rd.
Riverside, CA 92509
Rev. Victor Yap, Pastor
Tel: (909) 360-0113
Email: rcachurch@aol.com
Web: www.riversidealliance.com

ROCK KOREAN PRESBYTERIAN CHURCH
3219 Clairemont Mesa Blvd.
San Diego, CA 92117
Eugene Y. Kim, English Ministry Coordinator
Tel: (858) 273-9191
Email: cowman@rockkpc.com
Web: http://rockkpc.com

SACRAMENTO KOREAN PRESBYTERIAN CHURCH
9924 Mills Station Rd.
Sacramento, CA 95827
Tel: (916) 361-1019
Email: church@skpc.org
Web: www.skpc.org

SAN FRANCISCO CHINESE ALLIANCE CHURCH
1150 Vicente St.
San Francisco, CA 94116
Rev. Peter Wong, Senior Pastor
Tel: (415) 564-3301 Fax: (415) 564-3627
Email: sfcac@yahoo.com
Web: www.sfcac.org

SAN FRANCISCO CHINESE MENNONITE CHURCH
4021 California St.
San Francisco, CA 94118
David Lo, Pastor
Tel: (415) 221-7115 Fax: (415) 221-7115
Email: sf_cmc@yahoo.com

SAN JOSE CAMBODIAN BUDDHIST SOCIETY
840 Mervyn's Way
San Jose, CA 95127
Mr. Norind Su, President
Tel: (408) 251-4458
Email: norind.su@netapp.com
Web: www.wattkhmer.org

SHAAREY ZEDEK CONGREGATION
12800 Chandler Blvd.
Valley Village, CA 91607
Dr. Irving Steinberg, President
Tel: (818) 763-0560 Fax: (818) 763-8215
Email: president@valleyshul.com
Web: www.valleyshul.com

SINAI TEMPLE
10400 Wilshire Blvd.
Los Angeles, CA 90024
Brina Rosenbaum, President
Tel: (310) 474-1518 Fax: (310) 474-6801
Email: info@sinaitemple.org
Web: www.sinaitemple.org

ST. JAMES ARMENIAN CHURCH
4950 W. Slauson Ave.
Los Angeles, CA 90056
Tel: (323) 295-4588
Email: stjamesacla@earthlink.net
Web: http://home.earthlink.net/~stjamesacla

ST. MARY'S JACOBITE SYRIAN ORTHODOX CHURCH
P.O. Box 125
Downey, CA 90241
Fr. Sabu Thomas, Vicar
Email: sabuachen@hotmail.com
Web: http://sor.cua.edu/index.html

ST. PAUL ARMENIAN CHURCH
3767 N. 1st St.
Fresno, CA 93726
Rev. Fr. Arshen Avak Kahana Aivazian, Parish Priest
Tel: (559) 226-6343 Fax: (559) 226-1912
Email: derarshen@stpaulfresno.com
Web: www.stpaulfresno.com

ST. PETER ARMENIAN CHURCH
17231 Sherman Way
Van Nuys, CA 91406
Tel: (818) 344-4860 Fax: (818) 344-1926
Email: stpeterarm@earthlink.net
Web: www.stpeterarmenianchurch.org

TEMPLE BETH EL
2675 Central Ave.
Riverside, CA 92506
Alan Stein, President
Tel: (951) 684-4511 Fax: (951) 684-8437
Email: tbe2675@aol.com
Web: www.uahc.org/congs/ca/ca023

1435 W. 7th St.
San Pedro, CA 90732
Andrew Kauffman, President
Tel: (310) 833-2467 Fax: (310) 833-6504
Email: tbeoffice@bethelsp.org
Web: www.bethelsp.org

TEMPLE BETH EL JEWISH COMMUNITY CENTER
3055 Porter Gulch Rd.
Aptos, CA 95003-2703
Richard M. Litvak, Senior Rabbi
Tel: (831) 479-3444 Fax: (831) 475-7246
Email: rlitvak@sbcglobal.net
Web: www.templebethelaptos.org

TEMPLE BETH EL OF SOUTH ORANGE COUNTY
2A Liberty
Aliso Viejo, CA 92656
Cynthia Mirsky, President
Tel: (949) 362-3999
Email: dcmirsky@aol.com
Web: www.templebethelsoc.org

TEMPLE BETH ISRAEL
3033 N. Towne Ave.
Pomona, CA 91767
Linda Feinman, President
Tel: (909) 626-1277
Email: administrator@tbipomona.org
Web: www.tbipomona.org

TEMPLE BETH ISRAEL OF HIGHLAND PARK AND EAGLE ROCK
P.O. Box 421176
Los Angeles, CA 90042
Henry Leventon, President
Tel: (323) 255-5416
Email: tbi@tbila.org
Web: www.tbila.org

TEMPLE BETH SHOLOM
642 Dolores Ave.
San Leandro, CA 94577
Harry A. Manhoff, Rabbi
Tel: (510) 357-8505
Email: tbsweb@tbssanleandro.org
Web: www.tbssanleandro.org

2625 N. Tustin Ave.
Santa Ana, CA 92705
Sylvan Swartz, President
Tel: (714) 628-4600 Fax: (714) 628-4619
Email: information@tbsoc.com
Web: www.tbsoc.com

TEMPLE EMANU-EL
1010 University Ave.
San Jose, CA 95126
Dana Magat, Rabbi
Tel: (408) 292-0939 Fax: (408) 292-7625
Email: rabbimagat@templesanjose.org
Web: www.templesanjose.org

TEMPLE EMANUEL OF BEVERLY HILLS
8844 Burton Way
Beverly Hills, CA 90211
Gordon Cutler, President
Tel: (310) 274-6388 Fax: (310) 271-4976
Email: templeemanuelbh@aol.com
Web: www.templeemanuelbh.com

TEMPLE ISAIAH
10345 W. Pico Blvd.
Los Angeles, CA 90064
Terry Pullan, President
Tel: (310) 277-2772 Fax: (310) 277-4122
Email: tpullan@templeisaiah.com
Web: www.templeisaiah.com

TEMPLE SINAI
2808 Summit St.
Oakland, CA 94609
Steven Chester, Rabbi
Tel: (510) 451-3263 Fax: (510) 465-0603
Email: latricea@oaklandsinai.org
Web: www.oaklandsinai.org

73-251 Hovley Ln. West
Palm Desert, CA 92260
Jack Olshansky, President
Tel: (760) 568-9699 Fax: (760) 773-4883
Email: templesinai@dc.rr.com
Web: www.templesinaipd.org

THE AMERICAN/INTERNATIONAL GITA SOCIETY
Fremont, CA
Tel: (510) 791-6953 Fax: (630) 604-7512
Email: mail2@gita-society.com
Web: www.gita-society.com

THE DAVIS CHINESE CHRISTIAN CHURCH
536 Anderson Rd.
Davis, CA 95616
Philip Gee, Pastor
Tel: (530) 753-0500 Fax: (530) 753-0519
Email: office@d-ccc.org
Web: www.d-ccc.org

THE FIRST HOME OF CHRIST
Menlo Park
71 Bay Rd.
Menlo Park, CA 94025
Tel: (650) 323-5550 Fax: (650) 323-5560
Email: homeofchrist@yahoo.com
Web: www.hoc.org/hoc1/index.html

THE HOME OF CHRIST CHURCH IN FREMONT
4248 Solar Way
Fremont, CA 94538
Pastor Paul Lee, English Pastor
Tel: (510) 651-9937 Fax: (510) 651-0864
Email: paul.lee@hoc3.org
Web: www.hoc3.org

THE HOME OF CHRIST CHURCH IN SAN FRANCISCO
465 W. Portal Ave.
San Francisco, CA 94127
Tel: (415) 564-2099 Fax: (415) 564-2099
Web: www.hocsf.org

THE SIKH FOUNDATION
580 College Ave.
Palo Alto, CA 94306
Dr. Narinder Singh Kapany, Founder and Chairman
Tel: (650) 494-7454 Fax: (650) 494-3316
Web: www.sikhfoundation.org

THE VIETNAMESE AMERICAN BUDDHIST CONGREGATION
3222 W. 1st St.
Santa Ana, CA 92703
Tel: (714) 775-6799
Web: www.hoanghiem.com

THERAVADA BUDDHIST SOCIETY OF AMERICA
17450 S. Cabrillo Hwy.
Half Moon Bay, CA 94019-2518
U Myat Htoo, President
Tel: (650) 726-7604
Email: tbsa@tbsa.org
Web: www.tbsa.org

TURKISH CONNECTIONS INTERNATIONAL
1900 S. Western Ave.
San Pedro, CA 90732
Tel: (310) 833-4413 Fax: (310) 833-0386
Email: rich@turkishconnections.org
Web: www.turkishconnections.org

UNITED ARMENIAN CONGREGATIONAL CHURCH
3480 Cahuenga Blvd. West
Los Angeles, CA 90068
Rev. Ron Tovmassian, Senior Pastor
Tel: (323) 851-5265 Fax: (323) 851-6726
Email: uaccfamily@aol.com
Web: www.uacc-church.org

UPLAND INDONESIAN SEVENTH DAY ADVENTIST CHURCH
11100 Cedar Ave.
Bloomington, CA 92316-0301
Tel: (909) 874-7697 Fax: (909) 824-3989
Email: webmaster@uisda.org
Web: www.uisda.org

VAJRAYANA FOUNDATION
2013 Eureka Canyon Rd.
Corralitos, CA 95076
Josh Godine
Tel: (831) 761-6266 Fax: (831) 761-6284
Email: office@vajrayana.org
Web: www.vajrayana.org

VALLEJO NEW LIFE FILIPINO CHURCH OF THE NAZARENE
4200 Georgia St.
Vallejo, CA 94591
Rev. Ricarda Valenzuela
Tel: (707) 648-3774
Email: avalenzuela@norcal.org

VEDANTA SOCIETY OF SOUTHERN CALIFORNIA
Hollywood Center
1946 Vedanta Pl.
Hollywood, CA 90068-3996
Tel: (323) 465-7114
Email: hollywood@vedanta.org
Web: www.vedanta.org

Santa Barbara Center
927 Ladera Ln.
Santa Barbara, CA 93108
Tel: (805) 969-2903
Email: santabarbara@vedanta.org
Web: www.vedanta.org

South Pasadena Center
309 Monterey Rd.
South Pasadena, CA 91030
Tel: (323) 254-1546
Email: pasadena@vedanta.org
Web: www.vedanta.org

Trabuco Canyon Center
P.O. Box 408, 19961 Live Oak Canyon Rd.
Trabuco Canyon, CA 92678
Tel: (949) 858-0342
Email: rkmtrabuco@vedanta.org
Web: www.vedanta.org

VIETNAMESE ALLIANCE CHURCH OF NEWARK
38325 Cedar Blvd.
Newark, CA 94560
Tel: (510) 791-1537 Fax: (510) 623-9063
Web: www.vndistrict.org/newark

VIETNAMESE DISTRICT OF THE CHRISTIAN & MISSIONARY ALLIANCE
2275 W. Lincoln Ave.
Anaheim, CA 92801
Tel: (714) 491-8007
Email: giaohat@vndistrict.org
Web: www.vndistrict.org

WAT LAO BOUBPHARAM
San Diego CA
205 N. 65th St.
San Diego, CA 92114
Web: www.watlaoboubpharam.8k.com

WAT LAO NAVARAM BUDDHIST MONASTERY
6691 Manning St.
San Diego, CA 92111
Ajahn Benton Pandito
Tel: (619) 560-1185
Email: navaram@pacbell.net

WEST LOS ANGELES KOREAN CHURCH
3840 Grand View Blvd.
Los Angeles, CA 90066
Tel: (310) 397-2741 Fax: (310) 397-6202
Web: http://wlakc.org/

WESTERN DIOCESE OF THE ARMENIAN CHURCH OF NORTH AMERICA
3325 N. Glenoaks Blvd.
Burbank, CA 91504
Tel: (818) 558-7474 Fax: (818) 558-6333
Email: info@armenianchurchwd.com
Web: www.armenianchurchwd.com

WINTERSBURG PRESBYTERIAN CHURCH
2000 N. Fairview St.
Santa Ana, CA 92706
Ted Esaki, Senior Pastor
Tel: (714) 740-9400 Fax: (714) 740-9404
Web: www.wintersburg.org

RESEARCH

ASIA FOREST NETWORK
5266 Hollister Ave. #237
Santa Barbara, CA 93111
Dr. Mark Poffenberger, Executive Director
Tel: (805) 696-9087 Fax: (805) 696-9097
Email: mpoffen@aol.com
Web: www.mekonginfo.org/mrc_en/doclib.nsf/0/6B03C8D5D34B2B74802567740062FD73/$FILE/AFN.html

CENTER FOR THE FUTURE OF CHINA
3 Montague Pl.
San Francisco, CA 94133
Mary O'Hara-Devereaux, President
Tel: (415) 398-8816 Fax: (415) 398-8815
Email: mohara@china-future.org
Web: www.china-future.org

COMPARATIVE AND INTERDISCIPLINARY RESEARCH ON ASIA
University of California, Los Angeles

290 Royce Hall
Los Angeles, CA 90095-1540
Shu-mei Shih, Associate Professor
Tel: (310) 794-8944 Fax: (310) 825-8808
Email: shih@humnet.ucla.edu
Web: www.international.ucla.edu/cira

INSTITUTE FOR INTERNATIONAL STUDIES
Stanford University
616 Serra St. #C100
Stanford, CA 94305-6055
Coit D. Blacker, Director
Tel: (650) 723-4581 Fax: (650) 725-2592
Email: cblacker@stanford.edu
Web: http://iis.stanford.edu

INSTITUTE FOR TAIWANESE STUDIES
19511 Rainbow Ct.
Cerritos, CA 90703
Adolf Huang, President
Tel: (562) 809-1569
Email: info@its-usa.org
Web: www.its-usa.org

INTERNATIONAL ASSOCIATION OF CHINESE LINGUISTICS
University of Southern California
THH 226F, East Asian Languages and Cultures
Los Angeles, CA 90089-0357
Audrey Li, Contact
Email: iacl@usc.edu
Web: www.usc.edu/dept/LAS/ealc/IACL

JAPANESE AMERICAN HISTORY ARCHIVES
1840 Sutter St.
San Francisco, CA 94115
Seizo Oka, Executive Director
Tel: (415) 776-0661

JAPANESE AMERICAN NATIONAL LIBRARY
1619 Sutter St.
San Francisco, CA 94109
Karl Matsushipa, Director
Tel: (415) 567-5006

THE 1990 INSTITUTE
P.O. Box 1681
Burlingame, CA 94011
Hang-Sheng Cheng, President
Tel: (650) 558-9939 Fax: (650) 558-9499
Web: www.1990institute.org

THE VIETNAMESE AMERICAN MEDICAL RESEARCH FOUNDATION
14971 Brookhurst St.
Westminster, CA 92683
Tel: (714) 839-5898 Fax: (714) 839-5989
Web: www.vamrf.org

SCIENTIFIC

AMERICAN COMMITTEE FOR THE WEIZMANN INSTITUTE OF SCIENCE
300 Montgomery St. #615
San Francisco, CA 94104
Dr. Jay Levy, Regional Chair
Tel: (415) 981-4001
Email: bayarea@acwis.org
Web: www.weizmann-usa.org

9911 W. Pico Blvd. #900
Los Angeles, CA 90035
Lon Morton, Regional Chair
Tel: (310) 247-1016
Email: LA@acwis.org
Web: www.weizmann-usa.org

ASIAN PACIFIC AMERICAN NETWORK
231 E. 3rd St. #G104
Los Angeles, CA 90013
Wataru Ebihara, Project Coordinator
Email: ebihara@apanet.org
Web: www.apanet.org

TAIWAN-AMERICA BIOTECH ASSOCIATION
1120 N. Brookhurst St.
Anaheim, CA 92801
Tel: (714) 778-2377 Fax: (949) 725-0212
Email: taba_usa@taba-usa.org
Web: www.taba-usa.org

SPEC. INT., AIDS

ASIAN PACIFIC AIDS INTERVENTION TEAM
605 W. Olympic Blvd. #610
Los Angeles, CA 90015
Jury Candelario, Director
Tel: (213) 553-1830 Fax: (213) 553-1833
Email: apait@apaitonline.org
Web: www.apaitonline.org

ASIAN PACIFIC ISLANDER COMMUNITY AIDS PROJECT
4776 El Cajon Blvd. #204
San Diego, CA 92115
Jess San Roque, Executive Director
Tel: (619) 229-2822 Fax: (619) 229-2831
Email: apicap@aol.com
Web: www.apicap.org

ASIAN & PACIFIC ISLANDER WELLNESS CENTER
730 Polk St., 4th Fl.
San Francisco, CA 94109
John Manzon-Santos, Executive Director
Tel: (415) 292-3400 Fax: (415) 292-3404
Email: johnny@apiwellness.org
Web: www.apiwellness.org

FILIPINO TASK FORCE ON AIDS
109 Bartlett St. #204
San Francisco, CA 94110
Victor Hall, Executive Director
Tel: (415) 920-2630 Fax: (415) 920-0763
Email: dmallillin@filaids.org
Web: www.filaids.org

SPEC. INT., ALCOHOL/DRUG CENTER

ASIAN AMERICAN DRUG ABUSE PROGRAM
5318 S. Crenshaw Blvd.
Los Angeles, CA 90043
Mike Watanabe, Executive Director
Tel: (323) 293-6284 Fax: (323) 295-4075
Email: miwat@aadapinc.org
Web: www.aadapinc.org

PACIFIC ASIAN ALCOHOL AND DRUG PROGRAM
532 S. Vermont Ave. #102
Los Angeles, CA 90020
Leo Pandac, Director
Tel: (213) 738-3361 Fax: (213) 389-4512
Email: info@paadp.org
Web: www.paadp.org

SPEC. INT., CHILD CARE

AID TO CHILDREN WITHOUT PARENTS, INC.
P.O. Box 21066
San Jose, CA 95151
Benjamin Lee, Chairman
Tel: (408) 225-8302 Fax: (408) 884-2233
Email: benjaminlee@acwp.org
Web: www.acwp.org

AMERICANS HELPING ASIAN CHILDREN
500 W. Harbor Dr. #301
San Diego, CA 92101
Dr. Bruce Johnson, President
Tel: (619) 297-7575 Fax: (619) 239-3292
Email: ahac@cox.net
Web: www.ahac.org

ASIA INJURY PREVENTION FOUNDATION
1943 Talmadge St.
Los Angeles, CA 90027
Mary Nemick, Director
Tel: (323) 497-2245 Fax: (323) 934-9975

Email: msnemick@aol.com
Web: www.asiainjury.org

BIG BROTHERS BIG SISTERS OF LOS ANGELES
1055 Wilshire Blvd. #1950
Los Angeles, CA 90017
John Kobara, President/CEO
Tel: (213) 481-3611
Email: contactus@bigbrothersbigsisterslaie.org
Web: www.bigsistersla.org

CHINATOWN CHILD DEVELOPMENT CENTER
720 Sacramento St.
San Francisco, CA 94108
Nancy Lim-Yee, Program Director
Tel: (415) 392-4453 Fax: (415) 433-0953

CHINATOWN COMMUNITY CHILDREN'S CENTER
979 Clay St.
San Francisco, CA 94108
Lawrence Chang, Executive Director
Tel: (415) 986-2528 Fax: (415) 986-1136
Email: cccc@childrencenter.org
Web: www.childrencenter.org

HALF THE SKY FOUNDATION
764 Gilman St.
Berkeley, CA 94710
Jenny Bowen, President
Tel: (510) 525-3377 Fax: (510) 525-3611
Email: info@halfthesky.org
Web: www.halfthesky.org

LIVES OUT OF CHINA FOUNDATION
1187 Coast Village Rd. #1-503
Santa Barbara, CA 93108
Tel: (866) 566-2674
Email: info@looc.org
Web: www.looc.org

PEACH FOUNDATION
1098 Marlin Ave.
Foster City, CA 94404
Ruth Jeng, Chairperson/Founder
Tel: (650) 525-1188 Fax: (650) 525-9688
Email: staff@peachfoundationusa.org
Web: www.peachfoundationusa.org

PHILIP HAYDEN FOUNDATION
40335 Winchester Rd. #E115
Temecula, CA 92591
Tim Baker, Founder/President
Tel: (866) 526-3712 Fax: (951) 587-8558
Email: baker@philiphayden.org
Web: www.philiphayden.org

PHILIPPINE CHILDREN'S FUND OF AMERICA
Sacramento Office
7714 Elsie Ave.
Sacramento, CA 95828
Rafael Mercurio, President
Tel: (916) 688-1574 Fax: (916) 682-7936
Email: give@philippinechildrensfund.org
Web: www.philippinechildrensfund.org

PHILIPPINE INTERNATIONAL AID
1486 Huntington Ave. #300
South San Francisco, CA 94080
Mona Lisa Yuchengco
Tel: (650) 872-8661 Fax: (650) 872-8651
Email: m.yuchenco@filipinasmag.com
Web: www.phil-aid.org

VIETNAMESE PARENTS WITH DISABLED CHILDREN ASSOCIATION
7526 Syracuse Ave.
Stanton, CA 90680
Tien Thanh Nguyen, Secretary
Tel: (562) 427-5161
Email: contact@vpdca.org
Web: www.vpdca.org

WU YEE CHILDREN'S SERVICES
Administrative Office
831 Broadway St. 2nd Fl.
San Francisco, CA 94133
Lisa Le, President
Tel: (415) 391-4721 Fax: (415) 391-4716
Email: admin@wuyee.org
Web: www.wuyee.org

SPEC. INT., COUNSELING

APA COUNSELING & NETWORK CENTER
638 Clay St.
San Francisco, CA 94111
Mai Mai Ho, Executive Director
Tel: (415) 617-0061 Fax: (415) 617-0064
Email: apa@apasfgh.org
Web: www.apasfgh.org

ASIAN AMERICAN CHRISTIAN COUNSELING SERVICE
2550 W. Main St. #202
Alhambra, CA 91801
Tel: (626) 457-2900

ASIAN HELP LINE OF FAMILY COUNSELING SERVICES
10642 Lower Azusa Rd. #C
El Monte, CA 91731
Joana Chang, Director
Tel: (626) 350-4400 Fax: (626) 350-4499

ASIAN PACIFIC COMMUNITY COUNSELING
5330 Power Inn Rd. #A
Sacramento, CA 95820
Judy Fong Heary, Executive Director
Tel: (916) 383-6783 Fax: (916) 383-8488
Email: jheary@apccounseling.org
Web: www.apccounseling.org

COMMUNITY COUNSELING SERVICE
1200 Wilshire Blvd. #210
Los Angeles, CA 90017
Anne Warman, Director
Tel: (213) 481-1347 Fax: (213) 482-9466

JEWISH FAMILY AND CHILDREN'S SERVICES OF LONG BEACH
3801 E. Willow St.
Long Beach, CA 90815
Tel: (562) 427-7916 Fax: (562) 427-7910
Email: jfcs@jfcslongbeach.org
Web: www.jfcslongbeach.org

JEWISH FAMILY AND CHILDREN'S SERVICES OF SAN FRANCISCO
Marin Main Office
600 5th Ave.
Sun Rafael, CA 94901
Anita Friedman, Executive Director
Email: admin@jfcs.org
Web: www.jfcs.org

Peninsula Main Office
410 Sherman Ave.
Palo Alto, CA 94306
Anita Friedman, Executive Director
Email: admin@jfcs.org
Web: www.jfcs.org

San Francisco Main Office
2150 Post St.
San Francisco, CA 94115
Anita Friedman, Executive Director
Tel: (415) 449-1200
Email: admin@jfcs.org
Web: www.jfcs.org

Sonoma County Main Office
1360 N. Dutton Ave. #C
Santa Rosa, CA 95401
Anita Friedman, Executive Director
Email: admin@jfcs.org
Web: www.jfcs.org

JEWISH FAMILY AND CHILDREN'S SERVICES OF THE EAST BAY
Berkeley Office
2484 Shattuck Ave. #210
Berkeley, CA 94704
Tel: (510) 704-7475 Fax: (510) 704-7494
Email: information@jfcs-eastbay.org
Web: www.jfcs-eastbay.org

Oakland Office
2647 International Blvd. #220
Oakland, CA 94601
Tel: (510) 434-7585 Fax: (510) 434-7584
Email: information@jfcs-eastbay.org
Web: www.jfcs-eastbay.org

JEWS FOR JUDAISM, INC.
Los Angeles
P.O. Box 351235
Los Angeles, CA 90035-1235
Bentzion Kravitz, Director
Tel: (310) 556-3344 Fax: (310) 556-3344
Email: la@jewsforjudaism.org
Web: www.jewsforjudaism.org

SPEC. INT., EDUCATION

ACADEMY OF CHINESE CULTURE AND HEALTH SCIENCES
1601 Clay St.
Oakland, CA 94612
Wei Tsuei, President
Tel: (510) 763-7787 Fax: (510) 834-8646
Email: request@acchs.edu
Web: www.acchs.edu

AMERICAN ARABIC EDUCATIONAL FOUNDATION
387 Catalina Shore Dr.
Costa Mesa, CA 92627
Email: dhsimon@pacbell.net
Web: www.aaefonline.org

ARMENIAN ACADEMY OF LOS ANGELES
P.O. Box 812
Verdugo, CA 91046
Tel: (818) 293-0010
Email: contact@armenianacademyofla.org
Web: www.armenianacademyofla.org

ASHA FOR EDUCATION
Berkeley
University of California at Berkeley Anthony Hall
Berkeley, CA 94720-4500
Foster Gonsalves, Projects Coordinator
Tel: (510) 558-0104
Email: berkeley@ashanet.org
Web: www.ashanet.org/berkeley/

ASIA INSTITUTE
University of California, Los Angeles
11288 Bunche Hall
Los Angeles, CA 90095-1487
Minnie Chi, Editor
Tel: (310) 825-0007 Fax: (310) 206-3555
Email: asia@international.ucla.edu
Web: www.international.ucla.edu/asia

ASIA PACIFIC RESEARCH CENTER
Stanford University
Encina Hall #E301
Stanford, CA 94305-6055
Shiho Harada Barbir, Associate Director
Tel: (650) 723-9741 Fax: (650) 723-6530
Email: shiho.barbir@stanford.edu
Web: http://aparc.stanford.edu

ASIAN AMERICAN COMMUNITIES FOR EDUCATION
1596 Post St.
San Francisco, CA 94109
Emalyn Lapus, Project Director
Tel: (415) 921-5537 Fax: (415) 563-7109
Email: info@sfaacets.org
Web: www.sfaacets.org

ASIAN AMERICAN PARENT ASSOCIATION
P.O. Box 2275
Cupertino, CA 95015-2275
Michelle Hu, Co-President
Email: info@aapa.net
Web: http://aapa.net

ASIAN AMERICAN STUDIES
San Francisco State University
1600 Holloway Ave. PSY 103
San Francisco, CA 94132-4252
Marlon Hom, Chair
Tel: (415) 338-2698 Fax: (415) 338-0500
Email: aas@sfsu.edu
Web: www.sfsu.edu/~aas

University of California at Berkeley
506 Barrows Hall #2570
Berkeley, CA 94720-2570
Michael Omi, Chairperson
Tel: (510) 643-0796 Fax: (510) 642-6456
Email: ethnicst@socrates.berkeley.edu
Web: http://ist-socrates.berkeley.edu/~ethnicst/

University of California, Davis
3102 Hart Hall
Davis, CA 95616
Kathy Entao, Program Coordinator
Tel: (530) 752-3625 Fax: (530) 752-9260
Email: kmentao@ucdavis.edu
Web: http://asa.ucdavis.edu

University of California, Santa Barbara
5044 Humanities and Social Science Bldg.
Santa Barbara, CA 93106
Douglas H. Daniels, Chair
Tel: (805) 893-8039 Fax: (805) 893-7766
Email: daniels@blackstudies.ucsb.edu
Web: www.asamst.ucsb.edu

University of California, Los Angeles
3230 Campbell Hall, 405 Hilgard Ave.
Los Angeles, CA 90095-1546
Don Nakanishi, Director
Tel: (310) 825-2974 Fax: (310) 206-9844
Email: dtn@ucla.edu
Web: www.sscnet.ucla.edu/aasc/

ASIAN AMERICAN STUDIES DEPARTMENT
California State University, Northridge
18111 Nordhoff St.
Northridge, CA 91330-8251
Teresa Williams-Leon, Chair
Tel: (818) 677-4966 Fax: (818) 677-7094
Email: teresa.k.williams@csun.edu
Web: www.csun.edu/asianamericanstudies

ASIAN PACIFIC AMERICAN STUDENT SERVICES
University of Southern California
STU 410
Los Angeles, CA 90089-4851
Jeff Murakami, Director
Tel: (213) 740-4999 Fax: (213) 740-5284
Email: apass@usc.edu
Web: www.usc.edu/student-affairs/apass

ASIAN PACIFIC AMERICAN TEACHERS ASSOCIATION
750 Escondido Rd., Bldg. 136-B
Stanford, CA 94305
Christopher Chiang
Tel: (818) 378-5999
Email: ckchiang@stanford.edu
Web: www.apata.org

ASIAN PACIFIC AMERICANS IN HIGHER EDUCATION
Mira Costa College, 1 Barnard Dr.
Oceanside, CA 92056
Victoria Munoz Richart, President
Tel: (760) 795-6610 Fax: (760) 795-6758
Email: vrichart@miracostacollege.edu
Web: www.miracosta.edu

ASIAN PACIFIC ISLANDER FACULTY STAFF ASSOCIATION
333 Twin Oaks Valley Rd.
San Marcos, CA 92096-0001
Edward Pohlert, President
Email: apifsa@csusm.edu
Web: www.csusm.edu/apifsa

ASIAN PACIFIC ISLANDER RECRUITMENT & RETENTION CENTER
University of California Berkeley
515 Eshleman Hall
Berkeley, CA 94720
Vincent Toan, Executive Director
Tel: (510) 643-2934 Fax: (510) 642-2604
Email: reachinfo@uclink.berkeley.edu
Web: www.ocf.berkeley.edu/~reach

ASSOCIATION FOR THE PROTECTION OF AFGHAN ARCHAEOLOGY, INC.
P.O. Box 6798
San Rafael, CA 94903-0798
Zemaryalai Tarzi
Email: info@apaa.info
Web: www.apaa.info

ASSOCIATION OF NORTHERN CALIFORNIA CHINESE SCHOOLS
P.O. Box 2428
Cupertino, CA 95015-2428
Oliver Wan, President
Email: president@anccs.org
Web: www.anccs.org

BAY VALLEY CHINESE SCHOOL
P.O. Box 3351
Danville, CA 94526
Tel: (925)820-9702
Email: bayvalleychineseschool@yahoo.com
Web: www.bayvalleychineseschool.com

BRIDGE TO ASIA
665 Grant Ave.
San Francisco, CA 94108
Jeff Smith, President
Tel: (415) 678-2994
Email: asianet@bridge.org
Web: www.bridge.org

CALIFORNIA CIVIL LIBERTIES PUBLIC EDUCATION PROGRAM
P.O. Box 942837
Sacramento, CA 94237-0001
Diane Matsuda, Acting Program Director
Tel: (916) 653-9404 Fax: (916) 654-5829
Email: dmatsuda@library.ca.gov
Web: www.library.ca.gov/cclpep/

CALIFORNIA ETHNIC MULTICULTURAL ARCHIVES
University of California
Donald Davidson Library
Santa Barbara, CA 93106
Salvador Guerena, Director
Tel: (805) 893-8563 Fax: (805) 893-5749
Email: guerena@library.ucsb.edu
Web: cemaweb.library.ucsb.edu/cema_index.html

CALIFORNIA JAPANESE AMERICAN ALUMNI ASSOCIATION
P.O. Box 15235
San Francisco, CA 94115-0235
Trevor Nakagawa, President
Email: info@cjaaa.org
Web: www.cjaaa.org

CENTER FOR ASIAN PACIFIC AMERICANS
University of California Riverside
Fine Arts Bldg., Dept. of Music
Riverside, CA 92521
Deborah Wong, Director
Tel: (909) 787-3726 Fax: (909) 787-4651
Email: dwong@mail.ucr.edu
Web: http://ethnomus.ucr.edu/capa/CAPA98.html

CENTER FOR CHINESE STUDIES
University of California, Los Angeles
11381 Bunche Hall
Los Angeles, CA 90095-1487
Richard Baum, Director
Tel: (310) 825-8683 Fax: (310) 206-3397
Email: gunde@ucla.edu
Web: www.international.ucla.edu/ccs

CENTER FOR EDUCATIONAL TELECOMMUNICATIONS
1940 Hearst St.
Berkeley, CA 94709
Loni Ding, Founder
Tel: (510) 841-1263
Email: loniding@sonic.net
Web: www.cetel.org

CENTER FOR KOREAN STUDIES
University of California, Berkeley
2223 Fulton St. #2318
Berkeley, CA 94720
Clare You, Chair
Tel: (510) 642-5674 Fax: (510) 643-9787
Email: cks@socrates.berkeley.edu
Web: http://ieas.berkeley.edu/cks

University of California, Los Angeles
11371 Bunche Hall
Los Angeles, CA 90095-1487
Robert Buswell, Director
Tel: (310) 825-3284 Fax: (310) 206-3555
Email: koreanstudies@international.ucla.edu
Web: www.international.ucla.edu/korea

CENTER FOR KOREAN-AMERICAN AND KOREAN STUDIES
California State University, Los Angeles
Department of Sociology
Los Angeles, CA 90032
Dr. Eui-Young Yu, Director
Tel: (323) 343-2217
Email: eyu@calstatela.edu
Web: www.calstatela.edu/centers/ckaks

CENTER FOR MIDDLE EASTERN STUDIES
University of California
340 Stephens Hall #2314
Berkeley, CA 94720-2314
Nezar AlSayyad, Chair
Tel: (510) 642-8208 Fax: (510) 643-3001
Email: cmes@uclink4.berkeley.edu
Web: www.ias.berkeley.edu/cmes

CENTER FOR NEAR EASTERN STUDIES
University of California, Los Angeles
10286 Bunche Hall
Los Angeles, CA 90095-1480
Leonard Binder, Acting Interim Director
Tel: (310) 825-1181 Fax: (310) 206-2406
Web: www.isop.ucla.edu/cnes

CENTER FOR SOUTH ASIA STUDIES
University of California, Berkeley
10 Stephens Hall
Berkeley, CA 94720-2310
Raka Ray, Chair
Tel: (510) 642-3608 Fax: (510) 643-5793
Email: csasasst@berkeley.edu
Web: http://ias.berkeley.edu/southasia

CENTER FOR SOUTHEAST ASIA STUDIES
University of California, Berkeley
2223 Fulton St. #617 M/C 2318
Berkeley, CA 94720-2318
Peter Zinoman, Chair
Tel: (510) 642-3609 Fax: (510) 643-7062
Email: cseas@uclink.berkeley.edu
Web: http://ias.berkeley.edu/cseas/

University of California, Los Angeles
11387 Bunche Hall Box #951487
Los Angeles, CA 90095-1487
Geoffrey Robinson, Director
Tel: (310) 206-9163 Fax: (310) 206-3555
Email: cseas@isop.ucla.edu
Web: www.international.ucla.edu/cseas

CHINESE AMERICAN INTERNATIONAL SCHOOL
150 Oak
San Francisco, CA 94102
Heather Lin, Executive Assistant
Tel: (415) 865-6000 Fax: (415) 865-6006
Email: h_lin@cais.org
Web: www.cie-cais.org

CHINESE SCHOOL OF SAN DIEGO
8825 Aero Dr. #110
San Diego, CA 92123
Sally Wong-Abry, Principal
Tel: (858) 565-0068 Fax: (858) 571-6867
Email: admin@chineseschoolsd.com
Web: www.ChineseschoolSD.com

COMMUNITY EDUCATIONAL SERVICES
80 Fresno St.
San Francisco, CA 94133
Darin Ow-Wing, Executive Director
Tel: (415) 982-0615
Email: darin@cessf.org
Web: www.cessf.org

CONTRA COSTA CHINESE SCHOOL
123 Golf Rd.
Pleasant Hill, CA 94523
Judy Chen, Principal
Tel: (925) 472-3838
Email: info@contracostacs.org
Web: www.contracostacs.org

COUNCIL ON ISLAMIC EDUCATION
P.O. Box 20186
Fountain Valley, CA 92728
Shabbir Mansuri, Founding Director
Tel: (714) 839-2929 Fax: (714) 839-2714
Email: info@cie.org
Web: www.cie.org

DEPARTMENT OF ASIAN AMERICAN STUDIES
University of California, Irvine
300 Murray Krieger Hall
Irvine, CA 92697-6900
Ketu H. Katrak, Director
Tel: (949) 824-2746
Email: khkatrak@uci.edu
Web: www.humanities.uci.edu/aas/

DEPARTMENT OF ASIAN LANGUAGES
Stanford University
Main Quad, Bldg. 50
Stanford, CA 94305-2034
John Wang, Director
Tel: (650) 725-2742 Fax: (650) 725-8931
Email: asianlanguages@stanford.edu
Web: www.stanford.edu/dept/asianlang

DEPARTMENT OF ASIAN/ASIAN AMERICAN STUDIES
California State University, Long Beach
1250 Bellflower Blvd.
Long Beach, CA 90840
Kristene Lindert, Admin. Support Coordinator
Tel: (562) 985-4645 Fax: (562) 985-1535
Email: klindert@csulb.edu
Web: www.csulb.edu/depts/as/

DEPARTMENT OF ETHNIC STUDIES
University of California, San Diego
9500 Gilman Dr. M/C 0522
La Jolla, CA 92093-0522
Yen Le Espiritu, President
Tel: (858) 534-3276 Fax: (858) 534-8194
Email: ethnicstudies@ucsd.edu
Web: www.ucsd.edu

EDUCATIONAL SERVICES EXCHANGE WITH CHINA
444 E. Huntington Dr. #200
Arcadia, CA 91006
Tel: (626) 294-9400 Fax: (626) 821-2022
Email: esichina@aol.com
Web: www.esec.org

ETHNIC STUDIES LIBRARY
University of California, Berkeley
30 Stephens Hall #2360
Berkeley, CA 94720-2360
Wei-Chi Poon, Asian American Studies Librarian
Tel: (510) 643-1234 Fax: (510) 643-8433
Email: wcpoon@library.berkeley.edu
Web: http://eslibrary.berkeley.edu

EVERGREEN EDUCATION FOUNDATION
P.O. Box 5131
Richmond, CA 94805
Tel: (415) 602-4754 Fax: (510) 501-2714
Email: evergreenlibrary@yahoo.com
Web: www.evergreeneducation.org

FILIPINO AMERICAN EDUCATORS ASSOCIATION, INC.
3640 Burritt Way
Glendale, CA 91214
Arturo Pacho, President
Tel: (818) 249-4778
Email: apacho@earthlink.net
Web: www.faeainc.org

FILIPINO AMERICAN LIBRARY
3200 W. Temple St.
Los Angeles, CA 90026
Fritz Friedman, Chairman
Tel: (213) 382-0488 Fax: (213) 382-0878
Email: filamlibrary@earthlink.net
Web: www.filipinoamericanlibrary.org

GO FOR BROKE EDUCATIONAL FOUNDATION
370 Amapola Ave. # 110
Terrance, CA 90501
Christine Sato -Yamazaki, Executive Director/ President
Tel: (310) 328-0907 Fax: (310) 222-5700
Email: esoldier@goforbroke.org
Web: www.goforbroke.org

HEBREW UNION COLLEGE-JEWISH INSTITUTE OF RELIGION
Los Angeles Office
3077 University Ave.
Los Angeles, CA 90007-3796
David Ellenson, President
Tel: (213) 749-3424 Fax: (213) 747-6128
Email: admissions@huc.edu
Web: www.huc.edu

HMONG ORGANIZATION FOR PARENTS EDUCATORS AND STUDENTS, INC.
P.O. Box 188695
Sacramento, CA 95818
Tsia T. Xiong, Executive Director
Tel: (916) 951-5931
Email: hopes@lanset.com
Web: www.hopesinc.org

INDIA LITERACY PROJECT
California Chapter
P.O. Box 361143
Milpitas, CA 95035-9998
Senthilkumar Divariam
Tel: (408) 328-8826
Web: www.ilpnet.org

INLAND RIVERSIDE CHINESE SCHOOL
P.O. Box 56335
Riverside, CA 92517
Tel: (909) 798-0233

INSTITUTE OF EAST ASIAN STUDIES
University of California, Berkeley
2223 Fulton St. #2318
Berkeley, CA 94720-2318
T.J. Pempel, Director
Tel: (510) 642-2809 Fax: (510) 643-7062
Email: ieas@berkeley.edu
Web: http://ieas.berkeley.edu

INTERCOLLEGIATE DEPARTMENT OF ASIAN AMERICAN STUDIES
Pitzer College
1050 N. Mills Ave., Mead Hall 131

Claremont, CA 91711
Madeline Gosiaco, Administrative Assistant
Tel: (909) 607-9508
Email: idaas@pomona.edu
Web: www.idaas.pomona.edu

JAPAN FOUNDATION LOS ANGELES OFFICE & LANGUAGE CENTER
333 S. Grand Ave. #2250
Los Angeles, CA 90071
Hayato Ogo, Director
Tel: (213) 621-2267 Fax: (213) 621-2590
Email: hayato_ogo@jflalc.org
Web: www.jflalc.org

JAPAN PACIFIC RESOURCE NETWORK
310 8th St. #305
Oakland, CA 94607
Tomoji Ishi, Contact
Tel: (510) 891-9045 Fax: (510) 891-9047
Email: info@jprn.org
Web: www.jprn.org

JAPANESE EDUCATIONAL RESOURCE CENTER
23240 Hawthorn Blvd. #219
Torrance, CA 90505
Kaz Kishita, President
Tel: (310) 373-4888 Fax: (310) 373-0855
Email: jerc8@hotmail.com
Web: www.jerc.org

JAPANESE FRIENDSHIP GARDEN SOCIETY OF SAN DIEGO
Balboa Park Administration Bldg., 2125 Park Blvd.
San Diego, CA 92101-4792
Luanne Lao-Kanzawa, Executive Director
Tel: (619) 232-2721 Fax: (619) 232-0917
Email: jfgsd@niwa.org
Web: www.niwa.org

JAPANESE LANGUAGE SCHOLARSHIP FOUNDATION
3127 Nichols Canyon Rd.
Los Angeles, CA 90046
Akiko Agishi, President/Founder
Tel: (323) 882-6545 Fax: (323) 969-9425
Email: aurorafoundation@usa.net
Web: www.jlsf-aurora.org

JAPANESE LANGUAGE SCHOOL UNIFIED SYSTEM, INC.
Jr. and Sr. High School (Elementary, Jr. & Sr. High cultural Classes)
1218 Menlo Ave.
Los Angeles, CA 90006
Terue Seino, Principal
Tel: (213) 383-4706
Email: office@kyodosystem.org
Web: www.kyodosystem.org

Orange Coast Gakuen (Elementary, Jr. & Sr. High School)
21141 Strathmoor Ln.
Huntington Beach, CA 92646
Terue Seino, Principal
Tel: (714) 964-7446
Email: office@kyodosystem.org
Web: www.kyodosystem.org

Pasadena Gakuen (Elementary/Jr. High School)
595 Lincoln Ave.
Pasadena, CA 91103
Terue Seino, Principal
Tel: (626) 356-9061
Email: office@kyodosystem.org
Web: www.kyodosystem.org

Rafu Chuo Gakuen (Preschool, Elementary, Jr. & Sr. High School)
202 N. Saratoga St.
Los Angeles, CA 90033
Terue Seino, Principal
Tel: (323) 268-4955
Email: office@kyodosystem.org
Web: www.kyodosystem.org

Valley Gakuen (Elementary, Jr. & Sr. High School)
8850 Lankershim Blvd.
Sun Valley, CA 91352
Terue Seino, Principal
Tel: (818) 767-9921
Email: office@kyodosystem.org
Web: www.kyodosystem.org

JEWISH COMMUNITY HIGH SCHOOL OF THE BAY
1835 Ellis St.
San Francisco, CA 94115
Edward Harwitz, Head of School
Tel: (415) 345-9777 Fax: (415) 345-1888
Email: contact@jchsofthebay.org
Web: www.jchsofthebay.org

JEWISH LEARNING EXCHANGE
7223 Beverly Blvd. #201
Los Angeles, CA 90036
Avrohom Czapnik, Rabbi
Tel: (323) 857-0923 Fax: (323) 857-0619
Email: jleoutreach@yahoo.com
Web: www.holysparks.com/jle.html

JEWISH PARTISAN EDUCATIONAL FOUNDATION
2107 Van Ness Ave. #302
San Francisco, CA 94109
Mitch Braff, Executive Director
Tel: (415) 563-2244 Fax: (415) 563-2442
Email: info@jewishpartisans.org
Web: www.jewishpartisans.org

JEWISH STUDY NETWORK, INC.
2584 Leghorn St. #-A
Mountain View, CA
Joey Felson, Executive Director
Tel: (650) 961-4576 Fax: (650) 961-4572
Email: info@jsn.info
Web: www.jewishstudynetwork.com

KAI MING HEAD START
950 Powell St.
San Francisco, CA 94108
Karen Lam, Director
Tel: (415) 982-4777 Fax: (415) 982-4120
Email: asst@kaiming.org
Web: www.kaiming.org

KOREAN AMERICAN SCHOLARSHIP FOUNDATION
Western Region
3435 Wilshire Blvd. #2450-B
Los Angeles, CA 90010
Kay Kim, President
Tel: (213) 380-5273 Fax: (213) 380-5273
Email: western@kasf.org
Web: www.kasf.org

KOREAN CENTER, INC.
Intercultural Institute of California
1362 Post St.
San Francisco, CA 94109
Kimberly Long, Executive Director
Tel: (415) 441-1881 Fax: (415) 885-4155
Email: info_kci@koreannet.org
Web: www.koreannet.org/home/home.html

KOREAN CENTER OF SAN FRANCISCO
1362 Post St.
San Francisco, CA 94109
Sang Hwa Lee, Chairman of the Board
Tel: (415) 441-1881 Fax: (415) 885-4155
Email: info_kci@koreannet.org
Web: www.koreannet.org

KYOTO CENTER FOR JAPANESE STUDIES
Stanford Overseas Studies
P.O. Box 20346
Stanford, CA 94309
Tel: (650) 725-0233 Fax: (650) 725-7355
Email: kcjs@osp.stanford.edu
Web: http://kcjs.stanford.edu

LEADERSHIP EDUCATION FOR ASIAN PACIFIC'S, INC.
327 E. 2nd St. #226
Los Angeles, CA 90012
J.D. Hokoyama, President/CEO
Tel: (213) 485-1422 x4112 Fax: (213) 485-0050
Email: leap@leap.org
Web: www.leap.org

LEHRHAUS JUDAICA
The Reutlinger Ctr., Ground Fl., 2736 Bancroft Way
Berkeley, CA 94704
Jehon Grist, Executive Director
Tel: (510) 845-6420 Fax: (510) 845-6446
Email: info@lehrhaus.org
Web: www.lehrhaus.org

MILLS COLLEGE
Ethnic Studies Dept.
5000 MacArthur Blvd.
Oakland, CA 94613
Jean Wong, Administrative Assistant
Tel: (510) 430-2080 Fax: (510) 430-2067
Email: ethnic@mills.edu
Web: www.mills.edu/eths/eths.html

MILPITAS COMMUNITY CHINESE SCHOOL
P.O. Box 361856
Milpitas, CA 95036-1856
Tel: (408) 278-5080
Web: www.mccs-usa.org

NAHAAL SCHOLARSHIP FOUNDATION
P.O. Box 4060
San Rafael, CA 54913
Email: info@nahaal.org
Web: www.nahaal.org

NATIONAL ASIAN PACIFIC AMERICAN LAW STUDENT ASSOCIATION
Loyola Law School of Los Angeles
919 S. Albany
Los Angeles, CA 90015
Nedrudee Liu, Co-President
Tel: (213) 736-1006
Email: nedrudee@aol.com
Web: www.napalsa.org

NATIONAL ASSOCIATION FOR ASIAN AND PACIFIC AMERICAN EDUCATION
P.O. Box 3366
Daly City, CA 94015-3366
Janet Lu, Executive Manager
Tel: (650) 994-6020 Fax: (650) 991-4676
Web: www.naapae.net

NEAR EASTERN LANGUAGES & CULTURES
University of California, Los Angeles
376 Kinsey Hall, Box 951511
Los Angeles, CA 90095-1511
William M. Schniedewind, Chair
Tel: (310) 825-4165
Email: williams@humnet.ucla.edu
Web: www.humnet.ucla.edu/humnet/nelc

NORTH AMERICAN CHINESE EDUCATIONAL FOUNDATION
1450 Avila Ct.
Hayward, CA 94544
Mike Mao, President
Tel: (415) 509-1799 Fax: (510) 265-1195
Email: hope@nacef.org
Web: www.nacef.org

NORTH PENINSULA MANDARIN SCHOOL
1818 Gilbreth Rd. #139
Burlingame, CA 94010
Tel: (660) 692-6932
Web: www.npms.org

OAKLAND HEBREW DAY SCHOOL
5500 Redwood Rd.
Oakland, CA 94619
Mark Shinar, Director
Tel: (510) 531-8600 Fax: (510) 531-8686
Email: office@ohds.org
Web: www.ohds.org

POMONA COLLEGE
Asian American Resource Center, Smith Campus Center
170 E. 6th St. #240
Claremont, CA 91711-6364
Daren Rikio Mooko, Director
Tel: (909) 621-8639 Fax: (909) 607-8513
Email: dmooko@pomona.edu
Web: www.pomona.edu/directories/administrativedirectory.shtml

PROJECT DOSTI
Stanford University
562 Salvatierra Walk
Stanford, CA 94305
Amit Garg
Email: amgarg@stanford.edu
Web: www.stanford.edu/group/dosti/

SAN DIEGO CHINESE ACADEMY
P.O. Box 910093
San Diego, CA 92191-0093
Cindy Liao, Principal
Email: principal@sd-ca.org
Web: www.sd-ca.org

SANTA BARBARA CHINESE SCHOOL
3991 Primavera Rd.
Santa Barbara, CA 93110
Sean Lee, Principal
Email: sbchineseschool.org
Web: www.geocities.com/sbchineseschool/index.html

SOCIETY FOR OPEN NEPAL
3100 Rubino Dr. #320
San Jose, CA 95125
Dipesh Shrestha, Co-Founder
Email: dsshrestha@hotmail.com
Web: www.opennepal.org

SOUTH BAY CHINESE SCHOOL
600 Cloyden Rd.
Palos Verdes, CA 90274
Tel: (310) 534-5589
Email: info@southbaychineseschool.org
Web: www.southbaychineseschool.org

SOUTHEAST ASIA COMMUNITY RESOURCE CENTER
10836 Gadsten Way
Rancho Cordova, CA 95670
Judy Lewis, Chair
Tel: (916) 635-6815 Fax: (916) 635-0174
Email: jlewis@seacrc.org
Web: www.seacrc.org

SOUTHEAST ASIAN VISION OF EDUCATION
3429 San Bruno Ct.
Merced, CA 95348
Tel: (209) 261-2520 Fax: (209) 725-1637
Email: pmoua@save-edu.org
Web: www.save-edu.org

STANFORD CHINA EDUCATION FOUNDATION
P.O. Box 51806
Palo Alto, CA 94303
Jingjun Cao, President
Tel: (408) 505-4216
Email: info@scef.org
Web: www.scef.org

STANFORD CHINESE SCHOOL
1440 Middlefield Rd.
Palo Alto, CA 94301
Tel: (650) 566-8636
Email: scsquestions@juno.com
Web: www.mychineseschool.com

TEHIYAH DAY SCHOOL
2603 Tassajara Ave.
El Cerrito, CA 94530
Steve Tabak, Head Administration
Tel: (510) 233-3013 Fax: (510) 233-0171
Email: stabak@tehiyah.org
Web: www.tehiyah.org

THE FOUNDATION FOR EXCELLENCE
1850 Warburton Ave. #201
Santa Clara, CA 95051
Suresh A. Seshan, Executive Director
Tel: (408) 985-2001 Fax: (408) 985-2003
Email: saseshan@ffe.org
Web: www.ffe.org

THE MANZANAR COMMITTEE
1566 Curran St.
Los Angeles, CA 90026
Sue Embrey, Chair
Tel: (323) 662-5102 Fax: (323) 666-5161
Email: sueke@msn.com
Web: www.manzanarcommittee.org

THE UNIVERSAL INSTITUTE OF ISLAMIC EDUCATION
7902 Gerber Rd. #140
Sacramento, CA 95828
Zakiyyah Muhammad, Founding Director
Tel: (916) 689-8443 Fax: (916) 689-5977
Email: uiie@islam.org
Web: www2.islamicity.com/uiie

TIBETAN NYINGMA INSTITUTE
1815 Highland Pl.
Berkeley, CA 94709
Tel: (510) 843-6812
Email: Nyingma-Institute@nyingma.org
Web: www.nyingmainstitute.com

TORRANCE CHINESE SCHOOL
5028 Scott St.
Torrance, CA 90503
Mike Wang, Principal
Tel: (310) 316-6669
Email: masteer@torrancecs.com
Web: www.torrancecs.com

TURKISH EDUCATIONAL FOUNDATION, INC.
P.O. Box 623
Berkeley, CA 94701
Erdem Esengil, President
Tel: (831) 425-1145 Fax: (831) 425-1158
Email: erdem.esengil@tef-usa.org
Web: www.tef-usa.org

UNIVERSITY OF JUDAISM
15600 Mulholland Dr.
Bel Air, CA 90077
Dr. Robert Wexler, President
Tel: (888) 853-6763
Email: rwexler@uj.edu
Web: www.uj.edu

US CHINA PEOPLES FRIENDSHIP ASSOCIATION
Long Beach Chapter
P.O. Box 14617
Long Beach, CA 90853
Dr. Elizabeth Kraft, Contact
Tel: (562) 596-8748 Fax: (562) 430-6057
Web: www.uscpfa.org

Northern California Subregion
2871 Doidge Ave.
Pinole, CA 94564
Judy Lee, President
Tel: (510) 758-7355 Fax: (510) 262-9451
Email: shanguo@aol.com
Web: www.uscpfa.org

Sacramento Valley Chapter
1175 Volz Dr.
Sacramento, CA 95822
Ruby M. Fong, Contact
Tel: (916) 447-3313 Fax: (916) 444-2288
Web: www.uscpfa.org

San Diego Chapter
P.O. Box 26913
San Diego, CA 92196
Lilin Wang/Mary Nohrden, Contacts
Tel: (858) 578-0555
Web: www.uscpfa.org

San Francisco Chapter
1795 Cayuga St.
San Francisco, CA 94112
David Ewing, Contact
Tel: (415) 781-8182
Web: www.uscpfa.org

San Gabriel Valley Chapter
5313 Sheila St.
Commerce, CA 90040
Bill Chu, Contact
Web: www.uscpfa.org

Santa Barbara Chapter
1215 DeLaVina St. #J
Santa Barbara, CA 93101
Desmond O'Neill, Contact
Tel: (305) 966-2211 Fax: (305) 966-7815
Web: www.uscpfa.org

South Bay Chapter
843 Hydrangea Ct.
Sunnyvale, CA 94086
Dana Eaton/Jimmy Wong, Contact
Tel: (408) 733-3684 Fax: (408) 241-0674
Web: www.uscpfa.org

Southern California Subregion
7279 Mulholland Dr.
Los Angeles, CA 90068
Frank Pestana, President
Tel: (323) 850-8188 Fax: (323) 850-8259
Email: frankUSCPFA@aol.com
Web: www.uscpfa.org

Westside Los Angeles Chapter
732 Maltman Ave.
Los Angeles, CA 90026
Claire Hirsch, Contact
Tel: (323) 666-300
Web: www.uscpfa.org

WEST VALLEY CHINESE LANGUAGE SCHOOL
P.O. Box 2383
Sunnyvale, CA 94087
Adelaide Wong, Principal
Tel: (408) 839-7001

WISDOM CHINESE SCHOOL
P.O. Box 188308
Sacramento, CA 95818
Stephen Cho
Email: chophi@yahoo.com

SPEC. INT., EMPLOYMENT

ACCESS
2612 Daniel Ave.
San Diego, CA 92111
Dr. Kenneth Fawson, Director
Tel: (858) 560-0871 Fax: (858) 560-8135
Email: kfawson@access2jobs.org
Web: www.access2jobs.org

ARISE PROJECT/AFGHAN CENTER
37416 Joseph St.
Fremont, CA 94536
Tel: (510) 794-1050
Email: info@ariseproject.org
Web: www.ariseproject.org

ASIAN ADVANCEMENT ASSOCIATION, INC.
7240 E. Southgate Dr. #7
Sacramento, CA 95823
John Thao, President
Tel: (916) 424-8784 Fax: (916) 428-6832
Email: jthaoaaa@jps.net

ASIAN PACIFIC AMERICAN PROGRAM
Space and Missile Systems Center
Los Angeles Air Force Base
Los Angeles, CA 92683
Ching Shelton, President

Tel: (310) 363-2719 Fax: (310) 363-3931
Email: ching.shelton@losangeles.af.mil
Web: www.losangeles.af.mil/base-orgs/apap/
activities.html

CALIFORNIA INDIAN MANPOWER CONSORTIUM
738 N. Market Blvd.
Sacramento, CA 95834
Lorenda Sanchez, Executive Director
Tel: (916) 920-0285 Fax: (916) 641-6338
Email: cimcinfo@cimcinc.com

CALIFORNIA STATE EMPLOYEES ASSOCIATION
1108 O St.
Sacramento, CA 95814
Joseph Jelincic, President
Tel: (916) 444-8134 Fax: (916) 326-4215
Email: jjelincic@calcsea.org
Web: www.calcsea.org

CAMBODIAN FAMILY
1111 E. Wakeham Ave. #E
Santa Ana, CA 92705
Rifka Sirfcs, Administration
Tel: (714) 571-1966 x 2 Fax: (714) 571-1974
Email: cambodianfamily@sbcglobal.net
Web: http://pages.sbcglobal.net/
cambodianfamily/index.html

ECONOMIC AND EMPLOYMENT DEVELOPMENT CENTER
2200 W. Valley Blvd. #A,B
Alhambra, CA 91803
Thai Phuc, Executive Director
Tel: (626) 281-3792 Fax: (626) 281-8064
Email: eedc@aol.com

JEWISH VOCATIONAL AND CAREER COUNSELING SERVICE
225 Bush St. #400
San Francisco, CA 94104
Shari Freedman, President
Tel: (415) 391-3600 Fax: (415) 391-3617
Email: hire@jvs.org
Web: www.jvs.org

JEWISH VOCATIONAL SERVICE
City Headquarters
6505 Wilshire Blvd. #200
Los Angeles, CA 90048
Rick Powell, President
Tel: (323) 761-8888 Fax: (323) 761-8575
Email: askus@jvsla.org
Web: www.jvsla.org

Valley Headquarters
22622 Vanowen St.
West Hills, CA 91307
Rick Powell, President
Tel: (818) 464-3222 Fax: (818) 464-3375
Email: valley@jvsla.org
Web: www.jvsla.org

WorkSource Center
5757 Wilshire Blvd. Promenade 3
Los Angeles, CA 90036
Rick Powell, President
Tel: (323) 904-4900
Email: worksource@jvsla.org
Web: www.jvsla.org

LOS ANGELES COUNTY FILIPINO AMERICAN EMPLOYEES ASSOCIATION
532 S. Vermont Ave. #103
Los Angeles, CA 90020
Merce Gillo, Vice President
Tel: (213) 974-1390
Email: lacfaea123@aol.com
Web: www.lacfaea.org

PACIFIC ASIAN CONSORTIUM IN EMPLOYMENT
1055 Wilshire Blvd. #1475
Los Angeles, CA 90017
Kerry N. Doi, Executive Director

Tel: (213) 353-3982 Fax: (213) 353-1227
Email: admin@pacela.org
Web: www.pacela.org

SPEC. INT., FAMILY PLANNING

APA FAMILY SUPPORT CENTER
730 Commercial St.
San Francisco, CA 94110
Mai Mai Ho, Executive Director
Tel: (415) 616-9797 Fax: (415) 616-9796
Email: apa@apasfgh.org
Web: www.apasfgh.org

ASIAN PACIFIC FAMILY RESOURCE CENTER
625 Wool Creek Dr. #F
San Jose, CA 95112
Kim Vu, Supervisor
Tel: (408) 299-1500 Fax: (408) 298-2482
Email: huynhvuk@cws.co.santa-clara.ca.us

ASSOCIATION FOR CHINESE FAMILIES OF THE DISABLED
720 Sacramento St., 2nd & 3rd Fl.
San Francisco, CA 94108
Nancy Lim-Yee, Board Secretary
Tel: (415) 392-4453 Fax: (415) 433-0953
Email: nanlimyee@aol.com

SPEC. INT., GAY&LESBIAN

ASIAN PACIFIC CROSSROADS
c/o The Center Orange County
12832 Garden Grove Blvd. #A
Garden Grove, CA 92643
Jim D., Chair
Tel: (714) 534-0862 Fax: (714) 534-5491
Email: chair@apc-oc.org
Web: www.apc-oc.org

ASIAN PACIFIC GAYS & FRIENDS, INC.
7985 Santa Monica Blvd. #109
West Hollywood, CA 90046-5112
Bill Tom, President
Email: info@apgf.org
Web: www.apgf.org

ASIAN & PACIFIC ISLANDER FAMILY PRIDE
P.O. Box 473
Fremont, CA 94537
Belinda Dronkers-Laureta, Co-Coordinator
Tel: (510) 818-0887 Fax: (510) 742-1102
Email: info@apifamilypride.org
Web: www.apifamilypride.org

ASIAN & PACIFIC ISLANDER LESBIAN & BISEXUAL WOMEN & TRANSGENDER NETWORK
P.O. Box 210698
San Francisco, CA 94121
Email: info@aplbtn.org
Web: www.aplbtn.org

ASIAN PACIFIC ISLANDERS FOR HUMAN RIGHTS
6115 Selma Ave. #207
Los Angeles, CA 90028
Patrick Mangto, Executive Director
Tel: (323) 860-0876
Email: apihr@apihr.org
Web: www.apihr.org

CHINESE RAINBOW ASSOCIATION
P.O. Box 252181
Los Angeles, CA 90025
Email: chinarainbow@hotmail.com
Web: www.chinarainbow.org

COMMUNITY UNITED AGAINST VIOLENCE
160 14th St.
San Francisco, CA 94103
Terry Person-Harris, Executive Director
Tel: (415) 777-5500 Fax: (415) 777-5565
Email: terry@cuav.org
Web: www.cuav.org

GAY ASIAN MULTICULTURAL EXCHANGE
P.O. Box 15904
San Francisco, CA 94115-0904
Email: info@gamx.org
Web: www.gamx.org

GAY ASIAN PACIFIC ALLIANCE
P.O. Box 421884
San Francisco, CA 94142-1884
Gary Chen, Chair
Tel: (415) 826-6210
Email: gary@gapa.org
Web: www.gapa.org

GAY ASIAN PACIFIC SUPPORT NETWORK
P.O. Box 461104
Los Angeles, CA 90046-1104
Chan Timothy, Co-chair
Tel: (213) 368-6488
Email: gapsn@gapsn.org
Web: www.gapsn.org

PACIFIC FRIENDS
P.O. Box 591208
San Francisco, CA 94159-1208
Skip Moulton, Committee Chairman
Tel: (415) 221-7642
Email: skip@pacificfriends.org
Web: www.pacificfriends.org

SATRANG
1026 Concha St.
Altadena, CA 91001
Sanjay Chhugani, President
Tel: (626) 379-3649
Email: president@satrang.org
Web: www.satrang.org

SOUTH BAY QUEER AND ASIAN
938 The Alameda
San Jose, CA 95126
Tel: (408) 293-2429
Email: info@sbqa.com
Web: www.sbqa.com

TRIKONE
P.O. Box 14161
San Francisco, CA 94114
Tel: (415) 487-8778
Email: trikone@trikone.org
Web: www.trikone.org

SPEC. INT., HEALTH SERVICES

AFGHAN MEDICAL ASSOCIATION OF AMERICA
31063 E. Sunset Dr. North
Redlands, CA 92373
Khushal A. Stanisai
Tel: (909) 796 0363 Fax: (909) 796 0762
Email: Stanisai@AOL.Com
Web: www.afghanmed.org

AFGHANISTAN DENTAL RELIEF PROJECT, INC.
31 E. Canon Perdido St.
Santa Barbara, CA 93101
James Rolfe, President/CEO
Tel: (805) 963-2329 Fax: (805) 962-2466
Email: adrp@verizon.net
Web: www.adrpinc.org

AMERICAN CANCER SOCIETY
Eastern Division-Northern California Chinese Unit
39277 Liberty St. #D14
Fremont, CA 94538
Ming Der Chang, President
Tel: (888) 566-6222
Email: ming-der.chang@cancer.org
Web: www.cancer.org

ARMENIAN AMERICAN MEDICAL SOCIETY OF CALIFORNIA
P.O. Box 32
Glendale, CA 91209
Dr. Armen Cherik, President
Tel: (818) 980-7777

Email: hkeyrib@aol.com
Web: www.instantweb.com/a/aamsc

ASIAN AMERICAN CANCER SUPPORT NETWORK
P.O. Box 2919
Sunnyvale, CA 94087
May Bakken, President
Email: info@aacsn.org
Web: http://aacsn.xtensify.com

ASIAN AMERICAN DONOR PROGRAM
7700 Edgewater Dr. #265
Oakland, CA 94621
Jonathan Leong, President
Tel: (510) 568-3700 Fax: (510) 568-2700
Email: asamdonors@aadp.org
Web: www.aadp.org

ASIAN AMERICAN NETWORK FOR CANCER AWARENESS, RESEARCH AND TRAINING
University of California, Davis, Cancer Center
4501 X St. #3011
Sacramento, CA 95817
Moon S. Chen, Jr., Ph.D., Principal Investigator
Email: aancart@ucdavis.edu
Web: www.aancart.org

ASIAN HEALTH SERVICES
Main Office
818 Webster St.
Oakland, CA 94607
Sherry Hirota, CEO
Tel: (510) 986-6830 X300 Fax: (510) 986-6830
Email: skiani@ahschc.org
Web: www.ahschc.org

ASIAN LIVER CENTER AT STANFORD UNIVERSITY
300 Pasteur Dr. #H3680
Stanford, CA 94305
Eric Sue, Outreach Coordinator
Tel: (650) 724-2923 Fax: (650) 723-0006
Web: http://liver.stanford.edu

ASIAN PACIFIC HEALTH CARE VENTURE,INC.
1530 Hillhurst Ave. #200
Los Angeles, CA 90027
Kazue Shibata, Executive Director
Tel: (323) 644-3880 Fax: (323) 644-3892
Email: info@aphcv.org
Web: www.aphcv.org

ASIAN & PACIFIC ISLANDER AMERICAN HEALTH FORUM
Main Office
450 Sutter St. #600
San Francisco, CA 94108
Ho Luong Tran, MD, Executive Director
Tel: (415) 954-9988 Fax: (415) 954-9999
Email: info@apiahf.org
Web: www.apiahf.org

ASIAN & PACIFIC ISLANDERS FOR REPRODUCTIVE HEALTH
Main Office
310 8th St. #309
Oakland, CA 94607
Eveline Shen, Director
Tel: (510) 434-7900 Fax: (510) 434-7902
Web: www.reproductivejustice.org

ASIANS FOR MIRACLE MARROW MATCHES
231 E. 3rd St. #G107
Los Angeles, CA 90013
Sharon Sugiyama, Project Director
Tel: (888) 236-4673 Fax: (213) 473-1661
Email: a3m@ltsc.org
Web: www.asianmarrow.org

ASSOCIATION OF ASIAN PACIFIC COMMUNITY HEALTH ORGANIZATIONS
300 Frank H. Ogawa Plz. #620
Oakland, CA 94612
Jeffrey B. Caballero, Executive Director

Tel: (510) 272-9536 Fax: (510) 272-0817
Email: info@aapcho.org
Web: www.aapcho.org

CHINESE AMERICAN OPTHALMOLOGICAL SOCIETY
1401 Avocado #903
Newport Beach, CA 92660
Arlene Gwon, VP Corporate Relations
Tel: (949) 640-6661 Fax: (949) 640-6660
Email: agwon@oc-net.com
Web: www.caosmd.com/index.htm

CHINESE COMMUNITY HEALTH CARE ASSOCIATION
170 Columbus Ave. #210
San Francisco, CA 94133
Edward A. Chow, Executive Director
Tel: (415) 397-3190 Fax: (415) 421-1853
Email: info@cchca.com
Web: www.cchca.com

CHINESE HOSPITAL
845 Jackson St.
San Francisco, CA 94133
Brenda Yee, CEO
Tel: (415) 982-2400 Fax: (415) 677-2488
Email: brenday@chasf.org
Web: www.chasf.org

HAIGHT ASHBURY FREE CLINICS,INC.
1696 Haight St.
San Francisco, CA 94117
Magdalen Chang, Center Manager
Tel: (415) 565-1927 Fax: (415) 487-9606
Web: www.hafci.org

INTERNATIONAL THAI THERAPISTS ASSOCIATION, INC.
P.O. Box 1048
Palm Spring, CA 92263
Tel: (231) 343-6972
Email: itta@core.com
Web: www.thaimassage.com

ISRAEL CANCER RESEARCH FUND
8383 Wilshire Blvd. #341
Beverly Hills, CA 90211
Benjamin Bonavida, President
Tel: (323) 651-1200 Fax: (323) 782-0400
Email: email@icrfla.org
Web: www.icrfonline.org

JAPANESE COMMUNITY HEALTH, INC.
420 E. 3rd St. #1010
Los Angeles, CA 90013
Sakaye Shigekawa, M.D., President
Tel: (213) 626-6071
Email: jchi@jchi.org
Web: www.jchi.org

JEWISH HEALTHCARE FOUNDATION
8489 W. 3rd St.
Los Angeles, CA 90048
Tel: (323) 852-1900 Fax: (323) 852-0727
Email: info@bikurcholimonline.org
Web: www.bikurcholimonline.org

KHEIR - ADULT DAY HEALTH CARE CENTER
939 S. Western Ave.
Los Angeles, CA 90006
Peter Kim, Program Director
Tel: (323) 373-1088 Fax: (323) 373-1080
Email: kheirinfo@koreanhealth.org
Web: www.koreanhealth.org

KOREAN AMERICAN FAMILY SERVICE CENTER
3727 W. 6th St. #509
Los Angeles, CA 90020
Peter Chang, Executive Director
Tel: (213) 389-6755 Fax: (213) 389-5172
Email: info@kafscla.com
Web: www.kafscla.org

LAO REHABILITATION FOUNDATION INC.
86 El Nido Dr.
Napa, CA 94559
Luc Janssens, Contact

Tel: (707) 265-6555 Fax: (707) 265-6566
Email: janssens@sonic.net
Web: www.laofoundation.com

MEHR FOUNDATION
P.O. Box 294
Orinda, CA 94563
Minoo Omidian, Contact
Tel: (510) 223-8390
Email: houshang_pakpour@yahoo.com
Web: www.mehrfoundation.com

NATIONAL ASIAN WOMEN'S HEALTH ORGANIZATION
250 Montgomery St. #900
San Francisco, CA 94104
Mary C. Hayashi, Founder/President
Tel: (415) 989-9747 Fax: (415) 773-2872
Email: info@nawho.org
Web: www.nawho.org

NICOS CHINESE HEALTH COALITION
1208 Mason St.
San Francisco, CA 94108
Kent Woo, Executive Director
Tel: (415) 788-6426 Fax: (415) 788-0966
Email: kentwoo@aol.com
Web: www.nicoschc.com

NORTH EAST MEDICAL SERVICES
1520 Stockton St.
San Francisco, CA 94133
Sophie Wong, President/CEO
Tel: (415) 391-9686 Fax: (415) 433-4726
Email: administration@nems.org
Web: www.nems.org

PACIFIC CLINICS
909 S. Fair Oaks Ave.
Pasadena, CA 91105
Ann Mary Stephenson, Divisional Director
Tel: (626) 795-8471
Email: amstephenson@pacificclinics.org
Web: www.pacificclinics.org

SOUTH ASIAN NETWORK
18173 S. Pioneer Blvd. #I
Artesia, CA 90701
Pradeepta Upadhyay, Director of Programs
Tel: (562) 403-0488 Fax: (562) 403-0487
Email: pradeepta@southasiannetwork.org
Web: www.southasiannetwork.org

SOUTH ASIAN PUBLIC HEALTH ASSOCIATION
P.O. Box 5823
Berkeley, CA 94705
Reena Antony, Board Member
Email: info@sapha.net
Web: www.sapha.net

THAI HEALTH AND INFORMATION SERVICES, INC.
1717 N. Gramercy Pl.
Hollywood, CA 90028
Tel: (323) 466-5966 Fax: (323) 466-9964
Email: info@thaihealth.org
Web: www.thaihealth.org

VIETNAMESE AMERICAN CANCER FOUNDATION
11770 Warner Ave. #113
Fountain Valley, CA 92708
Tel: (714) 751-5805
Email: info@vacf.org
Web: www.ungthu.org

VIETNAMESE COMMUNITY HEALTH PROMOTION
44 Page St. #500
San Francisco, CA 94102
Thoa Nguyen, Program Director
Tel: (415) 476-0557 Fax: (415) 431-7700
Email: thoa@itsa.ucsf.edu
Web: www.healthisgold.com

WRAP FAMILY SERVICES
Main Office

8616 La Tijera Blvd. #200
Los Angeles, CA 90045
Nancy Au, Executive Director
Tel: (310) 337-1550 Fax: (310) 337-2805
Email: info@wrapfs.org
Web: www.wrapfs.org

SPEC. INT., HOUSING

ASIAN NEIGHBORHOOD DESIGN
Downtown San Francisco
1182 Market St. #300
San Francisco, CA 94102
Harry Ja Wong, Principal Architect & Program Director
Tel: (415) 593-0423 Fax: (415) 593-0424
Email: info@andnet.org
Web: www.andnet.org

TENDERLOIN NEIGHBORHOOD DEVELOPMENT CORPORATION
201 Eddy St.
San Francisco, CA 94102
Kelly Cullen, Executive Director
Tel: (415) 776-2151 Fax: (415) 776-3952
Email: info@tndc.org
Web: www.tndc.org

SPEC. INT., HUMAN RELATIONS

AFGHANISTAN RELIEF ORGANIZATION
P.O. Box 10207
Canoga Park, CA 91304
Abdul Satar
Tel: (818) 727-0430 Fax: (818)709-7011
Email: info@afghanrelief.com
Web: www.afghanrelief.com

ALLIANCE FOR PRESERVING THE TRUTH OF SINO-JAPANESE WAR
P.O. Box 2066
Cupertino, CA 950152066
Tel: (415) 398-7758
Email: info@sjwar.org
Web: www.sjwar.org

AMERICAN INDIA FOUNDATION
West Coast Office
647 E. Calaveras Blvd.
Milpitas, CA 95035
Lata Krishnan, President
Tel: (408) 934-1600 Fax: (408) 934-1612
Email: sujatha.alluri@aifoundation.org
Web: www.aifoundation.org

AMERICAN JEWISH WORLD SERVICE
Bay Area Office
388 Market St. #400
San Francisco, CA 94111
Elizabeth Friedman Branoff, Director
Tel: (415) 296-2533 Fax: (415) 296-2525
Email: ebranoff@ajws.org
Web: www.ajws.org

AMERICAN RED MAGEN DAVID FOR ISRAEL
Western Region
6345 Balboa Blvd. #112
Encino, CA 91316
Ellen Rofman, Director
Tel: (800) 323-2371 Fax: (818) 776-9005
Email: erofman@armdi.org
Web: www.armdi.org

ARMENIA FUND, INC.
111 N. Jackson St. #205
Glendale, CA 91206
Tel: (818) 243-6222 Fax: (818) 243-7222
Web: www.armeniafund.org

ARMENIA GUIDE FUND
1146 N. Central Ave.
Glendale, CA 91202-2502
Email: info@AGFweb.org
Web: www.agfweb.org

ASIA SOCIETY
505 S. Flower St., Level C

Los Angeles, CA 90071
Carie Cable, Executive Director
Tel: (213) 624-0945 Fax: (213) 624-0158
Email: aslastaff@asiasoc.org
Web: www.asiasociety.org

Northern California Chapter
500 Washington St. #350
San Francisco, CA 94111
Vishakha N. Desai, President
Tel: (415) 421-8707 Fax: (415) 421-2465
Email: sanfrancisco@asiasoc.org
Web: www.asiasociety.org/sanfrancisco

ASIAN AMERICANS FOR COMMUNITY INVOLVEMENT
Main Center
2400 Moorpark Ave. #300
San Jose, CA 95128
Josephine S. Hawkins, President/CEO
Tel: (408) 975-2730 Fax: (408) 975-2745
Email: info@aaci.org
Web: www.aaci.org

ASIAN AMERICANS/PACIFIC ISLANDERS IN PHILANTHROPY
National Office
88 Kearny St. #1850
San Francisco, CA 94108
Cristina Regalado, Chair
Tel: (415) 273-2760 Fax: (415) 273-2765
Email: aapip@aapip.org
Web: www.aapip.org

ASIAN, INC.
Headquarters
1670 Pine St.
San Francisco, CA 94109-4525
Michael Chan, President
Tel: (415) 928-5910 Fax: (415) 921-0182
Email: info@asianinc.org
Web: www.asianinc.org

Oakland Office
211 10th St. #300
Oakland, CA 94607-4431
Michael Chan, President
Tel: (510) 839-3991 Fax: (510) 839-3913
Email: info@asianinc.org
Web: www.asianinc.org

South California Office, Los Angeles
4605 Lankershim Blvd. #418
North Hollywood, CA 91602
Michael Chan, President
Tel: (800) 869-7385 Fax: (818) 623-9799
Email: info@asianinc.org
Web: www.asianinc.org

ASIAN PACIFIC AMERICAN COALITION
1615 Edgewood Dr.
Palo Alto, CA 94303
Allan Seid, National President
Tel: (650) 327-9181 Fax: (408) 277-1030

ASIAN PACIFIC AMERICAN DISPUTE RESOLUTION CENTER
1145 Wilshire Blvd. #100
Los Angeles, CA 90017
Shirlie-Mae P. Mamaril, Executive Director
Tel: (213) 250-8190 Fax: (213) 250-8195
Email: info@apadrc.org
Web: www.apadrc.org

ASIAN & PACIFIC ISLANDER INSTITUTE ON DOMESTIC VIOLENCE
Asian & Pacific Islander American Health Forum
450 Sutter St. #600
San Francisco, CA 94108
Firoza Chic Dabby, Director
Tel: (415) 954-9988 Fax: (415) 954-9999
Email: apidvinstitute@apiah.org
Web: www.apiahf.org/apidvinstitute/default.htm

ASSOCIATION OF KOREAN ADOPTEES OF SAN FRANCISCO
P.O. Box 926
San Francisco, CA 94122-2200
Julie H. Baron, Member
Email: akasf@excite.com
Web: www.geocities.com/tokyo/garden/3947

ASSOCIATION OF TURKISH AMERICANS OF SOUTHERN CALIFORNIA, SAN DIEGO
P.O. Box 12692
La Jolla, CA 92039
Tug S. Engul, President
Tel: (858) 349-2609
Email: sdturks@sdturks.org
Web: www.sdturks.org

BAY AREA FRIENDS OF TIBET
2288 Fulton St. #312
Berkeley, CA 94704
Giovanni Vassallo, President
Tel: (510) 548-1271 Fax: (510) 548-3785
Email: bafot@friends-of-tibet.org
Web: www.friends-of-tibet.org

BLACK MOON
P.O. Box 5751
Sherman Oaks, CA 91403
Mark Vallen, Founder
Email: blackmoon@theblackmoon.com
Web: www.theblackmoon.com

CAMBODIAN COMMUNITY DEVELOPMENT, INC.
1900 Fruitvale Ave. #3B
Oakland, CA 94601
Lucy Dul, Executive Director
Tel: (510) 535-6120 Fax: (510) 532-5839
Email: ccdi@ccdi.org
Web: www.ccdi.org

CAMBODIAN ETHNIC CHINESE ASSOCIATION
676 N. Spring St.
Los Angeles, CA 90012
Tel: (213) 628-8298

CAMBODIAN HUMANITARIAN ORGANIZATION FOR PEACE ON EARTH
P.O. Box 17621
Long Beach, CA 90807
Email: c-hope@c-hope.org
Web: www.c-hope.org

CHINA CONNECTION
458 S. Pasadena Ave.
Pasadena, CA 91105
Kathy Call
Tel: (626) 793-3737 Fax: (818) 793-3362

CHINESE PROGRESSIVE ASSOCIATION
1042 Grant Ave., 5th Fl.
San Francisco, CA 94133
Gordon Mar, Executive Director
Tel: (415) 391-6986 Fax: (415) 391-6987
Email: justice@cpasf.org

COUNCIL OF PHILIPPINE AMERICAN ORGANIZATIONS OF SAN DIEGO COUNTY, INC.
P.O. Box 1504
National City, CA 91951
Aurora S. Cudal, President
Tel: (619) 477-4090 Fax: (619) 477-6052
Email: ascudal_1@juno.com
Web: www.copao.org

COUNCIL ON AMERICAN-ISLAMIC RELATIONS
Central Coast Chapter
777 Camino Pescadero #6
Goleta, CA 93117
Tel: (805) 685-4042
Email: cair@cair-net.org
Web: www.cair-net.org

Northern California Chapter
3000 Scott Blvd. #212
Santa Clara, CA 95054

Safaa Ibrahim, Executive Director
Email: nocal@cair.com
Web: www.cair-net.org

Southern California Chapter
2180 W. Crescent Ave. #F
Anaheim, CA 92801
Hussam Ayloush, Executive Director
Tel: (714) 776-1847 Fax: (714) 776-8340
Email: socal@cair.com
Web: www.cair-california.org

EAST BAY ASIAN LOCAL DEVELOPMENT CORPORATION
310 8th St. #200
Oakland, CA 94607
Lynette Jung Lee, Executive Director
Tel: (510) 287-5353 Fax: (510) 763-4143
Email: info@ebaldc.com
Web: www.ebaldc.com

FAMILY VIOLENCE PREVENTION FUND
383 Rhode Island St. #304
San Francisco, CA 94103-5133
Esta Soler, President
Tel: (415) 252-8900 Fax: (415) 252-8991
Email: info@endabuse.org
Web: www.endabuse.org

FILIPINO AMERICAN DEVELOPMENT FOUNDATION
953 Mission St. #30
San Francisco, CA 94103
Bernadette Borja Sy, Executive Director
Tel: (415) 348-8042 Fax: (415) 974-0349
Email: info@bayanihancc.org
Web: www.bayanihancc.org

FILIPINO CIVIL RIGHTS ADVOCATES
310 8th St. #308
Oakland, CA 94607
Lillian Galedo, Chair
Tel: (510) 465-9876 Fax: (510) 465-7548

FILIPINO-AMERICAN SERVICE GROUP INC.
135 N. Park View St.
Los Angeles, CA 90026
Susan Espiritu-Dilkes, Executive Director
Tel: (213) 487-9804 Fax: (213) 487-9806
Email: fasgi@fasgi.org
Web: www.fasgi.org

FORMOSA FOUNDATION
350 S. Figueroa St. #505
Los Angeles, CA 90071
Tel: (213) 625-1991 Fax: (213) 625-1941
Email: formosa@formosafoundation.org
Web: http://formosafoundation.org/

FRESNO CENTER FOR NEW AMERICANS
4879 E. Kings Canyon Rd.
Fresno, CA 93827
Lue N. Yang, Executive Director
Tel: (559) 255-8395 Fax: (559) 255-1656
Email: info@fresnocenter.com
Web: www.fresnocenter.com

FRIENDS OF SOUTH ASIA
3375 Homestead Rd. #61
Santa Clara, CA 95051
Tel: (408) 244-6797 Fax: (408) 249-5169
Email: fosa@ektaonline.org
Web: www.friendsofsouthasia.org

INDIA DEVELOPMENT AND RELIEF FUND
California Chapter
4433 Othello Dr.
Fremont, CA 94555
Tel: (510) 797-5601
Email: sandt@wile.thetech.org
Web: www.indolink.com/Orgs/idrfHome.html#BeginIDRF

INDIA DEVELOPMENT SERVICE
1920 S. Highland Ave. #300
Lombard, CA 60148
Roli Prasad, President
Tel: (630) 495-4200
Email: roli@uic.edu
Web: www.he.net/~ids/

INTERNATIONAL DEVELOPMENT EXCHANGE
827 Valencia St. #101
San Francisco, CA 94110-1736
Pete Stanga, Executive Director
Tel: (415) 824-8384 Fax: (415) 824-8387
Email: info@idex.org
Web: www.idex.org

ISRAELI HUMANITARIAN FOUNDATION
Southeast Region Office
11400 W. Olympic Blvd., 2nd Fl.
Los Angeles, CA 90064
Shelly Levy, Executive Director
Tel: (310) 445-8801 Fax: (310) 445-8813
Email: shelly@ihf.net
Web: www.ihf.net

JAPANESE AMERICAN CITIZENS LEAGUE
Berkeley Chapter
P.O. Box 7609
Berkeley, CA 94707-0609
James Duff, Jr., President
Email: berkeley@jacl.org
Web: www.berkeleyjacl.org

Diablo Valley Chapter
P.O. Box 5386
Walnut Creek, CA 94596
Milo Yoshino
Email: miloyoshi@aol.com
Web: www.dvjacl.org

National Headquarters
1765 Sutter St.
San Francisco, CA 94115
John Tateishi, Executive Director
Tel: (415) 921-5225
Email: jacl@jacl.org
Web: www.jacl.org

Northern California-Western Nevada-Pacific District Office
1255 Post St. #727
San Francisco, CA 94109
Patty Wada, Regional Director
Tel: (415) 345-1075 Fax: (415) 345-1077
Email: jacl-ncwnpro@email.msn.com
Web: www.jacl.org

Pacific Southwest District Office
244 S. San Pedro St. #406
Los Angeles, CA 90012
Tel: (213) 626-4471 Fax: (213) 626-4282
Email: psw@jacl.org
Web: www.jacl.org

JEWISH COMMUNITY RELATIONS COUNCIL OF SAN FRANCISCO, THE PENINSULA, MARIN, SONOMA, ALMEDA AND CONTRA COSTA COUNTIES
East Bay Office
300 Grand Ave.
Oakland, CA 94610-4826
Dana Sheanin, Regional Director
Tel: (510) 839-2900 X211 Fax: (510) 839-3996
Email: dana@jfed.org
Web: www.jcrc.org

Main Office
121 Steuart St. #301
San Francisco, CA 94105
Douglas Kahn, Executive Director
Tel: (415) 957-1551 Fax: (415) 979-0981
Email: info@jcrc.org
Web: www.jcrc.org

Marin/Sonoma Office
200 N. San Pedro Rd.
San Rafael, CA 94903
Judy Penso, Regional Director
Tel: (415) 472-5128 Fax: (415) 499-0308
Email: jpenso@jcrc.org
Web: www.jcrc.org

Peninsula Office

5150 El Camino Real #D-15
Los Altos, CA 94022
Karen Stiller, Regional Director
Tel: (6) 961-1922 Fax: (650) 961-1909
Email: dana@jfed.org
Web: www.jcrc.org

JEWISH RECONSTRUCTIONIST FEDERATION
West Coast Region
5870 W. Olympic Blvd.
Los Angeles, CA 90036
Devorah Servi, Regional Director
Tel: (323) 933-7491 Fax: (323) 933-7498
Email: westcoast@jrf.org
Web: www.jrf.org

JHAI FOUNDATION
921 France Ave.
San Francisco, CA 94112
Lee Thorn, Chair
Tel: (415) 344-0360
Email: lee@jhai.org
Web: www.jhai.org

KATIPUNAN-USA
P.O. Box 8701
Fountain Valley, CA 92708
Ernie Delfin, Founder
Tel: (714) 839-2615
Email: info@katipunan-usa.org
Web: www.katipunan-usa.org

KOREA SOLIDARITY COMMITTEE
P.O. Box 3936
Oakland, CA 94609-9991
Email: info@koreasolidarity.org
Web: www.koreasolidarity.org

KOREAN RESOURCE CENTER
900 S. Crenshaw Blvd.
Los Angeles, CA 90019
Dae Yoon, Executive Director
Tel: (323) 937-3718 Fax: (323) 937-3526
Email: krcla@krcla.org
Web: www.krcla.org

KOREAN-AMERICAN COMMUNITY SERVICES, INC.
1800-B Fruitdale Ave.
San José, CA 95128
Young Shim, Executive Director
Tel: (408) 920-9733 Fax: (408) 920-9726
Email: yshim@kacs1.org
Web: www.kacs1.org

LAO FAMILY COMMUNITY DEVELOPMENT, INC.
1551 23rd Ave.
Oakland, CA 94606-5018
Choasarn Chao, Executive Director
Tel: (510) 533-8850 Fax: (510) 533-1516
Email: choasarnchao@laofamilynet.org

LAO FAMILY COMMUNITY OF FRESNO, INC.
4903 E. Kings Canyon Rd. #281
Fresno, CA 93727
Pao Ly, Project Coordinator
Tel: (559) 453-9775 Fax: (559) 453-9705
Email: info@laofamilyfresno.org
Web: www.laofamilyfresno.org

LAO FAMILY COMMUNITY OF STOCKTON, INC.
807 N. San Joaquin St. #211
Stockton, CA 95202
Pheng Lo, Executive Director
Tel: (209) 466-0721 Fax: (209) 466-6567
Email: plo@laofamilyofstockton.org
Web: www.laofamilyofstockton.org

LAO VETERANS OF AMERICA, INC.
1945 N. Fine Ave. #102
Fresno, CA 93727
LtCol Thai C. Vang, President
Tel: (559) 252-3921 Fax: (559) 252-3901
Email: office@laoveterans.com
Web: www.laoveterans.com

LAOTIAN ORGANIZING PROJECT
220 25th St.
Richmond, CA 94804
Torm Nompraseurp, Lead Organizer
Tel: (510) 236-4616 Fax: (510) 236-4572
Email: torm@apen4ej.org
Web: www.apen4ej.org/organize_lop.htm

MAZON: A JEWISH RESPONSE TO HUNGER
National Office
1990 S. Bundy Dr. #260
Los Angeles, CA 90025-5232
H. Eric Schockman, Executive Director
Tel: (310) 442-0020 Fax: (310) 442-0030
Email: mazonmail@mazon.org
Web: www.mazon.org

MEDIA ACTION NETWORK FOR ASIAN AMERICANS
P.O. Box 11105
Burbank, CA 91510
Jen Kuo, President
Tel: (213) 486-4433
Email: manaaletters@yahoo.com
Web: www.manaa.org

MERCED LAO FAMILY COMMUNITY, INC.
855 W. 15th St.
Merced, CA 95340-5822
Paul G. Yang, President
Tel: (209) 384-7384 Fax: (209) 384-1911
Email: mlcf@laofamilymerced.com
Web: www.laofamilymerced.com

NATIONAL ASIAN PACIFIC AMERICAN FAMILIES AGAINST SUBSTANCE ABUSE, INC.
Southern California Office
340 E. 2nd St. #409
Los Angeles, CA 90012
Ford Kuramoto, National Director
Tel: (213) 625-5795 Fax: (213) 625-5796
Email: napafasa@napafasa.org
Web: www.napafasa.org

NAUTILUS INSTITUTE
125 University Ave.
Berkeley, CA 94710
Peter Hayes, Co-Founder/Executive Director
Tel: (510) 295-6100 Fax: (510) 295-6130
Email: nautilus@nautilus.org
Web: www.nautilus.org

NETWORK OF IRANIAN AMERICAN SOCIETY
14252 Culver Dr. #406
Irvine, CA 92604
Mojgan Anvari, President
Email: niasinfo@niasnet.org
Web: www.niasnet.org

NEW ISRAEL FUND
San Francisco Office
785 Market St., 14th Fl.
San Francisco, CA 94103
Peter Edelman, President
Tel: (415) 543-5055 Fax: (415) 543-6066
Email: sf@nif.org
Web: www.nif.org

PACIFIC ISLANDER COMMUNITY COUNCIL
P.O. Box 11247
Carson, CA 90749
Kawaiopua Alo, President
Tel: (714) 968-1785 Fax: (714) 968-1785
Email: kaiwipang@qnet.com

SAHARA
18520 1/2 S. Pioneer Blvd. #204
Artesia, CA 90701
Tazeem Bhindi, President
Tel: (562) 402-4132 Fax: (562) 402-6093
Email: sahara_2@hotmail.com
Web: www.charityfocus.org/sahara

SAHAYA INTERNATIONAL,INC.
Koen Van Rompay
2949 Portage Bay Ave. #195

Davis, CA 95616
Koen Van Rompay, Founder
Tel: (530) 756-9074
Email: kkvanrompay@ucdavis.edu
Web: www.sahaya.org

SAN DIEGO FRIENDS OF TIBET
3551 Front St.
San Diego, CA 92103
Dorothy Berger, Coordinator
Tel: (619) 682-7188
Email: dberger558@aol.com
Web: www.sdtibet.org

SIERRA FRIENDS OF TIBET
P.O. Box 1594
Nevada City, CA 95959
Joseph Guida
Tel: (530) 272-4725
Email: sfjcc@nccn.net
Web: www.sierrafriendsoftibet.org

SIMON WIESENTHAL CENTER
International Headquarters
1399 S. Roxbury Dr.
Los Angeles, CA 90035
Rabbi Marvin Hier, Dean/Founder
Tel: (800) 900-9036 Fax: (310) 553-4521
Email: information@wiesenthal.net
Web: www.wiesenthal.net

SPECIAL SERVICES FOR GROUPS
605 W. Olympic Blvd. #600
Los Angeles, CA 90015
Herbert Hatanaka, Executive Director
Tel: (213) 553-1800 Fax: (213) 553-1822
Email: ssg@ssgmain.org
Web: www.ssgmain.org

SWEATSHOP WATCH
310 8th St. #303
Oakland, CA 94607
Nikki Fortunato Bas, Executive Director
Tel: (510) 834-8990 Fax: (510) 834-8990
Email: sweatinfo@sweatshopwatch.org
Web: www.sweatshopwatch.org

THAI COMMUNITY DEVELOPMENT CENTER
6376 Yucca St. #B
Los Angeles, CA 90028
Chanchanit Martorell, M.A., Executive Director
Tel: (323) 468-2555 Fax: (323) 461-4488
Email: chancee@thaicdc.org
Web: www.thaicdc.org

THE AMERICAN JEWISH COMMITTEE
Los Angeles Chapter
9911 W. Pico Blvd. #1602
Los Angeles, CA 90035-2701
Rabbi Gary Greenebaum, Chapter Director
Tel: (310) 282-8080 Fax: (310) 282-8668
Email: losangeles@ajc.org
Web: www.ajc.org

Orange County California Chapter
2222 Martin St. #150
Irvine, CA 92612
Rabbi Marc S. Dworkin, Executive Director
Tel: (949) 660-8525 Fax: (949) 660-0570
Email: orangecounty@ajc.org
Web: www.ajc.org

San Diego Chapter
5095 Murphy Canyon Rd. #360
San Diego, CA 92123-4346
Sam Sokolove, Chapter Director
Tel: (858) 278-5943 Fax: (858) 278-5994
Email: sandiego@ajc.org
Web: www.ajcsandiego.org

San Francisco Chapter
121 Steuart St. #405
San Francisco, CA 94105
Ernest Weiner, Chapter Director
Tel: (415) 777-3820 Fax: (415) 777-1018
Email: sanfrancisco@ajc.org
Web: www.ajc.org

THE DUI HUA FOUNDATION
450 Sutter St. #900
San Francisco, CA 94108
John Kamm, Executive Director
Tel: (415) 986-0536 Fax: (415) 986-0579
Email: duihua@duihua.org
Web: www.duihua.org

THE SPIRAL FOUNDATION
211 Vance St.
Pacific Palisades, CA 90272
Marichia Simcik Arese, Director
Tel: (310) 459-6671 Fax: (310) 454-0414
Email: info@spiralfoundation.org
Web: http://spiralfoundation.org

TIBET JUSTICE CENTER
2288 Fulton St. #312
Berkeley, CA 94704
Minnie Cancellaro, Executive Director
Tel: (510) 486-0588 Fax: (510) 548-3785
Email: tibetjustice@tibetjustice.org
Web: www.tibetjustice.org

TIBETAN LIVING COMMUNITIES
1531 Estee Ave.
Napa, CA 94558
Email: tlc@TibetanLivingCommunities.org
Web: www.tibetanlivingcommunities.org

TIBETAN NUNS PROJECT
2288 Fulton St. #312
Berkeley, CA 94704
Rinchen Khando Choegyal, Director
Tel: (510) 647-3423
Email: tnpusa@igc.org
Web: www.tnp.org

UNION OF PAN ASIAN COMMUNITIES
1031 25th St.
San Diego, CA 92102
Lailani Frerickf, Executive Assistant
Tel: (619) 232-6454 Fax: (619) 235-9002
Email: reception@upacsd.com
Web: www.upacsd.com

VIETNAM HUMAN RIGHTS NETWORK
12522 Brookhurst St. #23
Garden Grove, CA 92840
Tel: (714) 636-8895
Email: vnhrnet@vietnamhumanrights.net
Web: www.vietnamhumanrights.net

VISION NEW AMERICA
514 Valley Way
Milpitas, CA 95305
Anna Wang, Executive Director
Tel: (408) 941-0888 Fax: (408) 941-0095
Email: info@visionnewamerica.org
Web: www.visionnewamerica.org

WORLD AFFAIRS COUNCIL OF NORTHERN CALIFORNIA
World Affairs Center
312 Sutter St. #200
San Francisco, CA 94108
Jane Wales, President/CEO
Tel: (415) 293-4600 Fax: (415) 982-5028
Email: wacpress@wacsf.org
Web: www.wacsf.org

SPEC. INT., IMMIGRATION

ASIAN IMMIGRATION SERVICE CENTER
1932 Mission St.
San Francisco, CA 94103
Edward Ma, President
Tel: (415) 552-0888 Fax: (415) 552-0887
Web:

BURMESE AMERICAN WOMEN'S ALLIANCE
56 Mayfield Ave.
Daly City, CA 94015
Jean Gale, President
Tel: (650) 756-5887 Fax: (650) 756-5887
Email: office@burmesewomen.org
Web: www.burmesewomen.org

CHINESE NEWCOMERS SERVICE CENTER
777 Stockton St. #104
San Francisco, CA 94108
Julia Ling, Executive Director
Tel: (415) 421-2111 Fax: (415) 421-2323
Email: cnsc@chinesenewcomers.org
Web: www.chinesenewcomers.org

FILIPINO COMMUNITY SUPPORT
525 W. Alma Ave.
San Jose, CA 95125
Jay Mendoza, Executive Director
Tel: (408) 297-1977 Fax: (408) 297-1978
Email: focus@focusnow.org
Web: www.focusnow.org

IMMIGRANT AND REFUGEE OFFICE
P.O. Box 15095
Los Angeles, CA 90015
Loc Nam Nguyen, Director
Tel: (213) 251-3489 Fax: (213) 251-3444
Email: lnguyen@ccharities.org

INDOCHINESE IMMIGRATION RESETTLEMENT CULTURAL CENTER
422 Park Ave.
San Jose, CA 95110
Vu Van Loc, Executive Director
Tel: (408) 971-7878 Fax: (408) 971-7882
Email: locvu@irccsj.com
Web: www.irccsj.com

KOREAN IMMIGRANT WORKERS ADVOCATES
3465 W. 8th St.
Los Angeles, CA 90005
Danny Park, Executive Director
Tel: (213) 738-9050 Fax: (213) 738-9919
Email: kiwa@kiwa.org
Web: www.kiwa.org

NATIONAL NETWORK FOR IMMIGRANT AND REFUGEE RIGHTS
310 8th St. #303
Oakland, CA 94607
Catherine Tactaquin, Executive Director
Tel: (510) 465-1984 Fax: (510) 465-1885
Email: nnirr@nnirr.org
Web: www.nnirr.org

VIETNAM MUTUAL ASSOCIATION
7621 Westminster Ave.
Westminster, CA 92683
Nguyen Van Long, President
Tel: (714) 894-3120 Fax: (714) 898-0677

SPEC. INT., INFORMATION REFERRAL

BERKELEY APEC STUDY CENTER
University of California
802 Barrows Hall #1970
Berkeley, CA 94720-1970
Vinod Aggarwal, Director
Tel: (510) 643-1071 Fax: (510) 643-1746
Email: basc@globetrotter.berkeley.edu
Web: http://globetrotter.berkeley.edu/basc/

CHINESE INFORMATION AND NETWORKING ASSOCIATION
4675 Stevens Creek Blvd. #101
Santa Clara, CA 95051
Vicki Young, President
Tel: (408) 504-7177
Email: vicki_young@pacbell.net
Web: www.cina.org

KOREAN AMERICAN ADOPTEE ADOPTIVE FAMILY NETWORK
P.O. Box 5585
El Dorado Hills, CA 95762
Chris Winston, President
Tel: (916) 933-1447
Email: kaanet@aol.com
Web: www.kaanet.com

KOREAN AMERICAN LIBRARIANS AND INFORMATION PROFESSIONALS ASSOCIATION
3112 Emerald Isle Dr.
Glendale, CA 91206
Youngsil Lee, President
Tel: (213) 228-7102
Email: ylee@lapl.org
Web: http://kalipa.apanet.org

SOUTH ASIAN HELPLINE AND REFERRAL AGENCY
18520 1/2 S. Pioneer Blvd. #204
Artesia, CA 90701
Tazeem Bhindi, President
Tel: (562) 402-4132 Fax: (562) 402-6093
Email: sahara_2@hotmail.com
Web: www.charityfocus.org/sahara

VIETNAMESE CHRISTIAN RESOURCE CENTER
678 Portola Dr.
San Francisco, CA 94127
Rev. Samuel Hien Ong, Pastor
Tel: (415) 731-9430
Email: contact@vcrc.org
Web: www.vcrc.org

SPEC. INT., LEGAL ASSISTANCE

ARMENIAN BAR ASSOCIATION
P.O. Box 29111
Los Angeles, CA 90029
Lisa Boyadjian, Administrative Assistant
Tel: (323) 666-6288
Email: info@armenianbar.org
Web: www.armenianbar.org

ASIAN AMERICAN LAWYER REFERRAL
3530 Wilshire Blvd. #1020
Los Angeles, CA 90010
Christine Lee, Executive Director
Tel: (213) 384-8072 Fax: (213) 384-3546
Email: aatims@hotmail.com

ASIAN DOMESTIC VIOLENCE CLINIC
1212 Broadway #400
Oakland, CA 94612
Dean Taylor, Director
Tel: (510) 251-2846 Fax: (510) 763-1490
Email: info@apilegaloutreach.org
Web: www.apilegaloutreach.org

ASIAN LAW ALLIANCE
184 E. Jackson St.
San Jose, CA 95112
Richard Konda, Executive Director
Tel: (408) 287-9710 Fax: (408) 287-0864
Email: sccala@pacbell.net
Web: www.asianlawalliance.org

ASIAN LAW CAUCUS
939 Market St. #201
San Francisco, CA 94103
Philip Y. Ting, Executive Director
Tel: (415) 896-1701 Fax: (415) 896-1702
Email: philting@asianlawcaucus.org
Web: www.asianlawcaucus.org

ASIAN PACIFIC AMERICAN LABOR ALLIANCE
Alameda County Chapter
1357 5th St.
Oakland, CA 94607
Nicole Lee, President
Tel: (510) 451-5466 x311
Email: nicolerosina@aol.com
Web: www.apalanet.org

ASIAN PACIFIC AMERICAN LEGAL CENTER OF SOUTHERN CALIFORNIA
1145 Wilshire Blvd., 2nd Fl.
Los Angeles, CA 90017
Stewart Kwoh, Esq., President/Executive Director
Tel: (213) 977-7500 Fax: (213) 977-7595
Email: skwoh@apalc.org
Web: www.apalc.org

ASIAN PACIFIC BAR ASSOCIATION OF THE SILICON VALLEY
2 N. 2nd St. #1400
San Jose, CA 95113
Jeffrey Li, President
Tel: (408) 286-2700 Fax: (408) 282-7088
Email: li_jk@pillsburylaw.com
Web: www.sccba.com/apba/welcome.htm

ASIAN PACIFIC BAR OF CALIFORNIA
Orange County District Attorney's Office
401 Civic Center Dr.
Santa Ana, CA 92701
Andrew Hoang Do, President
Tel: (714) 834-3600
Email: andrew.do@da.ocgov.com

ASIAN PACIFIC ISLANDER COUNCIL OF NORTHERN CALIFORNIA
2800 Cottage Way, M/C 150
Sacramento, CA 95825
Leila Horibata, Chair
Tel: (916) 978-5032 Fax: (916) 978-5055
Email: lhoribata@mp.usbr.gov

ASIAN PACIFIC ISLANDER LEGAL OUTREACH
1188 Franklin St. #202
San Francisco, CA 94109
Dean Ito Taylor, Director
Tel: (415) 567-6255 Fax: (415) 567-6248
Email: info@apilegaloutreach.org
Web: www.apilegaloutreach.org

JEWISH LABOR COMMITTEE
California Chapter
8339 W. 3rd St. #2
Los Angeles, CA 90048
Cookie Lommel, Regional Director
Tel: (323) 658-5500 Fax: (323) 658-5079
Email: JLCLA2@aol.com
Web: www.jewishlabor.org

SOUTHWEST CENTER FOR ASIAN PACIFIC AMERICAN LAW
3675 Ruffin Rd. #115
San Diego, CA 92123
Sally Lorang, Executive Director
Tel: (858) 571-9070 Fax: (858) 571-9071
Email: info@scapal.org
Web: www.scapal.org

VIET BAO KINH TE
4660 El Cajón Blvd. #105
San Diego, CA 92115
Nam Lee, Director
Tel: (619) 584-4137 Fax: (619) 584-8647

VIETNAMESE IMMIGRANTS MUTUAL ASSISTANCE ASSOCIATION
3435 Camino Del Rio S. #108
San Diego, CA 92108
Sinh Pham, CEO
Tel: (615) 521-0181
Email: info@vimaa.org
Web: www.vimaa.org

SPEC. INT., MENTAL HEALTH

ASIAN COMMUNITY MENTAL HEALTH SERVICES
310 8th St. #201
Oakland, CA 94607
Sharron Sue, Interim Executive Director
Tel: (510) 451-6729 Fax: (510) 268-0202
Email: sharrons@acmhs.org
Web: www.acmhs.org

ASIAN PACIFIC COUNSELING & TREATMENT CENTER
San Fernando Valley Center
5900 Sepulveda Blvd. #425
Van Nuys, CA 91411
Dr. Chong Suh, Director
Tel: (818) 267-1114 Fax: (818) 267-1199
Web: www.apctc.org

Cerritos Center
11050 E. Artesia Blvd. #E
Cerritos, CA 90703
Soonja Lee, Supervisor
Tel: (562) 860-8838 Fax: (562) 860-0248
Email: cerritos@apctc.org
Web: www.apctc.org

Main Office
520 S. Lafayette Park Pl., 3rd Fl.
Los Angeles, CA 90057
Chong Suh, Director
Tel: (213) 252-2100 Fax: (213) 252-2199
Web: www.apctc.org

Long Beach Office
1040 E. Wardlow Rd.
Long Beach, CA 90807
Jatu Marino, Supervisor
Tel: (562) 988-8822 Fax: (562) 988-8877
Web: www.apctc.org

Metro Center/Indochinese Program
605 W. Olympic Blvd. #350
Los Angeles, CA 90015
Wendy Nguyen, Receptionist
Tel: (213) 553-1850 Fax: (213) 553-1864
Email: metro@apctc.org
Web: www.apctc.org

ASIAN PACIFIC MENTAL HEALTH
1975 Long Beach Blvd.
Long Beach, CA 90806
Tom Lawson, Director
Tel: (562) 599-9401 Fax: (562) 218-0402

ASIAN PACIFIC PSYCHOLOGICAL SERVICES
431 30th St. #6-A
Oakland, CA 94609
Vinita Lee, Program Manager
Tel: (510) 835-2777 Fax: (510) 835-0164
Email: vlee@appsweb.org
Web: www.appsweb.org

COASTAL ASIAN PACIFIC MENTAL HEALTH SERVICES
14112 S. Kingsley Dr.
Gardena, CA 90249
Mitauiu Kubota, Director
Tel: (310) 217-7312 Fax: (310) 352-3111

NATIONAL RESEARCH CENTER ON ASIAN AMERICAN MENTAL HEALTH
University of California, Department of Psychology
1 Shields Ave.
Davis, CA 95616-8686
Dr. Nolan Zane, Director
Tel: (530) 752-5419 Fax: (530) 752-5419
Email: nwzane@ucdavis.edu
Web: http://psychology.ucdavis.edu/nrcaamh

AGING INFORMATION CENTER
Region IX: AS, AZ, CA, CNMI, GU, HI, NV
50 United Nations Plz. #455
San Francisco, CA 94102
David Ishida, Regional Administrator
Tel: (415) 437-8780 Fax: (415) 437-8782
Email: David.Ishida@aoa.gov
Web: www.aoa.dhhs.gov

ASIAN AMERICAN SENIOR CITIZENS SERVICE CENTER
309 W. Civic Center Dr.
Santa Ana, CA 92701
Donna Lin, Executive Director
Tel: (714) 560-8877 Fax: (714) 836-8188
Email: info@aascsc.org
Web: www.aascsc.org

ASIAN AND PACIFIC COALITION ON AGING
1543 W. Olympic Blvd. #200-A1
Los Angeles, CA 90005
John Kim, Director
Tel: (213) 365-6252 Fax: (213) 365-6259

CAMBODIAN RECONCILIATION COMMITTEE
P.O. Box 1682
Fresno, CA 93717
Sopheaktra Nou, Founder/Executive Director
Tel: (559) 255-9241
Email: crcfresno@yahoo.com
Web: http://crc_1.tripod.com

FAMILY BRIDGES,INC.
168 11th St.
Oakland, CA 94607
Corinne Jan, Director
Tel: (510) 839-2022 Fax: (510) 839-2435
Email: info@fambridges.org
Web: www.fambridges.org

FILIPINO AMERICAN SENIOR CITIZENS ASSOCIATION
8460 Mira Mesa Blvd.
San Diego, CA 92126-2311
Antonio Bacala, President
Tel: (858) 271-9385

FORMOSA SENIORS ASSOCIATION
9746 Piazza Ct.
Cypress, CA 90630
Tom Laow, President
Tel: (714) 229-8168 Fax: (714) 229-8168

HAPPY SENIOR CITIZENS
19402 Moorshire Dr.
Cerritos, CA 90703
Pete Inserto, President
Tel: (562) 865-4933

IRANIAN JEWISH SENIOR CENTER
1019 S. Wooster St.
Los Angeles, CA 90035
Lida Zarafshan, Contact
Tel: (310) 470-1065

JAPANESE AMERICAN RELIGIOUS FEDERATION ASSISTED LIVING FACILITY, INC.
1881 Bush St.
San Francisco, CA 94109
Steve Suzuki, President
Tel: (415) 674-4276
Web: www.kokoroassistedliving.org

JAPANESE AMERICAN SERVICE OF THE EAST BAY
2126 Channing Way
Berkeley, CA 94704
Laura Takeuchi, Executive Director
Tel: (510) 848-3560 Fax: (510) 848-3631
Email: jaseb@igc.org
Web: www.jaseb.org

JEWISH HOME SAN FRANCISCO
302 Silver Ave.
San Francisco, CA 94112
Daniel Ruth, CEO
Tel: (415) 334-2500 Fax: (415) 334-4375
Email: druth@jhsf.org
Web: www.jhsf.org

KEIRO SENIOR HEALTH CARE
325 S. Boyle Ave.
Los Angeles, CA 90033
Shawn Miyake, President/CEO
Tel: (323) 980-7555 Fax: (323) 263-2163
Email: contact@keiro.org
Web: www.keiro.org

KIMOCHI, INC.
1715 Buchanan St.
San Francisco, CA 94115
Steve Nakajo, Executive Director
Tel: (415) 931-2294 Fax: (415) 931-2299
Email: kimochikai@kimochi-inc.org
Web: www.kimochi-inc.org

KOREAN AMERICAN SENIOR CITIZENS
1661 W. San Carlos St. #B
San Jose, CA 95128
Heui S. Chi, President
Tel: (408) 247-0605 Fax: (408) 288-9630
Email: jhsc@yahoo.com

ON LOK SENIOR HEALTH SERVICES
1333 Bush St.
San Francisco, CA 94109-5611
Jennie Chin-Hansen, Executive Director
Tel: (415) 989-2578 Fax: (415) 292-8745
Email: info@onlok.org
Web: www.onlok.org

SELF-HELP FOR THE ELDERLY
Main Office
407 Sansome St.
San Francisco, CA 94111-3122
Antonia Tu, Secretary
Tel: (415) 982-9171 Fax: (415) 296-0313
Email: she@selfhelpelderly.org
Web: www.selfhelpelderly.org

YU-AI KAI JAPANESE AMERICAN COMMUNITY SENIOR SERVICE
588 N. 4th St.
San Jose, CA 95112
Wesley Mukoyama, Executive Director
Tel: (408) 294-2505 Fax: (408) 294-0343
Email: staff@yuaikai.org
Web: www.yuaikai.org

SPEC. INT., SOCIAL INTEREST

AFGHAN ACADEMY OF HOPE
6396 Hollister Ave. #155
Goleta, CA 93117
Diana Haskins, Co-Founder/President
Tel: (805) 685-8634
Email: Dihaskins@aol.com
Web: www.aaoh.org

AFGHAN COALITION
39155 Liberty St. #D-400
Fremont, CA 94538
Tel: (510) 574-2184 Fax: (510) 574-2185
Email: afghancoal@aol.com
Web: www.afghancoalition.org

AFGHAN REFUGEE ISLAMIC COMMUNITY OF THE BAY AREA
29414 Mission Blvd.
Hayward, CA 94544
Tel: (510) 582-2730

AFGHANS FOR AFGHANS
P.O. Box 475843
San Francisco, CA 94147-5843
Ann Rubin
Email: afghans4Afghans@aol.com
Web: www.afghansforAfghans.org

ALBERT L. SCHULTZ JEWISH COMMUNITY CENTER
4000 Middlefield Rd.
Palo Alto, CA 94303
Tel: (650) 493-9400 Fax: (650) 493-1187
Email: info@paloaltojcc.org
Web: www.paloaltojcc.org

ASIAN AMERICAN RECOVERY SERVICES, INC.
Asian American Residential Recovery Services
2024 Hayes St.
San Francisco, CA 94117
Susan Okada, Program Manager
Tel: (415) 750-5111 Fax: (415) 386-2048
Email: info-aars@aars-inc.org
Web: www.aars-inc.org

San Francisco Central Office
965 Mission St. #325
San Francisco, CA 94103
Jeff Mori, Executive Director
Tel: (415) 541-9285 Fax: (415) 541-9986
Email: jmori@aars-inc.org
Web: www.aars-inc.org

ASIAN AMERICANS FOR COMMUNITY OUTREACH
P.O. Box 61384
Sunnyvale, CA 94088

Billy Lu, President
Email: info@aaco-sf.org
Web: www.aaco-sf.org

ASIAN COMMUNITY CENTER
7375 Park City Dr.
Sacramento, CA 95831
Donna L. Yee, Executive Director
Tel: (916) 393-9026 Fax: (916) 393-9128
Email: info@accsv.org
Web: www.accsv.org

ASIAN COMMUNITY SERVICE CENTER
14112 S. Kingsley Dr.
Gardena, CA 90249
Stephen Yong, Center Director
Tel: (310) 217-7300 Fax: (310) 516-9226
Web: http://dcss.co.la.ca.us/srvc/asiantxt.htm

ASIAN FAMILY INSTITUTE
4020 Balboa St.
San Francisco, CA 94121
Dr. Eddie Chiu, Director
Tel: (415) 668-5998 Fax: (415) 668-5996

ASIAN PACIFIC ENVIRONMENTAL NETWORK
Main Office
310 8th St. #309
Oakland, CA 94607
Vivian Chang, Interim Executive Director
Tel: (510) 834-8920 Fax: (510) 834-8926
Email: apen@apen4ej.org
Web: www.apen4ej.org

ASIAN PACIFIC FUND
225 Bush St. #590
San Francisco, CA 94104
Gail M. Kong, Executive Director/President
Tel: (415) 433-6859 Fax: (415) 433-2425
Email: info@asianpacificfund.org
Web: www.asianpacificfund.org

ASIAN PACIFIC ISLANDER SOCIAL WORK COUNCIL
P.O. Box 146
San Francisco, CA 94108
Janice Wong, Co-Coordinator
Tel: (415) 386-7128
Email: cmcwong@pacbell.net

ASIAN PACIFIC PARTNERS FOR EMPOWERMENT, ADVOCACY AND LEADERSHIP
300 Frank H. Ogawa Plz. #620
Oakland, CA 94612
Rod Lew, Executive Director
Tel: (510) 272-9536 Fax: (510) 272-0817
Email: appeal@aapcho.org
Web: www.appealforcommunities.org

ASIAN PACIFIC POLICY AND PLANNING COUNCIL
3727 W. 6th St. #405
Los Angeles, CA 90020
Jury Candelario, President
Tel: (213) 388-2834 Fax: (213) 388-3452
Email: info@a3pcon.org
Web: www.a3pcon.org

ASIAN PERINATAL ADVOCATES
1001 Potrero Ave., MS6E
San Francisco, CA 94110
Mai Mai Ho, Executive Director
Tel: (415) 206-5450 Fax: (415) 206-4778
Email: apa@apasfgh.org
Web: www.apasfgh.org

ASIAN REHABILITATION SERVICES
1701 E. Washington Blvd.
Los Angeles, CA 90021
Tom Chung, Executive Director
Tel: (213) 743-9242 Fax: (213) 743-9266
Web: www.asianrehab.org

ASIAN RESOURCES CENTER
5709 Stockton Blvd.
Sacramento, CA 95824
May Lee, Director

Tel: (916) 454-1892 Fax: (916) 454-1895
Email: mlee@delpaso.seta.net
Web: www.asianresources.org

ASSOCIATION OF TURKISH AMERICANS OF SOUTHERN CALIFORNIA
444 W. Ocean Blvd., 8th Fl.
Long Beach, CA 90802
John Cihangir Safyurtlu, President
Tel: (562) 624-2885 Fax: (562) 624-2881
Email: President@execom.atasc.org
Web: www.atasc.org

BAY AREA BANGLADESH ASSOCIATION
P.O. Box 641118
San Jose, CA 95164-1118
Jahangir Dewan, President
Email: baba@baba1.com
Web: www.baba1.com

BAY AREA WOMEN'S AND CHILDREN CENTER
318 Leavenworth St.
San Francisco, CA 94102
Midge Wilson, Executive Director
Tel: (415) 474-2400 Fax: (415) 474-5525
Web: www.bawcc.org

BERKELEY RICHMOND JEWISH COMMUNITY CENTER
1414 Walnut St.
Berkeley, CA 94709
Tel: (510) 848-0237 Fax: (510) 848-0170
Email: info@brjcc.org
Web: www.brjcc.org

BINALONAN ASSOCIATION OF NORTHERN CALIFORNIA
2 Cirrus Ct.
Redwood City, CA 94062
Nelly Reyes, President
Email: info@binalonians.com
Web: www.binalonians.com

CAMBODIAN ASSOCIATION OF AMERICA
2390 Pacific Ave.
Long Beach, CA 90806-2708
Him S. Chhim, Executive Director
Tel: (562) 988-1863 Fax: (562) 988-1475
Email: caa@cambodian.com

CAMBODIAN EDUCATIONAL NETWORK
3774 Castro Valley Blvd.
Castro Valley, CA 94546
Mr. Khoeum Sok
Tel: (510) 881-5977
Email: shoeumsok@excite.com
Web: www.efn.org/~bhavia

CAMERON HOUSE
920 Sacramento St.
San Francisco, CA 94108
Greg Chan, President
Tel: (415) 781-0401 Fax: (415) 781-0605
Email: cameronhouse@cameronhouse.org
Web: www.cameronhouse.org

CENTER FOR THE PACIFIC ASIAN FAMILY
543 N. Fairfax Ave. #108
Los Angeles, CA 90036
Debra Suh, Director
Tel: (323) 653-4045 Fax: (323) 653-7913
Email: contact@cpaf.info
Web: www.cpaf.info

CHAMORRO COMMUNITY COUNCIL
P.O. Box 11108
Carson, CA 90746
Mary Salas, President
Tel: (310) 830-1273 Fax: (213) 365-9042
Email: mtsalas@pacbell.net

CHARITY CULTURAL SERVICES CENTER
827 Stockton St.
San Francisco, CA 94108
Harrison B. Lim, Executive Director
Tel: (415) 989-8224 Fax: (415) 391-0525
Email: charitycultural@yahoo.com
Web: www.charitycultural.org

CHINATOWN ALLEYWAY IMPROVEMENT ASSOCIATION
Chinatown Community Development Center
1525 Grant Ave.
San Francisco, CA 94133-3323
Cathie Lam, Senior Community Organizer
Tel: (415) 984-1461 Fax: (415) 362-7992
Email: clam@chinatowncdc.org
Web: www.chinatowncdc.org

CHINATOWN COMMUNITY DEVELOPMENT CENTER
1525 Grant Ave.
San Francisco, CA 94133
Gordon Chin, Executive Director
Tel: (415) 984-1450 Fax: (415) 362-7992
Email: info@chinatowncdc.org
Web: www.chinatowncdc.org

CHINATOWN TEEN POST
600 N. Broadway #D
Los Angeles, CA 90012
Don Toy, Executive Director
Tel: (213) 680-0876 Fax: (213) 680-0863
Email: teenpost@pacbell.net

CHINESE AMERICAN ASSOCIATION OF SOUTHERN CALIFORNIA
12830 Arabella St.
Cerritos, CA 90703
Richard Yu, President
Tel: (562) 940-2097 Fax: (562) 402-5621
Email: ryu@isd.co.la.ca.us

CHINESE AMERICAN CITIZENS ALLIANCE
National Headquarters
1044 Stockton St.
San Francisco, CA 94108
Saykin Foo, president
Tel: (415) 434-2222 Fax: (415) 982-3728
Email: cacasf@yahoo.com
Web: www.cacanational.org

CHINESE AMERICAN VOTERS EDUCATION COMMITTEE
838 Grant Ave.
San Francisco, CA 94108
David Lee, Executive Director
Tel: (415) 397-8133 Fax: (415) 397-8153
Email: cavec1@aol.com
Web: www.ncmonline.com

CHINESE BAPTIST CHURCH OF CENTRAL ORANGE
12012 Yale Ct.
Irvine, CA 92620
Darryl Fong, Assistant English Pastor
Tel: (714) 699-1700 Fax:

CHINESE FRIENDSHIP ASSOCIATION
3876 50th St.
San Diego, CA 92105
Chou Janchyi, President
Tel: (619) 528-0765 Fax: (619) 528-9058

CHINESE OUTREACH
P.O. Box 1763
Arcadia, CA 91077
Peter Tsou, Executive Director
Tel: (626) 254-1551 Fax: (626) 254-1527
Web: www.co.org

COALITION TO ABOLISH SLAVERY AND TRAFFICKING
5042 Wilshire Blvd. #586
Los Angeles, CA 90036
Dr. Kathryn McMahon, Co-President
Tel: (213) 365-1906 Fax: (213) 365-5257
Email: info@castla.org
Web: www.castla.org

DUDJOM INTERNATIONAL FOUNDATION
P.O. Box 40155
Berkeley, CA 94704-0155
Tel: (510) 215-8989
Email: dudjominternational@msn.com
Web: www.dudjominternational.org

EAST MEETS WEST
P.O. Box 29292
Oakland, CA 94604
Peter A. Singer, M.D., President
Tel: (510) 763-7045 Fax: (510) 763-6545
Email: info@eastmeetswest.org
Web: www.eastmeetswest.org

EAST SAN GABRIEL VALLEY JAPANESE COMMUNITY CENTER
1203 W. Puente Ave.
West Covina, CA 91790
Hiroko Takemoto, Operations Manager
Tel: (626) 960-2566 Fax: (626) 960-0866
Email: esgvjcc@yahoo.com
Web: www.nikkeifederation.org

FEDERATION OF FILIPINO AMERICAN ASSOCIATIONS, INC.
2125 Santa Fe Ave.
Long Beach, CA
Leo P. Pandac, President
Tel: (562) 570-4489 Fax: (562) 495-7502
Email: fedfilamassn@aol.com
Web: www.ffaai.org

FILIPINO AMERICAN COALITION FOR ENVIRONMENTAL SOLUTIONS
P.O. Box 2597
El Cerrito, CA 94530
Tel: (866) 206-9067
Email: info@facessolutions.com

FILIPINO AMERICAN COMMUNITY CLUB
192 Paddon Pl.
Marina, CA 93933
Tel: (831) 384-5383
Email: filam192@aol.com

FILIPINOS FOR AFFIRMATIVE ACTION
310 8th St. #306
Oakland, CA 94607
Lillian Galedo, Executive Director
Tel: (510) 465-9876 Fax: (510) 465-7548
Email: faa@filipinos4action.org
Web: www.filipinos4action.org

FRIENDS OF VALLEY CITIES JEWISH COMMUNITY CENTER
13164 Burbank Blvd.
Sherman Oaks, CA 91401
Tel: (818) 786-6310 Fax: (818) 989-0643
Email: info@valleycitiesjcc.org
Web: www.valleycitiesjcc.org

GATHER THE PEOPLE
510 E. Foothill Blvd. #B1
San Luis Obispo, CA 93405
Rabbi Moshe Ben Asher, Contact
Tel: (805) 785-0793 Fax: (805) 785-0794
Email: kharakim@jps.net
Web: www.gatherthepeople.org

GIVE2ASIA
465 California St.
San Francisco, CA 94104
Michael Rea, Managing Director
Tel: (415) 743-3336 Fax: (415) 391-4075
Email: info@give2asia.org
Web: www.give2asia.org

HAPA ISSUES FORUM, INC.
Irvine Chapter
University of California, c/o Office of the Dean of Students
Irvine, CA 92697-5125
Brad Curry, Social Chair
Email: bcurry@uci.edu
Web: http://spirit.dos.uci.edu/ucihapa/index.html

Los Angeles Chapter
231 E. 3rd St. #G-104
Los Angeles, CA 90013-1493
Tel: (213) 694-0286
Email: socal@hapaissuesforum.org

Web: www.hapaissuesforum.org/chapters/socalifornia.html

San Francisco Chapter
1840 Sutter St.
San Francisco, CA 94115-3220
Wei Ming Dariotis, Chapter Facilitator
Tel: (415) 409-4272 Fax: (415) 567-4222
Email: sf@hapaissuesforum.org
Web: www.hapaissuesforum.org

Stanford University Chapter
P.O. Box 11562
Stanford, CA 94309
Jaci Lew, Contact
Email: stanford@hapaissuesforum.org
Web: www.hapaissuesforum.org

UCLA Chapter
Box 951361
Los Angeles, CA 90095-1361
Amber Bechtel, President
Email: abechtel@ucla.edu
Web: www.studentgroups.ucla.edu/hapa/

University of California Berkeley Chapter
400 Eshleman Hall, M/C 4500
Berkeley, CA 94720-4500
Paul Young, President
Tel: (510) 466-5859
Email: MrMuD@uclink.berkeley.edu
Web: www.ocf.berkeley.edu/~hapa/

HIDAYA FOUNDATION
1765 Scott Blvd. #115
Santa Clara, CA 95050
Waseem Baloch, President/CEO
Tel: (408) 244-3282 Fax: (866) 344-3292
Email: mail@hidaya.org
Web: www.hidaya.org

HMONG AMERICAN COMMUNITY, INC.
1044 Fulton Mall #207
Fresno, CA 93721
Pheng Lee, Chairman
Tel: (559) 237-4919 Fax: (559) 237-5905
Email: hmongamer@att.net
Web: http://lennon.pub.csufresno.edu/~vl059

HONG BANG, INC.
P.O. Box 862743
Los Angeles, CA 90086-2743
Email: info@hongbang.org
Web: www.hongbang.org

HUONG VIET COMMUNITY CENTER
P.O. Box 29936
Oakland, CA 94604
Ky Bo, Executive Director
Tel: (510) 835-9156
Email: info@huongviet.org
Web: www.huongviet.org

INDIAN ASSOCIATION OF INLAND EMPIRE
P.O. Box 5584
San Bernardino, CA 92412
Rameesh Patel, President
Tel: (909) 425-1914 Fax: (909) 425-1914

INDO-AMERICAN COMMUNITY
12453 Andy St.
Cerritos, CA 90703
Sue Jandial, President
Tel: (562) 402-1847 Fax: (562) 402-4233

IRANIAN PARENTS CLUB OF NORTHERN CALIFORNIA
191 E. El Camino Real
Mountain View, CA 94043
Tel: (408) 369-0307
Email: fariborzfarahmand@yahoo.com
Web: www.7rooz.com/archives/020545.html

JAPAN AMERICA SOCIETY OF SOUTHERN CALIFORNIA
505 S. Flower St., Level C
Los Angeles, CA 90071
Tel: (213) 627-6217 Fax: (213) 627-1353

Email: info@jas-socal.org
Web: www.jas-socal.org

JAPAN SOCIETY OF NORTHERN CALIFORNIA
San Francisco Office
312 Sutter St. #410
San Francisco, CA 94108
Christopher J. Sigur, President
Tel: (415) 986-4383 Fax: (415) 986-5772
Email: jsnc@usajapan.org
Web: www.usajapan.org

JAPAN-US COMMUNITY EDUCATION AND EXCHANGE
1440 Broadway #901
Oakland, CA 94612
Conrad Asper, Executive Director
Tel: (510) 267-1920 Fax: (510) 267-1922
Email: info-us@jucee.org
Web: www.jucee.org

JAPANESE AMERICAN COMMUNITY SERVICES
231 E. 3rd St. #G104
Los Angeles, CA 90013
Alan Kumamoto, President
Tel: (323) 223-6473
Email: jacsfund@yahoo.com
Web: www.jacsfund.org

JAPANESE AMERICANS COMMUNITY CENTER
415 S. Claremont St.
San Mateo, CA 94401-3324
Roz Enomoto, Director
Tel: (650) 343-2793 Fax: (650) 343-2881

JEWISH COMMUNITY AGENCY OF SONOMA COUNTY
3855 Montgomery Dr.
Santa Rosa, CA 95405
Carolyn Metz, Executive Director
Tel: (707) 528-4222 Fax: (707) 528-4288
Email: carolynm@sfjcf.org
Web: www.jcagency.org

JEWISH COMMUNITY CENTER OF CONTRA COSTA
2071 Tice Valley Blvd.
Walnut Creek, CA 94595
Jennifer Cohen, President
Tel: (925) 938-7800 Fax: (949) 435-3401
Email: jcohen345@aol.com
Web: www.jccoc.org

JEWISH COMMUNITY CENTER OF ORANGE COUNTY
1 Federation Way #300
Irvine, CA 92603
Tel: (949) 435-3400 Fax: (949) 435-3401
Web: www.jccoc.org

JEWISH COMMUNITY CENTER OF SAN FRANCISCO
3200 California St.
San Francisco, CA 94118
Sandee Blechman, CEO
Tel: (415) 292-1200 Fax: (415) 292-1280
Email: info@jccsf.org
Web: www.jccsf.org

JEWISH COMMUNITY CENTER OF SILICON VALLEY
14855 Oka Rd.
Los Gatos, CA 95032
Cheryl Weissbart, Program Director
Tel: (408) 358-3636 Fax: (408) 458-7311
Email: cheryl@sanjosejcc.org
Web: www.sanjosejcc.org

JEWISH COMMUNITY CENTER OF THE DESERT
69-930 Hwy. 111 #204
Rancho Mirage, CA 92270
Ally Zemelman, President
Tel: (760) 324-4737 Fax: (760) 324-3154
Email: info@desertjcc.com
Web: www.desertjcc.com

JEWISH COMMUNITY CENTERS ASSOCIATION
Western Services Office
1068 N. Palm Canyon Dr.
Palm Springs, CA 92262
Tel: (760) 327-0369 Fax: (760) 327-0370
Email: namak@jcca.org
Web: www.jcca.org

JEWISH COMMUNITY FEDERATION
121 Steuart St.
San Francisco, CA 94105
Phyllis Cook, Interim CEO
Tel: (415) 777-0411 Fax: (415) 495-6635
Email: info@sfjcf.org
Web: www.sfjcf.org

JEWISH COMMUNITY FEDERATION OF THE GREATER EAST BAY
300 Grand Ave.
Oakland, CA 94610-4826
Loren Basch, CEO
Tel: (510) 839-2900 Fax: (510) 839-3996
Email: info@jfed.org
Web: www.jfed.org

JEWISH FAMILY & CHILDREN'S SERVICES OF THE EAST BAY
Berkeley Office
2484 Shattuck Ave. #210
Berkeley, CA 94704
David Biale, President
Tel: (510) 704-7475 Fax: (510) 704-7494
Email: information@jfcs-eastbay.org
Web: www.jfcs-eastbay.org

Oakland Office
2647 International Blvd. #220
Oakland, CA 94601
David Biale, President
Tel: (510) 434-7585 Fax: (510) 434-7584
Email: information@jfcs-eastbay.org
Web: www.jfcs-eastbay.org

Walnut Creek Office
1850 Tice Valley Blvd.
Walnut Creek, CA 94595
David Biale, President
Tel: (925) 927-2000 Fax: (925) 927-3131
Email: information@jfcs-eastbay.org
Web: www.jfcs-eastbay.org

JEWISH FAMILY SERVICE OF LOS ANGELES
6505 Wilshire Blvd. #500
Los Angeles, CA 90048
Tel: (323) 761-8800 Fax: (323) 761-8801
Email: jfsla@jfsla.org
Web: www.jfsla.org

JEWISH FAMILY SERVICE OF ORANGE COUNTY
1 Federation Way #350
Irvine, CA 92603-0174
Mel Roth, Executive Director
Tel: (714) 445-4950 Fax: (714) 435-3460
Email: info@jfsoc.org
Web: www.jfsoc.org

JEWISH FAMILY SERVICE OF PALM SPRINGS AND DESERT AREA
255 N. El Cielo Rd. #430A
Palm Springs, CA 92262-6990
Tel: (760) 325-4088 Fax: (760) 325-2188
Email: jfspsda@aol.com

JEWISH FAMILY SERVICE OF SACRAMENTO
2862 Arden Way #103
Sacramento, CA 95825
Judith Turtletaub, Executive Director
Tel: (916) 484-4400 Fax: (916) 484-4401
Email: jturtletaub@
Web: www.jfssac.org

JEWISH FAMILY SERVICE OF SAN DIEGO
Main Office
Leichtag Family Bldg., 3715 6th Ave.
San Diego, CA 92103
Tel: (619) 291-0473 Fax: (619) 291-2419

Email: jfs@jfssd.org
Web: www.jewishfamilyservicesd.org

JEWISH FAMILY SERVICE OF SILICON VALLEY
1101 S. Winchester Blvd. #L-237
San Jose, CA 951
Rosalie Sogolaw, Board President
Tel: (408) 556-0600 Fax: (408) 556-0091
Email: jfs@jfssv.org
Web: www.jfssv.org

JEWISH FAMILY SERVICES OF THE INLAND COMMUNITIES
4133 10th St.
Riverside, CA 92501-3109
Tel: (951) 784-1212 Fax: (951) 369-6614
Email: jewishfamily2000@yahoo.com

JEWISH FEDERATION COUNCIL OF GREATER LOS ANGELES
6505 Wilshire Blvd. #1000
Los Angeles, CA 90048
Harriet Hochman, Chair of Board
Tel: (323) 761-8200
Email: webcoordinator@jewishla.org
Web: www.jewishla.org

South Bay Council
3701 Skypark Dr. #100
Torrance, CA 90505
Harriet Hochman, Chair of Board
Tel: (310) 375-0863 Fax: (310) 375-0921
Email: webcoordinator@jewishla.org
Web: www.jewishla.org

Valley Alliance
22622 Vanowen St.
West Hills, CA 91307
Harriet Hochman, Chair of Board
Tel: (818) 464-3200 Fax: (818) 464-3248
Email: webcoordinator@jewishla.org
Web: www.jewishla.org

JEWISH FEDERATION OF GREATER LONG BEACH & WEST ORANGE COUNTY
3801 E. Willow St.
Long Beach, CA 90815
Michael S. Rassler, Executive Director
Tel: (562) 426-7601 Fax: (562) 424-3915
Email: webmaster@jewishlongbeach.org
Web: www.jewishlongbeach.org

JEWISH FEDERATION OF GREATER SANTA BARBARA
524 Chapala St.
Santa Barbara, CA 93101
Shelly Katz, Executive Director
Tel: (805) 957-1115 Fax: (805) 957-9230
Email: sbjfed@silcom.com
Web: www.jewishsantabarbara.org

JEWISH FEDERATION OF ORANGE COUNTY
1 Federation Way #330
Irvine, CA 92603-0174
Tel: (949) 435-3484 Fax: (949) 435-3485
Email: info@jfoc.org
Web: www.jewishorangecounty.org

JEWISH FEDERATION OF SACRAMENTO REGION
2351 Wyda Way
Sacramento, CA 95825
Tel: (916) 486-0906 Fax: (916) 486-0816
Email: federation@jewishsac.org
Web: www.jewishsacramento.org

JEWISH FEDERATION OF SILICON VALLEY
P.O. Box 320070
Los Gatos, CA 95032-0100
Brian David Goldberg, Executive Director
Tel: (408) 358-3033 Fax: (408) 356-0733
Email: bgoldberg@jvalley.org
Web: www.jewishsiliconvalley.org

JEWISH FEDERATION OF THE GREATER SAN GABRIEL & POMONA VALLEY
258 W. Badillo St.
Covina, CA 91723-1906
Tel: (626) 967-3656 Fax: (626) 967-5135
Email: federation@sgpvfed.org
Web: www.jewishsgpv.org

JEWISH FREE LOAN ASSOCIATION
6505 Wilshire Blvd. #715
Los Angeles, CA 90048
Mark Meltzer, Executive Director/CEO
Tel: (323) 761-8830 Fax: (323) 761-8841
Email: jfla@ix.netcom.com
Web: www.jfla.org

KOREAN COMMUNITY CENTER OF THE EAST BAY
4390 Telegraph Ave. #A
Oakland, CA 94609
Hun Kim, Executive Director
Tel: (510) 547-2662 Fax: (510) 547-3258
Email: general@kcceb.org
Web: www.kcceb.org

KOREAN COMMUNITY SERVICES, INC.
East Office
12531 Harbor Blvd.
Garden Grove, CA 92840
Robin William, Director
Tel: (714) 638-5008 Fax: (714) 638-3802
Email: contact@kcservices.org
Web: www.kcservices.org

Headquarters
1060 Brookhurst Rd.
Fullerton, CA 92833
Ellen Ahn, Executive Director
Tel: (714) 449-1339 Fax: (714) 449-1289
Email: contact@kcservices.org
Web: www.kcservices.org

Irvine Office
14795 Jeffrey Rd. #206 A
Irvine, CA 92680
Cleophus Rawls, Coordinator
Tel: (949) 654-9163
Email: contact@kcservices.org
Web: www.kcservices.org

Los Angeles Office
4416 W. Beverly Blvd.
Los Angeles, CA 90004
Ji Youn Lee, Coordinator
Tel: (213) 668-9007 Fax: (213) 644-7530
Email: contact@kcservices.org
Web: www.kcservices.org

West Office
8265 Garden Grove Blvd.
Garden Grove, CA 92844
Ken Sheller, Director
Tel: (714) 539-4544 Fax: (714) 539-5483
Email: contact@kcservices.org
Web: www.kcservices.org

LAO VOLUNTEER ACTION CLUB
4014 Manzanita Dr.
San Diego, CA 92105
Souvanh Tirakul, Contact Person
Tel: (619) 280-7530

LAWRENCE FAMILY JEWISH COMMUNITY CENTER OF SAN DIEGO COUNTY
4126 Executive Dr.
La Jolla, CA 92037
David Geffen, President
Tel: (858) 457-3030 Fax: (858) 642-2692
Web: www.lfjcc.org

LITTLE TOKYO SERVICE CENTER
231 E. 3rd St. #G104
Los Angeles, CA 90013
Bill Watanabe, Executive Director
Tel: (213) 473-1602 Fax: (213) 473-1601
Email: billwatanabe@ltsc.org
Web: www.ltsc.org

MAITRI
234 E. Gish Rd. #200
San Jose, CA 95112
Sonya Pelia, President
Tel: (408) 436-8393 Fax: (408) 436-8381
Email: maitri@maitri.org
Web: www.maitri.org

MT. CARMEL CAMBODIAN CENTER
1851 Cerritos Ave.
Long Beach, CA 90806
Mary Blatz, Director
Tel: (562) 591-8477 Fax: (562) 591-1367
Email: ladyofmtcarmel@geocities.com
Web: http://ethnicministry.la-archdiocese.
org/Asia/cambodia/

NATIONAL ASSOCIATION OF JAPAN-AMERICA SOCIETIES
Japan Society of San Diego and Tijuana
1250 6th Ave. #226
San Diego, CA 92101-4377
Dave Tuites, Executive Director
Tel: (619) 233-6873 Fax: (619) 702-5035
Email: jssdt@sbcglobal.net
Web: www.japan-society.org

ORANGE COUNTY ASIAN AND PACIFIC ISLANDER COMMUNITY ALLIANCE
12900 Garden Grove Blvd. #214-A
Garden Grove, CA 92843
Mary Anne Foo, MPH, Executive Director
Tel: (714) 636-9095 Fax: (714) 636-8828
Email: ocapica@ocapica.org
Web: www.ocapica.org

ORANGE COUNTY JAPANESE AMERICAN ASSOCIATION
505 S. Villa Real Dr. #103A
Anaheim Hills, CA 92867
Ikuko Sheroder, Office Manager
Tel: (714) 283-3551 Fax: (714) 283-3423
Email: network@ocjaa.org
Web: www.ocjaa.org

OSHER MARIN JEWISH COMMUNITY CENTER
200 N. San Pedro Rd.
San Rafel, CA 94903
Becky Pell Kaplan, President
Tel: (415) 444-8000 Fax: (415) 491-1235
Email: info@marinjcc.org
Web: www.marinjcc.org

PACIFIC ASIAN LANGUAGE SERVICES
605 W. Olympic Blvd. #600
Los Angeles, CA 90015
Heng Foong, Program Director
Tel: (213) 553-1818 Fax: (213) 553-1822
Email: info@palsforhealth.org
Web: www.palsforhealth.org

PAKISTAN RELIEF
32970 Alvarado Niles Rd. #760
Union City, CA 94587
Vajin Khan, Founder/Board Member
Tel: (510) 476-1734
Email: info@pakistanrelief.org
Web: www.pakistanrelief.org

PENINSULA JEWISH COMMUNITY CENTER
800 Foster City Blvd.
Foster City, CA 94404
Judy Edelson, Executive Director
Tel: (650) 212-7522 Fax: (650) 378-2799
Email: jedelson@pjcc.org
Web: www.pjcc.org

RAFU
231 E. 3rd St. #G104
Los Angeles, CA 90013
Tel: (213) 680-3484
Email: ncrrla@yahoo.com
Web: www.ncrr-la.org

SACRAMENTO LAO FAMILY COMMUNITY
5840 Franklin Blvd.
Sacramento, CA 95824-1122
Xia Kao Vang, Executive Director

Tel: (916) 424-0864 Fax: (916) 424-1861
Email: saclao@yahoo.com

SAMOAN FEDERATION OF AMERICA
404 E. Carson St.
Carson, CA 90745
Pele Faletoco, Executive Director
Tel: (310) 834-6404 Fax: (310) 835-3871
Email: pele11545@aol.com
Web: www.samoanfederation.com

SAN FERNANDO VALLEY JAPANESE AMERICAN COMMUNITY CENTER
12953 Branford St.
Pacoima, CA 91331
Henry Yamamura, Volunteer
Tel: (818) 899-1989 Fax: (818) 899-0659

SAN JOAQUIN INDOCHINESE ASSOCIATION
4502 N. Pershing Ave. #C
Stockton, CA 95207
Sen Nguyen, Executive Director
Tel: (209) 472-7145 Fax: (209) 472-1107
Email: sennguyen1@juno.com

SEARCH TO INVOLVE FILIPINO AMERICANS
3200 W. Temple St.
Los Angeles, CA 90026
Joel Jacinto, Executive Director
Tel: (213) 382-1819 Fax: (213) 382-7445
Email: jjacinto@esipa.org
Web: www.esipa.org

SOUTH BAY CITIES COUNCIL OF GOVERNMENTS
5033 Rock Valley Rd.
Rancho Palos Verdes, CA 90275
Jacki Bacharach, Executive Director
Tel: (310) 377-8987 Fax: (310) 377-5790
Email: sbccog@southbaycities.org
Web: www.southbaycities.org

SOUTHEAST ASIAN COMMUNITY CENTER
875 O'Farell St.
San Francisco, CA 94109
Philip Tuong Ngyugen, Executive Director
Tel: (415) 885-2743 Fax: (415) 885-3253
Email: seaccphilip@juno.com

1415 Koll Cir. #108
San Jose, CA 95112
Megan Bui, Director
Tel: (408) 436-8438 Fax: (408) 436-8745
Email: eaccmegan@juno.com

SOUTHERN CALIFORNIA CHINESE-AMERICAN ENVIRONMENTAL PROTECTION ASSOCIATION
P.O. Box 90783
City of Industry, CA 91715
Jason Wen
Email: board@sccaepa.org
Web: www.sccaepa.org

SOUTHERN CALIFORNIA PHILIPPINE U.S. VETERANS ASSOCIATION
P.O. Box 3743
Cerritos, CA 90703
John Skiles, President
Tel: (909) 672-6831

THE HOUSE OF PACIFIC RELATIONS-INTERNATIONAL COTTAGES, INC.
2125 Park Blvd.
San Diego, CA 92101
Tel: (619) 234-0739
Email: info@sdhpr.org
Web: www.sdhpr.org

TIBET ENVIRONMENTAL WATCH
906 Indian Rock Ave.
Berkeley, CA 94707
Robert Z. Apte
Tel: (510) 526-3657 Fax: (510) 526-4238
Email: rapte@dnai.com
Web: www.tew.org

TIBETAN CULTURAL & COMMUNITY SERVICE CENTER OF SOUTHERN CALIFORNIA
2501 Redondo Beach Blvd. #315
Gardena, CA 90249
Tel: (310) 289-4302
Email: tccsc@aol.com
Web: www.members.aol.com/tccsc

UNITED CAMBODIAN COMMUNITY, INC.
2338 E. Anaheim St. #200
Long Beach, CA 90804
Sereivuth Prak, Executive Director
Tel: (562) 433-2490 Fax: (562) 433-0564
Email: sereivuthprak@yahoo.com

UNITED JEWISH FEDERATION OF SAN DIEGO COUNTY
4950 Murphy Canyon Rd.
San Diego, CA 92123
Steve Solomon, President
Tel: (858) 571-3444 Fax: (858) 571-0701
Email: fedujf@ujfsd.org

US CHINA PEOPLE'S FRIENDSHIP ASSOCIATION
Western Region
2534 Doidge Ave.
Pinole, CA 94564
Betty Boyle, President
Tel: (510) 758-2851
Email: shanguo@aol.com
Web: www.uscpfa.org

VENICE JAPANESE COMMUNITY CENTER
12448 Braddock Dr.
Los Angeles, CA 90066
John Ikegami, President
Tel: (310) 822-8885 Fax: (310) 822-8885
Email: webmaster@vjcc.com
Web: www.vjcc.com

VENTURA COUNTY JEWISH FAMILY SERVICE
1915 E. Main St.
Ventura, CA 93001
Edward Tennen, President
Tel: (805) 641-6565 Fax: (805) 641-6560
Email: jfsventura@aol.com
Web: www.jfsvc.org

VIETNAM HEALTH, EDUCATION AND LITERATURE PROJECTS
P.O. Box 1242
San Jose, CA 95108
Thu Do, Executive Director
Tel: (408) 885-1791 Fax: (408) 885-1721
Email: info@vnhelp.org
Web: www.vnhelp.org

VIETNAMESE COMMUNITY CENTER OF SAN FRANCISCO
766 Geary St.
San Francisco, CA 94109
Lan T. Le, Chairman
Tel: (415) 351-1038 Fax: (415) 351-1039
Email: info@vietccsf.org
Web: www.vietccsf.org

WANG AND LI ASIA RESOURCES
Office Location
2342 Shattuck Ave. #257
Berkeley, CA 94704
Caroline Chi, Branch Manager
Tel: (510) 233-4882 Fax: (510) 217-4395
Email: oakland@wang-li.com
Web: www.wang-li.com

SPEC. INT., SPORTS

AIKIDO INSTITUTE
5036 Telegraph Ave. at 51st St.
Oakland, CA 94609
Kim Peuser, Chief Instructor
Tel: (510) 658-2155

Email: info@aikidoinstitute.org
Web: www.aikidoinstitute.org

ASIAN AMERICAN TENNIS FOUNDATION
P.O. Box 2365
Cupertino, CA 95015-2365
Michael Chan Jessup, President
Email: info@aatf.org
Web: www.aatf.org

ASIAN SKI & BOARD CLUB OF LOS ANGELES
P.O. Box 5022
Redondo Beach, CA 90278
Andy Hone, Treasurer
Email: chasegawa@asbcla.org
Web: www.asbcla.org

BAY AREA ASIAN SPORTS
P.O. Box 31129
San Francisco, CA 94131-0129
Tel: (650) 997-3840 Fax: (650) 755-9943
Email: dragonbasketball@hotmail.com
Web: www.baasdragons.org

CALIFORNIA DRAGON BOAT ASSOCIATION
268 Bush St. #888
San Francisco, CA 94104
Hans Wu, President
Tel: (415) 285-4881
Email: hanswu@aol.com
Web: www.cdba.org

HOMENETMEN
Glendale Ararat Chapter
3347 N. San Fernando Rd.
Los Angeles, CA 90065
Armond Gorgorian, Executive Director
Tel: (323) 256-2564 Fax: (323) 256-0639
Email: info@ararat.org
Web: www.ararat.org

Los Angeles "Mayr" Chapter
1203 N. Vermont Ave.
Los Angeles, CA 90029
Mayda Shahinian, Secretary
Tel: (323) 663-9381 Fax: (323) 663-9385
Email: Info@LaHomenetmen.org
Web: www.lahomenetmen.org

Santa Clara Valley "ANI" Chapter
P.O. Box 70864
Sunnyvale, CA 94086-0864
Email: info@SantaClaraANI.org
Web: www.santaclaraani.org

Western US Regional Office
501 E. Colorado
Glendale, CA 91205
Rubiana, Executive Director
Tel: (818) 244-3868 Fax: (818) 507-6761
Email: office@homenetmen.net
Web: www.homenetmen.org

INTERNATIONAL SHOTOKAN KARATE CLUB
Southwest
1218 5th St.
Santa Monica, CA 90401
James Field, Instructor
Tel: (310) 395-8545 Fax: (310) 458-2603
Email: info@jkasm.com
Web: www.jkasm.com

MODERN ARNIS REMY P. PRESAS INTERNATIONAL ORGANIZATION
1169 Market St. #249
San Francisco, CA 94103
Email: marppio@modernarnis.com
Web: www.modernarnis.com

NORTHERN CALIFORNIA NAGINATA FOUNDATION
5552 Southcrest Way
San Jose, CA 95123
Owen Chiu, President
Tel: Fax: (408) 225-0707
Email: ochiu55527@aol.com
Web: www.naginata.org

SACRAMENTO ASIAN SPORTS FOUNDATION
P.O. Box 221838
Sacramento, CA 95822
Mamie Yee, Executive Administrator
Tel: (916) 684-6533 Fax: (916) 684-6482
Email: myee99@aol.com
Web: www.sasfquest.org

SACRAMENTO JAPANESE UNITED METHODIST CHURCH BASKETBALL PROGRAM
7485 Rush River Dr. #710 PMB 306
Sacramento, CA 95831
Stuart Satow, President
Email: wotas@sbcglobal.net
Web: www.sjumcbasketball.org

SACRAMENTO REBELS YOUTH ORGANIZATION
P.O. Box 22218
Sacramento, CA 95822-0218
Ken Tipon, Chairman
Email: jsencil@pacbell.net
Web: www.sacrebels.org

SOUTHERN CALIFORNIA NAGINATA FEDERATION
P.O. Box 11195
Torrance, CA 90510-9998
Helen Michiyo Nakano, Chief Instructor
Email: webmaster@scnf.org
Web: www.scnf.org

WORLD HAPKIDO ASSOCIATION
1789 Thousand Oaks Blvd.
Thousand Oaks, CA 91360
Master Tae Jung, President
Tel: (805) 495-9622 Fax: (805) 494-4554
Email: MasterJung@WorldHapkido.com
Web: www.worldhapkido.com

YONSEI BASKETBALL ASSOCIATION
P.O. Box 661484
Los Angeles, CA 90066
Tel: (310) 391-7829
Email: kikari526@aol.com
Web: www.yonseiyouth.com

SPEC. INT., VOLUNTARY SERVICE

CHINESE AMERICAN SERVICE ALLIANCE
720 S. Atlantic Blvd.
Monterey Park, CA 91745
Frank Wang, President
Tel: (818) 585-9148
Email: info@casa-la.org
Web: www.casa-la.org

SEVA FOUNDATION
1786 5th St.
Berkeley, CA 94710
Lois Moore, Director of Development
Tel: (510) 845-7382 Fax: (510) 845-7410
Email: admin@seva.org
Web: www.seva.org

SOCIAL ASSISTANCE PROGRAM FOR VIETNAM
12881 Knott St. #116
Garden Grove, CA 92841
Thanh Ngoc Nguyen, President
Tel: (714) 901-1997 Fax: (714) 901-1997
Email: sapvn@hotmail.com
Web: www.sap-vn.org

TIBETAN AID PROJECT
2910 San Pablo Ave.
Berkeley, CA 94702
Sandy Olney
Tel: (800) 338-4238 Fax: (510) 548-2230
Email: tap@tibetanaidproject.org
Web: www.tibetanaidproject.org

TRAVEL CHINA ROADS
182 Bellah
Lindsay, CA 93247
Dr. Kent Stinson
Tel: (559) 562-3409
Email: tchinaroads@yahoo.com
Web: www.tchinaroads.com

VOICE OF CHINA AND ASIA MISSIONARY SOCIETY
P.O. Box 15
Pasadena, CA 91102
Tel: (626) 441-0640 Fax: (626) 441-8124
Email: info@vocamissionarysociety.org
Web: www.vocamissionarysociety.org

SPEC. INT., WOMEN

AFGHAN WOMEN'S ASSOCIATION INTERNATIONAL
P.O. Box 637
Fremont, CA 94537-0637
Tel: (510) 574-2180 Fax: (510) 574-2185
Email: afghancoal@aol.com
Web: www.awai.org

AFGHAN WOMEN'S MISSION
2460 N. Lake Ave. PMB 207
Altadena, CA 91001
Tel: (626) 797-5571 Fax: (509) 756-2236
Email: info@afghanwomensmission.org
Web: www.afghanwomensmission.org

ARAB WOMEN'S SOLIDARITY ASSOCIATION
P.O. Box 14871
San Francisco, CA 94114
Email: awsasf@yahoo.com
Web: www.awsa.net

ASIAN IMMIGRANT WOMEN ADVOCATES
310 8th St. #301
Oakland, CA 94607
Young Shin, Executive Director
Tel: (510) 268-0192 Fax: (510) 268-0194
Email: info@aiwa.org
Web: www.aiwa.org

ASIAN PACIFIC AMERICAN WOMEN'S LEADERSHIP INSTITUTE
P.O. Box 2330
La Mesa, CA 91943-2330
Anni Y. Chung, Board Chair
Tel: (619) 698-3746 Fax: (619) 698-5834
Email: info@apawli.org
Web: www.apawli.org

ASIAN PACIFIC WOMEN'S CENTER
1145 Wilshire Blvd. #102
Los Angeles, CA 90017
Chun-Yen Chen, Executive Director
Tel: (213) 250-2977 Fax: (213) 250-2911
Email: apwc@apwcla.org
Web: www.apwcla.org

ASIAN WOMEN'S RESOURCE CENTER
940 Washington St.
San Francisco, CA 94108
Stephen Louie, President
Tel: (415) 788-1088 Fax: (415) 397-6836
Email: glotan@onebox.com
Web: www.gbgm-umc.org/awrc

ASIAN WOMEN'S SHELTER
3543 18th St. #19
San Francisco, CA 94110
Hediana Utarti, Volunteer Coordinator
Tel: (415) 751-7110 Fax: (415) 751-0806
Email: hediana@sfaws.org
Web: www.sfaws.org

FILIPINA WOMEN'S NETWORK
P.O. Box 192143
San Francisco, CA 94119
Tel: (415) 278-9410 Fax: (415) 840-0655
Email: info@ffwn.org
Web: www.ffwn.org

HADASSAH
Central Pacific Coast Region
1400 Coleman Ave. #F-15
Santa Clara, CA 95050
Rena Feuerstein, President
Tel: (408) 727-2707 Fax: (408) 727-2768
Email: cpcr@hadassah.org
Web: www.hadassah.org

Southern California Chapter
11500 W. Olympic Blvd. #501
Los Angeles, CA 90064
Sherry Altura, President
Tel: (310) 479-3200 Fax: (310) 444-0911
Email: info@hadassahsc.org
Web: www.hadassah.org

HMONG WOMEN'S HERITAGE ASSOCIATION
2251 Florin Rd. #104
Sacramento, CA 95822
May Ying Ly, Executive Director
Tel: (916) 394-1405 Fax: (916) 392-9326
Email: myxly@hmongwomenheritage.org
Web: www.hmongwomenheritage.org

INDIAN BUSINESS AND PROFESSIONAL WOMEN
P.O. Box 361036
Milpitas, CA 95036-1036
Deepka Lalwani, Director
Tel: (408) 741-9100 Fax: (408) 956-9115
Web: www.ibpw.net

INDUS WOMEN LEADERS
236 W. Portal Ave. #473
San Francisco, CA 94127
Shalini Verma, Executive Director
Email: info@induswomenleaders.org
Web: www.induswomenleaders.org

IRANIAN FEDERATED WOMEN'S CLUB
1582 S. Stelling Rd.
Cupertino, CA 95014
Fay Ehsan, Treasurer
Tel: (408) 381-4268
Email: ifwc@aol.com
Web: www.payvand.org/IFWC/index.html

JAGRITI FOUNDATION
950 Ladera Ln.
Santa Barbara, CA 93108
Michelle Andina, President
Tel: (805) 969-9092 Fax: (805) 969-4122
Email: info@jagritifoundation.org
Web: www.jagritifoundation.org

KOREAN AMERICAN PROFESSIONAL WOMEN'S ASSOCIATION
P.O. Box 9015
San Jose, CA 95157
Jennifer Lee, President
Email: president@kapwasv.org
Web: www.kapwasv.org

KOREAN AMERICAN WOMEN ARTISTS & WRITERS ASSOCIATION
745 Buchanan St.
San Francisco, CA 94102
Jin Hi Kim, President
Tel: (415) 252-5828 Fax: (415) 252-5829
Email: kawawa@kawawa.org
Web: www.kawawa.org

MUSLIM WOMEN'S LEAGUE
3010 Wilshire Blvd. #519
Los Angeles, CA 90010
Tel: (626) 358-0335
Email: mwl@mwlusa.org
Web: www.mwlusa.org

NARIKA
P.O. Box 14014
Berkeley, CA 94712
Saba Brelvi, President
Tel: (510) 540-0754 Fax: (510) 540-0201
Email: info@narika.org
Web: www.narika.org

NATIONAL COUNCIL FOR JEWISH WOMEN
Los Angeles
543 N. Fairfax Ave.
Los Angeles, CA 90036
Marsha Atkind, President
Tel: (323) 651-2930 Fax: (323) 651-5348
Email: development@ncjwla.org
Web: www.ncjwla.org

SAN DIEGO CHINESE WOMEN'S ASSOCIATION
P.O. Box 881882
San Diego, CA 92168-1882
Devin Chin-Lee, President
Email: jungwon@cox.net
Web: http://members.cox.net/jungwon

STAND AGAINST DOMESTIC VIOLENCE
1410 Danzing Plz., 2nd Fl.
Concord, CA 94520
Tel: (925) 676-2845 Fax: (925) 676-0532
Web: www.standagainstdv.org

WOMEN ORGANIZED TO MAKE ABUSE NONEXISTENT, INC.
333 Valencia St. #251
San Francisco, CA 94103
Margaret Kokka, Interim Executive Director
Tel: (415) 864-4777 Fax: (415) 864-1082
Email: info@womaninc.org
Web: www.womaninc.org

SPEC. INT., YOUTH

AFGHAN AMERICAN YOUTH COUNCIL
7657 Winnetka Ave. #450
Canoga Park, CA 91306
Nasima Karim
Tel: (818) 796-1128
Email: board@aayc.org
Web: www.aayc.org

ARMENIAN YOUTH FEDERATION
104 N. Belmont St. #206
Glendale, CA 91206
Tel: (818) 507-1933 Fax: (818) 240-3442
Email: ayf@ayfwest.org
Web: www.ayfwest.org

ASIAN & PACIFIC ISLANDER YOUTH VIOLENCE PREVENTION CENTER
1970 Broadway #500
Oakland, CA 94612
Vanessa Cunanan, Research Assistant
Tel: (510) 208-0500 Fax: (510) 208-0511
Email: info@api-center.org
Web: www.api-center.org

ASIAN PACIFIC YOUTH LEADERSHIP PROJECT
P.O. Box 22423
Sacramento, CA 95822
Agnes Lee, President
Tel: (916) 497-0776
Email: info@apylp.org
Web: www.apylp.org

ASIAN YOUTH CENTER
100 W. Clary Ave.
San Gabriel, CA 91776
Tel: (626) 309-0622 Fax: (626) 309-0717
Email: admin@asianyouthcenter.org
Web: wwww.asianyouthcenter.org

ASIAN YOUTH PREVENTION SERVICES
2012 Pine St.
San Francisco, CA 94115
Ramon Calubaquib, Program Director
Tel: (415) 563-8052 Fax: (415) 921-1841
Email: moncha2go@aol.com

COMMUNITY YOUTH CENTER
Main Office
1693 Polk St.
San Francisco, CA 94116
Sarah Wan, Executive Director
Tel: (415) 775-2636 Fax: (415) 775-1345
Email: sarah_wan@cycsf.org
Web: www.cycsf.org

EAST BAY ASIAN YOUTH CENTER
Main Office
2025 E. 12th St.
Oakland, CA 94606
David Kakishiba, Executive Director
Tel: (510) 533-1092 Fax: (510) 533-6825
Email: ebayc@ebayc.org
Web: www.ebayc.org

FILIPINO YOUTH COALITION
525 Los Coches St.
Milpitas, CA 95035
Sarah Gonzales, Executive Officer
Tel: (408) 262-1400 Fax: (408) 262-7500
Email: info@filipinoyouthcoalition.org
Web: www.filamcenter.com/fyc/

INDO-CHINESE YOUTH CENTER
14112 S. Kingsley Dr.
Gardena, CA 90247
Lee Nguyen, Program Coordinator
Tel: (310) 768-8064 Fax: (310) 768-2779
Web: www.aadapinc.com

IRANIAN CHILDREN'S RIGHTS SOCIETY
27881 La Paz #G PMB 220
Laguna Niguel, CA 92677
Jila Kashef, Executive
Tel: (949) 266-0323 Fax: (949) 266-0323
Email: info@iranianchildren.org
Web: www.iranianchildren.org

JAPANESE COMMUNITY YOUTH COUNCIL
Administration Office
1596 Post St.
San Francisco, CA 94109
Jon Osaki, Executive Director
Tel: (415) 202-7909 Fax: (415) 563-7109
Email: info@jcyc.org
Web: www.jcyc.org

Programs & Services Office
2012 Pine St.
San Francisco, CA 94115
Julie Matsueta, Deputy Director
Tel: (415) 563-8052 Fax: (415) 921-1841
Email: info@jcyc.org
Web: www.jcyc.org

KASIYAHAN
P.O. Box 1002
Port Hueneme, CA 93044-1002
Tel: Fax: (805) 240-9102
Email: info@kasiyahan.com
Web: www.kasiyahan.com

KOREAN AMERICAN MENTORSHIP PROGRAM
525 Monte Vista Ave. #10
Oakland, CA 94611
Julie Ryu, Board Member
Tel: (510) 421-0556
Email: kamponline@yahoo.com
Web: www.kamponline.org

KOREAN YOUTH AND COMMUNITY CENTER, INC.
680 S. Wilton Pl.
Los Angeles, CA 90005
Michael Chun, CPA, Executive President
Tel: (213) 365-7400 Fax: (213) 383-1280
Email: info@kyccla.org
Web: www.kyccla.org

KOREAN YOUTH CULTURAL CENTER
4216 Telegraph Ave.
Oakland, CA 94609
Kyung Jin Lee, Executive Director
Tel: (510) 652-4964 Fax: (510) 652-6442
Email: info@kycc.net
Web: www.kycc.net

MIDDLE EAST CHILDREN'S ALLIANCE
905 Parker St.
Berkeley, CA 94710
Eugene Newport, President
Tel: (510) 548-0542 Fax: (510) 548-0543
Email: meca@mecaforpeace.org
Web: www.mecaforpeace.org

NATIONAL CENTER FOR MISSING & EXPLOITED CHILDREN
California
18111 Irvine Blvd. #C
Tustin, CA 92780-3403
Tel: (714) 508-0150 Fax: (714) 508-0154
Web: www.missingkids.com

NEPALESE YOUTH OPPORTUNITY FOUNDATION
3030 Bridgeway #123
Sausalito, CA 94965
Olga Murray, President
Tel: (415) 331-8585 Fax: (415) 331-4027
Email: info@nyof.org
Web: www.nyof.org

OAKLAND ASIAN STUDENTS EDUCATIONAL SERVICES
University of California, Berkeley
196 10th St.
Oakland, CA 94607
Nhi Chau, Executive Director
Tel: (510) 891-9928 Fax: (510) 879-9418
Email: info@oases.org
Web: www.oases.org

OVERSEAS CHINESE YOUTH ASSOCIATION
471 W. Lambert Rd. #113
Brea, CA 92821
Tel: (626) 359-0889
Email: lulala@ocya.org
Web: www.ocya.org

TAIWANESE AMERICAN YOUTH LEADERSHIP
Redwood Glen Camp
1430 Wurr Rd.
Loma Mar, CA 94021
Ivy Chen, Co-counselor
Tel: (650) 879-0320
Email: hsin_i_huang@yahoo.com
Web: www.tayl.org

THE CHILDREN'S DEFENSE FUND
101 Broadway
Oakland, CA 94607
Deena Lahn, Policy Director
Tel: (510) 663-3224 Fax: (510) 663-1783
Email: dlahn@cdfca.org
Web: www.cdfca.org

THE CHILDREN'S DEFENSE FUND
3655 S. Grand Ave. #270
Los Angeles, CA 90007
Victoria Ballesteros, Communications Associate
Tel: (213) 749-8787 Fax: (213) 749-4119
Email: vballesteros@cdfca.org
Web: www.cdfca.org

VIETNAMESE AMERICAN CENTER
65 N. 8th St.
San Jose, CA 95151
The-Vu Nguyen, Director of Operations
Tel: (408) 294-1638 Fax: (408) 294-1638
Email: vacsj@yahoo.com
Web: www.vacsj.org

VIETNAMESE YOUTH DEVELOPMENT CENTER
150 Eddy St.
San Francisco, CA 94102
Glades Perreras, Executive Director
Tel: (415) 771-2600 Fax: (415) 771-3917
Email: info@vydc.org
Web: www.vydc.org

YOUTH FOR ASIAN THEATER
550 29th Ave.
San Francisco, CA 94121
Lauren d. Yee, Executive Director & Founder
Tel: (415) 831-5849
Email: why_fat@yahoo.com
Web: www.yfat.webhop.org

STUDENT ORGANIZATION

ARMENIAN GRADUATE STUDENTS ASSOCIATION
University of California, Los Angeles
Kerckhoff Hall #316, 308 Westwood Plz.
Los Angeles, CA 90024
Haig Hovsepian, Executive Officer
Tel: (310) 206-8512
Email: agsaucla@ucla.edu
Web: www.studentgroups.ucla.edu/agsa

ARMENIAN STUDENT ASSOCIATION
California State University, Los Angeles
University Student Union, 2nd Fl.
Los Angeles, CA 90032
Levon Badalyan, President
Tel: (323) 343-5471
Email: lbadalyan@yahoo.com
Web: www.calstatela.edu/orgs/asa

ARMENIAN STUDIES PROGRAM
5245 N. Backer Ave. PB4
Fresno, CA 93740-8001
Dr. Dickran Kouymjian, Director
Tel: (559) 278-2669 Fax: (559) 278-2129
Email: dickrank@csufresno.edu
Web: http://armenianstudies.csufresno.edu

ASIAN AMERICAN ASSOCIATION
University of California, Davis
457 Memorial Union
Davis, CA 95616-8706
Justin B. Lim, President
Email: president@davisaaa.org
Web: http://davisaaa.org

ASIAN AMERICAN STUDENTS' ASSOCIATION
Stanford University
c/o Asian American Activities Center, M/C
3064, Old Union Club House
Stanford, CA 94305
Jimmy Lu
Email: aasacore@lists.stanford.edu
Web: www.stanford.edu/group/AASA/

ASIAN LAW JOURNAL
University of California
Boalt Hall School of Law, 589 Simon Hall
Berkeley, CA 94720
Hyun Lee, Managing Editor
Tel: (510) 643-9643
Email: hyunlee@boalthall.berkeley.edu
Web: www.boalt.org/ALJ/main.html

ASIAN & PACIFIC-ISLANDER STUDENT ALLIANCE
UC San Diego
9500 Gilman Dr. #A-43
La Jolla, CA 92093-0077
Ian Almazan, President
Tel: (858) 534-2048
Email: apsa@ucsd.edu
Web: www-acs.ucsd.edu/~apsa/

ASSOCIATION OF ASIAN AMERICAN YALE ALUMNI
c/o LF International
360 Post St. #705
San Francisco, CA 94108
Harry Chang
Email: GrantDin@yahoo.com
Web: www.aaaya.org

ASSOCIATION OF CHINESE STUDENTS AND SCHOLARS
Stanford University
P.O. Box 19462
Stanford, CA 94309
Ye Tao, President
Email: acsss-public@lists.stanford.edu
Web: www.stanford.edu/group/acsss

BARKADA CLUB
Santa Clara University
Shapell Lounge, 500 El Camino Real
Santa Clara, CA 95053

Lance Dwyer, President
Tel: (408) 554-4926 Fax: (408) 554-1958
Email: ldwyer@scu.edu
Web: www.scu.edu

BERKELEY HILLE JEWISH STUDENT CENTER
2736 Bancroft Way
Berkeley, CA 94704
Adam Weisberg, Executive Director
Tel: (510) 845-7793 Fax: (510) 845-7753
Email: aweisberg@berkeleyhillel.org
Web: www.berkeleyhillel.org

BERKELEY SOUTHEAST ASIANISTS
University of California at Berkeley
Department of Environment Science, Policy,
and Management, 135 Giannini Hall #3312
Berkeley, CA 94720-3312
Dorian Fougeres, Doctoral Candidate
Tel: (510) 643-3110
Email: fougeres@nature.berkeley.edu
Web: www.OCF.Berkeley.EDU/~bsea

BERKELEY STUDENTS FOR A SOVEREIGN TAIWAN
University of California, Berkeley
300 Eshleman Hall
Berkeley, CA 94720-4500
Diana Cheng, Head
Email: dianac89@uclink.berkeley.edu
Web: www.ocf.berkeley.edu/~bst/

CHINESE CAMPUS FELLOWSHIP
San Jose State University
San Jose, CA 95192
Pastor David Hoi, Advisor
Email: contact@sjsuccf.org
Web: www.sjsuccf.org

CHINESE STUDENTS & SCHOLARS ASSOCIATION
University of California
405 Hilgard Ave., Box 951361
Los Angeles, CA 90095-1361
Ke Wei, President
Email: cssauclapresident@yahoo.com
Web: http://cssa.ucla.edu/

FILIPINO AMERICAN STUDENT ORGANIZATION
California State University, Chico
400 W. 1st St.
Chico, CA 95929
John Sunga
Tel: (530) 680-7355
Email: johnsunga@aol.com
Web: www.csuchico.edu/faso

HMONG STUDENT INTER-COLLEGIATE COALITION
2117 Haste St. #304
Berkeley, CA 94704
Xai Lee, President
Tel: (209) 988-5652
Email: xai_lee@hotmail.com
Web: www.hsiconline.org

HONG KONG STUDENT ASSOCIATION
University of California, Berkeley
400 Eshelman Hall
Berkeley, CA 94720
Email: officers@ucbhksa.com
Web: www.ucbhksa.com

University of California, Irvine
Office of the Dean of Students
Irvine, CA 92697-5125
Email: hksa@uci.edu
Web: http://spirit.dos.uci.edu/hksa

INDIAN STUDENTS CLUB
California State University
University Student Union, 5280 N. Jackson
Ave. #5036
Fresno, CA 93740-8023
Kiran Rao, President
Email: indyarocks@yahoo.com
Web: www.iscfresno.com

IRANIAN STUDENT GROUP
University of California, Los Angeles
324 Kerckhoff Hall
Los Angeles, CA 90095
Pegah Shahriari, Chair
Tel: (310) 825-1845
Web: www.studentgroups.ucla.edu/isg

JAPANESE STUDENTS NETWORK OF SOUTHERN CALIFORNIA
123 Onizuka St. #310
Los Angeles, CA 90012
Tel: (213) 626-2905
Email: info@jsnla.org
Web: www.jsnla.org

KA MANA'O O HAWAII
Santa Clara University
Shapell Lounge, 500 El Camino Real
Santa Clara, CA 95053
Gina Pio Roda, President
Tel: (408) 554-4926 Fax: (408) 554-1958
Web: www.scu.edu

KABABAYAN
University of California, Irvine
Cross Cultural Center
Irvine, CA 92614
Kevin Nadal
Tel: (949) 824-7215
Email: knadal@uci.edu
Web: http://members.tripod.com/~KabaUCI

KOREAN STUDENT ASSOCIATION
CSU Sacramento, 6000 J St.
Sacramento, CA 95819
Dr. Brian Lim, Faculty Advisor
Tel: (916) 278-4164
Email: ksacsus@hanmail.net
Web: www.csus.edu/org/ksa

KOREAN STUDENT ASSOCIATION
Stanford University
P.O. Box 20121
Stanford, CA 94309
Chang Hwan Sung, President
Tel: (650) 723-2300
Email: chsung@stanford.edu
Web: www.stanford.edu/group/ksas

KOREAN-AMERICAN STUDENTS ASSOCIATION
University of California, Los Angeles
UCLA Campbell Hall 3230, Box 951546
Los Angeles, CA 90095-1546
Daniel Cho, President
Email: ksa@ucla.edu
Web: www.studentgroups.ucla.edu/ksa/

LAO STUDENT ASSOCIATION
San Diego State University
5500 Campanile Dr.
San Diego, CA 92182
Maly N. Vongsenekeo, President
Email: vongsene@rohan.sdsu.edu

ORGANIZATION OF ARAB-AMERICAN STUDENTS IN STANFORD
Stanford University
Stanford, CA 94305
Tel: (650) 723-2300
Email: oasis-list-owner@stanford.edu
Web: www.stanford.edu/group/arab

ORGANIZATION OF IRANIAN SCHOLARS
San Diego State University
Aztec Center 168
San Diego, CA 92182-7800
Torang Asadi, President
Email: persians@rohan.sdsu.edu
Web: www-rohan.sdsu.edu/%7epersians

PAKISTAN STUDENTS ASSOCIATION
California State University, Chico
400 W. 1st St.
Chico, CA 95929
Usman Khurshid
Tel: (530) 342-9171

Email: PSAChico@hotmail.com
Web: www.csuchico.edu/pakistan

PAKISTANI STUDENT ASSOCIATION
San Jose State University
1 Washington Sq., Student Life Center Box #75
San Jose, CA 95192
Asim Siddique, President
Tel: (408) 557-8341
Email: PSA_SJSU@yahoo.com
Web: www2.sjsu.edu/orgs/psa/front.html

PAKISTANIS AT STANFORD
Stanford University
Stanford, CA 94309
Maham Abbas Mela, President
Email: pas-officers@lists.stanford.edu
Web: www.stanford.edu/group/pakistan/index.
htm

PILIPINO ACADEMIC STUDENT SERVICES
University of California at Berkeley
515 Eshelman Hall
Berkeley, CA 94720
Jennifer Tuazon, Executive Director
Tel: (510) 643-9302 Fax: (510) 642-7920
Email: pass_2004@uclink.berkeley.edu
Web: www.ocf.berkeley.edu/~pass

PILIPINO AMERICAN COALITION
California State University, Long Beach
University Student Union, Student Life and
Development, 1250 Bellflower Blvd.
Long Beach, CA 90840-0604
Cesille Basila, President
Tel: (310) 669-4786
Email: lbpac@yahoo.com
Web: www.geocities.com/lbpac/abcon

PILIPINO AMERICAN COLLEGIATE ENDEAVOR
San Francisco State University
Student Center-M100C,1600 Holloway
San Francisco, CA 94132
Tel: (415) 338-1918
Email: pacecore@sfsu.edu
Web: http://userwww.sfsu.edu/%7Epacecore

PILIPINO AMERICANS IN SCIENCE AND ENGINEERING
University of California, Davis
Student Programs and Activities Center, Box
300
Davis, CA 95616
Albert Robelo, Co-President
Email: pase@engr.ucdavis.edu
Web: http://pase.engineering.ucdavis.edu

PILIPINO ASSOCIATION OF SCIENTISTS, ARCHITECTS, AND ENGINEERS
University of California at Berkeley
220 Bechtel Engineering
Berkeley, CA 94720
Email: pasae-core@uclink4.berkeley.edu
Web: www.ocf.berkeley.edu/~pasae

SOUTHEAST ASIAN STUDENT COALITION
University of California at Berkeley
506 Barrows Hall
Berkeley, CA 94720-2570
Email: berkeleysasc@uclink.berkeley.edu
Web: www.geocities.com/berkeleysasc

SRI LANKAN STUDENT ASSOCIATION
California State University, Chico
400 W. 1st St.
Chico, CA 95929
Chaminda Jayakody
Tel: (530) 894-5879
Email: chami602@yahoo.com
Web: www.csuchico.edu/csusrisa/index1.html

STANFORD TAIWANESE STUDENT ASSOCIATION
Stanford University
Stanford, CA 94305
Weiting Lei, President
Tel: (408) 406-3948

Email: weitingl@stanford.edu
Web: www.stanford.edu/group/stsa

STRIVE
c/o ASUC Office of Student Affairs, University
of California, 400 Eshleman Hall
Berkeley, CA 94720-4500
Huy Chung, Program Manager
Tel: (510) 848-6067
Email: ning489@uclink.berkeley.edu
Web: www.ocf.berkeley.edu/~strive

TAIWANESE AMERICAN STUDENTS ASSOCIATION
University of California, Berkeley
Berkeley, CA 94720
Alina Chen, External Vice President
Email: evp@tasa.berkeley.edu
Web: http://tasa.berkeley.edu/index.htm

TAIWANESE AMERICAN UNION
University of California, Los Angeles
3230 Campbell Hall, Box 951546
Los Angeles, CA 90095
Ricky Chung, President
Email: tau@ucla.edu
Web: www.studentgroups.ucla.edu/tau

THAI AMERICAN INTERCULTURAL SOCIETY
Stanford University
P.O. Box 17341
Stanford, CA 94309
Tonkid Chantrasmi, President
Email: tonkid@stanford.edu
Web: www.sacot.org/thais

THE IRANIAN STUDENT ALLIANCE IN AMERICA
400 Eshleman Hall
Berkeley, CA 94720
Elnaz Manoucheri, Director
Email: isaa_officers@berkeley.edu

UNION OF VIETNAMESE STUDENT ASSOCIATIONS OF SOUTHERN CALIFORNIA
P.O. Box 2069
Westminster, CA 92684
Tel: (714) 890-1418 Fax: (714) 890-1518
Email: contact@thsv.org
Web: www.thsv.org

UNITED VIETNAMESE STUDENT ASSOCIATIONS
Northern California
P.O. Box 612635
San Jose, CA 95161
Tam Dang, Coordinator
Email: president@norcalUVSA.org
Web: www.norcaluvsa.org

VIETNAMESE STUDENT ASSOCIATION
California State University
1250 Bellflower Blvd.
Long Beach, CA 90840
Susan Thai, President
Email: hnv_thai@yahoo.com
Web: www.csulb.edu/org/vsa

Santa Clara University
Cesar Chavez Commons, 500 El Camino Real
Santa Clara, CA 95053
Pauline Nguyen, Advisor
Tel: (408) 551-7152 Fax: (408) 551-7170
Web: www.scu.edu

University of California, Davis
Student Programs & Activities Center Box 224
Davis, CA 95616
Susan Mai, President
Email: vsa@ucdavis.edu
Web: http://asucd.ucdavis.edu/organizations/cultural/vsa

VIETNAMESE STUDENT ASSOCIATION
University of Southern California
Los Angeles, CA 90089
Philip Duong, President

Tel: (213) 740-2311
Email: vsa@usc.edu
Web: www-scf.usc.edu/%7Evsa

VIETNAMESE STUDENT UNION
University of California
308 Westwood Plz., 412 Kerckhoff Hall
Los Angeles, CA 90095
David Do, Co-President
Tel: (310) 794-9546
Email: vsu@ucla.edu
Web: www.uclavsu.org

CHINESE STUDENT ASSOCIATION
Santa Clara University
Shapell Lounge, 500 El Camino Real
Santa Clara, CA 95053
Minh Nguyen, President
Tel: (408) 554-4926 Fax: (408) 554-1958
Email: neodominal@yahoo.com
Web: www.scu.edu

COLORADO

ARTISTIC

ASIAN ART COORDINATING COUNCIL
255 Detroit St. #300
Denver, CO 80206
Julie Segraves, Executive Director
Tel: (303) 329-6417 Fax: (303) 320-7597
Email: julie@asianartcc.org
Web: www.asianartcc.org

BUSINESS

CHINA DEVELOPMENT INSTITUTE
1441 Wazee St. #103
Denver, CO 80202
Angel Chi, President
Tel: (303) 871-8734 Fax: (303) 871-8890
Email: info@cdius.org
Web: www.cdius.org/default.asp

JAPAN EXTERNAL TRADE ORGANIZATION
Denver Chapter
1200 17th St. #1110
Denver, CO 80202
Toshiako Endo, Chief Executive Director
Tel: (303) 629-0404
Email: jetroden@quest.net
Web: www.jetro.go.jp/usa/denver

JEWISH BUSINESS ASSOCIATION OF COLORADO
P.O. Box 371516
Denver, CO 80237
Andrew Ehrnstein, President
Tel: (303) 836-1522
Email: membership@jbacolorado.org
Web: www.jbacolorado.org

CHAMBER OF COMMERCE

ASIAN CHAMBER OF COMMERCE
Colorado Branch
924 W. Colfax Ave.
Denver, CO 80204
John Wright, Executive Director
Tel: (303) 595-9737 Fax: (303) 595-8880
Email: asiancc@rmi.net
Web: www.asianchambercommerce.org

RUSSIAN-AMERICAN CHAMBER OF COMMERCE
1552 Pennsylvania St.
Denver, CO 80203
Dr. Deborah Anne Palmieri, President/CEO
Tel: (303) 831-0829 Fax: (303) 831-0830
Email: generalinfo@russianamericanchamber.org
Web: www.russianamericanchamber.org

CULTURAL

ACADEMY OF CHINESE MARTIAL AND CULTURAL ARTS
1750 38th St.
Boulder, CO 80301
Shifu H. Solow
Tel: (303) 507-3800
Email: shifu@academychinesearts.org
Web: www.academychinesearts.org

COLORADO CHINA COUNCIL
4556 Apple Way
Boulder, CO 80301
Alice Renouf, Director
Tel: (303) 443-11 Fax: (303) 443-1107
Email: alice@asiacouncil.org
Web: www.asiacouncil.org

COLORADO FRIENDS OF TIBET
7305 Grandview Ave.
Arvada, CO 80003
Dawn Engle, President
Tel: (303) 455-1532 Fax: (303) 455-3921
Web: www.tibet.org/cft/

DENVER CHINESE CULTURE CENTER
P.O. Box 3189
Littleton, CO 80161-3189
Naili Yee, President
Tel: (303) 770-7866
Email: NailiYee@comcast.net
Web: http://go2ccc.com/dccc/main.php

FILIPINO AMERICAN COMMUNITY OF COLORADO
1900 Harlan St.
Edgewater, CO 80214
Frances A. Campbell, President
Tel: (303) 233-6817
Email: fran@filam-colo.org
Web: www.filam-colo.org

KOREAN WAR VETERANS ASSOCIATION
Colorado Springs Chapter
1593 Cragin Rd.
Colorado Springs, CO 80920
Ltc. Ellsworth Dutch Nelsen, Founder/President
Email: b13thfield@pcisys.net
Web: www.dutchnelsen.org

PHILIPPINE AMERICAN SOCIETY OF COLORADO
17198 E. Dorado Cir.
Aurora, CO 80015
Edith Pasion, President
Tel: (303) 690-5686
Email: epasion@earthlink.net

TURKISH AMERICAN CULTURAL SOCIETY OF COLORADO
P.O. Box 371193
Denver, CO 80237
Erdal Ozkan, President
Tel: (303) 273-3188 Fax: (303) 273-3189
Email: eozkan@mines.edu
Web: www.colorado.turkleri.com

MULTI-PURPOSE

AURORA ASIAN/ PACIFIC COMMUNITY PARTNERSHIP
9915 E. Colfax Ave.
Aurora, CO 80010
Nancy Webster McKinney, Co- Chair
Tel: (303) 361-0847 Fax: (303) 361-2953
Email: nwebster@auroragor.org
Web: www.auroraasian.org

PROFESSIONAL

ASIAN PACIFIC AMERICAN BAR ASSOCIATION
Colorado Branch
P.O. Box 3011
Denver, CO 80201

Neeti Pawar, President
Tel: (303) 320-4848
Email: peggy.chiu@tpl.org
Web: www.apaba.8k.com

ASIAN PACIFIC AMERICAN BAR ASSOCIATION OF COLORADO
Davis Graham & Stubbs LLP
1550 Arapahoe St. #500
Denver, CO 80202
Byeong Sook Seo, President
Tel: (303) 376-5000 Fax: (303) 376-5001
Email: bseo@gorsuch.com
Web: www.apaba.8k.com

ROCKY MOUNTAIN CHINESE SOCIETY OF SCIENCE AND ENGINEERING
7236 W. 97th Pl.
Westminster, CO 80021
Han-Ching Wu, President
Email: wuh@rmpprestress.com
Web: www.rmcsse.org

RELIGIOUS

ALPHA OMEGA RELIEF NETWORK
P.O. Box 63343
Colorado Springs, CO 80962-3343
Tel: (719) 596-7531 Fax: (719) 596-7534
Email: info@aorelief.org
Web: www.aorelief.org

ASSOCIATION OF NORTH AMERICAN CHINESE EVANGELICAL FREE CHURCHES
988 Delta Dr.
Lafayette, CO 80026
Tel: (303) 494-4559
Email: webmaster@anacefc.net
Web: www.anacefc.net

CAMBODIAN OUTREACH PROJECT
P.O. Box 7034
Broomfield, CO 80021
Email: mail@cambodianoutreachproject.org
Web: www.cambodianoutreachproject.org

CHINA PARTNER INC.
Headquarters
14A W. Dry Creek Cir.
Littleton, CO 80120
Erik Burklin, President
Tel: (303) 795-3190 Fax: (303) 795-3176
Email: headquarters@chinapartner.org
Web: www.chinapartner.org

CHINESE EVANGELICAL CHURCH OF DENVER
1099 Newark St.
Aurora, CO 80010
Paul Epp, English Pastor
Tel: (303) 366-0303 Fax: (303) 366-5923
Email: eppistle@hotmail.com
Web: www.cecd.net

DENVER CHINESE EVANGELICAL FREE CHURCH
275 S. Hazel Ct.
Denver, CO 80219
Rev. Chi-Eng Yuan, Pastor
Tel: (303) 936-4321
Email: pastor_yuan@dcefc.org
Web: www.dcefc.org

IRANIAN CHRISTIAN INTERNATIONAL, INC.
P.O. Box 25607
Colorado Springs, CO 80936
Tel: (719) 596-0010 Fax: (719) 574-1141
Email: ici@myprimus.com
Web: www.iranchristians.org

JAPANESE CHRISTIAN FELLOWSHIP NETWORK
P.O. Box 260532
Highlands Ranch, CO 80126-0532
Maki Goto, Contact
Tel: (303) 730-4226 Fax: (303) 730-4221
Email: ushq@jcfn.org
Web: www.jcfn.org

KOREAN CHRISTIAN CHURCH
1495 S. University Blvd.
Denver, CO 80210
Rev. Randy S. Ju, Senior Pastor
Tel: (303) 777-6566 Fax: (303) 777-0050
Web: www.kccdenver.org

TEMPLE SINAI
3509 S. Glencoe St.
Denver, CO 80237
Rob Abramson, President
Tel: (303) 759-1827 Fax: (303) 759-2519
Web: www.americanet.com/sinai

THE FIL-AM CHURCH OF DENVER
15534 E. Hinsdale Cir.
Centennial, CO 80112
Rev. Carlos Bulalayao, Senior Pastor
Email: Cbjdenver@comcast.net
Web: www.fil-amchurchdenver.org

THE FORT COLLINS EVANGELICAL FREE CHURCH
2824 Claremont Dr.
Fort Collins, CO 80526
Pastor David Auyeung
Tel: (970) 204-4046
Email: auyeung@webaccess.net
Web: http://fccefc.ccim.org

THE JEWISH RENEWAL COMMUNITY OF BOULDER
P.O. Box 21601
Boulder, CO 80308-4601
Sheldon Romer, President
Tel: (303) 271-3540 Fax: (303) 499-0841
Email: info@neveikodesh.org
Web: www.neveikodesh.org

TURKISH WORLD OUTREACH
508 Fruitvale Ct.
Grand Junction, CO 81504
Tel: (970) 434-1942 Fax: (970) 434-1461
Email: TWO@onlinecol.com
Web: www.two-fot.org

RESEARCH

ASIAN PACIFIC CENTER FOR HUMAN DEVELOPMENT
1825 York St.
Denver, CO 80206
Carey Ann Tanaka, Director
Tel: (303) 393-0304 Fax: (303) 388-1172
Email: careyanntanaka@hotmail.com

INSTITUTE FOR NATIONAL SECURITY STUDIES, US AIR FORCE ACADEMY
2354 Fairchild Dr. #5L27
USAF Academy, CO 80840
James Smith, Director
Tel: (719) 333-2717 Fax: (719) 333-2716
Email: inss@usafa.af.mil
Web: www.usafa.af.mil

JEWISH GENEALOGICAL SOCIETY OF COLORADO
6965 E. Girard Ave.
Denver, CO 80224
Myndel Cohen, President
Tel: (303) 756-6028
Email: hermyn@aol.com
Web: www2.jewishgen.org/jgs-colorado/

NATIONAL JEWISH MEDICAL AND RESEARCH CENTER
1400 Jackson St.
Denver, CO 80206
Lynn M. Taussig, President/CEO
Tel: (800) 222-5864
Email: webmaster@njc.org
Web: www.njc.org

SPEC. INT., CHILD CARE

ASIAN HOPE
12675 Home Farm Dr.
Westminster, CO 80234
Web: www.asianhope.org

CHINESE CHILDREN ADOPTION INTERNATIONAL
Headquarters
6920 S. Holly Cir.
Centennial, CO 80112
Josh Zhong, Founder/President
Tel: (303) 850-9998 Fax: (303) 850-9997
Web: www.chinesechildren.org

UPLIFT INTERNATIONALE
P.O. Box 582
Wheat Ridge, CO 80034
Jaime Yrastorza, President
Tel: (303) 707-1361
Email: info@upliftinternationale.org
Web: www.upliftinternationale.org

SPEC. INT., EDUCATION

ASIA TRANSPACIFIC FOUNDATION
2995 Center Green Ct.
Boulder, CO 80301
Tel: (800) 642-2742 Fax: (303) 443-7078
Email: ravel@AsiaTranspacific.com
Web: www.asiatranspacific.com

COLORADO SCHOOL OF TRADITIONAL CHINESE MEDICINE
1441 York St. #202
Denver, CO 80206-2127
George Kitchie, President
Tel: (303) 329-6355 Fax: (303) 388-8165
Email: cstcm-admin@traditionalhealing.net
Web: www.traditionalhealing.net

COLORADO SPRINGS CHINESE CULTURAL INSTITUTE
P.O. Box 2625
Colorado Springs, CO 80901
Mali Hsu, Founder/Chairwoman
Tel: (719) 635-0024
Email: malihsu@aol.com
Web: www.cscci.org

DENVER CHINESE SCHOOL
P.O. Box 261175
Highlands Ranch, CO 80163
Huiliang Liu, Chair
Tel: (303) 471-5358 Fax: (800) 675-2158
Email: dcsc@yahoogroups.com
Web: www.denverchineseschool.org

NATIONAL ASIAN PACIFIC AMERICAN LAW STUDENT ASSOCIATION
University of Denver College of Law
2255 E. Evans
Denver, CO 80208
Joseph Chu, President
Tel: (303) 871-2000
Email: jchu06@law.du.edu
Web: www.law.du.edu/apalsa/

US CHINA PEOPLES FRIENDSHIP ASSOCIATION
Denver Chapter
1945 Hudson St.
Denver, CO 80220
George Tung, Contact
Tel: (303) 355-2523 Fax: (303) 355-2523
Web: www.uscpfa.org

SPEC. INT., HEALTH SERVICES

HELPING HANDS
948 Pearl St.
Boulder, CO 80302
Tel: (303) 448-1811 Fax: (303) 440-7328
Email: helpinghands@sannr.com

SPEC. INT., HUMAN RELATIONS

BURMA LIFELINE
P.O. Box 21146
Boulder, CO 80308
Email: info@burmalifeline.org
Web: www.burmalifeline.org

CENTER FOR CHINA-US COOPERATION
University of Denver
2201 S. Gaylord
Denver, CO 80208
Sam Suisheng Zhao, Executive Director
Tel: (303) 871-2401 Fax: (303) 871-2456
Email: szhao@du.edu
Web: www.du.edu/gsis/china/

COLORADO REFUGEE NETWORK
789 Sherman St. #250
Denver, CO 80203
Barbara Carr, Refugee Coordinator
Tel: (303) 863-8211 Fax: (303) 863-0838
Email: barbara.carr@state.co.us
Web: www.coloradorefugeenetwork.org

SURMANG FOUNDATION
13536 Gold Hill Rd.
Boulder, CO 80302
Dr. Juliet Carpenter, Executive VP
Tel: (303) 459-9030
Email: info@surmang.org
Web: www.surmang.org

THE AMERICAN JEWISH COMMITTEE
Colorado Chapter
300 S. Dahlia #201
Denver, CO 80246
Judy Altenberg, Chapter President
Tel: (303) 320-1742 Fax: (303) 320-1742
Email: colorado@ajc.org
Web: www.ajc.org

SPEC. INT., MENTAL HEALTH

NATIONAL ASIAN AMERICAN PACIFIC ISLANDER MENTAL HEALTH ASSOCIATION
1215 19th St. #A
Denver, CO 80202
DJ Ida, Ph.D, Executive Director
Tel: (303) 298-7910 Fax: (303) 298-8081
Email: info@naapimha.org
Web: www.naapimha.org

SPEC. INT., SENIORS

AGING INFORMATION CENTER
Region VIII: CO, MT, ND, SD, UT, WY
1961 Stout St. #1022, Federal Office Bldg.
Denver, CO 80294-3538
Percy Devine, Regional Administrator
Tel: (303) 844-2951 Fax: (303) 844-2943
Email: percy.divine@aoa.gov
Web: www.aoa.dhhs.gov

JEWISH SENIOR RECREATION NETWORK
51 Grape St.
Denver, CO 80220
Sue Grant, Coordinator
Tel: (303) 388-4013 X 348
Email: sgrant@jewishfamilyservice.org
Web: www.JewishSeniorRec.net

SPEC. INT., SOCIAL INTEREST

ALLIED JEWISH FEDERATION OF COLORADO
300 S. Dahlia St. #300
Denver, CO 80246
Doug Seserman, President/CEO
Tel: (303) 321-3399 Fax: (303) 322-8328
Email: information@ajfcolorado.org
Web: www.jewishcolorado.org

BOULDER JEWISH COMMUNITY CENTER
3800 Kalmia Ave.
Boulder, CO 80301
Linda Loewenstein, Executive Director
Tel: (303) 998-1900 Fax: (303) 998-1965
Email: linda@boulderjcc.org
Web: www.boulderjcc.org

CAMBODIAN ORGANIZATION OF COLORADO
14383 N. 83rd St.
Longmont, CO 80503-7885
Chanrith Oun
Tel: (303) 678-8879 Fax: (303) 581-5121
Web: www.boulderparenting.org/ParentGuide/culturaldiversity.html

INTERNATIONAL MOUNTAIN EXPLORERS CONNECTION
P.O. Box 3665
Boulder, CO 80307
Scott Dimetrosky, Founder/Executive Director
Tel: (303) 998-0101 Fax: (303) 998-1007
Email: info@mountainexplorers.org
Web: www.hec.org

JAPAN AMERICA SOCIETY OF COLORADO
1625 Broadway #680
Denver, CO 80202
Richard K. Clark, President
Tel: (303) 592-5768 Fax: (303) 592-5767
Email: jascolorado@att.net
Web: www.jascolorado.org

JEWISH FAMILY SERVICE OF COLORADO
1355 S. Colorado Blvd. #400
Denver, CO 80222
Tel: (303) 759-4890 X505 Fax: (303) 759-5998
Web: www.jewishfamilyservice.org

ROCKY MOUNTAIN FRIENDS OF NEPAL
8962 E. Hampden Ave. PMB 186
Denver, CO 80231
Kshitij Sharma, Secretary
Tel: (303) 338-0970
Email: secretary@rmfn.org
Web: www.rmfn.org

SPEC. INT., SPORTS

COLORADO DRAGON BOAT FESTIVAL
605 Parfet St. #200
Lakewood, CO 80215
John Chin, Board of Director
Tel: (303) 404-5466 Fax: (303) 438-5788
Email: john.chin@frontrange.edu
Web: www.coloradodragonboat.org

INTERNATIONAL SHOTOKAN KARATE CLUB
Mountain States Region
7852 W. Florida Dr.
Lakewood, CO 80226
Yutaka Yaguchi, Instructor
Tel: (303) 733-8326 Fax: (303) 733-1226
Web: www.uniques.com/shotokan

JAPAN AIKIDO ASSOCIATION USA, INC.
5752 S. Kingston Way
Englewood, CO 80111
Seiji Tanaka, Chairman/Director
Web: www.tomiki.org

MOSAIC OUTDOOR CLUBS OF AMERICA
Denver Chapter
P.O. Box 24772
Denver, CO 80224
Alison Wallis, Chapter President
Tel: (303) 836-6662
Email: colorado@mosaics.org
Web: www.mosaics.org

SPEC. INT., WOMEN

NATIONAL COALITION AGAINST DOMESTIC VIOLENCE
P.O. Box 18749
Denver, CO 80218-0749
Rita Smith, Executive Director
Tel: (303) 839-1852 Fax: (303) 831-9251
Email: mainoffice@ncadv.org
Web: www.ncadv.org

SPEC. INT., YOUTH

JEWISH CHILDRENS ADOPTION NETWORK
P.O. Box 147016
Denver, CO 80214-7016
Tel: (303) 573-8113 Fax: (303) 893-1447
Email: jcan@qwest.net
Web: www.users.uswest.net/~jcan/

STUDENT ORGANIZATION

ASIAN PACIFIC AMERICAN STUDENT SERVICES
Colorado State University
212 Lory Student Ctr.
Fort Collins, CO 80523
Tel: (970) 491-6154 Fax: (970) 491-2574
Web: www.colostate.edu/Depts/APASS

Cultural Unity Center
103 UCB, Willard Admin #18
Boulder, CO 80309
Dale Trevino, Director
Tel: (303) 492-5667 Fax: (303) 735-0321
Email: dale.trevino@colorado.edu
Web: www.colorado.edu/studentaffairs/cuc/

INDIAN STUDENTS ASSOCIATION
University of Colorado at Boulder
207 UCB #453
Boulder, CO 80309
Neha Ahuja, President
Tel: (303) 492-6430
Email: isa@colorado.edu
Web: www.colorado.edu/studentgroups/isa

MUSLIM STUDENT ASSOCIATION
Colorado State University
Lory Student Ctr., P.O. Box 204
Fort Collins, CO 80523
Tel: (970) 491-1477
Email: msa@lamar.colostate.edu
Web: www.colostate.edu/Orgs/MSA

CONNECTICUT

ARTISTIC

CHINESE HEALING ARTS CENTER
73-3 Great Plains Rd.
Danbury, CT 06811
Dr. T.K. Shih, Contact
Tel: (203) 748-8107 Fax: (203) 791-9980
Email: qihealer@aol.com
Web: www.qihealer.com

CULTURAL

ASIAN AMERICAN CULTURAL CENTER
University of Connecticut
364 Fairfield Rd., U-186
Storrs, CT 06269-2186
Jeetendra Joshee, President
Tel: (860) 486-0830 Fax: (860) 486-1606
Email: aacctr3@uconnvm.uconn.edu
Web: www.asacc.uconn.edu

Yale University
295 Crown St.
New Haven, CT 06511
Saveena Dhall, Director
Tel: (203) 432-2931
Email: saveena.dhall@yale.edu
Web: www.yale.edu/aacc

CONNECTICUT CHINESE CULTURE ASSOCIATION
178 Highland St.
New Haven, CT 06511
Tel: (203) 624-4036
Email: ccca9@yahoo.com
Web: www.ctchinese.org

EAST ROCK INSTITUTE
251 Dwight St.
New Haven, CT 06511

Dr. Hesung Chun Koh, Director
Tel: (203) 624-8619 Fax: (203) 624-8619
Email: erikoh@yale.edu
Web: http://pantheon.cis.yale.edu/~eri3

JEWISH HISTORICAL SOCIETY OF GREATER HARTFORD
335 Bloomfield Ave.
West Hartford, CT 06117
Marsha Lotstein, Executive Director
Tel: (860) 236-4571 X341 Fax: (860) 233-0802
Email: jhsgh@jhsgh.org
Web: www.jhsgh.org

KOREAN AMERICAN ACTUARIAL SOCIETY, INC.
P.O. Box 231663
Hartford, CT 06123
Timothy Yi, President
Tel: (860) 881-4222
Email: tim.yi@koreanactuary.org
Web: www.koreanactuary.org

THE PHILIPPINE-AMERICAN GROUP OF GREATER WATERBURY AREA
63 Dundee Dr.
Cheshire, CT 06410
Gloria Manaloto, Secretary
Email: paggawa-owner@yahoogroups.com
Web: www.paggawa.org

US-CHINA EDUCATION AND CULTURE EXCHANGE CENTER
600 University Ave., Rennell Hall #234
Bridgeport, CT 06601
Scott F. Williams, Contact
Tel: (203) 576-6709 Fax: (203) 576-6764
Email: sfwilliams@comcast.com
Web: www.uschinaedu.org

MULTI-PURPOSE

SOUTHERN NEW ENGLAND TURKISH AMERICAN ASOCIATION
4 Beech Tree Way
Milford, CT 06460
Tel: (203) 878-8025
Email: info@snetaca.org
Web: www.snetaca.org

POLITICAL ACTION

INDIAN POLITICAL FORUM
66 Ruff Cir.
Glastonbury, CT 06033
Dami Rambhial, Secretary
Tel: (860) 633-1392 Fax: (860) 659-1671
Email: drambhial@aol.com

PROFESSIONAL

ASSOCIATION OF FILIPINO ENGINEERS
National Federation of Filipino American Associations (NaFFAA)
P.O. Box 2276
Milford, CT 06460
Arnulfo Rosario, Chairman
Tel: (203) 877-7260 Fax: (203) 877-7260
Web: www.naffaa.org

CONNECTICUT ASIAN PACIFIC AMERICAN BAR ASSOCIATION
Bingham McCutchen LLP
1 State St.
Hartford, CT 06103
Susan Kim, President
Tel: (860) 240-2858 Fax: (860) 240-2818
Email: susan.kim@bingham.com
Web: www.ctbar.org

RELIGIOUS

ASIA EVANGELICAL CHURCH
55 Washington Pl.

Bridgeport, CT 06604
Tel: (203) 384-9870

BETH EL TEMPLE
2626 Albany Ave.
West Hartford, CT 06117
Jan Margolius, Executive Director
Tel: (860) 233-9696 Fax: (860) 233-9802
Email: jmargolius@bethelwh.org
Web: www.bethelwesthartford.org

CAMBODIAN NEW LIFE EVANGELICAL CHURCH
22 Maple Ave.
Danbury, CT 06810
Tel: (203) 798-8084
Web: www.churchangel.com/WEBCT/danbury.htm

CHABAD OF SHORELINE
618 Main St.
Branford, CT 06405
Tel: (203) 488-2263 Fax: (203) 488-8711
Email: chabad@jewishshoreline.org
Web: www.jewishshoreline.org

CONGREGATION AGUDATH SHOLOM
301 Strawberry Hill Ave.
Stamford, CT 06902
Howard Rothman, President
Tel: (203) 358-2200 Fax: (203) 358-2323
Web: www.congregationagudathsholom.org

CONGREGATION B'NAI ISRAEL
2710 Park Ave.
Bridgeport, CT 06604
Mark Schiff, President
Tel: (203) 336-1858 Fax: (203) 367-7889
Email: welcome@congregationbnaiisrael.org
Web: www.congregationbnaiisrael.org

CONGREGATION B'NAI JACOB
75 Rimmon Rd.
Woodbridge, CT 06525-2098
Alan V. Wunsch, Executive Director
Tel: (203) 389-2111 Fax: (203) 389-5293
Email: cbj.info@snet.net
Web: www.bnaijacob.org

CONGREGATION BETH EL-KESER ISRAEL
85 Harrison St.
New Haven, CT 06515-1724
Gila Reinstein, President
Tel: (203) 389-2108 Fax: (203) 389-5899
Email: gila.reinstein@yale.edu
Web: www.beki.org

CONGREGATION BETH SHALOM RODFE ZEDEK
P.O. Box 438
Chester, CT 06412
Louise Ross, Co-President
Tel: (860) 526-8920 Fax: (860) 526-8918
Email: bethshalom@snet.net
Web: www.cbsrz.org

CONGREGATION BIKUR CHOLIM SHEVETH ACHIM
112 Marvel Rd.
New Haven, CT 06515
Dr. Peter Rogol, President
Tel: (203) 387-4699 Fax: (203) 387-2780
Email: davigdor2@snet.net
Web: www.bikurcholimsyn.org

CONGREGATION MISHKAN ISRAEL
785 Ridge Rd.
Hamden, CT 06517
Mark Sklarz, President
Tel: (203) 288-3877 Fax: (203) 248-2148
Email: congregation@snet.net
Web: www.uahc.org/ct/cmi

CONGREGATION OR SHALOM
205 Old Grassy Hill Rd.
Orange, CT 06477
Tel: (203) 799-2341 Fax: (203) 799-0239
Web: www.orshalom.net

CONNECTICUT KOREAN PRESBYTERIAN CHURCH
450 Whitney Ave.
New Haven, CT 06511
Tel: (203) 497-9744 Fax: (203) 497-8266
Email: ckpcgod@aol.com
Web: www.connecticutkoreanchurch.org

FAIRFIELD COUNTY CHINESE COMMUNITY CHURCH
240 Wolfpit Rd.
Wilton, CT 06897
Albert Li, Pastor
Tel: (203) 324-7881
Email: pastorli@fcccc.net
Web: www.fcccc.net

KOL AMI FOR REGIONAL CONSERVATIVE JUDAISM
1484 Highland Ave.
Cheshire, CT 06410
Guy Darter, President
Tel: (203) 272-1006
Email: kolamicheshire@yahoo.com
Web: www.kolamicheshire.org

TEMPLE BETH DAVID
3 Main St.
Cheshire, CT 06410
Michael Laden, President
Tel: (203) 272-0037 Fax: (203) 272-6562
Email: templebd@tbd.com
Web: www.tbdcheshire.org

TEMPLE SHOLOM
P.O. Box 509
New Milford, CT 06776
Lou Simon, President
Tel: (860) 354-0273
Email: pres@tsholom.org
Web: www.tsholom.org

TEMPLE SINAI
458 Lakeside Dr.
Stamford, CT 06903
David M. Cohen, President
Tel: (203) 322-1649 Fax: (203) 329-7741
Email: president@templesinaistamford.org
Web: www.templesinaistamford.org

THE CARDINAL KUNG FOUNDATION
P.O. Box 8086, Ridgeway Ctr.
Stamford, CT 06905
Joseph Kung
Tel: (203) 329-9712 Fax: (203) 329-8415
Email: JMKUNG@aol.com
Web: www.cardinalkungfoundation.org

UNITED SYNAGOGUE OF CONSERVATIVE JUDAISM
Connecticut Valley Region
1800 Silas Deane Hwy. #171
Rocky Hill, CT 06067
Joseph Bacher, President
Tel: (860) 563-5531 Fax: (860) 563-5541
Email: joeb.nai@rcn.com
Web: http://uscj.org/ctvalley

WESTVILLE SYNAGOGUE
74 W. Prospect St.
New Haven, CT 06515
Michael Wiesner, President
Tel: (203) 389-9513 Fax: (203) 389-9514
Email: travel@callnet.com
Web: www.westvilleshul.org

YOUNG ISRAEL OF NEW HAVEN
292 Norton St.
New Haven, CT 06511
Joshua Cypess, Rabbi
Tel: (203) 776-4212 Fax: (203) 776-1805
Email: yinh@yinh.org
Web: www.yinh.org

YOUNG ISRAEL OF STAMFORD
69 Oaklawn Ave.
Stamford, CT 06905
Elie Fishman, President
Tel: (203) 348-3955

Email: efishman@mjhs.org
Web: www.yistamford.org

SPEC. INT., CHILD CARE

CHINA CARE FOUNDATION, INC.
P.O. Box 142
Greenwich, CT 06807
Matt Dalio, Founder and President
Tel: (203) 861-6395 Fax: (203) 618-0470
Email: mdalio@chinacare.org
Web: www.chinacare.org

SPEC. INT., COUNSELING

ASIAN FAMILY SERVICES, INC.
1921 Park St.
Hartford, CT 06106
Myron Congdon, President
Tel: (860) 951-8770 Fax: (860) 232-9049
Email: info@asianfamilyservices.org
Web: www.asianfamilyservices.org

SPEC. INT., EDUCATION

ASIAN AMERICAN STUDIES INSTITUTE
University of Connecticut, Storrs
354 Mansfield Rd., U-2091
Storrs, CT 06269-2091
Roger Buckley, Director
Tel: (860) 486-4751 Fax: (860) 486-2851
Email: asiadm01@uconnvm.uconn.edu
Web: http://asianamerican.uconn.edu/

CENTER FOR IRANIAN RESEARCH AND ANALYSIS
275 Mount Carmel Ave.
Hamden, CT 06518-1949
Mahmood Monshipouri, Executive Director
Tel: (203) 582-3356 Fax: (203) 582-3471
Email: mahmood.monshipour@quinnipiac.edu
Web: faculty.quinnipiac.edu/libarts/monshipouri/circ/

CHINESE LANGUAGE SCHOOL OF CONNECTICUT
P.O. Box 515
Riverside, CT 06878-0515
Wen Hsu, Principal
Tel: (866) 301-4906
Email: info@chineselanguageschool.org
Web: www.chineselanguageschool.org

COUNCIL ON EAST ASIAN STUDIES
Yale University
P.O. Box 208206
New Haven, CT 06520-8206
Abbey Newman, Council Manager and Administrator
Tel: (203) 432-3426 Fax: (203) 432-3430
Email: eastasian.studies@yale.edu
Web: www.yale.edu/ycias/ceas/

COUNCIL ON MIDDLE EAST STUDIES
Yale University
P.O. Box 208206
New Haven, CT 06520-8206
Abbas Amanat, Chair
Tel: (203) 432-5596 Fax: (203) 432-5963
Web: www.yale.edu/ycias/cmes

JAPANESE EDUCATIONAL INSTITUTE OF NEW YORK
54 Greenwich Ave.
Greenwich, CT 06831
Tel: (203) 629-5922 Fax: (203) 629-4743
Email: nyjec123@aol.com

LINGNAN FOUNDATION
P.O. Box 208340
New Haven, CT 06520-8340
Leslie B. Stone, Executive Director
Tel: (203) 432-1063 Fax: (203) 432-7246
Email: leslie.stone@yale.edu
Web: www.lingnanfoundation.org

WESTCHESTER FAIRFIELD HEBREW ACADEMY
300 E. Putnam Ave.
Greenwich, CT 06830
Nora Anderson, Head of School
Tel: (203) 863-9663 Fax: (203) 863-2076
Email: info@wfha.org
Web: www.wfha.org

YALE CENTER FOR INTERNATIONAL AND AREA STUDIES
P.O. Box 208206
New Haven, CT 06520-8206
Ian Shapiro, Director
Tel: (203) 432-3410 Fax: (203) 432-9383
Email: peg.limbacher@yale.edu
Web: www.cis.yale.edu

YALE-CHINA ASSOCIATION IN THE US
442 Temple St.
New Haven, CT 06520-8223
Nancy E. Chapman, Executive Director
Tel: (203) 432-0880 Fax: (203) 432-7246
Email: yale-china@yale.edu
Web: www.yalechina.org

SPEC. INT., HEALTH SERVICES

KHMER HEALTH ADVOCATES
29 Shadow Ln.
West Hartford, CT 06110
Theanvy Kuoch, Executive Director
Tel: (860) 561-3345 Fax: (860) 561-3538 .
Email: tkuoch@atmyhealthadvocates.org

SPEC. INT., HUMAN RELATIONS

COUNCIL ON AMERICAN-ISLAMIC RELATIONS
Connecticut Chapter
27 Oakridge Dr.
Old Lyme, CT 06371
Badar Malik, President
Tel: (860) 434-9099
Email: SanAntonio@cair-net.org
Web: www.cair-net.org

NORTH SOUTH FOUNDATION
Connecticut Region
10 Whitman Ln.
Old Lyme, CT 06371
Raghavendra Rao Paturi
Tel: (860) 434-9381
Email: paturir@yahoo.com
Web: www.northsouth.org

THE AMERICAN JEWISH COMMITTEE
Connecticut Chapter
733 Summer St. #403
Stamford, CT 06901-1081
Jann Renert, Chapter Director
Tel: (203) 965-0020 Fax: (203) 965-0040
Email: connecticut@ajc.org
Web: www.ajc.org

VIETNAMESE MUTUAL ASSISTANCE
143 Madison Ave.
Hartford, CT 06106-2540
Le Smith, Board Member
Tel: (860) 236-6452 Fax: (860) 236-6456
Email: vmaac2000@yahoo.com

SPEC. INT., MENTAL HEALTH

ASIAN FAMILY SERVICES
237 Hamilton St., 2nd Fl.
Hartford, CT 06106
Tel: (860) 951-8770 Fax: (860) 951-0347
Email: info@asianfamilyservices.org
Web: www.asianfamilyservices.org

SPEC. INT., SENIORS

JEWISH CARE NETWORK
18 Tower Ln. #301
New Haven, CT 06519
Tel: (203) 777-5002 Fax: (203) 777-5745
Email: contact@elderlyjcn.org
Web: www.elderlyjcn.org

JEWISH HOME FOR THE ELDERLY
175 Jefferson St.
Fairfield, CT 06825
Tel: (203) 365-6400 Fax: (203) 374-8082
Email: llockwood@jhe.org
Web: http://jhe.org

SPEC. INT., SOCIAL INTEREST

CHINESE ASSOCIATION OF FAIRFIELD COUNTY
P.O. Box 16492
Riverside, CT 06905
Jy-Hong Su, President
Email: Jy-Hong.Su@pb.com
Web: www.oca-fc.org/

EHDEN LEBANESE AMERICAN CLUB
3 Garthwait Rd.
Wolcott, CT 06716
Joseph R. Carrah, President
Tel: (203) 879-6955
Email: ehdenclub@yahoo.com
Web: www.ehden.org

JAPAN-AMERICA SOCIETY OF CONNECTICUT
P.O. Box 252
Plainville, CT 06062
Taka Yoneda, President
Email: info@japansocietyct.org
Web: www.japansocietyct.org

JEWISH CENTER FOR COMMUNITY SERVICES
4200 Park Ave.
Bridgeport, CT 06604
Eli Kornreich, President
Tel: (203) 372-6567 Fax: (203) 374-0770
Email: comments@jccs.org
Web: www.jccs.org

JEWISH COMMUNITY CENTER
P.O. Box 3326
Stamford, CT 06905
Gary S. Lipman, CEO
Tel: (203) 322-7900 Fax: (203) 329-7546
Email: gslipman@stamfordjcc.org
Web: www.stamfordjcc.org

JEWISH COMMUNITY CENTER OF GREATER HARTFORD
333 Bloomfield Ave.
West Hartford, CT 06117
Tel: (860) 232-4483 Fax: (860) 232-5221
Email: info@jewishhartford.org
Web: www.jewishhartford.org

JEWISH COMMUNITY CENTER OF GREATER NEW HAVEN
360 Amity Rd.
Woodbridge, CT 06525
Tel: (203) 387-2522 Fax: (203) 397-1162
Email: membership@jccnh.org
Web: www.jccnh.org

JEWISH FAMILY SERVICE
2370 Park Ave.
Bridgeport, CT 06604-1699
Harvey Paris, President
Tel: (203) 366-5438 Fax: (203) 366-1580
Email: info@jfsct.org
Web: www.jfsct.org

JEWISH FAMILY SERVICE OF GREATER HARTFORD
740 N. Main St.
West Hartford, CT 06117

Tel: (860) 236-1927 Fax: (860) 236-6483
Web: www.jfshartford.org

JEWISH FAMILY SERVICE OF NEW HAVEN, INC.
1440 Whalley Ave.
New Haven, CT 06515
Barney Yellen, Executive Director
Tel: (203) 389-5599 Fax: (203) 389-5904
Email: contact@jfsnh.org
Web: www.jfsnh.org

JEWISH FAMILY SERVICE OF STAMFORD, INC.
111 Prospect St.
Stamford, CT 06901
Tel: (203) 921-4161 Fax: (203) 921-4169
Web: www.stamfordjfs.org

JEWISH FAMILY SERVICES OF GREENWICH, INC.
1 Holly Hill Ln.
Greenwich, CT 06830
Tel: (203) 622-1881 Fax: (203) 622-1885
Email: mail@jfsgreenwich.org
Web: www.jfsgreenwich.org

JEWISH FEDERATION OF GREATER NEW HAVEN
360 Amity Rd.
Woodbridge, CT 06525
Tel: (203) 387-2424 Fax: (203) 387-1818
Email: marinak@megahits.com
Web: www.jewishnewhaven.org

JEWISH FEDERATION OF GREENWICH
1 Holly Hill Ln.
Greenwich, CT 06830
Pamela Ehrenkranz, Executive Director
Tel: (203) 552-1818 Fax: (203) 622-1237
Email: ujapamz@optonline.net
Web: www.ujafedgreenwich.org

JEWISH FEDERATION OF NORTHERN FAIRFIELD
62-69 Kenosia Ave.
Danbury, CT 06810
Judy Prager, Executive Director
Tel: (203) 792-6353 Fax: (203) 748-5099
Email: info@thejf.org
Web: www.thejf.org

JEWISH FEDERATION OF WESTERN CONNECTICUT
P.O. Box 657
Southbury, CT 06488
Robert Zwang, Executive Director
Tel: (203) 267-3177 Fax: (203) 267-3392
Email: rzwang@aol.com
Web: www.jfed.net

UJA/FEDERATION OF WESTPORT-WILTON-NORWALK
431 Post Rd. East
Westport, CT 06880
Tel: (203) 226-8197 Fax: (203) 226-5051
Email: webmaster@ujafederation.org
Web: www.ujafederation.org

UNITED JEWISH FEDERATION OF GREATER STAMFORD, NEW CANAAN AND DARIEN
1035 Newfield Ave. #200
Stamford, CT 06905-2591
Tel: (203) 321-1373 Fax: (203) 322-3277
Email: office@ujf.org
Web: www.ujf.org

SPEC. INT., WOMEN

HADASSAH
Connecticut Region
59 Amity Rd.
New Haven, CT 06515
Pennie Sessler Branden, President
Tel: (203) 389-6740 Fax: (203) 389-8758
Email: psbranden@aol.com
Web: www.hadassah.org

SNEHA, INC.
P.O. Box 271650
West Hartford, CT 06127-1650
Chelsey Ramesh, President
Tel: (860) 658-4615 Fax: (860) 521-1562
Email: sneha@sneha.org
Web: www.sneha.org

STUDENT ORGANIZATION

ARAB STUDENTS' ASSOCIATION OF YALE COLLEGE
Yale University
P.O. Box 202187
New Haven, CT 06520
Raja Shamas, President
Email: contactASA@yale.edu
Web: www.yale.edu/arab

KASAMA
Yale University
New Haven, CT 06520
Christina Chinloy, President
Email: christina.chinloy@yale.edu
Web: www.yale.edu/kasama/index.html

KOREAN AMERICAN STUDENTS CONFERENCE
P.O. Box 202616
New Haven, CT 06520-2616
Adrian Hong, Executive Director
Tel: (203) 980-6543 Fax: (270) 721-2121
Email: kascon@yale.edu

KOREAN AMERICAN STUDENTS OF YALE
Yale University
P.O. Box 203353
New Haven, CT 06520
Hydie Kim, President
Tel: (203) 436-1941
Email: hydie.kim@yale.edu
Web: www.yale.edu/kasy/

DELAWARE

CULTURAL

CHINESE AMERICAN COMMUNITY CENTER
P.O. Box 849
Hockessin, DE 19707
Juliet Hsiao, Chair
Tel: (302) 239-0432
Email: cacc_de@hotmail.com
Web: www.caccdelaware.org

JEWISH HISTORICAL SOCIETY OF DELAWARE
505 Market St. Mall
Wilmington, DE 19801
Tel: (302) 655-6232
Email: jhsdel@yahoo.com
Web: www.hsd.org/jhsd.htm

POLITICAL ACTION

ORGANIZATION OF CHINESE AMERICANS-DELAWARE
4404 Emerson Rd.
Wilmington, DE 19802
Theresa Lee, President
Tel: (302) 764-4260
Email: oca@ocanatl.org

RELIGIOUS

WILMINGTON COMMUNITY EVANGELICAL CHURCH
1512 Brackenville Rd.
Hockessin, DE 19707
Tel: (302) 239-4990 Fax: (302) 239-9094
Web: www.wcec-home.org

SPEC. INT., EDUCATION

CHINESE AMERICAN COMMUNITY CENTER MONTESSORI SCHOOL
1313 Little Baltimore Rd.
Hockessin, DE 19707
Elizabeth Simon, Administrator
Tel: (302) 239-2917 Fax: (302) 239-0184
Email: caccsimon@aol.com
Web: www.caccmont.org

SPEC. INT., SOCIAL INTEREST

DELAWARE CHINESE AMERICAN ASSOCIATION
P.O. Box 1677
Hockessin, DE 19707
Yong Tao, President/Activity Coordinator
Tel: (302) 234-4525
Email: yong.tao@udel.edu
Web: www.de-chineseamerican.org

JEWISH COMMUNITY CENTER OF WILMINGTON
101 Garden of Eden Rd.
Wilmington, DE 19803
David Bernstein, President
Tel: (302) 478-5660 Fax: (302) 478-6068
Email: jccinfo@jccdelaware.org
Web: www.jccdelaware.org

JEWISH FAMILY SERVICE
101 Garden of Eden Rd.
Wilmington, DE 19803
Dory Zatuchni, Executive Director
Tel: (302) 478-9411 Fax: (302) 479-9883

JEWISH FEDERATION OF DELAWARE
100 W. 10th St. #301
Wilmington, DE 19801
Dr. Barry S. Kayne, President
Tel: (302) 427-2100 Fax: (302) 427-2438
Email: ruth.rosenberg@shalomdelaware.org
Web: www.shalomdelaware.org

STUDENT ORGANIZATION

CHINESE STUDENTS & SCHOLARS ASSOCIATION
University of Delaware
Newark, DE 19716
Yun Zhuo, President
Tel: (302) 831-2791
Email: yzhuo@udel.edu
Web: http://copland.udel.edu/stu-org/CSSA/

DISTRICT OF COLUMBIA

ARTISTIC

ASIAN PACIFIC AMERICAN FILM
P.O. Box 18405
Washington, DC 20036
Benjamin Lee, President
Email: apafilm@yahoo.com
Web: www.apafilm.org

PHILIPPINE ARTS, LETTERS AND MEDIA COUNCIL
4715 47th St. NW
Washington, DC 20016
Arabella Harmon, President
Tel: (202) 364-8471 (h) Fax: (202) 364-8471

TSUNAMI THEATER COMPANY
P.O. Box 65059
Washington, DC 20835
J. Rebecca Taylor, Producing Artistic Director
Tel: (202) 299-0320
Email: jrstaylor@tsunamitheatre.org
Web: www.tsunamitheatre.org

BUSINESS

AMERICAN ASSOCIATION OF EXPORTERS AND IMPORTERS
1200 G St. #800
Washington, DC 20005
Hallock Northcott, President
Tel: (202) 661-2181 Fax: (202) 661-2185
Email: hq@aaei.org
Web: www.aaei.org

AMERICAN TURKISH COUNCIL
1111 14th St. NW
Washington, DC 20005
G. Lincoln McCurdy, President
Tel: (202) 783-0483 Fax: (202) 783-0511
Email: atc@the-atc.org
Web: www.americanturkishcouncil.org

CENTER FOR INTERNATIONAL PRIVATE ENTERPRISE
1155 15th St. NW #700
Washington, DC 20005
John Sullivan, Executive Director
Tel: (202) 721-9200 Fax: (202) 721-9250
Email: cipe@cipe.org
Web: www.cipe.org

HONG KONG ECONOMIC AND TRADE OFFICE
Washington, DC Office
1520 18th St. NW
Washington, DC 20036
Jacqueline Ann Willis, Commissioner
Tel: (202) 331-8947 Fax: (202) 331-8958
Email: jacqueline_willis@hketowashington.gov.hk
Web: www.hketowashington.gov.hk/washington_dc.htm

INTERNATIONAL BUSINESS ETHICS INSTITUTE
1725 K St. NW #1207
Washington, DC 20006
Ronald Riebl, Program Associate
Tel: (202) 296-6938 Fax: (202) 296-5897
Email: riebl@business-ethics.org
Web: www.business-ethics.org

INTERNATIONAL ENTERPRISE SINGAPORE
Washington, DC Office
3501 International Pl. NW
Washington, DC 20008
Balagopal Nair, Director
Tel: (202) 537-3100 Fax: (202) 537-0876
Email: enquiry@iesingapore.gov.sg
Web: www.iesingapore.gov.sg

JAPAN INFORMATION ACCESS PROJECT
2000 P St. NW #620
Washington, DC 20036
Mindy Kotler, Director
Tel: (202) 822-6040 Fax: (202) 822-6044
Email: mkotler@jiaponline.org
Web: www.jiaponline.org

NATIONAL ASSOCIATION OF MANUFACTURERS
1331 Pennsylvania Ave. NW #600
Washington, DC 20004-1790
Michael G. Aylward, Vice President
Tel: (202) 637-3000 Fax: (202) 637-3182
Email: manufacturing@nam.org
Web: www.nam.org

THE KOREA TRADE CENTER
1129 20th St. NW #410
Washington, DC 20036
Dong W. Kwak, Director General
Tel: (202) 857-7919 Fax: (202) 857-7923
Web: www.kotra.or.kr

US CHINA BUSINESS SOLUTIONS
1300 Pennsylvania Ave. NW #700
Washington, DC 20004
John Asher, Chairman
Tel: (202) 204-3055 Fax: (202) 204-3056

Email: info@uschinabiz.com
Web: www.uschinabiz.com

US INTERNATIONAL TRADE COMMISSION
500 E St. SW
Washington, DC 20436
Marilyn R. Abbott, Secretary
Tel: (202) 205-2000 Fax: (202) 205-2104
Email: webmaster@usitc.gov
Web: www.usitc.gov

US PAKISTAN BUSINESS COUNCIL
1615 H St. NW
Washington, DC 20062-2000
Esperanza Gomez, President
Tel: Fax: (202) 463-3114
Email: uspbc@uschamber.com
Web: www.uspakistan.org

US THAILAND BUSINESS COUNCIL
3050 K St. #205
Washington, DC 20007
Karl D. Jackson, President
Tel: (202) 337-5973 Fax: (202) 337-0039
Email: ustbc@ustbc.org
Web: www.ustbc.org

US-ASEAN BUSINESS COUNCIL
1101 17th St. NW #411
Washington, DC 20036
John Phipps, Director
Tel: (202) 289-1911 Fax: (202) 289-0519
Email: jphipps@usasean.org
Web: www.us-asean.org

US-CHINA BUSINESS COUNCIL
1818 N St. NW #200
Washington, DC 20036
Dr. Robert A. Kapp, President
Tel: (202) 429-0340 Fax: (202) 775-2476
Email: info@uschina.org
Web: www.uschina.org

US-INDIA BUSINESS COUNCIL
1615 H St. NW
Washington, DC 20062
Rick Rossow, Director of Operations
Tel: (202) 463-5323 Fax: (202) 463-3173
Email: usibc@uschamber.com
Web: www.usibc.com

US-QATAR BUSINESS COUNCIL
1341 Connecticut Ave. NW #4A
Washington, DC 20036
Elie Haddad, Managing Director
Tel: (202) 457-8555 Fax: (202) 457-1919
Email: info@qatarbusinesscouncil.org
Web: www.qatarbusinesscouncil.org

US-RUSSIA BUSINESS COUNCIL
1701 Pennsylvania Ave. NW #520
Washington, DC 20006
Eugene K. Lawson, President
Tel: (202) 739-9180 Fax: (202) 659-5920
Email: info@usrbc.org
Web: www.usrbc.org

US-SAUDI ARABIAN BUSINESS COUNCIL
1401 New York Ave. NW #720
Washington, DC 20005
Sheikh Abdulaziz, CEO
Tel: (202) 638-1212 Fax: (202) 638-2894
Email: ussaudi@us-saudi-business.org
Web: www.us-saudi-business.org

CHAMBER OF COMMERCE

AMERICAN UZBEKISTAN CHAMBER OF COMMERCE
1800 Massachusetts Ave. NW #600
Washington, DC 20036
Robert Pace, Executive Director
Tel: (202) 887-5300 Fax: (202) 659-7010
Email: aucc@erols.com
Web: www.aucconline.com

ARAB AMERICA CHAMBER OF COMMERCE OF WASHINGTON DC
4455 Connecticut Ave. NW #B550

Washington, DC 20008
Sharissi Mercer, Office Manager
Tel: (202) 364-7070 Fax: (202) 364-8997
Email: aaccghanim@hotmail.com
Web: www.dcaacc.org

ARAB AMERICAN CHAMBER OF COMMERCE

1050 17th St. NW #600
Washington, DC 20036
Deborah Campbell, President
Tel: (202) 347-5800 Fax: (202) 521-1806
Email: campbell@arabchamber.com
Web: www.arabchamber.org

FEDERATION OF INDIAN CHAMBERS OF COMMERCE

DC Office
1050 17th St. NW #600
Washington, DC 20036
Prasanta Bismal, President
Tel: (202) 776-7181 Fax: (202) 331-8703

NATIONAL US-ARAB CHAMBER OF COMMERCE

1023 15th St. NW #400
Washington, DC 20005
David Hamod, President
Tel: (202) 289-5920 Fax: (202) 289-5938
Email: nusacc@aol.com
Web: www.nusacc.org

RUSSIAN-AMERICAN CHAMBER OF COMMERCE

P.O. Box 15343
Washington, DC 20003
Dr. Igor S. Oleynik, President/CEO
Tel: (202) 546-2103 Fax: (202) 546-3275
Email: ibpusa@comcast.net

SAUDI ARABIAN COUNCIL OF CHAMBERS OF COMMERCE AND INDUSTRY

601 New Hampshire Ave. NW
Washington, DC 20037
Abraham Laseygh, Commercial Attaché
Tel: (202) 342-3800 Fax: (202) 342-0271
Email: saco@resa.org
Web: www.saudicommercialoffice.com

UNITED STATES-AZERBAIJAN CHAMBER OF COMMERCE

1212 Potomac St. NW
Washington, DC 20007
Seymour Khalilov, Executive Director
Tel: (202) 333-8702 Fax: (202) 333-8703
Email: chamber@usacc.org
Web: www.usacc.org

US PAN ASIAN AMERICAN CHAMBER OF COMMERCE

1329 18th St. NW
Washington, DC 20036
Susan Au Allen, President/CEO
Tel: (202) 296-5221 Fax: (202) 296-5225
Email: administrator@uspaacc.com
Web: www.uspaacc.com

CULTURAL

AMERICAN FRIENDS OF TURKEY

1111 14th St. NW #1050
Washington, DC 20005
G. Lincoln McCurdy, President
Tel: (202) 783-0483 Fax: (202) 783-0511
Email: info@afot.us
Web: www.afot.us

AMERICAN TURKISH ASSOCIATION OF WASHINGTON, DC

1526 18th St. NW
Washington, DC 20036
Email: info@atadc.org
Web: www.atadc.org

ASIAN PACIFIC AMERICAN PROGRAM

Smithsonian Institute
A&I #2467, MRC:440, P.O. Box 37012
Washington, DC 20013-7012

Franklin Odo, Director
Tel: (202) 786-2409 Fax: (202) 633-9047
Web: www.apa.si.edu

GUAM SOCIETY OF AMERICA

P.O. Box 1515
Washington, DC 20013-1515
Terri Guevara Smith, President
Tel: (301) 386-6025
Email: fuunaguam@aol.com
Web: www.guamsociety.org

IRANIAN AMERICAN CULTURAL ASSOCIATION

P.O. Box 5831
Washington, DC 20016
Farima Farzaneh, Board of Director
Tel: (301) 656-4222 Fax: (301) 299-8936
Email: iaca@iaca-dc.org
Web: www.iacadc.org

NATIONAL JAPANESE AMERICAN MEMORIAL FOUNDATION

1000 Connecticut Ave. NW #304
Washington, DC 20036
Warren N. Minami, Chairman
Tel: (202) 530-0015 Fax: (202) 530-0016
Email: info@njamf.com
Web: www.njamf.com

ROSHAN CULTURAL HERITAGE INSTITUTE

1101 30th St. NW #500
Washington, DC 20007
Elahe Omidyar Mir-Djalali, President/Director
Tel: (202) 625-8390 Fax: (202) 625-8395
Web: www.roshan-institute.org

VIETNAMESE CULTURE & SCIENCE ASSOCIATION

DC Chapter
P.O. Box 65872
Washington, DC 20035-5872
Tel: (301) 604-7533
Web: vcsa_dc@yahoo.com

GOVERNMENT

AMERICAN TASK FORCE ON PALESTINE

815 Connecticut Ave. NW #1200
Washington, DC 20006
Ziad J. Asali, President
Tel: (202) 887-0177 Fax: (202) 887-1920
Email: atfp@atfp.net
Web: www.americantaskforce.org

COALITION FOR ASIAN PACIFIC AMERICAN FEDERAL EMPLOYEE ORGANIZATION

P.O. Box 23772
Washington, DC 20026
Jasmine Choy, Chair
Email: aagen@earthlink.net
Web: www.aagen.org

FEDERAL ASIAN PACIFIC AMERICAN COUNCIL

National Chapter
P.O. Box 23184
Washington, DC 20026-3184
Linda Miller, President
Tel: (202) 418-2581 Fax: (202) 418-6369
Email: linda.miller@fcc.gov
Web: www.fapac.org

INTERNATIONAL MONETARY FUND

700 19th St. NW
Washington, DC 20431
Rodrigo de Rato, Managing Director
Tel: (202) 623-7000 Fax: (202) 623-4661
Email: webmaster@imf.org
Web: www.imf.org

OFFICE ON ASIAN & PACIFIC ISLANDER AFFAIRS

Government of the District of Columbia
1 Judiciary Sq. 441 4th St. NW #805S
Washington, DC 20001
Tel: (202) 727-3120 Fax: (202) 727-9655

Email: apia@dc.gov
Web: www.apia.dc.gov

THE BURMA FUND

1319 F St. NW #303
Washington, DC 20004
Tel: (202) 639-0636 Fax: (202) 639-0638
Email: mailbox1@burmafund.org
Web: www.burmafund.org

LAW ENFORCEMENT

ASIAN LIAISON UNIT-METROPOLITAN POLICE DEPARTMENT

611 H St. NW
Washington, DC 20001
Charles H. Ramsey
, Chief of Police
Tel: (202) 535-2522 Fax: (202) 535-2656
Email: ktemsupa@mpdc.org
Web: www.mpdc.org

CENTER FOR SECURITY POLICY

1920 L St. NW #210
Washington, DC 20036
Frank J. Gaffney, President/CEO
Tel: (202) 835-9077 Fax: (202) 835-9066
Email: info@centerforsecuritypolicy.org
Web: www.centerforsecuritypolicy.org

METROPOLITAN POLICE DEPARTMENT

Asian Liason Unit
616 H St. NW
Washington, DC 20001
Sgt. Kenny Temsupasiri
Tel: (202) 724-8009
Email: asian.liason@dc.gov

NATIONAL ASIAN PEACE OFFICERS ASSOCIATION

P.O. Box 50973
Washington, DC 20091-0973
George Kim, President
Tel: (202) 431-2175
Email: president@napoa.org
Web: www.napoa.org

MULTI-PURPOSE

ASIA FOUNDATION

1779 Massachusetts Ave. NW #815
Washington, DC 20036
Nancy Yuan, Vice President
Tel: (202) 588-9420 Fax: (202) 588-9409
Email: info@asiafound-dc.org
Web: www.asiafoundation.org

ASIAN AMERICAN LEADERSHIP, EMPOWERMENT AND DEVELOPMENT FOR YOUTH AND FAMILIES

1323 Girard St. NW
Washington, DC 20009
Sandy Hoa Dang, Executive Director
Tel: (202) 884-0322 Fax: (202) 884-0012
Email: sdang@aalead.org
Web: www.aalead.org

AZERBAIJAN-AMERICAN EDUCATIONAL, CULTURAL AND ECONOMIC CENTER, INC.

1615 New Hampshire Ave. NW #100
Washington, DC 20009
Tel: (240) 631-6051 Fax: (240) 631 7701
Email: mahir@erols.com
Web: www.civilsoc.org/announce/azeramer.htm

POLITICAL ACTION

AMERICAN ENTERPRISE INSTITUTE FOR PUBLIC POLICY RESEARCH

1150 17th St. NW
Washington, DC 20036
Christopher DeMuth, President
Tel: (202) 862-5800 Fax: (202) 862-7177
Email: info@aei.org
Web: www.aei.org

AMERICAN MUSLIM COUNCIL

721-R 2nd St. NE
Washington, DC 20002
Tel: Fax: (202) 543-0095
Email: amc@amconline.org
Web: www.amconline.org

AMERICAN MUSLIMS FOR JERUSALEM

208 G St. NE
Washington, DC 20002
Tel: (202) 548-4200 Fax: (202) 548-4201
Email: amj@amjerusalem.org
Web: www.amjerusalem.org

AMERICAN TASK FORCE OF LEBANON

2213 M St. NW, 3rd Fl.
Washington, DC 20037
The Hon. Edward M. Gabriel, President/COO
Tel: (202) 223-9333 Fax: (202) 223-1399
Web: www.atfl.org

AMERICAN-ARAB ANTI-DISCRIMINATION COMMITTEE

Headquarters
4201 Connecticut Ave. NW #300
Washington, DC 20008
Mary Rose Oakar, President
Tel: (202) 244-2990 Fax: (202) 244-3196
Email: moakar@adc.org
Web: www.adc.org

AMERICANS FOR PEACE NOW

National Headquarters
1101 14th St. NW 6th Fl.
Washington, DC 20005
Tel: (202) 728-1893 Fax: (202) 728-1895
Email: apndc@peacenow.org
Web: www.peacenow.org

ARAB AMERICAN INSTITUTE

1600 K St. NW #601
Washington, DC 20006
James Zogby
Tel: (202) 429-9210 Fax: (202) 429-9214
Email: jzogby@aaiusa.org
Web: www.aaiusa.org

ARMENIAN ASSEMBLY OF AMERICA

122 C St. NW #350
Washington, DC 20001
Ross Varitian, Executive Director
Tel: (202) 393-3434 Fax: (202) 638-4904
Email: info@aaainc.org
Web: www.aaainc.org

ARMENIAN NATIONAL COMMITTEE OF AMERICA

National Headquarters
888 17th St. NW #904
Washington, DC 20006
Aram S. Hamparian, Executive Director
Tel: (202) 775-1918 Fax: (202) 775-5648
Email: anca@anca.org
Web: www.anca.org

ASIAN AMERICAN ACTION FUND

707 H St. NW #200
Washington, DC 20001
Yeni Wong, Chair/Co-Founder
Tel: (202) 530-4702
Email: info@aaa-fund.org
Web: www.aaa-fund.org

ASIAN AMERICAN GOVERNMENT EXECUTIVES NETWORK

1001 Connecticut Ave. #601 NW
Washington, DC 20036
Peter Wong, Chair
Email: aagen@earthlink.net
Web: www.aagen.org

ASIAN PACIFIC AMERICAN INSTITUTE FOR CONGRESSIONAL STUDIES

1001 Connecticut Ave. NW #835
Washington, DC 20036
William Mo Marumoto, President/CEO
Tel: (202) 296-9200 Fax: (202) 296-9236
Email: apaics@apaics.org
Web: www.apaics.org

ASIAN PACIFIC AMERICAN LABOR ALLIANCE
National Office
815 16th St. NW
Washington, DC 20006-4101
Luisa Blue, National President
Tel: (202) 974-8051 Fax: (202) 974-8056
Email: apala@apalanet.org
Web: www.apalanet.org

ASIAN & PACIFIC ISLANDER AMERICAN VOTE 2004
1001 Connecticut Ave. NW #601
Washington, DC 20036
Janelle Hu, National Director
Tel: (202) 223-9170 Fax: (202) 296-0540
Email: info@apiavote.org
Web: www.apiavote.org

ATATURK SOCIETY OF AMERICA
4731 Massachusetts Ave. NW
Washington, DC 20016
Tel: (202) 362-7173 Fax: (202) 363-4075
Email: ataturksociety@earthlink.net
Web: www.ataturksociety.org

CENTER FOR STRATEGIC AND INTERNATIONAL STUDIES
1800 K St. NW
Washington, DC 20006
Sam Nunn, Chairman/CEO
Tel: (202) 887-0200 Fax: (202) 775-3199
Email: rexe@kslaw.com
Web: www.csis.org

COUNCIL FOR THE NATIONAL INTEREST
1250 4th St. SW #WG-1
Washington, DC 20024
Paul Findley, Founding Chairman
Tel: (202) 863-2951 Fax: (202) 863-2952
Email: count@igc.org
Web: www.cnionline.org

EAST TIMOR ACTION NETWORK
National Office
P.O. Box 15774
Washington, DC 20003-0774
Karen Orenstein, Representative
Tel: (202) 544-6911 Fax: (202) 544-6118
Email: karen@etan.org
Web: www.etan.org

INDIAN AMERICAN CENTER OF POLITICAL AWARENESS
1025 Connecticut Ave. NW #1000
Washington, DC 20036
Christopher Dumm, Executive Director
Tel: (202) 955-8338 Fax: (202) 327-5483
Email: iacfpa@iacfpa.org
Web: www.iacfpa.org

INSTITUTE FOR SCIENCE AND INTERNATIONAL SECURITY
236 Massachusetts Ave. NE #500
Washington, DC 20002
David Albright, President/Founder
Tel: (202) 547-3633 Fax: (202) 547-3634
Email: isis@isis-online.org
Web: www.isis-online.org

INTERNATIONAL CAMPAIGN FOR TIBET
1825 K St. NW #520
Washington, DC 20006
John Ackerly, President
Tel: (202) 785-1515 Fax: (202) 785-4343
Email: info@savetibet.org
Web: www.savetibet.org

IRANIAN AMERICAN POLITICAL ACTION COMMITTEE
729 15th St. NW, 3rd Fl.
Washington, DC 20005
Morad Ghorban, Political Director
Tel: (202) 824-0718 Fax: (202) 737-6063
Email: info@iranianamericanpac.org
Web: www.iranianamericanpac.org

JAPAN POLICY RESEARCH INSTITUTE
Washington, DC Office
1630 Connecticut Ave. NW, 7th Fl.
Washington, DC 20009
Steven C. Clemons, Co-Founding Director
Tel: (202) 986-0342 Fax: (202) 986-3696
Email: clemons@jpri.org
Web: www.jpri.org

JEWISH COUNCIL FOR PUBLIC AFFAIRS
Washington DC Office
1640 Rhode Island Ave.
Washington, DC 20036-3278
Tel: (202) 293-1649 Fax: (202) 293-2154
Email: contactus@the jcpa.org
Web: www.jewishpublicaffairs.org

JEWISH REPUBLICAN COALITION
50 F St. NW #100
Washington, DC 20001
Sam Fox, Chairman
Tel: (202) 638-6688 Fax: (202) 638-6694
Email: rjc@rjchq.org
Web: www.rjchq.org

JEWS UNITED FOR JUSTICE
2027 Massachusetts Ave. NW
Washington, DC 20036
Sheryl Adler, Board of Director
Tel: (202) 483-1945
Email: info@jufj.org
Web: www.jufj.org

KOREAN AMERICAN COALITION
Washington, DC
1140 Connecticut Ave. NW #1200
Washington, DC 20036
Thomas J. Han, Chair
Tel: (202) 296-6401 Fax: (202) 296-6407
Email: info@kacdc.org
Web: www.kacdc.org

KUWAIT INFORMATION OFFICE
2600 Virginia Ave. NW #404
Washington, DC 20037
Tareq Al-Mezrem, Director
Tel: (202) 338-0211 Fax: (202) 338-0957
Email: tareq@kuwait-info.org
Web: www.kuwait-info.org

MIDDLE EAST POLICY COUNCIL
1730 M St. NW #512
Washington, DC 20036
Richard Wilson, Executive Director
Tel: (202) 296-6767 Fax: (202) 296-5791
Email: info@mepc.org
Web: www.mepc.org

MUSLIM PUBLIC AFFAIRS COUNCIL
110 Maryland Ave. NE #304
Washington, DC 20002
Sarah Eltantawi, Communications Director
Tel: (202) 547-7701 Fax: (202) 547-7704
Email: sarah@mpac.org
Web: www.mpac.org

NATIONAL ASIAN PACIFIC AMERICAN LEGAL CONSORTIUM
1140 Connecticut Ave. NW #1200
Washington, DC 20036
Karen K. Narasaki, President/Executive Director
Tel: (202) 296-2300 Fax: (202) 296-2318
Email: info@napalc.org
Web: www.napalc.org

NATIONAL CONFERENCE ON SOVIET JEWRY
2020 K St. NW #7800
Washington, DC 20006
Joel M. Schindler, President
Tel: (202) 898-2500 Fax: (202) 898-0822
Email: ncsj@ncsj.org
Web: www.ncsj.org

NATIONAL COUNCIL OF PAKISTANI AMERICANS
236 Massachusetts Ave. NE #602
Washington, DC 20002
Faiz Rehman, Founder
Tel: (202) 675-2004 Fax: (202) 675-2006
Web: www.ncpa.info

NATIONAL FEDERATION OF FILIPINO AMERICAN ASSOCIATIONS
Headquarters
1444 N. St. NW
Washington, DC 20005
Armando Heredia, Chief of Staff
Tel: (202) 986-9330 Fax: (202) 478-5109
Email: admin@naffaa.org
Web: www.naffaa.org

NATIONAL JEWISH DEMOCRATIC COUNCIL
P.O. Box 75308
Washington, DC 20013-5308
Ambassador Arthur Schechter, Chair
Tel: (202) 216-9060 Fax: (202) 216-9061
Email: info@njdc.org
Web: www.njdc.org

NATIONAL ORGANIZATION OF PACIFIC ISLANDERS IN AMERICA
P.O. Box 70167, SW Station
Washington, DC 20024
Maria C. Teehan, Acting Executive Director
Tel: (301) 386-6025
Email: president@nopia.us
Web: www.nopia.us

NATIONAL ORGANIZATION OF REPUBLICAN ARMENIANS
1745 Pennsylvania Ave. NW #126
Washington, DC 20006
Email: info@nora-dc.org
Web: www.nora-dc.org

ORGANIZATION OF CHINESE AMERICANS
National Office
1001 Connecticut Ave. NW #601
Washington, DC 20036
Christine Chen, Executive Director
Tel: (202) 223-5500 Fax: (202) 296-0540
Email: oca@ocanatl.org
Web: www.ocanatl.org

PAKISTANI AMERICAN CONGRESS, USA
1717 K St. NW #600
Washington, DC 20036
Ashraf Abassi, President
Tel: (202) 973-0177 Fax: (202) 331-3759
Email: president@pacus.org
Web: www.pacus.org

PROJECT INTERCHANGE
1156 15th St. NW #1201
Washington, DC 20005
Carole Stern
Tel: (202) 833-0025 Fax: (202) 331-7702
Email: pi@ajc.org
Web: www.projectinterchange.org

SOUTH ASIAN AMERICAN LEADERS OF TOMORROW
4401-A Connecticut Ave. NW PMB 264
Washington, DC 20006
Jeet Bindra, Chairman Emeritus
Tel: (973) 220-9714
Email: saalt@saalt.org
Web: www.saalt.org

THE GROUP OF THIRTY CONSULTATIVE GROUP ON INTERNATIONAL ECONOMIC AND MONETARY AFFAIRS, INC.
1990 M St. #450
Washington, DC 20036
John Walsh, Executive Director
Tel: (202) 331-2472 Fax: (202) 785-9423
Email: info@group30.org
Web: www.group30.org

THE MAUREEN AND MIKE MANSFIELD FOUNDATION
Washington, DC Office
1401 New York Ave. NW #740
Washington, DC 20005-2102
L. Gordon Flake, Executive Director
Tel: (202) 347-1994 Fax: (202) 347-3941
Email: info@mansfieldfdn.org
Web: www.mansfieldfdn.org

THE WASHINGTON KURDISH INSTITUTE
611 4th St. SW
Washington, DC 20024
Tel: (202) 484-0140 Fax: (202) 484-0142
Email: wki@kurd.org
Web: www.kurd.org

US-AFGHANISTAN RECONSTRUCTION COUNCIL
2020 Pennsylvania Ave. NW #342
Washington, DC 20006
M. Omar Hadi, Interim Executive Director
Email: contact@us-arc.org
Web: www.us-arc.org

PROFESSIONAL

AMERICAN ASSOCIATION OF BANGLADESHI ENGINEERS AND ARCHITECTS-WASHINGTON DC
Washington DC Chapter
Washington, DC
Dr. Shah Mahmood, President
Email: Mahmoodsj@ih.navy.mil
Web: www.aabea.org/chapters/washington_dc.php

ASIAN PACIFIC AMERICAN BAR ASSOCIATION
1200 G St. NW
Washington, DC 20005
Anthony Tu-Sekine, President
Tel: (202)737-8833
Email: tu-sekine@sewkis.com
Web: www.napaba-dc.org

ASIAN PACIFIC AMERICAN BAR ASSOCIATION OF GREATER, DC
P.O. Box 23124
Washington, DC 20026
Eugene Chay, President
Tel: (202) 347-5634
Email: apaba@apaba-dc.org
Web: www.apaba-dc.org

ASIAN PACIFIC AMERICAN NETWORK IN AGRICULTURE
P.O. Box 44399
Washington, DC 20026
Ram Chandran, President
Tel: (202) 694-5446 Fax: (202) 720-3984
Email: chandran@ers.usda.gov
Web: www.apana-usda.org

CHINESE ECONOMISTS SOCIETY
733 15th St. NW #202
Washington, DC 20005
Polly He, Office Manager
Tel: (202) 347-8588 Fax: (202) 347-8510
Email: vmcorp@aol.com
Web: www.china-ces.org

INTERACTION
1717 Massachusetts Ave. NW #701
Washington, DC 20036
Mary McClymont, President/CEO
Tel: (202) 667-8227 Fax: (202) 667-8236
Email: ia@interaction.org
Web: www.interaction.org

INTERNATIONAL COUNCIL ON KOREAN STUDIES
407 6th St. SW
Washington, DC 20024-2705
Dr. Hang Yul Rhee, President
Tel: (202) 554-2105 Fax: (202) 550-2087
Email: info@icks.org
Web: www.icks.org

IRANIAN-AMERICAN BAR ASSOCIATION
1025 Connecticut Ave. NW #1012

Washington, DC 20036
Jamie Abadian, Director
Tel: (202) 828-1217 Fax: (202) 857-9799
Email: iaba@iaba.us
Web: www.iaba.us

NATIONAL ASIAN PACIFIC AMERICAN BAR ASSOCIATION

DC Chapter
910 17th St. NW #315
Washington, DC 20006
John Yang, President
Tel: (202) 719-4483 Fax: (202) 719-7207
Email: jyang@wrf.com
Web: www.napaba.org

Washington DC Office
733 15th St. NW #315
Washington, DC 20005
Parkin Lee, President
Tel: (202) 421-9039 Fax: (202) 393-0995
Email: foundation@napaba.org
Web: www.napaba.org

NETWORK OF SOUTH ASIAN PROFESSIONALS, DC

Network of Indian Professionals of North America
P.O. Box 1809
Washington, DC 20013
Salil Maniktahla, President
Email: president@netsap.org
Web: www.netsap.org

SOUTH ASIAN BAR ASSOCIATION OF GREATER DC

P.O. Box 65349
Washington, DC 20035
Rudhir B. Patel, Chairman/President
Email: sabadc@sabadc.org
Web: www.sabadc.org

THE SOCIETY OF IRANIAN PROFESSIONALS

P.O. Box 9645
Washington, DC 20016
Tel: (703) 471-4747 Fax: (703) 471-4747
Email: sip1367@yahoo.com
Web: http://iran270.tripod.com/sip/index.html

RELIGIOUS

ARABIC BAPTIST CHURCH

4605 Massachusetts Ave. NW
Washington, DC 20016
Esper Ajaj, Pastor
Tel: (202) 363-3911 Fax: (202) 244-8780
Email: pastor@abcdc.org
Web: www.abcdc.org

ARABIC CHURCH OF THE REDEEMER

4420 River Rd. NW
Washington, DC 20016
Rev. Fuad Khouri, Pastor
Tel: (202) 244-5100
Email: redeemerdc@aol.com
Web: www.forministry.com/usdcpcusaacotr

CHINESE COMMUNITY CHURCH

900 Massachusetts Ave.
Washington, DC 20001
Pastor Charles Koo, Senior Pastor
Tel: (202) 637-9852 Fax: (202) 637-9857
Email: cccdc@juno.com
Web: www.cccdc.com

RELIGIOUS ACTION CENTER OF REFORM JUDAISM

2027 Massachusetts Ave. NW
Washington, DC 20036
Rabbi David Saperstein, Director and Counsel
Tel: (202) 387-2800 Fax: (202) 667-9070
Email: rac@urj.org
Web: www.rac.org

RESEARCH

ARMENIAN NATIONAL INSTITUTE

122 C St. NW #360
Washington, DC 20001
Dr. Rouben P. Adalian, Director
Tel: (202) 383-9009 Fax: (202) 383-9012
Email: ani@aaainc.org
Web: www.armenian-genocide.org

BRITISH AMERICAN SECURITY INFORMATION COUNCIL

110 Maryland Ave. NE #205
Washington, DC 20002
Chris Lindborg, Analyst
Tel: (202) 347-8340 Fax: (202) 546-8056
Email: basicus@basicint.org
Web: www.basicint.org

CHEMICAL & BIOLOGICAL ARMS CONTROL INSTITUTE

1747 Pennsylvania Ave. NW, 7th Fl.
Washington, DC 20006
Michael L. Moodie, President
Tel: (202) 296-3550 Fax: (202) 296-3574
Email: cbaci@cbaci.org
Web: www.cbaci.org

ECONOMIC STRATEGY INSTITUTE

1401 H St. NW #560
Washington, DC 20005
Clyde V. Prestowitz, Jr., President
Tel: (202) 289-1288 Fax: (202) 289-1319
Email: presto@econstrat.org
Web: www.econstrat.org

INSTITUTE FOR INTERNATIONAL ECONOMICS

1750 Massachusetts Ave. NW
Washington, DC 20036-1903
Peter G. Peterson, Chairman
Tel: (202) 328-9000 Fax: (202) 659-3225
Email: ppeterson@iie.com
Web: www.iie.com

INSTITUTE FOR POLICY STUDIES

733 15th St. NW #1020
Washington, DC 20005
Robert Alvarez, Director
Tel: (202) 234-9382 Fax: (202) 387-7915
Email: kitbob@erols.com
Web: www.ips-dc.org

INTERNATIONAL RESEARCH & EXCHANGES BOARD

2121 K St. NW #700
Washington, DC 20037
Mark G. Pomar, President
Tel: (202) 628-8188 Fax: (202) 628-8189
Email: irex@irex.org
Web: www.irex.org

JAPAN SOCIETY FOR THE PROMOTION OF SCIENCE

Washington Office
1800 K St. NW #920
Washington, DC 20006
Tel: (202) 659-8190 Fax: (202) 659-8199
Email: webmaster@jspsusa.org
Web: www.jspsusa.org

LAOGAI RESEARCH FOUNDATION

1925 K St. NW #400
Washington, DC 20006
Harry Wu, Executive Director
Tel: (202) 833-8770 Fax: (202) 833-6187
Email: laogai@laogai.org
Web: www.laogai.org

MIDDLE EAST MEDIA RESEARCH INSTITUTE

P.O. Box 27837
Washington, DC 20038-7837
Tel: (202) 955-9070 Fax: (202) 955-9077
Email: memri@memri.org
Web: www.memri.org

MIDDLE EAST RESEARCH AND INFORMATION PROJECT

1500 Massachusetts Ave. NW #119

Washington, DC 20005
Jillian Schwedler, Chair
Tel: (202) 223-3677 Fax: (202) 223-3604
Email: merip@nb.net
Web: www.merip.org

PROGRESSIVE POLICY INSTITUTE

600 Pennsylvania Ave. SE #400
Washington, DC 20003
Will Marshall, President
Tel: (202) 547-0001 Fax: (202) 544-5014
Email: press@dlcppi.org
Web: www.ppionline.org

SIGUR CENTER FOR ASIAN STUDIES

George Washington University
1957 E St. NW #503
Washington, DC 20052
Mike Mochizuki, Director and Japan-US Relations Chair
Tel: (202) 994-5886 Fax: (202) 994-6096
Email: gsigur@gwu.edu
Web: www.gwu.edu/~sigur

SCIENTIFIC

AMERICAN COMMITTEE FOR THE WEIZMANN INSTITUTE OF SCIENCE

1730 Rhode Island Ave. NW #409
Washington, DC 20036
Shelly Kamins, Regional Chair
Tel: (202) 293-6883
Email: dc@acwis.org
Web: www.weizmann-usa.org

SPEC. INT., EDUCATION

AMERICA MIDEAST EDUCATIONAL AND TRAINING SERVICES, INC.

1730 M St. NW #1100
Washington, DC 20036
Theodore H. Kattouf, President & CEO
Tel: (202) 776-9600 Fax: (202) 776-7000
Email: inquiries@amideast.org
Web: www.amideast.org

AMERICAN COLLEGE PERSONNEL ASSOCIATION

1 Dupont Cir. #300
Washington, DC 20036
Donna Bourassa, Associate Executive Director
Tel: (202) 835-2272 Fax: (202) 296-3286
Email: dmb@acpa.edu
Web: www.acpa.nche.edu

AMERICAN COUNCIL ON EDUCATION

Center for Advancement of Racial and Ethnic Equity
1 DuPont Cir. NW #800
Washington, DC 20036
William B. Harvey, Vice President/Director
Tel: (202) 939-9395 Fax: (202) 785-2990
Email: caree@ace.nche.edu
Web: www.acenet.edu

ARI FOUNDATION

1455 F St. NW #225
Washington, DC 20005
Gunay Evinch, Director
Tel: (202) 737-7788 Fax: (202) 737-7122
Email: ari@ari-us.org
Web: www.ari-us.org

ASIAN PACIFIC AMERICAN BAR ASSOCIATION EDUCATIONAL FUND

P.O. Box 2209
Washington, DC 20013-2209
Jennifer D. Choe, President
Email: aef@vvault.com
Web: www.aef-apaba.org

CENTER FOR CONTEMPORARY ARAB STUDIES

Georgetown University
ICC 241
Washington, DC 20057-1020
Michael C. Hudson, Director

Tel: (202) 687-5793 Fax: (202) 687-7001
Email: ccasinfo@georgetown.edu
Web: www.ccasonline.org

CENTER FOR MUSLIM-CHRISTIAN UNDERSTANDING

Georgetown University
37th and O St. NW ICC 260
Washington, DC 20057
John L. Esposito, Founding Director
Tel: (202) 687-8375 Fax: (202) 687-8376
Email: cmcu@georgetown.edu
Web: http://cmcu.georgetown.edu

CENTER FOR THE STUDY OF ISLAM & DEMOCRACY

2121 K St. NW #700
Washington, DC 20037
Abdulaziz Sachedina, Chair
Tel: (202) 942-2183 Fax: (202) 628-8189
Email: feedback@islam-democracy.org
Web: www.islam-democracy.org

CONFERENCE ON ASIAN PACIFIC AMERICAN LEADERSHIP

c/o Summer Internship Application, P.O. Box 65073
Washington, DC 20035-5073
Cindy Han, Board Member
Tel: (877) 892-5427
Email: info@capal.org
Web: www.capal.org

ECONOMIC POLICY INSTITUTE

1660 L St. NW #1200
Washington, DC 20036
Larry Mishel, President
Tel: (202) 775-8810 Fax: (202) 775-0819
Email: epi@epinet.org
Web: www.epinet.org

EDWIN O. REISCHAUER CENTER FOR ASIAN STUDIES

Johns Hopkins University
1619 Massachusetts Ave. NW
Washington, DC 20036
Nathaniel B. Thayer, Senior Advisor
Tel: (202) 663-5815 Fax: (202) 663-5799
Email: fjshima@mail.jhuwash.jhu.edu
Web: www.sais-jhu.edu

FOREIGN POLICY INSTITUTE

Johns Hopkins University
1619 Massachusetts Ave. NW
Washington, DC 20036
Courtney Mata, Program Administrator
Tel: (202) 663-5773 Fax: (202) 663-5769
Email: fpi@jhu.edu
Web: www.sais-jhu.edu/centers/fpi/index.html

FORMOSAN ASSOCIATION FOR PUBLIC AFFAIRS

552 7th St. SE
Washington, DC 20003
.Dr. Ming-chi Wu, President
Tel: (202) 547-3686 Fax: (202) 543-7891
Email: president@fapa.org
Web: www.fapa.org

HERITAGE FOUNDATION

Asian Studies Center
214 Massachusetts Ave. NE
Washington, DC 20002-4999
Peter Brookes, Director
Tel: (202) 546-4400 Fax: (202) 546-8328
Email: info@heritage.org
Web: www.heritage.org

INSTITUTE OF TURKISH STUDIES

Georgetown University
Intercultural Center, Box 571033
Washington, DC 20057-1033
Sabri Sayari, Executive Director
Tel: (202) 687-0295 Fax: (202) 687-3780
Email: sayaris@turkishstudies.org

INTERNATIONAL FUND FOR CHINA'S ENVIRONMENT
2421 Pennsylvania Ave. NW
Washington, DC 20037
Dr. Ping He, President
Tel: (202) 822-2141 Fax: (202) 457-0908
Email: ifce@ifce.org
Web: www.ifce.org

IRAN TEACHERS ASSOCIATION, INC.
Washington, DC
Email: informgr@mehregan.org
Web: www.mehregan.org

IRANIAN ACADEMIC ASSOCIATION
Washington, DC
Mali Naghavi, President
Email: info@iaa-dc.org
Web: www.iaa-dc.org

JAPAN AMERICA STUDENT CONFERENCE
606 18th St. NW, 2nd Fl.
Washington, DC 20006
Robin L. White, President
Tel: (202) 289-4231 Fax: (202) 789-8265
Email: jascinc@jasc.org
Web: www.jasc.org

JAPAN EXCHANGE & TEACHING ALUMNI ASSOCIATION
Washington, DC Chapter
Embassy of Japan, 2520 Massachusetts Ave. NW
Washington, DC 20008
Susan Gundersen, President
Email: president@jetaadc.org
Web: http://jetaadc.org

JEWISH INSTITUTE FOR NATIONAL SECURITY AFFAIRS
1779 Massachusetts Ave. NW #515
Washington, DC 20036
Norman Hascoe, President
Tel: (202) 667-3900 Fax: (202) 667-0601
Email: info@jinsa.org
Web: www.jinsa.org

MIDDLE EAST INSTITUTE
1761 N St. NW
Washington, DC 20036-2882
Edward S. Walker, Jr., President
Tel: (202) 785-1141 Fax: (202) 331-8861
Email: mideasti@mideasti.org
Web: www.mideasti.org

NATIONAL ASSOCIATION FOR ASIAN AND PACIFIC AMERICAN EDUCATION
Region I
4400 Massachusetts Ave. NW
Washington, DC 20016
Joanne Yamauchi, Contact
Tel: (202) 885-2076
Email: dr-y@american.edu
Web: www.naapae.net

THE BROOKINGS INSTITUTION
1775 Massachusetts Ave. NW
Washington, DC 20036
Strobe Talbott, President
Tel: (202) 797-6000 Fax: (202) 797-6004
Email: webmaster@brookings.edu
Web: www.brookings.edu

THE WASHINGTON INSTITUTE FOR NEAR EAST POLICY
1828 L St. NW #1050
Washington, DC 20036
Patrick Clawson, Deputy Director
Tel: (202) 452-0650 Fax: (202) 223-5364
Email: info@washingtoninstitute.org
Web: www.washingtoninstitute.org

SPEC. INT., GAY&LESBIAN

ASIANS & FRIENDS - WASHINGTON
P.O. Box 18974
Washington, DC 20036
Tel: (202) 387-ASIA
Email: AfWash@aol.com
Web: www.afwashington.net

PARENTS, FAMILIES AND FRIENDS OF LESBIAN AND GAYS
1726 M St. NW #400
Washington, DC 20036
Ron Schlittler, Executive Director
Tel: (202) 467-8180 Fax: (202) 467-8194
Email: info@pflag.org
Web: www.pflag.org

SPEC. INT., HEALTH SERVICES

ASIAN & PACIFIC ISLANDER AMERICAN HEALTH FORUM Washington DC Office
1001 Connecticut Ave. NW #835
Washington, DC 20036
Dr. Ho L. Tran, President
Tel: (202) 466-7772 Fax: (202) 466-6444
Email: hforum@apiahf.org
Web: www.apiahf.org

ASIAN & PACIFIC ISLANDER PARTNERSHIP FOR HEALTH
3000 Connecticut Ave. NW #110
Washington, DC 20008
Joslyn Maula, Executive Director
Tel: (202) 986-2393
Email: info@apiph.org
Web: www.apiph.org

OFFICE OF MINORITY HEALTH RESOURCE CENTER
P.O. Box 37337
Washington, DC 20013-7337
J. Tarcisio M. Carneiro, Project Director
Tel: (800) 444-6472 Fax: (301) 251-2160
Email: info@omhrc.gov
Web: www.omhrc.gov

SPEC. INT., HUMAN RELATIONS

AGA KHAN FOUNDATION
1825 K St. NW #901
Washington, DC 20006
Iqbal Noor Ali, CEO
Tel: (202) 293-2537 Fax: (202) 785-1752
Email: info@akfusa.org
Web: www.akdn.org

AMERICAN JEWISH WORLD SERVICE
Washington, DC Office
2027 Massachusetts Ave. NW
Washington, DC 20036
Jacob Fain, Policy Associate
Tel: (202) 387-2800 Fax: (202) 667-9070
Email: jfain@ajws.org
Web: www.ajws.org

AMERICAN NEAR EAST REFUGEE AID
1522 K St. NW #202
Washington, DC 20005-1270
Peter Gubser, President
Tel: (202) 347-2558 Fax: (202) 682-1637
Email: paula@anera.org
Web: www.anera.org

ASIA SOCIETY
1800 K St. NW #1102
Washington, DC 20006
Joseph C. Synder, Director
Tel: (202) 833-2742 Fax: (202) 833-0189
Email: dcinfo@asiansoc.org
Web: www.asiasociety.org

ASIAN PACIFIC AMERICAN HERITAGE COUNCIL,INC.
1310 19th St. NW
Washington, DC 20005
Mary Lee Lau, President
Tel: (301) 983-1845 Fax: (301) 983-0042
Email: mlau2@aol.com
Web: www.apahcinc.org

ASPEN INSTITUTE
1 Dupont Cir. NW #700
Washington, DC 20036
James Spiegelman, Director
Tel: (202) 736-5800 Fax: (202) 467-0790
Email: jim.spiegelman@aspeninstitute.org
Web: www.aspeninstitute.org

ASSEMBLY OF TURKISH AMERICAN ASSOCIATIONS
1526 18th St. NW
Washington, DC 20036
Vural Cengiz, President
Tel: (202) 483-9090 Fax: (202) 483-9092
Email: assembly@ataa.org
Web: www.ataa.org

ATLANTIC COUNCIL OF THE UNITED STATES
910 17th St. NW #1000
Washington, DC 20006
Christopher Makins, President
Tel: (202) 778-4961 Fax: (202) 463-7241
Email: info@www.acus.org
Web: www.acus.org

CARNEGIE ENDOWMENT FOR INTERNATIONAL PEACE
1779 Massachusetts Ave. NW
Washington, DC 20036
Jessica Mathews, President
Tel: (202) 483-7600 Fax: (202) 483-1840
Email: info@ceip.org
Web: www.ceip.org

CATO INSTITUTE
1000 Massachusetts Ave. NW
Washington, DC 20001
Peter Ackerman, Board of Director
Tel: (202) 842-0200 Fax: (202) 842-3490
Email: packerman@cato.org
Web: www.cato.org

CENTER FOR DEFENSE INFORMATION
1779 Massachusetts Ave. NW
Washington, DC 20036-2109
Bruce Blair, President
Tel: (202) 332-0600 Fax: (202) 462-4559
Email: info@cdi.org
Web: www.cdi.org

CHARITY LOBBYING IN THE PUBLIC INTEREST
2040 S St. NW
Washington, DC 20009
Liz Baumgarten, President
Tel: (202) 387-2008 Fax: (202) 387-5149
Email: liz@clpi.org
Web: www.clpi.org

CONGRESSIONAL ASIAN PACIFIC AMERICAN CAUCUS
1713 Longworth House Office Bldg.
Washington, DC 20515
Michael Honda, Chairman
Tel: (202) 225-2631 Fax: (202) 225-2699
Email: mike.honda@mail.house.gov
Web: www.house.gov/wu/capacweb

COUNCIL ON AMERICAN-ISLAMIC RELATIONS
National Office
453 New Jersey Ave. SE
Washington, DC 20003
Nihad Awad, Executive Director
Tel: (202) 488-8787 Fax: (202) 488-0833
Email: cair@cair-net.org
Web: www.cair-net.org

EURASIA FOUNDATION
1350 Connecticut Ave. NW #1000
Washington, DC 20036
Charles William Maynes, President
Tel: (202) 234-7370 Fax: (202) 234-7377
Email: eurasia@eurasia.org
Web: www.eurasia.org

FOUNDATION FOR MIDDLE EAST PEACE
1761 N St. NW
Washington, DC 20036
Philip C. Wilcox, Jr., President
Tel: (202) 835-3650 Fax: (202) 835-3651
Email: pcwilcox@fmep.org
Web: www.fmep.org

HENRY L. STIMSON CENTER
11 Dupont Cir. #900
Washington, DC 20036
Ellen Laipson, President/CEO
Tel: (202) 223-5956 Fax: (202) 238-9604
Email: info@stimson.org
Web: www.stimson.org

HMONG NATIONAL DEVELOPMENT, INC.
1112 16th St. NW #110
Washington, DC 20036
Bo Thao, Executive Director
Tel: (202) 463-2118 Fax: (202) 463-2119
Email: info@hndlink.org
Web: www.hndlink.org

HUMAN RIGHTS WATCH
1630 Connecticut Ave. NW #500
Washington, DC 20009
Kenneth Roth, Executive Director
Tel: (202) 612-4321 Fax: (202) 612-4333
Email: hrwdc@hrw.org
Web: www.hrw.org

JAPAN-US FRIENDSHIP COMMISSION
1110 Vermont Ave. NW #800
Washington, DC 20005
Richard J. Samuels, Chairman
Tel: (202) 418-9800 Fax: (202) 418-9802
Email: jusfc@jusfc.gov
Web: www.jusfc.gov

JAPANESE AMERICAN CITIZENS LEAGUE
Washington, DC Office
1001 Connecticut Ave. NW #730
Washington, DC 20036
Floyd Mori, Director of Public Policy
Tel: (202) 223-1240 Fax: (202) 296-8082
Email: dc@jacl.org
Web: www.jacl.org

KOREA ECONOMIC INSTITUTE
1201 F St. NW #910
Washington, DC 20004
Joseph Winder, President
Tel: (202) 464-1982 Fax: (202) 464-1987
Email: jabw@keia.org
Web: www.keia.org

NATIONAL ASSOCIATION OF JAPAN-AMERICA SOCIETIES
733 15th St. NW #700
Washington, DC 20005
Samuel M. Shepherd, President
Tel: (202) 783-4550 Fax: (202) 783-4551
Email: contact@us-japan.org
Web: www.us-japan.org

NATIONAL COALITION FOR ASIAN PACIFIC AMERICAN COMMUNITY DEVELOPMENT
1001 Connecticut Ave. NW #730
Washington, DC 20036
Lisa Hasegawa, Executive Director
Tel: (202) 223-2442 Fax: (202) 223-4144
Email: lisa@nationalcapacd.org
Web: www.nationalcapacd.org

NATIONAL COUNCIL ON US-ARAB RELATIONS
1730 M St. NW #503
Washington, DC 20036
Dr. John Duke Anthony, Founder/CEO
Tel: (202) 293-6466 Fax: (202) 293-7770
Email: info@ncusar.org
Web: www.ncusar.org

NEW ISRAEL FUND
National Headquarters
1101 14th St. NW, 6th Fl.
Washington, DC 20005-5639
Peter Edelman, President
Tel: (202) 842-0900 Fax: (202) 842-0991
Email: info@nif.org
Web: www.nif.org

REFUGEES INTERNATIONAL
1705 N St. NW
Washington, DC 20036
Ken Bacon, President
Tel: (202) 828-0110 Fax: (202) 828-0819
Email: ri@refintl.org
Web: www.refugeesinternational.org

SOUTHEAST ASIA RESOURCE ACTION CENTER
1628 16th St. NW, 3rd Fl.
Washington, DC 20009-3099
KaYing Yang, Executive Director
Tel: (202) 667-4690 Fax: (202) 667-6449
Email: searac@searac.org
Web: www.searac.org

THE AMERICAN JEWISH COMMITTEE
Washington Chapter
1156 15th St. NW #1201
Washington, DC 20005
David Bernstein, Chapter Director
Tel: (202) 785-4200 Fax: (202) 785-0390
Email: washington@ajc.org
Web: www.ajcwashington.org

THE IRAQ FOUNDATION
1012 14th St. NW. #1110
Washington, DC 20005
Tel: (202) 347-4662 Fax: (202) 347-7897
Email: iraq@iraqfoundation.org
Web: www.iraqfoundation.org

THE NATIONAL IRANIAN AMERICAN COUNCIL
2451 18th St. NW, 2nd Fl.
Washington, DC 20009
Dokhi Fassihian, Executive Director
Tel: (202) 518-6187 Fax: (202) 518-5507
Email: info@niacouncil.org
Web: www.niacouncil.org

THE REFUGEE COUNCIL USA
3211 4th St. NE
Washington, DC 20017-1194
Sasha Bennet, Assistant Coordinator
Tel: (202) 541-5402 Fax: (202) 722-8805
Email: council@refugeecouncilusa.org
Web: www.refugeecouncilusa.org

THE WORLD BANK GROUP
1818 H St. NW
Washington, DC 20433
Sereen Juma, Communications Officer
Tel: (202) 473-1000 Fax: (202) 477-6391
Email: sjuma@worldbank.org
Web: www.worldbank.org

US INSTITUTE OF PEACE
1200 17th St. NW #200
Washington, DC 20036
Kuimba Boston, Public Outreach
Tel: (202) 457-1700 Fax: (202) 429-6063
Email: usip_requests@usip.org
Web: www.usip.org

US-CHINA POLICY FOUNDATION
316 Pennsylvania Ave. SE #201-202
Washington, DC 20003
Sarah Terbrueggen, Program Associate
Tel: (202) 547-8615 Fax: (202) 547-8853
Email: uscpf@uscpf.org
Web: www.uscpf.org

WORLD AFFAIRS COUNCIL OF WASHINGTON, DC
1800 K St. NW #1014
Washington, DC 20006
Katherine Wilkins, President
Tel: (202) 293-1051 Fax: (202) 293-3467
Email: info@worldaffairsdc.org
Web: www.worldaffairsdc.org

SPEC. INT., IMMIGRATION

NATIONAL IMMIGRATION FORUM
50 F St. NW #300
Washington, DC 20001

Frank Sharry, Executive Director
Tel: (202) 347-0040 Fax: (202) 347-0058
Email: info@immigrationforum.org
Web: www.immigrationforum.org

NEWCOMER COMMUNITY SERVICE CENTER
1628 16th St. NW
Washington, DC 20009
Vilay Chaleunrath, Executive Director
Tel: (202) 462-4330 Fax: (202) 462-2774
Email: vilay@newcomerservice.org
Web: www.newcomerservice.org

SPEC. INT., INFORMATION REFERRAL

CHINATOWN INFORMATION & REFERRAL CENTER
900 Massachusetts Ave. NW
Washington, DC 20001
John K. Lem, Director
Tel: (202) 898-0061 Fax: (202) 898-2519
Email: jlem@chinatownscdc.org

SPEC. INT., LEGAL ASSISTANCE

AMERICAN IMMIGRATION LAWYERS ASSOCIATION
918 F St. NW
Washington, DC 20004
Jeanne A. Butterfield, Executive Director
Tel: (202) 216-2400 Fax: (202) 783-7853
Email: executive@aila.org
Web: www.aila.org

ASIAN PACIFIC AMERICAN LEGAL RESOURCE CENTER
733 15th St. NW #315
Washington, DC 20005
Pauline Y. Poh, Development Associate
Tel: (202) 393-3572 Fax: (202) 393-0995
Email: info@apalrc.org
Web: www.apalrc.org

JEWISH LABOR COMMITTEE
Washington DC Chapter
815 16th St. NW
Washington, DC 20006
Nancy Mills, Chair
Email: washingtonJLC@aol.com
Web: www.jewishlabor.org

SPEC. INT., SENIORS

NATIONAL AGING INFORMATION CENTER
Administration on Aging
1 Massachusetts Ave. #4100 & 5100
Washington, DC 20201
Josefina G. Carbonell, Assistant Secretary
Tel: (202) 619-0724 Fax: (202) 357-3555
Email: aoainfo@aoa.gov
Web: www.aoa.dhhs.gov

THE ASSOCIATION OF JEWISH AGING SERVICES OF NORTH AMERICA
316 Pennsylvania Ave. SE #402
Washington, DC 20003
Harvey Tillipman, Executive Director
Tel: (202) 543-7500 Fax: (202) 543-4090
Email: harvey@ajas.org
Web: www.ajas.org

SPEC. INT., SOCIAL INTEREST

AFGHANISTAN - AMERICA FOUNDATION
209 Pennsylvania Ave. SE #700
Washington, DC 20003
Don Ritter, Chairman
Tel: (202) 543-1177 Fax: (202) 543-7931
Email: info@afghanistanfoundation.org
Web: http://burningbush.netfirms.com/afghan/foundation.htm

AMERICAN KURDISH INFORMATION NETWORK
2722 Connecticut Ave. NW #42
Washington, DC 20008-5316
Kani Xulam, Director
Tel: (202) 483-6444
Email: akin@kurdistan.org
Web: www.kurdistan.org

ARAB AMERICAN INSTITUTE FOUNDATION
1600 K St. NW #601
Washington, DC 20006
Helen Samhan, Executive Director
Tel: (202) 429-9210 Fax: (202) 429-9214
Email: hsamhan@aaiusa.org
Web: www.aaiusa.org/aaif.htm

ASIAN PACIFIC AMERICAN MUNICIPAL OFFICIALS
National League of Cities
1301 Pennsylvania Ave. NW #550
Washington, DC 20004
Mary Gordon, Manager
Tel: (202) 626-3000 Fax: (202) 626-3043
Email: gordon@nlc.org
Web: www.nlc.org

ASIAN SERVICE CENTER
417 G Pl. NW
Washington, DC 20001
Zoie Cheng, Director
Tel: (202) 842-4376 Fax: (202) 842-5437
Email: asc.dc@verizon.net

GRACE HERITAGE
P.O. Box 42267
Washington, DC 20015
Jasmine Wibisono, Co-Founder
Tel: (202) 262-3775 Fax: (703) 333-6079
Email: info@thegraceheritage.org
Web: www.thegraceheritage.org

INTERNATIONAL FOOD AND AGRICULTURAL TRADE POLICY COUNCIL
1616 P St. NW #100
Washington, DC 20036
Ann Tutwiler, President
Tel: (202) 328-5056 Fax: (202) 328-5133
Email: agritrade@agritrade.org
Web: www.agritrade.org

JAPAN AMERICA SOCIETY OF WASHINGTON DC
1020 19th St. NW #LL40
Washington, DC 20036
Laurel Lukaszewsky, Executive Director
Tel: (202) 833-2210 Fax: (202) 833-2456
Email: jaswdc@us-japan.org
Web: www.us-japan.org/dc

LAOTIAN AMERICAN NATIONAL ALLIANCE
Newcomer Community Service Center
1628 16th St. NW
Washington, DC 20009
Vilay Chaleunrath, Executive Director
Tel: (202) 462-4330 Fax: (202) 462- 2774
Email: vilay@newcomerservice.org

NATIONAL ALLIANCE OF LEBANESE AMERICANS
2020 Pennsylvania Ave. NW
Washington, DC 20006
Ziad Nassar, Founder
Tel: (202) 333-1722
Email: info@nala.com
Web: www.nala.com

NATIONAL COUNCIL OF ASIAN PACIFIC AMERICANS
1440 Connecticut Ave. NW #1200
Washington, DC 20036
Web: www.ncapaonline.org

NATIONAL MULTICULTURAL INSTITUTE
3000 Connecticut Ave. NW #438
Washington, DC 20008-2556
Elizabeth Pathy Salett, President
Tel: (202) 483-0700 Fax: (202) 483-5233

Email: nmci@nmci.org
Web: www.nmci.org

PHILIPPINE AMERICAN FOUNDATION FOR CHARITIES, INC.
DC Branch
1444 N St. NW
Washington, DC 20005
Mary Anne T. Fadul, President
Tel: (703) 624- 5685 Fax: (202) 986-9332
Email: info@pafc-inc.org
Web: www.pafc-inc.org

SPEC. INT., SPORTS

WONG CHINESE BOXING ASSOCIATION
218 Florida Ave. NW
Washington, DC 20001
Raymond Wong, Contact
Tel: (202) 234-1826 Fax: (202) 986-3586
Email: rwong@wongchineseboxing.com
Web: www.wongliondance.com

SPEC. INT., WOMEN

ASIAN PACIFIC ISLANDER DOMESTIC VIOLENCE RESOURCE PROJECT
P.O. Box 14268
Washington, DC 20044
Anjali Nagpaul, Executive Director
Tel: (202) 464-4477 Fax: (202) 986-9332
Email: info@dvrp.org
Web: www.dvrp.org

JEWISH WOMEN INTERNATIONAL
2000 M St. NW #720
Washington, DC 20036
Loribeth Weinstein, Executive Director
Tel: (800) 343-2823 Fax: (202) 857-1380
Email: lweinstein@jwi.org
Web: www.jewishwomen.org

MUSLIM WOMEN LAWYERS FOR HUMAN RIGHTS
1420 16th St. NW
Washington, DC 20036-2202
Azizah Y. Al-Hibri, President
Tel: (202) 234-7302 Fax: (202) 234-7304
Email: karamah@karamah.org
Web: www.karamah.org

NATIONAL ASIAN PACIFIC AMERICAN WOMEN'S FORUM
National Office
1001 Connecticut Ave. NW #730
Washington, DC 20036
Kiran Ahuja, National Director
Tel: (202) 293-2688 Fax: (202) 223-4144
Email: kahuja@napawf.org
Web: www.napawf.org

NATIONAL COUNCIL OF JEWISH WOMEN
Washington Office
1707 L St. NW #950
Washington, DC 20036-4206
Marsha Atkind, President
Tel: (202) 296-2588 Fax: (202) 331-7792
Email: action@ncjw.org
Web: www.ncjw.org

VIETNAM WOMEN'S MEMORIAL FOUNDATION, INC.
1735 Connecticut Ave. NW
Washington, DC 20009
Tel: (866) 822-8963
Email: vvmfdc@aol.com
Web: www.vietnamwomensmemorial.org

WOMEN'S ALLIANCE FOR PEACE AND HUMAN RIGHTS IN AFGHANISTAN
P.O. Box 77057
Washington, DC 20013-7057
Zieba Shorish-Shamley, Director/Founder
Email: info@wapha.org
Web: www.wapha.org

SPEC. INT., YOUTH

CAMPAIGN FOR TOBACCO FREE KIDS
1400 Eye St. NW #1200
Washington, DC 20005
William V. Corr, Executive Director
Tel: (202) 296-5469 Fax: (202) 296-5427
Email: info@tobaccofreekids.org
Web: www.tobaccofreekids.org

KESHER
Washington,DC Office
800 8th St. NW
Washington, DC 20001-3742
Rabbi Marc Israel, Director
Tel: (202) 449-6508
Email: misrael@urj.org
Web: www.keshernet.com

THE CHILDREN'S DEFENSE FUND
25 E St. NW
Washington, DC 20001
Marian Wright Edelman, President
Tel: (202) 628-8787 Fax: (202) 662-3510
Email: cdfinfo@childrensdefense.org
Web: www.childrensdefense.org

STUDENT ORGANIZATION

ASIAN PACIFIC AMERICAN LAW STUDENT ASSOCIATION
Georgetown University Law Center
Office of Student Affairs, 600 New Jersey
Ave. NW
Washington, DC 20001
Jenny Yoo, President
Tel: (202) 662-9000
Email: jjy4@law.georgetown.edu
Web: www.law.georgetown.edu

CHINESE AMERICAN STUDENT ASSOCIATION
George Washington University
800 21st St. #435
Washington, DC 20052
Thao To, Co-President
Email: bigto@gwu.edu
Web: www.gwu.edu/~casa

CHINESE STUDENTS & SCHOLARS ASSOCIATION
George Washington University
2231 Ontario Rd. NW
Washington, DC 20009
Miaoqing Huang, President
Tel: (202) 518-9242
Email: mghuang@gwu.edu
Web: www.gwu.edu/~cssa/

KOREAN-AMERICAN STUDENT ASSOCIATION
George Washington University
2121 Eye St. NW
Washington, DC 20052
Martin Kim, President
Email: kasa@gwu.edu
Web: www.gwu.edu/~kasa/

THE PHILIPPINE CULTURAL SOCIETY
George Washington University
2121 Eye St. NW #435
Washington, DC 20052
Christine Dela Rosa, President
Tel: (609) 439-1596
Email: pcsgwu@gwu.edu
Web: www.pcsgwu.org

THE TURKISH STUDENT ASSOCIATION
George Washington University
800 21st St. NW
Washington, DC 20052
Zeynep Guven, President
Tel: (202) 994-3709
Email: turkish@gwu.edu
Web: www.gwtsa.org

UNITED STATES STUDENT ASSOCIATION
1413 K St., 9th Fl. NW
Washington, DC 20005
Irene Schwoeffermann, Director
Tel: (202) 347-8772 Fax: (202) 393- 5886
Email: cdp@usstudents.org
Web: www.usstudents.org

FLORIDA

ARTISTIC

IKEBANA INTERNATIONAL
6545 SW 135th Dr.
Pine Crest, FL 33156
Mieko Kubota, Japanese Instructor/Ikebana Artist
Tel: (305) 665-2141 Fax: (305) 665-2141

PHILIPPINE DANCE TROUPE USA, INC.
4770 SW 152 Terr.
Miramar, FL 33027
Inday Abuan, President
Tel: (954) 441-2948 Fax: (954) 441-2948
Email: eda@csklegal.com

BUSINESS

FLORIDA/KOREA ECONOMIC COOPERATION COMMITTEE, INC.
2801 Ponce de Leon Blvd. #700
Coral Gables, FL 33134
Dave Woodward, Executive Director
Tel: (305) 569-2639 Fax: (305) 569-2649
Email: information@fl-seusjapan.org
Web: www.fl-seusjapan.org

HONG KONG TRADE DEVELOPMENT COUNCIL
Courvoisier Ctr. 2 #509
601 Brickkell Key Dr.
Miami, FL 33131
Winchell Cheung, Director
Tel: (305) 577-0414 Fax: (305) 372-9142
Email: miami.office@tdc.org.hk
Web: www.tdctrade.com

KOREA TRADE CENTER
2 S. Biscayne Blvd. # 3770
Miami, FL 33131
Ho-Won Chung, Director
Tel: (305) 374-4648 Fax: (305) 375-9332
Email: ktcmiami@aol.com

THAI TRADE CENTER MIAMI
200 S. Biscayne Blvd. #4420
Miami, FL 33131
Pensri Jutidharabongse, Director
Tel: (305) 379-5675 Fax: (305) 379-5677
Email: ttcmiami@earthlink.net
Web: www.thaitrade.com

CHAMBER OF COMMERCE

AMERICAN-ISRAEL CHAMBER OF COMMERCE
5944 Coral Ridge Dr. #180
Coral Spring, FL 33076
Chuck Ruddy, Executive Director
Tel: (561) 620-9288 Fax: (561) 892-2433
Email: info@aiccfl.org
Web: www.aiccfl.org

ASIAN-AMERICAN CHAMBER OF COMMERCE OF SOUTH FLORIDA
1250 E. Hallandale Beach Blvd. #405
Hallandale Beach, FL 33009
Ty Javellana, President
Tel: (954) 454-7478 Fax: (954) 454-7976
Email: info@aaccsfl.org

CHINESE AMERICAN CHAMBER OF COMMERCE
P.O. Box 1396
Miami, FL 33233

Judith Lai, President
Tel: (305) 588-8202 Fax: (954) 964-8220
Email: judylai@johndchang.org

KOREAN-AMERICAN CHAMBER OF COMMERCE OF GREATER MIAMI
7840 NW 56th St.
Miami, FL 33166
Jong Sun Kim, Director
Tel: Fax: (305) 592-3665
Email: kacc@abicc.org
Web: www.abicc.org/kaccmiami

PHILIPPINE AMERICAN CHAMBER OF COMMERCE OF TAMPA BAY
3105 W. Waters #107
Tampa, FL 33614
Paul Beraquit, President/Chairman
Tel: (813) 936-5100
Email: PBQT@bankonparagon.com
Web: www.paccoftampabay.com

CULTURAL

ASIAN CULTURAL ASSOCIATION
2759 Marsh Wren Cir.
Longwood, FL 32779-3004
Jasbir Mehta, Executive Director
Tel: (407) 333-3667 Fax: (407) 333-1692
Email: jasbirmehta@aca-florida.org
Web: www.aca-florida.org

ASIAN CULTURE SOCIETY
7832 W. Sample Rd.
Margate, FL 33065
Syed Jafri, Secretary
Tel: (954) 752-3028 Fax: (954) 752-2188

ASIAN PACIFIC AMERICAN HERITAGE
Eglin Air Force Base, Florida
Valparaiso, FL 32580
Olivia F. Adrian, Program Manager
Tel: (850) 882-0179 Fax: (850) 882-9685
Email: olivia.adrian@eglin.af.mil

CORAL SPRINGS CHINESE CULTURAL ASSOCIATION
8343 W. Atlantic Blvd.
Coral Springs, FL 33071
Carol Yuan, President
Tel: (954) 753-4788 Fax: (954) 753-0033
Email: cscca@bizland.com
Web: www.cscca.bizland.com

FILIPINO AMERICAN ASSOCIATION
3234 Abbot Ave. NE
Palm Bay, FL 32905
Romy DeLapaz, President
Tel: (321) 722-1780
Email: faabco@cfl.rr.com
Web: www.sfacef.org

FLORIDA TURKISH AMERICAN ASSOCIATION
P.O. Box 50021
Lighthouse Point, FL 33074
Ismael Ercan, President
Tel: (954) 975-3384
Web: www.ftaa.com

JAPAN AMERICA SOCIETY
4000 Morikami Park Rd.
Delray Beach, FL 33446
James Mihori, President
Tel: (561) 278-3614 Fax: (561) 278-1773

JEWISH MUSEUM OF FLORIDA, INC.
301 Washington Ave.
Miami Beach, FL 33139
Marcia Kerstein Zerivitz, Founding Executive Director
Tel: (305) 672-5044 Fax: (305) 672-5933
Email: director@jewishmuseum.com
Web: www.jewishmuseum.com

KOREAN CULTURAL FOUNDATION OF GREATER MIAMI, INC.
2754 NW 112th Ave. 33172

Miami, FL 33172
Daiyong Chong, President
Tel: (305) 665-1961 Fax: (305) 406-2010

KOREAN WAR VETERANS ASSOCIATION
Manasota Chapter
P.O. Box 3067
Oneco, FL 34264-3067
Gene Gillette, President
Tel: (941) 746-4440
Email: gillettedman@aol.com
Web: www.orgsites.com/fl/kwva

PHILIPPINE CULTURAL FOUNDATION, INC.
14301 Nine Eagles Rd.
Tampa, FL 33626
Tel: (813) 925-1232 Fax: (813) 818-9599
Web: www.bayanihanartscenter.org

TAMPA BAY CHINESE COMMUNITY
P.O. Box 46163
Tampa, FL 33647
Jim Chen
Tel: (813) 973-3579
Email: contact@tampabaychinese.s5.com
Web: www.tampabaychinese.s5.com

THAI AMERICAN ASSOCIATION OF SOUTH FLORIDA
12112 Lymestone Way
Cooper City, FL 33026
Khanya Moolsiri, President
Tel: (954) 431-7484 Fax: (954) 431-8573
Email: Kmoolsiri@aol.com

THE MORIKAMI MUSEUM AND JAPANESE GARDENS
4000 Morikami Park Rd.
Delray Beach, FL 33446
Kizzy Sanchez, Events Manager
Tel: (561) 495-0233 X226
Email: morikami@co.palm-beach.fl.us
Web: www.morikami.org

TURKISH AMERICAN CULTURAL ASSOCIATION OF FLORIDA
P.O. Box 3303
Brandon, FL 33509-3303
Aydin Sunol, President
Email: tacaf@tacaf.org
Web: www.tacaf.org

VIETNAMESE STUDENT ORGANIZATION AT THE UNIVERSITY OF FLORIDA
300-5 JWRU
Gainesville, FL 32611
Nam Luong, President
Tel: (352) 392-1665 ext.325
Email: vu-quoc@ufl.edu
Web: http://grove.ufl.edu/~vso

ENTERTAINMENT

ASIAN PACIFIC FILM FESTIVAL OF FLORIDA
P.O. Box 16515
Plantation, FL 33318
Beryl Williams, President
Tel: (954) 327-1810 Fax: (954) 327-1810
Email: apfff@juno.com
Web:

MULTI-PURPOSE

ASIAN AMERICAN FEDERATION OF FLORIDA
8445 S.W. 148 Dr.
Miami, FL 33158
Josephine Gordy, Secretary
Tel: (305) 235-5120 Fax: (305) 278-8775
Email: jgordy@alkalife.com

BIG BEND FILIPINO-AMERICAN ASSOCIATION
1307 Walden St.
Tallahassee, FL 32311
Clyde Diao, President
Email: ferdfrancis@comcast.net
Web: http://bbfaa.freeservers.com

CHINESE AMERICAN CLUB OF MIAMI
P.O. Box 430810
Miami, FL 33243
John Tsai, President
Tel: (305) 274-4915 Fax: (305) 274-1651
Email: tsai@ocn-miami.com
Web: www.ocn-miami.com

FLORIDA NEPAL ASSOCIATION
7458 Champagne Pl.
Boca Ratton, FL 33433
Bijaya Kattel, President
Email: sanjay@bajracharya.net
Web: www.floridanepal.org

PROFESSIONAL

AMERICAN SOCIETY OF ENGINEERS OF INDIAN ORIGIN-CENTRAL FLORIDA CHAPTER
P.O. Box 6223
Lakeland, FL 33807-6223
Vijay S. Sheth, Secretary
Tel: (407) 671-7832
Web: www.aseio.org

ASIAN AMERICAN JOURNALISTS ASSOCIATION
Florida Chapter
2121 SW 19th Ave.
Ocala, FL 34474
Ferdinand DeVega, President
Tel: (352) 671-6409 Fax: (352) 867-4018
Email: ferdinandmdevega@aol.com
Web: www.aaja.org/Chapters/Florida

JACKSONVILLE ASIAN AMERICAN BAR ASSOCIATION
126 W. Adams St.
Jacksonville, FL 32202
Maria Aguila, President
Tel: (904) 356-8371 Fax: (904) 356-8780
Email: maria.aguila@jaxlegalaid.org

NATIONAL ARAB AMERICAN MEDICAL ASSOCIATION
Central Florida Chapter
4106 W. Lake Mary Blvd. #325
Lake Mary, FL 32746
Dr. Ansara, Chapter President
Tel: (407) 333-1212
Email: naama@naama.com
Web: www.naama.com

Florida Chapter (Miami area)
3222 Tamiami Trail
Port Charles, FL 33952
Issa F. Baroudi, Chapter President
Tel: (941) 627-5155 Fax: (941) 235-3136
Email: naama@naama.com
Web: www.naama.com

NETWORK OF INDIAN PROFESSIONALS-MIAMI
Network of Indian Professionals of North America
Miami, FL
Malvi Patel, President
Email: www.netipmiami.org
Web: www.netipmiami.org

SIDDIQ KHAN & ASSOCIATION
7400 SW 50th Terr. #105
Miami, FL 33155
Mohannad Siddiq Khan, President
Tel: (305) 662-2301 Fax: (305) 661-3962
Email: skainc@bellsouth.net
Web: www.ska-engineering.com

RELIGIOUS

BETH AHM ISRAEL
9730 Stirling Rd.
Cooper City, FL 33024
Elaine Levine, Executive Director
Tel: (954) 431-5100 Fax: (954) 431-8204
Email: execsyn@aol.com
Web: www.bethahmisrael.com

CHABAD JEWISH CENTER OF JUPITER
156 Morning Dew Cir.
Jupiter, FL 33458
Berel Barash, Rabbi
Tel: (561) 694-6950
Email: rabbibarash@yahoo.com
Web: www.jewishjupiter.com

CHINA PARTNER, INC.
Florida Chapter
P.O. Box 880288
Boca Raton, FL 33488
Erik Burklin, President
Tel: (561) 482-2773 Fax: (561) 482-4476
Email: florida@chinapartner.org
Web: www.chinapartner.org

CHINESE BAPTIST CHURCH OF CORAL SPRINGS
200 Coral Ridge Dr.
Coral Springs, FL 33071
Linus Lau, Pastor
Tel: (954) 255-9910 Fax: (954) 344-1883
Email: cbccoralsprings@cbccoralsprings.org
Web: www.cbccoralsprings.org

CHINESE BAPTIST CHURCH OF MIAMI
595 SW 124th Ave.
Miami, FL 33184
David Chan, Senior Pastor
Tel: (305) 551-0138
Web: http://cbcmiami.org/miami

DAYTONA ARABIC EVANGELICAL CHURCH
3211 S. Peninsula Dr.
Daytona Beach, FL 32118
Tel: (386) 761-1383 Fax: (386) 788-0990
Email: webmaster@daytona-arabic-ministries.org
Web: www.daytona-arabic-church.org

JACKSONVILLE CAMBODIAN BUDDHIST SOCIETY INC.
4518 Clinton Ave.
Jacksonville, FL 32207
Tel: (904) 739-8137

JEWS FOR JESUS
South Florida
4654 N. University Dr.
Fort Lauderdale, FL 33351
Stan Meyer, Chief of Station
Tel: (954) 616-5050 Fax: (954) 616-5051
Email: florida@jewsforjesus.org
Web: www.jfjonline.org

KOREAN FIRST BAPTIST CHURCH
6018 N. Highland Ave.
Tampa, FL 33604
Paul Kim, Youth Minister
Tel: (813) 239-0213 Fax: (813) 239-0157
Email: pkjdsn@tampabay.rr.com
Web: www.kfbctampa.org

TEMPLE BETH DAVID
4657 Hood Rd.
Palm Beach Gardens, FL 33418
David L. Goldstein, Rabbi
Tel: (561) 694-2350 Fax: (561) 694-9518
Email: info@templebethdavidfl.org
Web: www.templebethdavidfl.org

TEMPLE BETH EL
1351 S. 14th Ave.
Hollywood, FL 33020-6499
Allan C. Tuffs, Rabbi
Tel: (954) 920-8225 Fax: (954) 920-7026
Email: rabbi@templebethelhollywood.org
Web: www.templebethelhollywood.org

16225 Winkler Rd.
Fort Myers, FL 33908
Larry Schoenfeld, President
Tel: (239) 433-0018 Fax: (239) 433-3235
Web: www.templebethel.com

400 Pasadena Ave.
St. Petersburg, FL 33707
Terry L. Hirsch, President

Tel: (727) 347-6136
Email: terryhirsch@templebeth-el.com
Web: www.templebeth-el.com

TEMPLE BETH ISRAEL
7100 W. Oakland Park Blvd.
Sunrise, FL 33313
Ron Rubinoff, President
Tel: (954) 742-4040 Fax: (954) 742-4480
Email: yaakovt@aol.com
Web: www.tbiftl.org

TEMPLE KOL AMI
8200 Peters Rd.
Plantation, FL 33324
Richard Lundy, President
Tel: (954) 472-1988 Fax: (954) 472-4439
Email: tka@templekolami.com
Web: www.templekolami.com

UNITED SYNAGOGUE OF CONSERVATIVE JUDAISM
Southeast Region
2600 N. Military Trail #248
Boca Raton, FL 33431
Sandy LeVine, President
Tel: (561) 372-0420 Fax: (561) 372-0424
Email: soeast@uscj.org
Web: http://uscj.org/soeast

VIETNAMESE BAPTIST CHURCH
4300 S. Manhattan Ave.
Tampa, FL 33611
Phan Hoa Hiep, Pastor
Tel: (813) 831-1951 Fax: (813) 832-3587
Email: vbctampa@yahoo.com
Web: www.manhattanbaptist.org/vbc.htm

SCIENTIFIC

AMERICAN COMMITTEE FOR THE WEIZMANN INSTITUTE OF SCIENCE
2300 Glades Rd. #210W
Boca Raton, FL 33431
Alex Bruner, Director
Tel: (561) 210-8440
Email: palmbeach@acwis.org
Web: www.weizmann-usa.org

200 S. Park Rd. #405
Hollywood, FL 33021
Melvin Allen Dick, Regional Chair
Tel: (954) 964-8071
Email: southflorida@acwis.org
Web: www.weizmann-usa.org

DAVE AND MARY ALPER JEWISH COMMUNITY CENTER
11155 SW 112th Ave.
Miami, FL 33176
Shelly Brodie, President
Tel: (305) 271-9000 Fax: (305) 595-1902
Email: info@alperjcc.org
Web: www.alperjcc.org

SPEC. INT., CHILD CARE

CHINESE CHILDREN ADOPTION INTERNATIONAL
Florida Chapter
1801 Miccosukee Commons Dr.
Tallahassee, FL 32308
Nancy Fontaine, Director
Tel: (850) 878-8788
Email: ccaifl@chinesechildren.org
Web: www.chinesechildren.org

ISRAEL CHILDREN'S CENTERS, INC.
2151 W. Hillsboro Blvd.
Deerfield Beach, FL 33442
Tel: (954) 480-6333 Fax: (954) 480-6611
Email: national@israelchildren.org

JEWISH ADOPTION AND FOSTER CARE OPTIONS, INC.
4200 University Dr.
Sunrise, FL 33351
Ronald D. Simon, Founder/President

Tel: (954) 749-7230
Email: info@jafco.org
Web: www.jafco.org

SOUTH-EAST ASIAN RELIEF, INC.
P.O. Box 15025
St. Petersburg, FL 33733
Rex Almquist, Director
Tel: (727) 321-1538 Fax: (727) 321-1538
Email: Searusa@yahoo.com
Web: http://searinc.tripod.com

THE FAR EAST HELP FOUNDATION
14543 SW 97th St.
Miami, FL 33186
Ngoc Anh Huynh
Tel: (305) 752-6954 Fax: (305) 387-1725
Email: fareasthelp@yahoo.com
Web: www.fareasthelp.org

SPEC. INT., EDUCATION

ARTHUR I. MEYER JEWISH ACADEMY
3261 N. Military Trail
West Palm Beach, FL 33409
Tel: (561) 686-6520 Fax: (561) 686-8522
Email: office@meyeracademy.com
Web: www.meyeracademy.com

BOYS TOWN JERUSALEM FOUNDATION OF AMERICA, INC.
Southeastern Region
5329 W. Atlantic Ave. #205-B
Delray Beach, FL 33484
Rabbi Simcha Freedman, Executive Director
Tel: (800) 738-6222 Fax: (561) 496-4842
Email: simfree@bellsouth.net
Web: www.boystownjerusalem.com

INSTITUTE FOR ASIAN STUDIES
Florida International University
University Park, DM 300-B
Miami, FL 33199
Steven Heine, Director
Tel: (305) 348-1914 Fax: (305) 348-6586
Email: asian@fiu.edu
Web: www.fiu.edu/~asian

JEWISH THEOLOGICAL SEMINARY
Florida Region
6100 Glades Rd. #205
Boca Raton, FL 33434
Helene Riffle, Director
Tel: (561) 852-3454
Web: www.jtsa.edu

LORRAINE AND JACK N. FRIEDMAN COMMISSION FOR JEWISH EDUCATION
Boynton Beach Office
8500 Jog Rd.
Boynton Beach, FL 33437
Steven Schauder, Executive Director
Tel: (561) 509-0110 Fax: (561) 752-8350
Email: info@cjepb.com
Web: www.cjepb.com

West Palm Beach Office
3267 N. Military Trail
West Palm Beach, FL 33409
Steven Schauder, Executive Director
Tel: (561) 640-0700 Fax: (561) 640-4304
Email: info@cjepb.com
Web: www.cjepb.com

THE CULTURAL AND EDUCATIONAL SCHOLARSHIP FOUNDATION OF CHINESE WOMEN'S CLUB
Greater Miami
13615 S. Dixie Hwy. #114 PMB 388
Miami, FL 33176-7252
Maria Lian, President
Email: maria.lian@alum.mit.edu

US CHINA PEOPLES FRIENDSHIP ASSOCIATION
Palm Beach County Chapter
7088 SE Rivers Edge
Jupiter, FL 33458

Marge Ketter, Contact
Tel: (561) 747-9487 Fax: (561) 747-9487
Web: www.uscpfa.org

Sarasota Chapter
295 Morningside Dr.
Sarasota, FL 34236
G. Duane Finger, Contact
Tel: (941) 388-5098
Web: www.uscpfa.org

SPEC. INT., EMPLOYMENT

US AIR FORCE ASIAN AMERICAN/ PACIFIC ISLANDER EMPLOYMENT PROGRAM
Dept. of the Airforce
205 W. D Ave. #467
Eglen AFB, FL 32542-6864
Olivia Adrian
Tel: (850) 882-0179 Fax: (850) 882-9685

SPEC. INT., FOOD

CHINESE FOOD SERVICE & RESTAURANT ASSOCIATION
14087 SW 48th Ln.
Miami, FL 33175
Abe Yu, President
Tel: (305) 221-9442 Fax: (305) 221-0360

SPEC. INT., HEALTH SERVICES

INTERNATIONAL INSTITUTE OF ISLAMIC MEDICINE
P.O. Box 160
Brandon, FL 33509-0160
Husain Nagamia, Chairman
Tel: (813) 661-6161 Fax: (813) 684-5500
Email: info.iiim@verizon.net
Web: www.iiim.org

SPEC. INT., HUMAN RELATIONS

ALPERT JEWISH FAMILY & CHILDREN'S SERVICE
4605 Community Dr.
West Palm Beach, FL 33417
Howard Levy, President
Tel: (561) 684-1991 Fax: (561) 684-5366
Web: www.jfcspb.org

AMERICAN RED MAGEN DAVID FOR ISRAEL
Southeast Region
2100 E. Hallandale Beach Blvd.
Hallandale, FL 33009
Stephen Slingbaum, President
Tel: (800) 626-0046 Fax: (954) 457-7705
Email: info@armdise.org
Web: www.armdi.org

COUNCIL ON AMERICAN-ISLAMIC RELATIONS
Main Office
12535 Orange Dr. #614
Davie, FL 33330
Altaf Ali, Executive Director
Tel: (954) 916-5661 Fax: (954) 916-5662
Email: info@cair-florida.org
Web: www.cair-florida.org

Regional Office
8056 N. 56th St.
Tampa, FL 33617
Altaf Ali, Executive Director
Tel: (813) 514-1414 Fax: (813) 514-1415
Email: tampa@cair-florida.org
Web: www.cair-florida.org

ISRAELI HUMANITARIAN FOUNDATION
Southeast Region Office
211 Goolsby Blvd.
Deerfield, FL 33442
Harlee Burger, Board of Director
Tel: (954) 426-3539 Fax: (954) 596-1011
Email: hlb305@aol.com
Web: www.ihf.net

Southeast Region Office
1835 E. Hallandale Beach Blvd. #333
Hallandale Beach, FL 33009
Susi Deneroff, Senior Director
Tel: (954) 455-2586 Fax: (954) 455-2677
Email: susi@ihf.net
Web: www.ihf.net

NEW ISRAEL FUND
Florida Office
1400 NW 107th Ave.
Miami, FL 33172
Peter Edelman, President
Tel: (305) 392-4021 Fax: (305) 392-4004
Email: florida@nif.org
Web: www.nif.org

SIMON WIESENTHAL CENTER
Boca Raton Office
2300 Glades Rd. #308-E
Boca Raton, FL 33431
Debra Rubenstein, National Director
Tel: (561) 367-0722 Fax: (561) 367-0556
Email: drubenstein@wiesenthal.com
Web: www.wiesenthal.com

Miami Office
4601 Sheridan St. #220
Hollywood, FL 33021
Robert L. Novak, National Director for Development
Tel: (954) 966-1118 Fax: (954) 966-1533
Email: swcsouthern@aol.com
Web: www.wiesenthal.com

THE AMERICAN JEWISH COMMITTEE
Miami Chapter
9200 S. Dadeland Blvd. #518
Miami, FL 33156-2717
Debbie Brodie-Weiss, Director of Development
Tel: (305) 670-1121 Fax: (305) 670-6252
Email: miami@ajc.org
Web: www.ajc.org

Palm Beach Chapter
1900 NW Corporate Blvd. #210W
Boca Raton, FL 33431-7320
William Gralnick, Chapter Director
Tel: (561) 994-7286 Fax: (561) 994-7294
Email: palmbeach@ajc.org
Web: www.ajc.org

West Coast Florida Chapter
2055 Wood St. #218
Sarasota, FL 34237-7903
Ruth Young, Chapter Director
Tel: (941) 365-4955 Fax: (941) 955-9116
Email: sarasota@ajc.org
Web: www.ajc.org

SPEC. INT., SENIORS

NATIONAL ALLIANCE TO NURTURE THE AGED AND THE YOUTH, INC.
The Asian Pacific American Community Center
659 NE 125th St.
N. Miami, FL 33161
Joy Bruce, President
Tel: (305) 981-3232 Fax: (305) 981-3231
Email: joybruce@aol.com
Web: www.nanay.com

SPEC. INT., SOCIAL INTEREST

ADOLPH AND ROSE LEVIS JEWISH COMMUNITY CENTER
9801 Donna Klein Blvd.
Boca Raton, FL 33428
Tel: (561) 852-3200 Fax: (561) 852-6019
Web: www.levisjcc.org

AMERICAN-LEBANESE ENGINEERING SOCIETY
P.O. Box 690785
Orlando, FL 32819

Sam Sebaali, President
Tel: (407) 422-6761 Fax: (407) 422-9664
Email: ssebaali@feg-inc.us

ASIAN FAMILY & COMMUNITY EMPOWERMENT CENTER INC.
2201 1st Ave. North
Saint Petersburg, FL 33713
Tel: (727) 321-8887 Fax: (727) 321-7176
Email: Info@asianface.org
Web: www.asianface.org

CENTRAL ASIAN FREE EXCHANGE
P.O. Box 60816
Fort Myers, FL 33906
Tel: (239) 561-5968 Fax: (239) 561-2981
Email: cafeuzbek@aol.com

CHINESE-AMERICAN ASSOCIATION OF TAMPA BAY
P.O. Box 47614
Tampa, FL 33647
Wang Ping, President
Tel: (813) 971-6781
Email: Contact-CAAT@yahoogroups.com
Web: http://caatfl.tripod.com/index.html

DAVID POSNACK JEWISH COMMUNITY CENTER
5850 S. Pine Island Rd.
Davie, FL 33328
Mark Sherman, Executive Director
Tel: (954) 434-0499 Fax: (954) 434-1741
Email: info@dpjcc.org
Web: www.dpjcc.org

FLANZER JEWISH COMMUNITY CENTER
582 S. McIntosh Rd.
Sarasota, FL 34232
Marshall Klein, President/CEO
Tel: (941) 378-5568 Fax: (941) 378-1681
Email: mklein@flanzerjcc.com
Web: www.flanzerjcc.com

GREATER MIAMI JEWISH FEDERATION
4200 Biscayne Blvd.
Miami, FL 33137-3279
Tel: (305) 576-4000 Fax: (305) 573-4584
Email: info@gmjf.org
Web: www.jewishmiami.org

GULF COAST JEWISH FAMILY SERVICES, INC.
14041 Icot Blvd.
Clearwater, FL 33760
Tel: (727) 538-7150 Fax: (727) 535-4774
Email: info@gcjfs.org
Web: www.gcjfs.org

ISRALIGHT
Florida Chapter
P.O. Box 880943
Boca Raton, FL 33488-0943
Susan Ruben, Office Manager
Tel: (561) 447-0592 Fax: (561) 447-8744
Email: susan@isralight.org
Web: www.isralight.org

JACKSONVILLE JEWISH FEDERATION
8505 San Jose Blvd.
Jacksonville, FL 32217
Tel: (904) 448-5000 Fax: (904) 448-5715
Email: info@jaxjewish.org
Web: www.jaxjewish.org

JAPAN AMERICAN SOCIETY OF NORTHWEST FLORIDA, INC.
11000 University Pkwy. Bldg. 87 #119
Pensacola, FL 32514-5750
Tel: (850) 474-3363 Fax: (850) 857-6024
Email: japan@uwf.edu

JEWISH ASSOCIATION FOR RESIDENTIAL CARE
21160 95th Ave. South
Boca Raton, FL 33428
Debra Hallow, Executive Director
Tel: (561) 558-2550 Fax: (561) 487-7840
Email: debrah@bocafed.org

JEWISH COMMUNITY ALLIANCE
8505 San Jose Blvd.
Jacksonville, FL 32217
Myron I. Flagler, Executive Director
Tel: (904) 730-2100 Fax: (904) 730-2444
Web: www.jcajax.org

JEWISH COMMUNITY CENTER OF GREATER ORLANDO
Maitland Campus
851 N. Maitland Ave.
Maitland, FL 32751
Marvin Friedman, Executive Director
Tel: (407) 645-5933 Fax: (407) 645-1172
Web: www.orlandojcc.org

South Orlando Campus
11200 Apopka Vineland Rd.
Orlando, FL 32836
Marvin Friedman, Executive Director
Tel: (407) 239-7411
Web: www.orlandojcc.org

JEWISH COMMUNITY CENTER OF GREATER PALM BEACH
Kaplan JCC
3151 N. Military Trail
West Palm Beach, FL 33409
Tel: (561) 689-7700 Fax: (561) 478-3060
Email: susan@kaplanjcc.com
Web: www.jcconline.org

Hochman JCC
8500 Jog Rd.
Boynton Beach, FL 33437
Tel: (561) 740-9000 Fax: (561) 478-3060
Email: susan@kaplanjcc.com
Web: www.jcconline.org

JEWISH COMMUNITY CENTER OF VENICE
600 N. Auburn Rd.
Venice, FL 34292
Joel S. Kreiss, President
Tel: (941) 484-2022 Fax: (941) 483-9043
Email: jccvenice@att.net
Web: www.jccv.org

JEWISH COMMUNITY SERVICES OF SOUTH FLORIDA, INC.
735 NE 125th St.
North Miami, FL 33161
David B. Saltman, President/CEO
Tel: (305) 899-1587 Fax: (305) 899-6367
Web: www.jcsfl.org

JEWISH FAMILY SERVICE, INC. OF BROWARD COUNTY
100 S. Pine Island Rd. #230
Plantation, FL 33324
Sandra S. Sundel, CEO
Tel: (954) 370-2140 Fax: (954) 916-1252
Email: info@jfsbroward.org

JEWISH FAMILY SERVICES OF GREATER ORLANDO, INC.
The George Wolly Ctr., 2100 Lee Rd.
Winter Park, FL 32789
Barry Kudlowitz, Executive Director
Tel: (407) 644-7593 Fax: (407) 628-0773
Email: info@jewishfamilyservicesorlando.org
Web: www.jewishfamilyservicesorlando.org

JEWISH FEDERATION OF COLLIER COUNTY
1250 Tamiami Trail North #202
Naples, FL 34102
Tel: (239) 263-4205 Fax: (239) 263-3813
Email: jfccfl@aol.com
Web: www.jewishnaples.org

JEWISH FEDERATION OF GREATER ORLANDO
851 N. Maitland Ave.
Maitland, FL 32751
Eric Geboff, Executive Director
Tel: (407) 645-5933 Fax: (407) 645-1172
Email: ericg@orlandojewishfed.org
Web: www.shalomorlando.org

JEWISH FEDERATION OF LEE AND CHARLOTTE COUNTIES
6237 E. Presidential Ct.
Fort Myers, FL 33919
Doug Gribin, President
Tel: (239) 481-4449 Fax: (239) 481-0139
Email: jfed@jewishfederationswfl.org
Web: www.jewishfederationswfl.org

JEWISH FEDERATION OF PALM BEACH COUNTY
4601 Community Dr.
West Palm Beach, FL 33417
Tel: (561) 478-0700 Fax: (561) 478-9696
Web: www.jewishpalmbeach.org

JEWISH FEDERATION OF PINELLAS COUNTY
13191 Starkey Rd. #8
Largo, FL 33773
Tel: (727) 530-3223 Fax: (727) 531-0221
Email: jpinellas@bssfl.com
Web: www.jewishpinellas.org

JEWISH FEDERATION OF SOUTH PALM BEACH COUNTY
9901 Donna Klein Blvd.
Boca Raton, FL 33428
Tel: (561) 852-3100 Fax: (561) 852-3150
Email: dstern@jewishboca.org
Web: www.jewishboca.org

JEWISH SOLIDARITY, INC.
100 Beacom Blvd.
Miami, FL 33135
Edie B. Levy, Founder
Tel: (305) 642-1600 Fax: (305) 642-1686
Email: jewishsolidarity@bellsouth.net
Web: www.jewishcuba.org

KOREAN AMERICAN COMMUNITY RELATIONS COUNCIL OF SOUTH FLORIDA
8445 SW 148th Dr.
Miami, FL 33158
Sang Whang, Chair
Tel: (305) 235-5120 Fax: (305) 278-8775
Email: sang@alkalife.com
Web: www.alkalife.com

MIAMI-DADE COUNTY ASIAN AMERICAN ADVISORY BOARD
Stephen P. Clark Ctr., 111 NW 1st St. # 660
Miami, FL 33128
Mohammad Shakir, Board Director
Tel: (305) 375-1570 Fax: (305) 375-5715
Email: morilla@co.miamidade.fl.us
Web: www.miamidade.gov

MICHAEL-ANN RUSSELL JEWISH COMMUNITY CENTER
18900 NE 25th Ave.
N. Miami Beach, FL 33180
Gary Bomzer, Contact
Tel: (305) 932-4200 Fax: (305) 932-9161
Email: info@marjcc.org
Web: www.marjcc.org

SARASOTA-MANATEE JEWISH FEDERATION
580 S. McIntosh Rd.
Sarasota, FL 34232
Tel: (941) 371-4546 Fax: (941) 378-2947
Email: info@smjf.org
Web: www.smjf.org

SOREF JEWISH COMMUNITY CENTER
6501 W. Sunrise Blvd.
Plantation, FL 33763
Tel: (727) 736-1494 Fax: (727) 736-5634
Web: www.sorefjcc.org

TAMPA JCC/FEDERATION, INC.
13009 Community Campus Dr.
Tampa, FL 33625
Dr. Barry B. Zeltzer, Executive Director
Tel: (813) 264-9000 Fax: (813) 265-8450
Email: info@jewishtampa.org
Web: www.jewishtampa.org

UNITED JEWISH COMMUNITY OF BROWARD COUNTY
5890 S. Pine Island Rd.
Davie, FL 33328
Tel: (954) 252-6900 Fax: (954) 252-6892
Email: info@jewishbroward.org
Web: www.jewishbroward.org

VIETNAMESE COMMUNITY ASSOCIATION OF CENTRAL FLORIDA
1210 E. Colonial Dr. #1
Orlando, FL 32803
Nguyen Lan, VP
Tel: (407) 896-3434 Fax: (407) 896-3437
Email: lan@teamscrub.com

SPEC. INT., SPORTS

CHINESE BOXING INSTITUTE INTERNATIONAL
P.O. Box 666957
Pompano Beach, FL 33066
Email: cbii@mac.com
Web: www.chineseboxing.com

FILIPINO COMBAT SYSTEMS
P.O. Box 1628
Auburndale, FL 33823
Ray Dionaldo, Founder
Email: ray@fcskali.com
Web: www.fcskali.com

INTERNATIONAL SHOTOKAN KARATE CLUB
South Atlantic
10810 Wiles Rd.
Coral Springs, FL 33071
Shigeru Takashina, Instructor
Tel: (954) 346-0035 Fax: (954) 733-7857
Email: saka@iskfsaka.org
Web: www.sakahonbu.org

MOSAIC OUTDOOR CLUBS OF AMERICA
South Florida Chapter
P.O. Box 810362
Boca Raton, FL 33481
Matthew Shuchman, Chapter President
Tel: (305) 650-2966
Email: sofla@mosaics.org
Web: www.mosaics.org

THE CHINESE KARATE FEDERATION
6077 Lake Worth Rd.
Greenacres, FL 33463
Web: www.chinesekaratefederation.com

SPEC. INT., WOMEN

HADASSAH
Florida Atlantic Region
5341 W. Atlantic Ave. #305
Delray Beach, FL 33484
Judy Greer, President
Tel: (561) 498-1012 Fax: (561) 498-1599
Email: floridaatlantic@hadassah.org
Web: www.hadassah.org

Florida Central Region
971 Virginia Ave. #E
Palm Harbor, FL 34683
Karen Eisler, President
Tel: (727) 772-0868 Fax: (727) 772-0968
Email: flcentralregion@hadassah.org
Web: www.hadassah.org

Florida-Broward County Region
6501 W. Sunrise Blvd.
Ft. Lauderdale, FL 33313
Rosalind Rosen, President
Tel: (954) 792-3258 Fax: (954) 792-5832
Email: floridabroward@hadassah.org
Web: www.hadassah.org

Greater Miami Region
4200 Biscayne Blvd.
Miami, FL 33137

Clara Gillman, President
Tel: (305) 576-4447 Fax: (305) 576-4448
Email: greatermiami@hadassah.org
Web: www.hadassah.org

SPEC. INT., YOUTH

NATIONAL CENTER FOR MISSING & EXPLOITED CHILDREN
Florida
9176 Alternate A1A #100
Lake Park, FL 33403
Tel: (561) 848-1900 Fax: (561) 848-0308
Email: flbranch@nencmec.org
Web: www.missingkids.com

STUDENT ORGANIZATION

ASIAN STUDENT UNION
Florida State University
A303B Old Union, A205 Oglesby Union
Tallahassee, FL 32306-4027
Alan Truong, Director
Tel: (850) 644-3909
Email: fsuasu@hotmail.com
Web: www.fsu.edu/~activity/ASU

University of Florida
300-5 JWRU
Gainesville, FL 32611
Mark Villegas, President
Tel: (352) 392-1665 x325
Email: asu@grove.ufl.edu
Web: http://grove.ufl.edu/~asu

INDIAN STUDENT ASSOCIATION
University of Central Florida
Student Union #305
Orlando, FL 32816
Pavan Talakala, President
Tel: (407) 616-2616
Email: sangam@mail.ucf.edu
Web: http://pegasus.cc.ucf.edu/%7Esangam

INDONESIAN STUDENT ASSOCIATION
Florida State University
318-4 Pennell Circle Dr.
Tallahassee, FL 32310
Deden Rukmana, President
Tel: (850) 576-6807
Email: permias_tlh@yahoo.com
Web: www.fsu.edu/~fsu-isc/permias

KOREAN STUDENT ASSOCIATION
University of Florida
Gainesville, FL 32611
Beomjin Park, President
Email: beomp@ufl.edu
Web: http://grove.ufl.edu/~ksa

KOREAN UNDERGRADUATE STUDENT ASSOCIATION
University of Florida
P.O. Box 118505
300 J Wayne Reitz Union
Gainesville, FL 32611
Catherine Yoon, President
Tel: (352) 262-9538
Email: kusa@grove.ufl.edu
Web: http://grove.ufl.edu/~kusa/

MUSLIM STUDENTS ASSOCIATION
Florida International University
GC 340, FIU South
Miami, FL 33199
Nour Kablawi, President
Web: www.msafiu.com

PAKISTANI STUDENTS ASSOCIATION
University of Central Florida
Orlando, FL 32801
Zeeshan Furqan, President
Tel: (407) 823-2000
Email: psa@pegasus.cc.ucf.edu
Web: http://pegasus.cc.ucf.edu/~psa/

GEORGIA

BUSINESS

JAPAN EXTERNAL TRADE ORGANIZATION
Atlanta Chapter
Marquis One Tower, 245 Peachtree Center Ave. #2208
Atlanta, GA 30303
Hirokaku Yamaoka, Chief Executive Director
Tel: (404) 681-0600 Fax: (404) 681-0713
Email: hirokaku_yamaoka@jetro.go.jp
Web: www.jetro.go.jp/usa/atlanta

JEWISH-BLACK BUSINESS COALITION
181 14th St. #500
Atlanta, GA 30309
Todd Zeldin, Co-Founder
Tel: (404) 653-0049 Fax: (404) 795-1098
Email: info@jbbcoalition.org
Web: www.jbbcoalition.org

CHAMBER OF COMMERCE

AMERICAN ISRAEL CHAMBER OF COMMERCE
Southeast Region
1150 Lake Hearn Dr. #130
Atlanta, GA 30342
Thomas Glaser, President
Tel: (404) 843-9426 Fax: (404) 843-1416
Email: tom@aiccse.org
Web: www.aiccse.org

ASIAN AMERICAN CHAMBER OF COMMERCE OF GEORGIA, INC.
P.O. Box 550113
Atlanta, GA 30355
John Lu, President
Tel: (770) 394-0970 Fax: (770) 394-9911
Email: aaccga@yahoo.com
Web: http://aaccga.org

GEORGIA INDO-AMERICAN CHAMBER OF COMMERCE
4780 Ashford Dunwoody Rd. #A-276
Atlanta, GA 30338
Tel: (678) 230-3283 Fax: (770) 381-9344
Email: info@giacc.org
Web: www.giacc.org

JAPANESE CHAMBER OF COMMERCE OF GEORGIA
Marquis One Tower, 245 Peachtree Center Ave. #2208
Atlanta, GA 30303
Hirokazu Yamaoka, Chair
Tel: (404) 522-0122 Fax: (404) 522-7524
Email: info@jccg.org
Web: www.jccg.org

PAKISTAN INTERNATIONAL CHAMBER OF COMMERCE, INC.
2495-A E. Gate Pl.
Snellville, GA 30078
Ashraf Gohar Goreja, President/CEO
Tel: (770) 982-1340 Fax: (770) 982-0273
Email: info@pakchamber.com
Web: www.pakchamber.com

PHILIPPINE AMERICA CHAMBER OF COMMERCE OF GEORGIA, INC.
1620 Manhasset Farm Ct.
Dunwoody, GA 30338
Didi O'Connor, President
Tel: (770) 396-1828 Fax: (770) 396-6695
Web: www.paccga.org

CULTURAL

ALIF INSTITUTE
P.O. Box 29067
Atlanta, GA 30359
Tel: (770) 936-8770 Fax: (770) 936-8769
Email: info@alifInstitute.org
Web: www.alifinstitute.org

ATLANTA ASSOCIATION FOR BHARATANATYAM
P.O. Box 923192
Norcross, GA 30010-3192
Chandrika Chandran, President
Email: contact@aabha.org
Web: www.ipnatlanta.net/aabha

BAL VIHAR
Interactive College of Technology
5303 New Peachtree Rd.
Chamblee, GA 30141
Prakash Gupta, Contact
Tel: (770) 216-2960
Email: mjain@balvihar.org
Web: www.balvihar.org

BRAHMIN SAMAJ OF GEORGIA, INC.
P.O. Box 80162
Atlanta, GA 30366
Pradipbhai Sevak, President
Tel: (770) 680-2741
Email: sevak4@juno.com
Web: http://members.tripod.com/~Brahmin_Samaj_of_GA

CHINESE CULTURE CENTER
5377 New Peachtree Rd.
Chamblee, GA 30341
Kuo Sun, President
Tel: (770) 451-4456 Fax: (770) 451-8119
Email: atltaipei@mindspring.com

FILIPINO AMERICAN ASSOCIATION OF GREATER ATLANTA
975 Cone Rd.
Forest Park, GA 30297
Willee Bonus, President
Email: nsalgado@atl-filam.org
Web: www.atl-filam.org

GREATER ATLANTA MALAYALEE ASSOCIATION
P.O. Box 931206
Norcross, GA 30003-1206
K.C. George, President
Tel: (770) 949-1373
Email: georgekc@hotmail.com
Web: www.gamaonline.org

INDIA AMERICAN CULTURAL ASSOCIATION
1281 Cooperlake Rd.
Smyrna, GA 30082
Paddy Sharma, President
Tel: (770) 436-3719 Fax: (770) 436-4272
Web: www.myiaca.org

JAPANESE EMBROIDERY CENTER, INC.
2727 Spalding Dr.
Dunwoody, GA 30350
Shuji Tamura, President
Tel: (770) 390-0617 Fax: (770) 512-7837
Email: info@japaneseembroidery.com
Web: www.japaneseembroidery.com

NEPALESE ASSOCIATION IN SOUTHEAST AMERICA
Prakash Malla, President
Tel: (478) 275-8342
Email: mallap@bellsouth.net
Web: www.nepal-america.org

SOUTHERN JEWISH HISTORICAL SOCIETY
P.O. Box 5024
Atlanta, GA 30302-5024
Email: info@jewishsouth.org
Web: www.jewishsouth.org

TELUGU ASSOCIATION OF METRO ATLANTA
11290 Donington Dr.
Duluth, GA 30097
Surender Reddy Mutyala, President
Tel: (770) 685-2020
Email: tama_mutyala@go.com
Web: www.tama.org

THE AFGHAN COMMUNITY FOUNDATION, INC.
P.O. Box 7870
Atlanta, GA 30357-0870
Web: www.afghancommunityfoundation.org

TURKISH AMERICAN CULTURAL ASSOCIATION OF GEORGIA
P.O. Box 190013
Atlanta, GA 31119
Fusun Ercan, President
Tel: (770) 442-9171
Email: info@tacaga.org
Web: www.tacaga.org

WILLIAM BREMAN JEWISH HERITAGE MUSEUM
1440 Spring St. NW
Atlanta, GA 30309
Jane D. Leavey, Executive Director
Tel: (678) 222-3700
Email: jleavey@thebreman.org
Web: www.thebreman.org

POLITICAL ACTION

AMERICAN-ARAB ANTI DISCRIMINATION COMMITTEE
Georgia Chapter
P.O. Box 467446
Atlanta, GA 31146
Akeel Hanano, President
Tel: (404) 575-4016 Fax: (404) 761-0507
Email: hanano@adcgeorgia.org
Web: www.adcgeorgia.org

INDIAN AMERICAN FORUM FOR POLITICAL EDUCATION
3310 Haver Hill Row
Lawrenceville, GA 30044
Narendra Reddy, President
Tel: (770) 921-8678
Email: ngreddy9@aol.com
Web: www.iafpe.org

INDO-AMERICAN DEMOCRATS OF GEORGIA
P.O. Box 1758
Mabledon, GA 30126
Mohinder M. Bajaj, Chairman
Tel: (770) 948-0020 Fax: (770) 948-0024
Email: mohbajaj@yahoo.com

KOREAN AMERICAN COALITION
Atlanta Chapter
4675 River Green Pkwy.
Duluth, GA 30096
Susan Kim, President
Tel: (404) 388-6560 Fax: (770) 232-9087
Email: info@kacatl.org
Web: www.kacatl.org

PROFESSIONAL

ASIAN AMERICAN HOTEL OWNERS ASSOCIATION
66 Lenox Pointe NE
Atlanta, GA 30324
Fred Schwartz, President
Tel: (800) 495-5958 Fax: (404) 816-6260
Email: info@aahoa.com
Web: www.aahoa.com

ASIAN AMERICAN JOURNALISTS ASSOCIATION
Atlanta Chapter
290 Sisson Ave. NE
Atlanta, GA 30317
Rodney Ho, President
Tel: (404) 526-5688
Email: rho@ajc.com
Web: www.aaja.org/chapters/atlanta/

INDIAN PROFESSIONALS NETWORK OF ATLANTA
P.O. Box 49494
Atlanta, GA 30359
Narsi Narasimhan, Founder

Tel: (770) 451-2299 Fax: (770) 451-2299
Email: narsi@mindspring.com
Web: www.ipnatlanta.net

NATIONAL ASSOCIATION OF ASIAN AMERICAN PROFESSIONALS
NAAAP-Atlanta
P.O. Box 620035
Atlanta, GA 30362
Jimmy Tai, President
Email: mail@naaapatlanta.org
Web: www.naaapatlanta.org

THE FEDERATION OF ASSOCIATIONS OF CHINESE PROFESSIONALS IN SOUTHERN USA
791 Atlantic Dr.
Atlanta, GA 30332-0269
Haibo Du, President
Email: haibod@applink.net

RELIGIOUS

AHAVATH ACHIM SYNAGOGUE
600 Peachtree Battle
Atlanta, GA 30327
Joel C. Lobel, Executive Director
Tel: (404) 355-5222 Fax: (404) 352-2831
Email: jlobel@aasynagogue.org
Web: www.aasynagogue.org

ARABIC BAPTIST CHURCH
3715 LaVista Rd.
Decatur, GA 30033
Rev. Nicholas Murr
Tel: (404) 325-4214
Email: nmurr@worldnet.att.net
Web: www.jesus-saves.org

ATLANTA CHINESE CHRISTIAN CHURCH
4434 Britt Rd.
Tucker, GA 30084
Rev. Jeffrey Lu, Senior Pastor
Tel: (770) 908-1972 Fax: (770) 908-1773
Email: info@accc.org
Web: www.accc.org

ATLANTA KOREAN MARTYRS CATHOLIC CHURCH
6003 Buford Hwy.
Doraville, GA 30340
Tel: (770) 455-1380 Fax: (770) 455-4262

ATLANTA TAMIL CHURCH
2534 Duluth Hwy.
Duluth, GA 30097
Rev. Palmer Paramadhas, Pastor
Tel: (404) 245-7674
Email: atlanta@atlantatamilchurch.org
Web: www.atlantatamilchurch.org

CAMBODIAN BUDDHIST SOCIETY
P.O. Box 48442
Atlanta, GA 30362
Tel: (770) 482-5563

CHINMAYA MISSION MIDDLE GEORGIA
129 Lake Front Dr.
Warner Robins, GA 31088
Dr. G.V. Raghu, Contact
Tel: (478) 922-9710
Email: atlanta@chinmayamission.org
Web: www.chinmaya-atlanta.com

CONGREGATION BETH SHALOM
5303 Winters Chapel Rd.
Atlanta, GA 30360
Mark H. Zimmerman, President
Tel: (770) 399-5300 Fax: (770) 399-0766
Email: shalom@bshalom.net
Web: www.bshalom.net

CONGREGATION BETH TEFILLAH
5065 Highpoint Rd.
Atlanta, GA 30342
Yossi New, Rabbi
Tel: (404) 843-2464 Fax: (404) 257-9306

Email: admin@bethtefillah.org
Web: www.bethtefillah.org

CONGREGATION ETZ CHAIM
1190 Indian Hills Pkwy.
Marietta, GA 30068
Allan H. Glazerman, Executive Director
Tel: (770) 973-0137 Fax: (770) 977-0829
Email: glaze@etzchaim.net
Web: www.etzchaim.net

CONGREGATION GESHER L' TORAH
4320 Kimball Bridge Rd.
Alpharetta, GA 30022
Albert Slomovitz, Rabbi
Tel: (770) 777-4009 Fax: (770) 777-4090
Email: info@gltorah.org
Web: www.gltorah.org

CONGREGATION OR VESHALOM
1681 N. Druid Hills Rd.
Atlanta, GA 30319
Jack A. Arogeti, President
Tel: (404) 633-1737 Fax: (404) 633-5938
Email: office@orveshalom.com
Web: www.orveshalom.com

CONGREGATION SHEARITH ISRAEL
1180 University Dr. NE
Atlanta, GA 30306
Karen Tashman, Executive Director
Tel: (404) 873-1743 Fax: (404) 873-6235
Email: shearithisrael@mindspring.com
Web: www.shearithisrael.com

FIRST ASIAN INDIAN BAPTIST CHURCH OF METRO ATLANTA
570 Piedmont Rd. NE
Marietta, GA 30066
Rev. Younis Farhat, Pastor
Tel: (770) 516-5751 Fax: (770) 423-0125
Email: aibc@mindspring.com
Web: www.ipnatlanta.net/aibc

FIRST INDIA BAPTIST CHURCH
1995 Clairmont Rd.
Decatur, GA 30033
Rev. Avinash Raiborde, Pastor
Tel: (404) 636-6595 Fax: (404) 634-6062
Email: pastor@firstindiabaptist.com
Web: www.firstindiabaptist.com

JAIN SOCIETY OF GREATER ATLANTA
669 S. Peachtree St.
Norcross, GA 30071-2438
Raju Shah, President
Tel: (770) 613-0103
Email: jaincenteratlanta@hotmail.com
Web: www.jsgatemple.org

NORTH AMERICA SHIRDI SAI TEMPLE OF ATLANTA
700 James Burgess Rd.
Suwanee, GA 30024
Ranga Rao Sunkara, President
Tel: (678) 455-7200
Email: webmaster@templeofpeace.org
Web: www.templeofpeace.org

TEMPLE BETH TIKVAH
9955 Coleman Rd.
Roswell, GA 30075
Robert Mittleman, Executive Director
Tel: (770) 642-0434 Fax: (770) 642-0647
Web: www.bethtikvah.com

TEMPLE EMANU-EL
1580 Spalding Dr.
Atlanta, GA 30350
Julie S. Schwartz, Rabbi
Tel: (770) 395-1340 Fax: (770) 395-1343
Email: jschwartz@temple-emanuel.net
Web: www.te-atl.com

TEMPLE KOL EMETH
1415 Old Canton Rd.
Marietta, GA 30062
Sharon Klein, Executive Director

Tel: (770) 973-3533 Fax: (770) 579-9707
Email: sharonklein@kolemeth.net
Web: http://kolemeth.net

TEMPLE SINAI
5645 Dupree Dr. NW
Atlanta, GA 30327-4399
Warren Zindler, President
Tel: (404) 252-3073 Fax: (404) 252-8570
Email: warren@zindlers.com
Web: www.templesinai.org

THE TEMPLE
1589 Peachtree St. NE
Atlanta, GA 30309-2401
Mark R. Jacobson, Executive Director
Tel: (404) 873-1731 Fax: (404) 873-5529
Email: office@the-temple.org
Web: www.the-temple.org

YOUNG ISRAEL OF TOCO HILLS
2074 LaVista Rd. NE
Atlanta, GA 30329
Jennifer Harris, Executive Director
Tel: (404) 315-1417 Fax: (404) 315-1417
Email: yithinfo@yith.org
Web: www.yith.org

RESEARCH

CENTER FOR INTERNATIONAL TRADE AND SECURITY
University of Georgia
120 Hunter Holmes Academic Bldg.
Athens, GA 30602
Gary Bertsch, Director
Tel: (706) 542-2985 Fax: (706) 542-2975
Email: gbertsch@uga.edu
Web: www.uga.edu/cits

JEWISH GENEALOGICAL SOCIETY OF GEORGIA, INC.
P.O. Box 681022
Marietta, GA 30068
Gary Palgon, President
Tel: (770) 458-6664
Email: jgsginc@hotmail.com
Web: www.jewishgen.org/jgsg/

SPEC. INT., CHILD CARE

CHINESE CHILDREN ADOPTION INTERNATIONAL
5825 Glenridge Dr., Bldg. 1 #126
Atlanta, GA 30328
Richard L. Dietz, Director
Tel: (404) 250-0055 Fax: (404) 250-0099
Email: ccaiga@chinesechildren.org
Web: www.chinesechildren.org

SPEC. INT., EDUCATION

ARAB AMERICAN FUND OF GEORGIA, INC.
P.O. Box 29067
Atlanta, GA 30359
R. Houssami, President
Tel: (404) 633-1161 Fax: (404) 228-4432
Email: info@alifInstitute.org
Web: www.alifInstitute.org

ASHA FOR EDUCATION
Athens
108 College Station Rd. #H108
Athens, GA 30605
Maria Chinwala, Treasurer
Tel: (706) 380-6959
Email: mariagc@uga.edu
Web: www.ashanet.org/athens/

Atlanta
2099 E. Lake Park Dr.
Smyrna, GA 30080
Ashok Narayan, Projects Coordinator
Tel: (404) 325-1415
Email: ashoknarayan_asha@yahoo.com
Web: www.ashanet.org/atlanta/

ASIAN AMERICAN LANGUAGE SERVICES
3575 River Summit Trail #B
Duluth, GA 30097
Garry Guan, President
Tel: (770) 623-6688 Fax: (770) 623-0078
Email: garry@aals.com
Web: www.aals.com

CENTER FOR JEWISH EDUCATION AND EXPERIENCES
1776 Old Springhouse Ln.
Atlanta, GA 30338
Paul A. Flexner, Executive Director
Tel: (770) 455-6565 Fax: (770) 455-6365
Email: flex@cjee.org
Web: www.jesatlanta.org

GREENFIELD HEBREW ACADEMY
5200 Northland Dr.
Atlanta, GA 30342
Tel: (404) 843-9900 Fax: (404) 252-0934
Email: langerm@ghacademy.org
Web: www.ghacademy.org

JEWISH EDUCATIONAL LOAN FUND
4549 Chamblee Dunwoody Rd.
Atlanta, GA 30338
Cheryl M. Eppsteiner, Executive Director
Tel: (770) 396--3080
Email: info@jelf.org
Web: www.jelf.org

US CHINA PEOPLES FRIENDSHIP ASSOCIATION
Atlanta Chapter
18 Fairfield Dr.
Avondale Estates, GA 30002
Peggy Roney, Contact
Tel: (404) 292-0714
Web: www.uscpfa.org

SPEC. INT., HUMAN RELATIONS

COUNCIL ON AMERICAN-ISLAMIC RELATIONS
Northern Georgia Chapter
3920 N. Peachtree Rd. #205
Atlanta, GA 30341
Yusof Burke, President
Tel: (770) 220-0082 Fax: (770) 220-0082
Email: cair@cair-northgeorgia.org
Web: www.cair-northgeorgia.org

NATIONAL ASSOCIATION OF CHINESE AMERICANS
Atlanta Chapter
5483 Redbark Way
Dunwoody, GA 30338
Wei Hu, President
Tel: (770) 394-6542
Email: weihu@troutmansanders.com
Web: www.naca-atlanta.org

THE AMERICAN JEWISH COMMITTEE
Atlanta Chapter
6 Piedmont Ctr. #510
Atlanta, GA 30305-1530
Elise Eplan, President
Tel: (404) 233-1530 Fax: (404) 261-2344
Email: info@ajcatlanta.org
Web: www.ajcatlanta.org

SPEC. INT., IMMIGRATION

ASIAN COMMUNITY SERVICES, INC.
4229 1st Ave. #B
Tucker, GA 30084
Tel: Fax: (770) 908-2678
Web: www.sph.emory.edu/
BUFORDHWYCORR/acs.html

SPEC. INT., SENIORS

AGING INFORMATION CENTER
Region IV: AL, FL, GA, KY, MS, NC, SC, TN

Atlanta Federal Ctr., 61 Forsyth St. SW
5M69
Atlanta, GA 30303-8909
Percy Devine, Regional Administrator
Tel: (404) 562-7600 Fax: (404) 562-7598
Email: Percy.Devine@aoa.gov
Web: www.aoa.dhhs.gov

SPEC. INT., SOCIAL INTEREST

ASIAN/PACIFIC- AMERICAN COUNCIL OF GEORGIA, INC.
c/o Center for Pan Asian Community, Inc.
3760 Park Ave.
Doraville, GA 30340
Chaiwon Kim, Executive Director
Tel: (770) 936-0969 Fax: (770) 458-9377
Email: cpacs@cpacs.org
Web: www.cpacs.org

CENTER FOR PAN ASIAN COMMUNITY SERVICES, INC.
3760 Park Ave.
Doraville, GA 30340
Chaiwon Kim, Executive Director
Tel: (770) 936-0969 Fax: (770) 458-9377
Email: cpacs@cpacs.org
Web: www.cpacs.org

HMONG CULTURAL ORGANIZATION, INC.
P.O. Box 925
Winder, GA 30680
Young Xiong, President
Tel: (770) 207-0769
Email: info@hmonggeorgia.org
Web: www.hmonggeorgia.org

JAPAN-AMERICAN SOCIETY OF GEORGIA
3121 Maple Dr. #224
Atlanta, GA 30305
Yuko Takahashi, Cultural Coordinator/Office Manager
Tel: (404) 842-1400 Fax: (404) 842-1415

JEWISH EDUCATIONAL ALLIANCE/ SAVANNAH JEWISH FEDERATION
P.O. Box 23527
Savannah, GA 31403
Susan Adler, Assistant Director
Tel: (912) 355-8111 Fax: (912) 355-8116
Web: www.savj.org

JEWISH FEDERATION OF GREATER ATLANTA
1440 Spring St. NW
Atlanta, GA 30309
Linda Selig, President
Tel: (404) 873-1661 Fax: (404) 874-7043
Email: webmaster@jfga.org
Web: www.shalomatlanta.org

MARCUS JEWISH COMMUNITY CENTER OF ATLANTA
5342 Tilly Mill Rd.
Dunwoody, GA 30338
Donald A. Jaslow, President
Tel: (770) 396-3250 Fax: (770) 698-2055
Web: http://marcusjcc.accrisoft.com

PAKISTANI AMERICAN SOCIETY OF ATLANTA
6013 Yellowood Ct.
College Park, GA 30349
Shahid Nawaz Qureshi, President
Tel: (404) 545-1387
Email: info@pasainfo.org
Web: www.pasainfo.org

RAKSHA, INC.
P.O. Box 12337
Atlanta, GA 30355
Aparna Bhattacharyya, Executive Director
Tel: (404) 876-0670 Fax: (404) 876-4525
Email: raksha@mindspring.com
Web: www.raksha.org

SPEC. INT., SPORTS

MOSAIC OUTDOOR CLUBS OF AMERICA
Atlanta Chapter
P.O. Box 8185
Atlanta, GA 31106-0185
Matt Gottlieb, Chapter President
Tel: (770) 263-8027
Email: atlanta@mosaics.org
Web: www.mosaics.org

SPEC. INT., WOMEN

ARAB AMERICAN WOMEN'S SOCIETY OF GEORGIA
P.O. Box 467152
Atlanta, GA 31146
Iman Abuaisheh, President
Tel: (404) 634-3807
Email: info@AAWSG.org
Web: www.aawsg.org

HADASSAH
Southern Region
2646 Weddington Pl.
Marietta, GA 30068
Susan Moye, President
Tel: (770) 578-0097
Email: susan.moye@hadassah.org
Web: www.hadassah.org

STUDENT ORGANIZATION

BANGLADESH STUDENT ASSOCIATION
Georgia Tech
Student Services #141, 353 Ferst Dr. NW
Atlanta, GA 30332-0289
Shubin Shahab, President
Email: bsa@gatech.edu
Web: www.cyberbuzz.gatech.edu/bsa/

KOREAN UNDERGRADUATE STUDENT ASSOCIATION
Georgia Institute of Technology
Atlanta, GA 30332
Sun Moon Kim, President
Tel: (404) 808-5573
Email: gtg253i@mail.gatech.edu
Web: www.cyberbuzz.gatech.edu/kusa

PAKISTAN STUDENT ASSOCIATION
University of Georgia
International Student Life Office
Athens, GA 30602
Sajid Ali Qureshi, President
Email: psa@listserv.uga.edu
Web: www.uga.edu/pakistan

UNIVERSITY OF GEORGIA HILLEL
1155 S. Milledge Ave.
Athens, GA 30605
Shawn Laing, Director
Tel: (706) 543-6393 Fax: (706) 543-2542
Email: hillel@uga.edu
Web: www.uga.edu/hillel

HAWAII

ARTISTIC

HUI NOEAU VISUAL ARTS CENTER
2841 Baldwin Ave.
Makawao, HI 96768
John Wilson, Interim Director
Tel: (808) 572-6560 Fax: (808) 572-2750
Email: info@huinoeau.com
Web: www.huinoeau.com

BUSINESS

JAPAN-AMERICAN INSTITUTE OF MANAGEMENT SCIENCE
6660 Hawaii Kai Dr.
Honolulu, HI 96825-1192
Dr. Glenn K. Miyataki, President
Tel: (808) 395-2314 Fax: (808) 396-7111
Email: info@jaims.org
Web: www.jaims.org

SAMOAN SERVICE PROVIDER'S ASSOCIATION
1208 N. King St.
Honolulu, HI 96817
William Emmsley, Executive Director
Tel: (808) 842-0218 Fax: (808) 847-6729
Email: sspa@hi.com

CHAMBER OF COMMERCE

CHINA HAWAII CHAMBER OF COMMERCE
55 Merchant St., Harbor Ct. #1813
Honolulu, HI 96813
Johnson Choi, President and Executive Director
Tel: (808) 222-8183 Fax: (808) 524-8063
Email: info@hkchcc.org
Web: www.hkchcc.org

CHINESE CHAMBER OF COMMERCE OF HAWAII
42 N. King St.
Honolulu, HI 96813
Terrill S. W. Chock, President
Tel: (808) 533-3181 Fax: (808) 533-6967
Email: info@chinesechamber.com
Web: www.ccchi.org

HAWAII KOREAN CHAMBER OF COMMERCE
1188 Bishop St. #811
Honolulu, HI 96813
Daniel J.Y. Pyun, President
Web: www.hkccweb.org

HONG KONG CHINA HAWAII CHAMBER OF COMMERCE
55 Merchant St. #1813
Honolulu, HI 96813
Johnson W. K. Choi, President & Executive Director
Tel: (808) 222-8183 Fax: (808) 524-8063
Email: johnsonchoi@johnsonchoi.com
Web: www.hkchcc.org

HONOLULU-JAPANESE CHAMBER OF COMMERCE
2454 S. Beretania St. #201
Honolulu, HI 96826-1596
Sharon Narimatsu, President
Tel: (808) 949-5531
Email: hjccserve@hula.net
Web: www.honolulujapanesechamber.org

VIETNAMESE AMERICAN CHAMBER OF COMMERCE OF HAWAII
P.O. Box 2011
Honolulu, HI 96805
Ralph Portmore, Chairman
Tel: (808) 545-1889 Fax: (808) 734-2315
Email: info@vacch.org
Web: www.vacch.org

COMMUNICATIONS

PACIFIC ISLANDERS IN COMMUNICATIONS
1221 Kapi'olani Blvd. #6A-4
Honolulu, HI 96814
Peter Kamamo Apo, President
Tel: (808) 591-0059 Fax: (808) 591-114
Email: info@piccom.org
Web: www.piccom.org

CULTURAL

BISHOP MUSEUM
1525 Bernice St.
Honolulu, HI 96817
Bill Brown, President
Tel: (808) 847-3511 Fax: (808) 841-8968
Web: www.bishopmuseum.org

FILIPINO COMMUNITY CENTER, INC.
94-428 Mokuola St. #302
Waipahu, HI 96797
Amy Agbayani, Chairman
Tel: (808) 680-0451 Fax: (808) 680-7510
Email: filcom@filcom.org
Web: www.filcom.org

HAWAI'I MUSEUMS ASSOCIATION
P.O. Box 4125
Honolulu, HI 96812-4125
Dolly Strazar, President
Email: info@hawaiimuseums.org
Web: www.hawaiimuseums.org

JAPANESE CULTURAL CENTER OF HAWAII
2454 S. Beretania St.
Honolulu, HI 96826
Kiko Bonk, President
Tel: (808) 945-7633 Fax: (808)944-1123
Email: info@jcch.com
Web: www.jcch.com

KONA HISTORICAL SOCIETY
P.O. Box 398
Captain Cook, HI 96704
Scott Seymour, President
Tel: (808) 323-3222 Fax: (808) 323-2398
Email: khs@konahistorical.org
Web: www.konahistorical.org

MAUI HISTORICAL SOCIETY
Bailey House Museum
2375-A Main St.
Wailuku, HI 96793
Roslyn Lightfoot, Executive Director
Tel: (808) 244-3326
Email: baileyh@aloha.net
Web: www.mauimuseum.org

POLYNESIAN CULTURAL CENTER
55-370 Kamehameha Hwy.
Laie, HI 96762
Tel: (800) 367-7060 Fax: (888) 722-7339
Email: internetrez@polynesia.com
Web: www.polynesia.com

THE NATIONAL KOREAN WAR MUSEUM
235 Kellog St.
Wahiawa, HI 96786
Kyle K. Kopitke, Founder
Tel: (808) 622-5100
Email: kkopitke@hotmail.com
Web: www.nkwm2.org

VIETNAMESE-AMERICAN CULTURE AND EDUCATION FOUNDATION
P.O. Box 2011
Honolulu, HI 96805
Thanh Lo Le Khac Sananikone, Executive Director
Tel: (808) 735-0238 Fax: (808) 734-2315
Email: vacefhawaii@yahoo.com
Web: www.vacef.us

MULTI-PURPOSE

AMICUS FOUNDATION
4217 Waipua St.
Kilauea, HI 96754
James Winkler, Chief Executive Director
Tel: (808) 828-2828 Fax: (808) 828-0119
Email: info@amicusfoundation.org
Web: www.amicusfoundation.org

HAWAII CHINESE ASSOCIATION
P.O. Box 27918
Honolulu, HI 96827
Judy Liu, President
Tel: (808) 946-4603 Fax: (808) 946-4603
Email: judyliu2003@yahoo.com
Web: www.hkchcc.org

POLITICAL ACTION

ASIAN PACIFIC AMERICAN LABOR ALLIANCE
Hawaii Chapter
888 Mililani St.
Honolulu, HI 96814
Joan Takano, President
Tel: (808) 543-0043
Web: www.apalanet.org

ORGANIZATION OF CHINESE AMERICANS-HAWAII
1585 Kapiolani Blvd. #1218
Honolulu, HI 96814
Alan Ho, President
Email: alanho68@yahoo.com

PACIFIC FORUM CSIS
1001 Bishop St. #1150, Pauaai Tower
Honolulu, HI 96813
Ralph Cossa, President
Tel: (808) 521-6745 Fax: (808) 599-8690
Email: pacforum@hawaii.rr.com
Web: www.csis.org

PROFESSIONAL

ASIAN AMERICAN JOURNALISTS ASSOCIATION
Hawaii Chapter
P.O. Box 22592
Honolulu, HI 96823
Jill Kuramoto, Chapter President
Tel: (808) 536-9979 Fax: (808) 525-8640
Email: aajahawaii@yahoo.com
Web: www.aajahawaii.org

FILIPINO AMERICAN LEAGUE OF ENGINEERS & ARCHITECTS
P.O. Box 4135
Honolulu, HI 96814
Marites Calad Shoji, President
Email: mshoji@norman-wright.com
Web: www.falea.org

HAWAII FILIPINO LAWYERS ASSOCIATION
707 Richard St. #710
Honolulu, HI 96813
Pablo P. Quiban, President
Tel: (808) 528-3955 Fax: (808) 523-9476
Email: ppq-esq@hawaii.rr.com

PACIFIC ISLAND HEALTH OFFICERS ASSOCIATION
1451 S. King St. #211
Honolulu, HI 96814
Dr. Robert V. Tucker, Executive Director
Tel: (808) 945-1555 Fax: (808) 945-1558
Email: pihoa@hawaii.edu

RELIGIOUS

CAMBODIAN MISSION OUTREACH
c/o Sandie Sveiven, 76-6196 Lehua Rd.
Kailua Kona, HI 96740
Tel: (808) 331-2371
Web: www.cambodiachurch.org

FIRST CHINESE CHURCH OF CHRIST IN HAWAII
1054 S. King St.
Honolulu, HI 96814
Dr. Samuel Ling, Head Pastor
Tel: (808) 593-9046 Fax: (808) 593-2145
Email: info@firstchinese.org
Web: www.firstchinese.org

VIETNAMESE CHRISTIAN FELLOWSHIP
720 N. King St.
Honolulu, HI 96817
Pastor Luu
Tel: (808) 842-1089 Fax: (808) 842-1089
Email: pjhonolulu@juno.com
Web: http://vietnamesechristian.hi.us.
mennonite.net/Home

RESEARCH

ASIA-PACIFIC CENTER FOR SECURITY STUDIES
2058 Maluhia Rd.
Honolulu, HI 96815
H.C. Stackpole, President
Tel: (808) 971-8900 Fax: (808) 971-8999
Email: executivestaffdivision@apcss.org
Web: www.apcss.org

HONOLULU COUNTY GENEALOGICAL SOCIETY
P.O. Box 235039
Honolulu, HI 96823-3500
Martha Reamy, President
Tel: (808) 695 5761
Email: wwreamy@hawaii.rr.com
Web: www.rootsweb.com/~hihcgs

SPARK M. MATSUNAGA INSTITUTE FOR PEACE
2424 Maile Way, Saunders Hall 717
Honolulu, HI 96822
Kem Lowry, Program Director
Tel: (808) 956-7427 Fax: (808) 956-5708
Email: uhip@hawaii.edu
Web: www.peaceinstitute.hawaii.edu/page12.html

UNIVERSITY OF HAWAII MANOA ETHNIC STUDIES
George Hall #301
Honolulu, HI 96822
Dean Alegado, Director
Tel: (808) 956-8086 Fax: (808) 956-9494
Email: alegado@hawaii.edu
Web: www.soc.hawaii.edu

SPEC. INT., AIDS

MALAMA PONO THE HIV SERVICE AGENCY OF KAUA'I
2970 Kele St. #104
Lihue, HI 96766
Tel: (808) 246-9577 Fax: (808) 246-9588
Email: info@malama-pono.org
Web: www.malama-pono.org

SPEC. INT., ALCOHOL/DRUG CENTER

COALITION FOR A DRUG FREE HAWAII
1130 N. Nimitz Hwy, #A259
Honolulu, HI 96817
Tel: (808) 545-3228 Fax: (808) 545-2686
Email: cdfh@pixi.com
Web: www.drugfreehawaii.org

SPEC. INT., EDUCATION

EAST-WEST CENTER
1601 East-West Rd.
Honolulu, HI 96848
Dr. Charles E. Morrison, President
Tel: (808) 944-7111 Fax: (808) 944-7106
Email: morrisoc@eastwestcenter.org
Web: www.eastwestcenter.org

NATIVE HAWAIIAN CENTER OF EXCELLENCE
University of Hawaii at Manoa, John A. Burns School of Medicine
1960 East-West Rd., Biomedical Bldg. B-205
Honolulu, HI 96822
Benajmin Young, Director & Principal Investigator
Tel: (808) 956-5826 Fax: (808) 956-6588
Email: youngben@hawaii.edu
Web: www.hawaii.edu/nhcoe/

NATIVE HAWAIIAN EDUCATION COUNCIL
1850 Makuakane St., Bldg. F
Honolulu, HI 96817
Peter Hanohano, Executive Director
Tel: (808) 842-8044 Fax: (808) 842-8662
Email: nhec@hawaii.rr.com
Web: www.nhec.us

THE CENTER FOR KOREAN STUDIES
School of Hawaiian, Asian & Pacific Studies
University of Hawaii at Manoa
1881 East-West Rd.
Honolulu, HI 96822
Ho-min Sohn, Director
Tel: (808) 956-7041 Fax: (808) 956-2213
Email: korstudy@hawaii.edu
Web: www.hawaii.edu/korea

US CHINA PEOPLES FRIENDSHIP ASSOCIATION

Hawaii Chapter
P.O. Box 133, Capt Cook
Kona, HI 96704
Brenda Lee, Contact
Web: www.uscpfa.org

Hawaii Subregion
2530 Ferdinand
Honolulu, HI 96822
Yun Soong Jim, President
Tel: (808) 949-8327
Email: vysjim@aloha.net
Web: www.uscpfa.org

Hilo Chapter
15-2721 Ohiki St.
Pahoa, HI 96778
Sara Burgess, Contact
Tel: (808) 965-8055 Fax: (808) 965-8055
Web: www.uscpfa.org

Honolulu Chapter
1717 Mott Smith Dr. #1706
Honolulu, HI 96822
Vernon W.C. Ching, Contact
Tel: (808) 524-2014
Web: www.uscpfa.org

Kailua-Kona Chapter
77-6555 Seaview Cir.
Kailua-Kona, HI 96740
Caroline L. Nakashima, Contact
Tel: (808) 329-6024
Web: www.uscpfa.org

Kauai Chapter
2735 Nokekula Cir.
Lihue, HI 96766-9603
Violet L. Hee, Contact
Tel: (808) 245-8166 Fax: (808) 245-8166
Web: www.uscpfa.org

Oahu Chapter
702 Kalalea St.
Honolulu, HI 96825
Daniel Yee, Contact
Tel: (808) 839-3772
Web: www.uscpfa.org

SPEC. INT., HEALTH SERVICES

ALOHA MEDICAL MISSION
1314 S. King St. #503
Honolulu, HI 96814
Dr. Reynold Feldman, Executive Director
Tel: (808) 593-9696 Fax: (808) 591-1266
Email: alohamm@lava.net
Web: www.alohamm.org

KOKUA KALIHI VALLEY HEALTH CENTER
2239 N. School St.
Honolulu, HI 96819
Geoffrey Pang, President
Tel: (808) 848-0976 Fax: (808) 847-6051
Email: kokua@kkv.net
Web: www.kkv.net

KOKUA NURSES
210 Ward Ave. #118
Honolulu, HI 96814
Tel: (808) 594-2326 Fax: (808) 592-1248
Email: cheryl@kokuanurses.com
Web: www.kokuanurses.com

PALOLO CHINESE HOME, INC.
2459 10th Ave.
Honolulu, HI 96816
Leigh Wai Doo, President
Tel: (808) 737-2555 Fax: (808) 735-1754
Email: info@palolohome.com
Web: www.palolohome.com

PAPA OLA LOKAHI
894 Queen St.
Honolulu, HI 96813

Hardy Spoehr, Executive Director
Tel: (808) 597-6550 Fax: (808) 597-6551
Email: hspoehr@papaolalokai.org

TRADITIONAL CHINESE MEDICAL COLLEGE OF HAWAII
P.O. Box 2288
Kamuela, HI 96743-2288
Jacqueline Hahn, President
Tel: (808) 885-9226 Fax: (808) 885-9226
Email: tcmch@tcmch.edu
Web: http://home.earthlink.net/~tcmch1/

WAIANAE COAST COMPREHENSIVE HEALTH CENTER
86-260 Farrington Hwy.
Waianae, HI 96792
Ginger Fuata, President
Tel: (808) 696-7081 Fax: (808) 696-7093
Email: wcchc@wcchc.com
Web: www.wcchc.com

WAIMANALO HEALTH CENTER
41-1347 Kalanianaole Hwy.
Waimanalo, HI 96795
Chuck Braden, Executive Director
Tel: (808) 259-7948 Fax: (808) 259-6449
Email: cbraden@waimanalohc.org
Web: www.waimanalohc.org

SPEC. INT., HOUSING

NANAKULI HOUSING CORPORATION
P.O. Box 17489
Honolulu, HI 96817-0489
Paige Barber, President
Tel: (808) 842-0770 Fax: (808) 842-0780
Email: baseyardhawaii@yahoo.com

SPEC. INT., HUMAN RELATIONS

ASSOCIATION OF CHINESE FROM VIETNAM, CAMBODIA, & LAOS
900 Maunakea St.
Honolulu, HI 96817
Thomas Fum, President
Tel: (808) 531-3012 Fax: (808) 550-2998

COUNCIL FOR NATIVE HAWAIIAN ADVANCEMENT
33 S. King St. #513
Honolulu, HI 96813
Robin Puanani Danner, CEO & President
Tel: (800) 709-2642 Fax: (808) 521-4111
Email: cnha@hawaiiancouncil.org
Web: www.hawaiiancouncil.org

HAWAI'I COMMUNITY FOUNDATION
1164 Bishop St. #800
Honolulu, HI 96813
Kelvin H. Taketa, President & CEO
Tel: (808) 537-6333 Fax: (808) 521-6286
Email: info@hcf-hawaii.org
Web: www.hawaiicommunityfoundation.org

THE CENTENNIAL COMMITTEE OF KOREAN IMMIGRATION TO THE UNITED STATES
1881 East-West Rd.
Honolulu, HI 96822
Donald C.W. Kim, General Chair
Tel: (808) 956-6385 Fax: (808) 956-2213
Email: dukhee@koreancentennial.org
Web: www.koreancentennial.org

SPEC. INT., LEGAL ASSISTANCE

CHINESE COMMUNITY ACTION COALITION
P.O. Box 90766
Honolulu, HI 96805
Bryan Man, President
Tel: (808) 735-4850 Fax: (808) 739-4614
Email: bman@chaminade.edu

SPEC. INT., SOCIAL INTEREST

ASSOCIATION OF HAWAIIAN CIVIC CLUBS
P.O. Box 1135
Honolulu, HI 96807
Tel: (808) 394-0050 Fax: (808) 394-0057
Email: hawaiimaoli@hawaii.rr.com
Web: www.aohcc.org

HAWAI'I PEOPLE'S FUND
810 N. Vineyard Blvd.
Honolulu, HI 96817
Nancy Aleck, Executive Director
Tel: (808) 845-4800 Fax: (808) 845-4800
Email: info@hawaiipeoplesfund.org
Web: www.hawaiipeoplesfund.org

JAPAN AMERICA SOCIETY OF HAWAII
P.O. Box 1412
Honolulu, HI 96806-1412
Earl Okawa, President
Tel: (808) 524-4450 Fax: (808) 524-4451
Email: admindir@jashawaii.org
Web: www.jashawaii.org

JEWISH COMMUNITY OF KAUAI, INC.
P.O. Box 3749
Lihue, HI 96766
Martin J. Kahn, President
Tel: (808) 822-5281
Email: kahn@hawaiian.net
Web: www.jewishcommunityofkauai.org

UNITED CHINESE SOCIETY
42 N. King St.
Honolulu, HI 96817
Henry Lee, Secretary
Tel: (808) 536-4621 Fax: (808) 536-7848
Email: ucs@lava.net

SPEC. INT., SPORTS

INTERNATIONAL SHOTOKAN KARATE CLUB
Pacific Shotokan Karate-Do
P.O. Box 61214
Honolulu, HI 96839
Harry Tagomori, Regional Director
Tel: (808) 956-7606
Email: iskfhawaii@aol.com
Web: www.psk-iskf-jka.org

PACIFIC AMERICAN FOUNDATION
33 S. King St. #205
Honolulu, HI 96813
David E.K. Cooper, President
Tel: (808) 533-2836 Fax: (808) 533-1630
Email: dekcooper@thepaf.org
Web: www.thepaf.org

SPEC. INT., WOMEN

ASIAN PACIFIC AMERICAN WOMEN'S LEADERSHIP INSTITUTE
89-051 Haleakala Ave.
Waianae, HI 96792
Kay Kiyomi Iwata, Board Chair
Tel: (808) 585-8558 Fax: (808) 668-9768
Email: info@apawli.org
Web: www.apawli.org

JAPANESE WOMEN'S SOCIETY FOUNDATION
P.O. Box 3233
Honolulu, HI 96801
Marjorie Yoshioka, President
Tel: (808) 943-6993

SPEC. INT., YOUTH

ASIAN PACIFIC ISLANDER YOUTH VIOLENCE PREVENTION CENTER
1441 Kapiolani Blvd. #1802
Honolulu, HI 96814
Gregory Y. Mark, Principal Investigator
Tel: (808) 945-1517 Fax: (808) 945-1506
Email: mayedad@dop.hawaii.edu
Web: www.api-center.org

SARILING GAWA YOUTH COUNCIL
P.O. Box 971225
Waipahu, HI 96797
Alma Trinidad, President
Email: info@sarilinggawa.org
Web: www.sarilinggawa.org

IDAHO

ARTISTIC

ASIAN AMERICAN COMPARATIVE COLLECTION
University of Idaho
P.O. Box 441111
Moscow, ID 83844-1111
Priscilla Wegars, Volunteer Curator
Tel: (208) 885-7075 Fax: (208) 885-2034
Email: pwegars@uidaho.edu
Web: www.uidaho.edu/ls/aacc/

RELIGIOUS

BOISE CHINESE CHRISTIAN CHURCH
3000 Esquire Dr.
Boise, ID 83704
Abraham Chen
Tel: (208) 938-7716
Email: jwaschen@yahoo.com
Web: www.boiseccc.org

SPEC. INT., CIVIL RIGHTS

JAPANESE AMERICAN CITIZENS LEAGUE
Intermountain District Council
381 Hyde Ave.
Pocatalo, ID 83201-3274
Silvana Watanabe, District Governor
Email: silvanawcu@jacl.org
Web: www.jacl.org

ILLINOIS

ARTISTIC

CENTER FOR ASIAN ARTS AND MEDIA
600 S. Michigan Ave.
Chicago, IL 60605
Nancy Tom, Executive Director
Tel: (312) 344-7870 Fax: (312) 344-8010
Email: asianarts@colum.edu
Web: www.asianartsandmedia.org

CHICAGO ASIAN AMERICAN JAZZ FESTIVAL
P.O. Box 1069
Oak Park, IL 60304
Tatsu Aoki, Founder
Tel: (708) 386-9349 Fax: (708) 488-9781
Email: promotions@asianimprov.com
Web: www.aajazz.org

RIKSHA
3062 S. Broad St.
Chicago, IL 60608
Alexander Yu, Executive Director
Tel: (773) 847-1753 Fax: (773) 594-9898
Email: editors@riksha.com
Web: www.riksha.com

STIR-FRIDAY NIGHT
P.O. Box 268560
Chicago, IL 60626
Jennifer Liu, Executive Director
Tel: (847) 663-9257 Fax: (847) 663-9257
Email: stirfridaynight@hotmail.com
Web: www.stirfridaynight.org

BUSINESS

ASIAN AMERICAN ALLIANCE
222 W. Cermak Rd. #303
Chicago, IL 60616-1986
Emir Abinion, President
Tel: (312) 326-2200 Fax: (312) 326-0399

Email: info@asianamericanalliance.com
Web: www.asianamericanalliance.com

ASIAN AMERICAN SMALL BUSINESS ASSOCIATION

5901 N. Cicero Ave. #205
Chicago, IL 60646
John S. Lee, Executive Director
Tel: (773) 545-0600 Fax: (773) 545-5449
Email: aasba5000@msn.com

ASIAN AMERICAN SMALL BUSINESS DEVELOPMENT CENTER

Asian American Alliance
222 W. Cermak Rd. #303
Chicago, IL 60616-1986
Mitch Chul Woo Schneider, Director
Tel: (312) 326-2200 Fax: (312) 326-0399
Email: mitch@asianamericanalliance.com
Web: www.asianamericanalliance.com/aasbdc

CHINAWISE

2126 W. Armitage Ave. #3
Chicago, IL 60647
Jing Zhao Cesarone, President
Tel: (773) 486-7705 Fax: (773) 442-0404
Email: info@chinawiseusa.com
Web: www.chinawiseusa.com

CHINESE BUSINESS STUDENTS ASSOCIATION

University of Chicago Graduate School of Business
1101 E. 58th St.
Chicago, IL 60637
Jason Yin, Primary Contact
Email: zyin1@gsb.uchicago.edu
Web: http://gsb.uchicago.edu

ENGINEERING EXPORT PROMOTION COUNCIL

333 N. Michigan Ave. #2014
Chicago, IL 60601
Ashish Mehra, Resident Director
Tel: (312) 236-2162 Fax: (312) 236-4625
Email: eepcchicago@worldnet.att.net
Web: www.eepc.gov.in

JAPAN EXTERNAL TRADE ORGANIZATION

Chicago Chapter
401 N. Michigan Ave. #660
Chicago, IL 60611
Tomoharu Washio, Chief Executive Director
Tel: (312) 832-6000 Fax: (312) 832-6066
Web: www.jetrocgo.org

KOREAN AMERICAN MERCHANTS ASSOCIATION OF CHICAGO

4300 N. California Ave.
Chicago, IL 60618
Charse Yun, Executive Director
Tel: (773) 583-5501 Fax: (773) 583-7009

CHAMBER OF COMMERCE

AMERICA-ISRAEL CHAMBER OF COMMERCE

180 N. Michigan Ave. #911
Chicago, IL 60601
Rabbi Yechiel Eckstein, Founder/President
Tel: (312) 641-2937 Fax: (312) 641- 2941
Email: info@americaisrael.org
Web: www.americaisrael.org

AMERICAN-RUSSIAN CHAMBER OF COMMERCE & INDUSTRY

200 World Trade Center, 1540 Mechandise Mart
Chicago, IL 60654
Helen Teplitskaia, President
Tel: (312) 494-6562 Fax: (312) 494-9840
Email: info@arcci.org
Web: www.arcci.org

CHICAGO CHINATOWN CHAMBER OF COMMERCE

2169B S. China Pl.

Chicago, IL 60616
Helen Lee, President
Tel: (312) 326-5320 Fax: (312) 326-5668
Email: info@chicagochinatown.org
Web: www. chicagochinatown.org

CHICAGO KOREAN AMERICAN CHAMBER OF COMMERCE

5601 N. Spaulding Ave.
Chicago, IL 60659
Jin Lee, Executive Director
Tel: (773) 583-1700 Fax: (773) 583-9724
Email: ckacc@aol.com

PHILIPPINE AMERICAN CHAMBER OF COMMERCE OF GREATER CHICAGO

Dr. Jose P. Rizal Heritage Ctr., 1332 W. Irving Park Rd.
Chicago, IL 60613
Luis C. Bautista, Executive Director
Tel: (773) 325-9650 Fax: (773) 325-9657
Email: luischito@ameritech.net
Web: www.paccgreaterchicago.com

UNITED STATES OF AMERICA-CHINA CHAMBER OF COMMERCE

55 W. Monroe St. #630
Chicago, IL 60603
Siva Yam, President
Tel: (312) 368-9911 Fax: (312) 368-9922
Email: info@usccc.org
Web: www.usccc.org

US PAN ASIAN AMERICAN CHAMBER OF COMMERCE

Midwest Chapter
5410 W. Roosevelt Rd. #231
Chicago, IL 60644
Chacko Varghese, Chapter President
Tel: (773) 626-3100 Fax: (773) 626-5541
Web: www.uspaacc.com

CULTURAL

CHICAGO ISLAMIC CULTURAL CENTER

P.O. Box 203
Oaklawn, IL 60454
Hasm Isa, Director
Tel: (773) 436-8083 Fax: (773) 436-8785

CHICAGO LEBANESE CLUB

P.O. Box 81584
Chicago, IL 60681-0584
Daisy Malek-Shadid, President
Tel: (847) 778-5197 Fax: (847) 778-5197
Email: clc@chicagolebaneseclub.org
Web: www.leb.net/clc

CHINESE AMERICAN CULTURAL BRIDGE CENTER

855 E. Golf Rd. #2126
Arlington Heights, IL 60005
Qiu Min Ji, President
Tel: (877) 592-7072 Fax: (847) 718-0279
Email: info@cacbc.org
Web: www.cacbc.org

CHINESE MUSEUM FOUNDATION

P.O. Box 167298
Chicago, IL 60616-7298
Kinman Auyeung, Board of Director
Tel: (312) 949-1000 Fax: (312) 949-1000
Email: office@ccamuseum.org
Web: www.ccamuseum.org

FILIPINO AMERICAN HISTORICAL SOCIETY OF CHICAGO

5472 S. Dorchester Ave.
Chicago, IL 60615
Estrella R. Alamar, Founding President
Tel: (773) 947-8696 Fax: (773) 955-3635
Email: ealamar@aol.com
Web: www.fahsc.org

FILIPINO-AMERICAN ASSOCIATION

Iowa-Illinois Quad-Cities

1223 34th Ave. Ct.
Rock Island, IL 61201
Cecilla Barnes, President
Tel: (309) 793-1855 Fax: (309) 794-0800
Email: toncyle@msn.com

INDO-AMERICAN CENTER

6328 N. California Ave.
Chicago, IL 60659
Chris Zala, Executive Director
Tel: (773) 973-4444 Fax: (773) 973-0157
Email: czala@indoamerican.org
Web: www.indoamerican.org

INTERNATIONAL RAMAYANA INSTITUTE OF NORTH AMERICA

799 Roosevelt Rd., Bldg. 6 #208
Glen Ellyn, IL 60137
Fax: (630) 858-8787

IRANIAN CULTURAL SOCIETY

P.O. Box 124
Hinsdale, IL 60522
M. Naficy, President
Email: webmaster@icsociety.com
Web: www.icsociety.com

KCC JAPAN EDUCATION EXCHANGE

188 W. Randolph #1809
Chicago, IL 60601
Tel: (312) 364-9336 Fax: (312) 364-9337
Email: kobecollegecorp@prodigy.net
Web: www.kccjee.org

KOREAN AMERICAN RESOURCE & CULTURAL CENTER

2701-A W. Peterson Ave.
Chicago, IL 60659
Kyung Nan Yu, Board President
Tel: (773) 506-9158 Fax: (773) 506-9159
Email: krcc@krccweb.org
Web: www.krccweb.org

KOREAN WAR EDUCATOR

111 E. Houghton St.
Tuscola, IL 61953
Lynnita Jean Brown, Founder/CEO
Tel: (217) 253-4620
Email: lynnita@koreanwar-educator.org
Web: www.koreanwar-educator.org

KOREAN WAR VETERANS NATIONAL MUSEUM AND LIBRARY

Tanger Outlet Ctr., Tuscola Blvd. #C-500
Tuscola, IL 61953
William F. O'Brien, President
Tel: (888) 295-7212
Email: scorum@theforgottenvictory.org
Web: www.theforgottenvictory.org

LEADERSHIP CENTER FOR ASIAN PACIFIC AMERICANS

P.O. Box 25465
Chicago, IL 60625
Chaffee Tran, President
Tel: (773) 293-8445
Email: lca@acon.org
Web: www.acon.org/lca/

PARS EDUCATIONAL AND CULTURAL SOCIETY

P.O. Box 9549
Naperville, IL 60567
Shahla Afshar, President
Tel: (877) 379-6519 Fax: (877) 379-6519
Email: president@parssociety.net
Web: www.parssociety.net

PINTIG CULTURAL GROUP

4750 N. Sheridan Rd. #418
Chicago, IL 60640
Allan Sargan, Executive Director
Tel: (773) 293-2787 Fax: (773) 293-2787
Email: info@pintig.org
Web: www.pintig.org

SPRINGFIELD CHINESE AMERICAN ASSOCIATION

3208 Forsythe Dr.
Springfield, IL 62704
Feng Huo, President
Tel: (217) 726-6638
Email: fendihuo@yahoo.com

THAI CULTURAL AND FINE ARTS INSTITUTE

1960 Oak Knoll Dr.
Lake Forest, IL 60045
Supachai Pongched, President
Tel: (847) 295-0346 Fax: (630) 455-9553
Email: contact@thai-culture.org
Web: www.thai-culture.org

THE JEWISH PRODUCTION ORGANIZATION FOR CULTURAL EVENTS AND THEATER

P.O. Box 5215
Skokie, IL 60076
Michael Lorge, Founder
Tel: (847) 933-3000
Email: info@pocet.0rg
Web: www.pocet.org

TURKISH AMERICAN CULTURAL ALLIANCE OF CHICAGO

3845 N. Harlem Ave.
Chicago, IL 60634
Mehmet Celebi, President
Tel: (773) 725-3655 Fax: (773) 725-3685
Email: info@tacaonline.org
Web: www.tacaonline.org

ENTERTAINMENT

3RD I CHICAGO

c/o Chicago Filmmakers, 5243 N. Clark St.
Chicago, IL 60640
Email: thirdi-chicago@thirdi.org
Web: www.thirdi.org/~chicago/

LAW ENFORCEMENT

ASIAN AMERICAN LAW ENFORCEMENT ASSOCIATION (MIDWESTERN STATES)

P.O. Box 56652
Chicago, IL 60656
Audie Manaois, President
Email: www.aaleachgo@aol.com
Web: www.aalea.org

MULTI-PURPOSE

ARAB AMERICAN ACTION NETWORK

3148 W. 63rd St.
Chicago, IL 60629
Tel: (773) 436-6060 Fax: (773) 436-6460
Email: aaan@aaan.org
Web: www.aaan.org

ASIAN AMERICAN NET

916 S. Taylor Ave.
Oak Park, IL 60304
M. Bazlul Karim, President
Tel: (708) 445-3975 Fax: (708) 445-3975
Email: info@asianamerican.net
Web: www.asianamerican.net

ISLAMIC COMMUNITY CENTER OF ILLINOIS

6435 W. Belmont
Chicago, IL 60634
Yousif Marei, Office Manager
Tel: (773) 637-3755 Fax: (773) 637-3892
Email: icci@cssn.net

PUNJABI CULTURAL SOCIETY OF CHICAGO

P.O. Box 1244
Palatine, IL 60078
Bhagwant S. Sandhu, President
Tel: (847) 359-5727 Fax: (847) 359-1107
Email: info@pcschicago.org
Web: www.pcschicago.org

TZU CHI
Chicago Office
6601 S. Cass Ave. #G
Westmont, IL 60559
Cheng Yen, Founder
Tel: (630) 963-6601 Fax: (630) 960-9360
Email: yahmei_hsieh@us.tzuchi.org
Web: http://chicago.us.tzuchi.org

VIETNAMESE ASSOCIATION OF ILLINOIS
5252 N. Broadway, 2nd Fl.
Chicago, IL 60640
Tom Nguyen, Executive Director
Tel: (773) 728-3700 Fax: (773) 728-0497
Email: tamduc9@aol.com
Web: www.v-a-i.net

XILIN ASIAN COMMUNITY CENTER
1163 E. Ogden Ave. #300-A
Naperville, IL 60563
Linda Yang, Director
Tel: (630) 355-4322 Fax: (630) 455-4326
Email: asiancommunitycenter@xilin.org
Web: www.xilin.org

POLITICAL ACTION

ASIAN PACIFIC AMERICAN LABOR ALLIANCE
Chicago/Illinois Pre-Chapter
c/o SEIU Local-20-HC 309 W. Washington St. #250
Chicago, IL 60606
Rex Lai, Organizing Director
Tel: (312) 641-1516 Fax: (312) 641-0773
Email: rexlai@juno.com

BRIT TZEDEK V'SHALOM
11 E. Adams #707
Chicago, IL 60603
Marcia Freedman, President
Tel: (312) 341-1205 Fax: (312) 341-1206
Email: info@btvshalom.org
Web: www.btvshalom.org

INDO-AMERICAN DEMOCRATIC ORGANIZATION, INC.
8026 N. Lawndale
Skokie, IL 60076
Selma D'Souza, President
Tel: (847) 622-5203
Email: iado@iado.org
Web: www.iado.org

MIDWEST ASIAN AMERICAN STUDENTS UNION
P.O. Box 2965
Champaign, IL 61825
Linda Luk, Director
Email: linda_luk@hotmail.com
Web: www.maasu.org

MUSLIM CIVIL RIGHTS CENTER
7667 W. 95th St. #8-B
Hickory Hills, IL 60457
Rasheed Ahmed, President
Tel: (708) 598-6640 Fax: (708) 598-5283
Email: info@mcrcnet.org
Web: www.mcrcnet.org

PROFESSIONAL

AMERICAN ASSOCIATION OF PHYSICIANS OF INDIAN
Illinois Chapter
17 W. 300 22nd St.
Oak Brook, IL 60181
Dhrumla Bhatt, Director
Tel: (216) 741-3900 Fax: (630) 530-2475
Email: dbhatt@aapiusa.net

AMERICAN ASSOCIATION OF THE PHYSICIANS OF INDIAN ORIGIN
Headquarters
17 W. 300 22nd St. #300-A
Oakbrook Terrace, IL 60181-449.

Sharad Lakhanpal, President
Tel: (630) 530-2277 Fax: (630) 530-2475
Email: info@aapiusa.net
Web: www.aapiusa.org

ARAB AMERICAN ASSOCIATION OF ENGINEERS & ARCHITECTS
P.O. Box 1536
Chicago, IL 60690-1536
Abder Rahman Ghouleh, President
Tel: (312) 409-8560
Email: aaaea@aaaea.org
Web: www.aaaea.org

ARAB AMERICAN BAR ASSOCIATION
P.O. Box 81093
Chicago, IL 60681
Rouhy J. Shalabi, President
Tel: (312) 946-0110 Fax: (312) 565-2070
Email: bar@arabbar.org
Web: www.arabbar.org

ASIAN AMERICAN BAR ASSOCIATION OF THE GREATER CHICAGO AREA
321 S. Plymouth Ct.
Chicago, IL 60604
Neera Walsh, President
Tel: (312) 554-2044 Fax: (312) 554-9843
Email: aabachicago1@aol.com
Web: www.aabachicago.com

ASIAN AMERICAN JOURNALISTS ASSOCIATION
Chicago Chapter
P.O. Box 577639
Chicago, IL 60657-9997
Lorene Yue, President
Email: chiaaja@yahoo.com
Web: www.aaja.org/Chapters/Chicago

ASSOCIATION OF CHINESE SCIENTISTS AND ENGINEERS
P.O. Box 59715
Shaumburg, IL 60159
Luan Wenqi, President
Email: acsemembers@acse.org
Web: www.acse.org

ASSOCIATION OF PAKISTANI PHYSICIANS OF NORTH AMERICA
6414 S. Cass Ave.
Westmont, IL 60559
Omar Atiq, President
Tel: (630) 968-8585 Fax: (630) 968-8677
Email: appna@appna.org
Web: www.appna.org

CHICAGO CHINESE COMPUTING PROFESSIONAL ASSOCIATION
740 Oakwood Ct.
Westmont, IL 60059
Ben Gao, Director
Tel: (847) 322-3124
Email: info@cccpa.org
Web: www.cccpa.org

COUNCIL OF AMERICAN MUSLIM PROFESSIONALS
6157 N. Sheridan #3C
Chicago, IL 60660
Danial Mohruddin, President
Tel: (773) 793-7752 Fax: (773) 793-1322
Email: info@chicago-il.campnet.net
Web: www.campnet.net

ISLAMIC MEDICAL ASSOCIATION OF NORTH AMERICA
Headquarters Office
950 75th St.
Downers Grove, IL 60516
Parvaiz A. Malik, M.D., President
Tel: (630) 852- 2122 Fax: (630) 435-1429
Email: hq@imana.org
Web: www.imana.org

NATIONAL ARAB AMERICAN JOURNALISTS ASSOCIATION
P.O. Box 2127

Orland Park, IL 60462
Ray Hanania, Executive Director
Tel: (708) 403-1203 Fax: (708) 575-9078
Email: rayhanania@aol.com
Web: www.hanania.com

NATIONAL ASSOCIATION OF ASIAN AMERICAN PROFESSIONAL
Chicago Chapter
P.O. Box 81138
Chicago, IL 60681
Roselle Olea, President
Tel: (773) 918-2454
Email: roselle_olea@yahoo.com
Web: www.naaapchicago.org

NETWORK OF INDIAN PROFESSIONALS
P.O. Box 642233
Chicago, IL 60664-2233
Ramya Bavikatte, President
Email: execboard@netip-chicago.org
Web: www.netip-chicago.org

NORTH AMERICAN CHINESE CLINICAL CHEMISTS ASSOCIATION
909 Bedford Ct.
Buffalo Grove, IL 60089
Wenzhi Li, President
Email: wzli@dpconline.com
Web: www.naccca.org

RELIGIOUS

ARMENIAN ALL SAINTS APOSTOLIC CHURCH
1701 Greenwood Rd.
Glenview, IL 60025
Tel: (847) 998-1989 Fax: (847) 998-3448
Web: www.accglenview.8k.com

ASIA REACHING MISSION
803 Poplar Ave.
Elmhurst, IL 60126
Richfield Cudal
Email: renfield@vitrtual.com.ph
Web: www.nfbc.net/Missions/Cudal.htm

BURMESE BUDDHIST ASSOCIATION
15 W. 110 Forest Ln.
Elmhurst, IL 60126
Email: mwbba_admin@email.com
Web: WWW.BBA.US

CHINESE BIBLE CHURCH OF OAK PARK
700 S. Ridgeland Ave.
Oak Park, IL 60304
Tel: (708) 383-6867
Email: cbcop@cbcop.org
Web: www.cbcop.org

CHINESE CHRISTIAN MANDARIN CHURCH
9 S. 565 Clarendon Hills Rd.
Willowbrook, IL 60521
Hsien-Hau Wang, Chairperson
Tel: (630) 655-1148 Fax: (630) 655-7078
Email: ccmc@chicagoccmc.org
Web: www.chicagoccmc.org

CHINESE CHRISTIAN UNION CHURCH
2301 S. Wentworth Ave.
Chicago, IL 60616
Stephen Ye, Sr., Chairman
Tel: (312) 842-8545 Fax: (312) 842-4304
Web: www.ccuc.net

CHINESE EVANGELICAL FREE CHURCH OF GREATER CHICAGO
P.O. Box 1129
Arlington Heights, IL 60006-1129
Simon Chung, Chair
Tel: (847) 918-1804
Email: slchung@cefcchicago.org
Web: www.cefcchicago.org

CONGREGATION KOL AMI
845 N. Michigan
Chicago, IL 60611

Larry Glickman, Executive Director
Tel: (312) 664-4775
Email: info@kol-ami.com
Web: www.kol-ami.com

DAWN R. SCHUMAN INSTITUTE
601 Skokie Blvd. #306
Northbrook, IL 60062
Lynn Fienberg, President
Tel: (847) 509-8282 Fax: (847) 509-8284
Email: info@dawnschuman.org
Web: www.dawnschuman.org

FIRST KOREAN PRESBYTERIAN CHURCH
900 N. Milwaukee Ave.
Glenview, IL 60025
Tel: (847) 299-1776
Web: www.fkpc.net

HAHNA KOREAN PRESBYTERIAN CHURCH
1485 Whitcomb Ave.
Des Plaines, IL 60018
Tel: (847) 803-1131
Email: hahnaem@yahoo.com
Web: http://hahnachurch.org

INTERFAITH REFUGEE IMMIGRATION MINISTRIES
4753 N. Broadway #401
Chicago, IL 60640
Melineh Kano, Program Director
Tel: (773) 989-5647 Fax: (773) 989-0484
Email: irim@irim.org
Web: www.irim.org

JEWISH RECONSTRUCTIONIST CONGREGATION
303 Dodge Ave.
Evanston, IL 60202-3252
Carole Caplan, President
Tel: (847) 328-7678 Fax: (847) 328-2298
Email: info@jrc-evanston.org
Web: www.jrc-evanston.org

JEWS FOR JESUS
Chicago
4118 Oakton St.
Skokie, IL 60076
Jhan Moskowitz, Chief of Station
Tel: (847) 679-2680 Fax: (847) 679-5845
Email: chicago@jewsforjesus.org
Web: www.jfjonline.org

KNIGHTS OF RIZAL
2043 N. Kostner Ave.
Chicago, IL 60639
Sir Ban Gallardo, Chapter Commander
Tel: (773) 227-8968
Web: www.thepinoy.com/kor

LAKEVIEW CHURCH
950 N. Brook Ave.
Northbrook, IL 60062
Joshua Kang, Lead Pastor
Tel: (847) 480) 2900 Fax: (847) 480-2901
Email: pastorjoshua@lakeview.org
Web: www.lakeview.org

NORTHWEST FILIPINO BAPTIST CHURCH
1900 Nerge Rd.
Elk Grove Village, IL 60007
Tel: (847) 352-1968
Web: www.nfbc.net

PALESTINE AMERICAN COMMUNITY CENTER
6000 W. 79th St.
Burbank, IL 60459
Abdel Ghafar Al-Arouri, President
Tel: (708) 233-6623
Email: pacc-chicago@hotmail.com

PEOPLE OF THE BOOK LUTHERAN OUTREACH
Illinois
405 Rush St.
Roselle, IL 60172
Samuel Nasir

Tel: (630) 894-3263
Email: pobloffice@sbcglobal.net
Web: www.poblo.org

TEMPLE B'NAI ISRAEL

400 N. Edgelawn Dr.
Aurora, IL 60506
Tel: (630) 892-2450 Fax: (630) 892-8317
Email: info@temple-bnai-israel.org
Web: www.temple-bnai-israel.org

TEMPLE BETH EL

3610 Dundee Rd.
Northbrook, IL 60062
Rosely Kaiser, President
Tel: (847) 205-9982 Fax: (847) 205-9921
Email: office@templebeth-el.org
Web: www.templebeth-el.org

TEMPLE SHOLOM OF CHICAGO

3480 N. Lake Shore Dr.
Chicago, IL 60657
Aaron Mark Petuchowski, Rabbi
Tel: (773) 525-4707 Fax: (773) 525-3502
Email: rabbiamp@sholomchicago.org
Web: www.sholomchicago.org

UNITED SYNAGOGUE OF CONSERVATIVE JUDAISM

Midwest Region
601 Skokie Blvd. #402
Northbrook, IL 60062
Robert Tecktiel, President
Tel: (847) 714-9130 Fax: (847) 714-9133
Email: midwest@uscj.org
Web: http://uscj.org/midwest

WHEATON CHINESE ALLIANCE CHURCH

1748 S. Blanchard Rd.
Wheaton, IL 60187
Pastor Green, English Pastor
Tel: (630) 462-0196 Fax: (630) 462-6992
Email: office@wcac-cma.org
Web: www.wcac-cma.org

RESEARCH

ASIAN AMERICAN INSTITUTE

4753 N. Broadway #904
Chicago, IL 60640
Tuyet Le, Executive Director
Tel: (773) 271-0899 Fax: (773) 271-1982
Email: tuyet@aaichicago.org
Web: www.aaichicago.org

SCIENTIFIC

AMERICAN COMMITTEE FOR THE WEIZMANN INSTITUTE OF SCIENCE

79 W. Monroe St. #111
Chicago, IL 60603
Marshall Bennett, Regional Chair
Tel: (312) 641-5700
Email: chicago@acwis.org
Web: www.weizmann-usa.org

SPEC. INT., AIDS

AIDS LEGAL COUNCIL OF CHICAGO

Main Office
188 W. Randolph #2400
Chicago, IL 60601-3005
Ann Hilton Fisher, Esq., Executive Director
Tel: (312) 427-8990 Fax: (312) 427-8419
Email: info@aidslegal.com
Web: www.aidslegal.com

SPEC. INT., CHILD CARE

JEWISH CHILDREN'S BUREAU

Central Office
216 W. Jackson Blvd. #800
Chicago, IL 60606
Tel: (312) 444-2090
Web: www.jcbchicago.org

JYOTI CHILDREN'S DEVELOPMENT FOUNDATION INC.

4015 Amalfi Dr.
Glenview, IL 60025
Saryu N. Dixit, Founder
Tel: (847) 299-5474
Email: info@jyotiforchildren.org
Web: www.jyotiforchildren.org

SPEC. INT., COUNSELING

ILLINOIS COUNCIL FOR VIOLENCE PREVENTION

220 S. State St. #1215
Chicago, IL 60604
Debbie Bretag, Executive Director
Tel: (312) 986-9200 Fax: (312) 922-2277
Email: icvp@icvp.org
Web: www.icvp.org

SPEC. INT., EDUCATION

AMERICAN INSTITUTE OF INDIAN STUDIES

1130 E. 59th St.
Chicago, IL 60637
Ralph W. Nicholas, President
Tel: (773) 702-8638
Email: aiis@uchicago.edu
Web: www.indiastudies.org

AMERICAN ISLAMIC COLLEGE

640 W. Irving Park Rd.
Chicago, IL 60613
Asad Husain, Ph.D., President
Tel: (773) 281-4700 Fax: (773) 281-8552
Email: info@aicusa.edu
Web: www.aicusa.edu

ASHA FOR EDUCATION

Carbondale
Student Development, SIU
Carbondale, IL 62901-4425
Anil S. Mehta, Co-coordinator
Tel: (618) 453-7040
Email: anil@siu.edu
Web: www.ashanet.org/carbondale/

ASIAN AMERICAN STUDIES PROGRAM

University of Illinois at Urbana-Champaign
1208 W. Nevada M/C 142
Urbana, IL 61801
Sharon Lee, Assistant Director
Tel: (217) 244-9530 Fax: (217) 265-6235
Email: aasp@uiuc.edu
Web: www.aasp.uiuc.edu

ASIAN EDUCATIONAL MEDIA SERVICE

805 W. Pennsylvania Ave. M/C 025
Urbana, IL 61801
Jenny Huang, Program Director
Tel: (217) 333-9597 Fax: (217) 265-0641
Email: aems@uiuc.edu
Web: www.aems.uiuc.edu

ASIAN STUDIES

Loyola University Chicago, Lake Shore Campus
History Dept., Crown Ctr. #505
Chicago, IL 60626
Ann Harrington, Director
Tel: (773) 508-2228 Fax: (773) 508-2153
Email: aharril@luc.edu
Web: www.luc.edu/depts/asian_st

ASIAN/ASIAN AMERICAN STUDENT SERVICES

Northwestern University
1936 Sheridan Rd., 1st Fl.
Evanston, IL 60208
Dimple Patel, Coordinator
Tel: (847) 467-7583 Fax: (847) 491-3128
Email: asian@northwestern.edu
Web: www.northwestern.edu/asian-american

CENTER FOR MIDDLE EASTERN STUDIES

University of Chicago
5828 S. University Ave.

Chicago, IL 60637
John E. Woods, Director
Tel: (773) 702-8297 Fax: (773) 702-2587
Email: cmes@uchicago.edu
Web: www.cmes.uchicago.edu

COMMUNITY FOUNDATION FOR JEWISH EDUCATION

618 S. Michigan Ave.
Chicago, IL 60605
Tel: (312) 913-1818 Fax: (312) 913-1763
Email: info@cfje.org
Web: www.cfje.org

FILIPINO AMERICAN NETWORK

P.O. Box 5711
Chicago, IL 60680-5711
Edgar Jimenez, President
Email: rvillar@mail.com
Web: www.fan-chicago.org

JAPAN AMERICA SOCIETY OF CHICAGO SCHOLARSHIP FOUNDATION

225 W. Wacker Dr. #2250
Chicago, IL 60606
Tel: (312) 263-3049 Fax: (312) 263-6120
Email: jasc@us_japan.org
Web: www.jaschicago.org

JAPAN CHRISTIAN ACADEMY ASSOCIATION

P.O. Box 905
Wheaton, IL 60189-0905
Web: www.caj.or.jp

JEWISH THEOLOGICAL SEMINARY

Midwest Region
65 E. Wacker Pl. #1200
Chicago, IL 60601
Nadine Sasson Cohen, Co-Director
Tel: (312) 606-9086
Web: www.jtsa.edu

NATIONAL ASSOCIATION FOR ASIAN AND PACIFIC AMERICAN EDUCATION

Region II
125 S. Clark, 8th Fl.
Chicago, IL 60603
Myrna Garcia, Contact
Tel: (773) 553-1834 Fax: (773) 553-1831
Email: mgarcia@cps.k12.il.us
Web: www.naapae.net

THE CHICAGO NORTH CHINESE SCHOOL

1600 E. Golf Rd.
Des Plaines, IL 60016
Rose Chang, Principal
Tel: (847) 635-1823
Email: jchang@tokoam.com
Web: www.cncschool.org

US CHINA PEOPLES FRIENDSHIP ASSOCIATION

Carbondale Chapter
1214 W. Schwartz
Carbondale, IL 62901
Kathleen Trescott, Contact
Tel: (618) 549-1555 Fax: (618) 549-9766
Web: www.uscpfa.org

Chicago Chapter
212 Sabin St.
Sycamore, IL 60178
Keith Krasemann, Contact
Tel: (815) 899-2908
Web: www.uscpfa.org

SPEC. INT., EMPLOYMENT

JEWISH VOCATIONAL SERVICE

216 W. Jackson Blvd. #700
Chicago, IL 60606
Richard M. Bendix Jr., President
Tel: (312) 673-3400 Fax: (312) 553-5544
Email: jvs@jvschicago.org
Web: www.jvschicago.org

SPEC. INT., GAY&LESBIAN

ASIANS & FRIENDS CHICAGO

P.O. Box A-3916
Chicago, IL 60690-3916
Brad H., President & Webmaster
Tel: (312) 409-1573
Email: info@afchicago.org
Web: www.afchicago.org

SANGAT CHICAGO

P.O. Box 268463
Chicago, IL 60626
Ifti Nasim, Co-Founder
Tel: (773) 506-8810 Fax: (773) 271-4024
Email: sangatchicago@aol.com
Web: http://members.aol.com/youngal/sangat.html

SPEC. INT., HEALTH SERVICES

ASIAN AMERICAN HEALTH

6212 N. Lincoln Ave.
Chicago, IL 60659
Dr. Sunbum Kim, President
Tel: (773) 588-5770 Fax: (773) 588-3100

ASIAN HEALTH COALITION OF ILLINOIS

4554 N. Broadway #305
Chicago, IL 60640
Joanna Su, MSW, Executive Director
Tel: (773) 878-3539 Fax: (773) 878-0783
Email: joanna@asianhealth.org
Web: www.asianhealth.org

CENTER FOR MINORITY HEALTH SERVICES

Illinois Department of Public Health
535 W. Jefferson St.
Springfield, IL 62761
Doris Turner, Chief
Tel: (217) 785-4311 Fax: (217) 558-7181
Email: dturner@idph.state.il.us
Web: www.idph.state.il.us

CHICAGO CENTER FOR JEWISH GENETIC DISORDERS

Ben Gurion Way, 1 S. Franklin St., 4th Fl.
Chicago, IL 60606
Karen Litwack, Director
Tel: (312) 357-4718
Email: jewishgeneticsctr@juf.org
Web: www.jewishgeneticscenter.org

ILLINOIS DEPARTMENT OF HUMAN SERVICES

401 S. Clinton
Chicago, IL 60607
Grace Hou, Assistant Secretary
Tel: (312) 793-2347 Fax: (312) 793-2351
Web: www.dhs.state.il.us

ISRAEL CANCER RESEARCH FUND

5200 Main St., 2nd Fl.
Skokie, IL 60077-2198
Jules Harris, President
Tel: (847) 568-1810 Fax: (847) 568-1805
Email: icrfchicago@yahoo.com
Web: www.icrfonline.org

MAGEN DAVID ADOM

8930 Gross Point Rd. #800
Skokie, IL 60077-1864
Tel: (847) 583-0664 Fax: (847) 583-8556
Email: magendavidadom@hotmail.com
Web: www.magendavidadom.org

SPEC. INT., HUMAN RELATIONS

AMERICAN FRIENDS SERVICE COMMITTEE

Great Lakes Region
637 S. Dearborn, 3rd Fl.
Chicago, IL 60605
Michael McConnell, Regional Director
Tel: (312) 427-2533 Fax: (312) 427-4171
Email: mmcconnell-glr@afsc.org
Web: www.afsc.org

AMERICAN JEWISH WORLD SERVICE
Midwest Office
320 W. Ohio St. North #650
Chicago, IL 60610-4116
Elizabeth Versten, Director
Tel: (312) 440-0787 Fax: (312) 440-1479
Email: bversten@ajws.org
Web: www.ajws.org

AMERICAN RED MAGEN DAVID FOR ISRAEL
Midwest Region
1 E. Wacker Dr. #2224
Chicago, IL 60601
Sandy Rosen, Director
Tel: (888) 674-4871 Fax: (312) 494-1903
Email: info@armdi.org
Web: www.armdi.org

AMERICAN ZIONIST MOVEMENT
Chicago Office
5200 Main St.
Skokie, IL 60077
W. James Schiller, President
Tel: (847) 677-5949
Web: www.azm.org

ARAB AMERICAN REPUBLICAN FEDERATION
9525 S. 79th Ave. #204
Hickory Hills, IL 60457
Andy Hassan, Chairman
Tel: (708) 430-7744 Fax: (708) 430-7825

ASIAN HUMAN SERVICES, INC.
4753 N. Broadway #700
Chicago, IL 60640
Abha Pandya, Executive Director
Tel: (773) 728-2235 Fax: (773) 728-4751
Email: info@asianhumanservices.org
Web: www.asianhumanservices.org

ASIAN HUMAN SERVICES OF CHICAGO INC.
4753 N. Broadway #700
Chicago, IL 60640
Sergey Sergeyev, Human Resource Manager
Tel: (773) 728-2235 Fax: (773) 728-4751
Email: info@asianhumanservices.org
Web: www.asianhumanservices.org

CAMBODIAN ASSOCIATION OF ILLINOIS
2831 W. Lawrence Ave.
Chicago, IL 60625
Kompha Seth, Executive Director
Tel: (773) 878-7090 Fax: (773) 878-5299
Email: cai@cambodian-association.org
Web: www.cambodian-association.org

CHICAGO COMMISSION ON HUMAN RELATIONS
Advisory Council on Asian Affairs
740 N. Sedgwick St. #300
Chicago, IL 60610
Naisy Dolar, Director/Community Liaison
Tel: (312) 744-4115 Fax: (312) 744-1081
Email: ndolar@cityofchicago.org
Web: www.cityofchicago.org/humanrelations

CHICAGO COUNCIL ON FOREIGN RELATIONS
116 S. Michigan Ave., 10th Fl.
Chicago, IL 60603
Marshall Bouton, President
Tel: (312) 726-3860 Fax: (312) 726-4491
Email: info@ccfr.org
Web: www.ccfr.org

COUNCIL ON AMERICAN-ISLAMIC RELATIONS
Chicago Chapter
7667 W. 95th St. #304
Hickory Hills, IL 60457
Sara Zarzour, Office Manager
Tel: (312) 922-4720 Fax: (708) 598-1389
Email: szarzour@hotmail.com
Web: www.cairchicago.org

HEARTLAND ALLIANCE FOR HUMAN NEEDS & HUMAN RIGHTS
208 S. LaSalle St. #1818
Chicago, IL 60604
Sid Mohn, President
Tel: (312) 660-1300 Fax: (312) 660-1500
Email: moreinfo@heartlandalliance.org
Web: www.heartlandalliance.org

ILLINOIS DEPARTMENT OF HUMAN SERVICES
100 S. Grand Ave. East
Springfield, IL 62762
Carol L. Adams, Secretary
Tel: (800) 843-6154 Fax: (217) 557-1647
Email: dhswbbt@dhs.state.il.us
Web: www.dhs.state.il.us

ISLAMIC ASSOCIATION FOR PALESTINE
P.O. Box 1163
Bridgeview, IL 60455
Rafeeq Jaber, President
Tel: (708) 974-1488 Fax: (708) 974-3265
Email: iapinfo@iap.org
Web: www.iap.org

JAPANESE AMERICAN CITIZENS LEAGUE
Midwest District Office
5415 N. Clark St.
Chicago, IL 60640
Bill Yoshino, Regional Director
Tel: (773) 728-7170 Fax: (773) 728-7231
Email: midwest@jacl.org
Web: www.jacl.org

JEWISH RECONSTRUCTIONIST FEDERATION
Midwest Region
P.O. Box 724
Lake Zurich, IL 60047-0724
Dina April, Regional Director
Tel: (847) 438-7728
Email: midwest@jrf.org
Web: www.jrf.org

KOREAN AMERICAN COMMUNITY SERVICES
4300 N. California Ave.
Chicago, IL 60618
Soyoung Kwon, President
Tel: (773) 583-5501 Fax: (773) 583-7009
Email: info@kacschgo.org
Web: www.kacschgo.org

NORTH SOUTH FOUNDATION
Illinois Region
2 Marissa Ct.
Burr Ridge, IL 60527
Dr. Ratnam Chitturi
Tel: (630) 323-1966 Fax: (630) 455-9008
Email: chitturi@northsouth.org
Web: www.northsouth.org

SIKH AMERICAN HERITAGE ORGANIZATION
P.O. Box 63
Wayne, IL 60184-0063
Raginder Singh Mago, Director
Tel: (630) 377-5893 Fax: (630) 377-5893
Email: sikhamerican@aol.com
Web: www.sikhamerican.org

UNITED HOLY LAND FUND
6000 W. 79th St. #200
Burbank, IL 60459
Mohammed Aburmisham, Executive Director
Tel: (708) 430-9731 Fax: (708) 430-9936
Email: uhlfusa@yahoo.com
Web: www.uhlfusa.org

SPEC. INT., IMMIGRATION

BUREAU OF REFUGEE AND IMMIGRANT SERVICES
Chicago Office
527 S. Wells St., 5th Fl.
Chicago, IL 60607
Edwin Silverman, Chief

Tel: (312) 793-7120 Fax: (312) 793-2281
Email: dhsd6024@dhs.state.il.us
Web: www.dhs.state.il.us

CHINESE MUTUAL AID ASSOCIATION
Main Office
1016 W. Argyle St.
Chicago, IL 60640
Denise Lam, Executive Director
Tel: (773) 784-2900 Fax: (773) 784-2984
Email: info@chinesemutualaid.org
Web: www.chinesemutualaid.org

COALITION OF AFRICAN, ASIAN, EUROPE AND LATINO IMMIGRANTS OF ILLINOIS
4300 N. Hermitage Ave.
Chicago, IL 60613
Dale Asis, Executive Director
Tel: (773) 248-1019 Fax: (773) 248-1179
Email: contact@caaelii.org
Web: www.caaelii.org

ILLINOIS COALITION FOR IMMIGRANTS AND REFUGEE RIGHTS
36 S. Wabash #1425
Chicago, IL 60603
Joshua W. Hoyt, Executive Director
Tel: (312) 332-7360 Fax: (312) 332-7044
Email: info@icirr.org
Web: www.icirr.org

LAO AMERICAN COMMUNITY SERVICES
4750 N. Sheridan #369
Chicago, IL 60640
Somlith Visaysouk, Executive Director
Tel: (773) 271-0004 Fax: (773) 271-1682
Email: somlith_lacs@yahoo.com

METROPOLITAN ASIAN FAMILY SERVICES, INC.
Head Office
7541 N. Western Ave.
Chicago, IL 60645
Santosh Kumar, Executive Director
Tel: (773) 465-3105 Fax: (773) 465-0158
Email: santosh1250@hotmail.com
Web: www.mafsinc.com

METROPOLITAN ASIAN FAMILY SERVICES, INC.
Schaumburg Office
127 E. Main St.
Schaumburg, IL 60172
Prem Jalota, Supervisor
Tel: (630) 307-6277 Fax: (630) 307-6477
Email: mafs2000@hotmail.com
Web: www.mafs.itgo.com

SPEC. INT., INFORMATION REFERRAL

JAPAN INFORMATION CENTER
Olympia Center
737 N. Michigan Ave. #1000
Chicago, IL 60611
Tel: (312) 280-0430 Fax: (312) 280-6883
Email: jicchicago@webkddi.com
Web: www.chicago.us.emb-japan.go.jp/jic.html

SPEC. INT., LEGAL ASSISTANCE

JEWISH LABOR COMMITTEE
Chicago Chapter
55 E. Monroe St. #2930
Chicago, IL 60603
Michael Perry, Chair
Tel: (312) 641-2960 Fax: (312) 251-8815
Email: JLCMidwest@aol.com
Web: www.jewishlabor.org

SPEC. INT., SENIORS

AGING INFORMATION CENTER
Region V: IL, IN, MI, MN, OH, WI
233 N. Michigan Ave. #790
Chicago, IL 60601-5519
Larry Brewster, Regional Administrator

Tel: (312) 353-3141 Fax: (312) 886-8533
Email: Larry.Brewster@aoa.gov
Web: www.aoa.dhhs.gov

CENTER FOR SENIORS
5320 N. Kedzie Ave.
Chicago, IL 60625
Jae Kwan Ha, Executive Director
Tel: (773) 478-1245 Fax: (773) 478-4070

KOREAN AMERICAN SENIOR CENTER
5008-14 N. Kedzie Ave.
Chicago, IL 60625
Paul Yun, Executive Director
Tel: (773) 478-8851 Fax: (773) 478-8552
Email: aging@chikasc.org
Web: www.chikasc.org

NATIONAL ASIAN- PACIFIC CENTER ON AGING- SENIOR ENVIRONMENTAL EMPLOYMENT PROGRAM
122 S. Michigan Ave.
Chicago, IL 60603
Mei Lin, Project Director
Tel: (312) 913-0979 Fax: (312) 913-0982
Email: web@napca.org
Web: www.napca.org

SPEC. INT., SOCIAL INTEREST

ARAB AMERICAN FAMILY SERVICES
10608 S. Roberts Rd.
Palos Hills, IL 60465
Itedal Shalabi, Coordinator
Tel: (708) 974-8084 Fax: (708) 974-8086
Email: itedals@yahoo.com
Web: www.aafamilyservices.com

BANGLADESH ASSOCIATION OF CHICAGOLAND
P.O. Box 59849
Chicago, IL 60659
Farhad Hossain, Moderator BACUSA
Tel: (773) 252-4050 (h)
Email: farhad@hossains.com

CHAMPAIGN-URBANA JEWISH FEDERATION
503 E. John St.
Champaign, IL 61820
Lee Melhado, Executive Director
Tel: (217) 367-9872 Fax: (217) 344-1541
Email: cujf@shalomcu.org
Web: www.cujf.org

CHINESE AMERICAN SERVICE LEAGUE
2141 S. Tan Ct.
Chicago, IL 60616
Bernarda Wong, President
Tel: (312) 791-0418 Fax: (312) 791-0509
Email: adminis@caslservice.org
Web: www.caslservice.org

Adult Day Care
2141 S. Tan Ct.
Chicago, IL 60616
Suelee Chang, Manager
Tel: (312) 808-7257 Fax: (312) 0509
Email: adminis@caslservice.org
Web: www.caslservice.org

2141 S. 10th Ct.
Chicago, IL 60616
Suey Lee Chang, Manager
Tel: (312) 808-7250 Fax: (312) 326-5244
Email: elderly@caslservice.org
Web: www.caslservice.org

HAMDARD CENTER
355 N. Wood Dale Rd.
Wood Dale, IL 60191
Tajwar Rizziudin, Director
Tel: (630) 860-2290 Fax: (630) 860-1918
Email: hamdardcenter@netzero.net
Web: www.hamdardcenter.org

JAPAN AMERICA SOCIETY OF CHICAGO
20 N. Clark St. #750

Chicago, IL 60602
Thomas P. McMenamin, President
Tel: (312) 263-3049 Fax: (312) 263-6120
Email: kono@jaschicago.org
Web: www.jaschicago.org

JAPANESE AMERICAN SERVICE COMMITTEE
4427 N. Clark St.
Chicago, IL 60640
Jean M. Fujiu, Executive Director
Tel: (773) 275-0097 Fax: (773) 275-0958
Email: jascinfo@jasc-chicago.org
Web: www.jasc-chicago.org

JAPANESE MUTUAL AID SOCIETY OF CHICAGO
2249 W. Berwyn Ave.
Chicago, IL 60625
Tel: (773) 907-3002

JEWISH COMMUNITY COUNCIL OF WEST ROGERS PARK
3003 W. Touhy Ave.
Chicago, IL 60645
Roberta Nechin, Contact
Tel: (773) 331-2503 Fax: (773) 761-8835
Email: jccwrp@aol.com

JEWISH COUNCIL ON URBAN AFFAIRS
618 S. Michigan Ave.
Chicago, IL 60605
Richard Rhodes, President
Tel: (312) 663-0960 Fax: (312) 663-5305
Email: jcuamail@jcua.org
Web: www.jcua.org

JEWISH FAMILY AND COMMUNITY SERVICES OF CHICAGO
Chicago City Office
3525 W. Peterson Ave.
Chicago, IL 60659
Tel: (773) 866-5035 Fax: (773) 866-1035
Web: www.jfcschicago.org

Executive Office
216 W. Jackson Blvd. #700
Chicago, IL 60606
Tel: (312) 357-4800 Fax: (312) 855-3750
Email: administration@jfcschicago.org
Web: www.jfcschicago.org

Hias Chicago
216 W. Jackson Blvd. #700
Chicago, IL 60606
Tel: (312) 357-4666 Fax: (312) 855-3291
Web: www.jfcschicago.org

Niles Township District
5150 Golf Rd. Goldie Bachmann Luftig Bldg.
Skokie, IL 60076
Tel: (847) 568-5200 Fax: (847) 568-5250
Email: ntdstaff@jfcschicago.org
Web: www.jfcschicago.org

North Suburban District
85 Revere Dr. #J
Northbrook, IL 60062
Tel: (847) 272-2882 Fax: (847) 272-1115
Email: nsd@jfcschicago.org
Web: www.jfcschicago.org

Northwest Suburban
1250 Radcliffe Rd.
Buffalo Grove, IL 60089
Tel: (847) 392-8820 Fax: (847) 392-3221
Email: nwsd@jfcschicago.org
Web: www.jfcschicago.org

South Suburban District
3649 W. 183rd St.
Hazel Crest, IL 60429
Tel: (708) 799-1869 Fax: (708) 798-9148
Web: www.jfcschicago.org

Virginia Frank Child Development Center
3033 W. Touhy
Chicago, IL 60645

Tel: (773) 761-4550 Fax: (773) 761-6426
Email: cdc@jfcschicago.org
Web: www.jfcschicago.org

West Suburban Office
10 E. 22nd St. #215
Lombard, IL 60148
Tel: (630) 932-7832
Web: www.jfcschicago.org

JEWISH UNITED FUND OF METROPOLITAN CHICAGO
1 S. Franklin St.
Chicago, IL 60606
Tel: (312) 357-4929 Fax: (312) 553-5486
Email: missions@juf.org
Web: www.juf.org

JORDAN ARAB AMERICAN ASSOCIATION
3206 W. Lawrence Ave.
Chicago, IL 60625
Mohana Shawahin, Treasurer
Tel: (773) 588-1098 Fax: (773) 267-6844

KOREAN AMERICAN ASSOCIATION OF CHICAGO
5941 N. Lincoln Ave.
Chicago, IL 60659
Gilyoung Kim, President
Tel: (773) 878-1900 Fax: (773) 878-9075
Email: kykim@koreachicago.org
Web: www.koreachicago.org

KOREAN SELF-HELP COMMUNITY CENTER
4934 N. Pulaski Rd.
Chicago, IL 60630
Joong K. Shin, Executive Director
Tel: (773) 545-8348 Fax: (773) 545-0054
Email: ckshc@msn.com

LAO AMERICAN COMMUNITY OF JOLIET
1614 Court Wright Dr.
Plainfield, IL 60544
Sithat Phomachanom, President
Tel: (815) 609-0753

PUI TAK CENTER
2216 S. Wentworth Ave.
Chicago, IL 60616
David Wu, Executive Director
Tel: (312) 328-1188 Fax: (312) 328-7452
Email: dwu@aol.com
Web: www.puitak.org

TIBETAN ALLIANCE OF CHICAGO
950-54 W. Carmen St.
Chicago, IL 60640
Tel: (773) 275-7454
Email: contact@tibetan-alliance.org
Web: www.tibetan-alliance.org

SPEC. INT., SPORTS

HOMENETMEN
Chicago
P.O Box 935
Glenview, IL 60025
Yeghpayr Krikor Kassarjian, Chairman
Email: Info@homenetmenchicago.org
Web: www.homenetmenchicago.org

MOSAIC OUTDOOR CLUBS OF AMERICA
Chicago Chapter
P.O. Box 47-6775
Chicago, IL 60647
Joel Berman, Chapter President
Tel: (773) 384-6436
Email: joel.berman@comcast.net
Web: www.mosaics.org

SPEC. INT., WOMEN

APNA GHAR, INC.
4753 N. Broadway #518
Chicago, IL 60640
Dr. Ashima Mehta, President
Tel: (773) 334-0173 Fax: (773) 334-0963

Email: info@apnaghar.org
Web: www.apnaghar.org

HADASSAH
Chicago Chapter
4711 Golf Rd. #600
Skokie, IL 60076
Bobbie Levin, President
Tel: (847) 675-6790 Fax: (847) 679-5286
Email: susan.rifkin@hadassah.org
Web: www.hadassah.org

KOREAN AMERICAN WOMEN IN NEED
P.O. Box 59133
Chicago, IL 60659
Inhe Choi, President
Tel: (773) 583-1392 Fax: (773) 583-2454
Email: kanwin@ameritec.net
Web: www.kanwin.org

NATIONAL COUNCIL FOR JEWISH WOMEN
Chicago North Shore Section
1107 Central Ave.
Wilmette, IL 60091
Tel: (847) 853-8889
Email: info@ncjwchicagonorthshore.org
Web: www.ncjwchicagonorthshore.org

SOCIETY OF WOMEN ENGINEERS
Headquarters
230 E. Ohio St. #400
Chicago, IL 60611-3265
Betty Shanahan, Executive Director
Tel: (312) 596-5223 Fax: (312) 596-5252
Email: hq@swe.org
Web: www.swe.org

SPEC. INT., YOUTH

ASIAN YOUTH SERVICES
4750 N. Sheridan Rd. #443
Chicago, IL 60640
Shari Fenton, Director
Tel: (773) 506-0766 Fax: (773) 506-0766
Email: sharifenton405@hotmail.com

CHINESE AMERICAN SERVICE LEAGUE YOUTH CENTER
2141 S. Tancourt
Chicago, IL 60616
Ivy Siu, Program Manager
Tel: (312) 808-0280 Fax: (312) 808-0277

JEWISH BIG SISTERS
1316 W. Fargo Ave. #303
Chicago, IL 60626
Ruth Rubin, Contact
Tel: (773) 764-4759 Fax: (773) 764-7567
Email: jbssisters@aol.com

JEWISH COUNCIL FOR YOUTH SERVICES
Central Office
100 N. LaSalle St. #400
Chicago, IL 60602
Marty Oliff, Executive Director
Tel: (312) 726-8891 Fax: (312) 726-8923
Email: moliff@jcys.org
Web: www.jcys.org

JCYS Adventure Education
1726 N. Orchard
Chicago, IL 60614
Andy Gehl, Program Director
Tel: (312) 482-9517
Email: agehl@jcys.org
Web: www.jcys.org

JCYS Camp Henry Horner
26710 W. Nippersink Rd.
Ingleside, IL 60041
Kenley Perry, Program Director
Tel: (847) 740-5010 Fax: (847) 740-5014
Email: kperry@jcys.org
Web: www.jcys.org

JCYS Camp Red Leaf
26710 W. Nippersink Rd.
Ingleside, IL 60041
Ashley Wilson, Director
Tel: (847) 740-5010 Fax: (847) 740-5014
Email: awilson@jcys.org
Web: www.jcys.org

JCYS George W. Lutz Family Center
800 Clavey Rd.
Highland Park, IL 60035
Brenda Weitzberg, Director
Tel: (847) 433-6001 Fax: (847) 433-6003
Email: bweitzberg@jcys.org
Web: www.jcys.org

JCYS Lakeview Family Ctr.
957 W. Grace
Chicago, IL 60613
Jean Losek, Director
Tel: (773) 281-2533 Fax: (773) 281-2403
Email: jlosek@jcys.org
Web: www.jcys.org

JCYS Max Davidson Tennis and Swim Ctr.
1195 Half Day Rd.
Highland Park, IL 60035
Heather Connolly, Site Director
Tel: (847) 432-6355 Fax: (847) 433-6003
Email: hconnolly@jcys.org
Web: www.jcys.org

JCYS North Shore Day Camp
2939 Summit Ave.
Highland Park, IL 60035
Micky Baer, Director
Tel: (847) 433-6732 Fax: (847) 433-5076
Email: mbaer@jcys.org
Web: www.jcys.org

JCYS Northwest Family Ctr.
1700 Weiland Rd.
Buffalo Grove, IL 60089
Michael Garlin, Director
Tel: (847) 279-0900 Fax: (847) 279-0909
Email: mgarlin@jcys.org
Web: www.jcys.org

OUR CHINESE DAUGHTERS FOUNDATION
P.O. Box 1243
Bloomington, IL 61702-1243
Dr. Jane Liedtke, CEO/Founder
Tel: (309) 830-0983
Email: jane@ocdf.org
Web: www.ocdf.org

SOUTH-EAST ASIA CENTER
5120 N. Broadway
Chicago, IL 60640
Peter R. Pott, Executive Director
Tel: (773) 989-6927 Fax: (773) 989-7755
Email: seac1134@yahoo.com

STUDENT ORGANIZATION

ASIAN AMERICAN ASSOCIATION
University of Illinois, Urbana Champaign
280 Illini Union #256
Urbana, IL 61801
Lisa Nonzee, President
Email: snonzee@uiuc.edu
Web: www2.uiuc.edu/ro/aaa

ASIAN AMERICAN COALITION COMMITTEE
University of Illinois Chicago
Campus Programs Box #A29, 750 S. Halsted St.
Chicago, IL 60607-7012
Sae-Rom Chae, Chair
Tel: (312) 355-5174
Email: schae2@uic.edu
Web: www2.uic.edu/stud_orgs/pol/aacc

ASIAN CULTURAL EXCHANGE
DePaul University
2250 N. Sheffield Ave. #201
Chicago, IL 60614
Jon Reinert, President

Tel: (773) 687-2000 x4003
Email: jreinert@acedpu.com
Web: www.acedpu.com

ASIAN PACIFIC AMERICAN LAW STUDENT ASSOCIATION
Northwestern University School of Law
357 E. Chicago Ave.
Chicago, IL 60611
Dane Choe, President
Tel: (312) 503-8649
Email: d-choe2006@law.nothwestern.edu
Web: www.law.northwestern.edu

CHINESE UNDERGRADUATE STUDENT ASSOCIATION
University of Wisconsin
222 Christine Way
Bolingbrook, IL 60440
Jingjing Wang
Tel: (630) 378-0359
Email: cusa@studentorg.wisc.edu
Web: www.sit.wisc.edu/~cusa/

COUNCIL OF PAN ASIAN AMERICANS
Loyola University Chicago
6525 N. Sheridan Rd.
Chicago, IL 60626
Rama Seedoo, Co-President
Tel: (773) 274-3000
Email: copaaluc@yahoo.com
Web: www.luc.edu/orgs/copaa/

FILIPINOS IN ALLIANCE
University of Illinois at Chicago
750 S. Halsted St. #300 CCC Box 11
Chicago, IL 60607-7012
Santi Khairassame, President
Tel: (312) 355-0619
Web: www2.uic.edu/stud_orgs/cultures/fia

HONG KONG STUDENT ASSOCIATION
Northwestern University
1936 Sheridan Rd.
Evanston, IL 60201
Chris Wong, President
Email: chriswong@northwestern.edu
Web: http://groups.northwestern.edu/hksa/

INDIAN STUDENT ASSOCIATION
University of Illinois, Urbana Champaign
280 Illini Union #272
Urbana, IL 61801
Shaan Kapoor, President
Tel: (217) 244-0775
Email: kapoor@uiuc.edu
Web: www2.uiuc.edu/ro/ISA

KOREAN STUDENT ASSOCIATION
Northwestern University
633 Clark St.
Evanston, IL 60208
Myung-Han Yoon, President
Tel: (847) 491-3741
Email: mhyoon @northwestern.edu
Web: http://groups.northwestern.edu/ksa/org.htm

Western Illinois University
Student Activities Department, 1 University Cir.
Macomb, IL 61455-1390
Jongnam Choi, Student Advisor
Tel: (309) 298-1414
Email: kosa@wiu.edu
Web: www.wiu.edu/users/mikosa/

KOREAN STUDENTS ORGANIZATION
University of Chicago
5454 S. Shore Dr. #1134
Chicago, IL 60615
Jeannie Kim, President
Tel: (773) 702-1234
Email: jeannie@uchicago.edu
Web: http://kso.uchicago.edu/

MALAYSIAN STUDENT ASSOCIATION
University of Illinois at Urbana-Champaign
408 E. Stoughton St. #6
Champaign, IL 61820

Ahmad Feizal Hazrik Ahmad Rosdi, President
Tel: (217) 352-2120
Email: rahmad@uiuc.edu
Web: www2.uiuc.edu/ro/MaSA

MUSLIM STUDENTS ASSOCIATION
University of Illinois, Urbana-Champaign
280 Illini Union
Urbana, IL 61801
Email: msa@uiuc.edu
Web: www2.uiuc.edu/ro/msa

PAKISTAN STUDENT ASSOCIATION
Southern Illinois University, Edwardsville
Campus Box 1168
Edwardsville, IL 62026
Farhan Adil, President
Email: fadil@siue.org
Web: www.siue.edu/STACTV/PSA

PERSIAN CULTURAL ASSOCIATION
University of Illinois at Urbana-Champaign
1401 W. Green St. #280 MB #82
Urbana, IL 61801
Farzad Moeinzadeh, President
Email: moeinzad@uiuc.edu
Web: www2.uiuc.edu/ro/pca

PHILIPPINE STUDENT ASSOCIATION
University of Illinois, Urbana Champaign
280 Illini Union #14
Urbana, IL 61801
Antoinette Fadera, President
Tel: (217) 333-1631
Email: psauiuc@hotmail.com
Web: www2.uiuc.edu/ro/psa

ROMANIAN STUDENT CLUB
University of Illinois at Urbana-Champaign
400 Student Services Bldg., 610 E. John St.
Champaign, IL 61820
Ruxandra M. Costescu, President
Email: rsc@uiuc.edu
Web: www2.uiuc.edu/ro/RomClub

SAMAHAN
University of Chicago
5706 S. University Ave.
Chicago, IL 60637
Melissa Quintos, President
Email: mquintos@uchicago.edu
Web: http://samahan.uchicago.edu

TAIWANESE AMERICAN STUDENTS CLUB
Northwestern University
Norris University Ctr., 1999 Campus Dr.
Evanston, IL 60208
Coco Shiao, President
Tel: (847) 491-2360
Email: shiao@northwestern.edu
Web: http://groups.northwestern.edu/tasc/index2.html

TURKISH STUDENT ASSOCIATION
Illinois Institute of Technology
3300 S. Federal St.
Chicago, IL 60616-3793
Mehmet Tolga Yildir, President
Tel: (312) 326-1345
Email: yildmeh@iit.edu
Web: www.iit.edu/~iittturk

VIETNAMESE STUDENT ASSOCIATION
University of Illinois Urbana Champaign
280 Illini Union #21
Urbana, IL 61801
Dung Quang, President
Email: quang@uiuc.edu
Web: www2.uiuc.edu/ro/vsa

INDIANA

ARTISTIC

INDIANAPOLIS MINYO DANCERS, INC.
8807 Madison Ave. #205-B
Indianapolis, IN 46227
Chieko Jacobs, Director
Tel: (317) 888-9568

BUSINESS

JAPANESE AMERICAN CONNECTION
8445 Castleton Corner Dr.
Indianapolis, IN 46250
Hannah Mayamoto Smith, Vice President
Tel: (317) 841-4161 Fax: (317) 841-4173
Email: hannah.smith@cbscompanies.com
Web: www.cbscompanies.com

CULTURAL

AMERICAN TURKISH ASSOCIATION OF INDIANA
5219 Wiltonwood Ct.
Indianapolis, IN 46254
Ahmet Fer, President
Tel: (317) 490-0752
Email: ata-in@ata-in.org
Web: http://ata-in.org

ASIAN CULTURE CENTER
Indiana University
807 E. 10th St.
Bloomington, IN 47408
Melanie Castillo-Cullather, Director
Tel: (812) 856-5361 Fax: (812) 856-5030
Email: acc@indiana.edu
Web: www.indiana.edu/~acc

INDIANA ASSOCIATION OF CHINESE AMERICANS, INC.
P.O. Box 18
Carmel, IN 46033
Agnes Yam Wolverton, Acting President
Email: info@iacaonline.org
Web: www.iacaonline.org

MINYO CLUB OF INDIANAPOLIS
3525 S. Mayflower Dr.
Indianapolis, IN 46221
Tokiko Gilson, Manager
Tel: (317) 241-7280

SOCIETY FOR PROMOTION OF PERSIAN CULTURE, INC.
P.O. Box 22381
Indianapolis, IN 46222
Behrooz Vakily, President
Tel: (317) 329-0520
Email: sppcindiana@yahoo.com
Web: www.sppcindiana.org

TAIWANESE AMERICAN ASSOCIATION OF INDIANAPOLIS
10387 Orchard Park South Dr.
Indianapolis, IN 46280
Julie Chang, Acting President
Tel: (317) 815-9011 Fax: (317) 815-9011
Email: c21juliechang@yahoo.com
Web: www.taaindy.org

TIBETAN CULTURAL CENTER
P.O. Box 2581
Bloomington, IN 47402
Sandy Belth, Contact Person
Tel: (812) 334-7046 Fax: (812) 335-9054
Email: tcc@tibetancc.com
Web: www.tibetancc.com

POLITICAL ACTION

INTERNATIONAL TIBET INDEPENDENCE MOVEMENT
P.O. Box 592
Fishers, IN 46038
Larry Gerstein, President
Tel: (317) 579-9015 Fax: (317) 579-0914
Email: rangzen@aol.com
Web: www.rangzen.org

PROFESSIONAL

ASSOCIATION OF MUSLIM SCIENTISTS AND ENGINEERS
P.O. Box 38

Plainfield, IN 46168
Tel: (517) 947-6338 Fax: (517) 947-6338
Email: office@amse.net
Web: www.amse.net

RELIGIOUS

ARAB INTERNATIONAL MINISTRIES
P.O. Box 50986
Indianapolis, IN 46250
Tel: (888) 446-5457 Fax: (317) 818-0888
Email: aim7@indy.net

CHINESE COMMUNITY CHURCH OF INDIANAPOLIS
3405 E. 116th St.
Carmel, IN 46033
Yun Han Gwo, Senior Pastor
Tel: (317) 706-0433 Fax: (317) 706-0434
Email: info@indychinesechurch.org
Web: www.indychinesechurch.org

CRESCENT PROJECT
P.O. Box 50986
Indianapolis, IN 46250
Tel: (888) 446-5457
Email: info@crescentproject.org
Web: www.arabim.org

INDIANA ASSEMBLY OF GOD KOREAN CHURCH
9605 E. 30th St.
Indianapolis, IN 46229
Paul Inho Cho, Pastor
Tel: (317) 898-1770 Fax: (317) 898-1770
Email: jbc6870@iquest.net
Web: www.inkoreanag.com

KOREAN PRESBYTERIAN CHURCH OF PURDUE
320 W. North St.
West Lafayette, IN 47906
Richard Kim, Pastor
Tel: (765) 743-8183
Email: taek.kim@verizon.net
Web: www.purduekoreanchurch.org

VIETNAMESE AMERICAN BUDDHIST ASSOCIATION
7410 Campfire Run
Indianapolis, IN 46236
Long Nguyen, Secretary
Tel: (317) 826-1716 Fax: (317) 327-8480
Email: lkhnguyen@cs.com

SPEC. INT., EDUCATION

ASSOCIATION FOR JAPANESE LITERARY STUDIES
Purdue University
1359 Stanley Coulter Hall
West Lafayette, IN 47907
Eiji Sekine, Associate Professor
Tel: (765) 494-2258 Fax: (765) 496-1700
Email: esekine@purdue@.edu
Web: www.sla.purdue.edu/fll/AJLS

DEPARTMENT OF NEAR EASTERN LANGUAGES AND CULTURES
Indiana University
Goodbody Hall 102, 1011 E. 3rd St.
Bloomington, IN 47405-7005
Salman H. Al-Ani, Professor
Tel: (812) 855-5993 Fax: (812) 855-7841
Email: nelcmesp@indiana.edu
Web: www.indiana.edu/~nelcmesp

INNER ASIAN & URALIC NATIONAL RESOURCE CENTER
Indiana University
Goodbody Hall #324
Bloomington, IN 47405
Tel: (812) 856-5263 Fax: (812) 855-8667
Email: iaunrc@indiana.edu
Web: www.indiana.edu/~iaunrc

THE SOCIETY FOR ASIAN AND COMPARATIVE PHILOSOPHY

Departments of Philosophy
746 Flanner Hall University of Notre Dame
Notre Dame, IN 46556
Fred Dallmayr, President
Tel: (574) 631-5491 Fax: (574) 631-9238
Email: dallmayr.1@nd.edu
Web: www.sacpweb.org

TRI-STATE ASSOCIATION OF PHYSICIANS FROM INDIAN

415 W. Columbia St.
Evansville, IN 47710
Satyam Tatineni, President
Tel: (812) 464-9133 Fax:
Email: drstatineni@yahoo.com
Web: www.tapiusa.org

US CHINA PEOPLES FRIENDSHIP ASSOCIATION

Central Indiana Chapter
8426 Viburnum Ct.
Indianapolis, IN 46260
Marion Harcourt, Contact
Tel: (317) 251-4436
Web: www.uscpfa.org

Midwest Region
402 E. 43rd St.
Indianapolis, IN 46205
Robert Sanborn, Jr., President
Tel: (317) 283-7735
Email: robert@thesanborns.com
Web: www.uscpfa.org

SPEC. INT., HUMAN RELATIONS

ISLAMIC SOCIETY OF NORTH AMERICA

P.O. Box 38
Plainfield, IN 46168
Sheikh Muhammed Nur Abdullah, President
Tel: (317) 839-8157 Fax: (317) 839-1840
Email: president@isna.net
Web: www.isna.net

JEWISH COMMUNITY RELATIONS COUNCIL OF INDIANAPOLIS

1100 W. 42nd St.
Indianapolis, IN 46208
Marcia Goldstone, Executive Director
Tel: (317) 926-2935 Fax: (317) 926-2952
Web: www.indyjcrc.org

TABITHA FOUNDATION USA

P.O. Box 272
Jamestown, IN 46147
Cathy Caldwell
Email: cathy@tabitha-usa.org
Web: www.tabitha-usa.org/Tabitha_Cambodia.shtml

SPEC. INT., SOCIAL INTEREST

ASIAN AMERICAN ALLIANCE

1000 E. 116th St.
Carmel, IN 46032
June Kiyomoto, Executive Administrator
Tel: (317) 818-6699 Fax: (317) 818-6788
Email: jkiyomoto@aaalliance.org
Web: www.aaalliance.org

FORT WAYNE JEWISH FEDERATION

227 E. Washington Blvd.
Fort Wayne, IN 46802-3121
Doris W. Fogel, President
Tel: (260) 422-8566 Fax: (260) 422-8567
Email: fwjewfed@aol.com
Web: www.shalomfw.org

INDIANA CHINESE AMERICAN PROFESSIONAL ASSOCIATION INC.

5812 E. Fallcreek Pkwy. North Dr.
Indianapolis, IN 46226
David Wong
Tel: (317) 254-8288 Fax: (317) 254-8688
Email: ttwong@comcast.net

JAPAN AMERICA SOCIETY OF INDIANA INC.

39 W. Jackson Pl. # 50
Indianapolis, IN 46225
Theresa A. Kulczak, Executive Director
Tel: (317) 635-0123 Fax: (317) 635-0452
Email: jasi@iquest.net
Web: www.japanindiana.org

JEWISH FEDERATION OF GREATER INDIANAPOLIS

6705 Hoover Rd.
Indianapolis, IN 46260
Tel: (317) 726-5450 Fax: (317) 205-0307
Email: info@jfgi.org
Web: www.jfgi.org

JEWISH FEDERATION OF GREATER LAFAYETTE

P.O. Box 3802
West Lafayette, IN 47996
Laura Starr, President
Tel: (765) 426-4724 Fax: (765) 426-4724
Email: jfgl1@juno.com
Web: www.jfgl.org

KAWAN INDONESIA

8310 Mockingbird Ln.
Indianapolis, IN 46256
Edwina MacDonald, President
Tel: (317) 578-3031 Fax: (317) 578-3502
Email: emacdo1015@aol.com

STUDENT ORGANIZATION

ASIAN AMERICAN ASSOCIATION

Indiana University
Indiana Memorial Union #672 & 673
Bloomington, IN 47405
Sung K. Ahn, President
Email: aaa@indiana.edu
Web: www.indiana.edu/~aaa

CHINESE STUDENTS AND SCHOLARS ASSOCIATION

Indiana University
807 E. 10th St.
Bloomington, IN 47408
Leon Li, President
Email: iucssa@indiana.edu
Web: www.indiana.edu/~iucssa/index.html

HONG KONG STUDENT ASSOCIATION

Indiana University
807 E. 10th St.
Bloomington, IN 47408
Samantha Chow, President
Email: hongkong@indiana.edu
Web: www.indiana.edu/~hongkong

INDIAN STUDENT ASSOCIATION

Indiana University
807 E. 10th St.
Bloomington, IN 47408
Nazia Khan, President
Email: isa@indiana.edu
Web: www.indiana.edu/~isa

INDONESIAN STUDENT ASSOCIATION - PERMIAS

Indiana University
807 E. 10th St.
Bloomington, IN 47408
Fredi Pribadi, President
Email: fpribadi@indiana.edu
Web: www.indiana.edu/~indo/

JAPANESE STUDENT ASSOCIATION

Indiana University
807 E. 10th St.
Bloomington, IN 47408
Shotaro Ishikawa, President
Email: shishika@indiana.edu
Web: www.indiana.edu/~jsa/index.htm

KOREAN STUDENT ASSOCIATION

Indiana University

P.O. Box 7842
Bloomington, IN 47407
Yongkuk Chung, President
Email: iuksa@indiana.edu
Web: www.indiana.edu/~iuksa

MONGOLIA SOCIETY, INC.

Indiana University
322 Goodbody Hall, 1011 E. 3rd St.
Bloomington, IN 47405-7005
Dr. Henry G. Schwarz, President
Tel: (812) 855-4078 Fax: (812) 855-7500
Email: monsoc@indiana.edu
Web: www.indiana.edu/~mongsoc

PURDUE SINGAPORE STUDENTS' ASSOCIATION

Purdue University
Stewart Ctr. #644
West Lafayette, IN 47905
Email: merlion@expert.ics.purdue.edu
Web: http://web.ics.purdue.edu/~merlion/

PURDUE TAIWAN STUDENT ASSOCIATION

Purdue University
West Lafayette, IN 47907
Eddy Chang, President
Email: chang6@purdue.edu
Web: www.purdue.edu/tsa

PURDUE TURKISH STUDENT ASSOCIATION

Purdue University
Stewart Ctr. #641
West Lafayette, IN 47907
Levent Gun, President
Email: lgun@mgmt.purdue.edu
Web: http://web.ics.purdue.edu/~turkiye/

PURDUE UNIVERSITY CHINESE STUDENT-SCHOLAR ASSOCIATION

Purdue University
Stewart Ctr., #616, 128 Memorial Mall
West Lafayette, IN 47907-2034
Zhi Qi, President
Tel: (765) 494-5325 (O)
Email: zhiqi@purdue.edu
Web: www.pucssa.org

SINGAPORE STUDENTS ASSOCIATION

Indiana University
807 E. 10th St.
Bloomington, IN 47405
Email: ssa@indiana.edu
Web: www.indiana.edu/~ssa

TAIWANESE AMERICAN FOUNDATION

Manchester College
604 E. College Ave.
North Manchester, IN 46962
Bernice Tsai, Executive Director
Email: bernicers@hotmaill.com
Web: www.tafworld.org

TAIWANESE STUDENT ASSOCIATION

Indiana University
807 E. 10th St.
Bloomington, IN 47408
Louis Liao, President
Email: loliao@indiana.edu
Web: www.indiana.edu/~taiwan/index.htm

TURKISH STUDENT ASSOCIATION

Indiana University
807 E. 10th St.
Bloomington, IN 47408
Emir Kaya, President
Email: ekaya@indiana.edu
Web: www.indiana.edu/~tsa/

VIETNAMESE STUDENT ASSOCIATION

Indiana University
807 E. 10th St.
Bloomington, IN 47408
Yen Do, President
Email: ydo@indiana.edu
Web: www.indiana.edu/~vsa/index.html

VIETNAMESE STUDENT ASSOCIATION OF NOTRE DAME

315 Lafortune Student Center
Notre Dame, IN 46556
Dr. Steven Brady, President
Tel: (574) 631-7421
Email: vsand@nd.edu
Web: www.nd.edu/~vsand

IOWA

BUSINESS

IOWA ASIAN ALLIANCE

1501 15th St., Regency 1 Bldg. #200
West Des Moines, IA 50266
Paul Shao, Chairman
Tel: (515) 309-6047 Fax: (515) 453-8539
Email: info@iowaasianalliance.com
Web: www.iowaasianalliance.com

CULTURAL

KADSAM THAIDAM SOCIETY

3216 42nd St. East
Des Moines, IA 50317
Thomas Baccam, Chair
Tel: (515) 263-0725
Email: tbaccam@efr.org

MULTI-PURPOSE

ASIAN AMERICAN COUNCIL

P.O. Box 1808
Des Moines, IA 50306-1808
Cyndi Chen, President
Tel: (515) 283-2388 Fax: (515) 284-5411
Email: aaciowa@yahoo.com

RELIGIOUS

ASSOCIATION OF MUSLIMS IN AMERICA

University of Iowa
P.O. Box 2501
Iowa City, IA 52244
Email: muslims@blue.weeg.uiowa.edu
Web: www.uiowa.edu/~muslims

CAMBODIAN BUDDHIST SOCIETY

1901 7th St.
Des Moines, IA 50314
Tel: (515-247-0189

SPEC. INT., EDUCATION

CENTER FOR ASIAN AND PACIFIC STUDIES

University of Iowa
276 International Center
Iowa City, IA 52242-1802
Stephen Vlastos, Director
Tel: (319) 335-1305 Fax: (319) 335-3345
Email: caps@blue.weeg.uiowa.edu
Web: www.uiowa.edu/~caps

US CHINA PEOPLES FRIENDSHIP ASSOCIATION

Quad Cities Chapter
5166 Century Heights
Bettendorf, IA 52722
Jin Qian, Contact
Tel: (563) 449-9877
Web: www.uscpfa.org

SPEC. INT., HUMAN RELATIONS

AMERICANS & PALESTINIANS FOR PEACE

P.O. Box 113
Muscatine, IA 52761
John Dabeet, President & Founder
Tel: (563) 263-8145 Fax: (563) 288-6074
Email: president@ampal.net
Web: www.muscanet.com/~ampal

SPEC. INT., IMMIGRATION

BUREAU OF REFUGEE SERVICES
Department of Human Services, State of Iowa
1200 University Ave. #D
Des Moines, IA 50314
Wayne Johnson, Bureau Chief
Tel: (515) 283-7999 Fax: (515) 283-9160
Email: refugee@dhs.state.ia.us
Web: www.dhs.state.ia.us/refugee

SPEC. INT., SOCIAL INTEREST

EMPLOYEE & FAMILY RESOURCES
505 5th Ave. #930
Des Moines, IA 50309-2316
Paul Hedquist, CEO
Tel: (515) 288-9020
Email: info@efr.org
Web: www.efr.org

JAPAN AMERICA SOCIETY OF IOWA
P.O. Box 12093
Des Moines, IA 50312
Polly Fortune, President
Tel: (515) 285-2464
Email: mp4chun@mchsi.com
Web: www.i-rule.net/jasi.org

JEWISH FEDERATION OF GREATER DES MOINES
910 Polk Blvd.
Des Moines, IA 50312
Tel: (515) 277-6321 Fax: (515) 277-4069
Email: jcrc@dmjfed.org
Web: www.dmjfed.org

TAIWANESE ASSOCIATION OF IOWA
811 Hickman Rd.
Des Moines, IA 50314
Ta-Yu Yang, Director
Tel: (515) 883-2940 Fax: (515) 226-9674
Email: tayuyang@cs.com

SPEC. INT., SPORTS

BREESE FAMILY TAE-KWON DO & FITNESS CENTER
2006 Indianola Ave.
Des Moines, IA 50315
Tony Breese, Owner
Tel: (515) 282-2040

STUDENT ORGANIZATION

MALAYSIAN STUDENT ASSOCIATION
Iowa State University
G37, E. Student Office Space, Memorial Union
Ames, IA 50010
Steven Loh, President
Email: amsisu@iastate.edu
Web: www.amsisu.iastate.edu

THAI STUDENT ASSOCIATION AT THE UNIVERSITY OF IOWA
University of Iowa
1015 Oakcrest St. #71
Iowa City, IA 52246
Puwat Charukamnoetkanok
Tel: (319) 887-1652
Email: puwat1998@hotmail.com

KANSAS

CULTURAL

FILIPINO ASSOCIATION OF GREATER KANSAS CITY
Cultural Center
9810 W. 79th St.
Overland Park, KS 66210
Neofito Rabang, President
Tel: (913) 381-1601 Fax: (913) 491-6981
Email: promedia@fagkc.org
Web: www.fagkc.org

POLITICAL ACTION

INDO-AMERICAN FORUM FOR POLITICAL EDUCATION
10551 Barkley #400
Oberlin Park, KS 66212
Sri Melethil, President
Tel: (913) 432-6656 Fax: (913) 432-6667
Email: smelethil@kc.rr.com

RELIGIOUS

LAO BUDDHIST ASSOCIATION
725 W. Spruce
Olathe, KS 66061
Ounthong Sengphokham, Contact
Tel: (913) 829-6647

LAO BUDDHIST ASSOCIATION OF KANSAS
2550 S. Greenwich rd.
Wichita, KS 67210
Tel: (316) 685-6360

PHILIPPINE EVANGELICAL ENTERPRISES INC.
15354 Quivira
Overland Park, KS 66221
Tel: (913) 897-4369 Fax: (913) 897-2099
Email: stanbuss@sbcglobal.net

TEMPLE CONGREGATION B'NAI JEHUDAH
12320 Nall Ave.
Overland Park, KS 66209
Rick Klein, Executive Director
Tel: (913) 663-4050 Fax: (913) 906-9544
Email: rklein@bnaijehudah.org
Web: www.bnaijehudah.org

WICHITA CAMBODIAN BUDDHIST SOCIETY, INC.
3190 S. Clifton Ave.
Wichita, KS 67210
Tel: (316) 684-9422

SPEC. INT., EDUCATION

CHINESE SCHOOL OF GREATER KANSAS CITY FOUNDATION
11401 Cedar Leawood
Overland Park, KS 66211
T'ai-ying Chiu, Principal
Tel: (913) 469-9318

KANSAS COLLEGE OF CHINESE MEDICINE
9235 E. Harry St.
Wichita, KS 67207
Qizhi Gao, President
Tel: (888) 481-5226 Fax: (316) 691-8868
Email: admin@kccm.edu
Web: www.kccm.edu

SPEC. INT., EMPLOYMENT

WICHITA ASIAN ASSOCIATION
2502 E. Douglas St.
Wichita, KS 67214-4514
Mohan Kambamtati, Director
Tel: (316) 689-8729 Fax: (316) 689-8274
Email: wichindo@earthlink.net

SPEC. INT., HUMAN RELATIONS

THE AMERICAN JEWISH COMMITTEE
Kansas City Chapter
5801 W. 115th St. #203
Overland Park, KS 66211-1824
Marvin Szneler, Chapter Director
Tel: (913) 327-8126 Fax: (913) 327-8110
Email: kansas@ajc.org
Web: www.ajc.org

SPEC. INT., SOCIAL INTEREST

JEWISH COMMUNITY CAMPUS OF GREATER KANSAS CITY, INC.
5801 W. 115th St.
Overland Park, KS 66211
Alan Bram, Contact
Tel: (913) 327-8200 Fax: (913) 327-8040
Email: alanb@jewishkc.org

JEWISH COMMUNITY CENTER OF GREATER KANSAS CITY
5801 W. 115 St.
Overland Park, KS 66211
Cary J. Minkoff, Executive Director
Tel: (913) 327-8000 Fax: (913) 327-8040
Email: carym@jewishkc.org
Web: www.jcckc.org

JEWISH COMMUNITY FOUNDATION OF GREATER KANSAS CITY
5801 W. 115th St., Koralchick Wing #202
Overland Park, KS 66211
Lauren Mattleman Hoopes, Executive Director
Tel: (913) 327-8100 Fax: (913) 327-8100
Email: support@jcfkc.org
Web: www.jcfkc.org

JEWISH FEDERATION OF GREATER KANSAS CITY
5801 W. 115th St. #201
Overland Park, KS 66211
Tel: (913) 327-8100 Fax: (913) 327-8110
Email: webmaster@jewishkc.org
Web: www.jewishkansascity.org

MID-KANSAS JEWISH FEDERATION
400 N. Woodlawn #8
Wichita, KS 67208
Tel: (316) 686-4741 Fax: (316) 686-6008
Email: jpress@mkjf.org
Web: www.mkjf.org

SPEC. INT., WOMEN

HADASSAH
Great Plains Region
7199 W. 98th Terr. #160
Overland Park, KS 66212
Sybil Kaplan, President
Tel: (913) 341-9996 Fax: (913) 341-9998
Email: greatplainsreg@aol.com
Web: www.hadassah.org

STUDENT ORGANIZATION

MALAYSIAN STUDENTS ASSOCIATION
University of Kansas
400 Kansas Union
Lawrence, KS 66045
Chu Shin Ying, President
Email: shinying@ku.edu
Web: www.msiaku.org

VIETNAMESE STUDENT ASSOCIATION
University of Kansas
400 Kansas Union #F
Lawrence, KS 66045
Tu Le, President
Email: vsa@ku.edu
Web: www.ku.edu/~kuvsa

KENTUCKY

CULTURAL

CRANE HOUSE, THE ASIA INSTITUTE, INC.
1244 S. 3rd St.
Louisville, KY 40203
Lisa K. Work, Executive Director
Tel: (502) 635-2240 Fax: (502) 635-7659
Email: lisawork@insightbb.com
Web: www.cranehouse.org

TREENANEEL OF KENTUCKY
3403 Hanover Ct.
Louisville, KY 40207
Subhashis Satpathy, President

Tel: (502) 893-1619
Email: ssatpathy_us@yahoo.com
Web: www.treenaneel.org

POLITICAL ACTION

ORGANIZATION OF CHINESE AMERICANS
Kentuckiana Chapter
P.O. Box 7526
Louisville, KY 40257
Yong You, President
Tel: (502) 339-0399 Fax: (502) 339-7560
Email: ocaky@yahoo.com
Web: www.ocaky.org

PROFESSIONAL

CHINESE PROFESSIONALS AND ENTREPRENEURS ASSOCIATION
P.O. Box 32362
Louisville, KY 40232
Tel: (502) 637-0280
Email: cpaeimg@cpaea.org
Web: www.cpaeimg.org

RELIGIOUS

GRACE FELLOWSHIP CHURCH OF LOUISVILLE
8025 La Grange Rd.
Louiseville, KY 40222-4799
James Santos, Pastor
Tel: (502) 394-0113
Email: info@filipinochristians.org
Web: www.filipinochristians.org

SPEC. INT., CHILD CARE

FAMILIES WITH CHILDREN FROM CHINA
Louisville Chapter
3602 Trail Creek Place
Louisville, KY 40241
Web: www.pelec.com/fcclou.htm

SPEC. INT., EDUCATION

JAPANESE LANGUAGE SCHOOL OF GREATER CINCINNATI
Northern Kentucky University, BEP 102 Nunn Dr.
Highland Heights, KY 41099
Haruo Ishikawa, Principal
Tel: (859) 572-6197 Fax: (859) 572-6198
Email: jls_cinci@nku.edu
Web: www.jls-cincinnati.edu

US CHINA PEOPLES FRIENDSHIP ASSOCIATION
Owensboro, KY/Evansville, IN Chapter
2253 Canonero Loop
Owensboro, KY 42301
Su-hwa Winny Lin, Contact
Tel: (270) 685-7045
Web: www.uscpfa.org

SPEC. INT., SOCIAL INTEREST

CENTRAL KENTUCKY JEWISH FEDERATION
1050 Chinoe Rd. #203
Lexington, KY 40502
Tel: (859) 268-0672 Fax: (859) 268-0775
Email: lexadmin@jewishlexington.org
Web: www.jewishlexington.org

JAPAN-AMERICA SOCIETY OF KENTUCKY
3070 Harrodsburg Rd.
Lexington, KY 40503
Tel: (859) 224-7001 Fax: (859) 224-7033
Email: info@jask.org
Web: www.jask.org

JEWISH COMMUNITY CENTER OF LOUISVILLE
3600 Dutchmans Ln.

Louisville, KY 40205
Gary Bernstein, Executive Director
Tel: (502) 459-0660
Email: jewishcenter@jccoflouisville.org
Web: www.jccoflouisville.org

JEWISH COMMUNITY FEDERATION OF LOUISVILLE, INC.

3630 Dutchmans Ln.
Louisville, KY 40205
Tel: (502) 451-8840 Fax: (502) 458-0702
Email: jfed@iglou.com
Web: www.jewishlouisville.org

JEWISH FAMILY & VOCATIONAL SERVICE

3587 Dutchmans Ln.
Louisville, KY 40205
Judy Freundlich Tiell, Acting Executive Director
Tel: (502) 452-6341 Fax: (502) 452-6718
Email: jfvs@jfvs.com
Web: www.jfvs.com

KENTUCKY TAI CHI CHUAN CENTER

P.O. Box 1053
Versailles, KY 40383
William Wojasinski, Instructor
Tel: (859) 879-9434
Email: bill@kentuckytaichi.com
Web: www.kentuckytaichi.com

SPEC. INT., WOMEN

NATIONAL COUNCIL FOR JEWISH WOMEN

Louisville Section
1250 Bardstown Rd., Midcity Mall
Louisville, KY 40204-1333
Sandy Friedson, President
Tel: (502) 458-5566 Fax: (502) 458-5516
Email: office@ncjwlou.org
Web: www.ncjwlou.org

LOUISIANA

ARTISTIC

JAPANESE GARDEN SOCIETY OF NEW ORLEANS, INC.

P.O. Box 850-465
New Orleans, LA 70185-0465
Jack P. Strong, President
Tel: (504) 568-6033
Email: president@jgsneworleans.org
Web: www.jgsneworleans.org

CULTURAL

FILIPINO AMERICAN ASSOCIATION OF ST. TAMMANY

P.O. Box 4107
Slidell, LA 70459
Zenaida Dhir, President
Email: webmaster@faast.itgo.com
Web: www.faast.itgo.com

INDONESIAN AMERICAN COMMUNITY ASSOCIATION

3837 Sue Ker Dr.
Harvey, LA 70058
Dr. Sofjan Lamid, President
Tel: (504) 245-1185 Fax: (504) 245-8144
Email: iacaneworleans@yahoo.com
Web: www.iacaneworleans.tripod.com

KOREAN WAR VETERANS ASSOCIATION

1144-A Jim Meyer Dr.
Alexandria, LA 71303
Louis T. Dechert, President
Tel: (318) 445-1035
Email: dechertusa@earthlink.net
Web: www.kwva.org

PROFESSIONAL

CHINESE PROFESSIONALS ASSOCIATION OF NEW ORLEANS

5205 Avron Blvd.

Metairie, LA 70006
Lucy Chun, Treasurer
Tel: (504) 455-8185 Fax: (504) 455-8185
Email: chun8@aol.com

NATIONAL ARAB AMERICAN MEDICAL ASSOCIATION

Southern Chapter/Alabama, Louisiana, Mississippi
5107 Mallard Dr.
Alexandria, LA 71303
Alaa Younes, Chapter President
Tel: (318) 767-0960 Fax: (318) 767-0610
Email: ayounes@bellsouth.net
Web: www.naama.com

SOCIETY OF IRANIAN ARCHITECTS AND PLANNERS

P.O. Box 241810
Los Angeles, LA 90024
Mohamad Reza Borghei, President
Tel: (310) 726-4411
Email: moborghei@yahoo.com
Web: www.siap.org

RELIGIOUS

ASIA BAPTIST CHURCH

1400 Sere St.
New Orleans, LA 70122-1506
Robert
Tel: (504) 283-9293 Fax: (504) 283-4292

CHINESE CHRISTIAN CHURCH OF BATON ROUGE

10011 Old Hammond Hwy.
Baton Rouge, LA 70816
Rev. K.C. Chen, Senior Pastor
Tel: (225) 927-3239 Fax: (225) 927-4392
Email: kli@selu.edu
Web: www.cccbr.org

CHINESE PRESBYTERIAN CHURCH

2901 W. Esplanade Ave.
Kenner, LA 70065
Lila Crotty, Interim Secretary
Tel: (504) 461-0702 Fax: (504) 461-5435
Email: cpc_nola@bellsouth.net
Web: www.cpcnola.org

CONGREGATION B'NAI ISRAEL

3354 Kleinert Ave.
Baton Rouge, LA 70806
Victor E. Sachse, President
Tel: (225) 343-0111 Fax: (225) 343-0653
Email: office@bnai-israel.com
Web: www.bnai-israel.com

KOREAN BAPTIST CHURCH OF BATON ROUGE

264 Burgin Ave.
Baton Rouge, LA 70808
Rev. Jae Hoon So, Pastor
Tel: (225) 768-7700
Email: jaehoonso@cox.net
Web: www.geocities.com/brkbc

TEMPLE SINAI

6227 St. Charles Ave.
New Orleans, LA 70118
Gene Fendler, President
Tel: (504) 861-3693 Fax: (504) 861-3102
Email: sinai@usa.net
Web: www.templesinaino.org

VIETNAMESE HOPE BAPTIST CHURCH

7133 Greenwell Springs Rd.
Baton Rouge, LA 70805
Vinh T. Nguyen, Pastor
Tel: (225) 926-0605
Email: viethope@vietnamesehope.org
Web: www.vietnamesehope.org

SPEC. INT., CHILD CARE

FAMILIES WITH CHILDREN FROM CHINA

Louisiana Chapter
P.O. Box 7362
Metairie, LA 70010-7362
Jean Porche, President
Email: Info@FCCL.org
Web: www.fccl.org

SPEC. INT., SOCIAL INTEREST

ASIAN PACIFIC AMERICAN SOCIETY

3500 N. Causeway Blvd. #1548
Metairie, LA 70002
Sun Kim, Chairman
Tel: (504) 231-3109
Email: sunmkim@aol.com
Web: www.apasneworleans.com

JAPAN SOCIETY OF NEW ORLEANS

P.O. Box 56785
New Orleans, LA 70156
Ken Magee, President
Tel: (504) 905-6179 Fax: (504) 833-9778
Email: ken@thegatlinggroup.com

JEWISH COMMUNITY CENTER

5342 St. Charles Ave.
New Orleans, LA 70115
Lisa Gurk Herman, President
Tel: (504) 897-0143 Fax: (504) 897-1380
Email: info@nojcc.com
Web: www.nojcc.com

JEWISH COMMUNITY CENTERS ASSOCIATION

Southern Services Office
8200 Hampson St. #301
New Orleans, LA 70118
Tel: (504) 866-5090 Fax: (504) 866-8164
Email: anneisen@jcca.org
Web: www.jcca.org

JEWISH FAMILY SERVICE

3330 W. Esplanade Ave. #600
Metairie, LA 70002
Tel: (504) 831-8475 Fax: (504) 831-1130
Email: jfs@jfsneworleans.org
Web: www.jfsneworleans.org

JEWISH FEDERATION OF GREATER NEW ORLEANS

3747 W. Esplande Ave.
Metairie, LA 70002
Tel: (504) 780-5600 Fax: (504) 780-5601
Email: shalom@jewishnola.com
Web: www.jewishnola.com

NORTH LOUISIANA JEWISH FEDERATION

4700 Line Ave. #117
Shreveport, LA 71106
Tel: (318) 868-1200 Fax: (318) 868-1272
Email: nljfed@bellsouth.net
Web: www.nljfed.org

PEOPLE HELPING PEOPLE OF THE PHILIPPINES FOUNDATION, INC.

301 Orchard Dr.
Lake Charles, LA 70605
Tel: (832) 640-3727
Email: PHP@PHPFoundation.org
Web: www.phpfoundation.org

SPEC. INT., WOMEN

LOUISIANA ASIAN AMERICAN WOMEN'S CAUCUS

5636 Janice Ave.
Kenner, LA 70065
Neela Kulkarni, Chairwoman
Tel: (504) 887-3100 Fax: (504) 887-5515
Email: neelak444@aol.com

SPEC. INT., YOUTH

JEWISH CHILDREN'S REGIONAL SERVICES

3500 N. Causeway Blvd. #1120

Metairie, LA 70002
Tel: (504) 828-6334 Fax: (504) 828-5255
Email: moreinfo@jcrsnola.org
Web: www.jcrs.org

MAINE

CULTURAL

MAINE FRIENDS OF TIBET

129 Smutty Ln.
Saco, ME 04072
Terry A. Frahlich, Administrative Contact
Tel: (207) 294-3377
Email: rebeccawing@reddawg.net
Web: www.mindfulnesscenter.org

VIETNAM TRIPLE DEUCE, INC.

P.O. Box 665
Norridgewock, ME 04957
Jim May
Tel: (207) 634-3355
Email: jlmay@tds.net
Web: www.vietnamtripledeuce.org

RELIGIOUS

TEMPLE BETH EL

400 Deering Ave.
Portland, ME 04103
Elaine Rosen, President
Tel: (207) 774-2649 Fax: (207) 774-7518
Web: www.templebethel-maine.org

SPEC. INT., CHILD CARE

MAINE FAMILIES WITH CHILDREN FROM ASIA

26 Hadfield Rd.
Minot, ME 04258
Susan Greenwood, President
Email: susangreenwood@mefca.org
Web: www.mefca.org

SPEC. INT., EDUCATION

CAMBODIAN ARTS AND SCHOLARSHIP FOUNDATION

P.O. Box 18186
Portland, ME 04112
Email: Info@cambodianscholarship.org
Web: www.cambodianscholarship.org

US CHINA PEOPLES FRIENDSHIP ASSOCIATION

Portland, Maine Chapter
18 Ocean View Rd.
Cape Elizabet, ME 04107
Ellen Van Fleet, Contact
Tel: (207) 767-4175
Web: www.uscpfa.org

SPEC. INT., SOCIAL INTEREST

JAPAN AMERICA SOCIETY OF MAINE

P.O. Box 8461
Portland, ME 04104-8641
Lucy Sloan, Contact
Tel: (207) 771-0224
Email: takara@prexar.com
Web: www.maine-japan.org

JEWISH COMMUNITY ALLIANCE OF SOUTHERN MAINE

57 Ashmont St.
Portland, ME 04103
Charlie Miller, President
Tel: (207) 772-1959 Fax: (207) 772-2234
Email: info@mainejewish.org
Web: www.mainejewish.org

JEWISH COMMUNITY COUNCIL OF BANGOR

6 State St. #314
Bangor, ME 04401

Tel: (207) 941-2950
Email: info@jccbangormaine.org
Web: www.jccbangormaine.org

MARYLAND

ARTISTIC

ANATOLIAN ARTISANS, INC.
11325 Empire Ln.
North Bethesda, MD 20852
Yildiz Yagci, President/CEO
Tel: (301) 231-8128 Fax: (301) 231-6668
Email: info@anatolianartisans.org
Web: www.anatolianartisans.org

CHINESE AMERICAN MUSIC SOCIETY
P.O. Box 922
Bowie, MD 20715
Robert Kwok, President
Tel: (301) 262-8012 Fax: (301) 262-1228

CHINESE HOLOCAUST MUSEUM IN THE UNITED STATES, INC.
10720 Tuckahoe
Gaithersburg, MD 20878
Email: rycgsh@ritvax.isc.rit.edu
Web: www.chineseholocaust.com

KOREAN CONCERT SOCIETY
P.O. Box 60341
Potomac, MD 20859
Dr. Benjamin Whang, President
Tel: (703) 821-2852
Email: ybbwhang@koreanconcertsociety.org
Web: www.koreanconcertsociety.org

WASHINGTON TOHO KOTO SOCIETY
10230 Green Forest Dr.
Silver Spring, MD 20903-1536
Kyoko Okamoto, President & Music Director
Tel: (301) 434-4487 Fax: (301) 431-3346
Email: info@kotosociety.org
Web: www.kotosociety.org

BUSINESS

ASIAN AMERICAN BUSINESS ROUNDTABLE
20224 Thunderhead Way
Germantown, MD 20874
Rawlein G. Soberano, Ph.D., President
Tel: (301) 601-9038 Fax: (301) 601-9430
Email: info@aabronline.org
Web: www.aabronline.org

MARYLAND-CHINA BUSINESS COUNCIL, INC.
7201 Wisconsin Ave. #703
Bethesda, MD 20814
Clay E. Hickson, President/Chairman
Tel: (410) 451-0025
Web: www.mcbc.net

METROPOLITAN WASHINGTON CHINESE RESTAURANTS ASSOCIATION
6701 Democracy Blvd. #300
Bethesda, MD 20817
Joseph Shao, President
Tel: (301) 365-9600 Fax: (301) 365-4218
Email: jws@dragonbridge.com

THE JEWISH CENTER FOR BUSINESS DEVELOPMENT
1515 Reisterstown Rd.
Baltimore, MD 21208
Tel: (410) 653-5763 Fax: (410) 486-0957
Email: info@jcbd.org
Web: www.jcbd.org

US ASIA COMMERCIAL DEVELOPMENT CORPORATION
P.O. Box 1290
Burtonsville, MD 20866
Joanne Littlefair, Contact
Tel: (202) 835-1735 Fax: (202) 835-1737
Web: www.usasia.com

WORLD TRADE CENTER INSTITUTE
401 E. Pratt St. #232
Baltimore, MD 21202
Deborah M. Kielty, President/Executive Director
Tel: (410) 576-0022 Fax: (410) 576-0751
Web: www.wtci.org

CHAMBER OF COMMERCE

ARAB AMERICAN CHAMBER OF COMMERCE, MARYLAND
972 Mount Holly Dr. #21401
Annapolis, MD 21401
Jessica Lee, Executive Director
Tel: (410) 757-5544 Fax: (202) 521-1806
Web: www.arabchamber.org

CULTURAL

CAMBODIAN AMERICAN HERITAGE, INC.
12911 Canoe Ct.
Fort Washington, MD 20744
Saroeum Tes, President
Tel: (301) 292-6862 Fax: (703) 370-8980
Email: saroeumtes@aol.com
Web: www.cambodianheritage.org

CHHANDAYAN - THE TEMPLE OF RHYTHM
11112 Candle Light Ln.
Potomac, MD 20854
Samir Chatterjee, Director
Tel: (301) 983-8870
Email: samir@tabla.org
Web: www.tabla.org

IRAN CULTURAL AND EDUCATIONAL CENTER
12030 Gatewater Dr.
Potomac, MD 20854
Tel: (301) 545-0143
Email: info@iraneducationalcenter.org
Web: www.iraneducationalcenter.org

IRANIAN-AMERICAN CULTURE SOCIETY OF MARYLAND
P.O. Box 9844
Towson, MD 21284-9844
Mahvash Shahegh, President
Tel: (410) 720-4507
Email: webmaster@iacs-md.org
Web: www.iacs-md.org

JEWISH HUMANISTS OF GREATER WASHINGTON CONGREGATION BETH CHAI
6301 River Rd.
Bethesda, MD 20817
Arthur Blecher
Tel: (301) 229-7400 Fax: (301) 255-8210
Email: info@bethchai.org
Web: www.bethchai.org

JEWISH MUSEUM OF MARYLAND, INC.
15 Lloyd St.
Baltimore, MD 21202
Tel: (410) 732-6400 Fax: (410) 732-6451
Email: info@jewishmuseummd.org
Web: www.jhsm.org

KET DOAN ASSOCIATION
P.O. Box 2452
Rockville, MD 20847-2452
La Hong Ly, President
Email: info@ketdoan.org
Web: ww.ketdoan.org

TAIWANESE ASSOCIATION OF AMERICA
P.O. Box 34563
West Bethesda, MD 20817
Tom Yang, President
Tel: (703) 333-5755 Fax: (703) 333-5755
Email: taagwc@yahoo.com
Web: www.taagwc.org

THE ASSOCIATIONS OF NEPALIS IN AMERICA
9114 Margo Rd.
Lanham, MD 20706

Krishna Nirola, President
Email: ana@ana-home.org
Web: www.ana-home.org

ENTERTAINMENT

ADVANCEMENT & PROMOTION OF CHARITABLE ACTIVITIES
7005 Brickyard Rd.
Potomac, MD 20854
Jatinder Kumar
Tel: (301) 299-6463
Email: kumar@apca-usa.org
Web: www.apca-usa.org

MULTI-PURPOSE

CHINA FOUNDATION, INC.
Washington DC Area Office
9216 Falls Chapel Way
Potomac, MD 20854
Jane H. Hu, Ph.D., Chairman
Tel: (301) 340-2065
Email: info@chinafoundation.net
Web: www.chinafoundation.net

THE ASSOCIATED: JEWISH COMMUNITY FEDERATION OF BALTIMORE
101 W. Royal Ave.
Baltimore, MD 21201-5728
Tel: (410) 727-4828 Fax: (410) 837-1327
Email: contact@associated.org
Web: www.associated.org

TIBETAN MEDITATION CENTER
9301 Gambrill Park Rd.
Frederick, MD 21702
Khenchen Konchog Gyaltshen, Spiritual Director
Tel: (301) 473-5750
Web: www.drikungtmc.org

POLITICAL ACTION

AFGHANS FOR CIVIL SOCIETY
806 N. Charles St.
Baltimore, MD 21201
Qayum Karzai, Founder & President
Tel: (410) 385-1445 Fax: (410) 385-1475
Email: baltimore@afghansforcivilsociety.org
Web: www.afghansforcivilsociety.org

INDO-AMERICAN FORUM FOR POLITICAL EDUCATION
13500 Stonebridge Terr.
Germantown, MD 20874
Y.N. Gupta, President
Tel: (301) 428-1783
Web: www.nfia.net

MARYLAND GOVERNOR'S OFFICE IN ASIAN PACIFIC AFFAIRS
311 W. Saratoga St. #278
Baltimore, MD 21201
Agnes M. Smith, Executive Administrator
Tel: (410) 767-7491 Fax: (410) 333-3980
Email: mdapa@dhr.state.md.us
Web: www.dhr.state.md.us

ORGANIZATION OF CHINESE AMERICANS- GREATER WASHINGTON D.C.
P.O. Box 34943
Bethesda, MD 20817
Sharon Wong, President
Tel: (703) 625-6197 Fax: (410) 798-9437
Email: oca-dc@att.net
Web: www.ocadc.org

PROFESSIONAL

ASIAN PACIFIC AMERICAN BAR ASSOCIATION
Maryland Chapter
6063 Charles Edward Terr.

Columbia, MD 21045
Melissa Shin, President
Tel: (410) 884-3527 Fax: (410) 884-3527
Email: melissashin@yahoo.com

ASSOCIATION OF NIST ASIAN-PACIFIC AMERICANS
National Institute of Standards and Technology
100 Bureau Dr., M/S #8520
Gaithersburg, MD 20899-8520
Wong-Ng, Doctor, Ph.D.
Tel: (301) 975-5791 Fax: (301) 975-5334
Email: winnie.wong-ng@nist.gov
Web: www.nist.gov/anapa

NATIONAL ASSOCIATON OF PROFESSIONAL ASIAN AMERICAN WOMEN (NAPAW)
18627 Carriage Walk Cir.
Gaithersburg, MD 20879
Tel: (301)869-8288
Web: www.napaw.com

PHILIPPINE AMERICAN ACADEMY OF SCIENCE AND ENGINEERING
16609 Cutlass Dr.
Rockville, MD 20853-1333
Prof. Carlito Lebrilla, Ph.D., President
Tel: (301) 924-2242
Email: hope.celso@verizon.net
Web: www.paase.org

PHILIPPINE AMERICAN BAR ASSOCIATION
5900 89th Ave.
New Carrolton, MD 20784-2820
Ed Edatienza, President
Tel: (301) 952-2622 Fax: (301) 952-2965
Email: ededatienza@dtscs.state.md.us
Web: www.paba-dc.org

THE CHINESE-AMERICAN PROFESSIONALS ASSOCIATION OF METROPOLITAN WASHINGTON D.C.
P.O. Box 341682
Bethesda, MD 20827
David Su, Board of Director
Tel: (301) 926-8450 Fax: (301) 590-0932
Email: dsu@nist.gov
Web: www.capadc.net

RELIGIOUS

BURMA AMERICA BUDDHIST ASSOCIATION
1708 Powder Mill Rd.
Silver Spring, MD 20903
Tel: (301) 439-4035
Web:

CAMBODIAN BUDDHIST SOCIETY, INC.
13800 New Hampshire Ave.
Silver Spring, MD 20904
Dr. Sovan Tun
Tel: (301) 622-6544
Email: sovantun@cambodian-buddhist.org
Web: www.cambodian-buddhist.org

CHINESE CHRISTIAN CHURCH OF GREATER WASHINGTON DC
7716 Piney Branch Rd.
Silver Spring, MD 20910
James Sun, Pastor
Tel: (3010 587-0033 Fax: (301) 587-0438
Email: info@cccgw.org
Web: www.forministry.com/ USMDINDPTCCCOG

CHINMAYA
Kailas Niwas
46 Norwood Rd.
Silver Spring, MD 20905
Swami Dheeranandaji, Resident Acharya
Tel: (301) 384-5009 Fax: (301) 384-1204
Email: anil.kishore@verizon.net
Web: www.chinmayadc.org

COMMITTEE FOR RELIGIOUS FREEDOM IN VIETNAM
8001 Bradley Blvd.
Bethesda, MD 20817
Shandon Phan, Staff
Tel: (301) 365-2489 Fax: (301) 365-5961
Email: crfv@crfvn.org
Web: http://crfvn.org

DHARMA REALM BUDDHIST ASSOCIATION
Avatamsaka Hermitage
11721 Beall Mountain Rd.
Potomac, MD 20854-1128
Tel: (301) 299-3693 Fax: (301) 299-3693
Web: www.drba.org/branches/

IRANIAN CHRISTIAN CHURCH
10613 Georgia Ave.
Silver Spring, MD 20902
Tel: (301) 649-7086 Fax: (301) 649-3053
Email: iccdc@farsinet.com
Web: www.farsinet.com/iccdc

JEWS FOR JESUS
Washington DC
11623 Nebel St.
Rockville, MD 20852
Stephen Katz, Chief of Station
Tel: (301) 770-4000 Fax: (301) 770-0900
Email: dc@jewsforjesus.org
Web: www.jfjonline.org

KOREAN BAPTIST CHURCH OF WASHINGTON
310 Randolph Rd.
Silver Spring, MD 20906
Tel: (301) 622-5375
Email: info@kbcw.org
Web: www.kbcw.org

KOREAN PRESBYTERIAN CHURCH OF ROCKVILLE
800 Hurley Ave.
Rockville, MD 20850
Rev. Jaemo Park, Pastor
Tel: (301) 838-0766 Fax: (301) 838-3060
Email: kpcrem@yahoo.com
Web: www.kpcr.org

KOREAN ZION PRESBYTERIAN CHURCH
9947 Harford Rd.
Baltimore, MD 21234
Tel: (410) 665-6432
Web: http://koreanzionpresbyterianchurch.cjb.net/

LAUREL FILIPINO CHURCH OF GOD
613 Montgomery St.
Laurel, MD 20707
Rev. Mariano Gabor, Pastor
Tel: (301) 839-6322
Web: www.filipinochristian.org

MISSIONARIES TO ASIA
16817 National Pike
Hagerstown, MD 21740
Billy Taylor, Bishop
Tel: (301) 665-9595
Email: missionaries@missionariestoasia.com
Web: www.missionariestoasia.com

SOUTHERN ASIA ADVENTIST ASSOCIATION
P.O. Box 4818
Silver Spring, MD 20914
Krupavaram Meesarapu, President
Tel: (301) 236-4741
Email: president@saaa.org
Web: www.saaa.org

ST. THOMAS SYRIAN ORTHODOX CHURCH
28201 Kemptown Rd.
Damascus, MD 20872
Tel: (301) 253-4300
Email: syrianorthodox@yahoo.com
Web: www.geocities.com/syrianorthodox

TEMPLE EMANUEL OF BALTIMORE
909 Berrymans Ln.
Reistertown, MD 21136
Richard A. Fishkin, Executive Director
Tel: (410) 526-3676
Web: www.templeemanuelofbaltimore.org

TEMPLE EMANUEL OF MARYLAND
10101 Connecticut Ave.
Kensington, MD 20895
Esther Starobin, President
Tel: (301) 942-2000 Fax: (301) 942-9488
Email: erstarobin@msn.com
Web: www.templeemanuelmd.org

UNITED SYNAGOGUE OF CONSERVATIVE JUDAISM
Seaboard Region
121 Congressional Ln. #210
Rockville, MD 20852
Jerold L. Jacobs, President
Tel: (301) 230-0801 Fax: (301) 816-2931
Email: jlj@cohnmarks.com
Web: www.uscj.org/seabd

RESEARCH

JEWISH GENEALOGICAL SOCIETY OF GREATER WASHINGTON
P.O. Box 31122
Bethesda, MD 20824-1122
Sharlene Kranz, President
Tel: (301) 365-4546
Email: skranz_99@yahoo.com
Web: www.jewishgen.org/jgsgw/

SCIENTIFIC

INSTITUTE FOR ENERGY AND ENVIRONMENTAL RESEARCH
6935 Laurel Ave. #201
Takoma Park, MD 20912
Arjun Makhijani, President
Tel: (301) 270-5500 Fax: (301) 270-3029
Web: www.ieer.org

NIH- KOREAN SCIENTISTS ASSOCIATION
6001 Executive Blvd.
Bethesda, MD 20892
Moo Park, President
Tel: (301) 443-9813
Email: moo_park@nih.gov

SCIENCE AND ARTS FOUNDATION
1010 Rockville Pike #506
Rockville, MD 20852
Tel: (301) 340-2525 Fax: (301) 340-6848
Email: info@safusa.org
Web: www.science-arts.org

SPEC. INT., CHILD CARE

CHILDREN OF PERSIA
P.O. Box 2602
Montgomery Village, MD 20886
Shiva Davoodpour, President
Tel: (301) 315-0750
Email: info@childrenofpersia.org
Web: www.childrenofpersia.org

TURKISH CHILDREN FOSTER CARE
730 Ticonderoga Ave.
Severna Park, MD 21146
Tel: (410) 647-1315
Email: TCFC76@aol.com
Web: www.turkishchildren.org

SPEC. INT., COUNSELING

JEWS FOR JUDAISM, INC.
Baltimore/Washington DC
P.O. Box 15059
Baltimore, MD 21282
Scott Hillman, Director
Tel: (410) 602-0276 Fax: (410) 602-0578
Email: baltimore@jewsforjudaism.org
Web: www.jewsforjudaism.org

SPEC. INT., EDUCATION

AHIMSA YOUTH ORGANIZATION
24 Rockcrest Cir.
Rockville, MD 20851
Email: ahimsayouth@hotmail.com
Web: www.ayo.org

ASIA PACIFIC LEGAL INSTITUTE
4432 Prancing Deer Dr.
Ellicott City, MD 21043-6785
Paul Chang-Bin Liu, President
Tel: (410) 480-4895 Fax: (410) 480-4896
Email: apli@apli.org
Web: www.apli.org

ASIAN AMERICAN STUDIES PROGRAM
University of Maryland
1122 Cole Field House
College Park, MD 20742
Seung-Kyung Kim, Director
Tel: (301) 405-0996 Fax: (301) 314-6575
Web: www.aast.umd.edu

ASIAN CLASSICS INPUT PROJECT
Washington DC Area Office
11911 Marmary Rd.
Gaithersburg, MD 20878-1839
Robert J. Taylor, Asst. Director
Tel: (301) 948-5569 Fax: (301) 349-2623
Email: acip@comcast.net
Web: www.asianclassics.org

BALTIMORE HEBREW UNIVERSITY
5800 Park Heights Ave.
Baltimore, MD 21215
Rela Mintz Geffen, Ph.D., President
Tel: (888) 248-7420
Email: bhu@bhu.edu
Web: www.bhu.edu

BOYS TOWN JERUSALEM FOUNDATION OF AMERICA, INC.
Baltimore Office
3823 Labyrinth Rd.
Baltimore, MD 21215
Rabbi David Herman, Director
Tel: (410) 358-3814 Fax: (410) 585-1513
Email: btjny@compuserve.com
Web: www.boystownjerusalem.com

CHINESE LANGUAGE SCHOOL OF COLUMBIA
P.O. Box 1292
Ellicott City, MD 21041
Richard Kuan, Principal
Email: rkuan@swales.com
Web: www.clscweb.org

FOUNDATION FOR IRANIAN STUDIES
4343 Montgomery Ave.
Bethesda, MD 20814
Tel: (301) 657-1990 Fax: (301) 657-1983
Email: fis@fis-iran.org
Web: www.fis-iran.org

GAITHERSBURG CHINESE SCHOOL
P.O. Box 83627
Gaithersburg, MD 20883
Principal Lin
Tel: (301) 519-1777
Email: gaithersburgchineseschool@yahoo.com
Web: www.gaithersburgchineseschool.org

HOPE CHINESE SCHOOL
College Park Campus
P.O. Box 881
College Park, MD 20741
Jizhong Chen, Principal
Tel: (410) 715-6870
Email: jizhongchen@hotmamil.com
Web: www.hopechineseschool.org

Gaithersburg Campus
Northwest High School, 13501 Richter Farm Rd.
Germantown, MD 20874

Yili Yang, Principal
Tel: (301) 980-4623
Email: yangyili@ncifcrf.gov
Web: www.hopechineseschool.org

Rockville Campus
11713 Tifton Dr.
Potomac, MD 20854
Shanying Li, Principal
Tel: (301) 765-9574
Email: lishanying@aol.com
Web: www.hopechineseschool.org

IRANIAN AMERICAN TECHNOLOGY COUNCIL, INC.
849 Quince Orchard Blvd. #C
Gaithersburg, MD 20878
Fred Korangy, Board Of Director
Tel: (800) 788-7824
Email: info@iatc.us
Web: www.iatc.us

JEWISH LITERACY FOUNDATION, INC.
17 Warren Rd. #18
Pikesville, MD 21208
Yigal Segal, Executive Director
Tel: (877) 554-8372 Fax: (410) 602-4033
Email: yigal@jewishliteracy.org
Web: www.jewishliteracy.org

MEI-HWA CHINESE SCHOOL
P.O. Box 10638
Silver Spring, MD 20914-4264
Yen-Wu Chen, Chairman
Tel: (301) 317-9455
Email: contact@meihwa.org
Web: www.meihwa.org

NEPAL EDUCATION AND CULTURAL CENTER
9114 Margo Rd.
Lanham, MD 20706
Tel: (301) 552-2299

PANIM: THE INSTITUTE FOR JEWISH LEADERSHIP AND VALUES
6101 Montrose Rd. #200
Rockville, MD 20852
Rabbi Sydney Schwarz, Founder/President
Tel: (301) 770-5070 Fax: (301) 770-6365
Email: info@panim.org
Web: www.panim.org

ROCKVILLE CHINESE SCHOOL
14501 Good Earth Ct.
Rockville, MD 20850
Lily Fang, Principal
Tel: (301) 738-8495
Email: rcsmd1@yahoo.com
Web: www.rcsmd.org

SPEC. INT., EMPLOYMENT

ASIAN AND PACIFIC ISLANDER AMERICAN ORGANIZATION
c/o NIH/NLM Bldg. 38A #B1 W08G, 8600 Rockville Pike
Bethesda, MD 20894
Dar-Ning Kung Ph.D., President
Tel: (301) 435-8628 Fax: (301) 480-3127
Email: kungd@mail.nlm.nih.gov
Web: www.recgov.org/r&w/apao/index.htm

GLOBAL ALLIANCE FOR WORKERS AND COMMUNITIES
32 S St. #500
Baltimore, MD 21202
Carol O' Laughlin, Executive Director
Tel: (410) 951-1500
Email: carol@iyfnet.org
Web: www.theglobalalliance.org

JEWISH VOCATIONAL SERVICE
1515 Reisterstown Rd.
Baltimore, MD 21208
Jennie Z. Rothschild, Executive Director
Tel: (410) 486-0099 Fax: (410) 486-0957

Email: careers@jvsbaltimore.org
Web: www.jvsbaltimore.org

SPEC. INT., HEALTH SERVICES

COUNSELORS HELPING ASIAN INDIANS
4517 Redleaf Ct.
Ellicott City, MD 21043
Razia F. Kosi, President
Tel: (410) 461-1634
Email: raziachai@hotmail.com
Web: www.geocities.com/raziachai/content.html

PAKISTAN PUBLIC HEALTH FOUNDATION
615 N. Wolfe St. #E8035
Baltimore, MD 21205
Rashid A. Chotani, President
Tel: (410) 614-8330 Fax: (410) 614-1419
Email: rchotani@jhsph.edu
Web: www.pphf.org

THE SOUTH ASIAN PUBLIC HEALTH ASSOCIATION
11200 Lockwood Dr. #1207
Silver Spring, MD 20901
Abhijit Ghosh, Co-Chair
Fax: (520) 844-1254
Email: info@sapha.net
Web: www.sapha.net

SPEC. INT., HOUSING

CALVERT FOUNDATION
4550 Montgomery Ave.
Bethesda, MD 20814
Shari Berenbach, Executive Director
Tel: (800) 248-0337 Fax: (301) 654-7820
Email: foundation@calvert.com
Web: www.calvertfoundation.org

SPEC. INT., HUMAN RELATIONS

COALITION OF ASIAN PACIFIC AMERICAN DEMOCRATS OF MARYLAND
9913 Dickens Ave.
Bethesda, MD 20814
Man Cho, Chairman
Tel: (301) 564-4592 Fax: (301) 564-4592
Email: capamd@yahoo.com

COUNCIL ON AMERICAN-ISLAMIC RELATIONS
Maryland Chapter
7752 Woodmont Ave. #213
Bethesda, MD 20814
Seyed Rizwan Mowlana, Executive Director
Tel: (301) 986-1900 Fax: (301) 986-8772
Email: info@cairmd.org
Web: www.cairmd.org

INDIA DEVELOPMENT AND RELIEF FUND
Maryland Chapter
5821 Mossrock Dr.
N. Bethesda, MD 20852-3238
Tel: (301) 984-2127 Fax: (301) 984-2127
Email: sandt@wile.thetech.org
Web: www.indolink.com/Orgs/idrfHome.html#BeginIDRF

ISLAMIC-AMERICAN ZAKAT FOUNDATION
4323 Rosedale Ave.
Bethesda, MD 20814
Imad A. Ahmad, President
Email: zakat@iazf.org
Web: www.iazf.org

JEWISH RECONSTRUCTIONIST FEDERATION
Chesapeake Region
8409 Snowden Loop Ct.
Laurel, MD 20708
Jackie Land, Regional Director
Tel: (301) 206-3332
Email: jland@jrf.org
Web: www.jrf.org

KOREAN AMERICAN COMMUNITY SERVICES, INC.
969 Thayer Ave.
Silver Spring, MD 20910
Tae Park, Executive Director
Tel: (301) 589-6470 Fax: (301) 589-4724

MARYLAND VIETNAMESE MUTUAL ASSOCIATION
11501 Georgia Ave. #312
Wheaton, MD 20902
Phu Le, Director
Tel: (301) 946-7911 Fax: (301) 942-1257
Email: president@mdvietmutual.org
Web: www.mdvietmutual.org

NATIONAL FEDERATION OF INDIAN-AMERICAN ASSOCIATIONS
9000 Acredale Ct.
College Park, MD 20740
Parthasarthy Pillai, President
Tel: (301) 935-5321 Fax: (301) 935-2627
Email: PPillai1@aol.com
Web: www.fiancr.org

NFIA- NATIONAL FEDERATION OF INDIAN-AMERICAN ASSOCIATIONS
Headquarters
319 Summit Hall Rd.
Gaithersburg, MD 20877
Niraj Baxi, President
Tel: (301) 926-3013 Fax: (301) 926-3378
Email: info@nfia.net
Web: www.nfia.net

NORTH SOUTH FOUNDATION
Maryland Region
6405 Brass Bucket Ct.
Laytonsville, MD 20882
Dr. Murali Gavini
Tel: (301) 947-2702
Email: mbg299@worldnet.att.net
Web: www.northsouth.org

PAKISTANI AMERICAN PUBLIC AFFAIRS COMMITTEE
7350 Vandusen Rd. #450
Laurel, MD 20707
Email: info@pakpac.net
Web: www.pakpac.net

SIKH MEDIAWATCH AND RESOURCE TASK FORCE
P.O. Box 1761
Germantown, MD 20875-1761
Manjeeet Singh
Tel: (877) 917-4547 Fax: (202) 318-4433
Email: info@sikhmediawatch.org
Web: www.sikhmediawatch.org

THE AMERICAN JEWISH COMMITTEE
Baltimore Chapter
20 S. Charles St., 4th Fl.
Baltimore, MD 21201-3220
Lois Rosenfield, Chapter President
Tel: (410) 539-4777 Fax: (410) 752-2905
Email: baltimore@ajc.org
Web: www.ajc.org

VIETNAM VETERANS OF AMERICA
8605 Cameron St. #400
Silver Spring, MD 20910
Tel: (800) 882-1316
Email: membership@vva.org
Web: www.vva.org

SPEC. INT., IMMIGRATION

NATIONAL ALLIANCE OF VIETNAMESE AMERICAN SERVICE AGENCIES
1010 Wayne Ave. #310
Silver Spring, MD 20910
Huy Bui, Executive Director
Tel: (301) 587-2781 Fax: (301) 587-2783
Email: navasa@navasa.org
Web: www.navasa.org

SPEC. INT., INFORMATION REFERRAL

CHINA NEWS DIGEST INTERNATIONAL, INC.
P.O. Box 10111
Gaithersburg, MD 20898-0111
Email: webmaster@cnd.org
Web: www.cnd.org

VIETNAMESE ASSOCIATION FOR COMPUTING, ENGINEERING, TECHNOLOGY AND SCIENCE
P.O. Box 2583
Silver Spring, MD 20915-2583
Hai Tran, President
Tel: (212) 387-9679 Fax: (212) 387-9679
Email: vacets-adcom@vacets.org
Web: www.vacets.org

SPEC. INT., SENIORS

PHILIPPINE HOME FOR SENIOR CITIZENS
6482 Bock Rd.
Oxon Hill, MD 20745
Abby Myers, Manager
Tel: (301) 567-9537 Fax: (301) 567-2000
Email: mrsphilippines@humphreycompanies.com

SPEC. INT., SOCIAL INTEREST

ASSOCIATION FOR INDIA'S DEVELOPMENT
Baltimore Chapter, Maryland
202, UC University of Maryland Baltimore County, 1000 Hilltop Cir.
Baltimore, MD 21250
Poonam Munshi, Contact
Email: aid_baltimore@yahoogroups.com
Web: www.aidindia.org/baltimore

College Park Chapter
P.O. Box F
College Park, MD 20741
Mohan Bhagat
Tel: (888) 825-5224 Fax: (301) 314-9465
Email: info@aidindia.org
Web: www.aidindia.org

BANGLADESHI-AMERICAN FOUNDATION, INC.
11021 Brent Rd.
Potomac, MD 20854
Badrul Haque, Chairperson
Tel: (301) 299-3770
Email: Badrulhaque@hotmail.com
Web: ww.bafi.org

CHESAPEAKE BAY AREA FRIENDS OF TIBET
P.O. Box 963
Havre de Grace, MD 21078
Davida Gypsy Breier, Contact
Tel: (410) 273-7146 Fax: (410) 273-7146
Email: davida@leekinginc.com
Web: www.leekinginc.com

CHINESE AMERICAN CITIZENS ALLIANCE
2421 Kaywood Ln.
Silver Spring, MD 20905
David Leong, President
Tel: (301) 236-9359 Fax: (775) 255-0368
Email: leong3us@starpower.net

CHINESE CULTURE AND COMMUNITY SERVICE CENTER, INC.
16039 Comprint Cir.
Gaithersburg, MD 20877
Linda Lee, Executive Director
Tel: (240) 631-1200 Fax: (240) 631-2468
Email: ccacc@ccacc-dc.org
Web: www.ccacc-dc.org

COUNCIL OF ASIAN INDIAN ASSOCIATIONS OF GREATER WASHINGTON, INC.
1021 University Blvd. East
Silver Spring, MD 20903

Koshy Samuel, President
Tel: (301) 384-2441 Fax: (301) 384-2441
Email: caia@caiawashington.org
Web: www.caiawashington.org

FILIPINO-AMERICAN ASSOCIATION
St. Mary's County
22688 Avenmar Dr.
Leonard Town, MD 20650
Jose Aguinaldo, President
Tel: (301) 475-2084

IRAN FREEDOM FOUNDATION, INC.
P.O. Box 3422
Bethesda, MD 20817
M.R. Tabatabai, President
Tel: (301) 907-8877
Email: tabamr@gte.net
Web: www.iffmrt.org

JEWISH COMMUNITY CENTER OF GREATER WASHINGTON
6125 Montrose Rd.
Rockville, MD 20852
Arnie Sohinki, CEO
Tel: (301) 881-0100
Email: asohinki@jccgw.org
Web: www.jccgw.org

Owing Mills
3506 Gwynnbrook Ave.
Owing Mills, MD 21117
Tel: (410) 356-5200
Web: www.jcc.org

Park Heights
5700 Park Heights Ave.
Baltimore, MD 21215
Tel: (410) 542-4900
Web: www.jcc.org

JEWISH COMMUNITY COUNCIL OF GREATER WASHINGTON
6101 Montrose Rd. #205
Rockville, MD 20852
Tel: (301) 770-0881 Fax: (301) 770-7553
Email: jcouncil@jcouncil.org
Web: www.jcouncil.org

JEWISH FAMILY SERVICES OF CENTRAL MARYLAND
5750 Park Heights Ave.
Baltimore, MD 21215
Barbara Levy Gradet, Executive Director
Tel: (410) 466-9200 Fax: (410) 664-0551
Email: jfs@jfs.org
Web: www.jfs.org

JEWISH FEDERATION OF GREATER WASHINGTON
6101 Montrose Rd.
Rockville, MD 20852
Tel: (301) 230-7200 Fax: (301) 230-7265
Email: info@shalomdc.org
Web: www.shalomdc.org

JEWISH FEDERATION OF HOWARD COUNTY
8950 Route 108 #115
Columbia, MD 21045
Ruth Naftaly, Executive Board President
Tel: (410) 730-4976 Fax: (410) 730-9393
Email: jfohc@starpower.net
Web: www.jewishhowardcounty.org

JEWISH FOUNDATION FOR GROUP HOMES
6010 Executive Blvd. #800
Rockville, MD 20852
Vivian Bass, Executive Director
Tel: (301) 984-3839 Fax: (301) 770-0442
Email: jfgh@jfgh.org
Web: www.jfgh.org

JEWISH SOCIAL SERVICE AGENCY
6123 Montrose Rd.
Rockville, MD 20852
Joan De Pontet, Executive Director
Tel: (301) 881-3700
Email: jdepontet@jssa.org
Web: www.jssa.org

KERALA ASSOCIATION OF GREATER WASHINGTON
3305 Dunnington Rd.
Beltsville, MD 20705
Benoy Thomas, President
Tel: (301) 572-7855
Email: info@kagw.com
Web: www.kagw.com

KOREAN SERVICE CENTER OF GREATER WASHINGTON
Branch Office
217 Muddy Branch Rd.
Gaithersburg, MD 20878
Key Young Kim, Chairman
Tel: (301) 933-7010 Fax: (301) 933-7336
Email: kcsc_md@kcscgw.org
Web: www.kcscgw.org

MARINDUQUENO ASSOCIATION OF THE CAPITAL AREA
9828 Bristol Ave.
Silver Spring, MD 20901
Gaudioso Sore, President
Tel: (301) 681-6751
Email: dio_loyda@hotmail.com
Web: www.macadc.org

MARYLAND AMERICAN TURKISH ASSOCIATION
10176 Baltimore National Pike #211
Ellicott City, MD 21042
Tel: (410) 750-7735 Fax: (410) 750-3158
Email: info@atamd.org
Web: www.atamd.org

PAKISTAN ASSOCIATION OF GREATER WASHINGTON METROPOLITAN AREA, INC.
P.O. Box 8466
Gaithersburg, MD 20898-8466
Mohammad Siddique, President
Email: pakistan_association@yahoo.com
Web: www.geocities.com/pakistan_association/Organization.htm

REPUBLICAN ASIAN AMERICAN ALLIANCE
118 Water St.
Gaithersburg, MD 20877
Dr. John Tzeng, CEO
Tel: (301) 330-0639
Email: johntzeng@aol.com

SIKH COUNCIL ON RELIGION AND EDUCATION
Washington DC Office
2466 Reedie Dr. #14
Wheaton, MD 20902
Sher Singh, Director of Community Relations
Tel: (301) 946-2800 Fax: (301) 946-2800
Email: info@sikhcouncilusa.org
Web: www.sikhcouncilusa.org

TAIWAN ENVIRONMENTAL ACTION NETWORK
2144 Plant Sciences Bldg.
College Park, MD 20742
Shenglin Chang, Contact
Email: tean-com@formosa.org
Web: http://tean.formosa.org

WHITE HOUSE INITIATIVE ON ASIAN AMERICANS AND PACIFIC ISLANDERS
5600 Fishers Ln. #10-42
Rockville, MD 20857
Betty Lam, Community Liaision
Tel: (301) 443-0949 Fax: (301) 443-0259
Email: aapi@hrsa.gov
Web: www.aapi.gov

SPEC. INT., SPORTS

HOMENETMEN
Greater Washington DC
4906 Flint Dr.
Bethesda, MD 20816
Email: HMEMDC@HOMENETMEN-DC.COM
Web: www.homenetmen-dc.com

SPEC. INT., WOMEN

ASHA, INC.
P.O. Box 2084
Rockville, MD 20847
Nandini Assar, Ph.D., Executive Director
Tel: (202) 207-1248 Fax: (202) 296-2318
Email: asha@ashaforwomen.org
Web: www.ashaforwomen.org

ASIAN WOMEN'S SELF-HELP ASSOCIATION
P.O. Box 34303
W. Bethesda, MD 20827
Sheila Kelkar, Services Coordinator
Tel: (301) 369-0134
Email: asha@ashaforwomen.org
Web: www.ashaforwomen.org

HADASSAH
Greater Baltimore Chapter
3723 Old Court Rd. #205
Baltimore, MD 21208
Sharona Hoffman, President
Tel: (410) 484-9590 Fax: (410) 484-0161
Email: andrea.weiss@hadassah.org
Web: www.hadassah.org

Greater Washington Area Chapter
1220 East-West Hwy. #120
Silver Spring, MD 20910
Jane Nyce, President
Tel: (301) 585-7772 Fax: (301) 585-7775
Email: susan.zeidman@hadassah.org
Web: www.hadassah.org

LAO AMERICAN WOMEN ASSOCIATION
6807 Ingraham St.
Riverdale, MD 20737
Bounheng Inversin, President
Tel: (301) 306-0345 Fax: (301) 306-0345
Email: hanumahn@tidalwave.net

NATIONAL COUNCIL FOR JEWISH WOMEN
Montgomery County Section
13802 Dowlais Dr.
Rockville, MD 20853
Norma Krupenie, President
Tel: (301) 460-8382
Email: normakrup@hotmail.com
Web: www.ncjw.org

ORGANIZATION OF CHINESE AMERICAN WOMEN
4641 Montgomery Ave. #208
Bethesda, MD 20814
Rosetta Lai, National President
Tel: (301) 907-3898 Fax: (301) 907-3899
Email: ocawwomen@ocawwomen.org
Web: www.ocawwomen.org

SAMHATI
6108 Robinwood Rd.
Bethesda, MD 20817
Jahanara Hasan
Tel: (202) 342-8393
Web: www.umiacs.umd.edu/users/sawweb/sawnet/samhati.html

SPEC. INT., YOUTH

JEWISH YOUTH PHILANTHROPY INSTITUTE
6101 Montrose Rd. #202
Rockville, MD 20852
Eytan Hammerman, Director
Tel: (301) 348-7346 Fax: (301) 230-7232
Email: jypi@shalomdc.org
Web: www.jypi.org

OVERSEAS YOUNG CHINESE FORUM
11423 Potomac Oaks Dr.
Rockville, MD 20850
Hao Zou, President
Email: info@oycf.org
Web: www.oycf.org

STUDENT ORGANIZATION

ASIAN AMERICAN STUDENT UNION
University of Maryland
3112 Stamp Student Union
College Park, MD 20742
Amy Wang, President
Tel: (301) 314-7121
Email: aasu-board@umail.umd.edu
Web: www.studentorg.umd.edu/aasu

MUSLIM STUDENTS' ASSOCIATION
University of Maryland at College Park
P.O. Box 44, Stamp Student Union
College Park, MD 20742
Mohamed Abutaleb, President
Tel: (301) 314-9545
Email: umcp_msa@yahoo.com
Web: www.msa-umd.org

VIETNAMESE STUDENT ASSOCIATION
University of Maryland
Stamp Student Union #75
College Park, MD 20742
Nhu-Uyen Cung, President
Email: vsa_umcp@yahoo.com
Web: www.vsa-umcp.com

MASSACHUSETTS

ARTISTIC

ASIAN AMERICAN ARTISTS ASSOCIATION
P.O. Box 856
Jamaica Plain, MA 02130
Elaine Yoneoka, President
Tel: (617) 524-4673 Fax: (617) 524-4673
Email: eyart@aol.com

CAMBODIAN MASTER PERFORMERS PROGRAM
44 Farnsworth St.
Boston, MA 02210
Elizabeth Chey, Program Development Officer, World Education
Tel: (617) 482-9485 Fax: (617) 482-0617
Email: echey@cambodianmasters.org
Web: www.cambodianmasters.org

DANCE PHILIPPINES PERFORMING ARTS COMPANY, INC.
51 Brazil St.
Melrose, MA 02176
Marijo Torres, Director
Tel: (617) 290-5104
Email: dppac@yahoo.com
Web: www.dancephilippines.com

FOUNDATION FOR CHINESE PERFORMING ARTS
3 Partridge Ln.
Lincoln, MA 01773
Catherine Tan Chan, President
Tel: (781) 259-8195 Fax: (781) 259-9147
Email: foundation@chineseperformingarts.net
Web: www.chineseperformingarts.net

HANDEL AND HAYDN SOCIETY
300 Massachusetts Ave.
Boston, MA 02115
Mary A. Deissler, Executive Director
Tel: (617) 262-1815 Fax: (617) 266-4217
Email: info@handelandhaydn.org
Web: www.handelandhaydn.org

NATIONAL CENTER FOR JEWISH FILM
Brandeis University
Lown 102, M/S 053
Waltham, MA 02454
Sharon P. Rivo, Executive Director
Tel: (781) 899-7044 Fax: (781) 736-2070
Email: ncjf@brandeis.edu
Web: www.jewishfilm.org

BUSINESS

CHINA FUND, INC.
225 Franklin St.
Boston, MA 02111
Gary L. French, President
Tel: (888) 246-2255
Web: www.chinafundinc.com

CHINESE ECONOMIC DEVELOPMENT COUNCIL
65 Harrison Ave., 7th Fl.
Boston, MA 02111
Edward Chiang, Chairman
Tel: (617) 482-1011 Fax: (617) 482-5289
Email: cedc@cedc-boston.org

ORGANIZATION OF PAKISTANI ENTREPRENEURS OF NORTH AMERICA
New England Chapter
4 Maxwell Cir.
Hudson, MA 01749
Imran Sayeed, President
Tel: (866) 290-7374 Fax: (866) 290-7374
Email: info@opennewengland.org
Web: www.open-us.org

US-CHINA EXCHANGE ASSOCIATION
Boston Office
4 Old Country Path
Ashland, MA 01721
Tel: (508) 243-6469 Fax: (781) 846-5932
Web: www.usachina.org

CULTURAL

AMERICAN COUNCIL FOR SOUTHERN ASIAN ART
Museum of Fine Arts, Boston
465 Huntington Ave.
Boston, MA 02115-5597
Joan Cummins, Secretary
Tel: (617) 267-9300
Email: webmaster@mfa.org
Web: www.mfa.org

ARMENIAN LIBRARY AND MUSEUM OF AMERICA, INC.
65 Main St.
Watertown, MA 02472
Sabine Chouljian, Office Manager
Tel: (617) 926-2562 X3 Fax: (617) 926-0175
Email: sabine@armenianlibraryandmuseum.org
Web: www.almainc.org

CAMPAIGN TO PROTECT CHINATOWN
33 Harrison Ave., 3rd Fl.
Boston, MA 02111
Suzanne Lee, Chairperson
Tel: (617) 426-0643 Fax: (617) 357-9611
Email: justice@cpaboston.org
Web: www.cpaboston.org

CHINESE CULTURAL CENTER
620 Massachusetts Ave.
Cambridge, MA 02139
Tel: (617) 876-0918 Fax: (617) 876-2067

CHINESE HISTORICAL SOCIETY OF NEW ENGLAND
2 Boylston St. #G-3
Boston, MA 02116
Lai Ying Yu, Administrative Office Manager
Tel: (617) 338-4339
Email: chsne@verizon.net

GREATER BOSTON CHINESE CULTURAL ASSOCIATION
437 Cherry St.
W. Newton, MA 02465
Christine Choate, President
Tel: (617) 332-0377 Fax: (617) 630-8192
Email: gbccaorg@aol.com
Web: www.gbcca.org

ISKWELAHANG PILIPINO
109 Davis Rd.
Bedford, MA 02730
Cristina S. Castro, Administrative Director
Tel: (781) 275-8225 Fax: (781) 275-8225

Email: criscastro@ipbahay.org
Web: www.ipbahay.org

JAPANESE ASSOCIATION OF MIT
77 Massachusetts Ave. #54-1711
Cambridge, MA 02139
Masahiro Sugiyama, Treasurer
Email: nihonjinkai-request@mit.edu
Web: http://web.mit.edu/jam

KOREAN INSTITUTE: CENTER FOR LANGUAGE AND CULTURE
1775 Massachusettts Ave. #4
Cambridge, MA 02140
Young Sook Kim, President
Tel: (617) 876-3540 Fax: (617) 661-6424

KOREAN WAR VETERANS OF MASSACHUSETTS, INC.
State House #546-4
Boston, MA 02133
Joseph P. McCallion, President
Tel: (617) 723-1716 Fax: (617) 723-1716
Web: http://koreanvetsofmass.org

PAKISTAN ASSOCIATION OF GREATER BOSTON
P.O. Box 412
Wayland, MA 01778
Dure Afzal, President
Email: info@pagb.org
Web: www.pagb.org

TAIWANESE AMERICAN FOUNDATION OF BOSTON
500 Lincoln St., 1st Fl.
Allston, MA 02134
Email: info@taf-boston.org
Web: www.geocities.com/taf_boston/TAFB_home.htm

TIBETAN ASSOCIATION OF BOSTON
P.O. Box 381256
Cambridge, MA 02139
Tashi Kamson, President
Tel: (617) 823-8710
Web: www.bostontibet.org

TURKISH AMERICAN CULTURAL SOCIETY OF NEW ENGLAND, INC.
P.O. Box 230162
Boston, MA 02123-0162
Ferhan Gomulu, Secretary General
Email: tacs@tacsne.org
Web: www.tacsne.org

TURKISH CULTURAL FOUNDATION
12 Elizabeth Dr.
Chelmsford, MA 01824
Tel: (301) 571-0980
Email: webmaster@turkishculture.org
Web: www.turkishculture.org

MULTI-PURPOSE

CHINA FOUNDATION, INC.
Eastern Regional Office
79 Claflin St.
Belmont, MA 02478
Yuanli Liu, MD, Ph.D, Regional Director
Tel: (617) 432-4623
Email: us-east@chinafoundation.net
Web: www.chinafoundation.net

GREAT WALL CENTER, INC.
110 Pleasant St., 3rd Fl.
Malden, MA 02148
Richard Cheng, Executive Director
Tel: (781) 388-6931
Email: wprichardcheng@juno.com
Web: www.greatwallcenter.org

SRI LANKA ASSOCIATION OF NEW ENGLAND
P.O. Box 442
North Chelmsford, MA 01863-0442
Akalusha Mutukumarana, President

Tel: (978) 275-4196 Fax: (978) 455-1552
Email: slaneusa2001@yahoo.com
Web: www.slaneusa.com

VIETNAMESE AMERICAN INITIATIVE DEVELOPMENT
42 Charles St. #E
Dorchester, MA 02122
Nhan Paul Ton That, Executive Director
Tel: (617) 822-3717 Fax: (617) 822-3718
Email: vietaidstaff@vietaid.org
Web: www.vietaid.org

POLITICAL ACTION

AFGHANS FOR CIVIL SOCIETY
30 Brattle St.
Cambridge, MA 02138
Qayum Karzai, Founder & President
Tel: (617) 576-7104
Email: acs@afghanpolicy.org
Web: www.afghansforcivilsociety.org

AMERICAN-ARAB ANTI-DISCRIMINATION COMMITTEE
Massachusetts Chapter
565 Boylston St.
Boston, MA 02116
Randa Shedid, VicePresident
Tel: (617) 262-8902
Email: info@adcma.org
Web: www.adcma.org

ARMENIAN NATIONAL COMMITTEE OF AMERICA
Eastern Region
80 Bigelow Ave.
Watertown, MA 02472
Doug Geogerian, Director
Tel: (617) 923-1918 Fax: (617) 926-5525
Email: ancaer@anca.org
Web: www.anca.org

ASIAN PACIFIC AMERICAN LABOR ALLIANCE
Boston
Asian American Construction Trades Association, 41 Seminole Rd.
Acton, MA 01720-2406
Kenneth Wing, Member
Tel: (978) 263-1001

INDIAN AMERICAN FORUM FOR POLITICAL EDUCATION
16 Downing Rd.
Lexington, MA 02421
Vanita Shastri, Ph. D., President
Tel: (781) 862-9648
Email: info@iafpe-ne.org
Web: www.iafpe-ne.org

PROFESSIONAL

ASIAN AMERICAN JOURNALISTS ASSOCIATION
New England Chapter
WCVB TV 5, 5 TV Pl.
Needham, MA 02494
Sangita Chandra, Chapter President
Tel: (781) 433-4217
Email: schandra@hearst.com
Web: www.aajane.org

ASSOCIATION OF KOREAN NEUROSCIENTISTS IN NORTH AMERICA
MRC 216, 115 Mill St.
Bellmont, MA 21201
Dr. Kwng-Soo Kim, President
Tel: (617) 855-2024
Email: kskim@mclean.harvard.edu
Web: http://research.mclean.org/departments/mrc/mneurobio/index.html

INDIAN MEDICAL ASSOCIATION OF NEW ENGLAND
P.O. Box 9132
Waltham, MA 02454-9132

Onaly A. Kapasi, M.D., President
Tel: (781) 893-4610 Fax: (781) 893-2105
Web: www.imanemd.org

NATIONAL ASSOCIATION OF ASIAN AMERICAN PROFESSIONALS
National Chapter
P.O. Box 52030
Boston, MA 02205
Vincent Yee, President & Chairman
Email: info@naaap.org
Web: www.naaap.org

NETWORK OF SOUTH ASIAN PROFESSIONALS-BOSTON
Network of Indian Professionals of North America
Boston, MA
Yash Chitre, President
Email: yashchitre@netsapboston.org
Web: www.netsapboston.org

NEW ENGLAND ASSOCIATION OF CHINESE PROFESSIONALS
375 Concord Ave. #003
Belmont, MA 02478
Shih-Huei Wang, President
Email: DrWang123@aol.com
Web: www.neacp.org

NATIONAL ASSOCIATION OF ASIAN AMERICAN PROFESSIONALS
NAAAP-Boston
P.O. Box 381435
Cambridge, MA 02238
Wanda Wong, President
Tel: (781) 937-7072
Email: naaap@naaapboston.org
Web: www.naaapboston.org

RELIGIOUS

ARABIC BIBLE OUTREACH MINISTRY
P.O. Box 486
Dracut, MA 01826
Email: info@arabicbible.com
Web: www.arabicbible.com

ARABIC EVANGELICAL BAPTIST CHURCH
21 Stratford St.
West Roxbury, MA 02132-2008
Rev. Khaled Ghobrial
Tel: (781) 329-6639
Email: info@arabicchurch.org
Web: www.arabicchuch.org

ASIAN AMERICAN CHRISTIAN FELLOWSHIP
Harvard-Radcliffe University
4 University Hall
Cambridge, MA 02138-0572
Jenny Davis, Contact
Email: exec@hraacf.org
Web: www.hcs.harvard.edu/~hraacf

BANGLADESH ISLAMIC SOCIETY OF NEW ENGLAND, INC.
114 Yorktown St.
Somerville, MA 02144-2435
Muhammad Yusuf Siddiq
Web: www.melissadata.com

BOSTON CHINESE EVANGELICAL CHURCH
249 Harrison Ave.
Boston, MA 02111
Daniel Eng, English Secretary
Tel: (617) 426-5711 Fax: (617) 426-0315
Email: english.sec@bcec.net
Web: www.bcec.net

Newton Campus
218 Walnut St.
Newtonville, MA 02460
Rev. Steven Chin, Senior Pastor
Tel: (617) 243-0100 Fax: (617) 243-0900
Email: newton.english.sec@bcec.net
Web: www.bcec.net

CHINESE BIBLE CHURCH OF GREATER BOSTON
149 Old Spring St.
Lexington, MA 02421
Steve Chang, Pastor
Tel: (781) 863-1755 Fax: (781) 674-2312
Email: info@cbcgb.org
Web: http://cbcgb.org

CHINESE GOSPEL CHURCH OF MASSACHUSETTS
60 Turnpike Rd.
Southborough, MA 01772
Tel: (508) 229-2299 Fax: (508) 303-9911
Email: cgcm@cgcm.org
Web: www.cgcm.org

CONGREGATION BETH EL
105 Hudson Rd.
Sudbury, MA 01776
David Thomas, Rabbi
Tel: (978) 443-9622 Fax: (978) 443-9629
Email: info@bethelsudbury.org
Web: www.bethelsudbury.org

HARVARD ISLAMIC SOCIETY
Harvard College
University Hall, 1st Fl. #61
Cambridge, MA 02145
Rameez Qudsi, President
Email: his@digitas.harvard.edu
Web: www.digitas.harvard.edu/~his

JEWS FOR JESUS
Boston
705 Cambridge St.
Boston, MA 02135
Garrett Smith, Chief of Station
Tel: (617) 782-6222 Fax: (617) 782-6333
Email: boston@jewsforjesus.org
Web: www.jfjonline.org

LYNN CAMBODIAN BAPTIST CHURCH
10 Kelar Ave.
Lynn, MA 01905
Rev. BunChhum E. Tuy, Pastor
Tel: (781) 581-6058
Email: csbflinks@hotmail.com
Web: http://cambodianchristian.com/site/lcbc/

SAINTS VARTANANTZ ARMENIAN CHURCH
180 Old Westford Rd.
Chelmsford, MA 01824
Tel: (978) 256-7234 Fax: (978) 256-3776
Email: office@stsvartanantz.com
Web: www.stsvartanantz.com

ST. GREGORY ARMENIAN APOSTOLIC CHURCH OF MERRIMACK VALLEY
158 Main St.
North Andover, MA 01845
Tel: (978) 685-5038 Fax: (978) 683-7177
Email: stgregory@saintgregory.org
Web: www.saintgregory.org

ST. JAMES ARMENIAN CHURCH
465 Mt. Auburn St.
Watertown, MA 02472
Tel: (617) 923-8860 Fax: (617) 926-5503
Email: info@sthagop.com
Web: www.sthagop.com

TAIWAN PRESBYTERIAN CHURCH OF GREATER BOSTON
1458 Great Plain Ave.
Needham, MA 02492
Kok-thai Lim, Pastor
Tel: (617) 795-1507 Fax: (617) 795-1507
Email: pastor@tpcgb.org
Web: www.tpcgb.org

TEMPLE BETH SHOLOM
50 Pamela Rd.
Framingham, MA 01701
Laurence Bazer, Rabbi
Tel: (508) 877-2540 Fax: (508) 877-8278
Email: admin@beth-sholom.org
Web: www.beth-sholom.org

TEMPLE EMANUEL
280 May St.
Worcester, MA 01602-2599
Carlton Watson, President
Tel: (508) 755-1257 Fax: (508) 795-0417
Email: president@temple-emanuel.org
Web: www.templeemanuel.org

385 Ward St.
Newton Centre, MA 02459
Barbara Ross, Executive Director
Tel: (617) 558-8100 Fax: (617) 558-8150
Email: info@templeemanuel.com
Web: www.templeemanuel.com

7 Haggetts Pond Rd.
Andover, MA 01810
Carrie A. Lavoie, Executive Director
Tel: (978) 470-1356
Email: info@templeemanuel.net
Web: www.templeemanuel.net

TEMPLE EMANUEL OF THE MERRIMACK VALLEY
101 W. Forest St.
Lowell, MA 01851
Blake Voss, President
Tel: (978) 454-1372
Email: office@temv.org
Web: www.temv.org

TEMPLE ISRAEL BOSTON
477 Longwood Ave.
Boston, MA 02215
Dean Richlin, President
Tel: (617) 566-3960 Fax: (617) 731-3711
Email: info@tisrael.org
Web: www.tisrael.org

TEMPLE SINAI OF SHARON
25 Canton St.
Sharon, MA 02067-1200
Aaron Sherman, Rabbi
Tel: (781) 784-6081 Fax: (781) 784-2616
Email: rabbi@temple-sinai.com
Web: www.temple-sinai.com

UNITED SYNAGOGUE OF CONSERVATIVE JUDAISM
New England Region
1320 Centre St. #304
Newton Centre, MA 02159-2400
Aaron Kischel, Executive Director
Tel: (617) 964-8210 Fax: (617) 964-0647
Email: neweng@uscj.org
Web: www.uscj.org/neweng

VIETNAMESE ALLIANCE CHURCH OF BOSTON
286 Ashmont St.
Boston, MA 02126
Rev. Thanh V. Le, Pastor
Tel: (617) 265-4296

WORCESTER KOREAN UNITED METHODIST CHURCH
114 Main St.
Worcester, MA 01608
Rev. Jin Young Choi, Pastor
Tel: (508) 799-4488
Email: pastor@workmc.org
Web: www.workmc.org

RESEARCH

AMERICAN CENTER OF ORIENTAL RESEARCH IN AMMAN
656 Beacon St., 5th Fl.
Boston, MA 02215-2010
Tel: (617) 353-6571 Fax: (617) 353-6575
Email: acor@bu.edu
Web: www.bu.edu/acor/

INSTITUTE FOR FOREIGN POLICY ANALYSIS
675 Massachusetts Ave., 10th Fl.
Cambridge, MA 02139
Robert L. Pfaltzgraff, Jr., President

Tel: (617) 492-2116 Fax: (617) 492-8242
Email: mail@ifpa.org
Web: www.ifpa.org

JEWISH GENEALOGICAL SOCIETY OF GREATER BOSTON
P.O. Box 610366
Newton, MA 02461-0366
Tel: (617) 796-8522
Email: info@jgsbg.org
Web: www.jewishgen.org/boston/

NATIONAL BUREAU OF ECONOMIC RESEARCH, INC.
Main Office
1050 Massachusetts Ave.
Cambridge, MA 02138
Martin Feldstein, President/CEO
Tel: (617) 868-3900 Fax: (617) 868-2742
Web: www.nber.org

THE KOREA INSTITUTE
303 Coolidge Hall, 1737 Cambridge St.
Cambridge, MA 02138
Carter J. Eckert, Director
Tel: (617) 496-2141 Fax: (617) 495-9976
Email: korea@fas.harvard.edu
Web: www.fas.harvard.edu/~korea/index.html

TRANS-ARAB RESEARCH INSTITUTE
P.O. Box 495
Boston, MA 02112
Naseer H. Aruri
Tel: (781) 648-1245
Email: naruri@aol.com
Web: http://tari.org

UNIVERSITY OF MASSACHUSETTS-INSTITUTE FOR ASIAN AMERICAN STUDIES
100 Morrissey Blvd.
Boston, MA 02125
Paul Watanabe, Director
Tel: (617) 287-5650 Fax: (617) 287-5656
Email: asianaminst@umb.edu
Web: www.iaas.umb.edu

SCIENTIFIC

AMERICAN COMMITTEE FOR THE WEIZMANN INSTITUTE OF SCIENCE
10 Nancy Ln.
Framingham, MA 01701
Deanne Stone, Director
Tel: (508) 788-3500
Email: boston@acwis.org
Web: www.weizmann-usa.org

NEW ENGLAND BIOSCIENCE SOCIETY
Whitehead Institute for Biomedical Research/
MIT, 9 Cambridge Center #605
Cambridge, MA 02142
Moonkyoung Um, Ph.D., President
Email: moonkyoung@wi.mit.edu
Web: www.nebskorea.org

SPEC. INT., CHILD CARE

ALLIANCE FOR CHILDREN FOUNDATION
55 William St. #G-10
Wellesley, MA 02481-3902
Howard M. Cooper,Esq., Chairman
Tel: (781) 431-7148 Fax: (781) 431-7474
Email: info@allforchildren.org
Web: www.afcfoundation.org

CHINA ADOPTION WITH LOVE, INC.
251 Harvard St. #17 & #19
Brookline, MA 02446
Tel: (800) 888-9812 Fax: (617) 232-8288
Email: info@cawli.org
Web: www.cawli.org

FAMILIES WITH CAMBODIAN CHILDREN
20 Oakhurst Ave.
Ipswich, MA 01938
Fax: (978) 356-5186

Email: laurie@emilysbooks.com
Web: www.famcam.org

FOUNDATION FOR CHINESE ORPHANAGES
8 Berkeley St.
Cambridge, MA 02138-3464
Shanti Fry, President
Tel: (617) 876-3042 Fax: (617) 441-5449
Email: md0050@yahoo.com
Web: www.thefco.org

VIETHOPE, INC.
423 Brookline Ave. #199
Boston, MA 02215
Nam Tran Nguyen, President
Email: info@viethope.org
Web: www.viethope.org

SPEC. INT., COUNSELING

CHILD AND FAMILY SERVICE
Counseling/Mental Health Clinic
479 Main St.
Athol, MA 01331
Eve Bogdanove, Clinic Director
Tel: (978) 249-0499 Fax: (978) 249-7504
Email: ebogdanove@cfs.org
Web: www.cfs.org

JEWISH FAMILY AND CHILDREN'S SERVICES OF BOSTON
31 New Chardon St.
Boston, MA 02114
Tel: (617) 227-6641
Web: www.jfcsboston.org

1340 Center St.
Newton, MA 02459
Tel: (617) 558-1278
Web: www.jfcsboston.org

198 Vanderbilt Ave.
Norwood, MA 02062
Tel: (781) 551-0405
Web: www.jfcsboston.org

SPEC. INT., EDUCATION

ACTON CHINESE LANGUAGE SCHOOL
P.O. Box 2239
Acton, MA 01720-6239
Email: faq@acls-ma.org
Web: www.acls-ma.org

AMERICAN INSTITUTE FOR SRI LANKAN STUDIES
Tufts University
Department of History
Medford, MA 02155
John Rogers, Professor
Tel: (617) 484-2427 Fax: (617) 627-3479
Email: jrogers@emerald.tufts.edu

AMOUZESH OMEED, INC.
290 Turnpike Rd., PMB 412
Westborough, MA 01581
Kaveh Azar, Founder
Tel: (781) 863-8263
Email: kazar@quats.com
Web: www.omeed.org

ARMENIAN SCHOLARSHIP FOUNDATION, INC.
14 Sandrick Rd.
Belmont, MA 02478
Leon Barsoum, Chairman of the Board
Email: info@armenianscholarships.org
Web: www.armenianscholarships.org

ASHA FOR EDUCATION
Boston/MIT
P.O. Box 391802
Cambridge, MA 02139
Ravi Shankar Mundoli, Coordinator
Email: ravim_asha@yahoo.com
Web: www.ashanet.org/mit/

ASIAN AMERICAN CIVIC ASSOCIATION
200 Tremont St.
Boston, MA 02116
Chau-Ming Lee, Executive Director
Tel: (617) 426-9492 Fax: (617) 482-2316
Email: alan@aaca-boston.org
Web: www.aaca-boston.org

ASIAN AMERICAN STUDIES
University of Massachusetts Boston
100 Morrissey Blvd.
Boston, MA 02125
Peter Kiang, Director
Tel: (617) 287-7614 Fax: (617) 287-5622
Email: peter.kiang@umb.edu
Web: omega.cc.umb.edu/~aast/

CENTER FOR MIDDLE EASTERN STUDIES
Harvard University
1430 Massachusetts Ave.
Cambridge, MA 02138
Tel: (617) 495-4055 Fax: (617) 496-8584
Email: mideast@fas.harvard.edu
Web: www.fas.harvard.edu

CENTRAL EURASIAN STUDIES SOCIETY
Harvard University
c/o Program on Central Asia and the Caucasus
625 Massachusetts Ave.
Cambridge, MA 02139
Gregory Gleason, President
Tel: (617) 496-2643 Fax: (617) 495-8319
Email: CESS@fas.harvard.edu
Web: http://cess.fas.harvard.edu

EDWIN O. REISCHAUER INSTITUTE OF JAPANESE STUDIES
Harvard University Eurasia Foundation
625 Massachusetts Ave., 2nd Fl.
Cambridge, MA 02139
Prof. Andrew Gordon, Director
Tel: (617) 495-3220 Fax: (617) 496-8083
Email: gamstutz@fas.harvard.edu
Web: www.fas.harvard.edu

FAIRBANK CENTER FOR EAST ASIAN RESEARCH
Harvard University
1737 Cambridge St.
Cambridge, MA 02138
Dr. Wilt Idema, Director
Tel: (617) 495-4046 Fax: (617) 495-9976
Email: fairbank@fas.harvard.edu
Web: www.fas.harvard.edu/~fairbank

FLETCHER SCHOOL OF LAW AND DIPLOMACY
Tufts University
169 Holland St.
Somerville, MA 02144
Tel: (617) 627-3376 Fax: (617) 627-3712
Email: fletcherweb@tufts.edu
Web: http://fletcher.tufts.edu

HARVARD-YENCHING INSTITUTE
2 Divinity Ave. & Vanserg Hall, 25 Francis Ave.
Cambridge, MA 02138
Tu Weiming, Director
Tel: (617) 495-4050 Fax: (617) 496-7206
Email: yenching@fas.harvard.edu
Web: www.harvard-yenching.org

JEWISH COMMUNITY DAY SCHOOL
25 Lenglen Rd.
Newton, MA 02458
Hamutal Gavish, Head of the School
Tel: (617) 965-5100 Fax: (617) 969-3237
Email: jcds@jcdsboston.org
Web: www.jcdsboston.org

JEWISH SPECIAL EDUCATION COLLABORATIVE
P.O. Box 63
Sharon, MA 02067
Sue Schweber, Program Coordinator
Tel: (781) 784-8201
Email: sschweber@jsec.info
Web: www.jsec.info

LEXINGTON CHINESE SCHOOL

221 Concord Ave.
Belmont, MA 02478
Joanne Sheu, Principal
Tel: (978) 250-3572 Fax: (978) 250-3572
Email: principal@lcs-chinese.org
Web: www.lcs-chinese.org

MIDDLE EAST INFORMATION NETWORK

197 Fairmount Ave. #2
Boston, MA 02136
Edward Graham, President
Email: info@mideastinfo.com
Web: www.mideastinfo.com

NATIONAL JEWISH COALITION FOR LITERACY

134 Beach St.
Boston, MA 02111
Leibel Fein, Director
Tel: (617) 423-0063
Web: www.njcl.net

NEPALESE CHILDREN'S EDUCATION FUND

P.O. Box 380061
Cambridge, MA 02238-0061
Omprakash Gnawali, Chairman
Email: contact@nepalchildren.org
Web: www.nepalchildren.org

NEWTON CHINESE LANGUAGE SCHOOL

P.O. Box 2661
Woburn, MA 01888-1261
Tel: (781) 690-1825
Email: principal@nclsboston.org
Web: www.nclsboston.org

THE CHINESE LANGUAGE SCHOOL

17 Stedman Rd.
Lexington, MA 02421
Email: tcls@thechineselanguageschool.org
Web: www.thechineselanguageschool.org

US CHINA PEOPLES FRIENDSHIP ASSOCIATION

New England Capter
720 Massachusetts Ave.
Cambridge, MA 02139
Richard Pendleton, Contact
Tel: (617) 491-0577 Fax: (617) 491-0594
Email: pinebush2002@yahoo.com
Web: www.uscpfa.org

SPEC. INT., EMPLOYMENT

JEWISH VOCATIONAL SERVICE OF GREATER BOSTON

105 Chauncy St.
Boston, MA 02111
Tel: (617) 542-1993 X3227 Fax: (617) 451-9973
Email: learning@jvs-boston.org
Web: www.jvs-boston.org

SPEC. INT., FAMILY PLANNING

CHILD AND FAMILY SERVICE OF PIONEER VALLEY

425 Union St., Level D
West Springfield, MA 01089
Randy Bradbury, Program Coordinator
Tel: (413) 737-4718 Fax: (413) 827-7817
Email: adiaz@cfs.org
Web: www.cfs.org

FAMILIES WITH CHILDREN FROM CHINA

New England Chapter
8 Berkley St.
Cambridge, MA 02138
Shanti Fry, President
Tel: (617) 876-3042 Fax: (617) 441-5449
Email: shantifry@aol.com
Web: www.thefco.org

SPEC. INT., GAY&LESBIAN

LONG YANG CLUB BOSTON

2 Ware St. #209
Cambridge, MA 02138
Ron Suleski, Treasurer
Tel: (617) 661-9165 Fax: (617) 661-9165
Email: boston@longyangclub.org
Web: www.longyangclub.org/boston

SPEC. INT., HEALTH SERVICES

ASIAN PEDIATRIC & ADOLESCENT CLINICAL SERVICES

New England Medical Center
750 Washington St. #351
Boston, MA 02111
Sue Chin Ponte, Director
Tel: (617) 636-1337 Fax: (617) 636-7719
Email: sponte@tufts-nemc.org
Web: www.tufts-nemc.org

CAMBODIAN HEALTH COMMITTEE

c/o Center for Blood Research, 800 Huntington Ave.
Boston, MA 02115
Tel: (617) 278-3464
Web: www.boston.com

CHILD AND FAMILY SERVICE

Valley Infant Development Service/Disability Resource Program
130 Maple St. #140
Springfield, MA 01103
Terri Cain, Director
Tel: (413) 739-3954 Fax: (413) 785-1728
Email: tcains@cfs.org
Web: www.cfs.org

JEWISH MEMORIAL HOSPITAL AND REHABILITATION CENTER

59 Townsend St.
Roxbury, MA 02119
Tel: (617) 442-8760 Fax: (617) 989-8214
Email: admin@jmhrc.com
Web: www.jmhrc.com

JORDAN HOSPITAL

275 Sandwich St.
Plymouth, MA 02360
Alan D. Knight, President/CEO
Tel: (508) 746-2000
Web: www.jordan.org

MASSACHUSETTS ASIAN AND PACIFIC ISLANDERS FOR HEALTH

59 Temple Pl. #406
Boston, MA 02111
Jacob Smith Yang, Executive Director
Tel: (617) 426-6755 Fax: (617) 426-6756
Email: mail@mapforhealth.org
Web: www.mapforhealth.org

NEPONSET HEALTH CENTER

398 Neponset Ave.
Dorchester, MA 02122
Mary Zapata, Social Services/Domestic Violence Coordinator
Tel: (617) 282-3200 Fax: (617) 825-8577
Email: mzapata@harborhealthinc.org

SOUTH COVE COMMUNITY HEALTH CENTER

145 S. St.
Boston, MA 02111
Eugene Welch, Executive Director
Tel: (617) 521-6700 Fax: (617) 457-6799
Email: ewelch@scchc.org
Web: www.scchc.org

SOUTHEAST ASIAN HEALTH PROGRAM FAMILY & SOCIAL SERVICE CENTER

26 Queen St.
Worcester, MA 01610
Tam Le, Program Coordinator
Tel: (508) 860-7700 Fax: (508) 860-7989

TUFTS-NEW ENGLAND MEDICAL CENTER FOR ASIAN ACCESS PROGRAM

750 Washington St. #790
Boston, MA 02111
May Wu, Program Director
Tel: (617) 636-6372 Fax: (617) 636-2579
Email: mwu@tufts-nemc.org
Web: www.tufts-nemc.org

SPEC. INT., HOUSING

ASIAN COMMUNITY DEVELOPMENT CORPORATION

888 Washington St. #102
Boston, MA 02111
Jeremy Liu, Executive Director
Tel: (617) 482-2380 Fax: (617) 482-3056
Email: info@asiancdc.org
Web: www.asiancdc.org

SPEC. INT., HUMAN RELATIONS

ARMENIAN RELIEF SOCIETY, INC.

80 Bigelow Ave.
Watertown, MA 02472
Hamesd Beugekian, Executive Secretary
Tel: (617) 926-5892 Fax: (617) 926-4855
Email: ARS1910@aol.com
Web: www.ars1910.org

BOSTON COMMITTEE FOR PALESTINIAN RIGHTS

P.O. Box 2433
Cambridge, MA 02138
Tel: (617) 292-6308
Email: info@bcpr.org
Web: www.bcpr.org

CHINESE CONSOLIDATED BENEVOLENT ASSOCIATION

90 Tyler St.
Boston, MA 02111
Roman Chan, President
Tel: (617) 542-2574 Fax: (617) 542-0926

JEWISH COMMUNITY RELATIONS COUNCIL OF GREATER BOSTON

126 High St.
Boston, MA 02110-2700
Nancy K. Kaufman, Executive Director
Tel: (617) 457-8600 Fax: (617) 988-6255
Email: executivedirector@jcrcboston.org
Web: www.jcrcboston.org

KOREAN-AMERICAN CITIZENS LEAGUE OF NEW ENGLAND

294 Washington St. #436
Boston, MA 02108
Song K. Kim, President
Tel: (617) 482-1300 Fax: (617) 482-3344
Email: songkim@winstarmain.com
Web: www.kaclne.org

THE AMERICAN JEWISH COMMITTEE

Boston Chapter
126 High St., 3rd Fl.
Boston, MA 02110
Larry Lowenthal, Chapter Director
Tel: (617) 457-8700 Fax: (617) 988-6252
Email: boston@ajc.org
Web: www.ajc.org

SPEC. INT., IMMIGRATION

OFFICE FOR REFUGEES AND IMMIGRANTS

Massachusetts Office
18 Tremont St. #600
Boston, MA 02108
Juliette Nguyen, Executive Director
Tel: (617) 727-7888 Fax: (617) 727-1822
Email: juliettenguyen@state.ma.us
Web: www.state.ma.us/org

SPRINGFIELD VIETNAMESE-AMERICAN CIVIC ASSOCIATION, INC.

433 Belmont Ave.
Springfield, MA 01108
Elizabeth Vo, Executive Director
Tel: (413) 733-9373 Fax: (413) 737-3419
Email: svaca@verizon.net

THE MASSACHUSETTS IMMIGRANT AND REFUGEE COALITION

105 Chauncy St. #901
Boston, MA 02111
Ali Noorani, Executive Director
Tel: (617) 350-5480 x210 Fax: (617) 350-5499
Email: flopez@miracoalition.org
Web: www.miracoalition.org

SPEC. INT., INFORMATION REFERRAL

SANGHA TIBET RESOURCE CENTER

237 Holland St. (Teele Square)
Somerville, MA 02144
Tom Digenti, Founder/Director
Tel: (617) 629 4674
Email: sangha-tibet@rcn.com
Web: www.sangha-Tibet.org

SPEC. INT., LEGAL ASSISTANCE

CAMBODIAN MUTUAL ASSOCIATION ASSISTANCE OF GREATER LOWELL, INC.

165 Jackson St.
Lowell, MA 01852
Tel: (978) 596-1000 Fax: (978) 454-1806
Email: vros@cmaalowell.org
Web: www.cmaalowell.org

INTERNATIONAL BRIDGES TO JUSTICE

198 Tremont St. #447
Boston, MA 02116
Karen I. Tse, Founder/Executive Director
Email: webmaster@ibj.org
Web: www.ibj.org

JEWISH LABOR COMMITTEE

New England Chapter
99 Chauncy St. #600
Boston, MA 02111
David Dolev, Regional Director
Tel: (781) 883-7117
Email: BostonJLC@aol.com
Web: www.jewishlabor.org

NATIONAL ASIAN PACIFIC AMERICAN BAR ASSOCIATION

Asian American Lawyers Association of Massachusetts
P.O. Box 5655
Boston, MA 02114
Myong J. Joun, President
Tel: (617) 742-4100 Fax: (617) 742-5858
Email: mjjoua@civil-rights-law.com
Web: www.aalam.org

SPEC. INT., MENTAL HEALTH

CHILD AND FAMILY SERVICE

Counseling & Mental Health Clinic
238 Main St. #4
Greenfield, MA 01301
Tel: (413) 774-6252 Fax: (413) 773-0477
Email: srhodes@cfs.org
Web: www.cfs.org

CHILD AND FAMILY SERVICE

Counseling/Mental Health Clinic
390 Main St. #939
Worcester, MA 001608
Tel: (508) 753-1260 Fax: (508) 831-9624
Email: dkott@cfs.org
Web: www.cfs.org

Counseling/Mental Health Clinic
39 Union St.

East Hampton, MA 01027
Chris Shanky, Supervisor
Tel: (413) 529-1764 Fax: (413) 529-9047
Email: sshanky@cfs.org
Web: www.cfs.org

SPEC. INT., SENIORS

AGING INFORMATION CENTER
Region I: CT, MA, ME, NH, RI, VTS.
John F. Kennedy Bldg. #2075
Boston, MA 02203
Robert O'Connell, Regional Administrator
Tel: (617)565-1158 Fax: (617) 565-4511
Email: aoainfo@aoa.gov
Web: www.aoa.gov

JEWISH GERIATRIC SERVICES, INC.
770 Converse St.
Longmeadow, MA 01106
Tel: (413) 567-6211 Fax: (413) 567-0175
Email: info@jewishgeriatric.org
Web: www.jewishgeriatric.org

JEWISH REHABILITATION CENTER FOR AGED OF THE NORTH SHORE, INC.
330 Paradise Rd.
Swampscott, MA 01907
Debbie Giovannucci, Admissions Coordinator
Tel: (781) 598-5310 Fax: (781) 598-8021
Email: info@jrcnorthshore.org
Web: www.jrcnorthshore.org

LEBANESE COMMUNITY HOUSING FOR THE ELDERLY, INC.
222 Pelham St.
Methuen, MA 01844-1467
Tel: (978) 681-8845

SPEC. INT., SOCIAL INTEREST

AMERICAN LEGION- BOSTON CHINATOWN POST #328
181 Brighton St.
Belmont, MA 02478
Dave Ching, Adjutant
Tel: (617) 489-1144

ARMENIA TREE PROJECT
65 Main St.
Watertown, MA 02472
Jeff Masarjian, Executive Director
Tel: (617) 926-8733 Fax: (617) 492-2020
Email: info@armeniatree.org
Web: www.armeniatree.org

ASIAN AMERICAN RESOURCE WORKSHOP
33 Harrison Ave., 3rd Fl.
Boston, MA 02111
Tel: (617) 426-5313 Fax: (617) 542-4900
Email: info@aarw.org
Web: www.aarw.org

ASIAN OUTREACH PROGRAM
197 Friend St.
Boston, MA 02114
Zenobia Lai, Managing Attorney
Tel: (617) 371-1270 x324 Fax: (617) 371-1222
Email: zlai@gbls.org
Web: www.gbls.org/asian/

ASIAN TASK FORCE AGAINST DOMESTIC VIOLENCE
Asian Shelter and Advocacy Project
P.O. Box 120108
Boston, MA 02112
Atsuko Fish, President Board of Directors
Tel: (617) 338-2350 Fax: (617) 338-2354
Email: asiandv@atask.org
Web: www.atask.org

ASSOCIATION FOR INDIA'S DEVELOPMENT
Boston Chapter, Massachusetts
P.O. Box 390884
Cambridge, MA 02139

Suresh Madhu, General Information
Tel: (617) 852-3851
Email: aid-boston@egroups.com
Web: www.aidboston.org

ASSOCIATION FOR THE DEVELOPMENT OF PAKISTAN
P.O. Box 990627
Boston, MA 02199
Omar Biabani, President
Tel: (617) 764-2441 Fax: (775) 257-9324
Email: contact@developpakistan.org
Web: www.developpakistan.org

BOSTON CHINATOWN NEIGHBORHOOD CENTER
885 Washington St.
Boston, MA 02111
David Y. S. Moy, Agency Director
Tel: (617) 635-5129 Fax: (617) 635-5132
Email: dysmoy@bcnc.net
Web: www.bcnc.net

CAMBODIAN AMERICAN LEAGUE OF LOWELL, INC.
60 Middlesex St.
Lowell, MA 01852
Bunroeun Thach, Acting Executive Director
Tel: (978) 454-3707 Fax: (978) 441-1781
Email: info@cambodianamerican.com
Web: www.cambodianamerican.com

CAMBODIAN COMMUNITY RESOURCE CENTER
43 Hulst Rd.
Amherst, MA 01002
Ronnie Booxbaum
Tel: (413) 256-0181
Email: rbooxbaum@gtcinternet.com
Web: www.comcol.umass.edu

CENTRAL MASSACHUSETTS FILIPINO-AMERICAN ASSOCIATION
139 Nugget Dr.
Charlton, MA 01507
Joseph Mahoney, President
Email: info@cmfaa.org
Web: www.cmfaa.org

CHINATOWN NEIGHBORHOOD SERVICE CENTER
200 Tremont St.
Boston, MA 02111
Chau Ming Lee, Director
Tel: (617) 426-9492
Web: www.bostonabcd.org/people/aaca.htm

CHINESE PROGRESSIVE ASSOCIATION
33 Harrison Ave., 3rd Fl.
Boston, MA 02111
Lydia Lowe, Staff
Tel: (617) 357-4499 Fax: (617) 357-9611
Email: justice@cpaboston.org
Web: www.cpaboston.org

COMBINED JEWISH PHILANTHROPIES
126 High St.
Boston, MA 02110
Tel: (617) 457-8500 Fax: (617) 988-6262
Email: info@cjp.org
Web: www.cjp.org

GREATER BOSTON ERUV CORPORATION
653 Chestnut Hill Ave.
Brookline, MA 02445-4148
Jesse Hefter, President
Email: j.hefter@verizon.net
Web: www.bostoneruv.org

HARVARD CHINA REVIEW
P.O. Box 380219
Cambridge, MA 02238-0219
Tel: (617) 249-1612 Fax: (617) 249-1612
Email: hcr@harvardchina.org
Web: www.harvardchina.org

IRANIAN ASSOCIATION OF BOSTON
P.O. Box 64
Newtonville, MA 02460

Amir Hooshang Hashemi, President
Tel: (617) 789-4426
Email: president@iaboston.org
Web: www.iaboston.org

JAPAN SOCIETY OF BOSTON
1 Milk St., 2nd Fl.
Boston, MA 02109
Yumiko Arimura, Membership Coordinator
Tel: (617) 451-0726 Fax: (617) 451-1191
Email: jsb@us-japan.org
Web: www.us-japan.org/boston

JAPANESE ASSOCIATION OF GREATER BOSTON
361 Massachusetts Ave.
Arlington, MA 02474
Tel: (781) 643-1061 Fax: (781) 648-8404
Email: info@jagb.org
Web: www.jagb.org

JEWISH COMMUNITY CENTER OF THE NORTH SHORE
4 Community Rd.
Marblehead, MA 01945
Diane Knoff, President
Tel: (781) 631-8330
Web: www.jccns.com

JEWISH COMMUNITY CENTERS OF GREATER BOSTON
333 Newton St.
Newton, MA 02459
Tel: (617) 558-6500 Fax: (617) 969-5115
Email: info@jccgb.org
Web: www.jccgb.org

JEWISH COMMUNITY OF AMHERST, INC.
742 Main St.
Amherst, MA 01002
David Dunn Bauer
Tel: (413) 256-0160 Fax: (413) 256-1588
Email: info@j-c-a.org
Web: www.j-c-a.org

JEWISH FAMILY SERVICE OF GREATER SPRINGFIELD, INC.
15 Lenox St.
Springfield, MA 01108
Wendy Sutter, Office Manager
Tel: (413) 737-2601 Fax: (413) 737-0323
Email: info@jfslink.org
Web: www.jfslink.org

JEWISH FAMILY SERVICE OF METROWEST
475 Franklin St. #101
Framingham, MA 01702-6265
Marc Jacobs, Executive Director
Tel: (508) 875-3100 Fax: (508) 875-4373
Email: info@jfsmw.org
Web: www.jfsmw.org

JEWISH FAMILY SERVICE OF THE NORTH SHORE, INC.
17 Front St.
Salem, MA 01970
Jon Firger, CEO
Tel: (978) 741-7878 Fax: (978) 741-8383
Email: jfirger@jfsns.org
Web: www.jfsns.org

New American Center
298 Union St.
Lynn, MA 01901-1318
Jon Firger, CEO
Tel: (781) 593-0100 Fax: (781) 599-3329
Email: jfirger@jfsns.org
Web: www.jfsns.org

JEWISH FAMILY SERVICE OF WORCESTER, INC.
646 Salisbury St.
Worcester, MA 01609
Stephen Slaten, Executive Director
Tel: (508) 755-3101 Fax: (508) 755-7460
Email: info@jfsworcester.org
Web: www.jfsworcester.org

JEWISH FEDERATION OF CENTRAL MASSACHUSETTS
633 Salisbury St.
Worcester, MA 01609-1120
Tel: (508) 756-1543 Fax: (508) 798-0962
Email: bluks@jfcm.org
Web: www.jewishcentralmass.org

JEWISH FEDERATION OF GREATER SPRINGFIELD
1160 Dickinson St. #2
Springfield, MA 01108-3198
Tel: (413) 737-4313 Fax: (413) 737-4348
Email: info@jewishspringfield.org
Web: www.jewishspringfield.org

JEWISH FEDERATION OF THE BERKSHIRES
196 South St.
Pittsfield, MA 01201
Arlene Schiff, Executive Director
Tel: (413) 442-4360 Fax: (413) 443-6070
Email: arlene.schiff@verizon.net
Web: www.jewishfederationberkshires.org

JEWISH FEDERATION OF THE NORTH SHORE
21 Front St.
Salem, MA 01970
Audrey Pransky, Foundation Director
Tel: (978) 745-4222 Fax: (978) 741-7507
Email: mail@jfns.org
Web: www.jewishnorthshore.org

LAO ASSOCIATION OF MASSACHUSETTS
23 Upham St.
Malden, MA 02148
Damdouame Ratanesone, Director
Tel: (781) 322-9754

LEVENTHAL-SIDMAN JEWISH COMMUNITY CENTER
445 Central St.
Stoughton, MA 02072
Barry Charton, Executive Director
Tel: (781) 341-2016 Fax: (781) 341-2340
Email: bcharton@striarjcc.org
Web: www.striarjcc.org

MERRIMACK VALLEY JEWISH FEDERATION
P.O. Box 937
Andover, MA 01810
Tel: (978) 688-0466 Fax: (978) 688-1097
Email: info@mvjf.org
Web: www.mvjf.org

MUSLIM COMMUNITY SUPPORT SERVICES, INC.
P.O. Box 850092
Braintree, MA 02185
Majid Palwala
Tel: (888) 773-3777
Email: mmuneeruddin@yahoo.com
Web: www.muslimsupport.org

PAKISTAN AMERICAN ASSOCIATION
Southern New England Chapter
P.O. Box 30
Sharon, MA 02067
Sohail Pirzada, President
Email: president@paasne.com
Web: www.paasne.com

PLANNING ACTION COUNCIL
Allston-Brighton Area
143 Harvard Ave.
Allston, MA 02134
Paul Creighton, Director
Tel: (617) 783-1485 Fax: (617) 783-0763
Web: www.bostonabcd.org

STRIAR JEWISH COMMUNITY CENTER OF GREATER BOSTON
445 Central St.
Stoughton, MA 02072
Barry Charton, Executive Director
Tel: (781) 341-2016 Fax: (781) 341-2340
Email: bcharton@striarjcc.org
Web: www.striarjcc.org

TIBETAN POVERTY ALLEVIATION FUND, INC.
663 Green St.
Cambridge, MA 02139
Arthur Holcombe, President
Tel: (415) 401-7371
Email: arthur@tpaf.org
Web: www.tpaf.org

VIETNAMESE AMERICAN CIVIC ASSOCIATION, INC.
1452 Dorchester Ave., 3rd Fl.
Dorchester, MA 02122
Duy V. Pham, Executive Director
Tel: (617) 288-7344 Fax: (617) 288-4860
Email: office@vacaboston.org
Web: www.vacaboston.org

SPEC. INT., SPORTS

BOSTON MUAY THAI ACADEMY
222 Broadway
Revere, MA 02151
Tel: (781) 284-5649
Email: staff@bostonmuaythai.com
Web: www.bostonmuaythai.com

DRAGON BOAT CLUB OF BOSTON
P.O. Box 380155
Cambridge, MA 02238-0155
Jonathan Scherer, President
Tel: (617) 441-0330
Email: redragon210@yahoo.com
Web: www.dbcb.org

HOMENETMEN
Boston
47 Nichols Ave.
Watertown, MA 02472
Yeghpayr Ara Barsoumian, Chairman
Tel: (617) 924-6992
Email: HomenetmenBoston@HomenetmenBoston.org
Web: www.homenetmenboston.org

Eastern Regional Executive
80 Bigelow Ave.
Watertown, MA 02472
Marcel Karian, Chairman
Tel: (617) 926-6380 Fax: (617) 926-6379
Email: homenetmeneusa@aol.com
Web: www.homenetmen.com

MOSAIC OUTDOOR CLUBS OF AMERICA
Massachusetts Chapter
P.O. Box 1821
Brookline, MA 02446-0015
Barry P., Chapter President
Tel: (866) 895-0615
Email: mosaic_mass@yahoo.com
Web: www.mosaics.org

SPEC. INT., WOMEN

ARMENIAN INTERNATIONAL WOMEN'S ASSOCIATION
P.O. Box 654
Belmont, MA 02478
Suzanne Moranian, President
Tel: (617) 926-0171
Web: www.aiwa-net.org

ASIAN AMERICAN SUPPORT AND RESOURCE AGENCY
54 Cummings Park #316
Woburn, MA 01801
Kamal Misra, Treasurer
Tel: (866) 922-2772 Fax: (781) 932-6664
Email: aasra@aasranewengland.org
Web: www.aasranewengland.org

ASIAN SISTERS IN ACTION
P.O. Box 380331
Cambridge, MA 02238
Email: asiainfo@yahoogroups.com
Web: www.asiasisters.org

COALITION AGAINST TRAFFICKING IN WOMEN
University of Massachusetts
P.O. Box 9338
N. Amherst, MA 01059
Dr. Janice Raymond, Co-Executive Director
Fax: (413) 367-9262
Email: info@catwinternational.org
Web: www.catwinternational.org

HADASSAH
Boston Chapter
2001 Beacon St.
Brighton, MA 02135
Valerie Lowenstein, President
Tel: (617) 566-0666 Fax: (617) 232-7946
Email: roberta.goldschneider@hadassah.org
Web: www.hadassah.org

Northern New England Region
19-A Crosby Dr. #210
Bedford, MA 01730
Fran Feldman, President
Tel: (781) 280-0663 Fax: (781) 280-0174
Email: region.nne@hadassah.org
Web: www.hadassah.org

Southern New England Region
220 Reservoir St. #23
Needham, MA 02494
Benita Ross, President
Tel: (781) 444-7676 Fax: (781) 444-1547
Email: region.sne@hadassah.org
Web: www.hadassah.org

IRANIAN WOMEN'S STUDIES FOUNDATION, INC.
P.O. Box 380882
Cambridge, MA 02238-0882
Golnaz Amin, Founder/Chairperson
Tel: (617) 492-9001 Fax: (617) 492-0111
Email: iranianwsf@aol.com
Web: www.iwsf.org

JEWISH WOMEN'S ARCHIVE
138 Harvard St.
Brookline, MA 02446
Gail Twersky Reimer, Executive Director
Tel: (617) 232-2258 Fax: (617) 975-0109
Email: webmaster@jwa.org
Web: www.jwa.org

SOUTH ASIAN WOMEN FOR ACTION
18 O'Rourke Path
Newton, MA 02459
Hardip Mann, Member
Tel: (617) 497-0316 Fax: (617) 497-0316
Email: sawa@way.net
Web: www.way.net/sawa

SPEC. INT., YOUTH

ARMENIAN YOUTH FEDERATION
80 Bigelow Ave.
Watertown, MA 02472
Tel: (617) 923-1933 Fax: (617) 924-1933
Email: ayf@ayf.org
Web: www.ayf.org

BOSTON ASIAN: YOUTH ESSENTIAL SERVICE, INC.
87 Tyler St.
Boston, MA 02111
Jane Leung, Executive Director
Tel: (617) 482-4243 Fax: (617) 482-3620
Email: janesleung@bostonasianyes.org
Web: www.bostonasianyes.org

COALITION FOR ASIAN PACIFIC AMERICAN YOUTH
100 Morrissey Blvd.
Boston, MA 02125
Sophia Kim, Coordinator
Tel: (617) 287-5658 Fax: (617) 287-5622
Email: capay@umb.edu
Web: www.capayus.org

JEWISH BIG BROTHER AND BIG SISTER ASSOCIATION OF GREATER BOSTON
333 Nahanton St.
Newton, MA 02459
Harvey D. Lowell, President/CEO
Tel: (617) 558-6535 Fax: (617) 332-9123
Email: info@jbbbs.org
Web: www.jbbbs.org

JEWISH ORGANIZING INITIATIVE
99 Chauncy St. #600
Boston, MA 02111
Michael Jacoby Brown, Executive Director
Tel: (617) 350-9994 Fax: (617) 350-9995
Email: joi@jewishorganizing.org
Web: www.jewishorganizing.org

NATIONAL BIG BROTHER BIG SISTER ASSOCIATION
Big Sister Association of Greater Boston
161 Massachusetts Ave., 2nd Fl.
Boston, MA 02115
Jerry Martinson, Executive Director
Tel: (617) 236-8060 Fax: (617) 236-8075
Email: bigsister@bigsister.org
Web: www.bigsister.org

THE SHARING FOUNDATION
P.O. Box 600
Concord, MA 01742
Nancy W. Hendrie, M.D., President
Tel: (978) 369-1120
Email: nhendrie@roteang.org
Web: www.sharingfoundation.org

STUDENT ORGANIZATION

ARMENIAN STUDENTS' ASSOCIATION OF AMERICA, INC.
Boston
P.O. Box 79019
Waverly, MA 02479-0019
Email: asa@asainc.org
Web: www.asainc.org/boston/

ASIAN AMERICAN ASSOCIATION
4 University Hall
Cambridge, MA 02138
Email: hraaa@hcs.harvard.edu
Web: www.hcs.harvard.edu/~hraaa

ASIAN AMERICAN STUDENTS IN ACTION AT WILLIAMS COLLEGE
Williams College Multicultural Center
Jenness House, 10 Morley Dr.
Williamstown, MA 01267
Lillian Chang, Co-Chair
Tel: (413) 597-3340
Email: lillian.chang@williams.edu
Web: http://wso.williams.edu/orgs/aasia/

ASIAN COMMUNITY
Tufts University
Mayer Campus Cir.
Medford, MA 02155
Kim Sue, President
Email: jleung02@tufts.edu
Web: http://ase.tufts.edu/act

CHINESE STUDENTS & SCHOLARS ASSOCIATION
Harvard University
Dudley House, Harvard University
Cambdridge, MA 02138
Kai Guo, President
Email: admin@hcssa.org
Web: www.hcssa.org

HANSORI
Massachusetts Institute of Technology
77 Massachusetts Ave.
Cambridge, MA 02139-4307
Jason Kim, Co-President
Web: www.mit.edu/activities/hansori/hansori-home.html

HARVARD PROJECT FOR ASIAN AND INTERNATIONAL RELATIONS
P.O. Box 380032
Cambridge, MA 02238
Yanjun Wang, Chief Executive Officer
Tel: (617) 384-1158 Fax: (617) 384-1158
Email: hpair@hcs.harvard.edu
Web: www.hpair.org

HARVARD SOCIETY OF ARAB STUDENTS
Harvard College
University Hall, 1st Fl., Students Activity Center
Cambridge, MA 02138
Noor Al-Dabbagh, President
Email: arabs@hcs.harvard.edu
Web: www.hcs.harvard.edu/~arabs

INTERCOLLEGIATE TAIWANESE AMERICAN STUDENTS ASSOCIATION
P.O. Box 961856
Boston, MA 02196
David K. Lee, President
Email: info@itasa.org
Web: www.itasa.org

KOREAN STUDENTS ASSOCIATION
Massachusetts Institute of Technology
77 Massachusetts Ave.
Cambridge, MA 02139-4307
Soojin Lee, President
Tel: (617) 253-1000
Email: ksa-exec@mit.edu
Web: http://web.mit.edu/ksa/www/intro.htm

MUSLIM STUDENTS' ASSOCIATION
Massachusetts Institute of Technology
Religious Activities Center, 77 Massachusetts Ave.
Cambridge, MA 02139
Omar Abdala, President
Tel: (617) 258-9285
Email: msa-ec@mit.edu
Web: http://mit.edu/mitmsa/www

Tufts University
44 Professors Row #92
Medford, MA 02155
Zaid Al-Hinai, President
Email: ist@tufts.edu
Web: www.ase.tufts.edu/msat

PAKISTANI STUDENTS AT MIT
Massachusetts Institute of Technology
77 Massachusetts Ave.
Cambridge, MA 02139
Asfandyar Qureshi, President
Tel: (617) 253-1000
Email: pakistanis@mit.edu
Web: http://web.mit.edu/paksmit/www/home.html

THAI STUDENT ASSOCIATION IN BOSTON
1085 Commonwealth Ave. #185
Boston, MA 02215-1023
Tel: Fax: (617) 787-4292
Email: twa@nwg.nectec.or.th
Web: www.nectec.or.th/users/pong/TSAB

THE ARABIC HERITAGE CLUB
Northeastern University
232A Curry Student Ctr.
Boston, MA 02115
Yarub Al-Yarubi, President
Tel: (617) 373-2637
Email: nuahc@mail2arab.com
Web: www.atsweb.neu.edu/arabsa

TUFTS ASSOCIATION OF SOUTH ASIANS
Tufts University
Medford, MA 02155
Roneel Punjabi, President
Tel: (617) 628-5000
Email: Roneel.Punjabi@tufts.edu
Web: http://ase.tufts.edu/tasa/

TURKISH STUDENT ASSOCIATION
Tufts University
29 Chetwynd Rd. #2

Somerville, MA 02144
Can Saydam, President
Tel: (617) 718-9671
Email: turkishstudenta@hotmail.com
Web: www.ase.tufts.edu/tsa

VIETNAMESE STUDENTS CLUB
Tufts University
Medford, MA 02155
David Nguyen, Co-President
Tel: (617) 628-5000
Email: david.nguyen@tufts.edu
Web: http://ase.tufts.edu/vsc/

MICHIGAN

ARTISTIC

ARAB THEATRICAL ARTS GUILD
1420 Dacosta St.
Dearborn, MI 48128
Tel: (313) 563-4126
Email: info@arabtheater.org
Web: www.arabtheater.org

JEWISH THEATER GRAND RAPIDS
160 Fountain NE
Grand Rapids, MI 49503
Tel: (616) 234-3946
Email: info@jtgr.org
Web: www.jtgr.org

BUSINESS

DETROIT CHINESE BUSINESS ASSOCIATION
P.O. Box 2769
Dearborn, MI 48123
Raymond Xu, President
Email: info@dcba.com
Web: www.dcba.com

CHAMBER OF COMMERCE

AMERICAN ARAB CHAMBER OF COMMERCE
4917 Schaefer #215
Dearborn, MI 48126
Nasser Beydoun, Executive Director
Tel: (313) 945-1700 Fax: (313) 945-6697
Email: nbeydoun@americanarab.com
Web: www.americanarab.com

CULTURAL

AMERICAN FEDERATION OF RAMALLAH PALESTINE
Michigan
27484 Ann Arbor Trail
Westland, MI 48185
Tel: (734) 425-1600 Fax: (734) 425-3985
Email: afrp@afrp.org
Web: www.afrp.org

AMERICAN ORIENTAL SOCIETY
University of Michigan
Hatcher Graduate Library
Ann Arbor, MI 48109-1205
Jonathan Rogers
Tel: (734) 647-4760
Email: jrodgers@umich.edu
Web: www.umich.edu/~aos

AMERICAN-ARAB ANTI-DISCRIMINATION COMMITTEE
Greater Detroit Chapter
P.O. Box 4227
Dearborn, MI 48121
Abed Ayoub, Chapter President
Tel: (313) 995-3333
Email: aayoub@adc.org
Web: www.adcmichigan.org

ARAB AMERICAN AND CHALDEAN COUNCIL
Administrative Office
28551 Southfield Rd. #204
Lathrup Village, MI 48076
Dr. Haifa Fakhouri, President/CEO
Tel: (248) 559-1990 Fax: (248) 559-9117
Email: acc@arabacc.org
Web: www.arabacc.org

ARAB COMMUNITY CENTER FOR ECONOMIC & SOCIAL SERVICES
Cultural Arts
2601 Saulino Ct.
Dearborn, MI 48120
Dr. Anan Ameri, Executive Director
Tel: (313) 843-2844 Fax: (313) 843-0097
Email: aameri@accesscommunity.org
Web: www.accesscommunity.org

ASIAN YOUNG PROFESSIONAL GROUP
7270 Finnegan Dr.
West Bloomfield, MI 48322
Iris Shen-Van Buren, President
Tel: (248) 737-5534
Email: aypg@yahoogroups.com

ASSOCIATION OF NEPALESE IN MIDWEST AMERICA
West Bloomfield, MI
Pradeep Dhital, President
Tel: (248) 738-0270
Email: pdhital@aol.com
Web: www.ansca.org

GREAT LAKES AMERICAN TURKISH CULTURAL ASSOCIATION
1956 Lac Du Mont Dr.
Haslett, MI 48840
Email: president@gatca.org
Web: www.gatca.org

JEWISH HISTORICAL SOCIETY OF MICHIGAN
6600 W. Maple Rd.
West Bloomfield, MI 48322-3003
Robert D. Kaplow, President
Tel: (248) 432-5600 X2517
Email: jhsofmichigan@msn.com
Web: www.michjewishhistory.org

LEBANESE AMERICAN HERITAGE CLUB
13530 Michigan Ave. #227
Dearborn, MI 48126
Ali Berry, President
Tel: (313) 846-8480 Fax: (313) 846-8480
Email: lahc@lahc.org

MAM NON ORGANIZATION
P.O. Box 8206
Ann Arbor, MI 48107
Linh Song, Director
Tel: Fax: (734) 527-6007
Email: info@mamnon.org
Web: www.mamnon.org

PHILIPPINE AMERICAN COMMUNITY CENTER OF MICHIGAN
17356 Northland Park Ct.
Southfield, MI 48075
Efren Platon, Chairperson
Tel: (248) 443-7037 Fax: (248) 443-7078
Email: paccm@paccm.org
Web: www.paccm.org

SHAKUNAGE CONSULTING, INC.
838 Stuart
East Lansing, MI 48823
Dianne Alexanian, Director
Tel: (517) 332-3221
Email: info@shakunage.org
Web: www.shakunage.org

TURKISH AMERICAN CULTURAL ASSOCIATION OF MICHIGAN
P.O. Box 3552
Farmington Hills, MI 48333
Canon Ozaktay, President

Tel: (248) 763-9544 Fax: (248) 626-8279
Email: tacam@tacam.org
Web: www.tacam.org

VIETNAMESE ASSOCIATION OF MICHIGAN
500 W. Lenawee St. #317
Lansing, MI 48933
Van Tien Le, President
Tel: (517) 485-9208 Fax: (517) 485-9224
Email: support@hoinguoivietmi.org
Web: www.hoinguoivietmi.org

POLITICAL ACTION

AMERICAN-ARAB ANTI-DISCRIMINATION COMMITTEE
Flint Chapter
414 Oldmill Dr.
Flushing, MI 48433
Khalil Khrais, Chapter President
Tel: (810) 659-2855
Email: rabbas@adc.org
Web: www.adc.org

Greater Michigan Office
13530 Michigan Ave. #329
Dearborn, MI 48126
Imad Hamad, Regional Director
Tel: (313) 581-1201 Fax: (313) 581-1604
Email: adcmichigan@adc.org
Web: www.adcmichigan.org

ARAB AMERICAN INSTITUTE
Michigan Chapter
4917 Schaefer Rd. #214
Dearborn, MI 48126
Tel: (313) 584-8868 Fax: (313) 584-1388
Email: aaimichigan@hotmail.com
Web: www.aaiusa.org

ASIAN PACIFIC AMERICAN LABOR ALLIANCE
Michigan Pre-Chapter
8731 E. Jefferson
Detroit, MI 48214
Ying Gee, Chapter Coordinator
Tel: (313) 926-5361 Fax: (313) 926-5708
Email: ygee@uaw.net
Web: www.apalanet.org

PROFESSIONAL

AMERICAN SOCIETY OF ENGINEERS OF INDIAN ORIGIN-MICHIGAN CHAPTER
P.O. Box 87676
Canton, MI 48187
Yogi Patel, Treasurer
Tel: (313) 393-3434
Email: info@aseimichigan.org
Web: www.aseimichigan.org

BANGLADESH MEDICAL ASSOCIATION OF NORTH AMERICA
Michigan Chapter
3376 Vineyardhill Dr.
Rochester, MI 48306
Dr. Sunil Das, President
Tel: (248) 475-9476
Web: www.ama-assn.org

NATIONAL ARAB AMERICAN MEDICAL ASSOCIATION
Michigan Chapter
801 S. Adams Rd. #208
Birmingham, MI 48009
Ellen R. Potter, Executive Director
Tel: (248) 646-3661 Fax: (248) 646-0617
Email: naama@naama.com
Web: www.naama.com

NETWORK OF INDIAN PROFESSIONALS-MICHIGAN
Network of Indian Professionals of North America
Jignesh Desai, President/Treasurer
Email: jdesai@yahoo.com
Web: www.netip-mi.org

RELIGIOUS

CAMBODIAN BUDDHIST SOCIETY OF MICHIGAN INC.
P.O. Box 1533
Holland, MI 49422-1533
Heng Van Mork

CAMBODIAN FELLOWSHIP CHRISTIAN REFORMED CHURCH
238 W. 15th St.
Holland, MI 49423
Socheth-Na
Tel: (616) 392-1014
Web: www.pathwaystudio.com/devo/churchdir/chdirpages/cambcrc.html

CHINESE CHRISTIAN FELLOWSHIP CHURCH IN ANN ARBOR
P.O. Box 3188
Ann Arbor, MI 48106
David Soemarko, Elder
Email: david@dsoemarko.us
Web: www.ccfcaa.org

CONGREGATION B'NAI MOSHE
6800 Drake Rd.
West Bloomfield, MI 48322
Dennis Deutsch, President
Tel: (248) 788-0600 Fax: (248) 788-0604
Email: cbminfo@bnaimoshe.org
Web: www.bnaimoshe.org

KOREAN PRESBYTERIAN CHURCH OF METRO DETROIT
27075 W. 9 Mile Rd.
Southfield, MI 48034
Rev. Kwan David Whang, Pastor
Tel: (248) 356-4488 Fax: (248) 356-6119
Web: www.kpcmd.org

KOREAN UNITED METHODIST CHURCH AT ANN ARBOR
1526 Franklin St.
Ann Arbor, MI 48103
Steve Khang, English Ministry Pastor
Tel: (734) 662-0660
Email: joon@kumcaa.org
Web: www.kumcaa.org

LANSING KOREAN UNITED METHODIST CHURCH
1120 S. Harrison Rd.
East Lansing, MI 48823
Tel: (517) 333-3633 Fax: (517) 669-1275
Email: Borincho@comcast.net
Web: www.lkumc.org

PEOPLE OF THE BOOK LUTHERAN OUTREACH
Dearborn Heights
922 N. Beech Daly Rd.
Dearborn Heights, MI 48127
Tel: (313) 563-2051
Email: pobloffice@sbcglobal.net
Web: www.poblo.org

Lansing
501 W. Saginaw
Lansing, MI 48933
Tel: (517) 372-1631
Email: shanti72r@yahoo.com
Web: www.poblo.org

ST. JOHN'S ARMENIAN CHURCH
22001 Northwestern Hwy.
Southfield, MI 48075
Rev. Garabed Kochakian, Pastor
Tel: (248) 569-3405 Fax: (248) 569-0716
Web: www.stjohnsarmenianchurch.org

ST. MARY'S SYRIAN ORTHODOX CHURCH
25566 Lahser Rd.
Southfield, MI 48034
Tel: (586) 779-2230
Email: morthmariyam@yahoo.com

ST. MICHAEL THE ARCHANGEL RUSSIAN ORTHODOX CHURCH
26355 W. Chicago Rd.
Redford, MI 48239
Rev. Michael E. Barna, Dean Emeritus
Tel: (313) 937-2120
Email: ftim@twmi.rr.com
Web: www.stmichaelroc.org

ST. SARKIS ARMENIAN APOSTOLIC CHURCH
19300 Ford Rd.
Dearborn, MI 48128
Rev. Fr. Daron Stepanian, Pastor
Tel: (313) 336-6200 Fax: (313) 336-4530
Email: rev.fr.daron@saintsarkis.org
Web: www.saintsarkis.org

TEMPLE B'NAI ISRAEL
4409 Grand Prairie Rd.
Kalamazoo, MI 49006
Ellen Winter, President
Tel: (269) 342-9170
Email: eflannerywinter@chartermi.com
Web: www.kzootemple.org

TEMPLE BETH EL
7400 Telegraph Rd.
Bloomfield, MI 48301
Daniel B. Syme, Rabbi
Tel: (248) 851-1100 Fax: (248) 851-1187
Email: rabbisstudy@tbeonline.org
Web: www.tbeonline.org

5150 Calkinds Rd.
Flint, MI 48532
Karen Companez, Rabbi
Tel: (810) 720-9494 Fax: (810) 720-1912
Email: rabbi@templebethelflint.org
Web: www.templebethelflint.org

TEMPLE EMANUEL
1715 E. Fulton St.
Grand Rapids, MI 49503
Tom Heitman, President
Tel: (616) 459-5976 Fax: (616) 459-6510
Email: president@templeemanuelgr.org
Web: www.templeemanuelgr.org

TEMPLE KOL AMI
5085 Walnut Lake Rd.
West Bloomfield, MI 48323
Norman T. Roman, Rabbi
Tel: (248) 661-0040
Email: temple@tkolami.org
Web: www.tkolami.org

SCIENTIFIC

AMERICAN COMMITTEE FOR THE WEIZMANN INSTITUTE OF SCIENCE
6735 Telegraph Rd. #365
Bloomfield Hills, MI 48301
Ira Mondry, Regional Chair
Tel: (248) 258-9890
Email: michigan@acwis.org
Web: www.weizmann-usa.org

SPEC. INT., COUNSELING

MICHIGAN ASIAN INDIAN FAMILY SERVICES
P.O. Box 252673
West Bloomfield, MI 48325
Kitty Prasad, chairperson
Tel: (248) 477-4985 Fax: (248) 477-2366
Email: info@maifs.org
Web: www.maifs.org

SPEC. INT., EDUCATION

ANN HUA CHINESE SCHOOL
P.O. Box 130212
Ann Arbor, MI 48113-0212
Tel: (734) 668-7659
Email: annhuaschool@yahoo.com
Web: www.annhua.org

ASHA FOR EDUCATION
Ann-Arbor
P.O. Box 130751
Ann Arbor, MI 48113
Kumar Velayudham, Publicity Co-ordinator
Tel: (586) 578-4354
Email: kumarvel@umich.edu
Web: www.ashanet.org/annarbor/

ASIAMERICA FOUNDATION DARUNEE FUND
P.O. Box 1184
Ann Arbor, MI 48106-1184
Tel: (734) 994-6106 Fax: (734) 998-0163
Email: usoffice@daruneefund.org
Web: www.daruneefund.org/asiamerica.htm

ASSOCIATION FOR ASIAN STUDIES
1021 E. Huron St.
Ann Arbor, MI 48104
Mary Elizabeth Berry, President
Tel: (734) 665-2490 Fax: (734) 665-3801
Email: meberry@socrates.berkeley.edu
Web: www.aasianst.org

CENTER FOR CHINESE STUDIES
University of Michigan
SSWB #3669, 1080 S. University Ave.
Ann Arbor, MI 48109-1106
James Lee, Director
Tel: (734) 764-6308 Fax: (734) 764-5540
Email: chinese.studies@umich.edu
Web: www.umich.edu/~iinet/ccs/

CENTER FOR SOUTHEAST ASIAN STUDIES
University of Michigan
1080 S. University Ave. #3640
Ann Arbor, MI 48109-1106
Judith O. Becker, Director
Tel: (734) 764-0352 Fax: (734) 936-0996
Email: csseas@umich.edu
Web: www.umich.edu/~iinet/cseas/

CHINA BLUE CHARITY FUND
University of Michigan
3909 Michigan Union 81
Ann Arbor, MI 48109
Email: chinablue@umich.edu
Web: www.chinabluecharity.org

JAPANESE TEACHERS ASSOCIATION OF MICHIGAN
8 Vernon Ave.
Battle Creek, MI 49014
Anne Hooghart, President
Tel: (616) 965-2326
Email: hooghart@msu.edu
Web: www.emich.edu/public/foreignlanguages/jpne/jtam.html

JEWISH THEOLOGICAL SEMINARY
Great Lakes Region
6735 Telegraph Rd. #310
Bloomfield Hills, MI 48301
Tom Wexelberg-Clouser, Director
Tel: (248) 258-0055
Web: www.jtsa.edu

NATIONAL ASIAN PACIFIC AMERICAN LAW STUDENT ASSOCIATION
Thomas M. Cooley Law School
300 S. Capitol Ave.
Lansing, MI 48933
Tel: (517) 334-5704 Fax: (517) 334-5772
Web: www.cooley.edu

US CHINA PEOPLES FRIENDSHIP ASSOCIATION
Greater Lansing Chapter
1019 Abbott Rd.
East Lansing, MI 48823
Rosemary Severance, Contact
Tel: (517) 351-6351
Web: www.uscpfa.org

SPEC. INT., EMPLOYMENT

ARAB COMMUNITY CENTER FOR ECONOMIC & SOCIAL SERVICES
Employment & Training
6451 Schaefer Rd., 2nd Fl.
Dearborn, MI 48126
Sonia Harb, Director
Tel: (313) 945-8159 Fax: (313) 624-9417
Email: sharb@accesscommunity.org
Web: www.accesscommunity.org

JEWISH VOCATIONAL SERVICE
29699 Southfield Rd.
Southfield, MI 48076-2063
Barbara Nurenberg, President/CEO
Tel: (248) 559-5000 Fax: (248) 559-0773
Email: info@jvsdet.org
Web: www.jvsdet.org

SPEC. INT., HEALTH SERVICES

ARAB COMMUNITY CENTER FOR ECONOMIC & SOCIAL SERVICES
Community Health & Research Center
6450 Maple St.
Dearborn, MI 48126
Dr. Adnan Hammad, Director
Tel: (313) 216-2200 Fax: (313) 584-3206
Email: ahammad@accesscommunity.org
Web: www.accesscommunity.org

SPEC. INT., HUMAN RELATIONS

AMERICAN FEDERATION OF MUSLIMS OF INDIAN ORIGIN
29008 W. 8th Mile Rd.
Farmington, MI 48336
Dr. Sayed Samee, National President
Web: www.afmi.org

ARAB COMMUNITY CENTER FOR ECONOMIC & SOCIAL SERVICES
Main Office
2651 Saulino Ct.
Dearborn, MI 48120
Ismael Ahmed, Executive Director
Tel: (313) 842-7010 Fax: (313) 842-5150
Email: iahmed@accesscommunity.org
Web: www.accesscommunity.org

ASIAN AMERICAN CITIZENS FOR JUSTICE
19111 W. 10 Mile Rd. #121
Southfield, MI 48075
Nati Jenks, Director
Tel: (248) 352-1020 Fax: (248) 352-1020
Email: travelsfun@mich.com

ASSOCIATION OF CHINESE AMERICANS
420 Peterboro
Detroit, MI 48201
Shenlin Chen, Director
Tel: (313) 831-1790 Fax: (313) 831-3156
Email: contactus@acadetroit.org
Web: www.acadetroit.org

COUNCIL ON AMERICAN-ISLAMIC RELATIONS
Michigan Chapter
28820 Southfield Rd. #126
Lathrup Village, MI 48076
Umar Abdur-Rahman, Director
Tel: (248) 569-2203 Fax: (248) 569-9748
Email: cairmichigan@yahoo.com
Web: www.cairmichigan.org

HOLOCAUST MEMORIAL CENTER
28123 Orchard Lake Rd.
Farmington Hills, MI 48334
Gail Cohen, Tour Coordinator
Tel: (248) 553-2400 Fax: (248) 553-2433
Email: info@holocaustcenter.org
Web: www.holocaustcenter.org

SOCIETY FOR HUMANISTIC JUDAISM
26811 W. 12 Mile Rd.
Farmington Hills, MI 48334

Rabbi Miriam Jerris, Contact
Tel: (248) 478-7610 Fax: (248) 478-3159
Email: info@shj.org
Web: www.shj.org

THE AMERICAN JEWISH COMMITTEE
Detroit Chapter
6735 Telegraph #320
Bloomfield Hills, MI 48301-3145
Sharona Shapiro, Michigan Area Director
Tel: (248) 646-7686 Fax: (248) 646-7688
Email: detroit@ajc.org
Web: www.ajc.org

THE IRAQI HUMAN RIGHTS SOCIETY
21505 John R. Rd.
Hazel Park, MI 48030
Tel: (248) 722-2907 Fax: (248) 398-4509
Email: ihrusa@yahoo.com
Web: www.geocities.com/iraqihumanrightsusa/00201.htm

SPEC. INT., LEGAL ASSISTANCE

JEWISH LABOR COMMITTEE
Detroit Chapter
8846 Robindale
Detroit, MI 48239
Selma Goode, Contact
Tel: (313) 534-0553
Email: DetroitJLC@aol.com
Web: www.jewishlabor.org

SPEC. INT., SENIORS

JEWISH HOME AGING SERVICES
6710 W. Maple Rd.
West Bloomfield, MI 48322
Tel: (248) 661-2999 Fax: (248) 661-1628
Web: www.jhas.org

SPEC. INT., SOCIAL INTEREST

ALPHA IOTA OMICRON FRATERNITY
Alpha Chapter
925 S. State St.
Ann Arbor, MI 48104
Neal Pancholi, Co-President
Tel: (281) 300-8974
Email: pancholi@umich.edu
Web: www.aio-um.com

ASIAN CENTER OF WEST MICHIGAN
401 W. Fulton St. #359C
Grand Rapids, MI 49504
Elizabeth MacLahlan, Office Manager
Tel: (616) 331-6570 Fax: (616) 331-6570
Email: centera@gvsu.edu
Web: www.asiancenter.info

BURMESE RELIEF CENTER-USA
1401 Woodlawn Park Dr.
Flint, MI 48503-2768
Tel: (810) 341-6960
Email: burmese@brelief.net
Web: www.brelief.net

FLINT JEWISH FEDERATION
619 Wallenberg St.
Flint, MI 48502
Tel: (810) 767-5922 Fax: (810) 767-9024
Email: fjf@tm.net
Web: http://users.tm.net/flint

HMONG AMERICAN COMMUNITY
2101 West Holmes Rd.
Lansing, MI 48911
Cheu Xiong, Director
Tel: (517) 272-1582 Fax: (517) 272-0853
Email: hmongamerican58@hotmail.com

JEWISH COMMUNITY CENTER OF METROPOLITAN DETROIT
D. Dan and Betty Kahn Bldg.
6600 W. Maple Rd.
West Bloomfield, MI 48322-3022

Hannan Lis, President
Tel: (248) 661-1000
Web: www.jccdet.org

JEWISH COMMUNITY CENTER OF METROPOLITAN DETROIT
Jimmy Prentis Morris Bldg.
15110 W. Ten Mile
Oak Park, MI 48237-1472
Hannan Lis, President
Tel: (248) 967-4030
Web: www.jccdet.org

JEWISH COMMUNITY CENTER OF WASHTENAW COUNTY
2935 Birch Hollow Dr.
Ann Arbor, MI 48108
David Segaloff, President
Tel: (734) 971-0990 Fax: (734) 677-0109
Email: jcc@jccfed.org
Web: www.jccannarbor.org

JEWISH COMMUNITY COUNCIL OF METROPOLITAN DETROIT
6735 Telegraph Rd. #100
Bloomfied Hills, MI 48301
David Gad-Harf, Executive Director
Tel: (248) 642-5393 Fax: (248) 642-6469
Email: council@jfmd.org
Web: www.jewishcommunitycouncil.org

JEWISH FAMILY SERVICE OF METROPOLITAN DETROIT
Southfield Office
24123 Greenfield Rd.
Southfield, MI 48075
Norman Keane, Executive Director
Tel: (248) 559-1500 Fax: (248) 559-9858
Email: jcranston@jfsdetroit.org
Web: www.jfsdetroit.org

West Bloomfield Office
6960 Orchard Lake Rd.
West Bloomfield, MI 48322
Norman Keane, Executive Director
Tel: (248) 737-5055 Fax: (248) 737-9858
Email: jcranston@jfsdetroit.org
Web: www.jfsdetroit.org

JEWISH FEDERATION OF GRAND RAPIDS
4127 Embassy Dr. SE
Grand Rapids, MI 49546
Tel: (616) 942-5553 Fax: (616) 942-5780
Email: jcfgr@iserv.net
Web: www.jewishgrandrapids.org

JEWISH FEDERATION OF METROPOLITAN DETROIT
P.O. Box 2030
Bloomfield, MI 48303-2030
Tel: (248) 642-4260 Fax: (248) 642-4985
Email: jfmd@jfmd.org
Web: www.thisisfederation.org

JEWISH FEDERATION OF WASHTENAW COUNTY
2939 Birch Hollow Dr.
Ann Arbor, MI 48108
Tel: (734) 677-0100 Fax: (734) 677-0109
Email: info@jewishannarbor.org
Web: www.jewishannarbor.org

THE JAPAN-AMERICA SOCIETY OF WEST MICHIGAN
Commerce Pt. #80, 77 E. Michigan Ave.
Battle Creek, MI 49017
Tel: (616) 962-4076 Fax: (616) 962-6309
Email: info@jaswm.org
Web: www.us-japan.org/jaswm

TIBET MICHIGAN
40 Monroe Ctr. NW #304
Grand Rapids, MI 49503
Glenn Freeman, Administrator
Tel: (616) 235-0284 Fax: (616) 235-0284
Email: tibetmichiganmain@yahoo.com
Web: www.tibetmichigan.home-page.org

UNITED AMERICAN LEBANESE FEDERATION
26331 Southfield Rd.
Lathrup Village, MI 48076
Warren David, President
Tel: (586) 979-3801 Fax: (810) 821-5970
Email: rahee@aheecommunications.com

SPEC. INT., WOMEN

ASIAN PACIFIC AMERICAN WOMEN'S ASSOCIATION
1138 Woodwind Trail
Haslett, MI 48840
Margo K. Smith, Chair
Tel: (517) 339-4170 (h)
Email: smithmk@msu.edu

HADASSAH
Greater Detroit Chapter
5030 Orchard Lake Rd.
West Bloomfield, MI 48323
Susan Luria, President
Tel: (248) 683-5030 Fax: (248) 683-1139
Email: ediskin@hadassah.org
Web: www.hadassah.org

MICHIGAN CHINESE WOMEN'S ASSOCIATION
1902 Old Orchard Ct.
Ann Arbor, MI 48103
Regin Yang, President
Tel: (734) 662-4992
Email: ayang@umic.edu
Web: www.mcwa.net

NATIONAL COUNCIL FOR JEWISH WOMEN
Greater Detroit Section
26400 Lahser Rd. #100
Southfield, MI 48034
Susan Gertner, President
Tel: (248) 355-3300 Fax: (248) 355-9951
Email: ncjwgds@earthlink.com
Web: www.ncjwgds.org

STUDENT ORGANIZATION

ARMENIAN STUDENTS' CULTURAL ASSOCIATION
University of Michigan, Ann Arbor
3909 Michigan Union, 530 State St.
Ann Arbor, MI 48109
Aram Gavoor, Co-President
Email: asca-info@umich.edu
Web: www.umich.edu/~armenia

CHINESE STUDENT ASSOCIATION
University of Michigan, Ann Arbor
4156 Michigan Union
Ann Arbor, MI 48109
Manling Tong, President
Email: manlingt@umich.edu
Web: www.umich.edu/~umcsa

FILIPINO STUDENT SOCIETY
Wayne State University
Student Center Bldg., 2nd Fl. #193
Detroit, MI 48202
Nanette Maranan, President
Email: filsoc@wayne.edu
Web: www.filsoc.uni.cc

INDIAN AMERICAN STUDENT ASSOCIATION
530 S. State St. #4347
Ann Arbor, MI 48104
Neal Pancholi, President
Tel: (281) 300-8974
Email: pancholi@umich.edu
Web: www.umich.edu/~iasa

INDIAN STUDENTS' ASSOCIATION
University of Michigan
4302 Michigan Union, 530 State St.
Ann Arbor, MI 48109

Parag Dixit, Member
Email: isa.contact@umich.edu
Web: www.umich.edu/~isa

KOREAN INTERNATIONAL STUDENT ASSOCIATION
University of Michigan, 603 Madison St.
Ann Arbor, MI 48109-1370
Tel: (734) 764-9310
Email: kisa.staff@umich.edu
Web: www.umich.edu/~icenter.intlstudents/
studentorgs/index.html

KOREAN STUDENTS UNITED
Michigan State University
101 Student Services Bldg.
East Lansing, MI 48824
Thomas Cho
Tel: (517) 980-4445
Web: www.msu.edu/~ksu/

LEBANESE STUDENT ASSOCIATION
University of Michigan
Ann Arbor, MI 48109
Yumna Mackie, President
Email: lsaeboard@umich.edu
Web: www.umich.edu/~lebanese

MUSLIM STUDENTS' ASSOCIATION
University of Michigan
530 S. State St.
Ann Arbor, MI 48104
Saif Omar, President
Email: saifomar@umich.edu
Web: www.umich.edu/~muslims

PAKISTANI STUDENTS' ASSOCIATION
University of Michigan, Ann Arbor
Ann Arbor, MI 48109
Sukaina Sangji, Execuive Chair
Tel: (734) 764-1817
Email: psa.board@umich.edu
Web: www.umich.edu/~pakistan

PERSIAN STUDENTS ASSOCIATION
University of Michigan
3909 Michigan Union, 530 S. State St.
Ann Arbor, MI 48109
Sonya Hovsepian, President
Email: persians.board@umich.edu
Web: www.umich.edu/~persians

PHILIPPINE STUDY GROUP STUDENT ASSOCIATION
University of Michigan
44124 Richmond
Canton, MI 48187
Tel: (313) 717-4083
Email: philippinestudygroup1@hotmail.com
Web: www.umich.edu/~psgsa

TAIWANESE STUDENT ASSOCIATION
Michigan Technological University
211 W. McNair Hall
Houghton, MI 49931
Chiang Wen-Po, President
Tel: (906) 483-6180
Email: tsa@mtu.edu
Web: www.sos.mtu.edu/tsa

THAI STUDENT ASSOCIATION
Western Michigan University
1903 W. Michigan Ave.
Kalamazoo, MI 49008
Anupon Naksut, President
Tel: (269) 387-1000
Web: www.rso.wmich.edu/thai/index.html

TURKISH STUDENT ASSOCIATION
University of Michigan
Michigan Student Assembly, 530 S. State St.
Ann Arbor, MI 48109-1349
Fatih Kocer, President
Email: turkishboard@umich.edu
Web: www.umich.edu/~umtsa

MINNESOTA

ARTISTIC

INDONESIAN PERFORMING ARTS ASSOCIATION OF MINNESOTA
P.O. Box 582133
Minneapolis, MN 55458-2133
John Brower, Executive Director
Tel: (651) 766-9377
Email: ipaam@ipaam.org
Web: www.ipaam.org

MIXED BLOOD THEATRE COMPANY
1501 S. 4th St.
Minneapolis, MN 55454
Christine Nelson, Production Manager
Tel: (612) 338-7892
Email: cnelson@mixedblood.com
Web: www.mixedblood.com

MU PERFORMING ARTS
2700 NE Winter St. #1A
Minneapolis, MN 55413
Rick Shiomi, Artistic Director
Tel: (612) 824-4804 Fax: (612) 824-3396
Email: info@muperformingarts.org
Web: www.muperformingarts.org

CHAMBER OF COMMERCE

AMERICAN-ISRAEL CHAMBER OF COMMERCE & INDUSTRY OF MINNESOTA, INC.
13100 Wayzata Blvd. #200
Minnetonka, MN 55305
Daniel Lieberman, President
Tel: (952) 593-8666
Email: info@aiccmn.org
Web: www.aiccmn.org

MINNESOTA HMONG CHAMBER OF COMMERCE
1885 University Ave. #20
St. Paul, MN 55104
Chengy Thao-Yang, Chair
Tel: (651) 645-6777 Fax: (651) 645-6784
Email: info@mnhmongchamber.com
Web: www.hmongchamber.com

VIETNAMESE AMERICAN CHAMBER OF COMMERCE
1159 University Ave. #106
St. Paul, MN 55104
Tyler Le, President
Tel: (651) 209-1708 Fax: (651) 209-1709
Email: info@vietnamesechamber.com
Web: www.vietnamesechamber.com

COMMUNICATIONS

ASIAN MEDIA ACCESS
3028 Oregon Ave. South
Minneapolis, MN 55426
Ange Hwang, Executive Director
Tel: (612) 376-7715 Fax: (612) 373-2751
Email: amamedia@amamedia.org
Web: www.amamedia.org

CHINESE COMMUNICATION ASSOCIATION
University of Minnesota
329 Murphy Hall
Minneapolis, MN 55455
Junhao Hong, President
Email: jhong@buffalo.edu
Web: http://sjmc.cla.umn.edu/cca/index.htm

CULTURAL

CENTER FOR ASIANS AND PACIFIC ISLANDERS
3702 E. Lake St. #200
Minneapolis, MN 55406
Vee Phan Nelson, Executive Director
Tel: (612) 721-0122
Web: www.capiusa.org

CHINESE AMERICAN ASSOCIATION OF MINNESOTA
P.O. Box 582584
Minneapolis, MN 55458
Vincent Mar, President
Email: info@caam.org
Web: www.caam.org

CULTURAL SOCIETY OF FILIPINO-AMERICANS
P.O. Box 2773
St. Paul, MN 55102
Glen King, President
Tel: (763) 571-7696
Web: www.csfamn.org

HMONG NATIONALITY ARCHIVES
775 N. Milton St. #109
St. Paul, MN 55104-1565
Tzianeng Vang, President
Tel: (651) 338-7443 Fax: (651) 293-3994
Email: hna1999@hmongarchives.org
Web: www.hmongarchives.org

INDIA ASSOCIATION OF MINNESOTA
P.O. Box 130158
St. Paul, MN 55113
Rabinder Bains, President
Tel: (651) 735-4322
Email: president@iamn.org
Web: www.iamn.org

KOREAN CULTURE CAMP, INC.
3424 Crost Dr.
St. Anthony, MN 55418
Joan Scipior, Contact
Tel: (612) 789-5288
Email: joan@donfred.com
Web: www.koreanculturecampmn.org

TAIWANESE ASSOCIATION OF AMERICA
Minnesota Chapter
19779 182nd Ave.
Big Lake, MN 55309
Ray Tsai, President
Tel: (763) 350-2106
Email: taamn@taamn.org
Web: www.taamn.org

THAI LANGUAGE AND CULTURE SERVICE
869 Westview Ct.
Shoreview, MN 55126
Kalong Sujjapunroj, Consultant
Tel: (651) 486-8286 Fax: (651) 486-8286
Email: sujja001@umn.edu

TURKISH AMERICAN ASSOCIATION OF MINNESOTA
P.O. Box 14704
Minneapolis, MN 55414
John Serim, President
Email: President@taam.org
Web: www.taam.org

MULTI-PURPOSE

ASIAN AMERICAN RENAISSANCE
P.O. Box 4154
Saint Paul, MN 55104
Tel: (651) 641-4040

GLOBAL COUNCIL OF PAKISTAN
609 Oak St. SE #2-10
Minneapolis, MN 55414
Email: info@gcpak.org
Web: www.gcpak.org

SOUTHEAST ASIAN COMMUNITY COUNCIL
555 Girard Terr. North #110
Minnneapolis, MN 55405
Cha Lee, Executive Director
Tel: (612) 342-1530 Fax: (612) 377-2163
Email: info@fafeacc-mn.org

POLITICAL ACTION

ASIAN PACIFIC AMERICAN LABOR ALLIANCE
Minnesota Pre-Chapter
c/o AFT, 2025 75th Ct. North
Brooklyn Park, MN 55444
Lyfu Vang, Contact Person
Tel: (612) 668-1934
Email: apala@apalanet.org
Web: www.apalanet.org

COUNCIL ON ASIAN-PACIFIC MINNESOTANS
658 Cedar St #160
Saint Paul, MN 55155
Kao Ly ILean Her, Executive Director
Tel: (651) 296-0538 Fax: (651) 297-8735
Email: kao.ly.her@state.mn.us
Web: www.state.mn.us/ebranch/capm

JEWISH COMMUNITY ACTION
2375 University Ave. West #150
St. Paul, MN 55114-1633
Suzanne Bring, Development Director
Tel: (651) 632-2184 Fax: (651) 632-2188
Email: suzanne@jewishcommunityaction.org
Web: www.jewishcommunityaction.org

PROFESSIONAL

ASIAN AMERICAN JOURNALISTS ASSOCIATION
Minnesota Chapter
345 Cedar St.
St. Paul, MN 55101
Nancy Ngo, President
Tel: (651) 228-5172 Fax: (651) 228-5177
Email: nngo@pioneerpress.com
Web: www.aaja.org

NATIONAL ASIAN PACIFIC AMERICAN BAR ASSOCIATION OF MINNESOTA
600 Nicollet Mall #380
Minneapolis, MN 55402
Dan Lew, President
Tel: (651) 215-0653 Fax: (651) 215-0673
Email: dan.lew@state.mn.us
Web: www.napaba.org

PHILIPPINE-MINNESOTAN MEDICAL ASSOCIATION
P.O. Box 25815
Woodbury, MN 55125
Bernard R. Quebral, President
Tel: (651) 739-4416 Fax: (651) 769-0571
Email: info@pmmamd.org
Web: www.pmmamd.org

RELIGIOUS

B'NAI ISRAEL SYNAGOGUE
621 2nd St. SW
Rochester, MN 55902
Tel: (507) 288-5825 Fax: (507) 288-8562
Email: bnaisrael@aol.com
Web: www.bnaisrael.org

CHINESE CHRISTIAN CAMPUS FELLOWSHIP
1795 Eustis St.
Lauderdale, MN 55113
Tel: (651) 644-9321
Email: cccf@umn.edu
Web: www.tc.umn.edu/~cccf

FILIPINO AMERICAN CHRISTIAN CHURCH
2025 Skillman Ave. West
Roseville, MN 55115
Sanny Olojan, Pastor
Tel: (651) 631-0211
Email: sanny.olojan@filamchurchmn.org
Web: www.filamchurchmn.org

JAPANESE FELLOWSHIP CHURCH
4217 Bloomington Ave.
Minneapolis, MN 55407
Tel: (612) 722-8315

KOREAN ADOPTEES MINISTRY
P.O. Box 130563
Roseville, MN 55113
Rev. Sung Chul Park, Director/Minister
Tel: (877) KAM-9294 Fax: (651) 647-6775
Email: scpark-kam@hotmail.com
Web: www.kam3000.org

KOREAN HOPE PRESBYTERIAN CHURCH
Mendota Heights, MN 55118
Fax: (651) 905-0360

TWIN CITY CHINESE CHRISTIAN CHURCH
1795 Eustis St.
Lauderdale, MN 55113
Samuel Ng, Elder
Tel: (651) 644-9321
Email: contact@tcccc.org
Web: www.tcccc.org

WAT LAO MINNESOTA
22605 Cedar Ave.
Farmington, MN 55024-9691
Tel: (952) 469-1692
Web: www.angelfire.com/mn2/watlao/

SPEC. INT., CHILD CARE

CHILDREN'S SHELTER OF CEBU
P.O. Box 247
Cambridge, MN 55008
Tel: (763) 689-6558
Email: cscusa@cscshelter.org
Web: www.cscshelter.org

CHINA AIDS ORPHAN FUND
The Minneapolis Foundation
800 IDS Ctr., 80 S. 8th St.
Minneapolis, MN 55402
Ms. Peg Helminski, Communication Coordinator
Email: PegHelminski@aol.com
Web: www.chinaaidsorphanfund.org

SPEC. INT., COUNSELING

JEWISH FAMILY AND CHILDREN'S SERVICE OF MINNEAPOLIS
13100 Wayzata Blvd. #400
Minnetonka, MN 55305
Tel: (952) 546-0616 Fax: (952) 593-1778
Email: jfcs@jfcsmpls.org
Web: www.jfcsmpls.org

SPEC. INT., EDUCATION

ASIAN PACIFIC AMERICAN LEARNING RESOURCE CENTER
185 Klaeber Ct., 320 16th Ave. SE
Minneapolis, MN 55455
Vang Lee, Coordinator
Tel: (612) 624-2317
Email: leexx048@umn.edu
Web: www.apalrc.umn.edu

FILIPINO AMERICAN WOMEN'S NETWORK
P.O. Box 16533
St. Paul, MN 55117
Kim Paray, Director
Tel: (763) 560-5858
Email: info@fawmn.org
Web: www.fawnmn.org

FREEMAN CENTER FOR INTERNATIONAL ECONOMIC POLICY
University of Minnesota
301 19th Ave. South
Minneapolis, MN 55455
G. Edward Schuh, Regents Professor
Tel: (612) 626-0564 Fax: (612) 625-3513
Email: geschuh@hhh.umn.edu
Web: www.hhh.umn.edu

FRIENDS OF CHINA- USA
14833 57th St. North

Stillwater, MN 55082
Email: friendsofchina@juno.com
Web: http://friendsofchina.net

MINNEAPOLIS JEWISH DAY SCHOOL
4330 Cedar Lake Rd.
Minneapolis, MN 55416
Dr. Ray Levi, Head of School
Tel: (952) 381-3500 Fax: (952) 381-3501
Email: apayton@mjds.net
Web: www.mjds.net

US CHINA PEOPLES FRIENDSHIP ASSOCIATION
Duluth Chapter
810 E. 4th St.
Duluth, MN 55880
Greg W. Stoewer, Contact
Tel: (218) 525-1577
Web: www.uscpfa.org

Minnesota Chapter
P.O. Box 251002
Woodbury, MN 55125
Mary Warpeha, President
Tel: (651) 638-0743
Email: info@uscpfa-mn.org
Web: www.uscpfa-mn.org

National Office
3000 Foxpoint Rd.
Burnsville, MN 55337
Barbara Harrison, National President
Tel: (952) 894-5745 Fax: (952) 894-5745
Email: harri089@tc.umn.edu
Web: www.uscpfa.org

SPEC. INT., EMPLOYMENT

JEWISH VOCATIONAL SERVICE
Minneapolis Office
430 1st Ave. North #620
Minneapolis, MN 55401
Terri Gordon, Chair
Tel: (612) 692-8920 Fax: (612) 692-8921
Email: jvs@jvsmn.org
Web: www.jvsmn.org

SPEC. INT., FAMILY PLANNING

ADOPTED KOREAN CONNECTION
12676 74th Ave. South
Maple Grove, MN 55369
Tawni Traynor, Board Member
Tel: (612) 532-9913
Email: contact@akconnection.com
Web: www.akconnection.com

FAMILY AND YOUTH ADVANCEMENT SERVICES, INC.
1031 Payne Ave.
St. Paul, MN 55101
T. Cher Moua, Founder/Executive Director
Tel: (651) 774-5567 Fax: (651) 774-5924
Email: info@hmongfamily.org
Web: www.hmongfamily.org

OMBUDSPERSON FOR ASIAN-PACIFIC FAMILIES
State of Minnesota
1450 Energy Park Dr. #106
St. Paul, MN 55108-5227
Bauz L. Nengchu, Ombuds Person for Asian Pacific Families
Tel: (651) 643-2514 Fax: (651) 643-2539
Email: bauz.nengchu@mnfamiliesombuds.org

SPEC. INT., HEALTH SERVICES

DISABLE HOME HEALTH CARE, INC.
1086 Race St. #2
St. Paul, MN 55117
Tong P. Yang, President
Tel: (651) 292-8705 Fax: (651) 488-7364
Email: yanglyfashions@cs.com

SPEC. INT., HUMAN RELATIONS

HMONG MUTUAL ASSISTANCE ASSOCIATION, INC.
1130 N. 7th St.
Minneapolis, MN 55411
Xang Vang, Executive Director
Tel: (612) 374-2694 Fax: (612) 374-5205
Email: admin@hamaa.org
Web: www.hamaa.org

HUMAN RIGHTS CENTER
University of Minnesota
N120 Mondale Hall, 229 19th Ave. South
Minneapolis, MN 55455
Jacqueline Romano, Office Manager
Tel: (612) 626-0041 Fax: (612) 626-7592
Email: humanrts@umn.edu
Web: www.umn.edu/humanrts

JEWISH COMMUNITY RELATIONS COUNCIL MINNESOTA AND THE DAKOTAS
12 N. 12th St. #480
Minneapolis, MN 55403
Julie Swiler, Director of Public Affairs
Tel: (612) 338-7816 Fax: (612) 349-6569
Email: info@minndakjcrc.org
Web: www.minndakjcrc.org

LAO FAMILY COMMUNITY OF MINNESOTA, INC.
320 W. University Ave.
St. Paul, MN 55103
Ying Vang, Executive Director
Tel: (651) 221-0069 Fax: (651) 221-0276
Email: admin@laofamily.org
Web: www.laofamily.org

ORGANIZATION OF CHINESE AMERICANS
Minnesota
P.O. Box 11146
St. Paul, MN 55111
Jeff Eng, President
Tel: (651) 633-0075

OUTREACH ASIA
5608 Benton Ave.
Edina, MN 55436
Mike Peck, President
Tel: (952) 922-8536
Email: outreachasia@msn.com
Web: www.outreachasia.org

PILLSBURY UNITED COMMUNITIES- THE WAITE HOUSE
2529 13th Ave. South
Minneapolis, MN 55404
Adri Fuel
Tel: (612) 721-1681 Fax: (612) 721-2752

THE CHILDREN'S DEFENSE FUND
200 University Ave. West #210
St. Paul, MN 55103
Jim Koppel, Director
Tel: (651) 227-6121 Fax: (651) 227-2553
Email: cdf-mn@cdf-mn.org
Web: www.cdf-mn.org

UNITED JEWISH FUND AND COUNCIL OF ST. PAUL
790 Cleveland Ave. South #227
St. Paul, MN 55116
Eli Skora, Executive Director
Tel: (651) 690-1707 Fax: (651) 690-0228
Email: webmaster@ujfc.org
Web: www.jewishminnesota.org

SPEC. INT., IMMIGRATION

INTERCULTURAL MUTUAL ASSISTANCE ASSOCIATION OF SOUTHEASTERN MINNESOTA
300 11th Ave. NW
Rochester, MN 55901
Ron Buzard, Executive Director
Tel: (507) 289-5960 Fax: (507) 289-6199
Email: imaa@imaa.net
Web: www.imaa.net

SPEC. INT., SOCIAL INTEREST

HMONG AMERICAN PARTNERSHIP
1075 Arcade St.
St. Paul, MN 55106
William Yang, Director
Tel: (651) 495-9160 Fax: (651) 495-1699
Email: hapmail@hmong.org
Web: www.hmong.org

Minneapolis
1121 Glenwood Ave. North
Minneapolis, MN 55405
Gaoxee Yang, Manager
Tel: (612) 377-6482 Fax: (612) 377-4633
Email: hapmail@hmong.org
Web: www.hmong.org

HMONG CULTURAL CENTER, INC.
995 University Ave. West #214
Saint Paul, MN 55104
Txong Pao Lee, Executive Director
Tel: (651) 917-9937 Fax: (651) 917-9978
Email: pao@hmongcenter.org
Web: www.hmongcenter.org

HMONG NATIONAL ORGANIZATION, INC.
501 N. Dale St. #106
St. Paul, MN 55103
Nou Yang, Associate Director
Tel: (651) 290-2343 Fax: (651) 228-7272
Email: nou@hmongnat.org
Web: www.hmongnat.org

JAPAN AMERICA SOCIETY OF MINNESOTA
Riverplace EH-131, 43 Main St.
SE Minneapolis, MN 55414
Takuzo Ishida, President
Tel: (612) 627-9357 Fax: (612) 379-2393
Web: www.mn-japan.org

JEWISH COMMUNITY SERVICES OF GREATER ST. PAUL AREA
1375 St. Paul Ave.
St. Paul, MN 55116
Dori Denelle, Executive Director
Tel: (651) 698-0751 Fax: (651) 698-8591
Email: info@stpauljcc.org
Web: www.stpauljcc.org

JEWISH FAMILY SERVICE OF ST. PAUL
1633 W. 7th St.
St. Paul, MN 55102
Rena Waxman, Executive Director
Tel: (651) 698-0767 Fax: (651) 698-0162
Email: info@jfssp.org
Web: www.jfssp.org

LAO ASSISTANCE CENTER OF MINNESOTA
503 Irving Ave. North #100A
Minneapolis, MN 55405
Sunny Chanthanovong, Executive Director
Tel: (651) 374-4967 Fax: (612) 374-4821
Email: laoassistance@qwest.net
Web: www.laocenter.org

MINNEAPOLIS JEWISH FEDERATION
13100 Wayzata Blvd. #200
Minnetonka, MN 55305
Joshua Fogelson, Executive Director
Tel: (952) 593-2600 Fax: (952) 593-2544
Email: webmaster@ujfc.org
Web: www.jewishminnesota.org

MINNESOTA INDONESIA SOCIETY
76010 7th Ct. NE
Minneapolis, MN 55434
Wiwiek Santoso, President
Tel: (763) 755-3894
Email: nefoea@yahoo

MOTHERS ASSOCIATION FOR KOREAN-AMERICANS
P.O. Box 32094
Fridley, MN 55432
Patricia O' Neill, President
Tel: (651) 454-1955
Email: info@imaka.org
Web: www.imaka.org

NATIONAL INSTITUTE OF ADMINISTRATION ALUMNI ASSOCIATION
P.O. Box 14572
Minneapolis, MN 55414
Thoi Xuan Tran, Chairman
Tel: (763) 783-9575 Fax: (763) 783-1864
Email: tom42tran@hotmail.com

PAN ASIAN AMERICAN VOICES FOR EQUALITY
8625 Hunters Way
Apple Valley, MN 55124
Karen Tanaka Lucas, Director
Tel: (952) 431-1740 Fax: (952) 431-1740
Email: lucasskgl@aol.com

SABES JEWISH COMMUNITY CENTER
4330 S. Cedar Lake Rd.
Minneapolis, MN 55416
Fred Leeb, Interim COO
Tel: (952) 381-3400 Fax: (952) 381-3401
Email: info@sabesjcc.org
Web: www.sabesjcc.org

UNITED CAMBODIAN ASSOCIATION
1101 N. Snelling Ave.
St. Paul, MN 55108
Sotheary Duong, Executive Director
Tel: (651) 222-3299 Fax: (651) 222-3599

VIETNAMESE BROADCASTING OF MINNESOTA
P.O. Box 40459
Saint Paul, MN 55104
Hoa Young, Chair
Tel: (651) 307-4283
Email: contact@vbmtv.com
Web: www.vbmtv.org

VIETNAMESE COMMUNITY OF MINNESOTA
P.O. Box 43939
Brooklyn Park, MN 55443
Thang Dinh Le, Board of Representatives
Email: thangle2007@aol.com

VIETNAMESE COMMUNITY OF THE USA
P.O. Box 14572
Minneapolis, MN 55414
Thoi Xuan Tran, President
Tel: (763) 783-9575 Fax: (763) 783-1864

VIETNAMESE SOCIAL SERVICES OF MINNESOTA
1159 University Ave. West
St. Paul, MN 55104
Yen Pham, Executive Director
Tel: (651) 641-8907 Fax: (651) 641-8908
Email: ypham@vssmn.org
Web: www.vssmn.org

SPEC. INT., WOMEN

ASIAN WOMEN UNITED OF MINNESOTA
1954 University Ave. #4
St. Paul, MN 55104
Sinuon Sin, Executive Director
Tel: (651) 646-2118 Fax: (651) 646-2284
Email: awum@awum.org
Web: www.awum.org

ASSOCIATION FOR THE ADVANCEMENT OF HMONG WOMEN IN MINNESOTA
4403 Lake St.
Minneapolis, MN 55406
Ly Vang, Director
Tel: (612) 724-3066 Fax: (612) 724-3098
Email: info@aahwm.org
Web: www.aahwm.org

BLACK, INDIAN, HISPANIC, AND ASIAN WOMEN IN ACTION
1830 James Ave. North
Minneapolis, MN 55411
Alice O. Lynch, Executive Director
Tel: (612) 521-2986 Fax: (612) 529-6745
Email: info@biha.net
Web: www.biha.net

HADASSAH
Upper Midwest Region
4820 Minnetonka Blvd. #305
Minneapolis, MN 55416
Deborah Bearman Jewett, President
Tel: (952) 924-4999 Fax: (952) 922-0929
Email: umregion@hadassah.org
Web: www.hadassah.org

LAO WOMEN ASSOCIATION
503 Irving Ave. North #100A
Minneapolis, MN 55405
Phouninh Vixayvong, Executive Director
Tel: (612) 374-4967 Fax: (612) 374-4821
Email: laoassistance@qwest.net
Web: www.laocenter.org

NATIONAL ASIAN PACIFIC AMERICAN WOMEN'S FORUM
Minnesota Chapter
P.O. Box 160032
St. Paul, MN 55116
Pacyinz Lyfound, Representative
Tel: (651) 296-9825
Email: manjusuri@yahoo.com
Web: www.napawf.org/mn

NATIONAL COUNCIL FOR JEWISH WOMEN
Greater Minneapolis Section
3000 S. Highway 100 #500
St. Louis Park, MN 55416
Soni Cohen, President
Tel: (952) 922-7900 Fax: (952) 922-7901
Email: tmgsoni@aol.com
Web: www.ncjwmpls.org

NATIONAL COUNCIL FOR JEWISH WOMEN
St. Paul Section
St. Paul, MN
Tel: (651) 768-0173
Email: Info@ncjwstpaul.org
Web: www.ncjwstpaul.org

SPEC. INT., YOUTH

LAO PARENTS AND TEACHERS ASSOCIATION
2648 W. Broadway Ave.
Minneapolis, MN 55411
Tel: (612) 302-9048 Fax: (612) 522-2431
Email: laoptamn@laopta.org
Web: www.laopta.org

STUDENT ORGANIZATION

ASIAN AMERICAN LAW STUDENTS ASSOCIATION
University of Minnesota
229 19th Ave. South
Minneapolis, MN 55455
Neng Vue, President
Tel: (651) 731-5953
Email: vuex0066@umn.edu

ASIAN AMERICAN STUDENT UNION
University of Minnesota
Coffman Memorial Union, 300 Washington Ave. SE #219
Minneapolis, MN 55455
Surya Sukumar, President
Tel: (612) 624-9824
Email: asu@umn.edu
Web: www.tc.umn.edu/~asu/

CAMBODIAN STUDENTS ASSOCIATION OF MINNESOTA
University of Minnesota
300 Washington Ave. SE
Minneapolis, MN 55455
Southear Ben, President
Tel: (612) 659-9176
Email: csam@umn.edu
Web: www.tc.umn.edu/~csam

CHINESE AMERICAN STUDENT ASSOCIATION
University of Minnesota
Coffman Union, 300 Washington Ave. SE #219
Minneapolis, MN 55455
Email: casa@umn.edu
Web: www.tc.umn.edu/~casa

HILLEL
University of Minnesota
1521 University Ave. SE
Minneapolis, MN 55414
Amy Olson, Director
Tel: (612) 379-4026 Fax: (612) 379-9004
Email: hillel@umn.edu
Web: www.tc.umn.edu/~hillel

HMONG MINNESOTA STUDENT ASSOCIATION
University of Minnesota
300 Washington Ave. #226-C
Minneapolis, MN 55455
Tel: (612) 624-9749
Email: hmsa@umn.edu
Web: www.tc.umn.edu/~hmsa/

INDIAN STUDENT ASSOCIATION
University of Minnesota
900 Washington Ave. SE
Minneapolis, MN 55414
Anuratha Elayaperumal, President
Tel: (763) 360-4795
Email: indians@umn.edu
Web: www.tc.umn.edu/~indians

KOINONIA
University of Minnesota
701 8th Ave. NW
New Brighton, MN 55112
Young Park, President
Tel: (651) 633-2434
Email: park0594@mn.edi
Web: www.mnkoinonia.com

KOREAN CHRISTIAN CAMPUS FELLOWSHIP
University of Minnesota
300 Washington Ave. SE #126
Minneapolis, MN 55455
Jin Choi, President
Tel: (612) 801-0974
Email: choi0126@umn.edu

KOREAN GRADUATE STUDENT ASSOCIATION
University of Minnesota
1622 Carl St. #215
St. Paul, MN 55108
Jaewon Kim, President
Tel: (612) 220-0683
Email: jwkim@ece.umn.edu

KOREAN INTERNATIONAL STUDENT ORGANIZATION
University of Minnesota
1112 8th St. SE #15
Minneapolis, MN 55414
Kyom Bae, President
Tel: (612) 623-0478
Email: kiso@umn.edu
Web: www.tc.umn.edu/~kiso

KOREAN STUDENT ASSOCIATION IN COMPUTER SCIENCE
University of Minnesota
414 7th Ave. SE #B304
Minneapolis, MN 55414
Sungil Hong, President
Tel: (612) 379-2561
Email: hong0098@umn.ed

MALAYSIAN STUDENTS ASSOCIATION
University of Minnesota
220 Delaware St. SE #173
Minneapolis, MN 55455
Munir Sulaiman, President
Tel: (612) 301-4226

Email: persisma@tc.umn.edu
Web: www.tc.umn.edu/~persisma

MINNESOTA CHINESE STUDENT ASSOCIATION
University of Minnesota
825 Washington Ave. SE #201
Minneapolis, MN 55414
Colin Lin, President
Tel: (612) 379-3992
Email: mcsa@tc.umn.edu
Web: www.tc.umn.edu/~mcsa

NEPALESE STUDENT ORGANIZATION
Minnesota State University
International Students Office, P.O. Box 8400
Mankato, MN 56002
Email: nsc_mankato@yahoo.com
Web: http://krypton.mnsu.edu/~nestcom

PAKISTAN STUDENT ASSOCIATION
Minnesota State University
1904 Warren St. #107
Mankato, MN 56001
Momen Sajjad, President
Tel: (507) 382-7596
Email: momen.sajjad@mnsu.edu
Web: http://krypton.mnsu.edu/~psa

PAKISTANI STUDENT ASSOCIATION
University of Minnesota
University of Minnesota
Minneapolis, MN 55455
Usman Anwer, President
Email: anwe0004@umn.edu
Web: www.tc.umn.edu/~psa

PHILIPPINE STUDENTS' ASSOCIATION
University of Minnesota
300 Washington Ave. SE
Minneapolis, MN 55455
Email: philsa@umn.edu

THAI STUDENT ASSOCIATION OF THE UNIVERSITY OF MINNESOTA
University of Minnesota
700 5th Ave. SE
Minneapolis, MN 55414
Anjalee Tangjaturonrusamee, President
Tel: (612) 378-9402
Email: tang0160@umn.edu
Web: www.umn.edu/~thaisa

VIETNAMESE STUDENT ASSOCIATION
University of Minnesota
Asian American Student Union
300 Washington Ave. SE #219
Minneapolis, MN 55455
Lan Nguyen, Secretary
Email: vsa@umn.edu
Web: www.tc.umn.edu/~vsa

MISSISSIPPI

CULTURAL

THE BENEVOLENT ASIAN JADE SOCIETY OF NEW ENGLAND
P.O. Box 6061
Boston, MS 02114
Benjamin Leong, President

POLITICAL ACTION

INDIAN AMERICAN FORUM FOR POLITICAL EDUCATION
Mississippi Chapter
23 Moss Forest Cir.
Jackson, MS 39211
Shampat Shivangi, Chapter President
Tel: (601) 956-2301 Fax: (601) 956-2301
Email: drssshivangi@aol.com
Web: www.iafpe.org

SPEC. INT., EDUCATION

US CHINA PEOPLES FRIENDSHIP ASSOCIATION
Hazlehurst Chapter
413 Pine Ridge Dr.
New Albany, MS 38652
Margaret McLemore, Contact
Tel: (662) 539-0886
Web: www.uscpfa.org

SPEC. INT., HUMAN RELATIONS

SOUTHERN FEDERATION OF SYRIAN LEBANESE AMERICAN CLUBS
P.O. Box 12848
Jackson, MS 39236-2848
Email: sfslac@cs.com
Web: www.sfslac.org

THE CHILDREN'S DEFENSE FUND
P.O. Box 11437
Jackson, MS 39283
Tel: (601) 321-1966 Fax: (601) 321-8736
Web: www.childrensdefense.org

SPEC. INT., SOCIAL INTEREST

JAPAN-AMERICA SOCIETY OF MISSISSIPPI
P.O. Box 16884
Jackson, MS 37236-6884
Kazuko White, President
Tel: (601) 354-1652 Fax: (601) 353-0641
Email: jasmis@bellmouth.net
Web: www.jasmis.us

MISSOURI

BUSINESS

JAPANESE BUSINESS ASSOCIATION AT KANSAS CITY
c/o SONY WRPC, 8281 NW 107th Terr.
Kansas City, MO 64153
Shun Fujishima, President
Tel: (816) 880-6802
Email: Shun.Fujishima@am.sony.com

CHAMBER OF COMMERCE

AMERICA-ISRAEL CHAMBER OF COMMERCE OF ST. LOUIS
12400 Olive Blvd. #246
St. Louis, MO 63141
Allyn Aach, Executive Director
Tel: (314) 205-9400 Fax: (314) 205-9402
Email: email@aiccstl.org
Web: www.aiccstl.org

CULTURAL

CHINESE CULTURE AND EDUCATION FOUNDATION
8601 Olive Blvd., Jeffrey Plz.
St. Louis, MO 63132
Joel Glassman, Director
Tel: (314) 432-3858 Fax: (314) 432-1217
Email: info@ccefoundation.org
Web: www.ccefoundation.org

GREATER KANSAS CITY JAPAN FESTIVAL
P.O. Box 22487
Kansas City, MO 64113-2487
Andrew T. Tsubaki, Executive Director
Tel: (785) 842-3923
Email: atsubaki@sunflower.com
Web: www.gkcjapanfestival.com

INDIA ASSOCIATION OF ST. LOUIS
12808 Stopping Meadows
St. Louis, MO 63131
Shri Thanedar, Board Member
Tel: (314) 432-7878 Fax: (314) 432-2126
Email: sthanedar@aol.com

ST. LOUIS PHILIPPINE-AMERICAN 1904 WORLD'S FAIR CENTENNIAL CELEBRATION, LTD.
P.O. Box 15009, Manchester Rd. #333
Ballwin, MO 63011
Tel: (314) 739-4009
Email: steering@stlphilam.com
Web: www.stlphilam.com

GOVERNMENT

WORLD UNITED FORMOSANS FOR INDEPENDENCE
P.O. Box 411442
Kansas City, MO 64141-1442
Tel: (559) 278-2392 Fax: (559) 278-4911
Email: info@wufi.org
Web: www.wufi.org

MULTI-PURPOSE

JAPAN SOCIETY
14130 Baywood Villages Dr.
St. Louis, MO 63017
Yoshiaki Shibusawa, President
Tel: (314) 453-0690 Fax: (314) 453-0776
Email: shibu@accessus.net

POLITICAL ACTION

INDIAN AMERICAN FORUM FOR POLITICAL EDUCATION
Missouri Chapter
823 White Rock Dr.
St. Louis, MO 63131
Swaren Saxena, President
Tel: (314) 966-6188 Fax: (314) 821-7448
Email: saxenamwi@aol.com
Web: www.iafpe.org

ORGANIZATION OF CHINESE AMERICANS
St. Louis Chapter
P.O. Box 4151
Chesterfield, MO 63006
Matthew Yu, President
Email: president@oca-stl.org
Web: http://oca-stl.org

PROFESSIONAL

NATIONAL ARAB AMERICAN MEDICAL ASSOCIATION
St. Louis Chapter
12825 Dubon Ln.
St. Louis, MO 63131
Dr. Shubany, Chapter President
Tel: (314) 362-2317
Email: naama@naama.com
Web: www.naama.com

NETWORK OF SOUTH ASIAN PROFESSIONALS-ST. LOUIS
Network of Indian Professionals of North America
P.O. Box 170194
St. Louis, MO 63117
Avi Mazumdar, President
Tel: (314) 910-0479
Email: netsap_stl@yahoo.com
Web: www.netsap.net

RELIGIOUS

ASIAN CHRISTIAN MISSION
111 W. 3rd St.
Joplin, MO 64801
Melissa Brown, Secretary
Tel: (417) 782-1381
Email: jyangmi@loxinfo.co.th
Web: www.cartervillecc.org/Missions/Missions_Asian_Christian_Mission.htm

VIETNAMESE BUDDHIST ASSOCIATION OF ST. LOUIS
5234 Bulwer Ave.

St. Louis, MO 63147
Tel: (314) 421-3450 Fax: (618) 621-0109
Email: vienminhtemple@msn.com

RESEARCH

JEWISH GENEALOGICAL SOCIETY OF ST. LOUIS
2203 Seven Pines Dr.
St. Louis, MO 63146
Ilene Wittels, Co-President
Tel: (314) 275-7136
Email: igwittel@artsci.wustl.edu
Web: www.jewishgen.org/jgs-StLouis/

SPEC. INT., COUNSELING

JEWISH FAMILY AND CHILDREN'S SERVICES OF SAINT LOUIS
10950 Schuetz Rd.
St. Louis, MO 63146
Tel: (314) 993-1000 Fax: (314) 812-9398
Email: jfcs@jfcs-stl.org
Web: www.jfcs-stl.org

SPEC. INT., EDUCATION

RIME BUDDHIST CENTER
700 W. Pennway
Kansas, MO 64108
Chuck Stanford, Lama
Tel: (816) 471-7073
Email: Lama108@aol.com
Web: www.rimecenter.org

ST. LOUIS MODERN CHINESE SCHOOL
167 Lamp and Lantern Village #151
Chesterfield, MO 63017-8208
Tel: (314) 779-4270
Email: contact@slmcs.org
Web: www.slmcs.org

US CHINA PEOPLES FRIENDSHIP ASSOCIATION
Kansas City Chapter
201 Woodbridge Ln.
Kansas City, MO 64145
Joyce W. Cox, Contact
Tel: (816) 942-6307
Web: www.uscpfa.org

SPEC. INT., HUMAN RELATIONS

CHINESE AMERICAN FORUM, INC.
P.O. Box 719
St. Charles, MO 63302-0719
Harold Y.H. Law, President
Email: cafpeng@earthlink.net
Web: www.cafmag.org

COUNCIL ON AMERICAN-ISLAMIC RELATIONS
St. Louis Chapter
14366 Manchester #200
St. Louis, MO 63011
James Hacking, Director
Tel: (636) 207-8882 Fax: (314) 754-8117
Email: admin@cair-stl.org
Web: www.cair-stl.org

JEWISH COMMUNITY RELATIONS COUNCIL OF ST. LOUIS
12 Millstone Campus Dr.
St. Louis, MO 63146
Tel: (314) 432-0020 Fax: (314) 989-1361
Email: jcrcstl@jcrcstl.org
Web: www.jcrcstl.org

THE AMERICAN JEWISH COMMITTEE
St. Louis Chapter
7730 Carondelet Ave. #417
St. Louis, MO 63105-3329
Betsy Gallop Dennis, Chapter Director
Tel: (314) 721-8866 Fax: (314) 721-8626
Email: stlouis@ajc.org

Web: www.ajc.org

SPEC. INT., IMMIGRATION

REFUGEE AND IMMIGRATION SERVICES
Diocese of Jefferson City
P.O. Box 417, 1130 E. Elm St.
Jefferson City, MO 65102
Alice Wolters, Director
Tel: (573) 635-9127 Fax: (573) 635-3659
Email: risdjc@mchsi.com

SPEC. INT., SOCIAL INTEREST

JEWISH COMMUNITY ARCHIVES OF GREATER KANSAS CITY
302 Newcomb Hall, UMIC
Kansas City, MO 64110
David Boutros, Associate Director
Tel: (816) 235-1543
Email: whmckc@umkc.edu
Web: www.umkc.edu/whmckc/JCA/JCA.htm

JEWISH FEDERATION OF ST. LOUIS
12 Millstone Campus Dr.
St. Louis, MO 63146
Tel: (314) 432-0020 Fax: (314) 432-1277
Email: jfedstl@jfedstl.org
Web: www.jewishinstlouis.org

JEWISH HERITAGE FOUNDATION OF GREATER KANSAS CITY
1 Ward Pkwy. #234
Kansas City, MO 64112
Steve Israelite, Executive Director
Tel: (816) 561-0563 Fax: (816) 561-0687
Email: jhfsteve@crn.org
Web: www.jhf-kc.org

ST. LOUIS CHRISTIAN CHINESE COMMUNITY SERVICE CENTER
8225 Olive Blvd.
St. Louis, MO 63132
Rev. David Cheung, Board of Director
Tel: (314) 989-1220 Fax: (314) 989-1220
Email: stl-cccsc@sbcglobal.net
Web: www.stl-cccsc.org

SPEC. INT., WOMEN

NATIONAL COUNCIL FOR JEWISH WOMEN
St. Louis Section
8350 Delcrest Dr.
St. Louis, MO 63124
Nancy Siteman, President
Tel: (314) 993-5181 Fax: (314) 993-5362
Email: mail@ncjwstl.org
Web: www.ncjwstl.org

SPEC. INT., YOUTH

NATIONAL CENTER FOR MISSING & EXPLOITED CHILDREN
Kansas City
1018 W. 39th St. #B
Kansas City, MO 64111
Tel: (816) 756-5422 Fax: (816) 756-1804
Web: www.missingkids.com

STUDENT ORGANIZATION

CHINESE STUDENTS AND SCHOLARS ASSOCIATION
University of Missouri-Rolla
Rolla, MO 65409
Feng Liu, President
Tel: (573) 341-6177
Email: flq22@umr.edu
Web: http://web.umr.edu/~cssa/

FRIENDSHIP ASSOCIATION OF CHINESE STUDENTS & SCHOLARS
University of Missouri -Columbia-
International Affairs
A022 Brady Commons

Columbia, MO 65211
Han Xiangyong, President
Tel: (573) 882-3780
Email: xhtxb@mizzou.edu
Web: www.missouri.edu/~facss

THAI STUDENT ASSOCIATION
Southwest Missouri State University
Springfield, MO 65804
Tel: (417) 831-7843
Email: tsa2002n@hotmail.com
Web: http://studentorganizations.smsu.edu/tsa

MONTANA

SPEC. INT., EDUCATION

MAI WAH SOCIETY, INC.
P.O. Box 404
Butte, MT 59703
Jim Griffin, President
Tel: (406) 723-3231
Email: info@maiwah.org
Web: www.maiwah.org

TIBETAN CHILDREN'S EDUCATION FOUNDATION
210 N. Higgins Ave. #336
Missoula, MT 59802
Roy Andes
Tel: (406) 728-7295 Fax: (406) 721-7364
Email: RoyHAndes@aol.com

SPEC. INT., HUMAN RELATIONS

REFUGEE ASSISTANCE CORPORATION
1280 S. 3rd West
Missoula, MT 59801
Mary Yang, Executive Director
Tel: (406) 721-5052 Fax: (406) 721-5055
Email: refugee@centric.net
Web: www.spahs.umt.edu/sw/agencies/
refugeeassist.htm

SPEC. INT., SOCIAL INTEREST

JEWISH COMMUNITY OF FLATHEAD VALLEY BET HARIM, INC.
P.O. Box 364
Kalispell, MT 59903-0364
LeAnn Kalstein, President
Tel: (406) 756-5159
Email: info@betharim.com
Web: www.betharim.com

STUDENT ORGANIZATION

MALAYSIAN STUDENT ASSOCIATION
University of Montana
C201A, University Center
Missoula, MT 59812
Steven Kwan, President
Email: malay@selway.umt.edu
Web: www2.umt.edu/asum/msa

NEBRASKA

CULTURAL

ASIAN COMMUNITY AND CULTURAL CENTER
2615 O St.
Lincoln, NE 68510
Modesta Putla, Executive Director
Tel: (402) 477-3446 Fax: (402) 477-4508
Email: modesta@lincolnasiancenter.org
Web: www.lincolnasiancenter.org

SPEC. INT., FAMILY PLANNING

HEARTLAND FAMILIES WITH CHILDREN FROM CHINA CHAPTER
701 S. 182nd St.
Elkhorn, NE 68022

Kathy Bernal, Leader
Tel: (402) 498-9140

CATHOLIC SOCIAL SERVICES REFUGEE RESETTLEMENT PROGRAM
123 N. 25th St.
Lincoln, NE 68503
Curt Krueger, Resettlement Director
Tel: (402) 474-1600 Fax: (402) 474-1612
Email: ckrueger@csshope.org

HMONG INTERNATIONAL HUMAN RIGHTS WATCH
P.O. Box 4965
Omaha, NE 68104
Laura Xiong, Executive Director
Email: info@hmongihrw.org
Web: www.hmongihrw.org

SPEC. INT., SOCIAL INTEREST

AFGHAN RENASCENT YOUTH ASSOCIATION
6316 Tanglewood Ln.
Lincoln, NE 68516
Farida Ebrahim, President
Tel: (402) 890-7018
Email: febrahim2@unl.edu
Web: www.aryahelps.org

INDIAN ASSOCIATION OF LINCOLN
5430 Bison Dr.
Lincoln, NE 68516
Sudesh Batra, President
Tel: (402) 423-5568
Email: jagsudesh@yahoo.com

JEWISH FEDERATION OF OMAHA
333 S. 132nd St.
Omaha, NE 68154-2198
Tel: (402) 334-8200 Fax: (402) 334-1330
Email: pmonsk@top.net
Web: www.jewishomaha.org

NATIVE AMERICAN PUBLIC TELECOMMUNICATIONS, INC.
P.O. Box 83111
Lincoln, NE 68501
Frank Blythe, Executive Director
Tel: (402) 472-3522 Fax: (402) 472-8675
Email: native@unl.edu
Web: www.nativetelecom.org

NEVADA

CULTURAL

CHINESE CULTURAL FOUNDATION
8808 Canyon Springs Dr.
Las Vegas, NV 89117
Frank Tsou, President
Tel: (702) 255-8788 Fax: (702) 255-8656
Web: www.lvcc.org

LAS VEGAS HAWAIIAN CIVIC CLUB
P.O. Box 29237
Las Vegas, NV 89126-9237
Helene K. Pierce, President
Tel: (702) 382-6939
Email: info@lvhcc.org
Web: www.lvhcc.org

SINGAPORE ASSOCIATION OF NEVADA
1930 Village Center Cir. #3-281
Las Vegas, NV 89134
K.C. Tan, President
Email: info@singaporenevada.org
Web: www.singaporenevada.org

VIETNAMESE COMMUNITY ASSOCIATION
2951 Copper Beach Ct.
Las Vegas, NV 89117
Long Pham, Contact
Tel: (702) 734-3804 Fax: (702) 240-0928

LAW ENFORCEMENT

NEVADA ASIAN PACIFIC POLICE OFFICERS ASSOCIATION
3141 E. Sunrise
Las Vegas, NV 89101
Gary Schofield, President

MULTI-PURPOSE

ASIAN PACIFIC AMERICAN FORUM
2983 Pinehurst Dr.
Las Vegas, NV 89101
Rozita Lee, Chairwoman
Tel: (702) 739-9311 Fax: (702) 732-3313
Email: rozitalee@aol.com

CHUNG YING TANG FOUNDATION
3773 Howard Hughes Pkwy. #350 North
Las Vegas, NV 89109
Merlinda Gallegos, Program Director
Tel: (702) 734-3700 Fax: (702) 734-6766
Email: mgallegos@tangfoundation.org
Web: www.tangfoundation.org

PROFESSIONAL

ASIAN CHINESE ACADEMIC ASSOCIATION
2245 Homeland St.
Las Vegas, NV 89128
Tony Lei, Chairman
Tel: (702) 255-9058 Fax: (702) 255-9058
Email: tojulei@yahoo.com

ISLAMIC TRAINING FOUNDATION
P.O. Box 3443
Sparks, NV 89432-3443
Rafik Beekun, Contact
Tel: (775) 355-1461 Fax: (775) 355-0393
Email: info@islamist.org
Web: www.islamist.org

VIETNAM HELICOPTER PILOTS ASSOCIATION
Nevada
8420 Culver Ct.
Las Vegas, NV 89117
Email: President@VHPALasVegas.org
Web: www.vhpalasvegas.org

RELIGIOUS

JAPANESE CHRISTIAN CHURCH OF LAS VEGAS
5720 Surfside Ct.
Las Vegas, NV 89110
Tel: (702) 437-5633

TEMPLE BETH SHOLOM
10700 Havenwood Ln.
Las Vegas, NV 89135
Laura Sussman, Executive Director
Tel: (702) 804-1333
Email: lsussman@bethsholomlv.org
Web: www.bethsholomlv.org

TEMPLE SINAI
3405 Gulling Rd.
Reno, NV 89503
Jeff Blanck, President
Tel: (775) 747-5508 Fax: (775) 747-1911
Email: temple.sinai@juno.com
Web: www.uahcweb.org/nv/nv001

SPEC. INT., EDUCATION

LAS VEGAS CHINESE ACADEMY
2120 Waterbury Ln.
Las Vegas, NV 89134
Mei Tang, Manager Principal
Tel: (702) 242-0708 Fax: (702) 242-0708
Email: mwtang@earthlink.net

US CHINA PEOPLES FRIENDSHIP ASSOCIATION
Las Vegas Chapter

1905 Wengert Ave.
Las Vegas, NV 89104
Edna Zhuo, Contact
Tel: (702) 387-6151
Web: www.uscpfa.org

SPEC. INT., HUMAN RELATIONS

JAPANESE AMERICAN CITIZENS LEAGUE
P.O. Box 14458
Las Vegas, NV 89114-4458
Jason Schuck, President
Tel: (702) 655-2561
Email: miyukicats@aol.com

SPEC. INT., LEGAL ASSISTANCE

JEWISH LABOR COMMITTEE
Nevada Chapter
1701 Whitney Mesa #102
Henderson, NV 89014
Gail Tuzzolo
Tel: (702) 933-2140 Fax: (702) 452-9537
Email: tuzzolo@aol.com
Web: www.jewishlabor.org

SPEC. INT., SOCIAL INTEREST

ASIAN SERVICE CENTER
5300 Springmountain Rd. #212E
Las Vegas, NV 89146
Patrick Lau, Manager
Tel: (702) 893-1768 Fax: (702) 893-1782
Email: plau1@aol.com

CHINESE AMERICAN BENEVOLENT ASSOCIATION
3863 S. Valley View Dr. #4
Las Vegas, NV 89103
Alex Young, Former President
Tel: (702) 368- 3332 Fax: (702) 368-2125

ILOCANO AMERICAN ASSOCIATION
5600 Grossmont Ave.
Las Vegas, NV 89110
Fely Dumo, President
Tel: (702) 699-3034
Email: fpdumo@aol.com

JAPAN AMERICA SOCIETY OF NEVADA
P.O. Box 81287, 6882 Edna Ave.
Las Vegas, NV 89180-1287
Tel: (702) 252-0277 Fax: (702) 253-0075
Email: kkb@co.clark.nv.us

JEWISH FEDERATION OF LAS VEGAS
2317 Renaissance Dr.
Las Vegas, NV 89119
Tel: (702) 732-0556 Fax: (702) 732-3228
Web: www.jewishlasvegas.com

SPEC. INT., WOMEN

KOREAN AMERICAN WOMEN'S ASSOCIATION
2708 Faiss Dr.
Las Vegas, NV 89134
Chon Edwards, Founder
Tel: (702) 242-6640
Email: jce15@juno.com

SPEC. INT., YOUTH

PHILIPPINE AMERICAN YOUTH ORGANIZATION
3701 W. Charleston Blvd.
Las Vegas, NV 89102
Janice Aranas, President
Tel: (702) 878-5504 Fax: (702) 878-8206

NEW HAMPSHIRE

CULTURAL

INDIAN ASSOCIATION OF NEW HAMPSHIRE
P.O. Box 3132
Manchester, NH 03105
Prithvi Kumar, President
Email: president@ianh.org
Web: www.ianh.org

SCIENTIFIC

THE JORDAN INSTITUTE
18 Low Ave., 2nd Fl.
Concord, NH 03301
Patrick Miller, Executive Director
Tel: (603) 226-1009 Fax: (603) 226-0042
Email: info@thejordaninstitute.org
Web: www.thejordaninstitute.org

SPEC. INT., SOCIAL INTEREST

JAPAN AMERICAN SOCIETY OF NEW HAMPSHIRE
P.O. Box 1226
Portsmouth, NH 03802-1226
Charles Doleac, Director
Tel: (603) 433-1360 Fax: (603) 433-1360
Email: cdoleac@nhlawfirm.com
Web: www.us-japan.org

JEWISH FEDERATION OF GREATER MANCHESTER
698 Beech St.
Manchester, NH 03104
Marc S. Gilman, President
Tel: (603) 627-7679 Fax: (603) 627-7963
Email: office@jewishnh.org
Web: www.jewishnh.org

STUDENT ORGANIZATION

CHINESE STUDENTS AND SCHOLARS ASSOCIATION
University of New Hamshire
Durham, NH 03824
Jiebing Sun, President
Tel: (603) 862-1393
Email: jsun@cisunix.unh.edu
Web: www.unh.edu/cssa/

NEW JERSEY

ARTISTIC

JAPANESE ARTISTS ASSOCIATION OF NEW YORK, INC.
175 Maplewood Ave.
Bogota, NJ 07603
Keiko Koshimitsu, President
Tel: (201) 457-1030
Email: koshimitsu@jaa-ny.org
Web: www.jaa-ny.org

KOLODZEI ART FOUNDATION, INC.
123 S. Adelaide Ave. #1N
Highland Park, NJ 08904
Tel: (732) 545-8425 Fax: (732) 545-8428
Email: kolodzei@kolodzeiart.org
Web: www.kolodzeiart.org

NATYALAYA, THE ASIAN INDIAN SCHOOL FOR CLASSICAL & FOLK DANCES
208 Powder Mill Rd.
Morris Plains, NJ 07950
Lakshmi Anand, Founder/Director
Tel: (973) 285-0311 Fax: (973) 292-2637
Email: laxmianand@aol.com

BUSINESS

US-CHINA EXCHANGE ASSOCIATION
Headquarters

16 Bridge St.
Metuchen, NJ 08840
Tel: (732) 494-2724 Fax: (732) 494-5802
Web: www.usachina.org

CHAMBER OF COMMERCE

NEW JERSEY CHINESE AMERICAN CHAMBER OF COMMERCE
216 W. State St.
Trenton, NJ 08608
Joan Verplanck, President
Tel: (609) 989-7888 Fax: (609) 989-9696
Email: joan@njchamber.com
Web: www.njchamber.com

NEW JERSEY CHINESE-AMERICAN CHAMBER OF COMMERCE
2147 Route 27, 1st Fl.
Edison, NJ 08817
John Lau, President
Tel: (732) 650-1618 x128 Fax: (732) 650-9668
Email: info@njcacc.org
Web: www.njcacc.org

NEW YORK KOREAN-AMERICAN JUNIOR CHAMBER OF COMMERCE
P.O. Box 256
Palisades Park, NJ 07650
Tel: (201) 941-5441 Fax: (201) 941-5443
Email: info@kajaycees.org
Web: www.kajaycees.com

CULTURAL

AZERBAIJAN SOCIETY OF AMERICA
New Jersey
P.O. Box 69
Lodi, NJ 07644
Web: www.usa.azeris.org

GARDEN STATE CULTURAL ASSOCIATION
P.O. Box 308
Scotch Plains, NJ 07076
Alok Mittra, General Secretary
Tel: (609) 897-9221
Web: www.gsca.us

INDO-AMERICAN CULTURAL SOCIETY
1412 Oak Tree Rd.
Iselin, NJ 08830
Pradeep Kothari, President
Tel: (732) 283-9696 Fax: (732) 283-1091
Email: indoamerican@hotmail.com

JEWISH CULTURAL SCHOOL AND SOCIETY
P.O. Box 3365, Memorial Station
Upper Montclair, NJ 07043
Email: membership@jcss-nj.com
Web: www.jcss-nj.com

JEWISH HISTORICAL SOCIETY OF CENTRAL JERSEY
228 Livingston Ave.
New Brunswick, NJ 08901
Tel: (732) 249-4894
Email: jhscj@cs.com
Web: www.jewishgen.org/jhscj/

JEWISH HISTORICAL SOCIETY OF METROWEST
901 Route 10
Whippany, NJ 07981-1156
Robert R. Max, President
Tel: (973) 929-2995 Fax: (973) 428-8237
Email: jmcgillan@jhsmw.org
Web: www.jhsmw.org

KHMER KAMPUCHEA KROM ASSOCIATION
3405 Federal St.
Camden, NJ 08105
Linh C. Thach, Case Manager
Tel: (856) 488-7979 Fax: (856) 614-0750
Email: khmerkromassociation@comcast.net

KOREAN CULTURAL OUTREACH NETWORK
1562 Lemoine Ave., 2nd Fl.
Fort Lee, NJ 07024
Chris Choe, Contact
Email: info@kcon.org
Web: www.kcon.org

LAND AND CULTURE ORGANIZATION
P.O. Box 1386
Hoboken, NJ 07030
Sylvie Khayat
Tel: (888) LCO-1555
Email: sylvie@landandculture.org
Web: www.lcousa.org

NEW JERSEY CHINESE COMMUNITY CENTER
17 School House Rd.
Somerset, NJ 08854
Tel: (732) 377-0011 Fax: (732) 377-0017
Email: nj@chinese-community-center.org
Web: www.chinese-community-center.org

NEW JERSEY CHINESE CULTURAL STUDIES FOUNDATION
P.O. Box 543
Princeton Junction, NJ 08550
Lily Griggs, Chairman
Tel: (609) 374-2008 Fax: (732) 821-1885
Email: info@njccsf.org
Web: www.njccsf.com

PERSIAN CULTURAL FOUNDATION
210 Cedar St.
Garfield, NJ 07026
Tel: (973) 772-0702 Fax: (973) 772-5858
Email: info@persiancultural.org
Web: http://persiancultural.org

PERSIAN CULTURAL & HUMANITARIAN ASSOCIATION, INC.
P.O. Box 80
Clifton, NJ 07011
Zaman Zamanian, President
Email: pcha@pchanj.com
Web: www.pchanj.com

PHILIPPINE-AMERICAN FRIENDSHIP COMMITTEE, INC.
157A Mallory Ave.
Jersey City, NJ 07304
Lourdes P Corrales, Chairperson
Tel: (201) 332-4711 Fax: (201) 333-6891
Web: www.pafcom.org

SOMERSET COUNTY CULTURAL DIVERSITY COALITION
P.O. Box 5082
Somerville, NJ 08876
Dr. Tulsi R. Maharjan, Chair
Tel: (908) 369-4318
Email: interfaith@raritanval.edu
Web: www.sccdiversity.org

SUMEI MULTIDISCIPLINARY ARTS CENTER
19 Liberty St.
Newark, NJ 07102
Yolan Skeete, Executive Director
Tel: (973) 643-7883 Fax: (973) 242-7914
Email: sumeiart@aol.com
Web: www.sumei.org

TAIWANESE ASSOCIATION OF AMERICA
New Jersey Chapter
P.O. Box 604
Princeton Junction, NJ 08550
Pin Shuo Liu, President
Email: taanjboard@yahoo.com
Web: http://taa.formosa.org/local/nj

LAW ENFORCEMENT

NEW JERSEY ASIAN AMERICAN LAW ENFORCEMENT OFFICERS ASSOCIATION
P.O. Box 958
Old Bridge, NJ 08857
Robert May, President
Email: NJASIANLAW@hotmail.com
Web: www.njaalea.org

MULTI-PURPOSE

PHILIPPINE-AMERICAN COMMUNITY OF BERGEN COUNTY
156 W. Bridle Way
Paramus, NJ 07652
Tel: (201) 845-9674
Email: pacbc@pacbc.org
Web: www.pacbc.org

TZU CHI
New Jersey Office
150 Commerce Rd.
Cedar Grove, NJ 07009
Cheng Yen, Founder
Tel: (973) 857-8666 Fax: (973) 857-9555
Email: info@us.tzuchi.org
Web: http://nj.us.tzuchi.org

POLITICAL ACTION

AMERICAN IRANIAN COUNCIL
20 Nassau St. #111
Princeton, NJ 08542
Hooshang Amirahmadi, Founder/President
Tel: (609) 252-9099 Fax: (609) 252-9698
Email: aic@american-iranian.org
Web: www.american-iranian.org

AMERICAN-ARAB ANTI-DISCRIMINATION COMMITTEE
New Jersey Chapter
P.O. Box 531
West Caldwell, NJ 07007-0531
Aref Assaf, President
Tel: (201) 225-0067
Email: adc@adcnj.us
Web: www.adcnj.us

ARAB AMERICAN INSTITUTE
New Jersey Chapter
390 George St. #409
New Brunswick, NJ 08901
Tel: (732) 246-1254 Fax: (973) 253-6101
Email: aai_newjersey@yahoo.com
Web: www.aaiusa.org

PACIFIC ASIAN COALITION
5 Stonehenge Ln.
Bridgewater, NJ 08807-2063
C. S. Yang, President
Tel: (908) 875-8004
Email: suepaiyang@att.net

PROFESSIONAL

ASIAN INDIAN PROFESSIONALS
64 Regan Ln.
Voorhees, NJ 08043
Dr. Sunder Mansukhani, Founding President
Tel: (856) 751-6342
Email: smansuk@comcast.net

ASIAN PACIFIC AMERICAN LAWYERS ASSOCIATION OF NEW JERSEY, INC.
, NJ
Vimal K. Shah, President
Email: president@apalanj.com
Web: www.apalanj.com

ASSOCIATION OF THAI PROFESSIONALS IN AMERICA AND CANADA
14 Doric Ave.
Parsippany, NJ 07054
Dr. Methi Wecharatana, President
Tel: (973) 299-7992 Fax: (973) 299-1117
Email: mail@atpac.org
Web: www.atpac.org

CHINESE AMERICAN MEDICAL SOCIETY
281 Edgewood Ave.
Teaneck, NJ 07666
Tak Kwan, President
Tel: (201) 833-1506 Fax: (201) 833-8252
Email: hw5@columbia.edu
Web: www.camsociety.org

DASTAK- NETWORK OF PAKISTANI PROFESSIONALS
67 Joni Ave.
Hamilton, NJ 08690
Ahsan Naqvi, President
Email: info@dastak.org
Web: www.dastak.org

INDIAN DENTAL ASSOCIATION OF NORTH AMERICA NEW JERSEY
110 Bergen St. #D-830
Newark, NJ 07103
Asha Samant, President
Tel: (973) 972-4615 Fax: (973) 972-0370
Email: samantas@umdnj.edu

IRANIAN AMERICAN MEDICAL ASSOCIATION
397 Haledon Ave.
Haledon, NJ 07508
Amir Zamani, President
Tel: (973) 595-8888 Fax: (973) 790-7755
Email: info@iama.org
Web: www.iama.org

MONTE JADE SCIENCE AND TECHNOLOGY ASSOCIATION
East Coast Chapter
330 Macland
Keasbey, NJ 08832
William Yeh, Chairman
Tel: (732) 346-0200 Fax: (732) 346-0209
Email: yeh@csico.com
Web: http://cht1.endiva.net/mjeast

Mid Atlantic Chapter
3120 Fire Rd.
Egg Harbor Township, NJ 08234
Dr. James Yoh, Chairman
Tel: (609) 645-0900 Fax: (609) 645-3316
Email: jimmy.yoh@galaxyscientific.com
Web: www.mjma.org

PHILIPPINE NURSES ASSOCIATION OF AMERICA
60 Kingsbridge Dr., Lumberton Township
Mount Holly, NJ 08060-5034
Seny Lipat, President
Tel: (609) 262-9383
Email: PNAA2003@yahoo.com
Web: www.pnaa03.org

PHILIPPINE NURSES ASSOCIATION OF NEW JERSEY
850 Maple Ave.
Piscataway, NJ 08854
Iluminada C. Jurado, President
Email: rpestrada@yahoo.com
Web: www.pnanj.org

RELIGIOUS

ANSHE EMETH MEMORIAL TEMPLE
222 Livingston Ave.
New Brunswick, NJ 08901
Gail R. Kroop, Executive Director
Tel: (732) 545-6484 Fax: (732) 745-7448
Email: exec@aemt.info
Web: http://aemt.net

ARMENIAN MISSIONARY ASSOCIATION OF AMERICA, INC.
31 W. Century Rd.
Paramus, NJ 07652
Ara Balian, President
Tel: (201) 265-2607 Fax: (201) 265-6015
Email: amaa@amaa.org
Web: www.amaa.org

ARMENIAN PRESBYTERIAN CHURCH
140 Forest Ave.
Paramus, NJ 07652
Rev. Berj Gulleyan, Pastor
Tel: (201) 265-8585
Email: apcherald@armenianpresbyterianchurch.org
Web: www.armenianpresbyterianchurch.org

ASIAN INDIAN CHRISTIAN CHURCH (NEW JERSEY)
301 Chestnut St.
Roselle Park, NJ 07204
Rev. B.B.C. Kumar
Tel: (908) 688-8426
Email: pastors@aiccnj.org
Web: www.aiccnj.org

CHINESE CHRISTIAN CHURCH OF NEW JERSEY
232 S. Beverwyck Rd.
Parsippany, NJ 07054
Rev. Paul Siu, Consulting Senior Pastor
Tel: (973) 335-0183
Email: paul.siu@cccnj.org
Web: www.cccnj.org

FIRST FILIPINO BAPTIST CHURCH
65 W. 15th St.
Bayonne, NJ 07002
Rev. Ulysses Marino, Senior Pastor
Tel: (201) 823-0858
Email: ffbcnj@ffbcnj.com
Web: www.ffbcnj.com

HOUSE OF PRAYER FOR ALL NATIONS CHURCH
925 5th Ave.
River Edge, NJ 07661
Brian S. Lee, Senior Pastor
Tel: (201) 576-9110
Email: admin@hop-church.org
Web: www.hop-church.org

JAPANESE CHRISTIAN CHURCH OF NEW JERSEY
120 E. Pleasant Ave.
Maywood, NJ 07607
Manabu Nishikori
Tel: (201) 712-9833 Fax: (201) 251-7977
Web: www.jccofnj.org

KOREA CAMPUS CRUSADE FOR CHRIST IN AMERICA
New Jersey Office
215 Main St.
Fort Lee, NJ 07024
Tel: (201) 947-4145 Fax: (201) 947-3820
Email: nyoffice@kcccusa.org
Web: www.kcccusa.org

KOREAN PRESBYTERIAN CHURCH OF ELIZABETH
700 Bayway Ave.
Elizabeth, NJ 07202
Rev. Isaac Ahn, Pastor
Tel: (908) 354-8848
Email: info@kpce.org
Web: www.kpce.org

MONMOUTH CHINESE CHRISTIAN CHURCH
1209 W. Front St.
Lincroft, NJ 07738
Rev. Paul Chang, Pastor
Tel: (732) 842-2174 Fax: (732) 842-1315
Email: webservant@mccc.org
Web: www.mccc.org

RIVERSIDE CHURCH
925 5th Ave.
River Edge, NJ 07661
Brian Lee, Senior Pastor
Tel: (201) 576-9110
Email: admin@hop-church.org
Web: www.hop-church.org

TAIWANESE AMERICAN FELLOWSHIP PRESBYTERIAN CHURCH
100 Livingston Ave.
New Brunswick, NJ 08901
Rev. Ben Hsieh
Tel: (732) 937-9227 Fax: (732) 937-5119
Email: bhsieh@tafpc.org
Web: www.tafpc.org

TEMPLE BETH EL
2419 Kennedy Blvd.

Jersey City, NJ 07304
Kenneth Brickman, Rabbi
Tel: (201) 333-4229
Email: bethel@betheljc.org
Web: www.betheljc.org

TEMPLE BETH SHOLOM

1901 Kresson Rd.
Cherry Hill, NJ 08003-2580
Jerry Ackerman, Executive Director
Tel: (856) 751-6663 Fax: (856) 751-2369
Email: jerrya@tbsonline.org
Web: www.tbsonline.org

TEMPLE EMANU-EL

180 Piermont Rd.
Closter, NJ 07624
Ilene Anesini, Executive Director
Tel: (201) 750-9997 Fax: (201) 750-1894
Email: info@templeemanu-el.org
Web: www.templeemanu-el.com

TEMPLE EMANU-EL OF WEST ESSEX

264 W. Northfield Rd.
Livingston, NJ 07039
Mary Ann Ferber Levine, President
Tel: (973) 992-5560 Fax: (973) 992-4428
Email: info@emanuel.org
Web: www.emanuel.org

TEMPLE EMANUEL

1101 Springdale Rd.
Cherry Hill, NJ 08003
Ken Korach, President
Tel: (856) 489-0029 Fax: (856) 489-0032
Email: kakorach@traonline.com
Web: www.templeemanuel.org

TEMPLE EMANUEL OF NORTH JERSEY

151 E. 33rd St.
Paterson, NJ 07514
Marc Schwartz, President
Tel: (973) 684-5565 Fax: (973) 279-4123
Email: office@templeemanuelnj.org
Web: www.tenjfl.org

TEMPLE EMANUEL OF THE PASCACK VALLEY

87 Overlook Dr.
Woodcliff Lake, NJ 07677
Andre Ungar, Rabbi
Tel: (201) 391-0801
Email: info@temple-emanuelpv.org
Web: www.temple-emanuelpv.org

TEMPLE SHOLOM

760 Pompton Ave.
Cedar Grove, NJ 07009
Stephen Siegel, President
Tel: (973) 239-1321
Email: ssiegel111@aol.com
Web: www.shalom.net

P.O. Box 539
Scotch Plains, NJ 07076
Susan Weiseman, President
Tel: (908) 889-4900 Fax: (908) 889-9920
Email: temple@sholomnj.org
Web: www.sholomnj.org

P.O. Box 6007
Bridgewater, NJ 08807
Ruth Zelig, President
Tel: (908) 722-1339 Fax: (908) 253-0878
Email: temple.sholom@verizon.net
Web: www.temple-sholom.net

TEMPLE SINAI

208 Summit Ave.
Summit, NJ 07901
Tel: (908) 273-4921 Fax: (908) 273-3653
Email: tempo@templesinainj.org
Web: www.templesinainj.org

THE FIRST FILIPINO AMERICAN UNITED METHODIST CHURCH

110 Hancock Ave.
Jersey City, NJ 07307
Rev. Patria Agustin-Smith, Pastor
Tel: (201) 216-0206

Email: Administration@ffaumc.org
Web: www.ffaumc.org

THE KOREAN FIRST PRESBYTERIAN CHURCH OF TRENTON
Bethany Presbyterian Church Building
400 Hamilton Ave.
Trenton, NJ 08609
Rev. Sang Hak Yu, Pastor
Tel: (609) 730-0028 Fax: (609) 730-0030
Email: KoreanChurch@AsianLink.Net
Web: www.firstkorean.com

THE KOREAN LOGOS PRESBYTERIAN CHURCH

3575 Valley Rd.
Liberty Corner, NJ 07938
Tel: (908) 542-1003
Email: namyoungyoon@yahoo.com
Web: www.klogos.org

UNITED SYNAGOGUE OF CONSERVATIVE JUDAISM
New Jersey Region
P.O. Box 390
Linden, NJ 07036-0390
David Schechner, President
Tel: (908) 925-8725 Fax: (908) 486-8725
Email: njersey@uscj.org
Web: http://uscj.org/njersey

VISHWA HINDU PARISHAD OF AMERICA, INC.

P.O. Box 611
Iselin, NJ 08830
Sushim Mukherji, National Office Manager
Tel: (732) 744-0851 Fax: (732) 744-0847
Email: office@vhp-america.org
Web: www.vhp-america.org

RESEARCH

JIVA USA

1565 Lemoine Ave. #1J
Fort Lee, NJ 07024
Rishi Pal Chauhan, President, Jiva Institute
Tel: (201) 242-9676 Fax: (201) 224-5202
Email: info@jiva.org
Web: www.jiva.org/jivausa

SCIENTIFIC

KOREAN-AMERICAN SCIENTISTS AND ENGINEERS ASSOCIATION
New Jersey Chapter
, NJ
Keyong Ho Yang, President
Tel: (732) 216-6280
Email: khyang@geointeract.com
Web: www.ksea-nj.org

SPEC. INT., CHILD CARE

FILIPINO CHILDREN'S FUND

P.O. Box 452
Cliffwood, NJ 07721-0452
Kristine Carranceja, Executive Director
Email: kristine@fcfinc.org
Web: www.fcfinc.org

VIBHA

P.O. Box 372
Berkeley Heights, NJ 07922-0372
Vijay Vemulapalli, Steering Committee
Tel: (877) 233-3222
Web: www.atlanta.vibha.org

SPEC. INT., COUNSELING

JEWISH FAMILY AND CHILDREN'S SERVICES OF GREATER MERCER COUNTY

707 Alexander Rd. #102
Princeton, NJ 08540-6331
Linda Meisel, Executive Director
Tel: (609) 987-8100 Fax: (609) 987-0574
Email: jfcs@pluto.njcc.com
Web: www.jfcsonline.org

JEWISH FAMILY AND CHILDREN'S SERVICES OF NEW JERSEY

705 Summerfield Ave.
Asbury Park, NJ 07712
Melvin Cohen, Executive Director
Tel: (732) 774-6886 Fax: (732) 774-8809

JEWISH FAMILY AND CHILDREN'S SERVICES OF NORTH JERSEY

1 Pike Dr.
Wayne, NJ 07470
Abraham Davis, Executive Director
Tel: (973) 595-0111
Email: info@jfcsnj.org
Web: www.jfcsnj.org

JEWISH FAMILY AND CHILDREN'S SERVICES OF NORTH JERSEY
Fair Lawn Branch Office
17-10 River Rd.
Fair Lawn, NJ 07410
Abraham Davis, Executive Director
Tel: (201) 796-5151
Email: info@jfcsnj.org
Web: www.jfcsnj.org

SPEC. INT., EDUCATION

ARAB STUDENT AID INTERNATIONAL

P.O. Box 10
Fanwood, NJ 07023
Tel: Fax: (908) 654-3940
Email: info@asai2000.org
Web: www.xramps.com

ASHA FOR EDUCATION
Central NJ
P.O. Box 285
New Brunswick, NJ 08903
Anil S. Mehta, Co-coordinator
Tel: (618) 453-7040
Email: anil@siu.edu
Web: www.ashanet.org/carbondale/

CHINESE HERITAGE SCHOOL OF NEW JERSEY

P.O. Box 127
Monmouth Junction, NJ 08852
Yatsing Chu, Chairman
Email: info@chsnj2000.org
Web: www.chsnj2000.org

JEWISH EDUCATION ASSOCIATION OF METROWEST

901 Route 10 East
Whippany, NJ 07981
Linda C. Lum, Managing Director
Tel: (973) 428-7400 Fax: (973) 428-4720
Email: ljum@jeametrowest.org
Web: www.jeametrowest.org

JEWISH LEARNING EXPERIENCE OF BERGEN COUNTY, INC.

1600 Queen Anne Rd.
Teaneck, NJ 07666
Baruch Price, Director
Tel: (201) 833-1328
Email: jlerabbi@jle.org
Web: www.jle.org

LIVINGSTON CHINESE SCHOOL

P.O. Box 179
Livingston, NJ 07039
Mickey Lam, Principal
Email: LivingstonChineseSchool@yahoo.com
Web: www.livingstonchineseschool.org

MURRAY HILL CHINESE SCHOOL

P.O. Box 4322
Warren, NJ 07059
Eric Sun, Principal
Tel: (848) 219-3694
Email: principal@mhcs-nj.org
Web: www.mhcs-nj.org

NORTHERN NEW JERSEY CHINESE ASSOCIATION CHINESE SCHOOL

P.O. Box 721
Pine Brook, NJ 07058
Tel: (973) 517-2392
Email: nnjcacs@hotmail.com
Web: www.nnjcacs.org

PRINCETON CHINESE LANGUAGE SCHOOL

P.O. Box 185
Princeton Junction, NJ 08550
Wen Chyi Shyu, Chairperson
Tel: (609) 279-0058
Email: pcls_org@yahoo.com
Web: www.pcls.org

SEABROOK EDUCATIONAL AND CULTURAL CENTER, INC.
Upper Deerfield Township Municipal Bldg.
P.O. Box 5041
Seabrook, NJ 08302
John N. Fuyuume, Project Director
Tel: (856) 451-8393 Fax: (856) 451-1379
Email: seabrookeducation@juno.com

SOCIETY OF INDIAN ACADEMICS IN AMERICA

86 Wortendyke Ave.
Emerson, NJ 07630
Rishi Raj, President
Tel: (201) 262-2356 Fax: (201) 262-2345
Email: rishisraj@cs.com

THE CHINESE SCHOOL OF SOUTH JERSEY

P.O. Box 2024
Cherry Hill, NJ 08003
Email: plo@cssj.org
Web: www.cssj.org

TIBETAN BUDDHIST LEARNING CENTER

93 Angen Rd.
Washington, NJ 07882-9767
Tel: (908) 689-6080
Email: setabit@njskylands.com
Web: www.njskylands.com/clbuddhist.htm

UNION CHINESE SCHOOL
Thomas Alva Edison Intermediate High School
800 Rahway Ave.
Westfield, NJ 07090
Email: ucs@westfieldnj.com
Web: www.westfieldnj.com

US-CHINA EDUCATIONAL EXCHANGE

15 Locust St.
Jersey City, NJ 07305
Tel: (201) 432-6861 Fax: (201) 432-6861
Email: hsintl@aol.com
Web: www.us-chinaedexchange.org

YINGHUA LANGUAGE SCHOOL

P.O. Box 3004
Princeton, NJ 08543-3004
Tel: (609) 530-0399 Fax: (775) 262-7968
Email: info@yinghua.org
Web: www.yinghua.org

SPEC. INT., GAY&LESBIAN

LONG YANG CLUB
New Jersey Chapter
P.O. Box 5130
New Brunswick, NJ 08903
Tel: (732) 247-0515
Email: newjersey@longyangclub.org
Web: www.longyangclub.org/newjersey/

SPEC. INT., HEALTH SERVICES

AMERICAN CANCER SOCIETY
Eastern Division-New Jersey Chinese Unit
669 Littleton Rd.
Parsippany, NJ 07054
Ming Der Chang, President
Tel: (973) 334-2249

Email: ming-der.chang@cancer.org
Web: www.cancer.org

JEWISH RENAISSANCE FOUNDATION, INC.
149 Kearny Ave.
Perth Amboy, NJ 08861
Tel: (732) 325-2114 Fax: (732) 325-0256
Email: jrfmed@aol.com
Web: www.jrfmed.org

RAZI HEALTH FOUNDATION
930 Clifton Ave.
Clifton, NJ 07013
Tel: (718) 980-1708 Fax: (973) 470-9858
Email: help@razihealthfoundation.org
Web: http://razihealthfoundation.org

SPEC. INT., HUMAN RELATIONS

ASSOCIATION OF JEWISH FAMILY & CHILDREN'S AGENCIES
557 Cranbury Rd. #2
East Brunswick, NJ 08816-5419
Bert J. Goldberg, President/CEO
Tel: (800) 634-7346 Fax: (732) 432-7127
Email: ajfca@ajfca.org
Web: http://ajfca.org

COUNCIL ON AMERICAN-ISLAMIC RELATIONS
New Jersey Chapter
265-A Route 46 W. #3 E-1
Totowa, NJ 07512
Magdy Mahmoud, President
Tel: (973) 785-3050 Fax: (877) 875-0826
Email: cair@cair-nj.org
Web: www.cair-nj.org

DITH PRAN HOLOCAUST AWARENESS PROJECT, INC.
P.O. Box 1616
Woodbridge, NJ 07095
Email: dithpran@aol.com
Web: www.dithpran.org

INTERNATIONAL CAMPAIGN ON DALIT HUMAN RIGHTS
70 Maple Ave.
Morristown, NJ 07960-5293
Kitty Ferguson, Chairperson/Volunteer
Tel: (973) 538-0555 X14 Fax: (973) 538-7790
Email: dalitusa@aol.com

THE AMERICAN JEWISH COMMITTEE
Central New Jersey
225 Millburn Ave. #301
Millburn, NJ 07041-1694
Allyson Gall, Director
Tel: (973) 379-7844 Fax: (973) 379-2036
Email: newjersey@ajc.org
Web: www.ajc.org

SPEC. INT., MENTAL HEALTH

NATIONAL ALLIANCE FOR THE MENTAL ILL
Chinese American Mental Health Outreach Program
1562 US Hwy. 130
North Brunswick, NJ 08902
Maggie Luo, Program Coordinator
Tel: (732) 940-0991 Fax: (732) 940-0355
Email: namichinesegroup@yahoo.com
Web: www.naminj.org/programs/camhop/camhop.html

SOUTH ASIAN MENTAL HEALTH AWARENESS IN JERSEY
1652 Route 130
North Brunswick, NJ 00820
Tel: (732) 940-0991 Fax: (732) 940-0355
Email: naminj@optonline.net
Web: www.naminj.org

SPEC. INT., SENIORS

JEWISH COMMUNITY HOUSING CORPORATION
750 Northfield Ave.
West Orange, NJ 07052
Martin Kalishman, President
Tel: (973) 731-2020 Fax: (973) 731-2225
Email: susanl@jchcorp.org

JEWISH HOME OF BERGEN ROCKLEIGH
10 Link Dr.
Rockleigh, NJ
Charles P. Berkowitz, Executive VP
Tel: (201) 784-1414
Email: cberkowitz@jewishhomerockleigh.org
Web: www.jewishhomerockleigh.org

SPEC. INT., SOCIAL INTEREST

BAPS CARE INTERNATIONAL
195 Main St. #304
Metuchen, NJ 08840
Swaminarayan Sanstha, Board of Director
Tel: (888) 227-3881 Fax: (732) 744-1171
Email: info@bapscare.org
Web: www.bapscare.org

COALITION OF INDIAN ORGANIZATIONS OF NEW JERSEY, INC.
208 Powder Mill Rd.
Morris Plains, NJ 07950
Lakshmi Anand, President
Tel: (973) 285-0311 Fax: (973) 292-2637
Email: laxmianand@aol.com

FILIPINO AMERICAN SOCIETY OF TEANECK
P.O. Box 2001
Teaneck, NJ 07666
Email: fast@fastnj.org
Web: www.fastnj.org

JEWISH ASSOCIATION FOR DEVELOPMENTAL DISABILITIES, INC.
190 Moore St. #410
Hackensack, NJ 07601
Errol Seltzer, Executive Director
Tel: (201) 457-0058 Fax: (201) 457-0025
Email: ujaadd@aol.com
Web: www.j-add.com

JEWISH CENTER OF TEANECK
70 Sterling Pl.
Teaneck, NJ 07666
Richard Tannenbaum, Executive Director
Tel: (201) 833-0515
Email: execdir@aol.com
Web: www.jewishcenterofteaneck.org

JEWISH COMMUNITY CENTER OF ATLANTIC COUNTY
501 N. Jerome Ave.
Margate, NJ 08402
Jack I. Fox, Executive Director
Tel: (609) 822-1167 Fax: (609) 822-9419
Email: info@jccatlantic.org
Web: www.jccatlantic.org

JEWISH COMMUNITY CENTER OF PARAMUS
E. 304 Midland Ave.
Paramus, NJ 07652
Gary Hutmatcher, President
Tel: (201) 262-7691 Fax: (201) 262-6516
Web: www.jccparamus.org

JEWISH COMMUNITY CENTER OF THE DELAWARE VALLEY
999 Lower Ferry Rd.
Ewing, NJ 08628-3297
Robert Frey, Executive Director
Tel: (609) 883-9550 Fax: (609) 883-9113
Email: rgfrey@jcctoday.org

Web: www.jcctoday.org

JEWISH COMMUNITY CENTER OF WESTERN MONMOUTH COUNTY
100 Route 9 North
Manalapan, NJ 07726
Shelley Feingold, Outreach Director
Tel: (732) 683-9300 Fax: (732) 683-9301
Web: www.jccwm.com

JEWISH FAMILY SERVICE
1485 Teaneck Rd.
Teaneck, NJ 07666
Jeff Lampl, Executive Director
Tel: (201) 837-9090 Fax: (201) 837-9393
Email: jeffl@jfsbergen.org
Web: www.jfsbergen.org

JEWISH FAMILY SERVICE OF METROWEST
256 Columbia Turnpike #105
Florham Park, NJ 07932
Tel: (973) 765-9050 Fax: (973) 765-0195
Web: www.jfs-metronj.org

JEWISH FAMILY SERVICE OF SOMERSET HUNTERDON AND WARREN COUNTIES, INC.
150-A W. High St.
Somerville, NJ 08876
Tova Friedman, CEO
Tel: (908) 725-7799 Fax: (908) 725-0284
Email: jfsofshw@verizon.com

JEWISH FAMILY SERVICE OF SOUTHERN MIDDLESEX COUNTY
East Brunswick Office
517 Ryders Ln.
East Brunswick, NJ 08816
Sara Levine, CEO
Tel: (732) 257-4100 Fax: (732) 257-0955
Email: jfsofsmc@aol.com
Web: www.jfsofsmc.org

JEWISH FAMILY SERVICE OF SOUTHERN MIDDLESEX COUNTY
Monroe Office
Concordia Shopping Ctr., #52
Monroe, NJ 08831
Sara Levine, CEO
Tel: (609) 395-7979 Fax: (609) 395-7129
Email: jfsmonroe@aol.com
Web: www.jfsofsmc.org

JEWISH FEDERATION OF ATLANTIC AND CAPE MAY COUNTIES
501 N. Jerome Ave.
Margate, NJ 08402
Tel: (609) 822-4404 Fax: (609) 822-4426
Email: karen@jewishbytheshore.org
Web: www.jewishbytheshore.org

JEWISH FEDERATION OF CENTRAL NEW JERSEY
1391 Martine Ave.
Scotch Plains, NJ 07076
Tel: (908) 889-5335 Fax: (908) 889-5370
Email: community@jfedcnj.org
Web: www.jewishjerseycentral.org

JEWISH FEDERATION OF CUMBERLAND COUNTY
1063 E. Landis Ave. #B
Vineland, NJ 08360
Tel: (856) 696-4445 Fax: (856) 696-3428
Email: questions@jfedcc.org
Web: www.jfedcc.org

JEWISH FEDERATION OF GREATER MIDDLESEX COUNTY
230 Old Bridge Turnpike
South River, NJ 08882-2000
Tel: (732) 432-7711 Fax: (732) 432-0292
Email: middlesexfed@aol.com
Web: www.jfgmc.org

JEWISH FEDERATION OF GREATER MONMOUTH COUNTY
100 Grant Ave.

Deal, NJ 07723
Tel: (732) 531-6200 Fax: (732) 531-9518
Email: info@jewishmonmouth.org
Web: www.jewishmonmouth.org

JEWISH FEDERATION OF SOMERSET, HUNTERDON & WARREN COUNTIES
775 Talamini Rd.
Bridgewater, NJ 08807
Tel: (908) 725-6994 Fax: (908) 725-9753
Email: info@jfedshaw.org
Web: www.jfedshaw.org

JEWISH FEDERATION OF SOUTHERN NEW JERSEY
1301 Springdale Rd. #200
Cherry Hill, NJ 08003
Neal A. Cupersmith, President
Tel: (856) 751-9500 Fax: (856) 751-1697
Web: www.jfedsnj.org

PRINCETON IN ASIA
Princeton University
83 Prospect Ave. #202
Princeton, NJ 08544
Anastasia Vrachnos, Executive Director
Tel: (609) 258-3657
Email: pia@princeton.edu
Web: www.princeton.edu/~pia

SRI LANKA WILDLIFE CONSERVATION SOCIETY
127 Kingsland St.
Nutley, NJ 07110
Ravi Corea, President
Email: info@slwcs.org
Web: www.slwcs.org

UJA/FEDERATION OF NORTHERN NEW JERSEY
111 Kinderkamack Rd.
River Edge, NJ 07661
Howard E. Charish, Executive VP
Tel: (201) 488-6800 Fax: (201) 488-1507
Email: welcome@ujannj.org
Web: www.ujannj.org

UNITED JEWISH COMMUNITIES OF METROWEST
901 Route 10
Whippany, NJ 07981-1156
Tel: (973) 929-3000 Fax: (973) 884-7361
Web: www.ujfmetrowest.org

UNITED JEWISH FEDERATION OF PRINCETON MERCER BUCKS
4 Princess Rd. #206
Lawrenceville, NJ 08648
Kenneth H. Mack, President
Tel: (609) 219-0555 Fax: (609) 219-9040
Email: mailbox@ujfpmb.org
Web: www.ujfpmb.org

WINDSOR AREA TAIWANESE AMERICAN ASSOCIATION
P.O. Box 272
Princeton Junction, NJ 08550
Wen Ching Leu, President
Tel: (732) 225-2887
Email: WATAA@hotmail.com
Web: www.wataa.org

SPEC. INT., SPORTS

HOMENETMEN
New Jersey
P.O. Box 614
Cliffside Park, NJ 07010
Maral Apkarian, Secretary
Email: vick@deltaprinting.com
Web: www.homenetmen-nj.com

SPEC. INT., WOMEN

ASIAN WOMEN'S CHRISTIAN ASSOCIATION
333 Grand Ave.
Palisades Park, NJ 07650
Barbara Jun, Executive Director
Tel: (201) 461-9125 Fax: (201) 461-7518
Email: awca.nj@verizon.net

HADASSAH
Northern New Jersey Region
1005 Clifton Ave.
Clifton, NJ 07013
Debra Mazon, President
Tel: (973) 472-1401 Fax: (973) 472-1364
Email: hadassahnnj@aol.com
Web: www.hadassah.org

Southern New Jersey Region
3301 Route 66, Bldg. C
Neptune, NJ 07753
Rita Millen, President
Tel: (732) 643-1100 Fax: (732) 643-1199
Email: region.southernnj@hadassah.org
Web: www.hadassah.org

MANAVI, INC.
P.O. Box 3103
New Brunswick, NJ 08903-3103
Maneesha Kelkar, Program Director
Tel: (732) 435-1414 Fax: (732) 435-1411
Email: manavi@att.net
Web: www.manavi.org

SPEC. INT., YOUTH

SUMISIBOL
72 Van Reipen Ave. PMB 292
Jersey City, NJ 07306
Rolando Lavarro, Executive Director
Email: sumisibol@sumisibol.org
Web: www.sumisibol.org

STUDENT ORGANIZATION

ARMENIAN STUDENTS' ASSOCIATION OF AMERICA, INC.
New Jersey
441 Jersey Ave.
Fairview, NJ 07022
Email: asa@asainc.org
Web: www.asainc.org/newjersey/

ASIA CENTER OF SETON HALL UNIVERSITY
The Asia Center FH, 128 Seton Hall University
South Orange, NJ 07079
Father Laurence T. Murphy, Director
Tel: (973) 761-9072 Fax: (973) 275-2383
Email: oip@shu.edu
Web: http://academic.shu.edu/asiacenter

ASIAN AMERICAN STUDENTS ASSOCIATION
Princeton University
24 1st Campus Ctr. #2408
Princeton, NJ 08544
Grace Chang, Co-President
Email: aasa@princeton.edu
Web: www.princeton.edu/~aasa

NEW MEXICO

ARTISTIC

JAPANESE SWORD SOCIETY OF THE UNITED STATES, INC.
P.O. Box 513
Albuquerque, NM 87103-0513
Barry Hennick
Email: barry@hennick.ca
Web: www.jssus.org

CULTURAL

IRANIAN CULTURAL SOCIETY OF NEW MEXICO
Albuquerque, NM
Jilla Salari, President
Email: ics@icsnm.org
Web: www.icsnm.org

NEW MEXICO CHINESE ASSOCIATION
6400 Glen Oak NE
Albuquerque, NM 87111
Paul H. Lee, Advisor
Tel: (505) 275-1055 Fax: (505) 883-9092
Email: puhsuan@aol.com

RIO GRANDE FILIPINO AMERICAN NATIONAL HISTORICAL SOCIETY
P.O. Box 80241
Albuquerque, NM 87198
Evelio A. Sabay, President
Email: eveliosabay12@earthlink.net
Web: www.fanhs-riogrande.org

GOVERNMENT

FEDERAL ASIAN PACIFIC AMERICAN COUNCIL
New Mexico Chapter
P.O. Box 5400
Albuquerque, NM 87185-5400
Ashok Kapoor, Chairman
Tel: (505) 845-4574 Fax: (505)-845-5508
Email: akapoor@doeal.gov
Web: www.doeal.gov/apap/fapac-nm.htm

POLITICAL ACTION

PROJECT TIBET
403 Canyon Rd.
Santa Fe, NM 87501
Paljor Thundup, Administrator
Tel: (505) 982-3002 Fax: (505) 988-4142

PROFESSIONAL

BURMESE MEDICAL ASSOCIATION OF NORTH AMERICAN
1141-A Mall Dr.
Las Cruces, NM 88011
Stanislaus Ting, MD, President
Tel: (505) 522-2400
Web: www.ama-assn.org

RELIGIOUS

CONGREGATION ALBERT
3800 Louisiana Blvd. NE
Albuquerque, NM 87110
Gary Singer, President
Tel: (505) 883-1818 Fax: (505) 883-1814
Email: admin@congregationalbert.org
Web: www.congregationalbert.org

KOREAN PRESBYTERIAN GALILEE CHURCH
2200 Chelwood Park Blvd. NE
Albuquerque, NM 87122
Rev. Won Dae Lee, Pastor
Tel: (505) 291-1292 Fax: (505) 291-1297
Email: galileecrc@email.msn.com
Web: www.jesuskorea.org/kpc

KOREAN UNITED METHODIST CHURCH OF ALBUQUERQUE
601 Tyler Rd. NE
Albuquerque, NM 87113
Rev. Ki Cheon Kim, Pastor
Tel: (505) 341-0205 Fax: (505) 266-7288
Email: boskee@post.harvard.edu
Web: www.gbgm-umc.org/kumc-albuquerque

RESEARCH

NEW MEXICO US-JAPAN CENTER
1400 Central Ave. SE #2300

Albuquerque, NM 87106
Wallace Lopez, Director
Tel: (505) 842-9020 Fax: (505) 766-5166
Email: info@nmjc.org
Web: www.nmjc.org

SPEC. INT., EDUCATION

ARAB WORLD AND ISLAMIC RESOURCES
P.O. Box 174
Abiquiu, NM 87510
Rahman Lutz
Tel: (505) 685-4533 Fax: (505) 685-4533
Email: requests@AWAIRonline.org
Web: www.awaironline.org

FRIENDS OF TIBETAN WOMEN'S ASSOCIATION
P.O. Box 31307
Santa Fe, NM 87594
Sarah Lukas, President
Tel: (505) 988-1938 Fax: (505) 988-1938
Email: fotwa2@fotwa.org
Web: www.fotwa.org

THE PRANAYAMA INSTITUTE
P.O. Box 1103
Peralta, NM 87042
Web: www.pranayama.org

US CHINA PEOPLES FRIENDSHIP ASSOCIATION
Albuquerque Chapter
11329 Woodmar Ln. NE
Albuquerque, NM 87111
Elena Lu, Contact
Tel: (505) 296-6481 Fax: (505) 332-3206
Web: www.uscpfa.org

SPEC. INT., SOCIAL INTEREST

GREEN TARA FOUNDATION
P.O. Box 91676
Albuquerque, NM 87199-1676
Gerry Laidlaw, President
Tel: (505) 878-9225
Email: gl@green-tara.org
Web: www.green-tara.org

JAPAN AMERICA SOCIETY OF NEW MEXICO
P.O. Box 6541
Albuquerque, NM 87197-6541
Yosh Akutagawa, President
Tel: (505) 242-5676 Fax: (505) 830-0988
Email: jasnm@att.net
Web: www.us-japan.org/jasnm/

JEWISH COMMUNITY CENTER OF GREATER ALBUQUERQUE, INC.
5520 Wyoming Blvd. NE
Albuquerque, NM 87109
Michelle Schipper, Executive Director
Tel: (505) 332-0565 Fax: (505) 275-1307
Email: jccabq@jccabq.org
Web: www.jccabq.org

JEWISH FAMILY SERVICE OF ALBUQUERQUE, INC.
5520 Wyoming Blvd. NE #200
Albuquerque, NM 87109
Erika Rimson, President
Tel: (505) 291-1818 Fax: (505) 291-0322
Email: jfsabq@jfsabq.org
Web: www.jfsabq.org

JEWISH FEDERATION OF GREATER ALBUQUERQUE
5520 Wyoming Blvd. NE
Albuquerque, NM 87109
Toby Simon, President
Tel: (505) 821-3214 Fax: (505) 821-3351
Email: info@jewishnewmexico.org
Web: www.jewishnewmexico.org

KOREAN AMERICAN ASSOCIATION OF NEW MEXICO
7212 Menaul Blvd. NE
Albuquerque, NM 87110
Jen Choi, Associate President
Tel: (505) 883-5755 Fax: (505) 881-4045

NEW YORK

ARTISTIC

ASIAN AMERICAN ARTS ALLIANCE
74 Varick St. #302
New York, NY 10013
Lillian Cho, Executive Director
Tel: (212) 941-9208 Fax: (212) 941-7978
Email: info@aaartsalliance.org
Web: www.aaartsalliance.org

ASIAN AMERICAN ARTS CENTRE
26 Bowery, 3rd Fl.
New York, NY 10013
Tel: (212) 233-2154 Fax: (212) 766-1287
Email: aaac@artspiral.org
Web: www.artspiral.org

ASIAN AMERICAN WOMEN ARTISTS ALLIANCE
136 15th St., Basement
Brooklyn, NY 11215
Yan Kong, Executive Director
Tel: (718) 788-6170 Fax: (718) 788-6170
Email: info@aawaa.org
Web: www.aawaa.org

CENTER FOR US-CHINA ARTS EXCHANGE
Columbia University
423 W. 118th St. #1E
New York, NY 10027-7247
Dr. Ken Hao, Assistant Director
Tel: (212) 280-4648 Fax: (212) 662-6346
Email: us_china_arts@yahoo.com
Web: www.columbia.edu/cu/china

CHINESE AMERICAN ARTS COUNCIL, INC.
456 Broadway, 3rd Fl.
New York, NY 10013
Alan Chow, Executive Director
Tel: (212) 431-9740 Fax: (212) 431-9789
Email: info@gallery456.org
Web: www.gallery456.org

CHINESE FOLK DANCE COMPANY
390 Broadway, 2nd Fl.
New York, NY 10013
Xiaoling Yang, CFDC Artistic Director
Tel: (212) 334-3764 Fax: (212) 334-3768
Email: info@chinesedance.org
Web: www.chinesedance.org

CHINESE-AMERICAN ARTISTS SOCIETY OF NEW YORK CORPORATION
142-37 59th Ave.
Flushing, NY 11355
Chor Foo Choi, Chairman
Tel: (718) 321-7812
Email: contact@choichorfoo.com
Web: www.choichorfoo.com

DISHA THEATER COMPANY
108-17 72nd Ave. #3B
Forest Hill, NY 11375
Purva Bedi, Board of Directors Member
Tel: (212) 502-7973 Fax: (212) 894-3794
Email: info@dishatheatre.org
Web: www.dishatheatre.org

EN FOCO, INC.
32 E. Kingsbridge Rd.
Bronx, NY 10468
Charles Biasiny-Rivera, Executive Director
Tel: (718) 584-7718 Fax: (718) 584-7718
Email: info@enfoco.org
Web: www.enfoco.org

H.T. CHEN & DANCERS
70 Mulberry St., 2nd Fl.
New York, NY 10013

Dian Dong, Associate Director
Tel: (212) 349-0126 Fax: (212) 349-0494
Email: info@htchendance.org
Web: www.htchendance.org

IN MIXED COMPANY
125 W. Duke Ellington Blvd. #2A
New York, NY 10025-3725
Maura Donohue, Artistic Director
Tel: (917) 207-5373
Email: info@inmixedcompany.com
Web: www.inmixedcompany.com

INDO AMERICAN ARTS COUNCIL, INC.
118E 25th St., 3rd Fl.
New York, NY 10010
Aroon Shivdasani, President/Executive Director
Tel: (212) 529-2347 Fax: (212) 477-4106
Email: aroon@iaac.us
Web: www.iaac.us

INDO CENTER OF ART AND CULTURE
530 W. 25th St.
New York, NY 10001
Email: info@indocenter.com
Web: www.indocenter.com

INTERNATIONAL SEJONG SOLOISTS
37 W. 65th St., 3rd Fl.
New York, NY 10023
Hyo Kang, Artistic Director
Tel: (212) 580-5494 Fax: (212) 580-5337
Email: sejong@sejongsoloists.org
Web: www.internationalsejongsoloistc.org

IRANIAN ART FOUNDATION
124 E. 79th St. #4A
New York, NY 10021
Maryam Horri, Contact
Tel: (212) 472-9856
Email: info@iranianartfoundation.org
Web: www.iranianartfoundation.org

JAPANESE FOLK DANCE INSTITUTE OF NY, INC.
568 Grand St. J-1206
New York, NY 10002
Momo Suzuki, Director
Tel: (212) 982-6952 Fax: (212) 982-2415
Email: momosuzuki@nyc.com

KINDING SINDAW
201 E. 19th St. #8L
New York, NY 10003
Potri Ranka Manis, Artistic Director
Tel: (212) 982-2158 Fax: (212) 982-2158
Email: inquiries@kindingsindaw.org
Web: www.kindingsindaw.org

KOREAN AMERICAN CONTEMPORARY ART, LTD.
100 W. 32nd St.
New York, NY 10001
Tel: (212) 643-2988 Fax: (212) 643-2988
Web: www.kacal.org

MA-YI THEATER COMPANY
520 8th Ave. #309
New York, NY 10018
Jorge Z. Ortoll, Executive Director
Tel: (212) 971-4862
Email: info@ma-yitheatre.org
Web: www.ma-yitheatre.org

NATIONAL ASIAN AMERICAN THEATER COMPANY
520 8th Ave. #316
New York, NY 10018
Mia Katiabak, Artistic Producing Director
Tel: (212) 244-0447 Fax: (212) 244-0448
Email: info@naatco.org
Web: www.naatco.org

NYJPW CHINESE-AMERICAN ARTS & CULTURE ASSOCIATION, INC.
30 E. 20th St. #302
New York, NY 10003
John & Penny Cheng-Hua Wang, Founder

Tel: (201) 262-4338
Email: penny.wang@nyjpw.org
Web: www.nyjpw.org

PAN ASIAN REPERTORY THEATRE
520 8th Ave., 3rd Fl. #314
New York, NY 10018
Tisa Chang, Artistic/Producing Director
Tel: (212) 868-4030 Fax: (212) 868-4033
Email: panasia@aol.com
Web: www.panasianrep.org

SECOND GENERATION
100 Lafayette St. #800
New York, NY 10013
Welly Yang, Founder
Tel: (212) 334-4777 Fax: (831) 597-4099
Email: info@2g.org
Web: www.2g.org

SOUTH ASIAN LEAGUE OF ARTISTS IN AMERICA
16 W. 32nd St. #10C
New York, NY 10001
Geeta Citygirl, Artistic Director/Founder
Tel: (212) 330-8097 Fax: (212) 579-5537
Email: submissions@salaamtheatre.org
Web: www.salaamtheatre.org

TIBETAN LIBERATION THEATRE
P.O. Box 1082
New York, NY 10013
Virginia Henes
Tel: (212) 995-8578 Fax: (212) 260-9454
Email: info@tibetanliberation.org

WORLD ARTISTS FOR TIBET
142-20 84th Dr.
Briarwood, NY 11435
Ronit Herzfeld, President
Tel: (718) 658-0906 Fax: (718) 206-1851
Email: art4tibet@aol.com
Web: www.art4tibet1998.org

ZAMIR CHORAL FOUNDATION
120 Riverside Dr. #1
New York, NY 10024
Matthew Lazar, Founder
Tel: (212) 362-3335 Fax: (212) 362-4662
Email: information@zamirfdn.org
Web: www.zamirfdn.org

BUSINESS

AMERICA CHINA EXCHANGE SOCIETY
120 W. 75th #5A
New York, NY 10023
Tel: (917) 299-4949
Email: info@acescenter.com
Web: www.acescenter.com

ARAB BANKERS ASSOCIATION OF NORTH AMERICA
420 Lexington Ave. #43
New York, NY 10170-0002
Samer S. Khanachet, President
Tel: (212) 599-3030 Fax: (212) 599-3131
Email: skhanachet@arabbankers.org
Web: www.arabbankers.org

ASIAN AMERICAN ADVERTISING FEDERATION
286 Spring St. #201
New York, NY 10013
Bill Imada, President
Tel: (212) 242-3351 Fax: (212) 691-5969
Email: info@3af.org
Web: www.3af.org

ASIAN AMERICAN BUSINESS DEVELOPMENT CENTER, INC.
150 Lafayette St. #901
New York, NY 10013
John Wang, President
Tel: (212) 966-0100 Fax: (212) 966-2786
Email: general.info@aabdc.com
Web: www.aabdc.com

CENTER FOR JAPAN-US BUSINESS AND ECONOMIC STUDIES
Leonard N. Stern School of Business, New York University
44 W. 4th St. #7-190
New York, NY 10012-1126
Henry Kaufman, Management Center
Tel: (212) 998-0750 Fax: (212) 995-4219
Email: rramacha@stern.nyu.edu
Web: www.stern.nyu.edu

CENTER ON JAPANESE ECONOMY AND BUSINESS
Columbia University
322 Uris Hall M/C 5998, 3022 Broadway
New York, NY 10027
Hugh Patrick, Director
Tel: (212) 854-3976 Fax: (212) 678-6958
Email: cjeb@columbia.edu
Web: www-1.gsb.columbia.edu/japan

CHINESE ASSOCIATION FOR SCIENCE AND BUSINESS, INC.
19 W. 34th St. #603
New York, NY 10001
Tel: (212) 736-1104 Fax: (212) 736-1117
Web: info@casbi.org

HONG KONG ECONOMIC AND TRADE OFFICE
New York Office
115 E. 54th St.
New York, NY 10022
Sarah P.C. Wu, Director
Tel: (212) 752-3320 Fax: (212) 752-3395
Email: sarah_wu@hketony.gov.hk
Web: www.hketony.gov.hk/new_york.htm

INDIAN TRADE PROMOTION ORGANIZATION
60 E. 42nd St. #863
New York, NY 10165
D S. Chadha, Director
Tel: (212) 370-5262 Fax: (212) 370-5250
Email: ltpony@hotmail.com
Web: www.indiatradepromotion.org

INTERNATIONAL ENTERPRISE SINGAPORE
New York Office
55 E. 59th St. #21A
New York, NY 10022
Hoo Hoe Keat, Center Director
Tel: (212) 421-2207 Fax: (212) 888-2897
Email: enquiry@iesingapore.gov.sg
Web: www.iesingapore.gov.sg

JAPAN EXTERNAL TRADE ORGANIZATION
New York Chapter
McGraw Hill Bldg., 42nd Fl., 1221 Ave. of the Americas
New York, NY 10020-1079
Jun Okumura, President
Tel: (212) 997-0400 Fax: (212) 997-0464
Web: www.jetro.org

TURKISH AMERICAN BUSINESS FORUM
51 E. 42nd St. #510
New York, NY 10017
Victor Baruh, Chairman
Tel: (212) 599-1192 Fax: (212) 599-2565
Email: info@forum.org
Web: www.forum.org

UNITED STATES COUNCIL FOR INTERNATIONAL BUSINESS
1212 Ave. of the Americas
New York, NY 10036
Thomas M.T. Niles, President
Tel: (212) 354-4480 Fax: (212) 575-0327
Email: info@uscib.org
Web: www.uscib.org

CHAMBER OF COMMERCE

AMERICA-ISRAEL CHAMBER OF COMMERCE & INDUSTRY
120 W. 45th St., 18th Fl.
New York, NY 10036

Max Brandsdorfer, President
Tel: (212) 819-0430 Fax: (212) 819-0431
Email: info@aicci.org
Web: www.aicci.org

AMERICAN INDONESIAN CHAMBER OF COMMERCE
317 Madison Ave. #520
New York, NY 10017
Wayne Forrest, Executive Director
Tel: (212) 687-4505 Fax: (212) 687-5844
Email: aiccny@bigplanet.com
Web: www.aiccusa.org

INDIA-AMERICAN CHAMBER OF COMMERCE
263-10 Hillside Ave.
Florel Park, NY 11004
Kay Kapur, President
Tel: (718) 343-6976 Fax: (718) 343-6938
Web: www.indiaweeklyusa.com

JAPANESE CHAMBER OF COMMERCE AND INDUSTRY IN NEW YORK, INC.
145 W. 57th St., 6th Fl.
New York, NY 10019
Tsutomu Karino, Executive Director
Tel: (212) 246-8001 Fax: (212) 246-8002
Email: membership@jcciny.org
Web: www.jcciny.org

NATIONAL US-ARAB CHAMBER OF COMMERCE
New York Office
420 Lexington Ave. #2034
New York, NY 10170
Gilbert Hage
Tel: (212) 986-8024 Fax: (212) 986-0216
Email: nusacc@aol.com
Web: www.nusacc.org

PHILIPPINE AMERICAN CHAMBER OF COMMERCE
317 Madison Ave. #520
New York, NY 10017
Wayne Forrest, Executive Director
Tel: (212) 972-9326 Fax: (212) 687-5844
Email: philamcham@prodigy.net
Web: www.philamchamber.com

TURKISH AMERICAN CHAMBER OF COMMERCE
730 5th Ave., 9th Fl.
New York, NY 10019
Mustafa Merc, Director
Tel: (212) 659-7720 Fax: (212) 659-7805
Email: info@turkishuschamber.org

US PAN ASIAN AMERICAN CHAMBER OF COMMERCE
East Coast Chapter
135 W. 36th St., 4th Fl.
New York, NY 10018
Howard Li, Chapter President
Tel: (212) 967-8100 Fax: (212) 967-8180
Email: howardli@waitex.com
Web: www.uspaacc.com

COMMUNICATIONS

AFGHAN COMMUNICATOR
41-36 College Point Blvd. #2A
Flushing, NY 11355
Rameen Moshref Javid, Executive Director
Tel: (718) 445-6438
Email: rameen@afghancommunicator.com
Web: www.afghancommunicator.com

AMERICAN JEWISH HISTORICAL SOCIETY
15 W. 16th St.
New York, NY 10011
David Solomon, Interim Executive Director
Tel: (212) 294-6160 Fax: (212) 294-6161
Email: info@ajhs.org
Web: www.ajhs.org

ASIAN MEDIA WATCHDOG
676A 9th Ave. #193
New York, NY 10036

Colleen Eustice-Sakai, Co-Founder
Tel: (212) 560-5683 Fax: (212) 957-9191
Email: contact@asianmediawatchdog.com
Web: www.asianmediawatchdog.com

JEWISH FUNDERS NETWORK
330 7th Ave., 18th Fl.
New York, NY 10001
Mark Charendoff, President
Tel: (212) 726-0177 Fax: (212) 594-4292
Email: jfn@jfunders.org
Web: www.jfunders.org

SOUTH ASIAN JOURNALISTS ASSOCIATION
Columbia Graduate School of Journalism
2950 Broadway
New York, NY 10027
Sreenath Sreenivasan, Co-founder
Tel: (212) 854-5979
Email: sree@sree.net
Web: www.saja.org

CULTURAL

AFGHAN HINDU ASSOCIATION, INC.
261 Madison Ave., 26th Fl.
New York, NY 10016
Balram Kakkar
Tel: (212) 867-2969
Web: www.afghanhindu.com

AMERICA ISRAEL CULTURAL FOUNDATION
51 E. 42nd St. #400
New York, NY 10017
Tel: (212) 557-1600 Fax: (212) 557-1611
Email: info@aicf.org
Web: www.aicf.org

AMERICAN FEDERATION OF RAMALLAH PALESTINE
560 Uniondale Ave.
Uniondale, NY 11553
Tel: (516) 481-2404
Web: www.afrp.org

ARMENIAN GENERAL BENEVOLENT UNION
55 E. 59th St.
New York, NY 10022-1112
Tel: (212) 319-6383 Fax: (212) 319-6507
Email: agbuwb@agbu.org
Web: www.agbu.org

ASIAN CULTURAL COUNCIL
437 Madison Ave., 37th Fl.
New York, NY 10022-7001
Ralph Samuelson, Director
Tel: (212) 812-4300 Fax: (212) 812-4299
Email: acc@accny.org
Web: www.asianculturalcouncil.org

BANGLADESHI CULTURAL CENTER
82-59 247th St.
Bellerose, NY 11426
Nayeema Khan, President
Tel: (718) 470-0337 Fax: (718) 347-7768

CENTER FOR JEWISH HISTORY
15 W. 16th St.
New York, NY 10011
Bruce Slovin, Chairman
Tel: (212) 294-8301 Fax: (212) 294-8302
Email: development@cjh.org
Web: www.cjh.org

CENTER FOR KOREAN AMERICAN CULTURE
136-70 Roosevelt Ave., 2nd Fl.
Flushing, NY 11354
Tel: (718) 535-6469 Fax: (718) 939-2712
Email: ckac@interport.net

CHINA INSTITUTE
125 E. 65th St.
New York, NY 10021
Jack Maisano, President
Tel: (212) 744-8181 Fax: (212) 628-4159
Email: info@chinainstitute.org
Web: www.chinainstitute.org

CHINESE CLUB OF WESTERN NEW YORK
105 Cherrywood Dr.
Williamsville, NY 14221
Mae Huo, President
Tel: (212) 689-6891
Email: huo2@adlphia.net
Web: www.cc-wny.org

CHINESE INSTITUTE OF ROCHESTER
P.O. Box 25303
Rochester, NY 14625-0303
Dr. Pinyen Lin, President
Tel: (585) 264-9625
Email: administration@nycir.org
Web: www.nycir.org

CLUB ZAMANA
Columbia University
401 Lerner
New York, NY 10027
Darshan Doshi, President
Email: zamana@columbia.edu
Web: www.columbia.edu/cu/zamana/contact.html

COMMITTEE OF 100 CULTURAL INSTITUTE
677 5th Ave., 3rd Fl.
New York, NY 10022
Shirley Young, President
Tel: (212) 371-6565 Fax: (212) 371-9009
Email: c100@committee100.org
Web: www.ci.committee100.org

CRIMSON KINGS DRUM, FIFE & BUGLE CORPS
New York Chinese School
62 Mott St. #408
New York, NY 10013
Anna Fu, Director
Tel: (212) 226-5346 Fax: (212) 625-8664
Email: info@crimsonkings.com
Web: www.crimsonkings.com

INDOCHINA SINO-AMERICAN COMMUNITY CENTER
170 Forsyth St., 2nd Fl.
New York, NY 10002
Thang Thai, President
Tel: (212) 226-0317 Fax: (212) 925-0327
Email: isacenter@netzero.net

INSTITUTE FOR KOREAN-AMERICAN CULTURE
141-30 33rd Ave.
Flushing, NY 11354
Damian B. Kim, President
Tel: (718) 460-5190 Fax: (718) 616-5314
Email: kimd@nychhc.org

JAPAN AMERICA SOCIETY ITHACA AREA, INC.,
P.O. Box 4012
Ithaca, NY 14852-4012
Tel: (607) 266-0721 Fax: (607) 266-0721
Email: jasiaithaca@hotmail.com

JAPAN PERFORMING ARTS
152 W. 57th St., 39th Fl.
New York, NY 10019
Tel: (212) 489-0299 Fax: (212) 489-0409
Email: info@jfny.org
Web: www.jfny.org

KAYA
224 Riverside Dr. #1B
New York, NY 10025
Soo Kyung Kim, Founding Publisher
Tel: (212) 229-1445
Email: kaya@kaya.com
Web: www.kaya.com

KOREAN CULTURAL SERVICE
460 Park Ave., 6th Fl.
New York, NY 10022
Yangwoo Park, Director
Tel: (212) 759-9550 Fax: (212) 688-8640
Email: nykocus@koreanculture.org
Web: www.koreanculture.org

MUSEUM OF CHINESE IN THE AMERICAS
70 Mulberry St., 2nd Fl.
New York, NY 10013
Charles Lai, CEO
Tel: (212) 619-4785 Fax: (212) 619-4720
Email: clai@moca-nyc.org
Web: www.moca-nyc.org

NATIONAL FOUNDATION FOR JEWISH CULTURE
330 7th Ave., 21st Fl.
New York, NY 10001
Richard A. Siegel, Executive Director
Tel: (212) 629-0500 Fax: (212) 629-0508
Email: nfjc@jewishculture.org
Web: www.jewishculture.org

NECHUNG FOUNDATION, NYC
110 1st Ave., 5th Fl.
New York, NY 10009
Ven. Pema Dorjee, Senior Monk
Tel: (212) 388-9784
Email: info@nechungnyc.org
Web: www.nechungnyc.org

NEW YORK CHINESE CULTURAL CENTER
390 Broadway, 2nd Fl.
New York, NY 10013
Amy Chin, Executive Director
Tel: (212) 334-3764 Fax: (212) 334-3768
Email: info@chinesedance.org
Web: www.chinesedance.org

NEW YORK METROPOLITAN JAPANESE SWORD CLUB
P.O. Box 1119, Rockfeller Ctr. Station
New York, NY 10185
Jim Gilbert, President
Tel: (212) 691-2891
Web: www.ny-tokenkai.org

NORTH AMERICAN SANKETHI ASSOCIATION
34 Longwood Dr.
Clifton Park, NY 12065
K.V. Srikantiah, President
Email: president@sankethi.org
Web: www.sankethi.org

NYEMA PROJECTS, INC.
247 Sheafe Rd.
Wappingers Falls, NY 12590
Pema Dorje, President
Tel: (845) 297-3843 Fax: (845) 297-5761
Email: office@nyema.org
Web: www.nyema.org

PHILIPPINE INDEPENDENCE DAY COUNCIL, INC.
133 W. 72nd St. #203
New York, NY 10023
Reuben S. Seguritan, Esq., President
Tel: (212) 799-1847 Fax: (212) 799-9423
Email: parade@philippineindependence.com
Web: www.philippineindependence.com

SEPHARDIC HOUSE
15 W. 16th St.
New York, NY 10011
Momie R. Yohai, President
Tel: (212) 294-8350 Fax: (212) 294-8348
Email: sephardichouse@cjh.org
Web: www.sephardichouse.org

TAIWANESE ASSOCIATION OF AMERICA
Greater NY Chapter
137-44 Northern Blvd.
Flushing, NY 11354
Tel: (646) 219-2036
Email: taa@taiwaneseny.com
Web: http://taa.taiwaneseny.com

THE CULTURAL DEVELOPMENT CENTER-PLAINVIEW CHINESE SCHOOL
1535 Old Country Rd.
Plainview, NY 11803
Tel: (516) 753-5616 Fax: (516) 753-5617
Web: plainview@lipvcs.org

THE GERE FOUNDATION
Initiatives Foundation
341 Lafayette St. #4416
New York, NY 10012
Kristina Kulin
Email: info@initiativesfoundation.org
Web: www.gerefoundation.org

THE JEWISH MUSEUM
1109 5th Ave., 92nd St.
New York, NY 10128
Helen Goldsmith Menschel, Director
Tel: (212) 423-3200
Email: info@thejm.org
Web: www.thejewishmuseum.org

THE TIBET CENTER
P.O. Box 1873, Murray Hill Station
New York, NY 10156
Tel: (212) 779-1841 Fax: (212) 779-3426
Email: info@thetibetcenter.org
Web: www.thetibetcenter.org

TIBET HOUSE
22 W. 15th St.
New York, NY 10011
Robert A. F. Thurman, President
Tel: (212) 807-0563 Fax: (212) 807-0565
Email: info@tibethouse.org
Web: www.tibethouse.org

TURKISH SOCIETY OF ROCHESTER
2841 Culver Rd.
Rochester, NY 14622
Huseyin Tekin, President
Tel: (585) 266-1980 Fax: (585) 266-1996
Email: hcan@rochester.rr.com
Web: www.tsor.org

VIRSA FOUNDATION
32 Jones St.
New York, NY 10014
Ishrat Ansari, President
Email: ishrat@virsaonline.com

WU TANG PHYSICAL CULTURE ASSOCIATION
9 2nd Ave.
New York, NY 10003
Frank Allen, Director
Tel: (212) 533-1751
Web: www.metal-tiger.com/wu_tang_pca/

YESHIVA UNIVERSITY MUSEUM
15 W. 16th St.
New York, NY 10011
Tel: (212) 294-8330 Fax: (212) 294-8335
Email: info@yum.cjh.org
Web: www.yumuseum.org

ENTERTAINMENT

3RD I NEW YORK
c/o Prerana Reddy 98 Graham Ave. #2
Brooklyn, NY 11206
Email: thirdi_ny@yahoo.com
Web: www.thirdi.org/~ny/index.html

ASIAN CINEVISION
133 W. 19th St. #300
New York, NY 10011
Risa Morimoto, Executive Director
Tel: (212) 989-1422 Fax: (212) 727-3584
Email: risa@asiancinevision.org
Web: www.asiancinevision.org

JEWISH MEDIA FUND, INC.
55 E. 59th St.
New York, NY 10022
Eli N. Evans, Chairman
Email: info@jvhc.org
Web: www.jewishmediafund.org

MUSIC FROM CHINA
170 Park Row #12D
New York, NY 10038
Susan Cheng, Executive Director

Tel: (212) 941-8733 Fax: (212) 625-8586
Email: muschina@echonyc.com
Web: www.musicfromchina.org

THE WORKSHOP: ASIAN AMERICAN FILMMAKERS COLLABORATIVE
928 Broadway #405
New York, NY 10010
Stephen Bai, Founder/President
Tel: (212) 388-9260
Email: workshopaafc@yahoo.com
Web: www.theworkshop.org

LAW ENFORCEMENT

ASIAN JADE SOCIETY
P.O. Box 969, Peck Slip Station
New York, NY 10272
Eugene Canapi, President
Email: ajs4nypd@aol.com
Web: www.nypdajs.org

ASIAN JADE SOCIETY (NASSAU COUNTY POLICE)
P.O. Box 2063
Massapequa, NY 11758
John Espina, President
Web: www.ncpdajs.org

PORT AUTHORITY POLICE OF NY&NJ
P.O. Box 866, Church St. Station
New York, NY 10008
Nicholas Yum, President

MULTI-PURPOSE

ASIAN AMERICAN COALITION OF STATEN ISLAND
688 Drungoole Rd. West
Staten Island, NY 10312
Syng Kwak, President
Tel: (718) 273-8052

ASIAN AMERICAN SUPPORT AND RELIEF ADVANCEMENT
86-34 Sutro St.
Holliswood, NY 11423
Ashi Chabra, President
Tel: (718) 479-5983
Email: support@aasra.net
Web: www.aasra.net

ASIAN AMERICANS FOR EQUALITY, INC.
Central Office
277 Grand St., 3rd Fl.
New York, NY 10002
Christopher Kui, Executive Director
Tel: (212) 680-1374 Fax: (212) 680-1815
Email: info@aafe.org
Web: www.aafe.org

CHINESE CULTURAL PROGRAM & CONFUCIUS PLAZA DAY CARE
40 Division St. #131
New York, NY 10002
Pauline Chen, Director
Tel: (212) 925-4325 Fax: (212) 274-0897
Email: pcchen@cpc-nyc.org

GREATER NEW YORK VIETNAMESE AMERICAN COMMUNITY ASSOCIATION
81 Ocean Pkwy. #1K
Brooklyn, NY 11218-1754
Dang Tran, President
Tel: (718) 633-6715 Fax: (718) 871-5908

ISLAMIC CIRCLE OF NORTH AMERICA
166-26 89th Ave.
Jamaica, NY 11432
Dr. Talat Sultan, President
Tel: (718) 658-1199 Fax: (718) 658-1255
Email: info@icna.org
Web: www.icna.org

JAMMA FOUNDATION
P.O. Box 30209
New York, NY 10011

Suzanne Meyers, Founder
Email: suzanne@jammafoundation.org
Web: www.jammafoundation.org

JAPAN SOCIETY
333 E. 47th St.
New York, NY 10017
Lori Hamamoto, Special Assistant to the
President/Director of Public Relations
Tel: (212) 832-1155 Fax: (212) 715-1262
Web: www.japansociety.org

KOREAN MUTUAL AID SOCIETY
37-06 111th St.
Corona, NY 11368
Tel: (718) 651-7373 Fax: (718) 478-6055
Web: www.kcsny.org

TRACE FOUNDATION
31 Perry St.
New York, NY 10014
Corinna Bordewieck, Executive Assistant
Tel: (212) 367-7380 Fax: (212) 367-7383
Email: info@trace.org
Web: www.trace.org

TRI-CITY INDIAN ASSOCIATION
P.O. Box 12094
Albany, NY 12212-2094
Seema Langer, President
Tel: (518) 383-7415
Email: president@tricityindia.org
Web: www.tricityindia.org

TZU CHI
Long Island Office
350 Jericho Turnpike #004
Jericho, NY 11753
Cheng Yen, Founder
Tel: (516) 935-5170 Fax: (516) 935-5175
Email: info@us.tzuchi.org
Web: http://li.us.tzuchi.org

ULSTER COUNTY JEWISH FEDERATION
159 Green St.
Kingston, NY 12401
Lisa Baker Brill, Executive Director
Tel: (845) 338-8131 Fax: (845) 338-8134
Email: info@ucjf.org
Web: www.ucjf.org

UNITED SRI LANKA SOCIETY OF NEW YORK
FDR Station, P.O. Box 7295
New York, NY 10150
Waruna Buwaneka, President
Tel: (718) 261-4586
Email: info@uslsny.org
Web: www.uslsny.org

VIETNAMESE AMERICAN CULTURAL ORGANIZATION, INC.
113 Baxter St.
New York, NY 10013
Joseph Hein, Executive Director
Tel: (212) 343-0762 Fax: (212) 343-0822
Email: vacuosa@hotmail.com
Web: www.dvguide.com/newyork/vietnamese.html

POLITICAL ACTION

AMERICANS FOR PEACE NOW
New York Office
114 W. 26th St. #1000
New York, NY 10001
Tel: (212) 627-3223 Fax: (212) 627-3225
Email: apndc@peacenow.org
Web: www.peacenow.org

ASIAN AMERICAN FEDERATION OF NEW YORK
120 Wall St., 3rd Fl.
New York, NY 10005
Cao K. O, Executive Director
Tel: (212) 344-5878 Fax: (212) 344-5636
Email: info@aafny.org
Web: www.aafny.org

ASIAN AMERICAN REPUBLICAN COMMITTEE
35 Stonehouse Rd.
Scarsdale, NY 10582
Priscilla Parameswaran, Chairman
Email: vpwaren@aol.com

ASIAN PACIFIC AMERICAN LABOR ALLIANCE
New York Chapter
20 Confucius Plz. #28L
New York, NY 10002
Marian Thom, President
Tel: (212) 598-6807
Email: mariancthom@hotmail.com
Web: www.apalanet.org

IRANIAN-AMERICAN ANTI-DISCRIMINATION COUNCIL
Persian Watch Center
23 Leatherstocking Ln.
Scarsdale, NY 10583
Email: mail@antidiscrimination.org
Web: www.antidiscrimination.org

ISRAEL POLICY FORUM
165 E. 56th St., 2nd Fl.
New York, NY 10022
Debra Wasserman, Executive Director
Tel: (212) 245-4227 Fax: (212) 245-0517
Web: www.israelpolicyforum.org

JAPAN CENTER FOR INTERNATIONAL EXCHANGE, INC.
1251 Ave. of Americas #810
New York, NY 10020
James Gannon, Executive Director
Tel: (212) 921-4260 Fax: (212) 921-4356
Email: info@jcie.org
Web: www.jcie.org

JEWISH COUNCIL FOR PUBLIC AFFAIRS
New York Office
443 Park Ave. South
New York, NY 10016
Tel: (212) 684-6950 Fax: (212) 686-1353
Email: contactus@the jcpa.org
Web: www.jewishpublicaffairs.org

JEWISH POLITICAL EDUCATION FOUNDATION, INC.
P.O. Box 4458
Great Neck, NY 11023-4458
Tel: (516) 487-2990 Fax: (516) 487-2530
Email: info@jpef.net
Web: www.jpef.net

JEWS FOR RACIAL AND ECONOMIC JUSTICE
135 W. 29th St. #600
New York, NY 10001
Dara Silverman, Executive Director
Tel: (212) 647-8966 Fax: (212) 647-7124
Email: jfrej@igc.org
Web: www.jfrej.org

KOREAN AMERICAN ADVISORY COMMITTEE (NASSAU COUNTY LEGISLATURE)
9 Cherry Ln.
Syosset, NY 11791
Fred Lee, President
Tel: (212) 480-3200 X13 Fax: (516) 496-7215
Email: busan9@yahoo.com

KOREAN AMERICAN LEAGUE FOR CIVIC ACTION, INC.
Greeley Square Station
149 W. 24th St., 6th Fl.
New York, NY 10001
Veronica S. Jung, Executive Director
Tel: (212) 633-2000 Fax: (212) 633-1627
Email: info@kalca.org
Web: www.kalca.org

MILAREPA FUND
P.O. Box 1678

New York, NY 10013
Andrew Bryson
Tel: (212) 226-4739 Fax: (212) 226-0326
Email: milarepa@milarepa.org
Web: www.milarepa.org

NATIONAL COMMITTEE FOR LABOR ISRAEL
275 7th Ave. #1501
New York, NY 10001
Tel: (212) 647-0300 Fax: (212) 647-0308
Email: ncli.info@laborisrael.org
Web: www.laborisrael.org

NATIONAL FEDERATION OF FILIPINO AMERICAN ASSOCIATIONS
Region 1-Eastern Region
Empire State Bldg., 350 5th Ave. #10009
New York, NY 10118
Loida Nicolas Lewis, CEO
Tel: (212) 714-2277 Fax: (212) 714-9331
Email: tlcbih@aol.com
Web: www.naffaa.org

STUDENTS FOR A FREE TIBET
602 E. 14th St., 2nd Fl.
New York, NY 10009
Lhadon Tethong, Director
Tel: (212) 358-0071 Fax: (212) 358-1771
Email: info@studentsforafreetibet.org
Web: www.studentsforafreetibet.org

UNITED STATES TIBET COMMITTEE
241 E. 32nd St.
New York, NY 10016
Sarah Hoffman, National Coordinator
Tel: (212) 481-3569 Fax: (212) 779-9245
Email: ustc@igc.org
Web: www.ustibet.org

WORLD CAMBODIAN CONGRESS
103 N. Harrison Ave.
Congers, NY 10920
Komen Ear
Tel: (503) 654-9983 Fax: (845) 356-6820
Email: info@wccpd.org
Web: www.wccpd.org

PROFESSIONAL

ASIAN AMERICAN BAR ASSOCIATION OF NEW YORK
P.O. Box 3656, Grand Central Station
New York, NY 10163-3656
Pui Cheng, President
Tel: (212) 557-4040
Email: aabanyissues@verizon.net
Web: www.aabany.org

BANGLADESH MEDICAL ASSOCIATION OF NORTH AMERICA
4250 Hempstead Turnpike #17
Bethpage, NY 11714-5707
Ziauddin Ahmed, M.D., President
Tel: (516) 796-4245 Fax: (516) 731-1683
Email: editor@bmana.com
Web: www.bmana.com

CHINESE AMERICAN ASSOCIATION FOR ENGINEERING
P.O. Box 869
New York, NY 10268
Beile Yin, Chairman
Tel: (718) 591-6012
Email: suggestion@caae.org
Web: www.caae.org

CHINESE LANGUAGE TEACHERS ASSOCIATION OF GREATER NEW YORK
125 E. 65th St.
New York, NY 10021
Yong Ho, President
Tel: (212) 744-8181 Fax: (212) 628-4159
Email: exec@clta-gny.org
Web: http://clta-gny.org

JAPANESE MEDICAL SOCIETY OF AMERICA
345 E. 37th St.
New York, NY 10016

Mitsugu Shimmyo, President
Tel: (212) 867-5700

JEWISH COMMUNAL SERVICE ASSOCIATION OF NORTH AMERICA, INC.
15 E. 26th St. #917
New York, NY 10010
Jay Spector, President
Tel: (212) 532-0167 Fax: (212) 532-1461
Email: info@jcsana.org
Web: www.jcsana.org

JEWISH PROFESSIONALS INSTITUTE
1638 E. 21st St.
Brooklyn, NY 11210-5038
Rabbi Rudomin
Tel: (718) 382-8058 Fax: (718) 382-3508
Email: rudomin@jpi.org
Web: www.jpi.org

NATIONAL ARAB AMERICAN MEDICAL ASSOCIATION
New York Chapter
8000 4th Ave. #118
Brooklyn, NY 11209
Henry Habib, Chapter President
Tel: (718) 833-8136
Email: naama@naama.com
Web: www.naama.com

NETWORK OF INDIAN PROFESSIONALS
P.O. Box 3165
New York, NY 10163
Sandeep Dutta, President
Fax: (212) 702-9121
Email: president@netip-ny.org
Web: www.netip-ny.org/newsite

SOUTH ASIAN BAR ASSOCIATION OF NEW YORK
P.O. Box 841
New York, NY 10163
Rosena P. Rasalingam, Esq., Secretary
Tel: (212) 880-6228 Fax: (212) 682-0200
Email: info@sabany.org
Web: www.sabany.org

SRI LANKA MEDICAL ASSOCIATION OF NORTH AMERICA, INC.
2500-16 Nesconset Hwy.
Stony Brook, NY 11790
Sandran Para Waran, President
Tel: (631) 246-5454 Fax: (631) 246-5902
Web: www.slmana.org

THE ASIAN AMERICAN WRITERS' WORKSHOP
16 W. 32nd St. #10A
New York, NY 10001
Quang Bao, Executive Director
Tel: (212) 494-0061 Fax: (212) 494-0062
Email: desk@aaww.org
Web: www.aaww.org

THE NATIONAL ASSOCIATION OF ASIAN AMERICAN PROFESSIONALS
NAAAP-New York
P.O. Box 772, KnickerBocker Station
New York, NY 10002
Trusha Mehta, President
Tel: (866) 841-9139 X3037
Email: naaapny@naaapny.org
Web: www.naaapny.org

RELIGIOUS

AFGHAN ISLAMIC CENTER
87 Brandywine Ave.
Schenectady, NY 12307
Tel: (518) 374-2364

AMERICA BURMA BUDDHIST ASSOCIATION, INC.
619 Bergen St.
Brooklyn, NY 11238
U Han Kyu, President
Tel: (718) 622-8019 Fax: (718) 622-8019
Web: www.mahasiusa.org

AMERICAN SRI LANKA BUDDHIST ASSOCIATION
115 John St.
Staten Island, NY 10302
Heenbunne Kondanna
Tel: (718) 556-2051
Email: heenko@yahoo.com
Web: www.sibv.org

ANANDA MARGA
97-38 42nd Ave. #1-F
Corona, NY 11368
Tel: (718) 898-1603 Fax: (718) 898-1604
Email: sos@nys.amps.org
Web: www.anandamarga.org

ASIAN CLASSICS INSTITUTE
P.O. Box 144
New York, NY 10276
Tel: (212) 475-7752
Email: aci@world-view.org
Web: www.world-view.org/aci/index.html

B'NAI ISRAEL REFORM TEMPLE
67 Oakdale-Bohemia Rd.
Oakdale, NY 11769
Brian Linehan, President
Tel: (631) 563-1660 Fax: (631) 563-9816
Email: president@bnai-israel.org
Web: www.bnai-israel.org

BANGLADESH HINDU MANDIR
9439 44th Ave.
Elmhurst, NY 11373
Tel: (718) 446-6727

BROOKLYN FILIPINO CHRISTIAN CHURCH
24 Washington Ave.
Valley Stream, NY 11580
Dante Ramiro, Pastor
Tel: (516) 285-1308
Email: dsramiro@msn.com
Web: www.filipinochristian.org/brooklyn/

CENTER CONFERENCE OF AMERICAN RABBIS
355 Lexington Ave.
New York, NY 10017
Janet Marder, President
Tel: (212) 972-3636
Email: info@ccarnet.org
Web: www.ccarnet.org

CHINESE CHRISTIAN YOUTH FELLOWSHIP
549 W. 123rd St.
Manhattan, NY 10027
Email: ccyf@ccyf-ny.org
Web: www.ccyf-ny.org

CHINESE EVANGEL MISSION CHURCH
97 Madison St.
New York, NY 10002
John Eng, Pastor
Tel: (212) 571-1083
Email: info@cemc-m.org
Web: www.cemc-m.org

CHINESE EVANGEL MISSION CHURCH OF QUEENS
203-02 Rocky Hill Rd.
Bayside, NY 11361
Tel: (718) 352-9570 Fax: (718) 352-9571
Web: http://cem.xboxplayer.com/index.php

CHINESE UNITED METHODIST CHURCH
69 Madison St.
New York, NY 10002
Mey Joy Choy, Executive Director
Tel: (212) 349-2703 Fax: (212) 349-0702
Email: cmcc@cumc-nyc.org
Web: www.cumc-nyc.org

ELAT CHAYYIM: THE JEWISH RENEWAL RETREAT CENTER
99 Mill Hook Rd.
Accord, NY 12404
Rabbi Howard Avruhm Addison
Tel: (800) 398-2630 Fax: (845) 626-2037

Email: info@elatchayyim.org
Web: www.elatchayyim.org

FILIPINO AMERICAN UNITED CHURCH OF CHRIST
Union Congregational Church
86-15 114th St.
Richmond Hill, NY 11418
Tel: (718) 847-7982
Web: http://members.aol.com/filamucc/home/

FIRST CHINESE PRESBYTERIAN CHURCH
61 Henry St.
New York, NY 10002
Tel: (212) 964-5488 Fax: (212) 566-2974
Email: office@fcpc.org
Web: www.fcpc.org

FIRST KOREAN BAPTIST CHURCH OF NEW YORK
87-37 Whitney Ave.
Elmhurst, NY 11373
Rev. Benjamin Hou, Senior Clergy
Tel: (718) 803-6378

FIRST KOREAN PRESBYTERIAN CHURCH OF L.I.
36 Center St.
Williston Park, NY 11596
Rev. John H.K. Chung, Senior Clergy
Tel: (718) 445-6856

GRACE KOREAN PRESBYTERIAN CHURCH OF NEW YORK
240-54 69th Ave.
Little Neck, NY 11362
Rev. Chung Kuk Kim, Senior Clergy
Tel: (718) 672-3806

IRANIAN ZOROASTRIAN ASSOCIATION
106 Pomona Rd.
Suffern, NY 10901
Shirin Kiamanesh, President
Tel: (845) 362-2104
Email: skiamane@anchor-computer.com
Web: www.fezana.org

ISRAEL HASBARA COMMITTEE
P.O. Box 4484, Grand Central Station
New York, NY 10163
Email: infosubmit@infoisrael.net
Web: www.infoisrael.net

JEWISH APPLESEED FOUNDATION, INC.
P.O. Box 308
New York, NY 10021
Rabbi Jo David, Executive Director
Tel: (212) 249-0799 Fax: (212) 249-5142
Email: rabbidavid@jewishappleseed.org
Web: www.jewishappleseed.org

JEWISH AWARENESS MINISTRIES
4431 Union Rd.
Buffalo, NY 14225
Tel: (716) 635-9337 Fax: (716) 635-9353
Email: jewishawareness@cs.com
Web: www.jewishawareness.org

JEWS FOR JESUS
New York
109 E. 31st St.
New York, NY 10016
Karol Joseph, Leadership Team
Tel: (212) 683-7077 Fax: (212) 683-2661
Email: ny@jewsforjesus.org
Web: www.jfjonline.org

KOREA BUDDHISM JO-GEI TEMPLE OF AMERICA INC.
45-18-48th Ave.
Woodside, NY 11377
Tel: (718) 706-1749 Fax: (718) 392-3011
Email: info@nychogyesa.org
Web: www.nychogyesa.org

KOREAN AMERICAN PRESBYTERIAN CHURCH OF QUEENS
143-17 Franklin Ave.
Flushing, NY 11355

Rev Young Choon Chang, Senior Clergy
Tel: (718) 886-4040

KOREAN CENTRAL CHURCH OF NEW YORK
32-71 41st St.
Long Island City, NY 11103
Rev. Calvin Kim, Pastor
Tel: (718) 956-4923
Email: nyhope123@yahoo.com
Web: www.nyhope.org

KOREAN CENTRAL PRESBYTERIAN CHURCH
58-06 Springfield Blvd.
Oakland Gardens, NY 11364
Rev. Chang Eui Ahn, Senior Clergy
Tel: (718) 229-9191 Fax: (718) 229-3159

KOREAN CHURCH OF ETERNAL LIFE
34-03 57th St.
Woodside, NY 11377
Rev. Mini Il Lim, Senior Clergy
Tel: (718) 335-8818

KOREAN CHURCH OF QUEENS
89-00 23rd Ave.
East Elmhurst, NY 11369
Rev. Jin Kwan Han, Senior Clergy
Tel: (718) 672-1150

KOREAN METHODIST CHURCH AND INSTITUTE
633 W. 115th St.
New York, NY 10025
Rev. Sung Soo Hahn, Senior Pastor
Tel: (212) 662-1422 Fax: (212) 662-9696
Email: nykchurch@aol.com
Web: www.gbgm-umc.org/kmciny

KOREAN FILIPINO PRESBYTERIAN CHURCH
40-11 29th St.
Long Island City, NY 11101
Rev. Sung Nung Shin, Senior Clergy
Tel: (718) 786-9721

KOREAN PRESBYTERIAN CHURCH OF FOREST HILL
70-35 112th St.
Forest Hills, NY 11375
Rev. Hi Chul Yang, Senior Clergy
Tel: (718) 263-3633

KOREAN PRESBYTERIAN CHURCH OF NEW YORK
21-70 Hazen St.
East Elmhurst, NY 11370
Rev. Hee So Park, Senior Clergy
Tel: (718) 728-9197

KOREAN PRESBYTERIAN CHURCH OF QUEENS
46 Cambridge St.
Deer Park, NY 11729
Rev. Young Choon Kim, Senior Clergy
Tel: (718) 961-7975

KOREAN PRESBYTERIAN CHURCH OF SOUTHERN NY
51-05 Queens Blvd.
Woodside, NY 11377
Rev. Sang Il Park, Senior Clergy
Tel: (718) 639-8309

KOREAN PRESBYTERIAN CHURCH OF WESTCHESTER
901 Pelhamdale Ave.
Pelham, NY 10803
Tel: (914) 738-3076 Fax: (914) 632-5229
Email: kpcow@hotmail.com
Web: www.kpcow.org

KOREAN SEVENTH-DAY ADVENTIST CHURCH
45-11 21st St.
Long Island City, NY 11101
Rev. Keun Suk Ok, Senior Clergy
Tel: (718) 796-9883

KOREAN TRINITY PRESBYTERIAN CHURCH
5701 246th Pl.
Little Neck, NY 11362-2029
Heung Ik Cha, Pastor
Tel: (718) 476-3201
Email: alphamedico@aol.com

KOREAN UNITED METHODIST CHURCH IN GREATER NY
46-16 Little Neck Pkwy.
Little Neck, NY 11362
Rev. Paul Kim, Senior Clergy
Tel: (718) 631-2300

MID-HUDSON KOREAN UNITED METHODIST CHURCH
38 Jackson Rd.
Poughkeepsie, NY 12603
Rev. Seong In Jin, Pastor
Tel: (845) 463-0027 Fax: (845) 463-1114
Web: www.gbgm-umc.org/midhudson

NATIONAL ASSOCIATION OF TEMPLE EDUCATORS
633 3rd Ave., 7th Fl.
New York, NY 10017-6778
Stanley Schickler, Executive Director
Tel: (212) 452-6510 Fax: (212) 452-6512
Email: nateoff@aol.com
Web: http://rj.org/nate

NEW HOPE FELLOWSHIP
242 N. Broadway
Sleepy Hollow, NY 10591
Tel: (914) 332-0447
Email: info@newhopefellowship.org
Web: www.newhopefellowship.org

NEW HOPE KOREAN BAPTIST CHURCH OF NEW YORK
56-09 Bell Blvd.
Oakland Gardens, NY 11364
Rev. James B. Chun, Senior Clergy
Tel: (714) 468-1867

NEW YORK DONG WON KOREAN PRESBYTERIAN CHURCH
21-01 124th St.
College Point, NY 11356
Rev. David Heegurn Park, Senior Clergy
Tel: (718) 321-9199 Fax: (718) 446-8467

NEW YORK JAPANESE CHURCH
26 Cameron Pl.
Tuckahoe, NY 10523
Joe Suzuki, Pastor
Email: info@nyjc.org
Web: www.nyjc.org

NEW YORK KOREAN CHURCH OF THE NAZARENE
45-05 48th Ave.
Woodside, NY 11377
Rev. James K. Lee, Senior Clergy
Tel: (718) 786-1577

NORTHEAST QUEENS JEWISH COMMUNITY COUNCIL
58-20 Little Neck Pkwy.
Little Neck, NY 11362
Jeffrey Gurdus, President
Tel: (718) 225-6750 Fax: (718) 423-8276
Email: president@northeastqueensjewish.org
Web: www.northeastqueensjewish.org

PHILIPPINE JESUIT FOUNDATION
130 Beekman St. #4A
New York, NY 10038
Fr. Noel Vasquez, Chairman/President
Tel: (212) 385-1589 Fax: (212) 964-2558
Email: exsec@philjesuit.net
Web: www.philjesuit.net

QUEENS CHINESE PRESBYTERIAN CHURCH
98-54 Horace Harding Expressway
Rego Park, NY 11374
Rev. Matthew Lui, Senior Clergy
Tel: (718) 271-8505

ROCHESTER CHINESE CHRISTIAN CHURCH
1524 Jackson Rd.
Penfield, NY 14526
Pastor Herman Tang
Tel: (585) 872-6708
Web: www.rochesterccc.org

TAIWAN UNION CHRISTIAN CHURCH
30-55 31st St.
Astoria, NY 11102
Tel: (718) 278-0408
Web: www.tuccny.org

TAIWANESE AMERICAN REFORMED CHURCH OF QUEENS
P.O. Box 610512
Bayside, NY 11361
Rev. Chung-Huei Cho, Senior Clergy
Tel: (718) 281-1267

TEMPLE BETH EL
402 N. Tioga St.
Ithaca, NY 14850
Richard Polenberg, President
Tel: (607) 273-5775
Email: secretary@tbeithaca.org
Web: www.tbeithaca.org

411 Hoosick St.
Troy, NY 12180
Reeva Nowitz, President
Tel: (518) 272-6113
Email: info@betheloftroy.org
Web: www.betheloftroy.org

TEMPLE BETH EL OF NORTHERN WESTCHESTER
220 S. Bedford Rd.
Chappaqua, NY 10514
David Ruzow, President
Tel: (914) 238-3928 Fax: (914) 238-4030
Email: temple@bethelnw.org
Web: www.bethelnw.org

TEMPLE BETH SHOLOM
401 Roslyn Rd.
Roslyn, NY 11577
Alan B. Lucas, Rabbi
Tel: (516) 621-2288 Fax: (516) 621-0417
Web: www.bethsholom.com

TEMPLE BETH-EL OF GREAT NECK
5 Old Mill Rd.
Great Neck, NY 11023
Jerome K. Davidson, Rabbi
Tel: (516) 487-0900 Fax: (516) 487-6941
Email: jdavidson@tbegreatneck.org
Web: www.tbegreatneck.org

TEMPLE EMANUEL
243 Albany Ave.
Kingston, NY 12401
Phil Rose, President
Tel: (845) 338-4271 Fax: (845) 338-0506
Email: templeemanuel@hvc.rr.com
Web: www.templeemanuelkingston.org

TEMPLE EMANUEL AT PARKCHESTER
2000 Benedict Ave.
Bronx, NY 10462
Miriam Korman, President
Tel: (718) 828-3400 Fax: (718) 828-3401
Email: office@templeparkchester.org
Web: http://templeparkchester.org

TEMPLE EMANUEL OF GREAT NECK
150 Hicks Ln.
Great Neck, NY 11024
Steven Boughner, Co-President
Tel: (516) 482-5701
Email: info@emanuelgn.org
Web: www.emanuelgn.org

TEMPLE SHOLOM
2075 E. 68th St.
Brooklyn, NY 11234
Barry Weintrob, President
Tel: (718) 251-0370
Email: office@temsholom.org
Web: http://temsholom.org

TEMPLE SHOLOM OF FLORAL PARK
263-10 Union Turnpike
Floral Park, NY 11004
Ruth Gerver, President
Tel: (718) 343-8660
Email: info@templesholom.info
Web: www.templesholom.info

TEMPLE SINAI
363 Penfield Rd.
Rochester, NY 14625
Jerry Elman, President
Tel: (585) 381-6890
Web: www.tsinai.org

50 Alberta Dr.
Amherst, NY 14226-2087
Roger Cominsky, President
Tel: (716) 834-0708 Fax: (716) 834-0708
Email: templesinai@juno.com
Web: www.jrf.org/templesinai

425 Roslyn Rd.
Roslyn Heights, NY 11577
Ethel Liebeskind, Executive Director
Tel: (516) 621-6800
Email: generalmail@templesinairoslyn.com
Web: www.templesinairoslyn.com

P.O. Box 1045
Saratoga Springs, NY 12866
Steve Selig, President
Tel: (518) 584-8730
Email: sselig@nycap.rr.com
Web: www.templesinai-saratogasprings.org

THE RAMAKRISHNA-VIVEKANAND CENTER OF NEW YORK
17 E. 94th St.
New York, NY 10128
Tel: (212) 534-9445 Fax: (212) 828-1618
Web: www.ramakrishna.org

THE ROCHESTER KOREAN UNITED METHODIST CHURCH
1274 Penfield Center Rd.
Penfield, NY 14526
Tom Muratore, Pastor
Tel: (585) 872-0188
Web: www.rkumc.org

TIBETAN YOUTH CONGRESS
32-11 42nd St. #B
Astoria, NY 11103
Kunga Thinley, President
Tel: (718) 545-0113
Email: info@tibetanyouthcongress.us
Web: www.tibetanyouthcongress.us

TURKISH ISLAMIC CULTURAL CENTER
4506 Skillman Ave.
Sunnyside, NY 11104-2117
Tel: (718) 433-4298

UNITED SYNAGOGUE OF CONSERVATIVE JUDAISM
Empire Region
P.O. Box 8687
Albany, NY 12208
Ann Dozoretz Earne, President
Tel: (518) 438-2052 Fax: (518) 438-2053
Email: empire@uscj.org
Web: http://uscj.org/empire

International Headquarters
155 5th Ave.
New York, NY 10010-6802
Carole Korowitz, President
Tel: (212) 353-9439 Fax: (212) 260-7442
Email: info@uscj.org
Web: www.uscj.org

RESEARCH

APEC STUDY CENTER
Columbia University
321 Uris Hall, 3022 Broadway
New York, NY 10027-7004
Tel: (212) 854-3976 Fax: (212) 678-6958
Email: aw2040@columbia.edu
Web: www.columbia.edu/cu/business/apec

ASIAN AMERICAN CENTER AT QUEENS COLLEGE
65-30 Kissena Blvd. Temp #23
Flushing, NY 11367-1597
Dr. Madhulika Khandelwal, Director
Tel: (718) 997-3050 Fax: (718) 997-3055
Email: aac@qc.edu
Web: http://qcpages.qc.edu/asian_american_center

ASIAN AMERICAN CENTER BRIDGE
University at Stony Brook
245 Harriman Hall
Stony Brook, NY 11794-3750
Gary Mar, Director
Tel: (631) 632-7582
Email: gary.mar@sunsysb.edu
Web: aacws.har.sunysb.edu

JEWISH GENEALOGICAL SOCIETY, INC.
15 W. 16th St.
New York, NY 10011
Tel: (212) 294-8326
Email: info@jgsny.org
Web: www.jgsny.org

JEWISH GENEALOGICAL SOCIETY OF LONG ISLAND
37 Westcliff Dr.
Dix Hills, NY 11746
Sandy Masnick, President
Email: sandymasnick@aol.com
Web: www.jewishgen.org/jgsli/

THE AMERICAN INSTITUTE OF IRANIAN STUDIES
118 Riverside Dr.
New York, NY 10024
Dr. Erica Ehrenberg, Executive Director
Email: aiis@nyc.rr.com
Web: www.simorgh-aiis.org

THE NATIONAL INSTITUTE OF JUDAISM AND MEDICINE
P.O. Box 1244, 450 Clarkson Ave.
Brooklyn, NY 11203
Michael Moshe Akerman, Program Director
Tel: (718) 270-2422
Email: ocme@downstate.edu
Web: www.nijm.org

SCIENTIFIC

AMERICAN COMMITTEE FOR THE WEIZMANN INSTITUTE OF SCIENCE
633 3rd Ave., 20th Fl.
New York, NY 10017
Martin Kraar, Executive Vice President
Tel: (212) 895-7900 Fax: (212) 895-7999
Email: info@acwis.org
Web: www.weizmann-usa.org

KOREAN-AMERICAN MATERIALS, METALS AND MINERALS SOCIETY
36 Mayberry Rd.
Chappaqua, NY 10514
Sung-Kwon Kang, President
Tel: (914) 945-3932
Email: kang@watson.ibm.com

SPEC. INT., AIDS

ASIAN & PACIFIC ISLANDER COALITION ON HIV/AIDS
150 Lafayette St., 6th Fl.
New York, NY 10013
Therese Rodriguez, Executive Director
Tel: (212) 334-7940 Fax: (212) 334-7956
Email: apicha@apicha.org
Web: www.apicha.org

SOUTH ASIA AGAINST AIDS FOUNDATION, INC.
303 Park Ave. South #1080
New York, NY 10010
Asha Olivia, President/Founder
Tel: (646) 729-3962
Email: asha@saaaids.org
Web: www.saaaids.org

SPEC. INT., ALCOHOL/DRUG CENTER

CHINATOWN ALCOHOLISM SERVICES/ HAMILTON-MADISON HOUSE
253 S St., 2nd Fl.- 3rd Fl.
New York, NY 10002
May Lai, Director
Tel: (212) 720-4520 Fax: (212) 732-9754/732-9774
Email: cas@hmh100.com/ asian american organization recovery
Web: www.hmh100.com

SPEC. INT., CHILD CARE

CHILDREN OF ARMENIA FUND
630 5th Ave. #2100
New York, NY 10111
Mary Ann Kibarian, Executive Director
Tel: (212) 994-8250 Fax: (212) 994-8299
Email: makibarian@coafkids.org

CHILDREN OF CHINA PEDIATRICS FOUNDATION
P.O. Box 5594
New York, NY 10185
Hong Haiyang, Board of Director
Email: info@china-pediatrics.org
Web: www.china-pediatrics.org

CHILDREN'S DEFENSE FUND-NEW YORK
Albany Office
119 Washington Ave., 3rd Fl.
Albany, NY 12210
Jennifer Post, Project Coordinator
Tel: (518) 449-2830 Fax: (518) 449-2846
Email: jpost@cdfny.org
Web: www.cdfny.org

Main Office
420 Lexington Ave. #655
New York, NY 10170-0699
Donna A. Lawrence, Executive Director
Tel: (212) 697-2323 Fax: (212) 697-0566
Email: messages@cdfny.org
Web: www.cdfny.org

CHINATOWN DAYCARE CENTER, INC.
35 Division St.
New York, NY 10002
Gary Wan, Executive Director
Tel: (212) 431-3845 Fax: (212) 431-3893

FAMILIES WITH CHILDREN FROM CHINA
Central New York Chapter
P.O. Box 5558
Syracuse, NY 13220
Email: fcccny@yahoo.com
Web: http://home.twcny.rr.com/fccofcny/index.html

HOMELAND CHILDREN'S FOUNDATION
121 New York Ave.
Congens, NY 10920
Dr. Hong Haiyang, Board of Director
Tel: (845) 268-0222 Fax: (845) 268-9078
Email: homelandchina@aol.com
Web: http://hometown.aol.com/homelandchina/index.html

ISRAEL CHILDREN'S CANCER FOUNDATION
7 Penn Plz. #1602
New York, NY 10001-3977
Michael B. Harris, Chairman
Tel: (212) 768-4447 Fax: (212) 768-8927
Email: info@israelcancer.org
Web: www.israelcancer.org

JEWISH CHILD CARE ASSOCIATION
120 Wall St.
New York, NY 10005
Leonard S. Elman, President
Tel: (212) 425-3333 Fax: (212) 425-9397
Email: jcca@jccany.org
Web: www.jccany.org

THE GRACE CHILDREN'S FOUNDATION
697 W. End Ave. #14E
New York, NY 10025
Nancy Robertson, President
Tel: (212) 662-1143 Fax: (212) 362-3850
Email: tgcfny@aol.com
Web: www.gracechildren.org

SPEC. INT., COUNSELING

BANGLADESH ASSOCIATION OF NEW YORK
45 Kirkwood
Locust Valley, NY 11542
Tel: (516) 674-0648
Email: info@bany-ny.org
Web: www.bany-ny.org

JEWS FOR JUDAISM, INC.
New York
P.O. Box 117
Forest Hills, NY 11375
Gerry Sigal, Director
Email: newyork@jewsforjudaism.org
Web: www.jewsforjudaism.org

KOREAN AMERICAN COUNSELING CENTER, INC.
35-26 Union St.
Flushing, NY 11354
Giho Kim, Executive Director
Tel: (718) 939-7214 Fax: (718) 939-2586

SPEC. INT., EDUCATION

AA SQUARED
P.O. Box 4093
Stony Brook, NY 11790
John Cordero, Co-Chair
Tel: (631) 831-6062
Email: board@aasquared.org
Web: www.aasquared.org

ALBANY CHINESE SCHOOL
Shaker Junior High
475 Watervliet-Shaker Rd.
Latham, NY 12110
Ming Xu, Principal
Tel: (518) 475-0165
Email: principal@albanychineseschool.org
Web: www.albanychineseschool.org

AMERICAN FRIENDS OF WUJS INSTITUTE
2562 Broadway #116
New York, NY 10025-5657
Rebecca Schweiger, North American Director
Tel: (888) 985-7467
Email: wujsusa@prodigy.net
Web: www.wujs-arad.org

ARABIAN F.O.A.L. ASSOCIATION
P.O. Box 198
Parksville, NY 12768-0198
Frederick Metcalf, President
Tel: (505) 531-2977 Fax: (505) 531-2978
Email: elizabethanarab@hotmail.com
Web: www.foal.org

ASIAN AMERICAN LEGAL DEFENSE AND EDUCATION FUND
99 Hudson St., 12th Fl.
New York, NY 10013
Margaret Fung, Executive Director
Tel: (212) 966-5932 Fax: (212) 966-4303
Email: info@aaldef.org
Web: www.aaldef.org

ASIAN AMERICAN STUDIES PROGRAM
Cornell University

420 Rockefeller Hall
Ithaca, NY 14850
Sunn Shelley Wong, Director
Tel: (607) 255-3320 Fax: (607) 254-4996
Email: apa1@cornell.edu
Web: www.aasp.cornell.edu

ASIAN CLASSICS INPUT PROJECT
New York Area Office
P.O. Box 20373
New York, NY 10009
John Brady, Director
Tel: (212) 475-8935 Fax: (212) 477-7176
Email: acip@well.com
Web: www.asianclassics.org

ASIAN/PACIFIC/AMERICAN STUDIES PROGRAM & INSTITUTE
New York University
269 Mercer St. #609
New York, NY 10003
Jack Tchen, Founding Director
Tel: (212) 998-3700 Fax: (212) 995-4705
Email: apa.studies@nyu.edu
Web: www.apa.nyu.edu

BHARATIYA VIDYA BHAVAN
305 7th Ave., 17th Fl.
New York, NY 10001
P. Jayaraman, Director
Tel: (212) 989-8383 Fax: (212) 989-6482
Email: info@bhavanus.com
Web: www.bhavanus.com

BOYS TOWN JERUSALEM FOUNDATION OF AMERICA, INC.
National Office
12 W. 31st St. #300
New York, NY 10001
Rabbi Ronald L. Gray, Executive Vice President
Tel: (800) 469-2697 Fax: (212) 244-2052
Email: btjny@compuserve.com
Web: www.boystownjerusalem.com

CENTER FOR INDIA STUDIES
SUNY at Stony Brook
E-5350 Melville Library
Stony Brook, NY 11794-3386
Nirmal Mattoo, President
Tel: (631) 632-9742 Fax: (631) 751-7050
Email: indiastudies@stonybrook.edu
Web: http://naples.cc.sunysb.edu/cas/india.nsf

CENTER FOR JEWISH EDUCATION OF ROCKLAND
900 Route 45 #1
New City, NY 10956-1140
Laurie A. Hoffman, Executive Director
Tel: (845) 362-4200 Fax: (845) 362-4282
Email: cjerock@aol.com
Web: www.cjerock.org

CENTER FOR KOREAN LEGAL STUDIES
Columbia University School of Law
435 W. 116th St.
New York, NY 10027
Jeong-Ho Roh, Director
Tel: (212) 854-5759 Fax: (212) 854-4980
Email: jr253@columbia.edu
Web: www.law.columbia.edu/center_program/korean_legal

CENTER ON CHINESE EDUCATION
Teachers College Columbia University
525 W. 120th St., Box 211C
New York, NY 10027
Mun C. Tsang, Director
Tel: (212) 678-3814
Web: www.tc.columbia.edu/centers/coce

CHIANG CHING-KUO FOUNDATION CENTER FOR CHINESE CULTURAL AND INSTITUTIONAL HISTROY
Columbia University
Department of East Asian Languages and Cultures, 406 Kent Hall, M/C 39007
New York, NY 10007
Prof. David Wang, Director

Tel: (212) 854-5631 Fax: (212) 678-8629
Email: jbw15@columbia.edu
Web: www.cckf.org

COALITION FOR THE ADVANCEMENT OF JEWISH EDUCATION
261 W. 35th St., 12th Fl.
New York, NY 10001
Eliot G. Spack, Executive Director
Tel: (212) 268-4210 Fax: (212) 268-4214
Email: cajeny@caje.org
Web: www.caje.org

DONALD KEENE CENTER OF JAPANESE CULTURE
Columbia University
507 Kent Hall M/C 3920
New York, NY 10027
Donald Keene, Professor
Tel: (212) 854-5036 Fax: (212) 854-4019
Email: donald-keene-center@columbia.edu
Web: www.columbia.edu/cu/ealac/dkc

DRISHA INSTITUTE FOR JEWISH EDUCATION
37 W. 65th St., 5th Fl.
New York, NY 10023
David Silber, Founder/Dean
Tel: (212) 595-0307 Fax: (212) 595-0679
Email: info@drisha.org
Web: www.drisha.org

FOREIGN POLICY ASSOCIATION
470 Park Ave. South
New York, NY 10016
Noel V. Lateef, President
Tel: (212) 481-8100 Fax: (212) 481-9275
Email: info@fpa.org
Web: www.fpa.org

GURUKUL, INC.
20 Thames Ct.
Getzville, NY 14068
Email: setlur@cedar.buffalo.edu
Web: www.acsu.buffalo.edu/~setlur/gurukul.html

HARRIMAN INSTITUTE
Columbia University
420 W. 118th St. M/C 3345
New York, NY 10027
Gordon N. Bardos, Assistant Director
Tel: (212) 854-4623 Fax: (212) 666-3481
Email: gnb12@columbia.edu
Web: www.columbia.edu/cu/sipa/regional/hi

HEBREW UNION COLLEGE-JEWISH INSTITUTE OF RELIGION
New York Office
1 W. 4th St.
New York, NY 10012-1186
David Ellenson, President
Tel: (212) 674-5300 Fax: (212) 388-1720
Email: admissions@huc.edu
Web: www.huc.edu

HENRY LUCE FOUNDATION, INC.
111 W. 50th St.
New York, NY 10020
Michael Gilligan, President
Tel: (212) 489-7700 Fax: (212) 581-9541
Email: hlf@hluce.org
Web: www.hluce.org

JAPAN FOUNDATION OF NEW YORK
152 W. 57th St., 17th Fl.
New York, NY 10019
Masaru Susaki, Director General
Tel: (212) 489-0299 Fax: (212) 489-0409
Email: info@jfny.org
Web: www.jfny.org

JAPAN ICU FOUNDATION, INC.
475 Riverside Dr. #439
New York, NY 10115-0439
David W. Vikner, President
Tel: (212) 870-3386 Fax: (212) 870-2696

Email: info@jicuf.org
Web: www.jicuf.org

JEWISH BOOK COUNCIL
15 E. 26th St.
New York, NY 10010
Carolyn Starman Hessel, Executive Director
Tel: (212) 532-4949 X297 Fax: (212) 481-4174
Email: carolynhessel@jewishbookcouncil.org
Web: www.jewishbookcouncil.org

JEWISH EDUCATION SERVICE OF NORTH AMERICA INC.
111 8th Ave.
New York, NY 10011
Jonathan Woocher
Tel: (212) 284-6950 Fax: (212) 284-6951
Email: jwoocher@jesna.org
Web: www.jesna.org

JEWISH HERITAGE DAY SCHOOL OF BUFFALO
411 John James Audubon
Amherst, NY 14228
Shmuel Schanowitz, Principal
Tel: (716) 568-0226
Email: jhds@buffalo.com

JEWISH NATIONAL FUND
National Office
42 E. 69th St.
New York, NY 10021
Ronald S. Lauder, President
Tel: (212) 879-9305 Fax: (212) 570-1673
Email: communications@jnf.org
Web: www.jnf.org

JEWISH TEACHERS CORPS
45 W. 36th St.
New York, NY 10018
Rabbi Uri Gordon, Director
Tel: (888) 582-6777 Fax: (212) 244-7855
Email: uri@jtcorps.org
Web: www.jtcorps.org

JEWISH THEOLOGICAL SEMINARY
Long Island and Queens Region
575 Underhill Blvd. #168
Syosset, NY 11791
Jacqueline Glodstein, Director
Tel: (516) 496-9525
Web: www.jtsa.edu

Northeast Region
3080 Broadway
New York, NY 10027
David-Seth Kirshner, Senior Director
Tel: (212) 678-8057
Web: www.jtsa.edu

KARMA KAGYU INSTITUTE
335 Meads Mountain Rd.
Woodstock, NY 12498
Dr. Williard Roth, President
Email: pres@karmakagyu.org
Web: www.karmakagyu.org

KOREAN AMERICAN SCHOLARSHIP FOUNDATION
Northeastern Region
51 W. Overlok
Port Washington, NY 11050
Woon-Kun Jae, Chairman
Tel: (718) 353-6921 Fax: (516) 883-1964
Email: northeastern@kasf.org
Web: www.kasf.org

LEO BAECK INSTITUTE
15 W. 16th St.
New York, NY 10011
Carol Kahn Strauss, Executive Director
Tel: (212) 744-6400 Fax: (212) 988-1305
Email: carol@lbi.cjh.org
Web: www.lbi.org

NATIONAL ASIAN PACIFIC AMERICAN LAW STUDENT ASSOCIATION
Touro College

300 Nassau Rd.
Huntington, NY 11743
Wook Chung, President
Tel: (631) 421-2244 Fax: (631) 421-2675
Email: tourolaw_apalsa@hotmail.com
Web: www.napalsa.org

NATIONAL JEWISH CENTER FOR LEARNING AND LEADERSHIP
440 Park Ave., 4th Fl. South
New York, NY 10016-8012
Rabbi Irwin Kula, President
Tel: (212) 779-3300 Fax: (212) 779-1009
Email: info@clal.org
Web: www.clal.org

NORTHERN WESTCHESTER CHINESE SCHOOL
P.O. Box 52
Yorktown Heights, NY 10598
Juliet Candee, Principal
Email: principal@nynwcs.org
Web: www.nynwcs.org

OHASHI INSTITUTE
New York
147 W. 25th St., 8th Fl.
New York, NY 10001
Wataru Ohashi, Co-Director
Tel: (646) 486-1187 Fax: (646) 486-1409
Email: info@ohashiatsu.org
Web: www.ohashiatsu.org

PAKISTAN LITERACY FUND
301 E. 38th St. #8A
New York, NY 10016
Tel: (212) 937-3621 Fax: (212) 937-3616
Email: info@pakfund.org
Web: www.pakfund.org/pef

PARDES INSTITUTE OF JEWISH STUDIES
136 E. 39th St.
New York, NY 10016
Rabbi Elisha Ancelovits, Faculty
Tel: (888) 875-2734 Fax: (212) 447-4315
Email: info@pardesusa.org
Web: www.pardes.org.il

PLAINVIEW CHINESE SCHOOL
1535 Old Country Rd.
Plainview, NY 11803
Tel: (516) 753-5616 Fax: (516) 753-5617
Email: plainview@lipvcs.org
Web: www.lipvcs.org

PROBINI FOUNDATION, INC.
80-56 251st St.
Bellerose, NY 11426
Dr. Sachi Dastidar, Chair of Trustee
Tel: (718) 343-0189 Fax: (718) 343-0189
Email: probini@hotmail.com
Web: www.probini.org

PROMOTION OF EDUCATION IN PAKISTAN FOUNDATION, INC.
166 5th Ave., 5th Fl.
New York, NY 10010
Rudina Xhaferri, Executive Director
Tel: (212) 255-5399 Fax: (212) 633-2220
Email: info@pepfoundation.org
Web: www.pepfoundation.org

SENIORNET LEARNING CENTER AT THE JEWISH COMMUNITY CENTER OF STATEN ISLAND
475 Victory Blvd.
Staten Island, NY 10301
Tel: (718) 720-7965
Email: info@seniornetsi.org
Web: www.seniornetsi.org

STATEN ISLAND CHINESE SCHOOL
P.O. Box 492
Staten Islang, NY 10309
Tel: (718) 938-1489
Email: sichinese@hotmail.com
Web: www.sichinese.org

THE INSTITUTE FOR VIETNAMESE CULTURE & EDUCATION
131 Lexington St.
Westbury, NY 11590
Tran Thang, President
Tel: (516) 334-7399
Email: nhipsong@ivce.org
Web: www.ivce.org

UNITED BOARD FOR CHRISTIAN HIGHER EDUCATION IN ASIA
475 Riverside Dr. #1221
New York, NY 10115
Richard J. Wood, President
Tel: (212) 870-2600 Fax: (212) 870-2322
Web: www.unitedboard.org

US CHINA PEOPLES FRIENDSHIP ASSOCIATION
Eastern Region
112 Chestnut St.
Albany, NY 12210
Rezsin Adams, President
Tel: (518) 462-0891 Fax: (518) 436-1935
Email: pinebush2002@yahoo.com
Web: www.uscpfa.org

New York City Chapter
122 W. 27th St., 10th Fl.
New York, NY 10001
Irving Zuckerman
Tel: (212) 989-5152
Web: www.uscpfa.org

Northeastern Albany New York Chapter
9 Hunters Run Blvd.
Cohoes, NY 12047
Kirk Huang, Chapter President
Tel: (518) 782-0746
Email: kkhbravo@yahoo.com
Web: www.uscpfany.org

WEATHERHEAD EAST ASIAN INSTITUTE
Columbia University
420 W. 118th St. M/C 3333
New York, NY 10027
Charles Armstrong, Acting Director
Tel: (212) 854-2592 Fax: (212) 749-1497
Email: cra10@columbia.edu
Web: www.columbia.edu

WESTCHESTER CHINESE SCHOOL
P.O. Box 435
Scarsdale, NY 10583
Philip Chen, Principal
Email: yude_school@excite.com
Web: www.yude.org

SPEC. INT., EMPLOYMENT

CHINATOWN MANPOWER PROJECT
70 Mulberry St.
New York, NY 10013
James Melendez, Executive Director
Tel: (212) 571-1690 Fax: (212) 571-1686
Email: jamesjmelendez@aol.com
Web: www.chinatownweb.com/cmp

SPEC. INT., FAMILY PLANNING

COALITION FOR ASIAN AMERICAN CHILDREN & FAMILIES
50 Broad St. #1701
New York, NY 10004
Myra Liwanag, Interim Executive Director
Tel: (212) 809-4675 Fax: (212) 785-4601
Email: cacf@cacf.org
Web: www.cacf.org

LOWER EAST SIDE FAMILY UNION
Manhattan Office
84 Stanton St.
New York, NY 10002
Darryl A. Chisolm, Executive Director
Tel: (212) 260-0040 Fax: (212) 529-3244
Email: dchisolm@lesfu.org

Web: www.lesfu.org

SPEC. INT., GAY&LESBIAN

GAY ASIAN & PACIFIC ISLANDER MEN OF NEW YORK
Old Chelsea Station, P.O. Box 1608
New York, NY 10113
Glenn Magpantay, Co-Chair
Tel: (212) 802-7423
Email: gapimny@gapimny.org
Web: www.gapimny.org

IBAN/ QUEER KOREANS OF NEW YORK
Audrey Lord Project, Inc.
85 S. Oxford St.
Brooklyn, NY 11217-1607
Kris Hayashi, Executive Director
Tel: (718) 596-0342 Fax: (718) 596-1328
Email: alpinfo@alp.org
Web: www.alp.org

LESBIAN AND GAY IMMIGRATION RIGHTS TASK FORCE
350 W. 31st St. #505
New York, NY 10001
Victoria Neilson, Legal Director
Tel: (212) 714-2904 Fax: (212) 714-2973
Email: info@immigrationequality.org
Web: www.lgirtf.org

SOUTH ASIAN LESBIAN & GAY ASSOCIATION OF NEW YORK CITY
Old Chelsea Station, P.O. Box 1491
New York, NY 10113
Asnetta Seecharras, Executive Director
Tel: (212) 358-5132
Email: salganyc@hotmail.com
Web: www.salganyc.org

SPEC. INT., HEALTH SERVICES

AMERICAN CANCER SOCIETY
Eastern Division-New York Chinese Unit
41-60 Main St. #206
Flushing, NY 11355
Ming Der Chang, President
Tel: (718) 886-8890 Fax: (718) 886-8981
Email: ming-der.chang@cancer.org
Web: www.cancer.org

Eastern Division-Queens Regional Office
Korean Outreach Program
97-77 Queens Blvd. #1110
Rego Park, NY 11374
Ming Der Chang, President
Tel: (718) 263-1532
Email: ming-der.chang@cancer.org
Web: www.cancer.org

ASIAN BICULTURAL CLINIC- GOUVERNEUR HOSPITAL
Department of Psychiatry
227 Madison St. #382
New York, NY 10002
Diana Chan, Coordinating Manager
Tel: (212) 238-7332 Fax: (212) 238-7399
Email: info@asianmentalhealth.org
Web: www.asianmentalhealth.org/aabhsd.asp?orgid=4

CAMMY LEE LEUKEMIA FOUNDATION, INC.
16 W. 32nd St. #10-D
New York, NY 10001-3808
Ann Yang, Program Director
Tel: (646) 473-0044 Fax: (646) 473-0045
Email: cllforg@yahoo.com
Web: www.cllf.org

CENTER FOR IMMIGRANT HEALTH
NYU School of Medicine
550 1st Ave.
New York, NY 10016
Francesca Gany, Chair/Executive Director
Tel: (212) 263-8783 Fax: (212) 263-8234
Web: www.med.nyu.edu/cih

CHARLES B. WANG COMMUNITY HEALTH CENTER
Flushing Office
136-26 37th Ave., 2nd Fl.
Flushing, NY 11354
Betty Cheng, Associate Executive Director
Tel: (718) 886-1212 Fax: (718) 886-2568
Web: www.cbwchc.org

Manhattan Chapter
268 Canal St. #6F
New York, NY 10013
Jane T. Eng, Executive Director
Tel: (212) 379-6988 Fax: (212) 379-6936
Web: www.cbwchc.org

CHARLES B. WANG COMMUNITY HOUSE CENTER
125 Walker St., 2nd Fl.
New York, NY 10013
Jane Eng, Executive Director
Tel: (212) 226-3888 Fax: (212) 226-2289

FILIPINO-AMERICAN MEDICAL, INC.
P.O. Box 161
New York, NY 10101
Niles Perlas, Chair
Tel: (212) 582-3304 Fax: (212) 582-6809
Email: nperlas@att.net
Web: www.ifami.com

GRACIE SQUARE HOSPITAL ASIAN PROGRAM
420 E. 76th St.
New York, NY 10021
Raymond Tam, Assistant Director
Tel: (212) 434-5577 Fax: (212) 434-5578
Email: info@nygsh.org
Web: www.nygsh.org

INDO-AMERICAN PSYCHIATRIC ASSOCIATION
855 Bruce Dr.
East Meadow, NY 11554-5148
Anjali Pandya, Executive Director
Tel: (516) 292-9741
Email: apandya880@yahoo.com
Web: www.myiapa.org

ISRAEL CANCER RESEARCH FUND
1290 Ave. of the Americas #550
New York, NY 10104
Yashar Hirshaut, President
Tel: (212) 969-9800 Fax: (212) 969-9822
Email: mail@icrfny.org
Web: www.icrfonline.org

JEWISH GUILD FOR THE BLIND
15 W. 65th St.
New York, NY 10023
Tel: (800) 284-4422 Fax: (212) 769-6266
Email: info@jgb.org
Web: www.jgb.org

KOREAN AMERICAN FAMILY SERVICE CENTER
P.O. Box 541429
Flushing, NY 11354
Hye-Suk Theresa Chong, Executive Director
Tel: (718) 539-7682 Fax: (718) 460-3965
Email: contact@kafsc.org
Web: www.kafsc.org

LANTERN LUPUS NETWORK
535 E. 70th St.
New York, NY 10021
Karen Ng
Tel: (866) 505-2253 Fax: (212) 472-6530
Email: ngk@hss.edu
Web: www.hss.edu/departments/specialties/rheumatology

LOWER EAST SIDE SERVICE CENTER
Chinese Continuing Day Treatment Program
157 Chambers St., 8th Fl.
New York, NY 10007
Alan Mathis, President/CEO
Tel: (212) 566-5372 Fax: (212) 732-5224

Email: amathis@lesc.org
Web: www.lesc.org

SOUTH ASIAN MARROW ASSOCIATION OF RECRUITERS
55-13 96th St.
Rego Park, NY 11368
Vikramjit Chhabra, Coordinator
Tel: (718) 592-0821 Fax: (718) 592-5848
Email: samarinfo@aol.com
Web: www.samarinfo.org

TIBETAN REFUGEE HEALTH CARE PROJECT
101 W. 23rd St. #158
New York City, NY 10011
Email: info@tibetanrefugeehealth.org
Web: www.tibetanrefugeehealth.org

SPEC. INT., HOUSING

AAFE COMMUNITY DEVELOPMENT FUND, INC.
111 Division St.
New York, NY 10002-6103
Christopher Kui, Executive Director
Tel: (212) 964-2288 Fax: (212) 964-6003
Email: info@aafecdf.org
Web: www.aafecdf.org

ASIAN AMERICAN HOUSING MANAGEMENT COMPANY
50 Norfolk St.
New York, NY 10002
Don Hong, President
Tel: (212) 475-7730 Fax: (212) 475-7802
Email: aahmc@erols.com

ASIAN AMERICANS FOR EQUALITY FAIR HOUSING CENTER
40-34 Main St.
Flushing, NY 11354
Tel: (718) 539-7290 Fax: (718) 539-5706
Email: fairhousing@aafe.org
Web: http://aafe.org/fair_housing/

HAMILTON MADISON HOUSE SUPPORTED HOUSING PROGRAM
108-11 48th Ave.
Corona, NY 11368
Linda Tung, Director
Tel: (718) 760-3810 Fax: (718) 760-0890
Email: linda@hmh100.com
Web: www.hmh100.com

RENAISSANCE ECONOMIC DEVELOPMENT CORPORATION
1 Pike St.
New York, NY 10002
Benjamin Warnki, Managing Director
Tel: (212) 964-6022 Fax: (212) 964-6022
Email: info@renaissance-ny.org
Web: www.renaissance-ny.org

SPEC. INT., HUMAN RELATIONS

AMERICAN INDIA FOUNDATION
55 E. 52nd St., 29th Fl.
New York, NY 10022
Lata Krishnan, President
Tel: (212) 891-4654 Fax: (212) 891-4717
Email: nandini.ansari@aifoundation.org
Web: www.aifoundation.org

AMERICAN JEWISH WORLD SERVICE
National Office
45 W. 36th St., 10th Fl.
New York, NY 10018-7904
Ruth Messinger, President
Tel: (800) 889-7146 Fax: (212) 736-3463
Email: ajws@ajws.org
Web: www.ajws.org

AMERICAN RED MAGEN DAVID FOR ISRAEL
National Headquarters
888 7th Ave. #403
New York, NY 10106

Emanuel Celler, Director
Tel: (866) 632-2763 Fax: (212) 757-4662
Email: info@armdi.org
Web: www.armdi.org

AMERICAN ZIONIST MOVEMENT
National Office
633 3rd Ave.
New York, NY 10017
W. James Schiller, President
Tel: (212) 318-6100
Web: www.azm.org

ANTI-DEFAMATION LEAGUE
823 United Nations Plz.
New York, NY 10017
Graham Cannon, Head of Marketing
Tel: (212) 885-7700 Fax: (212) 885-5855
Email: webmaster@adl.org
Web: www.adl.org

ARMENIA FUND USA, INC.
152 Madison Ave. #803
New York, NY 10016-5424
Irina Lazarian, Executive Director
Tel: (212) 689-5307 Fax: (212) 689-5317
Email: info@armeniafundusa.org
Web: www.armeniafundusa.org

ASIA SOCIETY
Headquarters
725 Park Ave.
New York, NY 10021
Vishakha N. Desai, President
Tel: (212) 288-6400 Fax: (212) 517-8315
Email: info@asiasoc.org
Web: www.asiasociety.org

ASSOCIATION OF INDIANS IN AMERICA
166 W. 22nd St. #1G
New York, NY 10011
Nalini Shah, President
Tel: (212) 647-9131
Email: nshah_8155@hotmail.com
Web: www.aianewyork.com

BREAKTHROUGH
34-36 85th St.
Jackson Heights, NY 11372
Mallika Dutt, Executive Director
Tel: (718) 457-4300 Fax: (718) 457-4307
Email: contact@breakthrough.tv
Web: www.breakthrough.tv

BROOKLYN CHINESE AMERICAN ASSOCIATION
5002 8th Ave.
Brooklyn, NY 11220
Paul Mak, President
Tel: (718) 438-9312 Fax: (718) 438-8303
Email: bcaspirit@aol.com

BURMA PROJECT/SOUTHEAST ASIA INITIATIVE
Open Society Institute
400 W. 59th St.
New York, NY 10019
Maureen Aung-Thwin, Director
Tel: (212) 548-0632 Fax: (212) 548-4655
Email: maungthwin@sorosny.org
Web: www.burmaproject.org

CARNEGIE COUNCIL ON ETHICS AND INTERNATIONAL AFFAIRS
170 E. 64th St.
New York, NY 10021-7478
Joel H. Rosenthal, President
Tel: (212) 838-4120 Fax: (212) 752-2432
Email: info@cceia.org
Web: www.cceia.org

CHINESE AMERICAN PLANNING COUNCIL
150 Elizabeth St.
New York, NY 10012
David Chen, Executive Director
Tel: (212) 941-0920 Fax: (212) 966-8581
Email: cpccentral@cpc-nyc.org
Web: www.cpc-nyc.org

CHINESE CONSOLIDATED BENEVOLENT ASSOCIATION
New York Chapter
62-64 Mott St.
New York, NY 10013
Tel: (212) 226-6280
Web: www.chinatownweb.com/ccba

CHINESE STAFF AND WORKERS' ASSOCIATION
P.O. Box 130401
New York, NY 10013-0995
Wing Lam, Executive Director
Tel: (212) 619-7979 Fax: (212) 374-1506
Email: cswa@cswa.org
Web: www.cswa.org

COALITION ON THE ENVIRONMENT AND JEWISH LIFE
443 Park Ave., 11th Fl. South
New York, NY 10016
Adam C. Stern, Executive Director
Tel: (212) 684-6950
Email: info@coejl.org
Web: www.coejl.org

COMMITTEE OF 100
677 5th Ave., 3rd Fl.
New York, NY 10022
Alice Mong, Executive Director
Tel: (212) 371-6565 Fax: (212) 371-9009
Email: c100@committee100.org
Web: www.committee100.org

COUNCIL ON AMERICAN-ISLAMIC RELATIONS
New York Chapter
475 Riverside Dr. #246
New York, NY 10115
Nasir Gondal, President
Tel: (212) 870-2002 Fax: (212) 870-2020
Email: cair-ny@cair-ny.com
Web: www.cair-ny.com

DRUM MAJOR INSTITUTE FOR PUBLIC POLICY
110 E. 59th St., 28th Fl.
New York, NY 10022
Steve Presser, Assistant to the President
Tel: (212) 909-9663 Fax: (212) 909-9493
Email: dmi@drummajorinstitute.org
Web: www.drummajorinstitute.org

EAST WEST INSTITUTE
700 Broadway
New York, NY 10003
Adam Albion, Project Manager
Tel: (212) 824-4100 Fax: (212) 824-4149
Email: aalbion@ewi.info
Web: www.iews.org

FILIPINO AMERICAN HUMAN SERVICES, INC.
185-14 Hillside Ave.
Jamaica, NY 11432
Vanessa G. Manzano, Executive Director
Tel: (718) 883-1295 Fax: (718) 523-9606
Email: fahsi@fahsi.org
Web: www.fahsi.org

FUND FOR ARMENIAN RELIEF
630 2nd Ave.
New York, NY 10016
Khajag Barsamian, President
Tel: (212) 889-5150 Fax: (212) 889-4849
Web: www.farusa.org

HARVARD ARAB ALUMNI ASSOCIATION
P.O. Box 2324
New York, NY 10108
Ahmad Anani, Co-President
Email: ahmad@harvardarabalumni.org
Web: www.harvardarabalumni.org

HUMAN RIGHTS IN CHINA
350 5th Ave. #3309
New York, NY 10118
Tel: (212) 239-4495 Fax: (212) 239-2561

Email: hrichina@hrichina.org
Web: http://iso.hrichina.org

IRANIAN AMERICAN SOCIETY OF NEW YORK
P.O. Box 306
Greenvale, NY 11548
Dr. Farhad Talebian, President
Tel: (516) 773-0720 Fax: (516) 624-0135
Email: mail@iasny.com
Web: www.iasny.com

IRANIAN REFUGEES ALLIANCE, INC.
P.O. Box 316
New York, NY 10276-0316
Tel: (212) 260-7460 Fax: (212) 260-7460
Email: irainc@irainc.org
Web: www.irainc.org

ISRAELI HUMANITARIAN FOUNDATION
National Office
276 5th Ave. #901
New York, NY 10001
Stanley J. Abrams, Executive Vice President
Tel: (212) 683-5676 Fax: (212) 213-9233
Email: stanley@ihf.net
Web: www.ihf.net

JAPAN FOUNDATION CENTER FOR GLOBAL PARTNERSHIP
152 W. 57th St., 39th Fl.
New York, NY 10019
Akihiko Murata, Director
Tel: (212) 489-1255 Fax: (212) 489-1344
Email: info@cgp.org
Web: www.cgp.org

JEWISH COMMUNITY RELATIONS COUNCIL OF NEW YORK
70 W. 36th St. #700
New York, NY 10018
Elana Bekerman, Program Director
Tel: (212) 983-4800 Fax: (212) 983-4084
Email: info@jcrcny.org
Web: www.jcrcny.org

JEWISH FUND FOR JUSTICE
330 7th Ave. #1401
New York, NY 10001
Marlene Provizer, Executive Director/CEO
Tel: (212) 213-2113 Fax: (212) 213-2233
Email: jfjustice@jfjustice.org
Web: www.jfjustice.org

JEWISH RECONSTRUCTIONIST FEDERATION
New York Region
475 Riverside Dr. #1367
New York, NY 10115
Melanie Schneider, Regional Director
Tel: (212) 870-2483 Fax: (212) 870-2862
Email: jrf-ny@jrf.org
Web: www.jrf.org

JEWISH SURVIVORS OF LATVIA, INC.
74 Short Way
Roslyn Heights, NY 11577
Steven Springfield, President
Tel: (516) 625-0210
Email: stevenriga@aol.com

MUSLIM PEACE FELLOWSHIP
P.O. Box 271
Nyack, NY 10960
Rabia Harris, Coordinator
Tel: (845) 358-4601 Fax: (845) 358-4924
Email: mpf@mpfweb.org
Web: www.mpfweb.org

NATIONAL COMMITTEE ON US CHINA RELATIONS
71 W. 23rd St. #1901
New York, NY 10010-4102
John L. Holden, President
Tel: (212) 645-9677 Fax: (212) 645-1695
Email: info@ncuscr.org
Web: www.ncuscr.org

NEW ISRAEL FUND
165 E. 56th St.
New York, NY 10022-2746
Peter Edelman, President
Tel: (212) 750-2333 Fax: (212) 750-8043
Email: ny@nif.org
Web: www.nif.org

NODUTDOL FOR KOREAN COMMUNITY DEVELOPMENT
37-48 61st St., 2nd Fl.
Queens, NY 11377
John Choe, Steering Committee Member
Tel: (718) 335-0419 Fax: (718) 335-0419
Email: nodutdol@egroups.com
Web: www.nodutdol.com

PHILIPPINE FORUM
8708 Justice Ave. #2E
New York, NY 11373
Robert Roy, Executive Director
Tel: (718) 565-8862 Fax: (718) 565-8856
Email: info@philippineforum.org

SERVICE AND EDUCATION FOR KOREAN AMERICANS, INC.
40-11 149th Pl.
Flushing, NY 11354
Tel: (718) 961-4117
Email: info@seka.org
Web: www.seka.org

SIMON WIESENTHAL CENTER
New York Office
50 E. 42nd St. #1600
New York, NY 10017
Rhonda Barad, Eastern Director
Tel: (212) 370-0320 Fax: (212) 883-0895
Email: rbarad@swcny.com
Web: www.wiesenthal.com

THE ABRAHAM FUND INITIATIVES
477 Madison Ave., 4th Fl.
New York, NY 10022
Ami Nahshon, President/CEO
Tel: (800) 301-3863 Fax: (212) 935-1834
Email: info@abrahamfund.org
Web: www.abrahamfund.org

THE AMERICAN JEWISH COMMITTEE
P.O. Box 705
New York, NY 10150
E. Robert Goodkind, President
Tel: (212) 751-4000 Fax: (212) 891-1492
Email: pr@ajc.org
Web: www.ajc.org

Buffalo/Niagara Chapter
805 Delaware Ave.
Buffalo, NY 14209
Stephen L. Yonaty, Chapter President
Tel: (716) 819-1213 Fax: (716) 819-1215
Email: buffalo@ajc.org
Web: www.ajc.org

Long Island Chapter
375 N. Broadway #205
Jericho, NY 11753
Ellen Israelson, Chapter Director
Tel: (516) 942-2651 Fax: (516) 942-4759
Email: longisland@ajc.org
Web: www.ajc.org

Westchester Chapter
235 Mamaroneck Ave. #301
White Plains, NY 10605
Laura Lewis, Chapter Director
Tel: (914) 948-5585 Fax: (914) 948-8711
Email: westchester@ajc.org
Web: www.ajc.org

THE FEDERATION OF TURKISH AMERICAN ASSOCIATIONS, INC.
821 United Nations Plz., 2nd Fl.
New York, NY 10017
Ata Erim, President
Tel: (212) 682-7688 Fax: (212) 687-3026
Email: tadfoffice@tadf.org
Web: www.tadf.org

THE TIBET FUND
241 E. 32nd St.
New York, NY 10016
Rinchen Dharlo, President/Director
Tel: (212) 213-5011 Fax: (212) 213-1219
Email: tibetfund@tibetfund.org
Web: www.tibetfund.org

TIBET AID
Tibetan Sponsorship Project
34 Tinker St.
Woodstock, NY 12498
Steve Drago, President
Tel: (845) 679-6973 Fax: (845) 679-6973
Email: sponsor@tibetaid.org
Web: www.tibetaid.org

TOLENTINE-ZEISER/ST. RITA'S
Center for Immigrant and Refugee Services
2342 Andrews Ave.
Bronx, NY 10468
Jean Marshall, Director
Tel: (718) 365-4390 Fax: (718) 295-8729
Email: stritacenter@aol.com

UNITED JEWISH COMMUNITIES
P.O. Box 30, Old Chelsea Station
New York, NY 10113
Tel: (212) 284-6500
Email: info@ujc.org
Web: www.ujc.org

US COMMITTEE FOR A FREE LEBANON
445 Park Ave., 9th Fl.
New York, NY 10022
Ziad K. Abdelnour, President
Fax: (212) 202-6166
Email: info@freelebanon.org
Web: www.freelebanon.org

WORLD UNION FOR PROGRESSIVE JUDAISM
633 3rd Ave.
New York, NY 10017-6778
Tel: (212) 452-6530 Fax: (212) 452-6585
Email: wupj@urj.org
Web: www.wupj.org

SPEC. INT., IMMIGRATION

CHINESE IMMIGRANT SERVICES
133-54 41st. Ave., 4th Fl.
Flushing, NY 11355
Susan Wu Rathbone, Chairperson
Tel: (718) 353-0195 Fax: (718) 359-5065

HEBREW IMMIGRANT AID SOCIETY
333 7th Ave., 17th Fl.
New York, NY 10001-5004
Leonard S. Glickman, President/CEO
Tel: (212) 967-4100 Fax: (212) 967-4483
Email: info@hias.org
Web: www.hias.org

KOREAN IMMIGRANT SERVICE OF NEW YORK
136-65 Roosevelt Ave. #200
Flushing, NY 11354
Suk Hee Kang, Executive Director
Tel: (718) 359-5400 Fax: (718) 539-5492
Email: kisny@aol.com
Web: www.kisny.org

NEW YORK IMMIGRANT COALITION
275 7th Ave., 9th Fl.
New York, NY 10001
Margie McHugh, Executive Director
Tel: (212) 627-2227 Fax: (212) 627-9314
Email: eseliz@thenyic.org
Web: www.thenyic.org

SPEC. INT., LEGAL ASSISTANCE

CHINA LABOR WATCH
P.O. Box 4134, Grand Central Station
New York, NY 10163-4134
Li Qiang, Executive Director
Tel: (917) 257-8589

Email: qiang@chinalaborwatch.org
Web: www.chinalaborwatch.org

COMMITTEE AGAINST ANTI- ASIAN VIOLENCE
2473 Valentine Ave.
Bronx, NY 10458
Tel: (718) 220-7391 Fax: (718) 220-7398
Email: justice@caaav.org
Web: www.caaav.org

DRUM
72-76 Broadway, 4th Fl.
Jackson Heights, NY 11372
Tel: (718) 205-3036 Fax: (718) 205-3037
Email: drum@drumnation.org
Web: www.drumnation.org

JEWISH LABOR COMMITTEE
25 E. 21st St.
New York, NY 10010
Stuart Appelbaum, President
Tel: (212) 477-0707 Fax: (212) 477-1918
Email: jlcexce@aol.com
Web: www.jewishlabor.org

THE ARAB AMERICAN JUSTICE PROJECT
80 Wall St. #718
New York, NY 10005
Dahlia Eissa, Director
Tel: (212) 480-2955 Fax: (212) 480-2956
Email: info@aajp.org
Web: www.aajp.org

WORKER'S AWAAZ
P.O. Box 471
Jackson Heights, NY 11372
Satwant Kukreja
Tel: (718) 565-0801 Fax: (718) 565-0836
Email: workersawaaz@yahoo.com
Web: www.workersawaaz.org

SPEC. INT., MENTAL HEALTH

ASIAN AMERICAN MENTAL HEALTH SERVICES/HAMILTON MADISON HOUSE
253 S St., 3rd Fl. West
New York, NY 10002
Deborah Lee, Director
Tel: (212) 720-4540 Fax: (212) 732-9297
Web: www.hmh100.com

ASIAN LIFENET
Mental Health Association of NYC
666 Broadway #200
New York, NY 10012
Tracy Luo, Director
Tel: (877) 990-8585 Fax: (212) 529-1959
Email: asianlifenet@hotmail.com
Web: www.mhaofnyc.com

ASIAN-AMERICAN MENTAL HEALTH HAMILTON-MADISON HOUSE
Korean Unit
78-14 Roosevelt Ave., 2nd Fl. #204
Jackson Heights, NY 11372
Inok Kim, Supervisor
Tel: (718) 899-8918 Fax: (718) 426-2219

ELMHURST HOSPITAL CENTER ASIAN MENTAL HEALTH CLINIC
79-01 Broadway
Elmhurst, NY 11373
Steven Zhou, Coordinator
Tel: (718) 334-3902 Fax: (718) 334-5721

JEWISH BOARD OF FAMILY AND CHILDREN'S SERVICES
120 W. 57th St.
New York, NY 10019
Email: admin@jbfcs.org
Web: www.jbfcs.org

NY COALITION FOR ASIAN AMERICAN MENTAL HEALTH
253 S St.
New York, NY 10002
Peter Yee, President
Tel: (212) 720-4522

Email: info@asianmentalhealth.org
Web: www.asianmentalhealth.org/aboutus.asp

SPEC. INT., SENIORS

AGING INFORMATION CENTER
Regions II & III: NY, NJ, PR, VI, DC, DE, MD, PA, VA, WV
26 Federal Plz. #38-102
New York, NY 10278
Robert O'Connell, Regional Administrator
Tel: (212) 264-2976 Fax: (212) 264-0114
Email: robert.o'connell@aoa.gov
Web: www.aoa.dhhs.gov

CHINATOWN SENIOR CITIZEN CENTER
70 Mulberry St.
New York, NY 10013
Mojang Tran, Director
Tel: (212) 233-8930 Fax: (212) 233-8932

GREATER CHINATOWN COMMUNITY ASSOCIATION
105 Mosco St.
New York, NY 10013
Tommy Tam, Executive Director
Tel: (212) 374-1311 Fax: (212) 374-1314
Email: graterchinatown@aol.com

HOMECAST COMMUNITY SERVICES, INC.
1413 Ave. T
Brooklyn, NY 11229
Tel: (718) 376-4036 Fax: (718) 376-4124

JEWISH ASSOCIATION FOR SERVICES FOR THE AGED
132 W. 31st St., 15th Fl.
New York, NY 10001
David Warren, President
Tel: (212) 273-5272 Fax: (212) 695-4206
Web: www.jasa.org

JEWISH HOME AND HOSPITAL FOR AGED
Bronx Division
100 W. Kingsbridge Rd.
Bronx, NY 10468
Tel: (718) 410-1500
Email: bronx_admissions@jewishhome.org
Web: www.jewishhome.org

Manhattan Division
120 W. 106th St.
New York, NY 10025
Tel: (212) 870-5919
Email: manhattan_admissions@jewishhome.org
Web: www.jewishhome.org

Westchester/Sarah Neuman Center
845 palmer Ave.
Mamaroneck, NY 10543
Tel: (914) 698-6005
Email: westchester_admissions@jewishhome.org
Web: www.jewishhome.org

KOREAN AMERICAN SENIOR CITIZENS COUNSELING CENTER
35-26 Union St.
Flushing, NY 11354
Giho Kim, Executive Director
Tel: (718) 939-7214 Fax: (718) 939-2586
Email: gihokim@helpneedy.org
Web: www.helpneedy.org

KOREAN AMERICAN SENIOR CITIZENS SOCIETY OF GREATER NEW YORK
149-18 41st Ave.
Flushing, NY 11355
Michael Chiew, Executive Director
Tel: (718) 461-3545 Fax: (718) 359-6024
Email: kascs@email.com

KOREAN AMERICAN SENIOR MUTUAL ASSOCIATION, INC.
35-30 Union St.
Flushing, NY 11354
Yunsuk Shim, President
Tel: (718) 762-6440 Fax: (718) 762-7757

LAGUARDIA SENIOR CENTER
New York Foundation for Senior Citizens, Inc.
280 Cherry St.
New York, NY 10002
David Mei, Director
Tel: (212) 732-3656 Fax: (212) 227-6410

NATIONAL INDO-AMERICAN ASSOCIATION FOR SENIOR CITIZENS
7 Roberta Ave.
Farmingville, NY 11738
Rajeshwar Prasad, Executive Director
Tel: (631) 698-0512
Email: niaasc@aol.com
Web: www.niaasc.org

SPEC. INT., SOCIAL INTEREST

A NEW HERITAGE OF GIVING-PHILANTHROPY IN ASIAN AMERICA
120 Wall St., 3rd Fl.
New York, NY 10005
Kristin Hokoyama
Tel: (212) 344-5878 x24 Fax: (212) 344-5636
Email: info@asianamericanphianthropy.org
Web: www.asianamericanphilanthropy.org

ALSO-KNOWN-AS, INC.
P. O. Box 6037
New York, NY 10150
Joy Lieberthal-Rho, President
Email: jlieberthal@mail.alsoknownas.org
Web: www.alsoknownas.org

ASIAN AMERICAN ALLIANCE
Columbia University
401 Lerner, M/C 2602
New York, NY 10027
Valerie Arboleda, Chair
Email: vaa2001@columbia.edu
Web: www.columbia.edu/cu/aaa/

ASIAN CHILDREN SERVICES VIETNAM HUMANITARIAN, CORP.
83 Prospect St.
Little Falls, NY 13365
Rose Marie Battisti
Tel: (315) 823-3165
Email: info@asianchildrenservices.org
Web: www.asianchildrenservices.org

ASIAN FINANCIAL SOCIETY
P.O. Box 568, Bowling Green Station
New York, NY 10274
Email: afswww@yahoo.com
Web: www.asianfinancialsociety.org

ASIAN OUTREACH PROGRAM
Queens Child Guidance Center
87-88 Justice Ave. #C-7
Elmhurst, NY 11373
Agenelo Digg, Clinic Administrator
Tel: (718) 899-9910 x211 Fax: (718) 899-9699
Email: asian11552@yahoo.com
Web: www.qcgc.org

ASIAN PACIFIC ALLIANCE OF NEW YORK
61-15 98th St. #10E
Rego Park, NY 11374-1409
Ed Remo
Email: apany@aol.com
Web: http://members.aol.com/apany/

ASIANS COMING TOGETHER
245 Park Ave., 21st Fl.
New York, NY 10167
Ronna Treier, National President
Tel: (585) 423-1173 Fax: (585) 423-5449
Email: pinyo.bhulipongsanon@usa.xerox.com
Web: www.asianscomingtogether.com

BABYLONIAN JEWISH CENTER
P.O. Box 220224
Great Neck, NY 11022-0224
Nir Shalom

Tel: (516) 773-9876
Email: info@bjcny.org
Web: www.bjcny.org

BANGLADESHI & AMERICAN SOCIAL DEVELOPMENT INSTITUTE, INC.
71-26 Roosevelt Ave.
Jackson Heights, NY 11372-6137
Abdul Martin Talukder
Web: www.melissadata.com

CHHAYA CDC
40-34 Main St., 2nd Fl.
Flushing, NY 11354
Vandana Chak, Esq., Director
Tel: (718) 463-6615 Fax: (718) 463-7006
Email: vandana@chhayacdc.org
Web: www.chhayacdc.org

CHINESE AMERICAN PLANNING COUNCIL-BROOKLYN
6022 7th Ave.
Brooklyn, NY 11220
Chang Xie, Director
Tel: (718) 492-0409 Fax: (718) 567-0397
Email: ppcbroklynchang@hotmail.com
Web: www.chinatownweb.com/CPC/

CHINESE AMERICAN PLANNING COUNCIL-HOME ATTENDANT PROGRAM
55 Ave. of the Americas #501
New York, NY 10013
Ling Ma, Program Director
Tel: (212) 219-8100 Fax: (212) 966-7371
Web: www.cpc-nyc.org

CHINESE COMMUNITY CENTER
Capital District of New York
P.O. Box 13951
Albany, NY 12212-3951
Hongyi Zhou, President
Tel: (518) 533-2424
Email: zhouh@crd.ge.com
Web: www.cccalbany.org

CHINESE PROGRESSIVE ASSOCIATION
83 Canal St. #304-305
New York, NY 10002
Mae Lee, Executive Director
Tel: (212) 274-1891 Fax: (212) 274-1891
Email: cpanyc@worldnet.att.net
Web: www.aafny.org/directory/new/search.asp?agencyid=46

CHINESE-AMERICAN PLANNING COUNCIL, INC.
150 Elizabeth St.
New York, NY 10012
David Chen, Executive Director
Tel: (212) 941-0920 Fax: (212) 966-8581
Email: cpc@cpc-nyc.org
Web: www.cpc-nyc.org

COALITION OF ASIAN PACIFIC AMERICANS
12 W. 18th St. #3-E
New York, NY 10011
James Yee, President
Tel: (212) 989-3610 Fax: (212) 206-9329
Email: jyee@capaonline.org
Web: www.capaonline.org

COALITION OF KOREAN AMERICAN SOCIAL SERVICES
35-20 147th St. #2F
Flushing, NY 11354
Myoung Ja Lee, Director
Tel: (718) 445-3929 Fax: (718) 661-4429
Email: kaard@verizon.net

COUNCIL OF PAKISTAN ORGANIZATION
1081 Coney Island Ave.
Brooklyn, NY 11230
Moe Razvi, Executive Director
Tel: (718) 859-2266
Email: copousa@copousa.org
Web: www.copousa.org

EAST MEADOW JEWISH CENTER
1400 Prospect Ave.
East Meadow, NY 11554
Ronald Androphy
Tel: (516) 483-4205 Fax: (516) 489-3354
Web: www.eastmeadowjc.org

FEDERATION OF JEWISH MEN'S CLUBS, INC.
475 Riverside Dr. #832
New York, NY 10115-0022
Daniel Stern, President
Tel: (212) 749-8100 Fax: (212) 316-4271
Email: international@fjmc.org
Web: www.fjmc.org

FILIPINO-AMERICANS IN LONG ISLAND, INC.
P.O. Box 145
Holbrook, NY 11741
Dr. Rene Gega, President
Tel: (631) 472-6619
Email: info@familii.org
Web: http://familii.org

HAMILTON-MADISON HOUSE
50 Madison St.
New York, NY 10038
Debra A. Thompson, President
Tel: (212) 349-3724 Fax: (212) 791-7540
Email: hmh@hmh100.com
Web: www.hmh100.com

HAWAI'I CULTURAL FOUNDATION
P.O. Box 250050
New York, NY 10025-0050
Michelle Akina, Co-President
Tel: (212) 966-3378 Fax: (609) 279-2897
Email: hcf@hcfnyc.org
Web: www.hawaiiculturalfoundation.org

ISRAEL COMMUNITY CENTER OF LEVITTOWN
3235 Hempstead Turnpike
Levittown, NY
Tel: (516) 731-2580
Email: webmaster@levittown-icc.com
Web: www.levittown-icc.com

ISRALIGHT
505 8th Ave. #2503
New York, NY 10018
Samuel A. Shor, Director of Community/Leadership Development
Tel: (212) 947-4911 Fax: (212) 947-4998
Email: sam@isralight.org
Web: www.isralight.org

JAPANESE AMERICAN ASSOCIATION OF NEW YORK
15 W. 44th St., 11th Fl.
New York, NY 10036
Toshio Kiso, President
Tel: (212) 840-6942 Fax: (212) 840-0616
Email: info@jaany.org
Web: www.jaany.org

JAPANESE AMERICAN SOCIAL SERVICES, INC.
275 7th Ave., 12th Fl.
New York, NY 10001
Peter D. Lederer, President
Tel: (212) 255-1881 Fax: (212) 255-3281
Email: info@jassi.org
Web: www.jassi.org

JEWISH COMMUNAL FUND
575 Madison Ave. #703
New York, NY 10022
Susan F. Dickman, Executive Vice President
Tel: (212) 580-4523 Fax: (212) 319-6963
Email: info@jewishcommunalfund.org
Web: www.jewishcommunalfund.org

JEWISH COMMUNITY CENTER IN MANHATTAN
334 Amsterdam Ave.
New York, NY 10023

David Black, Executive Director
Tel: (646) 505-4444 Fax: (212) 799-0254
Email: info@jccmanhattan.org
Web: www.jccmanhattan.org

JEWISH COMMUNITY CENTER OF DUTCHESS COUNTY, INC.
110 Grand Ave.
Poughkeepsie, NY 12603
Tel: (845) 471-0430 Fax: (845) 471-0659
Email: jccpok@aol.com
Web: www.jccdutchess.org

JEWISH COMMUNITY CENTER OF GREATER BUFFALO, INC.
2640 N. Forest Rd.
Getzville, NY 14068
Alan Feldman, Executive Director
Tel: (716) 688-4033 Fax: (716) 688-3572
Web: www.jccbuffalo.org

JEWISH COMMUNITY CENTER OF ROCHESTER
1200 Edgewood Ave.
Rochester, NY 14618
Leslie Berkowitz, Executive Director
Tel: (585) 461-2000
Web: www.jccrochester.org

JEWISH COMMUNITY CENTER OF SCHENECTADY
2565 Balltown Rd.
Niskayuna, NY 12309
Alex Hallenstein, Executive Director
Tel: (518) 377-8803 Fax: (518) 377-5530
Email: info@schenectadyjcc.org
Web: www.centers.jcca.org

JEWISH COMMUNITY CENTER OF WEST HEMPSTEAD
711 Dogwood Ave.
West Hempstead, NY 11552
David Weiss, President
Tel: (516) 481-7448
Email: eagai@optonline.net
Web: www.myshul.com

JEWISH COMMUNITY CENTERS ASSOCIATION
New York Office
15 E. 26th St.
New York, NY 10010-1579
Tel: (212) 532-4949 Fax: (212) 481-4174
Email: info@jcca.org
Web: www.jcca.org

JEWISH COMMUNITY COUNCIL OF GREATER CONEY ISLAND, INC.
3001 W. 37th St.
Brooklyn, NY 11224
Tel: (718) 449-5000 Fax: (718) 946-8240
Email: jcc@coney-island.org
Web: www.coney-island.org

JEWISH COMMUNITY COUNCIL OF THE ROCKAWAY PENINSULA
1525 Central Ave.
Far Rockaway, NY 11691-4001
Harvey Gordon, Executive Director
Tel: (718) 327-7755 Fax: (718) 327-4903
Email: hgordon@jccrp.org
Web: www.jccrp.org

JEWISH COMMUNITY FEDERATION OF GREATER ROCHESTER
441 East Ave.
Rochester, NY 14607-1932
Howard J. Grossman, President
Tel: (585) 461-0490 Fax: (585) 461-0912
Email: info@jewishrochester.org
Web: www.jewishrochester.org

JEWISH COMMUNITY FOUNDATION OF CENTRAL NEW YORK, INC.
5655 Thompson Rd.
Dewitt, NY 13214
Linda Alexander, Executive Director
Tel: (315) 445-2040 X130 Fax: (315) 234-4350

Email: lalexander@jewishfoundationcny.org
Web: www.jewishfoundationcny.org

JEWISH DISCOVERY CENTER
212 Exeter Rd.
Williamsville, NY 14221
Heschel Greenberg, Founder/Director
Tel: (716) 639-7600 Fax: (716) 631-0527
Email: greenbergy@cs.com
Web: www.jewishdiscovery.org

JEWISH FAMILY SERVICE OF BUFFALO AND ERIE COUNTY
70 Barker St.
Buffalo, NY 14209

Tel: (716) 883-1914 Fax: (716) 883-7637
Email: generalinfo@jfsbuffalo.org
Web: www.jfsbuffalo.org

JEWISH FAMILY SERVICE OF ROCHESTER, INC.
441 E. Ave.
Rochester, NY 14607
Barry Stein, Executive Director
Tel: (585) 461-0110 Fax: (585) 461-9658
Web: www.jfsrochester.org

JEWISH FAMILY SERVICE OF ROCKLAND COUNTY, INC.
900 Route 45 #2
New City, NY 10956
Sylvia Kaufman, Executive Director
Tel: (845) 354-2121 Fax: (845) 354-2928
Email: jfsrockland@aol.com
Web: www.jewishfamilyservice.net

JEWISH FAMILY SERVICES OF NORTHEASTERN NEW YORK
877 Madison Ave.
Albany, NY 12208
Anschel O. Weiss, CEO
Tel: (518) 482-8856 Fax: (518) 489-5839
Email: info@jfsneny.org
Web: www.jfsneny.org

JEWISH FEDERATION OF DUTCHESS COUNTY
110 Grand Ave.
Poughkeepsie, NY 12603
Alan N. Zucker, President
Tel: (716) 886-7750 Fax: (716) 886-1367
Email: info@jewishdutchess.org
Web: www.jewishdutchess.org

JEWISH FEDERATION OF GREATER BUFFALO
787 Delaware Ave.
Buffalo, NY 14209
Tel: (716) 886-7750 Fax: (716) 886-1367
Email: info@jfedbflo.org
Web: www.jfedbflo.com

JEWISH FEDERATION OF GREATER ORANGE COUNTY
68 Stewart Ave.
Newburgh, NY 12550
Raena Korenman, President
Tel: (845) 562-7860 Fax: (845) 562-5114
Email: info@jewishorangeny.org
Web: www.jewishorangeny.org

JEWISH OUTREACH INSTITUTE
1270 Broadway #609
New York, NY 10001
Dr. Kerry M. Olitzky, Executive Director
Tel: (212) 760-1440 Fax: (212) 760-1569
Email: info@joi.org
Web: www.joi.org

KOREAN AMERICAN ASSOCIATION FOR REHABILITATION OF THE DISABLED
35-20 147th St. Annex #2F
Flushing, NY 11354
Myoungja Lee, Director
Tel: (718) 445-3929 Fax: (718) 661-4429
Email: kaard@verizon.net
Web: www.kaard.org

KOREAN AMERICAN ASSOCIATION OF GREATER NEW YORK
149 W. 24th St., 6th Fl.
New York, NY 10011
Kichol Kim, President
Tel: (212) 255-6969 Fax: (212) 633-1627
Email: kckim@nykorean.org
Web: www.nykorean.org

KOREAN AMERICAN COMMUNITY FOUNDATION
213 W. 35th St.
New York, NY 10001
Tel: (212) 736-5223 Fax: (212) 736-5228
Email: info@kacfny.org
Web: http://kacfny.org

KOREAN COMMUNITY SERVICES OF METROPOLITAN NEW YORK
149 W. 24th St., 6th Fl.
New York, NY 10011
Kwang S. Kim, President
Tel: (212) 620-5284 Fax: (212) 463-8347
Email: kcs@kcsny.org
Web: www.kcsny.org

KOREAN SOCIAL SERVICE CENTER
16 W. 32nd St. #301
New York, NY 10001
Ha Ockchul, President
Tel: (212) 564-2772 Fax: (212) 564-2788

METROPOLITAN NEW YORK COORDINATING COUNCIL ON JEWISH POVERTY
80 Maiden Ln., 21st Fl.
New York, NY 10038
Joseph C. Shenker, President
Tel: (212) 453-9500 Fax: (212) 453-9600
Email: info@metcouncil.org
Web: www.metcouncil.org

NA'AMAT USA
350 5th Ave. #4700
New York, NY 10118
Tel: (212) 563-5222 Fax: (212) 563-5710
Email: naamat@naamat.org
Web: www.naamat.org

NATHAN CUMMINGS FOUNDATION
475 10th Ave., 14th Fl.
New York, NY 10018
Lance E. Lindblom, President/CEO
Tel: (212) 787-7300 Fax: (212) 787-7377
Email: info@nathancummings.org
Web: www.nathancummings.org

NAV NIRMAAN
87-08 Justice Ave. #CS
Elmhurst, NY 11373-4575
Jugrag Kour, President
Tel: (718) 478-4588 Fax: (718) 476-5959
Email: navnirmaan@yahoo.com

NORTH AMERICAN FEDERATION OF TEMPLE BROTHERHOODS
633 3rd Ave.
New York, NY 10017
Stuart Aaronson, President
Tel: (800) 765-6200 Fax: (212) 650-4189
Email: contact@nftb.org
Web: www.nftb.org

QUEENS CHILD GUIDANCE CENTER- ASIAN OUTREACH
Asian Outreach
87-08 Justice Ave. #C7
Elmhurst, NY 11373
Agnelo Dias, Clinic Administrator
Tel: (718) 899-9810 Fax: (718) 899-9699
Email: agnelodias@qcgc.org
Web: www.qcgc.org

REBUILD CHINATOWN INITIATIVE
277 Grand St., 3rd Fl.
New York, NY 10002
Email: info@rebuildchinatown.org
Web: www.rebuildchinatown.org

SOUTH ASIAN-AMERICAN WOMEN'S ASSOCIATION
60 E. 4th St.
Corning, NY 14830
Dr. Ishrat Mustafa, President/Founder
Tel: (585) 872-7545 Fax: (607) 962-3277
Email: sawweb@umiacs.umd.edu
Web: www.umiacs.umd.edu/users/sawweb/sawnet/saawa.html

SYRACUSE JEWISH FAMILY SERVICE
4101 E. Genesee St.
Syracuse, NY 13214
Tel: (315) 445-0820 Fax: (315) 445-0859
Email: admin@sjfs.org
Web: www.sjfs.org

SYRACUSE JEWISH FEDERATION
5655 Thompson Rd. South
Dewitt, NY 13214-0511
Michael Balanoff, President
Tel: (315) 445-2040 Fax: (315) 445-1559
Web: www.sjfed.org

TECHBANGLA
P.O. Box 382
Lagrangeville, NY 12540
Email: info@techbangla.org
Web: www.techbangla.org

THAI USA ASSOCIATION
628 10th Ave.
New York, NY 10036
Sara S. Paleewong, Secretary
Tel: (212) 245-4660 Fax: (212) 245-8844
Email: info@thai-usa.org
Web: www.thai-usa.org

THAILINKS
c/o Asian American Arts Alliance
74 Varick St. #302
New York, NY 10013
Anjana Suvarnananda, Founder
Email: info@thailinks.org
Web: www.thailinks.org

THE AMERICAN TURKISH SOCIETY
New York
305 E. 47th St. at 2nd Ave., 8th Fl.
New York, NY 10017
Ahmet M. Ertegun, Chairman
Tel: (212) 583-7614 Fax: (212) 583-7615
Web: www.americanturkishsociety.org

THE KOREA SOCIETY
950 3rd Ave., 8th Fl.
New York, NY 10022-2705
Hon. Donald P. Gregg, President/Chairman
Tel: (212) 759-7525 Fax: (212) 759-7530
Email: genna.ny@koreasociety.org
Web: www.koreasociety.org

UJA/FEDERATION OF NEW YORK
130 E. 59th St.
New York, NY 10022-1302
Morris W. Offit, President
Tel: (212) 980-1000 Fax: (212) 888-7538
Email: contact@ujafedny.org
Web: www.ujafedny.org

UNITED JEWISH FEDERATION OF NORTHEASTERN NEW YORK
800 New Loudon Rd.
Latham, NY 12210
Tel: (518) 783-7800 Fax: (518) 783-1557
Email: info@jewishfedny.org
Web: www.jewishfedny.org

UNITED STATES-JAPAN FOUNDATION
Headquarters
145 E. 32nd St.
New York, NY 10016
George R. Packerd, President
Tel: (212) 481-8753 Fax: (212) 481-8762
Email: info@us-jf.org
Web: www.us-jf.org

VIETNAMESE ADOPTEE NETWORK
333 Mamaroneck Ave. #183
White Plains, NY 10605-1313

Christopher Brownlee, President
Tel: (203) 530-5340
Email: chris@van-online.org
Web: www.van-online.org

YMCA OF GREATER NEW YORK
Flushing Korean Program
138-46 Northern Blvd.
Flushing, NY 11354
Helen Kang, International Program Coordinator
Tel: (718) 961-6880 Fax: (718) 461-4691
Email: hkang@ymcanyc.org
Web: www.ymcanyc.org

YOUNG KOREAN AMERICAN SERVICE & EDUCATION CENTER
National Korean American Service & Education Consortium
139-19 41st Ave., 3rd Fl.
Flushing, NY 11355
Yu Soung Mun, Executive Director
Tel: (718) 460-5600 Fax: (718) 445-0032
Email: ykasec@ykasec.org
Web: www.ykasec.org

ZIGEN FUND
38-27 217th St.
Bayside, NY 11361
Lily Waiyee Lee, President
Tel: (718) 233-2722 Fax: (718) 233-2722
Email: zigen@zigen.org
Web: www.zigen.org

SPEC. INT., SPORTS

FILIPINO AMERICAN GOLFERS ASSOCIATION, INC.
84-20 Charlecote Ridge
Jamaica, NY 11432
Web: www.filamgolfers.com

HOMENETMEN
New York
P.O. Box 872
Woodside, NY 11377
Email: vicken@nyc.rr.com
Web: www.geocities.com/homenetmenNY

UNITED STATES MUAY THAI ASSOCIATION
6535 Broadway Riverdale #1K
New York, NY 10471
Clint Heyliger, President/Founder
Email: usmta@usmta.com
Web: www.usmta.com

SPEC. INT., VOLUNTARY SERVICE

FALUN DAFA INFORMATION CENTER
331 W. 57th St., PMB 409
New York, NY 10019
Tel: (888) 842-4797
Email: contact@faluninfo.net
Web: www.faluninfo.net

MAHARASHTRA FOUNDATION
P.O. Box 2287, Church St. Station
New York, NY 10008-2287
Email: info@indiancharity.org
Web: www.indiancharity.org

NEPAL FORWARD FOUNDATION
445 Park Ave., 10th Fl.
New York, NY 10022
Eric J. Urbani, Staff
Tel: (212) 255-0809 Fax: (212) 255-0811
Email: eric.urbani@nepalforward.org
Web: www.nepalforward.org

NY DE VOLUNTEER, INC.
601 W. 110th St. #10K5
New York, NY 10025
Noriko Hino, Executive Director
Tel: (212) 932-7208
Email: staff@nydevolunteer.org
Web: www.nydevolunteer.org

PROJECT BY PROJECT
New York

P.O. Box 689, Radio City Station
New York, NY 10101
Jeremy Zhu, Chairperson
Tel: (917) 678-6148
Email: info@projectbyproject.org
Web: www.projectbyproject.org

SPEC. INT., WOMEN

AASRA OR SHELTER
127-04 111th Ave.
S. Ozon Park, NY 11420
Jasbir Bhatia, Executive Director
Tel: (510) 651-0178 Fax: (510) 657-6661

ASIAN AMERICAN WOMEN'S ASSOCIATION
P.O. Box 2004
Williamsville, NY 14221
Shobha Bhandary, President
Tel: (716) 626-4833
Email: tyson5246@hotmail.com
Web: www.projectflight.org/Directoryofwomen3.htm

ASIAN WOMEN IN BUSINESS
358 5th Ave. #504
New York, NY 10001
Bonnie Wong, President
Tel: (212) 868-1368 Fax: (212) 868-1373
Email: info@awib.org
Web: www.awib.org

GABRIELA NETWORK
P.O. Box 403
Times Square Station, NY 10036
Tel: (212) 592-3507 Fax: (651) 321-1845
Email: gabnet@gabnet.org
Web: www.gabnet.org

HADASSAH
Brooklyn Region
1416 Ave. M #302
Brooklyn, NY 11230
Roni Schwartz, President
Tel: (718) 382-6454 Fax: (718) 375-2596
Email: region.brooklyn@hadassah.org
Web: www.hadassah.org

Lower New York State Region
900 Route 45 #4
New York, NY 10956
Sharon Cadoff, President
Tel: (845) 362-2134 Fax: (845) 362-2287
Email: region.lowernys@hadassah.org
Web: www.hadassah.org

Nassau Region
430 De Mott Ave.
Rockville Centre, NY 11570
Gloria Kramer, President
Tel: (516) 766-2725 Fax: (516) 678-7212
Email: nassauregion@hadassah.org
Web: www.hadassah.org

New York Chapter
25 W. 45th St. #808
New York, NY 10036
Jill J. Prosky, President
Tel: (212) 575-8193 Fax: (212) 575-2631
Email: carolyn.kamlet@hadassah.org
Web: www.hadassah.org

Queens Region
211-06 48th Ave.
Bayside, NY 11364
Deborah Wohl, President
Tel: (718) 225-0999 Fax: (718) 225-2112
Email: region.queens@hadassah.org
Web: www.hadassah.org

Suffolk Region
74 Hauppauge Rd. #44
Commack, NY 11725
Karen Feit, President
Tel: (631) 499-3999 Fax: (631) 499-4035
Email: region.suffolk@hadassah.org
Web: www.hadassah.org

Upper New York State Region
1716 Central Ave.
Albany, NY 12205
Dorothy Ganz, President
Tel: (518) 452-5857 Fax: (518) 452-0373
Email: allgees@aol.com
Web: www.hadassah.org

Westchester Region
10 Midland Ave.
Port Chester, NY 10573
Lisa Davidson, President
Tel: (914) 937-3151 Fax: (914) 937-3852
Email: westchesterregion@hadassah.org
Web: www.hadassah.org

JEWISH FOUNDATION FOR EDUCATION OF WOMEN
135 E. 64th St.
New York, NY 10021
Marge Goldwater, Executive Director
Tel: (212) 288-3931 Fax: (212) 288-5798
Email: fdnscholar@aol.com
Web: www.jfew.org

JEWISH ORTHODOX FEMINIST ALLIANCE
15 E. 26th St. #915
New York, NY 10010
Robin Bodner, Executive Director
Tel: (212) 679-8500 Fax: (212) 679-7428
Email: jofa@jofa.org
Web: www.jofa.org

JEWISH RENAISSANCE CENTER
441 W. Ave.
New York, NY 10024
Leah Kohn, Co-Founder/Director
Tel: (212) 580-9666 Fax: (212) 799-1355
Email: learning@jewishrenaissance.org
Web: www.jewishrenaissance.org

NATIONAL COUNCIL FOR JEWISH WOMEN
Peninsula Section
342 Central Ave.
Lawrence, NY 11559
Robin Ivler, President
Tel: (516) 569-3660 Fax: (516) 569-3634
Email: info@ncjwpeninsulasection.org
Web: www.ncjwpeninsulasection.org

South Shore Section
P.O. Box 544
Rockville Center, NY 11571
Robin Ivler, President
Tel: (800) 829-6259 Fax: (516) 569-3634
Email: info@ncjwsouthshore.org
Web: www.ncjwsouthshore.org

NATIONAL COUNCIL OF JEWISH WOMEN
New York Headquarters
53 W. 23rd St., 6th Fl.
New York, NY 10010-4204
Marsha Atkind, President
Tel: (212) 645-4048 Fax: (212) 645-7466
Email: action@ncjw.org
Web: www.ncjw.org

NEW YORK ASIAN WOMEN'S CENTER
39 Bowery, PMB 375
New York, NY 10002
Tuhina De O'Conner, Executive Director
Tel: (212) 732-5230 Fax: (212) 587-5731
Email: contact@nyawc.org
Web: www.nyawc.org

NEWFILIPINA, INC.
50 Grand St. #F
New York, NY 10013
Perla Daly, President
Tel: (860) 350-2535
Email: perladaly@newfilipina.com
Web: www.newfilipina.com

SAKHI FOR SOUTH ASIAN WOMEN
P.O. Box 20208, Greeley Square Station
New York, NY 10001-0006
Purvi Shah, Executive Director
Tel: (212) 868-6741 Fax: (212) 564-8745

Email: sakhiny@aol.com
Web: www.sakhi.org

SOUTH ASIAN WOMEN'S CREATIVE COLLECTIVE
16 W. 32nd St. #10A
New York, NY 10001
Tel: (212) 494-0061 Fax: (212) 494-0062
Email: sawccmail@yahoo.com
Web: www.sawcc.org

SOUTH ASIAN WOMEN'S LEADERSHIP FORUM
Dobshinky & Priya, LLC
61 Broadway, 30th Fl.
New York, NY 10006
Judy Vincent, Director of New York Programs
Tel: (917) 375-0422
Email: sawlf@yahoo.com
Web: www.southasianwomen.org

TAIWAN WOMEN
P.O. Box 74-7943
Rego Park, NY 11374
Pei-Ti, General Administration
Fax: (435) 603-4971
Email: tw_women@ms92.url.com.tw
Web: http://tw-women.formosa.org

TIBETAN WOMEN'S ASSOCIATION
c/o Office of Tibet, 241 E. 32nd St.
New York, NY 10016
Tenzing Bhuti, President
Tel: (718) 739-6021
Email: tibwomen@yahoo.com
Web: www.tibetanwomen.org

WOMEN FOR AFGHAN WOMEN
35-32 Union St., 2nd Fl.
Flushing, NY 11354
Tel: (718) 321-2434
Email: office@womenforafghanwomen.org
Web: www.womenforafghanwomen.org

WOMEN'S LEAGUE FOR CONSERVATIVE JUDAISM
475 Riverside Dr. #820
New York, NY 10115
Gloria B. Cohen, International President
Tel: (800) 628-5083 Fax: (212) 870-1261
Email: womensleague@wlcj.org
Web: www.wlcj.org

YOUNG WOMEN'S CHRISTIAN ASSOCIATION
NYC Flushing Branch
42-07 Parsons Blvd.
Flushing, NY 11355
Roeme Kim, Branch Director
Tel: (718) 353-4553 Fax: (718) 353-4044
Email: rkim@ywcanyc.org
Web: www.ywca-flushing.org

SPEC. INT., YOUTH

AMIT
National Office
817 Broadway
New York, NY 10003
Jan Schechter, President
Tel: (800) 989-2648 Fax: (212) 353-2312
Email: info@amitchildren.org
Web: www.amitchildren.org

ASIAN AMERICAN COALITION FOR CHILDREN AND FAMILIES
c/o Asian Family Services- Chinatown Planning Council
365 Broadway, Ground Fl.
New York, NY 10013
David Chen, Executive Director
Tel: (212) 941-0030 Fax: (212) 226-5351

ASIAN PROFESSIONAL EXTENSION, INC.
64 Fulton St. #302
New York, NY 10038

Amy Mak, Program Director
Tel: (212) 748-1225 Fax: (212) 748-1250
Email: info@apex-ny.org
Web: www.apex-ny.org

CHINATOWN YMCA OF GREATER NEW YORK

Association Office
333 7th Ave., 15th Fl.
New York, NY 10001
Jack Lund, President/CEO
Tel: (212) 630-9600 Fax: (212) 630-9604
Web: www.ymcanyc.org

GERSHERCITY

15 E. 26th St. #916
New York, NY 10010
Ben Gordon, Founder/Chairman
Tel: (212) 786-5130 Fax: (212) 481-4174
Email: geshercity@geshercity.org
Web: www.geshercity.org

JEWISH CHILDREN'S LEARNING LAB, INC.

515 W. 20th St. 4 East
New York, NY 10011
Aviva Sussman, President
Tel: (212) 924-4500 Fax: (212) 924-9908
Email: jcllcm@aol.com
Web: www.jcllcm.com

KESHER

New York Office
633 3rd Ave.
New York, NY 10017
Lisa David, Assistant Director
Tel: (212) 650-4070 Fax: (212) 650-4199
Email: kesher@urj.org
Web: www.keshernet.com

KOREAN YOUTH CENTER OF NEW YORK

35-34 Union St.
Flushing, NY 11354
Dr. Francis Kim, Executive Director
Tel: (718) 321-1010 Fax: (718) 321-8282
Email: nykyc@msn.com

MYANMAR YOUTH ASSOCIATION, INC.

P.O. Box 398
New York, NY 10150
Kyaw Myaing, Chairman/Director
Email: kyawmyaing@hotmail.com
Web: www.myanmaryouth.org

NATIONAL CENTER FOR MISSING & EXPLOITED CHILDREN

New York
275 Lake Ave.
Rochester, NY 14608
Tel: (585) 242-0900 Fax: (585) 242-0717
Web: www.missingkids.com

New York/Manhattan Affiliate
395 Hudson St., 10th Fl.
New York, NY 10014
Tel: (212) 366-7880 Fax: (212) 366-7881
Web: www.missingkids.com

New York/Metropolitan New York
769 Elmont Rd.
Elmont, NY 11003
Tel: (718) 222-5888 Fax: (718) 222-5889
Web: www.missingkids.com

New York/Mohawk Valley
934 York St.
Utica, NY 13502
Tel: (315) 732-7233 Fax: (315) 732-2465
Web: www.missingkids.com

NATIONAL COUNCIL OF YOUNG ISRAEL

3 W. 16th St.
New York, NY 10011
Shlomo Z. Mostofsky, President
Tel: (800) 617-6294 Fax: (212) 727-9526
Email: ncyi@youngisrael.org
Web: www.youngisrael.org

NORTH AMERICAN FEDERATION OF TEMPLE YOUTH

633 3rd Ave., 7th Fl.
New York, NY 10017
Danny Zadoff, President
Tel: (212) 650-4070 Fax: (212) 650-4199
Email: nfty@urj.org
Web: www.rj.org/nfty

QUEEN AFTER SCHOOL YOUTH PROGRAM

136-26 37th Ave., 3rd Fl.
Flushing, NY 11354
Dominic Yip, Branch Director
Tel: (718) 358-8899 Fax: (718) 762- 6672
Web: www.cpc-ny.org/queens.htm

SOUTH ASIAN YOUTH ACTION, INC.

54-05 Seabury St.
Elmhurst, NY 11373
Annetta Seecharran, Executive Director
Tel: (718) 651-3484 Fax: (718) 651-3480
Email: saya@saya.org
Web: www.saya.org

YOUNG JUDAEA

National Office
50 W. 58th St.
New York, NY 10019
Tel: (212) 303-8014 Fax: (212) 303-4572
Email: info@youngjudaea.org
Web: www.youngjudaea.org

YOUNG KOREAN AMERICAN NETWORK

P.O. Box 6777, Yorkville Station
New York, NY 10128
Jayne Jun, President
Tel: (212) 229-8282
Web: www.ykan.org

YOUNG KOREANS UNITED

136-19 41st Ave., 3rd Fl.
Flushing, NY 11355
Young Sook Na, President
Tel: (718) 460-8474 Fax: (718) 445-0032
Email: ny@ykuusa.org
Web: www.ykuusa.org

STUDENT ORGANIZATION

ARMENIAN STUDENTS' ASSOCIATION OF AMERICA, INC.

New Jersey
P.O. Box 7876
New York, NY 10116-4634
Email: nyasa@asainc.org
Web: www.asainc.org/newyork/

ASIAN COLUMBIA ALUMNI, ASSOCIATION INC.

Columbia University
c/o First American International Bank
29 Bowery
New York, NY 10002
Yiting Shen, Vice President
Email: acaa@columbia.edu
Web: www.acaa95.org

CHINESE STUDENT ASSOCIATION

Teachers College Columbia University
525 W. 120th St.
New York, NY 10027
Tel: (212) 222-1899
Web: www.tc.columbia.edu/students/chisa

HAGOP KEVORKIAN CENTER

New York University
50 Washington Sq. South
New York, NY 10012
Shiva Balaghi, Associate Director/Outreach Coordinator
Tel: (212) 998-8877 Fax: (212) 995-4144
Email: kevorkian.center@nyu.edu
Web: www.nyu.edu/gsas/program/neareast

KOREAN GRADUATE STUDENT ASSOCIATION

State University of New York

1400 Washington Ave.
Albany, NY 12222
Tel: (518) 442-3300
Email: bl8692@albany.edu
Web: www.uakorea.org

Stoney Brook University, State University of New York

Graduate School, Computer Science Bldg., #2401
Stony Brook, NY 11794
Taewon Lee, President
Tel: (631) 632-6492
Email: kgsa@ic.sunysb.edu
Web: www.ic.sunysb.edu/Clubs/kgsa/

KOREAN STUDENT ASSOCIATION

State University of New York at Stoney Brook
Stoney Brook University
Stoney Brook, NY 11794
Tel: (631) 632-6000
Web: www.sinc.sunysb.edu/Clubs/ksa/

MUSLIM STUDENT ASSOCIATION

Binghamton University
P.O. Box 2000
Binghamton, NY 13902
Fahad Pervez, President
Tel: (607) 777-4282
Email: fahad2100@yahoo.com
Web: www.sa.binghamton.edu/~msa

University of Buffalo
320 Student Union
Amherst, NY 14260
Amil Sarfarz, President
Tel: (716) 645-2950 Fax: (716) 645-2112
Email: muslim-sa@buffalo.edu
Web: http://wings.buffalo.edu/student-life/sa/muslim/msa

Baruch College
360 Park Ave. South #1441
New York, NY 10010
Web: www.geocities.com/Heartland/Estates/4653/index

Rensselaer Polytechnic Institute
Rensselaer Union #126, 110 8th St.
Troy, NY 12180
Jawad R. Beg, President
Email: msa@rpi.edu
Web: http://msa.union.rpi.edu

SOUTH ASIAN GRADUATE ASSOCIATION

420 W. 118th St.
New York, NY 10027
R. Vijayaraghavan, President
Email: sagayale@hotmail.com
Web: http://yale.edu/saga/index.html

TAIWANESE STUDENT ASSOCIATION

Rensselaer Polytechnic Institute
110 8th St.
Troy, NY 12180-3590
Ching-Po Chen, President
Tel: (518) 276-6000
Email: chenc@rpi.edu
Web: http://tsa.union.rpi.edu/

NORTH CAROLINA

ARTISTIC

FARVAN INTERNATIONAL GALLERY

119 E. 17th St.
Charlotte, NC 28202
Farida T. Sweezy, President
Tel: (704) 375-1424 Fax; (704) 375-1488
Email: farvan@bellsouth.net
Web: www.farvan.com

BUSINESS

CAROLINA ASIAN INDIAN BUSINESS ASSOCIATION

319 S. Sharon Amity Rd. #300
Charlotte, NC 28204
Ravi Patel, President
Tel: (704) 364-6008 Fax: (704) 364-9293
Email: ravi@sree.com

CULTURAL

AMERICAN TURKISH ASSOCIATION OF NORTH CAROLINA

P.O. Box 31761
Raleigh, NC 27622-1761
Emin Pamucak, President
Email: webmaster@ata-nc.org
Web: www.ata-nc.org

CAMBODIAN CULTURAL CENTER

185 Pine Lodge Rd.
Lexington, NC 27292
Tel: (336) 357-5769
Web: www.unc.edu/courses/2001spring/reli/006j/001/Publish/page22.html

CHINESE AMERICAN ASSOCIATION OF CHARLOTTE

1615-G Deergreen Ln.
Charlotte, NC 28262
Jian Zhang, President
Tel: (704) 510-8888
Email: jxzhang@email.uncc.edu
Web: www.charlottechinese.8m.net

HMONG SOUTHEAST PAUV PHEEJ, INC.

216 2nd St. NW #209
Hickory, NC 28601
Vang Neng Xiong, President
Tel: (828) 267-0020
Email: info@hmongsoutheastpuavpheej.org
Web: www.hmongsoutheastpuavpheej.org

INDIA ASSOCIATION OF CHARLOTTE

2401 Fernbank Dr.
Charlotte, NC 28226
Prabal Roy, External Personnel Relation
Tel: (704) 424-3504 Fax: (704) 424-3500
Email: proy2@csc.com
Web: www.festivalindia.org

LAOTIAN CULTURE CENTER

5601 Rowan Way
Charlotte, NC 28214
Tel: (704) 393-3588

MONTAGNARD DEGA ASSOCIATION

611 Summit Ave. #10
Greensboro, NC 27405
Louis Bing, Director
Tel: (336) 373-1812 Fax: (336) 373-1832
Email: mda-lbing@triad.rr.com
Web: www.angelfire.com/dc/dega/

PAKISTANI AMERICAN ANJUMAN

P.O. Box 1825
Raleigh, NC 27602
Bilal Agha, President
Email: info@ncpaa.org
Web: www.ncpaa.org

TRIANGLE GUJARATI ASSOCIATION

P.O. Box 228
Morrisville, NC 27560
Pramila Damodia, President
Tel: (919) 469-3592
Web: www.nctga.org

VIETNAMESE COMMUNITY SERVICES CENTER

338 S. Sharon Amity #305
Charlotte, NC 28211
Michael Long Nguyen, President
Tel: (704) 568-8744 Fax: (704) 542-1698
Email: michaellong51@yahoo.com

MULTI-PURPOSE

PHILIPPINE AMERICAN ASSOCIATION OF NORTH CAROLINA, INC.
1309 Spring Forest Rd.
Raleigh, NC 27615
Henry Estrada, President
Tel: (919) 493-1933 Fax: (919) 684-3265
Email: hestrada@nc.rr.com
Web: www.paanc.org

UNITED HMONG ASSOCIATION OF NORTH CAROLINA
3354 16th Ave. SE
Conover, NC 28613
Tel: (828) 465-6288
Email: uha@unitedhmongassociation.org
Web: www.unitedhmongassociation.org

POLITICAL ACTION

ADVOCACY FOR NORTH CAROLINA ASIAN PACIFIC AMERICANS
1308 Ruffin St.
Durhan, NC 27701
Milan Pham, Chair
Tel: (919) 960-3877 Fax: (919) 960-3879
Email: email@ancapa.org
Web: www.ancapa.org

PROFESSIONAL

ASIAN LIBRARY
1339 Baxter St. #200
Charlotte, NC 28204
Ki-Hyun Chun, Publisher
Tel: (704) 334-3450 Fax: (704) 332-9373
Email: ki-hyun@chungroup.com
Web: www.chungroup.com

NATIONAL ASSOCIATION OF ASIAN AMERICAN PROFESSIONALS
NAAAP-North Carolina
3912-M Knickerbocker Pkwy.
Raleigh, NC 27612
Hector Javier, President
Tel: (919) 783-7482
Email: naaap_nc@yahoo.com
Web: www.naaap-nc.org

NETWORK OF INDIAN PROFESSIONALS-CHARLOTTE
Network of Indian Professionals
Charlotte, NC 28235
Rishi Zaveri, President
Email: rishi@netipcharlotte.org
Web: www.netipcharlotte.org

PHILIPPINE NURSES ASSOCIATION OF NORTH CAROLINA
P.O. Box 91224
Raleigh, NC 27675
Email: info@pnanc.org
Web: www.pnanc.org

RELIGIOUS

CAMBODIAN BUDDHIST SOCIETY
219 Owen Blvd.
Charlotte, NC 28213
Penny Lang
Tel: (704) 596-6628
Web: www.unc.edu/courses/2001spring/reli/006j/001/Publish/page25.html

CAMBODIAN METHODIST MISSION CHURCH OF CHARLOTTE
401 N. Tryon St.
Charlotte, NC 28202
Rev. Samuel Om, Pastor
Tel: (704) 334-8431 Fax: (704) 333-8807
Email: cambodianmissionchurch@yahoo.com
Web: http://cmccharlotte.tripod.com/main.html

FIRST KOREAN BAPTIST CHURCH
8905 Ray Rd.
Raleigh, NC 27613
Tel: (919) 870-9070 Fax: (919) 870-0291
Email: baekhap@nc.rr.com
Web: www.fkbc.org

GREENSBORO KOREAN UNITED METHODIST CHURCH
2504 E. Woodlyn Way
Greensboro, NC 27407
Jerry Lee, Youth Pastor
Tel: (336) 852-8535 Fax: (336) 852-8575
Email: willsu0005@yahoo.com
Web: www.gkumc.org

KOREAN CENTRAL BAPTIST CHURCH
6881 Cliffdale Rd.
Fayetteville, NC 28314
Kyung Chan Kim, Pastor
Tel: (910) 867-5118

NORTH CAROLINA BUDDHIST ASSOCIATION
4220 Forestville Rd.
Raleigh, NC 27616
Thich Thien Tam, Master
Tel: (919) 266-4230

NORTH CAROLINA KOREAN PRESBYTERIAN CHURCH
116 Tom Wilkinson Rd.
Durham, NC 27712
Rev. Joshua Moon, Pastor
Tel: (919) 471-1168 Fax: (919) 620-1598
Email: yjmoon@liberty.edu
Web: www.nckpc.org

TEMPLE EMANUEL
1129 Jefferson Rd.
Greensboro, NC 27410
Dr. Sherry Dickstein, President
Tel: (336) 292-7899 Fax: (336) 292-6527
Email: ters@templeemanuelgso.org
Web: www.templeemanuelgso.org

SPEC. INT., EDUCATION

CHINESE SCHOOL AT CHAPEL HILL
P.O. Box 3214
Chapell Hill, NC 27515
Shang Yin, Principal
Email: info@csch-nc.org
Web: www.csch-nc.org

JUNG TAO SCHOOL OF CLASSICAL CHINESE MEDICINE
207 Dale Adams Rd.
Sugar Grove, NC 28679
Sean C. Marshall, President
Tel: (828) 297-4181 Fax: (828) 297-4161
Email: info@jungtao.edu
Web: www.jungtao.edu

NC RALEIGH CHINESE LANGUAGE SCHOOL
P.O. Box 33426
Raleigh, NC 27636
Le Huynh, Principal
Email: info@ncrcls.org
Web: www.ncrcls.org

SPEC. INT., FAMILY PLANNING

FAMILIES WITH CHILDREN FROM VIETNAM
10009 Whitestone Rd.
Raleigh, NC 27615
Allison Martin, Director
Email: fcv-director@fcvn.org
Web: www.fcvn.org/trianglenc.htm

SPEC. INT., GAY&LESBIAN

ASIANS & FRIENDS - NORTH CAROLINA
P.O. Box 1863
Cary, NC 27512
Email: info@asiansandfriends.org
Web: www.asiansandfriends.org

SPEC. INT., HUMAN RELATIONS

NORTH CAROLINA JAPAN CENTER
705 Barbour Dr.
Raleigh, NC 27603
Tony Moyer, Director
Tel: (919) 515-3450 Fax: (919) 515-3686
Email: tony_moyer@ncsu.edu
Web: www.ncsu.edu

SPEC. INT., SENIORS

BHARATIYA SENIOR CITIZENS OF NORTH CAROLINA
303 Monty Bello Dr.
Cary, NC 27513
Dhirubhai Desai, President
Tel: (919) 677-8513

SPEC. INT., SOCIAL INTEREST

CHRISTIAN FRIENDS OF KOREA
P.O. Box 936
Black Mountain, NC 28711
John Akers, Chair
Tel: (828) 669-2355 Fax: (828) 669-2357
Email: cfk@cfk.org
Web: www.cfk.org

GREENSBORO JEWISH FEDERATION
5509C W. Friendly Ave.
Greensboro, NC 27410
Nancy Brenner, President
Tel: (336) 852-5433 Fax: (336) 852-4346
Email: mchandler@shalomgreensboro.org
Web: www.shalomgreensboro.org

HERITAGE FOUNDATION OF NORTH CAROLINA
1200 Mason Farm Rd.
Chapel Hill, NC 27514
Tel: (919) 932-1844 Fax: (919) 932-1844
Email: info@jhfnc.org
Web: www.jhfnc.org

HMONG-LAO ASSISTANCE ASSOCIATION, INC.
124 Logan Dr.
Mt. Gilead, NC 27306
Geu Vang, President
Tel: (910) 439-9533 Fax: (910) 439-9596
Email: geuvang@yahoo.com

JAPAN-AMERICA SOCIETY OF CHARLOTTE
105 W. Morehead St.
Charlotte, NC 28202
Maria Domoto, Executive Director
Tel: (704) 332-3800 Fax: (704) 332-3800
Email: jasc@bellsouth.net
Web: www.us-japan.org/jascharlotte

JAPANESE ASSOCIATION IN CHARLOTTE
322 Hawthorne Ln.
Charlotte, NC 28204
Tel: (704) 333-2775 Fax: (704) 333-0862
Email: nihonjinkai03@ctc.net

JEWISH FEDERATION OF DURHAM-CHAPEL HILL
3622 Lyckan Pkwy. #3003
Durham, NC 27707
Orit Ramler Szulik, Director
Tel: (919) 489-5335 Fax: (919) 489-5788
Email: federation@shalomdch.org
Web: http://shalomdch.org

JEWISH FEDERATION OF GREATER CHARLOTTE
5007 Providence Rd.
Charlotte, NC 28226
Tel: (704) 944-6760 Fax: (704) 944-6766
Email: jfgc@shalomcharlotte.org
Web: www.jewishcharlotte.org

RALEIGH-CARY JEWISH FEDERATION
8210 Creedmoor Rd. #104
Raleigh, NC 27613

Judah Segal, Executive Director
Tel: (919) 676-2200 Fax: (919) 676-2122
Email: info@rcjf.org
Web: www.rcjf.org

THAI ASSOCIATION OF NORTH CAROLINA
104 Beechtree Ct.
Apex, NC 27523
Surapon Sujjavanich, President
Tel: (919) 362-0470 Fax: (919) 362-3729
Email: psujj@aol.com

SPEC. INT., WOMEN

KIRAN: DOMESTIC VIOLENCE AND CRISIS SERVICES FOR SOUTH ASIANS IN NORTH CAROLINA
P.O. Box 3513
Chapel Hill, NC 27515-3513
Bianca Spencer, Co-Founder
Tel: (919) 865-4006
Email: kiraninc@hotmail.com
Web: www.kiraninc.org

STUDENT ORGANIZATION

ASIAN STUDENT ASSOCIATION
Duke University
101-3 Bryan Ctr.
Durham, NC 27708
Aileen Shiue, President
Email: aileen.shiue@duke.edu
Web: www.duke.edu/asian/

CHINESE STUDENT AND SCHOLARS FRIENDSHIP ASSOCIATION
North Carolina State University
Raleigh, NC 27695
Ruiqi Ma, President
Tel: (919) 515-2011
Email: rma@ncsu.edu

INDIAN STUDENTS ASSOCIATION
University of North Carolina
9621 A Vinca Cir.
Charlotte, NC 28213
Amol Kedar, President
Tel: (704) 548-8793
Email: ajkedar@uncc.edu
Web: http://triveni.info/mambo/index.php

KOREAN-AMERICAN STUDENT ASSOCIATION
University of North Carolina
9201 University City Blvd.
Charlotte, NC 28223-0001
Andrew Song Ju Kim, President
Tel: (704) 687-2000
Email: uncckasa@hotmail.com
Web: www.uncc.edu/stud_organ/ksa/

TAIWANESE STUDENT ASSOCIATION
Duke University
Durham, NC 27708
Hsu Chia-Yu, President
Tel: (919) 684-8111
Email: ch38@duke.edu
Web: www.duke.edu/csa/

TAIWANESE STUDENT ASSOCIATION
North Carolina State University
2320-307 Crescent Creek Dr.
Raleigh, NC 27606
Chin-Ling Ho, President
Tel: (919) 851-7478
Email: genny963@hotmail.com
Web: www.ncsu.edu/stud_orgs/tsa/

NORTH DAKOTA

RELIGIOUS

TEMPLE BETH EL
809 11th Ave. South
Fargo, ND 58103-3199
Bev Jacobson, President
Tel: (701) 232-0441 Fax: (701) 297-9144
Email: tbe@corpcomm.net
Web: www.kobrinsky.com/tbe.htm

STUDENT ORGANIZATION

CHINESE STUDENT & SCHOLARS ASSOCIATION
University of North Dakota
Grand Forks, ND 58202
Dr. Luke Huang, Advisor
Tel: (701) 777-2011
Email: luke_huang@und.nodak.edu
Web: www.und.edu/misc/cssatund/home/

OHIO

ARTISTIC

ASIAN ARTS CENTER
27 W. Whipp Rd.
Dayton, OH 45459
Debbie Spiegel
Tel: (937) 312-0333 Fax: (937) 312-0334
Email: asian_arts@hotmail.com
Web: www.asianartscenter.org

CHINESE MUSIC SOCIETY OF GREATER CINCINNATI
1115 Brayton Ave.
Cincinnati, OH 45215
Lizbie Lin
Tel: (513) 761-6397 Fax: (513) 761-6395
Email: lizbielin@hotmail.com

BUSINESS

ASIAN AMERICAN COMMERCE GROUP
4367 Wingate Dr.
Delaware, OH 43045
Dr. Sankar Sankarappa, President
Tel: (614) 881-6516 Fax: (614) 881-6516
Email: msankarappa@cs.com
Web: www.aacg.org

NATIONAL ARAB AMERICAN BUSINESS ASSOCIATION
26167 Euclid Ave. Arcade
Euclid, OH 44132
Tel: (216) 731-1776 Fax: (216) 731-1773
Web: www.naaba.com

CHAMBER OF COMMERCE

OHIO-ISRAEL CHAMBER OF COMMERCE
1801 E. 9th St. #1105
Cleveland, OH 44114
Howard Gudell, President
Tel: (216) 621-6832 Fax: (216) 621-6862
Email: hgudell@aol.com
Web: www.ohioisraelchamber.com

PHILIPPINE CHAMBER OF COMMERCE USA, INC.
5509 Ridge Rd.
Parma, OH 44129
Yolanda Salviejo, President
Tel: (440) 885-4000 Fax: (440) 888-7188
Web: www.pcci-oh.org

CULTURAL

ASIA FOR KIDS
4480 Lake Forest Dr. #302
Cincinnati, OH 45242
Tel: (513) 563-3100 Fax: (513) 563-3105

Email: info@afk.com
Web: www.afk.com

ASIAN AMERICAN COMMUNITY SERVICE COUNCIL & FESTIVAL
1881 Brandywine Dr.
Columbus, OH 43220
Yung Chen Lu, President
Tel: (614) 451-3550 Fax: (614) 451-2924
Email: lu@math.ohio-state.edu
Web: www.asian-festival.org

ASIAN CULTURAL SOCIETY
3133 Ludlow Rd.
Shaker Heights, OH 44120
Frances Namkoong, President
Tel: (216) 921-3217 Fax: (216) 751-5244
Email: dfnkg@att.net

BURMESE ASSOCIATION IN OHIO
626 Deering Dr.
Akron, OH 44313
Tel: (330) 864-6805
Email: mhtun@ideastar.com
Web: www.burmeseohio.com

CHINESE AMERICAN ASSOCIATION
P.O. Box 8305
West Chester, OH 45069
Richard Wang, President
Tel: (513) 622-3668
Email: rw0070@aol.com
Web: www.caacoh.org

CHINESE AMERICAN ASSOCIATION OF CINCINNATI
P.O. Box 8305
West Chester, OH 45069
Jay Shi, President
Tel: (513) 755-2723
Email: jayshi@fuse.net

CLEVELAND CONTEMPORARY CHINESE CULTURAL ASSOCIATION
28950 Naylor Dr.
Solon, OH 44139
Liming Wang, President
Tel: (440) 519-8895
Web: www.cccca.org

COLUMBUS CHINESE CULTURAL EXCHANGE
6897 Spruce Pine Dr.
Columbus, OH 43235
Ralph Chiao, President
Tel: (614) 792-6200 Fax: (614) 792-6200
Email: cxc003@yahoo.com

CONGRESS OF SECULAR JEWISH ORGANIZATIONS
320 Claymore Blvd.
Richmond Heights, OH 44143
Karen Knecht, Chair
Tel: (866) 333-2756
Email: knechtfour@aol.com
Web: www.csjo.org

FILIPINO AMERICAN MEMORIAL ENDOWMENT, INC.
535 Rolling Rock Ln.
Cincinnati, OH 45255
Alex Keller, Advisory Council
Fax: (513) 231-8763
Email: onibe@aol.com
Web: www.amchamphilippines.com/amcham/fame.html

GREATER TOLEDO ASSOCIATION OF ARAB AMERICANS
2909 W. Central Ave.
Toledo, OH 43606
Nader Qaimari, President
Tel: (419) 537-9014 Fax: (419) 537-9014
Email: comments@gtaaa.org
Web: www.gtaaa.org

IRANIAN CULTURAL ASSOCIATION OF GREATER COLUMBUS
P.O. Box 3434
Columbus, OH 43210

Dr. M. Mohktari, Board Member
Web: www.pazhvak.org

JAPANESE SPEAKING & CULTURAL INITIATIVE
P.O. Box 09428
Columbus, OH 43209
Yasue Sakaoka, Director
Tel: (614) 253-7741

NEPALI AMERICAN ORGANIZATION OF OHIO
1109 Fair Ave.
Columbus, OH 43205
Mary K. Rose, Secretary
Tel: (614) 253-3445
Email: admin@naoo.org
Web: www.naoo.org

PHILIPPINE AMERICAN SOCIETY OF GREATER DAYTON
10194 Cherrytree Terrace
Dayton, OH 45458
Gil Cruz, President
Tel: (937) 885-4960
Email: virgilcruz@yahoo.com

THE COLUMBUS JEWISH HISTORICAL SOCIETY
1175 College Ave.
Columbus, OH 43209-2890
Skip Yassenoff, President
Tel: (614) 238-6977 Fax: (614) 237-2221
Email: cjhsl@tcjf.org
Web: www.columbusjewishhistoricalsociety.org

TURKISH AMERICAN SOCIETY OF NORTHEASTERN OHIO
P.O. Box 22121
Cleveland, OH 44122
Suleyman Gokoglu, President
Email: tasno@tasno.org
Web: www.tasno.org

TURKISH-AMERICAN ASSOCIATION OF CENTRAL OHIO
P.O. Box 3566
Dublin, OH 43016
Cem Ozmeral, President
Email: cozmeral@columbus.rr.com
Web: www.taaco.org

VIETNAMESE ASSOCIATION OF GREATER DAYTON
P.O. Box 2154
Dayton, OH 45401-2154
Quang Pham, President
Tel: (937) 236-1103
Email: quangvp@aol.com

MULTI-PURPOSE

ASIA WIND
3959 Ritamarie Dr.
Columbus, OH 43220
Dr. Siuleung Lee, President
Tel: (614) 326-0888 Fax: (614) 326-0888
Email: itti@asiawind.com
Web: www.asiawind.com

ASIAN AMERICAN COMMUNITY SERVICES
4100 N. High St. #301
Columbus, OH 43214
Phyllis Law, Executive Director
Tel: (614) 220-4023 Fax: (614) 220-4024
Email: aacs@asiancomsv.org
Web: www.asiancomsv.org

ASIAN AMERICAN COUNCIL
4211 Wallington Dr.
Dayton, OH 45440
Ronald Katsuyama, President
Tel: (937) 294-8815 Fax: (937) 294-8815
Email: rkatsuyama@voyager.net
Web: http://iis.stat.wright.edu/aac-dayton/

ASIAN PACIFIC AMERICAN FEDERATION OF GREATER CLEVELAND
5340 Oberlin Ave. #1
Lorain, OH 44053
Dr. Masao S. Yu, President
Tel: (440) 988-9600 Fax: (440) 282-8289
Email: masaoyu@aol.com

CAMBODIAN MUTUAL ASSISTANCE ASSOCIATION
19 S. Monroe Ave.
Columbus, OH 43205
Chanrithy Uong, President
Tel: (614) 224-8888
Web: www.asianabc.com/users/cmaa

DAYTON AREA KOREAN ASSOCIATION
978 Marycrest Ln.
Centerville, OH 45429
Sung Ok Hong, President
Tel: (937) 260-2233
Email: peter.woo@lexis-nexis.com
Web: www.daka.org

DAYTON ASSOCIATION OF CHINESE AMERICANS
2226 Wedgewood Dr.
Dayton, OH 45434-8011
Junghsen Lieh (Lai), President
Tel: (937) 431-1096
Email: jlieh@cs.wright.edu

PHILIPPINE COMMUNITY IN CENTRAL OHIO
454 E. Clearview Ave.
Worthington, OH 43205
Cora Munoz
Tel: (614) 888-0734 (h)
Email: cmunoz@capital.edu

THE INDIA FOUNDATION
895 Kentshire Dr.
Dayton, OH 45459
Harish Trivedi, Chairman
Tel: (937) 433-4879 Fax: (937) 433-5748
Email: indiafound@earthlink.net

POLITICAL ACTION

ORGANIZATION OF CHINESE AMERICANS
Columbus Chapter
P.O. Box 20623
Columbus, OH 43220
Theresa Lee, President
Tel: (614) 624-7645 Fax: (614) 326-0888
Email: twlee1@yahoo.com
Web: www.asiawind.com

ORGANIZATION OF CHINESE AMERICANS OF GREATER CLEVELAND
1265 W. 106th St. #1
Cleveland, OH 44102
Johnny Wu, President
Tel: (216) 373-3278 Fax: (917) 591-4748
Email: president@ocagc.org
Web: www.ocagc.org

PROFESSIONAL

AMERICAN SOCIETY OF ENGINEERS OF INDIAN ORIGIN-OHIO CHAPTER
P.O. Box 21307
Cleveland, OH 44121
Satish Parikh, Chairman of Membership Committee
Tel: (440) 572-3144 Fax: (216) 321-1129
Email: satish.parikh@wgint.com
Web: www.aseio.org

MONTE JADE SCIENCE AND TECHNOLOGY ASSOCIATION
Ohio Monte Jade Club
1275 Kinnear Rd.
Columbus, OH 43212
Philip Chu, Chairman
Tel: (614) 340-1808 Fax: (614) 487-3704
Email: chu@aqualinks.com

NATIONAL ARAB AMERICAN MEDICAL ASSOCIATION
Ohio Chapter
20997 Lorain Rd.
Cleveland, OH 44126
Basem Droubi, Chapter President
Tel: (440) 356-1009
Email: naama@naama.com
Web: www.naama.com

NETWORK OF INDIAN PROFESSIONALS-CINCINNATI
Network of Indian Professionals
5484 Erie Station Ln. #3
Cincinnati, OH 45227
Komal Patel, President
Tel: (513) 627-5729
Email: netipcinti@yahoo.com
Web: www.netipcincinnati.org

NETWORK OF INDIAN PROFESSIONALS-CLEVELAND
Network of Indian Professionals of North America
Cleveland, OH
Web: www.netipcleveland.org

NETWORK OF INDIAN PROFESSIONALS-COLUMBUS
Network of Indian Professionals
P.O. Box 20671
Columbus, OH 43220-0671
Shobha Narayanan, President
Email: netipcmh@yahoo.com
Web: www.netipcolumbus.org

OHIO CHINESE AMERICAN PROFESSIONAL ASSOCIATION
Department of Chemical Engineering
Ohio State University
Athens, OH 45701
Wen-Jai Chen, Executive Director
Tel: (740) 592-2618
Email: chenw@ohio.edu
Web: www.ocapa-ohio.org

RELIGIOUS

ANSHE CHESED FAIRMOUNT TEMPLE
23737 Fairmount Blvd.
Beachwood, OH 44122-2296
Howard H. Ruben, Rabbi
Tel: (216) 464-1330 Fax: (216) 464-3628
Email: mail@fairmounttemple.org
Web: www.fairmounttemple.org

CHINA NOW MINISTRIES
3150 Ryan Meadows Pl.
Galena, OH 43021
Brent Ferguson
Email: tbf@ferguson.cc
Web: www.rioranchochristian.org/index.html

KOREAN CENTRAL PRESBYTERIAN CHURCH OF GREATER CLEVELAND
8220 Brecksville Rd.
Brecksville, OH 44141
Rev. David Kang, Senior Pastor
Tel: (440) 838-1066 Fax: (440) 838-1067
Email: kcpckang@sbcglobal.net
Web: www.clevelandkcpc.org

KOREAN-MADISONVILLE UNITED METHODIST CHURCH
6130 Madison Rd.
Cincinnati, OH 45227
Rev. Yijoon Chang, Pastor
Tel: (513) 271-1434 Fax: (513) 271-0424
Web: www.kmumc.org

SUBURBAN TEMPLE KOL AMI
22401 Chagrin Blvd.
Beachwood, OH 44122
Eric J. Bram, Rabbi
Tel: (216) 991-0700 Fax: (216) 991-0705
Email: dbram@suburbantemple.org
Web: www.suburbantemple.org

TEMPLE EMANU EL
2200 S. Green Rd.
University Heights, OH 44121
Renee Higer, Executive Director
Tel: (216) 381-6600 Fax: (216) 381-5509
Email: rhiger@teecleve.org
Web: www.teecleve.org

TEMPLE SHOLOM
3100 Longmeadow Ln.
Cincinnati, OH 45236
Steve Stein, President
Tel: (513) 791-1330 Fax: (513) 792-5792
Email: stemple@cinci.rr.com
Web: www.templesholom.net

UNITED SYNAGOGUE OF CONSERVATIVE JUDAISM
Great Lakes & Rivers Region
3645 Warrensville Center Rd. #220
Shaker Heights, OH 44122
Dr. Richard Lederman, Executive Director
Tel: (216) 751-0606 Fax: (216) 751-0607
Email: glr@uscj.org
Web: http://uscj.org/glr

SCIENTIFIC

KOREAN-AMERICAN SCIENTISTS AND ENGINEERS ASSOCIATION
Ohio Chapter
Columbus, OH
Byung Kwan Chun, President
Tel: (614) 451-8330 X101
Email: bchun@deform.com
Web: www.ksea-oh.org

SPEC. INT., CHILD CARE

CENTRAL OHIO FAMILIES WITH CHILDREN FROM CHINA
P.O. Box 554
Hilliard, OH 43026-0054
Fil Folden, President
Tel: (614) 470-3870
Email: kellerg@columbus.rr.com
Web: http://cofwcc.tripod.com/index.html

SPEC. INT., EDUCATION

ASIAN AMERICAN STUDIES PROGRAM
Ohio State University
Department of Comparative Studies
451 Hagerty Hall, 1775 College Rd.
Columbus, OH 43210-1340
Judy Wu, Coordinator
Tel: (614) 292-2559 Fax: (614) 292-6707
Email: wu.287@osu.edu
Web: http://asianam.osu.edu

CINCINNATI CONTEMPORARY CHINESE SCHOOL
P.O. Box 62090
Cincinnati, OH 45262
Charlie Chang, Principal
Tel: (513) 369-5841
Email: czhang39@yahoo.com
Web: www.cccschool.org

DEPARTMENT OF EAST ASIAN LANGUAGES AND LITERATURES
Ohio State University
204 Cunz Hall, 1841 Millikin Rd.
Columbus, OH 43210-1229
James Marshall Unger, Professor
Tel: (614) 292-5816 Fax: (614) 292-3225
Email: unger.26@osu.edu
Web: http://deall.osu.edu

HEBREW UNION COLLEGE-JEWISH INSTITUTE OF RELIGION
Cincinnati Office
3101 Clifton Ave.
Cincinnati, OH 45220-2488
David Ellenson, President
Tel: (513) 221-1875 Fax: (513) 221-0321

Email: admissions@huc.edu
Web: www.huc.edu

JAPAN UNITED STATES TEACHING, INC.
5295 Olentangy River Rd.
Columbus, OH 43235
Tel: (614) 326-3130

JEWISH EDUCATION CENTER OF CLEVELAND
2030 S. Taylor Rd.
Cleveland Heights, OH 44118
Seymour Kopelowitz, Executive Director
Tel: (216) 371-0446 Fax: (216) 371-2523
Email: sajbd@jecc.org
Web: www.jecc.org

MULTICULTURAL RESOURCE CENTER
Oberlin College
135 W. Lorain St.
Oberlin, OH 44074
Tracy Ng, Asian/Pacific American Community Coordinator
Tel: (440) 775-8802 Fax: (440) 775-6848
Email: mrc@oberlin.edu
Web: www.oberlin.edu/mrc

SPEC. INT., EMPLOYMENT

JEWISH VOCATIONAL SERVICE
4300 Rossplain Rd.
Cincinnati, OH 45236-1208
Peter Blocht
Tel: (513) 985-0515 Fax: (513) 793-5211
Email: info@jvscinti.org
Web: www.jvscinti.org

SPEC. INT., GAY&LESBIAN

ASIANS & FRIENDS CLEVELAND, INC.
P.O. Box 29031
Cleveland, OH 44129
Tel: (216) 226-6080 X3
Email: afcleveland@aol.com
Web: http://members.aol.com/afcleveland/index.html

SPEC. INT., HEALTH SERVICES

ASIAN HEALTH INITIATIVE
Ohio State University Medical Center
4100 N. High St. #301
Columbus, OH 43214
Frank Chi, Coordinator
Tel: (614) 220-4023 Fax: (614) 220-4024

FILIPINO AMERICAN DIETETIC ASSOCIATION
Sinclair Community College
27 Mann Ave.
Fairborn, OH 45324
Beatriz Dykes, President
Tel: (937) 754-1211 Fax: (937) 512-2546
Email: betty.dykes@sinclair.edu

SPEC. INT., HOUSING

ASIAN EVERGREEN HOUSING CORPORATION
3843 Payne Ave.
Cleveland, OH 44114
Tel: (216) 426-1363 Fax: (216) 426-1357

SPEC. INT., HUMAN RELATIONS

COUNCIL ON AMERICAN-ISLAMIC RELATIONS
Ohio Chapter
4700 Reed Rd. #B
Columbus, OH 43220
Jad Humeidan, Director
Tel: (614) 451-3232 Fax: (614) 451-3222
Email: ohio@cair-net.org
Web: www.cair-ohio.com

FRIENDSHIP FOUNDATION OF AMERICAN-VIETNAMESE, INC.
2238 W. Blvd.
Cleveland, OH 44102
Gia Hoa Ryan, Executive Director/Founder
Tel: (216) 651-6748
Email: friendshipfounda@msn.com

JAPANESE AMERICANS CITIZENS LEAGUE
4211 Wallington Dr.
Dayton, OH 45440
Ronald M. Katsuyama, President
Tel: (937) 294-8815
Email: rkatsuyama@voyager.net
Web: www.jacl.org

LEBANON RELIEF, INC.
1325 Virginia Trail
Youngstown, OH 44505
Tel: (330) 747-1954 Fax: (330) 759-3893
Email: feedback@lebanonrelief.com
Web: www.lebanonrelief.com

THE AMERICAN JEWISH COMMITTEE
Cincinnati Chapter
105 W. 4th St. #1008
Cincinnati, OH 45202-2766
Barbara Glueck, Chapter Director
Tel: (513) 621-4020 Fax: (513) 621-0703
Email: cincinnati@ajc.org
Web: www.ajc.org

Cleveland Chapter
1422 Euclid Ave. #625
Cleveland, OH 44115-1952
John Hexter, Chapter Director
Tel: (216) 781-6035 Fax: (216) 781-7519
Email: cleveland@ajc.org
Web: www.ajc.org

THE CHILDREN'S DEFENSE FUND
52 E. Lynn St. #400
Columbus, OH 43215
Ron Browder, Director
Tel: (614) 221-2244 Fax: (614) 221-2247
Email: cdfohio@cdfohio.org
Web: www.cdfohio.org

SPEC. INT., IMMIGRATION

COMMUNITY IMMIGRATION SERVICIES OF OHIO
4889 Sinclair Rd. #103
Columbus, OH 43229
Angie Plummer, Executive Director
Tel: (614) 840-9705 Fax: (614) 849-9718
Email: cirs@computernet.com
Web: www.cris-ohio.com

COMMUNITY REFUGEE AND IMMIGRATION SERVICE
3624 Bexvie Ave.
Columbus, OH 43227
Angela Plummer, Director
Tel: (614) 235-5747 Fax: (614) 235-6127

SPEC. INT., INFORMATION REFERRAL

ASIAN SERVICES IN ACTION, INC.
730 Carroll St.
Akron, OH 44304
May Chen, Executive Director
Tel: (330) 535-3263 Fax: (330) 535-3338
Email: asia@asiainc-ohio.org
Web: www.asiainc-ohio.org

SPEC. INT., LEGAL ASSISTANCE

ASIAN LEGAL SUPPORT CENTER
Richard T. Herman & Associates
815 Superior Ave. #1910
Cleveland, OH 44114
Richard T. Herman, Founder
Tel: (216) 696-6170 Fax: (216) 696-0104
Email: law@asklawyer.net
Web: www.asklawyer.net

SPEC. INT., SOCIAL INTEREST

AMERICAN JEWISH ARCHIVES
3101 Clifton Ave.
Cincinnati, OH 45220
Gary P. Zola, Executive Director
Tel: (513) 221-1875 Fax: (513) 221-7812
Email: aja@huc.edu
Web: www.huc.edu/aja

ASSOCIATION FOR INDIA'S DEVELOPMENT
Columbus Chapter
P.O. Box 3446
Columbus, OH 43210-3446
Tel: (614) 298-0512
Web: www.aidindia.org/columbus

CANTON JEWISH COMMUNITY CENTER
2631 Harvard Ave. NW
Canton, OH 44709
Tel: (330) 453-0132 Fax: (330) 452-4487
Email: poscjfed@neo.rr.com
Web: www.jewishcanton.org

CLEVELAND HILLEL FOUNDATION
11291 Euclid Ave., University Cir.
Cleveland, OH 44106
Tel: (216) 231-0040 Fax: (216) 231-0256
Email: info@clevelandhillel.org
Web: www.clevelandhillel.org

COLUMBUS JEWISH FEDERATION
1175 College Ave.
Columbus, OH 43209
Tel: (614) 237-7686 Fax: (614) 237-2221
Email: webmaster@tcjf.org
Web: www.jewishcolumbus.org

JAPAN AMERICA SOCIETY OF CENTRAL OHIO (COLUMBUS & AREA)
325 Oxley Hall, 1712 Neil Ave.
Columbus, OH 43210
Janet Stuckey, Executive Director
Tel: (614) 292-3345 Fax: (614) 292-4273
Web: www.oia.osu.edu/japan/japanamerica/

JAPAN SOCIETY OF CLEVELAND
2999 Payne Ave.
Cleveland, OH 44114
Tel: (216) 694-4774 Fax: (216) 622-6009
Email: jsc@us-japan.org
Web: www.us-japan.org/cleveland

JAPAN-AMERICA SOCIETY OF GREATER CINCINNATI
300 Carew Tower, 441 Vine St.
Cincinnati, OH 45202
Barry Scott Myers, Executive Director
Tel: (513) 579-3114 Fax: (513) 579-3101
Email: bmyers@gccc.com
Web: www.cincinnatijas.com

JEWISH COMMUNITY BOARD OF AKRON, INC.
750 White Pond Dr.
Akron, OH 44320
Robert Minster, President
Tel: (330) 869-2424 Fax: (330) 867-8498
Email: rminster@neo.rr.com
Web: http://jewishakron.org

JEWISH COMMUNITY CENTER
7420 Montgomery Rd.
Cincinnati, OH 45236
Roz Kaplan
Tel: (513) 761-7500 Fax: (513) 761-0084
Email: info@jcc-cinci.com
Web: www.jcc-cinci.com

JEWISH COMMUNITY CENTER OF AKRON
750 White Pond Dr.
Akron, OH 44320
Todd Rockoff, Center Director
Tel: (330) 867-7850
Email: todd_rockoff@jewishakron.org
Web: www.jewishakron.org

JEWISH COMMUNITY FEDERATION OF CLEVELAND
1750 Euclid Ave.
Cleveland, OH 44115
Tel: (216) 566-9200 Fax: (216) 861-1230
Email: webmaster@jcfcleve.org
Web: www.jewishcleveland.org

JEWISH FAMILY SERVICE
6525 Sylvania Ave.
Sylvania, OH 43560
Nancy Newbury, Interim Executive Director
Tel: (419) 885-2561 Fax: (419) 885-7427
Email: toljfs@aol.com

JEWISH FAMILY SERVICE ASSOCIATION
24075 Commerce Park Rd.
Beachwood, OH 44122
Robert Shakno, President/CEO
Tel: (216) 292-3999
Web: www.jfsa-cleveland.org

JEWISH FAMILY SERVICE OF AKRON
83 N. Miller Rd. #202
Akron, OH 44333
Esther Morris Cooper, President
Tel: (330) 867-3388 Fax: (330) 867-3396
Email: akronjfs@ald.net
Web: www.jewishakron.org/jfs.cfm

JEWISH FAMILY SERVICE OF CINCINNATI AREA
11223 Cornell Park Dr.
Cincinnati, OH 45242
Howard Schulltz, Executive Director
Fax: (513) 469-1195
Email: skaplan@jfscinti.org
Web: www.jfscinti.org

JEWISH FAMILY SERVICE OF COLUMBUS
1151 College Ave.
Columbus, OH 43209-2827
Chuck Weiden, Executive Director
Tel: (614) 231-1890 Fax: (614) 231-4978
Email: cweiden@jfscolumbus.org
Web: www.jfscolumbus.org

JEWISH FEDERATION OF CINCINNATI
4380 Malsbary Rd. #200
Cincinnati, OH 45242
Tel: (513) 985-1502 Fax: (513) 985-1503
Email: sklebanow@jfedcin.org
Web: www.jewishcincinnati.org

JEWISH FEDERATION OF GREATER DAYTON
4501 Denlinger Rd.
Dayton, OH 45426-2395
Peter Wells, Executive Vice President
Tel: (937) 854-4150 Fax: (937) 854-2850
Email: pwells@jfgd.net
Web: www.jewishdayton.org

JEWISH FOUNDATION OF CINCINNATI
8044 Montgomery Rd.
Cincinnati, OH 45236
Connie M. Hinitz
Tel: (513) 792-2715 Fax: (513) 792-2716
Email: jdfncin@supern.com

TAIWAN MERCHANTS ASSOCIATION OF OHIO
854 Werner Way
Worthington, OH 43085
Nelson Kuo, Director
Tel: (614) 785-0705 Fax: (614) 846-1486
Email: kentexcorp@hotmail.com

UNITED JEWISH COUNCIL OF GREATER TOLEDO
6505 Sylvania Ave.
Sylvania, OH 43560
Tel: (419) 885-4461 Fax: (419) 885-3207
Email: contact@jewishtoledo.org
Web: www.jewishtoledo.org

UNIVERSITY SETTLEMENT
4800 Broadway Ave.
Cleveland, OH 44127
Tracy Mason, Executive Director
Tel: (216) 641-8948 Fax: (216) 641-7971
Email: tracymason@universitysettlement.net
Web: www.universitysettlement.net

SPEC. INT., VOLUNTARY SERVICE

THE BON FOUNDATION
P.O. Box 181148
Cleveland Heights, OH 44118-7148
Kit Sawyer, President
Email: info@bonfoundation.org
Web: www.bonfoundation.org

SPEC. INT., WOMEN

HADASSAH
Central States Region
P.O. Box 190
New Albany, OH 43054
Esther Bleiweiss, President
Tel: (614) 402-8483 Fax: (614) 855-4338
Email: esther.bleiweiss@hadassah.org
Web: www.hadassah.org

NATIONAL COUNCIL FOR JEWISH WOMEN
Cleveland Section
26055 Emery Rd.
Warrensville Heights, OH 44128
Susan C. Levine, President
Tel: (216) 378-2204 Fax: (216) 378-2205
Email: infoncjwcs@adelphia.net
Web: www.ncjwcleveland.org

SPEC. INT., YOUTH

JEWISH BIG BROTHER AND BIG SISTER ASSOCIATION
22001 Fairmount Blvd.
Shaker Heights, OH 44118
Pam Davis, Secretary
Tel: (216) 320-8310 Fax: (216) 320-8759
Email: davisp@bellefairejcb.org
Web: www.bellefairejcb.org

THE CHILDREN'S DEFENSE FUND
629 Oak St. #400
Cincinnati, OH 45206
Eileen Cooper Reed, Director
Tel: (513) 751-2332 Fax: (513) 751-2003
Email: info@cdfcinti.org
Web: www.cdfcinti.org

STUDENT ORGANIZATION

ASIAN AMERICAN STUDENT SERVICES
Ohio State University
1739 N. High St.
Columbus, OH 43210
Tel: (614) 688-4449
Email: khan.162@osu.edu
Web: http://multiculturalcenter.osu.edu/asam

BANGLADESH STUDENTS ASSOCIATION
Ohio State University
504 Baker Systems Engineering Bldg., 1971 Neil Ave.
Columbus, OH 43210-1210
Mohammad Faisal Karim, President
Email: bsa-osu@lists.acs.ohio-state.edu
Web: www.acs.ohio-state.edu/students/bsa

CHINESE STUDENTS AND SCHOLARS SOCIETY
Ohio State University
P.O. Box 3599
Columbus, OH 43210
Liu Jinjun, President
Email: csss@osu.edu
Web: www.osu.edu/students/csss

INDIAN STUDENTS ASSOCIATION
University of Cincinnati
ML #136
Cincinnati, OH 45221
Mihir Phadke, President
Email: isa2@email.uc.edu
Web: www.soa.uc.edu/org/isa

JAPANESE CLUB
Ohio State University
211 Ohio Union, 1739 N. High St.
Columbus, OH 43210
Kelly Lichoff, President
Email: japaneseclub@osu.edu
Web: www.service.ohio-state.edu/students/j-club

KOREAN STUDENT ASSOCIATION
The Ohio State University
Columbus, OH 43210
James Baek, President
Tel: (614) 688-8449
Email: baek.23@osu.edu
Web: http://kusa.org.ohio-state.edu/

MUSLIM STUDENT ASSOCIATION
Cleveland State University
UC 102 Box #29
Cleveland, OH 44115
Ayesha Zafar, President
Email: zayeshaz@aol.com
Web: www.csuohio.edu/msa

Ohio University
13 Stewart St.
Athens, OH 45701
Ziad Akir, President
Tel: (740) 594-3890 Fax: (740) 594-3890
Email: muslimst@ohiou.edu
Web: http://cscwww.cats.ohiou.edu/~muslimst

THAI STUDENT ASSOCIATION
Kent State University
124 Bowmal Hall
Kent, OH 44243
Web: http://dept.kent.edu/stuorg/thaiclub

OKLAHOMA

ARTISTIC

THE WORLD ORGANIZATION OF CHINA PAINTERS
2641 NW 10th
Oklahoma City, OK 73107-5400
Tel: (405) 521-1234 Fax: (405) 521-1265
Email: wocporg@theshop.net
Web: www.theshop.net/wocporg

CHAMBER OF COMMERCE

AMERICAN INDIAN CHAMBER OF COMMERCE OF OKLAHOMA
5103 S. Sheridan Rd. #695
Tulsa, OK 74145
Dan Bigbee Jr., President
Tel: (918) 665-7087 Fax: (918) 298-1652
Email: chamber@aicco.org
Web: www.aicco.org

CULTURAL

INDIA ASSOCIATION OF OKLAHOMA
P.O. Box 720529
Oklahoma City, OK 73172
Gopal Ranebenur, President
Tel: (405) 843-3500

VIETNAMESE AMERICAN ASSOCIATION
Refugee Center
2316 NW 23rd St.
Oklahoma City, OK 73107
Cuong Van Nguyen, Executive Director
Tel: (405) 524-3088 Fax: (405) 524-2932
Email: vaaokc@vaaokc.org
Web: www.vaaokc.org

AMERICAN ASSOCIATION OF THE PHYSICIANS OF INDIAN ORIGIN
4200 Memorial Rd. #301
Oklahoma City, OK 73120
Avani P. Sheth, M.D., President
Tel: (405) 841 7899 Fax: (405) 330 6969
Email: info@aapiusa.net
Web: www.aapiusa.net

NATIONAL ARAB AMERICAN MEDICAL ASSOCIATION
Oklahoma Chapter
6303 Waterford Blvd. #200
Oklahoma City, OK 73118
Edward Shadeed, Chapter President
Tel: (405) 840-5100 Fax: (405) 840-5102
Email: naama@naama.com
Web: www.naama.com

RELIGIOUS

CHINA CALL, INC.
P.O. Box 700515
Tulsa, OK 74170-0515
Tel: (918) 359-4000 Fax: (918) 369-2772
Email: info@chcall.org
Web: www.chcall.org

SOUTHERN OKLAHOMA CHINESE BAPTIST CHURCH
625 E. Frank St.
Norman, OK 73071
Tel: (405) 360-0123
Email: friend@socbc.org
Web: www.socbc.org

TEMPLE B'NAI ISRAEL
4901 N. Pennsylvania
Oklahoma City, OK 73112
Larry Davis, President
Tel: (405) 848-0965 Fax: (405) 848-0966
Email: tbi@coxinet.net
Web: www.thetempleokc.org

SPEC. INT., CHILD CARE

CHINA HARVEST MINISTRIES
P.O. Box 2074
Broken Arrow, OK 74013
Rick Haynes, President
Tel: (918) 438-4464 Fax: (918) 438-4494
Email: chm@chinaharvest.com
Web: http://chinaharvest.org

NEW LIFE CHILDREN'S HOME, INC.
P.O. Box 700567
Tulsa, OK 74170-0567
Nolan Vockrodt, Founder
Tel: (918) 493-2287
Email: nlch@nlch.org
Web: www.nlch.org

SPEC. INT., EDUCATION

OKLAHOMA CHINESE SCHOOL
117 Pueblo
Edmund, OK 73013
Larry Lee, President
Tel: (405) 340-8173 Fax: (405) 340-8173
Email: okchinese@yahoo.com

SPEC. INT., HEALTH SERVICES

ASSOCIATION OF AMERICAN INDIAN PHYSICIANS
1225 Sovereign Row #103
Oklahoma City, OK 73108
Dr. Ben Muneta, M.D., President

Tel: (405) 946-7072 Fax: (405) 946-7651
Email: aaip@aaip.com
Web: www.aaip.com

SHIC, INC.: ASIAN HEALTH SERVICES EXCHANGE
P.O. Box 702194
Tulsa, OK 74170
Tel: (918) 523-7373 Fax: (918) 523-7373
Email: shic-usoffice@global-pc.net
Web: www.shicasianhealth.org

SPEC. INT., SOCIAL INTEREST

JEWISH FEDERATION OF GREATER OKLAHOMA CITY
710 W. Wilshire #C
Oklahoma City, OK 73116-7736
Tel: (405) 848-3132 Fax: (405) 848-3180
Email: okcfed@flash.net
Web: www.jfedokc.org

JEWISH FEDERATION OF TULSA
2021 E. 71st St.
Tulsa, OK 74136
Tel: (918) 495-1100 Fax: (918) 495-1220
Email: federation@jewishtulsa.org
Web: www.jewishtulsa.org

SPEC. INT., WOMEN

LAOTIAN WOMEN ASSOCIATION
2308 NW 19th St.
Oklahoma City, OK 73107
Vasithy Sandara, Founder
Tel: (405) 587-0478

STUDENT ORGANIZATION

MUSLIM STUDENTS ASSOCIATION
University of Oklahoma
900 Asp #370, Box #115
Norman, OK 73019-4058
Akbar Siddiqui, President
Email: msa_ou2001@yahoo.com
Web: www.ou.edu/student/oumsa

SRI LANKA STUDENT ASSOCIATION
Oklahoma State University
College of Arts and Sciences, 202 Life Sciences East
Stilwater, OK 74078
Arthur Webb, Staff Advisor
Tel: (405) 744-5658
Email: awebb@okway.okstate.edu
Web: www.okstate.edu/osu_orgs/ssa/ssa99.htm

VIETNAMESE AMERICAN STUDENT ASSOCIATION
Oklahoma State University
045 Student Union
Stillwater, OK 74078
Pauline Pham, President
Tel: (405) 744-6617
Email: paulinp@okstate.edu
Web: www.okstate.edu/osu_orgs/vasa

OREGON

ARTISTIC

JAPANESE GARDEN SOCIETY OF OREGON
P.O. Box 3847
Portland, OR 97208-3847
Tel: (503) 223-1321 Fax: (503) 223-8303
Email: japenesegarden@japanesegarden.com
Web: www.japanesegarden.com

KALAKENDRA SOCIETY FOR THE PERFORMING ARTS OF INDIA
P.O. Box 655
Portland, OR 97207
David Savage, President
Tel: (503) 233-8838 Fax: (503) 228-4065
Email: info@kalakendra.org
Web: www.kalakendra.org

TEATRO BAGONG SILANGAN
5520 SE Boise St.
Portland, OR 97216
Tel: (503) 771-9701
Email: mannys@asianavenue.com
Web: www.teatroportland.com

CHAMBER OF COMMERCE

PHILIPPINE AMERICAN CHAMBER OF COMMERCE OF OREGON
5424 N. Michigan St.
Portland, OR 97217
Jaime Lim, President
Tel: (503) 285-1994 Fax: (503) 283-4445
Email: emailus@paccoregon.net
Web: www.paccoregon.net

CULTURAL

ANDISHEH CENTER
PMB 121, 6327-C SW Capital Hwy.
Portland, OR 97239-1937
Tel: (503) 998-6816
Email: andisheh@andisheh.org
Web: www.andisheh.org

ASIAN FAMILY CENTER
4424 NE Glisan St.
Portland, OR 97213
Lee Po Cha, Family Center Coordinator
Tel: (503) 235-9396 Fax: (503) 235-0341
Web: www.irco.org

FILIPINO AMERICAN NATIONAL HISTORICAL SOCIETY
Oregon Chapter
6020 SW Corbett Ave.
Portland, OR 97239
Simeon D. Mamaril, Treasurer
Tel: (503) 246-7720 Fax: (503) 246-7720
Email: sidamae@juno.com

KOREAN WAR VETERANS ASSOCIATION
Iron Triangle Chapter
465 46th Ct. SE
Salem, OR 97301
Kenneth Crawford, President
Tel: (503) 588-0757
Web: http://home.teleport.com/~gsjones/kwva/kwva2.htm

NEPALI ASSOCIATION OF OREGON
5232 NE Irving St.
Portland, OR 97213
Daya Shakya, President
Tel: (503) 282-0447
Email: drasha@aol.com
Web: www.nepaloregon.org

NORTHWEST TIBETAN CULTURAL ASSOCIATION
P.O. Box 13120
Portland, OR 97213
Tsering Choephel, Chair
Tel: (503) 222-7172 Fax: (503) 222-1582
Email: info@nwtca.org
Web: www.nwtca.org

OREGON NIKKEI LEGACY CENTER
117 NW 2nd Ave.
Portland, OR 97209
June Arima Schumann, Executive Director
Tel: (503) 224-1458 Fax: (503) 224-1459
Email: onlc@oregonnikkei.org
Web: www.oregonnikkei.org

PHILIPPINE AMERICAN ASSOCIATION, INC.
840 Hughes St.
Eugene, OR 97402
Melissa Christoffels, Chairman
Tel: (541) 688-7758
Email: paa_chair2003@ix.netcom.com

PORTLAND CLASSICAL CHINESE GARDEN
NW 3rd & Everett
Portland, OR 97208

Tel: (503) 228-8131
Web: www.portlandchinesegarden.org

SAI LEUAD LAO ORGANIZATION
5233 NE Roselawn
Portland, OR 97218
Chandy Phanthavong, President
Tel: (503) 287-0907 Fax: (503) 287-0907

LAW ENFORCEMENT

OREGON ASIAN PEACE OFFICERS ASSOCIATION
3117 NE 32nd Ave.
Portland, OR 97212
John Rasmussen, President

POLITICAL ACTION

ASIAN PACIFIC AMERICAN LABOR ALLIANCE
Oregon Chapter
P.O. Box 23555
Tigard, OR 97281
Jeff McDonald
Tel: (503) 598-6342
Email: apala@apalanet.org
Web: www.apalanet.org

PROFESSIONAL

ASIAN PACIFIC AMERICAN NETWORK OF OREGON
4424 NE Glisan St.
Portland, OR 97213
Nathan Thuan Nguyen
Tel: (503) 235-9396 Fax: (503) 235-0341
Email: apanocommunity@yahoo.com

ASIAN PACIFIC LABOR ALLIANCE
c/o UFCW 555
7095 SW Sand Durg
Tigard, OR 97281
Jeff McDonald, President
Tel: (503) 598-6342 Fax: (503) 620-3816
Email: jeff.mcdonald@ufcw555.com

CHINESE AMERICAN SEMICONDUCTOR PROFESSIONAL ASSOCIATION
Portland Chapter
Portland, OR
Peir Chu, Chair of Portland Branch
Email: chair@caspa-portland.org
Web: www.objectis.net

RELIGIOUS

CAMBODIAN BUDDHIST SOCIETY OF OREGON
19940 SW Stafford Rd.
West Linn, OR 97068
Tel: (503) 638-3700

CHINESE EVANGELICAL CHURCH OF HILLSBORO
5529 Five Oaks Dr.
Hillsboro, OR 97124
Rev. Robert Altstadt, Senior Minister
Tel: (503) 466-2762 Fax: (503) 466-2762
Email: info@cechurch.org
Web: www.cechurch.org

CHINESE FAITH BAPTIST CHURCH
2830 NE Flanders St.
Portland, OR 97232
William Ki, Lead Pastor
Tel: (503) 236-8225
Email: wki@chinesefaith.org
Web: www.chinesefaith.org

MARPA FOUNDATION
1537 Lilac Cir.
Ashland, OR 97520
Judith Sundaram, Director
Tel: (541) 488-9702 Fax: (541) 488-9706
Email: marpafnd@ktgrinpoche.org
Web: www.ktgrinpoche.org

TEMPLE BETH ISRAEL
42 W. 25th St.
Eugene, OR 97405
Craig Starr, President
Tel: (541) 485-7218 Fax: (541) 485-7105
Email: info@tbieugene.org
Web: www.tbieugene.org

TIBETAN YOUTH CONGRESS
598 SE. 71st Ave.
Hillsboro, OR 97123
Wang Du, President
Tel: (503) 356-4582
Email: wangdu1@hotmail.com
Web: www.tibetanyouthcongress.com

RESEARCH

CENTER FOR ASIAN AND PACIFIC STUDIES
University of Oregon
110 Gerlinger Hall, 1246 University of Oregon
Eugene, OR 97403-1246
Jeffrey Hanes, Director
Tel: (541) 346-5068 Fax: (541) 346-0802
Web: http://darkwing.uoregon.edu/~caps

SPEC. INT., CHILD CARE

HOLT INTERNATIONAL CHILDREN'S SERVICES
P.O. Box 2880
Eugene, OR 97402
Gary Damar, President/CEO
Tel: (541) 687-2202 Fax: (541) 683-6175
Email: info@holtinternational.org
Web: www.holtintl.org

SPEC. INT., COUNSELING

JEWISH FAMILY AND CHILDREN'S SERVICES PORTLAND
1130 SW Morrison #316, Mayer Bldg.
Portland, OR 97205
Tel: (503) 226-7079 Fax: (503) 226-1130
Email: jfcs@jfcs-portland.org
Web: www.jfcs-portland.org

SPEC. INT., EDUCATION

AMERICAN CHINESE CULTURAL EXCHANGE, INC.
330 Morton Rd.
Oregon City, OR 97045
Paul Vasquez, President
Tel: (503) 656-7192 Fax: (503) 226-9991
Email: paulvasquez@acce-inc.org
Web: www.acce-inc.org

ASIAN AMERICAN FOUNDATION
P.O. Box 51117
Eugene, OR 97405
Web: www.aaforegon.com

EUGENE SPRINGFIELD ASIAN COUNCIL
P.O. Box 51117
Eugene, OR 97405
Brent Tokita, President
Tel: (541) 686-2014

MOMENI FOUNDATION
12190-B SW Longhorn Ln.
Beaverton, OR 97008
Moji Momeni, President
Tel: (503) 524-8280 Fax: (503) 524-3757
Email: momenifoundation@aol.com
Web: http://members.aol.com/
momenifoundation/myhomepage

MUSLIM EDUCATIONAL TRUST
P.O. Box 283
Portland, OR 97207
Tel: (503) 228-3754 Fax: (503) 228-1273
Email: metpdx@metpdx.org
Web: www.metpdx.org

PORTLAND CHINESE SCHOOL
P.O. Box 9767

Portland, OR 97228
Sheng Lin Ting, Principal
Tel: (503) 720-5367
Email: principal@portlandchineseschool.org
Web: www.portlandchineseschool.org

US CHINA PEOPLES FRIENDSHIP ASSOCIATION
Portland Chapter
2234 NE 25th Ave.
Portland, OR 97212
Paul Morris
Tel: (503) 249-3965 Fax: (503) 493-8621
Web: www.uscpfa.org

SPEC. INT., FAMILY PLANNING

ASSOCIATED SERVICES FOR INTERNATIONAL ADOPTION
5935 Willow Ln.
Lake Oswego, OR 97035-5344
Sandra Miller, Executive Director
Tel: (503) 697-6863 Fax: (503) 697-6957
Email: sandram@asiadopt.org
Web: www.asiadopt.org

SPEC. INT., HEALTH SERVICES

ASIAN HEALTH AND SERVICE CENTER
3633 SE 35th Pl.
Portland, OR 97202
Holden Leung, Executive Director
Tel: (503) 872-8822 Fax: (503) 872-8825
Email: csclink@teleport.com
Web: www.ahscpdx.org

SPEC. INT., HUMAN RELATIONS

ASSOCIATION FOR COMMUNAL HARMONY IN ASIA
4410 Verda Ln. NE
Keizer, OR 97303
Dr. Pritam K. Rohila, Ph.D., Executive Director
Tel: (503) 393-6944
Email: pritamr@open.org
Web: www.asiapeace.org

INDIA PARTNERS
P.O. Box 5470
Eugene, OR 97405
Tel: (541) 683-0696 Fax: (541) 683-2773
Email: info@indiapartners.org
Web: www.indiapartners.org

THE AMERICAN JEWISH COMMITTEE
Portland Chapter
1220 SW Morrison #828
Portland, OR 97205-2227
Emily Georges Gottfried, Area Executive Director
Tel: (503) 295-6761 Fax: (503) 497-9054
Email: portland@ajc.org
Web: www.ajc.org

SPEC. INT., IMMIGRATION

INTERNATIONAL REFUGEE CENTER OF OREGON
10301 NE Glisan St.
Portland, OR 97220
Tim Hertel, President
Tel: (503) 234-1541 Fax: (503) 234-1259
Email: admin@mail.irco.org
Web: www.irco.org

THE HONG KONG CLUB OF OREGON
P.O. Box 66758
Portland, OR 97290
Paul Ip, Chairman
Tel: (503) 771-3721
Email: pauli@hkclub-or.com
Web: www.hkclub-or.com

SPEC. INT., SENIORS

ASIAN PACIFIC AMERICAN SENIOR COALITION
4937 SE Woodstock Blvd.
Portland, OR 97206
Narcisa Pimentel, President
Tel: (503) 289-0963 Fax: (503) 775-0004
Email: apasc@qwest.net

SPEC. INT., SOCIAL INTEREST

ASIAN PACIFIC AMERICAN CONSORTIUM ON SUBSTANCE ABUSE
4937 SE Woodstock Blvd.
Portland, OR 97206
Lorrie Piatt-Montry, Executive Director
Tel: (503) 775-2458 Fax: (503) 775-0004
Email: services@apacsa.org
Web: www.apacsa.org

CHINESE AMERICAN CITIZENS ALLIANCE
Portland Lodge
11453 SE Hazel Hill Rd.
Clackamas, OR 97015
Ming Ming Tung-Edleman, President
Tel: (503) 698-2315 Fax: (503) 698-3488
Email: discover2000@juno.com
Web: www.cacaportland.com

CHRISTIAN FELLOWSHIP FOUNDATION FOR MINDANAO
63635 Boyd Acres Rd.
Bend, OR 97701
Bob Folkstead, Financial Officer
Email: brucencindy@mindspring.com
Web: www.visionaryfolks.com/cffm/

JAPAN-AMERICA SOCIETY OF OREGON
312 2nd Ave. NW
Portland, OR 97209
Dixie McKeel, Executive Director
Tel: (503) 552-8811 Fax: (503) 552-8815
Email: info@jaso.org
Web: www.jaso.org

JAPANESE AMERICAN ASSOCIATION OF LANE COUNTY
1978 W. 27th Pl.
Eugene, OR 97405
Seiko Kikuta, President
Tel: (541) 484-4656
Email: kikuta_lns@msn.com

JAPANESE ANCESTRAL SOCIETY OF PORTLAND
1550 SE Oak Grove Blvd.
Milwaukee, OR 97267
Tel: (503) 241-4527

JEWISH COMMUNITY OF CENTRAL OREGON
P.O. Box 1773
Bend, OR 97709-1773
Lester Friedman, President
Tel: (541) 385-6421
Email: info@jccobend.com
Web: www.jccobend.com

JEWISH FEDERATION OF PORTLAND
6680 SW Capitol Hwy.
Portland, OR 97219
N. Dickson Davis, President
Tel: (503) 245-6219 Fax: (503) 245-6603
Email: federation@jewishportland.org
Web: www.jewishportland.org

NORTHWEST CHINA COUNCIL
127 NW 3rd Ave.
Portland, OR 97209
Rosario Aglialoro, Executive Director
Tel: (503) 973-5451 Fax: (503) 973-5431
Email: nwchina@spiritone.com
Web: www.nwchina.com

OREGON COAST FILIPINO AMERICAN ASSOCIATION
93545 Shady Ln.
North Bend, OR 97459

Helen Coughlin, President
Tel: (541) 756-7437
Email: info@ocfaa.org
Web: www.ocfaa.org

OREGON JEWISH COMMUNITY FOUNDATION
610 SW Broadway #407
Portland, OR 97205
Stan Blauer, President
Tel: (503) 248-9328 Fax: (503) 248-9323
Email: questions@ojcf.org
Web: www.orjcf.org

WONG FAMILY ASSOCIATION
1941 SE 31st Ave.
Portland, OR 97214
Norman Wong, President
Tel: (503) 233-3600 Fax: (503) 230-9432
Email: maotd@msn.com

SPEC. INT., WOMEN

SOUTH ASIAN WOMEN'S EMPOWERMENT AND RESOURCE ALLIANCE
P.O. Box 91242
Portland, OR 97291-0242
Renee Wilder, Program Manager
Tel: (503) 641-2425
Email: sawera@sawera.org
Web: www.sawera.org

SPEC. INT., YOUTH

FILIPINO YOUTH AND FRIENDS COALITION FOR PROGRESS
17063 SE Pleides St.
Clackamas, OR 97015
Richard Dandasan, President
Tel: (503) 658-2048
Email: flip_richd@yahoo.com
Web: www.kpkoregon.cjb.net

STUDENT ORGANIZATION

CHINESE STUDENTS & SCHOLARS ASSOCIATION
University of Oregon
Erb Memorial Union #4, 1228 University of Oregon
Eugene, OR 97403-1228
Wang Yongjun, Chair
Email: ywang2@oregon.uoregon.edu
Web: http://gladstone.uoregon.edu/~cssa/

ISANG BANSANG PILIPINO-FILIPINO AMERICAN STUDENT ASSOCIATION
Oregon State University
149 Memorial Union E.
Corvallis, OR 97331-1610
Cliff Alagar, President
Tel: (541) 737-2101 Fax: (541) 737-7504
Email: ibp-officers@yahoogroups.com
Web: www.oregonstate.edu/groups/filipino

JAPANESE STUDENT ORGANIZATION
University of Oregon
Evb Memorial Union #202
Eugene, OR 97401
Sayuri Satofuka, Co-Director
Tel: (541) 346-4389
Email: jso@uoregon.edu
Web: http://gladstone.uoregon.edu/~jso

KAIBIGAN-FILIPINO AMERICAN STUDENT ASSOCIATION
Portland State University
P.O. Box 751-SALP
Portland, OR 97207-0751
Patrick B. Villaflores, President
Email: kaibigan@pdx.edu
Web: www.kaibigan.pdx.edu

PERSIAN STUDIES AND PERSIA HOUSE
Portland State University

P.O. Box 751
Portland, OR 97207
Tel: (503) 725-5214
Email: tehrank@pdx.edu
Web: www.persia.pdx.edu

SAMAHAN
Filipino American Student Association at
Portland Community College
1200 SW 49th Ave., CC202
Portland, OR 97219
Patrick Villaflores
Tel: (503) 977-4112
Email: pcc-samahan@yahoogroups.com

SINGAPORE STUDENTS ASSOCIATION
University of Oregon
Erb Memorial Union #202
Eugene, OR 97403
Tel: (541) 346-4368
Email: ssa@gladstone.uoregon.edu
Web: http://gladstone.uoregon.edu/~ssa

TURKISH AMERICAN STUDENT CULTURAL
ASSOCIATION
Portland State University
Student Development Service
P.O. Box 751
Portland, OR 97207
Sevket Numanoglu, President
Tel: (503) 725-7659 Fax: (503) 725-7659
Email: tasca@mail.pdx.edu
Web: www.ess.pdx.edu/tasca

VIETNAMESE STUDENT ASSOCIATION
Portland State University
704 SW Harrison St.
Portland, OR 972067
Totam Pham, President
Tel: (503) 702-3903
Email: vietnampsu@yahoo.com
Web: www.vsa.pdx.edu

PENNSYLVANIA

BUSINESS

CHINESE ENTREPRENEUR ASSOCIATION
882 S. Matlack St. #105
West Chester, PA 19382
Dr. Chris Pak, Chairman
Tel: (610) 738-7938 Fax: (610) 738-7928
Email: kyp7878@aol.com
Web: www.ceaa.org

MID-ATLANTIC RUSSIA BUSINESS
COUNCIL
1760 Market St. #1100
Philadelphia, PA 19103
Val Kogan, President/CEO
Tel: (215) 708-2628 Fax: (215) 963-9104
Email: info@ma-rbc.org
Web: www.ma-rbc.org

CHAMBER OF COMMERCE

AMERICA ISRAEL CHAMBER OF
COMMERCE
200 S. Broad St. #700
Philadelphia, PA 19102-3869
Debbie Buchwald, Executive Director
Tel: (215) 790-3722 Fax: (215) 790-3600
Email: aicc@gpcc.com
Web: www.americaisraelchamber.com

CHINESE JUNIOR CHAMBER OF
COMMERCE IN WESTERN COUNTRIES
Greater Philadelphia Chapter
140 W. Master St.
Philadelphia, PA 19122
Donald Chen, President
Tel: (215) 341-6762 Fax: (267) 989-7177
Email: america@cjcc.mailme.org
Web: www.cjcc.cn.st

CULTURAL

AMERICAN INSTITUTE OF BANGLADESH
STUDIES
Pennsylvania State University
111 Sowers St. #501
State College, PA 16801
Syedur Rahman, President
Tel: (814) 865-0436 Fax: (814) 865-8299
Email: sxr17@psu.edu
Web: www.aibs.net

AMERICAN-ARMENIAN SOCIETY
P.O. Box 9
Newtown Square, PA 19073
Daniel Terhanian, Public Relations
Tel: (215) 848-8714 Fax: (610) 359-8811
Email: info@american-armenian.org
Web: www.american-armenian.org

ASIAN ARTS INITIATIVE
1315 Cherry St., 2nd Fl.
Philadelphia, PA 19107
Gayle Isa, Executive Director
Tel: (215) 557-0455
Email: info@asianartsinitiative.org
Web: www.asianartsinitiative.org

INDIAN AMERICAN ASSOCIATION OF THE
LEHIGH VALLEY
P.O. Box 20002
Lehigh Valley, PA 18002-0002
Ashim Bhowmick, Spokesperson
Tel: (610) 439-8654 Fax: (610) 533-0416
Email: abhowmick95@cs.com
Web: www.iaalv.org

JAPAN ASSOCIATION OF GREATER
PITTSBURGH
3112 Ponderosa Dr.
Allison Park, PA 15101-3950
A. Saito
Tel: (412) 486-6052 Fax: (412) 486-6052
Email: jagp@jagp.org
Web: www.jagp.org

JEWISH PUBLICATION SOCIETY OF
AMERICA
2100 Arch St., 2nd Fl.
Philadelphia, PA 19103
Ellen Frankel, Editor-in-Chief/CEO
Tel: (215) 832-0608 Fax: (215) 568-2017
Email: jewishbook@jewishpub.org
Web: www.jewishpub.org

KOREAM FOUNDATION
P.O. Box 604
Gwynedd Valley, PA 19437
Jungsoo George Choe, President
Tel: (215) 699-9559 Fax: (215) 699-9550
Email: choes@koream.com
Web: www.koream.com

KOREAM INSTITUTE, INC.
P.O. Box 707
Gwynedd Valley, PA 19437
Sullae Choe, Executive Director
Tel: (215) 699-9559 Fax: (215) 699-9550
Email: choes@koream.com
Web: www.koream.com

MUSLIM COMMUNITY CENTER OF
GREATER PITTSBURGH
233 Seaman Ln.
Monroeville, PA 15146
Sayed Hamid Jafri, President
Tel: (412) 373-0101 Fax: (412) 373-0101
Email: admin_sec@mccgp.org
Web: www.mccgp.org

NATIONAL MUSEUM OF AMERICAN
JEWISH HISTORY
55 N. 5th St.
Philadelphia, PA 19106-2197
Tel: (215) 923-3811 Fax: (215) 923-0763
Email: nmajh@nmajh.org
Web: www.nmajh.org

PHILADELPHIA PERSIAN SOCIETY
P.O. Box 862
Bala Cynwyd, PA 19004
Narguess Askari, Board of Director
Tel: (215) 690-0501
Email: directors@persiansociety.org
Web: www.persiansociety.org

TURKISH AMERICAN SOCIETY OF UNITED
STATES
PMB 198, 761 W. Sproul Rd.
Springfield, PA 19064
Ibrahim Onaral, President
Tel: (215) 922-3262
Email: tafsus@tafsus.org
Web: www.geocities.com/tafsus/index.html

LAW ENFORCEMENT

PHILADELPHIA POLICE DEPARTMENT
COMMUNITY RELATIONS UNIT
1328 Race St., 2nd Fl.
Philadelphia, PA 19107
Sylvester Johnson, Police Commissioner
Tel: (215) 686-3380 Fax: (215) 686-3399
Web: www.ppdonline.org/ppd2_commrel.htm

MULTI-PURPOSE

ICON I PHILADELPHIA
Philadelphia, PA
Mike Chen
Email: icon@iconphiladelphia.org
Web: www.iconphiladelphia.org

JEWISH EMPLOYMENT AND VOCATIONAL
SERVICE
1845 Walnut St., 7th Fl.
Philadelphia, PA 19103
Ned J. Kaplin, Chairman
Tel: (215) 854-1800
Email: jevs@jevs.org
Web: www.jevs.org

PHILADELPHIA CHINATOWN
DEVELOPMENT CORPORATION
301-305 N. 9th St.
Philadelphia, PA 19107
John W. Chin, Executive Director
Tel: (215) 922-2156 Fax: (215) 922-7232
Email: info@chinatown-pcdc.com
Web: www.chinatown-pcdc.com

UNITED CAMBODIAN AMERICAN
ASSOCIATION
5402 B St.
Philadelphia, PA 19120
Son Thay Hien, President
Email: khmerinfo@khmerucaa.org
Web: www.khmerucaa.org

YORK JEWISH COMMUNITY CENTER
2000 Hollywood Dr.
York, PA 17403
Randy Freedman, Executive Director
Tel: (717) 843-0918 Fax: (717) 843-6988
Email: jcc@yorkjcc.org
Web: www.yorkjcc.org

POLITICAL ACTION

ASIAN AMERICAN CONGRESS
4934 Old York Rd.
Philadelphia, PA 19141
Binh Dao, Chairman
Tel: (610) 337-1245 Fax: (610) 337-1245
Email: btdao@comcast.net
Web:

ORGANIZATION OF CHINESE AMERICANS
Greater Philadelphia Chapter
1875 Jenkintown Rd. #D103
Jenkintown, PA 19046
Hsin-I C. Russell, Co-President
Tel: (215) 884-8124
Email: hcrussell@verizon.net
Web: www.oca-gp.org

Pittsburgh Chapter
4530 William Penn Hwy.
Murrysville, PA 15660
Dorothy Lee Green, President
Email: wtg1@adelphia.net
Web: www.ocapgh.org

PROJECT IMPACT FOR SOUTH ASIAN-
AMERICANS
P.O. Box 2070
Philadelphia, PA 19103
Kalpana Bhandarkar, Chair
Email: kalpana@project-impact.org
Web: www.project-impact.org

PROFESSIONAL

ASIAN AMERICAN JOURNALISTS
ASSOCIATION
Philadelphia Chapter
400 N. Broad St.
Philadelphia, PA 19101
Murali Balaji, President
Tel: (302) 324-2553
Email: aajaphilly@yahoo.com
Web: www.aaja.org/Chapters/Philadelphia/

CAMBODIAN AMERICAN NATIONAL
COUNCIL
5412 N. 5th St.
Philadelphia, PA 19120
Vi Houi, President
Tel: (215) 324-4070 Fax: (215) 324-2995
Email: canc@cancweb.org
Web: www.cancweb.org

MONTE JADE SCIENCE AND TECHNOLOGY
ASSOCIATION
Great Pittsburgh Chapter
4311 Michel Ct.
Murrysville, PA 15668
Rita M. Liu, Chairman
Tel: (724) 325-3279 Fax: (724) 325-3279
Email: thritaliu@aol.com

NETWORK OF INDIAN PROFESSIONALS-
PHILADELPHIA
Network of Indian Professionals of North
America
Philadelphia, PA
Shruti Singhal, National Liaison
Tel: (610) 662-3356
Email: shruti@netipphiladelphia.org
Web: www.netipphiladelphia.org

NETWORK OF INDIAN PROFESSIONALS-
PITTSBURGH
Network of Indian Professionals of North
America
Pittsburgh, PA
Sheel Mohnot, President
Email: info@netip-pittsburgh.org
Web: www.netip-pittsburgh.org

RELIGIOUS

ADATH ISRAEL
250 N. Highland Ave.
Merion Station, PA 19066
Len Bernstein, President
Tel: (610) 934-1919 Fax: (610) 664-0959
Email: info@adathisrael.org
Web: www.adathisrael.org

ALLIANCE FOR JEWISH RENEWAL
700 Lincoln Dr. #B2
Philadelphia, PA 19119-3046
Debra Kolodny, Executive Director
Tel: (215) 247-0210
Email: alephajr@aol.com
Web: www.aleph.org

ARAB WORLD MINISTRIES
P.O. Box 96
Upper Darby, PA 19082
Robert Sayer, Director
Tel: (800) 447-3566

Email: usa@awm.org
Web: www.gospelcom.net/awm/site/index.php

ASIAN CHRISTIAN FELLOWSHIP
Carnegie Mellon University
Box 1 University Ctr., 5000 Forbes Ave.
Pittsburgh, PA 15230
Tim Chen, Ministry Team
Email: acf@andrew.cmu.edu
Web: www.timothychen.com/acf/index.php

ASSOCIATION OF ISLAMIC CHARITABLE PROJECTS
4431 Walnut St.
Philadelphia, PA 19104
Tel: (215) 387-8888 Fax: (215) 387-3815
Web: www.aicp.org

BETH DAVID REFORM CONGREGATION
1130 Vaughans Ln.
Gladwyne, PA 19035
Jeffrey Saltz, President
Tel: (610) 896-7485 Fax: (610) 642-5406
Email: office@bdavid.org
Web: www.bdavid.org

BETH TIKVAH-B'NAI JESHURUN
1001 Paper Mill Rd.
Erdenheim, PA 19038
David Abernethy, President
Tel: (215) 233-5356 Fax: (215) 836-0211
Email: office@btbj.org
Web: www.btbj.org

CHINA AID ASSOCIATION
P.O. Box 263
Glenside, PA 19038
Tel: (215) 886-5210 Fax: (215) 886-1668
Email: bobfu@chinaaid.org
Web: www.chinaaid.org

CHINA OUTREACH MINISTRIES, INC.
P.O. Box 35
Mechanicsburg, PA 17055
Tel: (717) 591-3500 Fax: (717) 591-0412
Email: chinaout@aol.com
Web: www.chinaoutreach.org

CHINESE CHRISTIAN CHURCH AND CENTER
225 N. 10th St.
Philadelphia, PA 19107
Rev. Leslie Leung, Pastor
Tel: (215) 627-2360 Fax: (215) 627-1325
Email: info@cccnc.org
Web: www.cccnc.org

CHRISTIAN EVANGELICAL ARABIC CHURCH
338 E. Walnut St.
Allentown, PA 18103
Rev. Barty Abdelnour, Pastor
Email: ibrahimdds@aol.com
Web: www.ceachurch.homestead.com/ceachurch.html

CONGREGATION ADATH JESHURUN
7763 Old York Rd.
Elkins Park, PA 19027
Gavi Miller, Executive Director
Tel: (215) 635-6611 Fax: (215) 635-6165
Email: millerg@adathjeshurun.info
Web: www.adathjeshurun.info

CONGREGATION BETH AHAVAH
8 Letitia St.
Philadelphia, PA 19106-3050
Shelly Komito, President
Tel: (215) 923-2003 Fax: (215) 873-0108
Email: bethahavah@aol.com
Web: www.bethahavah.org

CONGREGATION BETH CHAIM
350 E. St.
Feasterville, PA 19053
Maurice Novoseller, Rabbi
Tel: (215) 355-3626 Fax: (215) 355-6907
Email: info@bethchaimpa.org
Web: www.bethchaimpa.org

CONGREGATION BETH EL
375 Stony Hill Rd.
Yardley, PA 19067
Lanny Blyweiss, Co-President
Tel: (215) 493-1707 Fax: (215) 493-7717
Email: info@bethelyardley.org
Web: www.bethelyardley.org

CONGREGATION BETH EL-NER TAMID
715 Paxon Hollow Rd.
Broomall, PA 19008
Barry Blum, Rabbi
Tel: (610) 356-8700 Fax: (610) 356-9248
Web: http://cbent.org

CONGREGATION BETH ISRAEL
542 S. New Middletown Rd.
Media, PA 19063
John Greenstine, President
Tel: (610) 566-4645 Fax: (610) 566-2240
Email: info@bethisraelmedia.org
Web: www.bethisraelmedia.org

CONGREGATION BETH OR
P.O. Box 660
Spring House, PA 19477
Ellen Svitek, President
Tel: (215) 646-5806 Fax: (215) 646-0173
Email: bethor@bethor.org
Web: www.bethor.org

CONGREGATION OHEV SHALOM
2 Chester Rd.
Wallingford, PA 19086
Andy Szabo, President
Tel: (610) 874-1465 Fax: (610) 874-1466
Email: info@ohev.net
Web: www.ohev.net

CONGREGATION OR AMI
708 Ridge Pike
Lafayette Hill, PA 19444
Tel: (610) 828-9066 Fax: (610) 828-3731
Email: office@or-ami.org
Web: www.or-ami.org

CONGREGATION OR SHALOM
835 Darby Paoli Rd.
Berwyn, PA 19312
Todd Chusid, President
Tel: (610) 644-9086 Fax: (610) 644-7405
Email: orshalom@earthlink.net
Web: www.orshalom.com

CONGREGATION RODEPH SHALOM
615 N. Broad St.
Philadelphia, PA 19123-2495
Roy H. Feinberg, Executive Director
Tel: (215) 627-6747 Fax: (215) 627-1313
Email: rfeinberg@rodephshalom.org
Web: www.rodephshalom.org

CONGREGATION SHAARAI SHOMAYIM
75 E. James St.
Lancaster, PA 17602
Randi Jacobson, President
Tel: (717) 397-5575 Fax: (717) 397-5599
Email: office@shaarai.org
Web: www.shaarai.org

CONGREGATION SONS OF ISRAEL
2715 Tilghman St.
Allentown, PA 18104
Arthur Hochhauser, President
Tel: (610) 433-6089 Fax: (610) 433-6080
Web: www.sonsofisrael.net

CONGREGATION TIFERES B'NAI ISRAEL
2478 Street Rd.
Warrington, PA 18976
Louis Cohen, President
Tel: (215) 343-0155 Fax: (215) 343-8136
Web: www.tbiwarrington.org

CONGREGATION TIFERETH ISRAEL
2909 Bristol Rd.
Bensalem, PA 19020
Ed Saks, President
Tel: (215) 752-3468 Fax: (215) 757-8660

Email: tiferethisrael-pa@comcast.net
Web: www.tiferethisrael-pa.org

FIRST KOREAN PRESBYTERIAN CHURCH OF PHILADELPHIA
770-800 W. Tabor Rd.
Philadelphia, PA 19120
Rev. Manwoo Kim, Senior Pastor
Tel: (215) 549-6880 Fax: (215) 549-6880
Email: info@fkpcp.org
Web: www.fkpcp.org

GERMANTOWN JEWISH CENTRE
400 W. Ellet St.
Philadelphia, PA 19119
Rachel Falkove, President
Tel: (215) 844-1507 Fax: (215) 844-8309
Email: office@germantownjewishcentre.org
Web: www.germantownjewishcentre.org

HAR ZION TEMPLE
1500 Hagys Ford Rd.
Penn Valley, PA 19072
Howard Griffel, Executive Director
Tel: (610) 667-5000 Fax: (610) 667-2032
Email: hzt@harziontemple.org
Web: www.harziontemple.org/harzion

KEHILAT HANAHAR
85 W. Mechanic St.
New Hope, PA 18938
Ed Tetelman, President
Tel: (215) 862-1912 Fax: (215) 862-6891
Email: khn@tradenet.net
Web: www.kehilathanahar.org

KESHER ISRAEL CONGREGATION
1000 Pottstown Pike
West Chester, PA 19380
Morrie Gold, President
Tel: (610) 696-7210 Fax: (610) 696-7107
Email: shalom@kesher-israel.org
Web: www.kesher-israel.org

KOREAN UNITED CHURCH OF PHILADELPHIA
Philadelphia, PA 19126-2116
Fax: (215) -0643
Email: kucp@kucp.org

KOREAN UNITED PRESBYTERIAN CHURCH OF PITTSBURGH
7600 Ross Park Dr.
Pittsburgh, PA 15237
Tel: (412) 369-9470
Email: pastor@pittsburgh-korean-church.org
Web: www.pittsburgh-korean-church.org

LEYV HA-IR, HEBREW FOR HEART OF THE CITY
P.O. Box 15836
Philadelphia, PA 19103
Joanne Perilstein, President
Tel: (215) 629-1995
Email: leyv-ha-ir@excite.com
Web: http://leyvhair.org

LOVE TRUTH CHINESE MENNONITE CHURCH
600 W. Chew Ave.
Philadelphia, PA 19120
Lemuel So, Pastor
Tel: (215) 924-2248 Fax: (215) 924-2248
Email: lemuelso@netscape.net

MAINE LINE REFORM TEMPLE
410 Montgomery Ave.
Wynnewood, PA 19096
Harry Goldberg, President
Tel: (610) 649-7800 Fax: (610) 642-6338
Email: info@mlrt.org
Web: www.mlrt.org

MESSIANIC JEWISH ALLIANCE OF AMERICA
P.O. Box 274
Springfield, PA 19064
Charles Kluge, President
Tel: (800) 225-6522 Fax: (610) 338-0471

Email: info@mjaa.org
Web: www.mjaa.org

MISHKAN SHALOM
4101 Freeland Ave.
Philadelphia, PA 19128
Jeff Sultar, Rabbi
Tel: (215) 508-0226 Fax: (215) 508-0932
Email: office@mishkan.org
Web: www.mishkan.org

OHEV SHALOM OF BUCKS COUNTY
944 2nd St. Pike
Richboro, PA 18954
Natalie Brooks, President
Tel: (215) 322-9595 Fax: (215) 322-8253
Email: ohev@ohev.org
Web: www.ohev.org

OLD YORK ROAD TEMPLE
971 Old York Rd.
Abington, PA 19001
Steve Pollock, President
Tel: (215) 886-8000 Fax: (215) 886-8320
Email: oyrtbetham@oyrtbetham.org
Web: www.oyrtbetham.org

PHILADELPHIA BUDDHIST ASSOCIATION
3741 Walnut St. PMB 512
Philadelphia, PA 19104
Tel: (610) 660-9269
Email: info@philabuddhistassoc.org
Web: www.philabuddhistassoc.org

PHILADELPHIA CAMBODIAN MENNONITE CHURCH
711-715 Snyder Ave.
Philadelphia, PA 19148
Tel: (610) 463-4677
Email: cindy_lay@netzero.net
Web: http://philadelphiacambodian.pa.us.
mennonite.net/

PHILADELPHIA KOREAN METHODIST CHURCH
1460 Limekiln Pike
Dresher, PA 19025
Young Shoon, English Ministry
Tel: (484) 716-4759
Web: www.pkmc.org

PITTSBURGH CHINESE CHURCH
8711 Old Perry Hwy.
Pittsburgh, PA 15237
Caleb Cheng, Board of Elders
Tel: (412) 366-9770 Fax: (412) 366-9771
Email: calebpc@comcast.net
Web: www.pghchinesechurch.org

REFORM CONGREGATION KENESETH ISRAEL
8339 Old York Rd.
Elkins Park, PA 19027
Janet Luterman, Director
Tel: (215) 887-8700 Fax: (215) 887-1070
Email: kifty@kenesethisrael.org
Web: www.kenesethisrael.org

SOCIETY HILL SYNAGOGUE
418 Spruce St.
Philadelphia, PA 19106
Lori Dafilou, Executive Director
Tel: (215) 922-6590 Fax: (215) 922-6599
Email: receptionist@societyhillsynagogue.org
Web: www.societyhillsynagogue.org

ST. GREGORY THE ILLUMINATOR ARMENIAN APOSTOLIC CHURCH
8701 Ridge Ave.
Philadelphia, PA 19128
Nerses Manoogian, Pastor
Tel: (215) 482-9200 Fax: (215) 482-7460
Email: stgregphil@aol.com
Web: www.saintgregory-phily.org

ST. MARKS' ARMENIAN CATHOLIC CHURCH
400 Haverford Rd.
Wynnewood, PA 19096

Rev. Armenag Bedrossain, Pastor
Tel: (610) 896-7789
Email: revabedrossian@yahoo.com
Web: www.smacc.org

SUBURBAN JEWISH COMMUNITY CENTER B'NAI AARON

560 Mill Rd.
Havertown, PA 19083
Lisa Malik, Rabbi
Tel: (610) 446-1967
Web: www.sjccba.org

TEMPLE BETH HILLEL-BETH EL

1001 Remington Rd.
Wynnewood, PA 19096
Ellen Moscow, President
Tel: (610) 649-5300 Fax: (610) 649-0948
Email: info@tbhbe.org
Web: www.tbhbe.org

TEMPLE BETH ISRAEL

2090 Hollywood Dr.
York, PA 17403
Leonard Berkowitz, President
Tel: (717) 843-2676 Fax: (717) 843-2676
Email: secretary@tbiyork.org
Web: www.tbiyork.org

TEMPLE BETH ZION-BETH ISRAEL

300 S. 18th St.
Philadelphia, PA 19103
Marianne Ruby Emmett, President
Tel: (215) 735-5148 Fax: (215) 735-7838
Email: president@bzbi.org
Web: www.bzbi.org

TEMPLE JUDEA OF BUCKS COUNTY

300 Swamp Rd.
Doylestown, PA 18901
Gary Pokras, Rabbi
Tel: (215) 348-5022 Fax: (215) 489-1188
Email: judea@templejudea.org
Web: www.templejudea.org

TEMPLE SHOLOM IN BROOMALL

55 N. Church Ln.
Broomall, PA 19008
David Berkowitz, President
Tel: (610) 356-5165 Fax: (610) 356-6713
Email: info@temple-sholom.org
Web: www.temple-sholom.org

TEMPLE SINAI

5505 Forbes Ave.
Pittsburgh, PA 15217
Rita L. Pollock, President
Tel: (412) 421-9715 Fax: (412) 421-8430
Email: office@templesinaipgh.org
Web: www.templesinaipgh.org

THE PHILADELPHIA MEDITATION CENTER, INC.

8 E. Eagle Rd.
Haverton, PA 19083
Email: phlmedctr@aol.com
Web: www.philadelphiameditation.org

TIBETAN BUDDHIST CENTER OF PHILADELPHIA

134 Heather Rd.
Upper Darby, PA 19082
Venerable Losang Samten, Spiritual Director
Email: tibetbc@yahoo.com
Web: www.libertynet.org/tibetan/

YOUNG ISRAEL OF ELKINS PARK

7715 Montgomery Ave.
Elkins, PA 19027
Edward MacConnell, President
Tel: (215) 635-3152
Email: president@yiep.org
Web: www.yiep.org

RESEARCH

JEWISH GENEALOGICAL SOCIETY OF GREATER PHILADELPHIA

P.O. Box 335
Exton, PA 19341-0335
Mark Halpern, President
Tel: (215) 918-0326 Fax: (610) 363-7956
Email: jgsgp@comcast.com
Web: www.jewishgen.org/jgsp/

SCIENTIFIC

AMERICAN COMMITTEE FOR THE WEIZMANN INSTITUTE OF SCIENCE

, PA
Judith B. Sherwood, Regional Chair
Tel: (202) 544-4757
Email: micky@acwis.org
Web: www.weizmann-usa.org

CHINESE AMERICAN CHEMICAL SOCIETY

2680 Monterey Dr.
Pittsburgh, PA 15241
Shiaw Tseng, President
Tel: (412) 854-6604 Fax: (412) 854-6613
Email: shiawtseng@yahoo.com

SPEC. INT., AIDS

AIDS SERVICES IN ASIAN COMMUNITIES

1201 Chestnut St. #501
Philadelphia, PA 19107
Ronald Sy, Executive Director
Tel: (215) 563-2424 Fax: (215) 563-1296
Email: info@asiac.org
Web: www.asiac.org

SPEC. INT., COUNSELING

JEWISH FAMILY AND CHILDREN'S SERVICES OF GREATER PHILADELPHIA

2100 Arch St., 5th Fl.
Philadelphia, PA 19103
Drew J. Staffenberg, President/CEO
Tel: (215) 496-9700 Fax: (215) 496-6622
Email: info@jfcsphil.org
Web: www.jfcsphil.org

JEWISH FAMILY AND CHILDREN'S SERVICES OF PITTSBURGH

5743 Bartlett St.
Pittsburgh, PA 15217
Tel: (412) 422-7200 Fax: (412) 422-9540
Email: info@jfcspgh.org
Web: www.jfcspgh.org

SPEC. INT., EDUCATION

AMERICAN INSTITUTE FOR PAKISTAN STUDIES

Department of Anthropology University of Pennsylvania Museum
3260 S. St. University of Pennsylvania
Philadelphia, PA 19104
Dr. Brian Spooner
Tel: (215) 746-0250 Fax: (215) 898-7462
Email: spooner@sas.upenn.edu
Web: www.pakistanstudies-aips.org

ASIAN AMERICAN STUDIES PROGRAM

University of Pennsylvania
166 McNeil Bldg.
Philadelphia, PA 19104-6299
Dr. Grace Kao, Director
Tel: (215) 898-1782 Fax: (215) 898-0988
Email: asam@ccat.sas.upenn.edu
Web: http://paachweb.vpul.upenn.edu/asamnew/

BOYS TOWN JERUSALEM FOUNDATION OF AMERICA, INC.

Mid-Atlantic Office
P.O. Box 745
Jenkintown, PA 19046
Henri Levitt, President

Tel: (800) 783-0947 Fax: (215) 887-1595
Email: phillybtj@nex-i.com
Web: www.boystownjerusalem.com

CENTER FOR THE ADVANCED STUDY OF INDIA

University of Pennsylvania
3600 Market St. #560
Philadelphia, PA 19104-2653
Francine R. Frankel, Director
Tel: (215) 898-6247 Fax: (215) 573-2595
Email: casi@sas.upenn.edu
Web: www.sas.upenn.edu/casi

COUNCIL OF INDIAN ORGANIZATIONS IN GREATER PHILADELPHIA

5901 Castor Ave.
Philadelphia, PA 19149
Suda Kartha, President
Tel: (215) 831-1095 Fax: (215) 831-1096
Email: sudakartha@aol.com
Web: www.ciophila.org

GRATZ COLLEGE

7605 Old York Rd.
Melrose Park, PA 19027
Jonathan Rosenbaum, Ph.D., President
Tel: (800) 475-4635 Fax: (215) 635-7320
Email: jrosenbaum@gratz.edu
Web: www.gratz.edu

JAPANESE LANGUAGE SCHOOL OF PHILADELPHIA

1445 City Line Ave.
Wynnewood, PA 19096
Tel: (610) 642-1202
Email: staff@jlsp.us
Web: www.jlsp.us/jsl/

JEWISH HERITAGE PROGRAMS

4032 Spruce St.
Philadelphia, PA 19104
Menachem Schmidt, Executive Director
Tel: (215) 222-9618
Email: jheritage@aol.com
Web: www.jhp.org

JEWISH THEOLOGICAL SEMINARY

Mid-Atlantic Region
261 Old York Rd. #617
Jenkintown, PA 19046
Rickey Goodman, Director
Tel: (215) 376-0474
Web: www.jtsa.edu

NATIONAL HAVURAH COMMITTEE

7135 Germantown Ave.
Philadelphia, PA 19119-1842
Sherry Israel, Vice President
Tel: (215) 248-1335 Fax: (215) 248-9760
Email: institute@havurah.org
Web: http://havurah.org

RECONSTRUCTIONIST RABBINICAL COLLEGE

1299 Church Rd.
Wyncote, PA 19095
Rabbi Dan Ehrenkrantz, President
Tel: (215) 576-0800 Fax: (215) 576-6143
Web: www.rrc.edu

YARDLEY CHINESE LANGUAGE SCHOOL

Newton Junior High School
116 Richboro Rd.
Newton, PA 18940
Chuan-Feng Shih, Principal
Tel: (215) 497-0864
Email: yclsmail@yahoo.com
Web: www.ycls.org

SPEC. INT., GAY&LESBIAN

ASIANS & FRIENDS-PITTSBURGH

P.O. Box 99191
Pittsburgh, PA 15233-4191
Paul Alarcon, President
Tel: (412) 521-5451 Fax: (412) 521-1368

Email: afpgh@hotmail.com
Web: www.afpgh.org

LONG YANG CLUB

Philadelphia
P.O. Box 475
Philadelphia, PA 19105
Ed Chen, President
Tel: (215) 339-1749
Email: philadelphia@longyangclub.org
Web: www.longyangclub.org/philadelphia/

SPEC. INT., HEALTH SERVICES

ASIAN AMERICAN HEALTH CARE NETWORK

Drexel University College of Medicine
2900 Queen Ln.
Philadelphia, PA 19129
Vincent Zarro, Faculty Advisor
Tel: (215) 991-8515
Email: zarro@drexel.edu

JEWISH HEALTHCARE FOUNDATION OF PITTSBURGH

650 Smithfield St. #2330
Pittsburgh, PA 15222
Karen Wolk Feinstein, President
Tel: (412) 594-2550 Fax: (412) 232-6240
Email: info@jhf.org
Web: www.jhf.org

SPEC. INT., HOUSING

JEWISH RESIDENTIAL SERVICES, INC.

5743 Bartlett St.
Pittsburgh, PA 15217
Tel: (412) 422-5560 Fax: (412) 422-5567
Email: info@jrspgh.org
Web: www.jrspgh.org

SPEC. INT., HUMAN RELATIONS

CAMBODIAN ASSOCIATION OF GREATER PHILADELPHIA

5412 N. 5th St.
Philadelphia, PA 19120
Cindy Suy, Executive Director
Tel: (215) 324-4070 Fax: (215) 324-2995
Email: cagp@cagp.org
Web: www.cambodianassociation.org

COUNCIL ON AMERICAN-ISLAMIC RELATIONS

Central Pennsylvania Chapter
P.O. Box 4516
Harrisburg, PA 11711
Saleh Malik, Director
Tel: (717) 730-4400
Email: samalik1@aol.com
Web: www.cair-net.org

JEWISH RECONSTRUCTIONIST FEDERATION

Central Office
7804 Montgomery Ave. #9
Elkins Park, PA 19027
Carl Sheingold, Executive Vice President
Tel: (215) 782-8500 Fax: (215) 782-8805
Email: info@jrf.org
Web: www.jrf.org

LEBANON AMERICAN RED CROSS

1220 Miflin St.
Lebanon, PA 17046
Dawn Vitez
Tel: (717) 273-2671 Fax: (717) 273-4201
Web: http://chapters.redcross.org/pa/lebanon

PAN ASIAN ASSOCIATION OF GREATER PHILADELPHIA

6705 Old York Rd.
Philadelphia, PA 19126
Jenny Shim, Manager
Tel: (215) 224-2000 Fax: (215) 224-8651
Email: info@jaisohn.org
Web: www.jaisohn.org

SOUTHEAST ASIAN MUTUAL ASSISTANCE ASSOCIATION COALITION, INC.
4601 Market St.
Philadelphia, PA 19139
Thim Prak, Office Manager
Tel: (215) 476-9640 Fax: (215) 471-8029
Email: trak@seamaac.org
Web: www.seamaac.org

THE AMERICAN JEWISH COMMITTEE
Philadelphia Chapter
42 S. 15th St. #1150
Philadelphia, PA 19102
Marc Shrier, President
Tel: (215) 665-2300 Fax: (215) 665-8737
Email: philadelphia@ajc.org
Web: www.ajc.org

Pittsburgh Chapter
2345 Murray Ave. #210
Pittsburgh, PA 15217
David Shtulman, Chapter Director
Tel: (412) 421-7927 Fax: (412) 421-7929
Email: pittsburgh@ajc.org
Web: www.ajc.org

SPEC. INT., IMMIGRATION

INDOCHINESE AMERICAN COUNCIL
4934-36 Old York Rd.
Philadelphia, PA 19141
Vuong Thuy, Executive Director
Tel: (215) 457-6666 Fax: (215) 457-0770

INTERNATIONAL SERVICE CENTER
21 S. River St.
Harrisburg, PA 17101
Truong Ngoc Phoung, Executive Director
Tel: (717) 236-9401 Fax: (717) 236-3821
Email: tnp@isc1976.com
Web: www.isc1976.com

SPEC. INT., INFORMATION REFERRAL

AMERICAN INSTITUTE FOR YEMENI STUDIES
P.O. Box 311
Ardmore, PA 19003-0311
Tel: (610) 896-5412 Fax: (610) 896-9049
Email: aiys@aiys.org
Web: www.aiys.org

SPEC. INT., LEGAL ASSISTANCE

JEWISH LABOR COMMITTEE
Philadelphia Chapter
1816 Chestnut St.
Philadelphia, PA 19103
Rosalind Spigel, Regional Director
Tel: (215) 587-6822 Fax: (215) 587-6823
Email: jlcras@aol.com
Web: www.jewishlabor.org

KOREAN AMERICAN LAWYERS' ASSOCIATION OF THE DELAWARE VALLEY
6625 Castor Ave.
Philadelphia, PA 19149
Kevin Kim, President
Tel: (215) 745-1768 Fax: (215) 745-1769
Email: kevinkimesquire@yahoo.com

SPEC. INT., SENIORS

CAMBODIAN AMERICAN SENIOR ASSOCIATION, INC.
1622 S. 7th St.
Philadelphia, PA 19148
Vanna Nguon, Outreach Worker
Tel: (215) 218-0585 Fax: (215) 218-0585

JEWISH ASSOCIATION ON AGING
200 JHF Dr.
Pittsburgh, PA 15217
Ed Szczypinski, Vice President
Tel: (412) 420-4000 Fax: (412) 521-0932

Email: eszczypinski@jaapgh.org
Web: www.jaapgh.org

SPEC. INT., SOCIAL INTEREST

ASIAN AMERICAN COUNCIL OF GREATER PHILADELPHIA
P.O. Box 29234
Philadelphia, PA 19125
Elias Dungca, President
Tel: (215) 634-6893

ASIAN AMERICAN FOUNDATION
1135 W. Cheltenham Ave. #2
Elkins Park, PA 19027
Tel: (215) 635-9052

ASIAN AMERICANS UNITED
Bok High School
1900 S. 8th St. #B3
Philadelphia, PA 19148
Ed Nakawatase, President
Tel: (215) 925-1538 Fax: (215) 925-1539
Email: aaunited@critpath.org

HMONG UNITED ASSOCIATION OF PENNSYLVANIA
4837 N. Mascher St.
Philadelphia, PA 19120
Shong Chai Hand
Tel: (215) 455-8490 Fax: (215) 455-8499
Email: hmongunaop@juno.com

INTERNATIONAL ASSOCIATION OF JEWISH VOCATIONAL SERVICES
1845 Walnut St. #640
Philadelphia, PA 19103
Genie Cohen, Executive Director
Tel: (215) 854-0233 Fax: (215) 854-0212
Email: coheng@iajvs.org
Web: www.iajvs.org

ISRAEL GUIDE DOG CENTER FOR THE BLIND
732 S. Settlers Cir.
Warrington, PA 18976
Tel: (267) 927-0205
Email: igdcb@nni.com
Web: www.israelguidedog.org

JAPAN AMERICA SOCIETY OF GREATER PHILADELPHIA
200 S. Broad St. #700
Philadelphia, PA 19102
Peter Sears, Board of Director/Co-Chair
Tel: (215) 790-3810 Fax: (215) 790-3805
Email: jasgp@philachamber.com
Web: www.jasgp.org

JAPAN AMERICA SOCIETY OF PENNSYLVANIA
600 Grant St. #444
Pittsburgh, PA 15219-2703
Tel: (412) 433-5021 Fax: (412) 433-5020
Email: jasp@us-japan.org
Web: www.us-japan.org

JAPANESE ASSOCIATION OF GREATER PHILADELPHIA
P.O. Box 31806
Philadelphia, PA 19104
Tel: (215) 840-4645
Email: info@jagphilly.org
Web: www.jagphilly.org

JEWISH COMMUNITY CENTER OF ALLENTOWN
702 N. 22nd St.
Allentown, PA 18104
Terry David Neff, Executive Director
Tel: (610) 435-3571 Fax: (610) 435-2859
Email: jccleadership@lvjcc.org
Web: www.allentownjcc.org

JEWISH COMMUNITY CENTER OF GREATER PHILADELPHIA
Central Office

401 S. Broad St.
Philadelphia, PA 19147
Judy Wortman, Site Director
Tel: (215) 545-4400 Fax: (215) 790-1040
Email: jwortman@phillyjcc.com
Web: www.phillyjcc.com

Jacob and Esther Stiffel Center
604 Porter St.
Philadelphia, PA 19148
Marcia Helfant, Site Director
Tel: (215) 468-3500 Fax: (215) 468-6767
Email: stiffel@phillyjcc.com
Web: www.phillyjcc.com

Kevy K. and Hortense M. Kaiserman Branch
45 Haverford Rd.
Wynnewood, PA 19096
Rabbi Marc Margolius, Site Director
Tel: (610) 896-7770 Fax: (610) 896-5808
Email: kaiserman@phillyjcc.com
Web: www.phillyjcc.com

Raymond and Miriam Klein Branch
10100 Jamison Ave.
Philadelphia, PA 19116
Gil August, Site Director
Tel: (215) 698-7300 Fax: (215) 673-7442
Email: info@phillyjcc.com
Web: www.phillyjcc.com

JEWISH COMMUNITY CENTER OF SCRANTON
601 Jefferson Ave.
Scranton, PA 18505
Ed Basan, Executive Director
Tel: (570) 346-6595
Email: mail@scrantonjcc.com
Web: www.scrantonjcc.com

JEWISH FAMILY SERVICE OF GREATER HARRISBURG
3333 N. Front St.
Harrisburg, PA 17110
Robert Caplan, President
Tel: (717) 233-1681 Fax: (717) 234-8258
Email: jfsofhbg@aol.com

JEWISH FAMILY SERVICE OF LACKAWANNA COUNTY
615 Jefferson Ave. #204
Scranton, PA 18510
Sheila J. Nudelman, Executive Director
Tel: (570) 344-1186
Email: jfsoflackawanna@aol.com
Web: www.jfednepa.org

JEWISH FAMILY SERVICE OF LANCASTER COUNTY
1120 Columbia Ave.
Lancaster, PA 17603
Phil Starr, CEO
Tel: (717) 293-1928 Fax: (717) 293-5070
Email: jfs-lncs@juno.com

JEWISH FAMILY SERVICE OF THE LEHIGH VALLEY
2004 Allen St.
Allentown, PA 18104
Phyllis Ringel, Executive Director
Tel: (610) 821-8722 Fax: (610) 821-8925
Email: info@jewishfamilyservice-lv.org
Web: www.jewishfamilyservice-lv.org

JEWISH FEDERATION OF GREATER PHILADELPHIA
2100 Arch St.
Philadelphia, PA 19103
Tel: (215) 832-0500 Fax: (215) 832-0510
Email: lyouman@phljnet.org
Web: www.jewishphilly.org

JEWISH FEDERATION OF NORTHEASTERN PENNSYLVANIA
601 Jefferson Ave.
Scranton, PA 18510
Mark Silverberg, Executive Director
Tel: (570) 961-2300 Fax: (570) 346-6147

Email: jfednepa@epix.net
Web: www.jfednepa.org

JEWISH MEMORIAL CENTER OF ALTOONA
1308 17th St.
Altoona, PA 16601
Sherry Thaler, Executive Director
Tel: (814) 944-4072 Fax: (814) 944-9874
Email: jmcalt@aol.com
Web: www.webalias.com/jmcalt

KOREAN AMERICAN ASSOCIATION OF GREATER PHILADELPHIA
6101 Rising-Sun Ave.
Philadelphia, PA 19111
Miho Chung, President
Tel: (215) 457-8343 Fax: (215) 827-2143
Email: koreanincphila@hotmail.com

KOREAN COMMUNITY DEVELOPMENT SERVICES CENTER
6055 N. 5th St.
Philadelphia, PA 19120
Jin Yu, President
Tel: (215) 276-8830 Fax: (215) 224-8150
Email: kcdsc@socky.com

READING JEWISH FEDERATION
1700 City Line St.
Reading, PA 19604
Tel: (610) 921-2766 Fax: (610) 929-1345
Email: stanr@epix.net
Web: www.readingjewishcommunity.com

SHEFA FUND
8459 Ridge Ave.
Philadelphia, PA 19128
Tel: (215) 483-4004
Email: info@shefafund.org
Web: www.shefafund.org

UNITED JEWISH COMMUNITY OF GREATER HARRISBURG
3301 N. Front St.
Harrisburg, PA 17110-1436
Tel: (717) 236-9555 Fax: (717) 236-8104
Email: communityreview@desupernet.net
Web: www.hbgjewishcommunity.com

UNITED JEWISH FEDERATION OF PITTSBURGH
234 McKee Pl.
Pittsburgh, PA 15213-3916
Tel: (412) 681-8000 Fax: (412) 681-3980
Email: information@ujf.org
Web: www.ujf.org

SPEC. INT., SOCIAL SERVICES

VIETNAMESE UNITED NATIONAL ASSOCIATION OF GREATER PHILADELPHIA
1033 S. 8th St.
Philadelphia, PA 19147
Loi Ma, Executive Director
Tel: (215) 923-3430 (h) Fax: (215) 293-4074
Email: loima@worldnet.att.net

SPEC. INT., SPORTS

INTERNATIONAL SHOTOKAN KARATE CLUB
East Coast
222 S. 45th St.
Philadelphia, PA 19104
Teruyuki Okazaki, Instructor
Tel: (215) 222-9382 Fax: (215) 222-7813
Email: pskc@iskf.com
Web: www.iskf.com

SPEC. INT., WOMEN

ASIAN AMERICAN WOMEN'S COALITION
301-305 N. 9th St.
Philadelphia, PA 19107
Tel: (215) 922-2156 Fax: (215) 922-7232
Web: www.homestead.com/aawc1/homepage.html

HADASSAH
Greater Philadelphia Chapter
1518 Walnut St. #1518
Philadelphia, PA 19102-3419
Lynn Gold-Benjamin, President
Tel: (215) 732-7100 Fax: (215) 732-7245
Email: barbara.nussbaum@hadassah.org
Web: www.hadassah.org

Greater Pittsburgh Chapter
1824 Murray Ave.
Pittsburgh, PA 15217
Susan Mazer, President
Tel: (412) 421-8919 Fax: (412) 421-0535
Email: sminkoff@hadassah.org
Web: www.hadassah.org

KOREAN AMERICAN WOMEN'S ASSOCIATION OF GREATER PHILADELPHIA
1135 W. Cheltenham Ave. #200
Melrose Park, PA 19027
Michealla Song, President
Tel: (215) 635-5158 Fax: (610) 353-5399
Email: ymshim8@hotmail.com

NATIONAL COUNCIL FOR JEWISH WOMEN
Pittsburgh Section
1620 Murray Ave.
Pittsburgh, PA 15217
Cynthia Busis, Executive Director
Tel: (412) 421-6118 Fax: (412) 421-1121
Email: info@ncjwpgh.org
Web: www.ncjwpgh.org

SPEC. INT., YOUTH

JEWISH CHILDREN'S FOLKSHUL
P.O. Box 25316
Philadelphia, PA 19119-5316
Mindy Blatt, Director
Tel: (215) 248-1550
Email: mblatt29@comcast.net
Web: www.folkshul.org

PITTSBURGH ASIAN AMERICAN YOUNG PROFESSIONAL ASSOCIATION
P.O. Box 2392
Pittsburgh, PA 15230
Joanne LaRose, President
Tel: (412) 355-6799
Email: info@paaypa.org
Web: www.paaypa.org

STUDENT ORGANIZATION

ASIAN STUDENTS ASSOCIATION
Carnegie Mellon University
University Ctr. Box 158
Pittsburgh, PA 15213
Ran Yi, President
Email: asa@andrew.cmu.edu
Web: www.andrew.cmu.edu

JAPANESE FRIENDSHIP ASSOCIATION
Pennsylvania State University
HUB/Robeson Cultural Ctr..
University Park, PA 16802
Kengo Nakamura, President
Email: kin100@psu.edu
Web: www.clubs.psu.edu/up/jfa

KOREAN STUDENT ASSOCIATION
University of Pennsylvania
3451 Walnut St.
Philadelphia, PA 19104
Gil Lee, President
Tel: (215) 898-5000
Email: gillee728@hotmail.com
Web: http://dolphin.upenn.edu/~ksagroup/

MUSLIM STUDENT ASSOCIATION
Temple University
Student Activities Ctr. #201
Philadelphia, PA 19122
Shahid Mohiuddin, President
Tel: (215) 204-2499

Email: shahidm@temple.edu
Web: www.temple.edu/msa

PAN-ASIAN AMERICAN COMMUNITY HOUSE
University of Pennsylvania
3601 Locust Walk
Philadelphia, PA 19104-6224
Dharma Naik, Director
Tel: (215) 746-6046 Fax: (215) 746-6047
Email: dnaik@pobox.upenn.edu
Web: www.vpul.upenn.edu/paach

PENN PAKISTAN SOCIETY
University of Pennsylvania
Meyerson Hall #B-1, 210 S. 34th St.
Philadelphia, PA 19104
Hasham Mehmood, President
Email: paksoc@dolphin.upenn.edu
Web: http://dolphin.upenn.edu/~paksoc

SINGAPORE STUDENTS' ASSOCIATION
Carnegie Mellon University
UC Mailbox 118, 5000 Forbes Ave.
Pittsburgh, PA 15213
Email: ssa@andrew.cmu.edu

TURKISH STUDENT ASSOCIATION
Penn State University Park
0810 Beaver Hall
University Park, PA 16802
Melike Etem, President
Tel: (814) 862-7866
Email: mxe181@psu.edu
Web: www.clubs.psu.edu/up/tsa

RHODE ISLAND

BUSINESS

JAPAN AMERICAN SOCIETY
28 Pelham St.
Newport, RI 02840
David Rosenberg, Festival Director
Tel: (401) 846-2720 Fax: (401) 846-5600
Web: www.blackshipsfestival.com

CULTURAL

RHODE ISLAND STATE ETHNIC HERITAGE COMMISSION
Chinese Subcommittee
134 High School Ave.
Cranston, RI 02910
Debra Leong, Chair
Tel: (401) 941-2497 Fax: (401) 941-2497
Web: www.rihphc.state.ri.us/

MULTI-PURPOSE

ASSOCIATION OF CHINESE AMERICANS
48 Blackstone Ave.
Pawtucket, RI 02860
Jonathan Yit, Director
Tel: (401) 722-6433 Fax: (401) 722-6433

RELIGIOUS

SAINTS SAHAG & MESROB ARMENIAN CHURCH
70 Jefferson St.
Providence, RI 02908
Hayr Simeon, Pastor
Tel: (401) 272-7712
Email: office@stsahmes.org
Web: www.stsahmes.org

TEMPLE BETH-EL
70 Orchard Ave.
Providence, RI 02906
Kenneth C. Kirsch, President
Tel: (401) 331-6070
Email: kkirsch@cox.net
Web: www.temple-beth-el.org

TEMPLE SINAI
30 Hagen Ave.
Cranston, RI 02920
Barry Rose, President
Tel: (401) 942-8350
Email: therosebud@cox.net
Web: www.templesinairi.org

WAT LAO BUDDHOVATH OF RHODE, ISLAND INC.
88 Limerock Rd.
Smithfield, RI 02917
Thongkhoun Pathana, President
Tel: (401) 232-7696 Fax: (978) 441-2878
Email: contact@watlaori.org
Web: www.watlaori.org

RESEARCH

ASIAN AMERICAN STUDIES/AMERICAN CIVILIZATION DEPARTMENT
Brown University
82 Waterman St.
Providence, RI 02912
Robert Lee, Professor
Tel: (401) 863-1693 Fax: (401) 863-1385
Email: robert_lee@brown.edu

SPEC. INT., HUMAN RELATIONS

HMONG UNITED ASSOCIATION
340 Lockwood St.
Providence, RI 02907
Sue Khang, Executive Director
Tel: (401) 455-0847 Fax: (401) 621-5631
Email: huari@huari.org
Web: www.huari.org

SPEC. INT., SENIORS

JEWISH SENIOR AGENCY OF RHODE ISLAND
229 Waterman St.
Providence, RI 02906
Susette Rabinowitz, Executive Director
Tel: (401) 351-4750 Fax: (401) 421-4905
Email: srabinowitz@jsari.org
Web: www.jsari.org

SPEC. INT., SOCIAL INTEREST

H.O.P.E. FOUNDATION INTERNATIONAL
162 E. Hilldrive
Cranston, RI 02920
Aramando Heredia, President
Tel: (401) 848-0622
Email: admin@hope-foundation.org
Web: www.hope-foundation.org

JEWISH FEDERATION OF RHODE ISLAND
130 Sessions St.
Providence, RI 02906-3497
Janet Engelhart, Executive Vice President
Tel: (401) 421-4111 Fax: (401) 331-7961
Email: shalom@jfri.org
Web: www.jfri.org

SOCIO ECONOMIC DEVELOPMENT CENTER FOR SOUTHEAST ASIANS
Main Office
270 Elmwood Ave.
Providence, RI 02907
Joseph R. Le, Executive Director
Tel: (401) 274-8811 Fax: (401) 274-8877

SPEC. INT., WOMEN

HADASSAH
Western New England Region
911 Pontiac Ave.
Cranston, RI 02920
Lorraine Rappoport, President
Tel: (401) 461-4480 Fax: (401) 461-4482
Email: wner@hadassah.org
Web: www.hadassah.org

STUDENT ORGANIZATION

ARMENIAN STUDENTS' ASSOCIATION OF AMERICA, INC.
National
333 Atlantic Ave.
Warwick, RI 02888
Tel: (401) 461-6114
Email: asa@asainc.org
Web: www.asainc.org

ASIAN AMERICAN STUDENTS ASSOCIATION
Brown University
P.O. Box 1930
Providence, RI 02912
Harold Lee, President
Email: juhyung_lee@brown.edu
Web: www.brown.edu/students/ssian_
american_students_association

BROWN TAIWAN SOCIETY
Brown University
Providence, RI 02912
Will Leung, Co-chair
Tel: (401) 863-1000
Email: taiwan@brown.edu
Web: http://students.brown.edu/bts/

KOREAN AMERICAN STUDENTS ASSOCIATION
Brown University
75 Waterman St.
Providence, RI 02912
Christine Chung, President
Tel: (401) 863-2341
Email: contact@brownkasa.com
Web: www.brownkasa.com

SOUTH CAROLINA

BUSINESS

INTERNATIONAL ENTERPRISE SINGAPORE
Charleston Office
2412 High Hammock Rd.
Seabrook Island, SC 29455
Stephen D. Ward, Honorary Business
Representative
Tel: (843) 768-4212 Fax: (843) 768-0179
Email: enquiry@iesingapore.gov.sg
Web: www.iesingapore.gov.sg

CULTURAL

FILIPINO AMERICAN ASSOCIATION OF GREATER COLUMBIA, SOUTH CAROLINA
P.O. Box 24112
Columbia, SC 29224
Peter Liunoras, President
Tel: (803) 699-1214
Email: faagc@hotmail.com
Web: www.filamsc.org

MULTI-PURPOSE

CAMBODIAN ASSOCIATION OF SOUTH CAROLINA
231 Norris Rd.
Spartanburg, SC 29303
Ching Mang, Vice Chairperson
Tel: (864) 439-3487

RELIGIOUS

CAROLINA KOREAN PRESBYTERIAN CHURCH
1712 Barbara Dr.
Columbia, SC 29223
Jae S. Choi, Pastor
Tel: (803) 788-5570
Email: myi@sc.edu
Web: www.midnet.sc.edu/ckpc/

KAHAL KADOSH BETH ELOHIM
90 Hasell St.
Charleston, SC 29401
Anthony David Holz, Rabbi
Tel: (843) 723-1090 Fax: (843) 723-0537
Email: office@kkbe.org
Web: www.kkbe.org

SPEC. INT., EDUCATION

US CHINA PEOPLES FRIENDSHIP ASSOCIATION
Charleston Chapter
18 Arabian Dr.
Charleston, SC 29407-9678
Violetta Czepowicz
Web: www.uscpfa.org

SPEC. INT., HUMAN RELATIONS

COUNCIL ON AMERICAN-ISLAMIC RELATIONS
South Carolina Chapter
221 Rolling Roch Rd.
Columbia, SC 29212
Minhaj Arastu, Chairman
Tel: (803) 750-1236
Email: cair-sc@cair-net.org
Web: www.cair-net.org

SPEC. INT., IMMIGRATION

SOUTH CAROLINA REFUGEE RESETTLEMENT PROGRAM
South Carolina Department of Social Services
P.O. Box 1520
Columbia, SC 29202-1520
Phane Phomsavanh, State Coordinator
Tel: (803) 737-9241 Fax: (803) 737-9296
Email: askdss@dss.state.sc.us
Web: www.state.sc.us/dss/

SPEC. INT., SOCIAL INTEREST

CHARLESTON JEWISH FEDERATION
P.O. Box 31298
Charleston, SC 29417
Tel: (843) 571-6565 Fax: (843) 556-6206
Email: ellenk@jewishcharleston.org
Web: www.jewishcharleston.org

COLUMBIA JEWISH FEDERATION
4540 Trenholm Rd.
Columbia, SC 29260
Frank Lourie, President
Tel: (803) 787-2023 Fax: (803) 787-0475
Email: info@jewishcolumbia.org
Web: www.jewishcolumbia.org

FILIPINO COMMUNITY CENTER
Charleston South Carolina
P.O. Box 1271
Goose Creek, SC 29445
Regina Veloso, President
Email: filipinocommunitycenter@yahoo.com
Web: http://filipinocommunitycenter.org

THE INDIAN-AMERICAN ASSOCIATION OF SOUTH CAROLINA
P.O. Box 25739
Columbia, SC 29224-5739
Web: www.indiausa-sc.org

SPEC. INT., YOUTH

NATIONAL CENTER FOR MISSING & EXPLOITED CHILDREN
South Carolina
2008 Marion St. #I
Columbia, SC 29201-2151
Tel: (803) 254-2326 Fax: (803) 254-4299
Web: www.missingkids.com

THE CHILDREN'S DEFENSE FUND
117 Cheraw St.
Bennettsville, SC 29512
Robin Sally, Director
Tel: (843) 479-5310 Fax: (843) 479-0605
Email: cdfinfo@childrensdefense.org
Web: www.childrensdefense.org

SOUTH DAKOTA

SPEC. INT., SPORTS

INTERNATIONAL SHOTOKAN KARATE CLUB
North Central
805 Bayberry Cir.
Sioux Falls, SD 57108
Lee Doohen, Instructor
Tel: (605) 332-6572
Email: sfshotokan@sio.midco.net
Web: www.iskf.com

STUDENT ORGANIZATION

CHINESE STUDENTS AND SCHOLARS ASSOCIATION
South Dakota School of Mines and Technology
501 E. Saint Joseph St.
Rapid City, SD 57701
Li Ping, Executive Officer
Email: ping.li@gold.sdsmt.edu
Web: www.sdsmt.edu/student-orgs/csa/

TENNESSEE

CULTURAL

LEUVA PATIDAR SAMAJ OF USA
716 Sweetwater Cir.
Old Hickory, TN 37138
Ramanbhai V. Patel, President
Tel: (615) 391-4577 Fax: (615) 391-4578
Email: info@leuvapatidarsamaj.com
Web: www.leuvapatidarsamaj.com

TAIWANESE ASSOCIATION OF AMERICA
712 Gracewood Way
Knoxville, TN 37922
Dr. Henry Hsu, President
Tel: (865) 966-2965
Email: hueyhsu@aol.com

MULTI-PURPOSE

ASIAN AMERICAN ORGANIZATION
4333 Park Forest Dr.
Memphis, TN 38141
Dr. N.K. Lakshmanan, Chairman
Tel: (901) 363-4105 Fax: (901) 761-2616

EAST TENNESSEE CHINESE ASSOCIATION
Guan Bo, Member
Email: etca@kornet.org
Web: www.kornet.org/etca/

POLITICAL ACTION

ORGANIZATION OF CHINESE AMERICANS
East Tennessee Chapter
Jack Kam, President
Web: www.kornet.org/oca-et

PROFESSIONAL

AMERICAN ASSOCIATION OF THE PHYSICIANS OF INDIAN ORIGIN
6918 Shallowford Rd. #200
Chattanooga, TN 37421
Vijaya L. Appareddy, Chairwoman
Tel: (423) 499-6165 Fax: (423) 499-0693
Email: appareddyvh@ramtec.com
Web: www.aapiusa.org

RELIGIOUS

ASIA INTERIOR MISSION
P.O. Box 21449
Chattanooga, TN 37424
Tel: (423) 313-2523
Email: asiainterior@aol.com
Web: www.asiainterior.org

KOREAN BAPTIST CHURCH OF MEMPHIS
9650 E. Shelby Dr.
Collierville, TN 38017
Jacob Park, Youth Pastor
Tel: (901) 755-5737
Email: jacob_park@koreanbaptist.org
Web: www.koreanbaptist.org

KOREAN UNITY BAPTIST CHURCH OF NASHVILLE
240 Tusculum Rd.
Antioch, TN 37013
Rev. Haeng Bo Lee, Senior Pastor
Tel: (615) 781-4949 Fax: (615) 781-9010
Email: pastor@koreanunity.org
Web: http://koreanunity.org

SPEC. INT., EDUCATION

ASIAN STUDIES AT UNIVERSITY OF TENNESSEE
1015 Volunteer Blvd.
Knoxville, TN 37996
Miriam Levering, Chair
Tel: (423) 974-6979
Email: mleverin@utk.edu
Web: www.utk.edu/~asc/

US CHINA PEOPLES FRIENDSHIP ASSOCIATION
Chattanooga Chapter
#12 N. Lynncrest Dr.
Chattanooga, TN 37411
Bob (Chang) Edwards
Tel: (423) 698-7339
Web: www.uscpfa.org

Memphis Chapter
2024 Old Lake Pike
Memphis, TN 38119-5518
Ann Freeman
Tel: (901) 754-0049
Web: www.uscpfa.org

Nashville Chapter
496 Ellenwood Dr.
Nashville, TN 37211
Barbara Cobb
Tel: (615) 833-9512 Fax: (615) 833-9512
Web: www.uscpfa.org

SPEC. INT., HUMAN RELATIONS

INDIA ASSOCIATION OF NASHVILLE
P.O. Box 22811
Nashville, TN 37202
Chander Kanal, President
Tel: Fax: (615) 794-8714
Email: primetec@comcast.net
Web:

THE CHILDREN'S DEFENSE FUND
Haley Farm, P.O. Box 840
Clinton, TN 37717-0840
Tel: (865) 457-6466 Fax: (865) 457-6464
Email: cdfhaley@childrensdefense.org
Web: www.haleyfarm.org

SPEC. INT., SOCIAL INTEREST

JAPAN AMERICA SOCIETY OF TENNESSEE
P.O. Box 190476
Nashville, TN 37219
Tel: (615) 532-8901 Fax: (615) 741-5829
Email: jastninfo@jastn.com
Web: www.jastn.com

JEWISH COMMUNITY FEDERATION OF GREATER CHATTANOOGA
P.O. Box 8947
Chattanooga, TN 37414
Stuart Bush, President
Tel: (423) 493-0270 Fax: (423) 493-9997
Email: president@jcfgc.org
Web: www.jcfgc.com

JEWISH FAMILY SERVICE OF NASHVILLE AND MIDDLE TENNESSEE, INC.
801 Percy Warner Blvd. #103
Nashville, TN 37205
Tel: (615) 356-4234 Fax: (615) 353-2652
Email: jfs@jfsnashville.org
Web: www.jfsnashville.org

KNOXVILLE JEWISH ALLIANCE
6800 Deane Hill Dr.
Knoxville, TN 37919
Marilyn Liberman, President
Tel: (865) 690-6343 Fax: (865) 694-4861
Email: kja@jewishknoxville.org
Web: www.jewishknoxville.org

MEMPHIS JEWISH FEDERATION
6560 Poplar Ave.
Germantown, TN 38138
Jeffrey Feld, Executive Director
Tel: (901) 767-7100 Fax: (901) 767-7128
Email: jfeld@memjfed.org
Web: www.korrnet.org/mjf

NORTH AMERICAN BANGLADESHI ISLAMIC COMMUNITY
P.O. Box 6631
Oak Ridge, TN 37831
Dr. Abu Bakar Ahmed, Executive Secretary
Tel: (465) 483-8189
Email: nabic-info@globalfront.com

SPEC. INT., VOLUNTARY SERVICE

PHILIPPINE OUTREACH
The Hope Foundation of America, Inc.
6576 E. Brainerd Rd. #201
P.O. Box 21449
Chattanooga, TN 37424
Ricky Fowler, Founder
Tel: (423) 893-5481 Fax: (423) 893-8097
Email: hope@thehopefoundation.com
Web: www.thehopefoundation.com/philippine_outreach.asp

SPEC. INT., WOMEN

NATIONAL COUNCIL FOR JEWISH WOMEN
Memphis Section
P.O. Box 17921
Memphis, TN 38187-0921
Email: info@ncjwmemphis.org
Web: www.ncjwmemphis.org

STUDENT ORGANIZATION

MUSLIM STUDENTS ASSOCIATION
Middle Tennessee State University
1301 E. Main St. Box #603
Murfreesboro, TN 37132
Zaid Altalib, President
Email: msa@mtsu.edu
Web: http://mtsu.edu/~msa

TEXAS

ARTISTIC

INDIAN CLASSICAL MUSIC CIRCLE OF AUSTIN
11958 Dorsett Rd.
Austin, TX 78727
Ramdas Sunder, President
Tel: (512) 448-6740
Email: ramdas@icmca.org
Web: www.icmca.org

BUSINESS

GREATER HOUSTON PARTNERSHIP
1200 Smith #700
Houston, TX 77002-4400
Jim C. Kollaer, President/CEO
Tel: (713) 844-3600 Fax: (713) 844-0200
Email: ghp@houston.org
Web: www.houston.org

JAPAN EXTERNAL TRADE ORGANIZATION
Houston Chapter
1221 McKinney St. #4141
Houston, TX 77010
Hitoshi Hasegawa, Chief Executive Director
Tel: (713) 759-9595 Fax: (713) 759-9210
Web: www.jetro.org

CHAMBER OF COMMERCE

ALL ASIAN AMERICAN CHAMBER OF COMMERCE
Headquarters
P.O. Box 37241
Haltom City, TX 76117
Judy Wang
Tel: (817) 475-4783 Fax: (817) 485-1061
Email: aaachamber@yahoo.com
Web: www.aaachamber.com

ASIAN CHAMBER OF COMMERCE
8557 Research Blvd. #140
Austin, TX 78758
Mai Nguyen, Executive Director
Tel: (512) 302-0016 Fax: (512) 302-4184
Email: mai@austinasianchamber.org

7457 Harwin Dr., Plaza II #146
Houston, TX 77036
Elsie Huang, President
Tel: (713) 782-7222 Fax: (713) 782-8676
Email: elsiehuang@asianchamber-hou.org
Web: www.asianchamber-hou.org

AUSTIN ASIAN CHAMBER OF COMMERCE
8557 Research Blvd. #140
Austin, TX 78758
Mai Nguyen, Executive Director
Tel: (512) 873-8288 Fax: (512) 873-8228
Email: mai@austinasianchamber.org
Web: www.austinasianchamber.org

GREATER DALLAS ASIAN AMERICAN CHAMBER OF COMMERCE
11171 Harry Hines Blvd. #115
Dallas, TX 75229
Les Tanaka, Executive Director
Tel: (972) 241-8250 Fax: (972) 241-8270
Email: info@gdaacc.com
Web: www.gdaacc.com

GREATER DALLAS KOREAN AMERICAN CHAMBER OF COMMERCE
11441 N. Stemmons Fwy. #219
Dallas, TX 75229
Sook Hee Jung, President
Tel: (972) 488-2224 Fax: (978) 488-2226
Email: gdkacc@yahoo.com
Web: www.koreanchamber.org

HOUSTON ASIAN JUNIOR CHAMBER OF COMMERCE
P.O. Box 42610
Houston, TX 77242-2610
Christine Tran, President
Tel: (713) 219-1632
Email: christine.tran@jpmchase.com
Web: www.hajcc.org

INDO-AMERICAN CHAMBER OF COMMERCE OF GREATER HOUSTON
1535 W. Loop South #200
Houston, TX 77027
Deepa Thakur, President
Tel: (713) 624-7131 Fax: (713) 624-7132
Email: info@iaccgh.com
Web: www.iaccgh.com

NATIONAL US-ARAB CHAMBER OF COMMERCE
Houston Office
1330 Post Oak Blvd. #1600
Houston, TX 77056
Rand Zalzala
Tel: (713) 963-4620 Fax: (713) 963-4609
Email: nusacc@aol.com
Web: www.nusacc.org

PAN AMERICAN CHAMBER OF COMMERCE
97400 Harwin Dr. #262
Houston, TX 77036
Tasleem Siediqui, Senior VP
Tel: (281) 236-7597 Fax: (713) 914-0906
Email: pakchamber@aol.com

TAIWANESE CHAMBER OF COMMERCE
4005 Manchaca Rd. #118
Austin, TX 78704
Lisa Lin, Chairperson
Tel: (512) 707-8898 Fax: (512) 707-8866
Email: lisalin@texastcn.edu

TAIWANESE CHAMBER OF COMMERCE OF ARLINGTON
711 Linda Vista Ave.
Arlington, TX 76013
Alex Lin, President
Tel: (817) 860-4228 Fax: (817) 276-9110
Email: lindavista@aol.com

TAIWANESE CHAMBER OF COMMERCE OF GREATER HOUSTON
P.O. Box 772881
Houston, TX 77215
Jackson Chang, Chairperson
Tel: (713) 965-9060 Fax: (713) 965-9069

TAIWANESE CHAMBER OF COMMERCE OF SAN ANTONIO
900 N. Main Ave.
San Antonio, TX 78212
James C. Hu, Chairperson
Tel: (210) 223-2951 Fax: (210) 223-9064
Web:

TARRANT COUNTY ASIAN AMERICAN CHAMBER OF COMMERCE
711 Houston St.
Ft. Worth, TX 76102
Tel: (817) 212-2690 Fax: (817) 212-2697
Web: http://members.tripod.com/~xirnet/Commerce/main.html

TEXAS ASIAN CHAMBER OF COMMERCE
8222 Jamestown Dr. #A-113
Austin, TX 78758
Clyde Prestwood, Jr., Executive Director
Tel: (512) 420-8777 Fax: (512) 339-4600
Email: tacc@txasianchamber.org
Web: www.txasianchamber.org

THAI AMERICAN CHAMBER OF COMMERCE
P.O. Box 681277
Houston, TX 77268-1277
Pat S. Charnveja, President
Tel: (281) 477-8803 Fax: (281) 970-5070
Email: tacc@thaiamcc.org
Web: www.thaiamcc.org

US PAN ASIAN AMERICAN CHAMBER OF COMMERCE
Southwest Chapter
505 E. Border St.
Arlington, TX 76010
Grace McDermott, Chapter President
Tel: (817) 543-4299 Fax: (817) 261-7389
Web: www.uspaacc.com

VIETNAMESE AMERICAN CHAMBER OF COMMERCE
2924 Milam St.
Houston, TX 77006
Hal N. Nguyen, Chair
Tel: (713) 526-8368 Fax: (713) 520-7633
Email: ls_hnnguyen@yahoo.com

CULTURAL

ACADEMY OF BANGLA ARTS AND CULTURE
3333 N. MacArthur Blvd. #300
Irving, TX 75062
Tariq Yasin Uzzal, President
Tel: (214) 770-4273
Email: info@abac-usa.org
Web: www.abac-usa.org

AMERICAN TURKISH ASSOCIATION OF HOUSTON
P.O. Box 61002
Houston, TX 77208
Tanju Obut, President
Email: president@atahouston.org
Web: www.atahouston.org

ASIAN AMERICAN CULTURAL CENTER
11713 Jollyville Rd.
Austin, TX 78759
Tel: (512) 336-5069 Fax: (512) 336-5075
Web: www.asianamericancc.org

ASIAN CULTURES MUSEUM
1809 N. Chaparral St.
Corpus Christi, TX 78401
Catherine LaCroix, Executive Director
Tel: (361) 882-2641 Fax: (361) 882-5718
Email: asianculturalmuseum@sbc.global.net
Web: www.geocities.com/asiancm

ASIAN FESTIVAL
801 S. Bowie
San Antonio, TX 78205
Diana Smith, Coordinator
Tel: (210) 458-2227 Fax: (210) 458-2218
Email: diana.smith@utsa.edu

ASIAN PACIFIC AMERICAN HERITAGE ASSOCIATION
6220 Westpark #245-B
Houston, TX 77057
Munir Ibrahim, President
Tel: (713) 784-1112 Fax: (832) 201-8228
Email: apaha@apaha.org
Web: www.apaha.org

BANGLADESH AMERICAN CENTER
13415 Renn Rd.
Houston, TX 77083
Azadul Haq, Center Director
Email: azadul_haq@kindermorgan.com
Web: www.bangladesh-association.com/bac

CHINESE CULTURAL CENTER
10303 W. Office Dr.
Houston, TX 77042
Shu-Ling Lee, Director
Tel: (713) 789-4995 Fax: (713) 789-4755
Email: hccc@houstanocac.org
Web: www.ocac.gov.tw/houston

DALLAS-FORT WORTH MAHARASHTRA MANDAL
17616 Squaw Valley Dr.
Dallas, TX 75252-5756
Sanjay Date, President
Tel: (972) 735-9357 Fax: (972) 391-4148
Email: committiee@dfwmm.org
Web: www.dfwmm.org

HOUSTON TAIPEI SOCIETY, INC.
4041 Richmond Ave. #200
Houston, TX 77027
Jackson Chang, Vice President
Tel: (713) 965-9060 Fax: (713) 965-9069
Email: pjwd1@aol.com

INDIA ASSOCIATION OF NORTH TEXAS
777 S. Central Expwy. #7C
Richardson, TX 75080
Shabnam Modgil, President
Tel: (972) 234-4268 Fax: (972) 234-4262
Email: info@iant.org
Web: www.iant.org

INDIA COMMUNITY CENTER OF AUSTIN
P.O. Box 27891
Austin, TX 78755
Debasree Dasgupta, Board Member
Tel: (512) 349-0403
Email: sdasgupta@austin.rr.com
Web: www.iccaustin.org

INDO-AMERICAN ASSOCIATION
3722 Latma Dr.
Houston, TX 77025
Hari Dayal, President
Tel: (281) 648-0422 Fax: (281) 648-2490
Email: info@iaahouston.com
Web: www.iaahouston.com

INSTITUTE OF CHINESE CULTURE
10550 Westoffice
Houston, TX 77042
Tel: (713) 339-1992
Email: info@icc-houston.org
Web: www.icc-houston.org

INTERNATIONAL NETSUKE SOCIETY
P.O. Box 833272
Richardson, TX 75083-3272
Tel: (972) 596-8250 Fax: (972) 866-9946
Web: www.netsuke.org

IRANIAN ISLAMIC AND CULTURAL FOUNDATION
2620 Tanglewilde
Houston, TX 77063
Tel: (713) 952-4726 Fax: (713) 977-5868
Email: bonyad@persianvillage.com

KOREAN WAR PROJECT
P.O. Box 180190
Dallas, TX 75218-0190
Hal Barker, Director
Tel: (214) 320-0342
Email: hbarker@kwp.org
Web: www.koreanwar.org

KOREAN WAR VETERANS ASSOCIATION
Lone Star Chapter
P.O. Box 802541
Houston, TX 77280-2541
Charlie Ehrlund, President
Tel: (713) 774-3662 Fax: (713) 774-3662
Email: webmaster@kwvahouston.com
Web: www.kwvahouston.org

LAO AMERICAN ASSOCIATION
1023 Castolan Dr.
Houston, TX 77038
Pon Chantharag, President
Tel: (281) 931-7394 Fax: (281) 447-7771

NEPALESE ASSOCIATION OF HOUSTON
Houston, TX
Rajendra Shrestha, President
Tel: (281) 376-6382
Email: rajshrestha01@hotmail.com
Web: www.houstonnepalese.org

PAKISTAN ASSOCIATION OF GREATER HOUSTON
9644 S. Kirkwood Rd.
Houston, TX 77099
Ghulam Bombaywala, President
Tel: (281) 933-0786
Email: pagh@sbcglobal.net

PAKISTAN SOCIETY OF NORTH TEXAS
P.O. Box 151863
Arlington, TX 76015
Dr. Raiz Haider, President
Email: rhaider@psntonline.com
Web: www.psntonline.com

TAIWANESE ASSOCIATION OF AMERICA
Dallas-Fort Worth Chapter
P.O. Box 110402
Carrollton, TX 75011-0402
George Yeh, President
Email: taa_dfw@yahoo.com
Web: www.taadfw.org

TAIWANESE HERITAGE SOCIETY OF HOUSTON
5885 Point West
Houston, TX 77036
Zen-Yu Chang, Chairman
Tel: (713) 271-5885
Web: www.houston-taiwanese.org

TEXAS TAIWAN CULTURE AND HERITAGE ASSOCIATION OF HOUSTON
5885 Point W.
Houston, TX 77036
Linda Wu, Chairman
Tel: (713) 271-5885 Fax: (713) 271-9229
Web: www.houston-taiwanese.org

THAI ARTS AND CULTURE OF HOUSTON
P.O. Box 681277
Houston, TX 77268-1277
Pat S. Charnveja, President
Tel: (713) 530-2486 Fax: (281) 893-9562
Email: prapatip@att.net

THE ARAB AMERICAN CULTURAL & COMMUNITY CENTER
10555 Stancliff Rd.
Houston, TX 77099
Tel: (832) 351-3366 Fax: (832) 351-3378
Email: acc-houston@ev1.net
Web: www.acc-houston.com

TURKISH AMERICAN ASSOCIATION OF NORTHERN TEXAS
P.O. Box 802995
Dallas, TX 75380
Aylin Gomez, President
Email: turant@turant.org
Web: www.turant.org

TURKISH AMERICAN ASSOCIATION OF SAN ANTONIO
P.O. Box 780523
San Antonio, TX 78278
Muge Wilson, President
Tel: (210) 764-8100
Email: cimenr@juno.com
Web: www.taa-sa.org

VIETNAMESE CULTURE & SCIENCE ASSOCIATION
Austin Chapter
P.O. Box 80802
Austin, TX 78708
Tel: (512) 670-5056
Web: vcsa_austin@yahoo.com

Houston Chapter
P.O. Box 741301
Houston, TX 77274
Nguyen P. Anhlan, President
Tel: (713) 406-3030 Fax: (281) 847-4264
Web: vhkh@vhkhvn.org

ENTERTAINMENT

SAN ANTONIO DANCE UMBRELLA
P.O. Box 830634
San Antonio, TX 78283
Rene'e Park, President
Tel: (210) 212-7775 Fax: (210) 212-9087
Email: sadu@sadu.org
Web: www.sadu.org

LAW ENFORCEMENT

LAW ENFORCEMENT ASSOCIATION OF ASIAN PACIFICS
P.O. Box 131672
Houston, TX 77219
Dennis Domagas, President
Web: www.napoa.org

MULTI-PURPOSE

AUSTIN-OITA SISTER CITY COMMITTEE
c/o Tokyo Electron America, Inc., 2400 Grove Blvd.
Austin, TX 78741
Zoltan Papp, Chairperson
Tel: (512) 292-6335
Email: zpapp@aus.telusa.com
Web: http://austinoita.tripod.com

DALLAS-FORT WORTH ASIAN-AMERICAN CITIZENS COUNCIL
4530 W. Buckingham Rd.
Garland, TX 75042
Dr. Keh-Shew Lu, Founding Chair
Email: info@dfwaacc.org
Web: www.dfwaacc.org

PHILIPPINE-AMERICAN SOCIETY OF AUSTIN
P.O. Box 270048
Austin, TX 78727-0048
Jimmy Boado, President
Email: pasatexas@yahoo.com
Web: www.pasa-tx.com

POLITICAL ACTION

80-20 INITIATIVE
Houston Chapter
8300 Bender Rd.
Houston, TX 77396
Rogene Gee Calvert, President
Tel: (713) 247-2013
Email: rgcalvert@earthlink.net
Web: www.80-20initiative.net

AMERICAN-ARAB ANTI-DISCRIMINATION COMMITTEE
Houston Chapter
P.O. Box 542000
Houston, TX 77254-2000
Tel: (713) 532-4232 Fax: (713) 532-4232
Email: email@adchouston.org
Web: www.adchouston.org

MUSLIM PUBLIC AFFAIRS COUNCIL
MPAC Houston
P.O. Box 6778
Houston, TX 77265
Hannah Hawk, Spokesperson
Tel: (713) 797-6722 Fax: (713) 665-2660
Email: mpachouston@mpac.org
Web: www.mpac.org

ORGANIZATION OF CHINESE AMERICANS-DALLAS/FT.WORTH
P.O. Box 1281
Rockwall, TX 75087
Susan Lu, President
Tel: (972) 772-3883
Email: info@ocadfw.org
Web: www.ocadfw.org

PROFESSIONAL

AMERICAN ASSOCIATION OF BANGLADESHI ENGINEERS AND ARCHITECTS-NORTH TEXAS
North Texas Chapter
, TX
Kem M. Rahman, President
Email: kemrahman@yahoo.com
Web: www.aabea.org/chapters/north_texas.php

ASIAN AMERICAN JOURNALISTS ASSOCIATION
Texas
508 Young St.
Dallas, TX 75202
Maricar Estrella, President
Tel: (214) 977-8635 Fax: (214) 977-8321
Email: maricar@star-telegram.com
Web: www.aaja.org

ASIAN AMERICAN PROFESSIONALS OF DALLAS
13237 Montford Rd. #417
Dallas, TX 75380
Justin Hung, President
Tel: (972) 378-3070 Fax: (972) 378-3070
Email: pa2@pa2.org

ASSOCIATION OF CHINESE AMERICAN PROFESSIONALS
10303 Westoffice Dr., Box #194
Houston, TX 77042
Michael Liu, President
Tel: (281) 491-4770 Fax: (281) 491-0772
Web: www.acaphouston.org

ASSOCIATION OF CHINESE PROFESSIONALS/DFW
ACP-Dallas Fort Worth
P.O. Box 832865
Richardson, TX 75083
Detian Cao (Bill)
Fax: (972) 692-7607
Email: acpdfw@hotmail.com
Web: www.acpdfw.org

ASSOCIATION OF IRANIAN PROFESSIONALS OF AUSTIN
P.O. Box 90218
Austin, TX 78709-0218
Esmaeil Talle, President
Email: info@aipa.net
Web: www.aipa.net

ASSOCIATION OF SCIENTISTS OF INDIAN ORIGIN IN AMERICA, INC.
7703 Floyd Curl Dr.
San Antonio, TX 78229-3900
Pudur Jagadeeswaran, President
Tel: (210) 567-3848 Fax: (210) 567-3803
Email: jagadeeswar@uthscsa.edu
Web: www.asioa.com

AUSTIN SOCIETY OF ASIAN AMERICAN PROFESSIONALS
, TX
James Shieh, Public Affairs Liason
Email: info@asaap.net
Web: www.asaap.net

CHINA-BURMA-INDIA HUMP PILOTS ASSOCIATION, INC.
720 S. Tyler St. #B132
Amarillo, TX 79101
Tel: (806) 331-1160 Fax: (806) 331-1160
Email: cbihpa@nts-online.net

CHINESE AMERICAN SEMICONDUCTOR PROFESSIONAL ASSOCIATION
CASPA Austin
Austin, TX
Jimmy Qin, Chair of Austin Branch
Tel: (512) 241-3810
Email: lingcen@yahoo.com
Web: www.caspa-austin.com

CHINESE DOCTORS ASSOCIATION OF HOUSTON
9630 Clarewood Dr. #A6
Houston, TX 77036
Jane Hsieh, Executive Director
Tel: (713) 270-8989 Fax: (713) 981-8978
Email: hihftexas@cs.com

DALLAS ASIAN AMERICAN BAR ASSOCIATION
901 Main St. #3100
Dallas, TX 75202-3789
Wilson Chu, President
Tel: (214) 651-5088 Fax: (214) 200-0588
Email: chuw@haynesboone.com
Web: www.daaba.org

NETWORK OF INDIAN PROFESSIONALS OF NORTH AMERICA
Network of Indian Professionals-Dallas, Inc.
Dallas, TX

Saurabh Modi, President
Email: info@netip-dallas.org
Web: www.netip-dallas.org

NETWORK OF INDIAN PROFESSIONALS-AUSTIN
5114 Balcones Woods Dr. #307, PMB 136
Austin, TX 78759
Naveen Valluri, President
Email: president@netip-austin.org
Web: www.serve.com/netipaus/

NETWORK OF INDIAN PROFESSIONALS-HOUSTON
Network of Indian Professionals of North America
P.O. Box 37376
Houston, TX 77237-7376
Mahima Khanna, President
Email: mahima@netiphouston.org
Web: www.netiphouston.org

NORTH TEXAS CHINESE ENGINEERS & ARCHITECTS
3204 Canton St.
Dallas, TX 75226
Alex Wong, President
Tel: (214) 670-4654 Fax: (214) 670-4808
Email: awong@ci.dallas.tx.us

SOUTH ASIAN AMERICAN BAR ASSOCIATION OF HOUSTON
P.O. Box 4178
Houston, TX 77210-4178
Vijay Kale, President
Tel: (281) 701-4516 Fax: (216) 225-0940
Email: kalelaw@sbcglobal.net
Web: www.saaba.net

THE NATIONAL ASSOCIATION OF ASIAN AMERICAN PROFESSIONALS
NAAAP-Houston
P.O. Box 540601
Houston, TX 77254-0601
Daniel Chen, President
Email: danielchen@naaaphouston.org
Web: www.naaaphouston.org

THE SOCIETY OF IRANIAN PROFESSIONALS OF TEXAS, INC.
P.O. Box 441602
Houston, TX 77244-1602
Dr. Mohammad Delshad, President
Tel: (281) 596-9283
Email: info@siptx.org
Web: www.siptx.org

VIETNAMESE PROFESSIONALS SOCIETY
Dallas Chapter
P.O. Box 631566
Irving, TX 75063-1566
Ai-Chang Pham, President
Tel: (214) 448-9138
Email: contact@vpsdallas.org
Web: www.vpsdallas.org

RELIGIOUS

ARAB VISION, INC.
Trinity Episcopal Church
12727 Hillcrest Rd.
Dallas, TX 75230
Bobby Adams, Former President
Tel: (214) 693-6867
Email: curator@gospelcom.net
Web: http://arabvision.gospelcom.net/int/index.html

ARLINGTON CHINESE CHURCH
805 Oakwood Ln.
Arlington, TX 76012
Rev. Edward Leung, Senior Pastor
Tel: (817) 277-7556 Fax: (817) 459-1560
Email: acc@accdfw.org
Web: www.accdfw.org

ASIA HARVEST
P.O. Box 901
Palestine, TX 75802
Tel: (877) 868-5025 Fax: (877) 868-5025
Email: office@asiaharvest.org
Web: www.asiaharvest.org

ASIAN AMERICAN BAPTIST CHURCH
801 W. Campbell Rd.
Richardson, TX 75080
Arnold Wong, Senior Pastor
Tel: (972) 994-9558 Fax: (972) 994-0050
Web: www.aabcdallas.org

ASIAN AMERICAN CHURCH OF HOUSTON
7887 Beechnut
Houston, TX 77074
Augustine Kim, Pastor
Tel: (713) 779-2224
Email: info@aach.org
Web: www.aach.org

AUSTIN CHINESE CHURCH
11118 Dessau Rd.
Austin, TX 78754
Rev. Gaylord Tsuei, English Pastor/Coordinating Pastor
Tel: (512) 339-8675 Fax: (512) 339-9556
Email: contact@austinchinesechurch.org
Web: www.austinchinesechurch.org

CAMBODIAN BUDDIST TEMPLE OF DALLAS
5701 Crystal Lake Blvd.
Dallas, TX 75236
Tel: (972) 709-5300

CHINESE BAPTIST CHURCH
900 Brogden Rd.
Houston, TX 77024
Dr. James Wong, Senior Pastor
Tel: (713) 461-0963 Fax: (713) 461-5186
Email: webmaster@cbchouston.org
Web: www.cbchouston.org

CLEAR LAKE CHINESE CHURCH
503 N. Austin St.
Webster, TX 77598
James Hwang, Pastor
Tel: (281) 338-1929 Fax: (281) 338-0435
Email: james_hwang@compuserve.com
Web: www.clearlakechinesechurch.org

CONGREGATION BETH ISRAEL
3901 Shoal Creek Blvd.
Austin, TX 78756
Theressa Lyons, President
Tel: (512) 454-6806 Fax: (512) 454-9493
Email: office@bethisrael.org
Web: www.bethisrael.org

CONGREGATION BETH ISRAEL
5600 N. Braeswood Blvd.
Houston, TX 77096
Sheldon Oster, President
Tel: (713) 771-6221
Email: info@beth-israel.org
Web: www.beth-israel.org

DALLAS CHINESE BIBLE CHURCH
1707 Campbell Trail
Richardson, TX 75082
Dr. William Ho, Senior Pastor
Tel: (972) 437-3466 Fax: (972) 437-3467
Email: office@dcbconline.org
Web: www.dcbconline.org

DALLAS CHINESE FELLOWSHIP CHURCH
2640 Glencliff Dr.
Plano, TX 75075
Rev. Nelson Lin, Pastor
Tel: (972) 612-7227
Email: nelson@dcfc.org
Web: www.dcfc.org

DENTON CHINESE CHURCH
409 Fulton St.
Denton, TX 76201
Tel: (940) 898-1511
Web: www.bibledcc.org

EL PASO CHINESE BAPTIST CHURCH
2030 Grant Ave.
El Paso, TX 79930
Rev. George Neri, Pastor
Tel: (915) 532-7153
Email: epcbc@yahoo.com
Web: www.elpasochinesebaptist.com

FIRST CHINESE BAPTIST CHURCH
5481 W. Prue Rd.
San Antonio, TX 78240
Rev. Tim Yin, Pastor
Tel: (210) 558-6393
Email: fcbcsa@juno.com
Web: www.fcbcsa.org

FIRST CHINESE BAPTIST CHURCH OF DALLAS
17817 Hillcrest Rd.
Dallas, TX 75252
Rev. Isaac Chu, Senior Pastor
Tel: (972) 931-5500 Fax: (972) 931-5500
Email: office@fcbcd.org
Web: www.fcbcd.org

FIRST PHILIPINE BAPTIST CHURCH
8809 Bissonnet St.
Houston, TX 77074
Rev. Ernest Dagohoy, Senior Pastor
Tel: (713) 541-1962 Fax: (713) 541-4253
Email: info@fpbchouston.org
Web: www.fpbchouston.org

GOSPEL MISSIONS PAKISTAN
P.O. Box 542442
Grand Praire, TX 75054-2442
Samson Timus
Tel: (972) 641-7451
Email: gospelmissionpak@aol.com

HOUSTON CHINESE CHURCH
10305 S. Main
Houston, TX 77025
William Hsueh, Senior Pastor
Tel: (713) 663-7550 Fax: (713) 663-6896
Email: hccoffice@hcchome.org
Web: www.hcchome.org

HYDE PARK CHINESE BAPTIST CHURCH
3901 Speedway
Austin, TX 78751
Rev. Caleb Tang, Pastor
Tel: (512) 465-8385 Fax: (512) 459-0248
Email: hpcbc@hpcbc.org
Web: www.hpcbc.org

ISLAMIC ASSOCIATION OF NORTH TEXAS
P.O. Box 833010
Richardson, TX 75083-9576
Nadiya Iqbao, Administrator
Tel: (972) 231-5698 Fax: (972) 231-6707
Email: board@iant.com
Web: www.iant.com

KOREAN PRESBYTERIAN CHURCH OF HOUSTON
9002 Rulan Rd.
Houston, TX 77055
Rev. Joseph Myung, Pastor
Tel: (713) 973-1123 Fax: (713) 365-0329
Email: info@twfhouston.org
Web: www.twfhouston.org

LUBBOCK CHINESE CHURCH
P.O. Box 4277
Lubbock, TX 79409
Robert Sea, Pastor
Tel: (806) 687-3968 Fax: (806) 687-3968
Email: webmaster@lubbockchinesechurch.org
Web: www.lubbockchinesechurch.org

PLANO CHINESE ALLIANCE CHURCH
1615 Dorchester Dr.
Plano, TX 75075
Rev. Andrew Tsai, Senior Pastor
Tel: (972) 867-2990
Email: revtsai2004@yahoo.com
Web: www.pcactexas.org

REFORMED KOREAN PRESBYTERIAN CHURCH
1400 W. Frankfurt Rd.
Carrollton, TX 75007
Rev. Jeong Yeop, Pastor
Tel: (214) 534-7141
Email: jyleepeace@msn.com
Web: www.olcc.org/inmission/national/reformedkorean.html

SOUTHWEST CHINESE BAPTIST CHURCH
12525 Sugar Ridge Blvd.
Stafford, TX 77477
Rev. Peter Tuck Soon Leong, Senior Pastor
Tel: (281) 495-1511 Fax: (281) 495-2170
Email: office@swcbc.org
Web: www.swcbc.org

TEMPLE BETH-EL
211 Belknap Pl.
San Antonio, TX 78212
David Oppenheimer, President
Tel: (210) 733-9135 Fax: (210) 737-8946
Email: president@beth-elsa.org
Web: www.beth-elsa.org

TEMPLE EMANU-EL
8500 Hillcrest Rd.
Dallas, TX 75225
Robert M. Cohan, President
Tel: (214) 706-0000 Fax: (214) 706-0025
Email: info@tedallas.org
Web: www.tedallas.org

TEMPLE SHALOM DALLAS
6930 Alpha Rd.
Dallas, TX 75240
Debbi K. Sorrentino, President
Tel: (972) 661-1810 Fax: (972) 661-2636
Email: dksorren@hotmail.com
Web: www.templeshalomdallas.org

TEMPLE SINAI
13875 Brimhurst Dr.
Houston, TX 77077
David Simon, President
Tel: (281) 496-5950 Fax: (281) 496-3436
Email: admin@temple-sinai.org
Web: www.temple-sinai.org

TEXAS CAMBODIAN BUDDHIST SOCIETY, INC.
15211 Sellers Rd.
Houston, TX 77060
Tel: (281) 999-8678

THE KOREAN GOSPEL CHURCH
11100 Beamer Rd.
Houston, TX 77089
David Kwan Woo Lim, Pastor
Tel: (281) 481-9433
Email: kmlimtx@yahoo.co.kr

VIETNAM BAPTIST CHURCH
Houston
1907 Dairy Ashfold
Houston, TX 77077
Hai Hoang Nguyen, Executive Director
Tel: (281) 752-5685
Web: www.vbchouston.org

VIETNAMESE BAPTIST CHURCH
Houston
6100 Ridgemont St.
Houston, TX 77087
Tel: (713) 645-7766
Web: www.vbcweb.org

VIETNAMESE EUCHARISTIC YOUTH SOCIETY IN THE USA
Christ the King Chapter
6550 Fairbanks North
Houston, TX 77040
Peter Thien Hoang, Pastor
Tel: (713) 939-1906 Fax: (713) 939-0771
Email: tong@aimagination.com
Web: www.loduc.org

RESEARCH

JEWISHGEN, INC.
2951 Marina Bay Dr. #130-472
League City, TX 77573
Tel: (281) 535-2200 Fax: (281) 535-2204
Email: support@jewishgen.org
Web: www.jewishgen.org

SCIENTIFIC

KOREAN-AMERICAN SCIENTISTS AND ENGINEERS ASSOCIATION
Austin Chapter
P.O. Box 812
Cedar Park, TX 78630
Wonhui Cho, President
Tel: (512) 656-2998 Fax: (512) 258-2654
Email: whcho@austin.rr.com
Web: www.ksea-austin.org

SPEC. INT., CHILD CARE

GREAT WALL CHINA ADOPTION
248 Addie Roy Rd. #A102
Austin, TX 78746
Snow Wu, President
Tel: (512) 323-9595 Fax: (512) 323-9599
Email: info@gwcadopt.org
Web: www.gwcadopt.org

SPEC. INT., COUNSELING

JEWISH FAMILY AND CHILDREN'S SERVICES OF SAN ANTONIO
12500 NW Military Hwy. #250
San Antonio, TX 78231
Chuck Barksdale, Interim Executive Director
Tel: (210) 302-6920 Fax: (210) 302-6952
Email: jfs@jfs-sa.org

SPEC. INT., EDUCATION

ASHA FOR EDUCATION
Austin
P.O. Box 319 The University of Texas at Austin, Student Organization Ctr., 1 University Station A6220
Austin, TX 78712-0181
Ravi Kokku, Projects Coordinator
Tel: (512) 451-8356
Email: r_koku@yahoo.com
Web: www.ashanet.org/austin/

ASIA HOUSTON NETWORK
P.O. Box 130676
Houston, TX 77219
Gigi Lee, President
Tel: (713) 385-8123 Fax: (713) 862-1709
Email: asiahouston@aol.com
Web: www.asiahouston.org

ISLAMIC EDUCATION CENTER OF HOUSTON, TEXAS
2313 S. Voss Rd.
Houston, TX 77057
Tel: (713) 787-5000 Fax: (281) 754-4430
Email: alim@iec-houston.org
Web: www.iec-houston.org

JORDAN SCHOOL
1303 E. Houston Ave.
Crockett, TX 75835
Debbie Kelly, Head of School
Tel: (936) 544-4049 Fax: (936) 546-0034
Email: debbiekelly@jordanschool.org
Web: www.jordanschool.org

MERIT CHINESE SCHOOL
1112 W. Parker Rd. #212
Plano, TX 75075
Frances Man Lee Leung, Principal
Tel: (972) 517-9382
Email: meritchineseschool@yahoo.com
Web: www.meritchineseschool.org

NATIONAL ASIAN PACIFIC AMERICAN LAW STUDENT ASSOCIATION
South Texas College of Law
1303 San Jacinto
Houston, TX 77002
Helene Nguyen, President
Tel: (713) 646-1732
Email: helenenguyen@hotmail.com
Web: www.napalsa.org/

OVERSEAS CHINA EDUCATION FOUNDATION
P.O. Box 772436
Houston, TX 77215-2436
Prof. Gan Liang, President
Tel: (281) 364-0055
Email: ocef@ocef.org
Web: www.ocef.org

SOCIETY OF IRANIAN AMERICAN WOMEN FOR EDUCATION
P.O. Box 572371
Houston, TX 77257
Tel: (713) 532-6666
Email: info@siawe.org
Web: www.siawe.org

SUN RAY CHINESE SCHOOL
Arlington Campus
1417 Chesterton
Richardson, TX 76011
Helen Lee, Principal
Tel: (972) 671-8234
Email: principal_arlington@sunraychinese.org
Web: www.sunraychinese.org

Carrollton Campus
2703 Quail Ridge Dr.
Carrollton, TX 75006
Zin Fan, Principal
Tel: (972) 931-5486 Fax: (972) 247-3539
Email: principal_carrollton@sunraychinese.org
Web: www.sunraychinese.org

Plano Campus
13019 Burninglog Ln.
Dallas, TX 75243
Jack Ting, Principal
Tel: (469) 789-6020
Email: principal_plano@sunraychinese.org
Web: www.sunraychinese.org

SUNFLOWER MISSION
P.O. Box 421448
Houston, TX 77242
Tuan Dao, Chariman
Tel: (713) 927-6235
Email: info@sunflowermission.org
Web: www.sunflowermission.org

THE ARAB-AMERICAN EDUCATIONAL FOUNDATION
P.O. Box 270333
Houston, TX 77277-0333
Samer Al-Azem, Boad Member
Tel: (713) 266-2390
Email: aaef@aaefhouston.org
Web: www.aaefhouston.org

THE HOUSTON KOREAN SCHOOL
10410 Clay Rd.
Houston, TX 77041
Tel: (713) 983-7441 Fax: (713) 460-9358
Email: contact@houstonkoreanschool.com
Web: www.houstonkoreanschool.com

US CHINA PEOPLES FRIENDSHIP ASSOCIATION
Austin Chapter
705 E. 3rd St.
Georgetown, TX 78626
George Meyer
Tel: (512) 863-4930
Web: www.uscpfa.org

Houston Chapter

c/o Eastern Resource Development, 5433
Westheimer Rd. #415
Houston, TX 77056
Nancy J. LiEaston
Tel: (281) 240-3588
Email: juanjli@aol.com
Web: www.uscpfa.org

Houston-Galleria Chapter
3711 San Felipe Rd.
Houston, TX 77027
Dr. Marilyn Wilhelm, Contact
Web: www.uscpfa.org

Southern Region
#3 Gessner Rd.
Houston, TX 77024
A. Cresali LaWell, President
Tel: (713) 722-9960 Fax: (713) 722-9960
Email: cresali@texas.net
Web: www.uscpfa.org

SPEC. INT., FAMILY PLANNING

DAYA
P.O. Box 571774
Houston, TX 77257
Lakshmy Parameswaran, President
Tel: (713) 914-1333
Email: info@dayahouston.org
Web: www.dayahouston.org

DAYA SOUTH ASIAN FAMILIES IN CRISIS
P.O. Box 571774
Houston, TX 77257
Viji Raman, Secretary of the Board
Tel: (713) 914-1333 Fax: (713) 467-9510
Email: viji-raman@yahoo.com
Web: www.dayahouston.org

FAMILIES WITH CHILDREN FROM CHINA
Hill Country Texas Chapter
2249 S. Abbey Loop
New Braunfels, TX 78130
Jeff Slomka
Tel: (830) 625-1718
Email: fcc@imalittle.com
Web: www.fwcc.org

SPEC. INT., GAY&LESBIAN

ASIANS & FRIENDS HOUSTON, INC.
P.O. Box 667100
Houston, TX 77266-7100
Chris K., President
Tel: (713) 626-6300
Email: chris@asiansandfriendshouston.com
Web: http://asiansandfriendshouston.com

TRIKONETEJAS
P.O. Box 4589
Austin, TX 78765-4589
Tel: (512) 560-9017
Email: trikone_tejas@yahoo.com
Web: www.main.org/trikonetejas

SPEC. INT., HEALTH SERVICES

ASIAN AMERICAN HEALTH COALITION OF THE GREATER HOUSTON AREA
c/o MGDI, P.O. Box 272804
Houston, TX 77277-2804
Beverly J. Gor, EdD, RD, LD, CDE, President
Tel: (713) 792-7802 Fax: (713) 794-5553
Email: asianhealthhouston@yahoo.com
Web: www.asianhealthhouston.org

HOUSTON INTERNATIONAL HEALTH FOUNDATION
9630 Clarewood Dr. #A6
Houston, TX 77036
Jane Hsieh, Executive Director
Tel: (713) 981-8989 Fax: (713) 981-8978
Email: hihftexas@cs.com

SPEC. INT., HOUSING

ASIAN REAL ESTATE ASSOCIATION OF AMERICA
17424 W. Grand Pkwy. #405
Sugar Land, TX 77479
Email: info@areaa.org
Web: www.areaa.org

SPEC. INT., HUMAN RELATIONS

ASIA SOCIETY
Texas
4605 Post Oak Pl. #205
Houston, TX 77027
Vishakha N. Desai, President
Tel: (713) 439-0051 Fax: (713) 439-1107
Email: txcenter@asiasoc.org
Web: www.asiasociety.org

COUNCIL ON AMERICAN-ISLAMIC RELATIONS
Austin Chapter
P.O. Box 12201
Austin, TX 78711
Tel: (512) 577-2247
Email: info@cair-austin.org
Web: www.cair-austin.org/

Dallas/Fort-Worth Chapter
3010 LBJ Frwy. #100
Dallas, TX 75234
Saffia Meek, Office Manager
Tel: (972) 241-7233 Fax: (972) 241-7466
Email: info@cairdfw.org
Web: www.cairdfw.org

Houston Chapter
5821 SW Fwy.
Houston, TX 77057
Tarek Hussein, President
Tel: (713) 838-2247 Fax: (713) 838-2250
Email: cair@cairhouston.org
Web: www.cairhouston.org

San Antonio Chapter
3358 Tavern Oaks
San Antonio, TX 78247
Sarwat Hussain, President
Tel: (210) 378-9528 Fax: (210) 494-4129
Email: sanantonio@cair-net.org
Web: www.cair-net.org

IC2 INSTITUTE
University of Texas, Austin
2815 San Gabriel
Austin, TX 78705
John Sibley Butler, Director
Tel: (512) 475-8900 Fax: (512) 475-8901
Email: info@icc.utexas.edu
Web: www.ic2.org

JAPANESE AMERICAN CITIZENS LEAGUE
5766 Kuldell Dr.
Houston, TX 77096
George Hirasaki, President
Tel: (281) 788-9415 Fax: (713) 988-5767
Email: houston@jacl.org
Web: www.jacl-houston.org

JEWISH COMMUNITY RELATIONS COUNCIL OF DALLAS
7800 Northhaven Rd.
Dallas, TX 75230
Lawrence D. Ginsburg, Chair
Tel: (214) 615-5254 Fax: (214) 373-3186
Email: jcrcdallas@jfgd.org
Web: www.jcrcdallas.org

NATIONAL MEDITATION CENTER FOR WORLD PEACE
Rt. 10 Box 2523
Jacksonville, TX 75766
Master Hughes, Director
Tel: (903) 589-5706
Email: nmc@nationalmeditation.org
Web: www.nationalmeditation.org

PALESTINE AFFAIRS COUNCIL
P.O. Box 740943
Houston, TX 77274
Kamal Khalil
Tel: (713) 762-2228
Email: info@pac-usa.org
Web: www.pac-usa.org

THE AMERICAN JEWISH COMMITTEE
Dallas Chapter
12890 Hillcrest Rd. #103
Dallas, TX 75230
Darrel Strelitz, Chapter Director
Tel: (972) 387-2943 Fax: (972) 404-1913
Email: dallas@ajc.org
Web: www.ajc.org

Houston Chapter
3355 W. Alabama #930
Houston, TX 77098-1722
Linda L. Burger, Chapter Director
Tel: (713) 439-1202 Fax: (713) 439-1240
Email: houston@ajc.org
Web: www.ajc.org

THE CHILDREN'S DEFENSE FUND
316 W. 12th St. #105
Austin, TX 78701
Patti Everitt, Executive Director
Tel: (512) 480-0990 Fax: (512) 480-0995
Email: peveritt@childrensdefense.org
Web: www.cdftexas.org

4500 Bissonnet #260
Bellaire, TX 77401
Barbara Best, Assosiate Director
Tel: (713) 664-4080 Fax: (713) 664-3032
Email: bbest@childrensdefense.org
Web: www.cdftexas.org

944-A W. Nolana Loop
Pharr, TX 78577
Olga Gabriel, Director
Tel: (956) 782-4000 Fax: (956) 283-7975
Email: ogabriel@childrensdefense.org
Web: www.cdftexas.org

VIETNAMESE MUTUAL ASSISTANCE ASSOCIATION OF GREATER TEXAS
7015 Greenville Ave. #200
Dallas, TX 75231
Dominic Nohe, Executive Director
Tel: (214) 691-1704 Fax: (214) 696-0275
Email: vmaatx@aol.com
Web: http://hometown.aol.com/vmaatx/hist_mis.htm

SPEC. INT., MENTAL HEALTH

ASIAN AMERICAN FAMILY COUNSELING CENTER
6220 Westpark #228
Houston, TX 77057
Rogene Gee Calvert, President
Tel: (713) 339-3688 Fax: (713) 339-3699
Email: info@aafcc.org
Web: www.aafcc.org

SPEC. INT., SENIORS

AGING INFORMATION CENTER
Region VI: AR, LA, OK, NM, TX
1301 Young St. #736
Dallas, TX 75201
Larry Brewster, Regional Administrator
Tel: (214) 767-2971 Fax: (214) 767-2951
Email: aoainfo@aoa.gov
Web: www.aoa.dhhs.gov

THAI SENIOR CITIZENS ASSOCIATION
P.O. Box 681277
Houston, TX 77268
Kitipot Charnveja, President
Tel: (832) 457-4281 Fax: (281) 970-5070
Email: kitipot@att.net

SPEC. INT., SOCIAL INTEREST

BANGLADESH ASSOCIATION, HOUSTON
P.O. Box 440233
Houston, TX 77244-0233
Selina Rahman, Chairperson
Email: skrahman1@yahoo.com
Web: www.bangladesh-association.com

CHINESE CIVIC CENTER
10052 Harwin Dr.
Houston, TX 77036
Huai, Chair
Tel: (713) 772-1133 Fax: (713) 772-1399
Web: www.chinesecivicenter.org

CHINESE COMMUNITY CENTER
5855 Sovereign Dr. #150
Houston, TX 77036-2337
Cecil Fong, Chair
Tel: (713) 271-6100 Fax: (713) 271-3713
Email: cecilfond@ccchouston.org
Web: www.ccchouston.org

DALLAS CHINESE COMMUNITY CENTER
400 N. Greenville Ave. #12
Richardson, TX 75081
Tel: (972) 480-0311
Web: www.dallasccc.org

HOPE INITIATIVE, INC.
P.O. Box 66855
Houston, TX 77266-6855
Phi Nguyen, President/CEO
Tel: (713) 972-4562
Email: hope.initiative@hionline.org
Web: www.hionline.org

JAPAN-AMERICA SOCIETY
Dallas/Fort Worth Chapter
11615 Forest Central Dr. #206, LB26
Dallas, TX 75243
Mark G. Johnson, President
Tel: (214) 342-2022 Fax: (214) 342-1022
Email: jasdfw@us-japan.com
Web: www.jasdfw.org

JAPANESE AMERICAN SOCIETY OF HOUSTON
4801 Woodway #110W
Houston, TX 77056
John A. Elsner, Executive Director
Tel: (713) 963-0121 Fax: (713) 963-8270
Email: jash@wt.net
Web: www.jashouston.org

JAPANESE COMMUNITY
6910 Woodsprings
Garland, TX 75044
Makoto Ueda, Editor
Tel: (972) 414-1748 Fax: (972) 495-5590
Email: irohadfw@mac.com

JEWISH COMMUNITY ASSOCIATION OF AUSTIN
7300 Hart Ln.
Austin, TX 78731
Paul Saper, President
Tel: (512) 735-8000 Fax: (512) 735-8001
Email: info@jcaaonline.org
Web: www.jcaaonline.org

JEWISH COMMUNITY CENTER OF DALLAS
7900 Northhaven Rd.
Dallas, TX 75230
Jay Jacobs, Executive Vice President
Tel: (214) 739-2737 Fax: (214) 368-4709
Email: jjacobs@jccdallas.org
Web: www.jccdallas.org

JEWISH COMMUNITY CENTER OF HOUSTON
5601 S. Braeswood
Houston, TX 77096
Jerry Wische, Executive Vice President
Tel: (713) 729-3200 Fax: (713) 551-7233
Email: jwische@jcchouston.org
Web: www.jcchouston.org

JEWISH FAMILY SERVICE OF HOUSTON
P.O. Box 20548
Houston, TX 77225
Tel: (713) 667-9336 Fax: (713) 667-3619
Email: jfs@jfshouston.org
Web: http://jfshouston.org

JEWISH FEDERATION OF GREATER DALLAS
7800 Northhaven Rd.
Dallas, TX 75230-3226
Tel: (214) 369-3313 Fax: (214) 369-8943
Email: contact@jfgd.org
Web: www.jewishdallas.org

JEWISH FEDERATION OF GREATER HOUSTON
5603 S. Braeswood Blvd.
Houston, TX 77096-3998
Tel: (713) 729-7000 Fax: (713) 721-6232
Email: lwunsch@houstonjewish.org
Web: www.houstonjewish.org

JEWISH FEDERATION OF SAN ANTONIO
12500 NW Military Hwy. #200
San Antonio, TX 78231
Tel: (210) 302-6960 Fax: (210) 408-2332
Email: markfreedman@jfsatx.org
Web: www.jfsatx.org

JORDAN CHAPEL BUILDERS
P.O. Box 1355
Pampa, TX 79065
Email: staff@jordanchapel.org
Web: www.jordanchapel.org

KOREAN SOCIETY OF DALLAS
11500 N. Stemmons Fwy. #261
Dallas, TX 75229
Yun Won Kim, President
Tel: (972) 488-1114 Fax: (972) 488-1115
Email: president@kdallas.com
Web: www.kdallas.com

MALAYSIAN SINGAPORE ASSOCIATION OF HOUSTON
P.O. Box 772358
Houston, TX 77215-2358
Chris Chew, President
Email: chris@icekacang.com
Web: http://web.wt.net/~msah

PAKISTAN WELFARE ORGANIZATION
P.O. Box 20328
Houston, TX 77225-0328
Aeta Moin, Board of Director
Tel: (713) 530-0518 Fax: (713) 783-5519
Email: info@pakistanwelfare.org
Web: www.pakistanwelfare.org

THAILAND NEW LIFE FOUNDATION
9701 Hwy. 277 South
Abilene, TX 79606
Tel: (915) 695-7291 Fax: (915) 676-4084
Email: tnlf@thailandnewlife.org
Web: www.thailandnewlife.org

VIETNAMESE STUDENTS ASSOCIATED CHARITIES
P.O. Box 66855
Houston, TX 77266-6855
Phi Nguyen, Chief Executive Officer
Email: phi.nguyen@hionline.org
Web: www.vsaconline.org

SPEC. INT., WOMEN

COMMITTEE ON SOUTH ASIAN WOMEN
Texas A&M University
Department of Psychology #267
College Station, TX 77843
Dr. Jyotsna Vaid, Doctor
Tel: (979) 845-2576 Fax: (979) 845-4727
Email: jxv@psyc.tamu.edu
Web: http://http.tamu.edu/~e305jj/cosaw.html

DELTA PHI OMEGA
National Council

4204 Lyons
Houston, TX 77020
Leena Cherian, President
Email: national_dpo@hotmail.com
Web: www.deltaphiomega.org

HADASSAH
Greater Southwest Region
2650 Fountain View #127
Houston, TX 77057
Marlene Rosenthal, President
Tel: (713) 339-2255 Fax: (713) 339-2888
Email: marlene.rosenthal@hadassah.org
Web: www.hadassah.org

NATIONAL COUNCIL FOR JEWISH WOMEN
Austin Section
P.O. Box 26641
Austin, TX 78755-0641
Email: info@ncjwmemphis.org
Web: www.ncjwaustin.org

Greater Dallas Section
219 Preston Royal Shopping Ctr. #9
Dallas, TX 75230
Tel: (214) 368-4405 Fax: (214) 368-4753
Email: info@ncjwdallas.org
Web: www.ncjwdallas.org

Greater Houston Section
6102 Queensloch
Houston, TX 77096
Amy Grossman, President
Tel: (713) 667-5694 Fax: (713) 661-0180
Email: amyg@houston.rr.com
Web: www.ncjwhouston.org

San Antonio Section
10108 Sunflower Ln.
San Antonio, TX 78213
Barbara Slavin, Board Member
Email: babsmbsh@aol.com
Web: www.ncjw-sanantonio.org

SAHELI FOR ASIAN FAMILIES
P.O. Box 3665
Austin, TX 78764
Linda Phan, Executive Director
Tel: (512) 703-8745
Email: saheli@saheli-austin.org
Web: www.saheli-austin.org

SPEC. INT., YOUTH

YEE FAMILY ASSOCIATION OF HOUSTON
9015 Sterlingame Dr.
Houston, TX 77031
Frank Yu, President
Tel: (713) 771-3745 Fax: (713) 988-5851
Email: fyai@houston.vv.com
Web: www.yeehouston.org

STUDENT ORGANIZATION

ASIAN AMERICAN LEADERSHIP AND EDUCATIONAL CONFERENCE
Southern Methodist University
P.O. Box 750355
Dallas, TX 75275
Tel: (214) 768-4580
Web: http://people.smu.edu/aalec

CHINESE STUDENTS ASSOCIATION AND SCHOLAR ASSOCIATION
University of Texas Medical Branch
3315 Pharmacology Bldg.
Galveston, TX 77555
Zhenyu Ji, President
Tel: (409) 747-7406
Email: yvonji@hotmail.com
Web: http://studentlife.utmb.edu/csa

INDIA MUSIC ARTS AND CULTURAL SOCIETY
University of Texas at Arlington
P.O. Box 19350-72

Arlington, TX 76019
Swati Desoares, President
Email: swatidesoares@yahoo.com
Web: http://imacs.uta.edu

INDIA STUDENTS ASSOCIATION
University of North Texas
P.O. Box 305310
Denton, TX 76203-5310
Ajit Ranade, President
Tel: (940) 565-2381
Email: ajitranade@unt.edu
Web: http://orgs.unt.edu/isa

ISLAMIC COMMUNITY
Bryan/College Station
417 Stasney St.
College Station, TX 77840
Faisal Chaudhry, President
Tel: (979) 846-4222 Fax: (979) 846-2193
Email: ec@icbcs.org
Web: www.icbcs.org

KOREAN STUDENT ASSOCIATION
University of North Texas
P.O. Box 306482
Denton, TX 76203
Email: sin0001@unt.edu
Web: http://orgs.unt.edu/ksa

MALAYSIAN & SINGAPOREAN STUDENT ASSOCIATION
University of Houston
Campus Activities Mailbox #290, 4800
Calhoun Rd.
Houston, TX 77204
Ching Lee, President
Email: info@uhmssa.org
Web: www.uhmssa.org

SRI LANKAN STUDENTS ASSOCIATION
University of Texas at Arlington
UTA Box 19356-56
Arlington, TX 76019
Mishkath Misbah, President
Tel: (817) 861-5703
Email: slsa_uta@yahoo.com
Web: www.uta.edu/students_orgs/srilanka

TAIWANESE ASSOCIATION
Rice University
P.O. Box 1892
Houston, TX 77251-1892
Web: www.ruf.rice.edu/~rta

TAIWANESE STUDENT ASSOCIATION
University of Texas at Austin
1 University Station, Department of Civil Engineering
Austin, TX 78712
Chi-Chi Lin, President
Tel: (512) 771-8720
Email: r89541129@ntu.edu.tw
Web: http://studentorgs.utexas.edu/tsa

TEXAS A&M TAIWANESE STUDENT ASSOCIATION
P.O. Box 14612
College Station, TX 77841-14612
Tel: (979) 260-5692
Email: tsacom@tamu.edu
Web: www.tamutsa.com

TEXAS A&M UNIVERSITY CHINA CLUB
College Station, TX 77843
Haidong Liu, President
Tel: (979) 845-6413
Email: haidongliu@tamu.edu
Web: www.tamu.edu/cssa

TURKISH STUDENT ASSOCIATION
Southern Methodist University
SMU Student Activities, 3140 Dyer
P.O. Box 750436
Dallas, TX 75275
Ali Bahadir Olcay, President
Tel: (214) 692-1368
Email: aolcay@mail.smu.edu
Web: http://people.smu.edu/tsa/

VIETNAM CENTER
Texas Tech University
Math Room #4, Box 41045
Lubbock, TX 79409-1045
Tel: (806) 742-3742 Fax: (806) 742-8664
Email: vietnam.center@ttu.edu
Web: www.vietnam.ttu.edu/vietnamcenter

UTAH

CULTURAL

CHINESE CULTURAL EDUCATION CENTER & PERFORMING ARTS GROUP
2066 E. Rainbow Point Dr.
Salt Lake City, UT 84124
Rachel Yee, Coordinator
Tel: (801) 272-0518 Fax: (801) 272-0518
Email: hwa_e@yahoo.com

THAI ASSOCIATION
871 W. 500 North
Salt Lake City, UT 84116
Suri Suddhiphayak
Tel: (801) 595-6829 Fax: (801) 595-6829

MULTI-PURPOSE

ASIAN ASSOCIATION OF UTAH
1588 S. Major St.
Salt Lake City, UT 84115
Shu Cheng, Director
Tel: (801) 467-6060 Fax: (801) 486-3007
Email: aau@aau-slc.org
Web: www.aau-slc.org

ORGANIZATION OF CHINESE AMERICANS
976 S. Vialacosta Way
Kaysville, UT 84037
Rosa Shu, Board Member
Email: rt2kermit@yahoo.com

RELIGIOUS

FIRST VIETNAMESE BAPTIST CHURCH
1235 California Ave.
Salt Lake City, UT 84101
Tel: (801) 886-7292
Web: www.fvbcslc.org

KOREAN PRESBYTERIAN CHURCH OF SALT LAKE CITY
425 E. 700 South
Salt Lake City, UT 84111-3903
Tel: (801) 322-0222
Web: www.ohex.com/utkr/

SPEC. INT., EDUCATION

JORDAN EDUCATION FOUNDATION
9361 S. 300 East
Sandy, UT 84093
Peggy Jo Kennett, President
Tel: (801) 567-8100 Fax: (801) 567-8078
Email: pjkennett@juno.com
Web: www.jordandistrict.org

KOREAN COMMUNITY SCHOOL OF UTAH
333 S. 900 East #100
Salt Lake City, UT 84106
Samuel Noh, President
Tel: (801) 595-1004 Fax: (801) 523-6637
Email: school@utahkorean.com
Web: www.utahkorean.com/school

THE MIDDLE EAST CENTER
University of Utah
260 Central Campus Dr. #153
Salt Lake City, UT 84112-9157
Tel: (801) 581-6181 Fax: (801) 581-6183
Web: www.hum.utah.edu/mec

US CHINA PEOPLES FRIENDSHIP
Utah Chapter
2890 Hackney Ct.
Park City, UT 84060

Shirley Smith/Val Chin
Tel: (801) 649-2495
Web: www.uscpfa.org

SPEC. INT., HUMAN RELATIONS

JAPANESE AMERICAN CITIZENS LEAGUE
242 S. 400 East
Salt Lake City, UT 84111
Sylvana Watanabe
Tel: (801) 355-8040 Fax: (801) 521-4010
Email: idcgov@jacl.com

NATIONAL TONGAN AMERICAN SOCIETY
5258 S. Pinemont Dr. #100
Salt Lake City, UT 84123
Sione Kaisa Lui, President
Tel: (801) 264-1812 Fax: (801) 288-2687
Email: ntas@planet-tonga.com
Web: www.planet-tonga.com/ntas/

UTAH STATE OFFICE OF ASIAN AFFAIRS
324 S St., 5th Fl.
Salt Lake City, UT 84111-2321
Edith Mitko, Director
Tel: (801) 538-8883 Fax: (801) 538-8678
Email: emitko@utah.gov
Web: http://dced.utah.gov/asian/

SPEC. INT., SOCIAL INTEREST

JEWISH FAMILY SERVICE
#2 N. Medical Dr.
Salt Lake City, UT 84113
Tel: (801) 581-1330 Fax: (801) 581-1334
Email: jfs@jfs-ut. org
Web: www.jfs-ut.org

UNITED JEWISH FEDERATION OF UTAH
2 N. Medical Dr.
Salt Lake City, UT 84113
Jim Isaacson, President
Tel: (801) 581-0102 Fax: (801) 581-1334
Email: isaacson@prism.net
Web: www.ujfslc.org

US- CHINA PEOPLE FRIENDSHIP ASSOCIATION
P.O. Box 4168
Park City, UT 84060
Shirley Smith, Co-Chair
Tel: (435) 649-6015 Fax: (435) 649-9141
Email: shirley@meanderadventures.com

STUDENT ORGANIZATION

CENTER FOR ETHNIC STUDENT AFFAIRS
University of Utah
200 S. Central Campus Dr. #318
Salt Lake City, UT 84112
Karen Kwan, Advisor
Tel: (801) 581-8151 Fax: (801) 581-7119
Email: kkwan@sa.utah.edu
Web: www.utah.edu/cesa

VERMONT

CULTURAL

ARAB CULTURE AND CIVILIZATION
National Institute of Technology and Liberal Education
550 Hinesburg Rd. #302
South Burlington, VT 05403
Tel: (802) 660-9200 Fax: (802) 443-2053
Email: content@nitle.org
Web: http://arabworld.nitle.org

RELIGIOUS

VERMONT KOREAN-AMERICAN UNITED METHODIST CHURCH
130 Maple St.
Essex Junction, VT 05452
Rev. Charlie Yang, Pastor

Tel: (802) 899-4249
Email: cheolheeyang@msn.com
Web: www.gbgm-umc.org/vermont-korean-american-umc

SPEC. INT., EDUCATION

MONGOLIAN-AMERICAN FRIENDSHIP PROJECT
62 1/2 Main St.
Middlebury, VT 05753
A. Enhtur, Director
Email: toroo_a@yahoo.com
Web: www.brightworks.com/mongolamerican

SPEC. INT., SOCIAL INTEREST

JAPAN AMERICA SOCIETY OF VERMONT
29 Ethan Allen Ave.
Colchester, VT 05446
Milton Beard, President
Tel: (802) 655-4197
Email: info@jasv.org
Web: www.jasv.org

JEWISH COMMUNITY OF GREATER STOWE
P.O. Box 253
Stowe, VT 05672
Nancy Krakower, President
Tel: (802) 253-1800
Email: info@jcogs.org
Web: www.jcogs.org

VIRGINIA

BUSINESS

ASHOKA
1700 N. Moore St. #2000
Arlington, VA 22209
Email: info@ashoka.org
Web: www.ashoka.org

CENTRAL ASIAN AMERICAN ENTERPRISE FUND
17569 Old Stage Coach Rd. #A
Dumfries, VA 22026
Virginia Macfarlan, Business Manager
Tel: (703) 221-7501 Fax: (703) 221-7351
Email: vmacfarlan@caaef.com
Web: www.caaef.com

CONFEDERATION OF INDIAN INDUSTRY
1300 N. 17th St. #1847
Rosslyn, VA 22209
Kiran Pasricha, Senior Director
Tel: (703) 841-3209 Fax: (703) 841-3309
Email: kir_pasricha@nema.org
Web: www.ciionline.org

KOREAN AMERICAN CONTRACTORS ASSOCIATION
7901 Byarnwood Ct.
Springfield, VA 22153
Bruce Park, Vice President of Sales
Tel: (800) 978-3500 Fax: (703) 451-9255

NATIONAL COUNCIL OF PHILIPPINE AMERICAN CANADIAN ACCOUNTANTS
9311 Myra Dr.
Great Falls, VA 22066
Klaus Buntua, National President
Tel: (703) 759-3947 Fax: (703) 912-3707
Email: klaus.buntua@verizon.net
Web: www.ncpaca.com

PAKISTAN AMERICAN BUSINESS ASSOCIATION
9302 Old Keene Mill Rd. #B
Burke, VA 22015-4278
Siddique Sheikh, Executive Director/Founder
Tel: (703) 440-1111 Fax: (703) 451-7777
Email: founder@pabausa.com
Web: www.pabausa.com

US-CHINA EXCHANGE ASSOCIATION
Washington DC Office
10091 John Mason Pl.
Fairfax, VA 22030
Tel: (703) 383-7887 Fax: (703) 383-1628
Web: www.usachina.org

US-TAIWAN BUSINESS COUNCIL
1700 N. Moore St. #1703
Arlington, VA 22209
Rupert Hammond Chambers, President
Tel: (703) 465-2930 Fax: (703) 465-2937
Email: council@us-taiwan.org
Web: www.us-taiwan.org

VIRGINIA/CHINA BUSINESS AND TECHNOLOGY COUNCIL
1714 Great Falls St.
McLean, VA 22101
Julie Rao, Chair
Tel: (571) 426-8282 Fax: (703) 790-5571
Email: jhrao@aol.com
Web: www.vcbtc.us/

CHAMBER OF COMMERCE

AFGHAN AMERICAN CHAMBER OF COMMERCE
9293 Old Keene Mill RD.
Burke, VA 22015
Tel: (703) 440-4000 Fax: (703) 440-4002
Email: info@a-acc.org
Web: www.a-acc.org

COMMUNICATIONS

AL-HEWAR CENTER, THE CENTER FOR ARAB CULTURE AND DIALOGUE
P.O. Box 2104
Vienna, VA 22180
Soubhi Ghandour, Founder/Executive Director
Tel: (703) 281-6277 Fax: (703) 437-6419
Email: alhewar@alhewar.com
Web: www.alhewar.com

UNITY: JOURNALISTS OF COLOR, INC.
1601 N. Kent St. #1003
Arlington, VA 22209
Anna M. Lopez, Executive Director
Tel: (703) 469-2100 Fax: (703) 469-2108
Email: executive@unityjournalists.org
Web: www.unityjournalists.org

CULTURAL

AMERICAN TURKISH FRIENDSHIP ASSOCIATION
3873 Plaza Dr.
Fairfax, VA 22030
Tel: (571) 432-0777 Fax: (571) 432-0332
Email: info@atfa.us
Web: www.atfa.us

ASIAN PACIFIC LADIES
8340 Greensboro Dr. #1001
McLean, VA 22102
Angie Shasata, President

CENTENNIAL COMMITTEE OF KOREAN IMMIGRATION TO THE UNITED STATES-GREATER WASHINGTON
P.O. Box 1262
Falls Church, VA 22041-1262
Dr. Yoon Soo Park, President
Tel: (703) 938-8092 Fax: (703) 938-1162
Email: info@cckigw.org
Web: www.cckigw.org

CONSERVANCY FOR TIBETAN ART & CULTURE
P.O. Box 6598
McLean, VA 22106-6598
Rinchen Dharlo, President
Tel: (703) 755-1533 Fax: (703) 847-8805
Email: info@tibetanculture.org
Web: www.tibetanculture.org

HOUSE OF IRAN
P.O. Box 10665
McLean, VA 22102-8665
Tel: (703) 442-8100 Fax: (703) 442-8624
Email: info@houseofiran.org
Web: www.houseofiran.org

IRANIAN CULTURAL ASSOCIATION
4001 Woodland Rd.
Annandale, VA 22003
Aminzadeh Mansour, Board of Director
Tel: (703) 817-1651
Email: kanooneiranian@hotmail.com
Web: www.kanooneiranian.org

IRANIAN CULTURAL CENTER
1201 Dolly Madison Blvd.
Mclean, VA 22101
Web: www.interculturalcenter.org

MANJIRO SOCIETY FOR INTERNATIONAL EXCHANGE, INC.
11227 S. Shore Rd.
Reston, VA 20190
Walle Hargreaves, President
Tel: (703) 471-5466 Fax: (703) 456-0285
Email: manjiro@manjiro.org
Web: www.manjiro.org

SRI LANKA ASSOCIATION OF GREATER WASHINGTON, INC.
1820 N. Fort Mayer Dr. #600
Arlington, VA 22209
Nihal Goonewardene, President
Tel: (703) 807-2080

VIETNAMESE CULTURAL SOCIETY OF METROPOLITAN WASHINGTON
P.O. Box 5091
Falls Church, VA 22044
Thanh Bui, President
Tel: (703) 534-3859 Fax: (703) 534-3859
Email: info@vcsmw.org
Web: www.vcsmw.org

FILIPINO-AMERICAN ASSOCIATION OF STAFFORD, VIRGINIA
P.O. Box 594
Garrisonville, VA 22463
Yoly Cuccio, Director
Email: faasvgroup@filamofstafford.org
Web: www.filamofstafford.org

HAI-HUA COMMUNITY CENTER
P.O. Box 8723
Falls Church, VA 22041
Hank Chao, CEO
Tel: (703) 931-0583 Fax: (703) 931-0583
Email: hank.chao@mci.com
Web: www.capava.org/archive/vaab_forum_051504_hankchao.htm

NEPAL FOUNDATION FOR INDIGENOUS COMMUNITIES
P.O. Box 945
Alexandria, VA 22313
Netra Darai, Director
Tel: (617) 441-0771
Email: darai@att.net
Web: www.nepal-nfic.org

NOORISTAN FOUNDATION
5049A Backlick Rd.
Annandale, VA 22003
Tel: (703) 658-9100 Fax: (703) 658-9103
Email: info@nooristanfoundation.org
Web: www.nooristanfoundation.org

SOCIETY OF EX-BUDHANILKANTA STUDENTS
4512 S. 31st St. #202
Arlington, VA 22206
Tel: (703) 931-7878
Email: sebsna@sebsonline.org
Web: www.sebsonline.org

FEDERATION OF REPUBLICAN ASIAN PACIFIC AMERICANS
1714 Great Falls St.
McLean, VA 22101
Julie Rao, Chair
Tel: (703) 734-9463 Fax: (703) 790-9571
Email: jhrao@aol.com

FILIPINO AMERICAN REPUBLICANS OF VIRGINIA, INC.
6746 Andres Terrace, Mezzanine Fl.
Springfield, VA 22151
Vellie S. Dietrich-Hall, President
Tel: (703) 642-8425
Email: info@filamvagop.org
Web: www.filamvagop.org

INDIAN AMERICAN FORUM FOR POLITICAL EDUCATION
8210 Riverside Rd.
Alexandria, VA 22308
Sapish Korpe, Chapter President
Tel: (301) 336-6857 (w) Fax: (310) 336-6899
Email: satish.korpe@verizon.net
Web: www.iafpe.org

ORGANIZATION OF CHINESE AMERICANS
Central Virginia Chapter
P.O. Box 70111
Richmond, VA 23225
Jane Ching, President
Tel: (804) 269-4466
Email: oca_cvc@hotmail.com
Web: www.oca-cvc.org

Eastern Virginia Chapter
1393 London Bridge Rd. #117
Virginia Beach, VA 23453
Simon Lee, President
Tel: (757) 430-0014 Fax: (757) 427-6287
Web: www.oca-evc.org

Northern Virginia Chapter
P.O. Box 592
Merrifield, VA 22116
Jack Hom, Executive VP
Tel: (202) 223-5500
Email: oca_nova@yahoo.com
Web: http://ocanova.iwarp.com

SOUTHWEST VIRGINIA CHAPTER
1674 Saint Andrew Cir.
Blacksburg, VA 24060
Judy Walters, President
Tel: (540) 951-8057
Email: waltej13@hotmail.com

ORGANIZATION OF CHINESE AMERICANS-YOUNG PROFESSIONALS
1686 Waterhaven Dr.
Reston, VA 20190
Jenson Dunn, President
Web: www.ocayp.com

US INDIA POLITICAL ACTION COMMITTEE
P.O. Box 222424
Chantilly, VA 20153
Tel: (703) 488-6880 Fax: (703) 802-6125
Email: info@usinpac.com
Web: www.usinpac.com

AMERICAN SOCIETY OF AFGHAN PROFESSIONALS
P.O. Box 11911
Burke, VA 22009
Weis Sherdel, Executive Director
Tel: (866) 442-1932
Email: weis_sherdel@hotmail.com
Web: www.afghanprofessionals.org

KOREAN AMERICAN UNIVERSITY PROFESSORS ASSOCIATION
515 Chesapeake Dr.
Great Falls, VA 22066
Yoon Shik Park, President
Tel: (202) 994-8215
Email: info@kaupa.org
Web: www.kaupa.org

KOREAN TRANSPORTATION ASSOCIATION IN AMERICA
1800 Jefferson Park Ave. #5
Charlottesville, VA 22903
Seong-soon Yun, President
Tel: (434) 924-3383
Email: hjs4x@virginia.edu
Web: www.kotaa.org

MONTE JADE SCIENCE AND TECHNOLOGY ASSOCIATION
Great Washington Chapter
7926 Jones Branch Dr. #900
McLean, VA 22102
James Cheng, Chairman
Tel: (703) 883-1788 Fax: (703) 883-0218
Email: jcheng@chm.net
Web: www.mj-dc.org

NETWORK OF SOUTH ASIAN PROFESSIONALS-RICHMOND
Network of Indian Professionals of North America
Richmond, VA
Nutan Sinha, President
Email: president@netsaprichmond.org
Web: www.netsaprichmond.org

PHILIPPINE NURSES ASSOCIATION
1605 Rollins Dr.
Alexandria, VA 22307
Alice Andam, President
Tel: (703) 768-6762 Fax: (703) 768-6762
Email: pandam@aol.com

SOCIETY OF AFGHAN ENGINEERS
P.O. Box 11520
Burke, VA 22009-1520
Quasem Kadir, President
Tel: (703) 793-6265 Fax: (703) 793-6265
Email: info@afghan-engineers.org
Web: www.afghan-engineers.org

ASIA ALIVE, INC.
P.O. Box 7506
Falls Church, VA 22040-7506
Nita Edwards
Tel: (703) 642-0124 Fax: (703) 642-0125
Email: hope@asiaalive.org
Web: www.asiaalive.org

BETH EL HEBREW CONGREGATION
3830 Seminary Rd.
Alexandria, VA 22304
Jay Lucas, President
Tel: (703) 370-9400 Fax: (703) 370-7730
Email: office@bethelhebrew.org
Web: www.bethelhebrew.org

CAMBODIAN EVANGELICAL CHURCH OF ARLINGTON VIRGINIA
300 N. Montague St.
Arlington, VA 22203
Rev. Hiepson Kaysarn, Senior Pastor
Tel: (703) 968-8820
Web: www.nvacec.com

CHINA EDUCATIONAL EXCHANGE
1251 Virginia Ave.
Harrisonburg, VA 22802
Myrrl Byler, Director
Tel: (540) 432-6983 Fax: (540) 434-5556
Email: info@chinaedex.org
Web: www.chinaeducationalexchange.org

CONGREGATION BETH ISRAEL
P.O. Box 320
Charlottesville, VA 22902
Elayne Phillips, President
Tel: (434) 295-6382 Fax: (434) 296-6491
Email: pres@cbicville.org
Web: www.cbicville.org

FILIPINO INDEPENDENT BAPTIST CHURCH
5809 Chambers St.
Norfolk, VA 23502
Jose Ramirez, Pastor
Tel: (757) 461-1005

FIRST CHINESE BAPTIST CHURCH
228 Pritchard Rd.
Virginia Beach, VA 23452
Long Yip, Chairman
Tel: (757) 340-6069
Email: contact@fcbc-va.org
Web: www.fcbc-va.org

GEORGE MASON CHINESE CHRISTIAN FELLOWSHIP
10523 Main St. #11
Fairfax, VA 22030
Andrew Liu
Email: andyxliu@hotmail.com
Web: www.gmu.edu/org/ccf

HILTON KOREAN CHRISTIAN CHURCH
P.O. Box 1186, 100 James River Dr.
Newport News, VA 23601
Pastor Kyo D. Song
Tel: (757) 596-5969 Fax: (757) 599-5354
Email: pastor@hiltonchurch.org
Web: www.hiltonchurch.org

HOLY MARTYRS OF VIETNAM CHURCH
915 S. Wakefield St.
Arlington, VA 22204
Thu H. Bui, Chairman of the Parish Council
Tel: (703) 553-0370 Fax: (703) 553-0371
Email: cttd.vn@verizon.net
Web: www.cttdva.net

KOREAN UNITED METHODIST CHURCH OF GREATER WASHINGTON
1219 Swinka Mill Rd.
McLean, VA 22102
Tel: (703) 448-1131 Fax: (703) 448-5384
Email: info@kumcgw.org
Web: www.kumcgw.org

OHEF SHOLOM TEMPLE
530 Raleigh Ave.
Norfolk, VA 23507
Michael L. Joseph, Senior Rabbi
Tel: (757) 625-4295 Fax: (757) 625-3762
Email: office@ohefsholom.org
Web: www.ohefsholom.org

PENINSULA CHINESE BAPTIST CHURCH
3800 George Washington Memorial Hwy.
Grafton, VA 23692
Rev. Philip Chao, Pastor
Tel: (757) 877-9787
Web: http://members.cox.net/pcbc2002/

THAI BUDDHIST CENTER OF NORTHERN VIRGINIA
22147 Cedar Green Rd.
Sterling, VA 20164-5332
Tel: (703) 406-8290 Fax: (703) 406-4705
Email: admin@watyarn.com
Web: www.watyarn.com

THE MUSLIM AMERICAN SOCIETY
P.O. Box 1896
Falls Church, VA 22041
Souheil Ghannouchi, President
Tel: (703) 998-6525 Fax: (703) 998-6526
Email: mas@masnet.org
Web: www.masnet.org

VIETNAMESE INSTITUTE OF PHILOSOPHY AND RELIGION
1609 Lozano Dr.

Vienna, VA 22182
Email: vientrietdao@yahoo.com
Web: http://members.cox.net/vipr/

VIETNAMESE INSTITUTE OF PHILOSOPHY AND RELIGION

1074 Great Passage Blvd.
Great Falls, VA 22066
Thu H. Bui, Ph.D., President
Tel: (703) 281-7929
Email: vientrietdao@yahoo.com
Web: www.vientrietdao.org

WAT LAO BUDDHAVONG OF WASHINGTON DC

3043 Catlett Rd.
Catlett, VA 20119
Phra Acharn Bounmy, Member
Tel: (540) 788-4968 Fax: (540) 788-1219
Email: watlao2000@yahoo.com
Web: www.watlao.org

RESEARCH

ATLAS ECONOMIC RESEARCH FOUNDATION

4084 University Dr. #103
Fairfax, VA 22030
Alejandro Chafuen, President
Tel: (703) 934-6969 Fax: (703) 352-7530
Email: atlas@atlasusa.org
Web: www.atlasusa.org

CHINA INFORMATION CENTER

3056 Covington St.
Fairfax, VA 22031
Tel: (703) 280-2700 Fax: (703) 280-2709
Email: mei.chen@cicus.org
Web: www.cicus.org

KOREA-US SCIENCE COOPERATION CENTER

1952 Gallows Rd.
Vienna, VA 22182
Gill Seung Lee, Director
Tel: (703) 893-9772 Fax: (703) 847-8592
Email: kosef@mannam.com
Web: www.kusco.org

SCIENTIFIC

EDUCATION AND SCIENCE SOCIETY, INC.

P.O. Box 9525
McLean, VA 22101-0525
Dr. Mu-Ming Poo, President
Tel: (703) 893-6743
Email: info@esscare.org
Web: www.esscare.org

KOREAN TOXICOLOGISTS ASSOCIATION IN AMERICA

500-A Woodland Ct.
Vienna, VA 22180
Byong Han Chin, President
Tel: (703) 305-6376 Fax: (703) 305-5147
Email: chin.byong-han@epamail.epa.gov

KOREAN-AMERICAN SCIENTISTS AND ENGINEERS ASSOCIATION

1952 Gallows Rd. #300
Vienna, VA 22182
Ashley Kim, Administrative Manager
Tel: (703) 748-1221 Fax: (703) 748-1331
Email: sejong@ksea.org
Web: www.ksea.org

SPEC. INT., CHILD CARE

HELP THE AFGHAN CHILDREN

8603 Westwood Center Dr. #230
Vienna, VA 22182
Suraya Sadeed, Founder/Executive Director
Tel: (703) 848-0407 Fax: (703) 848-0408
Email: info@helptheafghanchildren.org
Web: www.helptheafghanchildren.org

KOREAN FOCUS FOR ADOPTIVE FAMILIES

1906 Sword Ln.

Alexandria, VA 22308
Debbie Dalton, President
Email: info@koreanfocus.org
Web: www.koreanfocus.org

VIETNAM CHILDREN'S FUND

P.O. Box 150
Unionville, VA 22567
Terry Anderson, Co-Chair
Tel: (202) 347-2422
Email: director@vietnamchildren.org
Web: www.vietnamchildren.org

SPEC. INT., EDUCATION

AFGHAN ACADEMY, INC.

5105 Backlick Rd.
Annandale, VA 22003
Nesar Zia, President
Tel: (703) 941-1495 Fax: (703) 941-1495

AMERICAN ASSOCIATION OF TEACHERS OF ARABIC

College of William and Mary
P.O. Box 8795
Williamsburg, VA 23187-8795
John Eisele, Executive Director
Tel: (757) 221-3145 Fax: (757) 221-3637
Email: aata@wm.edu
Web: www.wm.edu/aata

ASNEX

1601 Willow Lawn Dr. #601
Richmond, VA 23230
Akemi Earle, VP/General Manager
Tel: (804) 282-6377 Fax: (804) 282-6376
Email: asianexus@asnex.com
Web: www.asnex.com/

CHIANG CHING-KUO FOUNDATION FOR INTERNAL SCHOLARLY EXCHANGE

8361 B Greensboro Dr.
McLean, VA 22102
Hsing-wei Lee, Director
Tel: (703) 903-7460 Fax: (703) 903-7462
Email: cckfnao@aol.com
Web: www.cckf.org

HOPE CHINESE SCHOOL

Fairfax Campus
6622 Fairweather Ct.
Burke, VA 22015
Bin Duan, Principal
Tel: (571) 239-1868
Email: bduan@yahoo.com
Web: www.hopechineseschool.org

Herndon Campus
Herndon High School, 700 Bennett St.
Herndon, VA 20170
Junzhe Liu, Principal
Tel: (571) 215-0098
Email: junzheliu817@yahoo.com
Web: www.hopechineseschool.org

INTERNATIONAL NEPALI LITERARY SOCIETY

1727 Horner Rd.
Woodbridge, VA 22191
Purushottam Subedi, President
Tel: (703) 491-1014 Fax: (703) 491-1014
Email: info@inls.org
Web: www.inls.org

IRANIAN COMMUNITY SCHOOL

311 W. Maple Ave. #A
Vienna, VA 22180
Shantadj Deyhimi, Founder/Principle
Tel: (703) 255-4726 Fax: (703) 319-7721
Email: deyhimi@iraniancommunityschool.com
Web: www.iraniancommunityschool.com

MIDDLE EAST STUDIES PROGRAM

University of Virginia
P.O. Box 400167
Charlottesville, VA 22904-4167
David A. Waldner, Director

Tel: (434) 924-3033 Fax: (434) 924-7867
Email: daw4h@virginia.edu
Web: http://faculty.virginia.edu/mesp

NORTHERN VIRGINIA EXPERIMENTAL CHINESE SCHOOL

P.O. Box 3765
Reston, VA 20195
Li-Ping Wang, Principal
Tel: (703) 863-9623
Email: info@nvaecs.org
Web: www.nvaecs.org

PEACE CORPS ALUMNI FOUNDATION FOR PHILIPPINE DEVELOPMENT

P.O. Box 126
Arlington, VA 22210
Maureen Carroll, President
Email: board@rpcvphilippines.org
Web: www.rpcvphilippines.org

THE JEFFERSON TIBETAN SOCIETY

P.O. Box 874
Charlottesville, VA 22902
Geshe Jampel Thardo, Resident Lama
Tel: (434) 980-1752
Email: jts108va@aol.com
Web: http://monticello.avenue.org/jts

US CHINA PEOPLES FRIENDSHIP ASSOCIATION

Richmond Chapter
1720 Hanover Ave.
Richmond, VA 23220
Dr. Sheryl Baldwin
Tel: (804) 353-5805
Web: www.uscpfa.org

VIETNAMESE LANGUAGE SCHOOL

Holy Martyrs of Vietnam Church
915 S. Wakefield St.
Arlington, VA 22204
Thu H. Bui, Principal
Tel: (703) 553-0370 Fax: (703) 553-0371
Email: cttd.vn@verizon.net
Web: www.cttdva.net/lopvietngu.htm

SPEC. INT., HEALTH SERVICES

AFGHAN HEALTH & DEVELOPMENT SERVICES

8603 Westwood Center Dr. #230
Vienna, VA 22182
Aziz R. Qarghah, Director
Tel: (703) 848-9346 Fax: (703) 848-0408
Email: arq@ahds.org
Web: www.ahds.org

VIETNAMESE RESETTLEMENT ASSOCIATION

6131 Willston Dr. #6
Falls Church, VA 22044
Kim Oanh Cook, Executive Director
Tel: (703) 532-3716 Fax: (703) 532-3525
Email: kcvra1@aol.com

SPEC. INT., HUMAN RELATIONS

AMERICAN COALITION FOR FILIPINO VETERANS, INC.

841 S. Glebe Rd.
Arlington, VA 22204
Eric LaChica, Executive Director
Tel: (202) 246-1998
Email: us.filvets@verizon.net
Web: http://usfilvets.tripod.com

AMERICAN IRAQI COUNCIL

7263 Maple Pl. #210
Annandale, VA 22003
Aziz-Al-Taee
Tel: (877) 807-8700 Fax: (877) 803-1800
Email: iraq@al-iraq.org
Web: www.al-iraq.org

FAMILIES OF VIETNAMESE POLITICAL PRISONERS ASSOCIATION

3223 S. Utah St.
Arlington, VA 22206
Ngoc Dung Trinh, Project Director
Tel: (703) 820-3396 Fax: (703) 820-3396
Email: dung.trinh@att.net

KOREAN-AMERICAN SOCIETY OF GREATER RICHMOND

3912 Meadowdale Blvd.
Richmond, VA 23234
Hyun Sung Lim
Fax: (804) 275-6134
Web: www.kasgr.org

LEAGUE OF KOREAN AMERICANS, USA, INC.

P.O. Box 1072
5238 Port Royal Rd.
Springfield, VA 22151-0072
Peter Shin, National Chairman
Tel: (703) 494-5221
Email: peter.shin@mvp-construction.com
Web: www.loka-usa.org

LEAGUE OF VIETNAMESE ASSOCIATION OF WASHINGTON, DC

P.O. Box 5055
Springfield, VA 22150
Doan Huu Dinh, Chairman
Tel: (877) 263-6109 Fax: (877) 263-6109
Email: lhvn@ureach.com

NATIONAL ASSOCIATION OF KOREAN AMERICANS

3883 Plaza Dr.
Fairfax, VA 22030
William T. Cho, President
Tel: (703) 267-2388 Fax: (703) 267-2396
Email: nakausa@naka.org
Web: www.naka.org

NATIONAL CONGRESS OF VIETNAMESE AMERICANS

6433 Northanna Dr.
Springfield, VA 22150
Hung Nguyen, President/CEO
Tel: (877) 592-4140
Email: info@ncvaonline.org
Web: www.ncvaonline.org

SPEC. INT., IMMIGRATION

BOAT PEOPLE SOS

6400 Arlington Blvd. #640
Falls Church, VA 22042
Tin Vo, Office Manager
Tel: (703) 538-2190 Fax: (703) 538-2191
Email: bpsos@bpsos.org
Web: www.bpsos.org

NEWCOMER COMMUNITY SERVICE CENTER

Virginia Office
6131 Willston Dr. Rm. 8
Falls Church, VA 22044
Vilay Chaleunrath, Executive Director
Tel: (703) 241-0300 Fax: (703) 241-9546
Email: newcomer@newcomerservice.org
Web: www.newcomerservice.org

REFUGEE AND IMMIGRATION SERVICES

Catholic Diocese of Richmond
811 Cathedral Pl.
Richmond, VA 23220
Suwattana Sugg, Education Coordinator
Tel: (804) 355-4559 Fax: (804) 355-4697
Email: ssugg@richmonddiocese.org
Web: www.richmonddiocese.org

SPEC. INT., INFORMATION REFERRAL

AFGHANS4TOMORROW

P.O. Box 9071
Reston, VA 20195-2971
Tel: (703) 708-5684

Email: info@afghans4tomorrow.com
Web: www.afghans4tomorrow.com

VIETNAMESE ASSOCIATION FOR COMPUTING, ENGINEERING TECHNOLOGY, AND SCIENCE
P.O. Box 230358
Centreville, VA 20120
Tran Hai, President/Chair
Email: vacets-adcom@vacets.org
Web: www.vacets.org

ASSEMBLY OF THE RVN VETERANS
P.O. Box 5055
Springfield, VA 22150
MG Le Minh Dao, CEO
Tel: (877) 263-6109 Fax: (877) 263-6109
Email: ubphhd@ureach.com

KOREAN CENTRAL SENIOR CENTER
8526 Amanda Pl.
Vienna, VA 22182
Tel: (703) 876-5545 Fax: (703) 869-0117
Web: www.kcpc.org/senior/

NORTHERN VIRGINIA VIETNAMESE SENIOR CITIZENS ASSOCIATION
Holy Martyrs of Vietnam Church
915 S. Wakefield St.
Arlington, VA 22204
Mai Pham Bui, President
Tel: (703) 553-0370 Fax: (703) 553-0371
Email: thumaibui@yahoo.com
Web: www.cttdva.net/novasca

ASIAN AMERICAN SOCIETY OF CENTRAL VIRGINIA
P.O. Box 35194
Richmond, VA 23235
Suwattana Sugg, Chairperson
Tel: (804) 272-5758
Email: aasocv98@hotmail.com
Web: www.aasocv.org

BANGLADESH CENTER FOR COMMUNITY DEVELOPMENT, INC.
313 N. Glebe Rd. #209
Arlington, VA 22203
Tel: (703) 243-1500
Web: www.banglaschool.us

DRAGON BRIDGE, INC.
7531 Leesburg Pike #202
Falls Church, VA 22043
Patricia Shao, President
Tel: (703) 883-0888 Fax: (703) 883-0512
Email: pws@dragonbridge.com
Web: www.dragonbridge.com

JAPAN VIRGINIA SOCIETY
830 E. Main St. #304
Richmond, VA 23219
Tel: (804) 783-0740 Fax: (804) 643-3727
Email: Japan@richmond.infi.net

JAPANESE AMERICAN CARE FUND
4022 Hummer Rd. #B
Annandale, VA 22003
Noriko Iwase, President
Tel: (703) 256-5223 Fax: (703) 256-5611
Email: carefund@jacarefund.org
Web: www.jacarefund.org

JEWISH COMMUNITY CENTER OF NORTHERN VIRGINIA
8900 Little River Turnpike
Fairfax, VA 22031
Barbara Kaplowitz, Director
Tel: (703) 323-0880 Fax: (703) 323-1993
Email: barbarak@jccnv.org
Web: www.jccnv.org

JEWISH COMMUNITY CENTER OF TIDEWATER
7300 Newport Ave.
Norfolk, VA 23505
Marty Trachtenberg, Executive Vice President
Tel: (804) 489-1371
Web: www.jccshr.org

JEWISH COMMUNITY FEDERATION OF RICHMOND
5403 Monument Ave.
Richmond, VA 23226-7128
Tel: (804) 288-0045 Fax: (804) 282-7507
Email: jgelfand@jewishrichmond.com
Web: www.jewishrichmond.org

JEWISH FAMILY SERVICE OF TIDEWATER, INC.
7300 Newport Ave.
Norfolk, VA 23505
Betty Ann Levy, Executive Director
Tel: (757) 489-3111 Fax: (757) 451-1796
Web: www.jfshamptonroads.org

JEWISH FAMILY SERVICES OF RICHMOND
6718 Patterson Ave.
Richmond, VA 23226
Susan Meyers, President
Tel: (804) 282-5644 Fax: (804) 285-0006
Email: information@jfsrichmond.org
Web: www.jfsrichmond.org

KOREAN AMERICAN SOCIETY OF GREATER RICHMOND
2800 Aylesford Dr.
Richmond, VA 23113
Eun Ho Kim, President
Tel: (804) 225-1399 Fax: (804) 225-1399
Email: knike326@aol.com

KOREAN ASSOCIATION OF TIDEWATER
300 Wythe St.
Portsmouth, VA 23704
Hyun-Jong Chay, Past President
Tel: (757) 397-0771 Fax: (757) 397-5702
Email: towi@bellatlantic.net

KOREAN COMMUNITY SERVICES CENTER
7610 New Castle Dr.
Annandale, VA 22003
Esther Park, Executive Director
Tel: (703) 354-6345 Fax: (703) 354-6391
Email: kcsc_va@kcscgw.org
Web: www.kcscgw.org

KOREAN SERVICE CENTER OF GREATER WASHINGTON
7610 Newcastle Dr.
Annandale, VA 22003
Key Young Kim, Chairman
Tel: (703) 354-6345 Fax: (703) 354-6391
Email: kcsc_va@kcscgw.org
Web: www.kcscgw.org

PHILIPPINE AMERICAN FOUNDATION FOR CHARITIES, INC.
Virginia Branch
2639 Paddock Gate Ct.
Herndon, VA 20171-2900
Mary Anne T. Fadul, President
Tel: (703) 471-0775
Email: info@pafc-inc.org
Web: www.pafc-inc.org

ROKPA USA
c/o Virginia Dempsey, 6501 Gretna Green Way
Alexandria, VA 22312
Edith Irwin
Tel: (703) 642-2248 Fax: (703) 642-1591
Email: info@rokpausa.org
Web: www.rokpa.org

TAIWANESE AMERICAN ASSOCIATION
P.O. Box 654
McLean, VA 22101
Dr. George T. Chang, Chairman of the Board of Directors
Tel: (703) 893-6500 Fax: (703) 356-4422

THAI-AMERICAN ASSOCIATION OF HAMPTON ROADS
3076 Egyptian Ln.
Virginia Beach, VA 23456
Nickie Kennedy, President
Tel: (757) 427-4121
Email: nkennedy@vbgov.com

UNITED JEWISH COMMUNITY OF THE VIRGINIA PENINSULA, INC.
2700 Spring Rd.
Newport News, VA 23606
Tel: (757) 930-1422 Fax: (757) 930-3762
Email: unitedjc@erols.com
Web: www.ujcvp.org

UNITED JEWISH FEDERATION OF TIDEWATER
5000 Corporate Woods Dr. #200
Virginia Beach, VA 23462
Harry Graber, Executive Vice President
Tel: (757) 965-6100 Fax: (757) 965-6102
Email: ujft@ujft.org
Web: www.jewishva.org

THAI TENNIS ORGANIZATION IN AMERICA
13015 Dunhill Dr.
Fairfax, VA 22030
George Duangmanee, President
Tel: (703) 855-9499
Email: thanakorn@titanus.org

VIETNAM ASSISTANCE FOR THE HANDICAPPED
P.O. Box 6554
McLean, VA 22106
Ca Van Tran, President
Tel: (703) 847-9582 Fax: (703) 448-8207
Email: vnah1@aol.com
Web: www.vnah-hev.org

AFGHAN WIDOWS AND ORPHANS FUND
P.O. Box 8208
McLean, VA 22106
Gina Hamrah, Founder
Tel: (866) 718-3056
Email: gina@awof.org
Web: www.awof.org

HADASSAH
Southern Seaboard Region
P.O. Box 71955
Richmond, VA 23238-2901
Debbie Friedman, President
Tel: (866) 822-5494
Email: debbie.friedman@hadassah.org
Web: www.hadassah.org

ORGANIZATION OF KOREAN AMERICAN WOMEN, INC.
P.O. Box 1079
Springfield, VA 22151
Silvia Patton, President
Tel: (703) 573-9111 Fax: (703) 573-9210
Email: okaw@okaw.org
Web: www.okaw.org

RAPE AGGRESSION DEFENSE PROGRAM
Falls Church City Police Department
498-A Wythe Creek Rd.
Poquoson, VA 23662
Jan Barrymore, Executive Board Member
Tel: (757) 868-4400 Fax: (757) 868-4401
Email: radinfo@rad-systems.com
Web: www.rad-systems.com

KOREAN AMERICAN SHARING MOVEMENT, INC.
7004 Little River Turnpike #0
Annandale, VA 22003
Gilbert Oh, Program Manager
Tel: (703) 867-0846 Fax: (703) 354-0427
Email: office@kasm.org
Web: www.kasm.org

NATIONAL CENTER FOR MISSING & EXPLOITED CHILDREN
National Headquarters
Charles B. Wang Intl. Childrens Bldg.
699 Prince St.
Alexandria, VA 22314-3175
Ernie Allen, President/CEO
Tel: (703) 274-3900 Fax: (703) 274-2200
Web: www.missingkids.com

ASIAN STUDENT UNION
University of Virginia
P.O. Box 400715,SAC Box 39
Charlottesville, VA 22904-4715
Huong Huynh, President
Email: huong@virginia.edu
Web: www.uvaasu.org

CHINESE STUDENT AND SCHOLARS ASSOCIATION
George Mason University
4400 University Dr.
Fairfax, VA 22030
Yihua Song, President
Tel: (703) 298-8796
Email: ysong1@gmu.edu
Web: www.gmu.edu/org/China

CHINESE STUDENTS AND SCHOLARS SOCIETY
University of Virginia
Newcomb Hall, P.O. Box 400715, Center Box 92
Charlottesville, VA 22901
Zhanxiang Huang, President
Email: csss-owner@virginia.edu
Web: http://scs.student.virginia.edu/~csss

FILIPINO AMERICAN STUDENT ASSOCIATION
Virginia Tech University
Squires Student Ctr.
Blacksburg, VA 24060
Crystal Tanyag, President
Email: ctanyag@vt.edu
Web: http://vtfasa.dyndns.org

HONG KONG CLUB
Virginia Polytechnic Institute
123 Squires Student Ctr.
Blacksburg, VA 24060
Desmond Ho, President
Email: hkclub@vt.edu
Web: http://filebox.vt.edu/org/hkclub

MUSLIM STUDENTS ASSOCIATION
University of Virginia
P.O. Box 400715, SAC Box #222
Charlottesville, VA 22904-4701
Yusra Hafiz, Council
Email: uva-msa@virginia.edu
Web: www.student.Virginia.EDU/~islam

ORGANIZATION OF YOUNG FILIPINO AMERICANS
University of Virginia
P.O. Box 400715, Sac Box 239
Charlottesville, VA 22904-4715
Jenni Zamora, President
Email: jcz8b@virginia.edu
Web: www.oyfa.com

THAI STUDENT ASSOCIATION
Virginia Polytechnic Institute & State University
Virginia Polytechnic Institute & State University
Blacksburg, VA 24061

Nithiwat Kampanya, President
Tel: (540) 231-6000
Email: trungroj@vt.edu
Web: www.thai.org.vt.edu

VIETNAMESE STUDENTS ASSOCIATION
University of Virginia
P.O. Box 400536
Charlottesville, VA 22904
Lang Nguyen, President
Tel: (434) 296-8624
Email: lhn6f@virginia.edu
Web: www.student.virginia.edu/~vsa-uva

WASHINGTON

ARTISTIC

ASIAN ART COUNCIL
Seattle Art Museum
P.O. Box 22000
Seattle, WA 98122-9700
Paula Mcardle, Art Council/Adult Public
Programs Manager
Tel: (206) 654-3119 Fax: (206) 654-3135
Email: councils@seattleartmuseum.org
Web: www.seattleartmuseum.org

JAPANESE GARDEN SOCIETY OF SEATTLE
1811 Queen Anne Ave. North #200
Seattle, WA 98109
Tel: (206) 286-9644 Fax: (206) 286-0709

NORTHWEST ASIAN AMERICAN THEATER
409 7th Ave. South
Seattle, WA 98104
Chay Yew, Artistic Director
Tel: (206) 340-1445 Fax: (206) 682-4348
Email: admin@nwaat.org
Web: www.nwaat.co.

BUSINESS

FOUNDATION FOR RUSSIAN AMERICAN ECONOMIC COOPERATION
2601 4th Ave. #310
Seattle, WA 98121
Carol Vipperman, President
Tel: (206) 443-1935 Fax: (206) 443-0954
Email: fraec@fraec.org
Web: www.fraec.org

JAPAN BUSINESS ASSOCIATION OF SEATTLE
1305 4th Ave. #816
Seattle, WA 98101
Tel: (206) 624-9077 Fax: (206) 340-1691
Email: shunju@jbaseattle.org
Web: www.jbaseattle.org

NATIONAL CENTER FOR ASIA PACIFIC ECONOMIC COOPERATION
2200 Alaskan Way #420
Seattle, WA 98121
Monica Whaley, Executive Director
Tel: (206) 441-9022 Fax: (206) 441-1006
Email: info@ncapec.org
Web: www.ncapec.org

CHAMBER OF COMMERCE

JAPANESE AMERICAN CHAMBER OF COMMERCE
1416 S. Jackson St.
Seattle, WA 98144
Scott Oki, Chairman
Tel: (206) 320-1010 Fax: (206) 322-1898
Email: jachamber@jachamber.com
Web: www.jachamber.com

CULTURAL

ARAB AMERICAN COMMUNITY COALITION
P.O. Box 31642
Seattle, WA 98103
Tel: (206) 545-1735 Fax: (206) 547-8607

Email: info@theaacc.org
Web: www.theaacc.org

CENTER FOR ETHICAL LEADERSHIP
1404 E. Jefferson St. #505
Seattle, WA 98122
Steve Stapleton, Office Manager
Tel: (206) 328-3020 Fax: (206) 328-4570
Email: center@ethicalleadership.org
Web: www.ethicalleadership.org

CHINESE COMMUNITY GIRLS DRILL TEAM
6710 -127 Pl. SE
Bellevue, WA 98006
Arthur Lum, President/Director
Tel: (425) 401-1464 Fax: (425) 401-1464
Email: drill1952@aol.com
Web: www.sccgdt.org

DENSHO JAPANESE AMERICAN LEGACY PROJECT
1416 S. Jackson St.
Seattle, WA 98144
Tom Ikeda, Executive Director
Tel: (206) 320-0095 Fax: (206) 320-0098
Email: tom.ikeda@densho.org
Web: www.densho.org

FILIPINO AMERICAN NATIONAL HISTORICAL SOCIETY
National Office
810 18th Ave. #100
Seattle, WA 98122
Dorothy Laigo Cordova, Executive Director
Tel: (206) 322-0203 Fax: (206) 322-0204
Email: fanhsnational@earthlink.org
Web: www.fanhs-national.org

FILIPINO CULTURAL HERITAGE SOCIETY OF WASHINGTON
1710 N. 103rd St.
Seattle, WA 98133
Flori Montate, President/Founder
Tel: (206) 527-8605 Fax: (206) 527-8603
Email: fmontante@juno.com

FILIPINO-AMERICAN ASSOCIATION OF THE TRI-CITIES
P.O. Box 115
Richland, WA 99352
Tel: (509) 547-0557
Email: kniter@cbvcp.com
Web: www.cbvcp.com/filam/filam.htm

KOREAN AMERICAN HISTORICAL SOCIETY
10303 Meridian Ave. North #200
Seattle, WA 98133-9483
Ick-Whan Lee, President
Tel: (206) 528-5784 Fax: (206) 523-4340
Email: kahs@kahs.org
Web: www.kahs.org

NEPAL SEATTLE SOCIETY
20130 128th Ave. SE
Kent, WA 98031
Tirtha Khanal, President
Tel: (206) 310-5919
Email: info@nepalseattle.org
Web: www.nepalseattle.org

OLYMPIA-YASHIRO SISTER CITY ASSOCIATION
P.O. Box 11998
Olympia, WA 98508-1998
Bob Nakamura, Treasurer
Email: sgtmilehibob@att.net
Web: www.oysc.org

SEATTLE CHINATOWN/INTERNATIONAL DISTRICT PRESERVATION AND DEVELOPMENT AUTHORITY
409 Mayard Ave. #200 South
Seattle, WA 98104
Sue Taoka, Executive Director
Tel: (206) 624-8929 Fax: (206) 467-6376
Email: info@scidpda.org

TET IN SEATTLE
P.O. Box 2833

Seattle, WA 98111-2833
Andrew Mo Nguyen, Executive Director
Tel: (206) 706-2658
Email: executivedir@tetinseattle.org
Web: www.tetinseattle.org

TURKISH AMERICAN CULTURAL ASSOCIATION OF WASHINGTON
P.O. Box 357
Kirkland, WA 98083-0357
Gokce D. Sezgin, President
Tel: (425) 646-7793
Email: board@tacawa.org
Web: www.tacawa.org

VIETNAM WOODEN BOAT FOUNDATION
425 Washington St.
Port Townsend, WA 09368
John Doney, President
Email: webmaster@vietnamboats.org
Web: www.vietnamboats.org

WING LUKE ASIAN MUSEUM
407 7th Ave. South
Seattle, WA 98104
Ron Chew, Executive Director
Tel: (206) 623-5124 Fax: (206) 623-4559
Email: rchew@wingluke.org
Web: www.wingluke.org

ENTERTAINMENT

THE REPERTORY ACTORS THEATRE
Seattle's Multi-Ethnic Philanthropic Theatre Company
1122 E. Pike St. #1111
Seattle, WA 98122
David Hsieh, Managing Artistic Director
Tel: (206) 364-3283
Email: react.works@usa.net
Web: www.reacttheatre.org

MULTI-PURPOSE

COMMUNITY ACTION PROGRAMMING
409 Maynard Ave. South #P1-B
Seattle, WA 98104
Kristopher Proctor, Program Manager
Tel: (206) 621-1815 Fax: (206) 467-6376
Email: cap@scidpda.org

FILIPINO COMMUNITY OF SEATTLE
5740 MLK Jr. Way South
Seattle, WA 98118
Bert Caoili, President
Tel: (206) 722-9372 Fax: (206) 722-1060
Email: kuyabert@comcast.net
Web: www.filipinocommunityseattle.org

MEDICAL, EDUCATIONAL, AND DEVELOPMENT OF RESOURCES THROUGH INTERNATIONAL EXCHANGE
17311 135th Ave. NE #C100
Woodinville, WA 98072
Andrew Goh, Executive Advisor
Tel: (866) 463-3749
Email: office@medrix.org
Web: www.medrix.org

STATE OF WASHINGTON COMMISSION ON ASIAN PACIFIC AMERICAN AFFAIRS
1210 Eastside St. SE, 1st Fl.
Olympia, WA 98504
Ellen Abellera, Executive Director
Tel: (360) 586-9500 Fax: (360) 586-9501
Email: capaa@capaa.wa.gov
Web: www.capaa.wa.gov

UNITED CAMBODIAN DEVELOPMENT ASSOCIATION
1421 195th St. SW
Lynnwood, WA 98036
Sin Pakun, President
Tel: (425) 579-0960
Email: ucda@unitedcambodian.org
Web: http://unitedcambodian.org

WASHINGTON STATE COMMISSION ON ASIAN PACIFIC AMERICAN AFFAIRS
P.O. Box 40925
Olympia, WA 98405
Ellen Abellera, Executive Director
Tel: (360) 725-5667
Email: capaa@capaa.wa.gov
Web: www.capaa.wa.gov

POLITICAL ACTION

ASIAN PACIFIC AMERICAN LABOR ALLIANCE
Seattle Chapter
3214 24th Ave. South
Seattle, WA 98144
Tracy Lai, President
Tel: (206) 721-1128
Email: mpedregosa@seiu6.org
Web: www.apalanet.org

South Puget Sound Chapter
2700 Evergreen Pkwy. NW
Olympia, WA 98505
Lin Crowley, President
Tel: (360) 867-6239 Fax: (360) 753-1695
Email: crowleyl@evergreen.edu
Web: www.apalanet.org

CIVIL SOCIETY INTERNATIONAL
2929 Blakeley St.
Seattle, WA 98105
Holt Ruffin, Executive Director
Email: csi@civilsoc.org
Web: www.civilsoc.org

ORGANIZATION OF CHINESE AMERICANS
Greater Seattle Chapter
606 Maynard Ave. South #104
Seattle, WA 98104
Mei-Ling Hsu, President
Tel: (206) 682-0665
Email: ocaseattle@ocaseattle.org
Web: www.ocaseattle.org

PACIFIC AMERICAN EXECUTIVE COUNCIL
1606 Richview Ave. NE #J402
Issaquah, WA 98029
Reidar H. Smith, Director
Tel: (425) 392-8692
Email: reidarsmith@comcast.net

PROFESSIONAL

ASIAN AMERICAN JOURNALISTS ASSOCIATION
Seattle Chapter
P. O. Box 9698
Seattle, WA 98109
Sharon Chan, Co-President
Email: schan@aajaseattle.org
Web: www.aajaseattle.org

ASIAN BAR ASSOCIATION OF WASHINGTON
701 5th Ave. #6100
Seattle, WA 98104
Ken Payson, President
Tel: (206) 389-4222 Fax: (206) 447-0849
Email: kpayson@hewm.com
Web: www.abaw.org

FILIPINO AMERICAN CITY EMPLOYEES OF SEATTLE
P.O. Box 12337
Seattle, WA 98111
Victor Pineda
Tel: (206) 684-0535

FILIPINO-AMERICAN PHYSICIANS OF WASHINGTON STATE
P.O. Box 3444
Federal Way, WA 98063
Leonico Panlasigui, President
Email: panlasigui@aol.com
Web: www.fapwa.org

KOREAN AMERICAN PROFESSIONALS SOCIETY
P.O. Box 392
Seattle, WA 98111-0392
Janette Kwon, President
Tel: (206) 560-0201
Email: seattlekaps@hotmail.com
Web: www.seattlekaps.org

NORTHWEST CHINESE HI-TECH PROFESSIONALS ASSOCIATION
4621 88th Ave. SE
Mercer Island, WA 98040
Mary Tan, President
Tel: (206) 601-9878 Fax: (206) 318-3746
Email: nwchp@nwchp.org
Web: www.nwchp.org

THE NATIONAL ASSOCIATION OF ASIAN AMERICAN PROFESSIONALS
P.O. Box 14344, International Station
Seattle, WA 98104
Ken Lee, Chapter President
Tel: (425) 450-4882
Email: pr@naaapseattle.org
Web: www.naaapseattle.org

VIETNAMESE PROFESSIONALS SOCIETY
Washington Chapter
P.O. Box 152
Everett, WA 98206
Hy-Lan Nguyen, Chapter President
Email: washington@hcgvn.vps.org
Web: www.vpswa.org

WASHINGTON ASSOCIATION OF PHYSICIANS OF INDIAN ORIGIN
1560 N. 115th St. #108
Seattle, WA 98133
Raksha Trivedi, M.D., President
Tel: (206) 362-3113

RELIGIOUS

AGAPE PRESBYTERIAN CHURCH
726 S. 356th St.
Federal Way, WA 98003
Tel: (253) 815-7800 Fax: (253) 740-4572
Email: pastorpaul@agapepc.com
Web: www.agapepc.com

ASIAN OUTREACH USA
305 NE 192nd Ave.
Vancouver, WA 98684
Tel: (360) 883-2421

CAMBODIAN MINISTRIES FOR CHRIST
6511-25th Ave. SW
Seattle, WA 98106-1612
Tel: (206) 935-0577
Email: info@cmcnews.org
Web: www.cmcnews.org

CHINESE EVANGELICAL CHURCH OF VANCOUVER
900 SE Ellsworth Rd.
Vancouver, WA 98684
Tel: (360) 944-1556
Web: www.cecv.org

CONGREGATION BETH ISRAEL
2200 Broadway
Bellingham, WA 98225
Bruce VanGlubt, President
Tel: (360) 733-8890 Fax: (360) 733-9842
Email: vp@bethisrael.com
Web: www.bethisrael.com

CONGREGATION KOL AMI
16530 Avondale Rd. NE
Woodinville, WA 98072
Carolyn Hathaway, President
Tel: (425) 844-1604
Email: president@kolami.net
Web: www.kolami.net

DHARMA REALM BUDDHIST ASSOCIATION
Gold Summit Sagely Monastery
233 1st Ave. West

Seattle, WA 98119
Tel: (206) 284-6690 Fax: (206) 284-6918
Email: info@goldsummitmonastery.org
Web: www.goldsummitmonastery.org

EVANGELICAL CHINESE CHURCH
651 NW 81st St.
Seattle, WA 98117
Simon Chou, Pastor
Tel: (206) 789-6380 Fax: (206) 782-3684
Email: simonchou@eccseattle.org
Web: www.eccseattle.org

JAPANESE COMMUNITY CHURCH OF TACOMA
12213 Pacific Ave. South
Tacoma, WA 98444
Tel: (253) 536-2993

KENT FIRST KOREAN CHRISTIAN REFORMED CHURCH
300 W. Saar St.
Kent, WA 98032
Ho C. Sng, Pastor
Tel: (253) 850-9191 Fax: (253) 852-7566
Email: kentcrc@hotmail.com
Web: www.crchurches.net/kent/index.htm

KHMER EVANGELICAL CHURCH
1320 SW 102nd St.
Seattle, WA 98146
Tel: (206) 533-1291
Email: langseang@hotmail.com
Web: http://cambodianchristian.com/site/kec

KOREAN AMERICAN CALVARY BAPTIST CHURCH
7817 S. 125th St.
Seattle, WA 98178
Jim Bae, Pastor
Tel: (206) 772-4371
Email: jimbae@kacbc.org
Web: www.kacbc.org

KOREAN UNITED PRESBYTERIAN CHURCH
8506 238th St. SW
Edmonds, WA 98026
Sonya Cha
Tel: (425) 776-2711
Email: sonyahcha@yahoo.com
Web: www.seattlekupc.org

NALANDABODHI
3902 Woodland Park Ave. North
Seattle, WA 98103
Tel: (206) 525-6925
Email: seattle@nalandabodhi.org
Web: www.nbseattle.org

SAKYA MONASTERY OF TIBETAN BUDDHISM
108 NW 83rd St.
Seattle, WA 98117
Jigdal Dagchen Sakya, Founder
Tel: (206) 789-2573 Fax: (206) 789-3994
Email: monastery@sakya.org
Web: www.sakya.org

SEATTLE CHINESE ALLIANCE CHURCH
2803 S. Orcas St.
Seattle, WA 98108
Rev. Vincent Yeung, Associate Pastor
Tel: (206) 725-0771 Fax: (206) 725-1647
Email: scac@scacseattle.org
Web: www.scacseattle.org

SEATTLE CHINESE BAPTIST CHURCH
5801 Beacon Ave. South
Seattle, WA 98108-3103
Rev. Martin Leung, Interim Pastor
Tel: (206) 725-6363 Fax: (206) 725-6352
Email: mleung@seattlecbc.org
Web: www.seattlecbc.org

SEATTLE CHINESE GRACE EVANGELICAL FREE CHURCH
1420 NW 80th St.
Seattle, WA 98117
Pastor Lam

Tel: (206) 364-6372
Email: chinesegrace@addr.com
Web: www.chinesegrace.addr.com

SEATTLE TAIWANESE CHRISTIAN CHURCH
5019 Keystone Pl. North
Seattle, WA 98103
Tel: (206) 632-4020
Web: www.stcc.us

SOUTH ASIA ADVOCATES
P.O. Box 2993
Kirkland, WA 98083
Email: southasiaadvocates@hotmail.com
Web: www.southasiaadvocates.com

TACOMA FIRST BAPTIST CHURCH
1328 S. 84th St.
Tacoma, WA 98444
Chang S. Moon, Pastor
Tel: (253) 535-2240
Email: monn@tfbc.org
Web: www.tfbc.org

TEMPLE BETH EL
5975 S. 12th St.
Tacoma, WA 98465-1998
Glenn Lasko, President
Tel: (253) 564-7101 Fax: (253) 564-7103
Email: info@templebethel18.org
Web: http://templebethel18.org

TEMPLE DE HIRSCH SINAI
1511 East Pike
Seattle, WA 98122
Lawrence N. Broder, Executive Director
Tel: (206) 323-8486
Email: lbroder@tdhs-nw.org
Web: www.tdhs-nw.org

RESEARCH

NATIONAL BUREAU OF ASIAN RESEARCH
4518 University Way NE #300
Seattle, WA 908105
Dr. Richard J. Ellings, President
Tel: (206) 632-7370 Fax: (206) 632-7487
Email: nbr@nbr.org
Web: www.nbr.org

SPEC. INT., ALCOHOL/DRUG CENTER

ASIAN AMERICAN CHEMICAL DEPENDANCY TREATMENT SERVICES
24823 Pacific Hwy. South #108
Kent, WA 98032
Tae Son Lee, Executive Director
Tel: (253) 941-2287 Fax: (253) 946-1660
Web: www.iacts.net

SPEC. INT., CHILD CARE

CAMBODIA TOMORROW
1515 Madrona Dr.
Seattle, WA 98122
Email: cambodiatomorrow@yahoo.com
Web: www.cambodiatomorrow.org

CHILDREN OF SYRIA
17482 NE 40th Pl. #G5
Redmond, WA 98052
Anas Abbar
Tel: (425) 869-9093
Email: syriakids@aol.com
Web: www.childrenofsyria.org

SHARE IN ASIA
P.O. Box 815
Kirkland, WA 98083-0815
Tel: (425) 889-9587
Email: information@shareinasia.org
Web: www.shareinasia.org

SPEC. INT., COUNSELING

KOREAN COMMUNITY COUNSELING CENTER
23830 Hwy. 99 North #204A
Edmond, WA 98026
Jean K. Rhee, Executive Director
Tel: (206) 784-5691 Fax: (425) 697-5703
Email: kccc1983@aol.com

SPEC. INT., EDUCATION

APEC STUDY CENTER
University of Washington
4516 University Way NE, Box 354846
Seattle, WA 98195
Donald C. Hellmann, Director
Tel: (206) 616-9100 Fax: (206) 616-6982
Email: info@iip.washington.edu
Web: www.iip.washington.edu

ASIAN ADULT ADOPTEES OF WASHINGTON
P.O. Box 15346
Seattle, WA 98115
Tim Holm, President/Treasurer
Tel: (206) 378-6958 Fax: (425) 379-9336
Email: jennykelly123@msn.com
Web: www.aaawashington.org

ASIAN AMERICAN/PACIFIC ISLANDER FACULTY/STAFF ASSOCIATION
Washington State University
Multicultural Center #104, P.O. Box 642318
Pullman, WA 99164-2318
Anita Rao, Staff
Tel: (509) 335-1986 Fax: (509) 335-1525
Email: wsuapa@wsu.edu
Web: www.wsu.edu/~aapihome

ASIAN PACIFIC AMERICAN STUDENT COALITION
Compton Union Bldg., #51G
Pullman, WA 99163
Keo Southichack, President
Tel: (509) 335-1986 Fax: (509) 335-8368
Email: keokeyo@hotmail.com
Web: http://cub.wsu.edu/aswsu/apasc

CHINA TOMORROW EDUCATION FOUNDATION
P.O. Box 1103
Mercer Island, WA 98040
Waisiu Law
Tel: (425) 788-1812 Fax: (253) 862-8214
Email: w.law@ieee.org
Web: www.chinatomorrow.org

GLOBAL BUSINESS CENTER
University of Washington Business School
Lewis Hall 303, Box 353200
Seattle, WA 98195-3200
Kirsten Aoyama, Director
Tel: (206) 685-3432 Fax: (206) 685-4079
Email: uwciber@u.washington.edu
Web: http://depts.washington.edu/~ciberweb/

MIDDLE EAST CENTER
University of Washington
225 Thomson Hall Box
Seattle, WA 98195
Ellis Goldberg, Director
Tel: (206) 543-4227 Fax: (206) 685-0668
Email: goldberg@u.washington.edu
Web: http://jsis.artsci.washington.edu/programs/mideast

NITARTHA INTERNATIONAL
4822 38th Ave. NE
Seattle, WA 98105-3021
Martin Marvet
Tel: (206) 985-8887 Fax: (206) 985-8878
Email: mmarvet@nitartha.org
Web: www.nitartha.org

TIBET EDUCATION NETWORK
Global Source Network
P.O. Box 11316
Bainbridge Island, WA 98110

Jon Garfunkel, Director
Tel: (206) 780-5797 Fax: (206) 780-5797
Email: info@globalsourcenetwork.org
Web: www.globalsourcenetwork.org

US CHINA PEOPLES FRIENDSHIP ASSOCIATION
Northwest Subregion
7031 NE 175th, SP #46
Kenmore, WA 98028
Grace Johnson, President
Tel: (425) 482-9219
Email: sugarbee0@earthlink.net
Web: www.uscpfa.org

Seattle Chapter
4917 N. 15th St.
Tacoma, WA 98406
Nancy Moffett
Tel: (253) 752-5528
Web: www.uscpfa.org

SPEC. INT., EMPLOYMENT

CENTER FOR CAREER ALTERNATIVES
901 Rainier Ave. South
Seattle, WA 98144
Alan Sugiyama, Executive Director
Tel: (206) 322-9080 Fax: (206) 322-9084
Email: kingcca@ccawa.org
Web: www.ccawa.org

SPEC. INT., HOUSING

INTERNATIONAL DISTRICT HOUSING ALLIANCE
606 Maynard Ave. South #105
Seattle, WA 98104
Stella Chao, Executive Director
Tel: (206) 623-5132 Fax: (206) 623-3479
Email: stella@apialliance.org
Web: www.apialliance.org

SPEC. INT., HUMAN RELATIONS

ASIAN PACIFIC ISLANDER COALITION
Pierce County
123 E. 96th St.
Tacoma, WA 98445
Lua Pritchard, Executive Director
Tel: (253) 535-4202 Fax: (253) 535-4827
Email: luaprkwa@nwlink.com

CHINATOWN INTERNATIONAL DISTRICT BUSINESS IMPROVEMENT AREA
409 Maynard Ave. South #P-1
Seattle, WA 98104
Tim Wang, Executive Director
Tel: (206) 382-1197 Fax: (206) 382-9958
Email: info@cidbia.org
Web: www.cidbia.org

COUNCIL ON AMERICAN-ISLAMIC RELATIONS
Seattle Chapter
P.O. Box 7411
Bellevue, WA 98008
Michaela Corning, Director
Tel: (206) 367-4081 Fax: (206) 774-0436
Email: info@cair-seattle.org
Web: www.cair-seattle.org

FILIPINO-AMERICAN CIVIC EMPLOYEES OF SEATTLE
P.O. Box 21831
Seattle, WA 98111-3811
Eileen Newell, President
Tel: (206) 615-0809
Email: eileen.newell@seattle.org
Web: www.facesseattle.org

GREATER SEATTLE VIETNAM ASSOCIATION
P.O. Box 23282
Seattle, WA 98102
Son Michael Pham, Co-President
Tel: (206) 322-1178 Fax: (206) 374-2944

Email: info@seattlevietnam.org
Web: www.seattlevietnam.org

INTER*IM COMMUNITY DEVELOPMENT ASSOCIATION
308 6th Ave. South
Seattle, WA 98104
Bob Santos, Executive Director
Tel: (206) 624-1802 Fax: (206) 624-5859
Email: bsantos@interimicda.org
Web: www.interimicda.org

JAPANESE AMERICAN CITIZENS LEAGUE
Pacific Northwest District Office
671 S. Jackson St. #206
Seattle, WA 98104
Karen Yoshitomi, Regional Director
Tel: (206) 623-5088 Fax: (206) 623-0526
Email: jaclpnwro@msn.com
Web: www.jacl.org

Seattle Chapter
316 S. Maynard St.
Seattle, WA 98104
Ryan Minato, Webmaster
Tel: (206) 622-4098
Email: email@jaclseattle.org
Web: www.jaclseattle.org

JEWISH PRISONER SERVICES INTERNATIONAL
P.O. Box 85840
Seattle, WA 98145-1840
Chaplain Gary Friedman, Chairman
Tel: (206) 985-0577 Fax: (206) 985-0479
Email: jewishprisonerservices@msn.com
Web: www.jewishprisonerservices.org

THE AMERICAN JEWISH COMMITTEE
1402 3rd Ave. #1415
Seattle, WA 98101-2100
Rabbi Richard Harkavy, Chapter Director
Tel: (206) 622-6315 Fax: (206) 622-3015
Email: seattle@ajc.org
Web: www.ajc.org

VOICES OF PALESTINE
P.O. Box 17467
Seattle, WA 98127-4311
Fax: (702) 995-4311
Email: general@voicesofpalestine.org
Web: www.voicesofpalestine.org

WORLD AFFAIRS COUNCIL
2200 Alaskan Way #450
Seattle, WA 98121
Ian H. Moncaster, President
Tel: (206) 441-5910 Fax: (206) 441-5908
Email: wac@world-affairs.org
Web: www.world-affairs.org

SPEC. INT., IMMIGRATION

INDOCHINA CHINESE REFUGEE ASSOCIATION
418 1/2 8th Ave. South
Seattle, WA 98104
Joel Crane, Program Coordinator
Tel: (206) 625-9955 Fax: (206) 625-0883
Email: icra@icra-yscs.org
Web: www.icrawa.org

REFUGEE AND IMMIGRANT SERVICE CENTER
711 State Ave. NE
Olympia, WA 98506
Nouk Leap, Office Manager
Tel: (360) 754-7197 Fax: (360) 705-4398
Email: risc@refugeeimmigrant.org

SPEC. INT., INFORMATION REFERRAL

ASIAN COUNSELING & REFERRAL SERVICE
Main Office
720 8th Ave. South #200
Seattle, WA 98104-3006
Diane Narasaki, Executive Director
Tel: (206) 695-7600 Fax: (206) 695-7606

Email: dianen@acrs.org
Web: www.acrs.org

CHINESE INFORMATION AND SERVICE CENTER
409 Maynard Ave. South #203
Seattle, WA 98104
Alaric Bien, Executive Director
Tel: (206) 624-5633 Fax: (206) 382-2089
Email: info@cisc-seattle.org
Web: www.cisc-seattle.org

SPEC. INT., LEGAL ASSISTANCE

INTERNATIONAL RESCUE COMMITTEE
318 1st Ave. South #200
Seattle, WA 98104
Robert Johnson, Regional Director
Tel: (206) 623-2105 Fax: (206) 623-2289
Email: bobj@theirc.org
Web: www.theirc.org

SPEC. INT., SENIORS

AGING INFORMATION CENTER
Region X: AK, ID, OR, WA
Blanchard Plz., M/S RX-33 2201 6th Ave. #1202
Seattle, WA 98121-1828
Chisato Kawabori, Regional Administrator
Tel: (206) 615-2298 Fax: (206) 615-2305
Email: chisato.kawabori@aoa.gov
Web: www.aoa.dhhs.gov

KIN ON COMMUNITY CARE NETWORK
4416 S. Brandon St.
Seattle, WA 98118
Samuel Y. Wan, CEO
Tel: (206) 721-3630 Fax: (206) 721-1371
Web: www.kinon.org

NATIONAL ASIAN PACIFIC CENTER ON AGING
1511 3rd Ave. #914
Seattle, WA 98101-1626
Clayton Fong, Executive Director
Tel: (206) 624-1221 Fax: (206) 624-1023
Email: website@napca.org
Web: www.napca.org

NIKKEI CONCERNS
1601 E. Yesler Way
Seattle, WA 98122
Wendy Li, Social Worker
Tel: (206) 323-7100 Fax: (206) 325-1502
Email: wendyl@nikkeiconcerns.org
Web: www.nikkeiconcerns.org

SPEC. INT., SOCIAL INTEREST

AMERICAN RED CROSS LANGUAGE BANK
1900 25th Ave. South
Seattle, WA 98144
Annette Holland, Language Bank Manager
Tel: (206) 726-3554 Fax: (206) 325-8211
Email: languagebank@seattleredcross.org
Web: www.seattleredcross.org

HELPING LINK
P.O. Box 28068
Seattle, WA 98118
M.D. Nguyen, Executive Director
Tel: (206) 568-5160 Fax: (206) 568-5160
Email: helpinglink@cablespeed.com
Web: www.cityofseattle.net/helpinglink

JAPAN AMERICA SOCIETY OF THE STATE OF WASHINGTON
2200 Alaskan Way #400
Seattle, WA 98121
Jeff Demetrescu, President
Tel: (206) 374-0180 Fax: (206) 374-0175
Email: jassw@us_japan.org
Web: www.us-japan.org/jassw

JAPANESE COMMUNITY SERVICE OF SEATTLE
1414 S. Weller St.

Seattle, WA 98144
Tel: (206) 323-0250

JEWISH FAMILY SERVICE
15821 NE 8th St. #210
Bellevue, WA 98008
Tel: (425) 643-2221 Fax: (425) 644-8798
Email: mesc@jfsseattle.org
Web: www.jfsseattle.org

Kent Office
1215 Central Ave. South #131
Kent, WA 98032
Tel: (253) 850-4065 Fax: (253) 850-4070
Email: kent@jfsseattle.org
Web: www.jfsseattle.org

Main Office
1601 16th Ave.
Seattle, WA 98122
JaneDeer-Hileman, Director of Volunteer Services
Tel: (206) 461-3240 Fax: (206) 461-3696
Email: contactus@jfsseattle.org
Web: www.jfsseattle.org

JEWISH FEDERATION OF GREATER SEATTLE
2031 3rd Ave.
Seattle, WA 98121
Tel: (206) 443-5400 Fax: (206) 443-0303
Email: info@jewishinseattle.org
Web: www.jewishinseattle.org

NORTHWEST ASIAN WEEKLY
412 Maynard Ave. South
Seattle, WA 98104
Carol Vu, Editor
Tel: (206) 223-5559 Fax: (206) 223-0626
Email: carol@nwasianweekly.com
Web: www.nwasianweekly.com

STROUM JEWISH COMMUNITY CENTER
3801 E. Mercer Way
Mercer Island, WA
Dana Weiner, Director
Tel: (206) 232-7115 Fax: (206) 232-7119
Email: info@sjcc.org
Web: www.sjcc.org

Seattle Facility
8606 35th Ave. NE
Seattle, WA 98115
Kristin Partridge, Director
Tel: (206) 526-8073 Fax: (206) 526-9958
Email: info@sjcc.org
Web: www.sjcc.org

TAIWANESE AMERICAN FOUNDATION OF GREATER SEATTLE
Seattle Taiwanese American Community Center
4307 11th Ave. NE
Seattle, WA 98105
Dan Zhuibin, President
Tel: (206) 633-1211
Email: webmaster@seataiwancenter.org
Web: www.seataiwancenter.org

VIETNAMESE ADOPTEE NETWORK
1615 S. Lucile St.
Seattle, WA 98108
Christopher Brownlee, President
Email: info@van-online.org
Web: www.van-online.org

VIETNAMESE COMMUNITY ACTIVITY CENTER
P.O. Box 66141
Seattle, WA 98166
Ghi Dang, Vice President Outreach/Culture Affair
Tel: (206) 248-6826 Fax: (206) 246-5652
Email: danghi@vncac.org
Web: www.vncac.org

SPEC. INT., SPORTS

INTERNATIONAL SHOTOKAN KARATE CLUB
Northwest

10020-A Main St. #151
Bellevue, WA 98004
Lee Doohen, Instructor
Tel: (425) 451-8722 Fax: (425) 452-5214
Email: cathycine@worldnet.att.net
Web: www.iskf.com

JAPAN KARATE FEDERATION
2109 E. 4th Plain Blvd.
Vancouver, WA 98661
Ken Kraisler, Chief Instructor
Tel: (360) 687-8790
Email: kraisler@pacific.com
Web: www.pacifier.com/~kraisler

WORLD MODERN ARNIS COALITION AND NATURAL SPIRIT INTERNATIONAL
P.O. Box 64069
University Place, WA 98464-0069
Tel: (253) 564-2867 Fax: (253) 565-7108
Email: kellysworden@comcast.net
Web: www.kellyworden.com

SPEC. INT., WOMEN

ASIAN AND PACIFIC ISLANDER WOMEN AND FAMILY SAFETY CENTER
P.O. Box 14047
Seattle, WA 98114
Emma Catague, Executive Director
Tel: (206) 467-9976 Fax: (206) 467-1072
Email: apiwfsc@apialliance.org

ASSOCIATION OF PACIFIC AND ASIAN WOMEN
Washington State University
P.O. Box 7206
Pullman, WA 99164
Nina Kim, Co-Chair
Tel: (509) 335-1986 Fax: (509) 335-8368
Email: nyk1luvhh@yahoo.com

CHAYA
P.O. Box 22291
Seattle, WA 98122
Vega Subramaniam, Executive Director
Tel: (206) 568-7576 Fax: (206) 568-2479
Email: chaya@chayaseattle.org
Web: www.chayaseattle.org

HADASSAH
Pacific Northwest Region
1750 112th Ave. NE #C225
Bellevue, WA 98004
Michelle Goldberg, President
Tel: (866) 946-6476 Fax: (425) 467-9199
Email: seattle@hadassah.org
Web: www.hadassah.org

KOREAN WOMEN 'S ASSOCIATION
Centralia Chapter
417 N. Pearl St. #A
Centralia, WA 98531
Lua Pritchard, Executive Director
Tel: (360) 736-4310 Fax: (360) 736-4319
Email: luaprkwa@nwlink.com
Web: www.kwaoutreach.org

Federal Way Chapter
31218 Pacific Hwy. South #A
Federal Way, WA 98003
Lua Pritchard, Executive Director
Tel: (253) 946-1995 Fax: (253) 946-1997
Email: kwaking@kwaoutreach.org
Web: www.kwaoutreach.org

Lacey Chapter
4306 Pacific Ave. SE
Lacey, WA 98503
Lua Pritchard, Executive Director
Tel: (360) 455-4524 Fax: (360) 455-4525
Email: luapr@kwaoutreach.org
Web: www.kwaoutreach.org

Main Office
125 E. 96th St.
Tacoma, WA 98445
Lua Pritchard, Executive Director

Tel: (253) 535-4202 Fax: (253) 535-4827
Email: luapr@kwaoutreach.org
Web: www.kwaoutreach.org

Shelton Chapter
1131 E. Shelton Springs Rd.
Shelton, WA 98584
Lua Pritchard, Executive Director
Tel: (360) 426-9700 Fax: (360) 426-6688
Email: luapr@kwaoutreach.org
Web: www.kwaoutreach.org

NATIONAL COUNCIL FOR JEWISH WOMEN
Seattle Section
1011 Boren Ave. Box 804
Seattle, WA 98104
Lauren B. Simonds, Executive Director
Tel: (425) 558-1894 Fax: (425) 867-9808
Email: ncjw@ncjwseattle.org
Web: www.ncjwseattle.org

NORTHWEST WOMEN'S LAW CENTER
3161 Elliott Ave. #101
Seattle, WA 98121
Lisa M. Stone, Executive Director
Tel: (206) 682-9552 Fax: (206) 682-9556
Email: nwwlc@nwwlc.org
Web: www.nwwlc.org

SPEC. INT., YOUTH

FILIPINO YOUTH ACTIVITIES
810 18th Ave. #108
Seattle, WA 98122
John Ragudos, Executive Director
Fax: (206) 461-4879
Email: fya@fya-pinoy.org
Web: www.fya-pinoy.org

STUDENT ORGANIZATION

ASIAN AMERICAN STUDENT UNION
SAO Box 232, UW Box 352238
Seattle, WA 98195-2238
Anthony Wu, Director
Email: anthonyw@u.washington.edu
Web: http://students.washington.edu/aasu

ASIAN STUDENT COMMISSION
University of Washington
Husky Union Bldg. #204-Q Box 352238
Seattle, WA 98195-2238
Tel: (206) 685-1908 Fax: (206) 685-4310
Email: asuwasc@u.washington.edu
Web: http://depts.washington.edu/asuwasc

CHINESE AMERICAN STUDENT ASSOCIATION
Seattle University
Pavilion 180, 901 12th Ave.
Seattle, WA 98122
Kimberly Chun, Club Contact
Tel: (206) 296-2525 Fax: (206) 296-6054
Email: seattleu_casa@hotmail.com
Web: www.seattleu.edu/student/activities/clubs/reg_club0304/casa.asp

FILIPINO AMERICAN STUDENT ASSOCIATION
University of Washington
3931 Brooklyn Ave.
Seattle, WA 98105
Victor Flores, Staff Advisor
Email: fasa@u.washington.edu
Web: http://students.washington.edu/fasa

Western Washington University
Associated Student Services Box Z1
Bellingham, WA 98225
Ronald S. Reboja, President
Tel: (360) 650-7576
Email: fasawwu@cc.wwu.edu
Web: http://yorktown.cbe.wwu.edu/03Spring/meliuss/FASA

Portland State University
8006 NW 15th Ct.

Vancouver, WA 98665
Tel: (360) 574-6275

KHMER STUDENT ASSOCIATION
University of Washington
3931 Brooklyn Ave. NE
Seattle, WA 98105
Yarun Luon, President
Email: khmer@u.washington.edu
Web: http://uwkhsa.org
Western Washington University
516 High St. Y-195
Bellingham, WA 98225
Sochantha Meng, President
Tel: (360) 650-7574
Email: khsawwu@hotmail.com
Web: www.ac.wwu.edu/~khmer

LAOTIAN STUDENT ASSOCIATION
University of Washington
SAO Box 125, UW Box 352238
Seattle, WA 98195
Veda Sonexaysana, President
Email: lsa@u.washington.edu
Web: http://students.washington.edu/lsa

RAJANA SOCIETY
University of Washington
3931 Brooklyn Ave. NE, Box 355650
Seattle, WA 98105
Puthearorth R. Kov, President
Email: rodkov@u.washington.edu
Web: http://students.washington.edu/rajana

WEST VIRGINIA

CULTURAL

TRI-STATE FILIPINO AMERICAN ASSOCIATION
P.O. Box 1044
Charleston, WV 25324
Millie Pajarillo, President
Tel: (304) 925-6767 Fax: (304) 925-6767

PROFESSIONAL

NATIONAL ARAB AMERICAN MEDICAL ASSOCIATION
West Virginia Chapter
P.O. Box 566
Poca, WV 25159
Sami Ghareeb, Chapter President
Tel: (304) 755-3931 Fax: (304) 755-5070
Email: naama@naama.com
Web: www.naama.com

RELIGIOUS

CONGREGATION B'NAI ISRAEL
2312 Kanawha Blvd. East
Charleston, WV 25311
Susan Allen, President
Tel: (304) 342-5852 Fax: (304) 342-8612
Email: allenrsjj@aol.com
Web: www.templeisraelwv.org

STUDENT ORGANIZATION

MUSLIM STUDENTS ASSOCIATION
West Virginia University
441 Harding Ave.
Morgantown, WV 26505
Mohamed Salem, President
Tel: (304) 598-7396
Email: mssewalim@yahoo.com
Web: www.wvu.edu/~msa

WISCONSIN

CULTURAL

HMONG-LAO AMERICAN ASSOCIATION
316 Court St. #7
Oshkosh, WI 54901
Jack Chang, Director
Tel: (920) 235-5133 Fax: (920) 385-3386
Email: jackchang2000@hotmail.com

WAUSAU AREA HMONG MUTUAL ASSOCIATION
1109 6th St.
Wausau, WI 54403
Chang Yang, President
Tel: (715) 842-8390 Fax: (715) 842-9202
Email: info@wausauhmong.org
Web: www.wausauhmong.org

WISCONSIN ORGANIZATION FOR ASIAN AMERICANS - MILWAUKEE
P.O. Box 11754
Shorewood, WI 53211-0754
Tel: (414) 483-8530 Fax: (262) 364-3560
Email: woaamilw@execpc.com
Web: www.asianmoonfestival.com

LAW ENFORCEMENT

JEWS FOR THE PRESERVATION OF FIREARMS OWNERSHIP, INC.
P.O. Box 270143
Hartford, WI 53027
Aaron Zelman, Executive Director
Tel: (262) 673-9745 Fax: (262) 673-9746
Email: jpfo@jpfo.org
Web: www.jpfo.org

MULTI-PURPOSE

PHILIPPINE-AMERICAN ASSOCIATION OF MADISON AND NEIGHBORING AREAS
P.O. Box 5013
Madison, WI 53705-0013
Email: executiveboard@pamana-madison.org
Web: www.pamana-madison.org

SHEBOYGAN HMONG MUTUAL ASSISTANCE ASSOCIATION
2304 Superior Ave.
Sheboygan, WI 53081
ChaSong Yang, Executive Director
Tel: (920) 458-0808 Fax: (920) 458-0081
Email: mail@hmaaweb.org
Web: www.hmaaweb.org

POLITICAL ACTION

ARMENIAN NATIONAL COMMITTEE OF AMERICA
Wisconsin Chapter
4100 N. Newman Rd.
Racine, WI 53406
Zohrab Khaligian
Email: khaligian@netzero.net
Web: www.anca.org

RELIGIOUS

CAMBODIAN BUDDHIST SOCIETY
1848 County Rd. Mm
Fitchburg, WI 53575
Tel: (608) 835-8136
Web:

DEER PARK BUDDHIST CENTER
4548 Schneider Dr.
Oregon, WI 53575
Geshe Lhundub Sopa, Director
Tel: (608) 835-5572 Fax: (608) 835-2964
Email: deerpk@hotmail.com
Web: www.deerparkcenter.org

INTERVARSITY CHRISTIAN FELLOWSHIP/ USA
6400 Schroeder Rd.
Madison, WI 53707-7895
Stan Wallace, Faculty Ministries
Tel: (608) 274-9001 Fax: (608) 274-7882
Email: information@intervarsity.org
Web: www.ivcf.org

LUTHERAN SOCIAL SERVICES
Corporate Office
647 W. Virginia St. #300
Milwaukee, WI 53204
David Larson, President/CEO
Tel: (414) 281-4400 Fax: (414) 325-3124
Email: info@lsswis.org
Web: www.lsswis.org

RESEARCH

HMONG RESEARCH CENTER
Longfellow Middle School
1900 Denton St.
La Crosse, WI 54601
J. Halderson, Teacher
Tel: (608) 789-7670
Email: jhalders@mail.sdlax.k12.wi.us
Web: www.lacrosseschools.com/longfellow/ sc/hrc/

SPEC. INT., CHILD CARE

SENDING OUR LOVE DESTINATION CHINA
5831 Sandhill Dr.
Middletown, WI 53562
Email: info@sendingourlovechina.org
Web: www.sendingourlovechina.org

SPEC. INT., EDUCATION

ASIAN AMERICAN STUDIES PROGRAM
University of Wisconsin-Madison
303 Ingraham Hall, 1155 Observatory Dr.
Madison, WI 53706
Hemant Shah, Director
Tel: (608) 263-2976 Fax: (608) 263-5307
Email: hgshah@wisc.edu
Web: http://polyglot.lss.wisc.edu/aasp/

CAMBODIAN SCHOOL PROJECT
2022 E. Dayton St.
Madison, WI 53704
Sarith Ou
Tel: (608) 256-1255
Email: sou@madison.k12.wi.us
Web: www.khmerschool.com

CENTER FOR SOUTHEAST ASIAN STUDIES
University Wisconsin-Madison
207 Ingraham Hall, 1155 Observatory Dr.
Madison, WI 53706-1397
Ian Coxhead, Director
Tel: (608) 263-1755 Fax: (608) 263-3735
Email: seasia@intl-institute.wisc.edu
Web: www.wisc.edu/ctrseasia/

EAST ASIAN LEGAL STUDIES CENTER
University of Wisconsin Law School
975 Bascom Mall
Madison, WI 53706-1399
Ethel E. Pellett, Program Assistant
Tel: (608) 262-9120 Fax: (608) 265-2253
Email: ealsc@law.wisc.edu
Web: www.law.wisc.edu/ealsc/

HMONG EDUCATIONAL ADVANCEMENTS, INC.
2414 W. Vliet St.
Milwaukee, WI 53205
Lee Yang, Acting Director
Tel: (414) 931-8834 Fax: (414) 931-0545
Email: ly2815@hotmail.com

INDOCHINESE LEARNING CENTER
Milwaukee Area Technical College
639 N. 25th St.
Milwaukee, WI 53233
Marilyn Hegge
Tel: (414) 344-4777 Fax: (414) 344-7447
Email: ilcmilwaukee@hotmail.com
Web: www.matc.edu

PHILIPPINE STUDIES
St.Norbert College
100 Grant St.
DePere, WI 54115-2099
Tel: (920) 403-3104 Fax: (920) 403-4086
Email: philippines@snc.edu
Web: www.snc.edu/philippines

SPEC. INT., EMPLOYMENT

WISCONSIN JOB CENTER
325 N. Roosevelt St.
Green Bay, WI 54301
Hun Ho, Director
Tel: (920) 448-6460 X254 Fax: (920) 448-6465
Web: www.browncountyjobcenter.org

SPEC. INT., HUMAN RELATIONS

COMMUNITY ACTION PROGRAM SERVICES
5499 Hwy. 10 East
Stevens Point, WI 54481
Karl Pnazek, President/CEO
Tel: (715) 343-7500 Fax: (715) 343-7520
Email: kspnazek@capmail.org
Web: www.capserv.org

HABIBA CHAOUCH FOUNDATION
P.O. Box 124
Beloit, WI 53512-0124
Lisa Halaby
Email: habibafoundation@habiba.org
Web: www.habiba.org

HMONG MUTUAL ASSISTANCE ASSOCIATION, INC.
423 Wisconsin St.
Eau Claire, WI 54703
Linda Lidka, Acting Executive Director
Tel: (715) 832-8420 Fax: (715) 832-0612

LA CROSSE AREA HMONG MUTUAL ASSISTANCE ASSOCIATION, INC.
2613 George St.
La Crosse, WI 54603
Denis L. Tucker, Executive Associate Director
Tel: (608) 781-5744 Fax: (608) 781-5011
Email: denis.tucker.lhmaa@centurytel.net

LAO FAMILY COMMUNITY, INC.
2331 W. Vieau Pl.
Milwaukee, WI 53204
Shoua N. Xiong, Executive Director
Tel: (414) 383-4180 Fax: (414) 385-3386
Email: laofamily1@aol.com

LAO HUMAN RIGHTS COUNCIL, INC.
P.O. Box 1606
Eau Claire, WI 54702
Dr. Vang Pobzeb, Executive Director
Tel: (715) 831-8355 Fax: (715) 831-8563
Email: laohumrights@earthlink.net
Web: www.laohumrights.org

ORGANIZATION OF CHINESE AMERICANS
Wisconsin Chapter
9501 Watertown Plank Rd.
Wauwatosa, WI 53226
Clarence Chou, President
Tel: (414) 257-6957 Fax: (414) 257-7575
Email: cchou@wrapmilw.org

THE AMERICAN JEWISH COMMITTEE
Milwaukee Chapter
759 N. Milwaukee St. #600
Milwaukee, WI 53202-3797
Harriet Schachter McKinney, Chapter Director
Tel: (414) 291-2140 Fax: (414) 291-2145
Email: milwaukee@ajc.org
Web: www.ajc.org

WISCONSIN TIBETAN ASSOCIATION
P.O. Box 5406
Madison, WI 53705
Web: www.geocities.com/Tokyo/3528/

WISCONSIN UNITED REFUGEE SERVICE, INC.
312 N. 3rd St.
Madison, WI 53704
Thaj Ying Lee, Executive Director
Tel: (608) 256-6400 Fax: (608) 256-6501
Email: thajyinglee@tds.net
Web: www.ursw.org

SPEC. INT., LEGAL ASSISTANCE

ADVOCAP, INC.
Fond du Lac Office
P.O. Box 1108
Fond du Lac, WI 54936-1108
Michael Bonertz, Executive Director
Tel: (920) 922-7760 Fax: (920) 922-7214
Email: mikeb@advocap.org
Web: www.advocap.org

SPEC. INT., MENTAL HEALTH

HMONG MENTAL HEALTH INSTITUTE
705 S. 24th Ave. #400
Wausau, WI 54401
Tel: (715) 843-1882 Fax: (715) 848-2959

SPEC. INT., SOCIAL INTEREST

HMONG AMERICAN FRIENDSHIP ASSOCIATION
3824 W. Vliet St.
Milwaukee, WI 53208
Lo Neng Kiatoukaysy, Executive Director
Tel: (414) 344-6575 Fax: (414) 344-6581
Email: loneng@hmongamer.org
Web: www.hmongamer.org

HMONG AMERICAN PARTNERSHIP
2198 S. Memorial Dr.
Appleton, WI 54915
Lo Lee, Executive Director
Tel: (920) 739-3192 Fax: (920) 739-3687
Email: foxvalleyhmong@wmconnect.com

JAPAN AMERICA SOCIETY OF WISCONSIN, INC.
1110 N. Old World 3rd St. #420
Milwaukee, WI 53203
Tel: (414) 225-6220 Fax: (414) 225-6235
Email: aldurtka@execpc.com

JEWISH FAMILY SERVICES, INC.
1300 N. Jackson St.
Milwaukee, WI 53202
Phyllis Brenowitz, President
Tel: (414) 390-5800 Fax: (414) 390-5808
Email: info@jfsmilw.org
Web: www.jfsmilw.org

MADISON JEWISH COMMUNITY COUNCIL
6434 Enterprise Ln.
Madison, WI 53719-1117
Diane Seder, President
Tel: (608) 278-1808 Fax: (608) 278-7814
Email: mjcc@mjcc.net
Web: www.jewishmadison.org

MILWAUKEE JEWISH FEDERATION
1360 N. Prospect Ave.
Milwaukee, WI 53202-3094
Tel: (414) 390-5700 Fax: (414) 390-5782
Email: webmaster@milwaukeejewish.org
Web: www.milwaukeejewish.org

SPEC. INT., SPORTS

HMONG COMMUNITY CENTER, INC.
1517 Washington St.
Manitowoc, WI 54220
Viluck Kue, Director
Tel: (920) 684-1228 Fax: (920) 684-0461
Email: hmong@hmongcommunitycenter.org
Web: www.hmongcommunity.org

SPEC. INT., WOMEN

HMONG AMERICAN WOMEN'S ASSOCIATION
2414 W. Vliet St.
Milwaukee, WI 53205
Kay Vang, Coordinator
Tel: (414) 342-0858
Email: kay@hawa-inc.org

STUDENT ORGANIZATION

ASIAN PACIFIC AMERICAN COUNCIL
University of Wisconsin, Madison
716 Langdon St., 2nd Fl. Red Gym
Madison, WI 53706
Ellen Hwang, Chair
Tel: (608) 262-5169
Email: apacwi@yahoo.com
Web: www.sit.wisc.edu/~apac

CHINESE STUDENTS AND SCHOLARS ASSOCIATION
University of Wisconsin-Madison
501 N. Whitney Way #9
Madison, WI 53705
Lu Shang, President
Tel: (608) 256-3483
Email: lshang@wisc.edu
Web: www.uwcssa.net

INDIA STUDENTS ASSOCIATION
University of Wisconsin
716 Langdon St., 2nd Fl.
Madison, WI 53706
Sanmay Pati, President
Tel: (608) 262-5170
Email: joinisa@yahoo.com
Web: www.sit.wisc.edu/~isa

WYOMING

COMMUNICATIONS

TIBET INFORMATION NETWORK
P.O. Box 2270
Jackson, WY 83001
Tel: (307) 733-4670 Fax: (307) 739-2501
Email: tinusa@wyoming.com
Web: www.tibetinfo.net

SPEC. INT., EDUCATION

US CHINA PEOPLES FRIENDSHIP ASSOCIATION
Wyoming Chapter
2007 Pioneer Ave. #10
Cody, WY 82414
Phyllis Pond
Tel: (307) 527-7544
Web: www.uscpfa.org

2 ISSUES/WEEK

ASIAN JOURNAL - MAIN OFFICE
Asian Journal Publications, Inc.
1150 Wilshire Blvd.
Los Angeles, CA 90017-1904
Momar Visaya, Editor
Tel: (213) 250-9797 **Fax:** (213) 481-0854
Email: info@asianjournal.com
Web: www.asianjournal.com
Circ.: 35,000
Price: Free
Publication description: A website designed and developed for Filipinos living and working in North America and other parts of the world.
Date established: 1991

BUT VIET WEEKLY NEWS
9780 Walnut St. #180
Dallas, TX 75243
Duc Mai, Editor
Tel: (972) 808-9700 **Fax:** (972) 808-9701
Email: butviet@aol.com
Circ.: 17,500
Price: Free
Date established: 1989

NGUOI VIET TAY BAC NEWSPAPER (NORTHWEST VIETNAMESE WEEKLY NEWS)
6951 Martin Luther King Way South #205
Seattle, WA 98118
Kim Pham, Editor-in-Chief
Tel: (206) 722-6984 **Fax:** (206) 722-0445
Email: nvtbnews@aol.com
Web: www.nguoiviet-taybac.com
Circ.: 15,000
Price: Free **Subscription:** $98.00/year
Date established: 1986

NORTH WEST NIKKEI - HOKUBEI HOCHI SHIMBUN
North American Post Publishing, Inc.
P.O. Box 3173
Seattle, WA 98114
Tomio Moriguchi, Chairman
Tel: (206) 624-6248 **Fax:** (206) 625-1424
Email: info@napost.com
Web: www.napost.com
Circ.: 8,000 - 15,000
Price: $0.75 **Subscription:** $27/3 mos.
Date established: 1902

SAIGON USA NEWS
545 E. Saint John St.
San Jose, CA 95112
Cuong Le, Editor
Tel: (408) 998-0508 **Fax:** (408) 993-0527
Email: saigonusanews@yahoo.com
Web: www.saigonusanews.com
Circ.: 4,000

Price: Free
Date established: 1996

WASHINGTON CHINESE NEWS
5848 Hubbard Dr.
Rockville, MD 20852
Jing F. Lee, General Manager
Tel: (301) 984-8988 **Fax:** (301) 984-8806
Email: news@wchns.com
Web: www.washingtonchinesenews.com
Circ.: 15,000
Price: Free **Subscription:** $65.00/year
Publication description: Chinese community newspaper serving in the greater Washington DC metropolitan area.
Date established: 1990

2 ISSUES/YEAR

AFGHAN JOURNAL
Pacific News Service
275 9th St., 3rd Fl.
San Francisco, CA 94103
Mizgon Zahir, Founder
Tel: (415) 503-4170 **Fax:** (415) 503-0970
Email: mizgonz@aol.com
Web: www.pacificnews.org
Circ.: 3,000
Price: Free
Publication description: Afghan Journal is the state's first Afghan-American print publication with a dual audience of both Afghan- and mainstream Americans. The journal provides a much-needed outlet for Afghan-Americans to overcome their fears of being targeted or misrepresented in the public realm, an to share their unique stories and experiences, many of which challenge widespread stereotypes and assumptions about Arab-Americans in the U.S.
Date established: 2001

INFOCUS NEWSLETTER
Visual Communications
120 Judge John Aiso St., Basement
Los Angeles, CA 90012
Leslie Ito, Executive Director
Tel: (213) 680-4462 **Fax:** (213) 687-4848
Email: info@vconline.org
Web: www.vconline.org
Circ.: 10,000
Price: Free
Publication description: To promote intercultural understanding through the production, presentation and preservation of honest and sensitive stories about Asian Pacific people.
Date established: 1970

JOURNAL OF VIETNAMESE PHILOSOPHY AND RELIGION
Vietnamese Institute of Philosophy and Religion
1074 Great Passage Blvd.
Great Falls, VA 22066
Thu H. Bui, Ph.D., President
Tel: (703) 281-7929
Email: vientrietdao@yahoo.com
Web: www.vientrietdao.org
Circ.: 1,000
Publication description: It publishes essays in Vietnamese and other European languages that make significant contributions to the understanding of Vietnamese philosophy and religions.
Date established: 1998

KOREAN KOREAN AMERICAN STUDIES BULLETIN
East Rock Institute
251 Dwight St.
New Haven, CT 06511
Dr. Hesung Chun Koh, President
Tel: (203) 624-8619 **Fax:** (203) 624-7933
Email: eri3@pantheon.yale.edu
Web: www.eastrockinstitute.org
Circ.: 3,000
Price: $37.00 **Subscription:** $20.00/year
Date established: 1984

LAO VISION MAGAZINE
7788 Flanders Dr.
San Diego, CA 92126
Kag Khetsavanh, Founder
Email: staff@laovision.net
Web: www.laovision.net
Date established: 1996

MIZNA
P.O. Box 14294
Minneapolis, MN 55414
Lisa Adwan, Editor
Email: mizna@mizna.org
Web: www.mizna.org
Subscription: $15/year

PHILIPPINE FIESTA JOURNAL
Special Edition Press, Inc.
104 E. 40th St. #407
New York, NY 10016
Fernando Mendez, President
Tel: (212) 682-6610 **Fax:** (212) 682-2038
Email: info@philippinefiesta.com
Web: www.philippinefiesta.com
Circ.: 20,000
Price: Free
Date established: 1999

TEN MAGAZINE
The Asian American Writers' Workshop
16 W. 32nd St. #10A

New York, NY 10001
Quang Bao, Executive Director
Tel: (212) 494-0061 **Fax:** (212) 494-0062
Email: desk@aaww.org
Web: www.aaww.org
Circ.: 5,000
Price: $2.00
Publication description: Ten Magazine is the record of Asian American Literature and the writers that give life to it. In tune with the pitch of Asian American literature, Ten offers insightful interviews with established and emerging writers, powerful essays, transcripts of challenging Workshop roundtable discussions, thoughtful book reviews and much more. The result is a magazine that possesses undeniable vibrancy and immediacy.
Date established: 1991

3 ISSUES/WEEK

DALLAS CHINESE TIMES
12809 Audelia Rd.
Dallas, TX 75243
William Chang, Manager
Tel: (972) 907-1919 **Fax:** (972) 907-1867
Email: chinese9071919@yahoo.com
Web: www.scdaily.com
Circ.: 8,000
Price: Free
Date established: 1982

THU DO THOI BAO
P.O. Box 11180
Alexandria, VA 22312
Dien Nguyen, Publisher
Tel: (703) 876-1697 **Fax:** (703) 876-1698
Email: dnguyen647@aol.com
Circ.: 6,000
Price: Free **Subscription:** $100/year
Date established: 1987

3 ISSUES/YEAR

AMERASIA JOURNAL
3230 Campbell Hall, Box 951546
Los Angeles, CA 90095-1546
Russell Leong, Editor in Chief
Tel: (310) 825-3415 **Fax:** (310) 206-9844
Email: aascpress@aasc.ucla.edu
Web: www.sscnet.ucla.edu/aasc
Circ.: 1,500
Price: $15.00 **Subscription:** $35.00/year
Date established: 1971

FILIPINO CONSUMER DIRECTORY
1150 Wilshire Blvd.
Los Angeles, CA 90017-1904
Momar Visaya, Editor

Tel: (213) 250-9797 **Fax:** (213) 481-0854
Email: info@fcdonline.com
Web: www.fcdonline.com
Circ.: 30,000
Price: Free
Publication description: Business link to the filipino community
Date established: 1992

HINDU UNIVERSITY OF AMERICA NEWSLETTER

Hindu University of America
113 N. Econolockhatchee Trail
Orlando, FL 32825-3732
Jadeine Shives, Marketing Manager
Tel: (407) 275-0013 **Fax:** (407) 275-0014
Email: staff@hindu-university.edu
Web: www.hindu-university.edu
Circ.: 3,000
Price: Free
Date established: 1993

NUEVA LUZ PHOTOGRAPHIC JOURNAL

En Foco, Inc.
32 E. Kingsbridge Rd.
Bronx, NY 10468
Charles Biasiny-Rivera, Executive Director
Tel: (718) 584-7718 **Fax:** (718) 584-7718
Email: info@enfoco.org
Web: www.enfoco.org
Circ.: 10,000
Price: $7.00 **Subscription:** $30.00 / Year
Publication description: To promote minority photographers.
Date established: 1974

SONG MANH MAGAZINE

P.O. Box 21245
San Jose, CA 95151
Huy Trinh, Editor
Tel: (408) 605-0605 **Fax:** (408) 347-9004
Email: htrinhmd@bigfoot.com
Web: www.songmanh.org
Circ.: 5,000
Price: Free
Date established: 1997

6 ISSUES/YEAR

FREEDOM SOCIALIST NEWSPAPER

Freedom Socialist Party/Radical Women
5018 Rainier Ave. South, New Freeway Hall
Seattle, WA 98118
Andrea Bauer, Managing Editor
Tel: (206) 722-2453 **Fax:** (206) 723-7691
Email: fsnews@mindspring.com
Web: www.socialism.com
Price: $1.00 **Subscription:** $8.00/year
Publication description: Socialist Feminist political party dedicated to eradicating injustice and inequality and bigotry for all people.
Date established: 1965

9 ISSUES/YEAR

WASHINGTON REPORT ON MIDDLE EAST AFFAIRS

American Educational Trust
P.O. Box 53062
Washington, DC 20009
Richard Curtiss, Executive Editor
Tel: (202) 939-6050 **Fax:** (202) 265-4574
Email: executive_editor@wrmea.com
Web: www.wrmea.com
Circ.: 100,000
Price: $3.50 **Subscription:** $29.00/year
Publication description: The Washington Report on Middle East Affairs is a 100-page magazine published 10 times per year in

Washington, DC, that focuses on news and analysis from and about the Middle East and U.S. policy in that region.
Date established: 1983

ANNUALLY

ANNUAL OF URDU STUDIES, THE

University of Wisconsin Department of Languages & Cultures of Asia
1220 Linden Dr.
Madison, WI 53706
Muhammad Umar Memon, Editor
Tel: (608) 262-3418 **Fax:** (608) 265-3538
Email: editor@urdustudies.com
Web: www.urdustudies.com
Circ.: 250
Subscription: $18.00/year
Publication description: To provide scholars working on Urdu humanities in the broadest sense a forum in which to publish scholarly articles, translations, and views. The AUS will also publish reviews of books, an annual inventory of significant Western publications in the field, reports, research in progress, notices, and information on forthcoming events of interests to its readers.
Date established: 1981

ANNUAL REPORT

Asian Community and Cultural Center
2615 O St.
Lincoln, NE 68510
Modesta Putla, Executive Director
Tel: (402) 477-3446 **Fax:** (402) 477-4508
Email: modesta@lincolnasiancenter.org
Web: www.lincolnasiancenter.org
Date established: 1992

ASIAN AMERICAN POLICY REVIEW

Harvard University
79 JFK St.
Cambridge, MA 02138
Fred Wang, Chairman of Executive Advisory Board
Tel: (617) 496-8655 **Fax:** (617) 384-9555
Email: aapr@ksg.harvard.edu
Web: www.ksg.harvard.edu/aapr
Subscription: $20.00/year
Publication description: The Asian American Policy Review is the first non-partisan academic journal in the country dedicated solely to analyzing public policy issues facing the Asian Pacific American community.
Date established: 1989

ASIAN BUSINESS COMMUNITY DIRECTORY

ABC Publishing, Inc.
417 University Ave.
St. Paul, MN 55103
Nghi Huynh, Publisher/Editor
Tel: (651) 224-6570 **Fax:** (651) 224-7032
Email: aapress@aapress.com
Web: www.aapress.com
Circ.: 15,000
Subscription: $50.00/year
Date established: 1981

ASIAN-AMERICAN YEARBOOK

TIYM Publishing Company, Inc.
6718 Whittier Ave. #130
McLean, VA 22101
Angela E. Zavala, Editor
Tel: (703) 734-1632 **Fax:** (703) 356-0787
Email: asianamericanyearbook@tiym.com
Web: www.asianamericanyearbook.com
Circ.: 50,000
Price: $29.95
Publication description: The most com-

prehensive reference guide for and about Asian Americans and Pacific Islanders. The Yearbook is a unique resource in the areas of employment, business, education, and health, as well as a powerful tool for organizations seeking to reach the large Asian American and Pacific Islander market.
Date established: 2004

ASIANS COLLECTIONS MAGAZINE AT UTAH-AUSTIN

Geography Bldg. #220
Austin, TX 78705
Jamie Takaki, Editor in Chief
Tel: (512) 480-0641
Email: jamie26@mail.utexas.edu
Publication description: Asian Collections Magazine is the first Asian American awareness magazine at the University of Texas at Austin. The main goals are to dispel stereotypes about Asian Americans and spread awareness about important issues that affect the community.

BRIDGE TO ASIA NEWSLETTER

Bridge to Asia
665 Grant Ave.
San Francisco, CA 94108
Jeff Smith, President
Tel: (415) 678-2994
Email: asianet@bridge.org
Web: www.bridge.org
Circ.: 4,000

Date established: 1987 **CHARITY CALENDAR**

Hope Initiative, Inc.
P.O. Box 66855
Houston, TX 77266-6855
Phi Nguyen, President/CEO
Tel: (713) 972-4562
Email: hope.initiative@hionline.org
Web: www.hionline.org
Circ.: 3,000
Date established: 2002

CHICAGO CHINESE YELLOW PAGES

2155 S. China Pl., 2nd Fl.
Chicago, IL 60616
Danny Lee, Editor
Tel: (312) 326-2900 **Fax:** (312) 326-6787
Email: ccn1@chicagochinesenews.com
Web: www.chicagochinesenews.com
Circ.: 10,000
Price: Free
Date established: 1993

CHINESE YELLOW PAGES OF CHICAGO

2167-B S. China Pl.
Chicago, IL 60616
James Chang, Editor
Tel: (312) 225-3929 **Fax:** (312) 225-8849
Email: editor@canews.com
Circ.: 10,000
Price: $10.00
Date established: 1993

CINEVIEW

Asian Cinevision
133 W. 19th St. #300
New York, NY 10011
Risa Morimoto, Executive Director
Tel: (212) 989-1422 **Fax:** (212) 727-3584
Email: risa@asiancinevision.org
Web: www.asiancinevision.org
Price: Free

COME TO AMERICA

312 E. 1st St. #300
Los Angeles, CA 90012
Toshi Ootsuka, Editor
Tel: (213) 626-5001 **Fax:** (213) 613-1187
Email: la@usjbnews.com
Circ.: 30,000

Price: $25.00
Date established: 2001

HMONG AMERICAN RESIDENCE & BUSINESS DIRECTORY

L & W Communications
962 University Ave. West
St. Paul, MN 55104
Cheu Lee, Publisher
Tel: (651) 224-9395 **Fax:** (651) 228-9049
Email: dick@hmongtimes.com
Web: www.hmongtimes.com
Circ.: 25,000
Price: $5.00
Publication description: Hmong American Residence & Business Directory serves the greater Minnesota and Wisconsin business communities.
Date established: 1996

NATIONAL ASIAN AMERICAN TELECOMMUNICATIONS ASSOCIATION NEWSLETTER

National Asian American Telecommunications Association
145 9th St. #350
San Francisco, CA 94103
Eddie Wong, Executive Director
Tel: (415) 863-0814 **Fax:** (415) 863-7428
Email: eddie@naatanet.org
Web: www.naatanet.org
Circ.: 10,000
Price: Free
Date established: 1980

NEW YORK BENRICHO

Y's Publishing Company, Inc.
228 E. 45th St., 7th Fl.
New York, NY 10017
Jin Yoshida, Publisher
Tel: (212) 682-9360 **Fax:** (212) 682-3916
Email: info@us-benricho.com
Web: www.us-benricho.com
Circ.: 60,000
Price: $30.00
Publication description: This publication is an encyclopedia for living among Japanese communities in the US.
Date established: 1975

PORTLAND CHINESE YELLOW PAGES

7827 SE Powell Blvd.
Portland, OR 97206
Charles Hui, Director
Tel: (503) 771-9560 **Fax:** (503) 788-8900
Email: charles@portlandchinesetimes.us
Web: www.portlandchinesetimes.us
Circ.: 10,000
Price: Free
Publication description: The Portland Chinese Yellow Pages contains business listing as well as various information such as medical advice, travel tips, and immigration laws.
Date established: 1997

ST. LOUIS CHINESE AMERICAN YELLOW PAGES

8041 Olive Blvd.
St. Louis, MO 63130
Francis Yueh, Editor
Tel: (314) 432-3858 **Fax:** (314) 432-1217
Email: editor@scanews.com
Web: www.scanews.com/yp
Circ.: 4,000
Price: Free
Date established: 2000

THAI DIRECTORY

Thai Association of North Carolina
104 Beechtree Ct.
Apex, NC 27523
Surapn Sujjavanich, President
Tel: (919) 362-0470 **Fax:** (919) 362-3729

Email: psujj@aol.com
Date established: 1987

THAI YELLOW PAGES
1123 N. Vine St. #6A
Los Angeles, CA 90038
Sriwong Kozziel, Editor-in-Chief
Tel: (323) 464-1425 Fax: (323) 464-2312
Email: khaosod@earthlink.net
Circ.: 20,000
Price: Free
Date established: 1995

YEU MAGAZINE
Vien Thao Media
620 Quinn Ave.
San Jose, CA 95112
Lien Ho, Publisher
Tel: (408) 947-7517 Fax: (408) 947-0463
Email: vienthaomedia@aol.com
Web: www.vienthao.com
Circ.: 10,000
Price: Free
Date established: 1999

BIANNUALLY

LAOGAI HANDBOOK
Laogai Research Foundation
1925 K St. NW #400
Washington, DC 20006
Harry Wu, Executive Director
Tel: (202) 833-8770 Fax: (202) 833-6187
Email: laogai@laogai.com
Web: www.laogai.org
Price: $25.00
Date established: 1992

MINORITY STUDENT OPPORTUNITIES IN UNITED STATES MEDICAL SCHOOLS
Association of American Medical Colleges
2450 N St. NW
Washington, DC 20037
Laly May Johnson, Editor
Tel: (202) 828-0416 Fax: (202) 828-1123
Email: publications@aamc.org
Web: www.aamc.org
Circ.: 500
Price: $12.00
Publication description: The data published show the number of minority applicants, the number offered an acceptance, the number of matriculants, and the number of graduates by gender and racial/ethnic groups.
Date established: 1987

BIMONTHLY

ASIAN AMERICAN TIMES, THE
668 N. 44th St. #343
Phoenix, AZ 85008
Manny Wong, Publisher
Tel: (602) 685-1138 Fax: (602) 685-1137
Email: mannywong@cybertrails.com
Web: www.theasianamericantimes.com
Circ.: 10,000
Price: Free Subscription: $25.00/year
Publication description: Arizona's first Chinese-language newspaper, the newspaper contains news of Arizona's Chinese community.
Date established: 1990

ASIAN PAGES
P.O. Box 11932
St. Paul, MN 55111
Cheryl Weiberg, Editor-in-Chief
Tel: (952) 884-3265 Fax: (952) 888-9373
Email: asianpages@att.net

Web: www.asianpages.com
Circ.: 75,000
Subscription: $35.00/year
Publication description: Asian Pages is an award-winning biweekly newspaper serving seven Midwest states (Illinois, Iowa, Michigan, Minnesota, North and South Dakota, and Wisconsin.)
Date established: 1990

AUDREY MAGAZINE
Korean American Publications
17000 S. Vermont Ave. #A
Gardena, CA 90247
James Ryu, Publisher
Tel: (310) 769-4913 Fax: (310) 769-4903
Email: editor@audreymagazine.com
Web: www.audreymagazine.com
Circ.: 10,000
Price: $3.95 Subscription: $14.00/year
Publication description: Audrey is the premier bimonthly English-language magazine highlighting the stories that interest Asian American women nationwide.
Date established: 2002

BULLETIN NEWSLETTER
Chinese Historical Society of America
965 Clay St.
San Francisco, CA 94108
Sue Lee, Executive Director
Tel: (415) 391-1188 Fax: (415) 391-1150
Email: info@chsa.org
Web: www.chsa.org
Circ.: 600
Date established: 1963

FIL-AM COURIER
P.O. Box 17753
Honolulu, HI 96817
Mary Cordero, Editor
Tel: (808) 595-8787 Fax: (808) 595-6883
Email: courier@lava.net
Circ.: 24,000
Price: Free Subscription: $35.00/year
Date established: 1987

FILIPINO MARTIAL ARTS MAGAZINE
P.O. Box 413
East Meadow, NY 11554-0413
Eliot D. Shearer, Publisher
Tel: (516) 486-5167 Fax: (516) 486-2846
Email: Publisher@filipinomag.com
Web: www.filipinomag.com
Circ.: 25,000
Price: $3.75 Subscription: $21/year
Date established: 1999

INDIA NEW ENGLAND
The Mishra Group, Inc.
318 Bear Hill Rd. #6
Waltham, MA 02451
Upendra Mishra, Publisher
Tel: (781) 487-0555 Fax: (781) 487-9207
Email: info@mishragroup.com
Web: www.indianewengland.com
Circ.: 13,000
Subscription: $19.95 yr.
Date established: 1996

JEMS JOURNAL
Japanese Evangelical Missionary Society
948 E. 2nd St.
Los Angles, CA 90012
Stan Date, President
Tel: (213) 613-0022 Fax: (213) 613-0211
Email: info@jems.org
Web: www.jems.org
Circ.: 9,000
Price: Free
Date established: 1955

KEKUAHAU
Honolulu County Geneological Society
P.O. Box 235039
Honolulu, HI 96823
Joann Honely
Tel: 808 695 5761
Circ.: 100
Publication description: Donate over 1000 genealogical research books to the new library at Kapokei Branch of HAwaii State Library
Date established: 1990

LIGHT OF CORAL SPRINGS, THE
Chinese Baptist Church of Coral Springs
200 Coral Ridge Dr.
Coral Springs, FL 33071
Linus Lau, Pastor
Tel: (954) 255-9910 Fax: (954) 344-1883
Web: www.cbccoralsprings.org
Circ.: 400

NGAY NAY NEWSPAPER
Ngay Nay Media, Inc.
4500 Montrose Blvd. #C
Houston, TX 77006
Trac T. Truong, Publisher/Editor
Tel: (713) 526-5352 Fax: (713) 526-8637
Email: tractruong@aol.com
Circ.: 20,000
Publication description: National Vietnamese-language newspaper.

NIKKEI WEST
P.O. Box 22400
Sacramento, CA 95822
Jeffrey Kimoto, Chief Editor/President
Tel: (916) 837-4178 Fax: (775) 213-1773
Email: mail@nikkeiwest.com
Web: www.nikkeiwest.com
Circ.: 7,400
Price: Free Subscription: $35.00/year
Publication description: English-only language Japanese American newspaper.
Date established: 1992

OHANA FAMILY MAGZINE
P.O. Box 230910
Las Vegas, NV 89123
Mel Ozeki, Editor
Tel: (702) 434-0544 Fax: (702) 435-8561
Email: editor@ohanamagazine.com
Web: www.ohanamagazine.com
Circ.: 11,000
Subscription: $25/year
Date established: 1996

PACIFIC CITIZEN NEWSPAPER
Japanese American Citizens League
7 Cupania Cir.
Monterey Park, CA 91755
Brian Tanaka, Office Manager
Tel: (323) 725-0083 Fax: (323) 725-0064
Email: paccit@aol.com
Web: www.jacl.org
Circ.: 50,000
Price: $1.50 Subscription: $35.00/year
Publication description: Pacific Citizen (P.C.) is the national publication of the Japanese American Citizens League (JACL), a civil rights organization based in San Francisco.
Date established: 1929

SOY SOURCE
Japan Pacific Publications, Inc.
P. O. Box 3092
Seattle, WA 98114
Andrew Taylor, President
Tel: (206) 622-7443
Email: soysource@japanpacific.com
Web: www.japanpacific.com
Circ.: 8,000
Price: Free Subscription: $30.00/year

Publication description: One of the foremost resources of Japanese translations, typesetting, and marketing assistance outside of Japan.
Date established: 1992

THE NATIONAL KAGRO JOURNAL
National Korean American Grocers Association
3055 Wilshire Blvd. #680
Los Angeles, CA 90010
John Kim, Chairman
Tel: (213) 388-0114 Fax: (213) 388-2489
Email: info@kagro.org
Web: www.kagro.org
Circ.: 15,000
Price: Free for members
Publication description: The National KAGRO Journal is the single most important communication vehicle reaching the entire KAGRO membership key decision makers in the grocery retail industry.
Date established: 1989

TIEN PHONG MAGAZINE
15 N. Highland St.
Arlington, VA 22201
Anh Ho, Editor
Tel: (703) 522-7151
Email: tienphonginc@msn.com
Circ.: 9,000
Price: $3.99 Subscription: $95.00/year
Date established: 1976

BIWEEKLY

ACC NEWS
Asian Community Center
7375 Park City Dr.
Sacramento, CA 95831
Donna Yee, Executive Director
Tel: (916) 393-9026 Fax: (916) 393-9128
Email: info@accsv.org
Web: www.accsv.org
Circ.: 8,000
Date established: 1972

AD MAGAZINE
Asian Diversity, Inc.
1270 Broadway #703
New York, NY 10001
Thomas Lee, Editor
Tel: (212) 465-8777 Fax: (212) 465-8396
Email: editor@asiandiversity.com
Web: www.asiandiversity.com
Price: Online Only

BRIDGE USA MAGAZINE
20300 S. Vermont Ave. #200
Torrance, CA 90502
Yoshihiro Ishii, President
Tel: (310) 532-5921 Fax: (310) 532-1184
Email: info@bridgeusa.com
Web: www.bridgeusa.com
Circ.: 35,000
Price: Free Subscription: $84.00/year
Date established: 1989

CHINESE BUSINESS JOURNAL
Chinese Business Journal
659 S. Weller St.
Seattle, WA 98104
Hung Sceto, Publisher
Tel: (206) 624-8781 Fax: (206) 624-7899
Circ.: 10,000
Price: Free
Date established: 1982

EAST WEST JOURNAL
East West Journal Corporation
1150 S. King St. #1103

Honolulu, HI 96814
Yuji Nagai, Editor
Tel: (808) 596-0099 **Fax:** (808) 596-2292
Email: info@eastwest-journal.com
Web: www.eastwest-journal.com
Circ.: 8,000
Price: Free **Subscription:** $16.00/year
Date established: 1976

FILIPINO GUARDIAN

P.O. Box 16067
San Francisco, CA 94116-1067
George Nervez, Publisher
Tel: (650) 871-1558 **Fax:** (650) 273-1543
Email: filguard2004@rcn.com
Circ.: 18,000
Price: Free
Publication description: An English language newspaper with a Bay Area readership.
Date established: 1986

FILIPINO-ASIAN BULLETIN

78 Country Village Rd, #2
Jersey City, NJ 07030
Alberto Quisumbing, Editor
Tel: (201) 993-5023
Email: philasianbulletin@hotmail.com
Circ.: 5,000
Price: Free
Date established: 2000

GIOI MOI MAGAZINE

1700 Chippendale Dr.
Arlington, TX 76012
Luong Si Truong, Editor
Tel: (817) 265-6356 **Fax:** (817) 548-8563
Email: tapchitgm@comcast.net
Circ.: 12,000
Price: Free **Subscription:** $95.00/year
Date established: 1988

HAWAII FILIPINO CHRONICLE

94-356 Waipahu Depot Rd.
Waipahu, HI 96787
Charlie Y. Sonido, Publisher/Executive Editor
Tel: (808) 678-8930 **Fax:** (808) 678-1829
Email: hfci@hawaii.rr.com
Web: www.rrhi.com/hfci/media.htm
Price: $1.00 **Subscription:** $40/year
Publication description: The Hawaii Filipino Chronicle was created in response to the growing need to reach out to the Filipino community, to inform and to educated, and above all else, to provide the vehicle with which our community can grow and prosper.

HMONG TIMES

L & W Communications
962 University Ave. West
St. Paul, MN 55104
Cheu Lee, Publisher
Tel: (651) 224-9395 **Fax:** (651) 228-9049
Email: dick@hmongtimes.com
Web: www.hmongtimes.com
Circ.: 15,000
Price: Free **Subscription:** $75.00/year
Date established: 1998

INTERNATIONAL EXAMINER

622 S. Washington St.
Seattle, WA 98104
Nhien Nguyen, Editor
Tel: (206) 624-3925 **Fax:** (206) 624-3046
Email: editor@iexaminer.org
Web: www.iexaminer.org
Circ.: 10,000
Price: Free **Subscription:** $20.00/year
Publication description: The oldest and largest English-language Asian American newspaper in the Northwest, providing in-depth cover-

age of Asian American news, politics, social services and the arts.
Date established: 1974

JAPANESE BEACH PRESS

615 Piikoi St. #1411
Honolulu, HI 96814
Shanna Pollard, Publisher
Tel: (808) 245-3681 **Fax:** (808) 591-0753
Email: jbp@aloha.net
Web: www.japanesebeachpress.com
Circ.: 24,000
Price: Free
Date established: 1971

MANILA MAIL, THE

3302 Walnut Manor Way
Falls Church, VA 22042
Bert Alsaro, Publisher
Tel: (703) 532-1367 **Fax:** (703) 532-1367
Email: manilamaildc@erols.com
Web: www.manilamaildc.com
Circ.: 20,000
Price: Free **Subscription:** $20.00/year
Date established: 1990

MIAMI KOREAN AMERICAN NEWS WEEKLY

525 NW 27th St.
Miami, FL 33127
Jacob Lee, Publisher
Tel: (305) 576-9001 **Fax:** (305) 573-1230
Email: miamikorean@yahoo.com
Web: www.miamikoreannews.com
Circ.: 5,500
Price: Free **Subscription:** $70.00/year
Date established: 1999

NIKKEIWEST - SAN JOSE

123 E. San Carlos St. #521
San Jose, CA 95112
Jeffrey Kimoto, Publisher/CEO
Tel: (408) 998-0920 **Fax:** (775) 213-1773
Email: mail@nikkeiwest.com
Web: www.nikkeiwest.com
Circ.: 7,500
Price: Free **Subscription:** $35.00/year
Publication description: To inform Japanese-American community of Northern California of news/events.
Date established: 1992

OVERSEAS CHINESE NEWS

Overseas Chinese Publishing Company
P.O. Box 430810
Miami, FL 33243
Dr. John J. Tsai, Editor/Publisher
Tel: (305) 274-4915 **Fax:** (305) 274-1651
Email: editor@ocn-miami.com
Web: www.ocn-miami.com
Circ.: 8,000
Price: Free **Subscription:** $30.00/year
Date established: 1990

PHILIPPINE MABUHAY NEWS

3142 E. Plaza Blvd. #N
National City, CA 91950
Lito Flores, Editor
Tel: (619) 470-6373 **Fax:** (619) 470-0613
Email: pmneditor@aol.com
Circ.: 30,000
Price: Free **Subscription:** $35.00/year
Publication description: English
Date established: 1993

PLANET GURU

India HQ Solutions, Inc.
2018 156th Ave. NE #100
Bellevue, WA 98007
Upasana Gupta, Editor
Tel: (425) 748-5128 **Fax:** (425) 696-9222
Email: info@planetguru.com
Web: http://planetguru.com
Circ.: 25,000

Price: Free
Date established: 1997

PRACHACHON THAI NEWS

375 Lastrito Ave.
Sunnyvale, CA 94086
Jua Ratanaphun, Editor-in-Chief
Tel: (408) 773-1102 **Fax:** (408) 773-6880
Email: jusa2005@yahoo.com
Web: www.prachachonusa.com
Circ.: 5,000
Price: $0.50 **Subscription:** $35.00/year
Date established: 1987

SAMPAN NEWSPAPER

Asian American Civic Association, Inc.
200 Tremont St.
Boston, MA 02116
Adam Smith, English Editor
Tel: (617) 426-9492 **Fax:** (617) 482-2316
Email: englisheditor@aaca-boston.org
Web: www.sampan.org
Circ.: 8,000
Price: Free **Subscription:** $30.00/year
Publication description: Sampan is the oldest and only bilingual Chinese-English newspaper in New England since 1972. Born out of the need to educate and inform the Chinese population of Greater Boston, Sampan continues to be the only comprehensive chronicle of issues and events which uniquely affect the local. Asian population and represents the only printed voice in both Chinese and English for the community. Sampan is a non-partisan Chinatown community newspaper of Greater Boston.
Date established: 1971

SAN DIEGO INTERNATIONAL TIMES

4655 Ruffner St. #290
San Diego, CA 92111
Shinji Sahara, Editor
Tel: (858) 576-9016 **Fax:** (858) 576-7294
Email: yu-yu@pacbell.net
Circ.: 10,000
Price: $3.00 **Subscription:** $72.00/year
Publication description: Mostly in Japanese
Date established: 1987

SUNDAY TOPIC KOREAN NEWS

1260 B St. #325
Hayward, CA 94541
Dong Yull Kim, Editor
Tel: (510) 645-1111 **Fax:** (510) 728-1249
Email: sundaytopic@yahoo.com
Circ.: 10,000
Price: Free
Date established: 1993

TIENG VIET SAN DIEGO NEWS

4745 El Cajon Blvd. #103
San Diego, CA 92115
Truong Vu, Editor
Tel: (619) 282-9993 **Fax:** (619) 282-8388
Email: tiengvietusa@aol.com
Circ.: 5,000
Price: Free
Date established: 1992

TUDO

2905 Milam St.
Houston, TX 77006
Mac Bich, Editor
Tel: (713) 524-5652 **Fax:** (713) 529-0182
Circ.: 10,000
Price: Free **Subscription:** $110.00/year
Date established: 1990

VIET NAM TU DO MAGAZINE

9550 Bolsa Ave. #202
Westminster, CA 92683
Khoy Nguyen, Publisher/Editor
Tel: (714) 531-6020 **Fax:** (714) 531-6020

Circ.: 7,000
Price: Free **Subscription:** $108.00/year

YDAN

2306 S. Benton Ct.
Lakewood, CO 80227
Thang Nguyen, Director of Marketing
Tel: (303) 391-7183 **Fax:** (303) 374-3869
Email: ydannews@aol.com
Circ.: 5,000
Price: Free
Date established: 1989

DAILY

CALI TODAY

Vietnamese Communication Group
540 S. 10th St.
San Jose, CA 95112
Nam Nguyen, President
Tel: (408) 297-8271 **Fax:** (408) 297-3654
Email: vietcommunications@yahoo.com
Web: www.calitoday.com
Circ.: 7,000
Price: Free
Publication description: Vietnamese language newspaper and website with a Northern California readership.
Date established: 1998

CHINA PRESS, THE

15 E. 40th St. #600
New York, NY 10016
I-der Jeng, Editor
Tel: (212) 683-8282 **Fax:** (212) 679-8407
Email: tcpeditor@hotmail.com
Web: www.chinapress.net
Circ.: 100,000
Price: $0.50 **Subscription:** $155.00
Date established: 1990

CHINA PRESS/ASIA PACIFIC OF CALIFORNIA

2121 W. Mission Rd.
Alhambra, CA 91803
Xiaodong Liu, Editor-in-Chief
Tel: (626) 281-8500 **Fax:** (626) 281-8400
Email: reporter@cpwc.com
Circ.: 10,000
Price: $0.25 **Subscription:** $130.00/year

CHINESE DAILY NEWS

10415-A W. Park
Houston, TX 77042
Linda Lin, Manager
Tel: (713) 771-4363 **Fax:** (713) 270-8222
Email: wjhouston@cdnews.com
Web: www.chineseworld.com
Circ.: 25,000
Price: $0.50

CHINESE DAILY NEWS

1588 Corporate Center Dr.
Monterey Park, CA 91754
Jackie Hsu, Editor
Tel: (323) 268-4982 X201
Web: www.worldjournal.com
Price: $0.50 **Subscription:** $176.00/year

CHINESE TIMES

2585 3rd St. #100
San Francisco, CA 94107
Percy Tong, Editor
Tel: (415) 358-3616 **Fax:** (415) 826-2128
Email: editor@chinesetimes.us
Web: www.mingpaousa.com
Price: $0.50
Date established: 1924

DONG-A DAILY NEWS

1330 Willow Ave. #101
Elkins Park, PA 19027

David Bo H. Lim, President
Tel: (215) 935-5000 **Fax:** (215) 935-8888
Email: bohlim@dongausa.com
Web: www.dongausa.com
Circ.: 9,000
Subscription: $120.00/year
Date established: 1980

HAWAII HOCHI
917 Kokea St.
Honolulu, HI 96817
Mintsunori Shoji, Editor
Tel: (808) 845-2255 **Fax:** (808) 841-1357
Email: hawaiihon001@hawaii.rr.com
Circ.: 4,000
Price: $0.50 **Subscription:** $150.00/year
Date established: 1912

HAWAII TRIBUNE HERALD
Stephen Media Group
P.O. Box 767
Hilo, HI 96721
David Bock, Editor
Tel: (808) 935-6621 **Fax:** (808) 969-9100
Email: letters@hawaiitribuneherald.com
Web: www.hilohawaiitribune.com
Circ.: 19,900
Price: $0.60 **Subscription:** $120.00/year

HOKUBEI MAINICHI NEWSPAPER
1746 Post St.
San Francisco, CA 94115
JK Yamamoto, Editor in Chief
Tel: (415) 567-7323 **Fax:** (415) 567-3926
Email: editor@hokubei.com
Web: www.hokubei.com
Circ.: 7,500
Price: $0.50 **Subscription:** $138.00/year
Publication description: A Japanese and English language newspaper with a Northern and Central California readership.
Date established: 1948

INTERNATIONAL DAILY NEWS
International Daily News
870 Monterey Pass Rd.
Monterey Park, CA 91754
feiwen hung, ceo
Tel: (323) 265-1317 **Fax:** 269-4013
Email: admin@chinesetoday.com
Web: www.chinesetoday.com
Price: $0.25
Publication description: International Daily News was the first full-color Chinese newspaper to be distributed in the United States.

JAPAN JOURNAL
1661 W. 3rd St.
Los Angeles, CA 90017
Tel: (213) 273-8977
Fax: (213) 273-8979

JAPANESE DAILY SUN, THE
330 E. 2nd St. #B
Los Angeles, CA 90012
Yumiko Hashimoto, Editor
Tel: (213) 617-3670 **Fax:** (213) 687-0331
Email: jps753@aol.com
Circ.: 15,000
Price: Free
Date established: 1976

KOREA CENTRAL DAILY CALIFORNIA
8269 Garden Grove Blvd.
Garden Grove, CA 92844
Brian Choi, Editor
Tel: (714) 638-2341 **Fax:** (714) 638-1101
Email: info@joongangusa.com
Web: www.joongangusa.com
Circ.: 17,500
Price: .50

KOREA CENTRAL DAILY NEWS
43-27 36th St.
Long Island City, NY 11101
Hyun Kim, Editor-in-Chief
Tel: (718) 361-8989 **Fax:** (718) 937-1654
Email: nykhil@joongangusa.com
Web: www.joongangusa.com
Circ.: 33,000
Price: $0.50 **Subscription:** $15.00-20.00/month

KOREA CENTRAL DAILY NEWS
320 Ward Ave. #207
Honolulu, HI 96814
Jae Hanpark, Editor
Tel: (808) 591-1700 **Fax:** (808) 591-0018
Email: jsl@joonganghi.com
Web: www.joonganghi.com
Circ.: 3,000
Price: $1.00 **Subscription:** $165.00/year
Date established: 1974

KOREA CENTRAL DAILY NEWS
44C Four Seasons Shopping Center
Chesterfield, MO 63017
Tom Paik, Editor
Tel: (314) 878-2183 **Fax:** (314) 878-1661
Subscription: $15.00/yr

KOREA CENTRAL DAILY NEWS- LOS ANGELES
690 Wilshire Pl.
Los Angeles, CA 90005
Sung Chan Kim, Editor
Tel: (213) 368-2626 **Fax:** (216) 389-8384
Web: www.joongangusa.com
Circ.: 250,000
Price: $0.50 **Subscription:** $175.00
Date established: 1975

KOREA CENTRAL DAILY NEWSPAPER
33288 Central Ave.
Union City, CA 94587
Taegung Kim, Editor
Tel: (408) 985-6500 **Fax:** (408) 985-2078
Circ.: 10,000
Price: $0.50 **Subscription:** $145.00/year

KOREA DAILY
13749 Midvale Ave. North
Seattle, WA 98133
Min Choi, Editor
Tel: (206) 365-4000 **Fax:** (206) 365-2102
Email: kcdnw@hotmail.com
Web: www.joongangseattle.com
Circ.: 10,000
Price: $0.50 **Subscription:** $150.00/year
Date established: 1985

KOREA DAILY, THE
2222 S. Havana St. #D
Aurora, CO 80014
Mike Kang, Editor in Chief
Tel: (303) 338-1234 **Fax:** (303) 752-2200
Web: www.joongangdenver.com
Circ.: 1,000
Price: $1.00 **Subscription:** $180.00/year
Date established: 1992

KOREA DAILY, THE
690 Wilshire Pl.
Los Angeles, CA 90005
Won Young Lee, Administrator
Tel: (213) 368-2500 **Fax:** (213) 389-8384
Email: info@joongangusa.com
Web: www.joongangusa.com
Circ.: 70,000
Price: $0.50 **Subscription:** $175.00/year
Date established: 1974

KOREA DAILY, THE
512 W. Maple Ave.
Vienna, VA 22180
Yongyil Kim, President
Tel: (703) 281-9660 **Fax:** (703) 281-9523
Email: washingtondc@joongangusa.com
Web: www.joongangusa.com
Circ.: 30,000
Price: $0.50 **Subscription:** $150.00/year
Date established: 2000

KOREA DAILY, THE
790 Busse Rd.
Elk Grove Village, IL 60007
KJ Lee, Editor
Tel: (847) 228-7200 **Fax:** (847) 427-9627
Web: www.joongangusa.com
Circ.: 45,000
Price: $0.75 **Subscription:** $200.00/year
Date established: 1979

KOREA TIMES
1572 Los Padres Blvd. #201
Santa Clara, CA 95050
Ken Yoo, Editor
Tel: (408) 554-0523 **Fax:** (408) 244-1693
Email: kenyoo@cyberpacific.com
Web: www.koreatimes.com
Circ.: 29,000
Price: $0.50 **Subscription:** $145.00/year

KOREA TIMES ATLANTA, THE
The Korea Times
6087 Buford Hwy.
Doraville, GA 30340
Sunny Kim, Editor
Tel: (770) 248-9510 **Fax:** (770) 248-9511
Email: ktimes@koreatimesatl.com
Web: www.koreatimes.com
Circ.: 6,000
Price: $.50 **Subscription:** $145.00/year
Date established: 1996

KOREA TIMES CHICAGO, THE
Korea Times, The
4447 N. Kedzie Ave.
Chicago, IL 60625
Haewon Lee, Editor
Tel: (773) 463-1050 **Fax:** (773) 463-2345
Email: ktdesign1@koreatimes.com
Web: www.koreatimes.com
Circ.: 25,000
Price: $0.75 **Subscription:** $200.00/year
Date established: 1971

KOREA TIMES DALLAS, THE
Korea Times, The
11338 Emerald St.
Dallas, TX 75229
KC Chung, Chief Editor
Tel: (972) 243-0005 **Fax:** (972) 243-0157
Email: koreatimesdallas@yahoo.com
Web: www.koreatimes.com
Circ.: 4,000
Price: $0.50 **Subscription:** $155.00/year
Date established: 1969

KOREA TIMES HAWAII, THE
Korea Times, The
1839 S. King St.
Honolulu, HI 96826
Sheen Soo, Editor
Tel: (808) 955-1234 **Fax:** (808) 946-9637
Email: edit@koreatimeshawaii.com
Web: www.koreatimeshawaii.com
Circ.: 6,000
Price: $1.00 **Subscription:** $165.00/year
Date established: 1974

KOREA TIMES HOUSTON, THE
Korea Times, The

9873 Long Point Rd.
Houston, TX 77055
Jaemin Chang, Publisher
Tel: (713) 932-6696 **Fax:** (713) 932-6698
Email: koreatimeshouston@yahoo.com
Web: www.koreatimes.com
Circ.: 3,000
Price: $0.50 **Subscription:** $150.00/year
Date established: 1987

KOREA TIMES NEW YORK, THE
Korea Times, The
42-22 27th St.
Long Island City, NY 11101-4192
Inkyu Kim, Editor
Tel: (718) 482-1111 **Fax:** (718) 784-7381
Email: hankuk97@koreatimes.com
Web: www.koreatimes.com
Circ.: 50,000
Price: $0.50 **Subscription:** $165.00/year
Date established: 1967

KOREAN CENTRAL DAILY NEWS
8136 NW Overland Dr.
Kansas City, MO 64151
Chang Kim, Editor-in-Chief
Tel: (816) 741-8864 **Fax:** (816) 741-6679
Circ.: 30,000
Price: $0.75 **Subscription:** $180.00/year
Date established: 1978

LIBERTY TIMES USA, THE
NEO Asian American Times, Inc.
135-19 Roosevelt Ave., 2nd Fl.
Flushing, NY 11354
Gow Kuen Chen, Editor
Tel: (718) 461-2555 **Fax:** (718) 460-3533
Email: ko@libertytimes.com
Web: www.libertytimes.com
Circ.: 30,000
Price: $0.25 **Subscription:** $150.00/year
Date established: 1995

MING PAO DAILY NEWS
Ming Pao Enterprise Corporation, Ltd.
43-31 33rd St., 2nd Fl.
Long Island City, NY 11101
Hu Xiao, Editor
Tel: (718) 786-2888 **Fax:** (718) 504-3885
Email: mpny@mingpaousa.com
Web: www.mingpaousa.com
Circ.: 142,561
Price: $0.50 **Subscription:** $208.00/year
Date established: 1997

NEW KWONG TAI PRESS
940 Chung King Rd.
Los Angeles, CA 90012
Tel: (213) 624-8947 **Fax:** (213) 624-6365

NGUOI VIET DAILY NEWS
Nguoi Viet, Inc.
14771 Moran St.
Westminster, CA 92683
Anh B. Do, CFO
Tel: (714) 892-9414 **Fax:** (714) 894-1381
Email: nvnews@aol.com
Web: www.nguoi-viet.com
Circ.: 18,200
Publication description: To be the most vital and trusted source of news and information for Vietnamese Americans and to empower their community.
Date established: 1978

NHAT BAO VIEN DONG
14891 Moran St.
Westminster, CA 92683
Quang Nguyen, Editor
Tel: (714) 379-2851 **Fax:** (714) 379-2853
Email: viendong@aol.com

Web: www.viendongnews.com
Circ.: 15,000
Price: $0.25
Date established: 1989

NICHI BEI TIMES

P.O. Box 15666
San Francisco, CA 94115
Kenji Taguma, English Editor
Tel: (415) 921-6822 **Fax:** (415) 921-0770
Email: nikkei@nichibeitimes.com
Web: www.nichibeitimes.com
Circ.: 8,000
Price: $0.50 **Subscription:** $156.24/year
Publication description: An English and Japanese language newspaper and website with a global readership.
Date established: 1946

NIHON KEIAI SHIMBUN

1325 Ave. of the Americas #2500
New York, NY 10019
Hideo Kawai, Editor-in-Chief
Tel: (212) 261-6220 **Fax:** (212) 621-6208
Email: ecntct@nikkei.co.jp
Web: www.nikkei.co.jp
Circ.: 13,050
Price: $3.50 **Subscription:** $105.00/month
Publication description: They do not handle inserts/ the headquarters is in Japan
Date established: 1995

RAFU SHIMPO

259 S. Los Angeles St., 3rd Fl.
Los Angeles, CA 90012
Michael Komai, Publisher
Tel: (213) 629-2231 **Fax:** (213) 687-0737
Email: rafushimpo@aol.com
Circ.: 20,000
Price: $0.40 **Subscription:** $120.00/year
Publication description: Established in 1903 and based in Los Angeles, the Rafu Shimpo is the largest American daily newspaper.
Date established: 1903

SEGYE TIMES, THE

38-42 9th St.
Long Island City, NY 11101
Oakkie Kim, Executive Editor
Tel: (718) 361-2600 **Fax:** (718) 361-2368
Email: segye@sgtusa.com
Web: www.sgtusa.com
Circ.: 40,000
Price: Free **Subscription:** $100.00/year
Date established: 1982

SING TAO DAILY NEWSPAPER

5000 Marina Blvd.
Brisbane, CA 94005
Julie Tung, Director
Tel: (650) 808-8818 **Fax:** (650) 808-8819
Email: info@singtao.com
Web: www.singtaousa.com
Circ.: 40,000
Price: $0.50
Publication description: A Chinese language newspaper with a global readership.
Date established: 1975

SING TAO DAILY NEWSPAPER

188 Lafayette St.
New York, NY 10013
Louts Chau, Editor
Tel: (212) 699-3800 **Fax:** (212) 699-3830
Email: info@nysingtao.com
Web: www.singtaousa.com
Circ.: 55,000
Price: $0.50 **Subscription:** $198.00/year
Publication description: A Chinese language newspaper with a global readership.
Date established: 1938

SING TAO DAILY NEWSPAPER

2161-B S. China Pl.
Chicago, IL 60616
Limin Zheng, Editor
Tel: (312) 842-3955 **Fax:** (312) 842-3957
Email: chicago@nysinggao.com
Web: www.singtaousa.com
Circ.: 3,000
Price: $0.50
Publication description: A Chinese language newspaper with a global readership.
Date established: 1936

SING TAO DAILY NEWSPAPER

17059 Green Dr.
City of Industry, CA 91745
Tel: (626) 956-8210 **Fax:** (626) 282-1273
Email: advertisingla@singtaousa.com
Web: www.singtaousa.com

SOUTHERN CHINESE DAILY NEWS

11122 Bellaire Blvd.
Houston, TX 77072
Jun Gai, Editor
Tel: (281) 498-4310 **Fax:** (281) 498-2728
Email: editor@gedn.com
Circ.: 25,000
Price: Free
Date established: 1979

THE KOREA DAILY

The Korea Daily
2811 Adeline St.
Oakland, CA 94608
Andrew Lee, Administrator
Tel: (510) 272-4600 **Fax:** (510) 272-4606
Email: info@joongangusa.com
Web: www.joongangusa.com
Price: $0.50 **Subscription:** $17.50 / month

THE KOREA DAILY

The Korea Daily
32 W. 32nd St., Rm. 401
New York, NY 10001
Bong Lee, Administrator
Tel: (212) 239-1774 **Fax:** (212) 244-5286
Email: nymanp@joongangusa.com
Web: www.joongangusa.com
Price: $0.50

THE KOREA TIMES ARIZONA

The Korea Times
4318 N. Ranier Circle
Mesa, AZ 85215
Joon Cha, Gen Mgr.
Tel: (480) 610-1605
Email: Koreacha1@hotmail.com
Circ.: 1 million
Price: $0.50 **Subscription:** $21/Monthly
Date established: 30 yrs ago

THE KOREA TIMES SEATTLE

The Korea Times
12532 Aurora North
Seattle, WA 98133
Helen Kim, Editor
Tel: (206) 622-2229 **Fax:** (206) 622-5332
Email: ktimesad@hotmail.com
Web: www.koreatimes.com
Circ.: 10,000
Price: $0.75 **Subscription:** $160.00/year
Date established: 1970

THE KOREA TIMES WASHINGTON, DC

7601 Little River Turnpike
Annandale, VA 22003
Yang Ho Lee, General Manager
Tel: (703) 941-8001 **Fax:** (703) 941-8004
Email: ktdcad@aol.com
Web: www.koreatimes.com
Circ.: 25,000
Price: $0.50 **Subscription:** $150.00
Date established: 1971

THOI BAO DAILY NEWS

447 E. Santa Clara St.
San Jose, CA 95113
Mghinag Vu, Editor
Tel: (408) 292-2276 **Fax:** (408) 292-0346
Email: vnthoibao@aol.com
Circ.: 10,000
Price: Free
Date established: 1993

THOI LUAN NEWS

P.O. Box 65705
Los Angeles, CA 90065
Tracy Do, Publisher
Tel: (323) 221-5851 **Fax:** (323) 225-1343
Email: thoiluan@sbcglobal.net
Circ.: 15,000
Price: $0.25 **Subscription:** $170.00/year
Date established: 1985

VIET BAO DAILY NEWS

9393 Bolsa Ave. #E
Westminster, CA 92683
Nini Lee, Director
Tel: (714) 894-2500 **Fax:** (714) 418-0705
Email: info@vietbao.com
Web: www.vietbao.com
Circ.: 35,000
Price: $0.25

VIETNAM DAILY NEWS

2350 S. 10th St.
San Jose, CA 95112
Gwen Nguyen, Editor
Tel: (408) 292-3422 **Fax:** (408) 293-5153
Email: vnnb@vietnamdaily.com
Web: www.vietnamdaily.com
Circ.: 14,000
Price: $0.75
Publication description: A Vietnamese language magazine (with a bilingual weekend weekend edition) with a Northern California Readership. The oldest and largest Vietnamese daily newspaper in Northern California.
Date established: 1986

VIETNAM LIBERTY NEWS

980 S. 2nd St.
San Jose, CA 95112
Manh Nguyen, Publisher
Tel: (408) 275-9790 **Fax:** (408) 275-9666
Email: vlnnews@aol.com
Price: Free

WORLD JOURNAL

231 Adrian Rd.
Milbrae, CA 94030
Yuruthen Chen, Editor
Tel: (650) 692-9936 **Fax:** (650) 692-9961
Web: www.chineseworld.com
Circ.: 65,000
Price: $0.50 **Subscription:** $180.00/year
Publication description: A Chinese language newspaper with a global readership.

WORLD JOURNAL

141-07 20th Ave., 2nd Fl.
Whitestone, NY 11357
Marcus Liu, Editor
Tel: (718) 746-8889 **Fax:** (718) 746-6509
Email: webmaster@worldjournal.com
Web: www.worldjournal.com
Circ.: 135,000
Price: $0.50 **Subscription:** $188.00/year
Date established: 1975

WORLD JOURNAL

2116 S. Archer Ave.
Chicago, IL 60616
Kaiti Chang, Editor-in-Chief
Tel: (312) 842-8080 **Fax:** (312) 842-3749
Email: benchang@wjnews.com
Web: www.worldjournal.com

Circ.: 50,000
Price: $0.60 **Subscription:** $188.00/year
Date established: 1985

WORLD JOURNAL

41 Bridge St., Bldg. A
Metuchen, NJ 08840
Allen Chang, Manager
Tel: (732) 632-8890 **Fax:** (732) 632-9595
Email: allenchang@wjnews.com
Web: www.worldjournal.com
Price: $0.50 **Subscription:** $60.00-$188.00/year

WORLD JOURNAL

10415 Westpark Dr. #A
Houston, TX 77042
Estaller Hsu, Director
Tel: (713) 771-4363 **Fax:** (713) 270-8222
Email: wji@wt.net
Web: www.worldjournal.com
Circ.: 30,000
Price: $0.50

WORLD JOURNAL

827-A Rockville Pike
Rockville, MD 20852
Billy Chou, Director
Tel: (301) 309-1007 **Fax:** (301) 309-0299
Email: amytanglee@aol.com
Web: www.worldjournal.com
Circ.: 20,000
Price: $0.60 **Subscription:** $188.00/year
Date established: 1976

WORLD JOURNAL

5555 SW 61st Ave.
Davie, FL 33314
Annie Liu, Manager
Tel: (954) 583-5898 **Fax:** (954) 583-9125
Web: www.chineseworld.com
Circ.: 6,000
Price: $0.50

WORLD JOURNAL

1017 Arch St.
Philadelphia, PA 19107
Liu Lin, Manager
Tel: (215) 592-9666 **Fax:** (215) 592-6436
Web: www.chineseworld.com
Circ.: 10,000
Price: $0.60 **Subscription:** $128.00/year
Date established: 1975

WORLD JOURNAL - ATLANTA

5391 New Peachtree Rd.
Chamblee, GA 30341
Lily Lee, Director
Tel: (770) 451-4509 **Fax:** (770) 457-7964
Email: info@wjatl.com
Web: www.worldjournal.com
Circ.: 15,000
Price: $0.60 **Subscription:** $188.00/year
Date established: 1980

WORLD JOURNAL - BOSTON

216 Lincoln St.
Boston, MA 02111
Carrie Tang, Editor
Tel: (617) 423-3347 **Fax:** (617) 350-9984
Email: ads@wjboston.com
Circ.: 38,000
Price: $0.60 **Subscription:** $1.88 / year
Date established: 1990

WORLD JOURNAL-CHINESE DAILY

1334 Enterprise Dr.
Romeoville, IL 60446
Katie Chang, Manager
Tel: (630) 759-9880 **Fax:** (630) 759-9840
Web: www.worldjournal.com

MONTHLY

A GIA DINH MAGAZINE
P.O. Box 621
Orlando, FL 32802
Vu Tran, Advertising Manager
Tel: (407) 625-2512 **Fax:** (407) 851-5140
Email: gdmag@aol.com
Circ.: 5,000
Price: Free
Date established: 1988

ARAB AMERICAN BUSINESS
P.O. Box 753
Huntington Beach, CA 92648
Nidal M. Ibrahim, Editor/Publisher
Tel: (714) 893-0121 **Fax:** (714) 893-0083
Email: ibrahim@arabamericanbusiness.com
Web: www.arabamericanbusiness.com
Circ.: 10,000
Price: $4.95 **Subscription:** $39.95/year
Date established: 2000

ASIAN AMERICAN TIMES
Asian American Times
699 Serramonte Blvd.
Daly City, CA 94015
Jose T. Panganiban, Editor in Chief
Tel: (650) 992-2708 **Fax:** (408) 369-1701
Email: editor@aatimes.com
Web: www.aatimes.com
Circ.: 50,000
Subscription: $24.00/year

ASIAN ENTERPRISE MAGAZINE
Asian Business Ventures, Inc.
23824 Twin Pines Ln.
Diamond Bar, CA 91765
Gelly Borromeo, Publisher
Tel: (909) 860-3316 **Fax:** (909) 860-7054
Email: gelly@asianenterprise.com
Web: www.asianenterprise.com
Circ.: 100,000
Price: $2.95 **Subscription:** $30.00/year
Publication description: Asian Enterprise is the largest small-business-focus publication, serving the needs of Asian Pacific Americans nationwide.
Date established: 1996

ASIAN ENTERPRISE MAGAZINE- HAWAII OFFICE
79984 Kealaola St.
Kealakekua, HI 96750
Willy Boromeo, Co-Owner
Tel: (808) 322-2698 **Fax:** (808) 322-2702
Email: editor@asianenterprise.com
Web: www.asianenterprise.com
Circ.: 30,000
Price: $2.95 **Subscription:** $30.00/year
Publication description: Asian Enterprise is the largest small-business-focus publication, serving the needs of Asian Pacific Americans nationwide.
Date established: 1990

ASIAN ENTERPRISE MAGAZINE-LAS VEGAS OFFICE
1205 N. Buffalo Dr. #201
Las Vegas, NV 89128
Gelly Borromeo, Publisher
Tel: (702) 254-5805 **Fax:** (702) 254-5805
Email: editor@asianenterprise.com
Web: www.asianenterprise.com
Circ.: 33,000
Price: Free **Subscription:** $30.00/year
Publication description: Asian Enterprise is the largest small-business-focus publication, serving the needs of Asian Pacific Americans nationwide.
Date established: 1985

ASIAN FOCUS
Houston Chronicle
801 Texas Ave. #300
Houston, TX 77002
Christine McCreary
Tel: (713) 220-7171 **Fax:** (713) 354-3295
Email: christine.mccreary@chron.com
Web: http://webadv.chron.com/house/house_a/asianfocus/
Publication description: Asian Focus is a tabloid publication from the Houston Chronicle covering Houston's thriving Asian communities, businesses, upcoming cultural events and more.

ASIAN FORTUNE NEWSPAPER
P.O. Box 578
Haymarket, VA 20168
Jay Chen, President/Publisher
Tel: (703) 753-8295
Email: info@asianfortune.com
Web: www.asianfortune.com
Circ.: 25,000
Price: Free **Subscription:** $30.00/year
Publication description: Free for all Asians.
Date established: 1993

ASIAN HERALD
Chun Group, Inc.
1339 Baxter St. #200
Charlotte, NC 28204
Andrea Lee, Executive Director
Tel: (704) 334-3450 **Fax:** (704) 332-9373
Email: aherald2004@yahoo.com
Web: www.chungroup.com
Circ.: 2,500
Price: Free **Subscription:** $12.00/year
Date established: 1993

ASIAN PACIFIC AMERICAN TIMES
5674 S. Jericho Way
Aurora, CO 80015
Nestor Mercado, Editor in Chief
Tel: (303) 699-7294 **Fax:** (303) 427-8109
Email: apatimes@apatimes.com
Web: www.apatimes.com
Circ.: 10,000
Subscription: $12/year

ASIAN SUNEWS
Asian Chamber of Commerce
1219 E. Glendale Ave. #25
Phoenix, AZ 85020
James Rocky Tang, President
Tel: (602) 222-2009 **Fax:** (602) 870-7562
Email: asiansun@aol.com
Web: www.asianchamber.org
Circ.: 6,000
Price: Free **Subscription:** NA
Date established: 1994

ATLANTA VIET BAO
P.O. Box 723176
Atlanta, GA 31139
Bang Bui, Owner
Tel: (770) 432-8863 **Fax:** (770) 432-8836
Email: info@avb-online.com
Web: www.avb-online.com
Circ.: 5,000
Price: Free
Publication description: Our mission is to inform, educate and entertain our readers on current events as well as delve more deeply into topics that are of particular interest to the Vietnamese community.
Date established: 1994

BEAUTY TIMES
625 N. Euclid Ave. #210
St. Louis, MO 63108
Sohey Ahn, Editor
Tel: (314) 454-0707 **Fax:** (314) 454-1331

Email: sohey6397@aol.com
Web: www.beauty-times.com
Circ.: 5,500
Price: $5.00 **Subscription:** $50.00/year
Date established: 1991

CONG ONG
P.O. Box 690621
Houston, TX 77969-0621
Pham Thong, Owner
Tel: (281) 894-7780
Email: congongts-usa@yahoo.com
Circ.: 10,000
Price: $40.00
Date established: 1990

DIVERSITY NEWS
1400 112th Ave. SE #100
Bellevue, WA 98004
Anne Haenni, President/CEO
Tel: (425) 427-2656 **Fax:** (425) 427-1115
Email: diversity@diversitynews.com
Web: www.diversitynews.com
Circ.: 7,000
Price: Free **Subscription:** $19.95/year
Publication description: Diversity News is a monthly publication now in its tenth year. The paper has an estimated readership of 40,000 throughout Washington state as well as nation wide.
Date established: 1992

FILIPINAS MAGAZINE
GBM Bldg., 1580 Bryant St.
Daly City, CA 94015
Greg B. Macabenta, Publisher
Tel: (650) 985-2530 **Fax:** (650) 985-2532
Email: g.macabenta@filipinasmag.com
Web: www.filipinasmag.com
Circ.: 30,000
Price: $5.95 **Subscription:** $18.00/year
Publication description: An English-language Filipino Monthly magazine with a national readership.
Date established: 1992

FILIPINO-AMERICAN HERALD
120 Andover Park East #160
Seattle, WA 98188
Alma Kern, Publisher
Tel: (206) 242-3264 **Fax:** (206) 722-4914
Circ.: 7,000
Price: Free

FLORIDA VIETBAO
P.O. Box 277625
Miramar, FL 33027-7625
Yen Chu, Owner
Tel: (954) 436-1712 **Fax:** (954) 438-3448
Email: yenchu36@aol.com
Price: Free **Subscription:** $12.00 yr.

GEKKAN MON JAPANESE MAGAZINE
PMP Advertising, Inc.
1581 Webster St. #155
San Francisco, CA 94115
Shigeru Kimura, President
Tel: (415) 563-7656 **Fax:** (415) 567-5871
Email: info@pmpad.com
Web: www.pmpad.com
Circ.: 5,000
Price: $2.00
Date established: 1976

HAWAII PACIFIC PRESS
1306 Pali Hwy.
Honolulu, HI 96813
Kazuo Nakamine, Publisher
Tel: (808) 523-9049 **Fax:** (808) 531-5386
Email: hppkazu@lava.net
Circ.: 5,200
Price: $1.50 **Subscription:** $25.00/year
Date established: 1977

INDIA CURRENTS
P.O. Box 21285
San Jose, CA 95151
Vandana Kumar, Publisher
Tel: (408) 274-6966 **Fax:** (408) 274-2733
Email: publisher@indiacurrents.com
Web: www.indiacurrents.com
Circ.: 30,000
Price: Free **Subscription:** $19.95/year
Publication description: India Currents is an important facet of America's emerging multicultural identity, a monthly publication devoted to the exploration of the heritage and culture of India as it exists in the United States. The magazine covers a wide range of subjects, opinion, music, dance, film, literature, travel, recipes, business that are of interests to Indian Americans and Indophiles.
Date established: 1987

INDONESIAN JOURNAL
Desktop Design, Inc.
6673 Orly Ct.
Fontana, CA 92336
Emile Mailangkay, Editor-in-Chief
Tel: (909) 355-5474 **Fax:** (909) 355-4680
Email: indojournal@msn.com
Circ.: 10,000
Price: Free
Date established: 1988

INDUS BUSINESS JOURNAL
The Mishra Group, Inc.
318 Bear Hill Rd. #6
Waltham, MA 02451
Upendra Mishra, Publisher
Tel: (781) 487-0555 **Fax:** (781) 487-9207
Email: info@mishragroup.com
Web: www.indusbusinessjournal.com
Circ.: 20,000
Subscription: $24.95 /yr.
Date established: 2000

J MAGAZINE
Genki Publishing
476 Commonwealth Ave.
Boston, MA 02215
Ryu Fujiwara, Publisher
Tel: (617) 262-9390 **Fax:** (617) 262-8036
Email: jmagazine@earthlink.net
Web: www.jmag.com
Circ.: 15,000
Price: Free **Subscription:** $30/year
Publication description: J magazine is a virtual entertainment/information magazine for the young Japanese living in the United States.

JAPAN NEWS CLUB
P.O. Box 151
Trenton, MI 48183
Mark Masada, Owner/Editor
Tel: (734) 675-5060 **Fax:** (734) 675-5060
Email: markmasada@hotmail.com
Circ.: 5,000
Price: Free
Publication description: Japanese community newspaper.
Date established: 1992

KOREA MONITOR
7006-A Little River Turnpike
Annandale, VA 22003
Jimmy Lee, General Manager
Tel: (703) 750-9111 **Fax:** (703) 750-3141
Email: info@koreamonitor.net
Web: www.koreamonitor.net
Circ.: 10,000
Price: Free **Subscription:** $60.00/year
Date established: 2003

KOREA MONITOR
LA Office
3435 Wilshire Blvd. #1985
Los Angeles, CA 90010
SK Lim, Publisher
Tel: (213) 637-0880 **Fax:** (213) 637-0889
Email: info@koreamonitor.net
Web: www.koreamonitor.net
Subscription: $60/year

KOREA MONITOR
NY Office
45-78 162nd St., 1st Fl.
Flushing, NY 11358
SK Lim, Publisher
Tel: (718) 461-7770 **Fax:** (718) 461-8880
Email: info@koreamonitor.net
Web: www.koreamonitor.net
Subscription: $60/year

KOREAM JOURNAL
Korean American Publications
17000 S. Vermont Ave. #A
Gardena, CA 90247
James Ryu, Editor in Chief
Tel: (310) 769-4913 **Fax:** (310) 769-4903
Email: info@koreamjournal.com
Web: www.koreamjournal.com
Circ.: 30,000
Price: $3.95 **Subscription:** $28.00/year
Publication description: Provides depth and insight into the evolving Korean American experience.
Date established: 1990

KOREAN HERALD
1339 Baxter St. #200
Charlotte, NC 28204
Ki-Hyun Chun, CEO
Tel: (704) 334-3450 **Fax:** (704) 332-9373
Email: koreanherald@hotmail.com
Web: www.chungroup.com
Circ.: 2,000
Price: Free **Subscription:** $12.00/year
Publication description: The Korean Herald is the only English publication that is completely devoted to Korean issues in the Southeast.
Date established: 1993

KOREAN JOURNAL NATIONWIDE
Korean Journal Media Group
1241 Blalock Rd. #101
Houston, TX 77055-6424
Thomas Kim, President
Tel: (713) 973-8655 **Fax:** (713) 467-9241
Email: ekim@kjol.com
Web: www.kjol.com
Circ.: 100,000
Publication description: Provides US, Korean, Korean & world news, politics, sports, education, entertainment & lifestyle features and commentary relevant to the lives of Korean speaking Americans.
Date established: 1995

LIGHTHOUSE
Lighthouse Publishing
5334 Torrance Blvd.
Torrance, CA 90503
Komiyama Yoichi, President
Tel: (310) 944-3533 **Fax:** (310) 944-3633
Email: lighthouse@us-lighthouse.com
Web: www.us-lighthouse.com
Circ.: 50,000
Price: Free **Subscription:** $50.00/year
Date established: 1989

LITTLE INDIA
350 5th Ave. #1826
New York, NY 10118
Prashanth Lakhihal, Business Development Manager
Tel: (212) 560-0608 **Fax:** (212) 560-0609
Email: info@littleindia.com
Web: www.littleindia.com
Circ.: 140,000
Price: Free
Publication description: Little India is a general interest magazine targeted at South Asians in the United States. It publishes news, information, features and trenchant commentaries on overseas Indian life, trends and personalities. It covers the full spectrum of Indian life, including business, arts and entertainment, politics, etc. Little India is the largest Indian, as well as the largest Asian title published in the United States.
Date established: 1991

MARKETING TO EMERGING MAJORITIES
EPM Communications, Inc.
160 Mercer St., 3rd Fl.
New York, NY 10012
Ira Mayer, Publisher
Tel: (212) 941-0099 **Fax:** (212) 941-1622
Email: info@epmcom.com
Web: www.epmcom.com
Publication description: Newsletter on marketing to Hispanic, Black and Asian-Americans.
Date established: 1988

NEW ASIAN PACIFIC TIMES
940 S. Craycroft Rd.
Tucson, AZ 85711
Dorothy Lew, Editor
Tel: (520) 512-0144 **Fax:** (520) 512-0189
Email: pacacenter@aol.com
Circ.: 300
Price: Free **Subscription:** N/A
Date established: 1997

NGUOI VIET ILLINOIS
Vietnamese Association of Illinois
5252 N. Broadway
Chicago, IL 60640
Tam D. Nguyen, Editor
Tel: (773) 728-3700 **Fax:** (773) 728-0497
Email: vaichicago@ameritech.net
Web: www.v-a-i.net
Circ.: 2,000
Price: Free **Subscription:** $30.00 yr.
Date established: 1976

ORANGE NETWORK, THE
Orange County Japanese American Association
505 S. Villa Real Dr. #103A
Anaheim Hills, CA 92807
Tel: (714) 283-3551 **Fax:** (714) 283-3423
Email: network@ocjaa.org
Web: www.ocjaa.org
Circ.: 3,000
Price: Free
Publication description: Outreaches to those Japanese and Japanese Americans in the Orange county area who can not access newspapers, radio or television due to their inability to understand English. It also promotes small businesses in the JA Community by offering low advertisement rates.
Date established: 1986

PACIFIC ASIAN CURRENT
529 Bourdet Ave.
Walnut, CA 91789
Kris Ishige, Editor
Tel: (909) 594-0654 **Fax:** (909) 594-6241
Email: w.design@verizon.net
Circ.: 35,000
Price: Free **Subscription:** NA
Date established: 1994

PCDC NEWS CONNECTION
Philadelphia Chinatown Development Corporation
301-305 N. 9th St.
Philadelphia, PA 19107
John W. Chin, Executive Director
Tel: (215) 922-2156 **Fax:** (215) 922-7232
Email: info@chinatown-pcdc.com
Web: www.chinatown-pcdc.com
Circ.: 500
Date established: 1965

PEACE TIMES
Action for Peace through Prayer and Aid
319 R St. NW
Washington, DC 20001
Sang Yin Choi, Publisher/Editor
Tel: (202) 316-9466 **Fax:** (202) 939-0864
Email: appasc@aol.com
Web: www.iappa.net
Circ.: 5,000
Price: Free
Date established: 2000

PHILIPPINE ASIAN AMERICAN TIMES
5674 S. Jericho Way
Aurora, CO 80015
Nestor Mercado, Editor
Tel: (303) 699-7294 **Fax:** (303) 699-7725
Email: noli@apatimes.com
Web: www.apatimes.com
Circ.: 10,000
Price: $2.00 **Subscription:** $24.00/year
Date established: 1996

PHILIPPINE POST MAGAZINE
11406 La Docena Ln.
Santa Fe Springs, CA 90670
Marisse Abelgas, Editor
Tel: (562) 801-1681 **Fax:** (562) 801-9981
Email: rppost@aol.com
Web: www.philpost.com
Publication description: The Philippine Post Magazine is all about Filipino-Americans. It's about things they do and how they feel as they carve out a better future for themselves and their families in America.
Date established: 1993

RANG DONG MAGAZINE
P.O. Box 46754
Philadelphia, PA 19160-6754
Quang Hong Mac, Publisher/Editor
Tel: (215) 288-3036 **Fax:** (215) 288-5647
Email: rangdong@aol.com
Web: www.macadsllcrangdong.org
Circ.: +4,000
Price: Free
Publication description: Vietnamese-language community newspaper.
Date established: 1988

SILICONINDIA MAGAZINE
Siliconindia, Inc.
46560 Fremont Blvd. #413
Fremont, CA 94538
Karthik Sundaram, Managing Editor
Tel: (510) 440-8249 **Fax:** (510) 440-8276
Email: karthik@siliconindia.com
Web: www.siliconindia.com
Circ.: 71,000
Price: Free **Subscription:** $12.00/year
Publication description: Business and technology magazine.
Date established: 1997

SINO MONTHLY NEW JERSEY
Sino Media, LLC
18 Sheppard Pl.
Edison, NJ 08817-3166
Ivy Lee, Chief Editor
Tel: (732) 650-7466 **Fax:** (732) 650-7468

Email: info@sino-monthly.com
Web: www.sino-monthly.com
Circ.: 17,000
Price: $1.00 **Subscription:** $10.00/year
Publication description: Provide information to Chinese communities.

SOUTH ASIAN MAGAZINE
P.O. Box 6673
McLean, VA 22106-6673
Bala Chandran, Editor
Tel: (703) 319-0100 **Fax:** (703) 319-0111
Email: info@asianocean.com
Web: www.asianocean.com
Circ.: 10,000
Price: Free
Date established: 2000

SOUTHERN JOURNAL OF HOUSTON
9118 Burger Ln.
Houston, TX 77040
Norma Inafuku, Manager
Tel: (713) 937-9181 **Fax:** (713) 466-8735
Email: southernjournal@att.net
Circ.: 6,000
Price: Free **Subscription:** $12.00/year
Publication description: A Japanese Community Newspaper serving the southern US.
Date established: 1989

SUN YAT SEN NEWS
1109 Powell St.
San Francisco, CA 94108
Lily, Editor
Tel: (415) 391-3691
Web: http://www.222.to/sunyatsen/
Publication description: Chinese

THE EYE
The Eye International, Inc.
15 San Juan Ave.
Daly City, CA 94015
Willie Jurado, Editor
Tel: (650) 992-2411 **Fax:** (650) 992-2411
Email: theeyeinc@aol.com
Circ.: 5,000
Price: $0.75
Date established: 1954

TU DO DAN BAN
3503 Elysian
Houston, TX 77009
Mimh Phat Le, Publisher
Tel: (281) 820-6452
Email: tddban@lmdcvn.com
Web: www.lmdcvn.com
Circ.: 3,000
Price: free

TV FAN COMPANY
P.O. Box 49202
Los Angeles, CA 90049
Koichi Takechi, Editor
Tel: (310) 479-7803 **Fax:** (310) 479-7593
Email: mail@tvfanshop.com
Web: www.tvfanshop.com
Circ.: 22,000
Price: Free **Subscription:** $27.00/year
Date established: 1975

VIA TIMES NEWSMAGAZINE
3108 W. Belmont Ave.
Chicago, IL 60618
Joe Mauricio, Co-Publisher
Tel: (773) 866-0811 **Fax:** (773) 866-9207
Email: viatimes@sbcglobal.net
Web: www.viatimes.com
Circ.: 60,000
Price: Free **Subscription:** $20.00/year
Publication description: Monthly news-magazine.
Date established: 1984

VIET WEEKLY
12866 Main St.
Garden Grove, CA 92840
Vu Le, Editor in Chief
Tel: (714) 590-3082 **Fax:** (714) 590-3084
Email: vietweekly@vietweekly.com
Web: www.vietweekly.com
Circ.: 12,000
Price: $0.50 **Subscription:** $110.00/year
Date established: 2003

QUARTERLY

AALAM NEWS
Asian American Lawyers Association of
Massachusetts
P.O. Box 5655
Boston, MA 02114
Myong J. Joun, President
Tel: (617) 742-4100 **Fax:** (617) 742-5858
Email: mjjoua@civil-rights-law.com
Web: www.aalam.org
Circ.: 200
Date established: 1984

AL JADID MAGAZINE
P.O. Box 241342
Los Angeles, CA 90024-1342
Elie Chalala, Editor
Tel: (310) 470-6984
Email: aljadid@jovanet.com
Web: www.aljadid.com
Price: $6.95 **Subscription:** $18.00/year
Date established: 1995

API LEGAL OUTREACH NEWSLETTER
Asian Pacific Islander Legal Outreach
1188 Franklin St. #202
San Francisco, CA 94109
Victor Hwang, Manager
Tel: (415) 567-6255 **Fax:** (415) 567-6248
Email: info@apilegaloutreach.org
Web: www.apilegaloutreach.org
Price: Free
Publication description: Newsletter of the
Asian Pacific Islander Legal Outreach
Date established: 1975

CHINA FOR CHILDREN MAGAZINE
Our Chinese Daughters Foundation
P.O. Box 1243
Bloomington, IL 61702-1243
Dr. Jane Liedtke, Founder/CEO
Tel: (309) 830-0983
Email: jane@ocdf.org
Web: www.ocdf.org
Date established: 1995

COLORLINES MAGAZINE
Applied Research Center
4096 Piedmont Ave. PMB 319
Oakland, CA 94611-9924
Tram Nguyen, Executive Editor
Tel: (510) 653-3415 **Fax:** (510) 653-3427
Email: colorlines@arc.org
Web: www.colorlines.com
Circ.: 5,000
Price: $4.95 **Subscription:** $16.00/year
Publication description: ColorLines is the first
national, multiracial magazine devoted to
covering the politics and creations of com-
munities of color.
Date established: 1998

COMMITTEE BRIDGES NEWSLETTER
Committee of 100
677 5th Ave., 5th Ave.
New York, NY 10022
Alice Mong, Executive Director
Tel: (212) 371-6565 **Fax:** (212) 371-9009
Email: c100@committee100.org

Web: www.committee100.org
Circ.: 3,000
Price: Free
Publication description: Offering news about
Asian Americans with an emphasis to the
Chinese community.
Date established: 1990

DHAMMANANDA NEWSLETTER
Theravada Buddhist Society of America
17450 S. Cabrillo Hwy.
Half Moon Bay, CA 94019-2518
U. Myat Htoo, President
Tel: (650) 726-7604
Email: tbsa@tbsa.org
Web: www.tbsa.org
Circ.: 1,500
Date established: 1980

EAST WEST REPORT, NEWSLETTER
US Pan Asian American Chamber of Com-
merce
1329 18th St. NW
Washington, DC 20036
Susan Au Allen, President/CEO
Tel: (202) 296-5221 **Fax:** (202) 296-5225
Email: administrator@uspaacc.com
Web: www.uspaacc.com
Circ.: 10,000
Date established: 1984

HINDUISM TODAY MAGAZINE
107 Kaholalele Rd.
Kapaa, HI 96746
Paramacharya Palaniswami, Editor
Tel: (808) 822-7032 **Fax:** (808) 822-4351
Email: letters@hindu.org
Web: www.hinduismtoday.com
Circ.: 10,000
Price: $5.95 **Subscription:** $35.00/year
Date established: 1979

IMAGE MAGAZINE
Organization of Chinese Americans
1001 Connecticut Ave. #601
Washington, DC 20036
Christine Chen, Executive Director
Tel: (202) 223-5500 **Fax:** (202) 296-0540
Email: info@ocanatl.org
Web: www.ocanatl.org
Circ.: 1,500
Publication description: Serves as a commu-
nications link between chapter members as
well as an informative source on federal and
legislative initiatives and policies relevant to
the Chinese American and Asian American
communities
Date established: 1985

KOREAN JOURNAL
5505 Wilshire Blvd.
Los Angeles, CA 90036
Tel: (323) 936-7141 **Fax:** (323) 936-5712
Email: info@kccla.org
Web: www.kccla.org
Subscription: $12.00 yr.
Publication description: K.C. magazine
covers many aspects of Korean life, History,
archaeology, painting, architecture, religions,
literature, lifestyles, modern art: here is where
the unfolding panoply of life in Korea is at
your fingertips.

KOREAN QUARTERLY
P.O. Box 6789
St. Paul, MN 55106
Stephen Wunrow, Publisher
Tel: (651) 771-8164
Email: editor@koreanquarterly.org
Web: www.koreanquarterly.org
Circ.: 22,000
Price: Free **Subscription:** $18.00/year
Publication description: To unite and sup-

port the entire Korean American commu-
nity including, first and second generation
Korean Americans, adopted Koreans and
their families, hapa, and bicultural Korean
Americans.
Date established: 1997

LITERATI, THE
Chinese Journal Corporation
1600 Armstrong Ave.
San Francisco, CA 94124
Maurice H. Chuck, Editor
Tel: (415) 822-1155 **Fax:** (415) 822-2525
Email: publishing@chinesejournal.com
Web: www.chinesejournal.com
Circ.: 2,000
Price: Free **Subscription:** $25.00/year
Publication description: Bimonthly Chinese
Language Literary Magazine
Date established: 1975

MIDDLE EAST POLICY
Middle East Policy Council
1730 M St. NW #512
Washington, DC 20036
Anne Joyce, Editor
Tel: (202) 296--6767 **Fax:** (202) 296-5791
Email: info@mepc.org
Web: www.mepc.org
Circ.: 4,000
Price: $15.00 **Subscription:** $172.00/year
Publication description: Middle East Policy
(ISSN 1061-1924) provides a forum for
viewpoints on recent developments that
affect US-Middle East Policy. It is published
quarterly in March, June, September and
December.
Date established: 1982

MONITOR, THE
Center for International Trade and Security
120 Hunter Holmes Academic Bldg.
Athens, GA 30602
Gary Bertsch, Director
Tel: (706) 542-2985 **Fax:** (706) 542-2975
Email: gbertsch@uga.edu
Web: www.uga.edu/cits
Date established: 1995

**NATIONAL JAPANESE HISTORICAL
SOCIETY NEWSLETTER**
National Japanese Historical Society
1684 Post St.
San Francisco, CA 94115
Rosalyn Tonai, Executive Director
Tel: (415) 921-5007 **Fax:** (415) 921-5087
Email: njahs@njhas.org
Web: www.njahs.org
Circ.: 2,000
Price: $7.00
Date established: 1991

NEWS CIRCLE-ARAB AMERICAN AFFAIRS
The News Circle Publishing House
P.O. Box 3684
Glendale, CA 91201
Joseph R. Haiek, Publisher
Tel: (818) 507-0333 **Fax:** (818) 246-1936
Email: newscircle@sbcglobal.net
Web: www.arab-american-affairs.net
Circ.: 5,000
Price: $3.95 **Subscription:** $35.00/year
Publication description: The oldest Arab-
American independent magazine specializ-
ing in Arab-American affairs.
Date established: 1972

NEWSLETTER
National Association for Asian and Pacific
American Education
P.O. Box 280346
Northridge, CA 91328-0346
Robert Johnson, Editor

Tel: (818) 677-6853 **Fax:** (818) 366-2714
Email: bjohnson@hawaii.edu
Web: www.naapae.net
Date established: 1977

SULO- PAASE NEWSLETTER
Philippine American Academy of Science
and Engineering
16609 Cutlass Dr.
Rockville, MD 20853-1333
Prof. Carlito Lebrilla, Ph.D., President
Tel: (301) 924-2242
Email: hope.celso@verizon.net
Web: www.paase.org
Date established: 1980

TEA LEAVES/NEWSLETTER
Colorado Springs Chinese Cultural Institute
P.O. Box 2625
Colorado Springs, CO 80901
Mali Hsu, Founder/Chairwoman
Tel: (719) 635-0024
Email: malihsu@aol.com
Web: www.cscci.org
Circ.: 1,000
Date established: 2001

TIBET AID ELECTRONIC NEWSLETTER
Tibet Aid
34 Tinker St.
Woodstock, NY 12498
Steve Drago, President
Tel: (845) 679-6973 **Fax:** (845) 679-6973
Email: sponsor@tibetaid.org
Web: www.tibetaid.org
Circ.: 800

US CHINA REVIEW
US China People's Friendship Association
2534 Doidge Ave.
Pinole, CA 94564
Betty Boyle, Western Region President
Tel: (510) 758-2851
Email: shanguo@aol.com
Web: www.uscpfa.org
Date established: 1972

VOICE
National Coalition Against Domestic Vio-
lence
P.O. Box 18749
Denver, CO 80218
Rita Smith, Executive Director
Tel: (303) 839-1852 **Fax:** (303) 831-9251
Email: rsmith@ncadv.org
Web: www.ncadv.org

SEMI-ANNUAL

HELPING HANDS NEWSLETTER
Asian Perinatal Advocate
1001 Potrero Ave. MS6E
San Francisco, CA 94110
Mai-Mai Ho, Executive Director
Tel: (415) 206-5450 **Fax:** (415) 206-4778
Email: apa@apasfgh.org
Web: www.apasfgh.org
Circ.: 3,000
Date established: 1987

WEEKLY

**AMERICAN & CHINESE BUSINESS NEWS
(CHINESE) /CHINA BUSINESS NEWS
(ENGLISH)**
932 Hungerford Dr. #25A
Rockville, MD 20850
Xugeng Zhou, Chief Editor
Tel: (301) 424-5978 **Fax:** (301) 424-5979

Email: acgroup@acweb.org
Web: www.acweb.com.cn
Circ.: 15,000
Subscription: $52.00/year
Date established: 1997

AMERICAN CHINESE TIMES
5253 El Cajon Blvd. #B
San Diego, CA 92115
William Liu, Editor
Tel: (619) 286-0953 **Fax:** (619) 286-9035
Email: actimes@usa.com
Circ.: 6,000
Price: Free
Date established: 1993

ANG PERYODIKO
23746 S. Main St.
Carson, CA 90745
David Casuco, Editor
Tel: (310) 830-6033 **Fax:** (310) 830-6076
Email: info@peryodiko.net
Web: www.peryodiko.net
Circ.: 30,000
Price: Free
Date established: 2000

ARAB VOICE
956 Main St.
Paterson, NJ 07503
Walid Rabah, Chief Editor
Tel: (973) 523-7815 **Fax:** (973) 523-0351
Email: wrabah@arabvoice.com
Web: www.arabvoice.com
Circ.: 25,000
Price: Free **Subscription:** $100.00/year
Date established: 1993

ARIZONA CHINESE NEWS
7328 N. 7th Ave.
Phoenix, AZ 85021
Shou Quin, Editor
Tel: (602) 269-3062 **Fax:** (602) 269-0715
Email: acznews@cox.net
Circ.: 5,000
Price: $0.40 **Subscription:** $40.00/year
Date established: 1991

ASIA TODAY
17250 Bothell Way NE #B
Seattle, WA 98155
John Chou, Director
Tel: (206) 365-8807 **Fax:** (206) 367-6283
Email: asia_today@hotmail.com
Circ.: 10,000
Price: Free **Subscription:** $50.00/year
Date established: 1988

ASIAN AMERICAN PRESS
ABC Publishing, Inc.
417 University Ave.
St. Paul, MN 55103
Nghi Huynh, Publisher/Editor
Tel: (651) 224-6570 **Fax:** (651) 224-7032
Email: aapress@aapress.com
Web: www.aapress.com
Circ.: 15,000
Price: $0.83 **Subscription:** $50.00/year
Date established: 1982

ASIAN AMERICAN TIMES
135-258 40th Rd. #3F
Flushing, NY 11354
Michael Chu, Editor
Tel: (718) 358-6413 **Fax:** (718) 358-6501
Email: chuasian@aol.com
Circ.: 5,000
Price: Free **Subscription:** $40.00/year
Date established: 1987

ASIAN ENTERTAINMENT WEEKLY
396 Broadway #300
New York, NY 10013

Brian Au, Manager
Tel: (212) 226-3388 **Fax:** (212) 226-9857
Email: puilinlee@aol.com
Circ.: 15,000
Price: Free

ASIAN GAZETTE
5848 Hubbard Dr.
Rockville, MD 20852
Ching L. Shu, Manager
Tel: (301) 468-2310 **Fax:** (301) 984-8806
Email: news@wchns.com
Circ.: 15,000
Price: Free
Publication description: Published in simplified Chinese serving Chinese immigrants from mainland China.
Date established: 2002

ASIAN JOURNAL
San Diego Asian Journal
550 E. 8th St. #6
National City, CA 91950
Simeon G. Silverio, Jr., Publisher & Editor
Tel: (619) 474-0588 **Fax:** (619) 474-0373
Email: asianjournal@aol.com
Web: www.asianjournalusa.com
Circ.: 35,000
Price: Free **Subscription:** $15.00/year
Publication description: Asian Journal is the leading Asian American publication in Southern California today.
Date established: 1986

ASIAN JOURNAL - SAN FRANCISCO
Asian Journal Publications, Inc.
156 S. Spruce Ave. #213
South San Francisco, CA 94080
Joseph Peralta, Associate Editor
Tel: (650) 583-6818 **Fax:** (650) 583-6819
Email: jojo@asianjournal.com
Web: www.asianjournal.com
Circ.: 25,000
Price: Free
Date established: 2002

ASIAN PACIFIC NEWS
13815 Graystone Ave.
Norwalk, CA 90650
Paisan Promnoi, Editor
Tel: (562) 868-6339 **Fax:** (562) 863-7820
Email: apacnews@hotmail.com
Circ.: 20,000
Price: Free **Subscription:** $90.00/year
Date established: 2000

ASIAN REPORTER NEWSPAPER
922 N. Killingsworth St. #1-A
Portland, OR 97217-2220
Jaime Lim, Publisher
Tel: (503) 283-4440 **Fax:** (503) 283-4445
Email: news@asianreporter.com
Web: www.asianreporter.com
Circ.: 19,500
Price: Free **Subscription:** $40.00/year
Date established: 1990

ASIAN WEEK
809 Sacramento St.
San Francisco, CA 94108
Samson Wong, Editor-in-Chief
Tel: (415) 397-0220 **Fax:** (415) 397-7258
Email: asianweek@asianweek.com
Web: www.asianweek.com
Circ.: 50,000
Price: Free **Subscription:** $29.00/year
Publication description: A national English-language news weekly for Asian Pacific American community. A chronicle of the Asian American experience. Asian Week provides a national forum on issues important to Asian Americans.
Date established: 1979

ATLANTA CHINESE NEWS
5725 Buford Hwy. #221
Atlanta, GA 30340
Amy Sheu, Director
Tel: (770) 455-0880 **Fax:** (770) 452-0670
Email: info@atlantachinesenews.com
Web: www.atlantachinesenews.com
Circ.: 10,000
Price: Free
Date established: 1992

BALITA USA
Balita Media, Inc.
520 E. Wilson Blvd. #210
Glendale, CA 91206
Berna O. Mabunga, Editor
Tel: (818) 552-4503 **Fax:** (818) 552-4592
Email: editor@balita.com
Web: www.balita.com
Circ.: 80,000
Price: Free **Subscription:** $54.00/year
Date established: 1991

BOSTON CHINESE NEWS
29 Slade St.
Belmont, MA 02478
Janice Yu, Publisher
Tel: (978) 369-2362 **Fax:** (617) 484-2033
Email: bcns@gis.net
Circ.: 10,000
Price: Free
Date established: 1991

CALIFORNIA EXAMINER - LOS ANGELES
The First Tri Media
4515 Eagle Rock Blvd.
Los Angeles, CA 90041
Ella Madrigal, Editor
Tel: (323) 344-3500 **Fax:** (323) 344-3501
Email: calexaminr@aol.com
Web: www.californiaexaminer.net
Circ.: 50,000
Price: Free
Publication description: The leading Filipino-American newspaper in Southern California.
Date established: 1982

CALIFORNIA EXAMINER - SAN DIEGO
The First Tri Media
914 E. 8th St. #212
National City, CA 91950
Fe Arre, Advertising Manager
Tel: (619) 477-0080 **Fax:** (619) 477-0090
Email: fe_arre@hotmail.com
Web: www.californiaexaminer.net
Circ.: 30,000
Price: Free **Subscription:** $25.00/year
Date established: 1993

CALIFORNIA JOURNAL FOR FILIPINO-AMERICANS, THE
P.O. Box 8119
Torrance, CA 90504
Joey Quinto, Publisher
Tel: (310) 532-6238 **Fax:** (310) 532-6242
Email: cjfilam@earthlink.com
Web: www.cjfilam.com
Circ.: 25,000
Price: Free **Subscription:** $168.00/year
Publication description: CJFA provides readers news from the Philippines, consumer and business news, SBA updates, community events and going-ons.
Date established: 1994

CHI-AM DAILY NEWS
673 Monterey Pass Rd.
Monterey Park, CA 91754
Catherine Shih, Editor
Tel: (626) 281-8989 **Fax:** (626) 281-0859
Email: news@chiam.org
Circ.: 10,000

Price: Free
Date established: 1990

CHICAGO CHINESE NEWS
2155 S. China Pl., 2nd Fl.
Chicago, IL 60616
Danny Lee, Editor
Tel: (312) 326-2900 **Fax:** (312) 326-6787
Email: ccn1@chicagochinesenews.com
Web: www.chicagochinesenews.com
Circ.: 10,000
Date established: 1990

CHICAGO SHIMPO
Chicago Shimpo
4670 N. Manor Ave.
Chicago, IL 60625
Yoshiko Urayama, President
Tel: (773) 478-6170 **Fax:** (773) 478-9360
Email: shimpo@mc.net
Circ.: 5,000
Price: $0.85 **Subscription:** $66.00/year
Publication description: Japanese American newspaper.
Date established: 1945

CHINA JOURNAL
US Dragon, LLC
2146-A S. Archer Ave.
Chicago, IL 60616
May Zheng, President
Tel: (312) 326-3228 **Fax:** (312) 326-3503
Email: chinajournal@sbcglobal.net
Web: www.usdragon.com
Circ.: 20,000
Price: Free
Date established: 1991

CHINA STAR
China Star Media Corporation
2210 S. Michigan Ave.
Chicago, IL 60616
Da Way Chou, President
Tel: (312) 842-8944 **Fax:** (312) 225-7513
Email: editor@chinastarmedia.com
Web: www.chinastarmedia.com
Circ.: 10,000
Price: Free **Subscription:** $65.00/year
Date established: 1996

CHINESE AMERICAN NEWS
2167-B S. China Pl., 2nd Fl.
Chicago, IL 60616
James Chang, Chief Editor
Tel: (312) 225-5600 **Fax:** (312) 225-8849
Email: editor@canews.com
Web: www.canews.com
Circ.: 10,000
Price: Free **Subscription:** $80.00/year
Date established: 1978

CHINESE AMERICAN POST
11 Federal Blvd. #1
Denver, CO 80219
Harrison Tu, Chief Editor
Tel: (303) 934-1773 **Fax:** (303) 934-0262
Email: chinesepost@aol.com
Circ.: 200,000
Price: Free **Subscription:** $25.00/year
Date established: 1994

CHINESE NEWS
4463 University Ave.
San Diego, CA 92105
Stanley Ting, Editor
Tel: (619) 280-3388 **Fax:** (619) 280-9970
Email: chinesenews@cox.net
Circ.: 20,000
Price: Free
Date established: 1983

COLORADO CHINESE NEWS
1548 W. Alameda Ave. #A

Denver, CO 80223
Wendy Chao, President
Tel: (303) 722-8268 **Fax:** (303) 722-7861
Email: editor@cocnews.com
Web: www.cocnews.com
Circ.: 6,500
Price: Free
Date established: 1994

DEP WEEKLY MAGAZINE

12313 Bellaire Blvd. #D
Houston, TX 77072-2254
Tam Tran, Editor
Tel: (281) 568-7070 **Fax:** (281) 568-7071
Email: depmagazine@aol.com
Circ.: 10,000
Price: Free **Subscription:** $144.00/year
Date established: 1988

DESI TALK

News India-Times Group
43 W. 24th St.
New York, NY 10010
Veena Merchant, Editor
Tel: (212) 675-7515 **Fax:** (212) 675-7576
Email: editor@newsindia-times.com
Web: www.newsindia-times.com
Circ.: 30,000
Price: Free **Subscription:** $26.00 / year
Date established: 1975

DIARYO PILIPINO

Streetnews Publishing, Inc.
1000 S. Fremont Ave. #0008
Alhambra, CA 91803
Rhony F. Laigo, Editor-in-Chief
Tel: (626) 588-2414 **Fax:** (626) 588-2639
Email: info@diaryopilipino.net
Web: www.diaryopilipino.la
Circ.: 40,000
Price: Free **Subscription:** $120.00/year
Publication description: This is the only Filipino Online newspaper updated daily.
Date established: 1996

DOINAY NEWSPAPER

P.O. Box 5061
Falls Church, VA 22044
Le T. Hoang, Advertising Manager
Tel: (703) 748-1239 **Fax:** (703) 748-1664
Email: doinay@aol.com
Circ.: 8,000
Price: $1.00
Date established: 1989

EXPRESS INDIA

ADV Solutions, Inc.
7908 Kennewick Ave. #101
Takoma Park, MD 20912
Rajan George, Editor
Tel: (301) 445-3543 **Fax:** (301) 576-3731
Email: expressindiaweek@aol.com
Circ.: 10,000
Price: Free
Date established: 1989

FILIPINO PRESS

The Filipino Press
P.O. Box 2226
National City, CA 91950
Doris Malabad, Editor
Tel: (619) 477-0940 **Fax:** (619) 477-1024
Email: filpress@aol.com
Web: www.filipinopress.com
Circ.: 25,000
Price: Free
Date established: 1986

FILIPINO REPORTER

Filipino Reporter Enterprises, Inc.
Empire State Bldg., 350 5th Ave.
New York, NY 10118-0110
Libertito Pelayo, Editor in Chief/Publisher
Tel: (212) 967-5784 **Fax:** (212) 967-5848
Email: filipinoreporter@worldnet.att.net
Web: www.filipinoreporter.com
Circ.: 25,000
Price: $1.25 **Subscription:** $45.00/year
Date established: 1972

FLORIDA CHINESE NEWS

3325 Griffin Rd. #193
Ft. Lauderdale, FL 33312
Raymond Ching, Editor
Tel: (954) 966-5264 **Fax:** (954) 966-4142
Email: info@floridachinese.com
Web: www.floridachinese.com
Circ.: 10,000
Price: Free **Subscription:** $60.00/year
Date established: 1986

GLOBAL CHINESE TIMES

1945 Lincoln Hwy. #5
Edison, NJ 08817-3263
Chenli Fang, Editor
Tel: (732) 650-9888 **Fax:** (732) 650-9889
Email: chiweekly@aol.com
Circ.: 30,000
Price: Free

GUJARAT SAMACHAR

3 Lincoln Hwy. #307
Edison, NJ 08820
Shrian Shah, Founder & Editor
Tel: (732) 452-1755 **Fax:** (732) 452-1756
Email: editor@gujaratsamachar.com
Web: www.gujaratsamachar.com

GUJARAT TIMES

News India-Times Group
43 W. 24th St. 9th Fl.
New York, NY 10010
Hasmukh Barot, Editor
Tel: (212) 727-2523 **Fax:** (212) 727-3298
Email: email@gujarattimes.com
Circ.: 12,000
Price: $1.00 **Subscription:** $40.00 / year
Date established: 1999

HOA THINH DON VIET BAO

8394-C2 Terminal Rd.
Lorton, VA 22079
Suong Truong, Publisher
Tel: (703) 339-9852 **Fax:** (703) 339-9857
Email: htdvietbao@aol.com
Circ.: 11,000
Price: $1.00
Publication description: Vietnamese Newspaper
Date established: 1983

INDIA ABROAD

Rediff Publications
43 W. 24th St., 7th Fl.
New York, NY 10010
Palem Panicker, Editor
Tel: (212) 929-1727 **Fax:** (212) 627-9503
Email: prem@us.rediff.com
Web: www.indiaabroad.com
Circ.: 61,856
Price: $1.00 **Subscription:** $32.00 yr.
Publication description: India Abroad is the oldest Asian Indian publication in North America, and the largest published outside of India. It provides a comprehensive view of international, national, and local news, as well as business and political coverage,

entertainment and event listings and sports and community commentary.
Date established: 1970

INDIA HERALD

6610 Harwin Dr. #120
Houston, TX 77036
Rajeev Gadgil, Editor
Tel: (713) 782-2828 **Fax:** (713) 782-9810
Email: indiaherald@prodigy.net
Web: www.india-herald.com
Circ.: 3,000
Price: $0.25 **Subscription:** $20.00 / year
Date established: 1995

INDIA IN NEW YORK

Rediff Publications
43 W. 24th St., 7th Fl.
New York, NY 10010
Nikhil Laxman, Editor
Tel: (212) 989-1606 **Fax:** (212) 627-9503
Web: www.indiaabroad.com
Price: Free **Subscription:**

INDIA JOURNAL

15605 S. Carmenita Rd. #107
Santa Fe Springs, CA 90670-5648
Mohinder Singh, Editor
Tel: (562) 802-9720 **Fax:** (562) 802-9750
Email: singh@indiajournal.com
Web: www.indiajournal.com
Circ.: 21,000
Price: $0.50 **Subscription:** $30.00/year
Date established: 1984

INDIA POST

Post Media, Inc.
29274 Union City Blvd.
Union City, CA 94587
Dr. Romesh Japra, Publisher
Tel: (510) 429-2110 **Fax:** (510) 429-1413
Email: publisher@indiapost.com
Web: www.indiapost.com
Circ.: 133,000
Price: $0.50 **Subscription:** $30.00/year
Publication description: Asian Indian newspaper with a national readership.
Date established: 1993

INDIA THIS WEEK

ADV Solutions, Inc.
P.O. Box 3788
Silver Spring, MD 20918
Rajan George, Editor
Tel: (301) 445-3543 **Fax:** (301) 576-3731
Email: indiathisweek@gmail.com
Circ.: 10,000
Price: Free
Date established: 2003

INDIA TODAY MAGAZINE

Living Media India Ltd.
290 Park Ave. South 10th Fl.
New York, NY 10010
Chander Rai, Publisher
Tel: (212) 375-0584 **Fax:** (212) 375-0752
Email: lmilny@aol.com
Web: www.indiatoday.com
Circ.: 30,000
Price: $2.00 **Subscription:** $73.00 yr.
Date established: NA

INDIA TRIBUNE

3302 W. Peterson Ave.
Chicago, IL 60659
Prashant Shah, Editor
Tel: (773) 588-5077 **Fax:** (773) 588-7011
Email: prashant@indiatribune.com
Web: www.indiatribune.com
Circ.: 27,000

Price: $0.75 **Subscription:** $32.00/year
Publication description: India Tribune, a weekly journal of its kind for the family in the USA, is a household name for many Indians.
Date established: 1974

INDIA TRIBUNE

100 W. 32nd St., 6th Fl.
New York, NY 10001
Prashant Shah, Editor
Tel: (212) 564-7336 **Fax:** (212) 564-7118
Email: info@indiatribune.com
Web: www.indiatribune.com
Circ.: 11,746
Price: $0.75 **Subscription:** $32.00 / year
Date established: 1977

INDIA TRIBUNE

5675 Jimmy Carter Blvd. #540, Global Mall
Norcross, GA 30071
Mustafa Ajmeri, Editor
Tel: (678) 463-6613
Email: ajmerimk@aol.com
Web: www.indiatribune.com
Circ.: 50,000
Price: $0.75 **Subscription:** $32.00/year
Publication description: India Tribune, a weekly journal of its kind for the family in the USA, is a household name for many Indians.
Date established: 1977

INDIA WEST

India West Publications, Inc.
933 MacArthur Blvd.
San Leandro, CA 94577
Bina Murarka, Editor
Tel: (510) 383-1140 **Fax:** (510) 383-1154
Email: news@indiawest.com
Web: www.indiawest.com
Circ.: 30,000
Price: Free **Subscription:** $30.00/year
Publication description: An English language Indian newspaper with a national readership.
Date established: 1975

INDIA-WEST PUBLICATIONS INC.

9333 McArthur Blda
San Leandro, CA 94577
Tel: 510 383 1140
Circ.: 30.000
Publication description: Inidan Life and Style
Date established: 1975

INDIAN NEWS EXPRESS

12303 Woodrow Ave.
Downey, CA 90241
Tel: (562) 803-8781 **Fax:** (562) 803-5130

INDO-AMERICAN NEWS

7457 Harwin Dr. #262
Houston, TX 77036
Pramod Kulkarni, Editor
Tel: (713) 789-6397 **Fax:** (713) 789-6399
Email: indoamericannews@yahoo.com
Web: www.indoamerican-news.com
Circ.: 4,000
Price: Free **Subscription:** $30.00/year
Date established: 1981

INTERTHAI PACIFIC RIM

1123 N. Vine St. #7
Hollywood, CA 90038
Pat Super, Editor
Tel: (323) 871-1868 **Fax:** (323) 871-1812

Email: info@interthainews.com
Web: www.interthainews.com
Circ.: 15,000
Price: Free **Subscription:** $90.00/year
Publication description: To serve Thai American Community with accurate news.
Date established: 1996

KOMERICAN NEWS
2240 Royal Ln. #214
Dallas, TX 75229
Ilman Fung, Director
Tel: (972) 620-8421 **Fax:** (972) 620-8423
Email: kmpost00@yahoo.com
Circ.: 7,000
Price: Free
Date established: 1990

KOREAN CHRISTIAN JOURNAL
5235 N. Elston Ave.
Chicago, IL 60630
Samuel D. Park, Editor/Publisher
Tel: (773) 777-7779 **Fax:** (773) 777-0004
Email: kcj@kcj777.com
Web: www.kcj777.com
Circ.: 5,000
Price: Free **Subscription:** $50.00/year
Date established: 1977

KOREAN DENVER NEWS
9650 E. Colfax Ave.
Aurora, CO 80010
Ki Cho, Publisher
Tel: (303) 364-4500 **Fax:** (303) 366-1110
Email: hanin_sm@hotmail.com
Circ.: 5,000
Subscription: $30/year

KOREAN JOURNAL ATLANTA
Korean Journal Media Group
5455 Buford Hwy. #207-A
Doraville, GA 30340
Thomas Kim, President
Tel: (770) 451-6946 **Fax:** (770) 451-6955
Email: kjatl@kjol.com
Web: www.kjol.com
Circ.: 8,000
Price: Free
Date established: 1983

KOREAN JOURNAL DALLAS
Korean Journal Media Group
2639 Walnut Hill Ln. #144
Dallas, TX 75229
David Son, President
Tel: (972) 241-7907 **Fax:** (972) 241-7909
Email: kjdallas20@yahoo.com.kr
Circ.: 6,000
Price: Free
Date established: 1984

KOREAN JOURNAL HOUSTON
Korean Journal Houston, Inc.
1249-A Blalock Rd.
Houston, TX 77055
Dong Choi, Editor
Tel: (713) 467-4266 **Fax:** (713) 467-2657
Email: kjhou2000@yahoo.com
Circ.: 8,000
Price: Free **Subscription:** $25.00/year
Date established: 1982

KOREAN SOUTHEAST NEWS
Korean Southeast News Company
5725 Buford Hwy. #211
Doraville, GA 30340
Peter Lee, Editor
Tel: (770) 454-9655 **Fax:** (770) 454-6191
Email: info@seweekly.com
Circ.: 10,000
Price: Free **Subscription:** $30.00/year
Date established: 1989

KOREAN SUNDAY NEWS
4550 Wilshire Blvd. #200
Los Angeles, CA 90010
Joon H. Lee, Publisher
Tel: (323) 954-7500 **Fax:** (323) 954-7503
Email: admin@koreansundaynews.com
Web: www.koreansundaynews.com
Circ.: 48,000
Price: $0.75 **Subscription:** $50.00/year
Publication description: Providing the Korean American community with prompt, accurate, and unbiased information catering to all ages and generations.
Date established: 1984

LANG MAGAZINE
6930 65th St. #101
Sacramento, CA 95823
Tam Nguyen, Publisher
Tel: (916) 393-4500 **Fax:** (916) 393-6299
Email: lang_magazine@yahoo.com
Circ.: 10,000
Publication description: A Vietnamese language magazine, publish weekly on Friday. Contents: local, Vietnam news, national & world news; political point of view, entertainment, sports.
Date established: 1989

LITTLE SAIGON NEWS, THE
13861 Seaboard Cir.
Garden Grove, CA 92843
Brigitte Suynh, Editor
Tel: (714) 265-0800 **Fax:** (714) 265-0180
Email: saigon_nho@hotmail.com
Circ.: 4,000
Price: Free
Date established: 1985

MAI MAGAZINE
P.O. Box 10640
Westminster, CA 92685
Mai Tran, Editor
Tel: (714) 892-6465 **Fax:** (714) 892-6405
Email: tuambaomai@aol.com
Price: Free

MANILA MAIL NEWSPAPER
12 Avalon Dr.
Daly City, CA 94015
Ruben P. Bunag, President/Publisher
Tel: (650) 992-5474 **Fax:** (650) 997-0673
Email: manilamail@sbcglobal.net
Circ.: 25,000
Price: Free **Subscription:** $35.00/year
Publication description: An English language newspaper with a Northern California readership.
Date established: 1990

MANILA-US TIMES
416 S. Verdugo Rd.
Glendale, CA 91205
Johnny M. Pecayo, Publisher/Editor-in-Chief
Tel: (818) 637-8320 **Fax:** (818) 637-8320
Email: johnnypecayo@yahoo.com
Circ.: 25,000
Price: Free **Subscription:** $120/yr.
Publication description: It is the only Filipino American-owned newspaper that honors and recognizes outstanding individuals, professionals, businessmen, community leaders, students, police officers and parents through the annual presentation of the Eagle Award of Excellence. It is the only newspaper that features the lady of the week ever issue and the executive profile of the week every other issue.
Date established: 1991

MO MAGAZINE
774 Geary St.

San Francisco, CA 94109
Huynh Luong Thien, Publisher
Tel: (415) 673-8115 **Fax:** (415) 673-6925
Email: mosf@aol.com
Circ.: 10,000
Price: Free
Publication description: The first and largest weekly Vietnamese magazine, serving the Vietnamese communities in San Francisco, Oakland, the East Bay and North Bay areas.
Date established: 1987

MOI NEWSPAPER
8091 Bolsa Ave. #A
Midway City, CA 92665
David Tran, Editor
Tel: (714) 893-0310 **Fax:** (714) 894-3783
Email: baomoi@aol.com
Circ.: 10,000
Price: Free

MUSLIM OBSERVER, THE
Muslim Media Network
29004 W. 8th Mile Rd.
Farmington, MI 48336
A. Raheman Nakadar, CEO
Tel: (248) 426-7777 **Fax:** (248) 476-8926
Email: ceo@mmn-usa.com
Web: www.muslimobserver.com
Circ.: 25,000
Price: Free **Subscription:** $50.00/year
Publication description: To develop a bridge between Muslims and non-Muslims in the world of media. Through promoting harmony, pluralism, human dignity and tolerance for differences of opinion.
Date established: 1998

NEVADA EXAMINER
First Tri Media, The
4515 Eagle Rock Blvd.
Los Angeles, CA 90041
Ella Madrigal, Editor
Tel: (702) 671-4050 **Fax:** (323) 344-3501
Email: radiomla@aol.com
Subscription: $35.00/year
Publication description: A leading Filipino-American newspaper in Las Vegas, Nevada

NEW ASIAN WEEKLY
6418 Oak Ave.
Temple City, CA 91780
Freeman Huang, Editor
Tel: (626) 462-0075 **Fax:** (626) 462-0077
Email: naw@naw1.com
Web: www.naw1.com
Circ.: 10,000
Price: $0.25 **Subscription:** $100.00/year
Date established: 1993

NEW KHAO SOD
1123 N. Vine St. #6A
Los Angeles, CA 90038
Sriwong Koziel, Editor
Tel: (323) 464-1425 **Fax:** (323) 464-2312
Circ.: 10,000

NEW WORLD TIMES
15209 Frederick Rd. #208
Rockville, MD 20850
Frank Jinng, Editor
Tel: (240) 453-9808 **Fax:** (240) 453-9818
Email: newworldtm@yahoo.com
Price: Free **Subscription:** NA
Date established: 1997

NEW YORK AWAM
373 Broadway #5C
New York, NY 10013
Hameed Minhas, Publisher
Tel: (212) 219-1331 **Fax:** (212) 219-1335
Email: nypawam@aol.com

Web: www.newyorkawam.com
Circ.: 50,000
Price: Free **Subscription:** $120.00/year
Date established: 1995

NEWS INDIA TIMES
43 W. 24th St.
New York, NY 10010
Beena Merchant, Chief Editor
Tel: (212) 675-7515 **Fax:** (212) 675-7624
Email: editor@newsindia-times.com
Web: www.newsindia-times.com
Circ.: 13,000
Price: $.60 **Subscription:** $26/year
Date established: 1975

NEWS PAKISTAN
153-25 Hill Side Ave.#2A
Jamaica, NY 11432
Tel: (718) 558-6080 **Fax:** (718) 558-6079
Email: newspakistan@aol.com
Circ.: 55,000
Price: Free **Subscription:** NA
Date established: 1996

NEWSLETTER
Korean American Adoptee Adoptive Family Network
P.O. Box 5585
El Dorado Hills, CA 95762
Chris Winston, President
Tel: (916) 933-1447
Email: kaanet@aol.com
Web: www.kaanet.com
Circ.: 3,000
Date established: 1998

NGUOI VIET LIBERTY NEWS
4660 Elcajon Blvd. #105
San Diego, CA 92115
Nam Le, Manager
Tel: (619) 584-4137 **Fax:** (619) 584-8647
Circ.: 6,000
Price: Free
Date established: 1985

OMAID WEEKLY
P.O. Box 30818
Alexandria, VA 22310
Mohammad Qawi Koshan, Editor in Chief
Tel: (703) 922-6321 **Fax:** (703) 922-6322
Email: mail@omaid.com
Web: www.omaid.com
Subscription: $80.00/year
Publication description: Omaid Weekly is the most widely read international Afghan newspaper. By international it is meant that it is based outside of Afghanistan and the target audience is the Afghan diaspora. The newspaper is currently in its fourteenth year of publication, includes the latest news on Afghanistan from Omaid Weekly reporters and international news agencies, as well as articles, commentaries, professionals, educators, religious and tribal leaders, and patriots about Afghanistan current affairs, politics, society, religion, culture, traditions and history.
Date established: 1992

PACIFIC TIMES NEWSPAPER
37-19 Main St. #2B
Flushing, NY 11354
George Chan, President
Tel: (718) 353-7512 **Fax:** (718) 353-8247
Circ.: 30,000
Price: $0.25 **Subscription:** $100.00/year
Date established: 1987

PAKISTAN CHRISTIAN POST
Pakistan Christian Congress
815 Seneca Ave. PMB #58
New York, NY 11385

Nazir S. Bhatti, Editor
Email: editor@pakistanchristianpost.com
Web: www.pakistanchristianpost.com
Subscription: $60/year

PAKISTAN POST NEWSPAPER
PAK News Corporation
169-22 Hill Side Ave.
Jamaica, NY 11432
Mohammad Farooqi, Chief Editor
Tel: (718) 739-2976 **Fax:** (718) 739-3249
Email: postnewyork@aol.com
Web: www.pakistanpost.net
Circ.: 40,000
Price: Free **Subscription:** $75.00/year
Date established: 1992

PHILIPPINE NEWS- HEAD OFFICE
Philippine News, Inc.
235 Grand Ave., 2nd Fl.
South San Francisco, CA 94080
Lito V. Gutierrez, Editor-in-Chief
Tel: (650) 872-3000 **Fax:** (650) 872-0217
Email: info@philippinenews.com
Web: www.philippinenews.com
Circ.: 40,000
Price: $1.00 **Subscription:** $78.00/year
Publication description: An English language Filipino newspaper with a national readership.
Date established: 1961

PHILIPPINE WEEKLY
P.O. Box 68593
Schaumburg, IL 60618
Orlando Bernardino, Editor
Tel: (847) 352-3877 **Fax:** (847) 352-3878
Email: philweek@ameritech.net
Circ.: 15,000
Price: Free
Date established: 1985

PHO NHO WEEKLY NEWS
6269 Leesburg Pike #306
Falls Church, VA 22044
Anh Nguyen, Publisher
Tel: (703) 533-0264 **Fax:** (703) 532-7453
Email: phonho@aol.com
Circ.: 9,600
Price: $3.00 **Subscription:** $156.00/year
Date established: 1988

PHUONG DONG TIMES
Eastern Times, Inc.
6221 39th Ave. South
Seattle, WA 98118
Dong Vo, Editor
Tel: (206) 760-9168 **Fax:** (206) 760-9168
Email: phuongdong91@yahoo.com
Circ.: 18,000
Price: Free
Publication description: Tabloid Newspaper about the Vietnamese living in the Northwest area of the United States.
Date established: 1991

PHUONG DONG TIMES
Eastern Times, Inc.
8220 SE Harrison St. #235
Portland, OR 97216
Dong Vota, Editor
Tel: (503) 740-9202 **Fax:** (503) 777-8337
Email: phuongdongtimes@yahoo.com
Circ.: 15,000
Price: Free
Publication description: Tabloid Newspaper about the Vietnamese living in the Northwest area of the United States.
Date established: 1991

PORTLAND CHINESE TIMES
7827 SE Powell Blvd.
Portland, OR 97206

Charles Hui, Director
Tel: (503) 771-9560 **Fax:** (503) 788-8900
Email: pct@portlandchinesetimes.us
Web: www.portlandchinesetimes.us
Circ.: 8,000
Price: Free **Subscription:** $50.00/year
Publication description: Chinese community newspaper with free distribution in Oregon and southwest Washington area covering local news and events for Asian with oriental business directory .
Date established: 1997

ROCKY MOUNTAIN JIHO, THE
P.O. Box 1073
Denver, CO 80201
Yoriko Imada, Editor
Tel: (303) 295-1848 **Fax:** (303) 296-0518
Email: rocky@coloradojijo.com
Web: www.coloradojijo.com
Circ.: 2,000
Price: Free **Subscription:** $36.00/year
Date established: 1961

SAIGON TIMES
9234 E. Valley Blvd.
Rosemead, CA 91770
Ai Cam, Publisher
Tel: (626) 288-2696 **Fax:** (626) 288-2033
Email: sgtimes@aol.com
Web: www.saigontimes.net
Circ.: 25,000
Price: Free
Date established: 1986

SEATTLE CHINESE POST
412 Maynard Ave. South
Seattle, WA 98104
Carol N. Vu, Editor
Tel: (206) 223-5559 **Fax:** (206) 223-0626
Email: carol@nwasianweekly.com
Web: www.nwasianweekly.com
Circ.: 5,000
Price: $0.50 **Subscription:** $23.00/year
Publication description: Focuses on northwest news and Asian Americans, written all in Chinese
Date established: 1982

SEREECHAI NEWSPAPER
1253 N. Vine St. #16A
Los Angeles, CA 90038
Somchet Phayakarint, Editor
Tel: (323) 465-7550 **Fax:** (323) 465-7383
Email: sereechai@sbcglobal.net
Web: www.sereechai.com
Circ.: 15,000
Price: $0.50
Date established: 1975

SEREY PHEAP CAMBODIAN NEWS
P.O. Box 40178
Long Beach, CA 90804
Narin Kem, Editor
Tel: (562) 498-0309 **Fax:** (562) 684-4309
Email: narink@aol.com
Web: www.sereypheapnews.com
Circ.: 20,000
Price: Free
Date established: 1981

SHIN HAN MINBO
141 S. New Hampshire Ave.
Los Angeles, CA 90004
Tel: (213) 382-9345 **Fax:** (213) 382-1678

SIAM MEDIA WEEKLY NEWSPAPER
9264 Valley Blvd.
Rosemead, CA 91770
Tang Sripipat, Editor-in-Chief
Tel: (626) 307-9117/9 **Fax:** (626) 307-9040
Email: siammedianews@yahoo.com

Circ.: 12,000
Date established: 1981

ST. LOUIS CHINESE JOURNAL
8517 Olive Blvd.
St. Louis, MO 63132
Wen Hwang, Director
Tel: (314) 991-3747 **Fax:** (314) 991-2554
Email: slcj@sprintmail.com
Web: www.stlouischinesejournal.com
Circ.: 8,000
Price: Free
Date established: 1996

SUC SONG NEWS
14541 Brookhurst St. #C8
Westminster, CA 92683
Thomas Nguyen, Editor
Tel: (714) 531-6217 **Fax:** (714) 531-6248
Email: sucsong@sbcglobal.net
Circ.: 20,000
Date established: 1990

TALIBA FILIPINO NEWS
3325 Wilshire Blvd. #306
Los Angeles, CA 90010
Vic Billones, Editor
Tel: (213) 388-8377 **Fax:** (213) 388-8684
Email: taliba@sbcglobal.net
Circ.: 30,000
Price: Free
Date established: 1996

THAI L.A. NEWS NEWSPAPER
1100 N. Main St.
Los Angeles, CA 90012
Viraj Rojanapanya, Editor
Tel: (323) 276-5837 **Fax:** (323) 441-9989
Email: thaila@lax-c.com
Circ.: 8,000
Price: $0.25 **Subscription:** $120.00/year
Date established: 1975

THANG LONG NEWSPAPER
P.O. Box 220812
Boston, MA 02122
Cuong Nguyen, Editor
Tel: (617) 436-4036 **Fax:** (617) 822-3444
Email: nvietnam04@yahoo.com
Web: www.conong.com
Circ.: 20,000
Price: Free
Date established: 1989

THANG MO
918 S. 1st St.
San Jose, CA 95110
Andy Tran, Manager
Tel: (408) 297-0545 **Fax:** (408) 297-5220
Email: thangmo@sbcglobal.net
Web: www.thangmo.com
Circ.: 10,000
Price: Free
Date established: 1983

THE EPOCH TIMES
Epoch USA, Inc.
P.O. Box 1860
Union City, CA 94587
Tel: (510) 366-0915 **Fax:** (510) 751-5317
Email: sanfrancisco@epochtimes.com
Web: www.epochtimes.com
Circ.: 600,000
Date established: 2000

THE FILIPINO EXPRESS NEWSPAPER
The Filipino Express Newspaper
2711 Kennedy Blvd.
Jersey City, NJ 07306
Lito Gatilan, Editor
Tel: (201) 434-1114 **Fax:** (201) 434-0880
Email: Filexpress@aol.com
Web: www.filipinoexpress.com

Circ.: 22,000
Price: $1.00 **Subscription:** $40.00/year
Date established: 1986

THE INDIAN EXPRESS NORTH AMERICAN EDITION
The Indian Express North American Edition
146 W. 29th St., 5th Fl.
New York, NY 10001
Sujit Rajan, Editor
Tel: (212) 594-6000 x15 **Fax:** (212) 594-8848
Email: letters@iexpressusa.com
Web: www.iexpressusa.com
Circ.: 25,000-30,000
Price: $0.60 **Subscription:** $18.00 / year
Date established: 2000

THE KOREAN NEWS OF CHICAGO
4001 W. Devon Ave. #336
Chicago, IL 60646
Cheon Lee, Editor
Tel: (773) 736-8949 **Fax:** (773) 736-6105
Email: koreannews@yahoo.co.kr
Web: www.kcr.co.kr
Circ.: 8,000
Price: Free
Date established: 1987

THE KOREANA NEWS USA
3130 Wilshire Blvd. #315
Los Angeles, CA 90010-1206
Chai Jung, Editor
Tel: (213) 382-5200 **Fax:** (213) 382-4100
Email: kn@koreananews.com
Web: www.koreananews.com
Circ.: 10,000
Price: Free

THE LITTLE SAIGON NEWS DC
P.O. Box 9253
Silver Spring, MD 20916
Dam Ngo, General Manager
Tel: (301) 871-2328 **Fax:** (301) 460-9298
Email: saigonnhodc@comcast.net
Circ.: 3,000
Date established: 1993

THE MANILA BULLETIN USA
Advent Publications, Inc.
362 E. Grand Ave.
S. San Francisco, CA 94080
Patricia Garcia, Editorial Director
Tel: (650) 873-0750x3024 **Fax:** (650) 873-4335
Email: tricia@teamlbc.com
Web: www.mbulletin-usa.com
Circ.: 15,000
Date established: 1993

THOI BAO MAGAZINE
308 12th St.
Oakland, CA 94607
Anthony Dang, Editor
Tel: (510) 763-5255 **Fax:** (510) 763-3996
Email: tbthoibao@aol.com
Circ.: 12,000
Price: $2.50
Date established: 1992

THOI MOI
10387 Friar Rd. #205
San Diego, CA 92120
Tel: (619) 417-2923 **Fax:** (619) 265-8827

THUONG MAI NEWSPAPER
4787 El Cajon Blvd. #201
San Diego, CA 92115
Tel: (619) 582-4976 **Fax:** (619) 286-1271
Email: sdthuongmai@san.rr.com
Circ.: 6,000
Price: Free

The publication description is provided by a company representative or selected from information published on the company's web site.

THUONG MAI VIETNAM/THE VIETNAM POST

10515 Harwin Dr. #120
Houston, TX 77036
Angelo Hoang Ngoc An, Editor
Tel: (713) 777-2012 **Fax:** (713) 777-4848
Email: web@thevietnampost.com
Web: www.thevietnampost.com
Circ.: 28,000
Price: Free
Publication description: The most popular and widely accepted publication by the local community.
Date established: 1980

TIEU THUYET WEEKLY MAGAZINE

14541 Brookhurst St.
Westminster, CA 92683
Tel: (714) 531-6217 **Fax:** (714) 531-6248
Email: julienhaigcon@yahoo.com
Circ.: 25,000

TRIEU THANH

295 Kinney Dr.
San Jose, CA 95112
Sylvia Tang, Owner
Tel: (408) 993-1144 **Fax:** (408) 993-1146
Price: Free

URDU TIMES

16-20 Hillside Ave.
Jamaica, NY 11432
Khall Aehman, Editor
Tel: (718) 297-8700 **Fax:** (718) 297-0017
Email: urdutimesny@aol.com
Web: www.urdutimes.com
Circ.: 35,000
Price: Free **Subscription:** $45.00/year
Date established: 1980

VIET TIDE NEWSPAPER

15781 Brookhurst St. #101
Westminster, CA 92683
Kathleen Nguyen, Editor in Chief
Tel: (714) 918-4444
Email: viettide@viettide.net
Web: www.viettide.net
Circ.: 12,000

Publication description: Vietnamese bilingual newspaper.
Date established: 2001

VOICE OF ASIA

9730 Townpark Dr. #102
Houston, TX 77036
Koshy Thomas, Publisher
Tel: (713) 988-5140 **Fax:** (713) 988-3915
Email: voiceasia@aol.com
Circ.: 25,000
Price: Free **Subscription:** $30.00/year
Date established: 1987

WASHINGTON MEDIA

7263 Maple Pl. #203
Annandale, VA 22003
Soni Kim, Owner
Tel: (703) 750-0366 **Fax:** (703) 750-0368
Email: wmkacs@aol.com
Circ.: 3,000
Price: Free **Subscription:** $80.00/year
Publication description: A Korean weekly paper
Date established: 1997

WEEKEND BALITA

Balita Media, Inc.
520 E. Wilson Ave. #210
Glendale, CA 91206
Berna O. Mabunga, Editor
Tel: (818) 552-4503 **Fax:** (818) 552-4592
Email: editor@balita.com
Web: www.balita.com
Circ.: 80,000
Price: Free **Subscription:** $54.00/year
Date established: 1991

WEEKLY BANGALEE

The Weekly Bangalee, Inc.
86-16 Queens Blvd. #202
Elmhurst, NY 11373
Kowshik Ahmed, Editor
Tel: (718) 639-1177 **Fax:** (718) 565-8101
Email: bangalee@mindspring.com
Circ.: 12,000
Price: $1.00 **Subscription:** $50.00
Date established: 1991

WEEKLY BANGLA PATRIKA

29-11 39th Ave., 2nd Fl.
Long Island City, NY 11101
Mahbubur Rahman, Editor
Tel: (718) 482-9923 **Fax:** (718) 482-9935
Email: banglapatrika@aol.com
Circ.: 15,000
Price: $1.00 **Subscription:** $90.00 yr.
Date established: 1996

WEEKLY BANGLADESH

Sangbad International
85-59 168th St.
Jamaica, NY 11432
Mohammed Waged A. Khan, Editor
Tel: (718) 523-6299 **Fax:** (718) 523-6299
Email: weeklybangladesh@mindspring.com
Circ.: 8,000
Price: Free **Subscription:** $50.00/year
Date established: 1998

WEEKLY BULLETIN

Holy Martyrs of Vietnam Church
915 S. Wakefield St.
Arlington, VA 22204
Thu H. Bui, Chairman
Tel: (703) 553-0370 **Fax:** (703) 553-0371
Email: cttd.vn@verizon.net
Web: www.cttdva.net
Circ.: 2,400
Date established: 1979

WEEKLY NEWS PROBASHI

Probashi Asian Publishing
4142 Benham St.
Elmhurst, NY 11373
Sikder Kabir, Editor
Tel: (212) 808-4444 **Fax:** (718) 457-3549
Email: probashi@mindspring.com
Circ.: 6,000
Price: $1.00 **Subscription:** $50.00/year
Date established: 1985

WEEKLY THIKANA

11-35 45th Ave.
Long Island City, NY 11101
Sayeed-Ur-Rabb, Editor

Tel: (718) 472-9086 **Fax:** (718) 361-5356
Email: thikana@mindspring.com
Web: www.thikana.net
Circ.: 12,500
Price: $1.00 **Subscription:** $60.00/year
Date established: 1990

WEEKLY-THURSDAY

ASIAN JOURNAL- LAS VEGAS OFFICE

Asian Journal Publications, Inc.
2770 S. Maryland Pkwy. #404
Las Vegas, NV 89109
Robert Macabagdal, Editor
Tel: (702) 792-6678 **Fax:** (702) 792-6879
Email: robert@asianjournal.com
Web: www.asianjournal.com
Circ.: 18,000
Price: Free
Date established: 1996

KHAO SOD NEWSPAPER

1123 N. Vine St. #6A
Los Angeles, CA 90038
Sriwong Koziel, Editor
Tel: (323) 464-1425 **Fax:** (323) 464-2312
Email: khaosod@earthlink.net
Circ.: 10,000
Price: Free
Date established: 1985

NORTHWEST ASIAN WEEKLY

Seattle Chinese Post, Inc.
412 Maynard Ave. South
Seattle, WA 98072
Carol Vu, Editor
Tel: (206) 223-5559 **Fax:** (206) 223-0626
Email: scpnwan@nwlink.com
Web: www.nwasianweekly.com
Circ.: 10,000
Price: $0.50 **Subscription:** $23.00/year
Publication description: Focuses on northwest news and Asian Americans, written all in English.
Date established: 1983

Federal and State Departments of Health and Minority Health Offices
continued from p. 175

TEXAS

TEXAS DEPARTMENT OF STATE HEALTH SERVICES
Office for the Elimination of Health Disparities, Center for Program Coordination
1100 W. 49th St. #M-760
Austin, TX 78756
Tel: (512) 458-7629 Fax: (512) 458-7488
Web: www.dshs.state.tx.us

UTAH

UTAH DEPARTMENT OF HEALTH
Office of Multicultural Health
P.O. Box 142001
Salt Lake City, UT 84114-2001
Tel: (801) 538-9457 Fax: (801) 538-6591

VERMONT

VERMONT DEPARTMENT OF HEALTH
Office of Minority Health
P.O. Box 70
108 Cherry St.
Burlington, VT 05402
Tel: (802) 863-7273 Fax: (802) 651-1634

VIRGIN ISLANDS

VIRGIN ISLANDS DEPARTMENT OF HEALTH
Office of Minority Health
48 Sugar Estate
St. Thomas, VI 00802
Tel: (340) 776-8311 X5079 Fax: (340) 777-4001

VIRGINIA

VIRGINIA DEPARTMENT OF HEALTH
Office of Policy & Planning, Office of Minority Health
109 Governor St., Madison Bldg., 10th Fl.
Richmond, VA 23219

Tel: (804) 864-7432 Fax: (804) 864-7440
Web: www.vdh.state.va.us

WASHINGTON

WASHINGTON DEPARTMENT OF HEALTH
Office of Policy, Legislative & Constituent Relations
P.O. Box 47890
101 Israel Rd. SE, Town Ctr. 1
Olympia, WA 98501
Tel: (360) 236-4021 Fax: (360) 586-7424

WEST VIRGINIA

WEST VIRGINIA DEPARTMENT OF HEALTH & HUMAN RESOURCES
Bureau for Public Health, Office of Rural Health, Minority Health Programs
350 Capitol St. #515
Charleston, WV 25301-3716
Tel: (304) 558-7138 Fax: (304) 558-2183

WISCONSIN

DEPARTMENT OF HEALTH & FAMILY SERVICES
Division of Public Health, Minority Health Program
1 W. Wilson St. #665
Madison, WI 53701
Tel: (608) 267-2173 Fax: (608) 264-7720
Web: www.dhfs.state.wi.us/Health/MinorityHealth

WYOMING

WYOMING DEPARTMENT OF HEALTH
Office of Minority Health
6101 Yellowstone Rd. #510
Cheyenne, WY 82002
Tel: (307) 777-5601 Fax: (307) 777-8545
Web: http://wdh.state.wy.us

Asian Pacific American Radio Stations

CALIFORNIA

Chinese Outreach (1470 KHZ)
P.O. Box 1763
Arcaida, CA 91077
Dr. Peter Tsou, President
Tel: (626) 254-1551 Fax: (626) 254-1527
Email: cola@co.org
Web: www.co.org

Pacific News Service
275 9th St.
San Francisco, CA 94103
Sandy Cloose, Executive Director
Tel: (415) 503-4170 Fax: (415) 503-0970
Email: scloose@pacificnews.org
Web: www.pacificnews.org

Radio Manila
4515 Eagle Rock Blvd.
Los Angeles, CA 90041
Oscar Jornacion, President
Tel: (323) 344-3500 Fax: (323) 344-3501
Email: radiomla@aol.com
Web: www.radiomanila.net

San Francisco Radio Mainichi, Inc.
(1450 KHZ)
1746 Post St., 2nd Fl.
San Francisco, CA 94115
June-ko Nakagawa, News Director
Tel: (415) 931-7050 Fax: (415) 931-7122
Email: info@radiomainichi.com
Web: www.radiomainichi.com

Tieng Vong Tinh Thoung (1430 KHZ)
554 S. 9th St.
San Jose, CA 95112
Bai-an Tran, President
Tel: (408) 280-5101 Fax: (408) 280-6789
Email: baitran@ix.netcom.com
Web: www.chinhnghia.org/tvtt

CALI-FM (106.3 MHZ)
Saigon Radio Hai Ngoai
14541 Brookhust St. #C7
Westminster, CA 92683
Julie Nguyen, CFO
Tel: (714) 775-9042 Fax: (714) 531-6248
Email: sucsong@sbcglobal.net

KAAM-AM (1400 KHZ)
Korean-American Radio
475 El Camino Real #202
Millbrae, CA 94030
Chin Kim, General Manager
Tel: (650) 259-1400 Fax: (650) 259-1401
Email: karadio@sbcglobal.net
Web: www.hanmiradio.com

KALI-FM (106.3 MHZ)
Bridge USA
20300 S. Vermont Ave. #200
Torrance, CA 90502

Masako Kagasaki, General Manager
Tel: (310) 532-5921 Fax: (310) 532-1145
Email: radio@bridgeusa.com
Web: www.bridgeusa.com

KALI-FM (106.3 MHZ)
Radio Bolsa
15751 Brookhurst St. #133
Westminster, CA 92683
Thien Nguyen, General Manager
Tel: (714) 418-2120 Fax: (714) 418-2129
Email: bolsaradio@aol.com
Web: www.vnradiobolsa.com

KAZN-AM (1300 KHZ)
Radio Chinese
747 E. Green St. #101
Pasadena, CA 91101
Kelvin Chu, General Manager
Tel: (626) 568-1300 Fax: (626) 568-3666
Email: gm@am1300.com
Web: www.am1300.com

KBIF-AM (900 KHZ)
United Hmong Radio
3401 W. Holand
Fresno, CA 93722
Dana Kennon, General Manager
Tel: (559) 222-0900 Fax: (559) 222-1573
Email: dana@kbif900.com
Web: www.kbif900am.com

KBLA-AM (1230 KHZ)
Radio Korea, U.S.A.
626 S. Kingsley Dr.
Los Angeles, CA 90005
David Choi, Director
Tel: (213) 487-1300 Fax: (213) 487-7455
Web: www.radiokorea.com

KBNR-AM (1480 KHZ)
Liberman Broadcasting of Houston
License Corp.
15781 Brookhurst St. #101
Westminster, CA 92683
Nimh Vu, General Manager
Tel: (714) 918-4444 Fax: (714) 918-4445
Email: radio@littlesaigonradio.com
Web: www.littlesaigonradio.com

KEST-AM (1450 KHZ)
Multicultural Radio Broadcasting, Inc.
145 Natoma St. #400
San Francisco, CA 94105
Julie Re, General Manager
Tel: (415) 978-5378 Fax: (415) 978-5380
Email: kest1450@sbcglobal.net
Web: www.kestradio.com

KEST-AM (1450 KHZ)
San Francisco Chinese Radio/Sing Tao
Chinese Radio
5000 Marina Blvd. #338
Brisbane, CA 94005

Tim Lau, Vice President
Tel: (650) 808-8080 Fax: (650) 808-8001
Email: timlau@chineseradio.com
Web: www.chineseradio.com

KFOX-AM (1650 KHZ)
Chagal Communications, Inc.
501 Santa Monica Blvd. #501
Santa Monica, CA 90401
Warren Chang, President
Tel: (310) 395-1427 Fax: (310) 395-1527
Email: chagalcom@aol.com

KIRN-AM (670 KHZ)
Radio Iran
3301 Barham Blvd. #300
Los Angeles, CA 90068
John Paley, General Manager
Tel: (323) 851-5476 Fax: (323) 512-7452
Email: info@parsnational.com
Web: www.radioiranla.com

KMRB-AM (1430 KHZ)
Sino Radio Broadcast Corporation
747 E. Green St., 4th Fl.
Pasadena, CA 91101
Kevin Chu, General Manager
Tel: (626) 844-0088 Fax: (626) 844-0414
Email: info@am1430.net
Web: www.mrbi.net

KPCC-FM (89.3 MHZ)
KPCC Southern California Public Radio
1570 E. Colorado Blvd.
Pasadena, CA 91106
Mark Crawly, General Manager
Tel: (626) 585-7000 Fax: (626) 585-7916
Email: mail@kpcc.org
Web: www.kpcc.org

KPFA-FM (94.1 MHZ)
Pacifica Foundation
1929 Martin Luther King, Jr. Way
Berkeley, CA 94704
Roy Campanella, Jr., Interim General
Manager
Tel: (510) 848-6767 Fax: (510) 848-3812
Email: info@kpfa.org
Web: www.kpfa.org

KQED-FM (88.5 MHZ)
KQED, Inc.
2601 Mariposa St.
San Francisco, CA 94110
Joanne Wallace, General Manager
Tel: (415) 864-2000 Fax: (415) 553-2192
Email: fm@kged.org
Web: www.kqed.org

KSJX-AM (1050 KHZ)
RadioBolsa
10161 Bolsa Ave. #8208
Westminister, CA 92683

Tom Pham, General Manager
Tel: (714) 897-2754
Email: bolsaradio@aol.com
Web: www.vnradiobolsa.com

KSON-FM (97.3 MHZ)
Jefferson Pilot Communications
P.O. Box 889004
San Diego, CA 92108-9004
Darrel Goodin, General Manager
Tel: (619) 291-9797 Fax: (619) 543-1353
Email: darrel@jpc.com
Web: www.kson.com

KSQQ-AM (1450 KHZ)
San Francisco Chinese Radio/Sing Tao
Chinese Radio
5000 Marina Blvd. #338
Brisbane, CA 94005
Tim Lau, Vice President
Tel: (650) 808-8080 Fax: (650) 808-8001
Email: timlau@chineseradio.com
Web: www.chineseradio.com

KSQQ-FM (96.1 MHZ)
San Francisco Chinese Radio/Sing Tao
Chinese Radio
5000 Marina Blvd. #338
Brisbane, CA 94005
Tim Lau, Vice President
Tel: (650) 808-8080 Fax: (650) 808-8001
Email: timlau@chineseradio.com
Web: www.chineseradio.com

KSQQ-FM (96.1 MHZ)
Vietnam Broadcasting
1577 Alum Rock Ave.
San Jose, CA 95116
Tiffany Tran, General Manager
Tel: (408) 937-4698 Fax: (408) 937-5103
Email: vnfmradio@yahoo.com
Web: www.vnmedia.com

KVNR-AM (1480 KHZ)
Little Saigon Radio
15781 Brookhurst St. #101
Westminster, CA 92683
Nimh Vu, President
Tel: (714) 918-4444 Fax: (714) 918-4445
Email: radio@littlesaigonradio.com
Web: www.littlesaigonradio.com

KVTO-AM (1400 KHZ)
San Francisco Chinese Radio/Sing Tao
Chinese Radio
5000 Marina Blvd. #338
Brisbane, CA 94005
Tim Lau, Vice President
Tel: (650) 808-8080 Fax: (650) 808-8001
Email: timlau@chineseradio.com
Web: www.chineseradio.com

KWRM-AM (1370 KHZ)
LA English & Chinese Radio
719 N. Sunset Ave.
West Covina, CA 91790
Salina Su, General Manager
Tel: (626) 856-3889 Fax: (626) 856-3896
Email: mail@am1370-chinese.com
Web: www.am1370-chinese.com

KXMX-AM (1190 KHZ)
Salem Communications
701 N. Brand Blvd.
Glendale , CA 91203
Terry Fahy, General Manager
Tel: (818) 956-5552 Fax: (818) 551-1110
Email: info@kkla.com
Web: www.kkla.com

KZSJ-AM (1120 KHZ)
Que Huong Radio
2670 S. White Rd. #165
San Jose, CA 95148
Khoi Nguyen, General Manager
Tel: (408) 223-3130 Fax: (408) 223-3131
Email: qhradio@aol.com
Web: www.quehuongmedia.com

VCB-AM (1430 KHZ)
Vietnamese Christian Broadcast
P.O. Box 2468
Fullerton, CA 92837
Timothy Thi, General Manager
Tel: (714) 533-2278 Fax: (714) 491-8912
Email: radio@tinlanh.org
Web: www.tinlanh.org

DISTRICT OF COLUMBIA

WPFW-FM (89.3 MHZ)
Pacifica Radio
2390 Champlain St. NW
Washington, DC 20009
Ron Pinchback , General Manager
Tel: (202) 588-0999 Fax: (202) 588-0561
Email: pinchback_ron@wpfw.org
Web: www.wpfw.org

GEORGIA

WSSA-AM (1570 KHZ)
Sheridan Network
2424 Old Rex Morrow Rd.
Ellenwood, GA 30294
Tony Stcyr, General Manager
Tel: (404) 361-8843 Fax: (404) 366-9772
Email: wussa@juno.com

HAWAII

KNDI AM (1270 KHZ)
Asia Pacific News
#1501 Hawaii Tower Amfac Center, 745
Fort St.
Honolulu, HI 96813
Laisin Lee, Advertising/Sponsorship
Tel: (808) 533-3305 Fax: (808) 533-3305
Email: radiohost@hkbah.org
Web: www.hkbah.org

KNDI-AM (1270 KHZ)
Broadcast House of the Pacific
1734 S. King St.
Honolulu, HI 96826
Leona Jona, President/General Manager
Tel: (808) 946-2844 Fax: (808) 947-3531
Email: kndi.am@verizon.net
Web: www.kndi.com

ILLINOIS

CKBI-AM (1330 KHZ)
Chicago Korean Broadcasting, Inc.
4449 N. Kedzie Ave., 2nd Fl.
Chicago, IL 60625
Young W. Kim, General Manager
Tel: (773) 463-1125 Fax: (773) 463-1164
Email: kbi1330@hotmail.com

KCBS-AM (1590 KHZ)
Korean Christian Broadcasting
5817 W. Dempster St.
Morton Grove, IL 60053
Dr. Sun Chul Kim , Executive Director
Tel: (847) 583-0191 Fax: (847) 583-8295

Q101
Global Radio, Inc.
2126B S. Archer Ave.
Chicago, IL 60616
Anita Hsueh, General Manager
Tel: (312) 326-5363 Fax: (312) 326-5361
Email: chnmedia@ameritech.net

LOUISIANA

RFV-AM (9930 KHZ)
Radio Free Vietnam, Trung Tam
P.O. Box 29245
New Orleans, LA 70198
Kyson Vuong, Chief Director
Tel: (504) 254-2304 Fax: (504) 254-2305
Email: rfvla@aol.com
Web: www.radiofreevietnam.com

MARYLAND

Washington Christian Radio System,
(1600 KHZ)
1751 Elton Rd. #201
Silver Spring, MD 20903
Young H. Kim, President
Tel: (301) 439-5700 Fax: (301) 439-4187
Email: wcrslive@yahoo.com
Web: www.wcrs.org

MASSACHUSETTS

WJDA-AM (1300 KHZ)
Boston Chinese Radio
YAU's Marketing Services, 110 W.
Squantum St. #33
North Quincy, MA 02171
Betty Yau, General Manager
Tel: (617) 770-3310 Fax: (617) 472-2574
Email: yausmktg@aol.com
Web: www.bostonchineseradio.com

NEW JERSEY

WCNJ-FM (89.3 MHZ)
Mercury Broadcasting
505 Phornall St. #306
Edison, NJ 08837
Paul Suri, General Manager
Tel: (732) 516-1030 X204
Email: info@wcnj.com
Web: www.wcnj.fm

WRSU-FM (88.7 MHZ)
Rutgers University
126 College Ave.
New Brunswick, NJ 08901
Dan Strafford, General Manager
Tel: (732) 932-7800 Fax: (732) 932-1768
Email: gm@wrsu.org
Web: www.wrsu.org

WTTM-AM (1680 KHZ)
EBC Radio
2088 Rt. 130 North
Monmouth Junction, NJ 08852
Alka Agrawal , General Manager
Tel: (732) 821-6009 Fax: (732) 821-6003
Email: alka@ebcmusic.com
Web: www.ebcmusic.com

NEW YORK

Sino Radio Broadcast/Sinocast
449 Broadway
New York, NY 10013
Tony Wong, Manager
Tel: (212) 431-4300 Fax: (212) 431-5802

CWCB-FM (88.1 MHZ)
Chung Wah Commercial Broadcasting Co.
16 Bowery, 4th Fl.
New York, NY 10013
Jack Tam, General Manager
Tel: (212) 571-0491 Fax: (212) 571-2922
Email: radio@cwcb.com
Web: www.cwcb.com

WAXQ-FM (104.3 MHZ)
Chinese American Voice
41-25 Kissena Blvd. #131
Flushing, NY 11355
Richard Hsuah, President
Tel: (718) 961-6490 Fax: (718) 886-3563
Email: cavoice@cavoice.com
Web: www.cavoice.com

WGSM-AM (930 KHZ)
AM Korea
136-56 39th Ave.
Flushing, NY 11354
Jeemin Roh, General Manager
Tel: (718) 358-4219 Fax: (718) 460-2379
Email: seajee1015@hotmail.com
Web: www.newyork.radiokorea.com

WNSW-AM (1430 KHZ)
Multicultural Radio Broadcasting, Inc.
449 Broadway, 5th Fl.
New York, NY 10013
Gene Hein Eneyer, General Manager
Tel: (212) 966-1059 Fax: (212) 966-9580
Email: info@mrbi.net
Web: www.mrbi.net

WZRC-AM (1480 KHZ)
Multicultural Radio Broadcasting, Inc.
449 Broadway, 5th Fl.
New York, NY 10013
Gene Hein Eneyer, General Manager
Tel: (212) 965-1480 Fax: (212) 965-8917
Email: info@mrbi.net
Web: www.mrbi.net

PENNSYLVANIA

WNWR-AM (1540 KHZ)
New World Radio
200 Monument Rd. #6
Bala Cynwyd, PA 19004
Alan Pendleton, General Manager
Tel: (610) 664-6780 Fax: (610) 664-8529
Email: sam@wnwr.com
Web: www.wnwr.com

WPWA-AM (1590 KHZ)
Korean Christian Broadcasting Company
1330 Willow Ave.
Elkins Park, PA 19027
Jong Hwan Kim, General Manager
Tel: (215) 935-5000 X101 Fax: (215)
935-8888

TEXAS

Radio Korea
2240 Royal Ln. #215
Dallas, TX 75229
Bernardo Ahn, President
Tel: (972) 620-7111 Fax: (972) 620-7140
Email: radiokoreatexas@yahoo.com
Web: www.radiokorea.com

Zacarias Serrato (1500 MHZ)
P.O. Box 523
Merkel, TX 79536
Zacarias Serrato, President
Tel: (325) 928-3060 Fax: (915) 928-4683

KAAM-AM (770 KHZ)
Crawford Broadcasting
3201 Royalty Row
Irving, TX 75062
Don Crawford, Jr., General Manager
Tel: (972) 445-1700 Fax: (972) 438-6574
Email: kaamradio@aol.com
Web: www.kaamradio.com

KANM-FM (99.9 MHZ)
Texas A&M University
Student Services Bldg. 1236 TAMU
College Station, TX 77843-1236
Matt Bannon, Station Manager
Tel: (979) 862-2516 Fax: (979) 847-8854
Email: kanm@kanm.tamu.edu
Web: http://kanm.tamu.edu

KCHN-AM (1050 KHZ)
Houston Southern Chinese Radio Network
11122 Bellaire Blvd.
Houston, TX 77072
Jean Lin, General Manager
Tel: (281) 498-4310 Fax: (281) 498-2728
Email: gedn@gedn.com
Web: www.scdaily.com

KENR-AM (900 KHZ)
5821 SW Frwy. #610
Houston, TX 77057-7502
Thi Hong, General Manager
Tel: (713) 917-0050 Fax: (713) 917-0213
Web: www.radiosaigonhouston.com

KEOS-FM (89.1 MHZ)
Brazos Educational Radio
P.O. Box 78
College Station, TX 77841
Lance Parr, General Manager
Tel: (979) 779-5367 Fax: (979) 779-7259
Email: keos@keos.org
Web: www.keos.org

KGOL-AM (1180 KHZ)
Entravision Communications Corporation
5821 SW Frwy. #600
Houston, TX 77057-7502
Carmen Aguilar, General Manager
Tel: (713) 349-9880 Fax: (713)349-0647
Email: caguilar@entravision.com
Web: www.entravision.com

KHCB-FM (105.7 MHZ)
Houston Christian Broadcasters
2424 South Blvd.
Houston, TX 77098
Bruce Munsteman, General Manager
Tel: (713) 520-5200
Email: email@khcb.org
Web: www.khcb.org

continued on p. 310

Asian Pacific American TV Stations

CALIFORNIA

KOREAN GOSPEL BROADCASTING CO.
621 S. Virgil Ave. #400
Los Angeles, CA 90005
Charles Kim, Director
Tel: (213) 381-1190 Fax: (213) 381-6744
Web: www.kgbc.com

ADELPHIA, CHANNEL 63
Sky Link TV
500 W. Montebello Blvd.
Rosemead, CA 91770
Tango Tang, General Manager
Tel: (323) 888-0028 Fax: (323) 888-0029
Email: info@skylinktv.us
Web: www.skylinktv.us

ADELPHIA (EAST VALLEY), CHANNEL 98
Sky Link TV
500 W. Montebello Blvd.
Rosemead, CA 91770
Tango Tang, General Manager
Tel: (323) 888-0028 Fax: (323) 888-0029
Email: info@skylinktv.us
Web: www.skylinktv.us

ALTRIO, CHANNEL 207
Sky Link TV
500 W. Montebello Blvd.
Rosemead, CA 91770
Tango Tang, General Manager
Tel: (323) 888-0028 Fax: (323) 888-0029
Email: info@skylinktv.us
Web: www.skylinktv.us

CHANNEL 18
Korean Television America Network
4525 Wilshire Blvd.
Los Angeles, CA 90010
Youngsoo Shoi, Advertising Director
Tel: (323) 964-0101 Fax: (323) 964-0102
Email: webmaster@kwebtv.net
Web: www.kwebtv.net

CHANNEL 32 & CHANNEL 26 (GREATER BAY AREA AND NORTHERN CA)
Chinese Television Company, Inc.
100 N. Hill Dr. #26
Brisbane, CA 94005
Tel: (415) 468-5588 Fax: (415) 468-5566

CHANNEL 83
Korean American Cablevision
2975 Wilshire Blvd. #100
Los Angeles, CA 90010
Howard Kim, President
Tel: (213) 351-1080 Fax: (213) 351-1084
Email: kungseok90010@yahoo.com

CHARTER, CHANNEL 284
Sky Link TV
500 W. Montebello Blvd.
Rosemead, CA 91770
Tango Tang, General Manager
Tel: (323) 888-0028 Fax: (323) 888-0029
Email: info@skylinktv.us
Web: www.skylinktv.us

CTI ZHONG TIAN CHANNEL
PTB Network
1255 Corporate Center Dr. #212
Monterey Park, CA 91754
Andy Chuang, General Manager
Tel: (323) 415-0068 Fax: (323) 415-0038
Email: ctiusa@ctitv.com.tw
Web: www.ctitv.com.tw

KLTL CHANNEL 64
Vien Thao TV
995 E. Santa Clara St.
San Jose, CA 95116
Vivian Thoung, Station Manager
Tel: (408) 947-7517 Fax: (408) 947-0463
Email: vienthamedia@aol.com
Web: www.vienthao.com

KMTP-TV CHANNEL 32, 31
Minority Television Project and Company
1504 Bryant St., 1st Fl.
San Francisco, CA 94103
Booker Wade, General Manager
Tel: (415) 777-3232 Fax: (415) 552-3209
Email: kmtp@kmtp.org
Web: www.kmtp.org

KNXT CHANNEL 49
Diocese of Fresno
1550 N. Fresno St.
Fresno, CA 93703
Marvin Harrison, Station Manager
Tel: (559) 488-7440 Fax: (559) 488-7444
Email: knxt@pacbell.net
Web: www.dioceseoffresno.org

KSCI CHANNEL 18
United Television Broadcasting Systems
1622 N. Highrun St.
Hollywood, CA 90028
Shigeto Terasaka, General Manager
Tel: (323) 469-2929 Fax: (323) 460-7377

KSCI CHANNEL 18, VIA UHF
Kempo Television Corporation
23441 Golden Spring #470
Diamond Bar, CA 91765
Miyoko Hirabayashi, VP
Tel: (909) 594-9996 Fax: (909) 860-5014

KSCI INTERNATIONAL CHANNEL
Fujisankei Communications
10100 Santa Monica Blvd. #460
Los Angeles, CA 90067

Norio Iwahori, Manager
Tel: (310) 553-5828 Fax: (310) 553-2196
Web: www.fujisankei.com

KSCI-TV CHANNEL 18
KSCI-TV
1990 S. Bundy Dr. #850
Los Angeles, CA 90025
Gannon Gray, General Sales Manager
Tel: (310) 478-1818 Fax: (310) 479-8118
Email: ggray@kscitv.com
Web: www.kscitv.com

KTSF CHANNEL 26
Lincoln Broadcasting Company
100 Valley Dr.
Brisbane, CA 94005
Michael Sherman, General Manager
Tel: (415) 468-2626 Fax: (415) 467-7559
Email: msherman@ktsftv.com
Web: www.ktsf.com

KXLA
Korean Television Enterprises, Ltd.
625 S. Kingsley Dr.
Los Angeles, CA 90005
C.K.Han, Director/Administration Dept.
Tel: (213) 382-6700 X600 Fax: (213) 382-4265
Email: ckhan@ktela.com
Web: www.ktela.com

SATELLITE/CABLE
ABS-CBN International, The Filipino Channel
859 Cowan Rd.
Burlingame, CA 94010
Rafael Lopez, Manager Director
Tel: (650) 697-3700 Fax: (650) 697-3500
Email: rlopez@abs-cbn.com
Web: www.abs-cbn.com/international

TAN TV
The Asia Network Inc.
6430 Sunset Blvd. #1200
Los Angeles, CA 90028
Timothy Lee, Production Manager
Tel: (323) 465-1100 Fax: (323) 957-6583
Email: tantv@ahnmir.com
Web: www.tantv.com

TIME WARNER, CHANNEL 98
Sky Link TV
500 W. Montebello Blvd.
Rosemead, CA 91770
Tango Tang, General Manager
Tel: (323) 888-0028 Fax: (323) 888-0029
Email: info@skylinktv.us
Web: www.skylinktv.us

TVB USA JADE CHANNEL 34
TVB Group
39 Dorman Ave.
San Francisco, CA 94124

Karman Liu, Marketing Manager
Tel: (415) 282-8228 Fax: (415) 282-8226
Email: sfjade@tvbusa.com
Web: www.tvbusa.com

TVB USA JADE CHANNEL LA
TVB Group
15411 Blackburn Ave.
Norwalk, CA 90650
Lisa Wong, Station Manager
Tel: (562) 802-0220 Fax: (562) 802-5096
Email: jade@tvbusa.com
Web: www.tvbusa.com

COLORADO

INTERNATIONAL CHANNEL
International Channel Networks
8900 Liberty Cir.
Englewood, CO 80122
Teresa Wiedel, Executive Director of Communications
Tel: (303) 268-5455 Fax: (720) 873-2900
Email: icinfo@i-channel.com
Web: www.i-channel.com

HAWAII

CHANNEL 20-9
JN Productions Inc.
2828 Paa St. #2140
Honolulu, HI 96819
Joanne Ninomiya, President
Tel: (808) 836-0361 Fax: (808) 833-4621
Email: jnp@jnproductions.com
Web: www.jnproductions.com

GTE CHANNEL 699
Chinese Community Broadcasting, Inc.
100 N. Beretania St., Cultural Plz. #206
Honolulu, HI 96817
Larry Chiang, President
Tel: (808) 523-7623 Fax: (808) 521-0764

KBFD-TV CHANNEL 32
The Asia Network
1188 Bishop St. #PH-1
Honolulu, HI 96813
Mr. Kea Sung Chung, President/CEO
Tel: (808) 521-8066 Fax: (808) 521-5233
Email: operations@kbfd.com
Web: www.kbfd.com

KIKU-TV
737 Bishop St. #1430
Honolulu, HI 96813
Phyllis Kihara, General Manager
Tel: (808) 847-2021 Fax: (808) 841-3326
Email: pkihara@kikutv.com
Web: www.kikutv.com

ILLINOIS

CABLE TV
International Channel Networks
Regency Office Plz. #108, 2700 River Rd.
Des Plaines, IL 60018
Conrad Hirth, Director
Tel: (312) 297-1957 Fax: (847) 298-9491
Web: www.i-channel.com

MASSACHUSETTS

WHDH-TV CHANNEL 7
Beam Corporation
7 Bulfinch Pl.
Boston, MA 02114
Mike Carson, General Manager
Tel: (617) 725-0777 Fax: (617) 248-5420
Email: mcarson@whdh.com
Web: www.whdh.com

NEW JERSEY

WMBC-TV CHANNEL 63
Mountain Broadcasting Corporation
99 Clinton Rd.
West Caldwell, NJ 07006
Victor Joo, General Manager
Tel: (973) 852-0300 Fax: (973) 852-0377
Email: info@wmbctv.com
Web: www.wmbctv.com

NEW YORK

CHANNEL 510
Tv Japan
100 Broadway, 15th Fl.
New York, NY 10005
Yuichi Tat Sumi, General Manager
Tel: (212) 713-8417 Fax: (212) 262-5577
Email: tvjapan@tvjapan.net
Web: www.tvjapan.net

CHANNEL 63
Fujisankei Communications
150 E. 52nd St., 34th Fl.
New York, NY 10022
Hector Lanirez, Administration Department Manager
Tel: (212) 702-0464 Fax: (212) 688-0392
Email: webmaster@fujisankei.com
Web: www.fujisankei.com

CHANNEL 73
Japan Media Productions
521 5th Ave. #1700
New York, NY 10175
Mako Matsuda, President
Tel: (212) 292-4211 Fax: (212) 682-3771
Email: jmpnewyork@aol.com

CHANNEL 78
Sino TV
449 Broadway
New York, NY 11013
Tony Wang, Manager
Tel: (212) 965-1480 Fax: (212) 965-8917

CHANNEL 80 AND 95 ON TIME WARNER
Ruposhi Bangla TV
115-46 148th St.
Jamaica, NY 11436
Mr. Anisuzzaman, Producer
Tel: (718) 659-0437 Fax: (718) 322-6354
Email: banglatv@aol.com
Web: www.banglatv.com

DTV- CHANNEL 511
Korean Channel, Inc.
137-77 Northern Blvd., 3rd Fl.
Flushing, NY 11354
Hyun Wi, General Manager
Tel: (718) 353-8970 Fax: (718) 359-2067
Web: tkctv@hotmail.com

TKC-TV CHANNEL 76
Korean Channel, Inc.
137-77 Northern Blvd., 3rd Fl.
Flushing, NY 11354
Hyun Wi, General Manager
Tel: (718) 353-8970 Fax: (718) 359-2067
Email: tkctv@hotmail.com

TV ASIA
International Channel Networks
570 Lexington Ave., 36th Fl.
New York, NY 10022
Patty Alvia, Office Assistant
Tel: (212) 527-9917 Fax: (212) 527-9915
Email: patty.alvia@i-channel.com
Web: www.i-channel.com

WMBC-TV CHANNEL 63
Sinovision
15 E. 40th St., 11th Fl.
New York, NY 10016
Yann Chen, General Manager
Tel: (212) 213-6688 Fax: (212) 213-8882

WNXY-TV CHANNEL 26
Metro Studios
204 E. 23rd St., 2nd Fl.
New York, NY 10010
James Chladek, General Manager
Tel: (212) 686-5386 Fax: (212) 576-1839
Email: james.chladek@verizon.net

WNYN-TV CHANNEL 39
Metro Studios
204 E. 23rd St., 2nd Fl.
New York, NY 10010
James Chladek, General Manager
Tel: (212) 686-5386 Fax: (212) 576-1839
Email: james.chladek@verizon.net

WNYX-TV CHANNEL 35
Metro Studios
204 E. 23rd St., 2nd Fl.
New York, NY 10010
James Chladek, General Manager
Tel: (212) 686-5386 Fax: (212) 576-1839
Email: james.chladek@verizon.net
Web: www.tv35newyork.com

WXNY-TV CHANNEL 32
Metro Studios
204 E. 23rd St., 2nd Fl.
New York, NY 10010
James Chladek, General Manager
Tel: (212) 686-5386 Fax: (212) 576-1839
Email: james.chladek@verizon.net

VIRGINIA

WKTV-TV CHANNEL 254
Washington Korean TV
2931 Eskridge Rd. #G
Fairfax, VA 22031
David Chu, General Manager
Tel: (703) 560-1591 Fax: (703) 560-1593
Email: wktvchu@yahoo.com
Web: www.wktvusa.com

WNVC-TV CHANNEL 56
Commonwealth Public Broadcasting
8101-A Lee Hwy.
Falls Church, VA 22042
Frederick Thomas, General Manager
Tel: (703) 698-9682
Email: fthomas@mhznetworks.org
Web: www.mhznetworks.org

WNVC-TV CHANNEL 56
Image In Asian Television
P.O. Box 6673
McLean, VA 22106-6673
Bala Chandran, Producer
Tel: (703) 319-0100
Email: info@asianocean.com

WNVT-TV CHANNEL 53
Commonwealth Public Broadcasting
8101-A Lee Hwy.
Falls Church, VA 22042
Frederick Thomas, General Manager
Tel: (703) 698-9682
Email: fthomas@mhznetworks.org
Web: www.mhznetworks.org

WASHINGTON

INTERNATIONAL CHANNEL NETWORKS
18 W. Mercer #110
Seattle, WA 98119
Shelly Kurtz, Station Manager
Tel: (206) 282-2762 Fax: (206) 282-2763
Email: shelly.kurtz@i-channel.com
Web: www.i-channel.com

Asian Pacific American Radio Stations continued from p. 308

KNON-FM (89.3 MHZ)
KNON
4415 San Jacinto
Dallas, TX 75204
Dave Chaos, Business Assistant
Tel: (214) 828-9500 Fax: (214) 823-3051
Email: knonsm@acorn.org
Web: www.knon.org

KREH-AM (900 KHZ)
Entravision
5821 SW Frwy. #610
Houston, TX 77057-7502
Kim Le, Manager
Tel: (713) 349-9880 Fax: (713) 917-0213
Email: info@radiosaigonjouston.com
Web: www.radiosaigonhouston.com

KTEK-AM (1110 KHZ)
South Texas Broadcasting
6161 Savoy #1200
Houston, TX 77036
Chuck Jewell, General Manager
Tel: (713) 260-3600 Fax: (713) 260-3628
Email: webmaster@kkht.com
Web: www.kkht.com

KTEK-AM (1110 KHZ)
Voice of Vietnam

2900 Travis #A
Houston, TX 77006
Susie Thang, General Manager
Tel: (713) 523-0302 Fax: (713) 523-1805
Email: vovnradio@yahoo.com
Web: www.vovnradio.com

KUTX-FM (90.1 MHZ)
KUT Radio
University of Texas at Austin, 1 University
Station A0704
Austin, TX 78712
Stewart Vanderwilt, General Manager
Tel: (512) 471-1631 Fax: (512) 471-3700
Email: svanderwilt@kut.org
Web: www.kut.org

KXEB-AM (910 KHZ)
BMP
8828 N. Stemmons Frwy. #101
Dallas, TX 75247
Don Littlefield, General Manager
Tel: (214) 634-7780 Fax: (214) 634-7523

KYND-AM (1520 KHZ)
16620 Cypress Rosehill Rd.
Cypress, TX 77429-9886
Bill Turner, General Manager
Tel: (281) 373-1520 Fax: (281) 373-5599

VIRGINIA

Washington Korean Broadcasting Company
7004 K Little River Tnpk.
Annandale, VA 22003
Yong Lee, Station Manager
Tel: (703) 354-4900 Fax: (703) 658-1500
Email: lee@wkbc.biz

WDCT-AM (1310 KHZ)
Family Radio, Ltd.
3251 Old Lee Hwy. #506
Fairfax, VA 22030
Ken Shin, General Manager
Tel: (703) 273-4000 Fax: (703) 273-1015
Email: 1310@radiowashingtonnews.com
Web: www.radiowashingtonnews.com

WUST-AM (1120 KHZ)
New World Radio, Inc.
2131 Crimmins Ln.
Falls Church, VA 22043
Allen Pendleton, General Manager
Tel: (703) 532-0400 Fax: (703) 532-5033
Email: mail@wust1120.com
Web: www.wust1120.com

WASHINGTON

KSUH-AM (1450 KHZ)
Radio Hankook
807 S. 336th St.
Federal Way, WA 98003
Sung Hong, General Manager
Tel: (253) 815-1212 Fax: (253) 815-1913
Email: info@radiohankook.com
Web: www.radiohankook.com

KWYZ-AM (1230 KHZ)
Radio Hankook
807 S. 336th St.
Federal Way, WA 98003
Sung Hong, General Manager
Tel: (253) 815-1212 Fax: (253) 815-1913
Email: info@radiohankook.com
Web: www.radiohankook.com

KXPA-AM (1540 KHZ)
Multicultural Radio Broadcasting
114 Lakeside Ave.
Seattle, WA 98122
Julie Re, General Manager
Tel: (206) 292-7800 Fax: (206) 292-2140
Email: kxpa@quest.net
Web: www.kxpa.com

Readership Survey

By completing this survey, you will automatically receive a 50% discount on the 2007/2008 ASIAN-AMERICAN YEARBOOK.

Name: _____

☐ Male ☐ Female

DOB: _____

Address: _____

City, State, Zip: _____

Phone (optional): _____

E-mail (optional): _____

Profession/Occupation: _____

Salary (approximately):
☐ Under 24,000   ☐ 25-40,000   ☐ 41-55,000
☐ 56-75,000   ☐ 76-100,000   ☐ over 100,000

Educational Attainment:
☐ High School   ☐ Undergraduate
☐ Graduate Degree   ☐ Post-Graduate Degree
☐ Other

Languages: _____

I utilize the Yearbook to _____

I think the Yearbook should include more information about _____

_____

I learned about the Yearbook through:

☐ Library ☐ Bookstore ☐ Internet ☐ Friend ☐ Employer ☐ Conference/Convention
☐ Other _____

Please feel free to provide additional comments in the space below:

_____

_____

Thank you for your valuable feedback.
TIYM Publishing Co., Inc.
6718 Whittier Ave., #130 McLean, VA 22101 - Tel: (703) 734-1632 - Fax: (703) 356-0787
E-mail: tiym@tiym.com

Information Update

If your organization, agency, or publication has made changes during the past year, or if you know of one that does not appear within this edition, please take a few moments to let us know by filling out the form below and faxing to us at **(703) 356-0787** or mailing it to: TIYM Publishing Co., Inc. 6718 Whittier Ave., #130, McLean, VA 22101.

You may also e-mail the updated information by visiting **www.asianamericanyearbook.com.**

Please indicate listing preference:

☐ Career Opportunities for Asian Americans ☐ Federal/State   ☐ Private Sector
☐ Minority Business Opportunities
☐ Institution Offering Scholastic Financial Aid
☐ Asian American Company
☐ Asian American Organization
☐ Asian American Publication
☐ Asian American Radio Station
☐ Asian American TV Station
☐ Other

Agency/ Company/ Organization Name: _____
Date Founded: _____
If it is a ☐ Branch or ☐   Affiliate of a larger organization, What is the name of that organization?_____
_____
Address: _____
City: _____ State: _____ Zip Code: _____
Telephone 1:_____ Telephone 2: _____ Fax: _____
E-mail:_____ Web: _____
Name of the Principal Contact: _____
Title of the Principal Contact: _____
Chief Purpose of the Organization (☐ attached is a separate sheet with a detailed description, or organization brochure): _____
_____

Publication/Station Name: _____
Circulation: _____ Verified: _____
No. of Members: _____ Most Important Meeting: _____ Date Held: _____
How often is the Publication Produced: _____
Language: ☐ English   ☐ Other: _____
Other Specifications: _____
_____

Thank you for helping us keep the **ASIAN-AMERICAN YEARBOOK** up-to-date.